On the site behind this house stood until 1904 Broomwood House (formerly Broomfield) where WILLIAM WILBERFORCE resided during the ⁄⁄ CAMPAIGN against ⁄⁄ SLAVERY which he ⁄. successfully conducted in Parliament ⁄⁄⁄⁄⁄

WILLIAM PITT THE YOUNGER 1759–1806 lived here 1803–1804

Lived in a house on this site.

ICKENS,
st.
ere.
12.
70.

EDWARD JOHNSTON 1872–1944 Master Calligrapher lived here 1905–1912

LOUIS KOSSUTH 1802–1894 Hungarian Patriot stayed here

SITE OF SCOTLAND YARD FIRST HEADQUARTERS OF THE METROPOLITAN POLICE 1829–1890

ENGLISH HERITAGE Sir ALFRED HITCHCOCK 1899–1980 Film Director lived here 1926–1939

ENCAUSTIC · TABLET · FOR · AFFIXING · TO · FRONT · OF · BUILDINGS · OF · HISTORIC · INTEREST
LCC WILLIAM PITT 1759–1806 Lived Here

ANTONIO CANAL CALLED CANALETTO (1697–1768) Venetian Painter Lived here

MITH
45
d wit
ere

ENGLISH HERITAGE Madame MARIE TUSSAUD 1761–1850 Artist in Wax lived here 1838–1839

LCC JAMES WOLFE 1727–1759 Victor of Quebec Lived Here

LONDON COUNTY COUNCIL SAMUEL ~PEPYS~ 1633–1703 DIARIST AND SECRETARY OF THE ADMIRALTY lived here 1679–1688

LIVED IN LONDON

LIVED IN LONDON

BLUE PLAQUES AND THE STORIES BEHIND THEM

Edited by

EMILY COLE

With a foreword by

STEPHEN FRY

YALE UNIVERSITY PRESS
NEW HAVEN AND LONDON

ENGLISH HERITAGE

Designed by Emily Lees

Printed in China

Library of Congress Cataloging-in-Publication Data

Cole, Emily.
Lived in London : blue plaques and the stories behind them / Emily Cole.
p. cm.
Includes bibliographical references and index.
ISBN 978–0–300–14871–8 (cl : alk. paper)
1. Historical markers–England–London–Guidebooks. 2. Terra-cotta plaques–England–London–Guidebooks.
3. Historic buildings–England–London–Guidebooks. 4. London (England)–Buildings, structures, etc.–Guidebooks.
5. London (England)–Guidebooks. 6. London (England)–History. I. Title.

DA689.H5C65 2009
942.1–dc22
2008051541

A catalogue record for this book is available from The British Library

THIS BOOK IS DEDICATED TO THE MEMORY OF
SIR LAURENCE GOMME,
AND TO ALL THOSE OTHERS
WHO HAVE WORKED WITH SUCH DEVOTION
AND ENTHUSIASM ON BEHALF OF
THE BLUE PLAQUES SCHEME

It takes longer than might be expected to organise the installation of a blue plaque. So it has proved with this book, the production and writing of which has been spread over a number of years and has involved a great many people. The concept, raised in 1996, began to be discussed seriously in 2000. In the early stages, David Robinson, Roger Bowdler, Geoff Noble and Val Horsler all made important contributions, as did Joanna Griffiths, who produced a series of designs, and Victor Belcher, who wrote some sample entries. Thanks are also due to Celia Joicey and Rob Carr-Archer of the National Portrait Gallery, who discussed with us the possibility of a joint publication. Those English Heritage staff involved in ensuing discussions regarding the book's format and content included Robin Taylor, Adele Campbell, Rob Richardson, Tracy Borman, John Cattell, Edward Impey, Chris Scull, Pam Whiffin and Sarah Vidler. English Heritage's Blue Plaques Panel – under the successive chairmanship of Francis Carnwath, Loyd Grossman and David Cannadine – also provided invaluable advice.

Work on planning, writing and editing began in earnest in 2003–4. Liz Drury was involved in this process from the outset until the bitter end – copy-editing the text, assisting with research, the compilation of indexes and the search for illustrations, and generally giving generously of her time and expertise. I am enormously grateful to Liz, whose patience, experience and attention to detail has played a major part in the successful completion of this publication.

The original text was written by a team of authors from English Heritage, including – alongside myself – Roger Bowdler, Nick Chapple, Peter Guillery, Timothy Jones, Susan Skedd, Howard Spencer, Chris Sumner, Sarah Vidler and Simon Wartnaby. The Blue Plaques Team – the historians of which are Susan Skedd and Howard Spencer – then expanded and made consistent the text overall, with a division of responsibility by chapter. Susan and Howard have thus served as my lieutenants for the bulk of the work on the text – besides being notable authors in their own right – and I am hugely grateful to both of them for their dedication, support and time, which was given at the expense of other blue plaques work.

The first full draft of the text was read – outside the Blue Plaques Team – by David Cannadine, John Cattell and Peter Guillery, who most generously undertook the work in spite of already heavy schedules. Frank

Kelsall, who worked on the plaques scheme for many years, kindly read through the introduction, as did Edward Impey; meanwhile, Susan Ashworth – who, with her husband Frank, crafts English Heritage blue plaques – read through the section on design and manufacture. The comments that resulted have undoubtedly improved the book overall, and I owe each of them a debt of gratitude. A special thank you goes to Stephen Fry, a member of the Blue Plaques Panel since 2003, who somehow found time to pen a masterly foreword and thereby made a notable addition to the book.

Outline picture research was carried out by the authors, with further initial investigation by Emma Brown. However, the bulk of the research was completed by myself, in partnership with the brilliant June Warrington, whose thoroughness, patience and irrepressible enthusiasm played such an important part in the book's completion. Thanks are also due to Libby Wardle, who provided invaluable assistance in the job of picture research. Like June, she has been a model of thoroughness and capability. In terms of copyright and the use of particular images, I am grateful for the legal advice provided by Julian Hamblin and Antony Douglass of Bond Pearce, and the further assistance of my colleagues Charlotte Bradbeer and Aaron Donaldson.

Much of the new photography for this book is the work of Derek Kendall, whose instinctive feel for the buildings and atmosphere of London – and of the part that plaques play – has resulted in a fabulous collection of images. Other English Heritage photographs were taken by Nigel Corrie, whose experience of blue plaques goes back a number of years, while Charles Walker provided vital assistance, sharing his skills and being helpful and calm, even in the face of deadlines and frenzy. A few house owners and custodians generously allowed our photographers special access to their properties; I am especially grateful to Gillian Darley, Daniel Robbins, Sarah and David Chisnall, and Garry and Laura Choun.

The maps showing the locations of blue plaques, all painstakingly hand-drawn, are the work of Malcolm Fowler. I have admired Malcolm's art since the unveiling in 2000 of the plaque to Sylvia Plath – whose house he illustrated so beautifully – and I am delighted to have been able to work with him on this project. The production of Malcolm's maps was made possible by an external commissioning grant from English Heritage's Historic Environment Enabling Programme, and for this I would like to thank Barney Sloane, Caroline Howarth and David McOmish. Permission for the reproduction of these illustrations was kindly given by the Geographers' A–Z Map Co. Ltd.; for this, I am especially grateful to Jennie Fancett.

In terms of bringing this book to press, I owe a great debt to Gillian Malpass – whose encouragement and advice have made publication with Yale possible – and David Cannadine, for further support and enthusiasm. In practical terms, the partnership was enabled by financial assistance provided from within English Heritage, and for that I wish to thank, in particular, Edward Impey, Chris Scull, John Cattell and Claire Scoones. It has been a pleasure to work with Emily Lees, the designer of this book, and Katie Harris, Publicity Manager at Yale.

At English Heritage, I am lucky enough to have a number of enormously helpful and supportive colleagues, whose skills and knowledge I have drawn upon extensively. First of all my team, members of which – between 2003 and today – are Cathy Benson, Alison Frappell, Esther Godfrey, Caroline Howarth, Susan Skedd, Howard Spencer, Sarah Vidler, Libby Wardle and Pam Whiffin. Secondly, my manager, John Cattell, together with members of the Blue Plaques Panel (past and present) – especially Christopher Beauman, Celina Fox, Stephen Fry, Jane Ridley, Gavin Stamp and A. N. Wilson – and members of the wider Architectural Investigation Division, including Susie Barson, Elain Harwood, Gordon Higgott, Adam Menuge, Kathryn Morrison, Joanna Smith and June Warrington. Other colleagues whom I would like to thank are David Allen, Jane Ashworth, Roger Bowdler, Helen Bowman, Claire Broomfield, Duncan Brown, Sophie Clarke, Nicola Cryer, Andy Donald, Matthew Dunsdon, Anna Eavis, Nigel Fradgley, Emily Gee, Felicity Gilmour, Heather Gordon, Peter Guillery, Javis Gurr, Cynthia Howell, Helen Jurga, Richard Lea, Ian Leith, Beth McHattie, Irene Peacock, Tori Reeve, Aileen Reid, David Robinson, Alyson Rogers, Treve Rosoman, Amanda Rowan, Andrew Saint, Andrew Sargent, Philip Temple, Colin Thom, Eleanor Thornton, Lucinda Walker, Emma Whinton-Brown, Anne Wiggans, Nigel Wilkins and Patricia Yeomans.

Beyond English Heritage, so many individuals – together with libraries, archive centres, galleries and museums – have freely and enthusiastically offered help, advice and information, regarding both the text and illustrations, that it is impossible to acknowledge them all. Among those who have contributed, knowingly or otherwise, are: Hugh Alexander, Rita Apsan, Frank and Susan Ashworth, Georgia Atienza, Sylvia Backemeyer, Kaisey Baillie, Malcolm Baird, Rob Baker, Malcolm Barr-Hamilton, Steven Bateman, Jane Baxter, Charles Beddington, Victor Belcher, Chris Bennett, Richard Bowden, Simon Bradley, Lynda Brooks, Iain Gordon Brown, Neil Burton, Margaret Busby, Ernie Butler, John Callow, Helen Carey, Lionel Carley, Clarinda Chun, Andrew Churchill, Mike Claxton, John Cloake, Gail Collingburn, John Coulter, Jo Crocker, John Croft, Patricia Daniel, Gillian Darley, Christopher Denvir, Christine De Poortere, Eddie Derrick, Howard Doble, Phil Dunn, Alex Edouard, Verity Elson, Robert Elwall, Elizabeth Emerson, Sally England, Jonathan Evans, James Feltham, Olga Ferguson, Robert Fleming, John Forester, Andre Gailani, Mireille Galinou, Maurice Garvie, Mariëlle Gerittsen, Sally Gilbert, Jennie Goossens, Luci Gosling, Martin Hallam, James Hamilton, Frank Harding, Zoë Hendon, Caroline Herbert, David Hibberd, Bette Hill, Victoria Hogarth, John Holbrook, Keith Holdaway, Major and Mrs Holt, Nigel Hughes, Sam Hutt, Nicholas Jacobs, Sunder Katwala, Christopher Kearl, Linda Kelley, Tim Kerr, Cassandra King, Louise King, Richard Knight, Rory Lalwan, Gerry Lambert, Richard Langley, Marie-Lou Legg, Virginia Lewick, Shuk Kwan Liu, Voula Livani, Anne Locker, Clifford Manlow, Katherine Marshall, Dave McCall, Seamus McKenna, Linda Merman, Tanya Millard, Michael Mitzman, Chantal Morel, Karen Morgan, Simon Moss, Simon Murphy, John Neligan, Dawn Oei, Arike Oke, Sue Palmer, Melanie Parker, Frank Parlato Jr., Joshua Pearcey, Antony Penrose, Roxanne Peters, John Physick, Jan Picton, Stephen Poover, Neil Rhind, John Richardson, Brian Riddle, Claire Rider, Andrew Robinson, Toni Saint, Lucy Scrivener, Lucy Short, Catherine Sloan, John Saumarez Smith, Lucy Smith, Stacey Smithson, Audrey Snell, Rachel Sparks, Siren Steen, Steve Stephens, Demi Stephens, Barbara Stoney, Kezia Storr, Emma Stower, Rosamund Strode, Tony Summerfield, Janice Swanson, Terence Taylour, David Tennant, Catherine Theakstone, Anna Towlson, Helen Trompeteler, Lucy Waitt, Dave Walker, Hannah Walker, Cat Warsi, Anne Wheeldon, Laura Whitton, Richard Wildblood, Sarah Williams, Val Wilmer, Andy Wittrick, Maggie Wood and Giles Wright.

Finally, a special thanks to my friends (especially Emily and Hannah), my partner Matthew Spriggs and my family – my parents B. J. Cole and Drusilla Cole, and my sister Peggy Cole – for supporting me through the course of this project. There have been times when it felt like it would never end, but I have enjoyed (almost) every day.

EMILY COLE
Head of Blue Plaques Team
English Heritage
October 2008

CONTENTS

Many of us like to believe that we understand the point and purposes of history, that we have a high doctrine of its importance in the world; that history moves us and engages us. I wonder how fully true that is.

There is a character in a novel by Vladimir Nabokov for whom distance in time is no different from distance in space: he is therefore capable, like most of us, of weeping at the human tragedy of an earthquake that happened yesterday a thousand miles away in China, but he is also capable of weeping at an equally destructive one which happened a thousand years ago: for him past and present are emotionally one. I remember being extraordinarily excited by this idea. Suppose the people and events of history truly could live in our minds as closely as the people and events of today? We all pay lip service to the idea that yesterday makes today, but it is hard to make the imaginative leap which truly connects us to the past. It is as if we are forced to move forwards in such a narrow passageway of time that the act of stopping to look behind us is difficult. It doesn't matter how much we intellectually grasp history, we are human beings for whom emotional engagement is often more real than intellectual. Blue plaques, in their simple way, address this defect.

The obvious merits of the plaques as records and registers of the eminent are one thing, and alone justify their existence, but I find that they go deeper than that. For me, they are a unique imaginative portal into the past, for in my mind all blue plaques are contemporaneous, which is to say, the people commemorated by them are in their buildings *now*.

Go to Dean Street in Soho and you will see Karl Marx letting himself out of his rooms, crossing into Frith Street where he nods to the essayist William Hazlitt (who in fact died when Marx was twelve years old) before finding himself importuned by a disordered John Logie Baird, who needs money for his new invention, television. Marx avoids him and avoids too the opium addict Thomas de Quincey who is on his way to visit his friend Shelley in Poland Street. Crossing over Oxford Street and striding towards Bloomsbury, Marx cuts James Boswell dead, nods to Keynes the economist, executes a stiff bow to Bertrand Russell, stares with envy at Charles Darwin's luxurious beard and – shaking his head with frank disbelief at the sight of Jimi Hendrix in tight purple jeans – disappears into the reading rooms of the British Library to continue his work on *Das Kapital*. There is no part of London where this game cannot be played. London's layers of history melt into one and we can all participate in the collisions of talent, energy and ambition that have made this metropolis hum with life and achievement for a thousand years.

To say that blue plaques 'bring the past alive' sounds like a ghastly cliché, but to me plaques really do animate their environment like nothing else; an ordinary window in an anonymous Camden street becomes the window out of which George Orwell is looking while he dreams up Big Brother and the Ministry of Fear, a smart Mayfair jeweller's looks across to where Handel is writing the Hallelujah Chorus.

To a student of architecture a city is always a living record of its past and present, but the plaques add *people*. Short, haiku-like biographies tell you just enough about those of whom you haven't heard to give a picture, the rest is up to one's own imagination and follow-up enquiries whether by Wikipedia or the *Dictionary of National Biography*.

Soldiers and statesmen people the squares and streets all at once, hobnobbing with music-hall artists, novelists, composers, kings-in-exile and founders of religious sects. Blue plaques pierce windows through the modernity of our sweaty, suffocating and congested twenty-first-century city, windows through which we can see history alive with us. It may sound fanciful, but what else connects people with the past and the present so completely? Historical novels and costume dramas perhaps, but they always tell you so much more about the age in which they were created than the age they attempt to recreate. Aside from anything else, blue plaques are unique in being able to make a traffic jam endurable.

I have been lucky enough to serve on English Heritage's Blue Plaques Panel for some years now and have taken part in the difficult, sometimes stormy discussions which attend the nomination and consideration of new candidates. Many inside and outside the panel worry that the great cliffs of science, medicine, engineering, architecture, literature, music, entertainment, politics, soldiering, religion and social reform are in danger of being eroded by the scummy tide of celebrity that now washes up against us all. The constitution of the blue plaques scheme attempts to forestall the worst excesses of temporary fame: a candidate must have been dead for twenty years or have been born more than a hundred years ago (and be dead): it is hoped that those provisions are enough to exclude the short-term glamour of the more meretricious and fly-by-night personalities who take up so much newspaper and magazine room today, but who will be forgotten in a twinkling tomorrow. Blue plaques are only interested in recording the kind of life achievements that change the course of human history, understanding and culture. Those of us with less substance and significance will have to make do with *Desert Island Discs* and *This Is Your Life*. Not all those commemorated will necessarily be household names, however. Part of the sport of Plaque Spotting is to encounter remarkable men and women of whom one has not heard, but whose claim to greatness one can discover: patriots, Japanese novelists and US Presidents (Mazzini, Soseki and Van Buren, for example) with whose names the world may not ring today are worth discovering. The presence of their plaques tells us much about them but much also about the London they chose to stay in and which offered them refuge and hospitality.

This invaluable book, written with insight and exemplary scholarship, is a perfect companion for anyone who has ever looked up and wondered . . .

STEPHEN FRY

1   A passing milkman admires the plaque to the Prime Minister Neville Chamberlain at 37 Eaton Square, Belgravia, in 1963.
[© Getty Images]

London contains many thousands of commemorative plaques. This book focuses on exactly eight hundred of them, all put up as part of the official blue plaques scheme, run successively by the (Royal) Society of Arts, the London County Council, the Greater London Council and English Heritage. It tells the story not only of the people honoured, but also of the plaques themselves and the buildings to which they draw attention.

Despite the scheme's modern title, by no means all the plaques are blue; they vary in design, material and colour, and were installed under flexible criteria until formal rules were set down in 1954. The buildings which they mark are likewise of an enormous variety: from government offices to buildings on housing estates, suburban semis to smart town houses in the centre of London.

This book is the first published guide to London's plaques for over half a century to be compiled with the aid of the official local government and English Heritage files. Extensive library research has also been undertaken, in order to elucidate the precise connection between the various historical figures and the buildings they occupied. Periods of residence have been given, or at least estimated, in every case, infor-mation which has – in some instances – been discovered for the first time. Particular attention has been paid to the activities carried out by the commemorated person during his or her time at the commemorated address. Where appropriate, the names and life dates of significant others who lived in these buildings – such as wives and children – have also been included. The inscriptions of the plaques are faithfully represented in the forms of nomenclature of the various individuals, and their professions, as they have been introduced (in bold) at the start of the entries; only the life dates, where they have been found to be inaccurate, have been corrected. For ease of use, the names of those figures who have plaques – and are included in this book – have been set out in capitals.

All previous official guides having been dealt with alphabetically, this is the first attempt to group the scheme's plaques by geographical area. It divides first by borough and then – where necessary – into smaller areas, the boundaries of which are not always formalised. In approaching these areas, common sense has prevailed over official demarcations; this has resulted in some plaques, which officially fall within one borough, being listed under another. For example, the Fitzrovia and Regent's Park section takes in plaques from both Westminster and Camden, while West Kensington includes plaques from both Kensington and Chelsea and Hammersmith and Fulham.

As this book makes clear, the plaques erected under the scheme are overwhelmingly to be found in central London: Westminster has the highest tally (nearly 270 plaques), with Kensington and Chelsea and Camden running a close second and third (both have around 160 plaques). Of individual areas, Marylebone has the most (with 62 plaques), closely followed by Hampstead (51), Bloomsbury (47) and Mayfair (45), while London's most 'plaqued' thoroughfares include Cheyne Walk, Bedford Square, Queen Anne's Gate and Eaton Square. The reasons for these concentrations are varied, but it should be noted that it was only in 1965 – with the creation of the GLC – that the scheme took in the outer areas of the capital. As the number of plaques in the outer boroughs are comparatively few, they are grouped together here into one section: Outer London.

Naturally, buildings bearing plaques are subject to change, even where they are listed or form part of conservation areas. Every effort has been made to ensure that this book is up-to-date. However, readers may find that, following publication, some plaques – which are visible and in situ at the time of writing – have been obscured or even removed altogether. Queries about such plaques should be directed to English Heritage.

Finally, it should be noted that while some of the buildings included in this book are open to the public – for example, as museums, hotels, shops and restaurants – the vast majority are in private hands. The scheme could not operate without the goodwill of the owners and occupiers of these properties, and those interested in viewing the plaques detailed in this book are entreated to respect their privacy.

BBC	British Broadcasting Corporation		NTPL	National Trust Photo Library
BFI	British Film Institute		NPG	National Portrait Gallery
Bt.	Baronet		*ODNB*	*Oxford Dictionary of National Biography*
CH	Companion of Honour		OM	Order of Merit
DACS	Design and Artists Copyright Society		PRA	President of the Royal Academy
DNB	*Dictionary of National Biography*		RA	Royal Academy / Royal Academician
EH	English Heritage		RAF	Royal Air Force
GLC	Greater London Council		RIBA	Royal Institute of British Architects
KG	Knight of the Order of the Garter		RN	Royal Navy
LCC	London County Council		SJ	Society of Jesus (Jesuits)
LMA	London Metropolitan Archives		SoA	Society of Arts
LSE	London School of Economics		UCL	University College London
MC	Military Cross		V&A	Victoria and Albert Museum
NMR	National Monuments Record		VC	Victoria Cross

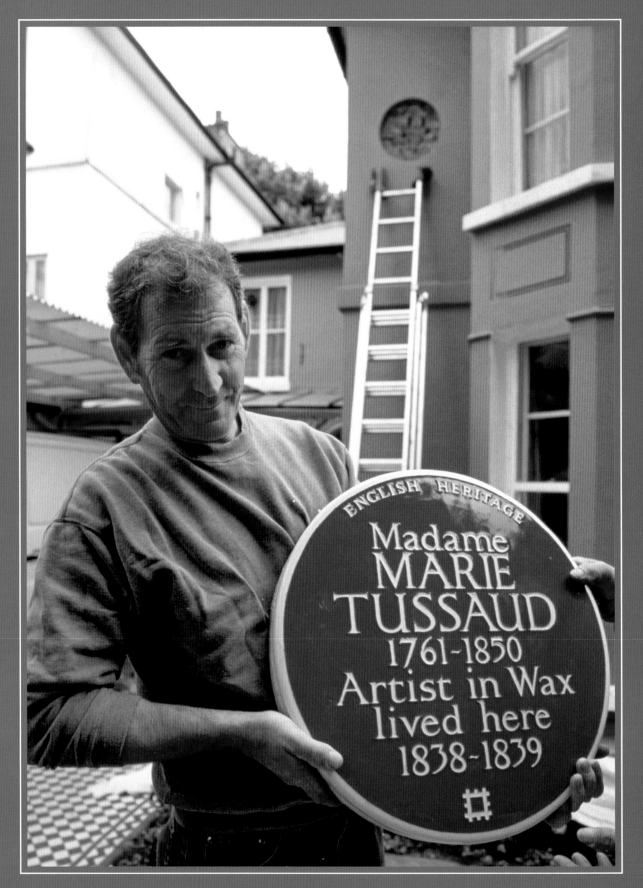

2   English Heritage contractor
Eddie Derrick installs the plaque to
Madame Marie Tussaud at 24
Wellington Road, St John's Wood,
in 2001. [© English Heritage.
Photograph by Nigel Corrie]

Blue plaques have long been a notable feature of London's streetscape, as familiar to us today as they were to figures such as LILLIE LANGTRY, JIMI HENDRIX and SIR WINSTON CHURCHILL (fig. 4). They adorn the façades of buildings in areas as different as Soho and Wimbledon, and awaken associations with times long past. A writer of 1952 spoke of coming across blue plaques 'in unexpected places, in streets mean and squalid, in jaded squares, and in fashionable thoroughfares; every Londoner knows them, springing up, as some of them appear to do, almost overnight'.[1]

London – described by BENJAMIN DISRAELI as a 'roost for every bird' and 'a nation, not a city' – includes plaques honouring a huge breadth of human endeavour: from politics to sculpture, religion to drama (figs 6 and 7).[2] Figures from countries as far-flung as New Zealand, Chile and Japan have been commemorated, together with people from London and across the British Isles. As the sculptor SIR WILLIAM REID DICK wrote in 1953, 'in their full range these plaques build up a many-sided picture of the city's achievements, bringing home to one a more complete idea of the activities of different ages'.[3] In honouring

the capital's buildings, the blue plaques scheme follows historical association rather than architectural merit or design; in few other ways could Nash terraces be grouped together with inter-war semis (figs 3 and 5). In a unique and successful fashion, plaques bring London to life, visibly demonstrating its remarkable historical significance and uniting past with present, people with place.

From the outset, the aim of the plaques scheme has been to celebrate the link between person and building, and to emphasise the social, human element of London's architecture which would not otherwise be widely recognised. As Reid Dick noted, perhaps the most absorbing thing about the plaques scheme 'is the way in which it brings us into direct contact with the lives of [notable] people'.[4] He had 'always found it interesting to consider the personalities together with the houses in which they lived' – a coupling which is often unexpected – and believed that 'by understanding the more personal side of great men, our appreciation of their achievements is enriched'.[5] Buildings are, after all, more than just bricks and mortar: they are the theatres in which our lives are enacted, and we can both be impressed by – and impress upon – these

1

noting that 'the great thing about it is that they never know they have it'.[8]

Driven largely by public suggestion, the blue plaques scheme has built up considerable momentum over the last 140 years, and has – since its founding in 1866 – been imitated across the world. Its huge popularity shows no sign of waning, there being a continual stream of new and interesting people that meet the scheme's selection criteria. Given the scale and density of London, there is always room for expansion; as this book makes clear, whole areas of the capital have yet to be marked with blue plaques, and there are likewise realms of endeavour that have yet to be represented adequately. In aiming to achieve such coverage, English Heritage does not work alone. Today, there are a number of well-established and successful plaques schemes which operate alongside – and are complementary to – English Heritage's own, including those run by the City of London Corporation, Westminster City Council, Southwark Council and the Ealing Civic Society. Fundamentally, all work to the same aims: to pay homage to the cosmopolitan history of London and to raise awareness about its special significance.

structures. WINSTON CHURCHILL famously stated that 'We shape our buildings, and afterwards our buildings shape us',[6] while LEONARD WOOLF wrote in 1975:

> what has the deepest and most permanent effect upon oneself and one's way of living is the house in which one lives. The house determines the day-to-day, hour-to-hour, minute-to-minute quality, colour, atmosphere, pace of one's life; it is the framework of what one does, of what one can do, and of one's relations with people . . . That is why looking back over my life I tend to see it divided into sections which are determined by the houses in which I lived, not by school, university, work, marriage, death, division, or war.[7]

By drawing attention to London's buildings, it has long been hoped that plaques can play a part in their preservation and, as we shall see (pp. 4–8), this has often proved to be the case. They also serve as educational tools and are a means of officially and visibly recognising the achievements of notable historical figures. The playwright Sir David Hare, in unveiling the plaque to the photographer LEE MILLER and the Surrealist SIR ROLAND PENROSE in 2003, described a blue plaque as 'the only distinction that anybody really wants in life',

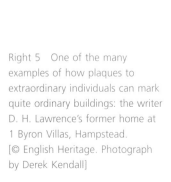

6   The LCC plaque to W. B. Yeats at 23 Fitzroy Road, Primrose Hill. [© English Heritage. Photograph by Derek Kendall]

7 The plaques to William Smith and Lord Fisher at 16 Queen Anne's Gate, Westminster. [© English Heritage. Photograph by Derek Kendall]

THE ROLE OF THE PLAQUES SCHEME

In 1863, when the politician and reformer WILLIAM EWART stood in the House of Commons to suggest a system of inscribing 'on those houses in London which have been inhabited by celebrated persons, the names of such persons', he did so against a background that was ideally suited to the birth of a plaques scheme.[9] The idea drew, most overtly, on the nineteenth-century enthusiasm for memorialisation; this is reflected in the term 'memorial tablets', used to describe plaques from the 1860s until at least the 1950s. The cult of Victorian hero worship peaked around the 1840s, yet the trend for commemoration continued right through the later part of the century and into the next. When Ewart gave his speech in the Commons in 1863, work was under-way on the sculpture surrounding Nelson's Column in Trafalgar Square (completed 1867), while work was just beginning on another of London's greatest monu-ments, the Albert Memorial in South Kensington, built in 1863–72 to designs by GEORGE GILBERT SCOTT (fig. 8). Such works were indicative of an increasing sense of nationalism and civic pride; public monuments cel-ebrating great men and women both reflected and encouraged patriotism, and had the power 'to focus public attention upon political and social values important in maintaining the status quo'.[10] Public monuments in the capital played a special role: they

were 'primarily symbols of national pride on view to the world and from which an understanding of the moral and physical achievements of the country could be ascertained'.[11]

Meanwhile, great men and women were also receiv-ing attention in the artistic and literary arenas; the National Portrait Gallery was founded in 1856, while the new enthusiasm for life history culminated in the *Dictionary of National Biography*, conceived by George Smith and LESLIE STEPHEN and begun in 1882. Inter-estingly, both public sculpture and the *DNB* involved the submission of nominations by the public at large, a process which continues to drive the plaques scheme; the final result was intended to be an 'expression of the consensus of public opinion'.[12]

Despite the success of the Victorians in the realm of commemoration, Ewart's contemporaries still felt that more needed to be done. In 1873 a correspondent to *The Times* wrote of there being 'scarcely a continental town in which a stranger could pass an hour without learning the names of its famous men from the street corners'. The writer bemoaned the fact that in London 'a man might pass a lifetime without knowing that the great city had ever given birth to any clay superior to that of which bricks are made'.[13] In 1903 the corre-spondent Algernon Ashton expressed similar senti-ments: 'we are, as a nation, singularly careless of the memory of our great men'.[14] The idea of a plaques scheme was thus strongly supported, it being felt that 'Nothing could be more fertile in interest than to make our houses their own biographers', a practice which 'would be instructive as well as interesting and graceful'.[15] In 1864 a writer, generally thought to be the architect GEORGE GODWIN – editor of *The Builder* from 1844 to 1883 – urged that 'the pleasures of memory and association connected with London houses' be awakened and maintained.[16]

But there was a second, even stronger, rationale behind the idea of a plaques scheme. From the outset, it was hoped that 'memorial tablets' would play a role in encouraging the preservation of houses of historical interest. In this regard, the plaques scheme forms an important part in the history of the conservation movement: it pre-dates by some years many other ini-tiatives, including the Society for Photographing Relics of Old London (founded 1875), the Society for the Protection of Ancient Buildings (founded 1877), the Survey of London (founded 1894) and The National

Trust (founded 1895). At the time Ewart voiced his idea, many Londoners were concerned about the future of the city's built environment, especially its domestic buildings. The fate of Northumberland House (fig. 9), a Jacobean mansion near Charing Cross, was a cause célèbre. In 1865, just a year before the plaques scheme was formally taken up, the Metropolitan Board of Works began moves to demolish the house as part of a new street development. The scheme was dropped after considerable protest, but was later revived; the house was demolished in 1874.

Aware of this and other imminent victims, writers set out the role they hoped the plaques scheme would

play. On 6 August 1864 'A London Wayfarer' wrote to *The Builder* in support of Ewart's idea, emphasising the 'duty which the society of the present generation owes to the next and succeeding ones, *and this is to endeavour to preserve the historical land-marks which now exist*'. The writer felt that if the example were to be set in London, 'there is the hope that throughout the provinces there may be a spirit of the same kind shown, and that in large towns notes of famous interest may in the same way be preserved'.[17] Another correspondent felt the value of marking 'in a permanent manner' the houses of notable persons would be 'the means of saving many a relic which will otherwise be ruthlessly swept away'.[18] In 1866 the Society of Arts stated that one of the benefits of a scheme 'may be a tendency to increase the public estimation for places which have been the abodes of men who have made England what it is'. Thus, 'some of the old haunts of London, teeming with historic interest, may be preserved from the ruthless hands of modern destroyers and improvers'.[19]

This did not immediately prove to be the case. For instance, although – as early as 1869 – the Society of Arts placed a tablet on 47 Leicester Square, the home for thirty-two years of SIR JOSHUA REYNOLDS (see fig. 450), the house was on the point of demolition in 1898. Algernon Ashton, a vociferous promoter of

10 Sir Isaac Newton's former home at 35 St Martin's Street, Leicester Square, in a photograph of 1898. It had been marked with a Society of Arts plaque in 1881 and was demolished in about 1913. [© City of London, LMA]

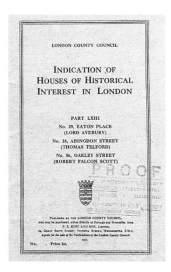

11 Cover of a booklet of 1935, belonging to the LCC's *Indication of Houses of Historical Interest in London* series. [Reproduced by permission of English Heritage]

Right 12 A photograph by John Summerson showing the Adam brothers' Adelphi Terrace, south of the Strand, during demolition in 1936. [Reproduced by permission of English Heritage. NMR]

memorial tablets, quickly defended the house as 'one of London's most precious relics', and asked, 'Why cannot such unique houses as these, where great and illustrious men have worked and died, be purchased by the nation, and thus protected for ever from ruthless destruction?'.[20] Number 47 was finally demolished in 1937, about twenty years after its near neighbour, 35 St Martin's Street, the last home of SIR ISAAC NEWTON (fig. 10), which had been marked with a plaque by the Society of Arts in 1881. Other losses include the birthplace of Lord Byron in Holles Street, Cavendish Square – marked by the Society of Arts in 1867 with its first blue plaque and demolished just over twenty years later – and the house of JOHN DRYDEN in Gerrard Street, Soho, demolished in about 1902.

There were concerns when in 1901 the plaques scheme passed into the hands of the LCC. Algernon Ashton saw this transfer of responsibility as a 'somewhat grim joke, seeing that the London County Council, so far from guarding famous buildings from destruction, seems ever to have been bent upon demolishing as many historical houses and streets in the Metropolis as its sacrilegious hands could possibly accomplish'.[21] However, the council – perhaps more than any other of

the scheme's administrators – emphasised the part played by plaques in preserving and promoting historic buildings; from 1901 until around the 1940s, it termed the scheme the 'Indication of Houses of Historical Interest in London' (fig. 11). An LCC booklet of the 1950s described the role of plaques as a reminder 'of distinguished contributors to London's life and of the need to preserve our visible heritage from the past which all too easily tends to disappear'.[22]

Although the demolition of the residences of great men and women has continued – victims of the twentieth century included Broomfield, the Clapham home of WILLIAM WILBERFORCE (see fig. 309), demolished in 1904, and ADELPHI TERRACE, south of the Strand (fig. 12 and see fig. 338), the home of figures such as DAVID GARRICK – it is possible to detect a gradual increase in the appreciation of such buildings and their associations. In 1954, when the selection criteria for blue plaques were formalised, Sir Howard Roberts – Clerk of the LCC – noted that 'the presence of a tablet can serve as an incentive to the preservation of a building of historical interest threatened with demolition'.[23] Four years later, the owner of 100 Bayswater Road wrote to inform the LCC of the historic associations of his residence – it was the house in which SIR JAMES BARRIE

A number of buildings – comparatively unexceptional from an architectural perspective – have been listed on account of the associations commemorated by the plaques that they bear. For instance, VAN GOGH's residence in Stockwell (fig. 14), JOHN LOGIE BAIRD's workshop in Soho, FANNY BURNEY's house in Mayfair (see fig. 394), OSCAR WILDE's Chelsea home (see fig. 189), D. H. LAWRENCE's house in Hampstead (see fig. 5), ERNEST SHACKLETON's house in Sydenham and the Lisson Grove residence of B. R. HAYDON and CHARLES ROSSI (see fig. 431). But there is still a long way to go before all buildings with important historical associations are fully appreciated, and while plaques may generate interest, they cannot actually prevent demolition. Over the history of the scheme about a hundred houses bearing plaques have been lost, many of immense significance on account of their associations and influence on a person's life and career. These include the homes of the artist Sir John Tenniel, the sculptor John Flaxman, the scientific writer Mary Somerville (fig. 15), the composer Sir Arthur Sullivan, the actor Edmund Kean and the founders of the Salvation Army, William

13 A photograph of 1975 with the proposed position of the plaque commemorating the site of the Cato Street Conspiracy in Marylebone. [© City of London, LMA]

Left 14 Vincent van Gogh's house at 87 Hackford Road, Stockwell, is among those London buildings bearing plaques which have been listed on account of their special historic interest. [© English Heritage. Photograph by Derek Kendall]

wrote *Peter Pan*. The building was then threatened with redevelopment, and he hoped that a plaque 'might give a little bit of added protection', as indeed it did.[24] Remarkable though it may seem today, JOHN KEATS's house in Hampstead (see fig. 100) and CHARLES DICKENS's house in Bloomsbury were both threatened with demolition in the early twentieth century; in both cases, it was their associations (and their plaques) that led to their preservation and conversion to museums. Likewise, the modest stable building in Marylebone in which the CATO STREET CONSPIRACY was discovered in 1820 must surely owe its survival to its associations, as described by the plaque (fig. 13).

15　Number 12 Hanover Square, Mayfair – the former home of the scientific writer Mary Somerville – is one of about a hundred buildings marked with plaques and then subsequently demolished. In this case, the building – shown here in a photograph of 1942 – was redeveloped in 1968. [Reproduced by permission of English Heritage. NMR]

and Catherine Booth. Over the course of the last ten years alone, redevelopment has claimed the homes (and plaques) of the Polar explorer Captain Lawrence Oates, the pioneer of cinematography William Friese-Greene and the music-hall comedian Harry Tate.

The educational role of plaques was recognised early on. Speaking at the unveiling of the first LCC plaque in 1903, Lord Rosebery stated that, 'for the young, who need to have their imaginations turned in a more worthy direction than the Olympian Games, it is not a bad thing to have it forced on their minds . . . that there are other avenues of fame, and that great cities gratefully remember those who have honoured them by living in their midst'.[25] Plaques draw the attention of the public not only to historical figures of fame and/or importance, but to the style and form of the buildings they mark. The latter role was, for a comparatively short time, undermined by the practice of installing plaques on 'sites', resulting in a steady stream of protest. The ever-vocal Algernon Ashton felt that it was 'surely the height of reverential folly and absurdity to erect tablets on new houses, merely because they happen to stand upon spots where notable personages lived in days gone by'; he continued that it was 'also misleading to the last degree, as people of future generations will, as a natural consequence, be utterly unable to tell whether such houses thus tableted are genuine or not'.[26] The early twentieth-century Clerks of the LCC, Sir Laurence Gomme and Sir James Bird, were also opponents of the creation of what they termed 'false history'. In 1954 the practice of erecting plaques on sites was stopped altogether, and this policy has been defended ever since, partly on educational grounds. In 1967 the GLC reiterated that 'while the actual house in which a person lived can, through its appearance and architectural features, afford some guide to that individual's personality and the nature of the age in which he lived, when it is replaced by a modern building all such historical connections are destroyed, and a plaque becomes in effect a substitute for a memorial to the person concerned'.[27]

Another interesting aspect of the plaques scheme is the way in which it encapsulates the values and interests of particular generations. As the scheme has long been run by public bodies, even though driven by public suggestion, existing plaques also – to a certain extent – signify what authority *wants* society to value. A list of figures (and houses) commemorated, when organised by date of plaque, presents an intriguing his-

torical tool. What this book makes clear is that notions of celebrity, and spheres of interest, have changed radically from generation to generation. Some of the people commemorated – for instance, Sir Charles Santley, Dame Clara Butt, Dan Leno and G. A. Henty – were enormously popular in their day, though their names mean little to most people now.

The way in which the representation of different professions within the scheme has changed over time is especially intriguing. In 1952 it was noted that existing plaques overwhelmingly commemorated figures 'distinguished in some branch of letters', statesmen, artists and scientists; no other group (medicine, music, architecture, exploration, etc.) was represented by more than ten plaques.[28] In 1983 the GLC could still note that the list of plaques was 'dominated by names from literature, the arts and politics; there are relatively few plaques to scientists and even fewer to those technical innovators who were at the centre of British economic development in the eighteenth and nineteenth centuries. Hardly any plaques relate to businessmen, unless they were also in politics or distinguished by their philanthropy'.[29] Before 1986 only one plaque commemorated a sports figure: that to W. G. Grace. This balance has already shifted noticeably in the past twenty years – the list of those honoured now includes engineers such as W. H. Barlow and J. H. Greathead, the businessman Harry Gordon Selfridge, popular musicians as diverse as Bert Ambrose and Jimi Hendrix and the football manager Herbert Chapman – and will no doubt continue to do so in the future.

As one might expect, politics has sometimes entered into decisions regarding commemoration, special weight being placed on figures who represented the views of the body administering the scheme at a given time. In 1966 the GLC reworked the 'twenty-year rule' to enable a plaque to be installed to Albert Mansbridge, a proposal made by the council's Chairman Sir Harold Shearman, and eleven years later broke the rule altogether in erecting a plaque to Herbert Morrison, a former leader of the LCC (see p. 18). On the other hand, the scheme has also been used as a way of changing political outlook and promoting social inclusion, drawing wider public attention to the historical importance of noteworthy women and figures from minority groups. While only four of the thirty-five plaques erected by the Society of Arts commemorated women – those to Mrs Sarah Siddons (lost through

demolition), JOANNA BAILLIE (fig. 16), ELIZABETH BARRETT BARRETT (see fig. 367) and FANNY BURNEY (see fig. 394) – the LCC made an early effort to redress the gender imbalance. The council installed its first plaque to a woman (also the first plaque in South London) – that commemorating the Wandsworth home of GEORGE ELIOT – in 1905, and continued to work concertedly in this area. Instead of waiting for the submission of nominations by the public, SIR LAURENCE GOMME took matters into his own hands in 1907, writing a paper on 'Notable Women' and presenting it to the Historical Records and Library Sub-Committee; it resulted in plaques to JENNY LIND (see fig. 234), MRS MARY GASKELL (see fig. 181) and Mary Somerville (see fig. 15), the last since lost through demolition. Similar initiatives have been taken ever since; for instance, a paper on women active in the suffrage movement was considered in 2000, and has resulted in

plaques to figures such as EMMELINE and DAME CHRISTABEL PANKHURST (see fig. 224).

The LCC first honoured a person from a non-white background in 1954, when a plaque was erected in Bow commemorating the stay of MAHATMA GANDHI; a plaque to MOHAMMED ALI JINNAH was installed in 1955 (see fig. 192), and plaques to RABINDRANATH TAGORE and LOKAMANYA TILAK followed in 1961. The council's successor, the GLC, was particularly active in this area, erecting plaques to figures including SAMUEL COLERIDGE-TAYLOR, Mary Seacole, RAM MOHUN ROY and SOLOMON T. PLAATJE. There are now over twenty-five plaques to black and Asian figures, including those to DR HAROLD MOODY (fig. 17), C. L. R. JAMES (see fig. 271), PAUL ROBESON, MAHARAJAH DULEEP SINGH and KWAME NKRUMAH. However, there is still much to be done in recognising London's great ethnic and cultural diversity; for example, as yet only two plaques honour figures from the Far East, those marking the homes of NATSUME SOSEKI and LAO SHE (see fig. 216).

It has been mentioned above that plaques, like other memorials, are a key means of promoting civic pride. Most perceive them as ornaments to London's buildings, and as points of interest and familiarity in an otherwise changing streetscape. In 1866 George Bartley – who had a hand in establishing the scheme under the Society of Arts – hoped that 'To travellers up and down in omnibuses, &c., [plaques] might sometimes prove an agreeable and instructive mode of beguiling a somewhat dull and not very rapid progress through the streets'.[30] LORD ROSEBERY, speaking at the unveiling of the plaque to the historian LORD MACAULAY – since lost through demolition – recalled the London thoroughfares he knew during his youth as being 'long wastes of yellow brick and dreary stucco in which we should have welcomed any relief to the eye', and felt that plaques 'take off the intolerable pressure of the monotony of endless streets' (fig. 18).[31] In this – as in all of its other roles – it is to be hoped that the scheme remains successful.

HISTORY

The Founding of the Plaques Scheme and the (Royal) Society of Arts (1866–1901)

The idea of a plaques scheme for London was first raised in the House of Commons on 17 July 1863 by

natural reaction was that the Metropolitan Board of Works would be an appropriate body to carry out such work. However, Ewart's idea was not met with full-hearted enthusiasm by William Francis Cowper MP, the First Commissioner of the Public Works. Although generally in support of a plaques scheme, he pointed out that 'it was the right of the owner or occupier of a house to write upon it what he pleased, and it might not be desirable to compel a man to place upon his house the name of a person who did not then live there'. Cowper added that 'Some persons liked to put their own names on a brass plate upon their doors, and might not wish to have the name of an eminent departed person also there. Some owners, too, might object to having the antiquity of their houses so prominently revealed, especially if they were thinking of selling them'.[33]

Despite these practical concerns, Ewart's idea quickly attracted interest and enthusiasm. Within a week of the MP's speech, HENRY COLE wrote to the *Journal of the Society of Arts* – of which he had served as Chairman – expressing his support, and suggesting that it was 'a proper subject for the Society of Arts to consider'. Cole went on to make recommendations about procedure:

> The Council [of the Society] might communicate with the owner or occupier of the premises, and, having obtained his concurrence, might, from its own funds, provide the necessary tablet, which, I should recommend, should not be a brass plate on the door, such as Mr Cowper hints at, but some kind of decorative tablet, which might be executed in terra cotta. It might also be ornamental, and of a character which would decorate the outside of any house, and therefore desirable for the occupier to have.[34]

The issue was quickly taken up in *The Builder*, which served as a platform for expressions of support and for proposals. Over the following years, correspondents to the journal suggested general guidelines – one writer hoped that the proposed tablets would 'be honourable to those who erect, and pleasant and suggestive to those who read' – while the idea of the Society of Arts being 'a very proper body to undertake the work' was further endorsed.[35]

Finally, in April 1866, the Society of Arts – founded in 1754 and given royal patronage in 1908 – gave in to

19   Workman Francis Drayton installing the plaque to William Ewart at 16 Eaton Place, Belgravia, in August 1963 – almost a hundred years after Ewart had risen in the House of Commons to propose the founding of what became the blue plaques scheme. [© PA Photos]

WILLIAM EWART (fig. 19), who proposed inscribing 'on those houses in London which have been inhabited by celebrated persons, the names of such persons'. For Ewart, 'The places which had been the residences of the ornaments of history could not but be precious to all thinking Englishmen'. He reminded the House 'how rich the metropolis was in such associations', and emphasised how desirable it was that 'some record should be placed upon the respective localities'.[32] The

pressure and appointed a committee 'to consider and report how the Society may promote the erection of statues or other memorials of persons eminent in Arts, Manufactures and Commerce', with particular reference to 'memorial tablets to deceased individuals'.[36] The committee was a distinguished body, including among its members the Chairman (Sir John Thwaites), Chief Engineer (Sir J. W. Bazalgette) and Architect (George Vulliamy) of the Metropolitan Board of Works. Also represented were the Chief Commissioner of Works William Cowper, the architects G. E. Street and P. C. Hardwick, and Henry Cole.

At its first meeting, on 7 May 1866, the committee considered a report by George C. T. Bartley – Cole's son-in-law and colleague at South Kensington – which effectively set down the general aims and parameters of the future plaques scheme. Bartley, later appointed 'convener', included a list of suggested nominees, including Benjamin Franklin, Lord Byron, David Garrick and James Boswell. This, he hoped, would give some idea of the vast potential, and the 'interesting matter' which the 'labels would make known'.[37] Like others, Bartley readily saw the potential of plaques as a conservation tool. He informed the committee that one of the scheme's benefits 'may be a tendency to increase the public estimation for places which have been the abodes of men who have made England what it is'.[38]

The details of the design of 'memorial tablets' were recommended (see pp. 24–25) and Bartley suggested that, in selecting the first few houses to be 'labelled', attention should be paid where possible to those situated in principal thoroughfares. The committee, meanwhile, recommended that tablets should honour both individuals eminent in arts, manufacture and commerce, and 'places and persons connected with historical events'.[39] The lists of names were, at first, to be provided by Bartley. At its meeting on 25 June 1866, the committee agreed the inscriptions of plaques to Lord Nelson, Sir Joshua Reynolds, Benjamin Franklin and Lord Byron. The plaque to Byron was the first erected under the scheme; it was in position at 24 Holles Street, Cavendish Square, Byron's birthplace, by February 1867. Sadly the house was demolished in about 1889, and it is now the plaque to Napoleon III, installed in King Street, St James's, by September 1867, that is the earliest to survive (fig. 20).

The Society of Arts continued the work of installing plaques until 1901, but did not operate a monopoly over plaques per se. As early as September 1867, the *Journal of the Society of Arts* relayed the society's desire to see plaques installed by others, 'either by corporate bodies or individuals', the society being 'happy to be instrumental in procuring suitable tablets from the manufacturers'.[40] In 1879 the society entered into an arrangement with the Corporation of the City of London, by which names were suggested by the society and plaques erected by the corporation. Although the process of nominating may have broken down quite early on, the demarcation – related to the jurisdictional independence of the City – has served ever since, and is the reason why plaques belonging to the official scheme are (with the exception of that honouring Dr Johnson) not to be found within the square mile. During the early decades of the twentieth century, the LCC was also excluded from installing plaques on the Grosvenor estate and the Bedford estate, the Duke of Westminster and the Duke of Bedford preferring their own plaques to those of the council.

21 The Society of Arts plaque to Michael Faraday at 48 Blandford Street, Marylebone, in an undated photograph, probably of the early twentieth century. [© City of London, LMA]

Benjamin Whitworth and H. D. Pochin, were willing to provide £50 for plaques. The 'donors' presented the society with a list of suggested names, given in order of priority.[41] The offer was accepted, and it is interesting to note that many of the fifteen suggestions made – for instance, Mrs Siddons, EDMUND BURKE (see fig. 453), DR JOHNSON (see fig. 71), THOMAS GAINSBOROUGH, SIR ROBERT WALPOLE and MICHAEL FARADAY (fig. 21) – resulted in early plaques. Algernon Ashton was another source of suggestions; his letters to the press urged the commemoration of figures including JOHN RUSKIN, CHARLES DICKENS (see fig. 64), BENJAMIN DISRAELI (see fig. 67) and THOMAS HOOD (see fig. 455), all commemorated with early plaques.[42]

In 1899 the great early champion of blue plaques – SIR LAURENCE GOMME, then Statistical Officer of the LCC – turned his attentions on the society's scheme. Even by that time, the scheme appears to have been remarkably popular – Gomme stated that the 'public press frequently draws attention to the subject'.[43] By 1901 thirty-five plaques had been erected by the Society of Arts – an average of one a year – of which only fifteen survive today; they honoured figures including JOHN RUSKIN, SIR ROWLAND HILL, W. M. THACKERAY, FANNY BURNEY, William Hogarth and GEORGE CRUIKSHANK. Although the society expressed itself 'perfectly ready and willing to carry on the work, and to bear the small expenses involved', it was acknowledged that 'the County Council, with its great organization and ample resources, can do work of this sort much better than any private institution'.[44] Gomme's recommendation was that the LCC, formed in 1889 on the abolition of the Metropolitan Board of Works, 'take up the matter systematically'; he expressed himself 'quite sure that a very valuable piece of work could in time be accomplished all over London'.[45] Following an approach to the Secretary of the Society of Arts, Sir Henry Trueman Wood, Gomme was able to report on 28 May 1900 that 'the Society would be likely to welcome this work being taken over by the Council'.[46] A formal agreement was entered into the following year, and the scheme duly transferred to the LCC in December 1901.

Little is known about the detailed working of the scheme under the Society of Arts. It is clear that there were procedures in place for the undertaking of research and the gaining of consents – the information transferred from the society to the LCC in 1901 included lists of cases for which permission had been refused and houses which could not be firmly identified – but the approach to suggestions was somewhat flexible. In 1872 the society was approached by a William Newmarch, who stated that two of his friends,

The London County Council (1901–65)

From the beginning, SIR LAURENCE GOMME (fig. 22) – who from 1900 to 1914 served as Clerk of the LCC –

was clear about the value and aim of plaques, and encouraged the body to see them as 'one of the most important matters in which the Council, under the powers of two Acts of Parliament authorising such work, can with advantage take action'.[47] By November 1901 the scheme was known as the Indication of Houses of Historical Interest in London, a name by which it remained known until at least the time of the Second World War (see fig. 11). In his speech at the unveiling of the first LCC plaque, installed in 1903 in honour of LORD MACAULAY, the council's first Chairman – LORD ROSEBERY – gave three reasons why the LCC undertook the work: first, that the tablets added to the amenities of London streets by calling attention to houses or places with interesting associations; second, that they provided a means of honouring famous Londoners or famous visitors to London; and third, that they could give accurate information about London history based on official records. Recalling these reasons in 1954, Sir Howard Roberts – Clerk of the LCC – felt them 'to be still valid', and added a fourth: 'the presence of a tablet can serve as an incentive to the preservation of a building of historical interest threatened with demolition'.[48]

In the LCC, the scheme gained a democratic base for the first time in its history, though the earliest con-

tenders for the council's plaques appear to have been drawn from a list of forty-nine houses, 'the residences of 32 individuals', supplied by the Society of Arts. Gomme reported that although the list had 'some remarkable omissions', it could 'be taken as a nucleus for the Council to work on'.[49] The list contained, amongst others, the names of JOSEPH BANKS, BENJAMIN DISRAELI, SAMUEL TAYLOR COLERIDGE, LORD MACAULAY, LORD PALMERSTON, SAMUEL PEPYS, PITT THE YOUNGER, ROBERT STEPHENSON and WILLIAM WILBERFORCE, all of whom were awarded plaques during the first two decades of the twentieth century.

As to the future means of canvassing nominations, Gomme recommended that 'a register should be kept of suggested houses, including therein any suggestions from members of the Council or the public press, or which might occur to myself or to the librarian in the course of investigations into the history of a particular locality'. Gomme suggested that 'until the Survey of London is at the Council's disposal for this among other purposes, a systematic investigation would probably be too laborious a proceeding for the object in view'.[50] A report of 1954 stated that the majority of suggestions had come in the past from 'private individuals, professional and learned societies, metropolitan borough councils, ambassadors or other representatives of foreign countries, etc.', although a number had come from members and officers of the LCC itself.[51] As Gomme had predicted, work on the Survey of London – associated with the LCC from 1910 and wholly taken over in 1952 – provided 'a systematic, if slow and piecemeal, topographical survey of houses with historical associations'.[52] Research resulted in plaques such as those to SAMUEL PEPYS and WILLIAM BLIGH, and the joint plaque to LILIAN BAYLIS and EMMA CONS, since lost through demolition. Like Gomme, Sir Howard Roberts felt the compilation of a complete list of famous Londoners – 'or, to approach it from the other angle, of a complete list of buildings which have formed the residences of famous persons' – would 'entail the expenditure of an unjustifiable amount of time of skilled technical staff', and would ultimately be impossible, as 'each generation of Londoners produces its own modicum of outstanding personalities'.[53]

Proposals for plaques, and related issues, were considered by a succession of different LCC committees, which met at the council's offices, firstly in Spring

Gardens, off Trafalgar Square, and from soon after the First World War at County Hall on the South Bank (see fig. 262). Initially, the Historical Records and Buildings Committee dealt with plaques; responsibility subsequently passed to groups including the Local Government (Records & Museums) Sub-Committee, the Parks Committee, the Town Planning Committee and the Planning and Communications Committee.

Although criteria for the plaques scheme were not formalised until 1954, there were general rules and regulations in place from an early date. Over the course of the scheme's history, only one plaque – that put up in 1867 to mark the home of Napoleon III (see figs 20 and 421) – has honoured a figure still living. In 1903 Lord Rosebery expressed his opinion that 'Celebrated dead persons should be . . . the limitation'. He reasoned that 'in the case of living persons of any public note, [a plaque] might induce crowds hostile or friendly to congregate round their houses, and disturb the repose and seclusion of many eminent and titled men'.[54] Draft regulations set down in 1903 proposed that no tablet be erected within twenty-five years of death. After debate, the relevant committee decided not to adopt any hard and fast lines regarding plaques until further experience had been gained; each case was to be dealt with on its merits. However, in 1912 there is a reference to what remains known as the 'twenty-year rule', and by 1947 a report could state that 'it has not generally been the practice to erect a memorial tablet to any person within twenty years of his death'.[55] Exceptions were, however, made in cases where figures were of undoubted distinction: plaques erected to figures not yet dead for twenty years included those to W. E. Gladstone (installed 1908), John Ruskin (1909), T. H. Huxley (1910) and Earl Roberts (1922).

The draft regulations of 1903 also proposed that no person be commemorated by more than one tablet. Thirty years later, the Clerk of the LCC wrote, 'Although it is not usual for the Council to commemorate more than one residence of any individual, this has been done in fifteen instances, generally (though not exclusively) in the case of persons of exceptional distinction'.[56] The figures who were bracketed in this category included Charles Dickens, W. E. Gladstone, D. G. Rossetti and Joseph Chamberlain, who were each commemorated with three plaques. The rule that only one plaque could be awarded per

person was made formal in 1954, though it is interesting to note that as late as 1977 a second plaque to an exceptional individual was considered, as long as it led 'to an increase in the number of plaques in outer boroughs and where the claims of the second address for commemoration are particularly strong'.[57]

Despite the LCC's emphasis on houses of historical interest, there were instances when plaques were placed on sites formerly occupied by the residences of famous or eminent individuals. The council seems always to have known that the practice was open to question; it resulted in a tirade of abuse from the correspondent Algernon Ashton, who asserted that plaques 'intentionally placed on wrong houses' made his 'blood boil'.[58] In relation to the re-erection of the plaque to John Dryden on a new building, Ashton wrote, 'It is an insane practice, and ought to be stopped forthwith, as it only tends to entirely mislead future generations, who will naturally believe these houses to be the actual historical ones'.[59] When an LCC officer pointed out that supplementary tablets were often added recording the history of building and plaque (see fig. 25), Ashton was still not appeased; 'to my mind', he wrote, 'this later tablet is just as absurd as the replacing of the old one'.[60] In 1903, with regard to the re-erection of the plaque to James Boswell, yet another writer complained that the LCC's 'crass folly and abject stupidity . . . in affixing memorial tablets to recently-constructed edifices are as apparent to the merest child as to the ordinary common-sense man', and hoped that they would 'repent of their folly, and not do anything so palpably incongruous in the future'.[61]

Perhaps with the words of these critics in mind, the LCC made an effort to create a different design for both 'site of residence' and 'historic site' plaques, signifying their separate purpose. Those commemorating Bow Street (see fig. 347), The Theatre (see fig. 147), William Wilberforce (see fig. 310) and Samuel Pepys and other residents of 14 Buckingham Street (fig. 23) take the form of rectangular tablets – as did that to Strype Street, Whitechapel, erected in 1929 and since lost through demolition (fig. 24) – while that on the site of Tyburn, first installed in 1909, was originally triangular. Especially notable is the plaque installed in 1922 in memory of the sixteenth-century navigators who set sail from Ratcliff; a series of tiles bearing coloured ships in sail, it was designed by the LCC's architect, G. Topham-Forrest (see fig. 291).

23   The LCC generally used rectangular tablets to signify sites of residence and sites of historic significance. An example is this plaque to Samuel Pepys and other residents of 14 Buckingham Street, south of the Strand. Erected in 1908, it is made up of a series of tiles crafted by Minton, Hollins & Co. [© English Heritage. Photograph by Derek Kendall]

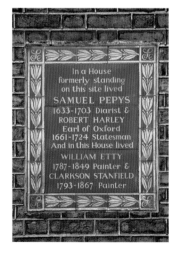

and JAMES BOSWELL (see figs 146 and 466) – it essentially began at this date, ushering in a phase during which a series of new plaques were placed on sites of residences. These commemorated figures such as SIR JOSHUA REYNOLDS (installed 1947), THOMAS EARNSHAW (1948), JOSEPH NOLLEKENS (1954) and FLORENCE NIGHTINGALE (1955) (fig. 26).

It was partly with this change in mind that formal selection criteria were set down and approved in 1954, though the move was also related to a larger reorganisation of the LCC's historical work at the time, possibly precipitated by the council taking over full control of the Survey of London. In his report to the Town Planning Committee, Sir Howard Roberts wrote that in recent years he had witnessed 'a subtle but definite shifting of emphasis from the idea of indicating houses and places of historical interest to that of honouring famous individuals'. He suggested this change be corrected, and emphasised the reasons why the practice of marking sites was undesirable. By seeing 'the actual residence of a well-known person', Roberts stated, the passer-by 'would gain some knowledge of the architecture prevalent in that person's time and of the background against which he lived'. He asserted that it was 'much more difficult to justify the erection of a commemorative plaque on a large modern block of flats or offices stating that X lived there in the 17th, 18th or 19th century. In effect, the plaque becomes a substitute for a statue or memorial'.[63] Roberts recommended that as a general rule plaques were not to be placed on the sites of former residences, and that more consideration was to be given to the intrinsic interest of the house being marked, a policy which was agreed by the committee. Since 1954 only twelve site plaques have been erected: five of these replace plaques which marked the original structures pre-demolition (for instance, those to CHARLES DARWIN, SAMUEL TAYLOR COLERIDGE and CAPTAIN JAMES COOK), and five commemorate buildings or events of historic interest (such as SCOTLAND YARD, MILLBANK PRISON and the founding of the FABIAN SOCIETY); the final two – commemorating WILLIAM CASLON and EDWARD GIBBON – can only be ascribed to momentary lapses on the part of the LCC.

In his report of 1954, Roberts sought also to formalise the twenty-year rule, which had been applied inconsistently; he pointed out that 'a number of plaques have been erected to persons who have but recently died', including those to JOHN BURNS, JOHN

24   Another example of the LCC's rectangular series of plaques, used to mark sites of historic interest. This white rectangular tablet – shown in a photograph of 1929 – commemorated the associations of Strype Street, Whitechapel, but was lost through demolition. [© City of London, LMA]

However, for a relatively brief period, the aims and rules of the scheme became confused. On account of war damage and high rates of demolition, the LCC found that a number of its plaques were without homes, and adopted a standard procedure of re-erecting them on the buildings which replaced the originals, together with rectangular supplementary tablets explaining their history. Examples of such plaques include those to SIR ISAAC NEWTON (fig. 25), JOHN HUNTER and LORD PALMERSTON (in Carlton Gardens). In 1938 the LCC decided that the practice should cease, and that 'the Clerk of the Council should report in each case on the question of fixing a new tablet on the new building'.[62] Although this approach had already been followed in a few instances – for example, in the case of the plaques to DANIEL DEFOE

Right 25   For a time, the LCC adopted the procedure of re-erecting plaques on the sites of the buildings they had once adorned, together with supplementary tablets explaining their history. An example is the plaque to Sir Isaac Newton, re-installed in 1915 at 87 Jermyn Street, St James's. [© English Heritage. Photograph by Derek Kendall]

Above 26   A brief period of commemorating with roundels the sites of the residences of notable people resulted in plaques such as that to Florence Nightingale, erected in 1955 at 10 South Street, Mayfair. It was such cases that led to the formalisation of selection criteria in 1954, which ended the practice of marking sites. [© English Heritage. Photograph by Derek Kendall]

Right 27   Notes made in c.1908 by an LCC historian using rate books to elucidate Napoleon III's supposed residence in Circus Road, St John's Wood. [Reproduced by permission of English Heritage]

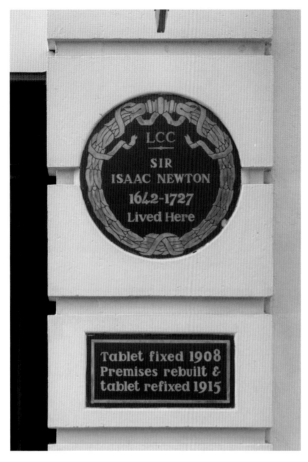

popular, as opposed to famous, figures – an interesting distinction – he recommended 'an even longer lapse of time than 20 years after death before reaching a decision'; the duration of fifty years was mentioned, though does not seem to have been formalised.[64] The suggested criteria were approved in October 1954, and were later adopted with only minor changes by the GLC and English Heritage.

A huge quantity of surviving paperwork, together with designs and photographs, reflects the vast amount of work the LCC dedicated to the plaques scheme. The research notes made during the first half of the twentieth century are meticulous, often including sketches of renumbering plans and – as a matter of course – detailed analyses of rate books and directories (fig. 27). Such research was overseen throughout the LCC's administration by the Clerk of the Council. Those closely involved in the daily work of the scheme included the staff of the council's library division. In 1953 it was noted that the business of the plaques scheme 'involves quite an amount of labour, amounting now to about $2/3$ of a historical research assistant's time'.[65] Especially significant was Miss Ida Darlington, who joined the LCC as a historical research assistant in 1926, was later Head of the LCC Record Office and Library and was active until the mid-1960s; in addition to her involvement with blue plaques, Ida Darlington worked for twenty years on the Survey of London.

The practice of holding unveiling ceremonies, usually organised by third parties and overseen by LCC staff, seems to date back to 1903. In May of that year, the council considered a paper on 'ceremonial precedents',

GALSWORTHY, JOHN LOGIE BAIRD, GUGLIELMO MARCONI, MAHATMA GANDHI and SIR FLINDERS PETRIE. For Roberts, the rule allowed 'a breathing space in which a man's reputation and achievement can be considered dispassionately', and he strongly recommended that figures who had not been dead for twenty years should be ineligible for consideration. In addition, Roberts recommended the setting down of rules by which a figure's significance could be measured. He pointed out that 'The Dictionary of Biography casts its net too wide to be of much use for this purpose', and suggested three pointers: '(a) that it is a *sine qua non* that the person should be recognised by members of his own profession or in his own sphere as being of outstanding eminence in his own life . . . (b) that he should have made some important and positive contribution to the welfare or happiness of humanity; (c) that his name should be known to the man in the street of the succeeding generation'. With regard to the last, Roberts acknowledged that there were instances when a figure might be more significant than well known, and that these should still be viewed favourably. For

which included an account of the unveiling of a plaque to WILLIAM PITT THE ELDER in Bath in 1899.[66] The ceremony, involving a 'curtain concealing the tablet' and the 'pulling of the cord', was performed by LORD ROSE-BERY, who was, interestingly, also responsible for unveiling the LCC's first plaque in November 1903. Although many plaques continued to be installed without fanfare, unveiling ceremonies became increasingly regular over the next sixty years. It was standard practice, by at least the 1950s, for plaques to be covered with a Union Jack which was then pulled away; this tradition continued until about the late 1970s (fig. 28). Until the time of the Second World War, leaflets were issued at every unveiling (indeed, at the installation of any plaque), detailing the story of person and house. These were published, two or three together, in booklet form (see fig. 11).[67]

The abolition of the LCC in 1965 marked the end of an era, not least for blue plaques. The council's sixty-four years as administrators of the scheme – it was run continuously, with the exception of the periods 1915–19 and 1940–47 – saw the installation of 268 plaques, a third of which were erected over the last twelve years of the council's life. It was the LCC that formulated the scheme's aims and procedures, both for research and administration, created fixed selection criteria,

designed the blue plaque as we know it today and gave the scheme its international profile. It is on this foundation that all later work has been built.

The Greater London Council (1965–86)

By early 1965 responsibility for what were by then familiarly known as 'blue plaques' had passed to the Planning and Communications Committee of the GLC. The council was formally informed of its inheritance of the scheme on 11 May 1965, and – having installed four plaques handed over by the LCC – erected its first plaque, that to SIR JOHN LAVERY, on 1 June 1966. At the outset, the GLC re-emphasised the primary purpose of plaques: 'to mark buildings or places with interesting associations, not to commemorate famous people'.[68] At its first meeting, the GLC committee noted that 'Suggestions for the erection of plaques come from many sources and will be considered on their merits'.[69] In order to ensure a consistent approach, certain principles were adopted; these followed, more or less exactly, the selection criteria operated by the LCC, including the twenty-year rule, the limitation of one plaque per person and the ruling out of 'sites of former houses'. Suggestions for plaques in the City of London continued to be referred to the City Corporation. Administrative processes were also much as before: 'If it is decided to erect a plaque, the consent of the owner, of the occupier and of any other person with an interest in the premises concerned will be sought before any publicity is given to the decision and before a design is prepared'.[70] The Historic Buildings Sub-Committee was authorised to deal with proposals for plaques, the council simply substituted its own name for that of the LCC on the plaque design, and matters carried on as before (fig. 29).

Under pressure from the public, the GLC put considerable vigour into its defence of the principle of non-commemoration of sites. Emphasis was given to the educational role of plaques, which was considered to be undermined when a building had been demolished. It was also noted that the scale of modern redevelopment schemes restricted the possibilities of erecting plaques on sites. A paper of 1967 stated, 'In the 1920s and 1930s new development was in the main confined to the erection of new buildings on the old building plots. Present-day schemes often involve large areas in which the old street lines are obliterated and the new

GREATER LONDON COUNCIL

SIR
GERALD
DU MAURIER
1873~1934
ACTOR~MANAGER
lived here from
1916
until his death

large blocks bear little or no relation to the position of former houses'.[71] At one point, the council considered operating a separate plaques scheme, under which sites could be commemorated by a different form of tablet, but this came to nothing.

One criterion that was relaxed by the GLC for a time was the twenty-year rule. In 1966 a suggestion made by the GLC's Chairman that a plaque be awarded to ALBERT MANSBRIDGE – who died in 1952 – precipitated a debate about the rule. An analysis of the plaques erected between 1950 and 1965 showed that twelve exceptions had been made (out of 177 plaques erected), and it was therefore decided that in future the qualifying period be reduced to ten years from death. This allowed the commemoration of three figures; MANSBRIDGE, SIR MAX BEERBOHM and SIR HARRY LAUDER. Three years later, in 1969, the principles were considered once again. No record of the discussion has survived, but the decision of the Historic Buildings Board – members of which included Sir John Betjeman and Sir John Summerson – was unequivocal: that the twenty-year rule be reinstated, with the addition of the words 'without exception'. It was, however, breached one final time, in order to allow the installation of a plaque in 1977 to HERBERT MORRISON.

By 1971 officers could comment on 'the great practical usefulness' of the twenty-year rule, but recommended that some relaxation of the criterion might be desirable in the case of a person of indisputable fame and of exceptional longevity, so that they could be commemorated after the centenary of their birth had passed. This amendment was adopted and the 'centenary provision' essentially took on its present form at that date. Meanwhile – for reasons that are now unclear – it was made more difficult for overseas visitors to be awarded plaques. Special principles were established for such cases; among other things, the proposed person could not be commemorated until fifty years after death, the better to assess the durability of his or her reputation. This criterion resulted in the rejection of figures such as the theologian and anti-fascist Dietrich Bonhoeffer, who died in 1945 and was thrown out by the GLC in May 1975. In October of that year, the Historic Buildings Board reconsidered this area of the criteria, with the result that fifty years from death was reduced to the standard twenty.

A report of 1984, by which time the burden of the work was handled by the historians' section of the Historic Buildings Division (Architect's Department), set out the various stages of the plaques scheme. It shows that procedures remained much the same as those followed by the LCC, and as those which are in operation today. The key difference during the GLC's tenure was that initial proposals joined 'a growing queue which receives attention at irregular intervals', historians being able to deal with cases only sporadically.[72] There were possible delays of up to eighteen months at this stage. Once reports had been written, proposals for plaques were considered by the Historic Buildings Board. It was noted that it was difficult to predict the amount of time required for each stage; experience had shown that it was rarely possible 'even when all circumstances are favourable, to complete all the processes in less than 9 months from suggestion to final erection'.[73] For the year 1977, it was recorded that around sixty suggestions for plaques had been made, more than a quarter from GLC members, and that an average of 55 per cent of cases had been shortlisted. The same year saw the installation of more than twenty plaques, then a record number for the scheme. While the LCC had erected a maximum of eighteen (in 1959) and an average of around six plaques per year, the GLC installed a minimum of five (in 1965–66 and 1970–71) and an average of twelve per year.

The outlay of staff time remained high during the GLC's administration. As before, plaques work was overseen by the Clerk's (later Director-General's) Department, in collaboration with the Architect's

FREDERICK GEORGE CREED and CLEMENT ATTLEE. The council – led by the Labour MP Ken Livingstone from 1981 to 1986 – also made a conscious effort to broaden representation, especially after January 1984, when concern was expressed about 'the extent to which the scheme endorses conventional views of who should be commemorated, and fails to reflect the current political priorities of the Council'.[74] Persons commemorated who perhaps more nearly represented those priorities include SYLVIA PANKHURST, VINAYAK DAMODAR SAVARKAR and SIR JACK HOBBS, all awarded plaques in 1985–86. The GLC was also active in commemorating sites of historical significance, such as ALEXANDRA PALACE, SCOTLAND YARD (fig. 30) and COUNTY HALL.

ENGLISH HERITAGE AND THE WORKING OF THE BLUE PLAQUES SCHEME

In April 1986, on the abolition of the GLC, the plaques scheme – then comprising 530 plaques – passed to English Heritage, formally known as the Historic Buildings and Monuments Commission for England. The continuance of this aspect of the GLC's work was permitted under Schedule 2 of the Local Government Act of 1985. It was noted that the selection criteria of 1954, with their various amendments, 'have proved their value', and they were adopted with only minor change; the twenty-year rule and the policy of not commemorating sites were both later reconsidered but, after discussion, were retained.[75] The transfer of responsibility included many of the staff who had previously worked on the scheme. Additionally, English Heritage agreed to put up five plaques which had been left in the GLC's offices on 31 March 1986. As to the installation of new plaques, eighteen per year was set as a reasonable target. The first English Heritage plaque, commemorating the artist OSKAR KOKOSCHKA, was installed on 6 August 1986.

Today, English Heritage receives about a hundred suggestions for blue plaques each year, nearly all of which come from members of the general public. It is a tribute to the popularity of the scheme that suggestions come not only from London but also from the rest of the British Isles and even from Europe, America and further afield. Proposers include experts in particular fields, members of professional and learned societies,

Department, which was responsible for the design, positioning, installation and maintenance of plaques. In 1974 responsibility for the whole scheme passed to the Architect's Department, which included the Historic Buildings Division. Following the retirement of Ida Darlington in the mid-1960s, the bulk of the work on blue plaques passed to a succession of members of GLC staff, including Arthur Percival, Victor Belcher, John Phillips, John Earl and Frank Kelsall, the last of whom saw through the transition of the scheme from the council to English Heritage. Notable assistance was provided by Miss E. Doris Mercer, Head Archivist of the GLC during the 1960s and 1970s.

Although, as has been seen, the GLC generally followed the procedures set down by its predecessor, it made great strides in certain areas. What stands out most is the council's achievement in widening the range of figures and buildings commemorated. Geographically, the GLC covered a broader area than its predecessor, which had been focused solely on central London boroughs. The GLC took on what was, for the plaques scheme, uncharted territory – for instance, Richmond, Croydon and Redbridge – erecting plaques including those to DAVID GARRICK, J. M. W. TURNER, LEONARD and VIRGINIA WOOLF, SIR ARTHUR CONAN DOYLE,

31 The plaque to Sir Nigel Gresley is one of comparatively few that commemorate places of work. It was erected on the Pancras Road side of King's Cross Station in 1997. [© English Heritage]

32 The selection criteria allow for the commemoration of figures whose names may not be widely known, but who nonetheless deserve national recognition. For example, David Edward Hughes, the inventor of the microphone. Hughes's three-nail microphone shown here dates from c.1878, and was so sensitive that it could detect a fly's footstep. [© Science Museum / Science & Society Picture Library]

relatives of a suggested person and individuals who own or occupy a house once lived in by a notable historical figure. Proposals are occasionally inspired by significant anniversaries or other commemorative events; the plaque to the Greek poet GEORGE SEFERIS, for example, was installed during the centenary of his birth.

All proposals that meet the basic selection criteria are considered by English Heritage's Blue Plaques Panel. This panel was formed in 1989 as the Commemorative Plaques Working Group, in order to ease the burden of work handled by the London Advisory Committee, which previously considered suggestions. The panel's original members included the historians David Starkey and Professor F. M. L. Thompson, and it was chaired for six years by the conservationist William ('Willie') Bell, who had previously chaired the Historic Buildings Board of the GLC and was a member of English Heritage's London Advisory Committee. Subsequent chairmen of the panel have included Francis Carnwath, former Deputy-Director of the Tate Gallery, the broadcaster and writer Loyd Grossman and the historian David Cannadine. The panel is composed so as to bring a variety of expertise to bear on the consideration of cases; members have included the actor and writer Stephen Fry, the historian Celina Fox, the writer and critic A. N. Wilson, the architectural historian Gavin Stamp and the Poet Laureate Andrew Motion.

On average, around a third of all suggestions are shortlisted (that is, approved pending detailed research). No quota system is operated, which means that there is often a quantity of detailed ('final') research waiting to be carried out. Where a proposal is rejected, ten years must elapse before the nominated person can be reconsidered. Sometimes – especially where a person has only recently died, even though their centenary may have passed – it pays to wait a little longer before agreeing to a plaque, ensuring that a person's name and reputation will stand the test of time. Figures to have been rejected in the past – and later commemorated – include WILKIE COLLINS, SYLVIA PLATH and EZRA POUND.

Selection Criteria

The scheme is governed by selection criteria, the history and development of which have already been discussed (see pp. 14–16). In order to be eligible for consideration, a person must have been dead for twenty years or have passed the centenary of their birth, whichever is the earlier. This delay allows a person's reputation to mature and ensures that their fame is long-lasting. Crucially, a building associated with them must survive largely unaltered, and must be visible from the public highway. English Heritage abides by this rule without exception, though consideration may be given to cases where reconstructed buildings present an exact facsimile frontage on the identical site. The nominated building is most often a residence, but significant places of work are sometimes also suggested. Plaques commemorating workplaces include those to OCTAVIA HILL, FRANCES MARY BUSS, NANCY MITFORD and SIR NIGEL GRESLEY (fig. 31). Unless a case is deemed exceptional, plaques are not erected on educational or ecclesiastical buildings, or Inns of Court. Whitehall (so rich in historical association) and the City of London (where an active plaques scheme is run by the City of London Corporation) are ruled out completely. The practice of installing plaques on gateposts – long considered a last resort – was formally excluded under the criteria in 2006.

In order to be approved for a plaque, nominated figures must meet the following criteria. They should:

- be regarded as eminent by a majority of members of their own profession or calling
- have made an important positive contribution to human welfare or happiness
- have resided in London for a significant period, in time or in importance, within their life and work
- have had such exceptional and outstanding personalities that the well-informed passer-by immediately recognises their names

  or

- deserve national recognition

The last point allows for people such as inventors and pioneers, whose names are not necessarily well known to the public at large but who are of key historical significance. Examples include DAVID EDWARD HUGHES, the inventor of the microphone (fig. 32), and ADA, COUNTESS OF LOVELACE, the pioneer of computing. In the case of overseas visitors, candidates should be of international reputation and should have spent a significant period in London, either in time or importance. Although famous people may have moved house regularly, it should be noted that only one plaque is allowed per person. Much thought is therefore given to establishing which address was most important to the life and work of a subject.

From time to time, plaques are put up to commemorate famous buildings and historical events, though these have to be of outstanding significance in order to be approved. In all, the scheme includes just over fifteen such plaques, including those honouring the ADELPHI, the RED HOUSE, ALEXANDRA PALACE, the first flight of the AVRO No. 1 TRIPLANE, COUNTY HALL and the founding of the PRE-RAPHAELITE BROTHERHOOD. The term 'historical site', as set down in the selection criteria, was interpreted flexibly – particularly by the GLC – leading to plaques such as those to SCOTLAND YARD, the FABIAN SOCIETY and the first FLYING BOMB on London. Today, a building must – as with a residence or workplace – be the original structure in which the work or event occurred.

Research

Research has always underpinned the work of the blue plaques scheme; it ensures accuracy and an upholding of standards, and is undertaken by professional historians who have a specialist knowledge of both architecture and biography. Two levels of research are carried out: the first focuses on a nominated figure's achievements and lasting significance, and leads to a so-called 'preliminary report', which forms the basis for the Blue Plaques Panel's initial recommendation. Where appropriate, experts in the relevant subject area are consulted, largely with the aim of establishing whether a suggested figure is indeed considered eminent by others of their profession or calling. The second level of research, carried out only for those cases shortlisted for commemoration, focuses on a person's various addresses and their significance within a person's life and work, and results in a 'final report'. Typically, a historian will consult primary sources such as rate books (see fig. 27), post office directories, electoral registers, census returns, letters, journals, autobiographies, historic maps, plans and photographs, and certificates of birth, marriage and death.

Particular care is taken when identifying residences with surviving buildings; as this book demonstrates, a great many of London's streets have been renamed and renumbered at various times. Such changes have to be carefully unpicked and analysed, or mistakes can easily be made. Experience has shown that errors can have serious implications. For instance, the house of BENJAMIN FRANKLIN in Craven Street, Charing Cross, was identified in the 1860s as number 7. Before SIR LAURENCE GOMME showed that the Society of Arts had commemorated the wrong building – Franklin did indeed live at 7 Craven Street, but the house had subsequently been renumbered as 36 – there were plans to turn number 7 (the imposter) into a museum. It is likely that, were it not for Gomme's additional research, the museum would have been created, and might even have continued to exist to this day.

Although, at the initial stage, each proposer is required to give evidence of at least one surviving building, a process of research, identification and selection is always undertaken. As has been stated, only one plaque can be awarded per person, which means that a historian has to consider a number of factors in choosing the building to be commemorated: how long a person lived in a house, the importance of this period to a person's life and work (naturally, birthplaces and places of death have special resonance), and the physical setting and integrity of the building concerned. Often, a favourite emerges quite quickly: it may be that a house was a person's home for much of their life, or is the only one of their residences to survive in London. In order to select one building, a process of elimination is usually required; other residences may be of lesser duration, may be out of sight from the public way and may have been altered or even demolished. Where all of a person's home addresses have gone, or have been ruled out, then attention may turn towards places of work. On rare occasions, it may be found that there are no addresses suitable for commemoration; this has proved the case, for instance, with the writer and pioneer of inoculation Lady Mary Wortley Montagu, the scientist Sir Humphry Davy, the artist Sir Edwin Landseer and the writer and artist Beatrix Potter.

In selecting an address for commemoration, the pre-existence of a plaque commemorating another individual does not work as a deterrent, though in no instance have more than two blue plaques been placed on a single property. It is, perhaps, rather remarkable that of London's 800 plaques only about ten pairings exist, including those to R. B. SHERIDAN and GENERAL JOHN BURGOYNE in Mayfair (see fig. 396), HILAIRE BELLOC and WALTER GREAVES in Chelsea (fig. 33), THOMAS WAKLEY and THOMAS HODGKIN in Bloomsbury (see fig.

33 Pairings of blue plaques are surprisingly rare. These two, commemorating Walter Greaves and Hilaire Belloc, were both erected on 3 July 1973 at 104 Cheyne Walk, Chelsea. [© English Heritage. Photograph by Derek Kendall]

48) and Andres Bello and Francisco de Miranda in Fitzrovia (see fig. 83). Where a link between a person and a building is already explicit – for instance, due to the presence of a museum, a private plaque or other record – a blue plaque may be deemed unnecessary.

The outlay of time and effort required by this part of the research process, which leads to a 'final report', is unpredictable. Some notable historical figures lived at a surprising number of houses; Agatha Christie, for example, lived in at least seven different buildings in London, nearly all of which survive. Where too much choice can therefore be a problem in some cases, insufficient information is an impediment in others. Overseas visitors are an especially challenging subject of research, since they are almost invariably not listed in directories, electoral registers and other such sources. Historians have sometimes had to feel their way with clues, relying on scraps of information. Today, English Heritage insists that a connection between a person and a building be clearly documented, even where the dates of residence are somewhat unclear.

Once a building has been selected, the historian considers the plaque's inscription. The final report will include a recommended wording – to be discussed by the Blue Plaques Panel – and a recommended position, though both may require amendment following consultation with house owners and occupiers. There are standard procedures for both of these elements: inscriptions will usually end with 'lived here in x–x', 'was born here' or 'lived and died here', though alternatives may be considered in special cases. In terms of positioning, plaques are usually placed – where possible – at ground-floor level. If a person lived in a flat, either in a house or a block, then the plaque will be placed as close as possible to the relevant area of residence, while not compromising visibility. A building's design and symmetry is, however, always borne in mind, and may necessitate adaptation.

Administration

Once research has been finalised, and a report has been approved by the Blue Plaques Panel, a case enters the administrative side of the blue plaques process. The installation of any plaque requires the consent of the relevant house owner and occupier. Where a building is listed, Listed Building Consent is also necessary, as plaques are rightly considered to represent a permanent alteration to a building's appearance. Once installed, they tend to remain. In only one known instance has a house owner requested that a plaque be removed: this was the case of Karl Marx, whose final address, 41 Maitland Park Road, Chalk Farm, was commemorated in 1935; shortly afterwards, following repeated vandalism, the plaque was taken down.

The consent process is handled in two stages: first, outline consent is sought in principle; if this is granted, a house owner is then asked to consider the plaque design and proposed position before giving final approval. As this part of the plaques process relies entirely on the goodwill of building owners, it is extremely unpredictable. Although most are happy for plaques to be erected, there are instances when owners refuse to give their consent. Their reasons vary: some do not wish attention to be drawn to their properties, while others are not in sympathy with the nature of the person suggested for commemoration. Where an owner refuses to allow the installation of a plaque, there is no option but to close a case, hoping that it might be reopened in the future. Examples of plaques now installed, but which originally met with resistance, include those to Lord Clive, Edward Gibbon and D. G. Rossetti.

When considering where a plaque should be placed on a building, the ability of the fabric to hold the plaque is carefully assessed. In rare cases, it is decided that a plaque might adversely affect the architectural integrity of a particular building. Under these circum-

stances, an alternative address is sought or a surface-mounted plaque might be considered, as was the case with 15 Poland Street, Soho, the home of PERCY BYSSHE SHELLEY. Once all consents have been gained, the plaque is ordered from one of English Heritage's manufacturers, and is normally ready within two months. Standard plaques are set into the fabric of the building, flush with the wall face, by one of English Heritage's specialist contractors (see figs 2 and 494). The costs of plaque manufacture and installation are borne entirely by English Heritage.

Plaques are often unveiled, events which are organised by a third party – such as the original proposer – with assistance from English Heritage. Unveiling ceremonies may be attended by the family, friends and colleagues of the person being commemorated; they are always enjoyable occasions, and can be emotional ones too. Some ceremonies attract a great deal of publicity, owing to the popularity of the person being honoured and/or the individual performing the unveiling. The unveiling of the plaque to JIMI HENDRIX was one of the most notable events of its type; the eastern end of Brook Street, Mayfair, was closed, allowing a huge crowd of invitees and onlookers to watch as the cord was pulled by Pete Townshend of The Who and Hendrix's co-band member Noel Redding. Others who have performed unveilings over the last hundred years include: the 5TH EARL OF ROSEBERY (LORD MACAULAY); Queen Elizabeth, The Queen Mother (P. G. WODEHOUSE; GENERAL CHARLES DE GAULLE); SYBIL THORNDIKE (SIR PHILIP BEN GREET; see fig. 263); Harold Wilson (WALTER BAGEHOT); KWAME NKRUMAH (LOKAMANYA TILAK; fig. 34); Margaret Thatcher (NANCY ASTOR); John Gielgud (EDITH EVANS); SIR ARTHUR BLISS (RALPH VAUGHAN WILLIAMS); Neil Kinnock (CLEMENT ATTLEE; see fig. 508); Sir John Mills (VIVIEN LEIGH); John Cleese (SIGMUND FREUD); Nelson Mandela (RUTH FIRST and JOE SLOVO; see fig. 72); Roy Hudd (WILL HAY; BUD FLANAGAN); Damon Hill (GRAHAM HILL); Alan Bennett (WILLIAM ROBERTS) and Charles, Prince of Wales (the EARL AND COUNTESS OF MOUNTBATTEN; see fig. 318).

Owing to the care and rigour that goes into each stage of the scheme, it generally takes between two and six years to progress from initial suggestion to plaque installation. In rare cases, where difficulties arise, the process may take even longer. However, once a plaque is up, it has the capacity to last for hundreds of years.

Aside from the process of installing new plaques, English Heritage is also responsible for the maintenance and promotion of the existing plaques detailed in this book. As a part of living buildings, they are naturally subject to change, a process which needs to be carefully monitored. As a result of architectural alterations, plaques may be moved or taken down altogether. In cases of demolition, a fresh process of research is carried out in the hope of identifying an alternative address at which the plaque can be placed. In the absence of any surviving buildings associated with a person, plaques are either offered to relevant museums or bodies – those commemorating Mrs Sarah Siddons and W. C. Macready form part of the collections of the Victoria and Albert Museum, for example – or are added to English Heritage's small collection.

DESIGN AND MANUFACTURE

The design of commemorative tablets was one of the first issues considered by the special committee of the Society of Arts. At its first meeting, on 7 May 1866, George Bartley – later the committee's convener – submitted a report asserting that tablets should 'differ as far as is possible from monumental or funeral tablets, as the public would certainly not like or tolerate the chief thoroughfares being converted into streets of tombs of a cheap and modern style'. In terms of practicalities, 'imperishability and ease in cleaning from deposits of soot, &c.' formed essential elements, as did moderate cheapness. Bartley suggested the inclusion of mosaic – 'either a plain polished marble or red granite slab, with an ornamental border of mosaic, or perhaps mosaic letters and a gold background with geometric border of the same material' – but made no prescriptions on the subject.[76]

Bartley felt the matter of inscription to be one of importance, stating that 'it appears to me that all terms of praise, or otherwise, should be omitted, and merely the plain statement of the facts given, consisting of names – for what celebrated – and dates of birth and death. The whole to be as concise and distinct as possible, to enable all who run to read'. The height of the tablets on the façade of a building was to be 'settled by circumstances, but should generally be . . . about 12 or 14 feet [3.6 or 4.2 m] from the ground'.[77]

In the end, the society decided to hold a competition for the design of its tablets, the winning entry to be offered a premium of £10. Tablets were to be 'capable of being executed in terra cotta, iron, or other enduring material', and were not to exceed in dimensions three feet (91.4 cm). They were to allow room for an inscription along the following lines: 'This tablet is erected to record that A. B. inventor, or, sculptor, painter (as the case may be) was born, lived or died (as the case may be) in this house. Placed by the Society of Arts 1866'.[78] The committee recommended that experiments with various types of tablets be made, and that 'designs be produced for that purpose'.[79] On these tablets was to be inscribed concise information relative to the individual or the fact commemorated, and the name of the Society of Arts.

In June 1866 the committee was presented with a specimen tablet and asked that four others be made according to this prototype, which seems to have been a roundel of encaustic ware. It was resolved that 'on every tablet be recorded the name, profession or occupation, date of birth and death and reason for placing the tablet'.[80] By February 1867, the first tablets had been made – by Minton, Hollins & Co. – and that to Lord Byron had been installed. Clearly, there was some initial experimentation; in June 1868 it was reported that progress in installing certain tablets had been delayed due to 'experiments in the manufacturing, which Messrs. Minton, Hollins, & Co., have been making'.[81]

However, on the whole, the design of the Society of Arts's plaques remained consistent throughout its administration of the scheme. They were – with one exception (an oblong plaque to John Milton) – roundels of encaustic ware, and were typically chocolate-brown in hue (fig. 35). Blue was used for the first plaques, those to Lord Byron and NAPOLEON III (see fig. 20), but the manufacturers found it 'difficult to produce tablets in that colour'.[82] Inscriptions were, as had been set out by the committee, extremely simple. Space was limited due to the plaque's design, the name of the Society of Arts being incorporated in a decorative border around the plaque's edge. In 1902 Sir Henry Trueman Wood – Secretary of the Society of

from some distance, therefore the letters must be large and distinct, and the whole inscription therefore extremely short . . . You will notice that the name of the Society of Arts is worked into the pattern around the edge. The idea of this was that the name of the Society should not be very conspicuous, but that it should be in evidence . . . It might be an advantage to have tablets of different sizes to allow for a longer inscription in some cases. But I have myself always held the view, and have impressed it on my Council, though not very strongly, that it was rather better that all the tablets put up should be uniform.[83]

In 1900, in advance of its formal adoption of the plaques scheme, the LCC began to investigate the question of design and material. Designs – which have unfortunately not survived – were submitted for consideration in that year and in 1901. Four more options were prepared by the Architect's Department and considered in June 1902. Clearly, none were particularly successful, for it was finally decided to follow the design used by the Society of Arts, simply substituting the council's own name (fig. 36). The LCC had to defend this inclusion of its title – or, more often, its initials – on several occasions, as a number of house owners objected to it. In 1903 Gomme explained to the rather tempestuous owner of 11 Berkeley Square, Mayfair, the former home of SIR HORACE WALPOLE, that:

> The object of the inclusion of the design of the letters 'L.C.C.' is to give some sort of guarantee of the authenticity of the statement contained on the tablet. Owing to changes in the numbering of houses and many other causes, it is exceedingly difficult to establish satisfactory identification of the premises in the majority of cases, and it is essential, therefore, that the public should be protected by knowing upon whose authority the tablets are erected. The letters, moreover, serve to indicate that the Council, which is the governing body in London, is of the opinion that the premises on which the tablet appears are deserving of commemoration.[84]

Despite Gomme's eloquent and clear explanation, the owner continued to object and ended up installing a plaque privately. Another critic, the owner of the

35 The plaque to Sir Harry Vane – installed in 1898 and now on a marooned gatepier in Rosslyn Hill, Hampstead – is an excellent example of the form of tablet used by the Society of Arts between 1867 and 1901. [© English Heritage. Photograph by Derek Kendall]

Arts – wrote to SIR LAURENCE GOMME on the subject of plaque design:

> The design of the tablets is perhaps not very attractive. It has often been criticised by members of my own Council, but none of them have ever been able to suggest an improvement. The tablet must of necessity be small. The inscription has to be read

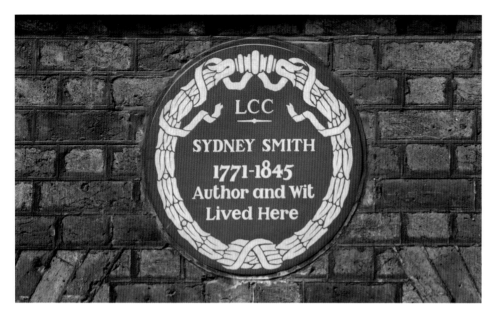

Mayfair house in which CHARLES JAMES FOX had formerly lived, forced the LCC into agreeing to cover the offending initials over altogether, with a piece of blue glass (see fig. 395).

Tenders were submitted for the manufacture of the LCC's plaques, it having been stipulated that 'the tablets are to be circular, 21 inches [53 cm] in diameter, and 1 inch [2.5 cm] thick with simple ornamental border and plain lettering in white upon an approved coloured ground . . . The edges of tablets to be slightly splayed from front to back and the back to be left rough and with proper keys formed in same for cement'. The plaques were to be of encaustic ware, 'thoroughly burnt and free from cracks or other defects', and of uniform texture and colouring.[85] The tender eventually accepted was that of Minton, the firm which had made all of the thirty-five plaques installed by the Society of Arts. Minton argued that plaques of a diameter of nineteen inches (48.3 cm) – as had been produced for the Society of Arts – would be cheaper, any larger size risking failure in the kiln, and told the LCC that a red or salmon background would be considerably cheaper than blue or green. The tender was accepted, and Minton continued to make plaques until 1921.

The first two decades of the twentieth century saw considerable variation in the design of LCC plaques. The roundel was standard, though there was no consistency in colour; despite the 1903 report by the LCC's architect that 'from the nature of the facings and finishing of the various fronts, tablets with the blue ground would be more suitable than those with the red ground', colours varied between chocolate-brown, green and blue.[86] These early roundels, with their characteristic laurel-wreath border – representing achievement, honour, glory and immortality – are said to have been designed by Arthur Halcrow Verstage, a member of the LCC's Architects' Department, and remained the standard model until the time of the Second World War. However, plaques could also take the form of rectangles, made up of smaller tiles – a form used specifically for plaques on sites, such as those to WILLIAM WILBERFORCE and SAMUEL PEPYS et al. (see figs 23 and 310) – and a series of monumental tablets were used at about the time of the First World War. These, made in Hopton Wood stone, lead and bronze, commemorate figures including THOMAS STOTHARD, W. M. THACKERAY, THOMAS HOOD (see fig. 445), HEINRICH HEINE (fig. 37), MICHAEL WILLIAM BALFE, MRS ELIZABETH GASKELL (see fig. 181), ANTHONY TROLLOPE and CHARLES HADDON SPURGEON.

In January 1921 a detailed report by the council's architect, G. Topham Forrest, set out experiences to date, with the aim of improving plaque appearance

and cost-effectiveness. It was stated that the design of plaques aimed: at permanence ('a surface that is impervious and does not materially change in colour'); an inscription that could be easily read, and, if necessary, easily cleaned; and dignity and simplicity of character. The architect added that plaques 'should be in keeping with the surroundings and, if possible, have some mark or reference applicable to the person memorialized'.[87] Bronze tablets were found to be expensive and, when bearing raised or incised lettering, not very legible, unless the lettering was enamelled; also, in one case (that of W. M. THACKERAY in Onslow Square, Kensington) the bronze caused staining on the building, and there were concerns about theft. Cast lead was cheaper and had more flexibility, but – like bronze and Hopton Wood stone – did not wear well. The favourites were encaustic ware, as had been used hitherto, or glazed Doulton Ware tablets, which had the great benefit of being comparatively cheap and easy to clean. A 'circular blue tablet in Doulton glazed ware' was ultimately chosen as the LCC's standard model, though it could be 'varied in any special case'.[88] The first of Doulton's plaques was erected on 28 February 1923 in honour of JOHN CONSTABLE, though the manufacturing process was only perfected in 1924; plaques installed in that year included those commemorating ALFRED STEVENS and LORD KITCHENER.

Over the next thirty years (until 1955), the artists and craftsmen of Royal Doulton produced – from a special studio at their Lambeth Works – a stream of plaques 'of unquestionably high quality', all with a protective coating of glaze.[89] Each plaque was individually designed, hand-lettered and coloured, and then fired at a temperature of around 1250°C. Perhaps most memorable are a series of highly coloured plaques with raised wreathed borders, produced in 1925–26 in a style inspired by the work of the della Robbias, an Italian family of sculptors and potters active in the fifteenth and sixteenth centuries. Of the seven plaques made only five survive: those commemorating CANALETTO (see fig. 461), W. E. GLADSTONE (see fig. 427), JAMES MCNEILL WHISTLER, SIR WALTER BESANT (fig. 38) and JOHN WESLEY (see fig. 159); two others, honouring Lord Byron and G. F. Watts, were removed due to demolition.

In 1938 a new plaque design was approved, based on drawings made by an unnamed student of the LCC's

Central School of Arts and Crafts, who was paid four guineas for the work (fig. 39). This omitted the wreathed border, was 'warm sepia-brown in place of the blue hitherto used for the majority of the Council's memorial tablets', had cream lettering and followed the traditional size – nineteen inches (48.3 cm) in diameter.[90] It was noted that the omission of the wreath 'enables a bolder spacing and arrangement of the lettering to be adopted'.[91] The design was made standard for all plaques, which were to be brown, though the colour would 'vary with the type of house on which the tablets are placed'.[92] The prototype was the plaque commemorating MOZART, erected in March 1939. The press reported that its design depended 'entirely for its distinctiveness on a studied setting out of the wording and proportioning of the characters'.[93] Shortly after

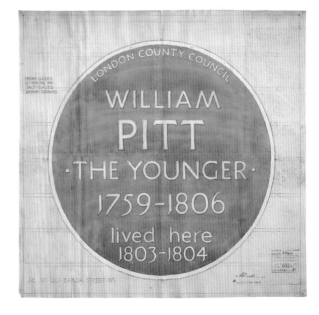

40   The LCC continued to use different forms of plaque even after the adoption of the blue roundel as standard. This rectangular tablet, commemorating Hubert Parry's residence at 17 Kensington Square, South Kensington, was put up in 1949. [© English Heritage. Photograph by Derek Kendall]

41   The plaque to Henry Gray at 8 Wilton Street, Belgravia. One of the series of brown plaques made to the new design, it was erected in 1947, after the war years. [© English Heritage. Photograph by Derek Kendall]

this plaque was erected, a narrow white edging was added to the design format.

A total of five other plaques, brown in colour and of the new design, were made immediately before the Second World War; these – two of which were later replaced with blue roundels – commemorated THOMAS HARDY, RUDYARD KIPLING, SIR JOSHUA REYNOLDS, SAMUEL PEPYS (see fig. 337) and HENRY GRAY (fig. 41), and were put up between 1940 and 1947. However, after establishing the scheme once again after the war, the LCC seems to have undergone something of a change of heart. Although it installed the brown plaques which had already been manufactured, new plaques – still to the new design – were coloured blue. The earliest of these, installed in March 1948, commemorated AUBREY BEARDSLEY; it quickly became the model for all others subsequently erected under the scheme, though shape continued to be altered in a few instances (fig. 40). Since the 1940s, the colour blue has only rarely been departed from for standard roundels: exceptions include the plaques to J. B. PRIESTLEY (see fig. 124) and VITA SACKVILLE-WEST and HAROLD NICOLSON (fig. 42), both of which were designed to blend in with existing plaques (bronze and brown respectively).

In 1952 the LCC considered the issue of design once again. The council's architect, Robert H. Matthew, reported on work which had been carried out on the plaques' lettering, 'having regard to the material used and the purpose and location of the tablets'.[94] A revision had been made following consultation with Sir Francis Meynell, typographical adviser to HM Stationery Office, resulting in lettering which was admired – and recommended to others – by Royal Doulton. Matthew concluded his report by stating:

The circular blue and white tablets erected by the Council year by year have become a feature of the London scene. They have attracted inquiries from all over the country from local authorities and private bodies which desire to erect tablets of their own, with a view to their adopting the Council's methods. The Committee may therefore consider that what has in effect become something of a tradition should not be departed from except for some very good reason.[95]

As recommended, the design was left unchanged, though three years later – when Doulton's works moved from Lambeth to the Midlands – the LCC was forced to find a new manufacturer. Doulton helpfully offered their mixes, glaze and technical data to Messrs Carter's Tile Co. Ltd, of Poole, Dorset. In December 1956 Carter's delivered its first plaque – that to the Australian novelist Henry Handel Richardson (fig. 44; installed in May 1957 but lost through demolition six years later). The company, of which Poole Pottery was

42 Very occasionally, English Heritage has varied the design and colour of a plaque to suit particular circumstances. In the case of Vita Sackville-West and Harold Nicolson, the plaque – erected in 1993 at 182 Ebury Street, Belgravia – was coloured brown to match the neighbouring LCC tablet to Mozart. [© English Heritage. Photograph by Derek Kendall]

43 The GLC plaque to George Orwell, erected in 1980 at 50 Lawford Road, Kentish Town. [© English Heritage. Photograph by Derek Kendall]

44 The first plaque made by Carter's of Poole commemorated the Australian novelist Henry Handel Richardson. It was unveiled in 1957 at 90 Regent's Park Road, but was lost through demolition six years later. [© PA Photos]

a subsidiary, was entrusted with plaque manufacture from early 1957 and continued to make plaques until 1981, when it was forced to cease production due to the comparatively small demand.

On taking over the plaques scheme in 1965, the GLC adopted the standard design, simply substituting the LCC's name with its own (fig. 43 and see fig. 29). In May of that year, it was noted that the colour combination of plaques 'assists legibility and blends happily with most London buildings'.[96] In early 1966 the council considered using a range of colours, but it was stated that 'blue has proved the most successful' and 'is associated in the minds of the general public with commemorative plaques'.[97] In 1986 English Heritage considered what its own course of action should be. The Head of London Division reported that the familiar blue and white design had been found to be 'very satisfactory . . . legible and readily identifiable'. He noted that the LCC and GLC 'used a house style of lettering which also contributed to the identity of the scheme', and concluded by recommending only minor change, emphasising the continuity between the GLC scheme and English Heritage.[98] He suggested that the words 'English Heritage' be placed at the upper edge; this was acted upon, and the organisation's logo was added at the bottom.

The approach to plaque inscription has remained largely consistent over the scheme's history. Details are brief, including the name by which a figure is best known and their dates of birth and death. The design of plaques – and their positioning, sometimes of necessity at a high level or at a distance from the public way – means that they can contain a maximum of nineteen words (including dates). The composition of

esting information (e.g. if a man in a long life lived only for one year in a London house) and if the facts are absolutely certain'.[99] As late as 1983, residency dates were still not always given; a GLC officer explained that this was 'partly to make plaques reusable if they have to be salvaged when buildings are demolished, and partly to avoid establishing misleading precedents on the length of stay necessary to establish a firm association between the person commemorated and the building for which the plaque is erected'.[100] Only in rare instances has a profession or other descriptor been omitted from a plaque inscription; examples include the plaque to MAHATMA GANDHI at Bow, it being felt that his name should 'stand alone', and the plaques to JOHN WESLEY (see fig. 159), SIR JOHN LUBBOCK and KARL MARX.[101]

The principal manufacturer of plaques between 1982 and his death in 1994 was Alan Dawson (fig. 45), based in Staffordshire; his first plaque was installed in November 1982 in honour of EDWARD IRVING and his last commemorated EDWARD WOOD, LORD HALIFAX. Thereafter, following a short delay during which processes were tested and perfected, manufacture was placed in the hands of Richard Wildblood (of Staffordshire) and Frank and Susan Ashworth (of London), who continue to make plaques for English Heritage today. It is an extremely skilled and time-consuming business; each plaque takes about two months to complete.

For most of the scheme's history, plaque designs have been produced by hand; early designs, especially when

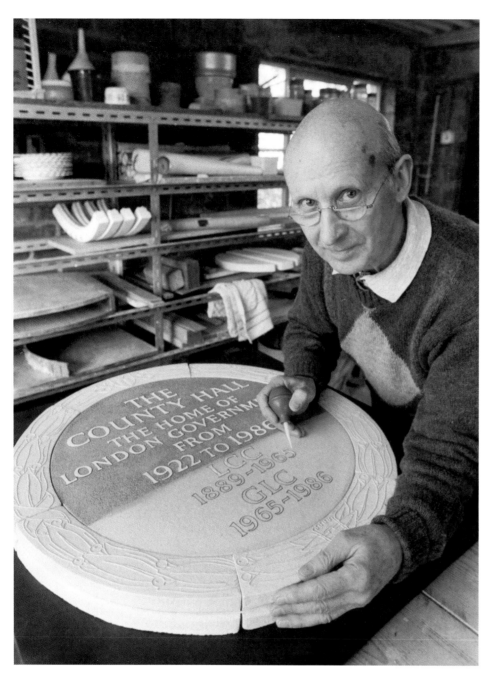

45 Alan Dawson, the principal manufacturer of plaques between 1982 and 1994, with the plaque commemorating County Hall. [© Sunday Telegraph]

46 The design for the LCC plaque to Sir Ernest Shackleton, erected in 1928 at 12 Westwood Hill, Sydenham. [Reproduced by permission of English Heritage]

an inscription consequently involves considerable thought, and is often only finalised after consultation with family members and experts. It is the practice of English Heritage always to include dates of residence where they are known with certainty. Such information was not generally included on plaques installed by the Society of Arts (plaques which do feature residency dates include that to ELIZABETH BARRETT BARRETT; see fig. 367), and the LCC and GLC were inconsistent in their approach. In 1953 it was noted that dates of residence 'should not be given unless they add some inter-

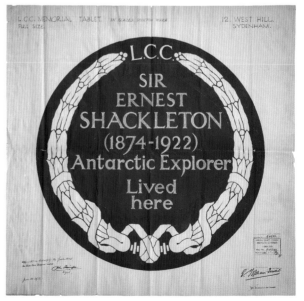

coloured, are works of some beauty (fig. 46 and see figs 29 and 38). From 1901 they were produced by the Architect's Department; the chief designer of plaques from 1955 until 1985 was a member of that department, Henry (Harry) Hooper, who was also responsible for a large amount of the signage produced by the LCC and GLC. He followed a set method of layout and lettering, only varying forms in special instances; for example, in the case of the plaques to JOHN WALTER, FRANK PICK, EDWARD JOHNSTON and LORD ASHFIELD, which employed special font types in honour of the person commemorated. It has been said that Harry Hooper, who died in 2005, 'was proud that in his tenure every aspect of the plaques' design and manufacture, from drawing the letters to the final fixing, was done by hand'.[102] For the past twenty years designs have been produced on computer, using a font that is unique to English Heritage. They are used as templates by the manufacturers, and are circulated to house owners and (where relevant) local authorities for approval.

Today, blue plaques are, after firing, nineteen inches (48.3 cm) in diameter and about two inches (5 cm) thick, their backs being partially hollowed out to reduce their weight and facilitate fixing to buildings. Smaller roundels are sometimes used to meet special circumstances, as in the case of the plaque to MARGARET RUTHERFORD. Manufacture is undertaken by the mixing and pouring of a thick clay slip into a casting mould. When sufficiently dry, the cast is removed and the outline of the inscription and border are piped onto the face of the plaque (fig. 47). The plaque is fired at a temperature of about 1230°C, and glaze is applied: white for the letters and border, and blue for the background. The plaque is then fired a second and final time, at a slightly lower temperature. The process produces characters and border which are in low relief, a special feature of English Heritage plaques. Due to their slightly domed design, modern plaques are self-cleansing and require virtually no maintenance. As this book so clearly illustrates, they have been known to last decades without deterioration or loss of impact – 'still standing, still bright, and still inciting to emulation'.[103]

NOTES

1 *The Times*, 1 April 1952, p. 8

2 Benjamin Disraeli, *Lothair* (London, 1877 edn), p. 48 and p. 111

3 Victor Burrows, with intro. by Sir William Reid Dick, *The Blue Plaque Guide to Historic London Houses and the Lives of their Famous Residents* (London, 1953), p. 7

4 Ibid

5 Ibid, p. 9

6 *The War Speeches of the Rt. Hon. Winston S. Churchill*, comp. Charles Eade, vol. III (London, 1952), p. 56 (28 October 1943)

7 Leonard Woolf, *Downhill All the Way: An Autobiography of the Years 1919–1939* (London, 1975), p. 14

8 Speech at plaque unveiling on 20 June 2003

9 Hansard, *Parliamentary Debates*, 17 July 1863 ('Residences of Deceased Celebrities')

10 Alison Yarrington, *The Commemoration of the Hero, 1800–1864: Monuments to the British Victors of the Napoleonic Wars* (New York and London, 1988), p. xi

11 Ibid, p. viii

12 Ibid, p. xi

13 *The Times*, 4 September 1873, p. 5

14 Algernon Ashton, *Truth, Wit, and Wisdom: A Mine of Information: 525 Letters to the Press, 1887–1903* (London, 1905), p. 404 (30 September 1903)

15 *The Times*, 4 September 1873, p. 5

16 *The Builder*, vol. XXII, 2 July 1864, pp. 485–86

17 Ibid, vol. XXII, 6 August 1864, p. 588

18 Ibid, vol. XXII, 16 July 1864, p. 533

19 *Journal of the Society of Arts*, vol. XIV, 11 May 1866, p. 437

20 Ashton, *Truth, Wit, and Wisdom: A Mine of Information*, p. 154 (22 August 1898) and p. 153 (18 August 1898)

21 Ibid, p. 371 (25 May 1903)

22 LCC, *Commemorative Tablets on Houses of Historical Interest* (London, 1956 edn), p. 3

23 Report on 'general principles involved in selection of buildings or persons for commemoration by plaques', 24 September 1954 (presented to Town Planning Committee on 1 October): Town Planning Committee Papers, LMA; copy on blue plaque file.

24 Letter of 10 November 1958 on blue plaque file.

25 Speech made by Lord Rosebery at the unveiling of the plaque to Lord Macaulay at Holly Lodge, Campden Hill, on 26 November 1903 (transcription on blue plaque file).

26 Ashton, *Truth, Wit, and Wisdom: A Mine of Information*, p. 90 (11 March 1897)

27 Report by the Architect and Clerk to the Council, 'Erection of Commemorative Plaques on Sites of Buildings Occupied by Famous Persons', considered by the Planning and Communications (Historic Buildings) Sub-Committee on 24 February 1967; copy on blue plaque file.

28 Report by the Clerk of the Council, 'Proposed Memorial Tablets to Three Eminent Surgeons', 7 January 1952; copy on blue plaque file.

29 Note of 28 March 1983 (re. plaque to Sir Richard Arkwright) on blue plaque file.

30 Committee Minutes of the Society of Arts, 2 May 1866

31 Speech made by Lord Rosebery at the unveiling of the plaque to Lord Macaulay, 26 November 1903 (op. cit.)

32 *Parliamentary Debates*, 17 July 1863 (op. cit.)

33 Ibid

34 *Journal of the Society of Arts*, vol. XI, 24 July 1863, p. 606

35 *The Builder*, vol. XXII, 23 July 1864, p. 537; ibid, vol. XXII, 16 July 1864, p. 533

36 Committee Minutes of the Society of Arts, 2 May 1866

37 *Journal of the Society of Arts*, vol. XIV, 11 May 1866, p. 437

38 Ibid

39 Ibid

40 Ibid, vol. XV, 20 September 1867, p. 774

41 Ibid, vol. XX, 26 April 1872, pp. 491–92

42 Ashton, *Truth, Wit, and Wisdom: A Mine of Information*, pp. 57, 63–64, 65, 91–92, 188, 241, 262–63, 273

43 Report of 17 July 1899 by Statistical Officer, 'Tablets upon Houses of Historic Interest', presented to the Historic Buildings Sub-Committee; copy on blue plaque file.

44 *The Times*, 19 December 1901, p. 11

45 Report of 17 July 1899 (op. cit.). See also LCC, *Indication of Houses of Historical Interest in London*, vol. I (London, 1915 edn), preface

46 Report of 28 May 1900 by Statistical Officer, 'Wall-Plates on Houses of Historic Interest', presented to Historic Buildings Sub-Committee; copy on blue plaque file.

47 Report of 22 November 1901 by Clerk of the Council, 'Indication of houses of historical interest in London', presented to the Historical Records and Buildings Committee; copy on blue plaque file.

48 Report of 24 September 1954 (op. cit.)

49 Report by Clerk of Council, 18 July 1902: Historical Records and Buildings Committee Papers (July–December 1902), LMA.

50 Ibid

51 Report of 24 September 1954 (op. cit.)

52 Ibid

53 Ibid

54 Speech made by Lord Rosebery at the unveiling of the plaque to Lord Macaulay, 26 November 1903 (op. cit.)

55 Quoted in paper by Victor Belcher, 'Commemorative Plaque Criteria: The Twenty-Year Rule', presented to the London Advisory Committee on 3 July 1992; copy on blue plaque file.

56 Report by Clerk of the Council, 31 January 1933; copy on blue plaque file.

57 Report of 22 June 1977; copy on blue plaque file.

58 Ashton, *Truth, Wit, and Wisdom: A Mine of Information*, p. 272 (29 November 1900) and p. 90 (11 March 1897)

59 Ibid, p. 295 (27 May 1902)

60 Algernon Ashton, *More Truth, Wit, and Wisdom: Another Mine of Information: 656 Letters to the Press, 1905–1907* (London, 1908), p. 21 (9 January 1906)

61 Letter in the *London Argus*, 8 October 1903, by Mr O. Mouat Balthasar; copy on blue plaque file.

62 Decision by Parks Committee, 24 June 1938, cited in report of 22 February 1947 by Acting Clerk and Architect of the Council, 'Erection of Commemorative Tablets on Buildings and Places of Historical Interest', considered by Town Planning Committee; copy on blue plaque file.

63 Report of 24 September 1954 (op. cit)

64 Ibid

65 Draft report and notes on 'Commemorative Tablets', 16 July 1953; copy on blue plaque file.

66 Paper on 'Ceremonial Precedents', 22 May 1903: Historical Records and Buildings Committee Papers (April–June 1903), LMA.

67 The substance of many of these leaflets found its way into the LCC's six-volume series, *Indication of Houses of Historical Interest in London* (London, 1904–38)

68 GLC Minutes, report of the Planning and Communications Committee ('Commemorative Plaques'), 11 May 1965, p. 393

69 Ibid

70 Ibid

71 Paper of 24 February 1967 (op. cit.)

72 Report by Director of Architecture and Controller of Transportation and Development, considered by the Policy Co-ordinating Committee on 18 January 1984; copy on blue plaque file.

73 Ibid

74 Report of 27 January 1984 by Director of Architecture and Controller of Transportation and Development, 'PCC: Blue Plaques', considered 1 February 1984; copy on blue plaque file.

75 Report by Head of London Division, 'Proposals for the Continuation of the GLC Scheme by the Commission [Historic Buildings and Monuments Commission for England]', considered by the London Advisory Committee on 2 April 1986; copy on blue plaque file.

76 *Journal of the Society of Arts*, vol. XIV, 11 May 1866, p. 437

77 Ibid

78 Committee Minutes of the Society of Arts, 9 May 1866

79 *Journal of the Society of Arts*, vol. XIV, 11 May 1866, p. 437

80 Committee Minutes of the Society of Arts, 25 June 1866

81 *Journal of the Society of Arts*, vol. XVI, 26 June 1868, p. 584

82 Letter of 25 June 1902 from Henry Trueman Wood, Secretary of the Society of Arts, to Laurence Gomme: Historical Records and Buildings Committee Papers (July–December 1902), LMA; copy on blue plaque file.

83 Ibid

84 Letter by Clerk of the Council, 8 December 1903; copy on blue plaque file.

85 Specification for manufacture, November 1902: Historical Records and Buildings Committee Papers (July–December 1902), LMA.

86 Report by the Architect, 22 May 1903: Historical Records and Buildings Committee Papers (April–June 1903), LMA.

87 Report by the Architect, 'Memorial Tablets: As to Design generally', 28 January 1921 (presented to Committee 18 February): Local Government Committee Papers (April–June 1921), LMA; copy on blue plaque file.

88 Note of committee decision, 4 March 1921; copy on blue plaque file.

89 Report of 23 June 1952 by the Architect, 'Design of Memorial Tablets'; copy on blue plaque file.

90 Papers of Parks Committee, 1938; copy on blue plaque file.

91 Ibid

92 Ibid

93 *The Builder*, vol. CLVI, 24 March 1939, p. 561

94 Report of 23 June 1952 (op. cit.)

95 Ibid

96 Report of 17 May 1965 by Clerk to the Council, Architect to the Council and Director of Planning and Valuer to the Council, 'Historic Buildings', p. 9; copy on blue plaque file.

97 Paper of 24 February 1967 (op. cit.)

98 Report considered 2 April 1986 (op. cit.)

99 Draft report and notes of 16 July 1953 (op. cit.)

100 Report of 14 June 1983 by Director of Architecture re. Sir Moses Montefiore; copy on blue plaque file.

101 Letter of 27 June 1953 (from the Clerk of the LCC) on blue plaque file.

102 *The Independent*, 11 December 2003

103 Speech made by Lord Rosebery at the unveiling of the plaque to Lord Macaulay, 26 November 1903 (op. cit.)

CAMDEN

In 1965 the old boroughs of Holborn, St Pancras and Hampstead were amalgamated to form the borough of Camden. With more listed buildings than any other borough apart from the City of Westminster, Camden also has the third highest tally of blue plaques in the capital. They are concentrated in two historic cores – Hampstead to the north and Bloomsbury to the south – and commemorate an eclectic selection of people, from the painter JOHN CONSTABLE to the mechanical engineer SIR HARRY RICARDO. Camden rises up from the medieval hamlet of St Giles in the Fields to as far north as the heights of Hampstead and Highgate. The

southern area, where much outstanding Georgian domestic architecture survives, was largely developed by 1830. The arrival of the railways transformed the central area: main-line stations arose on former meadows, and the 'march of bricks and mortar' continued inexorably northwards, past Camden Town, Primrose Hill and Belsize Park. One of the oldest of all London churches, St Pancras, was left marooned in its wake. So relentless was this tide of suburbanisation that one of the earliest – and greatest – of all London's battles for open spaces was waged over the preservation of Hampstead Heath, between 1831 and 1871.

Cannon Place, Hampstead, and the blue plaque to Sir Flinders Petrie at number 5 (see p. 104). [© English Heritage. Photograph by Derek Kendall]

48   The west side of Bedford Square, with the plaques to Thomas Wakley and Thomas Hodgkin at number 35. [© English Heritage. Photograph by Nigel Corrie]

BLOOMSBURY AND HOLBORN

Bloomsbury, a roughly rectangular area bounded by Tottenham Court Road to the west and Gray's Inn Road to the east, was developed from the late seventeenth century onwards. It has become most closely associated with the bohemian set of twentieth-century artists, writers and intellectuals known as the Bloomsbury Group, several of whom have plaques. Much of the area was – and remains – part of the Duke of Bedford's estate, and the ornate bronze plaques erected by the Estate in the early twentieth century – several of which have since been incorporated into the official plaques scheme – are a unique feature. Although wartime bombing and the develop-ment of the London University precinct has inter-rupted Bloomsbury's grid-like plan of squares and streets – most of which were gated until the late nine-teenth century – the area still has some of the finest Georgian houses in London. Further south, Kingsway is a modern thoroughfare – opened as recently as 1905 – but High Holborn was a medieval road into the City. Either side of it lie two great Inns of Court, Gray's Inn and Lincoln's Inn, both founded in the late Middle Ages. Nearby Lincoln's Inn Fields was first developed as a fashionable place of residence in the mid-seven-teenth century.

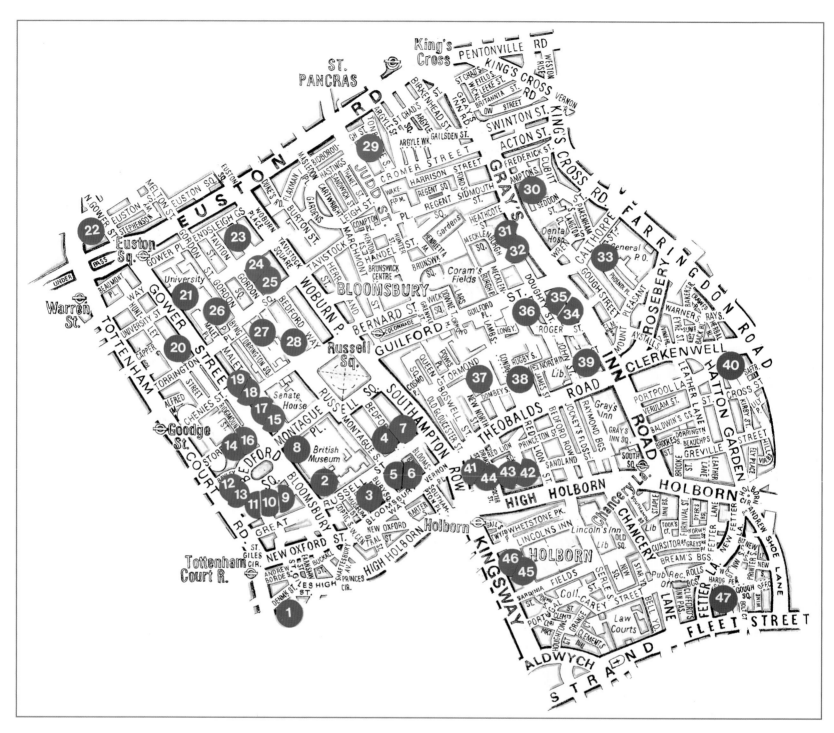

BLOOMSBURY AND HOLBORN

49   Portrait by George Beechey showing Augustus Siebe and his closed diving helmet, c.1840. [© Science Museum Pictorial / Science & Society Picture Library]

design of 1840 – the first in which the helmet was sealed to a diving suit, then made of canvas – remained in use for over a century; it was a vital enabling technology for many of the great Victorian civil engineering projects that required underwater foundation or investigative work, such as bridges, tunnels and lighthouses. Other machines designed or manufactured by Siebe were a dial weighing machine, a rotary water pump, a papermaking machine, and the world's first commercially viable ice-making machine, which he built under licence. For his successes, Siebe was awarded medals at the Great Exhibition of 1851 and the Paris Exhibition of 1855. After Siebe's retirement in 1868, his business passed to his son Henry and his son-in-law William Gorman. As Siebe Gorman, the company supplied both diving equipment and submarine engineers, and continued in existence until the 1990s. Siebe's plaque was put up at the suggestion of the Historical Diving Group and was unveiled in 2000 by Loyd Grossman, then Chairman of the Blue Plaques Panel and a keen scuba diver.

At 91 (formerly 46) Great Russell Street, WC1, close to the junction with Bloomsbury Street, a plaque commemorates **George du Maurier** (1834–1896) ❷ (see also pp. 107–8), the artist and writer. George Louis Palmella Busson du Maurier was born in Paris; his family's supposed French aristocratic pedigree was in fact the invention of his grandfather, a truth only discovered – by George's granddaughter, the novelist Daphne du Maurier – in 1962. Du Maurier himself set up house in Great Russell Street on his marriage to Emma Wightwick (1840/1–1915) in 1863, having previously shared bachelor quarters in Newman Street, north of Oxford Street, with WHISTLER. The du Mauriers paid twenty-five shillings a week for the second-floor apartment, which they furnished largely with wedding presents, including a new piano and 'a splendid sofa from Emma's uncle Noel'. 'Our lodgings are very nice and the studio will be a beauty in time', du Maurier told his mother.[1] The studio in question cost him an additional £25 a year, and was on the ground floor, behind a shop selling Pears soap. In 1864 du Maurier became a staff artist at *Punch*, in which capacity his satirical take on contemporary manners brought him to prominence. His work for the magazine included the cartoon that spawned the expression 'a curate's egg' (fig. 50). Du Maurier was blind in one

At the south-western corner of Bloomsbury, in the shadow of Centre Point, lies Denmark Street, WC2, nicknamed 'Tin Pan Alley' for its strong associations with the British music industry. By way of a contrast, at number 5, is the plaque to **Augustus Siebe** (1788–1872) ❶ , the pioneer of the diving helmet (fig. 49). Born in Saxony, Siebe moved to London in 1814, after having served in the Prussian Army. He spent nearly fifteen years as a watchmaker and silversmith at 145 High Holborn before moving in 1828 to late seventeenth-century premises at 5 Denmark Street; here, he lived and ran his engineering firm and died forty-four years later. Siebe's closed diving-helmet

TRUE HUMILITY.

Right Reverend Host. "I'M AFRAID YOU'VE GOT A BAD EGG, MR. JONES!"
The Curate. "OH NO, MY LORD, I ASSURE YOU! PARTS OF IT ARE EXCELLENT!"

50   The cartoon 'True Humility' by George du Maurier. Published in *Punch* on 9 November 1895, it introduced the expression 'a curate's egg'. [Reproduced with the permission of Punch Ltd]

51   The plaque to Randolph Caldecott at 46 Great Russell Street, in a photograph of 1980. [Reproduced by permission of English Heritage. NMR]

eye, and it was his concern at the possibility of losing his sight completely that led him to embark upon a second career as a writer; among his gifts to the lexicon, taken from his novel *Trilby* (1894), were 'trilby hat' and 'Svengali'. Three children were born to the du Mauriers before they moved on to 12 Earls Terrace, Kensington, W8 (see WALTER PATER) in March 1868, by which time George had also illustrated an eight-volume edition of the works of ELIZABETH GASKELL, regarded by some as his finest achievement. The plaque, which is at first-floor level, was unveiled by Daphne du Maurier in 1960.

Opposite the British Museum, at 46 Great Russell Street, can be found the plaque to **Randolph Caldecott** (1846–1886) ❸ , the artist and book illustrator (fig. 51). Caldecott had a great aptitude for creating pictures of animals and birds, though he is best known as an illustrator of children's books. He lived and worked at number 46 from 1872 to 1879, apparently as a lodger of a Mrs Spencer; among the works he executed here were the drawings for his book *The House That Jack Built* (1878) and commissions for *Punch* and the *Illustrated London News*. Thereafter Caldecott lived in Kent and Surrey, before travelling in 1885 to the United States, where he died. The original suggestion to commemorate Caldecott, at 24 Holland Street, Kensington, W8 – where he stayed in the 1880s – had been made in 1910, and was forestalled by the

First World War. When the suggestion was revived in 1974 by the occupant of 46 Great Russell Street, it was with the recommendation that 'we ... possess a charming ghost who must be Randolph Caldecott'.[2] The plaque was affixed three years later, at a time when the building was under threat of demolition for the proposed development of a new British Library. Fortunately for the house – which dates from the mid-nineteenth century – a new site for the library was found.

On the opposite side of Great Russell Street, at number 77, is a GLC plaque to the architect **Thomas Henry Wyatt** (1807–1880) ❹ . Wyatt, who belonged to a noted family of architects, was primarily a designer of country houses and churches – the most remarkable of which is the parish church at Wilton, Wiltshire, in a Romanesque basilica style; this, at its completion in 1845, was the largest Anglican church to have been built for a hundred years. Wyatt's Garrison Church of St George in Woolwich (1863) was built in a similar style, being likewise influenced by the architect's sketching tours of Europe; it is preserved as a fragmentary ruin,

having been largely destroyed in the Second World War. The church at Wilton was later criticised as 'un-English', and many of Wyatt's numerous subsequent ecclesiastical commissions were executed in the Gothic style. A contemporary account of a speech he gave to the RIBA – 'absolutely devoid of all affectation and pretentiousness – without a word that glittered – full of simple sound sagacity and everyday information' – might be just as aptly applied to Wyatt's workmanlike, efficient architectural compositions, suggests his modern biographer.[3] Wyatt lived at number 77 for most of his career as an architect, from the late 1840s until his death here over thirty years later. The house dates from the seventeenth century, but was extensively remodelled in the mid-1800s; it is probable that Wyatt himself designed the iron-roofed balcony on the Montague Street side. The plaque's installation was timed to mark the centenary of Wyatt's death.

At Russell Chambers, Bury Place, WC1, an English Heritage plaque marks the residence of **Bertrand Russell** (1872–1970) **5** , the philosopher and campaigner for peace. Russell, the best-known British philosopher of the twentieth century, moved to Flat 34 of Russell Chambers in autumn 1911 in order to be close to LADY OTTOLINE MORRELL, with whom he had a tempestuous love affair. 'How much emotion those little rooms in Bury Street held – intense and burning and very tragic!', she later wrote, though she had enjoyed making the place 'pretty and nice for him' and supplied many of the furnishings.[4] *Principia Mathe-*

matica (1911–13), written with A. N. Whitehead and perhaps Russell's most significant work, was published while he lived at this address, though most of his writing was done in Cambridge. His pacifist stance during the First World War lost him his Trinity College fellowship, however, and Russell let the flat at Bury Place in summer 1916 to save money, staying instead with his brother Frank in Gordon Square. He spent an unproductive few months in early 1917 back at Bury Place, 'brooding on the odiousness of the human race', and was here again intermittently in the months following his release in September 1918 from Brixton prison, where he had been incarcerated for a libellous article on the United States Army.[5] Russell finally gave up the lease on Flat 34 in 1922. The Russell Chambers block was built in the last decade of the nineteenth century on the estate of the Duke of Bedford, to whose family Bertrand Russell belonged – hence the coincidence of names between address and resident. T. S. ELIOT stayed here with Russell – the priapic philosopher began an affair with Eliot's wife Vivien – while another guest was Ludwig Wittgenstein, whose criticism of 'The Theory of Knowledge', a work-in-progress, led Russell to abandon the project.

Bloomsbury Square, WC1, dates originally from the early 1660s, when the Earl of Southampton's mansion, Southampton House (demolished), stood on its north side (fig. 52). Once one of the most magnificent squares in London, it has been extensively developed and is now overshadowed by the offices of an insurance company. The square has multiple medical associations: it formerly housed the headquarters of the Pharmaceutical Society, and was once home to JOHN RADCLIFFE, sometime physician to Queen Anne. Number 10 Bloomsbury Square is marked with a plaque of 1949 commemorating the dermatologist **Dr Robert Willan** (1757–1812) **6** ; it was his home from 1800 until 1811, when he left London for Madeira. Yorkshire born, Willan was in 1783 appointed physician to the Public Dispensary in London, then located in Carey Street, just south of Lincoln's Inn Fields. His reputation rests on his early classification of diseases of the skin, as described in *On Cutaneous Diseases* (1808). Willan's texts have been cited as the first of their kind to feature colour illustrations. An advocate of mineral-water cures, Willan was also an early chronicler of London's poor housing conditions and their links to

52   An aquatint showing Bloomsbury Square in 1787. The home of Dr Robert Willan forms part of the west side of the square, on the left of the picture, while Southampton House dominates the north side. [Reproduced by permission of English Heritage. NMR]

BLOOMSBURY AND HOLBORN

diseases; his *Reports on the Diseases in London* (1801) includes the luridly titled *An Account of the Dreadful Effects of Dram-Drinking*, issued separately in 1803. Number 10 Bloomsbury Square is part of a terrace of five houses dating from the 1660s but much altered since: among the additions are the pedimented attic storey and an Italianate stucco frontage.

At 4 Bloomsbury Place, WC1, part of a short thoroughfare which leads from Bloomsbury Square to Southampton Row (formerly Southampton Street), is a plaque to one of the area's most renowned residents, **Sir Hans Sloane** (1660–1753) ❼ , the physician and benefactor of the British Museum. Sloane was born in County Down, of Scottish-Irish ancestry, and studied medicine in France before setting up his practice in London. As a physician, he extolled the benefits of inoculation, the use of quinine and – more surprisingly – the consumption of milk chocolate. It is as a collector, however, that Sloane is remembered: his miscellanea of flora, fauna, manuscripts and some 30,000 books became, shortly after his death, the foundation of the collections of the British Museum, housed in nearby Montagu House from 1759. Sloane took up residence at 4 Bloomsbury Place in 1695, shortly after his marriage to Elizabeth, née Langley (d. 1724); apparently, the street was then unnamed, letters being addressed to him 'at the corner of Southampton Street, towards Bloomsbury Square'.[6] By 1708 the size of his collection was such that he was impelled to acquire additionally the house next door, the present number 5. Sloane remained here until 1742, when he retired to Chelsea; there, he was Lord of the Manor, and Sloane Square was named after him. The terrace of which numbers 4 and 5 form a part was refaced in an Italianate style in about 1860, but retains the essential structure of Sloane's time. The plaque, erected in 1965, was one of the last put up by the LCC.

Bedford Square, WC1, was laid out between 1775 and 1786 and has been attributed to the architect Thomas Leverton; it is undoubtedly one of the most magnificent and architecturally intact squares in London (see fig. 48). The square was long coveted as a place of residence by persons of distinction, a fact illustrated by the presence of eight official plaques. Each side of the square has a central focus: a large and imposing house with a stuccoed double frontage and pilasters. The cen-

trepiece on the east side, numbered 6, bears an LCC plaque commemorating the Lord Chancellor **John Scott, Lord Eldon** (1751–1838) ❽ (fig. 53). Born in Newcastle upon Tyne and called to the Bar in 1776, Scott – ennobled in 1801 – was implacably opposed to almost all legal and political reform, from the abolition of slavery to the outlawing of the employment of boy chimney-sweeps. Yet the length of Eldon's tenure on the Woolsack, which was almost unbroken between 1801 and 1827, has not since been equalled. George IV nicknamed him 'Old Bags'; it was at this house that George – as Prince Regent – forced Eldon to ratify the appointment of a royal favourite, Sir Joseph Jekyll, as a Master in Chancery, by threatening not to leave Eldon's bedroom, where he lay stricken with gout, until he acquiesced. Another soubriquet, bestowed on the Lord Chancellor by Jeremy Bentham, was 'Lord Endless', on account of the ponderousness of his deliberations before he reached a judgement. Eldon was a hate-figure for reformers: the house in Bedford Square, in which he lived from 1798 with his wife Elizabeth, née Surtees (1754–1831), was besieged by a mob during the

Corn Law riots of March 1815. The rioters broke all the windows, and used the railings to force their way into the hall, where they destroyed all the furniture. Eldon's family made good their escape to the British Museum to the rear; the Lord Chancellor later protested that he had not even voted for the parliamentary bill in question. Three years later, he moved to Hamilton Place, Mayfair, where he died in 1838.

On the south side of Bedford Square, at number 49, a GLC plaque marks the residence of **Ram Mohun Roy** (1772–1833) 9 , the Indian scholar and reformer. Born in Bengal, Ram Mohun (otherwise rendered as Rammohun) was among the early practitioners of journalism in India, founding Bengali and Persian newspapers in 1822, and was a pioneer in exploring the common ground between Christianity and Hinduism. His rejection of the Holy Trinity and of image worship made him enemies among both faiths, but gave him much in common with the Unitarians. Ram Mohun was also a campaigner against the practice of suttee, the (notionally voluntary) burning of widows on their husbands' funeral pyres. It was as an emissary of the Mughal Emperor that he arrived in England in April 1831; he attended the coronation of King William IV that year and witnessed the passage of the 1832 Reform Act, as well as the renewal of the East India Company's charter, the terms of which were a disappointment to him. Ram Mohun enjoyed the company of such political luminaries of the left as Robert Owen and Jeremy Bentham, and considered standing for Parliament himself. After spells in Regent Street and Cumberland Terrace, Regent's Park, he lodged at 49 Bedford Square from January 1832 with one Joseph Hare, brother of a Calcutta acquaintance, the watchmaker and philanthropist David Hare. From here, Ram Mohun travelled to Bristol in late summer 1833, where he died soon after and was buried. The plaque, erected in 1985, is of enamelled steel and surface-mounted, owing to concerns about the condition of the building's brickwork.

At 42 Bedford Square is a GLC plaque to **William Butterfield** (1814–1900) 10 , an architect best known for his ecclesiastical work. All Saints, Margaret Street (1849–59), his most famous London church, lies just north of Oxford Street. It is notable for its unabashed use of unadorned brick, a stylistic touch that has led

Butterfield to be described as 'a New Brutalist a hundred years ahead of his time'.[7] Perhaps Butterfield's best-known building is Keble College, Oxford (1868–83); its centrepiece, the chapel, features brick patterns that were designed, it is said, to lift the beholder's eyes heavenwards. Such triumphs were achieved at a price of alienating those whose standards did not match his own; Butterfield's perfectionism was such that he is supposed to have put his umbrella point through stained-glass work of which he did not approve. A tall, ascetic bachelor, he lived a fairly quiet and circumscribed existence between home, office and the Athenaeum club. For much of his active career Butterfield worked at 4 Adam Street, Adelphi, and lived, for a time, in the house next door; had it not been demolished, this would have been the obvious site for his plaque. Butterfield is commemorated instead at number 42, a classical three-bay Georgian town house of about 1775, where he lived from 1886 until his death here at the age of eighty-five. Among his last commissions was restoration work on All Saints, Margaret Street, over which – characteristically – he clashed with the vicar.

Next door, at number 41, is a metal plaque to the novelist **Sir Anthony Hope Hawkins** (1863–1933) 11 . Under the pen name of **Anthony Hope**, he is best known for the swashbuckling novel *The Prisoner of Zenda* (1894), a bestseller in its day and filmed several times since; the book has given to the world the word 'Ruritania' to denote a faraway romantic country. In summer 1903, Hope married Betty Sheldon (1885/6–1946) and moved to Bedford Square that September from his bachelor apartments in Savoy Mansions (now Savoy Hill), off the Strand. 'Recalcitrant impulses recalcitrate', he admitted to a friend just before embarking on married life at his smart new address, venturing a deadpan prediction that he would 'die a Tory and a Churchman and a Publisher'.[8] Hope, who did no such thing, came to relish the 'spaciousness and dignity' of number 41, especially its billiard room and squash court.[9] While he struggled to replicate the enormous success of his early novels, he nonetheless earned over £40,000 during his time at Bedford Square, and achieved belated critical recognition for *Sophy of Kravonia* (1906). During the First World War, Hope worked for the Ministry of Information to counter German propaganda, and was knighted for his services in 1918. In March the previous year he had moved to a smaller house in Gower Street, thinking it prudent to have 'a smaller shell to carry on my back'.[10] At the same time he bought a country retreat at Heath Farm, Walton-on-Thames, Surrey, whence Hope moved permanently in 1927 and where he died six years later. Like that which commemorates RAM MOHUN ROY (see p. 43), the plaque is a surface-mounted enamelled-steel model, because of similar concerns about the condition of the façade; it went up in 1976.

Two plaques are to be found at 35 Bedford Square (fig. 48), the offices since 1917 of the Architectural Association. The first commemorates **Thomas Wakley** (1795– 1862) **12** , the reformer and founder of *The Lancet*, the title of the periodical neatly encapsulating his double-pronged career as a medic and incisive political campaigner. Wakley, who was born in Devon and moved to London at the age of twenty, founded *The Lancet* in 1823, partly as a forum for medical innovations and partly to expose quackery and nepotism in medical appointments. In Parliament, which he entered at the third attempt in 1835 as a Member for Finsbury, he was known for his radical views: he campaigned against punishment by flogging in the Army and supported the cause of the Tolpuddle Martyrs. Wakley also served as West Middlesex coroner, becoming the first medic to hold the office; traditionally, it had been the preserve of lawyers. Of general service to posterity was his suggestion that all poison bottles should be made identifiable by touch. Wakley moved to Bedford Square in 1828, having lived previously in Thistle Grove (now Drayton Gardens), Chelsea. Number 35 – where he remained for twenty years, the most important of his professional and public life – was the setting for fortnightly whist or chess gatherings, attended by 'a large number of staunch friends who were attracted by his eloquence, his audacious defence of popular rights, his determination, self-confidence, and kindliness of manner'.[11] A plaque to Wakley was proposed as early as 1916; it was delayed by the First World War, and – having later encountered resistance from the building's owners – was not erected until 1962. Wakley's successor in the editor's chair of *The Lancet*, Dr Thomas Fox, presided at the unveiling.

The second plaque at 35 Bedford Square (see fig. 48) was put up by the GLC in 1985, at the suggestion of the Medical School of Guy's Hospital; it marks the residence of **Thomas Hodgkin** (1798–1866) **13** , the physician, reformer and philanthropist. In his lifetime, Hodgkin cut a lower profile than WAKLEY, although his social conscience was no less of a motive force: a devout Quaker, he was an active opponent of slavery and a strong supporter of the rights of indigenous peoples, notably of North America. Hodgkin's medical work has had a lasting influence on our understanding of the function of the body's immune system, and a disease of the lymphatic system is named after him. He lived at 35 Bedford Square after his marriage in January 1850 to Sarah Scaife (1804–1875), whose first husband had once been his patient; they moved into number 35 on 1 February – there having been no permanent occupant since Wakley's departure – and remained here for the duration of their sixteen-year marriage. This ended with Hodgkin's death while on a mission to Palestine to investigate the plight of oppressed Jewish people; he was an inveterate traveller in the promotion of philanthropic causes.

On the north side of Bedford Square, at number 13, is a plaque to the mechanical engineer **Sir Harry Ricardo** (1885–1974) **14** . Ricardo was the only son of Halsey Ralph Ricardo (1854–1928), the Arts and Crafts architect, and the great-great-nephew of David Ricardo, the MP and economist. Harry was born at number 13 and, when not away at school, lived here until his marriage in 1911 to Beatrice Hale; the house was kept on by the Ricardo family until the 1920s, by which time their main residence was in Sussex. Harry later recalled that the Bloomsbury of his childhood was 'inhabited for the most part by professional men . . . many of whom, like my architect father, carried out their professional work in their own homes'.[12] Ricardo's interest in mechanics developed in the basement workshop at the house. He built his first internal combustion engine in 1902, and in 1907 joined the company owned by his maternal grandfather, Sir Alexander Meadows Rendel, a civil engineer who was instrumental in the late nineteenth-century expansion of the port of London and was heavily involved in railway construction in India. In 1917 Ricardo launched his own company, which was – and remains – based at Shoreham-by-Sea, Sussex, in which county he later lived. Ricardo's petrol and diesel engines were used for aircraft, tanks and cars; he was responsible for an engine for London buses that halved existing fuel consumption, and for the design of a governor and fuel control for the first Whittle jet engine. Ricardo was knighted in 1948, and his plaque was erected in 2005.

The eighth plaque in Bedford Square, at number 11, commemorates **Henry Cavendish** (1731–1810) 15 , the natural philosopher, a term that was once the usual description of a scientist. Cavendish was the foremost experimental physicist of the age; among his discoveries were hydrogen, nitric acid and the relative density of the earth. He moved to Bedford Square in 1784, and established here his collection of minerals and a semi-public library of some 12,000 volumes, from which he never removed a book without leaving a receipt; books filled the entire first floor of the house, and a large part of the other storeys too. Cavendish retained the house – along with another, at Clapham Common, that held his laboratory – until his death. A valuer then declared of number 11 that he had 'scarce ever met with a more substantial or better built House'; it was finished, he continued, with 'the best materials', which included floors of Norway oak and a staircase of Portland stone.[13] The interior decor was uniformly green. Cavendish was taciturn to the point of Trappism; partly, it is said, because he had a high-pitched voice. He lived here with three servants, with whom he usually communicated by written note. The house, which was probably designed by Robert Palmer, agent to the 4th Duke of Bedford, is at the north-east corner of the square, where Gower Street meets Montague Place. The handsome bronze plaque is on the Montague Place elevation between two blind windows. It was put up by the Bedford Estate in 1904 in response to an LCC suggestion, and was incorporated into the official plaques scheme in 1983.

Several plaques may be seen in Gower Street, WC1, which runs north-east from Bedford Square and is named in honour of Gertrude Leveson-Gower – widow of the 4th Duke of Bedford – who oversaw its development in the late eighteenth century. The thoroughfare, with its long brick terraces, was described by RUSKIN as 'the ne plus ultra of ugliness in street architecture'.[14] At 7 (formerly 83) Gower Street, on the corner of Gower Mews, a plaque records the founding in 1848 of **The Pre-Raphaelite Brotherhood** 16 (fig. 54). The nucleus of this group consisted of the painters

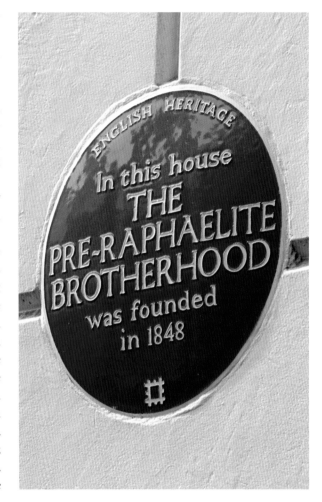

JOHN EVERETT MILLAIS, WILLIAM HOLMAN HUNT and DANTE GABRIEL ROSSETTI. Other members were the painter James Collinson (1825–1881), the sculptor Thomas Woolner (1825–1892), and the art critics Frederic George Stephens (1827–1907) and William Michael Rossetti (1829–1919), Dante Gabriel's younger brother. The crucial meeting of the 'brotherhood', at which they drew up their manifesto, took place at this house – then the Millais family home – in September 1848. The group's first paintings were exhibited the following year, signed 'PRB'; colourful and naturalistic, they were inspired by the unaffected simplicity of early Italian art. For their defiance of the conventional wisdom of the time – that the work of Raphael was peerless, and that of his antecedents indubitably inferior – they earned the opprobrium of, among others, DICKENS, but were defended by Ruskin. Although their youthful idealism brought them into conflict with the art establishment, the three leading Pre-Raphaelites went on to enjoy great success, and the foundation of the group is

55   A drawing of the interior of 2 Gower Street, taken from Rhoda and Agnes Garrett's *Suggestions for House Decoration in Painting, Woodwork and Furniture* (1876). Agnes lived at the house with her sister Millicent Garrett Fawcett for many years.

now seen as a seminal moment in British art history. The house, which is part of a terrace of eight dating from about 1780, was numbered 83 during the occupancy of the Millais family (1845–54). The unveiling of the plaque in 1998, timed to coincide with the 150th anniversary of the brotherhood's foundation, was attended by great-grandchildren of Millais, Rossetti and Hunt.

The rendered frontage of 2 Gower Street bears a plaque to **Dame Millicent Garrett Fawcett** (1847–1929) **17** , the pioneer of women's suffrage. Born in Suffolk, Millicent Garrett – the younger sister of ELIZABETH GARRETT ANDERSON – gave her first public speech in favour of votes for women in 1869 and presided over the campaign leading up to the foundation of the National Union of Women's Suffrage Societies in 1897. She took a gradualist approach to promoting the cause, and her attitude to the more militant suffragettes led by the PANKHURSTS was ambivalent. Fawcett was a more conservative figure, being opposed to Home Rule for Ireland and a strong supporter of the war effort in 1914–18; a moralist in personal matters, she once tore up a 'mischievous and objectionable' pamphlet advocating free love, though came to advocate divorce by mutual consent.[15] Millicent moved to Gower Street in 1884 – following the death of her husband, Henry Fawcett, who had been a Liberal minister – and died at the address forty-five years later. When she moved in – together with her daughter Philippa (1868–1948), a fellow suffrage campaigner – it was already the residence of her sister Agnes (1845–1935), who was well known as an interior designer, and was responsible for two decorated ceilings at the house (fig. 55). She proved a supportive and strong companion for the widowed Millicent, who, in her own words, 'always loved the Gower Street house and all its associations'.[16] The plaque was proposed by the Fawcett Society, which continues Millicent Fawcett's work of promoting equality between men and women, and was erected by the LCC in 1954.

At 10 Gower Street – part of the same terrace, dating from about 1780 – is the plaque to **Lady Ottoline Morrell** (1873–1938) **18** , the literary hostess and patron of the arts (fig. 56). Born Ottoline Cavendish-Bentinck in Portman Square, Marylebone, she married Philip Morrell (1870–1943), a Liberal politician and

member of the Oxford brewing dynasty, at the age of twenty-eight. The marriage was not, conventionally speaking, a success – Philip Morrell was an incorrigible philanderer – but the couple became renowned for their literary and artistic parties both at Garsington, their Oxfordshire home until 1928, and in London. In 1906 the Morrells moved to 44 Bedford Square; Ottoline's famous Thursday soirées began the following year – a tangible expression of her desire to live life 'on the same plane as poetry and as music'.[17] They were revived at the couple's home from 1927, 10 Gower Street, where guests included Stephen Spender, W. B. YEATS, LYTTON STRACHEY, SIEGFRIED SASSOON and T. S. ELIOT. It was also at this address, where Lady Ottoline spent the rest of her life, that she wrote her memoirs. Standing at almost six feet (183 cm) tall, she had a penchant for eccentric period costumes and outsize headdresses. Some of the artists and writers who benefited from her patronage – who included

56   Lady Ottoline Morrell and her young daughter, Julian [*sic*], stroll along the south side of Bedford Square in 1909. [© National Portrait Gallery, London]

Jacob Epstein, Mark Gertler and many of the Bloomsbury Group – were unable to restrain themselves from sniggering behind their hands at her appearance, her strange, nasal voice and peculiar mannerisms. Lady Ottoline was used as a literary archetype by, among others, D. H. Lawrence, with whom – as with Bertrand Russell – she had a tortured love affair. Her plaque was put up on the house – now owned by the University of London – in 1986.

Two doors up in the same terrace, at 14 (formerly 7) Gower Street, is the plaque to **James Robinson** (1813–1862) 19 , the pioneer of anaesthesia and dentistry. Robinson wrote a groundbreaking text on dental treatments, *The Surgical, Mechanical and Medical Treatment of the Teeth* (1846), and was the first person to use anaesthetic in Britain. This breakthrough was made at 52 Gower Street, the now-demolished home of Dr Francis Boott. There, on 19 December 1846, a lucky patient named Miss Lonsdale received an early Christmas present: the painless extraction of a molar while she slumbered under ether. Robinson wrote a treatise on the subject in 1847. His own practice was based at his town house, then numbered 7 Gower Street, from 1842 until his death, which took place at his country residence at Kenton, Middlesex, following an accident with a pruning knife. Among Robinson's other achievements were the publication of a journal, *Forceps* (1844–45), and the part he took in founding what became the Royal Dental Hospital and the University College Hospital Dental School. He was the first President of the College of Dentists (1856–58), but his efforts to forge a single professional association were not advanced by his prickly, intense personality. This may account too for the relative obscurity of Robinson's pioneering work, which the erection of this plaque, in 1991, has done something to rectify.

At 91 Gower Street (formerly 29 Upper Gower Street) is a plaque to **George Dance the Younger** (1741–1825) 20 , a successful and highly influential architect for more than fifty years. Among his commissions were the Church of All Hallows, London Wall (1765–67), Newgate Prison (1770–84; demolished 1902) and the Royal College of Surgeons building at Lincoln's Inn (1806–13). He was also responsible for the embellishment of the Guildhall (1788–89) and the layout of Finsbury Circus (1802); like his architect father,

George Dance the Elder, he held the office of Clerk of Works to the City of London. Dance lived at this address – a four-storey house built in 1789 which was then known as 29 Upper Gower Street – from 1790 until his death. The house was one of the many to take account of the London Building Act of 1774, legislation that set down minimum building standards and which Dance had helped to draft. A GLC historian commented that 'it is no doubt fitting that the architect should have chosen as his London home for many years one of the simple but excellently proportioned brick-built terrace houses that were such an important contribution to the Georgian townscape'.[18] The plaque, which was put up in 1970, was suggested by the architectural historian Dorothy Stroud; in her 1971 biography of Dance, Stroud suggested that he may have been responsible for some surviving internal details 'of very restrained design, including two chimney pieces on the first floor'.[19]

The northern portion of Gower Street has long been dominated by the buildings of University College London (founded 1827). Fixed to the college's modern Biological Sciences Building – which occupies the site of 110 Gower Street (formerly 12 Upper Gower Street) – is a plaque to the naturalist **Charles Darwin** (1809–1882) 21 . Erected in 1961, the plaque records Darwin's residence in the house on this site between 1838 and 1842, during which time he wrote *The Structure and Distribution of Coral Reefs* (1842), inspired by his five-year voyage on the *Beagle*, and sketched out his developing evolutionary theories; these, published as *On the Origin of Species* (1859), won him international acclaim. Darwin moved to number 110 during the very last days of 1838, barely two weeks before he married Emma Wedgwood (1808–1896); her pleasure at his having secured a lease on the yellow-curtained house – which, from its riotous decorative colour scheme, they nicknamed 'Macaw Cottage' – was tempered with an expression of hope that the previous occupants had 'discarded that dead dog out the garden'.[20] Darwin's son Francis – who was born after the family left Gower Street – described it as 'a small common-place London house, with a drawing room in front and a small room behind, in which [the family] lived for the sake of quietness'. He remembered how in after years 'my father used to laugh over the surpassing ugliness of the furniture, carpets, etc. . . . The only redeeming feature

address most readily associated with him: Down House, Kent. A plaque was originally installed on number 110 by the LCC in 1906, but the house was seriously damaged in the Second World War and demolished soon afterwards (fig. 57). Its successor, the Biological Sciences Building, dates from 1959–64.

Just north of the Euston Road, at 183 North Gower Street (formerly 9 George Street), NW1, an LCC plaque commemorates the Italian patriot **Giuseppe Mazzini** (1805–1872) ㉒ . The building – which, being double-fronted, is now incorporated with number 185 – is part of a Georgian terrace of five houses that narrowly escaped demolition in the 1960s as part of the redevelopment of Tolmers Square just to the west. As well as being a patriot, Mazzini – born in Genoa – was a republican and a democrat, in the European meaning of those terms, whose political aim of forming a single Italian state led to his exile from his homeland. In his absence, he was sentenced to death, and in 1837 moved to England. He lived at what was then known as 9 George Street from March of that year until March 1840. During this time, Mazzini earned a living from literary journalism and made contacts with, among others, JOHN STUART MILL and several leading Chartists. In a characteristic large-hearted gesture, he took in a young foundling called Susannah, who became his housekeeper. Mazzini went on to lead a short-lived radical administration in Rome during 1849; after its demise he returned to London, where he spent a large part of the rest of his life. He often went under an alias, and at most addresses his stay was brief. An exception was the now-demolished 2 Onslow Terrace, Fulham; this was known as 18 Fulham Road during his residence, which lasted for most of the 1860s. In 1872 Mazzini returned incognito to Italy, where he died shortly afterwards.

At 8 Taviton Street, WC1, is the plaque to **Hugh Price Hughes** (1847–1902) ㉓ , the Methodist preacher. Welsh by birth, Hughes spent most of his life in London. In 1884 he became the minister at Brixton Hill, and founded the *Methodist Times* a year later. He continued to edit this weekly paper until his death, which occurred in his study at Taviton Street. Hughes moved here in September 1887, having taken up a new post as Superintendent of the West London Methodist Mission, based in Holborn; with him came his children

57 Number 110 Gower Street and its LCC plaque to Charles Darwin in a photograph of autumn 1940, showing the scale of the bomb damage to the building. [Reproduced by permission of English Heritage]

was a better garden than most London houses have, a strip as wide as the house and thirty yards long'.[21] Somewhat to his surprise, Darwin took to London life: 'there is a grandeur about its smoky fogs, and the dull, distant sounds of cabs and coaches; in fact you may perceive I am becoming a thorough-paced Cockney', he told a friend in 1839.[22] He began to suffer from poor health, however, and on 14 September 1842 moved with his family and their butler, Joseph Parslow, to the

advancing time'.[23] Yet he refused to join a petition against the removal of the gates a few years later, on the grounds that Jesus would not have approved such a course 'when hundreds of people have to go a mile out of their way because half a dozen of us do not want to be disturbed'.[24] Hughes was behind the 'Forward Movement' in Methodism, which combined evangelism with social work, and he was made the first President of the National Free Church Council in 1896 – an illustration of his commitment to Nonconformist unity. A plaque to Hughes was first proposed in 1933, but the Taviton Street premises – which are part of a mid-1820s terrace designed by Thomas Cubitt – were at that time earmarked for demolition by the Bedford Estate. The building's future was secure by 1989, when a plaque was set up by English Heritage.

Gordon Square, WC1, was laid out by Thomas Cubitt in the mid-1820s, though some of the buildings of this 'Georgian' square were not completed until 1857. One of the earlier builds was number 46, which bears a plaque to the economist **John Maynard Keynes** (1883–1946) **24** (fig. 58). Arguably the most influential economist since Adam Smith, Keynes is remembered for the system of deficit finance that bears his name – Keynesianism – as described in his best-known book, *The General Theory of Employment, Interest and Money* (1936). He moved to 46 Gordon Square in 1916 as a tenant of the art critic Clive Bell (1881–1964) and his wife, the artist Vanessa Bell (1879–1961); earlier, the house had been occupied by Vanessa and her siblings, who included Virginia Woolf. Like them, Keynes belonged to the Bloomsbury Group; according to his biographer, 'most of the practical arrangements for Bloomsbury's collective London life were concentrated in his hands'.[25] Clive Bell called the house the group's '*monument historique*', and its several Bloomsbury connections led to consideration being given to commemorate the group as a whole.[26] However, unlike, for example, the Pre-Raphaelites, they were considered too amorphous a collection to merit such treatment. Keynes took over the lease of number 46 in 1918, and remained at the house until his death. Clive Bell kept a pied-à-terre here until 1924, and their periods of cohabitation were occasionally fractious: one unedifying dispute about an uncomfortable bed ended with Bell suggesting – in unvarnished language – that Keynes ought to take it because he was the less sexu-

58　The former home of John Maynard Keynes, seen from the garden of Gordon Square. [© English Heritage. Photograph by Derek Kendall]

and wife Mary, née Barrett (1853–1948), herself an active participant at the mission. Taviton Street was then gated, and a sabbatarian stillness reigned: 'We might be in the midst of the most delicious rural retreat', Hughes observed to his family, comparing the distant sound of the Euston Road to 'the roar of

BLOOMSBURY AND HOLBORN

ally active. Keynes worked for the Treasury during the early part of his time at Gordon Square before becoming, in 1924, Bursar of King's College, Cambridge. His wife, the ballet dancer Lydia Vasilievna Lopokova (1892–1981), remained at the address until 1948, and the plaque was put up in 1975.

At 51 Gordon Square is the plaque to a more flamboyant 'Bloomsburyite', **Lytton Strachey** (1880–1932) 25 , the critic and biographer. Strachey is best known for *Eminent Victorians* (1918), his pungent account of the lives of Florence Nightingale, General Gordon, Thomas Arnold and Cardinal Manning, which contrasted with the uncritical, magisterial biographies that were then the norm. In the preface, he recommended that 'a becoming brevity . . . is the first duty of the biographer'.[27] What he would have made of the exhaustive treatment since afforded to most of the Bloomsbury Group can only be a matter for speculation. Strachey's mother, the suffragist Jane Strachey (1840–1928), secured the house in Gordon Square in 1919 and appears to have moved in early the following year. Also based at number 51, which dates from 1857, were the unmarried Strachey sisters: Pippa (1872–1968), Marjorie (1882–1964) and Pernel (1876–1951). The terrace was already home to many of the Bloomsbury Group, causing Strachey to observe to Virginia Woolf, 'Very soon I foresee that the whole square will become a sort of college, and the rencontres in the garden I shudder to think of'.[28] It was his own chief London residence from 1921; he deemed it 'a great deal more comfortable & convenient' than the family's previous address in Belsize Park Gardens, and he had a self-contained flat on the ground floor – where the plaque is situated – from 1929 until his death.[29] Parts of *Queen Victoria* (1921) and *Elizabeth and Essex* (1928) were written at the house. Strachey's biographer Michael Holroyd, who proposed the plaque, discovered his subject's lost fellowship dissertation on Warren Hastings, the controversial Governor-General of Bengal, in the basement of number 51 during a visit in 1963, the family having given up the lease on the increasingly decrepit house not long before. An 'In/Out' board still stood in the entrance hall: deceased members of the Strachey family, some of whom had been dead for half a century, were marked as 'out'. The plaque was unveiled in 1971 by the historian Lord (Noel) Annan, whose early work on the Bloomsbury

Group was followed, appropriately, by his becoming Provost of nearby University College.

By the door of 14 Gordon Square, the home since 1890 of the Dr Williams's Library, is a plaque installed in 1990 in honour of **Robert Travers Herford** (1860–1950) 26 , the Unitarian minister, scholar and interpreter of Judaism. Herford both lived and worked at this address from 1914 to 1925: he was Secretary of the library, whose collection is devoted to the study of religious Nonconformity. The library building – constructed in a Tudor revival style in 1848–49 – had previously been a university hall of residence, in which Herford had lodged in his student days. A pioneering scholar of Judaism and a promoter of Judaeo-Christian relations, Herford explored the common heritage of the two traditions in works such as *Judaism in the New Testament Period* (1928) and *Talmud and Apocrypha* (1933); in lighter moments he referred to himself as a 'Jewnitarian'.[30] His work confronted some of the deepest-rooted assumptions of anti-Semitism; this – particularly at the time when he was writing – was of more than merely academic significance. Herford made the acquaintance of many Jewish scholars in London, and was able to trace several of his continental contacts after the Second World War.

On a truncated six-house terrace south of Gordon Square – all that remains of Torrington Square, WC1, following the development of the London University precinct – is an ornate bronze plaque erected by the Bedford Estate in about 1913. It is at number 30, and records the residence of **Christina Georgina Rossetti** (1830–1894) 27 , who is quaintly described thereon as 'poetess' (figs 59 and 60). The sister of Dante Gabriel Rossetti and William Michael Rossetti, Christina's reputation and influence as a poet have grown with the passage of time. Some of her earliest verses were published under the pseudonym Ellen Alleyn in the short-lived Pre-Raphaelite journal *The Germ*. Perhaps her best-known literary work is the collection *Goblin Market and other Poems* (1862), though Christina's name has come before a wider public through her authorship of the words of the Christmas carol 'In the Bleak Midwinter'; published posthumously, this is supposed to have been written before 1872. Christina Rossetti moved to Torrington Square – 'Torrington oblong', in brother Dante Gabriel's sceptical view –

59 The elaborate bronze plaque to Christina Rossetti at 30 Torrington Square. Erected by the Bedford Estate in c.1913, it was incorporated into the London-wide scheme by the GLC in 1974. [© English Heritage. Photograph by Derek Kendall]

HERE
LIVED AND DIED
CHRISTINA GEORGINA
ROSSETTI
POETESS
BORN 1830·DIED 1894

BLOOMSBURY AND HOLBORN

from the nearby Euston Road in 1876.[31] She shared the house – which was built by James Sim in the early 1820s – with her widowed mother Frances Rossetti (1800–1886) and two maternal aunts, Eliza Polidori (1809/10–1893) and Charlotte Polidori (1797/8–1890). As a home it was both expensive and gloomy, being darkened by soot-blackened trees that then stood in the square in front. 'Entering it you felt the presence of very old age, a silence that draped and muffled the house', remarked one visitor.[32] Certainly, Christina Rossetti's life was much restricted by the needs of her elderly relatives, who became bedridden in their later years: her nephew FORD MADOX FORD thought that her existence must have been 'extremely tragic' and detected in her poems 'a passionate yearning for the country'.[33] Christina's own health was failing by the time her aunt Eliza died in 1893, and her last companion was an indomitable Persian cat named Muff, who travelled around the house draped around her shoulders. A deeply religious High Anglican, her verse was chiefly devotional in her

later years, an exception being the sonnet sequence *Monna Innominata* (1881). Christina Rossetti died in the front drawing room at 30 Torrington Square. She was proposed for commemoration by her early biographer, Mackenzie Bell; the plaque was incorporated into the official scheme in 1974.

At 21 Russell Square, WC1, another bronze plaque erected by the Bedford Estate marks the residence of the law reformer **Samuel Romilly** (1757–1818) **28** . Romilly was indefatigable in his efforts to soften the savage eighteenth-century penal code; among his achievements was the abolition of the death penalty for pickpockets in 1808. A Whig, Romilly was elected to Parliament in 1806, and served as Solicitor-General in the short-lived 'talents' ministry of 1806–7; he was also an active campaigner for the abolition of slavery. When a plaque for Romilly was first suggested in 1904, the LCC contemplated marking his birthplace, 18 Frith Street, Soho, W1, but were rebuffed by the occupier. The Duke of Bedford then agreed to a plaque in Russell Square, where Romilly lived for the most active part of his career, from 1805 – when the square was newly laid out – until his death. This, however, was blocked by the

lessee – the fact of Romilly's having committed suicide here, in a fit of grief following the death of his wife Anne (*c.* 1773–1818), seems to have been the cause of this reluctance. Attention switched to a third address, 54 Gower Street (formerly 27 Lower Gower Street), on which the Bedford Estate fixed a tablet in 1906. This had disappeared by 1912, the house having been rebuilt. Rather than mark the new structure, the Bedford Estate preferred to erect a plaque at the Russell Square address, where a new tenant proved amenable. This was done in 1919, and the plaque was brought into the official scheme in 1983. Number 21 is an imposing four-storey three-bayed house, part of a terrace of four by James Burton. It dates from the first years of the nineteenth century but was considerably altered ninety years later.

Close to Bloomsbury's northern extent is the English Heritage plaque to the artist **Paul Nash** (1889–1946) **29** , who lived in Flat 176, Queen Alexandra Mansions, Bidborough Street, WC1. Nash moved here upon his marriage to Margaret Odeh (d. 1960) in 1914, and it remained his London base for the next twenty-two years. One of his most famous pictures was *Northern Adventure* (1929) (fig. 61), a Surrealist take on the

62 Thomas Carlyle's house at 33 Ampton Street in a photograph of 1949. [Reproduced by permission of English Heritage. NMR]

view of St Pancras Station from the small fifth-floor flat occupied by Nash and his wife – a prospect now impeded by Camden Town Hall. It was one of a series that he painted of the station – which also included the more conventional *St Pancras Lilies* (1927) – after a visit to several historic Italian cities drew him to architecture as a subject. A landscape painter of distinction, Nash was an official war artist in both world wars, and famously produced the stark battlescape *The Menin Road* (1918–19) and *Totes Meer* (1940–41), which depicts the twisted wreckage of German planes. He was dogged by asthma, and his search for a cure took him out of London to country retreats on the borders of Sussex and Kent, and in Dorset. Nash finally moved away from Queen Alexandra Mansions – to the fresher air of Hampstead – in 1936. The Queen Anne-style block, which dates from 1912, was chosen over his Kensington birthplace – Ghuzree Lodge, 2 Sunningdale Gardens, W8 – on account of the significance of his time in Bloomsbury to his artistic career.

East of Gray's Inn Road lies Ampton Street, WC1, once part of the Calthorpe estate. Set into the distinctive stucco frontage of 33 (formerly 4) Ampton Street is a brown wreathed LCC plaque to **Thomas Carlyle** (1795–1881) **30** , the essayist and historian (fig. 62 and see fig. 18). Carlyle, best known for his history of the French Revolution, was generally venerated as an intellectual colossus by his contemporaries. He and his wife Jane, née Welsh (1801–1866), whose tortured marriage lasted for nearly forty years, lodged at the Ampton Street address – then numbered 4 – for about six months from September 1831. It was the first London address that they shared; Thomas Carlyle, bedevilled by bedbugs in his previous lodgings near Tavistock Square, reported to his mother that the house's owners, a family named Miles, were 'cleanly, orderly and seem honest: no noises, no bugs disturb one through the night'. He complained, however, of its '*hamperedness . . .* I have a sort of feeling as if I were tied up in a *sack*, and could not get my fins stirred'.[34] He nonetheless wrote the philosophical essay *Characteristics* (1831) and a piece on Dr Johnson while living here. In March 1832 the Carlyles left London for a spell in their native Scotland, but Thomas returned to Ampton Street briefly in May 1834, before securing on 10 June 1834 their long-term London residence at 24 (then 5) Cheyne Row, Chelsea, SW3. This house, now

owned by The National Trust, became a museum to the prominent literary couple – through her letters and journal, Jane Carlyle rose to equal fame with her husband – and was therefore not considered for commemoration by the LCC. The plaque at number 33, installed in 1907, may be regarded as something of a lucky charm: the house – built in the 1820s – was one of the few in Ampton Street to survive the Second World War.

Only the north and east terraces of Mecklenburgh Square, WC1, survive from the original design of *c.* 1808 by Joseph Kay. On the square's east side, two plaques frame the doorway of number 21, part of a terrace built by George Payne, which features a notable stucco frontage (fig. 63). The first to go up was that to **R. H. Tawney** (1880–1962) **31** , the historian, teacher and political writer. A Christian Socialist and a professor at the London School of Economics, Richard Henry Tawney was one of the leading left-wing thinkers of the twentieth century, and exerted a strong influence on the philosophy and policy of post-war Labour governments. His best-known books were a critique of contemporary capitalism, *The Acquisitive Society* (1921), and a historical investigation into its origins, *Religion and the Rise of Capitalism* (1926). Tawney lived at four separate addresses in Mecklenburgh Square: he was at number 17 in 1913–15, and moved to number 44 in 1922, staying there until the early years of the Second World War. After the war, Tawney returned to the square, in which opulent surroundings he always considered himself 'a displaced peasant'; slippers and an old First World War army tunic were his familiar attire, and he was constantly wreathed in pipe smoke.[35] When not at their home in Stroud, Gloucestershire, he and his wife Jeannette (d. 1958) – sister of the social reformer William Beveridge, a friend of Tawney's at Balliol College, Oxford – lived at 26 Mecklenburgh Square (now rebuilt) from about 1947. They settled at number 21 – the commemorated address – in 1951; here, Tawney remained until very shortly before his death. He had refused a peerage in 1933 and, when the plaque was unveiled in 1980 on the centenary of his birth, it was pointed out that he might not have appreciated it.

The second plaque at 21 Mecklenburgh Square (see fig. 63) was erected by English Heritage and commemorates an earlier resident, **Sir Syed Ahmed Khan** (1817–1898) **32**, the Muslim reformer and scholar. Syed Ahmed lived in the house for seventeen months during 1869 and 1870, along with his sons Syed Mahmud and Syed Hamed – he had been widowed about eight years previously – and another compatriot, Khudadad Beg. As a magistrate in the service of the East India Company, Syed Ahmed (otherwise rendered as Saiyid Ahmad) saved thousands of British lives during the Great Rebellion in 1857 (formerly known as the Indian Mutiny), and in 1888 became one of the first Indians – and the first Muslim – to be knighted. On arriving in London in May 1869, the Syed party stayed briefly at the Charing Cross Hotel before taking furnished rooms at 21 Mecklenburgh Square, which then belonged to a Mr and Mrs Ludlam. The notion of living as a tenant was unfamiliar to him, but Syed Ahmed found the arrangement 'extremely comfortable' and his hosts charming yet unobtrusive; the four members of the party occupied six rooms and were attended by two servants.[36] While here, Syed Ahmed watched the Epsom Derby and witnessed the opening of the Holborn Viaduct; he also responded in print to hostile treatments of the prophet Mohammed and studied the English university system: the appetite for

adult education of the British public – especially British women – impressed him greatly. On his return to India he founded the Muhammadan Anglo-Oriental College at Aligarh (1877), which continues today as the Aligarh Muslim University. Sir Syed Ahmed was a pioneer of Islamic modernism, developing a theology that took account of European science; his approach can be gauged from the title of the periodical he founded, the *Mohammedan Social Reformer*. The plaque was unveiled in 1997 by its proposer, Syed Ahmed's modern biographer Dr Mohamed Abudulla Pasha.

At 20 Calthorpe Street, WC1, is a plaque to the architect **William Richard Lethaby** (1857–1931) **33** (see also pp. 59–60). During his time at the house – where he lived from 1880 to 1891 – Lethaby worked in the office of Richard Norman Shaw, and assisted in the design of New Scotland Yard (1888–90) on Victoria Embankment, now known as the 'Norman Shaw Building'. In 1883, Lethaby designed what was, by his later minimalist standards of decoration, a very ornate fireplace for Shaw's country-house masterpiece, Cragside, Northumberland. In 1889 he set up his own practice, and completed six large building commissions – five country houses and a church, All Saints, Brockhampton, Herefordshire (1901–2) – before devoting himself to teaching and scholarship. As well as his role at the Central School of Arts and Crafts – for which Shaw recommended him – Lethaby acted as art adviser to the LCC and was from 1900 to 1918 the first Professor of Design at the Royal College of Art. Although raised as a Bible Christian, he served as Surveyor of Westminster Abbey from 1906 to 1928 and wrote on its history. Number 20 is part of an early nineteenth-century yellow-brick terrace on the Calthorpe estate development overseen by Thomas Cubitt. The terrace only narrowly escaped demolition in the years just before the plaque went up in 1979.

Doughty Street, WC1, takes its name from the family that once owned the area, while its construction dates from the first two decades of the nineteenth century. At number 58, a plaque commemorates the joint residence of **Vera Brittain** (1893–1970) and **Winifred Holtby** (1898–1935) **34**, the writers and reformers. Brittain is renowned for her autobiographical *Testament of Youth* (1933), which deals with the devastating

63 The plaques to R. H. Tawney and Sir Syed Ahmed Khan framing the doorway of 21 Mecklenburgh Square. [© English Heritage. Photograph by Derek Kendall]

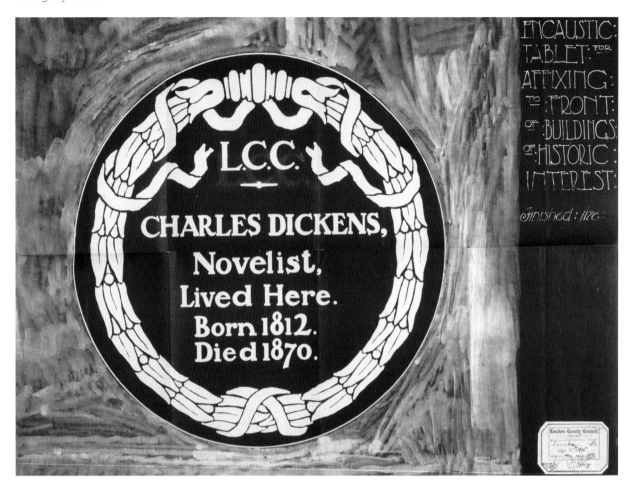

blow dealt to her generation by the First World War, in which she lost her fiancé. Holtby, a prolific author and journalist during her short life, is probably best known for the posthumously published *South Riding* (1936). The pair met at Somerville College, Oxford, both having worked as nurses during the war. Doughty Street, then a far more bohemian place than it is today, was their first London address; they lived in a tiny flat at the rear of number 52, to which they moved in December 1921, before transferring to a top-floor flat at number 58 in September 1922. 'In Doughty Street we had few comforts and no luxuries except a tortoise called Adolphus', Brittain later recalled; the flat was infested with mice, though its windows caught the afternoon sun, and it was cheerfully furnished in blue and mauve.[37] Both women had their first novels published in 1923: Holtby's *Anderby Wold* and Brittain's *The Dark Tide*, the latter an unflattering depiction of college life at Oxford; they also worked as freelance journalists, and took teaching jobs to make ends meet. Brittain and Holtby moved to Maida Vale

in autumn 1923, and continued to live under the same roof after Brittain's marriage to George Catlin in 1925. Brittain's biography of Holtby, *Testament of Friendship*, was published in 1940. Number 58 Doughty Street was selected for commemoration after the owners of Brittain and Holtby's residence in Glebe Place, Chelsea – where they lived after 1930 – refused to allow a plaque on their house. The plaque was unveiled by Brittain's daughter, the politician Shirley Williams, in 1995.

In the same terrace of sixteen houses, built between 1807 and 1809, is 48 Doughty Street, which bears a plaque to the novelist **Charles Dickens** (1812–1870) 35 . The blue wreathed tablet of 1903 was only the second installed by the LCC, and is the earliest of the council's plaques to survive (fig. 64). It pre-dates the opening of the house as a museum to Dickens in 1925, prior to which it had been under threat of demolition. Dickens moved to number 48 from Furnival Chambers, Holborn, in March 1837 on a three-year lease,

65 The garden of 14 Doughty Street, the former home of Sydney Smith, in a photograph of June 2005. [© English Heritage. NMR. Photograph by Derek Kendall]

1896) and Kate (1839–1929) – were born to Charles and Catherine Dickens in Doughty Street, and during his time here Charles forged friendships with several important figures in the arts, including the actor William Charles Macready and Thomas Carlyle, and secured election to both the Garrick and Athenaeum clubs. It was the favourable sales of *Nickleby* that enabled him to move his growing family in December 1839 to a larger house – 1 Devonshire Terrace, Marylebone – which was controversially demolished in 1958, along with its LCC plaque. Externally, 48 Doughty Street remains substantially as it was during Dickens's time; internally, the museum contains much to interest the Dickens aficionado, including the desk at which he wrote many of his books.

At 14 (formerly 8) Doughty Street, a brown wreathed LCC plaque marks the home of **Sydney Smith** (1771–1845) **36**, the author and wit (fig. 65). Smith was a clergyman by profession, but it is for his irreverent bon mots that he is remembered: his response to the suggestion that St Paul's Cathedral be surrounded by wooden paving was 'Let the Dean and Canons lay their heads together and the thing will be done'.[38] Smith and his wife Catharine, née Pybus (1768–1852) settled at number 14, which is part of a terrace of nineteen houses, shortly after their arrival in London in August 1803. Previously, they had lived in Edinburgh, where he worked as a personal tutor and – more importantly – co-founded a vastly influential literary journal, the *Edinburgh Review*. The house in Doughty Street was then numbered 8, and had been built not long before. The Smiths' first months here were marred by the fatal illness of their infant son, Noel; Saba (1802–1866), their daughter, recalled the period as one of 'considerable anxiety and a severe and courageous struggle with poverty'.[39] Part of the reason for this was Smith's unwillingness to trim his liberal views to gain clerical preferment; among the then-controversial causes Smith supported were Catholic emancipation and women's education. A regular preaching engagement at the nearby Foundling Hospital eventually came in March 1805, and others followed, partly as a result of his lectures on moral philosophy – delivered at the Royal Institution – that set London buzzing. In the meantime, Smith continued to write for the *Edinburgh Review*, and became part of the whiggish Holland House Set. In 1806 he moved to 18 Orchard Street, just

paying the substantial sum of £80 a year in rent. He lived at the house with his wife Catherine (1816–1879) and her younger sister, Mary Hogarth (1820–1837); Mary's sudden death at the age of seventeen – which took place at number 48, in Dickens's arms – brought about the only hiatus in his prolific writing career. While living here he nonetheless completed *The Pickwick Papers* (1837–38), *Oliver Twist* (1837–39) and *Nicholas Nickleby* (1838–39), and made a start on *Barnaby Rudge* (1841). Two daughters – Mary (1838–

north of Oxford Street, which he left for Yorkshire in 1809. Smith later returned to London, telling a correspondent, 'I have no relish for the country; it is a kind of healthy grave'.[40] His plaque in Doughty Street was put up in 1905, but it proved faulty and was replaced the following year.

Number 23 (formerly 29) Great Ormond Street, WC1, was the home of the prison reformer **John Howard** (1726–1790) ㊲ . Left a substantial fortune by his father, Howard found his calling as a result of his own imprisonment in Brest, France, after an ambush by privateers. As High Sheriff of Bedfordshire during 1773, he was aghast to find that many acquitted prisoners were kept locked up until such time as they had paid a release fee to their gaolers. Howard secured Acts of Parliament to prohibit this, and to improve health and sanitation in prisons. Despite his own persistent ill-health, he visited nearly every county gaol in England, and published his findings as *The State of the Prisons in England and Wales, with Preliminary Observations, and an Account of some Foreign Prisons* (1777). This catalogue of iniquities had a great influence on the next generation of penal reformers, such as Sir Samuel Romilly and Jeremy Bentham. Howard's house in Great Ormond Street – then numbered 29 – was left to him in August 1777 by his sister, and was his London base for the rest of his life. It dates from the early eighteenth century, though the stucco facing was added in about the 1850s. In his lifetime, Howard, a deeply religious Nonconformist, scorned all tokens of acclaim: he never sat for a portrait, and once put a stop to a subscription for a statue in his honour. It is therefore likely that he would not have been gratified by the blue wreathed plaque placed on his old house by the LCC in 1908, though he surely would have been pleased that his cause is perpetuated by the Howard League for Penal Reform, founded as the Howard Association in 1866.

At 24 Great James Street, WC1, a plaque honours **Dorothy L. Sayers** (1893–1957) ㊳ , the writer of detective stories. Sayers moved here on Christmas Eve 1921, having told her parents that she had found three 'small but very pretty rooms'; previously, she had lived in nearby Mecklenburgh Square, in such artistic poverty that she could only afford to eat 'if she dispensed with curtains'.[41] The newly decorated, white-panelled flat in Great James Street cost her £70 a year,

on an initial three-year lease. It was while living here, in January 1924, that Sayers gave birth to an illegitimate son, a fact she concealed from most of her family. In 1926 she married a journalist, Oswald Atherton 'Mac' Fleming (1881–1950), who – like her most famous literary creation, Lord Peter Wimsey – suffered from the after-effects of his experiences in the First World War. The couple shared their Great James Street home with a series of cats brought in to combat a mouse infestation. In 1929 they moved to Witham, Essex, but kept on the London flat as a pied-à-terre. Among the works Sayers wrote here were her first novel, *Whose Body?* (1923), which introduced the character of Lord Peter Wimsey, *Clouds of Witness* (1926), *Unnatural Death* (1927) and *The Unpleasantness at the Bellona Club* (1928). Meanwhile, in her day job at Benson's, an advertising agency, she devised the immortal slogan 'My Goodness, My Guinness'. Number 24 was the setting for her short story 'The Vindictive Story of the Footsteps that Ran', published in *Lord Peter Views the Body* (1928). Dating originally from the early eighteenth century, the house has been rebuilt since Sayers's residence, and is now incorporated into a single unit with number 23 next door. Her rooms would have been on the left-hand side of the present frontage, though the plaque is on the right.

At 22 Theobald's Road (formerly 6 King's Road), WC1, a brown wreathed LCC plaque marks the birthplace of the Conservative Prime Minister **Benjamin Disraeli, Earl of Beaconsfield** (1804–1881) ㊴ (see also pp. 435–6) (figs 66 and 67). The son of Isaac D'Israeli (1766–1848), a writer and historian, Benjamin Disraeli was a self-made man, and not averse to a little self-mythology: at various times he reportedly claimed to have been born in the Adelphi, where his father lived prior to his marriage; in the parish of St Mary Axe in the City; and at 6 Bloomsbury Square, to which his family moved in 1817. There is also a story that he was delivered at his grandparental home in Trinity Row, Islington – now 215 Upper Street, N1. However, it is all but certain that Disraeli was born at the commemorated address, then numbered 6 King's Road, in the early morning of 21 December 1804. Isaac D'Israeli and his wife Maria, née Basevi (1775–1847) were living at the house by 1802, and it was here – under the aegis of the Bevis Marks Synagogue – that the ceremony of circumcision took place, a week after young Benjamin

Above 67 The plaque to Benjamin Disraeli at 22 Theobald's Road. Erected in 1904, the plaque was destroyed during the Second World War and was replaced with a replica in 1948. [© English Heritage. Photograph by Derek Kendall]

Below 68 Sir Hiram Maxim with his famous invention, the Maxim gun, in a photograph of c.1880. [© Roger Viollet / Getty Images]

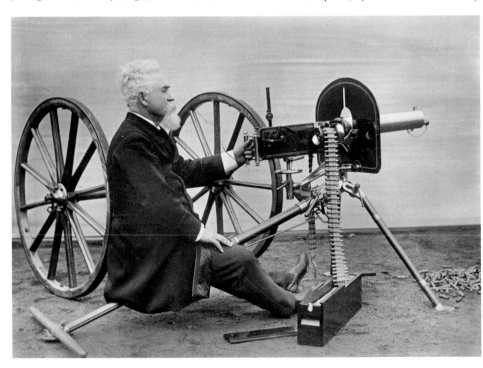

first drew breath. Disraeli went on to attend a school in Islington kept by a Miss Roper, before moving on to another in Blackheath run by the Rev. John Potticary. There he was given separate instruction in Judaism; his baptism into the Church of England took place at St Andrew's Holborn in July 1817, just before the family

left number 22, but it was not until 1822 that he dropped the apostrophe from the family name. The plaque was put up in 1904, amid fears that the house was to be pulled down. It was damaged by enemy action during the Second World War and the plaque was destroyed; an exact replica of the original design was used when the plaque was replaced in 1948. The house, which is part of a terrace of five built in about 1775, was once more earmarked for demolition in the late 1950s, and fell into decay before being restored in 1989.

At the corner of Hatton Garden and Clerkenwell Road lies Hatton House, 57D Hatton Garden, EC1. Commemorated here is **Sir Hiram Maxim** (1840–1916) **40**, the inventor and engineer who designed the eponymous Maxim gun, the first fully automatic machine gun, capable of firing off a devastating 500 rounds a minute (fig. 68). Maxim, who was born in Maine, USA, arrived in England in 1881 and soon afterwards took a business lease on these premises, which were built in 1880 and are outwardly little changed. Maxim perfected his gun by 1883 and set up the Maxim Gun Company the following year. The weapon soon attracted notice – HENRY MORTON STANLEY carried a Maxim gun on his mission to rescue David Livingstone in 1887 – and was adopted as standard by the British Army in 1889 and the Royal Navy in 1892. In 1888 Maxim's firm merged with Nordenfeldt and, having outgrown Hatton House, moved to Crayford, Kent. Eight years later, the business was absorbed by Vickers, the arms and aerospace firm, though Maxim – who became a naturalised British citizen in 1900 and was knighted in 1901 – remained a director until 1911. As an inventor, he was indefatigable: among his other, more benign, innovations were pre-Edisonian electric lights, an improved mousetrap and an expensive aeroplane that refused to become airborne. The proposal to honour Maxim came originally from the Norwood Society, which suggested marking his residence at 431 Norwood Road, Lambeth, a house that was demolished in the 1960s; he also lived in Bexleyheath and Streatham. The plaque was affixed to the workshop building in 1966.

On the Central School of Arts and Crafts (now Central St Martins) in Southampton Row, WC1, is a plaque to the architect **William Richard Lethaby** (1857–1931) **41** (see also p. 54), who served as first Principal of

At 17 Red Lion Square, WC1, a plaque commemorates three artists: the poet and painter **Dante Gabriel Rossetti** (1828–1882) (see also p. 191 and p. 518), the poet and artist **William Morris** (1834–1896) (see also pp. 567–8), and the painter **Sir Edward C. Burne-Jones** (1833–1898) (see also pp. 262–3) **42** (fig. 70). Rossetti took a lease on the first floor of this house with the painter Walter Howell Deverell (1827–1854) early in 1851, and stayed until May of that year. He is not known to have executed a major work during his brief stay but, five years later, recommended the place to Morris and Burne-Jones, in spite of its increasing dampness and decrepitude. The pair moved in during the summer of 1856 and remained here until the spring of 1859. The first-floor room at the front served as their studio, with its central window cut to the ceiling to optimise the light for painting, a feature since removed. Burne-Jones ('Ned') worked here on his early commissions, which included a collaboration with Rossetti and Morris on a scheme of murals for the Oxford Union building (1857–58). Meanwhile, Morris ('Topsy') embarked on his early ventures in interior decoration, producing for use in number 17 rough-hewn 'medieval' furniture that was notable more for its visual impact than for its ergonomics: 'If you want to be comfortable, go to bed', was his peremptory advice.[46] The young artists were attended by a housekeeper, Mary Nicolson, known as 'Red Lion Mary', who was also an able needleworker and contributed to Morris's designs. The house, designed by Nicholas Barbon and dating originally from the mid-1680s, was re-fronted in the early nineteenth century. The plaque, which is rectangular and of Hopton Wood stone, was affixed in 1911.

the school from 1896 to 1911. Born in Barnstaple, Devon, Lethaby was best known for his teaching and for his books on art and architecture, which exerted enormous influence on the development of twentieth-century British design; the art college he headed was soon hailed as 'a school of University rank for the artistic crafts'.[42] Anxious to promote good design to benefit British industry, Lethaby defined art simply as 'a well made thing'.[43] The teaching methods he promoted were correspondingly practical, with skilled craftsmen recruited to the college staff, among them the calligrapher EDWARD JOHNSTON. Lethaby was an active Principal, making stately progresses through classrooms 'like a white moustached rabbit, with a quick, dark eye'; his students felt themselves 'to be pioneers taking part in an exciting experiment'.[44] The plaque was put up in 1957 to mark the centenary of his birth; it would have gone on 111 Inverness Terrace, Bayswater, his residence in 1903–31, had it not been demolished shortly before. Originally, the Central School was based at Morley Hall in Regent Street, but in 1903 a site for the college was purchased in Southampton Row. In 1905–8, a classically influenced college building was constructed; Lethaby stipulated that it should be 'plain, reasonable and well-built', without ornamental flourish, and had a hand in its design, which was carried out by a former Central student, A. Halcrow Verstage (fig. 69).[45] The southern part of the building, on which the plaque was placed, was not part of the Central School at the time of Lethaby's stewardship, being occupied by the London Day Training College. This oversight influenced the later decision to commemorate Lethaby with a second plaque at his residence in Calthorpe Street, Bloomsbury.

The second plaque in Red Lion Square is on the Dane Street (formerly Leigh Street) elevation of number 12, a post-war office block named Summit House. It marks the site of the house occupied by **John Harrison** (1693–1776) 43 , the inventor of the marine chronometer. Harrison's achievement was the design of a timepiece that maintained sufficient accuracy on a long sea voyage to enable a ship's longitude to be calculated accurately. Reliable navigation was the basis of advantageous trade and imperial expansion, as well as being a matter of life and death for seafarers; in 1937 the proposer of the plaque, an LCC employee, made the astringent observation that 'surely an inventor who has saved hundreds or thousands of lives is as much worth attention as the scribblers whom the council delights to honour'.[47] Harrison was eventually awarded a plaque in 1954, war having intervened. The story of how this self-taught clockmaker from Lincolnshire came to make his chronometers, and of his subsequent battle with the Admiralty to obtain the full promised award of £20,000, has been the subject of a bestseller, Dava Sobel's *Longitude* (1995). Harrison moved to Red Lion Square in 1752, and the successful sea trials of his chronometers took place in 1761 and 1765; it was in the latter year too, and at this address, that he made the final disclosure and explanation of his H4 prototype design. Harrison's own room was on the second floor of the house; his first three experimental chronometers ticked away on the floor below, much as they do today at the Royal Observatory in Greenwich. Final settlement of his financial claims eventually came in 1773, just three years before his death, which occurred at number 12, a house that had been built about ninety years earlier. Between 1739 and 1752, Harrison was based nearby at 11 Orange Street, a now-vanished thoroughfare that ran westwards from the north side of Red Lion Square.

JOHN HARRISON's case for commemoration was enhanced by the fact that the LCC had already, in 1948, put up a plaque at nearby 119 High Holborn, WC1 – where the road joins Southampton Row – to **Thomas Earnshaw** (1749–1829) 44 , the watchmaker and chronometer maker. Earnshaw could not make the same claims to originality as Harrison, though the refinements he made to the marine chronometer were of sufficient importance for the British Horological Institute to suggest that Harrison could be credited as the 'orig-

inator' rather than the 'inventor' of the instrument, a distinction that the LCC judged would be lost on the public at large. Earnshaw's plaque – which was proposed by the Horological Institute and the Clockmakers' Company – is situated on an office building dating from the turn of the twentieth century, and marks the site of his workshop (he lived variously at addresses in Clerkenwell, St Pancras, Kennington and Greenford). Earnshaw was first apprenticed at 119 High Holborn to William Hughes; he inherited the business in 1792 and carried it on until about 1815, when it passed to his son Thomas (bap. 1774), who traded from the same High Holborn address until 1854. Like Harrison, Earnshaw wrestled with the problems of how to compensate for the effects of motion and temperature change on the mechanism of a timepiece. He possessed a combative – even rebarbative – personality, and carried on a long-running pamphleteering feud with a fellow clockmaker, John Arnold, over which of them deserved credit for one innovation, the spring-detent escapement. The Board of Longitude eventually awarded Earnshaw £3,000, in response to repeated petitioning; Earnshaw's mechanism, which ran without lubricating oil, was still in use over a century later.

Lincoln's Inn Fields, WC2, was developed from the mid-seventeenth century onwards around what is now the largest public square in London. Of the original houses, the sole survivor is number 59–60, on the square's west side, where a plaque commemorates the Prime Minister **Spencer Perceval** (1762–1812) 45 , who holds the unwanted record of being the only Prime Minister to be assassinated. This imposing building is known as Lindsey House, from the residence here in the early eighteenth century of the 4th Earl of Lindsey. Built in 1639–41, the house was divided in two in 1751–52. Spencer Perceval took up residence at number 59 in the early 1790s and reunited the two halves of the house with the purchase of number 60 in 1802. Short in stature, he was described by SYDNEY SMITH as having 'the head of a country parson, and the tongue of an Old Bailey Lawyer'.[48] Perceval became a King's Counsel and MP in 1796, and was Attorney-General in the Tory governments of Addington and PITT THE YOUNGER (1802–6). He left Lincoln's Inn Fields in 1807, shortly after accepting the post of Chancellor of the Exchequer in the Duke of Portland's administration. In 1809 Perceval became premier, but

BLOOMSBURY AND HOLBORN

his time at the top was abruptly terminated on 11 May 1812, when he was shot at point-blank range in the lobby of the House of Commons by one John Bellingham, a ruined merchant with a grudge. Perceval's dying words were reputed to have been, 'Oh, I am murdered!'. Cynics acclaimed this as a rare example of an unambiguous truth being uttered within the walls of Parliament. The house is set back at some distance from the pavement, and it is easy to miss the bronze LCC plaque with its dark patina; it was set up in 1914.

A few doors away, at 65 Lincoln's Inn Fields, there is a plaque to **William Marsden** (1796–1867) **46** , the surgeon and founder of the Royal Free and Royal Marsden hospitals. After having been unable to find a hospital bed for a desperately sick young woman he had found in a churchyard, Marsden opened a free dispensary at 16 Grenville Street, Hatton Garden, in 1828. During the 1832 cholera epidemic, it was the only foundation in London to admit sufferers; soon after, Marsden wrote a treatise on the disease. Thanks to the munificence of several wealthy backers, the dispensary became the Royal Free Hospital, which was situated in Gray's Inn Road until its move to Hampstead in 1978. This was not Marsden's only legacy: following the death of his first wife, Elizabeth Ann, from cancer in 1846, Marsden founded in 1851 the Free Cancer Hospi-

tal, dedicated to the study and treatment of the disease and based initially in Canon Row, Westminster. This became the Royal Marsden Hospital in Fulham Road, Brompton, the original part of which was completed in 1862. Marsden lived in Lincoln's Inn Fields from 1846 until his death; the square was then a popular address for surgeons, and has been the location since the early nineteenth century of the profession's Royal College. Number 65, a four-storey house designed by Thomas Leverton, dates from 1772. The plaque, embedded in its stone façade at first-floor level in 1986, was erected at the suggestion of the Royal Free Hospital and the Worshipful Company of Cordwainers, of which Marsden was a liveryman.

Just south of Holborn Circus, the author **Dr Samuel Johnson** (1709–1784) **47** is commemorated at 17 Gough Square, EC4 (see also pp. 378–9 and p. 381) (fig. 71). The brown encaustic-ware plaque is one of the earliest to survive, having been erected by the Society of Arts in 1876. It is an anomaly in that it lies within the City of London, where the Corporation of London has generally been responsible for commemorating historic sites. Dr Johnson's House, as it is known, is now a museum dedicated to the great lexicographer. It dates from the late seventeenth century, and has three storeys, a basement and a garret. It was in the building's attic rooms that Johnson worked on his famous *Dictionary of the English Language*, which was eventually published in two volumes in April 1755. This genre-defining work was completed with the help of five or six assistants who, despite Johnson's well-advertised prejudices, were mostly Scots. He presided precariously over their endeavours from a derelict armchair that was missing an arm and a leg. Johnson had moved to this address in 1746, just after he was contracted to produce the dictionary, in order to be closer to his printers in Fleet Street. It was in Gough Square that he suffered the loss of his wife Elizabeth, née Jervis (1689–1752); in after years, he could not bear to sit in the downstairs rooms that he associated with her. Among Johnson's many visitors was the actor DAVID GARRICK, who presented Johnson's tragedy *Irene* at Drury Lane in 1749. After the dictionary was finished, the house was deemed too large for his needs, and by March 1759 Johnson had moved into lodgings at Staple Inn, Holborn.

71   An etching of Dr Johnson's house at 17 Gough Square – with its plaque installed by the Society of Arts in 1876 – published in W. Monk's *Calendar* of 1931. [Courtesy of the Dr Johnson's House Trustees]

1 *The Young George du Maurier: A Selection of his Letters, 1860–67*, ed. Daphne du Maurier (London, 1951), p. 192 (12 January 1863)

2 Letter of 11 April 1974 on blue plaque file.

3 John Martin Robinson, *The Wyatts: An Architectural Dynasty* (Oxford, 1979), p. 226

4 Ray Monk, *Bertrand Russell: the Spirit of Solitude* (London, 1996), pp. 237–38

5 Ibid, p. 490

6 G. R. de Beer, *Sir Hans Sloane and the British Museum* (Oxford, 1953), p. 52. This work identifies Sloane's houses as numbers 3 and 4, failing to take into account the demolition of the original house at the eastern end of the terrace.

7 Paul Thompson, *William Butterfield* (London, 1971), p. 3

8 Sir Charles Mallet, *Anthony Hope and his Books* (London, 1935), p. 173 (September 1903)

9 Ibid, p. 183

10 Ibid, p. 232

11 S. S. Sprigge, *The Life and Times of Thomas Wakley* (London, 1897), p. 233

12 Sir Harry Ricardo, *Memories and Machines: The Pattern of my Life* (London, 1968), p. 13

13 Christa Jungnickel and Russell McCommach, *Cavendish: The Experimental Life* (Lewisberg, 1999), p. 315

14 Bridget Cherry and Nikolaus Pevsner, *The Buildings of England, London 4: North* (London, 1998), p. 325

15 R. Strachey, *Millicent Garrett Fawcett* (London, 1931), p. 236

16 Millicent Garrett Fawcett, *What I Remember* (London, 1924), p. 136

17 *Lady Ottoline's Album* (London, 1970), ed. C. G. Heilburn, intro. by Lord David Cecil, p. 14

18 Report of 16 September 1968 on blue plaque file.

19 Dorothy Stroud, *George Dance: Architect* (London, 1971), p. 170

20 *The Correspondence of Charles Darwin*, eds F. Burkhardt and S. Smith, vol. II (Cambridge, 1986), p. 149 (29 December 1938)

21 *The Life and Letters of Charles Darwin*, ed. Francis Darwin, vol. I (London, 1887), p. 299

22 Ibid, p. 299 (October 1839)

23 D. P. Hughes, *The Life of Hugh Price Hughes* (London, 1904), pp. 209–10

24 Ibid, p. 215

25 Robert Skidelsky, *John Maynard Keynes: Hopes Betrayed* (London, 1983), p. 332

26 Ibid

27 Lytton Strachey, *Eminent Victorians* (London, 1986 edn), p. 10

28 Michael Holroyd, *Lytton Strachey* (London, 1995), p. 462 (28 September 1919)

29 Barbara Caine, *Bombay to Bloomsbury: A Biography of the Strachey Family* (Oxford, 2005), p. 384

30 H. Maclachlan, *Robert Travers Herford: A Brief Sketch of his Life and Work* (London, *c.* 1951), p. 18

31 Kathleen Jones, *Learning not to be First: The Life of Christina Rossetti* (Moreton-in-Marsh, 1991), p. 175

32 Georgina Battiscombe, *Christina Rossetti: A Divided Life* (London, 1981), p. 189

33 Jones, *Learning not to be First*, p. 213

34 *The Collected Letters of Thomas and Jane Carlyle*, ed. C. R. Sanders (North Carolina, 1977), vol. VI, p. 23 (22 October 1831)

35 *ODNB*, vol. LIII, p. 849

36 G. F. I. Graham, *The Life and Work of Sir Syed Ahmed Khan* (London, 1909), p. 127

37 Vera Brittain, *Testament of Friendship* (London, 1941), p. 97

38 Hesketh Pearson, *The Smith of Smiths* (London, 1934), p. 237

39 Saba Holland, *Memoir of Sydney Smith*, vol. I (London, 1855), p. 108

40 *Letters of Sydney Smith*, ed. N. C. Smith, vol. II (Oxford, 1953), p. 668 (?July 1838)

41 David Coomes, *Dorothy L. Sayers: Careless Rage for Life* (Oxford, 1992), pp. 77–78 (21 November 1921)

42 Andrew Saint, 'Technical Education and the early LCC', in *Politics and the People of London: The London County Council 1889–1965*, ed. Andrew Saint (London, 1989), p. 80

43 Theresa Gronberg, 'William Richard Lethaby and the Central School of Arts and Crafts', in *W. R. Lethaby 1857–1931: Architecture, Design and Education*, eds Sylvia Backmeyer and Theresa Gronberg (London, 1984), p. 17

44 Ibid, p. 19

45 Ibid, p. 20

46 Fiona McCarthy, *William Morris: A Life for our Time* (London, 1994), p. 122

47 Note of 8 February 1937 on blue plaque file.

48 Denis Gray, *Spencer Perceval: The Evangelical Prime Minster* (Manchester, 1963), p. 15

72   Nelson Mandela unveils the
English Heritage plaque to his
friends and colleagues Ruth First
and Joe Slovo at 13 Lyme Street,
Camden, in 2003.
[© Troika Photos]

CAMDEN TOWN AND KENTISH TOWN

These parts of the parish of St Pancras began to be developed in the late eighteenth century, although the name Kentish Town dates back to medieval times. Camden Town was in existence by 1791, and took its title from the landowner Charles Pratt, 1st Earl Camden. The growth of both areas was affected by the completion of the Regent's Canal in 1816–20 and, in particular, by the coming of the railways in the mid-nineteenth century. Railway activity led to a loss of social cachet, and the two towns were overwhelmed by people seeking cheap housing; West Kentish Town and Agar Town, a squalid settlement to the east of St Pancras Way, were among the worst slums in London. Nonetheless, low costs and intense industrial activity had their benefits, attracting entrepreneurs, business-men, émigrés and artists, among others. The development of public housing estates in the post-war years was closely followed by gentrification, and the 1980s saw the transformation of Camden into a thriving centre of commerce and leisure.

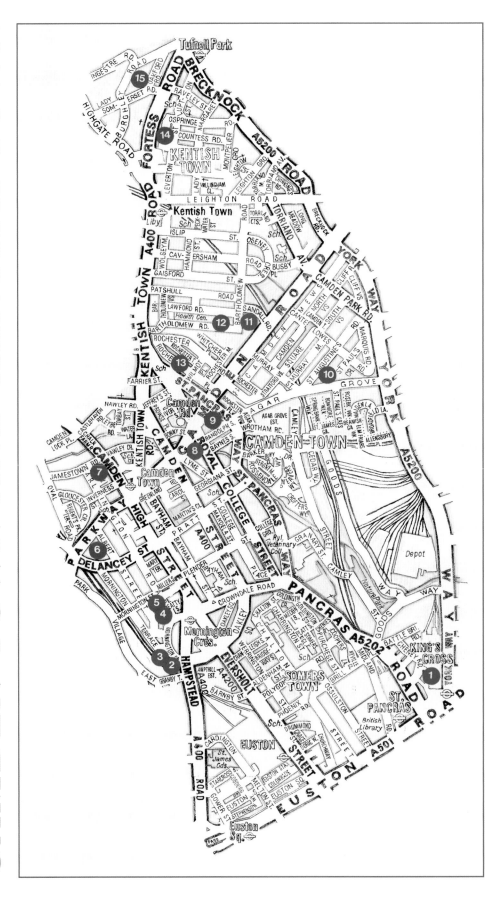

73 Sir Nigel Gresley at the Doncaster Works in 1938. He stands next to a train of his own design, the A4 Pacific No. 4498, which was named after him. [© National Railway Museum / Science & Society Picture Library]

74 A view of Mornington Crescent in c.1905, with 263 Hampstead Road and the Society of Arts plaque to George Cruikshank on the left of the picture. [Courtesy of Historical Publications Ltd]

Just north of the Euston Road, N1, on a wall of King's Cross Station – facing west towards Pancras Road – is the plaque to the locomotive engineer **Sir Nigel Gresley** (1876–1941) ❶ (fig. 73 and see fig. 31). As Chief Mechanical Engineer of the London and North Eastern Railway (LNER) from 1923 until his death in April 1941, Gresley worked from an office in the block on which the plaque has been placed; his room is believed to have been at first-floor level, to the right of the entrance. Born in Edinburgh, Gresley served part of his engineering apprenticeship at Crewe, a railway hub, and went on to design some of the most magnificent locomotives of the steam age, including the renowned 'Pacifics', which dramatically speeded up passenger services on the East Coast line in the 1930s. In 1934 the *Flying Scotsman* became the first steam engine to break the 100 mph speed barrier, an achievement bettered by the *Mallard*, which in 1938 clocked up a world record speed of 126 mph. Perhaps Gresley's best-known design, the *Mallard* is on display at the National Railway Museum in York. Gresley pushed the technology of steam engines to its limit, but he recognised where the future lay, and had a hand in the plans for the electrification of the line between Sheffield and Manchester. He was knighted in 1936, and LNER

named one of its engines after him the following year. The decision to commemorate Gresley at his workplace was made because his principal London residence – Camlet House, 53 Beech Hill, Hadley Wood, EN4, where he lived in 1923–29 – was found to be set back from the road. The plaque was unveiled in 1997 by Gresley's grandson, Tim Godfrey. At the time of writing, it has unfortunately been wholly obscured as a result of recent construction work.

The artist **George Cruikshank** (1792–1878) ❷ lived at 263 Hampstead Road (formerly 48 Mornington Place), NW1, between March 1850 and his death here twenty-eight years later (fig. 74). The house – which had earlier been the home of CLARKSON STANFIELD and boasted an artist's studio – was marked with a chocolate-coloured plaque by the Society of Arts in 1885. Born in London, the son of a caricaturist, Cruikshank's own artistic abilities were well developed by the age of ten and he was widely celebrated by the time he reached his twentieth birthday. He is remembered as the illustrator of *Oliver Twist* (1837–39) and other works by DICKENS, but Cruikshank made his name as a satirist whose distinctive drawings lampooned such figures as Napoleon and George IV, the latter as both Prince Regent and King. The ten years following his first encounter with Dickens in 1835 are generally thought to have been his most creative. Cruikshank's time at number 263 – a house of c. 1830 to which he moved on marrying his second wife, Eliza Widdison (1807–1890) – was marked by persistent debt and, despite sporadic success, a failure to live up to his former greatness. On the surface, the bohemian lifestyle of Cruikshank's youth gave way to sobriety – the artist was an avid promoter of temperance – though all was not what it seemed: while at number 263, Cruikshank seduced one of the young housemaids, Adelaide Attree (d. 1914),

CAMDEN TOWN AND KENTISH TOWN

with whom he had a number of children. The scale of Cruikshank's double life – and his maintenance of two households, one in Hampstead Road and the other close by at 31 Augustus Street – was not fully revealed until after his death.

The houses of Mornington Crescent, NW1, built in 1821–32, originally enjoyed clear views towards Regent's Park, but since the mid-nineteenth century have backed onto railway lines. Such a prospect does not seem to have concerned the painter and etcher **Walter Sickert** (1860–1942) ❸ , who is honoured with a GLC plaque at 6 Mornington Crescent, where he lived and worked in a two-room lodging from 1905 to *c.* 1908. In a letter to the GLC, a local resident (born in 1904) recalled that 'the inside hall or passage was tiled, and a wide, stone staircase curved round . . . up to the first floor, where Sickert lived, his studio being in the front room, which was lofty, with an ornately plastered ceiling and deep mouldings in the cornice, and with the usual big marble fireplace'.[1] WILLIAM ROTHENSTEIN commented that Sickert had a penchant for seediness, and Camden Town was certainly notorious at that time; in 1907, while Sickert was living here, the 'Camden Town Murder' of the prostitute Emily Dimmock hit the national headlines, and inspired the artist to create a

series of paintings based on the subject. A hugely influential painter, Sickert was a founder member of both the Fitzroy Street Group and the Camden Town Group – the latter formed in 1911. Known especially for his music-hall paintings of the 1880s and 1890s, Sickert produced a number of important works at number 6; these included the *Mornington Crescent Nude* series and portrait studies of the model 'Little Rachel' (fig. 75). Sickert was peripatetic by nature, living or working at more than thirty addresses in London during the course of his life. He was based in Camden until 1915, and spent the period 1924–34 in Islington.

At 20 (formerly 1A, then 4) Albert Street, NW1, a handsome Gothic-style house built in 1843–44 for the painter Charles Lucy (1814–1873), an English Heritage plaque commemorates the storyteller **George MacDonald** (1824–1905) ❹ (fig. 76). Born in Aberdeenshire, MacDonald moved in 1859 to London, where he taught English at Bedford College. As an author, he is known especially for the 'fairy romance' *Phantastes* (1858) and for his children's stories, which include *At the Back of the North Wind* (1871), *The Princess and the Goblin* (1872) and *The Princess and Curdie* (1882). His works have proved widely influential, with G. K. CHESTERTON, W. H. Auden, J. R. R. Tolkein and C. S. Lewis all acknowledging a debt to MacDonald's imagination and writing. MacDonald and his wife Louisa (1822–1902) lived at number 20 – known as Tudor Lodge – from August 1860 until around July 1863, when their growing family forced a move to the larger 12 Earls Terrace, Kensington, W8 (see WALTER PATER). In his semi-autobiographical novel *The Vicar's Daughter* (1872), MacDonald described number 20 as being

'stuck on like a swallow's nest to the end of a great row of commonplace houses, nearly a quarter of a mile in length'.[2] He was struck by its romantic appearance – describing it as 'the only pretty house . . . in all London' – and also by its purpose-built studio, built out beyond the back of the building and accessible via its hall.[3] This was used by MacDonald as a study and lecture room. He was visited in Albert Street by such friends as RUSKIN and Lewis Carroll.

Albert Street's long terrace of houses, referred to by MACDONALD, post-dates number 20 by about a year. One of these, number 44, was the last home of **John Desmond Bernal** (1901–1971) 5 , the crystallographer. Bernal was born in Ireland and studied physics at Cambridge, where his impressive knowledge gave rise to the nickname 'Sage'. In 1938 he was elected to the chair of physics at Birkbeck College, London, and in 1963 became Professor of Crystallography, the science of analysing the crystalline structure of materials. Bernal transformed the understanding of the structure of genes, viruses, proteins, vitamins and hormones, and was also a pioneer of modern X-ray crystallography, the scattering of X-rays through crystalline solutions to photograph the structure of molecules. During the Second World War, he devised plans that contributed to the success of the D-Day landings,

including co-inventing the Mulberry floating harbour. The friend of such diverse figures as Mao, Khrushchev and Picasso, Bernal lived in Albert Street from about 1967 until his death here four years later; he also kept a private flat at 22 Torrington Square, Bloomsbury, which was destroyed as part of the building of Birkbeck's Clore Management Centre (opened 1997). An ardent Marxist – he was one of the first to write about science in a political context – Bernal also believed in sexual liberty; his wife Eileen (b. 1898/9) and his two mistresses knew each other well. At weekends, Bernal regularly visited one of these women, Margot Heinemann, at 30 Southwood Lane, Highgate, N6, her home from the mid-1950s.

The Welsh poet **Dylan Thomas** (1914–1953) 6 was commemorated in 1984 with a plaque at 54 Delancey Street, NW1 (fig. 77). He was originally proposed in 1967, but it took years of research and persuasion to convince the GLC that a plaque in London would be appropriate. Born in Swansea, Thomas moved to London in 1934, soon after the publication of his first collection of verse, *Eighteen Poems*. He returned to the capital for prolonged periods throughout his life, though he was based mainly at Laugharne in South Wales. In all, his London lodgings numbered at least eleven; his biographer, Paul Ferris, told the GLC that Thomas was 'a commuter – writing in Wales and travelling up to London to drink'.[4] Number 54 Delancey Street is one of only two London buildings in which Thomas can be said to have made a home; he lived here with his wife Caitlin, née Macnamara (1913–1994) – also a writer – and their young children in a three-room basement flat from about October 1951 until their departure for America in January 1952. In December 1951 Thomas wrote of 'our new London house or horror on bus and night lorry route and opposite railway bridge and shunting station'.[5] By this time, the poet was admired for works such as the verse collection *Deaths and Entrances* (1946), as well as for his acting and readings for radio. *Under Milk Wood*, his greatest work, was still in preparation; the final version was broadcast in January 1954, three months after Thomas's alcohol-related death in New York. The poet's daughter, Aeronwy (b. 1943), recalled that number 54 was 'decorated throughout . . . in a riot of chintz, a real floral cornucopia'.[6] The landlady was Thomas's friend and patron Margaret Taylor, wife of

77   Caitlin Thomas unveils the plaque to her late husband, Dylan Thomas, at 54 Delancey Street in 1984, in the presence of their daughter Aeronwy. [Reproduced by permission of English Heritage]

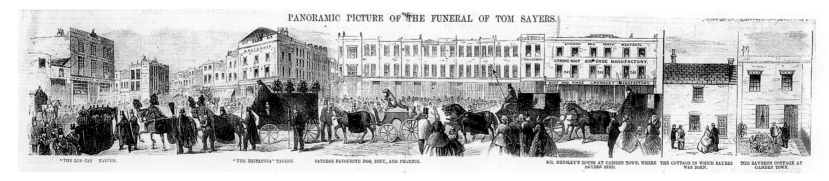

PANORAMIC PICTURE OF THE FUNERAL OF TOM SAYERS.

"THE RED CAP TAVERN.   "THE BRITANNIA" TAVERN.   SAYERS'S FAVOURITE DOG, TONY, AND PHAETON.   MR. MENSLEY'S HOUSE AT CAMDEN TOWN, WHERE SAYERS DIED.   THE COTTAGE IN WHICH SAYERS WAS BORN.   TOM SAYERS'S COTTAGE AT CAMDEN TOWN.

78   Detail from a panorama showing Tom Sayers's remarkable funeral procession, published in the *Illustrated Sporting News* on 13 January 1866. The building in which he died, 257 Camden High Street, is shown towards the right. [© Camden Local Studies and Archives Centre]

the historian A. J. P. Taylor; she provided a Romany caravan in the back garden so that Thomas could write away from the clamour of children, but he apparently found it too cold and damp. The caravan was still in existence at the time of the plaque's unveiling by Thomas's widow, Caitlin.

At 257 Camden High Street, NW1, a plaque honours the pugilist **Tom Sayers** (1826–1865) **7**, a sporting legend of the Victorian age, who died in the building at the age of thirty-nine (figs 78 and 79). Born in Brighton, Sayers moved to London in 1842 to take up work as a bricklayer, and made his first appearance in the boxing ring in 1849; weighing just under eleven stone (69 kg), and standing just five feet nine inches (175 cm) tall, he relied on his enormous strength and courage and his capacity to endure pain. A string of high-profile victories followed, and earned Sayers the chance of an encounter in 1853 with Nat Langham, then regarded as the most formidable prizefighter of his time. After sixty-one rounds, Sayers was beaten for the first and only time in his career. His final, and most famous, appearance in the ring was in Farnborough, Hampshire in April 1860, against the American John C. Heenan. This, 'the fight of the century', was attended by MPs and social commentators including THACK-ERAY, and was even followed by Queen Victoria. After over two hours and thirty-seven rounds, it ended in a draw; Sayers was badly hurt, and retired from the championship. The pugilist was closely associated with Camden Town, where he lived for about twenty years. His last permanent address was 51 Camden Street (formerly 10 Belle Vue Cottages; demolished), where Sayers lived from *c.* 1860 until 1864, when he was diagnosed with diabetes. His last days were spent at the home of his friend John Mensley, above the Mensley boot factory at 257 Camden High Street; he had intended merely to visit but, becoming extremely ill,

asked that his personal belongings be sent to him, and died here on 8 November 1865. It was from this address that Sayers's famous funeral procession, modelled on that of the Duke of Wellington, set out for Highgate Cemetery. The plaque was unveiled in 2002 by the British heavyweight champion Sir Henry Cooper.

At 13 Lyme Street, NW1, just off Camden Road, is the plaque to the South African freedom fighters **Ruth First** (1925–1982) and **Joe Slovo** (1926–1995) **8** (fig. 72). Both First and Slovo were at the forefront of the

79   Portrait of Tom Sayers, painted by an artist of the English School in *c.* 1840. [© Compton Verney]

struggle against apartheid for more than forty years. They met at the University of Witwatersrand in Johannesburg – where their fellow students included Nelson Mandela – and married in 1949. In the years that followed, both First and Slovo became prominent white activists in the Defiance Campaign, and helped to develop the Freedom Charter of the African National Congress (ANC); this began with the words 'South Africa belongs to all who live in it, black and white'. In 1956 the couple were charged with high treason; although charges were later dropped, they continued to suffer for their views, and in 1963 First was detained in prison. On her release she fled to England, where the account of her experience, *117 Days* (1965), brought her fame. From July 1966 to the end of 1978, the Slovos made 13 Lyme Street their base, while Ruth's parents – Julius and 'Tilly' First – lived in a separate basement flat, numbered 13A. During these twelve critical years First taught, and wrote works such as *The Barrel of a Gun: Political Power in Africa* (1970); the sound of her typewriter is said to have been heard day and night. Slovo, meanwhile, worked full-time for the ANC. In 1982 First – by then living in Mozambique – was tragically killed by a letter bomb sent by agents of the South African government. Slovo continued the fight, and was to play a vital role in bringing about the peaceful transfer of power in South Africa. The plaque was unveiled in 2003 by Nelson Mandela, the couple's close friend and comrade.

The suggestion to commemorate the artist and engraver of Indian scenes **William Daniell** (1769–1837) ⑨ at 135 St Pancras Way (formerly 7 Brecknock Terrace), NW1, followed consideration of his uncle, THOMAS DANIELL. The two were associated for much of their careers; in 1785 William accompanied Thomas to India, where he made drawings and sketches of the Indian subcontinent. These, worked up as engravings, were published in *Oriental Scenery* (1795–1808), the finest visual record of the East then available (see fig. 256). William was, in particular, a master of the aquatint; this process of making prints that resemble watercolours was pioneered by Thomas, but William took it to new heights of sophistication and refinement, as shown by works such as his *View of London* (1812), *Voyage round Britain* (1814–25) and *Views of Windsor, Eton, and Virginia Water* (1827–30). Daniell lived at 135 St Pancras Way – then known as 7 Brec-

knock Terrace and later as 135 King's Road – during the few months before his death here on 16 August 1837. The early nineteenth-century building was badly damaged during the Second World War and rebuilt in facsimile in the years that followed. It is the only one of Daniell's London addresses to survive at all, his four homes in Fitzrovia having been demolished. The plaque was erected by English Heritage in 2000.

In 2005 an English Heritage plaque was erected – and unveiled by the German Ambassador, Thomas Matussek – at 6 (formerly 52) St Augustine's Road, NW1, the former home of **Theodor Fontane** (1819–1898) ⑩ , the German writer and novelist. Fontane grew up in the state of Brandenburg, and moved to Berlin at the age of thirteen. By 1840, he had tried his hand at writing both verse and fiction, though he made his name as a journalist. In 1844 Fontane made the first of three journeys to England, home of his idols DICKENS and THACKERAY; the country, which he described as the 'model or, better, the essence of the whole world', was to influence his work deeply.[7] Fontane's stay of 1852 resulted in his *A Summer in London* (1854). During his last trip, of 1855–59, Fontane worked as a foreign correspondent for newspapers including *The Times* and also kept a diary, which he filled with observations on mid-Victorian society. His most significant residence during these years was 52 St Augustine's Road, an end-of-terrace house in which he and his family lived from August 1857 until their return to Germany at the end of 1858. Fontane wrote of the front aspect of the house as 'pleasant, the roof is flat, the plaster greyish-brown, the windows wide, with Venetian blinds'.[8] He went on to describe how he had 'deconsecrated' the back drawing room at ground-floor level 'by depriving it of its representative high status by moving in a big long table and making it into my study'; it apparently made 'an excellent workplace'.[9]

Fronting onto Sandall Road, NW5, is Camden School for Girls, which bears a plaque to **Frances Mary Buss** (1827–1894) ⑪ , the pioneer of education for women and the school's Headmistress in 1879–94. Born at 46 (later 12) Camden Street, Buss worked as a teacher from her teens in order to help support her family. In the 1840s, she taught at a private school founded by her mother in Kentish Town, and in 1850 she decided to open a school of her own; this, the North London Col-

80   Number 50 Lawford Road and its GLC plaque to George Orwell. [© English Heritage. Photograph by Derek Kendall]

founding of independent schools around the country, many under the auspices of the Girls' Public Day School Trust (founded 1872). In 1871 Buss opened a second school, the Camden School for Girls; this occupied premises in Prince of Wales Road, before transferring after the Second World War to nearby Sandall Road, then recently vacated by the NLCS, which had moved to Canons in Edgware. Buss proved herself a pioneer both through these initiatives and through her wider work. The first woman to describe herself as a headmistress, she dedicated herself to the improvement of teacher training for women, campaigned for the entitlement of women to sit public examinations and was an early supporter of women's admission to universities. The plaque, unveiled in 2000, marks the part of the Sandall Road building that dates from 1880. All of Buss's own residences – including 46 Camden Street and 89 King Henry's Road, Primrose Hill – have been demolished.

Number 50 Lawford Road, NW5, a house of the 1860s, bears a plaque erected in 1980 in honour of the novelist and political essayist **George Orwell** (1903–1950) 12 , born Eric Arthur Blair in India and brought up in England (fig. 80 and see fig. 43). It was around 1927 that he resolved to become a writer; *Down and Out in Paris and London* (1933) – published under his pseudonym – was the first in a series of autobiographical and semi-autobiographical works written before the Second World War. On the outbreak of the Spanish Civil War in 1936, Orwell joined the republican forces and became a dedicated socialist; his experiences in Spain are described in *Homage to Catalonia* (1938). Further experiences, not least more war, tempered Orwell's convictions; wariness of the threat of tyranny and scepticism of dogma characterise his two best-known works, *Animal Farm* (1945) and *Nineteen Eighty-Four* (1949). The writer lived at a number of addresses in London, many of them in Hampstead, where he worked in 1934–35 as an assistant in a bookshop. From August 1935 until January 1936 he lived on the top floor of 50 Lawford Road, which he shared with his friends and fellow writers Rayner Heppenstall (1911–1981) and Michael Sayers (b. 1912). It was during this time that Orwell wrote the bulk of his novel *Keep the Aspidistra Flying* (1936). Lawford Road features in the book as 'Willowbed Road', a street that 'contrived to keep up a kind of mingy, lower-middle-class decency'.[10]

legiate School for Ladies (NLCS), provided the middle classes with good tuition at moderate fees, and was based firstly in Camden Street and – from 1879 – in purpose-built premises in Sandall Road. Supervised by Buss for over forty years, it set the standard for a new kind of girls' education and, by 1900, had inspired the

81 'Father' Henry Willis sitting at the console of the Blenheim Palace organ, restored and rebuilt by his firm in 1891. [Courtesy of the British Organ Archive]

Orwell's own room, 'a top floor back', contained his writing table, while 'on the window-sill there was a sickly aspidistra in a green-glazed pot'.[11] The plaque's proposer, the writer and journalist Paul Barker, commented, 'I think that Kentish Town is *echt* Orwell territory – "marginal territory" – and it seemed especially apt to have a plaque there'.[12]

At 9 Rochester Terrace, NW1, a GLC plaque commemorates '**Father**' **Henry Willis** (1821–1901) 13 , the organ builder (fig. 81). The son of a carpenter, Willis was apprenticed in 1835 to John Gray, a London organ builder, and a decade later set up in business on his own. His 1847 commission to rebuild the organ of Gloucester Cathedral proved his 'stepping stone to fame'.[13] A steady stream of commissions followed; they included the organ for the 1851 Great Exhibition, later moved to Winchester Cathedral, together with those for St George's Hall, Liverpool (1854–55), the Royal Albert Hall (1871) and St Paul's Cathedral (1872). Over the course of his career, Willis built or rebuilt over 2,000 organs, and his works – known for their durability, and richness and clarity of sound – are to be found in such cathedrals as Durham, Lincoln, Salisbury, Truro and Wells. His firm – based from 1866 at The Rotunda, 67–71 Rochester Place – also produced small 'Scudamore' organs, specifically designed for small country churches. Willis – dubbed 'Father' in 1898 in a complimentary allusion to the famous seventeenth- and early eighteenth-century organ builder 'Father' (Bernard) Smith – lived from 1867 until 1895 at 9 Rochester Terrace, a semi-detached property of *c.* 1840; he could have seen his organ works from the rear windows of the house. Willis lived in Kentish Town – an area known more generally for piano making – for the rest of his life: first at 57 Lawford Road and from 1899 at 2 Bartholomew Road.

The painter **Ford Madox Brown** (1821–1893) 14 lived at 56 Fortess Road, NW5 – then known as 13 Fortess Terrace – from September 1855 until autumn 1862; the outlook from his first-floor studio was captured in *Hampstead – A Sketch from Nature* (1857) (fig. 82). By this time, Brown was already an artist of repute and was closely connected with the PRE-RAPHAELITE BROTHERHOOD. His most famous paintings date from the 1850s; they include *The Last of England* (1852–55), *An English Autumn Afternoon* (1852–55) and *Work* (1852–63), an innovative and complex image set in Hampstead that shows how the work ethic affects every level of society. In the 1860s, Brown also made a name for himself as an accomplished designer of furniture and stained glass, and was a partner in WILLIAM MORRIS's company – Morris, Marshall, Faulkner & Co. – from its foundation in 1861; some of Brown's furniture was designed specifically for his home in Fortess Terrace. In 1878 Brown began his last major work, twelve paintings on panel for Manchester's new town hall; these, illustrating the town's history, occupied him until his death in Primrose Hill. Brown lived at number 56 with his second wife, Emma (1829–1890) – formerly his model – and was visited here by friends such as

D. G. ROSSETTI, Morris and HOLMAN HUNT. The plaque was erected in 1976 at Fortess Road, Brown's later and more significant London home – 37 Fitzroy Square – having been destroyed during the war.

At 60 Burghley Road, NW5 – a typical terraced house of the late nineteenth century – is an English Heritage plaque to **Kwame Nkrumah** (1909–1972) ⑮ , the first President of Ghana (see fig. 34). Born in what was then known as the Gold Coast, Nkrumah moved to London in spring 1945, and began to study philosophy and law. However, this academic work was soon eclipsed by his political activities; by autumn 1945, Nkrumah had been elected Vice-President of the West African Student Union, Regional Secretary of the Pan-African Federation, and was made joint Secretary of the organising committee of the fifth Pan-African Congress, held in Manchester in October of that year. Initially, Nkrumah had found it hard to find accommodation; he recalled that, because of his colour, countless doors were slammed in his face. Eventually, he found a room at 60 Burghley Road, his home from June 1945 until November 1947, when he returned to the Gold Coast. Nkrumah's time here was happy; his landlady, Mrs Florence Manley, looked upon him 'as a member of my family', and made a point of opening her home to his friends.[14] It was also productive; here, he was 'always working, till 3 or 4 in the morning'.[15] Back in Africa, Nkrumah's charisma and visionary ideas led him to become a figure of major significance. In 1957, when – partly through his campaigning – the Gold Coast (renamed Ghana) became the first black African colony to achieve independence, Nkrumah was made the country's first Prime Minister; three years later, he became President. This period of his career was fraught with controversy, and ended in 1966 with his dismissal from office. Nkrumah did, however, leave a lasting legacy, providing Ghana with benefits such as free elementary education and a network of roads.

NOTES

1. Letter of 3 December 1974 on blue plaque file.
2. George MacDonald, *The Vicar's Daughter: An Autobiographical Story*, vol. I (London, 1872), p. 49
3. Ibid, p. 50
4. Undated note of 1976 on blue plaque file.
5. *The Collected Letters of Dylan Thomas*, ed. Paul Ferris (new edn, London, 2000), p. 914 (3 December 1951)
6. *The Times*, 10 January 1984, p. 3
7. Rüdiger Görner, 'The Passion for Wisdom – on Theodor Fontane', *Encounter* (February 1989), p. 53
8. *Fontanes Briefe in Zwei Bänden* (Berlin and Weimar, 1980), p. 214 (23 August 1857), English trans. by Nicholas Jacobs on blue plaque file
9. Ibid, p. 216
10. *The Complete Works of George Orwell*, ed. Peter Davison, vol. IV: *Keep the Aspidistra Flying* (London, 1987), p. 23
11. Ibid, p. 28
12. Letter of 7 November 1980 on blue plaque file.
13. *ODNB*, vol. LIX, p. 380
14. Marika Sherwood, *Kwame Nkrumah: The Years Abroad, 1935–1947* (Legon, Ghana, 1996), p. 165
15. Ibid, p. 166

83 Number 58 Grafton Way and its paired blue plaques to Francisco de Miranda and Andres Bello. Now known as Casa Miranda, the building is also marked with a stone tablet erected by the British Council in 1942. [© English Heritage. Photograph by Derek Kendall]

FITZROVIA AND REGENT'S PARK

The name 'Fitzrovia' – which derives from the Fitzroy Tavern in Charlotte Street – was coined as recently as 1940 by a journalist and has supplanted 'North Soho' as the term in general use for the area between Oxford Street and the Euston Road; here, it is taken to denote the part that lies within the modern borough of Camden. Starting with Rathbone Place in about 1720, Fitzrovia was developed in piecemeal fashion over the following century, mostly on a modest scale; an exception to this is the imposing Fitzroy Square, which was planned and partly built by ROBERT ADAM in 1790–94. The relentless move westwards of fashionable London meant that even these fine houses were soon subdivided, and the district became a favourite low-rent refuge for artists, craftsmen and writers. Fitzrovia has been extensively redeveloped since the Second World War, and the Post Office Tower (1961–64) is a dominating presence. By way of a contrast, Regent's Park – to the north – is ringed with palatial stuccoed terraces laid out from 1811, each constructed by a single builder under the supervision of John Nash, the mastermind of the scheme and the Prince Regent's favourite architect. In spite of war damage so extensive that there were voices urging total redevelopment, the restored Nash terraces still present some stunning urban vistas. Regent's Park straddles the modern boroughs of Westminster and Camden, with the area east of Park Square Gardens and the Outer Circle forming a part of the latter; both, however, are dealt with here.

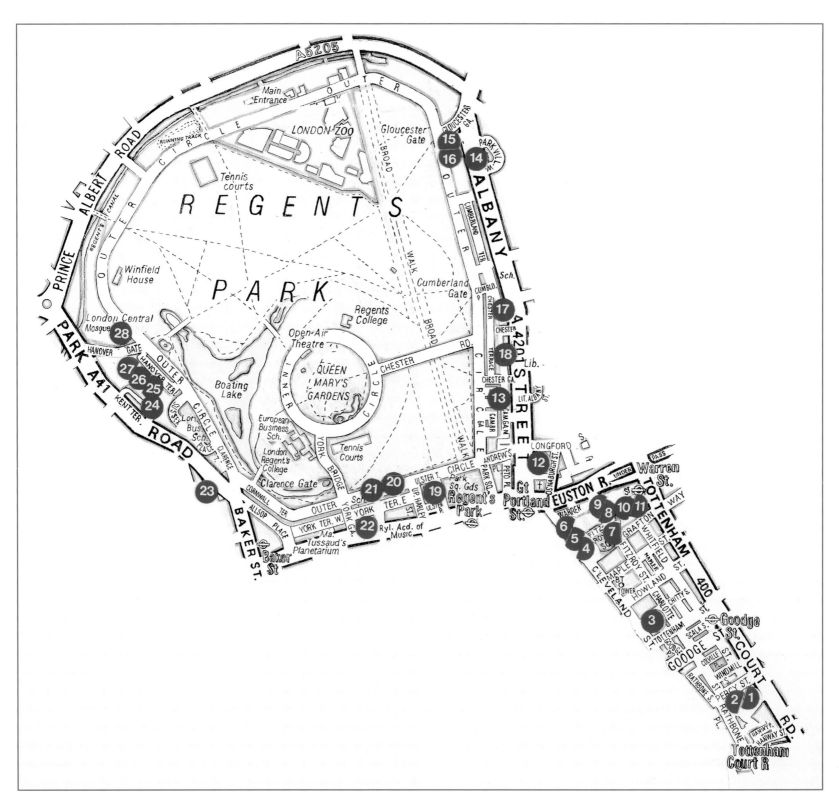

FITZROVIA AND REGENT'S PARK

FITZROVIA

Percy Street, W1, has two plaques on adjacent houses in the surviving southern terrace, which dates from the 1760s. At number 15 is that to **Charles Laughton** (1899–1962) ❶, the actor best known for his definitive portrayal of CAPTAIN WILLIAM BLIGH in the film *Mutiny on the Bounty* (1935) (fig. 84). He was described by a friend of his youth as 'the ungainliest of schoolboys, very fat with a huge head', but what Laughton lacked in looks he made up for with stage and screen presence, and he became known for his portrayals of sinister villains.[1] He moved to Percy Street with the actress Elsa Lanchester (1902–1986) – best remembered for playing the title role in *Bride of Frankenstein* (1935) – in 1928, when he was starring in the play *Alibi*; they were married the following year, though Laughton was essentially homosexual. The couple's second-floor flat was described by one biographer as 'a modest place for two such celebrated professionals, but salaries in those days were not high'.[2] They had two rooms knocked into one to maximise their living space, and also kept a cottage in the Surrey hills. Laughton and Lanchester moved out of Percy Street in 1931, when *Payment Deferred* – an adaptation of a novel by C. S. FORESTER in which they both appeared – transferred to New York. It was 'high time' that they moved out anyway,

Elsa later declared, 'because an Indian restaurant had opened underneath and the smell of garlic and curry which rose up was getting stronger and stronger'.[3] The couple settled in America in 1939, becoming American citizens in 1950. The plaque was proposed by the actor Simon Callow, who performed the unveiling in 1992 in the presence of many thespian luminaries, including Sir Alec Guinness.

Next door, at 14 Percy Street, is an LCC plaque to the poet and essayist **Coventry Patmore** (1823–1896) ❷. Patmore's essays range over art, architecture, philosophy and literature, but he is remembered chiefly for the series of four poems published between 1854 and 1863 known collectively as *The Angel in the House*. These are a paean to the virtues of married love and, by extension, to his first wife Emily Augusta, who died in July 1862. Patmore had taken rooms at number 14 just before this, and made it his principal home in 1863. He wrote *The Victories of Love* (1862–63) – the fourth and final part of the *Angel* series – while living here. Patmore's grief over his wife's death was prolonged, and he was apt to spend his evenings revisiting their old haunts. He was allowed leave from his post in the Department of Printed Books at the British Museum to go to Italy early in 1864, where he converted to Catholicism. His young daughter Emily, who was boarded out with friends, became an epistolary confidante for her father: 'My evenings are very dull', he told her, adding, 'I often want somebody to talk to . . . you must make haste and grow up, and then we will patch up another "home" '.[4] Patmore moved out of Percy Street not long after marrying his second wife, Marianne Byles, in July 1864, and lived for the latter part of his life in Sussex and Hampshire. A plaque was first suggested in 1911 by Patmore's son Tennyson – named after the Poet Laureate, a great family friend – but Patmore was then ineligible under the twenty-year rule; the existing plaque was erected almost half a century later.

Charlotte Street, W1, runs roughly north–south and is well known today as a 'restaurant row'. At number 81 – a much-altered house of the late eighteenth century, which was formerly known as 65 Upper Charlotte Street – is a GLC plaque to the architect **Sir Robert Smirke** (1780–1867) ❸.[5] This – the residence of his father, the painter Robert Smirke (1753–1845) – was his home in early life, from about 1786 to 1804. During

84 Charles Laughton and Elsa Lanchester 'at home'. Published in Lanchester's biography *Charles Laughton and I* (1938), the photograph probably shows the couple in their flat at 15 Percy Street.

this time, the younger Smirke studied under Sir John Soane and – more harmoniously – under GEORGE DANCE THE YOUNGER. Dance had a formative influence on the young architect, but perhaps more important to Smirke were the travels he made in Italy and Greece with his elder brother Richard between 1801 and 1804. Most of Smirke's work belongs to the Classical Revival. His most famous building is the British Museum (1823–46), which was completed in 1846–52 by his brother Sydney. Robert Smirke's repertoire extended to churches, country houses and bridges, though he is remembered above all as an architect of public buildings, for which his safe, solid style was well suited. He was, however, an innovator in his use of concrete and cast iron as construction materials. By the time of his retirement in 1846, at the age of sixty-five, Smirke had built up a substantial architectural practice – it was the largest in London at the time – and had completed around 130 commissions across Britain. His fortune must have made it easier to endure brickbats from those such as the arch-Goth A. W. N. Pugin, who opined that Smirke's career had already lasted too long.

Fitzroy Square, W1, the only London square to have been laid out by ROBERT ADAM, features five plaques. Two of these can be found at 29 Fitzroy Square – a building of the 1830s on the square's west side. The first, of bronze, commemorates the playwright and polemicist **George Bernard Shaw** (1856–1950) ④ (see also p. 376) (fig. 85). It was erected by St Pancras Borough Council in 1951, just a year after Shaw's death, and was incorporated into the official plaques scheme in 1975. It gives no vital dates or profession, but features the quotation 'From the coffers of his genius he enriched the world' – the text of the note written by Shaw's housekeeper, Mrs Laden, to announce his death. Shaw lived in the upper two storeys of this house – along with his mother, Lucinda, née Gurly (1830–1913), with whom his relations were cool – from March 1887 until his marriage to Charlotte Payne-Townshend in June 1898. During this time, Shaw cut his teeth as a theatre critic and playwright; among the works he wrote here was the collection *Plays: Pleasant and Unpleasant* (1898). In the 'unpleasant' category was *Mrs Warren's Profession* (1893), which was banned by the censor; 'My reputation as a dramatist grows with every play of mine that is not performed', he quipped.[6] A leading light of the FABIAN SOCIETY, Shaw also wrote

many polemical pieces, including *The Sanity of Art* (1895, 1908). His future wife Charlotte was shocked to find that he worked at Fitzroy Square in 'a very small room which was in a perpetual state of dirt and disorder', surrounded by 'heaps of letters, pages of manuscripts, books, envelopes, writing paper, pens ... butter, sugar, apples, knives, forks, spoons, sometimes a cup of cocoa or a half-finished plate of porridge, a saucepan and a dozen other things ... and all undusted, as his papers must not be touched'. The ungainly furniture obliged anyone who entered the room 'to move sideways like a crab', and occasional clean-up operations 'took two full days' hard work'.[7] After their marriage, the Shaws' London home was at the Adelphi, but his mother continued to live in Fitzroy Square until 1907.

The second plaque at 29 Fitzroy Square – erected in 1975 – honours the building's next occupant, **Virginia Stephen** (1882–1941) ⑤ , the novelist and critic better known by her married name **Virginia Woolf** (see also pp. 589–90). The daughter of LESLIE STEPHEN, Virginia became a leading light in the Bloomsbury Group of writers, artists and thinkers. She moved to Fitzroy

86 A view of the west side of Fitzroy Square in 1984, with the plaque to the 3rd Marquess of Salisbury on the right and the Post Office tower dominating the skyline. [Reproduced by permission of English Heritage. NMR]

later novel, *To the Lighthouse* (1927).[9] Finding the neighbourhood of Fitzroy Square to be noisy – Virginia complained of the vans 'which grind rough music beneath my window' – she was pleased to move to the quieter Brunswick Square in November 1911.[10]

The Prime Minster **Robert Gascoyne Cecil, 3rd Marquess of Salisbury** (1830–1903) ⑥ is commemorated with an LCC plaque of 1965 at 21 Fitzroy Square (fig. 86). This is set into the ground-floor stucco of the house, which is part of the western terrace and dates from the early 1830s. A direct descendant and namesake of the minister of Elizabeth I and James I, Robert Cecil married Georgina Alderson (1827–1899) in July 1857, but the union did not meet with his father's approval. Hence, when the couple moved into this house in late 1858 or early 1859, money was tight, especially given the recent birth of a daughter. Cecil took to journalism, and famously made an anonymous attack on the Conservative leader DISRAELI in *Bentley's Quarterly Review* of spring 1859 – at the time he was himself a Conservative MP, having been elected for Stamford in 1853. The Cecils moved to Duchess Street, Portland Place, in spring 1862, following the birth of another child. Soon Cecil was reconciled with his father, to whose title he succeeded in 1868, and he went on to serve as Prime Minister for three terms between 1885 and 1902, twice combining the office with that of Foreign Secretary. Tall and luxuriantly bearded, it has been said that – in the days before newspaper photography made the faces of celebrities so familiar – Salisbury was confused in the public mind with the cricketing hero W. G. GRACE, which was probably to his political benefit.

Square with her brother Adrian (1883–1948) in August 1907, taking number 29 on a five-year lease. 'We are having bright green carpets and I want to buy old furniture', she told a friend excitedly.[8] This was the siblings' first independent residence; despite their bohemian suppers of herrings and tripe, they still had servants to look after them. Virginia, who occupied the whole of the second floor, spent her time here writing articles for newspapers and began her first novel, *The Voyage Out*, published in 1915. This period of her life was also marked by trauma – in summer 1910 Virginia had her first experience of a sanatorium – and by an emotional entanglement with her brother-in-law, Clive Bell. Her trips to visit him and her sister Vanessa in St Ives caused her to wish that 'Bloomsbury was on the seashore', and provided the setting for Virginia's

At 7 Fitzroy Square – a late eighteenth-century house on the square's east side – a plaque of 1985 commemorates **Sir Charles Eastlake** (1793–1865) ⑦, the painter and first Director of the National Gallery (fig. 87). Charles Lock Eastlake made his name with *Napoleon Bonaparte on Board the 'Bellerophon'* (1815), which he painted from sketches made at his native Plymouth. The lucrative sale of this work enabled him to travel to Rome, and he did not return permanently to England until 1830. Eastlake settled at 13 Upper Fitzroy Street, and enjoyed some of his most productive years as a painter, before moving the short distance to Fitzroy Square in 1842. Here he excelled in his second career as an arts administrator; as Secretary of the Fine

87   The plaque to Sir Charles Eastlake at 7 Fitzroy Square and the fine fanlight of the late eighteenth-century house. [© English Heritage. Photograph by Derek Kendall]

was at this house that he recuperated after damaging an eye in a laboratory accident; at his insistence, students visited him here for tutorials during his convalescence. It has been said that Hofmann's two decades in London had a 'decisive impact on the teaching and practice of British laboratory science, as well as on British chemical technology'.[11] In 1865 Hofmann left Fitzroy Square and returned to Germany, where he played a part in the commanding lead that country subsequently built up in the chemical dyestuffs industry. The plaque was unveiled in 1995 by the German Ambassador, Dr Jürgen Oesterhelt.

At 56 Fitzroy Street (formerly 7 Upper Fitzroy Street), W1, is commemorated the explorer and navigator **Captain Matthew Flinders, RN** (1774–1814) ⑨ . Born near Boston, Lincolnshire, Flinders's pioneering survey of the coast of Australia, which he undertook between 1795 and 1803, was the basis for Admiralty charts for a century. He was the first to use the term 'Australia' for the new continent. Returning to England in 1810 – after release from a French prison in Mauritius – Flinders lived at several addresses in Fitzrovia, a reflection of his relative poverty. In May 1813 he was residing in Upper St John Street, now Whitfield Street. 'There have been many people calling at this house for money', Flinders wrote in his diary, and having found alternative accommodation at 56 Fitzroy Street – then 7 Upper Fitzroy Street – he 'agreed for 6 months at £100 a year, hired carts for the morrow, and packed up'.[12] In February 1814 Flinders moved again, to a house at nearby 14 London Street (now Maple Street; demolished), where he died that summer. Copies of his account of his adventures, *A Voyage to Terra Australis* (1814), were delivered by the publisher the day before his death. Flinders was first honoured with a plaque in 1961 at 53 Stanhope Street, north of the Euston Road, which was numbered 7 Mary Street when he lived there (1811–13). The plaque was recovered when the building was demolished in 1965, and was re-erected at its present site in 1973. Number 56 is the last of Flinders's London addresses to survive, and has been substantially altered, most obviously by the addition of a shop front.

Arts Commission, Eastlake worked alongside Prince Albert in supervising the interior decoration of the reconstructed Palace of Westminster (1841–63). He was elected President of the Royal Academy in 1850 and, having been Keeper of the National Gallery from 1843 to 1847, was appointed its first Director in 1855. Eastlake devoted the rest of his life to enlarging and improving the gallery's collection, and died while on a reconnoitring trip to Italy. His widow, Elizabeth, Lady Eastlake (1809–1893), a writer and journalist, lived on at number 7 until her death.

Two doors along, at 9 Fitzroy Square, is a plaque to another figure to enjoy the patronage of Prince Albert: it was due to the offices of the Prince Consort that the German chemist **A. W. Hofmann** (1818–1892) ⑧ was appointed Professor and Director of the newly established Royal College of Chemistry in London in 1845. Born near Frankfurt, August Wilhelm Hofmann studied at the universities of Giessen and Bonn, where he carried out investigative work into the organic chemistry of coal tar. Later he developed a lucrative sideline in applying fractional distillation techniques to the manufacture of artificial dyes based on magenta: two shades of synthetic dye are still known as 'Hofmann violets'. In London, Hofmann initially rented rooms in George Street, Hanover Square, and moved in 1854 to Fitzroy Square, close to the Royal College of Chemistry, then sited in Oxford Street. It

Two blue plaques adorn the frontage of 58 Grafton Way (formerly 27 Grafton Street), W1 (fig. 83). One commemorates **Francisco de Miranda** (1750–1816) ⑩ , who is described thereon as the 'Precursor of Latin

American Independence'. Miranda's campaign to throw off the Spanish yoke was inspired by the American War of Independence against the British; it is ironic, therefore, that he later came to live in London, having fled the Reign of Terror in revolutionary France. Miranda pleaded his cause with English politicians, including WILLIAM PITT THE YOUNGER, and unsuccessfully attempted to foment a rising in Venezuela in 1806. He tried again four years later, in collaboration with SIMÓN BOLÍVAR; on this occasion independence was actually declared, but Miranda was defeated and taken prisoner, and died in gaol at Cadiz. He lived in Grafton Way in 1802–10, apart from a two-year absence in New York from 1805. The house forms part of a terrace dating from 1792, and was then known as 27 Grafton Street. The upper floors were given over to Miranda's collection of books, prints and paintings – he was a formidable classical scholar – and the building served as an informal embassy and headquarters for the cause of Latin American self-determination. An Englishwoman, Sarah Andrews (d. 1847), Miranda's companion from 1799 and the mother of his two sons, lived on here until her death. Fittingly, the house is now owned by the Venezuelan government and, under the name of Casa Miranda, is used as a cultural centre. On it, a stone tablet commemorates Miranda, with a long inscription in both English and Spanish; this was installed by the British Council in 1942. The adjacent English Heritage plaque, which replaced one set up by Camden Council, was erected in 1996.

Also in 1996, a second plaque at 58 Grafton Way was erected in honour of **Andres Bello** (1781–1865) ⓫ , the poet, jurist, philologist and Venezuelan patriot (see fig. 83). Like MIRANDA, Bello was born in Caracas and collaborated with SIMÓN BOLÍVAR in the cause of South American independence. Bello stayed at 58 Grafton Way with Miranda soon after his arrival in Britain in 1810. He remained in the country until 1829, representing the new nations of Venezuela, Chile and Colombia to the British government; he married two Englishwomen in succession, fathered fifteen children, and became acquainted with such luminaries as the philosophers Jeremy Bentham and James Mill. Remarkably, he also found time to write poetry while resident in this country. The addresses in Somers Town, where he later enjoyed a more settled existence, are no longer extant; the fact of his living in what was

then a down-at-heel suburb is indicative of his financial circumstances. As well as being regarded as early Venezuela's foremost man of letters, he framed the civil code of Chile, which was widely imitated elsewhere in South America. As a philologist his greatest achievement was a grammar of Latin American Spanish, published in 1847.

REGENT'S PARK

Running north from the Euston Road, Osnaburgh Street, NW1, has been extensively redeveloped. Dominating its northern section is The White House, built in 1936 to designs by Robert Atkinson and now in use as a hotel; its main entrance faces onto Osnaburgh Terrace. On its rear service wing, embedded in the building's cream faience tiles, is a GLC plaque to the **Fabian Society** ⓬ , which was founded at a house on this site – 17 Osnaburgh Street, demolished in the 1930s. This was the home of Edward Pease (1857–1955), a solicitor, and was where a group of his friends met to discuss the ideas of the philosopher Thomas Davidson. The Fellowship of the New Life, as it was originally to be called, held its first meeting on 24 October 1883 (fig. 88) and became the Fabians on 4 January

88 A page from the handwritten minutes of the first meeting of the Fabian Society (here named 'The New Life'), held at 17 Osnaburgh Street on 24 October 1883. [Reproduced by kind permission of the LSE Archives and the Fabian Society]

89 Malcolm Muggeridge, editor of *Punch*, unveils the plaque to Henry Mayhew at 55 Albany Street in 1953. [© Getty Images]

while SIDNEY WEBB and ANNIE BESANT joined in 1885. The society's influence in the Labour Party has been considerable, and it continues to publish pamphlets on a wide variety of political topics. There has always been a strong Fabian presence in London local government, and the plaque was proposed by Andrew McIntosh (Lord McIntosh of Haringey), one-time leader of the Labour group on the GLC.

At 55 (formerly 129) Albany Street, NW1 – the main thoroughfare to the east of Regent's Park – is the plaque to **Henry Mayhew** (1812–1887) 13 , the founder of *Punch* and author of *London Labour and the London Poor*. Mayhew made his name from the late 1820s with popular magazines such as *Figaro in London*, which he edited in 1835–38, and also enjoyed success as a playwright. He became part-proprietor and founding editor of *Punch* in 1841, and was largely responsible for setting the journal's humorous, satirical tone. Mayhew's reputation as a social reformer rests on *London Labour and the London Poor* (1851), the definitive account of London street life of the era, which had a clear influence on DICKENS. Born in Great Marlborough Street, Westminster, Mayhew died in what is now Bedford Avenue, Bloomsbury, and – partly because he was perennially poor and occasionally bankrupt – lived at many different addresses in the intervening years. All were found to have been either demolished or radically altered, with the exception of 55 Albany Street, which was numbered 129 when Mayhew lived here during 1839 and 1840. He lodged with his brother Alfred, who threw him out of the house, so the story went, after he 'wrecked the kitchen and nearly killed the cook through an oxy-hydrogen experiment, which might have ended in a valuable discovery if it had not commenced with a terrific explosion'.[14] Mayhew's plaque was erected by the LCC in 1953, and unveiled by the then editor of *Punch*, Malcolm Muggeridge (fig. 89).

1884, with a stated aim of helping 'in the reconstruction of society in accordance with the highest moral possibilities'.[13] The principles of the society were – and remain – broadly socialist, and its name was taken from the Roman General Fabius Maximus, who adopted a famously cautious approach to masterminding the defeat of Hannibal – hence 'Fabian tactics'. The founder members included the pioneer sexologist HENRY HAVELOCK ELLIS; GEORGE BERNARD SHAW, an early recruit, soon became its motive force,

The composer **Constant Lambert** (1905–1951) 14 is commemorated with an English Heritage plaque at 197 Albany Street. The son of a painter, Lambert won a scholarship to the Royal College of Music, where he studied under VAUGHAN WILLIAMS, and was a reciter at early performances of William Walton's *Façade* (1926). Shortly afterwards, he was commissioned to write a ballet score for Diaghilev, *Romeo and Juliet*, and his most enduring work, *The Rio Grande* (1927), a jazz-

90 A detail of Richard Morris's aquatint *A Panoramic View round the Regent's Park* (1831). In the centre is Gloucester Terrace (renamed Gloucester Gate in 1913), designed by John Joseph Scoles, with St Katherine's Church and Hospital on the right. [Guildhall Library, City of London / The Bridgeman Art Library]

based setting of a poem by Sacheverell Sitwell. Lambert also worked as a conductor and critic: the provocative book *Music Ho! A Study of Music in Decline* (1934) was, like his early musical work, infused with verve and wit, but the suicide of two close friends, the painter Christopher Wood and the composer PETER WARLOCK, affected Lambert's state of mind, which was not improved by his heavy drinking. As far as his relationships with women were concerned, Constant was a misnomer: he was twice married, and numbered Margot Fonteyn among his lovers. His life was correspondingly unsettled, and he is reckoned to have had fourteen London addresses, most of short duration. Lambert lived at 197 Albany Street, which is part of a terrace of eight houses dating from the 1830s, from 1947 until his death. It was here that he wrote his last work, the ballet score *Tiresias*; this was performed at Covent Garden in July 1951, with choreography by Sir Frederick Ashton and decor by Lambert's second wife, Isabel (b. 1912).

A plaque at 15 Gloucester Gate, NW1, commemorates the author **W. W. Jacobs** (1863–1943) 15. William Wymark Jacobs was born in Wapping and worked initially as a clerk in the Civil Service; the success of his fiction – notably *The Skipper's Wooing* (1897) and *Sea Urchins* (1898) – enabled him to devote himself to writing full-time after 1899. Jacobs is best remembered today for his macabre tales, especially 'The Monkey's Paw', published in *The Lady of the Barge* (1902); the story was later adapted for stage and screen. Jacobs – who, ironically, was best known as a humorist in his day – went on to produce novels such as *Dialstone Lane* (1904) and short-story collections including *Night Watches* (1914). The plaque to 'W. W.', who lived in Gloucester Gate from 1928 to 1935, was proposed by one of Jacobs's granddaughters, Sarah Crowley, and was unveiled by another, the playwright Olwen Wymark; it is located on the house's Albany Street frontage in order to mark the entrance to 15A, where

Jacobs lived. This has now been re-integrated into the main body of the house, a detached villa of the late 1820s built to designs by John Joseph Scoles.

The architect John Joseph Scoles was also responsible for 6 Gloucester Gate, part of a terrace of eleven houses completed by 1828 (fig. 90). Here, an English Heritage plaque of 1989 commemorates **Sir Henry Wellcome** (1853–1936) 16, the pharmacist and founder of the Wellcome Trust and Foundation. Wellcome was born on a farm in Wisconsin, USA, where he later worked in his uncle's drugstore and gave an early hint of entrepreneurial flair by marketing his own invisible ink. He came to England in 1880 and set up a pharmacy business with fellow American Silas Mainville Burroughs. The company, Burroughs, Wellcome & Co., promoted a new form of compressed pill and became enormously successful. The fortune Wellcome made was ploughed into the founding of medical research laboratories and museums; these were consolidated as the Wellcome Foundation in 1924. About four years earlier, Gloucester Gate had been leased as his London base; it was, writes Wellcome's biographer, 'not luxurious and he spent relatively little time there', though it remained his home until his death.[15] Partly as a consequence of the failure of his marriage to Syrie, the daughter of DR BARNARDO – the couple had married in 1901 and divorced fifteen years later – he became reclusive, but still pursued the accumulation of medical books and artefacts with energy. Wellcome, who became a British citizen in 1910 and was knighted in 1932, hoped that his anthropological collections would form the basis of a 'Museum of Man'; this never came to pass, though much of the best material is now in the Science Museum, and his books form the basis of the Wellcome Library, housed by the Wellcome Trust.

Chester Terrace, NW1, designed by John Nash, has the longest unbroken façade of the Regent's Park development (fig. 91). It bears two official plaques. At number

FITZROVIA AND REGENT'S PARK

91 An undated photograph of the north entrance to Chester Terrace, designed by John Nash and built in c.1825. [Reproduced by permission of English Heritage. NMR]

27 is the English Heritage plaque to **Sir John Maitland Salmond** (1881–1968) ⓻ , Marshal of the Royal Air Force and RAF Commander. The son of a general, 'Jack' Salmond – as he was widely known – followed his father into the Army and served in Africa during the early years of the twentieth century. In 1910 he wrote a far-sighted essay entitled 'Airships and Aeroplanes in War', and transferred to the Royal Flying Corps two years later. In December 1913, Salmond set the British altitude record and, having served on the Western Front and reorganised air training at home, replaced Hugh Trenchard as Commander of the Flying Corps in France in January 1918. Promoted to major-general three months later, he transferred to the newly formed Royal Air Force and, in the years after the First World War, was able to resist calls to disband the RAF

by promoting its use as an imperial policing force – most notably in Iraq, then a British protectorate. It was while at the peak of his career – between 1928 and 1936 – that Salmond lived at 27 Chester Terrace. During his time at the house – where he lived with his wife Monica, née Grenfell (1893–1973) – Salmond became Chief of the Air Staff in 1929 and Marshal of the RAF in 1933. He retired from the air staff in the latter year, but returned to service during the Second World War as Director-General of Flying Control and Air–Sea Rescue (1941–43).

At 13 Chester Terrace a plaque of 1989 honours **C. R. Cockerell** (1788–1863) **18** , the architect and antiquary. Charles Robert Cockerell was educated in the office of Robert Smirke, a friend of his architect father. As a young man he made a circuit of the West Country and Wales with the artists Thomas Daniell and William Daniell, before spending the years 1810 to 1817 in Europe. This had a profound effect upon his architecture, which is unabashedly yet adventurously classical in style. An early commission was for the monument on Calton Hill in Edinburgh (built 1824–29; unfinished), but his best-known surviving building is the conjoined Ashmolean Museum and Taylor Institution in Oxford (1841–45), 'an unsightly pile of pagan details' according to the keenly Gothic A. W. N. Pugin.[16] Cockerell was Professor of Architecture at the Royal Academy in 1840–57; he was also Surveyor of St Paul's Cathedral, and became the first professional President of the Royal Institute of British Architects in 1860. After spending much of his professional life at Ivy House, North End Road, Hampstead, Cockerell moved to Chester Terrace in 1856 with his wife Anna, née Rennie (1803–1872). He retired from architectural practice three years later and died at number 13.

Just to the north of Marylebone Road lies Brunswick Place (formerly part of Upper Harley Street), NW1, which forms part of Nash's grand entrance to Regent's Park and was built in 1824. The imposing stuccoed house at 2 Brunswick Place was the last London home of **Frederick Denison Maurice** (1805–1872) **19** , the Christian philosopher and educationalist, who lived here from November 1862 until December 1866, when he moved to Cambridge to take up the Knightbridge chair of casuistry, moral theology and moral philosophy. The son of a Unitarian minister, F. D. Maurice

was ordained an Anglican priest in 1834 and, two years later, was appointed Chaplain of Guy's Hospital. In 1840 – having published one of his most significant works, *The Kingdom of Christ* (1838) – he became a professor at King's College London. However, his *Theological Essays* of 1853 led to accusations of heterodoxy, and his academic career was brought to a temporary close. Chaplain of Lincoln's Inn from 1846 to 1860, Maurice was a leader of the Christian Socialist movement – his colleagues included Charles Kingsley – and put his educational theories into action by helping to establish Queen's College at 43–49 Harley Street, Britain's first higher education college for women, in 1846; eight years later, he was a founder – and first Principal – of the Working Men's College at Red Lion Square, Holborn. During his time at number 2, Maurice was Chaplain of St Peter's in nearby Vere Street, a position he held until 1869. Maurice was first commemorated with a plaque by the LCC in 1906 at 21 Queen Square, Bloomsbury, his home from 1846 to 1856, but the building was demolished in 1960. The GLC plaque at 2 Brunswick Place was erected in 1977, following a suggestion made by the Working Men's College.

The actor-manager **Sir Charles Wyndham** (1837–1919) **20** has a plaque at 20 York Terrace East, NW1. This is the eastern half of Doric Villa by John Nash – built in 1822 and formerly known as 42 and 43 York Terrace – which has the external appearance of a mansion but is in fact a pair of semi-detached villas. Born Charles Culverwell in Liverpool, Wyndham qualified as a doctor, though his real passion was always for the theatre. He made his name in London's West End as a handsome, seductive leading man with an outstanding talent for comedy, and afterwards excelled as a manager. Wyndham's successes included the title role of T. W. Robertson's *David Garrick* (1886) and, like Garrick, he is distinguished in having a West End theatre named after him: Wyndham's Theatre in Charing Cross Road opened in 1899 (fig. 92), prior to which he managed the Criterion at Piccadilly Circus. In his theatrical heyday Wyndham lived at two addresses near the Finchley Road, both of which were flattened in the Second World War. So it was that the plaque was erected at Doric Villa in 1962, though the building was under some threat of demolition at the time. Wyndham died here, having taken up residence

FITZROVIA AND REGENT'S PARK

92   The auditorium of Wyndham's Theatre, Charing Cross Road, built by Sir Charles Wyndham in 1899. [© English Heritage. NMR. Photograph by Derek Kendall]

about a year before with Mary Charlotte Moore (1861–1931); once his leading lady and mistress, she was, by this time, his business partner and second wife.

CHARLES WYNDHAM's plaque, originally installed on the porch, was moved to its present position in order to match the site of a plaque put up in 1985 on the western half of Doric Villa – 19 York Terrace East. This commemorates the pioneer psychoanalyst **Dr Ernest Jones** (1879–1958) 21 . Jones grew up near Swansea, and practised as a neurologist before taking on the mantle of the chief English-language propagator of the ideas of SIGMUND FREUD. He set up in private practice as a psychoanalyst in 1913, and in the same year co-founded the London Psycho-Analytical Society; in 1920 Jones established the *International Journal for Psycho-*

Analysis and four years later co-founded the Institute of Psycho-Analysis in London. As well as producing books on psychoanalysis, he found time to write about his favourite hobby in *The Elements of Figure Skating* (1931). It was perhaps fortunate that this interest was shared by Sir Samuel Hoare, who was Home Secretary in 1938 when Jones applied for leave for Freud and his family to settle in this country. Earlier, Jones had been responsible for bringing MELANIE KLEIN to England. He lived at Doric Villa from 1921 to 1940, sharing the house with his Austrian wife Katherine, née Jokl and their four children. Since the installation of the plaque by the GLC, Jones's life and career have come in for some reappraisal, and his three-volume biography of his mentor, *Sigmund Freud: Life and Work* (1953–57), is now seen as overly uncritical.

At 5 York Gate, NW1, is a plaque of 1976 to **Francis Turner Palgrave** (1824–1897) **22** , the compiler of *The Golden Treasury*. It is for this anthology of English verse – fully entitled *The Golden Treasury of the Best Songs and Lyrical Poems in the English Language* (1861) – that Palgrave is best known, though he also wrote and published poetry of his own composition. Palgrave conceived the idea of a definitive collection of the best English verse while on a walking holiday in Cornwall with TENNYSON. The future Poet Laureate gave assistance and encouragement, though complained that Palgrave's chatter – which he compared to the noise of a bee in a bottle – was interfering with his own creative process. Palgrave's selection was confined to deceased writers, and was very much of its time, but this has scarcely dimmed the enduring popularity of the *Treasury*; Palgrave's subsequent anthology of living writers was less successful. In December 1862, Palgrave – who had been unrequitedly in love with Georgina Alderson, who became the wife of Lord Robert Cecil, later 3RD MARQUESS OF SALISBURY – married Cecil Greville Milnes (1834–1890) and moved to 5 York Gate. The couple's daughter recalled that their first year at the house was 'chiefly given up to seeing their many friends and relations', and the evenings to music, 'for my mother played the piano charmingly'.[17] They stayed for thirteen years at number 5, which lies at the corner with York Terrace East and forms part of a Nash terrace

of five built in the early 1820s; it has been gutted internally, but retains an authentic external appearance.

Number 23 Park Road (formerly 12 Park Place), NW1 – part of a terrace dating from about 1820 – bears an LCC plaque to the Argentine soldier and statesman **José de San Martín (The Liberator)** (1778–1850) **23** . Born in Yapeyú, San Martín spent his early life in Madrid, where he met and befriended BERNARDO O'HIGGINS. He returned to Argentina in 1812, and the following year led an army to victory against the Spanish at the Battle of San Lorenzo, the first victory of the Argentine War of Independence. Following a treacherous crossing of the Andes, San Martín entered Santiago in Chile with O'Higgins in February 1817, and subsequent victories helped to secure the liberation of Peru; San Martín was created Peru's 'Protector' in 1821. However, his encounter in 1822 with SIMÓN BOLÍVAR, the liberator of the northern states of South America, did not produce a meeting of minds, and San Martín effectively relinquished all claims to authority thereafter. On returning to Argentina he learned that his wife had died, and he left with his daughter for Europe, where he spent the rest of his life. San Martín lived at 23 Park Road – then 12 Park Place – in 1824. On 12 June of that year, he told James Paroissien, his English aide-de-camp, that the house had been obtained for him; '*Estoy con comodidad y en buena situacion*' ('I am comfortable and in a good location'), he added.[18] Paroissien's diary indicates that San Martín remained at the address until at least early September. He spent much time thereafter in Paris, and died at Boulogne-sur-Mer. The plaque was unveiled in 1953 by the Argentine Ambassador, Dr Domingo A. Derisi (fig. 93).

Kent Terrace, NW1, which dates from 1827, is the only Nash terrace not to face onto Regent's Park. At number 10 lived the painter and illustrator **E. H. Shepard** (1879–1976) **24** . Ernest Howard Shepard is celebrated as the illustrator of the Winnie the Pooh books of A. A. MILNE (fig. 94), a job he landed after illustrating Milne's children's poems while on the staff of *Punch* magazine; their first collaboration was *When We Were Very Young* (1924), the earliest of the Pooh series. Shepard's connection with *Punch* lasted nearly fifty years from 1906, and was strengthened by his marriage in 1904 to Florence Chaplin (d. 1927), the granddaughter of Ebenezer Landells, one of the magazine's

93 The unveiling of the plaque to José de San Martin at 23 Park Road in 1953. On the left is Mr W. G. Fiske, Chairman of the LCC Town Planning Committee; to his right are Viscount Davidson, Chairman of the Anglo-Argentine Society, and Dr Domingo Derisi, the Argentine Ambassador. The Peruvian Ambassador and the Chilean Chargé d'Affaires were also present. [© Getty Images]

FITZROVIA AND REGENT'S PARK

founders. Number 10 Kent Terrace was Shepard's childhood home from the age of about four; the notion was early instilled in him by his parents – the architect Henry Dunkin Shepard (d. 1902) and his wife Jessie – 'that he should always have a pencil in his hand, always have paper nearby and always be ready to draw anything that interested him'.[19] Later, he cheerfully described the house's garden as 'untidy, with some big trees and a lot of sooty shrubs, but it was an excellent place to play in'.[20] The idyll ended when his mother fell terminally ill, and he was sent to live with an aunt in 1890. When researching his autobiography after the Second World War, Shepard was pleased to find the house intact – 'ornamented with stucco columns in front and a small balcony to each drawing room window' – though in a somewhat shabby condition, with the front railings removed.[21] These have since been replaced, and the façade adorned with an English Heritage plaque, unveiled in 1993 by Shepard's daughter, Mary Knox.

Immediately behind Kent Terrace, facing Regent's Park, is the rather grander Hanover Terrace, NW1, another Nash design of the early 1820s. Under the pedimented centrepiece are numbers 10 and 11, both of which have plaques set behind the ground-floor colonnade. Number 10 was home to the composer **Ralph Vaughan Williams**, OM (1872–1958) 25 from 1953 until his death. Described by an obituarist as 'the first composer since the Elizabethans to reflect the spirit of all things English', Vaughan Williams's output ranged from sacred music to film scores.[22] He was renowned as a collector of English folk songs, yet was an internationalist by nature, with an eclectic range of musical influences. Vaughan Williams spent much of his life in the capital: from 1905 to 1929 he lived at 13 (later 12) Cheyne Walk, Chelsea (demolished), where he wrote *A London Symphony* (1914). He came to 10 Hanover Terrace in 1953 after marrying Ursula Penton Wood (b. 1911), his second wife. They 'enjoyed every minute of the time . . . in that beautiful house', she later remembered.[23] 'A big study on the first floor at the back gave Ralph a pleasant place for work, and a Steinway piano . . . allowed us to have plays-through of new works, parties with music and such luxuries'.[24] The octogenarian Vaughan Williams was astonishingly productive: works composed here included a setting of the verse of WILLIAM BLAKE and three symphonies. His sudden death at number 10 came barely a month after he had attended the premiere of his ninth symphony; an opera, *Thomas the Rhymer*, was left unfinished. The plaque was unveiled by SIR ARTHUR BLISS on the centenary of Vaughan Williams's birth, in the presence of his widow.

Next door, at number 11 Hanover Terrace, is an English Heritage plaque of 1990 to the architect **Anthony Salvin** (1799–1881) 26 . Salvin was a pioneering exponent of the Gothic and Tudor revivals; his best-known commissions were for country houses, such as the spectacular Harlaxton Manor, Lincolnshire (1831–37), and Scotney Castle, Kent (1835–43). He also undertook many well-regarded restorations, notably that of the Tower of London (1853–68), which secured him a commission to undertake similar work at Windsor Castle (1856–67). Salvin's labours were informed by a thorough knowledge of medieval buildings, though some of his church restorations – such as that at Durham Cathedral – are now regarded as less than sympathetic. Long resident in Finchley – at Elm House, East End Road (demolished) – Salvin moved to Hanover Terrace in 1858, along with his wife Anne (d. 1860), his architect son, also named Anthony (1827–1881), and two unmarried daughters. The move was prompted by medical advice: he had suffered a stroke and the omnibus commute was proving arduous. 'The irregularity of food was bad and he could never be sure of luncheon', one daughter explained.[25] After the death of his wife in 1860, Salvin sought solace in building himself a new house – Hawksfold at Fernhurst, Sussex – to which he moved in 1864. Meanwhile, his son kept up a connection with Regent's Park by designing buildings for London Zoo, including a lion house (1874–77; demolished 1975).

At 13 Hanover Terrace, a GLC plaque commemorates the writer **H. G. Wells** (1866–1946) 27 . Born in Bromley, Herbert George Wells studied at the Normal School (later Royal College) of Science, where he was strongly influenced by the teachings of T. H. HUXLEY. Turning to writing in the 1890s, he had his first success with *The Time Machine*, published in book form in 1895; film and radio adaptations have made *The War of the Worlds* (1898) his most famous work. As well as what would now be classed as science fiction, Wells wrote works of historical and social commentary, such

94   E. H. Shepard's design of
c.1928 for the cover to *The
Christopher Robin Story Book*,
showing the Winnie-the-Pooh
characters at the Enchanted Place.
[© 2009 Lloyds TSB Bank Plc.,
Executor of the Estate of E. H.
Shepard and the E. H. Shepard
Trust, reproduced by permission of
Curtis Brown Group Ltd, London.
Courtesy of V&A Images / Victoria
and Albert Museum, London]

as the best-selling *The Outline of History* (1920). He moved to Hanover Terrace in 1936, and composed his own obituary the following year: 'He occupied an old tumble-down house upon the border of Regent's Park and his bent, shabby, slovenly and latterly somewhat obese figure was frequently to be seen in the adjacent gardens, sitting and looking idly at the boats on the lake, or the flowers in the beds, or hobbling painfully about with the aid of a stick'.[26] The house was in fact very comfortable – its luxuries included a four-poster bed and a private telephone exchange – and Wells continued to write almost until the day he died. While his journalism remained sharp, most critics reckoned that the bleak commentary *Mind at the End of its Tether* (1945) unfortunately lived up to its title. Wells was one of the few residents of Hanover Terrace to stay put during the war, despite having windows shattered by flying bombs; he took particular delight in displaying a prominent number thirteen outside to deride superstition. His opinions remained as colourful – and colourfully expressed – as ever: he referred to the Royal Society as 'a lot of bastards' following their failure to offer him a fellowship, and to the Labour Party as his '*bête rouge*', though he nonetheless voted

for it in 1945.[27] Wells died at number 13 in 1946, and the plaque was unveiled twenty years later, on the centenary of his birth.

Further north lies Hanover Lodge, Outer Circle, NW1 – another part of Nash's development, which dates from 1822. Two admirals are here commemorated: **Thomas Cochrane**, **Earl of Dundonald** (1775–1860) and **David**, **Earl Beatty**, **OM** (1871–1936) 28 . A controversial figure, Cochrane won repute as a daring commander in the Napoleonic wars, but his career was stymied by his inability to hold his tongue – especially when he encountered incompetence in the senior ranks. He even vented his grievances in Parliament, where he sat for the constituency of Westminster as a radical. After being implicated – unfairly, it appears – in a financial scandal of 1814, Cochrane served a prison sentence; subsequently he was a successful mercenary naval commander for the liberationists in South America – where he fell out with SAN MARTÍN – and in Greece. Cochrane inherited the family title in 1831, and in the following year was pardoned and awarded the rank of rear admiral. He took up residence at Hanover Lodge not long afterwards, and remained here until about 1845, devoting much of his time to researching the maritime applications of steam power; his work resulted in the warship HMS *Janus* (1848). Less colourful – if only by comparison – is the career of David Beatty, who was promoted rear admiral at the age of only thirty-nine, appointed to command the Navy's battle-cruiser squadron in 1913, and took much credit for successful First World War engagements in the Heligoland Bight (1914). At the Battle of Jutland (1916), however, he saw the *Indefatigable* and the *Queen Mary* sunk before his eyes, and is supposed to have remarked, 'There seems to be something wrong with our bloody ships today'.[28] Appropriately, Beatty had acquired the former residence of Cochrane in late 1909; altered and enlarged for him by LUTYENS, Hanover Lodge – the walls of which were 'filled with portraits of old naval heroes and with pictures of the early battleships' – remained the home of Beatty and his wife Ethel (d. 1932) until the mid-1920s (fig. 95).[29] During this time Beatty was successively Commander-in-Chief of the Fleet (1916–19) and First Sea Lord (1919–27); his earldom and the Order of Merit came in 1919, and a blue plaque in 1974.

95   The interior of Admiral Beatty's writing room at Hanover Lodge, as it appeared in 1915. The walls of the house were 'filled with portraits of old naval heroes'. [© Country Life]

1   *The Times*, 17 December 1962, p. 12

2   Charles Higham, *Charles Laughton: An Intimate Biography* (London, 1976), p. 16

3   Elsa Lanchester, *Charles Laughton and I* (London, 1938), p. 93

4   Derek Patmore, *The Life and Times of Coventry Patmore* (London, 1949), p. 111

5   It is now accepted that Smirke was born in 1780, rather than in 1781, as is stated on the plaque.

6   *Daily Mail*, 15 May 1897

7   Janet Dunbar, *Mrs G. B. S.* (London, 1963), pp. 167–68

8   *The Letters of Virginia Woolf*, ed. Nigel Nicolson, vol. I: *The Flight of the Mind* (London, 1975), p. 291 (2 April 1907)

9   Ibid, p. 387 (11 March 1909)

10 Ibid, p. 291 (12 April 1907)

11 *ODNB*, vol. XXVII, p. 527

12 Miriam Estensen, *The Life of Matthew Flinders* (Crows Nest, Australia, 2002), p. 464 (27 May 1813)

13 Margaret Postgate, *The Story of Fabian Socialism* (London, 1961), p. 4

14 Athol Mayhew, *A Jorum of 'Punch' with those who Helped to Brew it* (London, 1895), p. 50

15 Robert Rhodes James, *Henry Wellcome* (London, 1994), p. 353

16 A. W. N. Pugin, *An Apology for the Revival of Christian Architecture in England* (London, 1843), p. 3

17 Gwenllian F. Palgrave, *Francis Turner Palgrave: His Journals and Memories of his Life* (London, 1899), p. 78

18 Copy of MSS letter from San Martín to James Paroissien on blue plaque file.

19 Arthur R. Chandler, *The Story of E. H. Shepard: The Man who Drew Pooh* (West Sussex, 2000), p. 14

20 E. H. Shepard, *Drawn from Memory* (London, 1957), pp. 14–15

21 Ibid, p. 14

22 *The Times*, 27 August 1958, p. 10

23 Letter from Ursula Vaughan Williams, 22 February 1872, on blue plaque file.

24 Ursula Vaughan Williams, *Paradise Remembered* (London, 2002), p. 173

25 Jill Allibone, *Anthony Salvin: Pioneer of Gothic Revival Architecture* (Columbia, USA, 1987), p. 149

26 Vincent Brome, *H. G. Wells: A Biography* (London, 1951), p. 3

27 Ibid, p. 10

28 S. Roskill, *Admiral of the Fleet Earl Beatty: The Last Naval Hero* (London, 1980), p. 160

29 Lawrence Weaver, 'Hanover Lodge, Regent's Park', *Country Life*, 1 May 1915, p. 600

96 The Freud Museum, 20 Maresfield Gardens, and its English Heritage plaques to Sigmund Freud (left) and Anna Freud (right). [© English Heritage. Photograph by Derek Kendall]

HAMPSTEAD

Hampstead was an ancient Middlesex settlement, its name meaning 'homestead'; it means rather more than that now. By Georgian times the area had become the Montpelier of London: its hilltop location gave it sweet airs and fine prospects, and City dwellers were duly enticed upwards. The chalybeate springs that rise here brought droves of Stuart and Georgian visitors up the hill to find a cure through the iron-rich waters, and from the seventeenth century onwards a growing number chose to retire to Hampstead. From the later 1700s, the woods and sprawling heath – not to men- tion the ever-changing skies – were increasingly ap- preciated by the town dweller eager to reconnect with his dwindling links to the countryside; London artists of the highest calibre were drawn to the place as well. In the popular mind, Hampstead is peopled with the intelligentsia, and given over to left-leaning politics, the arts, opulence and émigrés. On the evidence of the blue plaques put up so far, which are legion and densely clustered, the popular view is not far off the mark.

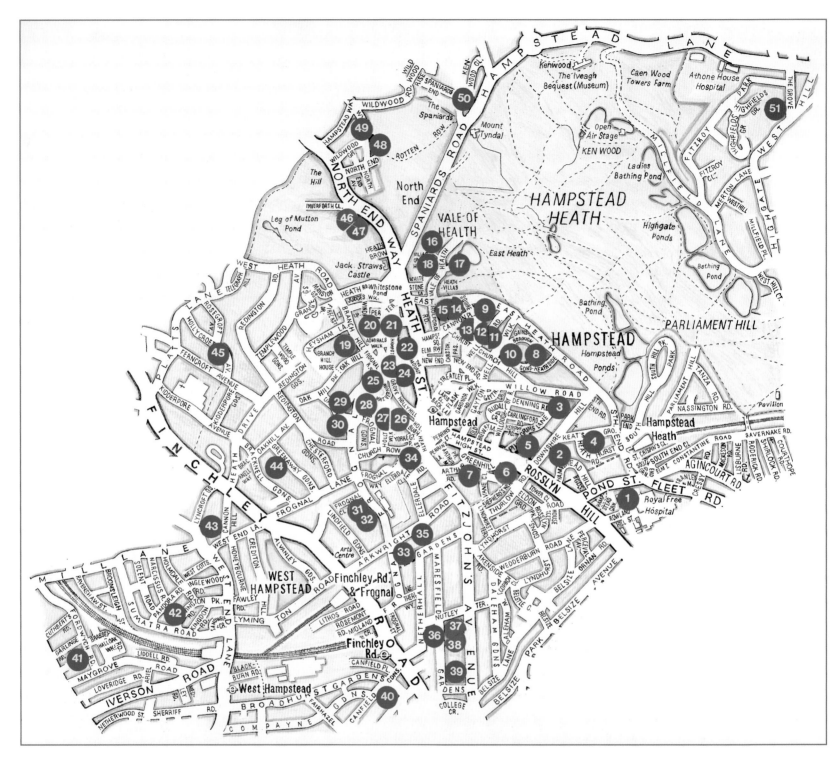

HAMPSTEAD

97 Bartram House, Pond Street – the former home of Sir Rowland Hill – in a watercolour of 1901 by Mary Anne Baily. By this time, the house formed part of the North Western Fever Hospital. [© Camden Local Studies and Archives Centre]

On a modern boundary wall of the Royal Free Hospital complex, facing down Rowland Hill Street, NW3, a chocolate-brown coloured plaque commemorates **Sir Rowland Hill**, KCB (1795–1879) ❶ (see also pp. 461–2), originator of the Penny Post. As a small supplementary tablet records, this plaque was installed by the Society of Arts in 1893 and was moved to its present position by the GLC in 1978.[1] It originally marked Bartram House, Pond Street, Hill's home from 1849 until his death (fig. 97). During his time here, Hill campaigned vigorously against the Hampstead Smallpox Hospital, located adjacent to his home. It was somewhat ironic, therefore, that soon after Hill's death his house was incorporated into the North Western Fever Hospital; this was replaced by the larger Hampstead General Hospital in 1905 and, once more, by the vast Royal Free Hospital, completed in 1975. Hill was already a national celebrity when he moved to Bartram House: his lifetime's preoccupation became apparent with the publication of *Post Office Reform: Its Importance and Practicability* (1837), and the introduction in 1840 of the Penny Post established his success. While in Hampstead, he served as Secretary to the Postmaster-General (1846–54) and Secretary to the Post Office (1854–64). Hill died at Bartram House and was buried in Westminster Abbey, a remarkable accolade for a sometimes controversial public servant.

Number 47 Downshire Hill, NW3 – an early nineteenth-century house in one of Hampstead's finest streets – is associated with a number of artists. In 1919–37 it was the home of the Carline family: Richard Carline (1896–1980) was a war artist of some repute, and his sister Hilda married Stanley Spencer (1891–1959), who spent some time here too. Next came the Uhlmans: a Jewish refugee himself, Fred Uhlman (1901–1985) opened his house to others fleeing the Nazis. Foremost among these house guests was the master of political photomontage, **John Heartfield** (1891–1968) ❷, whose plaque adorns the façade of number 47. Born Helmut Herzfeld in Germany, he anglicised his name during the First World War in a characteristically outspoken gesture of defiance. Together with Georg Grosz, he was one of the central figures in Berlin Dada. Heartfield's acerbic view of Weimar politics, combined with a strong commitment to communism, led him into the realm of political agitation. His weapon was photomontage, a new art form in which cut-out photographs were superimposed to create radical and disturbing images. Heartfield's anti-Nazi posters are some of the best-known images of inter-war political conflict; they include *Adolf the Superman: Swallows Gold and Spouts Junk* (1932) (fig. 98). Heartfield fled from the Nazis on their winning power

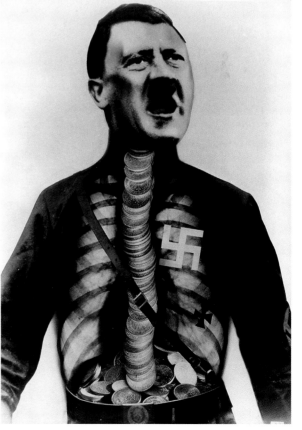

98 John Heartfield's iconic photomontage *Adolf the Superman: Swallows Gold and Spouts Junk* (1932; printed before 1942). [© The Heartfield Community of Heirs / VG Bild-Kunst, Bonn and DACS, London 2008. Courtesy of the National Gallery of Canada]

HAMPSTEAD

99 A photograph by David E. Scherman showing Lee Miller and Roland Penrose at home at 21 Downshire Hill in c.1943. [© Lee Miller Archives, England 2008]

Across the street, at 21 Downshire Hill, is the joint plaque to the photographer **Lee Miller** (1907–1977) and her husband, the Surrealist **Sir Roland Penrose** (1900–1984) ③ (fig. 99). New York-born Miller started her career as a model at the age of twenty. In 1929 she went to Paris, where her role as Man Ray's pupil, lover and muse led her to develop her own interest in photography. Miller's best-known work remains her reportage for *Vogue*: between 1942 and 1946 her coverage included the siege of Saint-Malo, Hitler's private apartments and the liberation of Paris; her images of the Dachau concentration camp were among the hardest hitting of the war. Miller had been involved in the Surrealist movement for some years before meeting, in 1937, Roland Penrose, a painter, art patron, friend of Picasso and founder in 1947 of the Institute of Contemporary Arts; he was a significant figure in the avant-garde British art scene, with exceptional contacts in Paris. Penrose formed the British Surrealist Group in 1935; in the following year, he organised the International Surrealist Exhibition in London and moved to 21 Downshire Hill. Miller joined him here three years later; the couple remained at number 21 until 1947, the year of their marriage, when they moved briefly to 36 Downshire Hill before shifting their base in 1949 to Farley Farm, Chiddingly, East Sussex, their home for the rest of their lives. Miller and Penrose were noted for their hospitality, and during their time at number 21 the house was a gathering point for artists, politicians and journalists: Man Ray and André Breton were both regular visitors. The plaque was unveiled in 2003 by their son Antony Penrose and the playwright Sir David Hare.

in 1933 and, after a period in Czechoslovakia, came to London in December 1938. Within a couple of weeks, he was taken in by the Uhlmans and given an upper room at number 47; the Artists' Refugee Committee – of which Uhlman's English wife Diana (1912–1999) was Secretary – was based in the house, as was the Free German League of Culture, founded by Fred Uhlman. The couple were much taken with 'Johnny', whom they found to be 'a charming, modest, meek and mild little man who only got excitable and fanatical when it came to politics'.[2] Heartfield shared the house with others including Gertrud Fietz, who later became his wife, and the art historian Francis Klingender (1907–1955). Leaving number 47 in January 1943, Heartfield and Gertrud moved to 1 Jackson's Lane, Highgate, N6, where they remained until they returned to Germany in 1950. The plaque in Downshire Hill was unveiled in 2004 by Fred and Diana Uhlman's daughter, Caroline Compton.

The poet **John Keats** (1795–1821) ④ lived at Wentworth Place, Keats Grove (formerly John Street), NW3, between 1818 and 1820 (fig. 100). The house had been built in 1815–16 by two literary men as a joint enterprise and shared residence: one was the antiquary, writer and critic Charles Wentworth Dilke (1789–1864), the other his friend Charles Armitage Brown (1789–1842). Dilke occupied the west (right) half and Brown the east (left); in 1838–39, the semi-detached pair were thrown into one house, which was named Lawn Cottage (later Lawn Bank). Keats, a Londoner, had been introduced to Hampstead in 1816 by LEIGH HUNT, whom he visited in the Vale of Health. He first took lodgings in Well Walk, but on his brother

100 An undated photograph of Keats House, Keats Grove, with its brown Society of Arts plaque erected in 1896. The building – originally a pair of semi-detached properties – opened to the public as a museum in 1925. [© City of London, LMA]

101 Ben Nicholson's *1934 (relief)*. One of a series of works which made his name, it was completed during the artist's first phase in Hampstead, when he lived with Barbara Hepworth at the Mall Studios. [© Angela Verren Taunt 2008. All rights reserved, DACS / Tate, London 2008]

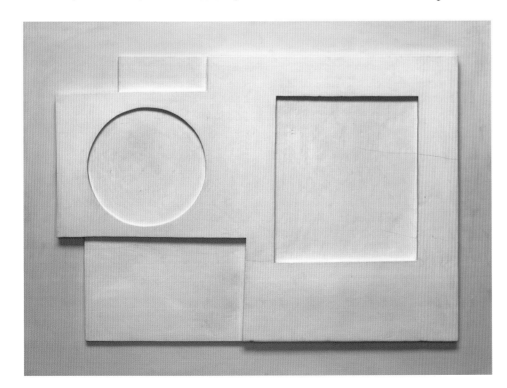

Tom's death in December 1818 he moved in with Brown at Wentworth Place. A number of his finest poems were composed at this time, including *The Eve of St Agnes* and 'La Belle Dame sans Merci'. In April 1819 the Brawne family rented Dilke's part of the house. By June, Keats was engaged to the daughter, Fanny Brawne (1800–1865), and the summer of that year marked the climax of his short life. He wrote 'Ode to a Nightingale' in May, seated beneath the plum tree in the garden. Keats was already suffering from tuberculosis, and even the much-vaunted Hampstead air was not sufficient cure; his health declined sharply after a freezing ride on a stagecoach from town to Hampstead in February 1820. In September of that year he left London for Rome, where he died. Wentworth Place was altered by a later resident, and enlarged. The plaque, chocolate-brown in colour, was erected by the Society of Arts in 1896, and may well have played a signal part in the 1920–21 campaign to save the house from demolition. Wentworth Place was purchased by donations, vested in Hampstead Borough Council and opened to the public in 1925 as Keats House, one of the first literary museums in the country.

At 2B Pilgrim's Lane, NW3, is the English Heritage plaque to the abstract artist **Ben Nicholson**, **OM** (1894–1982) **5** , who lived and died here. The son of the artist Sir William Nicholson, Ben lived with his family at another house in Pilgrim's Lane – number 1 – in 1904–6, and returned to spend two highly significant periods of his life in the area. The first was during the 1930s, when he occupied the Mall Studios, off Tasker Road, together with his equally distinguished second wife, the sculptor Barbara Hepworth, and their triplets; a secluded setting prevented the building from being commemorated. At this time, Nicholson was in the vanguard of progressive art in Britain. He belonged to Unit One, a collective of artists and architects that included PAUL NASH and HENRY MOORE; he also belonged to the French group Abstraction-Création, and was one of the international pioneers of Constructivism, editing the journal *Circle* with Naum Gabo and the architect Leslie Martin. Nicholson is renowned above all for his white and painted reliefs, produced from the 1930s onwards (fig. 101). His second period in Hampstead – the one commemorated with the blue plaque – was spent at 2B Pilgrim's Lane, his home from spring 1974 until his death. Number 2B, previously used as a studio by the abstract sculptor Robert Adams (1917–1984), was found for Nicholson by his dealers, the Marlborough Gallery. The building forms a twentieth-century addition to a handsome late Georgian house fronting onto Rosslyn Hill; it was substantially altered soon after the installation of the plaque in 2002.

On a marooned gatepier on the west side of Rosslyn Hill, NW3, a brown Society of Arts plaque honours

HAMPSTEAD

one of Hampstead's earliest notable residents: **Sir Harry Vane** (1613–1662) ⑥ (fig. 102 and see fig. 35).[3] Erected in 1898 at Vane House, Rosslyn Hill, it commemorates a remarkable (if maverick) statesman who ended his life on the block at Tower Hill. Henry Vane's early interest in republicanism prompted him to emigrate to the New World in 1635; within a year, at the age of twenty-three, he was Governor of Massachusetts. Having returned to England, he sat as an MP and played a leading part in the prosecution of the Earl of Strafford in 1641. Vane helped Cromwell manage the House of Commons during the Civil War, up to the execution of King Charles I in 1649, but won the sobriquet 'Sir Harry Weathervane' for his inconstancy thereafter. This shift of allegiance was not enough to save him from the vengeance of Charles II after the Restoration. 'He is too dangerous a man to let live, if we can honestly put him out of the way', remarked the King.[4] Arrested at his Hampstead home in July 1660, he was beheaded in 1662, as stated in the plaque's inscription. Vane House was later occupied by the noted moral philosopher Bishop Joseph Butler (1692–1752), and in 1855 became the Royal Soldiers' Daughters' Home. This important reminder of Hampstead's development as a place of elegant retirement was demolished as late as 1969, although the gatepost – on which the plaque is set – was retained.

The poet **Dame Edith Sitwell** (1887–1964) ⑦ spent most of her last years in Flat 42 of Greenhill, Hampstead High Street, NW3, a large Neo-Georgian apartment block of 1936 at the top of Rosslyn Hill. It was rather a 'normal' address for the strikingly singular-looking poet, who, with her equally celebrated brothers Osbert and Sacheverell, campaigned to promote interest in progressive literary and aesthetic endeavours among a rather suspicious British public.

Edith Sitwell wrote the words of *Façade* (1923), set to music by William Walton, and later won a reputation as a popular historian with works such as *The English Eccentrics* (1933) and *Victoria of England* (1936). It was as a poet, however, that Sitwell wished to be remembered. Her time at Greenhill was rather melancholy: when she arrived, in 1961, her health was failing, her reputation was beginning to be challenged, her finances were a cause of anxiety and her circle of friends was gradually passing away. The flat was small – Edith described it as 'just big enough for ghosts' – and was shared with her nurse, Doris Farquhar.[5] However, it was visited by many who trekked faithfully 'to that Greenhill far away' and witnessed Edith's triumphant seventy-fifth year, 1962, which saw the publication of *The Queens and the Hive*, her final collection of poetry, *The Outcasts*, and the reissue of *Fanfare for Elizabeth* (1946).[6] The 'Abbess of the Nightingales' moved to nearby 20 Keats Grove in spring 1964 and died soon after.

At East Heath Lodge, 1 East Heath Road, NW3, is an English Heritage plaque to the composer **Sir Arthur Bliss** (1891–1975) ⑧. Bliss was born in Barnes, the son of an American businessman. He lived in this fine semi-detached house of *c.* 1785 at the height of his career, between 1929 and 1939, when he and his wife Trudy (b. 1904) moved to America for a period before returning to an address in St John's Wood. One of the first works completed here was the choral symphony *Morning Heroes* (1930), his tribute to the dead of the Great War. Bliss had himself been gassed, and the piece, dedicated to his fallen brother, had considerable personal resonance. Here, he also wrote the stirring music to ALEXANDER KORDA's 1936 film *Things to Come*, after the book by H. G. WELLS, one of the most impressive early British film scores, and his music for the 1937 ballet *Checkmate*. Bliss, a cosmopolitan and innovative figure, came to be seen as the successor to ELGAR as a Romantic composer; knighted in 1950, he became Master of the Queen's Musick in 1953.

At 17 East Heath Road (formerly 2 Portland Villas) is a plaque of 1969 jointly commemorating the New Zealand-born writer **Katherine Mansfield** (1888–1923) and her husband, the critic **John Middleton Murry** (1889–1957) ⑨ (fig. 103). Fellow Hampstead writer D. H. LAWRENCE portrayed his sometime neigh-

103   Number 17 East Heath Road and its plaque to the writers Katherine Mansfield and John Middleton Murry. The couple named the house 'The Elephant' on account of its greyness and size. [© English Heritage. Photograph by Derek Kendall]

bours in *Women in Love* (1920) as Gudrun and Gerald, a couple of intensely connected fellow spirits. Mansfield's first collection of short stories, *In a German Pension* (1911), was written following a stay in Bavaria. Not long after its publication, she met Murry, with whom she settled; the couple were married in May 1918. Mansfield's all-too-short career was brought to an end by tuberculosis; it was in the vain hope that the Hampstead air might help her that she and Murry moved in late July 1918 to what was then 2 Portland Villas, a tall Italianate semi-detached house which they called 'The Elephant' on account of its greyness and size, but which commanded a superb view over the western heath.[7] Ida Baker, Mansfield's lifelong friend and Hampstead housekeeper, stated that 'Katherine saw in the house her last chance of a home of her own'.[8] A printing press was established in the base-ment, where small editions of the couple's works were produced. Visitors to the house included VIRGINIA WOOLF, WALTER DE LA MARE, T. S. ELIOT and OTTO-LINE MORRELL. Having wintered on the Italian Riviera, Mansfield returned to Hampstead in April to September 1920 before settling permanently on the Continent. There she was joined by Murry in early 1921, and there she died. Mansfield is remembered for her short stories: 'Prelude' (1916) is regarded as one of the finest in the genre. Her letters and journals also remain in high esteem; her husband published a notable collection of their correspondence in 1951. Murry edited a number of literary journals, including *The Athenaeum* and *The Adelphi*, and was a highly influential critic from the 1920s onwards. During the Second World War, he was one of the most prominent of pacifists.

HAMPSTEAD

104 *View over London from Hampstead Heath*, one of a series of watercolours painted by John Constable at his home at 40 Well Walk. The work – undated – was executed some time between 1830 and 1833. [© The Trustees of the British Museum]

Hampstead's best-known painter is **John Constable** (1776–1837) 🔟 , commemorated at 40 (formerly 6, later 26) Well Walk, NW3. In search of fresh air for his growing family and ailing wife, Maria, née Bicknell (1788–1828), he first moved from Fitzrovia to a now-demolished cottage in Whitestone Lane, close to Whitestone Pond, in the summer of 1819. Eight years later, the Constables moved to what was then 6 Well Walk, a late Georgian terraced house of *c*. 1820. 'We are at length fixed in our comfortable little house in Well Walk', he wrote shortly after moving here in the late summer; 'our little drawing-room commands a view unsurpassed in Europe, from Westminster Abbey to Gravesend'.[9] The great painter of the arable landscape lived in London for most of his adult life, and did much of his painting in the attic of his house at 35 (later 76) Charlotte Street, Fitzrovia; that building was marked with a plaque in 1906, but was demolished sixty years later. While living in Hampstead, Constable completed paintings such as *The Chain Pier, Brighton* (1826–27) and *Dedham Vale* (1828), as well as numerous *plein-air* sketches that capture the fleeting effects of weather and light over the Hampstead landscape (fig. 104). In November 1828, following the birth of their seventh child, Maria Constable died of tuberculosis at the Well Walk house. The family returned to Fitzrovia, though the Hampstead house was kept up as an occasional residence until at least 1834. A blue, wreathed Doulton plaque – the first of a series made by the Lambeth firm – was erected here in 1923.

Just across the road, at 13 Well Walk, is a plaque to another characteristic Hampstead resident: the socialist leader **Henry Mayers Hyndman** (1842–1921) 11️⃣ , who moved to number 13 in 1917 and died here four years later. He shared the house with his wife Rosalind, née Travers (1874–1923), a poet, and rented it from JOHN MASEFIELD, who lived here in 1912–17. Born in London, the son of a wealthy merchant, Hyndman became a socialist on reading MARX's *Das Kapital* in 1880 while crossing the Atlantic on business. This led to his 1881 publication *The Text-Book of Democracy: England for All*. In the same year, Hyndman helped to set up the Democratic Federation – one of the founding bodies of the Labour Party, its name was changed in 1884 to the Social Democratic Federation – and for many years edited its organ, *Justice*. Hyndman was also involved in the 1911 formation of the British Socialist Party; in 1916 – after a defeat in the party's leadership elections – he left it to found the National Socialist Party, which took on the name of the Social Democratic Federation in 1920. Number 13 is a handsome semi-detached house of the mid-1880s, embodying the familial respectability of Hampstead's late Victorian domestic architecture. The plaque was unveiled in 1972 by the historian Asa Briggs, who quoted Hyndman's quip 'there is no hope in this country but in the Labour Party. And there's not much hope in that'. Notably, a red flag – rather than the standard Union Jack – covered the plaque for the ceremony.

Another prominent socialist, the pioneer statistician **Karl Pearson** (1857–1936) 12️⃣ , is commemorated with a GLC plaque at 7 Well Road, NW3. The slightly technical nature of Pearson's achievement led to some hesitation over his fittingness for a plaque. Professors of statistics from around the world promptly leapt to his defence, emphasising his contribution to the evolution of modern statistical analysis, and duly carried the day. A protégé of SIR FRANCIS GALTON, Pearson is credited with establishing the modern discipline of mathematical statistics. He introduced a number of methods, including the chi-square test, was instrumental in the development of correlation theory, and – with W. F. R. Weldon – co-founded the discipline of biometry, the application of statistics to biology. Among his many published works are *The Grammar of Science* (1892), *Treasury of Human Inheritance* (1909–33) and a definitive biography of Galton (1914–30). 'K. P.' had worked

105 A photograph published in the *Strand Magazine* in 1929 showing the du Maurier family at home at Cannon Hall, 14 Cannon Place.

at University College London for many years before being appointed, in 1911, the college's first Galton Professor of Eugenics, a position he held until his retirement in 1933. The *Dictionary of National Biography* noted tersely that Pearson was 'admired and feared, rather than loved'.[10] The prickly professor's house, in which he lived from 1892 up to his death, is one of a procession of semi-detached red-brick pairs built in about 1880. It was the birthplace of his son Egon (1895–1980), also an eminent statistician.

At Cannon Hall, 14 Cannon Place, NW3, a GLC plaque honours the actor-manager **Sir Gerald du Maurier** (1873–1934) **13**, who lived here from 1916 until his death (fig. 105 and see fig. 29). The son of George du Maurier, Gerald was born in Hampstead and was connected with the area for much of his life. He made his stage debut in 1894 and was to become a hugely suc-

cessful actor, best remembered for his roles in plays by J. M. Barrie such as *The Admirable Crichton* (1902), *Peter Pan* (1904) and *Dear Brutus* (1917). From 1910 du Maurier turned to management, first at Wyndham's Theatre (see fig. 92) and from 1925 at the St James's Theatre. He was knighted in 1922. Cannon Hall dates from *c.* 1720 and ranks alongside Burgh House and Fenton House as one of Hampstead's most imposing early survivals of domestic architecture. Rather prosaically, it takes its name from the bollard outside, made from a piece of spent ordnance. Du Maurier's novelist daughter Daphne (1907–1989) wrote in 1934 of Sir Gerald's enthusiasm for Cannon Hall, which he shared with his wife, the actress Muriel Beaumont (1881–1957), and their children: 'He loved the garden and the view, and the rambling plan of the house – the lofty rooms, the old staircase, and especially the view from his bedroom window. He felt like a wanderer returned to

HAMPSTEAD

106 Sir Flinders Petrie during an expedition to Abydos, Egypt, in 1922. Behind him stands Mr G. W. H. Walker. [Reproduced with the permission of the Petrie Museum of Egyptian Archaeology, University College London]

the land of his birth . . . He would never want to move from Hampstead again. He would be a fixture now and for ever, part of the soil'.[11] Daphne herself grew up here; as she was still living when the plaque was erected in 1967, her name was omitted from its inscription.

The Egyptologist **Sir Flinders Petrie** (1853–1942) 14 is commemorated with an LCC plaque at 5 Cannon Place, one of two large houses built along this newly developed road in about 1875 (fig. 106). He moved here from nearby 8 Well Road in 1919, and remained until 1935, when he and his wife Hilda (1871–1957) moved to Jerusalem. Born in Charlton, Greenwich, William Matthew Flinders Petrie was the son of an electrical engineer and the grandson of the explorer CAPTAIN MATTHEW FLINDERS. He was interested in surveying by his twenties and in 1883, following work in Egypt, published *The Pyramids and Temples of Gizeh*. Over the next fifty-five years, Petrie led a number of pioneering excavations in Egypt and Palestine. He was one of the key figures to shift archaeology away from mere 'digging up' towards properly recorded investigations of sites, and established the British School of Archaeology in 1906. Among his many famous discoveries was the Palace of Apries, Memphis (1909). Between 1892 and 1933, Petrie served as the first Edwards Professor of Egyptology at University College London. His name lives on in the college's Petrie Museum in Malet Place, Bloomsbury, which houses a choice gathering of some of his finds.

The theologian **Baron Friedrich von Hügel** (1852–1925) 15 lived at 4 Holford Road, NW3, from 1882 to 1903. Born in Florence, the son of an Austrian diplomat and a Scottish mother who retired to Torquay in 1873, von Hügel followed his family to England and first settled in Hampstead in 1876, at 1 Heathfield Gardens (now 25 Cannon Place). He was a devoted heath walker, and was often accompanied by disputatious friends who shared his inquisitive piety and challenging stance on matters of religion. A pivotal figure in the formation of modern approaches to the study of the Bible, and – with CARDINAL NEWMAN – one of the key Catholic thinkers of his day, von Hügel combined an intellectual rigour towards the evidence with deep respect for religious faith, in such a way as to reconcile intellectual freedom with ecclesiastical authority. He went on to found the London Society for the Study of Religion in 1905, and to publish *The Mystical Element of Religion as Studied in St Catherine of Genoa and her Friends* (1908), generally regarded as his most important work. The Holford Road house is a large, gabled brick building; in 1903 von Hügel left it for 13 Vicarage Gate, Kensington, W8, where he died.

The Vale of Health, NW3, projects into the sloping heath like a remote hamlet of marooned town houses; sometime resident Compton Mackenzie found 'village life half an hour from Piccadilly Circus', while JOHN MIDDLETON MURRY referred to it rather more harshly as 'the Vale of Sickness'.[12] Popular with artists and writers, the cul-de-sac boasts three plaques. The first, at 3 Villas on the Heath – one of a row of mid-Victorian semi-detached houses with prominent bargeboarded gables – commemorates the Indian poet **Rabindranath Tagore** (1861–1941) 16 (fig. 107). Tagore, a Pirali Bengali Brahmin born in Calcutta, was a hugely productive and revered writer: he produced novels, short stories, dramas and essays, but is best remembered for his poetry, and for his sensitive plea for multiculturalism. Number 3 Villas on the Heath was his home for a few months in the summer of 1912, during Tagore's third visit to England. The lodgings were found for him by WILLIAM ROTHENSTEIN, who lived nearby at 11 Oak Hill Park (demolished). While at number 3, Tagore worked on translations of religious songs and lyrics, which were published in November 1912 by the India Society of London as *Gitanjali* ('Song Offerings'); the collection led to

107 A portrait of Rabindranath Tagore with Somendra Chandra Dev Burman, D. N. Maitra, John and William Rothenstein, and Rathindranath Tagore, the poet's son. The photograph was taken in Hampstead in 1912. [Courtesy of Andrew Robinson]

Tagore's becoming – in 1913 – the first non-European ever to win the Nobel Prize for Literature. The works greatly impressed Rothenstein, and on 7 July 1912 were read at his house by W. B. YEATS to an entranced audience that included ALICE MEYNELL and EVELYN UNDERHILL. Tagore told a friend that 'people here have taken to my work with such excessive enthusiasm that I cannot really accept it'.[13] Knighted in 1915, Tagore renounced the honour in protest at the Amritsar massacre of 1919. It was an Indian flag, and not a Union Jack, that was used at the plaque's unveiling in 1961.

The novelist and poet **D. H. Lawrence** (1885–1930) **17** lived at 1 Byron Villas, NW3, from August to December 1915. The only London address that Lawrence ever regarded as home (as opposed to temporary lodgings), number 1 forms the ground-floor flat of an unremarkable Edwardian house of about 1903 (see fig. 5); Lawrence lived here with his German wife Frieda, née Richthofen (1879–1956). Although brief, Lawrence's time at number 1 was significant: it saw the publication and suppression (on the grounds of obscenity) of one of his greatest works, *The Rainbow*, while Lawrence's experience of watching a Zeppelin raid from Hampstead Heath found its way into his 1923 novel *Kangaroo*. Shortly before Christmas 1915 – driven from London by depression following the ban of *The Rainbow* and the threat of air raids – Lawrence moved with Frieda to Cornwall, where he

wrote *Women in Love* (1920). There, the couple were suspected of being German spies and were forced to move yet again. The last decade of Lawrence's life – which saw the production of another controversial work, *Lady Chatterley's Lover* (1928) – was spent mostly on the Continent. Lawrence's stature as a novelist and poet soared after his early death, and remains huge to this day. The plaque was unveiled in 1969 by Montague Weekley, Frieda's son by her first husband (fig. 108); it was to be close to the children that the Lawrences had moved to Hampstead in the first place.

Rather less controversial in their day were the social historians **J. L.** (1872–1949) and **Barbara Hammond** (1873–1961) **18** , who lived from 1906 to 1913 at Hollycot in the Vale of Health, where they were commemorated by the GLC in 1972. (John) Lawrence Hammond and (Lucy) Barbara Bradby first met at Oxford University and were married in 1901; both were ardent Liberals. During most of their time at Hollycot, a semi-detached house of the late nineteenth century, Lawrence was employed as Secretary to the Civil Service Commission, having resigned his editorship of the weekly journal *The Speaker* in 1907. The couple were also starting to work closely together on a jointly written sequence of studies of eighteenth-century

108 Montague Weekley unveils the plaque to his stepfather, D. H. Lawrence, in 1969. On the left is Clare Mansel, a member of the GLC's Historic Buildings Board. [© City of London, LMA]

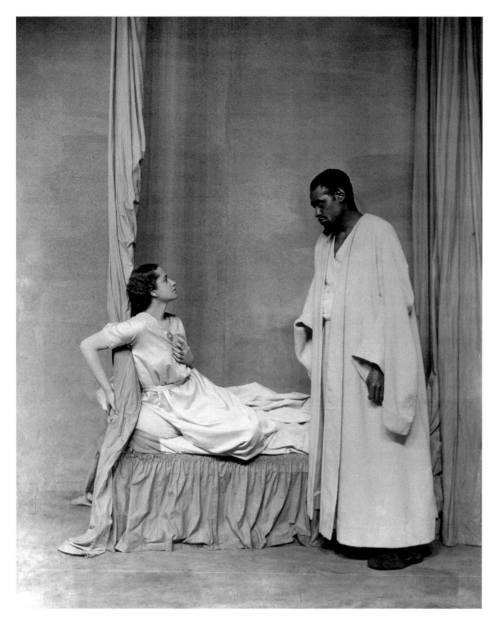

109 Paul Robeson as Othello, with Peggy Ashcroft playing Desdemona, 1930. [© Bettmann / CORBIS]

ing the American singer and actor **Paul Robeson** (1898–1976) ⑲ , one of the first black performers to achieve world renown (fig. 109). Robeson lived at this address in 1929–30, at the peak of his fame. His reputation was established with *Show Boat*, first performed in London in 1928, in which his commanding bass voice stood out, particularly with his rendition of 'Ol' Man River'. Robeson actually trained to be a lawyer and had already been called to the Bar in America before he took to the stage. London was important in his career: his performance of *Othello* at the Savoy Theatre in 1930 won many plaudits – the show moved to Broadway in 1943, where it became the longest-running Shakespearian production of all time – and he spent a number of years in the capital at the close of his working life. Robeson was highly engaged politically, and combined left-wing sympathies with open outrage at American race relations; through his performances and rallying broadcasts, he became a leading figure in the struggle against fascism, colonialism and racism. He enjoyed huge popularity in Soviet Russia, and he consequently suffered during the McCarthy years of the early 1950s. The first choice for a plaque was 19 Buckingham Street, Adelphi, WC2, Robeson's home from 1930 to 1937, but consent was refused by the building's owners. The plaque was unveiled at The Chestnuts by the singer Dame Cleo Laine in 2002. The house is part of a late nineteenth-century semi-detached pair now in use as a hotel.

The novelist and playwright **John Galsworthy** (1867–1933) ⑳ (see also pp. 376–7) was commemorated in 1950 at Grove Lodge, Admiral's Walk, NW3, his home from 1918 until 1933, very much his years of eminence (fig. 110). At the request of Galsworthy's widow, Ada (1866–1956), the plaque – installed by the LCC – does not mention that he died in the house. Galsworthy's earliest successful novel was *The Man of Property*, first published in 1906. This was the start of the renowned *Forsyte Saga* series, which continued with *In Chancery* (1920) and *To Let* (1921), both written during the author's time at Grove Lodge. Galsworthy's domestic chronicle attracted a huge following – Stalin was one of his many admirers – and was followed by two further trilogies: *A Modern Comedy* (1929) and *End of the Chapter* (1935). During his lifetime, Galsworthy was best known as a playwright, his works including *Strife* (1909), *The Skin Game* (1920) and *Escape* (1926). The

workers; this trilogy began with *The Village Labourer* (1911), a seminal study of the effect of enclosure on rural life, and was completed with *The Town Labourer* (1917) and *The Skilled Labourer* (1919). The Hammonds' aim was to awaken public conscience, and to inject a note of corrective realism into the complacent view of the Georgian age that was then widely prevalent. The trilogy established the Hammonds' reputations as leading social historians, and paved the way for further collaborations, including *The Age of the Chartists* (1930).

Beyond Whitestone Pond, at The Chestnuts, 1 Branch Hill, NW3, facing the West Heath, is a plaque honour-

110 A view of Admiral's Walk, with Admiral's House – the former home of Sir George Gilbert Scott – on the right and the plainer Georgian façade of Grove Lodge, the residence of John Galsworthy, beyond. [© English Heritage. Photograph by Derek Kendall]

Nobel Prize for Literature was awarded to Galsworthy in 1932; a delegation was sent to Hampstead from Sweden in order to make the presentation in Grove Lodge to the ailing author.

Next door to Grove Lodge is Admiral's House, 21 Admiral's Walk, which dates from about 1700 (see fig. 110). Another of the substantial first-generation suburban houses to be built in Hampstead, it takes its name from Fountain North, a naval officer who once lived here and who added a 'widow's walk' to the roofline, enabling him to look out across London and fire cannon in salute; that he was a lieutenant, not an admiral, is incidental. The house's most famous occupant, and recipient of the wreathed chocolate-brown plaque in 1910, was the architect **Sir George Gilbert Scott** (1811–1878) **21** . Scott lived here – in what was

then known as The Grove, Upper Heath – between 1856 and 1864, at the height of his career; he shared the house with his wife Caroline, née Oldrid (1811–1872) and their sons. Scott was one of the most industrious and successful of High Victorian architects; projects undertaken during his residence in Admiral's House included the Foreign Office in Whitehall (1862–75) and the Albert Memorial in Hyde Park (1863–72) (see fig. 8). His masterpiece, the Midland Grand Hotel at St Pancras Station (1868–74), came slightly later. The house, largely Georgian, is not evidently that of so eminent a Gothic Revivalist. A later occupant was the noted historian of the British Army, Sir John Fortescue (1859–1933).

Not far away, at New Grove House, 28 Hampstead Grove, NW3, is a plaque to the artist and writer **George du Maurier** (1834–1896) **22** (see also pp. 39–40) (fig.

111 The plaque to George du Maurier at New Grove House, 28 Hampstead Grove. Erected in 1900 by private subscribers, it mimics the design of the plaques installed by the Society of Arts. The plaque was incorporated into the official scheme by the LCC in 1959. [© English Heritage. Photograph by Derek Kendall]

111). Born in Paris, George Louis Palmella Busson du Maurier is remembered for his highly successful novel *Trilby* (1894), which he wrote while living at New Grove House. He was also celebrated for his satirical book illustrations; the best known of these appeared in *Punch* during the 1870s and 1880s (see fig. 50), but much of his finest work – such as his 1867 illustrations to Douglas Jerrold's *The Story of a Feather* – was carried out earlier in his career. Having established himself, and started a family – GERALD DU MAURIER was his son – he and his wife Emma, née Wightwick (1840/1–1915) moved in 1874 to this house, which is of eighteenth-century date with an added early Victorian 'Tudorbethan' exterior. Here he remained until 1895, the year before he died. It was said that the house's studio 'was the centre of the family life'. George 'was almost always sitting in the corner with the north light at his back, at work on his drawings, joining from time to time in the general conversation or interspersing a few comments'.[14] The plaque, brown in colour, was erected in 1900 by private subscribers; its design mimics the contemporary plaques of the Society of Arts. In 1959, after the novelist Daphne du Maurier – George's granddaughter – had expressed her concern about the plaque's condition and its being 'completely obscured by ivy', the LCC incorporated it into the official scheme.[15]

Another of Hampstead's earliest plaques, put up in 1900, is to be found at Bolton House, Windmill Hill, NW3. It honours the Scottish poet and dramatist **Joanna Baillie** (1762–1851) 23 , and was the fourth Society of Arts plaque to commemorate a woman (see fig. 16). Baillie was lionised in her day, and though her reputation has dipped subsequently, there can be little question as to her cultural interest. Several members of her family were prominent anatomists: her uncles

were JOHN HUNTER and WILLIAM HUNTER, and her brother Matthew was Physician-Extraordinary to George III. Joanna Baillie was drawn to the study of human character. Her most notable work was *Plays on the Passions*, a play cycle that appeared between 1798 and 1836. Scott, Wordsworth, Byron and KEATS each made the pilgrimage to Bolton House; Scott, in *Marmion* (1808), asserted that 'Avon's swans think Shakespeare lives again'.[16] Hyperbole perhaps, but Baillie was genuinely seen as the successor to Shake-speare in terms of her ability to infuse historical drama with a fitting measure of psychological intensity. Her 1800 play *De Montfort* was produced at Drury Lane by John Philip Kemble and Mrs Siddons; there too was performed in 1815 her most successful work, *The Family Legend* (1810). The chocolate-brown tablet, erected by the Society of Arts shortly before it handed over the plaques scheme to the LCC, blends in with the brick front of the house, one of a row of three built in about 1730. The inscription records that Baillie lived here for 'nearly 50 years'. In fact, it was just over thirty. Joanna first moved to Hampstead in 1791, but seems only to have taken up residence at Bolton House in 1820: in March of that year, she wrote of 'our new house . . . on what is called Holly Bush hill'.[17] She shared the house with her sister Agnes (1760–1861), and lived here until her death at the age of eighty-eight.

Across the green at 5 Holly Bush Hill, NW3, a wreathed LCC plaque of 1908 commemorates the painter **George Romney** (1734–1802) 24 , who was, with REYNOLDS and GAINSBOROUGH, one of the masters of Georgian portraiture (fig. 112). His classically inspired likenesses – especially of women, and most notably of Emma, Lady Hamilton – have enjoyed huge popular-ity. Romney followed his father's trade of cabinet-maker for the first ten years of his working life before becoming apprenticed to a local painter. His manual ability never deserted him: he made his own violin, and also designed his own studio extensions, first at his main London studio in Cavendish Square, and subse-quently at his home in Hampstead. This he bought in 1796 and extended by the addition of two huge rooms, the lower for teaching and painting and the upper for use as a studio and gallery (fig. 113); he took up resi-dence in 1798. His friend William Hayley described the artist in his new home: 'The singular fabrick, that Romney had now completed for his residence at

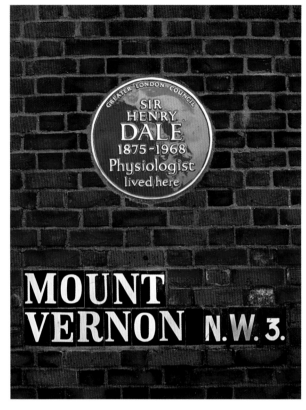

112 The wreathed LCC plaque to George Romney at 5 Holly Bush Hill, altered for the painter in c.1796–98. [© English Heritage. Photograph by Derek Kendall]

113 A photograph showing the interior of Romney's studio in 1931, as altered for his own use by the architect Clough Williams Ellis. [© Architectural Press Archive / RIBA Library Photographs Collection]

Above right 114 The plaque to Sir Henry Dale on the boundary wall of Mount Vernon House, Mount Vernon. [© English Heritage. Photograph by Derek Kendall]

Hampstead, was particularly suited to his own fancy. He had an excellent spacious gallery for the display of statues and pictures, and without moving from his pillow, he could contemplate from his own chamber window, a very magnificent view of the metropolis'.[18] Romney's life's work was largely over by the time he moved to Hampstead. Worn out by his hugely productive career as a portraitist, and frustrated by his inability to transfer success in this lesser genre of painting to the higher realm of history painting, in late summer 1799 he made the homeward journey back to Lancashire – whence he had set out for London in 1762 – and to his all but abandoned wife and son. After Romney's departure, the Hampstead house became assembly rooms in 1807, and was later a constitutional club. It was altered again by the architect, writer and conservationist Clough Williams Ellis (1883–1978), best remembered for establishing Portmeirion in Wales, who lived at number 5 from 1929 until the start of the Second World War.

The physiologist **Sir Henry Dale** (1875–1968) **25** was a distinguished figure in the medical world, and was commemorated in 1981 with a plaque on the boundary wall of Mount Vernon House, Mount Vernon, NW3 (fig. 114). Dale was elected a Fellow of the Royal Society in 1914, and served as its President in 1940–45. Knighted in 1932, he shared the Nobel Prize for Medicine in 1936 and received the Order of Merit in 1944.

Dale's contribution was not confined to medicine: he chaired the Scientific Advisory Committee to the War Cabinet, and was President of the British Council between 1950 and 1955. Medically, his specialism was the pharmacology of nervous impulses. From 1914, Dale worked for what in 1920 became the National Institute for Medical Research; he was its Director between 1928 and 1942. Mount Vernon House, a late Georgian building all but hidden by its boundary wall, stands close to the looming French Renaissance pile of Mount Vernon Hospital – converted to residential use in 1997 – which housed the National Institute. Dale lived in the house from 1919 until his retirement.

Frognal End, 18 Frognal Gardens, NW3, lies at the top of a private drive and is largely hidden from view. Laid out in the grounds of a much older building, the house was built in 1891–92 for the novelist and antiquary **Sir Walter Besant** (1836–1901) **26** . Besant, once a hugely popular writer and founder of the Society of Authors in 1884, is commemorated by the first of the building's two plaques. This, erected in 1925, is one the few surviving examples of Doulton's elaborate wreathed designs (see fig. 38). Besant – who was brother-in-law to the redoubtable reformer ANNIE BESANT – heightened public concern over the state of East London slums in his books *All Sorts and Conditions of Men* (1882) and *Children of Gibeon* (1886); one direct result of his campaigning was the opening in 1887 of the People's Palace in the Mile End Road, a huge complex devoted to popular entertainment and self-improvement. During Besant's time at Frognal End – from May 1892 until his death – he produced a large number of works, including the novels *The Rebel Queen* (1893), *The Master Craftsman* (1896) and *The Lady of Lynn* (1901). Most notable was his ambitious ten-volume version of Stow, *The Survey of London*, published posthumously between 1902 and 1912.

A second plaque at Frognal End, erected in 1986, records the residence of the statesman **Hugh Gaitskell** (1906–1963) ㉗ , the leader of the Labour Party whose early death probably deprived him of the office of Prime Minister. After Oxford, Gaitskell won his political spurs as a Workers' Educational Association lecturer in the Nottingham coalfields. Entering Parliament in 1945, he became a minister in the government of CLEMENT ATTLEE two years later and was appointed Chancellor of the Exchequer in 1950, at the young age of forty-four. He preferred to remain at 18 Frognal Gardens, however, having moved here in summer 1946, and did not occupy the Chancellor's official residence, 11 Downing Street. Number 18 was in its time 'as famous a political house as any in the country', and was the focus of an active social life, Gaitskell's group of friends and allies taking the name of the Hampstead or Frognal Set.[19] His feud with the left-winger Nye Bevan – who had fiercely opposed Gaitskell's proposals to introduce charges for some NHS services – culminated in Gaitskell's winning the Labour Party leadership contest against Bevan and HERBERT MORRISON in 1955. Gaitskell's modernising agenda sought to reposition Labour on the centre ground. One of his greatest struggles was with the radical disarmament lobby, which won a vote in favour of unilateral disarmament at the 1960 party conference that he refused to accept. The party was deeply divided over this, but Gaitskell's steadfastness won him the support of the majority of MPs. Gaitskell lived at number 18 until shortly before his death.

Number 108 Frognal, NW3, is an early eighteenth-century house that in all likelihood comprises three

small houses thrown together; a long-vanished tavern called the Three Pigeons was probably located here. The house's most distinguished resident was the ballerina **Tamara Karsavina** (1885–1978) ㉘ , who is commemorated with an English Heritage blue plaque (fig. 115). Born in St Petersburg, Karsavina was the daughter of a dancer and trained at the Imperial Russian Ballet School. She performed regularly at the Maryinsky Theatre, and in 1909 became one of the founder members of Diaghilev's Ballets Russes, taking leading parts alongside Vaslav Nijinsky. Karsavina was deeply influenced by the company's choreographer, Michel Fokine; she created a number of famous roles in Fokine's ballets, including the title role in *The Firebird* (1910) and the doll in *Petrouchka* (1911). In 1917 Karsavina married an English diplomat – Henry J. Bruce (1880–1951) – and the couple settled in London the following year. In 1920 she helped to found the Royal Academy of Dance, and from the early 1930s encouraged the development of British ballet, coach-

115   Tamara Karsavina in *c.*1912 playing the title role of *The Firebird*, choreographed by Michel Fokine. [© E. O. Hoppé / CORBIS]

ing dancers such as Margot Fonteyn. Karsavina's plaque was erected at number 108 in 1987, 102 years after her birth; she and her husband bought the house in 1950, and it remained her residence until 1974, when she moved to a nursing home in Buckinghamshire.

Frognal Mansions forms the southern half of 97 Frognal, an Edwardian five-storey block of flats. Here, at second-floor level, a plaque of 1979 marks Flat 2, where lived the contralto **Kathleen Ferrier** (1912–1953) ; the plaque is of enamelled steel, a material chosen as it fitted more comfortably into the available space on the building's façade. Lancashire-born, Ferrier's first job was as a telephone operator, a position which failed to make the best use of her remarkable voice. In 1937, accepting a wager from her husband, she won both singing and piano competitions at the Carlisle Festival. During the war she performed in factories and concerts, but her short professional career only took off in 1946, when she was cast in the title role of BENJAMIN BRITTEN's *The Rape of Lucretia*. Introduced to the conductor Bruno Walter in 1947, she gained world renown as an interpreter of Gustav Mahler, whose cause Walter did much to uphold. Ferrier's first performance of *Das Lied von der Erde* ('The Song of the Earth'), given at the Edinburgh

116 The exterior of Kate Greenaway's house at 39 Frognal, as it appeared in c.1905. The house was designed for her by Richard Norman Shaw in 1884.

Festival in 1947, cemented her reputation and led to many international performances. However, cancer was diagnosed in 1951, and her final appearance was given at Covent Garden in 1953, shortly after she was awarded the CBE. Ferrier lived at 2 Frognal Mansions from her arrival in London in December 1942 until April 1953, when failing health forced her to move to St John's Wood and, soon after, to a hospital.

The English Heritage plaque at 71 Frognal marks the residence of the pioneer plastic surgeon **Sir Harold Gillies** (1882–1960) . Born and raised in New Zealand, Gillies trained as a surgeon, and put his skills to work in seeking to make good the hideous damage done to soldiers' faces during the First World War. In so doing, he made considerable advances in the techniques of plastic surgery, which resulted in his 1920 work *Plastic Surgery of the Face*. 'This was a strange new art', he wrote, 'and unlike the student of today, who is weaned on small scar excisions and gradually graduated to a single hare-lip, we were suddenly asked to produce half a face'.[20] Two thousand casualties arrived at his ward in the military hospital at Aldershot with face and jaw wounds after the Battle of the Somme alone. This experience was to be called upon again: with the outbreak of the Second World War, Gillies was responsible for setting up a network of plastic surgery units across the country, where his groundbreaking techniques could be deployed in the reconstruction of smashed faces. He was also responsible for training his kinsman SIR ARCHIBALD MCINDOE. Inevitably, much of Gillies's work was devoted to the more mundane – and infinitely more lucrative – area of cosmetic surgery. Gillies lived at number 71 – an unusual corner house on a site bounded by Redington Road and Oak Hill Park – from 1921; bombing drove him out twenty years later.

At 39 (originally 50) Frognal, a plaque was erected in 1949 in honour of the Victorian artist **Kate Greenaway** (1846–1901) (figs 116 and 117). A neat rectangular panel of deep-blue Poole Pottery manufacture, with a coloured floral border, it was specially crafted so as to avoid diminishing the visual allure of her studio-house, which was designed in 1884 by RICHARD NORMAN SHAW. Greenaway's huge studio is clearly seen at second-floor level; placed at a 45° angle, so as to face north, it measures no less than twenty-seven feet by twenty-two feet (8 m by 6.7 m), which contrasts

117 The interior of Kate Greenaway's large second-floor studio at 39 Frognal, c.1905.

118 Dennis Brain and his horn, in a photograph taken by Howard Coster in 1956. [© National Portrait Gallery, London]

stead Cemetery, he had won a reputation as the outstanding horn-player of his generation in the world. Born in London, the third generation of a distinguished family of horn-players, Brain studied at the Royal Academy of Music, where he was taught by his father, Aubrey Brain. He made his name in the RAF Central Band and Orchestra during the Second World War, and at the peak of his career was in huge demand for concerts and recordings; Brain remains the most celebrated performer on the instrument to this day. He lived at number 37 during the period of his greatest fame, from 1952 until his untimely death, sharing the house with his wife Yvonne, née Coles and their two children.

The teacher and pianist **Tobias Matthay** (1858–1945) ③③, commemorated with a plaque of 1979 at 21 Arkwright Road, NW3, was born in London to German parents. He was associated with the Royal Academy of Music for over fifty years, between 1871, when he became a student there, and 1925, when he retired as Professor of Advanced Piano Playing. His principal

markedly with the intimate scale of most of her drawings; girls in mob caps were a speciality. Greenaway's reputation rests on her work for children's books; the Kate Greenaway Medal is still awarded for achievement in this field. Shaw's asymmetrical, tile-hung, gabled design, with a strikingly functional plan, shows to great effect the architect's inventiveness and confidence in handling his own interpretation of the English domestic tradition: 'To Kate Greenaway, Shaw plainly could not resist allotting the pert charm of a tile-hung house, small but high'.[21] Greenaway became extremely attached to JOHN RUSKIN, who visited her here regularly, lured by tea parties attended by just the sort of girls who featured in her watercolours. As Ruskin refused to write 'Frognal' every day of his life – 'It might as well be Dognal-Hognal-Lognal – I won't' – Greenaway was forced to keep him supplied with envelopes addressed to herself in her own handwriting.[22] She lived here from February 1885 until her death sixteen years later.

At 37 Frognal, a plaque of 1995 celebrates the residence of the horn-player **Dennis Brain** (1921–1957) ③② (fig. 118). Brain – like his fellow Hampstead blue plaque recipient MICHAEL VENTRIS – died in a car accident while still in his thirties. Before he was buried in Hamp-

published work was *The Act of Touch in all its Diversity* (1903): 'Mr Matthay has earned a place on a pedestal in a prominent position in the pantheon of pianoforte pedagogues', quipped a contemporary critic.[23] Perhaps his best-known pupil was MYRA HESS; others included Clifford Curzon and Moura Lympany. Matthay enjoyed a high reputation for his approach to learning, which laid stress on arm movement and muscular relaxation. To further his theories on piano technique, he established his own school at 309 Oxford Street; in 1910 it moved to 96 Wimpole Street, Marylebone. Matthay lived at Arkwright Road at the height of his career, from 1902 until 1909, when he left London for Surrey.

At 6 Ellerdale Road, NW3, a plaque commemorates the architect **Richard Norman Shaw** (1831–1912) 34 (see also pp. 548–9). This detached red-brick house was built in 1874–76 to Shaw's own design, and was his home from mid-1876 until his death here thirty-six years later; its irregular façade has been described by Shaw's biographer, Andrew Saint, as 'a topsy-turvy tease'.[24] Since 1954, the house has been in use as a convent. Commemoration of Shaw was first proposed in 1935, but – rather surprisingly – his case was rejected by the LCC. Reconsidered and approved in 1964, the suggestion went nowhere after the owners of number 6 declined to have a plaque; the existing blue roundel was installed only in 2006. Shaw was born in Edinburgh, and moved with his family to London at about the age of fourteen. In 1858 he became chief assistant to G. E. STREET, and four years later set up in practice on his own. Shaw rose quickly to the top of his profession, and enjoyed a long and highly successful career, during which he revolutionised English domestic architecture with his pioneering designs in the Queen Anne style. His country houses include Cragside, Northumberland (1870–85) and Bryanston, Dorset (1889–94). In London, he designed buildings such as Lowther Lodge, Kensington Gore (1873–75; the home since 1912 of the Royal Geographical Society) and artists' residences in Melbury Road, Holland Park, as well as elements of Bedford Park (1877–80), an early suburban development. Shaw had long been associated with Swiss Cottage and Hampstead before moving to 6 Ellerdale Road, which was described by his fellow architect Sir Reginald Blomfield as 'a house after his own heart, planned to suit himself with little regard to external appearance'.[25] Here, in his 'den', Shaw

executed many of his later architectural drawings, including those for New Scotland Yard (1887–90).

Netherhall Gardens, NW3, which was developed at about the time of the opening of Fitzjohn's Avenue in 1876, sports two blue plaques. That at number 51 honours **John Passmore Edwards** (1823–1911) 35 , the journalist, editor and builder of free public libraries. Passmore Edwards was a Cornishman, who spent his last sixty-five years in London amassing (and disbursing) a fortune made from publishing. Early ventures were not successful, and by the mid-1850s he was bankrupt and broken in health. However, his acquisition of the architectural journal *Building News* in 1862 led to a reversal of his fortunes, which continued with the *Mechanics Magazine* in 1869 and the first halfpenny newspaper, *The Echo*, in 1876. Passmore Edwards's origins were humble: his father had been a market gardener and carpenter. He remained mindful of the importance of philanthropic institutions, and embarked on one of Victorian England's most remarkable charitable sprees. He endowed art galleries, museums, hospitals and convalescent homes, but above all he is remembered for his singular charitable donations for public libraries. Of some seventy philanthropic foundations, over a third were libraries, many located in London and its suburbs. Architects such as Henry Hare and Maurice B. Adams were kept busy designing the buildings, all of which proudly proclaim Passmore Edwards's role in their establishment on their opulent late Victorian façades (see fig. 292). Passmore Edwards had at least six London addresses: this, his last, was his home from about 1908 until his death. The plaque was unveiled by his great-grandson, Alastair Ingham Clark, in 1988.

At 10 Netherhall Gardens – a block known as Fitzjohns Mansions – is a plaque of 1981 jointly commemorating the social scientists and political reformers **Sidney Webb** (1859–1947) and **Beatrice Webb**, née Potter (1858–1943) 36 . They occupied 'a cosy little flat' here for about a year after their marriage in July 1892, before moving to a more permanent home: 41 Grosvenor Road, Pimlico (demolished), their address from summer 1893 to 1929.[26] Remembered equally as historians and political activists, the couple were very much a unit: Beatrice referred to it as 'the firm of Webb'. From a relatively modest background, Sidney Webb

119   Sigmund Freud at work in his study at 20 Maresfield Gardens, 1939. [© Freud Museum, London]

was an early member of the FABIAN SOCIETY and made his name as a London County Councillor; in 1895 he helped to found the London School of Economics, and in 1913, with Beatrice and others, he launched the *New Statesman*. Beatrice was the daughter of a railway magnate, and thus brought private means to their partnership, as well as an equally determined commitment to social justice and applied research, to writing and to political engagement: she sat on the 1905 Royal Commission on the Poor Laws while beginning their major work, the nine-volume *English Local Government* (1906–29). Sidney subsequently entered national politics, serving as President of the Board of Trade in the first Labour government in 1924 and as Colonial Secretary (1929–31), having been raised to the peerage as Lord Passfield in 1929. During their later years, the Webbs became increasingly interested in Russia, and a long visit in 1932 led to the writing of *Soviet Communism: A New Civilisation?* (1935). Such was their stature at the time of their deaths that their ashes were interred in Westminster Abbey.

Two plaques are to be found at 20 Maresfield Gardens, NW3 (fig. 96). Erected by English Heritage, they are exceptional in commemorating a father and daughter: the psychiatrist and founder of psychoanalysis, **Sigmund Freud** (1856–1939) 37 , and the pioneer of child psychoanalysis, **Anna Freud** (1895–1982) 38 . Driven out of Vienna after the *Anschluss*, Sigmund Freud arrived in London in June 1938 – a move facilitated by his dedicated disciple, ERNEST JONES – and spent a short period in a flat at 39 Elsworthy Road, NW3, before moving in September to 20 Maresfield Gardens, a spacious brick-built house (fig. 119). It was here that Freud spent his final year before succumbing to his sixteen-year struggle with cancer, and here that he died. Freud brought much furniture from his Vienna consulting room, including various antiquities and his renowned couch; what had hitherto been a relatively ordinary detached house was thereby transformed into what, since its opening in 1986, has become one of London's most intriguing historic house museums. 'The fact that the house is here is one of the very few things we can thank the Nazis for', remarked John Cleese in his speech at the plaques' unveiling, which he performed with his psychoanalyst wife Alyce Faye Cleese.[27] Anna Freud lived and worked at number 20 for forty-four years, up to her own death.

She spent much time supporting her father, both domestically and professionally, and served for many years as the General Secretary of the International Psychological Association. A highly significant figure in her own right, Anna helped to establish modern approaches to child behaviour; in 1947 she founded the Hampstead Child Therapy Courses, and added the associated clinic five years later. Anna unveiled an LCC blue plaque to her father on the hundredth anniversary of his birth in 1956: a hitch with the suppliers meant that the plaque was a metal one. This was duly replaced – and the one to Anna added – in 2002.

The collector of English folk songs and dances **Cecil Sharp** (1859–1924) 39 is commemorated with a plaque at 4 Maresfield Gardens, a semi-detached house in which he lived from 1918 and died six years later; the house was shared with his wife, Constance (d. 1928), and his assistant, Maud Karpeles (1885–1976). Having spent a decade in Australia from 1882, Sharp became a music teacher – he was Principal of the Hampstead Conservatoire in 1896–1905. He first encountered folk music in 1899, and became a dedicated collector and promoter of its cause; Sharp sought out vernacular music survivals through a series of study tours, and in 1902 published *A Book of British Song for Home and School*. In 1911 he was instrumental in establishing the English Folk Dance Society, and thus for spearheading the morris-dancing revival. As summed up in the plaque unveiling speech, 'Most other collectors cherished their collections like a tray of butterflies and compared song varieties with somebody else's collection, but this man Sharp's idea was of giving the whole thing back to the people from whom it had come, beginning with the children'.[28] The unveiling took place in 1985, amid much music making and dancing. His living memorial is Cecil Sharp House in Camden, a large hall opened in 1930 as a centre for English folk dance, music and singing.

Martina Bergman Österberg (1849–1915) 40, the pioneer of physical education for women, is honoured with an English Heritage plaque at 1 Broadhurst Gardens, NW6. Madame Bergman-Österberg – as she was known after her marriage in 1886 – was born in Sweden, and trained at the Royal Central Gymnastics Institute, founded in Stockholm by Per Hendrick Ling. She was an early champion of 'Swedish drill', an approach to physical education that attracted considerable attention from the London School Board, which in 1879 appointed her countrywoman Concordia Löfving to develop this aspect of teaching. Bergman-Österberg took over in 1881, and soon embarked on the development of a course of instruction for teachers attached to the fast-expanding network of board schools. Number 1 Broadhurst Gardens, then known as Reremonde, was acquired in 1885 to serve as Bergman-Österberg's college for women, the Hampstead Physical Training College. The first of its kind in England, the college opened with just four students, but by 1895 had twenty-seven trainee teachers and had outgrown its premises. In that year, Bergman-Österberg and her flourishing institution transferred to Dartford, Kent; Dartford College, as it became known, merged with Thames Polytechnic in 1976, but was closed less than a decade later. Number 1 Broadhurst Gardens, a substantial corner building, dates from 1880; to its rear, visible from Greencroft Gardens, is the structure – dated 1885 – which probably served as the gymnasium.

One of England's most forceful twentieth-century painters, **David Bomberg** (1890–1957) 41 lived at 10 Fordwych Road, NW2, between 1928 and 1934. Born in Birmingham to Polish-Jewish parents, Bomberg studied at the Slade; he became close to leading figures in the English avant-garde, such as Jacob Epstein, Walter Sickert and Percy Wyndham Lewis, and

developed a powerful style akin to Vorticism. The outbreak of the First World War – in which he served – interrupted a fast-rising career, and the initial rejection of a major commission from Canada for a memorial painting led to disappointment, a recurring sentiment in his subsequent life. After a spell in Hampshire, away from the London art scene, Bomberg spent the mid-1920s in Palestine working for a Zionist organisation; this political engagement affected the development of his painting, which moved away from abstraction towards expressionistic realism. In November 1928, not long after his return, Bomberg moved to this unassuming late Victorian house in West Hampstead, sharing the house with the painter Lilian Mendelson (1898–1983) – later to become his wife – and her daughter Dinora. From here, he set out on numerous painting trips to Scotland, Russia and Spain; this last destination led to some of his most admired landscapes. Bomberg was hugely respected as a teacher; both Frank Auerbach and Leon Kossoff were pupils. A retrospective at the Tate in 1988 went some way towards establishing his reputation as one of the major figures of modern British painting. The plaque was unveiled in 1996 by Bomberg's stepdaughter, Dinora Davies-Rees.

At 31 Pandora Road, NW6, is the GLC plaque to the journalist and newspaper proprietor **Alfred Harmsworth, Viscount Northcliffe** (1865–1922) 42 (fig. 120). His connection with this late nineteenth-century terraced house was short but significant: Harmsworth moved here immediately after his marriage to Mary Milner (1867–1963) in April 1888 and left in 1891. During this time, working from the attic at number 31, he launched his first successful publishing venture, the magazine *Answers to Correspondents* (1888); he also established *Comic Cuts* and *Chips*, published by the Pandora Publishing Co., which he founded in 1890. Such was his success that Harmsworth was able to move the following year to an altogether grander residence near Broadstairs, Kent; most of his other London addresses were destroyed in the Blitz. Along with his younger brother and business manager Harold (later Lord Rothermere), Dublin-born Harmsworth was one of the dominant figures in the creation of the modern media. The pair founded the *Daily Mail* in 1896, and in 1903 – the year in which Harmsworth was made a baronet, before Balfour

120 A *Daily Mail* article of 3 September 1976 celebrating the installation of the plaque to Alfred Harmsworth, Viscount Northcliffe, at 31 Pandora Road. [© Daily Mail]

Northcliffe lived here

A PLAQUE is to be placed by the Greater London Council on a house that was once the home of Lord Northcliffe, founder of the Daily Mail.

Lord Northcliffe, then Alfred Harmsworth, moved to 31 Pandora Road, West Hampstead, N.W., in 1888 and there founded the publishing company that later took over the London Evening News and founded the Daily Mail in 1896.

The Mail then cost half an old penny and was the first national newspaper to bring the news to the masses.

Mr Robin Young, vice-chairman of the GLC's Historic Buildings Board, said that Lord Northcliffe, who died in 1922, was outstanding in the history of newspapers.

The council had searched for many years for a suitable site for a commemorative plaque. But several of Lord Northcliffe's London homes had been destroyed.

Sir Geoffrey Harmsworth, Lord Northcliffe's biographer, said

The Pandora Road house in Hampstead

last night: 'It is very good news that a plaque is at last to be put up to commemorate him.

'He was the greatest journalist who strode through Fleet Street. He was the father of modern journalism.

'He was a man of great foresight, understanding and compassion — a man who changed the face of newspapers.'

raised him to the peerage in 1905 – the brothers set up the first newspaper aimed at women, the *Daily Mirror*. Northcliffe took over the ailing *Times* in 1908, and used the paper as a platform for his political agenda, which included a scarcely concealed hunger for political office. Northcliffe's influence on popular opinion was very considerable during the First World War, which did not make for happy relations with the British premier, LLOYD GEORGE. Nonetheless, he was made Director of Propaganda in 1918. The plaque's unveiling was performed by Northcliffe's nephew, Sir Geoffrey Harmsworth, in 1979.

The conductor **Sir Adrian Boult**, **CH** (1889–1983) 43 occupied Flat 78 at Marlborough Mansions, Cannon Hill, NW6, between 1966 and 1977. The son of a Chester oil merchant, Boult studied at Oxford and joined the Royal Opera House, Covent Garden, in 1914. He conducted the first (private) performance of *The Planets* by HOLST in 1918, but the most important phase of his career opened in 1930 when he became Director of Music at the fledgling BBC, where he helped to create the BBC Symphony Orchestra. Knighted in 1937, he acquired an international reputation; in a field renowned for extravagance, Boult was a restrained conductor whose long recording career was notably successful. Created Companion of Honour in 1969, 'he was modest to a fault: he did not want a "fuss" made of him posthumously and donated his body to medical research'.[29] The plaque was unveiled by his fellow conductor Andrew Davis in 1998; the building on which it was placed is an otherwise unremarkable red-brick apartment block of about 1897, utterly representative of the late Victorian and early twentieth-century development of the western slopes of Hampstead. During the period he lived in Flat 78 – located at ground-floor level, to the left of the entrance, as marked by the plaque – Boult conducted the London Philharmonic Orchestra in a number of notable recordings for EMI; he gave his last performances in 1978.

At 16 Bracknell Gardens, NW3, a plaque of 1995 honours three members of the Huxley family: **Leonard Huxley** (1860–1933), and his sons **Julian Huxley** (1887–1975) and **Aldous Huxley** (1894–1963) 44 , men of science and letters. Leonard – the son of T. H. HUXLEY, whose biography he wrote – entered publishing after

an early teaching career and became the long-serving editor of the *Cornhill Magazine*, living in this conventional turn-of-the-century semi-detached house from 1916 until his death. He is better known today as the father of distinguished sons, neither of whom lived at number 16 for very long. Julian was a pioneer in the field of animal behaviour, and advanced theories of evolution through his own knowledge of genetics, statistics and behavioural analysis; he was elected to the Royal Society in 1938 and knighted in 1958. His concern for population growth, and interest in education, led to his being appointed in 1946 the first Secretary-General – and later Director-General – of UNESCO. He lived at nearby 31 Pond Street from 1943 to his death; a privately erected ceramic plaque, decorated with grebes in honour of his ornithological expertise, adorns the building's façade. Aldous Huxley was one of the most illustrious writers of the twentieth century. Near blind, he followed his father into literary journalism, and was able to devote himself to writing following the success of his first novel, *Crome Yellow*, in 1921. *Point Counter Point* (1928), *Brave New World* (1932) and *Eyeless in Gaza* (1936) constitute his best-known pre-war works. Huxley was restlessly inquiring, and his writing spans a wide range, from social commentary to mysticism, from scientific rationalism to experimentation with hallucinogenic drugs – his 1954 work *The Doors of Perception* did much to promote the later twentieth-century vogue for mind-expanding substances. Aldous lived intermittently at Bracknell Gardens from 1917 until 1919, the year of his marriage; he spent much of his later life abroad, mainly in America.

Number 24 Ferncroft Avenue, NW3, was the home of the Irish lyric tenor **John McCormack** (1884–1945) 45 . The son of an Athlone labourer, McCormack won Ireland's gold medal for tenors in the 1903 Feis Ceoil, and trained in Italy. He sang with NELLIE MELBA, and went on to enjoy huge popularity in America, becoming a naturalised US citizen in 1919. By the 1930s, McCormack was one of the world's highest-earning artists. His last operatic performance took place in 1923, after which he devoted himself to recitals and recordings, particularly of folk songs: his rendition of 'The Rose of Tralee' was hugely popular on both sides of the Atlantic. McCormack gave his farewell performance at the Royal Albert Hall in 1938, and died of pneumonia at his Irish home in Booterstown in 1945. The Ferncroft

Avenue house – which he named Rosaleen House, and which dates from about 1900 – was his first permanent London home after he found initial success, and was the one he lived at for the longest period: from 1908 to 1913. McCormack then moved to nearby 59 Netherhall Gardens, opposite the house where Sir Edward Elgar then lived, before departing for New York.

The sprawling brick mansion of Inverforth House, North End Way, NW3 – named after Lord Inverforth, a twentieth-century occupant – was originally built in about 1807, and was called Hill House; in 1896 it was substantially altered for the Fisher family, headed by George Fisher (1843–1920), a fine arts dealer. The house's gatepiers sport two English Heritage plaques, both erected in May 2002. The earlier resident was the statistician and geneticist **Sir Ronald Aylmer Fisher** (1890–1962) 46 , who lived here as a boy between 1896 and 1904, when financial collapse forced his family to move to Streatham. Fisher's future achievement lay in the same realm as that of his fellow Hampstead luminary, Karl Pearson. His most notable early work was carried out at the Rothamsted Experimental Station in Harpenden, Hertfordshire, where he was statistician in 1919–33; during this period, Fisher produced his classic texts *Statistical Methods for Research Workers* (1925) and *The Genetical Theory of Natural Selection* (1930), and invented statistical tests including the analysis of variation. Fisher left Rothamsted to succeed Pearson as Galton Professor of Eugenics at University College London, and in 1943 was appointed to the chair of genetics at Cambridge. Knighted in 1952, he is remembered as the most significant British statistician of the twentieth century.

The Fisher family was succeeded at Inverforth House – by then known as The Hill – by the soap-maker and philanthropist **William Hesketh Lever, 1st Viscount Leverhulme** (1851–1925) 47 . Lever came from Bolton shop-keeping stock, but moved into manufacturing. He made his fortune from soap: Sunlight soap, to be precise. Lever's technical innovation was to switch from making soaps based on tallow, or animal fats, to those based on vegetable oil; his great commercial innovation was to refine packaging and promotional advertising, and build up a brand profile. His success was prodigious – Lever Brothers was one of the largest British multinationals of the time – and he was soon

able to develop his interests in architecture and collecting. Port Sunlight, near Birkenhead, developed in the late nineteenth and early twentieth centuries near the Lever soapworks, ranks alongside Hampstead Garden Suburb as one of England's great experiments in town planning, and it is notable that the promoters of the two developments were near neighbours (see Henrietta Barnett). Curiously, another near neighbour was Thomas J. Barratt, proprietor of the Pears Soap Company, whose now-demolished house of Bellmoor stood at the top of East Heath Road. Lever and his wife Elizabeth, née Hulme (d. 1913) moved to Inverforth House in 1904; it remained Lever's London home until his death, and saw him created a baronet (1911), then a baron (1917), and advanced to a viscountcy (1922). The house and grounds were remodelled and extended in various phases throughout his residence, and covered a vast area by the time of his death. Early additions, including the music room wing and china wing, were carried out by the Liverpool firm of architects Grayson and Ould; they also designed the singular garden terrace that was built using spoil from the Hampstead Tube excavation, and to which the noted garden designer Thomas Mawson added a pergola.

Placed on the boundary wall of 19 North End, NW3 – a private drive on the north-western edge of Hampstead Heath – is an English Heritage plaque commemorating **Michael Ventris** (1922–1956) 48 , the short-lived architect whose immortality is assured through his work on deciphering Linear B. Ventris was able to demonstrate that this early script, uncovered in Crete by Sir Arthur Evans, was the true foundation of ancient Greek. This was a major breakthrough in establishing the connection between the Minoan civilisation and the subsequent development of cultures in mainland Greece. Ventris's interest had begun while a schoolboy; after wartime service in Bomber Command, he qualified as an architect and worked in the field of school design, but also devoted considerable energies to the issue of early Greek text analysis. His crucial 1953 article in the *Journal of Hellenic Studies*, co-authored with John Chadwick, drew on cryptographical techniques developed in wartime intelligence, but was essentially the product of sheer brilliance. Ventris did not live to see the publication of his key work (jointly written with Chadwick), *Documents in Mycenaean Greek* (1956); 'it is hardly possible to estimate the

HAMPSTEAD

121 The first-floor living room of Michael Ventris's house at 19 North End in a photograph of c. 2002. The Bauhaus furniture, brought from the Ventris family flat at Highpoint, is shown still in situ. [© Steve Stephens Photography]

importance of the contribution made by Michael Ventris to the understanding of the beginnings of Greek civilisation', commented Chadwick soberly in his obituary.[30] The plaque was erected at 19 North End in 1990. The house is a modest, but stylish, brick box, built in 1952–53 to designs by Ventris and his wife Lois (d. 1988). Marcel Breuer's fittings from the Ventris family flat at 47 Highpoint, Highgate, N6 – Michael's home from 1936 until 1953 – were incorporated into the interior (fig. 121).

Also at the northern edge of Hampstead Heath, just within the borough of Barnet, is the intriguing survival of Old Wyldes, North End, NW3, a seventeenth-century farmhouse – albeit altered – which is now a solitary reminder of the agricultural past of this corner of Middlesex. It was owned from 1820 by the Collins

family, who supplemented their living by taking in lodgers: DICKENS spent time here in 1837 following the death of his beloved sister-in-law Mary Hogarth. An oval blue plaque honours the landscape painter **John Linnell** (1792–1882) **49**, who lodged at Old Wyldes – then known as Collins's Farm or Heath Farm – in 1823 and, more permanently, from March 1824 to c. 1828; he rented the western half of the house for himself and his family (fig. 122). Linnell was utterly captivated by the elderly visionary poet and artist **William Blake** (1757–1827), whose frequent visits to Old Wyldes as the guest of Linnell are also commemorated on the plaque. Despite his advanced years, Blake would regularly undertake the seven-mile (11 km) uphill walk from Lambeth to Hampstead. He was often joined by Linnell's future son-in-law SAMUEL PALMER, who, together with Linnell and Edward Calvert, would form

118

122 A painting by John Linnell of *Collins's Farm*, now Old Wyldes, as it appeared in 1831. Part of Hampstead Hill is shown on the right. [© Museum of London]

the group of intensely lyrical painters of nature known as 'The Ancients', or the 'Shoreham Group', after the Kent village to which they gravitated from 1826 onwards. The plaque to Linnell and Blake, put up in 1975, is of fibre-glass: a conventional ceramic plaque would have been unsuitable for the weatherboarded wall. On the eastern half of the house, a private plaque of 1957 commemorates the architect and town planner Sir Raymond Unwin (1863–1940), who lived here from 1906 until his death.

The boundary wall of Heath End House (fig. 123) – a lonely villa in Spaniards Road, NW3, right at the top of the heath – is graced with a joint plaque to the founder of Hampstead Garden Suburb **Dame Henrietta Barnett** (1851–1936) and her husband, the social reformer **Canon Samuel Barnett** (1844–1913) 50 . The daughter of the wealthy businessman Alexander Rowland, Henrietta was the guiding spirit behind one of the pre-eminent developments of Edwardian London. The idea of a 'garden suburb' had first been mooted in 1898 by EBENEZER HOWARD; the first example to be laid out was at Letchworth, Hertfordshire, in 1903. A friend of OCTAVIA HILL, and interested similarly in the interrelationship of social and environmental factors, Mrs Barnett was the key figure behind the foundation of the Hampstead Garden Suburb Trust. A letter to a newspaper in 1903 suggested the creation of a garden suburb for the working classes, to be laid out on the area to the north of the Barnetts' Middlesex retreat. In 1905 Raymond Unwin began to advise on the layout of the suburb, and building work began two years later; at Henrietta's insistence, the new settlement was made up of mixed social classes. Canon Barnett, remembered for his work on behalf of the poor, became priest in charge of the deprived parish of St Jude's, Whitechapel, in 1873, shortly after his marriage to Henrietta. Samuel's awareness of the vast and growing chasm that separated the East End from better-off areas prompted him to found in 1884 the university settlement Toynbee Hall (see JIMMY MALLON). He also campaigned for significant welfare causes including Poor Law reforms and pensions. Heath End House – renamed St Jude's Cottage after Samuel's Whitechapel parish – was built in about 1788, and was occupied by the Barnetts between 1889 and 1913; it was largely rebuilt in 1923 by the novelist Sir Hall Caine (1853–1931). Here, Whitechapel girls would come and learn how to become servants, while 'restrooms' were provided for 'tired Toynbee men or

HAMPSTEAD

123 The rear of St Jude's Cottage (now Heath End House) in an early twentieth-century photograph, taken during the residence of the Barnetts. The house was a refuge for 'Whitechapel girls' and 'tired Toynbee men or workers'. In the foreground are Miss Gale and a group of the girls in training.

workers'.[31] In 1901 the Barnetts acquired the neighbouring mansion, and opened its doors to 'needy Whitechapel people' as the Erskine House Convalescent Home.[32] The home existed for fourteen years; Erskine House itself was demolished by Caine in 1923.

Across the heath, at 3 The Grove, Highgate, N6, is the plaque to the novelist, playwright and essayist **J. B. Priestley** (1894–1984) 51 (fig. 124). John Boynton Priestley was born in Bradford. After war service and Cambridge, he established himself as a literary journalist and made his reputation with the novels *The Good Companions* (1929) and *Angel Pavement* (1930). A hugely prolific playwright – no less than fifty plays flew

off his pen – Priestley is equally remembered for *Time and the Conways* (1937) and the enduring *An Inspector Calls* (1946). His commentaries – in particular the 1933 *English Journey* – won him considerable notice as a spokesman for England, and this led to his becoming a principal broadcaster during the Second World War. Never quite taken into the literary establishment, Priestley was nonetheless hugely successful and remains a celebrated figure. Late on, in 1977, he was admitted to the Order of Merit. Having spent the years 1928 to 1931 at 27 Well Walk, NW3, Priestley acquired 3 The Grove – a brick building of *c.* 1688 – in late 1931, and remained here until bombing forced him to leave ten years later. The house, which he shared with his wife Jane Wyndham Lewis (1892–1984), had strong literary connections: it was the last residence of SAMUEL TAYLOR COLERIDGE, commemorated here with a bronze tablet erected by St Pancras Borough Council in about 1950. Priestley wrote of number 3 as one 'of the loveliest things you ever saw. I sit in Coleridge's old room typing this letter; I see nothing from my window but Kenwood and the slope of the Heath, and our flower beds below, or our neighbour, Gladys Cooper, still beautiful, eating breakfast outside in pyjamas'.[33] Priestley's plaque, coloured brown so as not to overshadow the existing bronze tablet, was unveiled in the centenary year of his birth by his son Tom.

124 English Heritage contractor Ernie Butler cleans the newly installed, brown-coloured plaque to J. B. Priestley at 3 The Grove in 1994. [© Kippa Matthews / Guardian News & Media Ltd 1994]

NOTES

1 The supplementary tablet does, in fact, state that the plaque was originally installed by the Royal Society of Arts in 1892. This information is now known to be incorrect.

2 Fred Uhlman, *The Making of an Englishman* (London, 1960), p. 214

3 It is now accepted that Vane was born in 1613, rather than in 1612, as is stated on the plaque.

4 Christopher Wade, *Hampstead Past* (London, 1989), p. 16

5 Geoffrey Elborn, *Edith Sitwell: A Biography* (London, 1981), p. 259

6 Ibid

7 L. M. [Ida Baker], *Katherine Mansfield: The Memories of L. M.* [Leslie Moore] (London, 1971), p. 114

8 Ibid, p. 122

9 C. R. Leslie, *Memoirs of the Life of John Constable, RA,* ed. and enlgd Hon. Andrew Shirley (London, 1927), p. 220 (26 August 1827)

10 *DNB: 1931–1940* (repr., Oxford, 1985), p. 683

11 Daphne du Maurier, *Gerald: A Portrait* (London, 1934), pp. 186–87

12 Christopher Wade, *The Streets of Hampstead* (rev. edn, London, 1984), p. 81

13 *Selected Letters of Rabindranath Tagore*, eds Krishna Dutta and Andrew Robinson (Cambridge, 1997), p. 90 (28 June 1912)

14 C. C. Hoyer Millar, *George du Maurier and Others* (London, Toronto, Melbourne, Sydney, 1937), p. 19

15 Letter of 26 March 1959 on blue plaque file.

16 Wade, *Streets of Hampstead*, p. 31

17 *The Collected Letters of Joanna Baillie*, ed. Judith Bailey Slagle, vol. I (Cranbury, London, Ontario, 1999), p. 6, note 17 (29 March 1820)

18 William Hayley, *The Life of George Romney* (Chichester, 1809), p. 285

19 Brian Brivati, *Hugh Gaitskell* (London, 1996), p. 70

20 Leonard Mosley, *Faces from the Fire: The Biography of Sir Archibald McIndoe* (London, 1962), p. 57

21 Andrew Saint, *Richard Norman Shaw, RA* (New Haven and London, 1983 edn), p. 159

22 M. H. Spielmann and G. S. Layard, *Kate Greenaway* (London, 1905), p. 143

23 Jessie Henderson Matthay, *The Life and Works of Tobias Matthay* (London, 1945), p. 38

24 Saint, *Richard Norman Shaw*, p. 179

25 Sir Reginald Blomfield, *Richard Norman Shaw, RA* (London, 1940), p. 41

26 *The Diaries of Beatrice Webb*, eds Norman and Jeanne MacKenzie (London, 2000), p. 168 (1 December 1892)

27 *Camden New Journal*, 4 July 2002

28 Douglas Kennedy, 'Commemorative Plaque – Cecil J. Sharp', *English Dance and Song* (Autumn 1985), p. 33

29 Robert Ponsonby, 'Adrian Boult', *BBC Music Magazine*, January 1999, p. 39

30 *The Times*, 8 September 1956, p. 10

31 Henrietta Barnett, *Canon Barnett: His Life, Work, and Friends*, vol. II (London, 1918), p. 136

32 Ibid, p. 146

33 Judith Cook, *Priestley* (London, 1997), p. 115

125   Belsize Park Gardens, with,
in the foreground, number 44 and
its plaque to Frederick Delius.
[© English Heritage. Photograph
by Derek Kendall]

PRIMROSE HILL AND BELSIZE PARK

The ill-defined area to the south of Hampstead Village and to the north of Camden Town was largely open land until the nineteenth century. Primrose Hill itself – so-named from at least the sixteenth century – dominated the landscape, while other local landmarks included Belsize House and Chalcot's Farm, known as Chalk Farm House by the mid-eighteenth century. It was only following the development of neighbouring Regent's Park in the 1820s that the area's landowners maximised the potential of their plots. Throughout the middle decades of the century, fields gave way to long terraces of semi-detached and detached houses. 'The white cliffs of Belsize', with their stuccoed façades in the classical or Italianate styles, proved popular with the professional classes.[1] In Primrose Hill to the south, despite the all-too-evident presence of the railways, property was equally desirable, and attracted a slightly wider variety of residents. From the outset, the area proved particularly alluring to artists and writers, but it was in the inter-war years – with the arrival of figures such as Barbara Hepworth and HENRY MOORE – that it gained an international reputation.

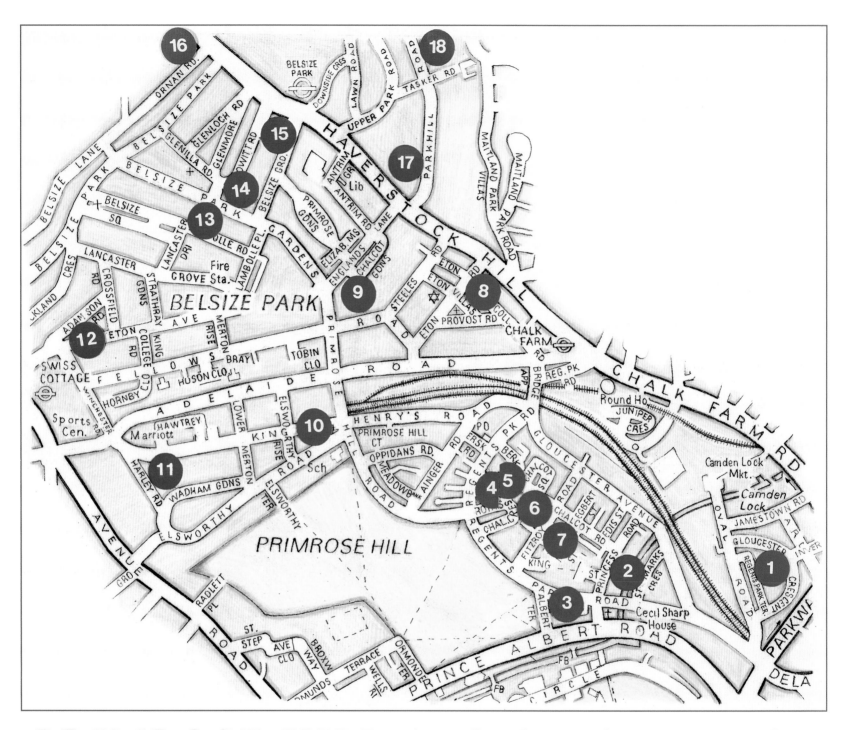

PRIMROSE HILL AND BELSIZE PARK

A plaque at 8 Regent's Park Terrace, NW1 – a house of the 1840s – commemorates the documentary film-maker **Humphrey Jennings** (1907–1950) **1**, described by the director Lindsay Anderson as 'the only real poet the British cinema has yet produced'.[2] Born in Suffolk, Jennings joined the GPO FILM UNIT – later the Crown Film Unit – in 1934, and there he learned his craft as an editor and director of short documentaries. In 1936, with ROLAND PENROSE and others, he organised London's International Surrealist Exhibition, and the following year co-founded Mass-Observation, a study of the everyday lives of ordinary people in Britain. In 1939 Jennings returned to film-making in earnest, and during the war years produced his finest and most influential work, all for the Crown Film Unit. This included *London Can Take It* (1940), *Listen to Britain* (1942), *Fires Were Started* (1943) and *A Diary for Timothy* (1945). Jennings lived at number 8 from January 1944 until his death; he rented part of the property from his friend Allen Hutt (1901–1973), the journalist, who lived here with his family. During Jennings's residence, Regent's Park Terrace was noisy and sooty: the proximity of the railway line to Euston meant that the house frequently shook, and the windows and books needed constant cleaning. Jennings commented that it was 'Rather noisy at times but extremely romantic'.[3] He originally lived in two rooms at ground-floor level but, on being joined by his wife Cicely (1908–1975) and two daughters in summer 1946, moved to the top two floors of the house. As space grew tighter, and interruptions more regular, Jennings acquired a room at 2 Regent's Park Terrace in which to paint. Throughout his time at number 8, Jennings worked on his great literary opus *Pandaemonium* (first published in 1985), an anthology that charted the Industrial Revolution through contemporary texts. The plaque was unveiled in 2006 by Marie-Lou Legg, Jennings's daughter.

Number 14 St Mark's Crescent, NW1 – one of a series of mid-nineteenth-century houses backing onto the Regent's Canal – was the home of the artist **William Roberts** (1895–1980) **2** (fig. 126). Roberts studied at the Slade, where his fellow pupils included MARK

126   The second-floor front room of William Roberts's house at 14 St Mark's Crescent in a photograph of 1998, taken three years after the death of Roberts's son John. The house was then left much as it had been during the artist's lifetime. [© Crown copyright. NMR. Photograph by Derek Kendall]

himself. Working from his studio in the ground-floor front room, the artist completed works such as *Trooping the Colour* (1958–59) and *The Lake* (1964) (fig. 127); it was at number 14 that he died at the age of eighty-four. The plaque was unveiled in 2003 by the writer and Camden resident Alan Bennett.

At 2 Albert Terrace, NW1, a plaque commemorates the eminent early photographer **Roger Fenton** (1819–1869) ❸ (fig. 128). Fenton lived in this imposing semi-detached house from 1847 until about 1863, while at the height of his career. Born in Lancashire, Fenton originally trained as a lawyer, but – on receiving a large inheritance – turned to painting, which he studied in Paris and London. Fenton was first drawn to the new art of photography in about 1852, and the following year helped to found the (Royal) Photographic Society; in the long term, he was to play a crucial part in promoting the standing of his profession. Fenton is remembered above all for his images of the Crimea; taken in 1855, these include *Valley of the Shadow of Death* and proved significant in educating the British public about the realities of war. Fenton's mastery of technique and his distinctive, imaginative style are also evident in his photographs of landscape, still life, architecture and the British royal family. Despite his success, Fenton suddenly and mysteriously abandoned photography in 1862, possibly disenchanted by the lowly status still accorded to the art form. Soon after,

GERTLER and PAUL NASH, and on leaving began a series of works influenced by Cubism and Post-Impressionism. With WYNDHAM LEWIS and others, Roberts was a founder in 1914 of the short-lived but influential Vorticist Group, which set out to free England from the legacy of the Victorian age. After serving as an official war artist from 1918, Roberts began the work for which he would become best known: studies of urban life, with people going about their daily activities. From 1925 to 1960, he taught at the Central School of Arts and Crafts. Roberts and his wife Sarah, née Kramer (1900–1992) moved to number 14 in 1946. At first, the couple lived in only one room – the 'ground floor front' of what was then a lodging-house – but gradually they took over the whole house as the sitting tenants dispersed. Eventually, the owner offered to sell the property to them for £1,200; desperately short of money, William and Sarah were offered the sum by a friend in exchange for some paintings. The couple, who lived here with their son John (1919–1995), set about decorating and furnishing number 14; many of the fittings were made by Roberts

129 A photograph of Friedrich Engels and Karl Marx (back right) – with Marx's daughters Laura, Eleanor and Jenny junior – during a picnic on Hampstead Heath, May 1864. [Courtesy of the Marx Memorial Library]

130 A watercolour by Malcolm Fowler painted shortly after the installation of the plaque to Sylvia Plath at 3 Chalcot Square. [© Malcolm Fowler]

he left his 'quiet nest in Albert Terrace' – at which his photographic studio was based – for Potters Bar, Hertfordshire, and returned to his career at the Bar.[4] The plaque was unveiled in 1991 by Fenton's great-grandniece, Dorothy Maud Ellis.

Regent's Park Road, NW1, is one of the most important and architecturally varied of the district's thoroughfares. A plaque at number 122, a mid-nineteenth-century terraced house at the foot of Primrose Hill, honours the political philosopher **Friedrich Engels** (1820–1895) **4** ; it was unveiled by the journalist Allen Hutt in 1972. Born in Germany, the son of a textile manufacturer, Engels came in 1842 to England, where he worked for the Manchester branch of his father's business. During this period, his interest in radicalism and socialism intensified, and he wrote influential works including *The Condition of the Working Class in England* (1845). In 1844 Engels met KARL MARX; thereafter, the pair's careers and writings were inseparably linked (fig. 129). Together, they wrote *The Communist Manifesto* (1848), and in 1849 both of them settled permanently

in England, where Engels provided Marx – whom he named 'the greatest living thinker' – with both intellectual and financial support.[5] In 1869 Engels retired from the family firm and the following year moved from Manchester to 122 Regent's Park Road. The house was chosen on account of its proximity to Marx's home – which was on the other side of Haverstock Hill, at 1 Maitland Park Road (demolished) – and was discovered by Marx's wife Jenny; she wrote that it 'delights us all with its wonderfully free setting'.[6] It was to be Engels's home until December 1894, when he moved east along the street to 41 Regent's Park Road.

Number 37 Chalcot Crescent, NW1, was the residence in 1888 of **Dr Jose Rizal** (1861–1896) **5** , the writer and national hero of the Philippines. Born in the province of Laguna, Rizal went to Spain in 1882 to study medicine and then travelled in Europe. He was a gifted linguist, musician, artist, historian, philosopher, naturalist and scientist, but it was in the literary and political realms that his influence was most felt. Rizal was an early leader of the Filipino movement for political, economic and social independence from Spain, then its colonial master. His first novel, *Noli Me Tangere* ('Touch Me Not'; 1887), quickly attracted the attention of the Spanish authorities, and was banned in the Philippines. Rizal was forced to travel abroad, and arrived in May 1888 in London, where he lodged in two rooms at number 37, the home of the Beckett family. During his stay, which lasted until early 1889, Rizal was occupied largely in scholarly research; at the British Museum, he discovered Antonio de Morga's *Sucesos de las Islas Filipinas*, an early seventeenth-century account evincing the rich history of the Philippines prior to Spanish rule. In 1890 Rizal published an edition of this work, and in 1891 followed it with *El Filibusterismo* ('The Subversive' or 'The Reign of Greed'), which further exposed the ills of the Spanish colonial government. In 1892 Rizal returned to the Philippines; there, he was accused – unjustly – of associating with a secret revolutionary society, and was executed by firing squad on 30 December 1896. The blue plaque was erected in 1983.

A plaque at 3 Chalcot Square, NW1, honours the great twentieth-century poet **Sylvia Plath** (1932–1963) **6** (fig. 130). Born in Boston, Massachusetts, Plath moved to England with her husband, the British poet Ted

131 The design for the LCC plaque to Alfred Stevens, installed at 9 Eton Villas in 1924.

Hughes (1930–1998), in December 1959. In January the following year, through the efforts of the American poet W. S. Merwin and his English wife, the couple found an unfurnished three-room flat on the top floor of number 3; it was to be their home until August 1961, when they moved to Devon. Plath's time at number 3 was happy and productive; here, she saw the publication of her first volume of poetry, *The Colossus* (1960), wrote her only novel, *The Bell Jar* (1963), and gave birth to her first child, Frieda. In December 1962, Plath left Devon with her children and returned to Primrose Hill, moving to 23 Fitzroy Road, '*the* street and *the* house . . . where I've always wanted to live . . . It is W. B. Yeats' house – with a blue plaque over the door, saying he lived there'.[7] However, she was soon overcome by the depression that dogged her throughout her life, and she committed suicide the following year, at the age of just thirty. The plaque at number 3 was unveiled in 2000 by Plath's children, Frieda and Nicholas Hughes. Asked why it did not mark 23 Fitzroy Road, Frieda replied, 'My mother died there . . . but she had *lived* here'.[8]

The plaque that attracted SYLVIA PLATH to 23 Fitzroy Road, NW1, was erected in 1957, and marks the boyhood home of the Irish poet and dramatist **William Butler Yeats** (1865–1939) **7** (see fig. 6). Born in Dublin, the son of the painter John Butler Yeats (1839–1922), William moved to London with his family in summer 1867. He lived at number 23 from that year until 1872, when he went on an extended stay to the Sligo home of his grandparents. The Yeats family later settled in Bedford Park in West London. In 1895 William moved to 5 Woburn Walk, Bloomsbury, WC1; the pre-existence of a plaque installed by St Pancras Borough Council meant that the building was not selected for commemoration by the LCC. Over the course of his long and distinguished career, Yeats was a prolific writer of poetry, plays and prose. It is, however, his poetry that places him in the first rank of writers. Yeats's first collection of verse, *The Wanderings of Oisin*, appeared in 1889, and was followed by works such as 'The Lake Isle of Innisfree' (1890), *The Wind among the Reeds* (1899), *The Wild Swans at Coole* (1919) and – the summit of his later achievements – *The Tower* (1928). His poetry, deeply influenced by mysticism and Gaelic legend, was to bring him international acclaim and, in 1923, the Nobel Prize for Literature. In London, where he lived for much of his life, Yeats was a prominent figure, and a friend of men such as OSCAR WILDE, WILLIAM MORRIS and GEORGE BERNARD SHAW.

The artist **Alfred Stevens** (1818–1875) **8** is honoured with a plaque at 9 Eton Villas, NW3, part of a terrace of three houses built in about 1849 (fig. 131).[9] Stevens gained his artistic training working with his father, a house painter and decorator, before studying in Italy from 1833 to 1842. The most important event in Stevens's career was the commission, in 1857, to design the Wellington Monument for St Paul's Cathedral (fig. 132). This work was to take up the remainder of his life, and was unfinished at the time of his death; it was later completed by JOHN TWEED. By the late 1850s, Stevens had settled in Eton Villas; he lived and died at number 9, and on the adjoining corner site – now occupied by Wellington House – began in 1866 to build a house and studio. While living in Eton Villas, Stevens was some-

132 A watercolour of 1877 showing the Wellington Monument in St Paul's Cathedral. This work dominated Alfred Stevens's years at Eton Villas, and was unfinished at the time of his death. [© City of London]

133 *Twilight Dreams* (1913) by Arthur Rackham, one of the many works the artist completed during his time at 16 Chalcot Gardens. [© University of Liverpool Art Gallery & Collections, UK / The Bridgeman Art Library]

thing of a recluse; it was said that, 'Engrossed with his work, he never went into society'.[10] In appearance, Stevens was formal – he was often mistaken by strangers for a Catholic priest – but in his habits he inclined to bachelor unconventionality; he apparently 'ate when he was hungry, and not always then, and went to bed when fatigue drove him there'.[11] The blue plaque – which bears the LCC's standard wreath border – was erected in 1924.

The illustrator **Arthur Rackham** (1867–1939) **9** , commemorated with a plaque at 16 Chalcot Gardens, NW3, was born in Lambeth and became a full-time artist in 1892. The publication of his illustrations for *Grimm's Fairy Tales* (1900) marked the beginning of Rackham's successful career. He was in particular demand as an illustrator of children's stories, and became renowned for his contributions to such works as *Rip Van Winkle* (1905), *Peter Pan in Kensington Gardens* (1906), *Alice in Wonderland* (1907) and *A Midsummer Night's Dream* (1908). His vivid depictions of fairies, witches, elves and other fantastical characters were known in households across Britain and America (fig. 133). Rackham lived at number 16 with his wife,

the painter Edyth Starkie (1867–1941), during the most important years of his career. The house, built in 1881 and enlarged in 1898 to the designs of C. F. A. Voysey, was altered by Maxwell Ayrton before the couple took up residence in 1906. Ayrton provided studios for both husband and wife; Arthur's, at first-floor level, was described in 1908 as 'a most delightful place, cool, airy and quiet'.[12] Number 16 remained the Rackhams' home until their removal to Sussex in 1920, though Arthur retained a workplace and pied-à-terre at 6 Primrose Hill Studios, NW1. The plaque was unveiled in 1981 by the illustrator's daughter, Barbara Edwards.

On the north side of Primrose Hill is Elsworthy Road, NW3, part of a leafy, late nineteenth-century development known locally as 'Elsworthy Village'. At number 4, a GLC plaque honours the musician **Sir Henry Wood** (1869–1944) **10** . Henry Joseph Wood was born in Oxford Street, and was to remain firmly connected with that area for much of his life. His greatest work, as a conductor and musical director, was carried out at the Queen's Hall, Langham Place (demolished); there, in 1895, Wood was the first conductor of the Promenade concerts (the 'Proms'), conceived by the venue's manager, Robert Newman. Wood was to conduct them for fifty consecutive seasons; his last Prom took place in 1944, by which time the concerts had transferred to the Royal Albert Hall. Knighted in 1911, Sir Henry hoped – through the Proms – to democratise the message of music, and disseminate more widely its beneficial effects. In this, he was eminently successful: by the time of his death, the Proms had become a British institution, and Wood was hailed as 'the most popular musical figure of his time'.[13] He lived at 4 Elsworthy Road from summer 1905 until autumn 1937, though not continuously; the house – built in about 1880 – was often let to friends, including DELIUS, who stayed here in 1918. Wood shared number 4 with his first wife Olga (1868–1909), a Russian-born soprano, and later with his second, Muriel Greatrex (1882–1967), a businesswoman. It was the third and last companion of his life, his ex-pupil Lady Jessie Wood (the names 'Lady' and 'Wood' both adopted by deed poll), who proposed the plaque, which was erected in 1969.

At 7 Harley Road, NW3, a plaque of 1969 commemorates another musical figure, the singer **Dame Clara Butt** (1872–1936) ⑪ .[14] Her period of residence, from 1901 to 1929, overlapped with that of SIR HENRY WOOD at Elsworthy Road. Clara's fine contralto voice was evident from her school years. In 1890 she won a scholarship to the Royal College of Music and moved from Bristol to London. She made her debut at the Royal Albert Hall in 1892, in Arthur Sullivan's cantata *The Golden Legend*. However, most of Butt's appearances were confined to the concert platform, where her powerful voice and striking presence – she was six feet two inches (188 cm) tall – made her one of the most popular singers of her day. Butt was particularly famous for the hymn 'Abide with me', while EDWARD ELGAR composed *Sea Pictures* (1899) with Clara's voice in mind; in 1902 she became the first singer to perform Elgar's 'Land of Hope and Glory'. She lived at number 7 with her husband, Robert Kennerley Rumford (1870–1957), a baritone singer with whom she performed regularly. This imposing house, at which the couple entertained some of the most notable personalities of the time, is now an old people's home known as Compton Lodge.

Robert Polhill Bevan (1865–1925) ⑫ , the Camden Town Group painter, lived at 14 Adamson Road, NW3

– a tall brick studio house of the late nineteenth century – from 1900 to 1925. Bevan studied art in London, Paris and Brittany, where he received encouragement from Gauguin and Renoir. He was one of the first painters to introduce Post-Impressionism to Britain, and in 1911 was a founder member of the Camden Town Group; he also played a key part in the founding of the London Group (1913) and the Cumberland Market Group (1915), the latter named after Bevan's studio at 49 Cumberland Market, near Regent's Park. It was while living at number 14 that he carried out much of the work for which he is best known: paintings of urban and country scenes which are characterised by strong colour, broad brushwork and simplified definition (fig. 134). At his first one-man show in 1905, Bevan exhibited what have been described as 'probably the most radical paintings by a British artist then to be seen in London'.[15] His work includes, most famously, views of cab horses and horse sales, and also many scenes of Hampstead and Belsize Park. Bevan's house in Adamson Road, in which he lived with his wife, the Polish painter Stanislawa de Karlowska (1876–1952), became a rendezvous for a group of artists that included WYNDHAM LEWIS. The plaque was unveiled in 1999 by Robert Baty, Bevan's grandson.

Belsize Park Gardens, NW3, with its lines of imposing semi-detached villas of the 1850s and 1860s, has been described by the architectural historian John Summerson as 'nothing if not robust'.[16] Number 37 was the home of **Henry Noel Brailsford** (1873–1958) ⑬ , described on the plaque as a writer and 'champion of equal and free humanity'. The son of a Wesleyan minister, Brailsford worked as a journalist from the late 1890s, and established himself as a writer for Liberal newspapers such as *The Echo* and the *Daily News*. However, he soon moved from liberalism to socialism, editing the paper of the Independent Labour Party, the *New Leader* (1922–26), and contributing regular columns to the *New Republic*, *Reynolds's News* and the *New Statesman*. Brailsford was known in particular as an expert on British imperial and foreign affairs. His work in this area included *The War of Steel and Gold* (1914), *A League of Nations* (1917) and *Rebel India* (1931), which supported Indian self-government. Throughout his career, Brailsford fought for the oppressed, and championed international concilia-

134 Robert Polhill Bevan's *From the Artist's Window* (1915–16), painted at 14 Adamson Road. [© Leicester Arts and Museums Service]

PRIMROSE HILL AND BELSIZE PARK

tion; his *Times* obituarist stated, 'Few men held more firmly or more consistently than Brailsford to an ideal of political and social justice'.[17] Number 37 Belsize Park Gardens was Brailsford's home from 1926 until his death; it was still the residence of his widow Evamaria (1914–1988) in 1983, when the GLC plaque was erected.

On the other side of the road, at 44 Belsize Park Gardens, an English Heritage plaque of 1999 commemorates the composer **Frederick Delius** (1862–1934) 14 (fig. 125). Delius was born in Bradford, Yorkshire, of German parents, and as a boy learned to play the piano and violin. Initially, his love of music was discouraged by his father, but – when it persisted – he was given support for a full musical education in Leipzig. Delius had lived for some time in France before 1897, when he settled in Grez-sur-Loing, near Fontainebleau, with the artist Helena 'Jelka' Rosen (1868–1935); the two were married in 1903. In the years that followed, Delius proved himself to be a highly prolific composer, comfortable working in a variety of musical forms, from chamber, choral and orchestral

works such as *On Hearing the First Cuckoo in Spring* (1912) to operas including *A Village Romeo and Juliet* (1899–1901). Towards the end of the First World War, at the height of his powers and public acclaim, Delius was forced to flee France for England. In early October 1918 he and Jelka moved into a large furnished flat at number 44, which featured 'a beautiful Bechstein grand'.[18] The couple remained here until May 1919, when they returned to their home in France. The period was not a productive one for Delius – Jelka said that he could never 'compose living in a town' – but was significant; the composer attended the first performances of two of his major works, his Violin Concerto (1916) and *Eventyr* (1917), and, 'disappointed with artistic London', set about creating a new concert society.[19]

The Prime Minister **Ramsay MacDonald** (1866–1937) 15 is honoured with a plaque at 9 Howitt Road, NW3, described in 1962 by the former Soviet Ambassador Ivan Maisky as 'one of those modest little villas favoured by middle-class English intelligentzia'.[20] Born

135 A photograph of 1924 showing the first Labour Cabinet in the garden of 10 Downing Street. Ramsay Macdonald appears fourth from the right in the bottom row. [Reproduced by kind permission of The National Archives UK (PRO30/69/1668)]

MR. CHARLES PHILIPS TREVELYAN, M.P.   LORD THOMSON.   MR. SIDNEY WEBB, M.P.   MR. JOHN WHEATLEY, M.P.   MR. F. W. JOWETT, M.P.   MR. THOMAS SHAW, M.P.
MR. STEPHEN WALSH, M.P.   VISCOUNT CHELMSFORD.   LORD OLIVIER.   COL. JOSIAH WEDGWOOD, M.P.   MR. VERNON HARTSHORN, M.P.
THE RT. HON. WILLIAM ADAMSON, M.P.   MR. PHILIP SNOWDEN, M.P.   MR. NOEL BUXTON, M.P.   THE RT. HON. JAMES HENRY THOMAS, M.P.
LORD PARMOOR, K.C.V.O.   VISCOUNT HALDANE, KT., O.M.   THE RT. HON. JAMES RAMSAY MACDONALD.   MR. JOHN R. CLYNES, M.P.   THE RT. HON. ARTHUR HENDERSON.

in Scotland, James Ramsay MacDonald was introduced to political life in the late 1880s as private secretary to a Liberal parliamentary candidate. His own political career only began after his marriage in 1896 to the socialist and feminist Margaret Gladstone – daughter of the chemist John Hall Gladstone – whose private income brought him financial independence. In 1900 MacDonald became Secretary of the newly founded Labour Representation Committee; in 1906 it became the Labour Party, and the same year MacDonald entered Parliament as MP for Leicester. He at once made his mark and, after the 1924 general election, formed the first Labour government (fig. 135), filling the office of Foreign Secretary as well as Prime Minister. In 1929 MacDonald regained the premiership as leader of another minority government; two years

later, amid the economic crisis of the Great Depression, he formed a national government with Liberal and Conservative support. This kept him in office until 1935, but earned him the lasting enmity of most of his former Labour colleagues. Number 9 Howitt Road is important both as MacDonald's residence – he lived here, a widower, from January 1916 to May 1925 – and as the place at which Britain's first Labour government was formed in 1924. The plaque was unveiled by Ramsay's son, Alister MacDonald, in 1963, at a ceremony attended by CLEMENT ATTLEE, SIR STANLEY UNWIN and LORD REITH.

Ornan Court (formerly Ornan Mansions), Ornan Road, NW3 – a mansion block on the corner of Haverstock Hill, at Belsize Park's northern limit – bears an

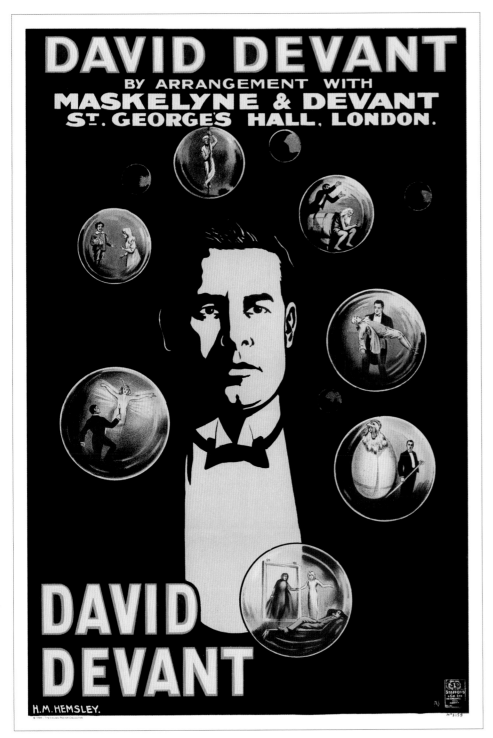

136 A promotional poster of c.1910 for David Devant's magic show at St George's Hall, Langham Place. The bubbles contain details of some of his most famous tricks, including 'The Mascot Moth' and 'The Artist's Dream'. [© Nielsen Magic Poster Collection]

today as the founding fathers of English conjuring. Based at St George's Hall in Langham Place (demolished), 'Maskelyne and Devant's Mysteries' wowed audiences with innovative and daring feats of illusionism. Devant's most famous tricks included 'The Mascot Moth', in which a winged woman seemingly dissolved in full view of the audience, and 'Biff', in which a motorcycle and its rider vanished from a crate suspended in mid-air (fig. 136). Devant was based in Belsize Park for about twenty-five years; of his three residences in the area – 2 Belsize Road, 1 Ornan Mansions and 17 Belsize Avenue – only Ornan Mansions (now Court) survives. Devant lived here in Flat 1 in 1915–17, when he was at the height of his fame. The plaque was unveiled in 2003 at an event organised by The Magic Circle, of which Devant became the first President in 1905.

The area around Parkhill Road, NW3, to the east of Haverstock Hill, was famously described by Herbert Read as 'a nest of gentle artists'.[21] In the 1930s, it housed a thriving community of writers and artists such as Read, PAUL NASH, Cecil Stephenson and Naum Gabo, together with Barbara Hepworth and BEN NICHOLSON, who were based at the Mall Studios off Tasker Road. One of the major figures of this artistic colony was the internationally renowned sculptor **Henry Moore, OM** (1898–1986) **17** , who lived and worked at 11A Parkhill Road (fig. 137). Henry Spencer Moore was born in Yorkshire, the son of a miner, and studied at the Leeds School of Art; there he met Barbara Hepworth, and was again a co-student of hers at the Royal College of Art. It was through Hepworth that Moore found number 11A, a two-storey extension to a Victorian house; it was his home from the time of his marriage in late July 1929 until 1940, when – after a few months at the Mall Studios – he and his wife Irina, née Radetzki (1907–1989) moved to Perry Green, Hertfordshire. Moore's time in Parkhill Road was one of productivity and innovation, during which he was greatly inspired by the local artistic circle; he produced twenty-two pieces in 1930 alone, most of them reclining figures and mother and child groups. This new and distinctive abstract style was to be further developed at Perry Green, where Moore produced works such as *Sheep Piece* (1971–72) and *Large Four Piece Reclining Figure* (1972–73). Moore's sketches and paintings are no less extraordinary; they include his series of 'shelter

English Heritage plaque to the magician **David Devant** (1868–1941) **16** . Born David Wighton in Holloway, he made his stage debut in 1893 at the Egyptian Hall in Piccadilly, England's 'Home of Mystery'. In 1905 Devant went into partnership with the great John Nevil Maskelyne; the pair were to dominate the world of magic for the next decade and are remembered

137 Henry Moore at work in his studio at 11A Parkhill Road in 1933. [© The Henry Moore Foundation archive]

Above right 138 A photograph of 1973 showing the proposed position of the plaque to Piet Mondrian, who lived at 60 Parkhill Road in 1938–40. It was installed in 1975. [© City of London, LMA]

drawings', inspired by a night spent in Belsize Park Underground station in 1940. The plaque was unveiled in 2004 by Moore's daughter, Mary.

Another artistic figure drawn to Parkhill Road was the painter **Piet Mondrian** (1872–1944) 18 , who lived at number 60 for nearly two years.[22] Born in Holland, Mondrian was a principal founding member of the Dutch art movement De Stijl ('The Style'). Between 1917 and 1920, he wrote a series of articles that introduced and discussed the philosophy known as Neo-Plasticism, which advocated abstraction and a simplified, reduced use of colour and form. This imbued his best-known paintings, called 'Compositions', which feature primary colours and rigorously geometric shapes and lines, and was to have a continuing influence on graphics and dress design, as well as on architectural and industrial design. Mondrian lived for many years in Paris, but in autumn 1938 the threat of war drove him to London, where he settled in a large first-floor room at the back of 60 Parkhill Road. Here, he became what Barbara Hepworth described as 'a most important focus'.[23] Mondrian's window overlooked a studio, to the rear of number 60, used by BEN NICHOLSON, while the garden connected via a gate to the Mall Studios. In a letter to the GLC, Hepworth wrote, 'We saw Mondrian nearly every day, communicating by the garden gates. He made his studio as exciting as the one in Montparnasse where he lived for so many years'.[24] Number 60 was Mondrian's base until late 1940, 'when a nearby bomb brought down his ceiling'.[25] He subsequently moved to New York, where he died four years later. The plaque was erected in 1975 (fig. 138).

NOTES

1 *The Streets of Belsize*, ed. Christopher Wade (London, 1991), p. 65

2 *Humphrey Jennings: Film-maker, Painter, Poet*, ed. Mary-Lou Jennings (London, 1982), p. 53

3 Kevin Jackson, *Humphrey Jennings* (London, 2004), p. 291

4 Letter of 18 May 1855 (from Roger to Grace Fenton). The letter forms part of the Annie Grace Fenton letter-book, Royal Photographic Society Collection, National Museum of Photography, Film & Television, Bradford. It has been published online at: www.rogerfenton.org.uk

5 *ODNB*, vol. XXXVII, p. 59

6 Heinrich Gemkow *et al.*, *Frederick Engels: A Biography* (Dresden, 1972), pp. 343–44

7 Sylvia Plath, *Letters Home: Correspondence, 1950–1963*, ed. Aurelia Schober Plath (London, 1975), p. 477 (7 November 1962)

8 *The Times Magazine*, 30 September 2000, p. 21

9 It is now accepted that Stevens was born in 1818, rather than in 1817, as is stated on the plaque.

10 LCC, *Indication of Houses of Historical Interest in London*, vol. V (London, 1930), pp. 58–59

11 Ibid, p. 59

12 James Hamilton, *Arthur Rackham: A Life with Illustration* (London, 1995), p. 80

13 *The Times*, 21 August 1944, p. 6

14 It is now accepted that Butt was born in 1872, rather than in 1873, as is stated on the plaque.

15 *ODNB*, vol. V, p. 582

16 *Belsize Park: A Living Suburb*, ed. Leonie Cohn (London, 1986), p. 25

17 *The Times*, 24 March 1958, p. 14

18 *Delius: A Life in Letters*, ed. Lionel Carley, vol. II (London, 1988), p. 195 (19 September 1918)

19 Ibid, p. 201 (20 December 1918); ibid, p. 200

20 Ivan M. Maisky, *Journey into the Past*, trans. Frederick Holt (London, 1962), p. 246

21 Herbert Read, 'A Nest of Gentle Artists', *Apollo*, vol. LXXVII (September 1962), pp. 536–38

22 The plaque incorrectly includes Mondrian's middle name. The artist was born Pieter Cornelis Mondriaan [*sic*], but was known as Piet Mondrian after 1911.

23 Letter of 16 February 1972 on blue plaque file.

24 Ibid

25 Ibid

139 Ranger's (or Chesterfield) House in a painting of 1884. The building bears stone plaques commemorating Philip, 4th Earl of Chesterfield and Garnet, 1st Viscount Wolseley. [© Museum of London]

THE BOROUGH OF

GREENWICH

The borough of Greenwich stretches along the south bank of the Thames to include Woolwich, and inland to embrace Charlton, much of Blackheath and Eltham. These localities have distinct historic identities, and blue plaques are to be found in all save Woolwich. The borough's historical focus is the former royal palace and park in Greenwich proper: the Tudor palace was rebuilt for the Navy as a magnificent home for its pensioners, while Greenwich Park, with the Old Royal Observatory on top of the hill, remains one of London's most sublime open spaces. The Navy and the observatory were both important in the part that the area, as a military-industrial metropolitan satellite,

contributed to the rise of British sea power. Eastwards, across former marshes, Woolwich had its own naval dockyard and the Royal Arsenal, long the nation's principal arms factory and a leading local employer of the skilled working classes. Blackheath was a forbidding expanse of open land on the main London–Dover road until it was made a genteel suburb in the later Georgian period. Eltham, which has a former royal palace of even greater antiquity than that at Greenwich, became a suburb in the decades around 1900, mixing terraces, semis and public housing, with one face looking to the Kent countryside.

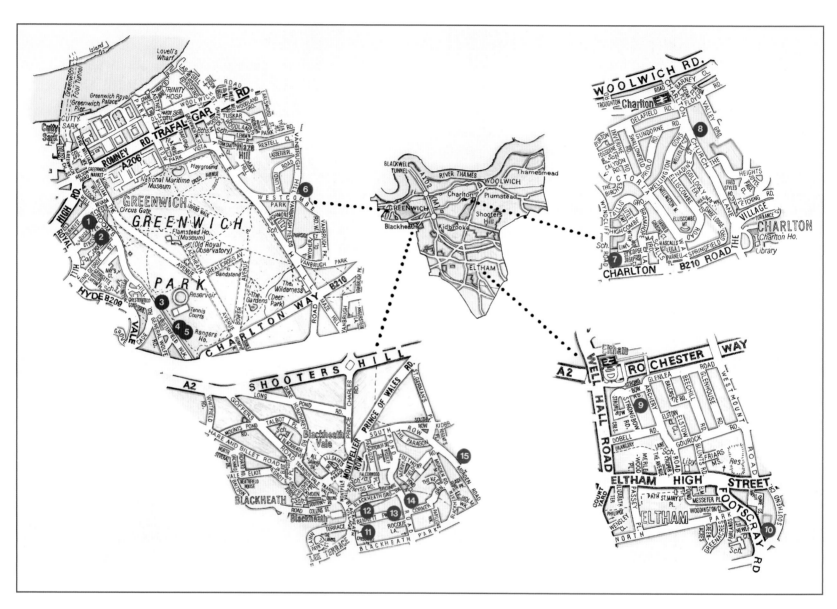

GREENWICH

140 C. Day-Lewis with his family – wife Jill, daughter Tamasin and son Daniel – at home at 6 Croom's Hill, reading one of the congratulatory letters sent on his appointment as Poet Laureate, 1968. [© Getty Images]

where he met the poet W. H. Auden, a major early influence; Day-Lewis came to prominence in the 1930s as a member of the left-wing 'Auden Gang'. In 1935 he published the first of a series of twenty detective stories, written under the pseudonym Nicholas Blake, and after a move to Devon in 1938 increasingly found his poetic voice. The year 1951 was a turning point for Day-Lewis: having left both his wife Mary and his mistress, the writer Rosamond Lehmann, he married the actress Jill Balcon (b. 1925), daughter of the film producer Sir Michael Balcon. He was also elected Oxford Professor of Poetry, a position Day-Lewis held until 1956. On 31 December 1957, eight months after the birth of his son, the actor Daniel Day-Lewis, he moved with his family to Croom's Hill. Number 6 remained Day-Lewis's home for the rest of his life, including the period when he was Poet Laureate, from 1968 to 1972. The house, and the area, occupied a firm place in Day-Lewis's affections; both were portrayed in his Nicholas Blake novel *The Worm of Death* (1961). In 1959 he wrote of being 'happy, living in this place where old and new can be focused together into a historic present'.[1] The English Heritage plaque was put up in 1998, without fanfare, as was the family's wish.

Further along, at 26 Croom's Hill, a plainer but no less grand later Georgian house, there is a GLC plaque to **Benjamin Waugh** (1839–1908) ❷ , the founder of the National Society for the Prevention of Cruelty to Children. The sylvan combes of Greenwich Park and polite Georgian residences of Croom's Hill belie the character of the wider area. Most of the population of Victorian Greenwich was poor. After the financial crash of 1866 that devastated shipbuilding on the Thames, poverty and brutalisation became acute. In that year, the Yorkshire-born Waugh moved to Greenwich to be a Congregationalist minister. He was shocked by what he saw on walks around east Greenwich, encountering children suffering not just from neglect and homelessness, but also from desperate cruelty. Waugh lived on Croom's Hill in about 1874–77, when his work to improve the lot of children began to attract notice. His efforts led to the establishment of the London Society for the Prevention of Cruelty to Children in 1884, on the centenary of which the plaque was unveiled; the society became national in scope in 1889, with Waugh continuing as its Director until his retirement in 1905. Whilst Waugh's contribution to history is well-estab-

On the west side of Greenwich Park is Croom's Hill, SE10. The houses become grander as the road rises away from the riverside town centre and the views grow more commanding, but this is not to say that the houses at the bottom are humble. Two plaques are to be found here, the first at 6 Croom's Hill, in a short row built by John Savory in 1718–21. It commemorates the last home of the Poet Laureate **C. Day-Lewis** (1904–1972) ❶ (fig. 140), who preferred 'C.' to his given name Cecil. Irish born, Day-Lewis was educated at Oxford,

lished, his connection with Croom's Hill has been the source of some confusion, and recent research has shown Waugh's plaque to be on the wrong building. The GLC, failing to allow for street renumbering, commemorated number 26 (originally number 13). The number 26 in which Waugh lived is, in fact, now 62 Croom's Hill, an idiosyncratic, bow-fronted house built in 1810 by Thomas Skinner.

Croom's Hill leads uphill to Chesterfield Walk, SE10, where several substantial houses back directly onto the park. Development here began in the late seventeenth century with a group of villas, the first hint of the suburb that the area was to become. One of these, enlarged in the early eighteenth century, came to be known as Macartney House. **General James Wolfe** (1727–1759) ③ , the victor of Quebec, lived here, as a wreathed LCC plaque testifies (fig. 141). This was erected in 1909 as part of a scheme to commemorate eminent military men; Wolfe's victory at Quebec (1759) was the battle that turned the Seven Years War. His father, Lieutenant-General Edward Wolfe (1685–1759), moved to Macartney House in 1751 from elsewhere in Greenwich, and the younger Wolfe lived here only occasionally. It was here – at what he described as 'the prettiest-situated house in England' – that he learned, in October 1757, that he had been promoted colonel.[2] Following his martyr's death at the moment of victory at Quebec, Wolfe's body was returned to his parents' house, where it lay in state until 20 November

1759, when Wolfe was buried beside his father at the parish church of St Alfege, Greenwich; his mother, Henrietta, lived on at the house until her death in October 1764. Unusually, the plaque is on the back wall, thus avoiding what the Clerk of the LCC termed 'false history' – a front extension of the house, designed by Sir John Soane, dates from 1802–5.[3] The plaque is also more easily visible here, as the back of the house overlooks the park.

Further along Chesterfield Walk towards Blackheath is Ranger's (or Chesterfield) House, built – as recent English Heritage research has revealed – in *c.* 1723 for Admiral Francis Hosier (d. 1727) and possibly designed by John James (fig. 139). This is now an English Heritage property, inherited – like the plaques scheme – from the LCC and GLC. Flanking the main entrance there are LCC commemorations of 1937, not blue plaques but twin inscriptions in Portland stone, recording the residences of **Philip, 4th Earl of Chesterfield** (1694–1773) ④ , the statesman and author, and **Garnet, 1st Viscount Wolseley** (1833–1913) ⑤ , the Field Marshal. These memorials, suggested by a local antiquary, A. R. Martin, were so made because the 'architectural features of the front elevation of the building are such that the affixing of a tablet of the usual design and colouring would not have been appropriate'.[4] Chesterfield inherited this villa on the death of his brother – John Stanhope – in December 1748, the year that he resigned as Secretary of State. It became his favourite summer residence and was named 'Babiole', as a compliment to his friend Madame de Monconseil. Chesterfield built the bow-windowed gallery wing on the south side of the 'very small' house in 1749–50, probably to designs by the Palladian architect Isaac Ware. Gradually retreating from public life, Chesterfield remained in what he called 'exile' in this 'hermitage' until autumn 1772, writing the letters for which he is chiefly remembered, gardening – 'I . . . converse with my vegetables d'égal à l'égal' – and reading, 'amusements, which my former youth and spirits would have despised, but which now stand in the stead of pleasures with me'.[5] The gallery housed his fine collection of art. Princess Sophia Matilda of Gloucester (1773–1844), niece of King George III, was the first Ranger of Greenwich Park to live here, from 1815 to 1844. In summer 1888 Field Marshal Lord Wolseley was offered Ranger's House by Queen Victoria, thus

141 The LCC plaque to General James Wolfe, erected in 1909 on the rear façade of Macartney House, Chesterfield Walk. [© English Heritage. Photograph by Derek Kendall]

becoming the last 'grace and favour' resident of the house before its municipalisation; he remained here until 1896. He was a reformer of army administration and training, and served in Burma, the Crimea, India, China, Canada and Africa, where he led the expedition to relieve General Gordon in Khartoum (1884–85).

On the east side of the park, access to the hillside district of Westcombe seems guarded by Vanbrugh Castle, the house of 1719 that Sir John Vanbrugh designed and built for himself, as a private plaque records. Behind lie the attractive streets of the Westcombe Park estate. Here, on a house of 1879–80 at 6 Vanbrugh Hill (formerly 3 Essex Villas), SE3, built by Joseph Bates as part of the first suburban development on the estate, a plaque honours **Sir Frank Dyson** (1868–1939) **6** . He was Astronomer Royal from 1910 to 1933, during which time he resided at the Royal Observatory in Greenwich Park. Dyson lived at 6 Vanbrugh Hill during the time he worked as chief assistant to his predecessor as Astronomer Royal, William Christie; he moved in after his marriage to Caroline Best (1867–1937) in June 1894 and left in January 1906, soon after being appointed Astronomer Royal for Scotland. Later, from 1933, Dyson lived at nearby 27 Westcombe Park Road. His achievements included the confirmation of the deflection of starlight in the sun's gravitational field, proposed by Einstein as part of his general theory of relativity. Dyson also constructed a free-pendulum clock of unprecedented accuracy that led the BBC in the 1920s to begin broadcasting accurate time signals from Greenwich, the origin of the 'pips'. The plaque was erected following a suggestion made to the GLC in 1981 by the residents of the house; set up in 1990, it was the first to honour an astronomer.

CHARLTON

Charlton has a great Jacobean mansion, Charlton House, and an attractive brick parish church of the 1630s in what was once the centre of a village. A short distance to the west there is an English Heritage plaque to the pioneering engineer **William Henry Barlow** (1812–1902) **7** at 145 Charlton Road, SE7, a detached double-fronted villa of *c.* 1810 formerly known as High Combe. The history of this house carries a rich testament to the area's importance as a nursery of engineering expertise. Born in Woolwich, Barlow was the son of a professor of mathematics at the Royal Military Academy, and trained as an engineer in the nearby royal dockyard. After early employ with Henry Maudslay, a renowned mechanical engineer whose roots were also in Woolwich, Barlow moved into railway work, and in 1851 he assisted with the ironwork for the Crystal Palace. Barlow is perhaps best known for his work for the Midland Railway. This included, most notably, the design and construction of the iron and glass train shed at St Pancras Station; when new in 1868, this was the world's largest clear-span roof, one of the great triumphs of Victorian structural engineering. Barlow moved to High Combe in 1857 with his wife Selina Crawford, née Caffin (d. 1903), also from Woolwich, and it continued to be his home until his death here at the age of ninety. The house was situated adjacent to East Combe, formerly the residence of his elder brother, Peter Barlow, also an engineer. William's son, Peter Crawford Barlow, likewise joined the profession, working in partnership with his father between 1874 and their retirement in 1896. High Combe, which now serves as the presbytery to the adjacent Roman Catholic Church of Our Lady of Grace, has also been associated with the rocket designer Sir William Congreve (1772–1828).

At 67 Charlton Church Lane, SE7, a bulky late Victorian house, a plaque of 1999 records the improbable residence here of the writer **Ettore Schmitz** (1861–1928) **8** , better known by his alias, **Italo Svevo**. This great Italian Modernist – friend of JAMES JOYCE, comic chronicler of the nature of consciousness and author, most famously, of *Confessions of Zeno* (1923) – lived at 67 Charlton Church Lane between 1903 and 1913, returning to the house regularly until the year before his death. He came from Trieste to Charlton to help set up a small riverside ships'-paint factory, part of his father-in-law Gioachino Veneziani's anti-corrosion composition works; the factory was in Anchor and Hope Lane, just to the north of Svevo's Church Lane base. As he travelled back and forth, 'finding myself awake, I had to collect myself in order to decide whether I was in Trieste, Murano or Charlton'. In less confused mind, he thought Charlton the 'drabbest and most out-of-the-way suburb', while also finding that 'my Church Lane is one of the most variegated streets in the Realm'.[6] He made up a violin trio with a workman from Woolwich Arsenal and a Charlton

GREENWICH

shopkeeper, and became a fanatical supporter of Charlton Athletic, English football champions in 1913. During his time in the capital, Svevo wrote – but never published – 'Soggiorno Londinese', which relates his experiences of Charlton, describing 'the absence of any and every kind of literature'.[7]

ELTHAM

In Eltham, **Herbert Morrison**, **Lord Morrison of Lambeth** (1888–1965) ❾ , the Cabinet minister and leader of the London County Council, is commemorated at 55 Archery Road, SE9 (fig. 142). He lived in this modest semi-detached house from 1929, soon after it was built, until 1960, during which time he was at the centre of English politics as a leading light in the Labour Party and the highly successful leader of the LCC (1934–40), with a parallel career as a parliamentarian and Cabinet minister. He rose to be Deputy Prime Minister, leader of the Commons and Foreign Secretary in CLEMENT ATTLEE's administration of 1945–51. Morrison counted his housing programmes and the introduction of the Green Belt among his greatest achievements. The year that he died, the LCC was wound up and replaced by the GLC. Contrary to

142 A portrait of Herbert Morrison and his second wife Edith in the front room of their home at 55 Archery Road. The photograph was chosen as the frontispiece for Morrison's *Autobiography* (1960).

the convention that twenty years should elapse after an individual's death before a plaque be considered, it was proposed that Morrison warranted immediate recognition. After deferral and much deliberation, the usual rules were set aside in order to recognise Morrison's 'outstanding and unique contribution to London, the London County Council and to London life'.[8] The plaque was unveiled in 1977 by the then leader of the GLC, Sir Reg Goodwin.

On the other side of Eltham High Street is another unassuming building, 59 Footscray Road (formerly 14 Victoria Road), SE9, which bears a GLC plaque to the naturalist and writer **Richard Jefferies** (1848–1887) ❿ . Humbly born in Wiltshire, Jefferies – a protégé of WILLIAM MORRIS – came to prominence with works such as *Wild Life in a Southern County* (1879), *The Amateur Poacher* (1879) and *Bevis* (1882), which has been described as 'the best boys' book ever written'.[9] Based on his memories of Wiltshire – a county Jefferies left in 1877 – these books established him as the foremost country writer of his day. Despite increasing ill-health, Jefferies kept up his literary output until his early death, at the age of thirty-eight. He lived at what was then 14 Victoria Road – a semi-detached house that was fairly newly built – from 24 June 1884 until April 1885, when he was compelled by illness to move to Sussex, where he died. During his time here, Eltham was an edge-of-town suburb, much more rural than is now readily recalled. This suburban identity, looking to both town and country, reflects Jefferies's outlook. He was a naturalist and a mystical chronicler of London's environs who, in 1885, wrote *After London*, an astonishing vision of an urban relapse into primitive wilderness. While here, Jefferies also penned a number of essays which were collected as *The Open Air* (1885). Later came *Amaryllis at the Fair* (1887), an autobiographical novel which was to be his final contribution to literature.

BLACKHEATH

In 'Blackheath Village', one road, Bennett Park, SE3 – a cul-de-sac just off Tranquil Vale – has three blue plaques. They could not be more diverse in their subjects. At number 4 lived the mathematician and astrophysicist **Sir Arthur Eddington**, **OM** (1882–1944) ⑪ (fig. 143). In February 1906 he succeeded SIR

143   The plaque to Sir Arthur Eddington at 4 Bennett Park. [© English Heritage. Photograph by Derek Kendall]

FRANK DYSON as chief assistant to the Astronomer Royal at the Royal Observatory, working first under William Christie and then, from 1910 until 1913, under Dyson. Throughout this period, Eddington rented rooms at 4 Bennett Park, a mid-nineteenth-century semi-detached building which then (with number 2 and later number 6) formed part of a boarding-house. In 1913 Eddington took up the Plumian chair of astronomy at Cambridge, a post that was joined the following year with the directorship of the university observatory; the latter served as his home for the rest of his life. At Cambridge, Eddington devised a mathematical method of analysing stellar movements, and went on to be a leading interpreter of Einstein's theory of relativity. The research that dominated the last two decades of his life appeared as *The Relativity Theory of Protons and Electrons* (1936) and *Fundamental Theory* (published posthumously in 1946). Eddington, who was knighted in 1930 and awarded the Order of Merit eight years later, also wrote popular scientific books including *The Nature of the Physical World* (1928). His plaque was erected by the GLC in 1974.

Almost opposite, at 5 Bennett Park, one of a group of semi-detached houses of 1869–70, there is a plaque to the postcard cartoonist **Donald McGill** (1875–1962) 12 . Active as a 'humour artist' from about 1904, McGill had a penchant for double entendre, large-bottomed women and weedy men. Called the 'king of the saucy postcard', his heyday was from the 1920s through to the 1950s. Brought up elsewhere in Blackheath, McGill lived and worked with his (respectable) family in a flat on the top two floors of this (respectable) house from 1932 to 1939, towards the middle of a (disrespectable) career during which he is said to have sold around 350 million cards. GEORGE ORWELL was sufficiently impressed by this 'harmless rebellion against virtue' to write an essay about McGill in 1941; in this, he enthused that McGill's cards, 'without being in the least imitative', were 'exactly what comic postcards have been any time these last forty years, and from them the meaning and purpose of the whole *genre* can be inferred'.[10] The plaque was proposed in 1975 on the centenary of McGill's birth. The owners of the house, who had suggested the plaque, organised the unveiling ceremony in 1977, substituting a pair of frilly knickers for curtains (fig. 144). The press predictably punned on the 'erection' of a 'blue' plaque, and a GLC officer com-

GREENWICH

Knickers off for postcards king

144   An article in the *South London Press* on 23 September 1977 celebrates the installation of a plaque to the postcard cartoonist Donald McGill at 5 Bennett Park. In honour of McGill's work, the plaque was unveiled from behind a pair of frilly knickers. [© South London Press]

mented that 'Possibly only Winston Churchill has beaten this for excitement'.[11]

The third of Bennett Park's blue plaques can be seen at the end of the cul-de-sac, at number 47 (formerly 45). It is on what was originally the Blackheath Art Club – residential studios and a gallery of 1885, designed by John C. P. Higgs and Frank Rudkin – the first of a clutch of Blackheath cultural institutions established by the philanthropist William Webster. Between 1933 and 1943, the building housed the studios of the pioneers of documentary film making, the **GPO Film Unit** ⑬ , later the Crown Film Unit, the offices of which were located at 21 Soho Square, W1. This is one of the few cases where a blue plaque commemorates a group rather than an individual. Here, under the leadership of John Grierson (1898–1972) – who is said to have coined the term 'documentary' – eloquent public-service left-wing social realism was given expression in films such as *Coal Face* (1935) and *Night Mail* (1936), which set verse specially commissioned from W. H. Auden to a score by Benjamin Britten. Talking pictures were then in their infancy, and the General Post Office Film Unit was noted for the accomplishment of its sound editing, the activity that

took place at Blackheath. When war broke out, the organisation was amalgamated under the Ministry of Information to form the Crown Film Unit, and turned its attention to fighting fascism with a string of outstanding documentaries produced by Humphrey Jennings. These films, all edited at Blackheath, include *Listen to Britain* (1942) and *Fires Were Started* (1943). The unit left London for Beaconsfield towards the end of the Second World War, and was disbanded in 1952. The Blackheath Preservation Trust restored the Bennett Park building in 1996–97 and proposed the plaque; it was unveiled in 2000 by Jennings's daughter, Marie-Lou Legg.

On the Cator estate on the east side of Blackheath Village there are two plaques, both to overseas visitors. In the summer of 1856, **Nathaniel Hawthorne** (1804–1864) ⑭ , the American author, stayed at 4 (formerly 6) Pond Road, SE3, one of a group of villas put up by Thomas Ross in 1829 (fig. 145). Having written his best-known books, *The Scarlet Letter* (1850) and *The House of the Seven Gables* (1851), in near-isolation in Salem, Massachusetts, Hawthorne came to England with his family in 1853 to earn a living as US Consul in Liverpool. The Hawthornes were invited to Black-

145   Number 4 Pond Road in a photograph of 1952, the year before the house was marked with a plaque commemorating Nathaniel Hawthorne. [© Getty Images]

heath to stay in the home of a friend, the poet and businessman Francis Bennoch (1813–1890). On taking up residence here in early July 1856, Hawthorne found 'Mr Bennoch's house not . . . so big as his heart'. Mrs Bennoch was 'somewhat put to her trumps by such an influx of guests', and the author had to find rooms nearby for his children and their nurse.[12] However, over the course of his three-month stay – Hawthorne left Pond Road on 8 September – the author found this 'little Cockney villa' to be 'very pleasant . . . very quiet, very homelike', and passed here 'some of the happiest hours that I have known since we left our American home'.[13] During his time in the country, Hawthorne wrote what were published in 1870 as his *English Notebooks*, edited by his widow Sophia (1809–1871) and dedicated by her to Bennoch. Number 4 Pond Road – known in the nineteenth century as Cosham Villa and Dinsdale Lodge, and numbered 6 until 1903 – was marked with a plaque in 1953. Hawthorne, not in his element in 'old' Europe, might have had fundamental objections; a visit to the British Museum prompted him to muse, 'The present is burthened too much with the past'.[14]

A short distance further east, at 15 (formerly 8) Morden Road, SE3, is another big villa, built in 1854 for the publisher and bookseller Pelham Richardson (1804–1860). His widow, Mary Jane (1813–1873), rented the house to the composer **Charles Gounod** (1818–1893) **15** for five weeks in 1870. Born in Paris, Gounod made his name with the opera *Faust* (1859); other operatic works included *Roméo et Juliette* (1867). He later turned to oratorios, composing works such as *La Rédemption* (1882) and *Mors et Vita* (1885), and also produced liturgical and orchestral music. Soon after the outbreak of the Franco-Prussian War, Gounod and his family fled to England, arriving in Liverpool in September 1870. The composer was resident in London for much of the period 1870–74, during which time – living mainly with Georgina Weldon at Tavistock House (demolished), Tavistock Square, Bloomsbury – he conducted concerts at the Crystal Palace, the Royal Albert Hall and elsewhere. Gounod stayed at Shirley Lodge, 15 Morden Road, shortly after his arrival in England, from early October until mid-November 1870. The house was marked with an LCC plaque in 1961.

NOTES

1 Sean Day-Lewis, *C. Day-Lewis: An English Literary Life* (London, 1980), p. 239
2 Beckles Willson, *The Life and Letters of James Wolfe* (London, 1909), p. 144 (9 June 1751)
3 Letter of 9 March 1910 on blue plaque file.
4 Letter of 26 November 1937 (from Clerk of the LCC) on blue plaque file.
5 *The Letters of Philip Dormer Stanhope, Earl of Chesterfield*, ed. Lord Mahon, vol. IV (London, 1892), p. 72 (6 April 1753); LCC leaflet, *London Houses of Historical Interest Marked by Memorial Tablets: Chesterfield (or Ranger's) House, Blackheath, SE10: Chesterfield*, New Series, no. 2 (1938); copy on blue plaque file.
6 John Gatt-Rutter, *Italo Svevo, A Double Life* (Oxford, 1988), pp. 204, 207, 212 and 213

7 Ibid, p. 302
8 Press release of 11 September 1974 on blue plaque file.
9 *ODNB*, vol. XXIX, p. 859
10 George Orwell, 'The Art of Donald McGill', *Horizon*, vol. IV, no. 21 (September 1941), p. 162
11 *Postcard Collectors Gazette*, November 1977, p. 18
12 *The Centenary Edition of the Works of Nathaniel Hawthorne: vol. XXII: The English Notebooks 1856–1860*, eds Thomas Woodson and Bill Ellis (Ohio, 1997), p. 66 (6 July 1856)
13 Ibid, p. 94 (2 August 1856); ibid, p. 149 (9 September 1856)
14 *The Centenary Edition of the Works of Nathaniel Hawthorne: vol. XXI*, eds Thomas Woodson and Bill Ellis (Ohio, 1997), p. 441 (27 March 1856)

GREENWICH

L.C.C.

DANIEL
DEFOE
(1661–1731)
Lived in a house
on this site.

146   The plaque to Daniel Defoe,
erected in 1932 on the side
elevation of 95 Stoke Newington
Church Street. [© English Heritage.
Photograph by Derek Kendall]

THE BOROUGH OF

THE BOROUGH OF

HACKNEY

Modern Hackney consists of the former metropolitan boroughs of Stoke Newington, Shoreditch and Hackney. Shoreditch, the southernmost district, lies just outside the boundaries of the City and from medieval times was a place of recreation for Londoners. Settlement and development had changed its character by the late seventeenth century, but Hackney remained a village for much longer; as such, it was popular as a place of retirement and as a destination for day trippers. Hackney and Stoke Newington were both notable centres of religious dissent: several sects set up meeting houses and colleges as they were close enough to the City to be convenient, yet beyond its jurisdiction. In the nineteenth century, speculative development covered the whole of modern Hackney with homes for clerks, artisans and small tradesmen. Over the last hundred years the district has seen depopulation, de-industrialisation and the demolition of swathes of its older housing stock. Efforts at regeneration are, however, bearing fruit, and today it is a vibrant area of great social and architectural diversity.

HACKNEY

147 The rectangular bronze LCC plaque commemorating the site of the Priory and The Theatre at 86–90 Curtain Road. [© English Heritage. Photograph by Derek Kendall]

At 86–90 Curtain Road, Shoreditch, EC2, at the corner with New Inn Yard, is a showroom-warehouse building of *c.* 1892. It bears an inconspicuous, rectangular bronze plaque erected by the LCC in 1920; this marks the site of both the **Priory of St John the Baptist**, Holywell, and **The Theatre** ❶ (fig. 147), the first London building specifically devoted to the performance of plays, which from 1577 to 1598 stood a short distance to the east. Holywell (or Haliwelle) Priory, founded in the mid-twelfth century in the fields north of London, was dissolved in 1539 and the land sold off. In 1576 a northern portion of the former priory precinct was leased to the actor James Burbage (d. 1597) and here, in partnership with his brother-in-law John Brayne (d. 1586), he erected a theatre. It was probably constructed of timber and was polygonal in shape, with an open courtyard at the centre. The site fell beyond the control of the City authorities, which viewed theatres as breeding grounds of disorder and disease, but could readily be reached by playgoers from London. Little is known about the works performed at The Theatre, but it is possible that some of Shake-speare's early plays were staged here, and more than likely that Shakespeare appeared here as a member of the Lord Chamberlain's company of players. Burbage's lease expired in 1597, and the following year The Theatre was broken up; its remains were carried across the river and used in the construction of the Globe Theatre, Southwark. The plaque was unveiled by the actress Lilian Braithwaite.

At 56 Mortimer Road (formerly 13 Trafalgar Terrace), De Beauvoir Town, N1, is a plaque put up in 1983 in memory of the zoologist **Philip Henry Gosse** (1810–1888) and his son, the writer and critic **Sir Edmund Gosse** (1849–1928) ❷ . P. H. Gosse was a self-trained naturalist and a great populariser of natural history in Victorian England. In November 1848 he married Emily Bowes (1806–1857), a writer of Christian tracts and fellow member of the Plymouth Brethren. 'Without a single day's honeymoon', the couple came to live in this modest terraced house, built a few years before and then known as 13 Trafalgar Terrace.[1] It belonged to Philip's formidable mother Hannah, who removed herself to nearby lodgings soon after. The couple's only child, Edmund, was born at the house the following year. Although it was not an easy birth, Philip's laconic diary entry reads, 'E. delivered of a son. Received green swallow from Jamaica'.[2] Edmund spent his early life at number 56 in an atmosphere of deep religious devotion and seclusion. In the early 1850s, the family spent time in south Devon, where P. H. Gosse turned his attention to marine biology. In May 1853 he helped to establish the world's first public aquarium at London Zoo, and in autumn of that year the family decamped to a larger house in Islington; Emily Gosse described their home in Mortimer Road as having been 'hallowed by many sweet associations'.[3] Edmund Gosse enjoyed a successful career as a biographer, literary critic and journalist. His most enduring work is the autobiographical *Father and Son* (1907), subtitled 'A Study of Two Temperaments', which recalls the difficult relationship between the two men named on the plaque.

The music-hall artiste **Marie Lloyd** (1870–1922) ❸ is commemorated at 55 Graham Road, Dalston, E8. Born Matilda Wood in Hoxton, in a house now demolished, Marie Lloyd made her stage debut at the age of four-teen and met with immediate success. During her career she inspired enormous affection in Hackney

HACKNEY

and beyond, performing songs such as 'My Old Man' and 'A Little of What you Fancy Does you Good'. In 1887, aged seventeen, she married a racecourse tout, Percy Courtenay (1862–*c*.1933), by whom she was already pregnant, and in 1888 they went to live at Graham Road. Courtenay relied on Lloyd to support him, which she was able to do thanks to her growing success. She typically performed in three shows a night in London; she also made long tours of the provinces, and played in New York in the autumn of 1890. Generous and gregarious, Lloyd filled her home with family, friends and fellow performers such as Dan Leno and Harry Relph, known as 'Little Tich'. Courtenay felt excluded from this extended 'family', and the marriage quickly fell apart. On the back of Lloyd's successful excursions into pantomime, they moved to a larger house in Lewisham in 1891, but separated three years later and were divorced in 1905. Her plaque, unveiled in 1977, was awarded by the GLC; ironically, Marie Lloyd had once been hauled before the Licensing Committee of its predecessor, the LCC, to answer the charge that her material was vulgar. Never short of repartee, she acquitted herself ably.

In Ram Place, off Chatham Place, Hackney, E9, is a row of workshop buildings in which are embedded the remains of the Old Gravel Pit Chapel, where a Presbyterian congregation met from 1715 to 1810 (fig. 148). On the north side of the building, close to its eastern end – and now obscured from its former sightline on Morning Lane by a block of housing – is a GLC plaque of 1985 commemorating the scientist, philosopher and theologian **Joseph Priestley** (1733–1804) **4** , who was minister here from 1791 to 1794.[4] Priestley was a major figure of the British Enlightenment, now remembered primarily for his discovery of oxygen, but better known in his day for his controversial views on theology and politics. His espousal of non-established religion and support for the French Revolution led to his being driven from his home in Birmingham by riots, from which Hackney provided a refuge. In London, where he lived from 1791, Priestley's notoriety caused him to be shunned by most members of the Royal Society – including Henry Cavendish, who had known him for a quarter of a century – though he was dined by the leading Whig parliamentarians Richard Brinsley Sheridan and Charles James Fox. His laboratory and library were reinstated at a new home in Clapton, which has been identified as the large house that stood on the southern corner of Lower Clapton Road and Clapton Passage until the 1880s. Priestley continued to publish theological and scientific pamphlets, and lectured on history and natural philosophy at Hackney New College. 'On the whole, I spent my time at Hackney even more happily than ever I had done before', he recalled.[5] After England went to war with revolutionary France – of which Priestley was an honorary citizen – he judged that 'my own situation, if not hazardous, was become unpleasant', and – having preached his last sermon on 30 March 1794 – he decamped with his family to the United States, where he spent the remainder of his life.[6]

A dissenter of an earlier generation was the novelist **Daniel Defoe** (1661–1731) **5** , who is commemorated by a plaque on the side (Defoe Road) elevation of 95 Stoke Newington Church Street, N16 (fig. 146). Defoe had enjoyed a varied career as businessman, journalist, spy and political agitator by the time he took a lease on the house that stood on this site, an event which

148   A view of the interior of the Old Gravel Pit Chapel before its mid-nineteenth-century alteration. Joseph Priestley was minister here between 1791 and 1794. [Courtesy of London Borough of Hackney Archives]

Far right 149   Daniel Defoe's Stoke Newington house in a view of 1724 by T. H. Crawford, executed during the novelist's time at the address. The building was demolished in about 1865. [Courtesy of London Borough of Hackney Archives]

DANIEL DEFOE'S HOUSE AT STOKE NEWINGTON, 1724.

most authorities date to 1708. His son-in-law Henry Baker called it 'a very handsome house', but most accounts tell of a nondescript building of barrack-like solidity in the Queen Anne style, to which Defoe's addition of two flat-roofed wings did no favours (fig. 149).[7] Here he wrote his first and most famous novel, *Robinson Crusoe* (1719), followed by *Captain Singleton* (1720) and *Moll Flanders* (1722), among others. In his spare time, Defoe experimented with pruning and grafting in his kitchen garden, beyond which a four-acre (1.6 ha) pleasure ground provided grazing for horses and – in 1709 – a place of encampment for Protestant refugees from Louis XIV, whose cause Defoe publicly pleaded. He remained in Stoke Newington until 1730, when, pursued for political reasons over a long-forgotten debt, he made over the lease of the house to Baker as a dowry for his daughter Sophia, and ended his days unhappily in City lodgings. The LCC erected the plaque in 1932 on number 95, then the North Star public house; it marks the approximate centre of Defoe's old home, which would have straddled the present Defoe Road and was demolished in about 1865.

At 50 Durley Road, N16, on the slopes of Stamford Hill at the far north of the borough, is a small house built in the 1880s that was once the home of **Ebenezer Howard** (1850–1928) **6** , the pioneer of the garden city movement. Howard had lived at several addresses in Stoke Newington and Stamford Hill before moving to number 50 in 1899, the year in which he formed the Garden City Association as a vehicle to promote his dream of a new form of settlement. This was intended to combine the best of town and country, and – more importantly – to embody service to community rather than self-interest. In 1898 Howard published *Tomorrow: A Peaceful Path to Real Reform*, which was reissued four years later under its better-known title of *Garden Cities of Tomorrow*. It summed up the ideas he had formed and expounded over the previous thirty years; his niece Ethel recalled that 'it was something of an affliction as a schoolgirl to be invited to go for a walk with an Uncle and then to have a Utopian town described at great length . . . I nobly tried to feel interested'.[8] In 1903 Howard's Garden City Pioneer Company purchased land at Letchworth, Hertfordshire, on which to build the first garden city. Howard moved into one of the newly built houses after the death of his wife Lizzie at Durley Road in the autumn of 1904. Other garden cities developed according to his principles included Welwyn Garden City (Howard's home from 1920), Wythenshawe, near Manchester, and Radburn, New Jersey, USA. Howard was knighted a year before his death; as he held this honour for such a brief period, it was omitted from the plaque, which was unveiled in 1991.

NOTES

1 Edmund Gosse, *Father and Son: A Study of Two Temperaments*, ed. James Hepburn (Oxford, 1974), p. 7. In a footnote (p. 179) Hepburn tentatively – but incorrectly – identifies the house as the present number 70.

2 Ibid, p. 7

3 Ibid, p. 10

4 An error in the manufacture of the plaque means that the date given is 1793, not 1791.

5 Joseph Priestley, *Autobiography of Joseph Priestley* (Bath, 1970), p. 130

6 Ibid, p. 132

7 Brian Fitzgerald, *Daniel Defoe: A Study in Conflict* (London, 1954), p. 214

8 Robert Beevers, *The Garden City Utopia* (London, 1988), p. 44

HACKNEY

150   The interior of the dining room of Sir Emery Walker's house at 7 Hammersmith Terrace, which remains much as he left it, with antique furniture, oriental rugs and ceramics, and Morris & Co. fabrics and wallpapers. [© Country Life]

HAMMERSMITH AND FULHAM

The borough of Hammersmith and Fulham stretches from Putney Bridge and Wandsworth Bridge in the south to Wormwood Scrubs, Old Oak Common and Kensal Green Cemetery – the final resting place of many eminent Londoners – in the north. Until 1834, Hammersmith was part of the single large parish of Fulham and was mainly agricultural, with built development only along King Street and on the riverside. Well into the nineteenth century, Fulham was still largely comprised of orchards and market gardens, with a scattering of older developments at New King's Road, Parsons Green and Walham Green, and a chain of substantial riverside mansions in large gardens, of which only Fulham Palace and Hurlingham House have escaped redevelopment. It is in the narrow strip of land running beside the Thames west of Hammersmith Bridge that much of the borough's architectural charm, and most of its blue plaques, are to be found. One prominent figure in the area's history, however, has been commemorated with a private – rather than a blue – plaque. This is WILLIAM MORRIS, who lived at Kelmscott House, 26 Upper Mall, from 1878 until his death. For eighteen years, this elegant late eighteenth-century house was the focus for many artistic, literary and political movements of Morris's day.

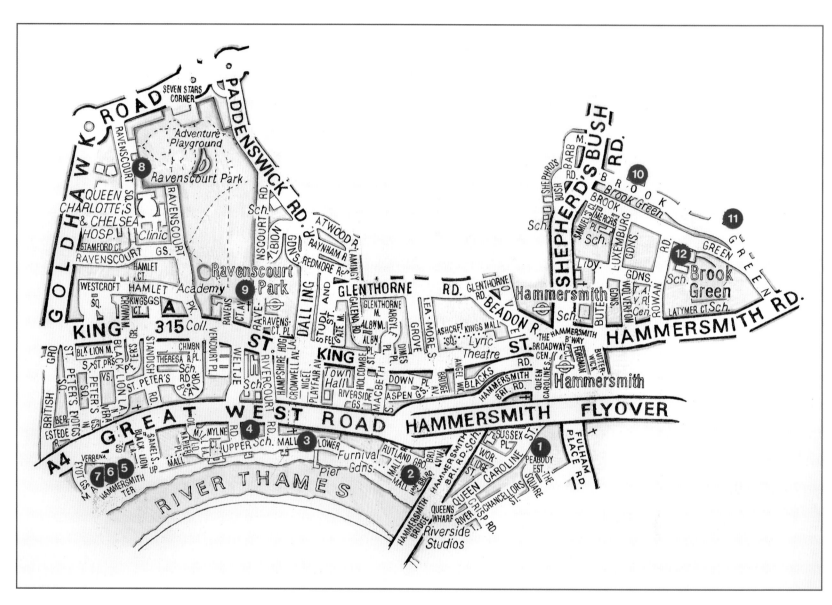

HAMMERSMITH AND FULHAM

Academy, felt able to say that 'no painter has been so internationally famous in his lifetime'.[1] Brangwyn, who was born in Bruges and was active as a painter from his teens, first leased Temple Lodge, a stuccoed Regency villa standing in a large garden, in 1900. In about 1908, having failed to persuade his alcohol-dependent wife Lucy (1875–1924) to move to the country, the painter built a double-height studio projecting forward to the right of the house; this was overlooked by a gallery from the first-floor room that Lucy used as a sitting room and where, according to Rodney Brangwyn, she sat 'feeling neglected, reading, sewing, or watching through a window her husband at work below'.[2] Here, in his studio, Brangwyn entertained eminent guests, such as the Crown Prince of Sweden, and produced some of his most important works; of special note are the British Empire Panels (1925–32), intended as murals for the House of Lords but rejected as being too colourful and flamboyant, and now on display in Swansea's Guildhall. In 1930 Brangwyn left London for good, moving to The Jointure in Ditchling – the Sussex home which he had bought in 1918. Temple Lodge was left in the hands of a caretaker until he gave up the lease in 1935.

To the west of Hammersmith Bridge – built in 1883–87 to the designs of SIR JOSEPH BAZALGETTE – is Lower Mall, W6. Its buildings, many with verandas and balconies, date from the seventeenth century and later, and face south across the Thames. Number 9 Lower Mall – an early nineteenth-century house, with tall French windows leading from the first-floor drawing room to the balcony – bears an English Heritage plaque put up in 1992. It commemorates the actor **George Devine** (1910–1966) ②, who was Artistic Director of the Royal Court Theatre, Chelsea, from 1956 to 1965. Devine lived here from 1954 until his separation from his wife Sophia, née Harris (1900–1966), in 1960. Sophia – who ran the theatrical design company Motley's with her sister Margaret and Elizabeth Montgomery – continued living at number 9 until her death. Born in Hendon, Devine began his theatrical career at Oxford University, where he appeared as Mercutio with John Gielgud and Peggy Ashcroft in a celebrated performance of *Romeo and Juliet* (1932). He went on to revolutionise stage training and production at the London Theatre Studio in Islington, which he ran with the French actor-director

151 Frank Brangwyn in his studio at Temple Lodge, 51 Queen Caroline Street, 13 October 1909. [© Hammersmith and Fulham Archives & Local History Collection]

At 51 Queen Caroline Street, W6, is a remnant of pre-twentieth-century Hammersmith: Temple Lodge, now The Gate Vegetarian Restaurant and Church of the Christian Community. Approached through a walled courtyard, Temple Lodge was once the house and studio of the artist **Sir Frank Brangwyn** (1867–1956) ①, whose residence here between 1900 and 1930 is marked by an English Heritage plaque erected in 1989 (fig. 151). Such was Brangywn's fame in his prime that SIR GERALD KELLY, President of the Royal

155

Michel Saint-Denis. As Artistic Director of the English Stage Company at the Royal Court Theatre, Devine encouraged a new generation of actors, directors and writers, and brought the theatre to international prominence. Between 1956 – when *Look Back in Anger* was first produced – and 1965, he staged 150 plays, nearly a hundred of them by young playwrights, such as John Osborne, Edward Bond and Arnold Wesker. The plaque was unveiled on Devine's birthday by the film and theatre director Lindsay Anderson; those present on the day included Sir John Gielgud, Billie Whitelaw, Alan Bates, Frank Finlay and others associated with Devine's work at the Royal Court. Also present was Devine's partner, Jocelyn Herbert, the daughter of SIR ALAN HERBERT; she lived with him from 1960 until his death and worked as designer on many of his productions.

Upper Mall, W6, begins with Sussex House, a building of *c*. 1726 set behind a high wall. Opposite, with gardens running down to the river's edge, is 15 Upper Mall, which bears a GLC plaque of 1974 commemorating **Thomas James Cobden-Sanderson** (1840–1922) ③ , who founded the Doves Bindery and Doves Press in this house and later lived and died here (fig. 152). Thomas Sanderson was born in Alnwick, Northumberland, and at the age of forty-two married Annie (1853–1926), the daughter of the Liberal MP RICHARD COBDEN, adding her name to his own. He trained initially in medicine and the law but, influenced by his suffragette wife and by the socialist views and artistic tastes of WILLIAM MORRIS and EDWARD BURNE-JONES, he established a reputation first as a binder and later as a printer of fine books of exemplary design in the Arts and Crafts manner, a term that Cobden-Sanderson is credited with coining. It was at number 15 – an early eighteenth-century house then joined to the neighbouring property, now number 13 – that the Doves Bindery was founded in March 1893, continuing in operation until 1921. From 1909 number 15 was also home to the Doves Press, which Cobden-Sanderson established with EMERY WALKER in 1900 at 1 Hammersmith Terrace; the press published fifty titles between 1901 and 1916. Although he leased 15 Upper Mall from 1893, Cobden-Sanderson did not reside permanently in the house until 1917; instead, he lived nearby at addresses including 7 Hammersmith Terrace (1897–1903) – which he sold to Walker – and 24 Upper

Mall (1908–9). Cobden-Sanderson's philosophical temperament, as indicated in his published journals, led him in search of a unifying principle in life and, tragically, to paranoia and religious zealotry. The Doves Press ceased production when in autumn 1916 he tipped the distinctive type into the river at Hammersmith Bridge to prevent Walker from making use of it. It took Cobden-Sanderson nearly a month of furtive nightly trips to 'bequeath' to the Thames the punches and matrices, as well as the type, thereby making it impossible for Walker to recast it.[3]

Number 48 Upper Mall, the end house of a short terrace built in 1880–83 facing the river, bears a plaque installed in 1991 in honour of the artist **Eric Ravilious** (1903–1942) ④ . The plaque – placed on the building's side elevation to Weltje Road, where the main entrance is located – commemorates the time he spent with his wife and fellow artist Tirzah Garwood (1908–1951) in the lower flat between 1931 and 1935, when they moved to Bank House, Castle Hedingham, Essex. Born in Acton, Ravilious trained at the Royal College of Art,

153 *The Stork at Hammersmith* (1932) – painted by Eric Ravilious during his time at 48 Upper Mall – depicts the view from the north side of the Thames east towards Hammersmith Bridge. [© Towner Art Gallery, Eastbourne, East Sussex, UK / The Bridgeman Art Library]

where his tutor was PAUL NASH. Like Nash, he became a war artist, but was also commissioned captain in the Marines and died at the age of thirty-nine in an air-sea rescue mission off Iceland. Ravilious is known as a watercolourist and an engraver, whose works are in an evocative English style and demonstrate a strong sense of design. In addition to his paintings of rural scenes, aeroplanes, battleships and the machinery of war, he produced wood engravings for the Golden Cockerell Press and designs for Josiah Wedgwood & Co., including a series based on his paintings of the Oxford and Cambridge Boat Race as seen from the Hammersmith riverside. While living at number 48, he spent many weekends at Brick House, Great Bardfield, Essex, which he shared with fellow artist Edward Bawden. Ravilious's work from this period includes many landscapes of Essex, as well as paintings of local scenes, such as *The Stork at Hammersmith* (1932) (fig. 153), and the murals that he and Tirzah painted for the Midland Hotel in Morecambe (1933; destroyed).

The mid-eighteenth-century buildings of Hammersmith Terrace, W6, have long gardens running down to the embankment wall, diverting the public path away from the riverside to run behind what were conceived as the backs of the properties. The first of the three houses in Hammersmith Terrace to have been commemorated is number 3, the home from 1905 to 1912 of **Edward Johnston** (1872–1944) **5** , the master calligrapher. The plaque, proposed by the Society of Scribes and Illuminators and erected in 1977, employs the style of lettering known as Johnston sans serif, commissioned in 1916 by FRANK PICK as a new and distinctive alphabet; it is familiar from its use for official signs and notices on the London Underground (figs 154 and 155). The font came to typify the calligraphy of the early twentieth century, and is still in use today. Johnston was born in Uruguay and trained initially in medicine, a career he abandoned in favour of the practice and teaching of lettering and illumination, in which he was encouraged by W. R. LETHABY. In 1899 Johnston started teaching at the Central School of Arts and Crafts; his students included Eric Gill and COBDEN-SANDERSON, for whose Doves Press he designed initials and headings. With his lectures, and the publication of works such as *Writing & Illuminating, & Lettering* (1906) and *Manuscript and Inscription Letters* (1909), Johnston proved influential in Europe and America,

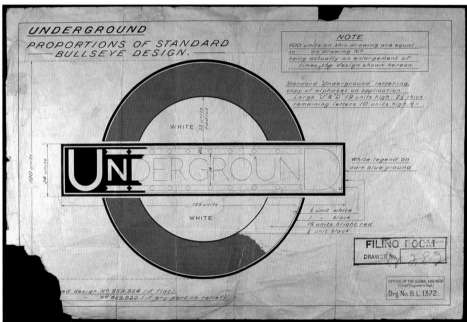

Top 154 The plaque to Edward Johnston, erected in 1977 at 3 Hammersmith Terrace. The distinctive Johnston sans serif was used for its inscription. [© English Heritage. Photograph by Derek Kendall]

Bottom 155 A design by Edward Johnston for the iconic London Underground roundel, c.1925. [London Transport Museum © Transport for London]

rapher and antiquary. It was unveiled in 1959 by his daughter Dorothy (1878–1963) – who lived here until her death – at a ceremony organised by the William Morris Society and the Kelmscott Fellowship. It is recorded that, at the age of five, Emery Walker formed 'a determination to live some day in one of those tall old houses that look upon the river between Hammersmith and Chiswick'.[5] In December 1879 he moved to 3 Hammersmith Terrace, and in 1903 succeeded COBDEN-SANDERSON at number 7, where he lived until his death thirty years later. Walker met WILLIAM MORRIS in 1883, and the pair became friends and associates, with shared interests in design and socialism. With Walker's advice and help, Morris founded the Kelmscott Press in 1890, which was run successively from three addresses in Upper Mall: numbers 16, 14 and (after 1894) 21. The press produced over fifty hand-printed works with type and ornaments designed by Morris. In 1900 Walker set up the Doves Press in partnership with Cobden-Sanderson, but increasingly suffered the consequences of his associate's paranoia. Walker enjoyed close ties with the Arts and Crafts movement in the Cotswolds, especially after 1922, when he spent much time at Daneway, his house in Gloucestershire. After his death, the interior and contents of 7 Hammersmith Terrace were lovingly preserved by his daughter Dorothy, and then after her own death by her nurse and companion, Elizabeth de Haas (1918–1999). In order to safeguard its future, Miss de Haas bequeathed the house to the Emery Walker Trust, which owns it today. As a consequence, number 7 remains much as it was left at Walker's death, replete with antique furniture, oriental rugs and ceramics, Morris & Co. fabrics, wallpapers and linoleum, pieces of furniture designed and formerly owned by Philip Webb, and items given by the Morris family (fig. 150). Walker and his wife Mary (1849/50–1920) were close friends of Morris's daughter, May, who lived next door at 8 Hammersmith Terrace from 1893 until 1923.

Number 12 Hammersmith Terrace, the home of the author, humorist and reformist MP **Sir Alan Herbert (A. P. H.)** (1890–1971) ❼ , was commemorated with a blue plaque in 1990, the centenary of Herbert's birth. Herbert signed the lease on number 12 in January 1916, while on leave from military service in France, and moved in with his wife Gwendolen (1894–1988) the fol-

and created a whole school of calligraphy in Britain. Gill – who from 1905 to 1907 lived at nearby 20 Black Lion Lane, Hammersmith (demolished) – later said of Johnston, 'He profoundly altered the whole course of my life and all my ways of thinking'.[4] In 1912 Johnston moved from Hammersmith Terrace to Ditchling, Sussex, where Gill had settled five years earlier and where FRANK BRANGWYN was later to live.

At 7 Hammersmith Terrace is a plaque erected by the LCC to **Sir Emery Walker** (1851–1933) ❻ , the typog-

lowing month, dying here fifty-five years later. He was called to the Bar in 1918, joined the staff of *Punch* – for which he wrote the notable series of articles 'Misleading Cases in the Common Law' – in 1924, and was elected as an Independent MP for Oxford University in 1935. Herbert's novel *Holy Deadlock* (1934) took as its theme the antiquated state of the law of divorce, and was instrumental in influencing public opinion, to the extent that his reforming Matrimonial Causes Bill became law in 1937. Herbert's novels include *The House by the River* (1920) and *The Water Gypsies* (1930), both clearly influenced by the area in which he lived. He also wrote lyrics, including those for the 1950 musical *Bless the Bride*. Herbert loved swimming in the Thames and preferred to commute to the House of Commons on his boat, *Water Gipsy*.

At 11 Ravenscourt Square, W6, an LCC plaque of 1952 honours the novelist Marie Louise de la Ramée (1839–1908), better known by her pen name 'Ouida' 8 , a childish corruption of the name Louise. Ouida was born in Bury St Edmunds, the only child of the Frenchman Louis Ramé and his English wife Susan, née Sutton (d. 1893). In 1857 she moved to London with her mother and grandmother and by 1859 they were living at Bessborough House, 11 Ravenscourt Square, an early Victorian semi-detached villa. It was while living here that Ouida published her first story, 'Dashwood's Drag' (1859), in *Bentley's Miscellany*. She made her reputation with *Under Two Flags* (1867), which sold millions of copies, earning the author a small fortune. A satirical attack on her output by Lord Strangford in the *Pall Mall Gazette* in 1867 paradoxically helped to establish a vogue for her stories, which were admired for their fast pace and romantic heroes. In all, Ouida produced forty-four works of fiction, including *Held in Bondage* (1863). After her grandmother's death in September 1866, she and her mother left Ravenscourt Square, and by the end of the year they were living in apartments at 51 Welbeck Street, Marylebone, W1. The following year Ouida moved to the newly opened Langham Hotel, where she entertained on a lavish scale and gleaned information for her novels from her guests, almost all of whom were men. The poet William Allingham described her as being 'dressed in green silk, with a clever, sinister face, her hair let down, small hands and feet, and a voice like a carving-knife'.[6] Ouida's extravagance, however,

outran her income, and in autumn 1871 she and her mother moved to Italy, where she declined into increasing eccentricity and poverty.

Number 19 Ravenscourt Road (formerly Shaftesbury Road), W6, the surviving half of a former pair of semi-detached mid-nineteenth-century houses, bears a GLC plaque to the stained-glass artist **Christopher Whitworth Whall** (1849–1924) 9 , who lived here from 1899 to 1921; between 1906 and 1924, his studio was based nearby at 1 Ravenscourt Park. Whall entered the Royal Academy Schools in 1867, where he came under the influence of LEIGHTON. He converted to Roman Catholicism in 1879, and in the same year gained his first commission designing windows for the Rosminian Order of Charity at the newly restored St Etheldreda's, Ely Place, Holborn; most of this work was destroyed during wartime bombing. In 1889 Whall joined the Art Workers' Guild and met the architect J. D. Sedding, who commissioned him to create windows for the Lady Chapel of St Mary's, Stamford; he later designed glass for Sedding's Holy Trinity Church, Sloane Street, Chelsea. Whall went on to become the leading stained-glass artist of the Arts and Crafts period, influential not only through his work, but also through his writing, his teaching and his association with the leading architects of the day. Perhaps his most outstanding achievement was the glass for the Lady Chapel and Chapter House at Gloucester Cathedral (1898–1913), which brought him commissions from South Africa and America. His work is distinguished by bold use of colour and contrasts, and his figures reflect his own character, 'gentle, friendly, great-hearted'.[7] In later years, Whall collaborated with his daughter Veronica (1887–1967), and – despite the onset of leukaemia – continued working right up to his death at his final home, 37 Harvard Road, Gunnersbury, W4.

A plaque commemorates 84 Brook Green, W6, a late Victorian red-brick house, both as the base of **the Silver Studio**, founded in 1880, and the home of its directors, **Arthur Silver** (1853–1896) and his sons **Rex Silver** (1879–1965) and **Harry Silver** (1881–1971) 10 (fig. 156). Over the course of eighty-three years, the Silver Studio produced nearly 30,000 designs, mainly for furnishing textiles and wallpapers, but also for complete interiors, dress fabrics, stencils, plaster-

work, metalwork, furniture, book jackets and advertisements. Its major customers were Liberty and Sanderson. Under the direction of Arthur – a friend and contemporary of WILLIAM MORRIS and WALTER CRANE – the Silver Studio became a major exponent of British Art Nouveau. However, the influences on its designs were always varied, and included the Japanese, Persian and Scandinavian styles. To accommodate the firm's increasing production, Arthur added a studio to

84 Brook Green in 1886, and in 1893 Rex bought the property immediately behind number 84, 3 Haarlem Road. These two properties were disposed of after the Silver Studio moved to the Corner House, 1 Haarlem Road, in 1912, where it remained until its closure in 1963. Number 1 Haarlem Road was also Rex's home and he continued to live there until his death. The plaque was proposed by Middlesex Polytechnic (now University), which holds the archive and research collection of the studio. It was manufactured by Neal French at the polytechnic's Ceramics Department, a unique departure, and was unveiled in January 1981, coinciding with the Silver Studio Centenary Exhibition held at the Museum of London.

The engraver and painter **Sir Frank Short** (1857–1945) 11 lived from 1893 to 1944 at 56 Brook Green, a mid-nineteenth-century terraced house. His plaque was installed by the LCC in 1951, the twenty-year rule having been waived when the proposer – Short's daughter, Dorothea – offered to pay for the plaque and its installation, which cost just under £32. After working initially as an engineer, Short studied at the National Art Training School (later the Royal College of Art), South Kensington, where he was encouraged by RUSKIN to revive the art of mezzotint engraving. His superb prints of works by J. M. W. TURNER quickly established his reputation, and regular visitors to his studios – first at 5, then at 8 Wentworth Studios, Manresa Road, Chelsea, and finally at Brook Green – included WHISTLER, who sought Short's advice on the technical aspects of etching and printing. Unlike previous practitioners of the art, Short often engraved outdoors, producing works such as *The Night Picket Boat at Hammersmith* (1916) and *Ebb Tide, Putney Bridge* (1925). From 1910 to 1938, he was President of the Society of Painter-Etchers, and for many years served as the Director of the Etching and Engraving School of the Royal College of Art.

Dominating the south side of Brook Green is St Paul's Girls' School, built in 1903 to designs by Gerald Horsley. From 1905 until the time of his death, the school served as the workplace of one of England's greatest composers, **Gustav Holst** (1874–1934) 12 . Born in Cheltenham, of Swedish ancestry, Holst was brought up in a musical environment. At the Royal College of Music, where he studied composition, his fellow students included Ralph Vaughan Williams. Finding that he needed an income to support his work as a composer, Holst took to teaching in 1903. Two years later, he was appointed Director of Music at St Paul's, a position he retained until the end of his life. At the school, he composed music for his pupils to perform, such as his well-known *St Paul's Suite* for strings (1912–13). In 1913 the Holst Wing was added to the right of the main school building. It was here – in a specially constructed soundproof music room, a haven of peace and solitude (fig. 157) – that Holst composed most of his works from *c.* 1914 to 1933, including his masterpiece, *The Planets* (1914–17). The plaque was unveiled in 2004 as part of the school's centenary celebrations.

NOTES

1 Rodney Brangwyn, *Brangwyn* (London, 1978), p. 302
2 Ibid, p. 158
3 *The Journals of Thomas James Cobden-Sanderson* (London, 1926), vol. II, p. 304
4 Eric Gill, *Autobiography* (London, 1940), pp. 118–19
5 *The Times*, 21 March 1958, p. 12
6 Elizabeth Lee, *Ouida: A Memoir* (London, 1914), p. 49
7 *ODNB*, vol. LVIII, p. 345

HAMMERSMITH AND FULHAM

158 The plaque to Caroline Chisholm, 'the emigrants' friend', at 32 Charlton Place, part of a terrace built in 1795. [© English Heritage. Photograph by Derek Kendall]

ISLINGTON

The borough of Islington was created in 1965 – an amalgamation of the metropolitan boroughs of Islington and Finsbury. It stretches from the northern edge of the City of London to the slopes of Highgate Hill and Crouch Hill some four miles (6.4 km) to the north. Old Islington village, together with north Clerkenwell – the western part of Finsbury – were once renowned as spas, and long maintained a reputation as places of recreation for Londoners. Being adjacent to the City, the southern part of Clerkenwell and the adjacent parish of St Luke's were built up early, but slum clearances brought a decline in population during the nineteenth century as offices and work-shops moved in. By contrast, north Clerkenwell and Islington saw a vast surge in its resident population; development of the area proceeded apace from the 1810s, and it became home to many professional artisans and City clerks, of whom Mr Pooter, the character invented by GEORGE GROSSMITH and his brother Weedon, was a fictitious embodiment. Following a long period of economic decline, Islington was 'rediscovered' in the 1960s, and has become a byword for gentrification. This is particularly true of the area around Islington Green, where many of the blue plaques are situated.

At 21–23 Chiswell Street, EC1, a modern office block close to the boundary with the City, there is a plaque to **William Caslon** (1692–1766) ❶ , the typefounder, whose distinctive Hebrew, Italic and Roman fonts were used for almost every book printed in English until about 1780; some are still in use today. A Worcestershire man, who was originally apprenticed as an engraver, Caslon opened his first type foundry in Clerkenwell in 1716, before moving to premises off Old Street in 1727. In 1737 he moved to what was then 62 Chiswell Street, a large, plain building with four principal storeys, where he lived as well as worked. Being fond of chamber music, Caslon installed an organ at the house, where parties were fuelled by his home-brewed ale. He retired in 1750, but his business was carried on in Chiswell Street by his son, the younger William Caslon (1720–1778), and transferred across the road to numbers 82–83 in 1909. During the Second World War, both the old and the new foundry buildings were destroyed. Caslon's plaque, which was put up by the LCC in 1958, was a late incidence of a site, rather than an original building, being marked. Following the demolition in 1989 of the anonymous office block that bore the LCC roundel, English Heritage oversaw the re-fixing of the plaque to its equally undistinguished successor.

A plaque at 47 City Road, EC1 – one of the few elaborate, highly coloured Doulton plaques to survive – commemorates **John Wesley** (1703–1791) ❷ , the

evangelist and founder of Methodism (figs 159 and 160). Wesley's home from 1779 to 1791, number 47 is substantially the same as when he lived here, and is preserved as a memorial to him, having been restored in 1897–98. Next door is Wesley's chapel (1777–78); this is the mother church of the denomination, though the formal separation of Methodism from the Anglican communion came after the death of its founder. Born in Lincolnshire, Wesley was ordained priest in 1728 and experienced a religious conversion ten years later, under the influence of Moravians he encountered in North America. Assisted by his brother CHARLES WESLEY, he oversaw the growth of Methodism, an evangelical movement that emphasised the role of personal salvation and appealed especially to the poorer classes; in 1739 a headquarters was established at the Foundry (demolished) in what is now Tabernacle Street, Shoreditch. In April 1777 Wesley laid the foundation stone of the new City Road chapel, which was designed by GEORGE DANCE THE YOUNGER, and spent his first night at the newly completed number 47 in October 1779. By then he was well into his seventies, yet there was little let-up in his life of itinerant, open-air preaching. 'I look upon all the world as my parish', he had said in 1739, when upbraided for trespassing on another parson's patch.[1] Wesley was notable as an early opponent of slavery, and for the dim view he took of conspicuous consumption; he was particularly vehement on the subject of elaborate hats worn by women. It was at City Road that Wesley died, with a final expression of confidence in the presence of his Maker; he was buried in a small graveyard behind the adjacent chapel. The plaque was proposed in 1925 by the then-

ISLINGTON

BLIND & CRIPPLED GIRLS AT WORK.

161 A contemporary postcard showing John Groom – wearing his habitual top hat – together with some of the disabled and blind girls who made artificial flowers from workshops in and around Sekforde Street. [Reproduced by permission of Livability / John Grooms (LMA collection)]

162 A coloured etching of the clown Joseph Grimaldi 'illuminating the entrance to Old Gutter Lane', 1833. [© V&A Images / Victoria and Albert Museum, London]

incumbent minister, the Rev. George H. McNeal. Problems in its manufacture meant that after the unveiling ceremony on Whit Monday in 1926 it was discreetly removed by the LCC for re-firing.

Strong religious impulses likewise motivated the philanthropist **John Groom** (1845–1919) ❸ , who founded workshops for disabled girls in the neighbourhood of his home at 8 Sekforde Street, EC1 (fig. 161). A devout Anglican, John Alfred Groom was born in Clerkenwell and, typically for the area, ran an engraving business from a glass-fronted shed in the garden of his house. He put his remaining energies into improving the lot of destitute, disabled and blind girls, whom he engaged to manufacture artificial flowers, an industry which was widespread in north Clerkenwell from the mid-nineteenth century. In the poorer districts, Groom cut a distinctive figure in his frock coat and top hat, though apparently he donned a flat cap when busy with his favourite recreation – watching Chelsea FC. Groom started his first charity – the Watercress and Flower Girls' Christian Mission – in 1866, and opened workshops in numerous houses in Sekforde Street before moving to the nearby Woodbridge Chapel in 1894. The purpose-built 'flower factory', constructed in 1908–10 at 1–7 Sekforde Street, was known – jarringly, to modern sensibilities – as the 'New Crippleage'. By 1913 there were nearly 260 girls at work there, earning between ten and fifteen shillings a week. Number 8 Sekforde Street forms part of a

terrace dating from 1826 and was Groom's home from 1875. It remained in his family when, for the last decade of his life, he moved to an orphanage he founded at Clacton, Essex. The English Heritage plaque was proposed by the charity John Grooms, which continues its founder's work and had its head office in Sekforde Street until 1967. It was unveiled in 1997 by the Lord Mayor of London; in attendance were Maud Waterer and Ruth Siddell, two former Grooms flower girls.

A plaque to the clown **Joseph Grimaldi** (1778–1837) ❹ (fig. 162) may be seen at 56 Exmouth Market, EC1 – formerly 8 Exmouth Street and, before 1819, 8 Braynes Row.[2] Born into a family of entertainers originally from Italy, 'Joey' Grimaldi made his professional debut – as Guzzle the Drinking Clown – in 1800. He became the unchallenged 'king of clowns' after eclipsing his rival and sometime sidekick, John Baptist Dubois; a vital figure in shaping pantomime as we know it, Grimaldi shone in serious roles too. He died at his home at 22 Calshot Street (formerly 33 Southampton Street), Islington; it was there that a plaque was erected by the LCC in 1938, but it was

MR GRIMALDI AS CLOWN.
ILLUMINATING THE ENTRANCE TO OLD GUTTER LANE.

removed when the area was cleared for new housing in 1960. A new plaque went up in 1989 in Exmouth Market, which had been Grimaldi's home from 1818 to 1829. DICKENS, who edited Grimaldi's voluminous memoirs, wrote that after 1820 his subject suffered 'little or nothing but one constant succession of afflictions and calamities, the pressure of which nearly bowed him to the earth'.[3] One of Grimaldi's remaining pleasures was to drink with friends at the Myddelton's Head, a pub that lay close to Sadler's Wells Theatre. The latter had been his stamping ground for more than thirty years; the ailing clown gave a farewell performance there on St Patrick's Day 1828, after which he wept 'with an intensity of suffering that it was painful to witness and impossible to alleviate'.[4] The following day, his home in Exmouth Market was besieged by fans. Apart from the addition of a shop front, it is the only early house on this side of the street to have retained most of its eighteenth-century character.

Edward Irving (1792–1834) **5** , the founder of the Catholic Apostolic Church, is commemorated at 4 Claremont Square (formerly 4 Myddelton Terrace), N1. Just as the followers of JOHN WESLEY were often known as Wesleyans, those who followed Irving were described as Irvingites; likewise, the formal establishment of a separate church body came after the founder's death. Unlike the Methodist Church, however, the Catholic Apostolic Church – which preached the imminence of Christ's second coming – has now all but vanished, though the influence of its teaching may be found in contemporary Pentecostalism. A tall, imposing figure, Irving was originally a Church of Scotland minister and first preached in London in 1822. His fiery sermons attracted many fashionable people to the Caledonian Chapel in Hatton Garden, including the Foreign Secretary GEORGE CANNING. Later, members of Irving's flock were known to swoon and speak in tongues, and in 1833 he was expelled from the Church of Scotland for heresy. Irving appears to have moved to number 4 early in 1824, not long after his marriage to Isabella Martin; the house, then newly built, formed part of Myddelton Terrace, which later became the west side of Claremont Square. As one biographer has remarked, the charismatic preacher chose an address 'far further from a fashionable neighbourhood than he need have done with his adequate stipend'.[5] One visitor was THOMAS CARLYLE, who commented on the prettiness of the

drawing-room furnishings; Isabella Irving seems to have been less enamoured, and had returned to Scotland with most of the household effects by September 1824. Irving himself kept number 4 as his London base until 1827, during which time he attended the first of the Albury conferences, held at the Surrey village of that name, which led in 1835 to the establishment of the Catholic Apostolic Church. From 1853 its main London church was in Gordon Square, Bloomsbury; today, it is known as the University Church of Christ the King. When, after some delay, the plaque was erected in 1982, it was felt that the original intention to call Irving a 'divine' was 'both archaic and vague', though the term does seem peculiarly appropriate to him.[6]

At 26 Batchelor Street (formerly Chapman Street), N1, a plaque honours the artist **Thomas Hosmer Shepherd** (1793–1864) **6** . Shepherd's artistic talent was apparent from an early age, as was that of his brother, George Sidney Shepherd, with whom he collaborated. Thomas soon became known for his lively drawings and watercolours of Regency and early Victorian London. His first and greatest success – *Metropolitan Improvements . . . London and its Environs in the Nineteenth Century* (1827), with text by James Elmes – was followed by contributions to works including Charles Frederick Partington's *Natural History and Views of London* (1835). Shepherd lived at number 26 from about 1819 to 1842, when the road was called Chapman Street. He never made a handsome living from his art; a surviving advertisement offers his services as a drawing master, and confirms that he worked as well as lived at this address. The house is part of a typical yellow-brick Regency terrace and was marked with a plaque in 1976, following a suggestion made by the Islington Society. At that time it belonged to the GLC, having once been scheduled for redevelopment. The inscription describes Shepherd as an 'artist who portrayed London'; his topographical views also covered Bristol, Bath and Edinburgh, but he spent most of his life in Islington, dying at 5 Cloudesley Street, just north of Batchelor Street.

In 1823 the essayist **Charles Lamb** (1775–1834) **7** (see also p. 561) – a leading figure in literary London, counting COLERIDGE and HAZLITT among his intimates – moved to 64 Duncan Terrace, N1 (fig. 163), then a part of Colebrooke Row. Charles lived here with

ISLINGTON

167

163 Number 64 Duncan Terrace and its LCC plaque to Charles Lamb in a photograph of April 1942. The house – which formerly fronted onto the New River – has been much altered since Lamb's day. [© City of London, LMA]

neither double coach-house nor wings', and added that 'like its tenant, it stood alone'.[8] Another visitor, the severely myopic writer George Dyer, fell into the adjacent – and now covered – New River; ironically, he was renowned for his poor personal hygiene. On the house – now named Colebrooke Cottage – is a terracotta-coloured LCC plaque dating from 1907. It includes the pen name 'Elia' that Lamb used for his contributions to the *London Magazine* during the period of his residence, which terminated when he and Mary moved to Enfield in 1827. Since that time, substantial changes have been made to number 64, which is no longer detached.

At 32 Charlton Place (formerly 3 Charlton Crescent), N1, a GLC plaque of 1983 commemorates **Caroline Chisholm** (1808–1877) ⑧ (fig. 158), a philanthropist and 'the emigrants' friend', who was born in Northampton and married a soldier, Captain Archibald Chisholm (1798–1877). He was stationed at Madras, where Caroline opened a school for the daughters of British soldiers, but it was in Sydney – whence the couple moved in 1838 – that she accomplished her major philanthropic work: the establishment of a home and employment agency for destitute girls. The Chisholms returned to England in 1846, and between 1849 and 1852 lived at what was then 3 Charlton Crescent. From this house, which is part of a terrace dated 1795, Caroline ran the Family Colonisation Society, which encouraged emigration to Australia – especially of women, in order to redress the gender imbalance in the colony. Prospective migrants were interviewed here by Caroline, who was described by a contemporary journalist as 'a sedate, matronly lady, with . . . a fascinating manner that at once seizes upon you', and were shown models of the berths in which they would sleep on the long voyage down under.[9] With five children, conditions can have been scarcely less cramped at the frugally furnished house, to which DICKENS – an active publicist of the scheme – was a visitor. Somewhat unflatteringly, it has been postulated that Caroline partly inspired him to create the character of Mrs Jellyby in *Bleak House* (1852–53). Caroline Chisholm travelled once more to Australia in 1854, returning to London twelve years later; she and her husband lived in humble circumstances in Highgate and in Fulham, where she died. The portrait of this self-effacing woman has since adorned Australian banknotes, and

his sister MARY LAMB, for whom he cared after her release from an asylum; together, the siblings had written *Tales from Shakespear* [sic] in 1807. Lamb described their Islington home as 'a cottage, for it is detached; a white house with six good rooms. The New River . . . runs . . . close to the foot of the house; and behind it is a spacious garden . . . You enter without passage into a cheerful dining-room . . . and above is a lightsome drawing-room, three windows, full of choice prints. I feel like a great lord, never having had a house before'.[7] Less flatteringly, THOMAS HOOD called it 'a cottage of Ungentility, for it had

as a Roman Catholic – an adherence that was held against her by many of her contemporaries – she has been nominated for beatification.

On the north side of Islington Green, N1, at number 10–11, a distinctive rectangular blue plaque is fixed above the shop sign of what is now a bookshop. It records the building's former incarnation as the **Collins Music Hall** 9 , an early and famous example of its kind (fig. 164). The first music hall on the site was built as the annexe to a public house, the Lansdowne Arms, in 1861–62; soon after this time, the premises were acquired by the singer and sometime bankrupt Samuel Thomas Collins Vagg (1826–1865), who performed as Sam Collins. Though he died barely eighteen months later, the venue – which was completely

rebuilt in 1897 – bore his name for most of its existence. The strict propriety observed during the hall's early years led to its being nicknamed 'the chapel on the Green'; nonetheless, its popularity was such as to cause complaints of overcrowding. The decline of music hall saw the building used from the 1930s for revue, repertory and strip shows, until a fire in 1958 ended its life as a performance venue. The plaque, unveiled in 1968, was erected at the suggestion of the architects who renovated the building as offices.

Among those who trod the boards at the COLLINS MUSIC HALL in its heyday were Charlie Chaplin, Gracie Fields, MARIE LLOYD and **George Leybourne** (1842–1884) 10 – otherwise known as 'Champagne Charlie', star of music hall (fig. 165). Leybourne's plaque is at 136 Englefield Road, N1, part of a terrace dating from the mid-1860s. Born in Gateshead, Leybourne began his performing career in the 'penny gaffs' of the East End. His defining moment came with the 1866 song 'Champagne Charlie', which he performed as a 'swell' in what was then regarded as a subversive imitation of upper-class dress and manners. Corporate sponsorship followed (from champagne

Below 164   A photograph by Donald Mcleish showing the exterior of the Collins Music Hall, Islington Green, in 1926. The building was damaged by fire in 1958, and – having been greatly remodelled – now houses a bookshop. [Courtesy of the Mander & Mitchenson Theatre Collection, London]

Below right 165   Cover of the music sheet for the hit song 'Champagne Charlie' (1866), made famous by George Leybourne. [© V&A Images / Theatre Collections]

ISLINGTON

makers), as did other hits, including 'The Daring Young Man on the Flying Trapeze' (1866). Leybourne has been described as Britain's first pop star, and his reported disillusionment with the emptiness of 'celebrity' has contemporary resonance. It is a grim irony that his early death at the age of just forty-two was probably drink-related; he died in Englefield Road, where, being in reduced circumstances, it appears that he had rented rooms. It is not known precisely how long he lived here, though a contemporary newspaper stated that it had been his home for some time. The 1944 film *Champagne Charlie* starred Tommy Trinder, another Collins Music Hall regular, and used plenty of dramatic licence in the portrayal of its eponymous hero. Leybourne's daughter Florence was married to another star of the music hall, ALBERT CHEVALIER.

At 52 Canonbury Park South, N1, is an English Heritage plaque to **Louis MacNeice** (1907–1963) ⑪ , the poet. Born in Belfast, into a family originally from Galway, MacNeice lived through the partition of his homeland and spent most of his time in England, a hybrid heritage that was reflected in his poetry. The MacNiece household – his wife, the singer and actress Hedli Anderson (1907–1990), two children and an Italian maid, Teresa – moved to Canonbury from Essex in 1947, while the poet was himself away in India on a production assignment for the BBC: his day job. In his absence, MacNeice urged his wife to 'shamelessly exploit all the chaps we know' in getting their furniture and effects shifted.[10] The family were delighted with the house, where MacNeice undertook collaborative work on a new translation of Goethe's *Faust* (1951); his rudimentary knowledge of German, he maintained, made for a freer, more readable rendition. DYLAN THOMAS was a house guest here in July 1948. For eighteen months during 1950 and 1951 the house was let, as MacNeice took a post at the British Institute in Athens; it was largely during this time that he wrote *Ten Burnt Offerings* (1952), a collection whose title readily evokes – as the poet intended – the ennui of middle age. In the summer of 1952, the family finally left Canonbury for Clarence Terrace, overlooking Regent's Park. First, it was intended to commemorate MacNeice there, but consent was not forthcoming; the plaque was put up instead at number 52, a semi-detached property of yellow brick dating from 1845.

Number 8 Canonbury Square, N1, bears a bronze LCC plaque to **Samuel Phelps** (1804–1878) ⑫ , the tragedian. Born in Devonport, Phelps made his London stage debut rather late in life, in 1837. His time in Canonbury – where he lived from *c.* 1845 until 1867, soon after the death of his wife Sarah – coincided with his stint as the highly successful actor-manager of Sadler's Wells Theatre (1844–62). It was during this time that he finally emerged from the shadow of William Charles Macready, the pre-eminent actor of his generation. Offstage, Phelps was noted for his 'retiring manner and modest mode of living', which did not prevent him suffering from the widespread contemporary prejudice against thespians when he found his daughter barred from admission to a nearby private school.[11] As a business manager, he made a commercial success of more than 1,600 Shakespeare productions at Sadler's Wells, a venue that had traditionally been known for its low-brow entertainment; many of these were plays that had not been seen for two hundred years. Their appeal crossed class boundaries, and the editor of the *Theatrical Journal* – an Islington neighbour of Phelps – paid tribute to the leading role he had taken in establishing the theatre 'in public favour for the acting of the legitimate drama'.[12] Number 8, which is part of a Georgian terrace of 1821, was marked with a plaque in 1911.

North of Highbury Corner is another bronze plaque: that to the statesman **Joseph Chamberlain** (1836–1914) ⑬ (see also pp. 313–14) (fig. 166). It marks his boyhood home, 25 Highbury Place, N5, the end house of a terrace developed by John Spiller in 1776–77. Chamberlain – who is best remembered for his

166   The bronze LCC plaque to Joseph Chamberlain at his boyhood home, 25 Highbury Place. [© English Heritage. Photograph by Derek Kendall]

achievements in social reform and for his stint as Colonial Secretary at the time of the Boer War – lived at this address from 1845 to 1854, together with his father Joseph (1796–1874), his mother Caroline (1808–1875) and seven younger siblings. During this time he first attended a school in nearby Canonbury Square run by the Rev. Arthur Johnson, 'an excellent teacher, and one to whom I owe much', Chamberlain reflected later.[13] In 1850 he progressed to University College School, then in Gower Street – an establishment favoured by Unitarians, the denomination to which the Chamberlain family belonged. There he excelled at mathematics and imbibed a lifelong distaste for sport; 'he possessed a good deal of individuality and a strong will, and always wanted to take the lead in anything that was going on among his companions', one contemporary recalled.[14] After leaving school, young Joseph was first set to work in the office of his father's shoemaking business in Milk Street in the City. Not long after his eighteenth birthday, he was sent to Birmingham, where the family held an interest in a screw manufacturing firm. Thus were Chamberlain's business and political careers fashioned in the Midlands; however, he demonstrated his enduring affection for his boyhood home by naming his Birmingham residence 'Highbury'. Three LCC plaques were raised to Chamberlain in the capital within six years of his death, of which two survive.

NOTES

1   *The Works of John Wesley*, ed. F. Baker, vol. XXV (Oxford, 1980), p. 616

2   It is now accepted that Grimaldi was born in 1778, rather than in 1779, as is stated on the plaque.

3   *Memoirs of Joseph Grimaldi*, ed. Charles Dickens (London, 1838, repr. 1968), p. 261

4   Richard Linklater, *Grimaldi: King of Clowns* (London, 1955), p. 196

5   Andrew Landale Drummond, *Edward Irving and his Circle* (London, 1937), p. 81

6   Report of 12 November 1981 on blue plaque file.

7   *The Letters of Charles Lamb*, ed. W. C. Hazlitt, vol. II (London, 1886), p. 132

8   E. V. Lucas, *Life of Charles Lamb*, vol. II (London, 1905), p. 116

9   Margaret Kiddle, *Caroline Chisholm* (London, 1950), p. 161

10 Jon Stallworthy, *Louis MacNeice* (London, 1995), p. 357

11 Shirley S. Allen, *Samuel Phelps and Sadler's Wells Theatre* (Middletown, Connecticut, 1971), p. 95

12 Ibid

13 N. Murrell Marris, *The Right Honourable Joseph Chamberlain: The Man and the Statesman* (London, 1900), p. 17

14 Ibid, p. 18

ISLINGTON

KENSINGTON AND CHELSEA

Of all the administrative amalgamations that accompanied the birth of the GLC in 1965, it was perhaps the forced marriage of Kensington and Chelsea that generated the most vociferous resentment. This emanated largely from the Chelsea side, possibly because it has the longer history as a place of significance, having been a fashionable riverside retreat since the sixteenth century. Kensington was little more than a small roadside village, albeit with a royal palace from the late 1600s, until its rapid nineteenth-century evolution into a fashionable suburb and – from the development of the museums precinct and the Royal Albert Hall – a centre for leisure and learning. As the birthplace of Queen Victoria, Kensington was awarded its royal prefix in 1901. Modern 'Chelsington' is the smallest London administrative district outside the City, and the most densely populated, with a high concentration of blue plaques; in terms of numbers, it runs neck and neck with Camden, behind only Westminster. Among the figures commemorated, the arts are well represented, bearing testament to the appeal of Kensington and Chelsea to writers, painters and musicians. Then as now, most denizens of the royal borough were comfortably off, though the bohemian atmosphere clings on in its northern and western reaches. Administratively, parts of West Kensington belong to the borough of Hammersmith and Fulham, but are treated under this chapter.

The blue plaque to George F. S. Robinson, Marquess of Ripon, at 9 Chelsea Embankment (see p. 196).
[© English Heritage. Photograph by Derek Kendall]

167 Cheyne Walk and its plaques
to the artists Philip Wilson Steer (at
number 109) and John Tweed (at
number 108). [© English Heritage.
Photograph by Derek Kendall]

CHELSEA

It has been said of Chelsea that 'No district of London has housed so many illustrious, brilliant, extraordinary characters'.[1] In the sixteenth and seventeenth centuries, people came to the area to 'take the air' and to enjoy boating, bathing and other riverside activities. The eighteenth and nineteenth centuries saw considerable development on both sides of King's Road, the loss of some of the early mansions that had dominated the banks of the Thames, and a dramatic increase in population. Still, for much of the 1800s, Chelsea retained its village atmosphere, and the picturesque, quiet streets stretching along and north of the river became a refuge for lovers of solitude and calm. The area's special connection with artists and writers began in the 1830s and lasted until after the Second World War, when property prices rose and the bohemian atmosphere was lost. The biggest change, however, had come in 1874, with the construction of the Embankment and the loss of many historic landmarks, including the ancient river wall. The parish of Chelsea is wedge-shaped. For the most part, its northern boundary is formed by the Fulham Road and its southern boundary by the Thames; to the east is Belgravia and to the west Fulham.

168 The installation of the plaque to Sir Charles Wentworth Dilke at 76 Sloane Street in October 1959. Dilke was born and died at this address, a remarkable connection of sixty-seven years. [© Getty Images]

1911) **1** (fig. 168). Born at number 76, Dilke inherited the house in 1869 from his father – Charles Wentworth Dilke (1810–1869), 1st baronet, a leading Commissioner of the Great Exhibition – and died here at the age of sixty-seven: a remarkable period of residence in the same building, and one that saw him rise to become one of the great Liberal thinkers of the later nineteenth century. Dilke's first book, *Greater Britain* (1868), was published in the year that he entered Parliament as Liberal MP for Chelsea. Dilke played a key part in the introduction of universal male suffrage, the legalisation of the position of trade unions and the limitation of hours of work. But for the fact that he was cited – it appears unjustly – in divorce proceedings in 1885, Dilke might well have gone on to become Liberal leader in the House of Commons. His importance continued to be felt into the early twentieth century, especially in the field of foreign and imperial affairs. Dilke – whose second wife was Emilia Francis, née Strong (1840–1904), a prominent art historian and trade unionist – was extremely well connected: 'I have known everyone worth knowing from 1850 until my death', he declared, when he knew his demise was imminent.[2]

Cadogan Place, SW1 – set back from Sloane Street behind gardens – was described by CHARLES DICKENS as the connecting link 'between the aristocratic pavements of Belgrave Square and the barbarism of Chelsea'.[3] The street bears blue plaques to two very different historical figures. The first, at 44 Cadogan Place, is one of three official London plaques to honour **William Wilberforce** (1759–1833) **2** (see also p. 295 and pp. 337–8), the opponent of slavery. Suffering the after-effects of a severe bout of influenza, Wilberforce came to London from Bath in order to consult a doctor. He arrived at number 44 – lent to him by his cousin, Mrs Lucy Smith – on 19 July 1833. Ten days later – on 29 July – Wilberforce died in the house. The installation of a plaque, unveiled in 1961, represented an exception to the LCC's rules: despite the fact that Wilberforce had already been commemorated, and that number 44 had been altered architecturally – its original plain early nineteenth-century façade was transformed in about 1850 – the council was won over by its significance as the place where Wilberforce died and one of the only surviving London houses associated with him. It was also noted

Chelsea's north-east corner was known in the late eighteenth century as Hans Town – in honour of its former landowner and resident, SIR HANS SLOANE – and later as Upper Chelsea. It forms the core of the Cadogan family's estate, and was built up in the 1770s by the architect Henry Holland and redeveloped from the 1870s. Sloane Street, SW1, stretching north from Sloane Square, is dominated today by modern blocks of flats, but number 76 is a reminder of late Victorian elegance. This house, on the corner of Sloane Street and Pavilion Street, bears a plaque erected in 1959 to the statesman and author **Sir Charles Wentworth Dilke** (1843–

CHELSEA

177

that, although Wilberforce's greatest work – his leadership of the campaign against slavery – was carried on while he was in Battersea Rise, it was completed – with the bill abolishing slavery in British territories – on 26 July 1833, during Wilberforce's brief time in Chelsea. He is said to have exclaimed, 'Thank God that I should have lived to witness [this] day'.[4] Visitors to number 44 in Wilberforce's final days included LORD MACAULAY and the young W. E. GLADSTONE.

Number 30 (formerly 3) Cadogan Place, a building of *c*. 1800, was the home from 1812 to 1815 of the actress **Dorothy Bland** (**Mrs Jordan**) (1762–1816) ❸ (fig. 169). Born in Ireland, Dora began her acting career in 1779 in Dublin, where she acquired a reputation for playing 'breeches' parts. In 1782, under the stage name of Mrs Jordan, she came to England, where her talents began to be fully recognised. Three years later, with her engagement at the Theatre Royal, Drury Lane, she entered the limelight. Over the course of her career, Mrs Jordan played a number of roles, but her forte was comedy. WILLIAM HAZLITT said that, 'Her face, her tears, her manners were irresistible. Her smile had the effect of sunshine, and her laugh did one good to hear

it'.[5] Jordan's domestic life was notorious: after several liaisons, she became in 1790 the mistress of the Duke of Clarence, later King William IV. During their twenty-year relationship, Dora bore him ten children, all given the surname FitzClarence. The couple lived together as husband and wife, mainly at Bushy House in Bushy Park, Surrey, of which William was Ranger, until they finally separated in 1811. Although Jordan's stage success continued, her final years were marked by tragedy: suffering increasingly from ill-health, she retired from the theatre in 1815, and left Cadogan Place for France, where she died alone and in poverty. The plaque was erected in 1975, at the suggestion of Jordan's great-great-grandson, Thomas Goff.

Analogous to MRS JORDAN is the late Victorian and Edwardian actress **Lillie Langtry** (1853–1929) ❹ , commemorated with a plaque at 21 Pont Street, SW1.[6] Born Emilie Charlotte Le Breton in Jersey – she later became popularly known as the 'Jersey Lily' – Langtry initially made her name as a 'professional beauty' and, more controversially, as the mistress of the future King Edward VII. In 1881 she made her professional stage debut in Oliver Goldsmith's *She Stoops to Conquer*. Although – unlike Mrs Jordan – she was never regarded as a great actress, Langtry was nonetheless immensely popular: HERBERT BEERBOHM TREE once told her, 'It doesn't matter what you play, Lillie. You hold all London in the palm of your white steel hand'.[7] She was also ambitious: in the 1880s she made extensive tours of America, and in 1900 took over the management of the Imperial Theatre, Westminster, which she rebuilt in magnificent style. By the time of her final stage appearance in 1918, Langtry had gained a reputation as an actress, writer and manager, and played a notable part in making the stage respectable for women. She lived at number 21, an elaborate brick building on the corner of Pavilion Road, from spring 1891 until spring 1897, when she moved to 2 Cadogan Gardens. Langtry shared the house with Jeanne-Marie (1881–1964), her daughter by Prince Louis of Battenberg, and decorated it sumptuously: a reporter described her bedroom as 'famous in its way, with its curtains, and draperies of pale-blue brocade, its toilet-table, gold-framed mirror, and its bed curtained with brocade and net, enriched with an appliqué of lace' (fig. 170).[8] On her marriage in 1899 to Hugo de Bathe, eighteen years her junior, Langtry went to live in

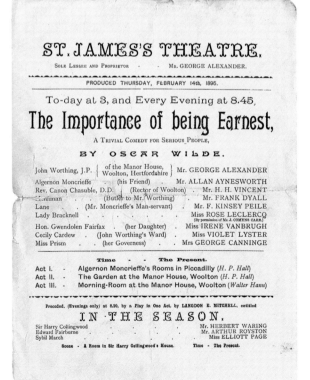

dermere's Fan (1892) and _The Importance of Being Earnest_ (1895) both premiered at the St James's (fig. 171). Alexander – together with his wife Florence, née Théleur (1857/8–1946), who assisted him in his work and acted as his fashion and artistic director – lived at 57 Pont Street, a large late nineteenth-century red-brick house, from 1895 until 1918; Sir George's death occurred at his country house, Little Court, Chorley Wood, Hertfordshire.

Number 8 Lennox Gardens, SW1 – an imposing corner house built in 1880–86 to designs by George Devey – was the home of the Polish statesman **Count Edward Raczyński** (1891–1993) ⑥ . Raczyński, a national hero, dedicated his life to the struggle for independence of the Polish people. Born in Zakopane into a prominent noble family, he joined the foreign service of the newly created Polish Republic in 1919. After distinguished service as his country's representative to the League of Nations, he was appointed Ambassador to the Court of St James's in November 1934. The apogee of his period in office came in 1939, with his involvement in the assistance pact that effectively brought Britain into the Second World War. After the fall of France in 1940, the Polish government-in-exile fled to London, and for

170 The interior of Lillie Langtry's bedroom at 21 Pont Street in a photograph of c.1895. The room was 'famous in its way, with its curtains, and draperies of pale-blue brocade'. [© Getty Images]

Monaco. In 1925 number 21 was incorporated into the Cadogan Hotel, which had been based at 75 Sloane Street since 1888; Langtry was allowed to stay in her old room whenever she was in London. It was at the hotel that Lillie's great friend and mentor Oscar Wilde was arrested in 1895. The unveiling of Langtry's plaque in 1980 was performed by her granddaughter, the television presenter Mary Malcolm, and was celebrated with 'a banquet of truly Edwardian proportions'.[9]

At 57 Pont Street, a plaque of 1951 honours another figure associated with the dramatic arts, the actor-manager **Sir George Alexander** (1858–1918) ⑤ , who was born George Alexander Gibb Samson in Reading. He was interested in the theatre from an early age, and made his professional stage debut in 1879. Soon after, he was engaged by Henry Irving, whose training was invaluable but arduous: 'five or six hours of rehearsing with Irving often left [Alexander] on the brink of tears'.[10] The most successful phase of Alexander's career began in 1890, when he signed the lease of the St James's Theatre, King Street, St James's; there – in the years before his death – he built up a reputation for his casting of talented actors and for promoting the work of British dramatists. He was closely associated with Arthur Pinero and Oscar Wilde: _Lady Win-_

171 Detail from a programme for the premiere (14 February 1895) of Oscar Wilde's _The Importance of Being Earnest_ at the St James's Theatre, managed by Sir George Alexander. [© V&A Images / Theatre Collections]

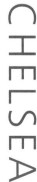

fifty years – while the Soviet-backed regime held sway in Warsaw – Raczyński was one of its key figures; he was never again to return to his native land, though he lived – just – to see Poland liberated from the Soviets. Between 1954 and 1972, Raczyński was one of the members of the Council of the Three, the presidential body of the Polish government-in-exile, and served as the exiled government's President from 1979 until his retirement in 1986. Raczyński – who lived for twenty-two years at 7 Armitage Road, Golders Green, NW11 – moved in 1967 to a flat at 8 Lennox Gardens. It remained his home until his death here at the age of 101, during which time heads of state, politicians, historians and writers all made their way to his door. It was at number 8 that Raczyński penned such works as his autobiography, *In Allied London* (1963). The English Heritage plaque was unveiled in 2004 by the Polish Ambassador, Stanislaw Komorowski.

Cadogan Square, SW1, was laid out in the 1880s in the grounds of Sloane Place, or The Pavilion, once the architect Henry Holland's own residence (demolished 1879). Number 75, on the square's south side, was the home from December 1922 until November 1930 of the novelist **Arnold Bennett** (1867–1931) **7** . Born in Staffordshire, Bennett spent his early life in the Potteries; these, described as the 'Five Towns', were to form the setting for many of his novels. In 1891 Bennett moved to Chelsea, where he spent some of his formative years with the Marriott family, who introduced him into literary and musical circles and encouraged him as a writer. Modelling his prose style on the work of the French masters, and in particular Flaubert and Balzac, Bennett wrote his first novel, *A Man from the North* (1898), while living in Chelsea. In the first decade of the twentieth century, based in France, he produced a steady stream of works, including *Anna of the Five Towns* (1902), *The Truth about an Author* (1903) and *The Old Wives' Tale* (1908). Bennett's second great period of productivity coincided with his return to Chelsea in the 1920s; works written in his flat at 75 Cadogan Square – which he described as 'a rather fine thing in houses' – include *Riceyman Steps* (1923), *Lord Raingo* (1926) and *Imperial Palace* (1930), as well as the weekly column for the *Evening Standard* that made him one of the most influential critics of the day.[11] The plaque – rectangular, so as to fit on the façade of the building – was erected by the LCC in 1958.

Avenue Court, an imposing apartment building of *c.* 1930 in Draycott Avenue, SW3, bears a plaque to the pioneering reconstructive surgeon **Sir Archibald McIndoe** (1900–1960) **8** , who lived in Flat 14 from about 1949 to 1955. Born in New Zealand, McIndoe worked as a surgeon in his home country and in America before coming to London in 1930. His cousin SIR HAROLD GILLIES, the pre-eminent plastic surgeon of the day, took McIndoe under his wing and helped him establish a practice in Harley Street. Soon after the outbreak of the Second World War, McIndoe was appointed consultant plastic surgeon to the RAF. In the following years – based at East Grinstead Hospital – McIndoe's unit carried out extensive surgery on some 3,600 airmen who had suffered severe burns. McIndoe undertook a series of painstaking operations, remodelling faces and reshaping limbs, but his work went beyond the physical; he also restored morale, and through encouragement gave his patients the strength to cope with life. In 1941 his grateful patients – the best known of whom was the airman and author Richard Hillary – formed the Guinea Pig Club. In 2000, on Battle of Britain Day (15 September), many members of the club attended the unveiling of McIndoe's plaque by his widow, Constance.

A plaque on the Blacklands Terrace façade of 25 Draycott Place, SW3, a late nineteenth-century building at the end of a row, honours the Admiral of the Fleet **Earl Jellicoe**, **OM** (1859–1935) **9** . John Rushworth Jellicoe was born in Southampton into a Hampshire family with a long seafaring tradition. He joined the Royal Navy in 1872, and was quickly recognised as a capable leader with a sound grasp of technology. At the gunnery school *Excellent* from 1884, and in subsequent years, Jellicoe was a firm favourite of LORD FISHER. During Jellicoe's time at this substantial house in Draycott Place, where he lived from about 1906 to 1908, he served as Director of Naval Ordnance and Controller at the Admiralty, and was promoted rear admiral (1907) and knighted (1908). On the outbreak of the First World War, he was made Commander-in-Chief of the Grand Fleet. Jellicoe is remembered especially for his direction of the British forces at the Battle of Jutland (31 May 1916), the principal naval engagement of the war. Criticised in some quarters for his choice of tactics – the battle was seen as something of a missed opportunity for the British – Jellicoe was promoted away from active command to become First Sea Lord in December 1916; he was made Admiral of the Fleet in 1919, and served as a popular Governor-General of New Zealand in 1920–24. Jellicoe's plaque was put up in October 1975, the day before a plaque to Fisher was erected in Westminster.

King's Road, SW3 – used from the late seventeenth century until 1830 as a private royal route between Whitehall and Hampton Court – is Chelsea's most important thoroughfare. It is architecturally varied, and in character shifts noticeably from the smart eastern end at Sloane Square to the more intimate western end near Battersea Bridge. The street's predominantly commercial identity explains the presence of only two blue plaques. The first, at 31 King's Road, commemorates the Australian composer, folklorist and pianist **Percy Grainger** (1882–1961) ❿ . One of the great eccentrics of twentieth-century classical music, Grainger grew up in Melbourne, where he made his debut as a pianist in 1894, and studied in Frankfurt. In 1901 he settled in London with his mother, Rose, née Aldridge (1861–1922), who was herself musically gifted. Grainger quickly made his name as a concert pianist, became a private teacher, and mixed with figures such as SIR CHARLES STANFORD, SIR HENRY WOOD and EDVARD GRIEG. The

quality of Grainger's innovatory compositions – his experiments in natural and synthetic sound were well ahead of their time – was quickly recognised by FREDERICK DELIUS. Grainger was also a pioneer folk-song collector and arranger, an aspect of his work that was to influence BENJAMIN BRITTEN. From late 1907 until autumn 1914 – the period of his most intense activity as a composer – Grainger lived above a tobacconist's shop at 31A King's Road; while here, he composed works including *Mock Morris* (1910) and *Handel in the Strand* (1911–12). At the outbreak of the First World War, he and his mother moved to the United States, where Grainger settled permanently in 1921.

The second blue plaque in King's Road is at number 152, a building known as The Pheasantry. Between 1881 and 1914 it formed the showroom of Joubert's, a firm of cabinetmakers and decorators; it was the Joubert family who reworked The Pheasantry in extravagant French style in the late nineteenth century, and they subsequently adapted the building for use as studios. The plaque commemorates the Jouberts' most famous tenant, the ballet dancer **Princess Seraphine Astafieva** (1876–1934) ⓫ , who lived and taught here from autumn 1916 until her death (fig. 172). The daughter of Prince Alexander Astafiev, Seraphine was born in Russia, where she attended the St Petersburg Imperial Ballet School. In 1910 she came to England with Serge Diaghilev's Ballets Russes. Three years later, she retired from the stage to teach ballet, establishing her first school in England in 1915. The following year, her dancing school – the Anglo-Russian Ballet – moved to 1 The Pheasantry, on the first floor of 152 King's Road. Here, Astafieva was to teach and influence countless ballet dancers; her students and visitors included Serge Diaghilev, Margot Fonteyn, Alicia Markova, Anna Pavlova, Anton Dolin and MARIE RAMBERT. The plaque – proposed by the then occupant of number 1, the painter Timothy Whidborne – was unveiled in 1968, in the presence of Markova, Dolin and other of her former pupils.

Number 6 Carlyle Square, SW3, immediately north of King's Road, was the home from 1921 to 1932 of the actress **Dame Sybil Thorndike** (1882–1976) ⓬ . Thorndike's professional debut of 1904 in a production by BEN GREET marked the beginning of a stage career that was to span six decades and result in her becom-

172 A photograph of 1922 showing Princess Seraphine Astafieva and some of her pupils in the studio at 152 King's Road. The young Alicia Markova – who was present at the unveiling of the blue plaque in 1968 – can be seen at the very centre. [© Getty Images]

ing one of the outstanding figures in British theatre. In 1908 – the year she married the actor and director Lewis Casson (1875–1969) – Thorndike first worked with GEORGE BERNARD SHAW, who in 1923 wrote for her the part of St Joan; it was to become her best-known role. Thorndike and Casson's period at 6 Carlyle Square, a house of *c.* 1860, encompassed some of their greatest achievements: while living here, the celebrated thespian couple managed the New Theatre, St Martin's Lane, and in 1931 Sybil was appointed DBE. In a specially extended drawing room on the first floor of number 6, Thorndike rehearsed her many parts, most notably St Joan, which she performed regularly from 1924 – when it opened at the New Theatre – until 1941. The affection in which the house was held by the family – including Sybil's son John Casson (1909–1999), who unveiled the plaque in 1998 – was a major consideration in its being selected for commemoration over 98 Swan Court, SW3, Casson and Thorndike's home from 1937 until their deaths.

St Luke's Rectory, 56 Old Church Street (formerly Church Street), SW3, partially hidden behind high brick walls, was the family home from 1836 to 1860 of **Charles Kingsley** (1819–1875) **13** , the writer. The son of a Church of England clergyman, Rev. Charles Kingsley (1781–1860), and his wife Mary, née Lucas (1787–1873), the younger Charles was born in Devon, and studied in London and at Cambridge. He resolved to become a curate in 1841 and married three years later; as a Christian Socialist who believed in the possibility of reconciling religion and science, Kingsley – a friend of F. D. MAURICE – published a number of controversial works in the decade that followed. He was also active as a teacher – he was Regius Professor of Modern History at Cambridge in 1860–69 – and was an active clergyman, enjoying royal favour. It is, however, for his fictional stories that Kingsley is chiefly remembered; notably, *Westward Ho!* (1855) and *The Water-Babies* (1863). Kingsley spent his adolescence and formative years at St Luke's Rectory; it was from here that he courted Fanny Grenfell (1814–1891), and here that the couple spent their honeymoon. The rest of his life was spent largely at Eversley, Hamshire, where he was rector for over thirty years. The plaque at the rectory – built in *c.* 1725 and much altered in subsequent centuries – was erected in 1979 beside the front door.

At 127 Old Church Street a plaque commemorates the ceramic artist and novelist **William De Morgan** (1839–1917) and his wife, the artist **Evelyn De Morgan** (1855–1919) **14** (figs 173 and 174). One of the most influential of all English ceramicists, famous for his beautiful patterns and richly coloured glazes, William De Morgan was born in Gower Street, Bloomsbury, and was admitted to the Royal Academy Schools in 1859. At first, he turned his attention to designing stained glass and tiles, but following the death of his father in 1871 he moved to 30 Cheyne Row (formerly 8 Great Cheyne Row), SW3, where he established the pottery that would make his name. In 1882 De Morgan moved his works to Merton Abbey, Surrey, where they remained until transferring to Fulham in 1889, two years after his marriage to Evelyn Pickering. For twenty years, the couple lived at 1 The Vale, Chelsea, but in the face of its imminent demolition moved in 1910 to 125 and 127 Church Street, two houses of *c.* 1804 which they set about converting into a single property. At second-floor level there was a large studio, while below was the study in which William – whose Fulham pottery had closed down in 1907 – turned out his literary works; these included the novels *A Likely Story* (1911) and *Ghost Meets Ghost* (1914). Evelyn, meanwhile, continued to paint, produc-

173   A portrait of William De Morgan painted by his wife Evelyn in 1909. The couple lived at 125–127 Old Church Street from 1910 until their respective deaths. [© National Portrait Gallery, London]

174 The exterior of 125–127 Old Church Street, the former home of William and Evelyn De Morgan, in a photograph of 1936. [© City of London, LMA]

ing – among other works – her series of fifteen 'war pictures', which included *The Red Cross* (1916). The couple lived in Old Church Street for the rest of their lives. The plaque was erected in 1937 at the suggestion of Evelyn's sister, Anna Maria Stirling; it features an unusual variant of the LCC's laurel-wreath border.

The sporting painter **John F. Sartorius** (*c.* 1779–1831) **15** was the first occupant of 155 Old Church Street – then also known as Church Lane West or Queen's Elms – one of a pair of houses built in 1806/7; the building later came to be known as 3 Upper Church Lane and 3 Upper Church Street, before being numbered 155 in 1868.[12] Born in London, John Francis was the last of four generations of the Sartorius family to enjoy popularity as a painter of racehorses, hunters and other sporting subjects. He followed the style and subject matter of his father, John Nost Sartorius, which belongs in the tradition of painters such as George Stubbs and Sir Edwin Landseer. Of the sixteen pictures Sartorius exhibited at the Royal Academy, the best known is *Coursing in Hatfield Park* (1806). Sartorius seems to have moved to Chelsea soon after the death of his grandfather, Francis Sartorius, in 1804. He was living at 155 Old Church Street by 1807, two years after his marriage to Zara Adamson, and left some time after 1812. The plaque was erected by the LCC in 1963.

In Elm Park Gardens, SW10, a large square of tall terraced houses laid out from 1875 to designs by GEORGE GODWIN, blue plaques on neighbouring properties commemorate two very different figures. At 32 Elm Park Gardens, a plaque marks the birthplace of the statesman **Sir Stafford Cripps** (1889–1952) **16** , a leading figure in the Labour government elected in 1945. Cripps was born into a political family: his father, Charles Alfred Cripps (1852–1941), later Baron Parmoor, served in the 1924 and 1929 Labour governments, while – on his mother's side – Stafford's uncle and aunt were SIDNEY and BEATRICE WEBB. Number 32 was the Cripps' family home from 1883 until 1900; Stafford's later life was spent mostly in official lodgings and in Gloucestershire. It was only after becoming Britain's youngest King's Counsel in 1927 that Cripps turned from a career in law to one in politics. He joined the Labour Party and became Solicitor-General in 1930. After serving with distinction in this and other positions – including British Ambassador to the Soviet Union (1940–42) – Cripps was made President of the Board of Trade in the 1945 government of CLEMENT ATTLEE, and two years later became Chancellor of the Exchequer. The stringent measures he enforced made his name a byword for post-war austerity. Ill-health forced Cripps's resignation in 1950, and he died two years later. His plaque was unveiled on 24 April 1989, the centenary of his birth.

Next door, at 34 Elm Park Gardens, an English Heritage plaque marks the residence of the entertainer and writer **Joyce Grenfell** (1910–1979) **17** . The only daughter of the architect Paul Phipps and Nora Langhorne, sister of NANCY ASTOR, Joyce was deeply attached to Chelsea and lived in the area for most of her life. She grew up performing at family gatherings and in her late teens began to take acting lessons, but in 1929 gave them up to marry Reginald Pascoe Grenfell (1903–1993), a chartered accountant. In the late 1930s, Grenfell once again began both to entertain and to write; after 1945, her reputation was established with a series of revues and a radio programme, and films that included *The Million Pound Note* (1953) and the St Trinian's series. In 1954 she reached the height of her career with the launch of her own show, *Joyce Grenfell Requests the Pleasure*. This featured some of her finest comic monologues, many of which were fuelled by the foibles and manners of the middle classes. In 1957 Joyce and Reggie

CHELSEA

moved from King's Road to Elm Park Gardens, where they remained until their respective deaths. When Grenfell first heard of the availability of Flat 8 – which occupied the third and attic floors of what had been two separate houses – she remarked, 'Nothing would make me live in Elm Park Gardens . . . where the Victorian houses, built at just the wrong period, are made of what I think of as public-lavatory yellow brick'.[13] Once inside, however, she 'liked it at once', and enlisted the help of her second cousin, Elizabeth Winn, an interior decorator.[14] During her time here, Grenfell remained hugely prolific, even after her retirement from the stage in 1973.

At 28 (formerly 5) Mallord Street, SW3, a GLC plaque marks the idiosyncratic little house built for the painter **Augustus John** (1878–1961) **18** (fig. 175). One of England's best-known twentieth-century artists – and the brother of another well-known painter, Gwen John – Augustus was born in Wales, and studied at the Slade. His work reflects an interest in a wide range of subjects, but it was in portraiture that he excelled, especially during the latter part of his career. Through-

175   Number 28 Mallord Street, built for Augustus John to designs by the Dutch architect Robert Van t' Hoff. The painter referred to the house as his 'damned Dutch shanty'. [© English Heritage. Photograph by Derek Kendall]

out his life, John was an individualist who defied social convention, and in the inter-war years he was taken up by fashionable society as the English bohemian par excellence. He was firmly associated with Chelsea during the early part of the century: in 1903, he founded – with William Orpen as Co-Principal – the Chelsea Art School, and in 1913 decided to build a house in Mallord Street, then a newly created thoroughfare. The designer of number 28 was the Dutchman Robert van 't Hoff; it is said that John went into a Chelsea pub in search of an architect and encountered van 't Hoff at the bar. John later described the house as 'a compromise', adding that van 't Hoff had gone 'as far as to import black Dutch pan-tiles for his high-pitched roof, but with his up-to-date passion for rectangles had eschewed the characteristic curved gable'.[15] Completed by May 1914, number 28 featured a staircase copied from Rembrandt's house in Amsterdam, while the focus was a large studio, where John completed works including the cartoon *Galway* (1916) and the portrait *The Marchesa Casati* (1919). The room, which extended into the garden, was the setting for many raucous parties; these typically included 'not one ugly girl' and ended in 'the most dreadful' orgies.[16] In the early 1930s, with the development of new buildings across the road, John began to feel claustrophobic in number 28, which he referred to as his 'damned Dutch shanty'.[17] The house – which John shared with Dorothy (Dorelia) McNeill (1881–1969), his artist's model and wife in all but name – was sold in 1934 to the singer Gracie Fields.

One of Augustus John's most notable neighbours was the author **A. A. Milne** (1882–1956) **19** , who lived at 13 (formerly 11) Mallord Street during the most creative years of his career (fig. 176). Alan Alexander Milne made his name at *Punch*, for which he worked from 1906 until the outbreak of the First World War. He published his first children's book while still in the Army, the light-hearted fairy story *Once on a Time* (1917), and after demobilisation devoted himself to stage comedy. Milne and his wife Daphne, née de Sélincourt (1889–1971) moved in summer 1919 to 11 Mallord Street (renumbered 13 in 1924) – 'the prettiest little house in London'.[18] Having lived in flats for many years, Milne found it thrilling to live in a house that had 'an outside personality as well as an inside one . . . Any of you may find himself some day in our quiet

176 A. A. Milne and his son Christopher Robin in a photograph of 1926 by Howard Coster. Christopher Robin was born at 13 Mallord Street, the Milnes' home from 1919, and – with his collection of toys – occupied a nursery on the top floor. [© National Portrait Gallery, London]

street, and stop a moment to look at our house; at the blue door with its jolly knocker, at the little trees in their blue tubs . . . at the bright-coloured curtains. We have the pleasure of feeling that we are contributing something to London'.[19] Mallord Street was until 1940 the Milnes' principal base – they also had a country home in Sussex – and it was here that their son Christopher Robin (1920–1996) was born. 'Billy', as he was known, lived in a nursery on the top floor of the house with his nanny, Olive Rand. Works completed during Milne's time here included *When We Were Very Young* (1924), *Winnie-the-Pooh* (1926), *Now We Are Six* (1927) and *The House at Pooh Corner* (1928); these were modelled on Christopher Robin and his toys, which became Pooh, Piglet, Eeyore, Kanga, Roo and Tigger. The works, which won their author international acclaim, were brought vividly to life by the illustrator E. H. Shepard and were later transferred to the screen by Disney.

The poet and novelist **George Meredith**, **OM** (1828–1909) 20 is commemorated with a GLC plaque at 7 Hobury Street, SW10, the end house of a short mid-nineteenth-century terrace. Born in Portsmouth, Meredith was articled to a London solicitor before turning to journalism. In 1849 he married Mary Ellen Nicolls – the widowed daughter of the novelist and poet Thomas Love Peacock – but the union was not happy, and the couple separated in 1857. By later that year, Meredith and his young son Arthur (b. 1853) were living at 7 Hobury Street, where they remained until moving to Esher, Surrey, in 1859. This was a significant period in the writer's life, during which he penned his

first major novel, *The Ordeal of Richard Feverel* (1859). By 1867, when he moved with his second wife to Flint Cottage, Box Hill, Surrey – his home for the remainder of his life – Meredith had achieved considerable literary success. His later works included *The Adventures of Harry Richmond* (1871), his acknowledged masterpiece, *The Egoist* (1879), *Poems and Lyrics of the Joy of Earth* (1883) and the successful *Diana of the Crossways* (1885). Meredith, appointed to the Order of Merit in 1905, was admired by figures such as Oscar Wilde and Thomas Hardy, and had a formative influence on the next generation of writers, including James Joyce and E. M. Forster.

Number 14 Gunter Grove, SW10, was the home of the composer **John Ireland** (1879–1962) 21 during some of the most productive years of his career. At the age of seventeen, Ireland became the youngest person ever to be awarded a fellowship of the Royal College of Organists. From 1904 to 1926, he was organist and choirmaster at St Luke's, Sydney Street, Chelsea, and it was through one of the church's choirboys that Ireland discovered 14 Gunter Grove. He rented a studio – now separately numbered 14A – and a flat here from 1908. In 1915 he purchased the whole house, in which he lived until his retirement in 1939 and which he kept on as his London base until 1953. Gunter Grove offered what Eugene Goossens described as 'the quiet haven of a few intimate friends' – Ireland was an intensely private person – and the detached studio was perfect for teaching and composing.[20] Works produced during Ireland's time here include the Second Violin Concerto (1915–17), *Songs Sacred and Profane* (1929–31), *A London Overture* (1936) and *These Things Shall Be*, a choral work composed for the 1937 coronation of King George VI. In the years 1923–39, Ireland was Professor of Composition at the Royal College of Music, where his pupils included Benjamin Britten.

Cheyne Walk, extending from Albert Bridge to Cremorne Road, bears a remarkable ten plaques. Until the construction of the Embankment in the 1870s, the thoroughfare overlooked the old river wall, a picturesque setting popular with artists and writers. Thomas Carlyle, a famous and long-standing Chelsea resident, described the road as 'a broad highway with shady trees', with 'boats lying moored, and a smell of shipping and tar' (see fig. 179).[21] The thoroughfare's

CHELSEA

177 Sylvia Pankhurst being taken into custody during a women's suffrage protest in Trafalgar Square, 1912. She was arrested and imprisoned on many occasions. [© Time & Life Pictures / Getty Images]

lure lasted into the twentieth century, when it attracted figures such as the campaigner for women's rights **Sylvia Pankhurst** (1882–1960) 22 , who lived at 120 Cheyne Walk, SW10, between 1906 and 1909. Sylvia was the second daughter of Richard Pankhurst, a Manchester lawyer and social reformer, and his wife EMMELINE, who was – with Sylvia and her elder sister CHRISTABEL – to become a major figure in the women's suffrage movement. In the early 1900s, Sylvia combined work for the Women's Social and Political Union, founded in 1903 by Emmeline and Christabel, with training as an artist: between 1903 and 1906 she studied at the Royal College of Art in Kensington. Pankhurst was known for her suffrage militancy – she was imprisoned for the first of many times in 1906, the year she moved to Cheyne Walk (fig. 177). In 1913 she founded the East London Federation of Suffragettes, and the following year launched a newspaper, the *Woman's Dreadnought*; Sylvia was later the author of several books, among them *The Suffragette Movement* (1931). In 1924 Pankhurst left Kensington and Chelsea for Woodford,

Essex, where she ran a tearoom with her partner, Silvio Corio. Her refusal to marry, and the birth of a child out of wedlock, widened a rift with her mother and sister, who were scandalised by the affair and never re-established contact. When Sylvia Pankhurst was first considered for commemoration by the GLC in 1980, her case was rejected, though two years later – the centenary of her birth – it was approved. The plaque was installed in 1985 at 120 Cheyne Walk, the most significant of her London residences to survive.

At 109 Cheyne Walk, another GLC plaque commemorates one of the many artistic figures associated with Chelsea, the painter **Philip Wilson Steer** (1860–1942) 23 (figs 167 and 178). Steer settled in the area in 1885, and was to remain here until his death at number 109, to which he had moved in 1898. A bachelor, he was looked after for much of this period by his devoted nurse and housekeeper, Margaret Raynes, née Jones (d. 1929), whose portrait he painted in 1922. Steer's work was first exhibited at the Royal Academy in 1883 and was initially much maligned by conservative critics. A central figure in the New English Art Club, which he co-founded in 1886 with the aim of encouraging young artists experimenting with new techniques, Steer – together with WALTER SICKERT – formed the nucleus of the 'English Impressionist' school. A breakthrough came in 1909, with the purchase by the Tate of his *Chepstow Castle* (1905) and the staging of a retrospective exhibition of his work. From that time on he was highly respected in the art world, and was a teacher at the Slade for nearly forty years. Steer spent his summers painting landscapes and his winters at his Chelsea home, working on portraits or studies from models. His biographer and fellow artist D. S. MacColl wrote that the 'Chelsea house was . . . one where Steer could set up his rest. Fronting all there was of sun from morning till night, it commanded a view of the river with its barges and old Battersea beyond. When darkness fell a Whistlerian nocturne succeeded'.[22] On the first floor, the front room with its three tall windows

served as 'sitting and painting-room combined', and can be glimpsed in the background of many of Steer's works.[23]

PHILIP WILSON STEER had for a neighbour the sculptor **John Tweed** (1863–1933) 24 , who lived at 108 Cheyne Walk (see fig. 167) from 1896 – the year after his marriage to Edith Clinton, Secretary to the Women's Suffrage Society – until shortly before his death. Born in Glasgow, Tweed studied in London and in Paris, where he met and became friends with Auguste Rodin, whose work he was later to promote. Tweed's career was characterised by a steady stream of portrait statues, and busts of soldiers and statesmen such as JOSEPH CHAMBERLAIN, KITCHENER and CLIVE OF INDIA; in 1912 he completed the monument to the Duke of Wellington in St Paul's Cathedral, which had been begun by ALFRED STEVENS. Originally proposed for commemoration by his daughter Ailsa, Tweed was rejected for a plaque by the LCC in 1952, and the GLC's

178 A tea party on Christmas Eve at 109 Cheyne Walk, the home of Sir Philip Wilson Steer, as depicted in the painting *Steer at Home* (c.1929–30) by Henry Tonks. [UCL Art Collections, University College London, UK / The Bridgeman Art Library]

CHELSEA

179 A nineteenth-century photograph taken from the Thames, showing Cheyne Walk before the creation of the Embankment. The Greaves boatyard is in the foreground and Lindsey House, 96–100 Cheyne Walk, can be seen beyond.
[© RBKC Libraries]

committee was similarly uncertain thirty years later. It was only after the President of the Royal Academy, Sir Hugh Casson, supported Tweed as a candidate for commemoration that a plaque was erected. While living at number 108, Tweed received visitors including BEERBOHM, BELLOC, WHISTLER and LUTYENS. Rodin was a frequent guest, staying at the house regularly between 1901 and 1914. Tweed's friend and patron Lady Marjorie Beckett wrote of 'The Chelsea house, so *perfect* in its modest beauty – with all those fine things,

bronzes and pictures about. What delicious evenings they were – Chelsea could never have excelled itself more in sheer conversation and art than at 108 Cheyne Walk'.[24] Tweed worked in studios nearby; these included 14A Cheyne Walk and, most importantly, 8 The Avenue Studios, Fulham Road.

Numbers 96–100 Cheyne Walk were originally a single property, rebuilt as Lindsey House in 1674 (fig. 179). In 1775 the building was divided into separate dwellings, and by the early 1800s it and the neighbouring properties were known as Lindsey Row; the stretch of road was incorporated into Cheyne Walk in 1876. Number 104 Cheyne Walk (formerly 10 Lindsey Row), on the corner of Milmans Street, formed part of the block, and bears two plaques, both erected on 3 July 1973 (see fig. 33). The first commemorates the artist **Walter Greaves** (1846–1930) 25 , who is remembered – with WHISTLER – as the Chelsea painter par excellence. Greaves was born at 31 (now 34) Cheyne Walk, the son of a boat builder – Charles William Greaves – who had rowed TURNER and other artists to beauty spots on the Thames. As boys, Walter and his brother Henry (1844–1904) decorated the prows of the City barges that were kept at Chelsea, and their father encouraged them to paint river scenes in their spare time. In 1847 the Greaves family moved to 9 Lindsey Row (now 103 Cheyne Walk), and in 1855 – in need of more space – they took on the neighbouring number 10, the building which now bears the plaque. In 1863, after Whistler moved to 7 Lindsey Row (now 101 Cheyne Walk), the brothers became the artist's devoted admirers and assistants, a relationship that was to last some twenty years. On occasion, 'the master' allowed the pair to exhibit their own work, which was clearly labelled 'by pupils of Whistler'. At first, Walter – always acknowledged as the more talented of the brothers – was dismissed as an imitator of Whistler. However, an exhibition of 1911 brought him overnight success. Walter's most famous works include *Hammersmith Bridge on Boat-Race Day* (*c.* 1862) and *Chelsea Regatta* (*c.* 1865). The Greaves brothers lived at 104 Cheyne Walk until 1897, when they moved to Fulham.

The second plaque at 104 Cheyne Walk commemorates one of the building's later residents, the poet, essayist and historian **Hilaire Belloc** (1870–1953) 26 , who lived here in 1900–5 (see fig. 33). Born near Paris to a French father and an English mother, Belloc moved to England early in his life and attended the Oratory School in Birmingham. It was at Oxford that he found his vocation as a writer; in 1896 Belloc published the collection *Sonnets and Verse*, as well as *The Bad Child's Book of Beasts*, characteristic of the comic and satirical verse for which he is best known. In after years he wrote in a variety of genres: fiction, biography, history, politics, travel and theology – he is remembered especially as a polemical apologist for Roman Catholicism.

In the winter of 1899–1900, Belloc and his wife Elodie, née Hogan (1868–1914) moved to London – and to 104 Cheyne Walk – where Belloc began to make the political contacts that would result in his being elected a Liberal MP in 1906. One of Belloc's earliest additions to number 104 was a telephone, the first in Cheyne Walk. Meanwhile, his literary work continued apace. In 1901 Belloc went on the 'pilgrimage' that resulted in one of his most successful books, *The Path to Rome* (1902), later described by its author as 'the only book I ever wrote for love'.[25] By 1905, the Bellocs were longing for open space and could no longer afford to keep the elegant house in Cheyne Walk. The following year they moved to King's Land, near Horsham, Sussex, which was to remain Belloc's home for the rest of his life. There, he continued to write, though his reputation – like that of his close associate G. K. CHESTERTON – was damaged by the anti-Semitic tone of some of his work.

Number 98 Cheyne Walk (formerly 4 Lindsey Row) was the home from 1807 to 1824 of **Sir Marc Isambard Brunel** (1769–1849) and his son **Isambard Kingdom Brunel** (1806–1859), the civil engineers 27 . At the time the plaque was erected, in 1954, it was the only address of the Brunels known to survive in London. Both father and son were immensely important in their field. Sir Marc is known above all for designing and building the first tunnel under the Thames, between Wapping and Rotherhithe, now part of the East London Line (fig. 180). This, the world's first underwater tunnel through soft ground, was begun in 1825 and – in spite of numerous difficulties and disasters – was completed in 1843. During his years at number 98, where he lived with his wife Sophia, née Kingdom (d. 1854), Brunel formed a company to finance the job, ran a mill at Battersea and supervised the education of his son Isambard Kingdom, who had learnt the rudiments of arithmetic and geometry by the age of four. It was in this riverside house that Isambard spent his boyhood, served as assistant to his father and developed the skills that were to result in his greatest achievements: the construction of the Great Western Railway (from 1833), the design of the Clifton Suspension Bridge, Bristol (1836–64) and the construction of ocean-going steamships, the most important of which was the *GREAT EASTERN*, launched in 1859 (see fig. 302). The Brunels moved from Chelsea

CHELSEA

180 A view of 1836 showing the entrance to the Thames Tunnel, designed and built by Sir Marc Isambard Brunel, with the assistance of his son Isambard Kingdom Brunel. The tunnel – which runs between Wapping and Rotherhithe – was the first tunnel under the Thames and opened in 1843. [© City of London]

Sunday 'breakfasts', attended by fellow artists. The art critic W. M. Rossetti wrote of the house in his diary, 'There are some fine old fixtures, such as doors, fireplaces, and Whistler has got up the rooms with many delightful Japanesisms'.[27] Whistler took pains over the house's interior decoration, and – assisted by WALTER GREAVES and his brother Henry – painted murals in the stairway and in some of the rooms. His studio, to the rear of the second floor, was depicted in the background of paintings such as the portrait – *Arrangement in Grey and Black* (1871–72) – of his mother Anna, née McNeill (1804–1881), with whom he lived. Among other works completed at number 96 were *Symphony in White No. III* (1867) and the series of Thames Nocturnes. When the artist left number 96, he was deeply in debt and already involved in a dispute with RUSKIN, who had denounced one of his Nocturnes as a 'pot of paint flung in the public face'.[28] The legal action Whistler v. Ruskin reached court in November 1878, by which time Whistler was living at the White House in nearby Tite Street, designed for him by E. W. Godwin. Whistler died at 74 Cheyne Walk, the address to which he had moved from Paris the previous year.

On 29 September 1810, the novelist **Mrs Gaskell** (1810–1865) **29** was born at 93 Cheyne Walk (originally 1 Belle Vue and later 12 Lindsey Row). The house was the home of Elizabeth Cleghorn Gaskell's parents, William (bap. 1770, d. 1829) and Elizabeth Stevenson (1771–1811), from 1809 until early 1811. They then moved around the corner to 3 Beaufort Row (later 7 Beaufort Street and since demolished). In October 1811 – when young Elizabeth was barely a year old – Mrs Stevenson died, and the child was taken to live with her maternal aunt, Hannah Lumb, in Knutsford, Cheshire; the town was later immortalised as Cranford in Gaskell's novel of that name (1851–53). Although Elizabeth returned to Chelsea to nurse her dying father in 1828–29, she later said – in the voice of one of her novel's narrators – 'I had vibrated all my life between Drumble [Manchester] and Cranford'.[29] Her stories began to appear in 1847, fifteen years after her marriage to the Rev. William Gaskell. Her first novel, *Mary Barton* (1848), with its depiction of the problems of industrial Manchester, brought its author instant fame. It was followed by other works including *Ruth* (1853), a second Manchester novel, *North and South* (1854–55), and a

to Blackfriars in 1824 in order to be closer to the tunnel, which was to make a heavy demand on their time for many years to come.

One of Chelsea's most flamboyant characters, the painter and etcher **James Abbott McNeill Whistler** (1834–1903) **28** , is honoured with an elaborate glazed-ware plaque of 1925 at 96 Cheyne Walk (formerly 2 Lindsey Row).[26] An American by birth, Whistler came to London in 1859 and lived in the capital for much of the remainder of his life. Of his various addresses – several in Chelsea – number 96 was the most significant: it was his home from late 1866 until October 1878, and was where he held his

biography (1856–57) of Gaskell's friend Charlotte Brontë. Elizabeth's last and greatest novel, *Wives and Daughters*, was left unfinished at the time of her death. A bronze plaque (fig. 181) was erected at number 93 in 1913 after Gaskell's biographer, Mrs Ellis H. Chadwick, disposed of the LCC's fears that the house had been rebuilt in the first half of the 1800s; she showed that it did, in fact, date from 1777.

Number 16 Cheyne Walk, SW3, has been known variously as Tudor House and Queen's House; it was once thought – mistakenly – that the house was of sixteenth-century origin and had been occupied by Catherine of Braganza, Queen of Charles II. In fact, the house was built in 1717–19 to the designs of John Witt. It was home to the poet and painter **Dante Gabriel Rossetti** (1828–1882) ③⓪ (see also p. 60 and p. 518), commemorated with a blue plaque in 1949 (figs 182 and 183). Rossetti was one of the foremost artists of the nineteenth century, who in 1848 helped to found the PRE-RAPHAELITE BROTHERHOOD. He settled at 16 Cheyne Walk on 24 October 1862, after the death of his wife and artist's model, Elizabeth Siddal. Some of his best work was produced during his time here, including the paintings *Beata Beatrix* (1864–70), *Monna Pomona* (1864) and *Monna Vanna* (1866), and his collected *Poems* (1870), which established his reputation as a writer. Rossetti invited his brother William Michael (1829–1919), an art critic and editor, to live

181 The design for the bronze LCC plaque to Mrs Gaskell, installed at her birthplace – 93 Cheyne Walk – in 1913.

Below 182 A painting by Henry Treffry Dunn showing D. G. Rossetti and his close friend Theodore Watts-Dunton in the richly coloured ground-floor drawing room of 16 Cheyne Walk, 1882. [© National Portrait Gallery, London]

Above right 183 A contractor installs the blue plaque at 16 Cheyne Walk, the former home of Dante Gabriel Rossetti, in November 1949. [© NI Syndication / The Times]

with him for a time, as well as the poet **Algernon Charles Swinburne** (1837–1909) (see also p. 343), who is commemorated on the plaque. Swinburne was at Cheyne Walk for just over a year – from late 1862 until 1864 – though he was often away. This was a productive time for him in terms of literary activity; he started work on a novel, *Lesbia Brandon* (unfinished), and on the play *Atalanta in Calydon* (1865), which was to become one of his most successful works. During the 1860s and 1870s, number 16 became a meeting place for poets and artists. Rossetti held regular dinner parties, and filled the house with antiques and works of art. In the garden he kept a small menagerie, which included wombats, a kangaroo and a Brahmin bull. Rossetti left Cheyne Walk in early 1882, shortly before his death. Not long afterwards, his former secretary, T. Hall Caine, wrote of the house's neglected appearance: the walls and reveals of doors and windows were covered with 'the tangled branches of the wildest ivy that ever grew untouched by shears', while the windows were 'dull with the accumulation of the dust of years'.[30] Needless to say, number 16 looks rather different today.

At 4 Cheyne Walk an LCC plaque of 1949 honours the novelist Mary Ann Cross, née Evans (1819–1880), better

CHELSEA

184 An etching of Monmouth House, which formerly stood at the north end of Lawrence Street. The building, which comprised four early eighteenth-century properties, accommodated the works of Chelsea China and was also the home of Tobias Smollett. [© RBKC Libraries]

known by her pseudonym, **George Eliot** 31 (see also pp. 342–3). Born in Warwickshire, Eliot moved in 1851 to London, where she wrote for the *Westminster Review* and tried her hand at novel-writing. *Adam Bede* (1859) was the first in a string of books that would establish her as a writer of the first rank; others were *The Mill on the Floss* (1860) and *Middlemarch* (1871–72). Eliot moved to Cheyne Walk with her new husband, the banker John Walter Cross (1840–1924) – more than twenty years her junior – on 3 December 1880. The couple were impressed by the prospect from the house, which had 'an outlook on the river and meadows beyond'.[31] Within days, the Crosses were holding 'little feasts of music' in the evenings, and were becoming reconciled to London life, 'notwithstanding the loss of country quiet light and beauty'.[32] This calm was, however, to be short-lived; Eliot soon fell seriously ill, and died here on 22 December 1880. The house, an imposing brick Queen Anne building, dates from 1718. In 1892 Alfred Beaver described the interior as having 'a wide well-staircase with handsome balustrade and frescoed walls and ceiling, in the style of Sir James Thornhill'.[33]

The discoverer of penicillin, **Sir Alexander Fleming** (1881–1955) 32 , lived from about 1920 until his death at 20A Danvers Street, SW3, a flat occupying the ground and basement floors of a large stuccoed house built in *c.* 1840; he shared the flat with his wife Sareen (1879/80–1949) and their son. Fleming was born in Scotland, the son of a farmer, and qualified as a doctor in 1906. His crucial work was carried out in the years after the First World War, when he served under Almroth Wright as a bacteriologist in the Inoculation Department of St Mary's Hospital, Paddington. Fleming's first notable discovery came in 1922, when he found and isolated a remarkable element that had the power of discovering bacteria; this he named lysozyme. Six years later, by a fortunate accident, Fleming discovered penicillin, a mould spore capable of inhibiting the growth of bacteria. Its practical application was not, however, developed until clinical tests were carried out in 1941 by Howard Florey and Ernst Chain. Once its potential was realised – penicillin saved the lives of thousands during the Second World War – Fleming was showered with honours, and in 1945 received the Nobel Prize jointly with Florey and Chain. Meanwhile, he continued to work in the Inoculation Department

185 The rectangular LCC plaque commemorating Monmouth House – the manufactory of Chelsea China and the former home of Tobias Smollett. It was installed at 16 Lawrence Street in 1950. [© English Heritage. Photograph by Derek Kendall]

– renamed the Wright-Fleming Institute of Microbiology – until his retirement in 1948. Fleming's residence in Danvers Street was not continuous – he also spent considerable time at his house in Barton Mills, Suffolk, especially during the war, when number 20 was damaged by bombs – but it was here that he died. His plaque was unveiled by his second wife, Amalia, in 1981, the centenary of Fleming's birth.

At the north end of Lawrence Street, SW3, stood Monmouth House, a building that comprised four early eighteenth-century properties and which survived until the early 1830s (fig. 184). As attested by a rectangular blue plaque on 16 Lawrence Street (fig. 185), part of a mid-eighteenth-century terrace, it was at Monmouth House that **Chelsea China** 33 was manufactured from 1745 to 1784, during which time the novelist **Tobias Smollett** (1721–1771) also lived here, from 1750 until mid-1763.[34] Smollett was one of London's leading literary men. Scottish by birth and a doctor by training, he became renowned as the author of works such as *The Adventures of Roderick Random* (1748), *The Adventures of Peregrine Pickle* (1751) and *The Expedition of Humphry Clinker* (1771). Smollett lived in the western portion of Monmouth House, while the Chelsea China factory – famous for its soft-paste porcelain – was based mainly in the eastern part of the building, but also spread into kilns and warehouses scattered between houses in the vicinity. It made its name under the management of Nicholas Sprimont (*c.* 1715–1771) from *c.* 1744 to 1769. By the early 1750s, a workforce of about a hundred people produced goods such as tea- and coffee-services and porcelain snuff-

186 The brown LCC plaque to Leigh Hunt at 22 Upper Cheyne Row, his home from 1833 until 1840. Hunt described the house as being 'of that old-fashioned sort which I have always loved best'. [© English Heritage. Photograph by Derek Kendall]

boxes bearing elaborate designs; some of the floral patterns were taken from flowers grown in the nearby Chelsea Physic Garden. The factory was closed and the firm wound up in 1784.

At 22 (formerly 4 and later 10) Upper Cheyne Row, SW3, a plaque of 1905 commemorates the essayist and poet **Leigh Hunt** (1784–1859) 34 (fig. 186). James Henry Leigh Hunt was born in Southgate, Middlesex, to American parents, and turned to literature at an early age; his first collection of poems, *Juvenilia*, was published in 1801. Seven years later, he became editor of *The Examiner*, set up by his brother John; part of

his life for thirteen years, the weekly newspaper became notorious for its reformist views and was the cause of Hunt's imprisonment in 1813–15. Meanwhile, Hunt had become part of the group that included Byron, SHELLEY, KEATS and LAMB – he was in Italy at the time of Shelley's death – and played a key part in promoting their work. As well as various journalistic endeavours, his own oeuvre included the narrative poems *The Story of Rimini* (1816) and 'Abou Ben Adhem' (1825), both much admired. Hunt was beset by debt throughout his life and, as a result, moved continually from one address to another; his London homes amounted to more than twenty. What was then

CHELSEA

numbered 4 Upper Cheyne Row, a building of *c.* 1716, was the home of Hunt and his wife Marianne, née Kent (1787–1857) from 1833 until 1840. In his autobiography, Hunt recalled that he was pleased to move to Chelsea, 'where the air of the neighbouring river was so refreshing . . . although our fortunes were at their worst, and my health almost of a piece with them, I felt for some weeks as if I could sit still for ever, embalmed in the silence'.[35] Hunt described his home as being 'of that old-fashioned sort which I have always loved best . . . It had seats in the windows, [and] a small third room on the first floor, of which I made a *sanctum*'.[36] His neighbour and friend Thomas Carlyle wrote in 1834 that Hunt's house – home to his seven children – 'excels all you have ever read of – *a poetical Tinkerdom*, without parallel even in literature'.[37] While here, Hunt wrote the protest ballad *Captain Sword and Captain Pen* (1835) and plays including *A Legend of Florence* (1840), and founded the short-lived *London Journal* (1834–35).

In 2000 a plaque was erected at 87 (formerly 146) Oakley Street, SW3, to the poet and essayist **Jane Francesca, Lady Wilde** (1821–1896) **35** – also known by her pen name '**Speranza**' – at the suggestion of her biographer, Joy Melville. Born in Dublin, Jane Elgee involved herself as a young woman in the nationalist cause, contributing inflammatory prose and verse as 'Speranza' to the Irish journal *The Nation*. At the age of thirty, she married William Wilde, a distinguished surgeon and folklorist; the couple – who had two sons, Oscar and William – were famed for the literary salons held at their Dublin home. Lady Wilde moved to London in 1879 following her husband's death, and quickly re-established her salons. These were the most notable feature of Jane's life at 87 Oakley Street, where she lived from 1887. 'Lady Wilde's crushes', as they were termed, were frequented by 'Ladies of high degree and Ladies of no degree – poets and painters, artists and critics, writers and scribblers', almost all of whom were anxious to make the acquaintance of Oscar, a regular attender at his mother's gatherings.[38] One visitor, the painter Herbert Schmalz, told how the atmosphere of Lady Wilde's rooms was 'made more mysterious by pastilles burning on the mantelpiece and by large mirrors being placed between the floor and the ceiling, with curtains at the edges, so that when crowded with people you could not see where the actual room left

off'.[39] Lady Wilde – who, like her famous son, was known for epigrammatic witticisms – published collections of her essays and editions of her husband's folklore works while living here. She died in Oakley Street in straitened circumstances during her son's imprisonment. Her plaque was unveiled by Vanessa Redgrave, who played Jane in the 1997 film *Wilde*.

Number 56 Oakley Street was the home of **Robert Falcon Scott** (1868–1912) **36** , the Antarctic explorer, as is evidenced by a wreathed plaque of 1935 (figs 187 and 188). Scott became a naval officer while in his teens and thereafter was more often at sea than ashore. In 1898 he was made torpedo-lieutenant on the flagship *Majestic* and two years later was placed in command of the National Antarctic Expedition. It was in August 1901 that Scott left England on the *Discovery*, leading what was to prove the first extensive land investigation of Antarctica. On his return to England in 1904, he was acclaimed as a national hero and promoted captain. The following year Scott moved to 56 Oakley Street, a Victorian terraced house, with his mother, Hannah, née Cuming, and his sisters. It is thought that part of his classic book *The Voyage of the 'Discovery'* (1905) was written in the house. While here, he courted his future wife, the artist Kathleen Bruce, who lived nearby at 133 Cheyne Walk. By January 1908, when number 56 was given up, Scott was already thinking of another Antarctic expedition. Two years later, with the sailing of the *Terra Nova*, the fateful journey began. On 18 January 1912 Scott and four others reached the South Pole, only to find that the Norwegian explorer Roald Amundsen had been there a month before. The disappointment and harsh conditions took their dreadful toll, and all of the party, including Scott, were dead by late March. Scott's wreathed blue plaque was conceived alongside, and erected a week before, that commemorating Edward Adrian Wilson, who died with Scott.

On the Phene Street side of 33 Oakley Gardens, SW3, a GLC plaque honours the novelist **George Gissing** (1857–1903) **37** , who lived here from September 1882 until May 1884; it was then 17 Oakley Crescent and a lodging-house, run by a Mrs Coward. Born in Wakefield, Yorkshire, Gissing made his name in London with a series of novels depicting the struggles of the lower-middle and working classes. The first of these,

187 The design for the wreathed LCC plaque to Robert Falcon Scott, erected in 1935 at 56 Oakley Street. [Reproduced by permission of English Heritage]

188 A photograph taken in Antarctica in April 1911, during the ill-fated *Terra Nova* Expedition of 1910–13. The two figures are Robert Falcon Scott and the physicist Charles Wright, with Tent Island in the distance. [© Royal Geographical Society]

Workers in the Dawn (1880), appeared shortly before his move to Chelsea. While living in Oakley Gardens, Gissing revised *Mrs Grundy's Enemies* (unpublished during his lifetime) and began *The Unclassed* (1884). His two rooms at number 33 provided a modicum of calm in which to write; in 1883 Gissing told his sister, 'There is only one place in the world wherein to live, and that is *Chelsea*!'.[40] Within months, however, the lodging-house had become too noisy, and he moved to a flat in Regent's Park. Gissing – who made his name with *Demos* (1886), subtitled 'A Story of English Social-ism' – lived largely outside London after 1890, and in 1899 settled in France, where he died. Works of this later period include *New Grub Street* (1891), the travel book *By the Ionian Sea* (1901) and the *Private Papers of Henry Ryecroft* (1903).

Number 9 Chelsea Embankment, SW3 – a tall red-brick house built in 1879 to designs by NORMAN SHAW – bears a plaque to the Viceroy of India, **George Frederick Samuel Robinson**, **Marquess of Ripon** (1827–1909) ㊳ . George was born at 10 Downing Street, the son of Viscount Goderich, Prime Minister in 1827–28. He began his own political life as attaché to a special mission to Brussels in 1849, and four years later entered Parliament as an advanced Liberal. In 1859 he succeeded to his father's title as Earl of Ripon, and to that of his uncle, Earl de Grey; he was elevated to a marquessate in 1871. At the age of thirty-nine, Ripon was appointed Secretary of State for India, and in 1880 GLADSTONE appointed him Viceroy of India. In this role, which he held until 1884, he initiated administrative, educational and political reforms to prepare India for self-government. Ripon felt that 'it is our duty to raise the people of this country politically and socially . . . making the educated natives the friends instead of the enemies of our rule'.[41] This approach won him widespread support among the Indian people, though it angered the English settlers. Having returned to England, Ripon served as First Lord of the Admiralty in 1886, and was Colonial Secretary from 1892 until the resignation of the government three years later. His final position was as Lord Privy Seal (1905–8). A plaque was set up in 1959 at number 9, the London home of Ripon – and his wife, Henrietta, née Vyner (1833/4–1907) – from 1890 until the time of his death, which occurred at Studley Royal, Yorkshire, his beloved country residence.

A plaque to the Dublin-born wit and dramatist **Oscar Wilde** (1854–1900) ㊴ was erected in 1954 – the centenary of his birth – at 34 (formerly 16) Tite Street, SW3 (fig. 189). It was at Oxford – where he studied in 1874–79 – that Wilde cultivated his pose of 'aesthete', and gained a reputation as a conversationalist and wit. In 1879 he moved to London, where he settled down to writing in earnest and met Constance Lloyd (1858–1898), the daughter of a successful Irish barrister. The couple married in May 1884, and arranged to lease 16 (now 34) Tite Street, a newly built house in the heart of Chelsea's fashionable artists' quarter; earlier, in 1880–81, Oscar had lived at Keats House, 1 (now 44) Tite Street. The Wildes took up residence in January 1885, after 'original and, as some visitors considered, bizarre' decorative work had been carried out by E. W. Godwin, a leading figure in the Aesthetic Movement; two years later, Oscar's mother, LADY WILDE, moved to nearby Oakley Street.[42] During his ten years at the house, Wilde enjoyed his greatest fame and success; his book of fairy stories, *The Happy Prince and Other Tales* (1888), was followed by a spectacular first novel, *The Picture of Dorian Gray* (1891), and a series of plays that included *Lady Windermere's Fan* (1892), *A Woman of No Importance* (1893), *An Ideal Husband* (1895) and *The Importance of Being Earnest* (1895). Number 34 Tite Street was famed for the eccentricity of its decor: the front door, entrance hall, staircase and dining room

189 Taken in 1953, this photograph shows the proposed position of the plaque to Oscar Wilde at 34 Tite Street; it was erected the following year, the centenary of Wilde's birth.
[© Getty Images / City of London, LMA]

were predominantly painted white – 'My eye requires in a room a resting-place of pure colour', Wilde wrote – while the drawing room had a ceiling by Godwin and WHISTLER.[43] Here, the Wildes entertained such well-known figures as Sarah Bernhardt, ELLEN TERRY, HENRY IRVING and D. G. ROSSETTI. Wilde wrote mainly in the library – at ground-floor level, facing onto the street – but he also worked in the exotic smoking room at the rear of the first floor; his bedroom was on the storey above, also to the rear. It was at Tite Street that the 8th Marquess of Queensberry – incensed by Wilde's association with his son, Lord Alfred Douglas ('Bosie') – made his unannounced appearance in 1894; after a row, he was thrown out, and Oscar sued him for libel. The action, which reached the courts in spring 1895, failed, and resulted in Oscar's prosecution and committal to prison for two years for homosexual practices. At the insistence of Wilde's creditors, the entire contents of his Tite Street home were sold; WILLIAM ROTHENSTEIN described how the house 'was filled with a jostling crowd, most of whom had come out of curiosity'.[44] In 1897, on his release from Reading Gaol, Wilde moved to the Continent, where he died a broken man.

A couple of doors away, at 30 (formerly 12) Tite Street, a plaque of 1984 commemorates the composer **Philip Arnold Heseltine** (1894–1930) ⑩ , better known by his pseudonym **Peter Warlock**. It was while he was at Eton, between 1908 and 1911, that Warlock's interest in music – specifically the music of FREDERICK DELIUS – was encouraged; Delius would become a major influence on Warlock's work, and a lifelong friend. During the First World War, he took up music journalism, and wrote a number of songs including 'As Ever I Saw' and 'Sweet Content'. Despite the success of his songs, of his books and editions of early English music, and especially of his own compositions – Warlock's masterpiece, the song-cycle *The Curlew* (1915–22), was followed by *An Old Song* (1917–23) and the popular *Capriol* suite (1927) – the composer was haunted by a lack of creative self-confidence. Prone to severe manic depression, he dabbled with the occult, and his wild, bohemian lifestyle formed the inspiration for fictional characters created by D. H. LAWRENCE and ALDOUS HUXLEY. Warlock, who had lived in various houses in Chelsea during the 1920s, moved in 1930 to the flat then numbered 12A Tite Street. In September of that year, he

wrote, 'I am full of hope for the future of my work if I can only manage to settle down in a quiet and secluded spot where I shall be undisturbed – and the flat I have found is just such a place'.[45] Being unable to fit his piano into the flat, he sold it and borrowed another of the appropriate size; by October, it was 'safely housed in a room with a gas fire'.[46] However, Warlock's inspiration soon seemed to dwindle, and the end came abruptly: he was found dead in his gas-filled flat in December; it is generally believed that he committed suicide.

The great American writer **Samuel L. Clemens** (1835–1910) ㊶ is known internationally as **Mark Twain**; he is honoured with a plaque at 23 Tedworth Square, SW3, a Victorian corner house that was his home from autumn 1896 until June 1897. Born in Florida, Samuel Langhorne Clemens tried his hand at various occupations – he served for a time as a steamboat pilot on the Mississippi – before turning to journalism. As Mark Twain, he first achieved literary fame with *The Innocents Abroad* (1869). This was followed by a string of successful books – *Roughing It* (1872), *The Adventures of Tom Sawyer* (1876), *The Prince and the Pauper* (1881), *Life on the Mississippi* (1883) – which culminated with *The Adventures of Huckleberry Finn* (1884). Between 1891 and 1900 Twain went on an extended lecture tour of Europe, and was in London for a good part of that period. Distressed at the death of his daughter Susy in August 1896, Twain maintained 'complete seclusion' in Chelsea – where he lived with his wife Olivia, née Langdon (1845–1904) – only receiving 'two or three intimate friends'; it has been said that 'Perhaps not a dozen people in London knew their address and the outside world was ignorant of it altogether'.[47] Still, his time at number 23 was productive; Clara Clemens described how her father 'used to rise sometimes as early as four or five o'clock in the morning. Never did he write more continuously'.[48] At the time the plaque was erected, in 1960, Clara recalled how her family had 'loved that little house and all the surrounding region . . . It is too bad that my father doesn't know about the tablet, but indeed he *may* know'.[49]

At 18 St Leonard's Terrace, SW3, a plaque commemorates **Bram Stoker** (1847–1912) ㊷ , the author of *Dracula*. Born in Dublin, Abraham Stoker was invited to London in 1878 by HENRY IRVING and took up work as business manager of the Lyceum Theatre. Stoker

CHELSEA

190 A view out of the turret window of Jerome K. Jerome's sixth-floor flat at Chelsea Gardens, looking along Chelsea Bridge Road towards the river. This view – less obstructed in Jerome's day – is said to have formed part of the inspiration for *Three Men in a Boat*, written at the address in 1889. [© English Heritage. Photograph by Derek Kendall]

rence, née Balcombe (1858–1935) became noted figures in Chelsea society. It was in 1890, while the couple were living at 17 St Leonard's Terrace – their home from *c*. 1885 – that Stoker began to make notes for a vampire story. Originally named *The Un-Dead*, the title *Dracula* was substituted shortly before its publication in May 1897; the book went through eleven editions in Stoker's lifetime and has become acknowledged as a classic. By the time of its publication, the Stokers had moved next door to 18 St Leonard's Terrace, their home from 1896 until about 1906. While living here, Stoker also produced the work of supernatural fiction *The Jewel of Seven Stars* (1903); *The Lair of the White Worm* followed in 1911. Stoker's plaque was unveiled in 1977, the eightieth anniversary of *Dracula*'s publication.

On the corner of Chelsea Bridge Road and Ebury Bridge Road, SW1, stands an imposing Victorian block of flats, Chelsea Gardens, which bears a plaque to the author **Jerome K. Jerome** (1859–1927) **43** . Born in Walsall, Staffordshire, Jerome Klapka Jerome worked successively as a railway clerk, schoolmaster and actor, before finding work as a journalist. It was his stage experience that led to his first book, *On the Stage – and Off* (1885). This was followed in 1886 by *The Idle Thoughts of an Idle Fellow* and in 1889 by Jerome's masterpiece, *Three Men in a Boat*, which depicts a series of comic episodes on a Thames riverboat trip. Other literary achievements included *Three Men on the Bummel* (1900) and Jerome's co-founding in 1892 of *The Idler*, a monthly magazine of wit whose contributors included ISRAEL ZANGWILL and MARK TWAIN. In his reminiscences, Jerome recalled, '*Three Men in a Boat. To say nothing of the dog* I wrote at Chelsea Gardens, up ninety-seven stairs. But the view was worth it. We had a little circular drawing-room . . . nearly all window, suggestive of a lighthouse, from which we looked down upon the river, and over Battersea Park to the Surrey Hills beyond, with the garden of old Chelsea Hospital just opposite' (fig. 190).[50] Jerome's flat – number 104, at sixth-floor level – consisted of two reception rooms, three bedrooms and a kitchen. He and his wife Georgina (1859–1938) moved in after their marriage in June 1888 and remained here until about 1894, when they moved to St John's Wood. The blue plaque was erected in 1989 next to the entrance to flats 91–104.

worked closely with Irving in establishing the theatre's success, only leaving the job when the theatre went into receivership in 1902. His many administrative innovations included the numbering of seats and promotion of advance reservations. Meanwhile, from the mid-1870s, Stoker became active as a writer, his early works including a book of fairy tales, *Under the Sunset* (1882). Based at 27 Cheyne Walk from 1880 – the Thames provided an invaluable artery linking his home and his area of work – Stoker and his wife Flo-

1   Thea Holme, *Chelsea* (London, 1972), p. xv
2   *ODNB*, vol. XVI, pp. 181–82
3   *The London Encyclopaedia*, eds Ben Weinreb and Christopher Hibbert (repr. London, 1990), p. 113
4   R. I. and S. Wilberforce, *The Life of William Wilberforce*, vol. V (London, 1838), p. 370
5   Claire Tomalin, *Mrs Jordan's Profession: The Story of a Great Actress and a Future King* (repr. London, 1995), p. 291
6   Due to a mistake on the plaque, Langtry's year of birth is given as 1852.
7   Noel B. Gerson, *Lillie Langtry* (London, 1972), p. 162
8   Ernest Dudley, *The Gilded Lily: The Life and Loves of the Fabulous Lillie Langtry* (London, 1958), pp. 116–17
9   *Sunday People*, 7 December 1980, p. 10
10 *ODNB*, vol. I, p. 667
11 Margaret Drabble, *Arnold Bennett* (London, 1974), p. 276
12 It is now known that Sartorius was baptised in 1779 and died in 1831; the plaque states that he was born *c.* 1775 and died *c.* 1830.
13 Joyce Grenfell, *In Pleasant Places* (repr. London, 1980), p. 21
14 Ibid
15 Augustus John, *Autobiography* (London, 1975 edn), p. 240
16 Michael Holroyd, *Augustus John* (London, 1996), p. 447
17 Ibid, p. 400
18 Ann Thwaite, *A. A. Milne: His Life* (London, 1990), p. 201
19 Ibid, p. 202
20 *The New Grove Dictionary of Music and Musicians*, ed. Stanley Sadie, vol. XII (2nd edn, London, 2001), p. 568
21 Richard Edmondes, *Chelsea* (London, 1956), p. 15
22 D. S. MacColl, *Life, Work and Setting of Philip Wilson Steer* (London, 1945), p. 54
23 Ibid
24 Lendal Tweed, *John Tweed, Sculptor: A Memoir* (London, 1936), p. 199
25 A. N. Wilson, *Hilaire Belloc* (London, 1984), p. 103
26 Whistler's name is incorrectly spelled 'McNeil' on the plaque.
27 Quoted in LCC, *Indication of Houses of Historical Interest in London*, vol. V (London, 1930), p. 89
28 Ibid, p. 90
29 Elizabeth Gaskell, *Cranford* (London, 1994 edn), p. 219
30 *The Bookman*, May 1904, p. 60
31 *George Eliot's Life as Related in Her Letters and Journals*, ed. J. W. Cross, vol. III (Edinburgh and London, 1885), p. 412 (2 August 1880)
32 Ibid, p. 437 (6 December 1880)
33 Alfred Beaver, *Memorials of Old Chelsea* (London, 1892), p. 208
34 The plaque states that Smollett lived at Monmouth House from 1750 to 1762, but the latter year is now known to be incorrect.
35 James Leigh Hunt, *Autobiography*, vol. III (London, 1850), pp. 223–24
36 Ibid, p. 226
37 Edmund Blunden, *Leigh Hunt: A Biography* (London, 1930), p. 253
38 Joy Melville, *Mother of Oscar: The Life of Jane Francesca Wilde* (London, 1994), pp. 209–10
39 Ibid, p. 211
40 *The Collected Letters of George Gissing: volume 2: 1881–1885*, eds Paul F. Mattheisen, Arthur C. Young and Pierre Coustillas (Athens, Ohio, 1991), p. 107 (15 September 1883)
41 Anthony Denholm, *Lord Ripon 1827–1909: A Political Biography* (London and Canberra, 1982), p. 161 (19 May 1883)
42 H. Montgomery Hyde, 'Oscar Wilde and His Architect', *Architectural Review*, vol. 109 (1951), p. 175
43 *The Complete Letters of Oscar Wilde*, eds Merlin Holland and Rupert Hart-Davis (London, 2000), p. 259 (16 May 1885)
44 Holme, *Chelsea*, p. 221
45 *The Collected Letters of Peter Warlock, 1922–30*, ed. Barry Smith, vol. IV (Woodbridge, 2005), p. 280 (10 September 1930)
46 Ibid, p. 282 (6 October 1930)
47 Clara Clemens, *My Father Mark Twain* (New York and London, 1931), p. 178; Albert Bigelow Paine, *Mark Twain: A Biography*, vol. II (New York and London, 1912), p. 1025
48 Clemens, *My Father Mark Twain*, p. 178
49 Letter of 25 May 1960 on blue plaque file.
50 Jerome K. Jerome, *My Life and Times* (London, 1926), p. 102

CHELSEA

191 The richly coloured interior of Leighton House, looking from the domed Arab Hall towards the hallway and staircase. [© English Heritage. Photograph by Derek Kendall]

HOLLAND PARK AND CAMPDEN HILL

Holland Park and Campden Hill lie within the area of Kensington that occupies rising ground between Kensington High Street and the old Uxbridge Road. They take their names from two important early seventeenth-century buildings: Holland House – the mansion of Sir Walter Cope (d. 1614), which survives in part – and Campden House, built for Sir Baptist Hicks (d. 1629), later Viscount Campden, and demolished in about 1900. To the east, the wider area is dominated by a third building dating originally from the Jacobean period: Kensington Palace, a royal residence since 1689. In the nineteenth century, these reminders of a largely rural past were swamped by mass development of housing aimed largely at the prosperous middle classes. By the early 1900s, this part of Kensington had become a favoured place of residence for painters and writers; Ezra Pound described it as 'SWARming with artistic types', while Ford Madox Ford named it 'a high class Greenwich Village'.[1] Today, Holland Park and Campden Hill retain an atmosphere of seclusion that is rare in modern Kensington.

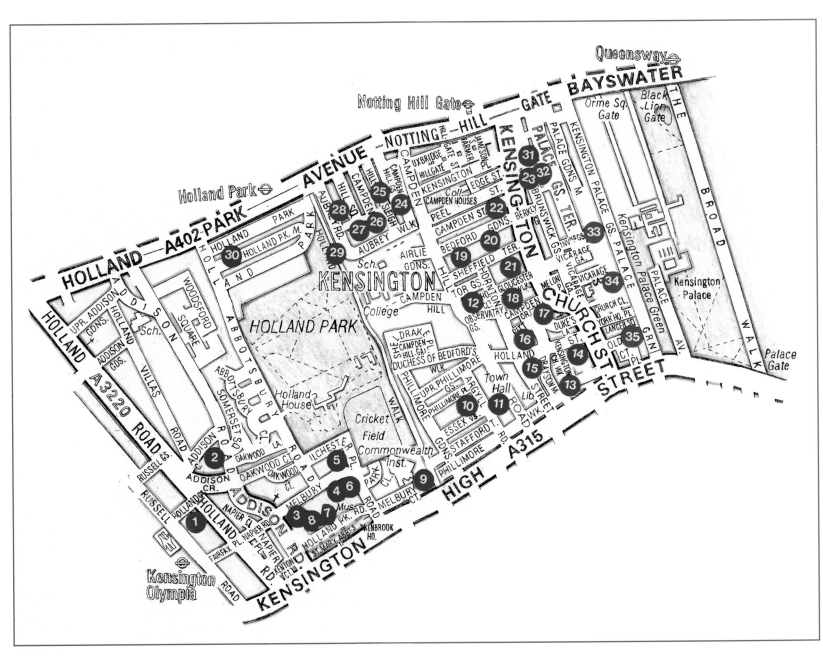

HOLLAND PARK AND
CAMPDEN HILL

192　A crowd gathers to see the unveiling of the plaque to Mohammed Ali Jinnah at 35 Russell Road, 1955. The unveiling was performed by the High Commissioner for Pakistan, with the Pakistan Police Pipe Band in attendance. [© RBKC Libraries]

The Holland estate, which originally comprised over 200 acres (81 ha) of land surrounding Holland House, was developed from the 1820s. Russell Road, W14, was built around the 1870s at the estate's western boundary, next to the railway. A former resident of number 35, one of a series of relatively modest terraced houses, was **Quaid i Azam Mohammed Ali Jinnah** (1876–1948) ❶ , the founder of Pakistan. Born in Karachi, Jinnah came to England in 1892 to study law at Lincoln's Inn and was called to the Bar four years later, at the age of just nineteen. During some of this time, and certainly in 1895, he occupied lodgings at 35 Russell Road, the home of a Mrs Page-Drake. When Jinnah returned to Bombay in 1896, he was already a convinced nationalist, and in the second decade of the twentieth century came to the forefront of Indian politics. In 1909 Jinnah was elected as the Bombay Muslims' representative on the legislative council, and four years later joined the All India Muslim League, with which he remained strongly connected for the rest of his life. He also played an important part in the founding of the All India Home Rule League in 1916. From 1937 Jinnah was increasingly known as 'Quaid-i-Azam', or 'Great Leader', and in 1947 was made the first Governor-General of Pakistan, the country he had helped to found. His imposing mau-

soleum, the Mazar-e-Quaid in Karachi, is one of Pakistan's national monuments. Jinnah's plaque, conceived alongside that for GANDHI at Kingsley Hall in Bow, was erected by the LCC in 1955. It was unveiled by M. Ikramullah, High Commissioner for Pakistan, with the Pakistan Police Pipe Band in attendance (fig. 192).

Addison Road, W14, was the first road to be built on the Holland estate, though number 67 – a stucco villa with a projecting porch – dates only from the early 1850s. It bears a plaque to **Chaim Weizmann** (1874– 1952) ❷ , the scientist and statesman, who served as first President of the state of Israel. Born in Pinsk, then part of the Russian Empire, Weizmann began his career as a chemist; he first came to England in 1904, taking up a lecturing post at Manchester University, and six years later became a naturalised British citizen. In 1915 Weizmann moved to London, where he was appointed Admiralty advisor on acetone supplies, which were essential to the wartime manufacture of explosives. In October of the following year, he and his wife Vera, née Khatzman (1881–1966) took up residence at number 67; it would remain their home until about the end of 1919, and was the birthplace of the couple's second son, Michael. During his years at number 67, Weizmann rose to become a major figure in the Zionist movement; his many achievements included the establishment of a firm understanding between Zionists and the British government, an accord that gave rise in 1917 to the Balfour Declaration, supporting a Jewish national home in Palestine. Weizmann described his residence of these years as 'a centre not only for the Zionists, but for a great many British political figures'.[2] As President of the World Zionist Organisation for much of the period 1920–46, Weizmann continued to be a figure of prominence in the later part of his life. He played an important part in negotiations over the partition of Palestine before British withdrawal in 1948 and, as soon as the state of Israel was proclaimed, was invited to become its President, a position he held until his death. It was originally hoped that Weizmann's plaque would be placed on 16 Addison Crescent, his home of 1920–39. However, consent was refused in 1974 by the building's owners – who cited concern regarding the recent oil crisis in the Middle East – and the GLC took the decision to commemorate 67 Addison Road instead. The plaque was unveiled in 1980.

193   The sculptor Sir Hamo Thornycroft at work in Melbury Road – probably in his studio at number 2B – in a photograph published in the *Strand Magazine* in 1893.

Melbury Road, W14, was – at the end of the nineteenth century – the mecca for London's artistic elite and the focus of the illustrious 'Holland Park Circle'; it was described in 1898 as 'a Kensington nook . . . altogether an ideal spot for the artist'.[3] Its earliest resident was the painter G. F. Watts, who had a house at number 6 from 1876 until shortly before his death in 1904; the building was demolished in 1964, and its fine LCC plaque of 1925 was retrieved. The presence of Watts – and LORD LEIGHTON – quickly attracted a group of highly successful Victorian artists, many of whom patronised their fellow Royal Academician, the architect RICHARD NORMAN SHAW. The sculptor **Sir Hamo Thornycroft** (1850–1925) ③ , however, chose to be more personally involved in the design of his house, which he completed in collaboration with the architect John Belcher. Numbers 2 and 4 Melbury Road, conceived as a semi-detached pair, were built in 1876–77: number 4 was a speculative property for sale or let, while number 2, to the west, formed the residence of the Thornycrofts. The family, who moved here in May 1877, comprised six artists and sculptors: Hamo, his parents – Thomas

(1815–1885) and Mary (1809–1895) – and three of his sisters. Number 2 – known as Moreton House after Little Moreton Hall, Cheshire, of which the family had been tenants in the 1700s – was decorated with the various Thornycrofts' works, and contained a complex of studios. The most important of these were situated within the house's south-west wing; this has since been subdivided as 2A Melbury Road and 24B Holland Park Road. In 1892 Belcher added a new studio house – now 2B Melbury Road – to which Thornycroft moved, letting number 2 (fig. 193); it was on 2B that the plaque was placed in 1957. During his time in Melbury Road, Thornycroft enjoyed a reputation as one of Britain's leading sculptors, and was noted for his dedication: in 1893 a journalist commented that 'He is always in his studio at half-past eight, and has, before now, held on to his mallet until two the next morning'.[4] His best-known works include the *Mower* (1884), the *Sower* (1886), and the portrait statues of General Gordon in Waterloo Place (1885–88), Oliver Cromwell in Old Palace Yard (1899) and W. E. GLADSTONE at the Aldwych (1900–5).

Number 8 Melbury Road was designed by NORMAN SHAW and built in 1875–76 for the artist **Marcus Stone** (1840–1921) 4 , once described as a 'dramatist in colour' (fig. 194).[5] The son of the artist Frank Stone, Marcus was educated and trained at home. The first of his works to attract widespread attention was *On the Road from Waterloo to Paris* (1863), a depiction of the defeated Napoleon. This was followed by a series of paintings, almost all of which are historical tableaux or picturesque costume pieces. The latter genre is especially well represented by the popular *In Love* (1888). Stone was also active as a book illustrator, and is particularly remembered for his contributions to the first edition of DICKENS's *Our Mutual Friend* (1864–65). Number 8 was Stone's principal residence from early 1877 until his death. The artist worked in a specially designed studio at first-floor level, 'one of the largest in London', lit by three huge oriel windows; there was a winter studio to the east, while the ground floor was a haven of domestic comfort.[6] In 1896 it was said that 'few artists' houses could pretend to serve to anything like the same extent the double purpose of a delightful dwelling and an ideal working place'.[7] Number 8 was divided into flats in about 1951 and marked with a plaque in 1994. Beneath it, a plaque to the film director Michael Powell (1905–1990) was subsequently erected by the Directors Guild of Great Britain.

MARCUS STONE's colleague and rival, the artist **Sir Luke Fildes** (1843–1927) 5 , also chose NORMAN SHAW as the architect of his new Holland Park home.[8] Number 31 (formerly 11) Melbury Road was built in 1876–77; Fildes wrote that it was the 'most superior

house of the lot. I consider it knocks Stone's to bits'.[9] Fildes began his artistic career as a book and magazine illustrator, and in 1870 collaborated with DICKENS in producing illustrations for his last, unfinished novel, *The Mystery of Edwin Drood*. Fildes's first major success came with his social realist painting *Applicants for Admission to a Casual Ward* (1874). This was followed by works in a similar vein, including *The Widower* (1876) and *The Doctor* (1891). From the late nineteenth century, Fildes was particularly popular as a portrait painter: his royal sitters included King Edward VII who, on visiting Fildes's Melbury Road studio, described it as 'one of the finest rooms in London'.[10] The plaque, erected in 1959, states that Fildes moved into number 31 in 1878. However, as the artist's son pointed out in a letter written to the LCC soon after the plaque's unveiling, Fildes did in fact take up residence in autumn 1877. He died here fifty years later.

Number 18 Melbury Road is a tall semi-detached house dated 1877, and is situated in the lower part of this artists' thoroughfare (fig. 195). It bears a wreathed LCC blue plaque commemorating the painter **William Holman Hunt, OM** (1827–1910) 6 . Born in the City of London, Holman Hunt met and befriended MILLAIS and DANTE GABRIEL ROSSETTI in the 1840s, and was part of the group that founded the PRE-RAPHAELITE

BROTHERHOOD in 1848. The works for which is he is best remembered – many of them inspired by his frequent visits to Jerusalem – include *The Light of the World* (1851–53), which has been described as 'arguably the most famous religious image of the nineteenth century', *The Scapegoat* (1854–55) and *The Finding of the Saviour in the Temple* (1854–60).[11] Holman Hunt's artistic output ended with his completion of *The Lady of Shalott* (c. 1888–1905), by which time he was suffering from glaucoma. The artist had long been resident of Holland Park and nearby Fulham by the time he moved in 1903 to 18 Melbury Road. Here, Holman Hunt dedicated himself to literary activities: he worked on his memoirs, and produced *Pre-Raphaelitism and the Pre-Raphaelite Brotherhood* in 1905, an account intended to propagate the principles of the group he had helped to found. In the same year, he was awarded the Order of Merit. Holman Hunt died at number 18; the house was still occupied by his widow, Edith, née Waugh (1846–1931), when the plaque was installed in 1923.

Lord Leighton (1830–1896) **7** , one of the most esteemed of late Victorian painters, is commemorated at 12 (formerly 2) Holland Park Road, W14. Born in Scarborough, Frederic Leighton studied art on the Continent and had his first success with *Cimabue's Madonna*; exhibited at the Royal Academy in 1855, the painting was purchased by Queen Victoria. From then on, his career was one of unbroken triumph, with works including *The Syracusan Bride* (1866), *Captive Andromache* (1886–88) and *Flaming June* (1895), his final masterpiece. Leighton was President of the Royal Academy in 1878–96, was created a baronet in 1886 and was raised to the peerage the day before his death. He was attracted to Holland Park in 1864 by the presence there of his friend G. F. Watts, and soon set about building a house in Holland Park Road. This, then numbered 2, was built to designs by George Aitchison with the close involvement of his client, and was ready for occupation by late 1866. The building's plain brick exterior – it was said on its completion that 'it expresses its purpose honestly to the casual passer-by, and no more' – belies what Nikolaus Pevsner has named 'the most sumptuous and colourful nineteenth-century artist's house in London' (fig. 191).[12] It was extended in phases throughout Leighton's residence, and features a vast studio at the rear of the first floor and, at the west, the domed Arab Hall, added in

1877–79 to house Leighton's collection of Middle Eastern tiles. There is only one main bedroom; the artist was a bachelor all his life, and also wanted to 'discourage long-term guests who might interfere with' his work.[13] On Leighton's death here, the house was bequeathed to the nation, and in 1926 transferred to the Royal Borough of Kensington. It was the local council, which runs Leighton House as a museum, that asked the LCC to install a plaque, duly erected in 1958.

Further along Holland Park Road, on the plain brick frontage of number 20 (formerly 3 The Studios), is a plaque put up in 1982 in honour of a rather different kind of artist: **Phil May** (1864–1903) **8** , a successful pen-and-ink illustrator. May, who was born in Leeds, came to public attention in London, where he worked for the *St Stephen's Review* and, from the 1890s, for *Punch*, among other magazines. He steadily acquired a name for his sympathetic comic delineations of low life – he was known especially for his drawings of 'guttersnipes', the urchins of the London streets; the volume *Guttersnipes: Fifty Original Sketches* appeared in 1896. By this time, the artist had established his own annual, *Phil May's Winter Annual*, which ran from 1892 until 1905 and proved highly popular. Indeed, such was his success that WHISTLER was able to state that 'modern black & white art could be summed up in two words – Phil May'.[14] May, whose simple, vigorous style influenced artists such as WALTER CRANE, DAVID LOW and Bert Thomas, lived and worked in Holland Park Road for some years: first, in around 1892–95, at number 65 (formerly 7; demolished), and from 1896 to 1899 at the commemorated address, Rowsley House, now number 20. Increasingly dependent on alcohol in his later years, May died at his home at 5 Melina Place, St John's Wood, NW8.

The single blue plaque in Kensington High Street, W8, commemorates the cartoonist **Sir David Low** (1891–1963) **9** . It marks the eastern end of Melbury Court, a block of 1928 that stands adjacent to the Commonwealth Institute (built in 1960–62). Here, in Flat 33, on the top floor of the building, Low lived from about 1956 until the time of his death seven years later. David Alexander Cecil Low was born in New Zealand, where – strongly influenced by the style of PHIL MAY (see above) – he developed a talent for political cartoons and caricatures. In 1919 he moved to London and, eight years later, was persuaded by Lord Beaverbrook to join the *Evening Standard*; Low's work appeared regularly in the newspaper until his resignation in 1949, and brought him to international attention. Low excelled as a satirist; his depictions of Hitler and Mussolini led to a ban on the *Standard* in both Germany and Italy. He was equally adept at inventing imaginary characters, of which Colonel Blimp – created in 1934 – is perhaps the best known. After leaving the *Standard*, Low moved on to the *Manchester Guardian*, for which he worked from 1952 until shortly before his death. Low's most significant London residence was 3 Rodborough Road, Golders Green, NW11, a modest detached house at which he lived in 1932–50. Consent for a plaque was, however, refused by the owners, and Melbury Court was selected instead. The plaque was unveiled in 1991 by the Home Secretary, Kenneth Baker, an admirer of Low's cartoons.

Number 16 Phillimore Place, W8 – formerly 16 Durham Villas – bears a plaque to **Kenneth Grahame** (1859–1932) **10** , the author of the children's classic *The Wind in the Willows*. Throughout the most important years of his life, Grahame, a Scot, enjoyed two careers: one, as an employee of the Bank of England – he entered the bank in 1879 and was appointed Secretary in 1898 – and another as a writer. In the latter capacity, Grahame first came to notice with *Pagan Papers* (1893), a collection of stories about a group of orphaned children. The work was followed in 1895 by *The Golden Age* and, four years later, by *Dream Days*. Grahame's lasting fame rests on *The Wind in the Willows* (1908). Supposedly based on a series of bedtime stories told by Grahame to his only child, Alastair (1900–1920), the work was written at number 16, the author's London home from the time of his marriage in July 1899 to Elspeth Thomson (1862–1946) until June 1908, when he retired from the Bank of England.[15] A friend and neighbour, Graham Robertson, wrote that Grahame's 'special room in No. 16 was most characteristic; it looked like a nursery. Books there were certainly, but they were outnumbered by toys . . . intriguing, fascinating toys which could hardly have been conducive to study'.[16] The plaque to Grahame was erected on this Victorian semi-detached house in 1959.

Towards the south end of Campden Hill Road, W8 – opposite the post-war civic centre and library – is number 29, the home of the poet **Sir Henry Newbolt** (1862–1938) **11** . Newbolt's first book was a novel, *Taken from the Enemy* (1892), but he is best remembered for his ballads, above all 'Drake's Drum' (1896) – published in the successful collection *Admirals All* (1897) – and 'Clifton Chapel' (1908), in which he recollected his happy schooldays at Clifton College, Bristol. After the outbreak of the First World War, Newbolt's literary output declined as he took on a succession of official posts. He is noted, in particular, for chairing the government committee that produced the innovative Newbolt Report (1921) on the teaching of English in England. For many years, Newbolt was part of a remarkable *ménage à trois*: he and his wife Margaret (b. 1867/8) shared a lover, Margaret's cousin Ella Coltman (b. 1863). Number 29 was Ella's home, and was used as a pied-à-terre by Newbolt from at least 1915. In autumn 1934 Newbolt and his wife moved in permanently. Margaret described how 'the Room of his Own in London which H. N. had used so constantly for twenty years past expanded into several rooms of our own. This was made possible by an ingenious architect who extended the little house for us – only a few feet – into its back garden'.[17] Newbolt died here in April 1938; the plaque was unveiled in 1994.

Number 80 Campden Hill Road is an 'unpretentious semi-detached villa' of 1848–49; it was formerly known as South Lodge – after the astronomer Sir James South, who had an observatory nearby – and bears a GLC plaque to the novelist and critic **Ford Madox Ford** (1873–1939) **12** .[18] Born Ford Hermann Hueffer to a German father and an English mother – he adopted the name Madox and in 1919 changed his surname to Ford – his first important publications were biographies of FORD MADOX BROWN (1896), his grandfather, and D. G. ROSSETTI (1902). In the first decade of the twentieth century, Ford came to prominence with a series of books co-authored with JOSEPH CONRAD, and with his founding in 1908 of the *English Review*. He had been based in Kensington for some time when he met the author Violet Hunt (1862–1942), who lived from 1896 until her death at South Lodge. Ford's wife refused his request for a divorce, and – amid scandal – he moved in about 1913 to South Lodge; here, he lived as Violet's 'paying guest' until August 1915 when, their affair more or less over, Ford joined the Army. Although his time at South Lodge was comparatively brief, Ford's presence was strongly felt; he and Violet – as 'Mr and Mrs Ford Hueffer' – held a series of salons that attracted friends including Ezra Pound, Wyndham Lewis and D. H. Lawrence. Ford's relationship with Violet gave rise to one of his greatest works, *The Good Soldier* (1915); this was followed in 1924–28 by four outstanding novels, known collectively as *Parade's End*, which drew on Ford's wartime experiences. Ford's pictures, books and furniture remained at South Lodge until after Violet's death, causing a friend to comment that 'in a queer, unaccountable way, he still dominated the house'.[19]

Another literary figure, the poet **Ezra Pound** (1885–1972) **13** , is commemorated nearby, at 10 Kensington Church Walk, W8, a quiet cul-de-sac behind Kensington High Street. Born in Idaho, USA, Pound arrived in 1908 in London, where he was to spend the formative – and most significant – years of his career. In the period up to his departure for Paris in 1921, Pound was productive as a writer – his collections of verse included *Personae* (1909), *Exultations* (1909), *Canzoni* (1911) and *Ripostes* (1912) – and he also worked to promote other, then little known, writers such as James Joyce and T. S. Eliot. In 1912 Pound invented the label 'imagism': imagist poetry stressed clarity, precision and economy of language, and was to have a profound influence on twentieth-century literature. Two years later, he named and was a founder of the Vorticist Group of artists and writers, which came to be led by Wyndham Lewis. Pound lived in a top-floor bed-sitting room at 10 Church Walk from 1909 until 1914, when his marriage necessitated larger quarters. The house was owned by a Mr and Mrs Langley, who were described by Pound as 'positively the best England can produce at ANY level'.[20] Here, Pound received visitors including Ford Madox Ford, D. H. Lawrence and Henri Gaudier-Brzeska. The later, controversial period of Pound's career was spent in Italy; his support for fascism led to his being indicted for treason in America, but he was instead certified insane and confined. It was partly for these unsavoury later associations that he died a semi-recluse in Venice. Pound was, in 1988, rejected for commemoration, but his literary importance and connection with London finally won through. A plaque was unveiled in 2004 in the presence of his daughter, Mary de Rachewiltz.

In 1952 a plaque was erected at 13 Holland Street, W8 – a property of *c.* 1760 known as The Old House – in honour of the artist **Walter Crane** (1845–1915) **14** . The son of a portrait painter, Crane first exhibited his work at the age of sixteen, but came to public notice from 1865 for his illustrations for a series of children's books – known as 'Toy Books' – printed by Edmund Evans; he was publicly acclaimed as 'the academician of the nursery'.[21] The 1870s saw Crane's increasing involvement in the decorative arts – he designed textiles, stained glass, tiles, wallpapers and plasterwork (fig. 196). In 1884 he was a founder member of the Art Workers' Guild and, four years later, founded the Arts and Crafts Exhibition Society, of which he served as President for many years; in 1898 he was appointed Principal of the Royal College of Art. By the turn of the twentieth century Crane was widely admired, and 13 Holland Street – his home from autumn 1892 until the year of his death – became a focus for an active social life; visitors included Burne-Jones and William Morris. The walls of number 13 were decorated with some of his celebrated wallpapers and textiles, while the collections it contained reflected the eclectic tastes of Crane and his wife Mary, née Andrews (*c.* 1846–1914).

At 37 Holland Street, part of an early twentieth-century terrace, an English Heritage plaque commemorates **Radclyffe Hall** (1880–1943) **15** , the novelist and poet. Marguerite Radclyffe-Hall began her literary

197 Radclyffe Hall (right) and Una, Lady Troubridge at a French bulldog show, 1928. [© Topfoto]

career writing verse, but it was her novel *The Well of Loneliness* (1928), together with her unconventional lifestyle and masculine appearance, that gained her notoriety and has, since then, made her an iconic figure (fig. 197). *The Well of Loneliness* – the fifth of seven novels written by Hall – is a largely autobiographical work in which a lesbian heroine, Stephen Gordon, searches for fulfilment and acceptance in the post-Victorian age. Its appearance scandalised 1920s society, and the book was quickly banned in Britain; it remained largely unavailable until its re-publication in 1949. Hall – known as 'John' to her friends – lived with Una, Lady Troubridge (1887–1963) from 1916 until her death. The couple – both women of considerable means – were inveterate movers-of-house, flitting from flat to flat with remarkable speed. Number 37 was their home from autumn 1924 until late 1928; Una described it as 'a charming house' in which they lived 'for four years. Something of a record for us, wander-

ing Gentiles that we were'.[22] It was while living here that Hall wrote *The Well of Loneliness*, and was besieged by the press and public when the scandal broke following its publication. Number 37 also saw the writing of the less controversial *Adam's Breed* (1926), a best-seller.

At 56 Hornton Street, W8, on the corner of Holland Street, a plaque marks the home of the musician **Sir Charles Stanford** (1852–1924) **16** (fig. 198). Born in Dublin, Charles Villiers Stanford had a keen interest in music from his youth and went to Cambridge as a choral scholar in 1870. Six years later, his incidental music to the drama *Queen Mary* by TENNYSON was performed at London's Royal Lyceum Theatre. Stanford's subsequent musical output included seven symphonies, nine operas – of which the most popular was *Shamus O'Brien* (1896) – and a large body of songs and choral works. He was influential as conductor of the

VAUGHAN WILLIAMS, SAMUEL COLERIDGE-TAYLOR, ARTHUR BLISS, FRANK BRIDGE, GUSTAV HOLST and JOHN IRELAND. Stanford settled in London in 1882, and lived from 1894 to 1916 at 50 Holland Street. The house was divided in two shortly before the western half – which became Holland Lodge, 56 Hornton Street – was marked with a plaque in 1961.

Number 28 Campden Grove, W8 – immediately to the west of Kensington Church Street – was, for a short period, the home of the Irish author **James Joyce** (1882–1941) 17 . Joyce was working on the first draft of *A Portrait of the Artist as a Young Man* when he met, in 1904, a chambermaid from Galway, Nora Barnacle (1884–1951). The couple eloped, and were to spend much of the rest of their lives in Trieste, Zurich and Paris. Joyce's first collection of poetry, *Chamber Music* (1907), was followed by *Dubliners* (1914) and the publication of *A Portrait of the Artist* (1916). The success of these books won him the support he needed to complete *Ulysses* (1922), among the greatest literary masterpieces of the time and one which brought Joyce both acclaim and infamy; its scatological wit meant that it was banned in America until 1934 and in Britain until 1936. A proposer of the plaque, Patrick Tierney, pointed out that 'when it came to accommodation, Joyce was a lifelong flea, leaping about between hotels and flats all over Europe'.[23] He lived in a flat at 28B Campden Grove from early May until early September 1931, during which time he was occupied with *Finnegans Wake* (1939); the sojourn was considered, in Joycean terms, to be remarkably settled. Joyce intended to make London his permanent home, and on 4 July married Nora Barnacle – long his wife in all but name – at Kensington Registry Office. However, hounded by the press, Joyce's view of London soured; his street, which he termed 'Campden Grave', he deemed to be inhabited by mummies. The flat was let, and the writer was never to set foot in England again. The plaque – slightly smaller than usual, so as to fit on the façade – was unveiled on the 112th anniversary of Joyce's birth.

London Bach Choir (1885–1902) and at the Leeds Festival (1901–10), as a writer on musical composition, and as a collector and editor of Irish folk music. Above all, he is remembered as a great teacher: a professor both at the Royal College of Music (1883–1924) and at Cambridge (1887–1924), Stanford's pupils included RALPH

Another short-term London resident, the Finnish composer **Jean Sibelius** (1865–1957) 18 , is commemorated at 15 Gloucester Walk, W8. Born in Hämeenlinna, Sibelius studied music in Helsinki, Berlin and Vienna; he began his musical life as a violinist but soon turned to composition. His first major success came with his *Kullervo* symphony (1892), which became a keystone of the Romantic nationalist movement in his homeland. In the following years, he produced many of his most famous works; these included the *Karelia* music and suite (1893), *Finlandia* (1899–1900) and *The Swan of Tuonela* (1893, rev. 1897, 1900). After 1900 Sibelius's fame spread abroad; in Britain, he was admired by figures such as the composer Granville Bantock and the conductor HENRY WOOD. Sibelius paid the first of five visits to Britain in 1905, largely to conduct. His longest visit was in 1909, when Rosa Newmarch – a writer and champion of east European music – found him accommodation at 15 Gloucester Walk. Sibelius lived in the house from February to March, during which time he composed his only published string quartet, *Voces Intimae*. Between 1910 and 1925 the composer concentrated mainly on symphonies, before giving up composition for the last three decades of his life. The English Heritage plaque, unveiled in 1995, was the first to honour a Finnish national.

Sheffield Terrace, W8, just north of the site of Campden House, has three plaques. The first, at number 58 – a detached, double-fronted house of the mid-1800s – commemorates the detective novelist and playwright **Dame Agatha Christie** (1890–1976) **19** , and was erected in 2001 (fig. 199). Born in Devon, Agatha wrote her first work of detective fiction, *The Mysterious Affair at Styles* (published 1920), in 1917, three years after her marriage to Archibald Christie. From 1920 to 1965, she produced at least one book every year. Christie's reputation was made with *The Murder of Roger Ackroyd* (1926), and her most famous characters – Hercule Poirot and Miss Marple – were

199   The plaque to Dame Agatha Christie at 58 Sheffield Terrace, erected by English Heritage in 2001. [© English Heritage. Photograph by Derek Kendall]

soon familiar to households across the world. Agatha Christie confessed that she had a 'passion' for houses.[24] Favouring Kensington and Chelsea, she lived at numerous addresses in London; so many, in fact, that the details became blurred. In her autobiography, she claimed to have lived at 48 Sheffield Terrace, while she actually lived several houses further west; the cause of confusion may have been her previous address, nearby 47–48 Campden Street, where she lived in 1930–34. Number 58 Sheffield Terrace was the home of Agatha and her second husband, the archaeologist Max Mallowan (1904–1978), from 1934 until 1941, when the couple were driven out by bombing. She described it as 'a happy house', and remembered that, 'When I saw it I wanted to live there as badly as I had ever wanted to live in any house. It was perfect, except perhaps for the fact that it had a basement. It had not many rooms, but they were all big and well-proportioned. It was just what we needed'.[25] It was the only address at which Christie had her own workroom; she declared that the room would contain 'a grand piano; large, firm table; a comfortable sofa or divan; a hard upright chair for typing; and one armchair to recline in, and there was to be nothing else'.[26] Here, at second-floor level, she completed some of her best-known stories, including *Murder on the Orient Express* (1934), *The ABC Murders* (1935) and *Death on the Nile* (1937).

At 34 (formerly 15) Sheffield Terrace a plaque marks the home of **Prebendary Wilson Carlile** (1847–1942) **20** , the founder of the Church Army. Born in Brixton, Carlile began his training to take holy orders in 1878. He was ordained deacon in 1880 and priest in 1881, and from 1880 to 1882 was curate of the Church of St Mary Abbots, Kensington. Later, from 1891 until his retirement in 1926, he was rector of St Mary-at-Hill in the City. Carlile was increasingly aware of the lack of contact between the established Church and the working classes, and in 1882 set up the Church Army, conceived along similar lines to the Salvation Army. The aim of the Church Army was to encourage and enable working people to carry out evangelical work; a training college for men was opened in Oxford in 1884, and one for women – run by Carlile's sister, Marie Louise – in West London in 1887. Despite its rather unconventional approach, the organisation grew rapidly, Carlile remaining strongly at its heart. By the early twentieth century, it was the largest lay society within the Church of England, and played an important part in rousing public social consciousness. Carlile lived at what was then 15 Sheffield Terrace – part of a row of houses built in *c*. 1850 – from about 1883 until 1891, when he moved to the City. The plaque was unveiled in 1972 by his grandson, Rev. Edward Wilson Carlile.

On the other side of the road, 19 Sheffield Terrace (formerly 29 Campden House Court) bears a plaque to **Sir Edward Henry** (1850–1931) 21 , Metropolitan Police Commissioner from 1903 to 1918 and the pioneer of fingerprint identification. Born in London, Henry entered the Indian Civil Service and by 1891 had risen to become Inspector-General of Police in Bengal. Building on the work on fingerprint identification carried out by Sir Francis Galton, Henry developed – between 1896 and 1897 – a new reference method for tracing individuals, and soon after published *Classification and Uses of Fingerprints* (1900). For the first time, the Henry system enabled fingerprints to be filed, searched, traced and compared with ease against thousands of others. In 1901 Henry was appointed Assistant Commissioner of Scotland Yard in charge of the Criminal Investigation Department, and set up the first fingerprint bureau in Britain; his system was soon adopted in countries around the world, and continues to be a vital element in police investigations today. In 1903 he became Commissioner, and moved to 19 Sheffield Terrace, a tall, red-brick house of *c*. 1898 that remained his home until he retired in 1920 to Ascot, Berkshire. It was on the steps of this house, in November 1912, that Henry survived an attempt on his life; the perpetrator, Alfred Bowes, had shot him over a failed attempt to obtain a cab-driver's licence (fig. 200). The plaque was unveiled in 2001 at a ceremony organised by the Metropolitan Police.

Number 4 Bedford Gardens, W8, was the London home of the composer and musician **Frank Bridge** (1879–1941) 22 from about 1914 until the time of his death, which occurred at his country home in Friston, Sussex. Originally proposed for commemoration in 1977 by Hiawatha, son of Samuel Coleridge-Taylor, Bridge was commemorated by English Heritage in 1989. He studied under Sir Charles Stanford at the Royal College of Music, and initially made his name as a viola player. However, he was also active as a com-

poser from 1900, producing chamber music and songs such as the Phantasie Piano Quartet (1910) and orchestral works including *Dance Rhapsody* (1908) and *The Sea* (1910–11). Bridge was a noted conductor – admired by, among others, Sir Henry Wood, for whom he took the baton at some of the Promenade concerts. From the early 1920s, Bridge virtually abandoned his activities as an instrumentalist in order to concentrate on composition. This phase of his career saw the production of works such as the Piano Sonata (1921–24), *Enter Spring* (1927), *Ovation* (1930), *Phantasm* (1931) and the Violin Sonata (1932). A popular teacher, Bridge's most famous pupil was Benjamin Britten, on whom he exerted a strong and lasting influence.

A composer of an earlier age, **Muzio Clementi** (1752–1832) 23 , known as 'the father of the pianoforte', was commemorated in 1963 at 128 Kensington Church Street, W8 (fig. 201). He lived at the house – then known as 1 High Row – from about 1818 until 1823. Born in Rome, Clementi found work as a church organist by the age of thirteen. In the following year, 1766, he came to England under the patronage of the businessman and politician Peter Beckford, on whose Dorset estate Clementi spent the next seven years. In

201   The rear of 128 Kensington Church Street, the former home of Muzio Clementi, in a photograph of the late nineteenth century. By this time, it was the residence of the artist John Callcott Horsley. [Reproduced by permission of English Heritage. NMR]

ing a performance by Isadora Duncan. In 1909 Marie moved to Geneva, where she studied eurhythmics with Émile Jaques-Dalcroze. It was during this period that Rambert met Serge Diaghilev, founder of the Ballets Russes, with which she subsequently collaborated. In 1914, having become passionate about classical ballet, Rambert settled in London, where she studied, performed and worked as a dance teacher for the rest of her life. She opened her first school in Bedford Gardens, Kensington, in 1920 and, six years later, founded a company which performed as Ballet Rambert from 1935; it is now the Rambert Dance Company, and continues to be respected throughout the world. Rambert is remembered as one of the most important figures of twentieth-century dance. She nurtured a generation of dancers and choreographers; these included Dame Alicia Markova, who danced with Ballet Rambert between 1930 and 1956 and unveiled the blue plaque in 1997. Number 19, a double-fronted house of the early 1870s, was the home of Rambert and her husband, the writer Ashley Dukes

1774 he moved to London, where his Opus 2 sonatas (1779) established his musical reputation. Clementi's success encouraged him to travel on the Continent. A highlight of these years was his famous musical 'competition' against MOZART; staged by Emperor Joseph II in Vienna in 1781, it resulted in a draw. From the 1790s, Clementi turned his attention from performing to composition, teaching and business, becoming involved with both music publishing and piano manufacture. Perhaps his most important work was his three-volume collection of études for the piano, *Gradus ad Parnassum* (1817–26); many of these pieces were written during his time in Kensington Church Street. Clementi was succeeded at number 128 – a house of the 1730s, altered in the mid-nineteenth century – by two other figures of note, neither of whom was considered quite important enough to be named on the plaque: the musician William Horsley (1774–1858) and his son, the painter John Callcott Horsley (1817–1903). The Horsleys were visited regularly at the house by yet another composer, Felix Mendelssohn.

On the west side of Campden Hill Road, in the area immediately to the south of Notting Hill Gate, is Campden Hill Gardens, W8. At number 19, an English Heritage plaque commemorates **Dame Marie Rambert** (1888–1982) **24** , the founder of Ballet Rambert (fig. 202). Born in Warsaw as Cyvia Ramberg, she is said to have been inspired to take up dance after watch-

202   Dame Marie Rambert strikes a pose for the camera at her home, 19 Campden Hill Gardens, in 1978. [© PA Photos]

(1885–1959), from 1920 until their respective deaths; they initially rented the top floor and gradually took possession of the whole house. For some of this period, Dame Marie's ballet company was based close by at the Mercury Theatre, Notting Hill Gate. This building was acquired – as Horbury Hall – for Rambert by her husband in 1925, was reworked as a theatre and renamed the Mercury in 1933. It ceased to be the company's base in 1966, though the school remained there until 1979.

Campden Hill Square, W8, was laid out in the 1820s by the property speculator Joshua Flesher Hanson. It was developed over a period of twenty-four years, beginning in 1827, and was – until 1893 – known as Notting Hill Square. At 9 Campden Hill Square – on the east side – a plaque marks the last home of **John McDouall Stuart** (1815–1866) 25 , a Scotsman who became the first explorer to cross Australia. Stuart qualified as a civil engineer before emigrating in 1838 to south Australia, where he worked as a surveyor and soon became involved in expeditions; in all, he undertook six journeys, between 1858 and 1862. On Stuart's first expedition, which aimed to find new pasture country, he discovered around 40,000 square miles (64,370 km) of new territory, including Chambers (now Stuart) Creek. In 1860, Stuart – a capable and caring leader – reached the centre of the continent, and two years later he finally set foot on its northern shore. For this remarkable achievement, he was awarded the highest honour of the Royal Geographical Society, the Patron's Medal. The route Stuart opened across Australia was used for the overland Adelaide–Darwin telegraph, and in 1942 formed the path of the Stuart Highway. Stuart never fully recovered from the privations he suffered during his rigorous journeys. In 1864 he returned to Britain on medical advice, and in that year moved to what was then 9 Notting Hill Square, where he died at the age of fifty. The LCC erected the plaque in 1962, one hundred years after Stuart's continental crossing, hoping that it would 'afford much pleasure both to visiting Australians and to Londoners themselves'.[27]

Number 16 Campden Hill Square was the home for over twenty-five years – from 1932 until his death – of the novelist and critic **Charles Morgan** (1894–1958) 26 ; his widow, the novelist Hilda Campbell Vaughan (1892–1985), and other family members continued to live here until 1974. Morgan joined the Navy in 1907, but resigned six years later in order to pursue a literary career, which was only interrupted by the First World War. In 1921 he joined the staff of *The Times*, and was the newspaper's drama critic from 1926 until 1939. His talents, however, were chiefly directed towards a sequence of novels, beginning with *The Gunroom* (1919) and ending with *Challenge to Venus* (1957). Many of his books – including the novels *Sparkenbroke* (1936), *The Voyage* (1940) and *The River Line* (1949) – were written during his time at number 16, which was bought largely with the proceeds of his successful work *The Fountain* (1932). The resident of the adjoining property, number 15, described Morgan as 'an intensely private neighbour, rarely exchanging words over the party-fence wall'. He apparently 'did not suffer young children lightly and found the boisterous family next door to be unacceptably disturbing to the process of creation; remonstrances followed and we all had to keep quiet'.[28] The plaque – proposed by Morgan's son Roger – was unveiled in 1992 at a ceremony attended by Sir Kingsley Amis, Ronald Harwood and Sir Isaiah Berlin.

In 1996 a plaque was erected to the writer **Siegfried Sassoon** (1886–1967) 27 at 23 Campden Hill Square, his last London home. Born in Kent, Sassoon lived the life of a country gentleman until the outbreak of the First World War, when he was commissioned into the Royal Welch Fusiliers; his exceptional courage earned him the MC and the nickname 'Mad Jack'. Recuperating from wounds in 1917, Sassoon spoke out in his writings against the futility of the slaughter on the Western Front and threw the ribbon of his MC into the Mersey. Soon after, at Craiglockhart War Hospital near Edinburgh, he met the young poet Wilfred Owen, on whom he was to prove a formative influence. In 1918 Sassoon returned to fight but, later that year, a serious wound ended his military career. His war poems, for which he is best remembered, were first published as a collection in 1919. Sassoon continued to write verse for the rest of his life, winning the Queen's Medal for Poetry in 1957. He is also known for his autobiographical works, two of which, *Memoirs of a Fox-Hunting Man* (1928) and *Memoirs of an Infantry Officer* (1930), were almost certainly written at number 23. Here, Sassoon had a flat – leased to him by the house's owner, the artist Harold Speed (1872–1957) – from 1925 until 1932, when he moved to Heytesbury, Wiltshire, his home for the rest of his life.

Number 50 Campden Hill Square, a house built in about 1835, bears an English Heritage plaque to **Evelyn Underhill** (1875–1941) 28 , the Christian philosopher and teacher. Underhill was born in Wolverhampton but spent her childhood – and almost all of her life – in Kensington. She was inspired to study medieval Christianity by a series of holidays in Italy, and by 1907 had become a convinced Christian. Her first major book, *Mysticism: A Study of the Nature and Development of Man's Spiritual Consciousness* (1911), was a pioneering study that asserted the continuing relevance of the Christian mystics. The work brought Underhill into contact with BARON FRIEDRICH VON HÜGEL; he became her spiritual director, and the pair remained close until his death in 1925, by which time Evelyn was a practising Anglican. Increasingly, readers of Underhill's books began to write asking for spiritual help and guidance, and by the early 1920s she was devoting much time to responding; in 1924 she began to conduct retreats, in which her talents were used to the full. Underhill moved to number 50 on her marriage in 1907 to Hubert Stuart Moore (1869–1951), a barrister and childhood friend, and it remained her home until summer 1939. In 1958 it was described as being 'in a very special sense the place of her ministry' and 'the friendliest of houses'.[29] The writer, a friend of Underhill, continued, 'Perhaps one day there will be a plaque to tell that a poet and a writer lived there, but only those who experienced her care for souls will know the real secret of the place'.[30] A plaque was duly erected by the GLC in 1975; it was made of fibreglass and was rectangular in shape, so as to fit on to the building's façade (fig. 203). By 1988 the plaque had become damaged and, two years later, it was replaced by English Heritage, who found that a standard roundel would fit after all.

A gatepost in Aubrey Walk, W8, bears a handsome rectangular LCC plaque commemorating **Aubrey House** (formerly Notting Hill House) 29 and its former residents, who included **Sir Edward Lloyd** (d. 1795), **Richard, 1st Earl Grosvenor** (1731–1802), the diarist **Lady Mary Coke** (1727–1811), the philanthropists **Peter** (1819–1891) and **Clementia Taylor** (1810–1908), and the art lover **William Cleverly Alexander** (d. 1916) (fig. 204). Aubrey House – which, as the plaque records,

occupies the site of Kensington Wells, an early eighteenth-century spa – was built mainly in the mid-1700s by Sir Edward Lloyd; it stands in substantial grounds to the west of Aubrey Walk, adjacent to Holland Park. The earliest notable resident of the house was Sir Richard Grosvenor, the 7th baronet, who lived here briefly in about 1767; a famous breeder of racing stock, he was created an earl in 1784. In June 1767 the house was taken, and subsequently altered, by Lady Mary Coke, née Campbell, who lived here until 1788. There are many references to what was then Notting Hill House in Coke's famous journal; written between

HOLLAND PARK AND CAMPDEN HILL

1766 and 1791, this provides a lively picture of the social life of her time. After a long period as a school, Aubrey House – so-named in the mid-nineteenth century – became the home of Peter Alfred Taylor and his wife Clementia, née Doughty. The couple took up residence in 1860, and remained here until 1873, when Peter's ill health prompted a move to Brighton. Both Taylors held advanced liberal views, and gave strong support to many movements for the promotion of political and social freedom. 'P. A. T.' (as he was known), who was MP for Leicester in 1862–84, was said by his detractors to be 'anti-everything', while Clementia was a notable activist for women's rights.[31] The first meeting of the Committee of the London National Society for Women's Suffrage was held at Aubrey House on 5 July 1867. Earlier, in 1863, Clementia had founded the Ladies' London Emancipation Society, the first national women's anti-slavery society. In 1869, in the grounds of Aubrey House, the Taylors opened the Aubrey Institute, an educational establishment. The house itself provided the setting for regular parties, and was known to be 'open to all, friend and stranger, black and white, rich and poor'.[32] Among frequent visitors was the Taylors' friend GIUSEPPE MAZZINI. The couple were succeeded at Aubrey House by William Cleverly Alexander, a collector and connoisseur of pictures and objets d'art, and a noted patron of WHISTLER. It was Alexander's daughters who agreed to the installation of the plaque in 1960. However, nine years later the house's principal owner asked the LCC to remove the plaque, which had become 'a perfect pest'.[33] He believed that the presence of the council's initials had led some to view the house as public property, and complained of 'drug sodden hippies and their attendant prostitutes' forcing their way into the grounds.[34] By 1972, the LCC had covered the plaque with a sign bearing the words: 'Aubrey House. Private', and it remained hidden from view for some thirty years.

Holland Park, W11, forms part of an estate built in 1860–79 – on ground that once belonged to Holland House – as a high-class development of substantial, detached villas. At number 53, built in 1862, a plaque of 2005 commemorates **Maharajah Duleep Singh** (1838–1893) **30** , the last ruler of Lahore (fig. 205). The extraordinary political career of Duleep Singh – a prince who became a pawn of the British government

– began in 1843: at the age of five, amidst chaos and disorder, he was declared Maharajah of the Punjab, and in the years that followed he witnessed the Anglo-Sikh Wars. As part of the Sikh surrender of 1849, Duleep Singh was dethroned, but was allowed to retain his title and was granted a pension on the condition that he remained obedient to the British government; his property, which included the famous Koh-i-noor diamond, was confiscated. In 1854 Duleep Singh – newly converted to Christianity – arrived in England, which was to remain his home for over thirty years. He soon became a favourite of Queen Victoria, and lived the life of an English country squire at Elveden Hall, Suffolk. Gradually, however, Duleep Singh became agitated by the refusal of the British to allow him to settle in India, and in 1886 attempted to return to his homeland; he was arrested on reaching Aden, where he was received back into the Sikh faith, and spent the rest of his life in Paris. It was in April 1881 that, forced through financial embarrassment to shut up Elveden, Duleep Singh took a lease of 53 Holland Park, where he planned to reside 'with my family as economically as possible'; it was from this house that he set out for the Punjab in 1886.[35] Number 53 remained the home of his children and his wife, Bamba, née Müller (1849–1887), until her death, and was sold in about 1890.

Palace Gardens Terrace, W8, runs parallel and to the east of Kensington Church Street on land that was formerly the glebe of the vicar of Kensington. It was developed from 1854, and is dominated by stuccoed terraced houses. The painter and writer **Percy Wyndham Lewis** (1882–1957) ③① had a furnished room at number 61 from May 1923 until March 1926. Lewis studied at the Slade, and became prominent in the London art world in the period before the First World War; he was closely associated with the Camden Town Group, and was – with Ezra Pound – a founder of Vorticism in 1914. After the war, Lewis turned increasingly from painting to writing. His first novel, *Tarr* (1918), heralded a stream of works on a variety of subjects; his novels included *Revenge for Love* (1937) and *Self Condemned* (1954). Lewis was closely connected with the area around Notting Hill Gate, which he termed 'Rotting Hill' on account of its decline in the post-war period. For the last twenty years of his life, he was based in a studio at 29 Notting Hill Gate (demolished). Lewis's time at number 61, at the end of a terrace, was productive. He was occupied, in particular, with 'The Man of the World', a work eventually published as a series of books that included *The Childermass* (1928) and *The Apes of God* (1930); 'I work incessantly at it', he told T. S. Eliot in a letter written from the house.[36] From 1923 until early 1925, Lewis had a studio nearby, at 44 Holland Street.

Sir Max Beerbohm (1872–1956) ③② , the artist and writer, was originally proposed for commemoration by the publisher and writer Rupert Hart-Davis; a plaque was erected in 1969 (only thirteen years after his death) at Beerbohm's birthplace, 57 Palace Gardens Terrace, a stuccoed house of *c.* 1860. The youngest child of Julius

(1810–1892) and Eliza Beerbohm (d. 1918) – and the half-brother of Herbert Beerbohm Tree – Henry Maximilian displayed a talent for drawing at an early age. Having attended a day school in Orme Square, near his family home, Beerbohm went to Charterhouse and then Oxford, where he met Oscar Wilde and William Rothenstein and, through them, Aubrey Beardsley. Beerbohm came to public attention with the launch in 1894 of *The Yellow Book*, to which he contributed essays and drawings. The year 1896 saw the publication of a collection of his essays and a volume of caricatures, both extremely well received: by 1898 he had, famously, been given the sobriquet 'the incomparable Max' by George Bernard Shaw. Beerbohm continued to be a prolific writer and artist – publishing works such as the novel *Zuleika Dobson* (1911), his best-known literary creation – but was known above all for his caricatures, the subjects of which included Thomas Hardy, W. B. Yeats and William Morris (see fig. 70). In 1898 Beerbohm became drama critic for the *Saturday Review*, a post he held until 1910, when he married and settled in Rapallo, Italy. Over the last twenty years of his life, having given up the art of caricature, he gave a series of popular broadcasts for BBC Radio. Beerbohm's residences in London were all short-lived. Number 57 – his birthplace and home of his earliest years – was felt to be the most suitable address for commemoration.

Number 16 (formerly 8) Palace Gardens Terrace bears an LCC plaque of 1923 to the physicist **James Clerk Maxwell** (1831–1879) ③③ . Born in Edinburgh, Maxwell was already an accomplished scientist by the time he went to Cambridge in 1850. Ten years later, he was appointed Professor of Natural Philosophy at King's College London; soon afterwards, in late 1860 or early 1861, he moved to number 16. This house of *c.* 1859 was to be his home until March 1866, a year after his resignation from King's. Maxwell's work was wide-ranging – his areas of special study included colour, molecular physics, thermodynamics and electromagnetism – and was of lasting significance in, among other fields, quantum mechanics, the development of electric power, telephony and radio. Albert Einstein said that 'one scientific epoch ended and another began with James Clerk Maxwell'.[37] Maxwell's time at what was then 8 Palace Gardens Terrace – a house he shared with his wife Katherine, née Dewar (1824–1886)

– saw the beginning and completion of some of his most valuable papers; these included 'A Dynamical Theory of the Electromagnetic Field' (1865) and 'On the Dynamical Theory of Gases' (1867). He carried out a number of his experiments in a large garret that ran the whole length of the house. For a time, the sill of one of the front windows bore a large colour box, painted black inside and out; this apparently 'excited the wonder of his neighbours, who thought him mad to spend so many hours in staring into a coffin'.[38] In 1871 Maxwell was appointed Cavendish Professor of Physics at Cambridge, where he supervised the design of the Cavendish Laboratory, opened in 1874. It was in Cambridge that he died at the age of forty-eight.

Palace Green, W8, adjacent to Kensington Palace, forms the southern end of Kensington Palace Gardens, an avenue that was known from the nineteenth century as 'Millionaires' Row'; by the 1990s it had become 'virtually an ambassadorial precinct'.[39] At 10 Palace Green, designed by E. N. May and built in 1905 – one of a series of detached houses on the west side of the road – a plaque honours **King Haakon VII** (1872–1957) ❸❹ , who led the Norwegian government-in-exile here between 1940 and 1945. Prince Carl of Denmark – as Haakon was originally known – joined the Danish Navy at the age of fourteen, and in 1896 married his first cousin, Princess Maud, daughter of King Edward VII. In 1905 he was invited to become constitutional monarch of a newly independent Norway and became Haakon VII, taking his regnal name from the medieval Norwegian rulers. His accession was confirmed, at his own insistence, by a national vote. The German invasion of Norway in April 1940 brought Haakon into greater personal prominence. He escaped capture, arriving in London in June 1940, and set up a base for the Norwegian Legation at 10 Palace Green. The government's headquarters was at Kingston House, Kensington Road, while Haakon's residential quarters were also elsewhere – first at Bowdown House, Berkshire, and from 1942 at Foliejon Park in Windsor; however, he commuted daily to Kensington, using number 10 as a base from which to make broadcasts and chair cabinet meetings. Haakon's contribution had a major impact on the war effort – by 1945, 25,000 Norwegians were fighting on behalf of the Allies – and his achievements ensured his long-term popularity. A plaque was erected at number 10, now the residence of the Norwegian Ambassador, in 2005, at a ceremony attended by Her Majesty Queen Elizabeth II, Prince Philip and the Norwegian royal family.

At 2 Palace Green, a chocolate-coloured plaque of 1887 is the earliest of the three in London to commemorate the novelist **William Makepeace Thackeray** (1811–1863) ❸❺ (see also p. 248 and 263–4). Set in an unusual position – above the central window at first-floor level – the plaque marks Thackeray's last, and favourite, home (fig. 206). He bought the house in May 1860 with money 'made out of the inkstand'; his most successful, and famous, book – *Vanity Fair* (1847–48) – had appeared nearly fifteen years earlier.[40] The structure, then dilapidated, was completely rebuilt at a cost of over £8,000. The work, undertaken by the architect Frederick Hering with the assistance of Thackeray himself, resulted in a handsome red-brick building in the Neo-Georgian style; it was described by Thackeray in 1861 as 'the reddest house in all the town'.[41] Despite the disapproval of friends and family – who suggested he

206   A sketch in a letter of 24 May 1861 by William Makepeace Thackeray showing his newly rebuilt house at 2 Palace Green. It was, he wrote, 'the reddest house in all the town'. [Henry W. and Albert A. Berg Collection of English and American Literature, The New York Public Library, Astor, Lenox and Tilden Foundations]

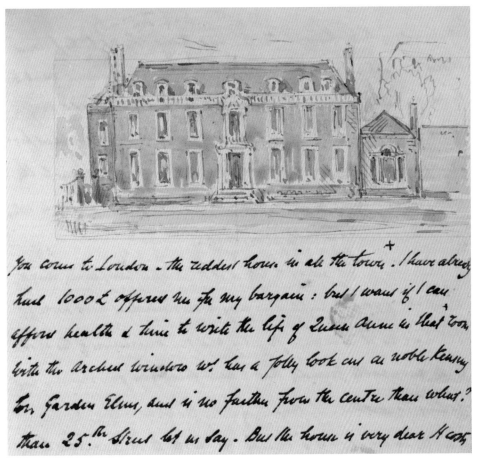

name the house 'Vanity Fair' on account of its lavishness – the novelist was delighted with his new home, moving in during March 1862, shortly after giving up the editorship of the *Cornhill Magazine*. Here, Thackeray spent his days relaxing, and overseeing the furnishing and decorating of what had become 'his principal pleasure'.[42] He wrote, 'it is one of the nicest houses I have ever seen', and had 'a strong idea that in the next world I shan't be a bit better off'.[43] Thackeray's last works, written from the study in the house, included *The Adventures of Philip* (1861–62) and *Denis Duval* (1864). He died at number 2 on Christmas Eve 1863; the house, which was altered in the 1880s, is now the Israeli Embassy.

NOTES

1   Humphrey Carpenter, *A Serious Character: The Life of Ezra Pound* (London, 1988), p. 130

2   Chaim Weizmann, *Trial and Error: The Autobiography* (London, 1949), p. 222

3   Caroline Dakers, *The Holland Park Circle: Artists and Victorian Society* (New Haven and London, 1999), p. 4

4   *Strand Magazine*, vol. VI (September 1893), p. 267

5   Ibid, vol. XVIII (August 1899), p. 123

6   Ibid, p. 131

7   Alfred Lys Baldry, *The Life and Work of Marcus Stone, RA* (London, 1896), p. 31

8   It is now accepted that Fildes was born in 1843, rather than in 1844, as is stated on the plaque.

9   Dakers, *The Holland Park Circle*, p. 159

10 L. V. Fildes, *Luke Fildes, RA: A Victorian Painter* (London, 1968), p. 46

11 *ODNB*, vol. XXVIII, p. 882

12 *Building News*, 9 November 1866, p. 747; Bridget Cherry and Nikolaus Pevsner, *The Buildings of England, London 3: North West* (London, 1991), p. 481

13 *Survey of London*, vol. XXXVII: *Northern Kensington*, ed. F. H. W. Sheppard (London, 1973), p. 140

14 *The Grove Dictionary of Art*, ed. J. Turner, vol. XX (London and New York, 1996), p. 880

15 The plaque, incorrectly, states that Grahame lived at the address in 1901–8.

16 Alison Prince, *Kenneth Grahame: An Innocent in the Wild Wood* (London, 1994), p. 178

17 Margaret Newbolt, *The Later Life and Letters of Sir Henry Newbolt* (London, 1942), p. 403

18 Douglas Goldring, *South Lodge: Reminiscences of Violet Hunt, Ford Madox Ford and the English Review Circle* (London, 1943), p. xix

19 Ibid, p. xii

20 Carpenter, *A Serious Character: The Life of Ezra Pound*, p. 127

21 *ODNB*, vol. XIII, p. 997

22 Una, Lady Troubridge, *The Life and Death of Radclyffe Hall* (London, 1961), p. 90

23 Letter of 17 September 1977 on blue plaque file.

24 Agatha Christie, *An Autobiography* (London, 1977), p. 426

25 Ibid, p. 467

26 Ibid

27 Letter of 30 April 1962 on blue plaque file.

28 Letter of 24 May 1991 on blue plaque file.

29 Margaret Cropper, *Evelyn Underhill* (London, New York, Toronto, 1958), p. 220

30 Ibid, p. 221

31 *ODNB*, vol. LIII, p. 963

32 Ibid, vol. LIII, p. 874

33 Letter of 19 August 1969 on blue plaque file.

34 Letter of 6 June 1972 on blue plaque file.

35 British Library, Asia, Pacific & Africa Collections, L/PS/3/231, p. 677 (4 February 1881)

36 *The Letters of Wyndham Lewis*, ed. W. K. Rose (London, 1963), p. 137 (October? 1923)

37 Basil Mahon, *The Man Who Changed Everything: The Life of James Clerk Maxwell* (Chichester, 2003), p. 1

38 Lewis Campbell and William Garnett, *Life of James Clerk Maxwell* (London, 1882), p. 318

39 Cherry and Pevsner, *London 3: North West*, p. 503

40 Ann Monsarrat, *An Uneasy Victorian: Thackeray, 1811–1863* (London, 1980), p. 409

41 *The Letters and Private Papers of William Makepeace Thackeray*, ed. Gordon N. Ray, vol. IV (London, 1945–46), p. 236 (24 May 1861)

42 *William Makepeace Thackeray: Memoirs of a Victorian Gentleman*, ed. Margaret Forster (London, 1978), p. 365

43 *The Letters and Private Papers of William Makepeace Thackeray*, ed. Ray, vol. IV, p. 264 (9 May 1862)

207   The LCC plaque to Francis
Place at 21 Brompton Square.
[© English Heritage. Photograph
by Derek Kendall]

KNIGHTSBRIDGE AND HYDE PARK GATE

Properly speaking, Knightsbridge is the thoroughfare running east-west from Hyde Park Corner to Kensington Road, though the name is more familiar as a description of the district as a whole. Here, the term is taken to denote the area to the west of Knightsbridge Underground station, including the portion of old Brompton that lies north-west of Brompton Road; it is a locality that straddles the City of Westminster and the Royal Borough of Kensington and Chelsea. Once a hamlet, and a favourite spot for duelling and highway robbery, Knightsbridge was said by 1840 to be 'as much London as Tottenham Court Road'.[1] Its present appearance and its social cachet owe much to the mid-

nineteenth-century development of estates adjoining Hyde Park that were designed with an exclusive market in mind; the lack of connecting roads to the older builds in Brompton was intentional. Westwards along Kensington Road, the area around Hyde Park Gate was developed at about the same time. Architecturally, it is much of a part with Knightsbridge and is therefore treated alongside it here. The wealth of the inhabitants in general is reflected in the plaques: some of the writers and painters honoured may have suffered for their art, but the cause of their suffering – at least while they lived in this district – was not poverty.

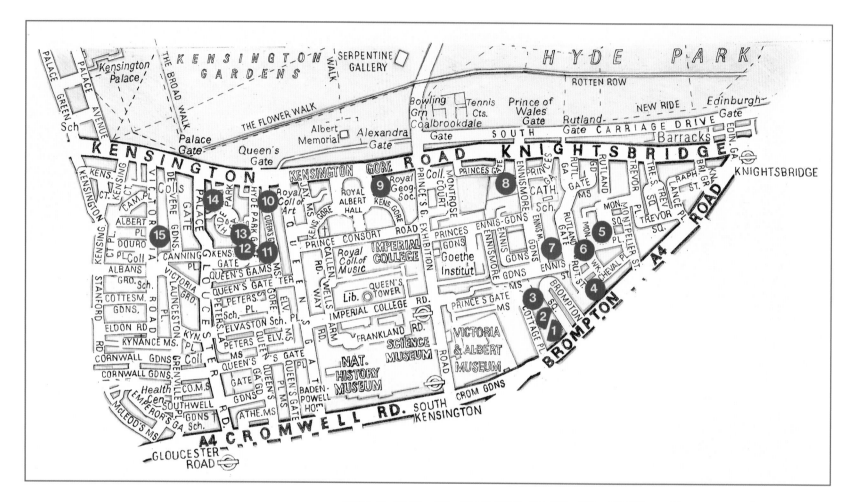

KNIGHTSBRIDGE AND
HYDE PARK GATE

Brompton Square, SW3, was laid out with terraced houses between 1821 and 1835 by William Farlar, an ironmonger; the west side, which has three plaques, was finished by 1826. Set into the first-floor brickwork of number 6 is an LCC plaque of 1959 to the French Symbolist poet **Stéphane Mallarmé** (1842–1898) ❶ , who stayed here during the spring and summer of 1863, when the building was a boarding-house. Born in Paris and orphaned at the age of seven, Mallarmé was a disciple of Baudelaire, but his work was also influenced by the English Romantics, KEATS, SHELLEY and COLERIDGE. His best-known work is *L'Après-midi d'un faune* (1865), which inspired Claude Debussy's prelude of 1894. Mallarmé came to London in autumn 1862, at the age of twenty, in order to learn English – partly to enable him to read the works of Edgar Allan Poe. As it transpired, he made a living teaching English – reluctantly – for most of his life, at *lycées* in Tournon, Besançon, Avignon and lastly in Paris, where he was part of the circle that included Manet, Gide, Proust and WHISTLER. Mallarmé considered London in the fog to be 'a town without peer', but he loathed the place in hot weather, and was completely dismissive of the city's male inhabitants: 'the English men, like the rooms of the Grand Hotel, strike me as being all alike'.[2] When Mallarmé met Marie Gerhard, a German governess and another alienated émigré, he hoped that 'from our two melancholies we could perhaps make a single happiness'.[3] They were duly married at a Catholic chapel in Kensington in August 1863, and left the country soon afterwards.

In the same terrace, at 21 Brompton Square, is the LCC plaque to **Francis Place** (1771–1854) ❷ , the political reformer (fig. 207). Place is best known as a political agitator in the City of Westminster – especially at the hotly contested general elections from 1806 onwards – and for his role in securing the repeal in 1824 of the Combination Laws, which had effectively prohibited trade unions. For many years he was known as the 'Radical tailor', his shop at 16 Charing Cross doubling as a library and a meeting place for reformers. Place's move to Brompton was prompted by a change in personal circumstances: in 1830, despite opposition from his family, he made a second marriage to Louisa Simeon Chatterley (b. 1797), an actress many years his junior. She was then residing at 15 Brompton Square, a house which then enjoyed, as Place noted, 'an unin-

terrupted view as far as Chiswick'. The square, he continued, 'was occupied by genteel quiet people, and was nicely kept'.[4] In 1833 he took a lease on number 21 for a relatively modest £60 per annum, a move in part prompted by financial considerations, Place having lost thousands of pounds through his lawyer's incompetence. He found the house to be 'sadly out of condition', and spent £360 that he could ill afford on its refurbishment.[5] Place had a hand in the reform of municipal corporations enacted in 1835 – the legislation that laid the foundations for modern local government. In 1838 he co-drafted the People's Charter, the founding document of Chartism, but became disillusioned with the movement and undertook little political activity after suffering a stroke in 1844. Seven years later, Place separated from his young wife and went to live with his daughter Annie in Hammersmith. He subsequently resided with two other daughters in Earls Court, where he died.

At 25 Brompton Square – the end house of the original terrace – is the English Heritage plaque to the writer **E. F. Benson** (1867–1940) ❸ (fig. 208). Edward Frederic Benson, known as 'Fred', belonged to an illustrious family: his father, Edward White Benson, was

208   A photograph of the writer E. F. Benson by Lafayette, taken at 25 Brompton Square in August 1926. [© National Portrait Gallery, London]

Archbishop of Canterbury, and his brothers were fellow writers R. H. Benson and A. C. Benson; the latter wrote the words to 'Land of Hope and Glory' (1902). Benson's first novel, *Dodo* (1893), was published when he was working at the British School of Archaeology in Athens; it proved an overnight success, and he soon dedicated himself to writing full-time. Benson was a prolific author, best known for the Mapp and Lucia series; these finely observed satires on the social whirl of the 1920s gained a new audience thanks to a successful television adaptation in the 1980s. Benson also wrote biographies and horror stories, including *The Room in the Tower* (1912). His first permanent address in London, from 1908, was 102 Oakley Street, Chelsea, SW3; in 1915 he took a lease on 25 Brompton Square, which remained his London home until his death. His move to number 25 was described in *Up and Down* (1918), while the house – which Sir Steven Runciman described as 'over-crowded with objects' – formed the setting for *Lucia in London* (1927), *Secret Lives* (1932) and a short story, 'Aunts and Pianos' (1928).[6] A talented pianist, Benson once accompanied DAME NELLIE MELBA in the large drawing room-cum-study on the first floor of the house; here, Benson 'poured tea for his guests out of a fine silver teapot, and loved to discuss, above all things, antiques'.[7] From 1918 he spent much time in Rye, Sussex – the Tilling of his novels. The blue plaque was unveiled in 1994 by Lord St John of Fawsley, a vice-president of the E. F. Benson Society.

Part of the old highway from London to Fulham, Brompton Road was so named in 1863. At 168 Brompton Road (formerly 45 Brompton Row), SW3, is an English Heritage plaque of 1999 to **Sir Benjamin Thompson**, **Count Rumford** (1753–1814) ④ (fig. 209). He is described thereon as an 'Inventor and Adventurer': inveterate in seeking to apply scientific principles to home improvement, Thompson made important modifications to cooking-stove and chimney design, invented a percolating coffee-pot, and still found time for military and political escapades in more than one country. Born in Massachusetts, he was loyal to the Crown and sailed for England in 1776. Here, Thompson's early experiments in cannonball ballistics led him to the conclusion that heat was not, as was then believed, a fluid; he was elected a Fellow of the Royal Society at the age of just twenty-six. He entered the military service of the Elector of Bavaria

in 1783, and rose to become a leading minister in the German state and a count of the Holy Roman Empire. As Count Rumford, he was back in London in 1798, where – after King George III refused him ambassadorial accreditation – he co-founded the Royal Institution with, among others, SIR JOSEPH BANKS and HENRY CAVENDISH. Rumford lodged for a time in Albemarle Street, Mayfair, while supervising the construction of the institution's building, though he had bought the house in old Brompton – then numbered 45 Brompton Row – in summer 1798. Here, his domestic improvements included the double-glazing of the front windows by means of three-sided projecting glass cases, in which there was space for ornamental plants. Rumford's study, on the third floor at the rear, then enjoyed a view of open country from its bay window. Having – quite characteristically – fallen out with his Royal Institution coadjutors, Rumford left both the house and the country in 1802.

At 1 Sterling Street, SW7, which lies at the corner of Montpelier Square, is the plaque to **Bruce Bairnsfather** (1888–1959) ⑤ , the cartoonist – he disliked the term 'cartoon', preferring to call his works 'drawings' or 'pictures'. Bairnsfather, a scion of the Raj, was born in the Punjab and set up as an artist in earnest after an early stint in the Army. He is widely remembered for the First World War cartoon of two beleaguered Tommies in a shell-hole, captioned 'Well, if you knows of a better 'ole, go to it', which first appeared in *The Bystander* in 1915. Much of Bairnsfather's work featured an archetypal soldier, the moustachioed, pipe-smoking 'Old Bill'; this salt-of-the-earth character became a household name, but was at first considered by some as insulting, and questions were even raised in Parliament. Bairnsfather – a machine-gun officer, later given the special rank of officer-cartoonist – was injured at the Second Battle of Ypres. His first settled home and studio after the war was the terraced house in Sterling Street, dating from the mid-1840s; he lived and worked here from 1919 until 1921, the year of his marriage. Bairnsfather was later involved in films and early television transmissions, and served as an artist for the US military during the Second World War. The plaque was suggested by his biographers Tonie and Valmai Holt, and was unveiled by Bairnsfather's daughter Barbara in 1981.

210   The rectangular marble plaque to Sir Francis Galton at 42 Rutland Gate. Erected in c.1931 by admirers of Galton, it was incorporated into the official scheme by the LCC in 1959. [© English Heritage. Photograph by Derek Kendall]

Rutland Gate, SW7, is built on the site of Rutland House, an eighteenth-century mansion; the lower part was developed with four-storey terraced town houses in the 1850s. At the south-east corner is number 42, once home to **Sir Francis Galton** (1822–1911) **6** , the explorer, statistician and founder of eugenics. After

studying mathematics and medicine at Cambridge, in 1850 Galton explored uncharted areas in south-west Africa. Memorably, his interest in statistics and human heredity was stimulated there by his observation that many indigenous women had unusually large breasts; he even devised a triangulation method for measuring their size. The extent to which traits and talents are inherited became his life's work, as summarised in *Natural Inheritance* (1889); *inter alia*, he contributed to the field of biostatistics and disproved the theory of pangenesis – that hereditary elements are carried in the bloodstream – as promulgated by his cousin CHARLES DARWIN. Following the marriage in 1853 of Francis to Louisa Butler (d. 1897), the Galtons lived in a flat in Victoria Street, Westminster, before buying the newly built house in Rutland Gate in 1858. Its elegance was said to be 'emblematic of the life they would lead in London for the next half century: active, central, wealthy and intellectual'; Galton lived here until his death.[8] The rectangular marble plaque was put up by admirers in about 1931 (fig. 210); the association of eugenics – Galton's neologism, meaning the scientific improvement of the human race – with the forced sterilisation programmes of the Nazis was, of course, a subsequent development. The house is now conjoined with number 41; the plaque was refurbished and re-sited by the LCC in 1959, and incorporated into the official scheme.

At 51 Rutland Gate is a plaque of 1972 to the colonial administrator **Lord Lugard** (1858–1945) **7** . Born in Madras, Frederick John Dealtry Lugard served in the Afghan, Sudan and Burmese wars before becoming High Commissioner of Northern Nigeria (1900–6). From 1907 to 1911 he was Governor of Hong Kong and from 1912 to 1919 served as Governor-General of Nigeria, the role for which he is best known; the country was formally united during his tenure, in 1914. During this period, on three-month furloughs, Lugard lived at number 51. It was his wife, Flora Louise, née Shaw (1852–1929) – the first woman on the permanent staff at *The Times*, and its sometime colonial editor – who found the house, being determined that when on home turf her husband should 'find his relations with the London world in proper trim'.[9] Her health prevented her from accompanying him to Nigeria, the name of which she had coined in a newspaper article of 1897. Flora bought the lease on 51 Rutland Gate for

KNIGHTSBRIDGE AND HYDE PARK GATE

£5,000, and spent nearly half that amount again on interior renovations; such was her reputation for hospitality that the house was dubbed 'The Lugard Arms'. Lugard himself, who sported what his biographer called a 'ferocious moustache', was known for his advocacy of eventual independence for African colonies.[10] His spell in Nigeria saw the country's two provinces united, but Lugard's administrative reforms sparked violence, and his relations with the Colonial Office were fractious. On his return in 1919, the Rutland Gate house was sold, and the Lugards moved to their country home, Little Parkhurst, Abinger Hammer, Surrey. Lugard was created Baron Lugard of Abinger in 1928.

Number 14 Princes Gate, SW1, was once the London home of the American-born international bankers **Junius S. Morgan** (1813–1890) and **John Pierpont Morgan** (1837–1913) **8** . Junius Spencer Morgan came to London from New England in the 1850s, and entered into partnership with the banker and philanthropist George Peabody. His negotiation of a loan to France during the Franco-Prussian War of 1870–71 put the firm, by then known as J. S. Morgan & Co., at the forefront of international investment banking. Renamed Morgan, Grenfell & Co., the firm acted for both the British and American governments during the First World War, and – as a subsidiary of Deutsche Bank – continues today. Junius first took a lease on 13 Princes Gate – the eastern half of the present house – in 1858, ten years after it had been completed by John Elger, the developer also responsible for Rutland Gate. Morgan bought the freehold in 1870 and came here regularly until retiring to Monte Carlo, where he died in a carriage accident. His son and successor John Pierpont Morgan acquired the adjacent property at number 14 in 1904 and threw the two buildings into one. This work was carried out in part to house his growing art collection: according to his wife Frances (b. 1845), he 'would collect anything from a pyramid to Mary Magdalene's tooth'.[11] Morgan shipped many of his treasures to New York in 1912, and died the following year. The conjoined houses were the scene of many meetings and entertainments at which important transatlantic social and business links were forged. King Edward VII and Queen Alexandra headed many guest lists; Pierpont even shared a mistress with the monarch – the actress Maxine Elliott. The present

front door dates from 1925–26, when the house was remodelled for use as the United States ambassador's residence, a purpose it served until 1955; the young John F. Kennedy (1917–1963) stayed here during his father's spell in that post, a fact commemorated by a private plaque. Since 1962, the building has been the premises of the Royal College of General Practitioners; the English Heritage plaque, positioned so as to balance the pre-existing plaque to Kennedy, was unveiled in 2004.

Albert Hall Mansions, Kensington Gore, SW7, is an imposing block designed by Richard Norman Shaw and built between 1880 and 1887. It bears a plaque to the conductor **Sir Malcolm Sargent** (1895–1967) **9** . Schooled at Stamford, and trained as an organist and composer, Sargent was appointed professor and conductor of orchestral classes at the Royal College of Music in 1923, and moved to London. A champion of contemporary classical music, he premiered works by, among others, Ralph Vaughan Williams and William Walton, and became a highly successful conductor, especially of choral music. Sargent lived in Belgravia, Bayswater and Kensington before settling in 1947 – the year of his knighthood – at Flat 9 Albert Hall Mansions, 'an eyrie dominating the Park and the Royal Albert Memorial; also the roof under which he was to die'.[12] Having conducted his first Prom concert in 1921, he went on to become as indelibly identified with the famous summer season as Sir Henry Wood himself. In addition, Sargent became known to the wider public for his contributions to BBC Radio's *Brains Trust*. Appropriately, the English Heritage plaque faces the concert hall where he enjoyed so many performing triumphs; its unveiling was organised in 1992 by the Malcolm Sargent Cancer Fund for Children.

Hyde Park Gate, SW7, is the name of two adjoining cul-de-sacs running south from Kensington Road, the easternmost of which boasts four plaques. At 9 Hyde Park Gate (formerly 1 Hyde Park Gate South) is a plaque to **Robert Baden-Powell** (1857–1941) **10** , who is described thereon, at the suggestion of the Scout Association, as the 'Chief Scout of the World', a title he was accorded in 1920 (fig. 211). This was his boyhood home, where he lived with his siblings and their widowed mother – Henrietta, née Smyth (1824–1914) – from the early 1860s until 1877 or 1878. The young Baden-Powell

211 The GLC plaque to Robert Baden-Powell on the boundary wall of 9 Hyde Park Gate. The 'chief scout of the world' lived here as a boy. [© English Heritage. Photograph by Derek Kendall]

KNIGHTSBRIDGE AND HYDE PARK GATE

– known as 'Stephe', pronounced 'Stevie', from his middle name of Stephenson – attended a dame school in Kensington Square before going on to prep school and Charterhouse. During school holidays, he enjoyed long walking tours and sailing expeditions on his eldest stepbrother's small yacht – the kind of healthy outdoor activities that he would later advocate in *Scouting for Boys* (1908). Baden-Powell held the first experimental scout camp in 1907 at Brownsea Island, Dorset, and saw the youth organisation he started grow into a world-wide phenomenon over the next decade – augmented by Girl Guides, Rosebuds (later Brownies), Wolf Cubs and Sea Scouts. In 1957, on the centenary of his birth, the proposal was made to commemorate his birthplace at 11 Stanhope Terrace (formerly 6 Stanhope Street), Paddington, but this was demolished shortly afterwards. Attention turned to 15 Knightsbridge (formerly 8 St George's Place), SW1, to which 'B-P' returned after the Siege of Mafeking in 1900, the escapade that first made his name. However, this building too was earmarked for demolition (it was later reprieved). So it was that the choice fell on 9 Hyde Park Gate, built between 1845 and 1847 by J. F. Hansom. Its ornate stucco decoration and pilasters are consistent with the

social pretensions of Baden-Powell's mother; it was she who, for spurious reasons, added Baden to the family name in 1869. Lack of space on the house's busy façade dictated that the plaque – erected in 1972 – be set on the boundary wall.

The scholar and writer **Sir Leslie Stephen** (1832–1904) ⑪ is commemorated at 22 (formerly 13) Hyde Park Gate. Stephen is chiefly remembered as editor of the *Cornhill Magazine* (1871–82), as an early publisher of works by THOMAS HARDY and HENRY JAMES, and for his founding editorship of the *Dictionary of National Biography* (*DNB*), begun in 1882. Stephen's connection with Hyde Park Gate was long-standing: he was born at number 42 and returned to number 20 in the same street – then numbered 11 Hyde Park Gate South – in June 1876, following the death of his first wife Minny, the daughter of THACKERAY. Two doors away lived the noted beauty Julia Duckworth (1846–1895), a widow, at what was then number 13; the address became number 22 in 1885. Stephen's friendship with her blossomed, and it was here that they set up house together after marrying in spring 1878. A two-storey upward extension was constructed (fig.

212 A photograph of c.1972 showing 22 Hyde Park Gate and the 'insensitive' two-storey extension added by Leslie Stephen in c.1878. [© City of London, LMA]

212); its brick facing jars with the stucco of the original house, and one critic has described it as 'insensitive'.[13] This contained Stephen's book-lined study on the fourth floor and extra accommodation above. Seven maids were crammed into the 'dark insanitary' basement, according to the recollection of the Stephens' daughter, VIRGINIA WOOLF; she, like her sister, the artist Vanessa Bell (1879–1961), was born in a first-floor bedroom.[14] Later, with their brothers Thoby (1880–1906) and Adrian (1883–1948), the daughters produced a family newspaper, the *Hyde Park Gate News*. Apart from the *DNB* – on which he often worked at home – Stephen's own publications included *An Agnostic's Apology and other Essays* (1893) and *The English Utilitarians* (1900). Stephen died at number 22; his plaque was erected in 1960, and has since been joined by two others, privately installed, commemorating his daughters Virginia and Vanessa.

The Prime Minister **Sir Winston Churchill**, **KG** (1874–1965) **12** has a plaque on his post-war town residence at 28 Hyde Park Gate (fig. 213). Churchill entered Parliament in 1900 as a Conservative, but joined the Liberals and served in the Cabinet of HERBERT ASQUITH. He resigned as First Lord of the Admiralty following the bloody fiasco of Gallipoli in May 1915, and afterwards commanded a battalion on the Western Front. Churchill rejoined the Conservatives in 1924, and was Chancellor of the Exchequer under STANLEY BALDWIN; as an opponent of the appeasement of Hitler, he spent many years in the political wilderness before replacing NEVILLE CHAMBERLAIN in 1940 as Prime Minister of the wartime coalition government. Churchill's legendary resolve – and his success in securing the support of the United States – was instrumental in the eventual Allied triumph. After his shock defeat at the general election of 1945, he bought number 28 as a London base, and had it redecorated at once. The general election of 1951 saw him return to 10 Downing Street, but he resigned in 1955 and returned to Hyde Park Gate, purchasing number 27, next door, as office accommodation. Out of government, Churchill travelled and lectured, took up painting again and revised his monumental *History of the English-Speaking Peoples* (1956–58) for publication. A crowd sang 'Happy Birthday' to him here on his ninetieth birthday in November 1964; Churchill replied with his familiar victory sign from the window,

213 Winston Churchill stands outside his house at 28 Hyde Park Gate in c.1951. [Churchill Archives Centre: Baroness Spencer Churchill Papers, CSCT 5/7/4. Reproduced by permission of the Master, Fellows and Scholars of Churchill College, Cambridge]

but – having suffered a series of strokes – he died at the house the following January. As well as being the London house where Churchill lived the longest, number 28 possesses intrinsic interest as a late Georgian survival amidst a sea of Victorian stucco. The GLC plaque was unveiled by Churchill's daughter, Mary, Lady Soames, in 1985.

Next door, at 29 Hyde Park Gate, lived the novelist and playwright **Enid Bagnold** (1889–1981) **13** . Born in Rochester, Bagnold first achieved literary notice with *A Diary without Dates* (1917). The frankness of this record of her experiences as a nurse during the First World War earned her an immediate exit from the profession by summary dismissal. Her subsequent novel, *Serena Blandish* (1924), subtitled 'The Difficulty of Getting Married', describes an impecunious woman's efforts to land a prize catch. Enid herself had no such trouble, having married Sir Roderick Jones (1877– 1962), the Chairman and Managing Director of the Reuters news agency, in 1920. Six years later they acquired number 29, an imposing three-storey stuccoed house dating from the early 1840s, and engaged Edwin Lutyens to remodel the interior. On the

second floor, Lutyens fashioned an enormous nursery for their children – reputed to be the largest in London, it doubled as a lecture hall – and created a square drawing room at garden level, reached by a magnificent oak staircase. For Enid there was a writing room 'like a ship's cabin'; this was approached by a short staircase, the newel of which was topped with a swivelling copper knob – the whimsical notion being that if inspiration struck during the night, she could run downstairs and vault straight to her desk.[15] *National Velvet* (1935), perhaps her best-known work, was an early success for Elizabeth Taylor in its screen adaptation (1944). Later, Enid turned to writing plays, including *Lottie Dundass* (1941) and *The Chalk Garden* (1955); the title of the latter derived from the couple's country home on the Sussex Downs at Rottingdean. Widowed in 1962, Enid Bagnold sold the house in Hyde Park Gate in 1970.

Number 2 Palace Gate, W8, was designed by P. C. Hardwick and built by Cubitt & Co. for the painter **Sir John Everett Millais**, **Bt**, **PRA** (1829–1896) **14** ; the house was substantially complete by April 1876, but the artist does not appear to have taken up residence until 1878 (fig. 214). By this time Millais, a member of the Pre-Raphaelite Brotherhood, had – having once been its scourge – become very much part of the artistic establishment; when he died at Palace Gate, it was as President of the Royal Academy. The house bears testament to his wealth and status; it was, said the art historian Sir Walter Armstrong, 'characteristic of the man . . . a great plain square house, with an excrescence here and there where demanded by convenience', with renaissance ornamental details 'of a rather severe type'.[16] For Millais, it was 'all that he desired', with the exception of there being no garden; he lived here for the rest of his life, sharing the house with his wife Euphemia ('Effie') (1828–1897), who was previously married to John Ruskin.[17] The large first-floor studio, hung with tapestries on three sides and with Van Dyck's *Time Clipping the Wings of Cupid* on the fourth wall, welcomed many distinguished sitters, including – in the single year of 1881 – Tennyson, Disraeli and Cardinal Newman; the latter was rated by Millais 'the most interesting sitter, except Mr Gladstone, who ever entered his studio'.[18] Perhaps to the overall detriment of his reputation, the painting for which Millais remains best known is *Bubbles* (1886); the model for the painting, which is

214 Sir John Everett Millais in his large first-floor studio at 2 Palace Gate, designed for him by P. C. Hardwick and completed in about 1876. [© Mary Evans Picture Library]

Sir J. E. Millais' Studio. Engraved by J. D. Cooper.

KNIGHTSBRIDGE AND HYDE PARK GATE

famed as an advertisement for Pears soap, was his grandson Willie. The plaque, made by Doulton, was placed to the left of the porch in 1926 at the suggestion of Lord Stuart of Wortley, the artist's son-in-law. Great consternation was caused when it was painted over during renovation of the building in 1983 for occupation by the Zambian High Commission; now restored, it is a fine example of the LCC's wreathed design.

An unusual rectangular plaque at 34 De Vere Gardens, W8, commemorates the writer **Henry James** (1843–1916) ⑮ ; it was put up by the LCC in 1949 (fig. 215). An American by birth, James is famous for his novels and short stories – and for his elaborate prose style. He moved to number 34 in March 1886 from a small flat in Mayfair, the darkness and mean dimensions of which contrasted sharply with the recently built fourth-floor flat at De Vere Gardens, which was 'like a photographer's studio'.[19] James's domestic needs were attended to by a live-in servant couple, and the writer jokingly vowed to a friend to be as 'bourgeoise as my means will permit, and have large fat sofas'.[20] To an aunt he proclaimed that 'my new quarters work beautifully and haven't a flaw', though with bachelor fastidiousness he complained of 'some romping little wretches of children overhead'.[21] James nonetheless enjoyed a productive spell here; among his successes were the novels *The Reverberator* (1888) and *The Tragic Muse* (1890) and, among other works for the stage, a dramatisation of his early novel *The American* (1877; stage version 1891). A book on plaques must mention his 1895 short story 'The Altar of the Dead', which tells of a man obsessed with the commemoration of those departed: James had been much affected by the loss of several close friends, including the actress Fanny Kemble and the writer Robert Louis Stevenson. From 1896 James based himself mostly in Rye, Sussex, where he settled permanently two years later. The London flat was sub-let, and James gave up the lease in 1902; it was at Rye that he produced many of his best-known works, including the sinister novella *The Turn of the Screw* (1898) and *The Wings of the Dove* (1902).

215   At 34 De Vere Gardens a rectangular LCC plaque commemorates Henry James, who lived in a flat on the fourth floor. [© English Heritage. Photograph by Derek Kendall]

NOTES

1 *London*, ed. Charles Knight, vol. I (London, 1841), p. 247
2 *Selected Letters of Stéphane Mallarmé,* ed. Rosemary Lloyd (Chicago, 1985), p. 23 (24 July 1863)
3 Ibid, p. 13 (4–5 August 1862)
4 *The Autobiography of Francis Place,* ed. Mary Thrale (Cambridge, 1972), p. 267
5 Ibid, p. 273
6 Tilling Society, newsletter no. 24 (February 1995), p. 5
7 Ibid
8 *ODNB*, vol. XXI, p. 346
9 Margery Perham, *The Life of Frederick Dealtry Lugard* (London, 1956), vol. II, p. 382
10 Ibid, vol. I, p. 170
11 Colin Thom, 'From Pierpont Morgan to the Kennedys and beyond: New Light on the Art and Architecture of No. 14 Princes Gate', *Apollo*, vol. CL, no. 448 (June 1999), p. 33
12 Charles Reid, *Malcolm Sargent* (London, 1968), p. 335
13 *Survey of London*, vol. XXXVIII: *The Museums Area of South Kensington and Westminster,* ed. F. H. W. Sheppard (London, 1975), p. 38
14 Noël Annan, *Leslie Stephen: The Godless Victorian* (London, 1984), p. 106
15 *Survey of London*, vol. XXXVIII, p. 37
16 John Guille Millais, *Life and Letters of Sir John Everett Millais,* vol. II (London, 1899), p. 93
17 Ibid
18 Ibid, p. 147
19 Fred Kaplan, *Henry James: The Imagination of Genius* (London, 1992), p. 296
20 Ibid, p. 297
21 Ibid

216　Number 31 St James's Gardens and its English Heritage plaque to the Chinese writer Lao She. It is the only plaque, thus far, to feature Chinese characters. [© English Heritage. Photograph by Derek Kendall]

NOTTING HILL AND LADBROKE GROVE

Two hundred years ago, the Notting Hill area was farmland, with the exception of the small settlement of Kensington Gravel Pits, now Notting Hill Gate. Development began on the estate of James Weller Ladbroke in the early 1820s, when Ladbroke Road was laid out, together with the arterial route of Ladbroke Grove, the name now applied to the northern part of the area. Economic recession slammed on the builders' brakes until the 1840s, when development began again, and proceeded additionally on the Norham estate to the west. The houses crept northwards, and by 1875 the area – including North Kensington, meaning broadly the district beyond today's Westway – was almost entirely built up. A number of speculators were ruined along the way, as the supply of houses outstripped middle-class demand, and much of the stock was soon subdivided. The penurious condition of many of the inhabitants is reflected in the stories behind several of the area's plaques. During the later twentieth century, Notting Hill became home to many immigrants from the West Indies; today, the district is known as much for its smart, if slightly louche, credentials as for its carnival.

NOTTING HILL AND
LADBROKE GROVE

217 A letter of 2 December 1872 from Hablot Knight Browne ('Phiz') to George Setten. At the top is a self-portrait and his Ladbroke Grove address, marked with a plaque by English Heritage in 2001. [Courtesy of the Beinecke Rare Book and Manuscript Library]

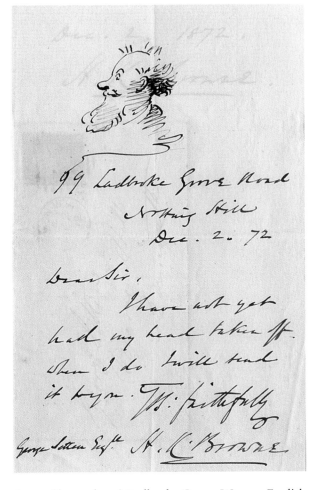

At 239 (formerly 99) Ladbroke Grove, W10, an English Heritage plaque commemorates **Hablot Knight Browne** (1815–1882) ❶ , alias '**Phiz**', the illustrator of DICKENS's novels (fig. 217). Born in Kennington and apprenticed as a line engraver, Browne soon moved into producing etchings and watercolours on his own account. He made his name when Dickens engaged him to illustrate *Pickwick Papers* (1836–37), taking the monicker 'Phiz' – signifying a depicter of physiognomies – as a counterpart to Dickens's 'Boz'. Browne used it for most of his professional work thereafter, and went on to produce the illustrations for nine more of Dickens's major novels, including *Nicholas Nickleby* (1838–39), *Martin Chuzzlewit* (1843–44), *David Copperfield* (1849–50) and *A Tale of Two Cities* (1859). According to G. K. CHESTERTON, 'no other illustrator ever created the true Dickens characters with the precise and correct quantum of exaggeration'.[1] Phiz also illustrated works by, among others, ANTHONY TROLLOPE, Edward Bulwer-Lytton and Harrison Ainsworth. Browne lived in Notting Hill from the early

1860s and moved to what was then 99 Ladbroke Grove in 1874, together with his wife Susannah, née Reynolds (1824–1902) and their children. The bow-fronted five-storey house was then of new construction; Phiz wryly dubbed it 'Bleak House' from its end-of-terrace location. By this time, his commissions were few and his health was failing, though in 1875 he published – under the pseudonym 'Damocles' – the ribald *All about Kisses*, which offered helpful advice about where, how and whom to kiss. An annuity granted to Phiz by the Royal Academy facilitated his move in 1880 to Clarendon Villas, Hove, where he died two years later.

Another story of genteel poverty lies behind the unusual plaque to the naturalist and writer **W. H. Hudson** (1841–1922) ❷ at 40 St Luke's Road, W11 (fig. 218). Born to American parents at Quilmes, near Buenos Aires, William Henry Hudson always regarded England as his spiritual home. He arrived by steamer in 1874, and moved to number 40 when his wife, Emily, née Wingrave (d. 1921), inherited the property in 1888; Hudson, who became a naturalised British citizen in 1900, spent the rest of his life here. It was at this address that he wrote the works that brought him to prominence as an early environmentalist: the collections of essays *The Naturalist in La Plata* (1892) and *Idle Days in Patagonia* (1893), the novel *Green Mansions* (1904), numerous books on the countryside and wildlife – especially the bird life of both England and Argentina – and an autobiography, *Far Away and Long Ago* (1918). The bronze tablet – executed by the celebrated sculptor Luis Perlotti of Buenos Aires – was commissioned by the Hudson's Friends Society of Quilmes, a body of his admirers in Argentina, and was erected in 1938 under the aegis of the LCC. It features an illustration in relief of his birthplace on the

218 The bronze plaque to W. H. Hudson at 40 St Luke's Road was erected in 1938 under the aegis of the LCC. Executed by Luis Perlotti of Buenos Aires, it features an illustration in relief of Hudson's birthplace on the Pampas. [© English Heritage. Photograph by Derek Kendall]

NOTTING HILL AND LADBROKE GROVE

floors and lived in the attic flat, 'the summit of their Cordillera . . . and year by year it became more of a toil to them to climb the sombre stairs. In the hall, and on the stairways and landings, there was no attempt at decoration: they were barely kept clean by the tenants and the housekeeper . . . in this grim jail was held . . . a prisoner of genius, whose only true home was under the open sky'.[3]

At 23 Aldridge Road Villas, W11, in the City of Westminster, is the plaque to the Indian statesman **Sardar Vallabhbhai Javerbhai Patel** (1875–1950) ③ (fig. 219).[4] Patel came to England to read for the Bar in 1910; after an initial burst of sightseeing, he threw himself wholeheartedly into his studies and – like GANDHI twenty years earlier – lived an ascetic existence. After a short spell in a hotel, Patel moved to number 23, then 'a moderately priced boarding-house', from which he walked the four-mile (6.4 km) distance to the Middle Temple every day.[5] He distinguished himself there, winning several prizes and completing his course of study early, and in 1912 returned home to Gujarat, where he set up in legal practice. A convert to the cause of independence, Patel went on to become Gandhi's chief lieutenant and, like him, spent time in prison for civil disobedience. He took a key part in the negotiations leading to independence in 1947, playing a leading role in the Indian National Congress, and later served as Minister for Home Affairs and Deputy Prime Minister under NEHRU. By the time of his death, which occurred in Bombay, Patel was widely addressed as 'Sardar', meaning 'chief'. Patel's plaque was erected by the GLC in 1986, at the suggestion of the MP Greville Janner. It was later damaged during building work, and replaced with an exact replica by English Heritage in 1991.

Appropriately, there is a plaque nearby – at 60 Elgin Crescent, W11, one of a pair of mid-nineteenth-century Italianate villas – to **Jawaharlal Nehru** (1889–1964) ④ , the first Prime Minister of India. Nehru, who came from a wealthy background, was educated at Harrow and Cambridge before going on to study law at the Inner Temple. In contrast to PATEL and GANDHI, Nehru lived what he later described as 'a soft and pointless existence' during his time at London's Inns of Court, developing expensive tastes and playing cards for money; a typical evening included a trip to

219 The plaque to Sardar Vallabhbhai Javerbhai Patel at 23 Aldridge Road Villas. Originally installed by the GLC, it was replaced with a replica by English Heritage in 1991. [© English Heritage. Photograph by Derek Kendall]

Pampas, which seems appropriate given that – despite the length of his residence here – Hudson's dislike of Tower House, as the building was then called, seems to have been matched only by his distaste for the area. The house was described by his biographer as 'stale and gloomy outside and dim with ancient paper and paint within'.[2] Hudson and his wife let out the lower

the theatre followed by a champagne supper at the Savoy.[6] 'Joe' Nehru – as his Harrovian friends addressed him – lived in Elgin Crescent from July 1910 to January 1911, and returned here when he was called to the Bar in the summer of 1912. Back in India, he joined Gandhi's campaign of civil disobedience in 1919, and became a leading figure of the Indian National Congress; presiding over its annual session in 1929, he declared himself a republican and a socialist. Like Gandhi and Sardar Patel, Nehru was frequently imprisoned by the British, but in 1947 became independent India's first Prime Minister. He held this office until his death, and his vision of a secular, democratic India is one that has endured. The plaque, suggested by the Indian High Commission, went up in 1989, in time for the centenary of Nehru's birth. It was unveiled by the Indian Vice-President, Dr Shankar Dyal Sharma.

Howard Staunton (1810–1874) **5** has a plaque at 117 Lansdowne Road, W11, on which he is described as 'British World Chess Champion' (fig. 220). While an official world chess championship did not then exist, Staunton was regarded as such in the years following his defeat of the French master Pierre Saint-Amant in 1843. Bobby Fischer, a world champion of more recent date, called him 'the most profound opening analyst of all time'.[7] The English Opening (given in chess notation as 1. c4) was named in Staunton's honour after he

220 Number 117 Lansdowne Road and its English Heritage plaque to the chess champion Howard Staunton, seen through the balustrade. [© English Heritage. Photograph by Derek Kendall]

used it with great success. He also gave his name to the 'Staunton pattern' of chess pieces, designed by his friend Nathaniel Cook in 1835, which is still the set most commonly used in the English-speaking world. Staunton was a prolific writer on the game; between 1840 and 1854 he owned and edited the monthly periodical the *Chess Player's Chronicle*, and from c. 1844 until his death edited the chess column of the *Illustrated London News*. Among the reference works he authored was *The Chess Player's Handbook* (1847). After 1854 Staunton played little chess, devoting his time instead to writing critical studies of Shakespeare. Of his several addresses in London, it was originally felt that 8 Sydney Place, South Kensington, SW7, where he lived in the years around 1850, was the best place for commemoration. However, the house already bore a plaque to the composer BÉLA BARTÓK, and the owners felt that another would be de trop. The choice fell instead on 117 Lansdowne Road, where Staunton lived from late 1871 until spring 1874, shortly before his death; the distinctive terrace has Dutch gables and a pierced parapet, and is unlike any other building in the area. The plaque was unveiled in 1999, in the presence of Julian Hodgeson, the reigning British champion.

At the south end of Lansdowne Road, on a site bounded by Ladbroke Road and Boyne Terrace Mews, is the extraordinary eight-storey brick edifice of Lansdowne House (fig. 221). Designed by William Flockhart in 1904, it was built to provide studio flats for artists through the munificence of Sir Edmund Davis, whose fortune derived from mining interests in South Africa. Six of Lansdowne House's artistic residents are commemorated on an unusual GLC plaque: **Charles Ricketts** (1866–1931), **Charles Shannon** (1863–1937), **Glyn Philpot** (1863–1937), **Vivian Forbes** (1891–1937), **James Pryde** (1866–1941) and **F. Cayley Robinson** (1862–1927) **6** . The erection of the plaque in 1979 was timed to coincide with a major retrospective of the two first named. Ricketts, a painter, book and stage designer who worked with OSCAR WILDE and GEORGE BERNARD SHAW, lived here with his lifelong partner Charles Shannon, a lithographer and painter, between 1904 – when the property was newly built – and 1923. Despite their relative poverty, they built up an impressive art collection that passed to the Fitzwilliam Museum and the British Museum after their deaths.

Philpot, a portraitist and sculptor who, like Ricketts, drew inspiration from the Old Masters, was one of their associates. Lansdowne House was variously his home and his studio from 1923 to 1935. With him lived his friend Vivian Forbes, another portrait painter, who tragically killed himself after Philpot's sudden death in 1937. James Pryde, a Scottish artist who had a studio here for nearly twenty-five years after 1915, is remembered as an innovative poster designer. Frederick Cayley Robinson, a Symbolist painter, was commissioned by Sir Edmund Davis to paint four murals of the Acts of Mercy for the entrance hall of the Middlesex Hospital, the first of which was completed in 1915. Robinson, who also taught and executed lithographic posters, had moved into Flat 1 at Lansdowne House the previous year, and stayed for a decade. The plaque, which was first suggested by a niece of Philpot, cost twice as much as the usual roundels. This was owing to the large number of characters on it, and the associated increased risk of problems in the firing process.

At 39 Chepstow Villas (formerly 11 Kensington Park Terrace), W11, is the plaque to **Louis Kossuth** (1802–1894) **7** , the Hungarian patriot (fig. 222). Once a political prisoner of the Austrians, Lajos ('Louis') Kossuth – leader of the revolution of 1848 – was Gov-

ernor of Hungary in 1849, after the country briefly threw off the yoke of the Habsburg Emperor of Austria. He was defeated and exiled later that year after Russian armies intervened on the Austrian side, and came to England in October 1851. He made a three-week tour of the country and met Mazzini, among others sympathetic to his cause; Kossuth was officially entertained by London's Lord Mayor, and at Copenhagen Fields in Islington addressed a gathering of tens of thousands representing the trade unions. From Britain, he visited the United States, returning to England in July 1852. It was from this date until March 1853 that he lived here, a house then known as 11 Kensington Park Terrace. Kossuth was widely fêted by English liberals, although some sections of the political establishment regarded him as a dangerous agitator. It has since been argued that his nationalism was so narrow as to be self-defeating – in, for example, his hostility to Slavic ambitions for self-determination. Kossuth made his living as a journalist before leaving England in 1859 for Italy, where he spent the rest of his life. The plaque to him went up exactly a hundred years after he left these shores – and barely three years after another popular uprising in Hungary was crushed.

There is a GLC plaque dating from 1967 at 7 Kensington Park Gardens, W11, the long-term residence of the scientist **Sir William Crookes** (1832–1919) **8** (fig. 223). The son of a tailor, Crookes attended the Royal College of Chemistry as a pupil and assistant of A. W. Hofmann. It was Crookes's discovery of the metallic element thallium in 1861 that brought about his early election as a Fellow of the Royal Society two years later. He moved in 1880 to number 7 – a stuccoed mid-Victorian house, with elaborate porch and balustrades, which he shared with his wife Ellen (d. 1916) – and died here nearly forty years later. A scientific colleague wrote, 'when one visited him . . . and saw his fine library with the well ordered though small laboratory opening out of it, and admired the neatness of his records and his untiring industry, one felt that here was a workshop from which phenomena of stimulating novelty might at any time emerge . . . It was a peaceful and secluded home of quiet research'.[8] Here, Crookes worked on the development of an incandescent lamp; the house was reputed to be one of the first in the country to be lit by electricity. His work on

222   The installation in June 1959 of the plaque to Louis Kossuth at 39 Chepstow Villas. [© NI Syndication / The Times]

223 A signed portrait photograph of the scientist Sir William Crookes in 1914. He lived for nearly forty years at 7 Kensington Park Gardens. [© Science Museum Pictorial / Science & Society Picture Library]

224 The campaigners for women's suffrage Emmeline and Christabel Pankhurst in a photograph of 1908. [© Illustrated London News Ltd / Mary Evans Picture Library]

volved in their mother's work, and became themselves leading figures in the fight for women's rights. In 1903 Emmeline and Christabel founded the Women's Social and Political Union, a militant group whose motto was 'Deeds, not words' and whose members were known as 'suffragettes'. While Emmeline played an active role – staging rallies and suffering repeated arrests – Christabel was known for her remarkable abilities as an organiser. The hardships took their toll on Emmeline; by 1916, when she took up residence at 50 Clarendon Road, her energies had been transferred to the care of 'war babies', children born out of wedlock as a result of the social upheaval. Four she adopted and brought to live with her at number 50, a stuccoed semi-detached house of the mid-1800s which she loved, and which was her home until her move to Canada in autumn 1919. Nearby, at Tower Cressy, Aubrey Road (demolished), Emmeline ran a day nursery and adoption home for female orphans. Meanwhile, at 50 Clarendon Road, Emmeline was joined by Christabel, who lived in the house for periods between 1917 and 1919. The right to vote was gained initially in 1918 and, on the same terms as men, in 1928, a crucial victory due in no small part to the Pankhursts. The plaque was unveiled in 2006 by Eveline Bennett, the last surviving war baby adopted by Emmeline.

cathode rays, and attendant success in producing a vacuum tube, was an important precursor for the discovery of X-rays and electrons; effectively, Crookes's work laid the ground for the entire new fields of nuclear physics and electronics. Later, his work on anti-polarising glass provided the basis for the development of sunglasses. Crookes, who was knighted in 1897, had a reputation for having a keen eye for the commercial application of science: two lucrative sidelines were the sodium amalgamation method of extracting gold and the use of sewage as fertiliser. Crookes's interest in psychic research, however, was an enthusiasm that somewhat imperilled his scientific reputation.

The campaigners for women's suffrage **Emmeline Pankhurst** (1858–1928) and her daughter **Dame Christabel Pankhurst** (1880–1958) ⑨ are honoured with an English Heritage plaque at 50 Clarendon Road, W11 (fig. 224). Emmeline Goulden was born in Manchester, and attended her first women's suffrage meeting at the age of fourteen. In 1879 she married Richard Pankhurst, a barrister and radical, who in 1870 had drafted the first women's suffrage bill in Britain. The couple had five children; the two eldest – Christabel and SYLVIA PANKHURST – were both closely in-

At 31 St James's Gardens (formerly St James's Square), W11, is an English Heritage plaque to the Chinese writer **Lao She** (1899–1966) ⑩ (fig. 216). Lao She is the pen name of Shu Qingchun, born in Beijing, one of the outstanding Chinese writers of the twentieth century: Robin Wood, a professor at China's Tsinghua University, described him – from his tendency towards humorous satire – as 'a Chinese Charles Dickens'.[9] A Christian convert, Lao She came to England in 1924 to teach Chinese at London University's School of Oriental Studies. His experiences resulted in the novel *The Two Mr Mas* (1929), an evocative account of London life in the 1920s from the viewpoints of a Chinese father and son. At St James's Gardens – then St James's Square – Lao She lodged between 1925 and 1928 with the scholar Clement Egerton, whom he assisted in his translation of *The Golden Lotus*, eventually published in 1939, one of the best-known Chinese erotic novels. In 1931 Lao She returned to China, where his literary successes included the novels *City of Cats* (1933) and *Rickshaw Boy* (1936) and the play *Teahouse* (1957). He was heavily involved in resistance against the Japanese after war broke out in 1937, and was initially well regarded in Maoist China. The Cultural Revolution changed all that, however, and he was hounded to the point of committing suicide in 1966. Lao She's rehabilitation was demonstrated by the presence of the Chinese Ambassador, Mr Zha Peixin, at the plaque's unveiling ceremony in 2003. It is the only plaque, thus far, to feature Chinese characters.

At 17 (formerly 21) St Ann's Villas, W11, a plaque marks the birthplace of **Albert Chevalier** (1861–1923) ⑪ , the music-hall comedian. At the age of eight he took part in 'penny readings' at a local hall, but his parents, who blessed him with the middle names of Onésime Britannicus Gwathveoyd Louis, wanted him to enter the priesthood. His father – Jean Onésime Chevalier, a language teacher – dabbled in spiritualism; for a time, Chevalier later recalled, the house 'became a happy hunting-ground for mystic waifs and strays. We held seances nightly'.[10] Despite these distractions, Chevalier made his professional stage debut in London in 1877, and spent fourteen years as an actor before turning to the music hall. His costermonger routine was soon a hit all over the country: such was his popularity that he performed at as many as five venues in a single night. Chevalier represented the respectable face of music-hall entertainment, and his name was commended to the LCC in 1963 with the observation that he 'never sang an offensive song'.[11] The plaque was unveiled two years later, to the strains of 'My Old Dutch', Chevalier's most readily recalled refrain, which he co-wrote in 1911 with his brother Auguste, whose pen name was Charles Ingle. The semi-detached house that bears the plaque was built in 1852; Chevalier had left here by 1894, the year he married Florrie, the daughter of George Leybourne, another star of the music hall.

NOTES

1 G. K. Chesterton, *Charles Dickens: A Critical Study* (London, 1906), p. 74

2 Morley Roberts, *W. H. Hudson: A Portrait* (London, 1924), p. 54

3 Ibid, p. 55

4 The third of Patel's names is more usually transliterated as 'Jhaverbhai'.

5 B. Krishna, *Sardar Vallabhbha Patel: India's Iron Man* (New Delhi, 1996), p. 28

6 Judith Brown, *Nehru* (New Haven and London, 2003), p. 41

7 D. Hooper and K. Whyld, *The Oxford Companion to Chess* (Oxford, 1992), p. 391

8 Edmund Edward Fournier d'Albe, *The Life of Sir William Crookes* (London, 1923), intro. by Oliver Lodge, p. xii

9 *Kensington & Chelsea News*, 27 November 2003, p. 5

10 Albert Chevalier, *Before I Forget* (London, 1901), p. 6

11 Report of 1963 on blue plaque file.

NOTTING HILL AND LADBROKE GROVE

225 A view which emphasises
the close relationship between
Sir Henry Cole – who lived at 33
Thurloe Square – and his place of
work: the Victoria and Albert
Museum (on the right of the
picture). [© English Heritage.
Photograph by Derek Kendall]

SOUTH KENSINGTON

The greater part of the area known as South Kensington is – in both bricks and mortar and in its very name – an invention of the later nineteenth century. Earlier buildings may be found in the old Brompton and Kensington High Street areas, but most of this fashionable suburb sprang up in the wake of the Great Exhibition of 1851, held in Hyde Park. The profits of the exhibition bankrolled the development of the museums on the land to the south, and high-class housing speculations were soon rife in the surrounding district. Sir Henry Cole – surely the single most influential figure in the area's development – was responsible for the modern name of what was previously regarded as part of Brompton. Once known for its nurseries and market gardens, the re-branded South Kensington rapidly gained social prestige on a par with Mayfair and Belgravia. Its houses were mostly large, stuccoed and Italianate, and their inhabitants almost invariably wealthy.

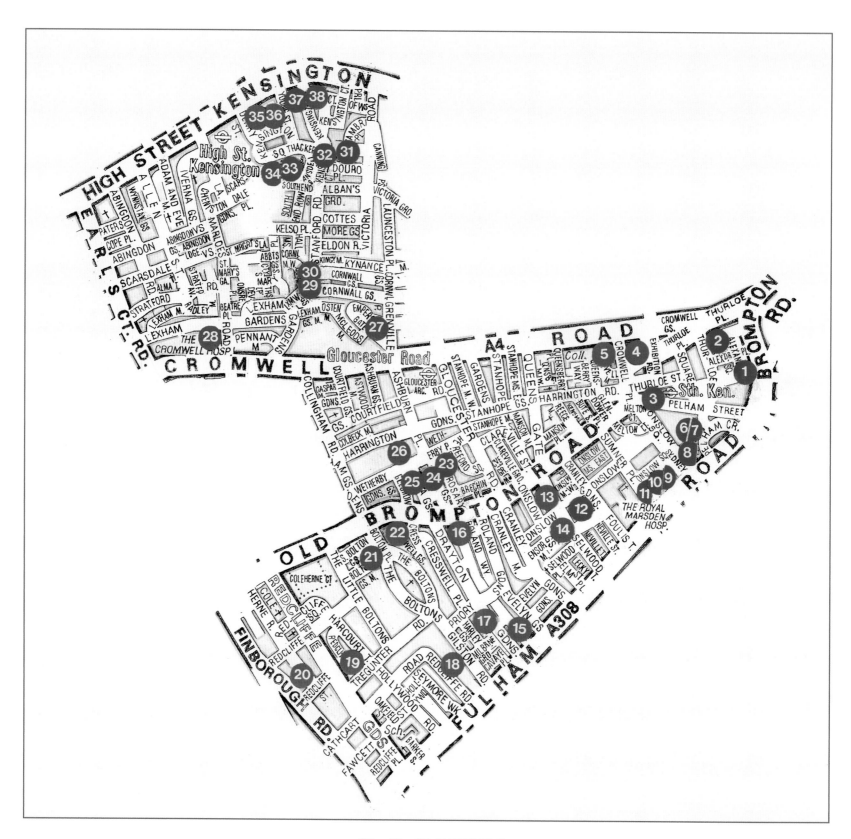

SOUTH KENSINGTON

The architect, journalist and social reformer **George Godwin** (1813–1888) ❶ is commemorated at 24 Alexander Square, SW3, an end-of-terrace house which forms a group with the adjacent South Terrace. Godwin was a pupil in the office of his architect father, George Godwin senior, and many of his buildings were collaborations with his brother Henry. Almost all were in Kensington, where Godwin lived for most of his life; his works in the area include Redcliffe Square (1869–76) and its church, St Luke's (1872–73). Godwin's wider significance owes more to his lengthy and highly successful stint as editor of *The Builder* (1844–83), which became noted for its campaigns for improved housing and public health; in this capacity, Godwin was also an early supporter of what became the blue plaques scheme (see p. 10). A recent commentator has hailed him as 'one of the few to perceive that London in this period was undergoing change equalled only by the rebuilding after the Great Fire'.[1] Godwin's vivid accounts of the evils of slum overcrowding were collected in three volumes, among them *Town Swamps and Social Bridges* (1859). Much of his editorial work was accomplished at the house in Alexander Square, which is part of a yellow-brick and stucco terrace of the late 1820s, and was his home from about 1850 until 1873. The unveiling of the plaque in 1969 was attended by Ian Leslie, then the editor of *Building* magazine, the successor to Godwin's *The Builder*.

At 33 Thurloe Square, SW7, lived **Sir Henry Cole** (1808–1882) ❷ , an influential member of the Society of Arts and another early proponent of 'memorial tablets' (see pp. 10–11); he is described on the plaque as 'Campaigner and Educator. First Director of the Victoria and Albert Museum' (fig. 225). An activist civil servant, Cole began his career in 1823 as a government clerk in the Record Commission; it was he who secured the building of the Public Record Office, begun in 1851, in Chancery Lane. The Great Exhibition in Hyde Park, held in the same year, was largely organised by Cole, who spent the next twenty years working on the development of the museums' precinct in South Kensington; such was his dominance of the project, which aimed to create a national centre for the arts and sciences, that he was dubbed 'King Cole'. Among his directorial responsibilities was the South Kensington Museum, opened in 1857; as this did not become the Victoria and Albert Museum until 1899, the inscription

on the plaque, erected in 1991, places ready public understanding before strict historical accuracy. Cole retired in 1873, and in December of that year went to live at 33 Thurloe Square, which faces the V & A, one wing of which is now named after Cole, its effective founder. The house, at the north-east corner of the square, forms the end of a terrace dating from about 1840, built to designs by GEORGE BASEVI. While here, Cole promoted the opening of the nearby National Training School for Music (1876), the predecessor of the Royal College of Music; among his earlier achievements – while on secondment to assist ROWLAND HILL in the introduction of a system of prepaid postage – was the commissioning of the first Christmas card (1843). Cole's driven nature sometimes gave offence; by way of reply, he asserted that 'if he had always waited for orders he would never have got anything done'.[2] He left Thurloe Square in 1877, and died five years later at 96 Philbeach Gardens, Earls Court, SW5.

At 18 Thurloe Street (formerly Alfred Place), SW7, is a plaque to the homoeopathic physician **Dr Margery Blackie** (1898–1981) ❸ . It was apparently at the age of five that Blackie – the niece of the leading homoeopath James Compton Burnett – decided that she wanted to become a doctor; she trained at the London School of Medicine for Women, and set up as a homoeopathic practitioner in 1926. Three years later, Blackie moved to number 18 – a mid-nineteenth-century stuccoed terraced house – and lived and worked here until 1980; it is said to have 'suited her to perfection'.[3] In her consulting room at the rear of the ground floor, patients were put at their ease by a blazing log fire and beautiful flower arrangements created by her long-term professional partner, Dr Helena Banks (d. 1971). By the time of the Second World War, Margery Blackie had gained international recognition, and was to play a major part in establishing the modern popularity of homoeopathy. She held several senior posts at the London Homoeopathic Hospital and encapsulated her medical ideas in a book, *The Patient, not the Cure* (1975). Blackie's clients included several members of the royal family, and in 1969 she was appointed Physician to Her Majesty Queen Elizabeth II. Among her students was Dr Sam Hutt – better known as the country and western singer Hank Wangford – who recalled her as 'a little woman with a classic grey bun who moved very fast, almost

SOUTH KENSINGTON

jerkily, like a wee bird whose eyes shone with an artless love of life: a born healer'.[4] Blackie's favourite television programme was *Match of the Day*, and she was wont to sing along with its signature tune in 'a sweet, pure singing voice', another friend remembered.[5] The English Heritage blue plaque to this improbable football fan was unveiled by Princess Alexandra, patron of the Blackie Foundation Trust, in 2004.

At 5 Cromwell Place, SW7, is a plaque to the painter **Sir John Lavery** (1856–1941) ④ (fig. 226). Born in Belfast, Lavery, who had lost both parents by the age of four, developed a sharp business sense to accompany his artistic flair. Much of his work was in the lucrative field of portrait painting: those who sat for him ranged from WINSTON CHURCHILL to Shirley Temple, though he was best known for his formal portrayals of the royal family. For one of his most successful genre paintings, *The Tennis Party* (1885), he chose a subject calculated to appeal to the middle-class mores of would-be patrons. Lavery had trained in Glasgow, and became associated with the Impressionist-inspired 'Glasgow

226 A cartoon by Powys Evans of Sir John Lavery. It was published in 1926, during the time the painter was living at 5 Cromwell Place. [© Estate of Powys Evans. Courtesy of National Portrait Gallery, London]

Boys'. With his second wife, the American-born society hostess Hazel Jenner Lavery (1880–1935), he had strong links with the cause of Irish self-determination; his painting *The Court of Criminal Appeal* (1916) depicted the notorious trial of Roger Casement, and in 1922 he painted Michael Collins – a visitor to 5 Cromwell Place, and the object of infatuation for Hazel Lavery – on his deathbed. Lavery, who was knighted in 1918, moved to the capital in 1896 and was living at Cromwell Place by 1899. After Hazel's death in 1935 he spent much time in the United States, but kept the house on until May 1940, when he left wartime London for Kilkenny. The handsome low-built Italianate house, which dates from the mid-nineteenth century, was adorned with a plaque – the first erected by the GLC – in 1966.

Opposite the Natural History Museum, 21 Cromwell Road, SW7, (formerly 1 Cromwell Houses), was originally the residence of **Sir Charles James Freake** (1814–1884) ⑤ , the builder and patron of the arts. Freake came of humble origins, but rose to became one of London's most successful speculative builders, employing nearly four hundred men by 1867. Early on, he worked with GEORGE BASEVI, whose stylistic influence was apparent in Freake's subsequent developments. The terrace on which he is commemorated was one of his own undertakings; he moved into the double-fronted house – which was originally numbered 1 – on its completion in 1860. Freake's houses were notably spacious, and his own establishment needed to be: in 1871 he was sharing it with his wife, daughter, three other female relations and ten servants. It was remarkable for its private theatre-cum-ballroom, contained within a large two-storey wing; the shows held here were attended by, among others, Edward, Prince of Wales and SIR HENRY COLE. It was Freake who financed the construction of the National Training School for Music (1874–75), a part of Cole's grand scheme; he also contributed to the construction of churches including St Paul's, Onslow Square (1859–60). Created a baronet in 1882, Freake never lost his cockney accent; his wife Eliza, née Wright (d. 1900) is reported to have dropped her aitches in solidarity. The plaque, on the Cromwell Place elevation of the house, was erected in 1981.

The stuccoed sweep of Pelham Crescent, SW7, was designed by the ubiquitous GEORGE BASEVI, and dates from around the mid-1820s (fig. 227). Number 21 was

227   A photograph of Pelham
Crescent in 1910. The street now
features blue plaques to François
Guizot (at number 21) and Sir
Nigel Playfair (at number 26).
[© RBKC Libraries]

the home of **François Guizot** (1787–1874) ⑥ , the French politician and historian. Once a celebrated professor of history at the University of Paris, Guizot was appointed Education Minister in 1832 by the 'citizen king', Louis-Philippe. He was briefly Ambassador to England in 1840, and his subsequent tenure as Foreign Minister was notable for a thaw in relations between the two countries. Having been the leading force in the French government for some time, Guizot became Prime Minister in 1847 but, like his royal master, he was forced to flee across the Channel with his family in the wake of the revolution of 1848. He took a lease on 21 Pelham Crescent, which was let furnished. 'I have found, close to London – at Brompton – a little house, which is almost in the country', he told a friend; 'it is good enough for us, and inexpensive'.[6] Having had his French property sequestered, Guizot made a living from writing, and produced several volumes on seventeenth-century England. To add to his woes, his elderly mother – a great influence on his life and character – died at number 21, and Guizot's refusal of a chair at Oxford betokened his desire to return to France as soon as was feasible. He did so in summer 1849, having – according to his landlord – clocked up an impressive list of damages, including the knob from a bedstead pole, a dustpan handle, and numerous items of crockery and glassware. The plaque was unveiled in 2001 by a Guizot descendant, Madame Catherine Coste.

At 26 Pelham Crescent lived the actor-manager **Sir Nigel Playfair** (1874–1934) ⑦ (see fig. 227). Educated at Harrow and Oxford, Playfair became a leading member of the University Dramatic Society, and proceeded to make his name as a versatile character actor with a reputation for 'good-humoured comedy, dry as the driest sherry'.[7] Playfair lived in Pelham Crescent

from about 1910 to 1922, during which time he made the transition to theatre management. During the First World War, a piece of Zeppelin shrapnel landed in the house's back garden; with admirable sangfroid, Playfair gave a tea party to celebrate. The adventurous interior decor was, according to his son, widely admired – especially the dining room, 'with its red carpet, its black table and sideboard, its yellow ceiling and walls'.[8] In 1918, along with ARNOLD BENNETT and his friend Alistair Tayler, Playfair bought the Lyric Theatre in Hammersmith. They transformed it from near dereliction to great prosperity, notably with a Playfair-directed revival of John Gay's *The Beggar's Opera* (1920). After 1925 Playfair lived at 24 Upper Mall, Hammersmith, W6 – where, given the strong local connection, his plaque would have been placed but for the owner's refusal to allow it. He was knighted in 1928 and later moved to Said House, Chiswick. 'Playfair popularized classics of English drama without debasing them', noted an LCC historian approvingly; his plaque went up in 1965.[9]

Number 7 Sydney Place, SW7, is part of another terrace designed by GEORGE BASEVI. Here, at the home of Sir Duncan Wilson (1875–1945), sometime Chief Inspector of Factories, the Hungarian composer and virtuoso pianist **Béla Bartók** (1881–1945) ⑧ often stayed when performing in London. Bartók visited Britain on at least sixteen occasions; his first visit was in 1904, when he gave a performance in Manchester of his symphonic poem *Kossuth* (1903), which commemorates the eponymous Hungarian national hero LOUIS KOSSUTH. For reasons of economy, he stayed with his friend Sir Duncan, and did so at least a dozen times between 1922 – when he gave his first London performance – and 1937. With Hungary's leaders allied to the Nazis, to whom Bartók was implacably opposed, he left his homeland for the USA during the Second World War, and died in New York at the age of sixty-four. A leading British admirer of Bartók's music – in which the Modernist influences of Stravinsky and Schönberg are leavened with inspiration from the eastern European folk tradition – was PETER WARLOCK, and it was the Peter Warlock Society that proposed the Bartók plaque. It was unveiled in 1997 by the then minister David Mellor and the music critic Felix Aprahamian, who had visited Bartók in Sydney Place some sixty years earlier. Proceedings were enlivened with a performance of Bartók's music by a chamber choir.

One of three plaques to the novelist **William Makepeace Thackeray** (1811–1863) ⑨ (see also pp. 218–19 and pp. 263–4) can be found at 36 Onslow Square, SW7 (fig. 228). Thackeray's move to the house in May 1854 was, he later recalled, 'awful to behold' – thanks to the volume of possessions he had accumulated in eight years at his previous address in Young Street.[10] The brick and stucco terraced house – one of the superior speculations of Sir Charles Freake – was then barely five years old. Here Thackeray completed *The New-comes* (1853–55) and wrote *The Virginians* (1857–59), with the able assistance of his daughter Anne (1837–1919), later Lady Ritchie, who had started to work as his literary secretary and went on to become a respected writer in her own right; his other daughter Minny (1840–1875) later married Leslie Stephen. Thackeray's mother and stepfather, Major and Mrs Carmichael-Smyth, also lived here for a spell in 1857, an experience that persuaded Thackeray not to make the arrangement permanent. With the exception of the fourth floor, which was added in 1907, the house remains much the same as when the Thackeray family left in March 1862. The LCC bronze plaque was put in place in 1912; its unusual position at worm's-eye level is the consequence of a request made in 1923 by the building's occupier, who found that in its original, more elevated, location it wept unsightly stains down the pristine stucco frontage. Nine years later, a new lessee requested that the tablet be moved to a more prominent spot on the building; she was wearily informed that she was free to do so at her own expense, and here the correspondence on file ceases. Thackeray would surely have enjoyed this small comedy.

At 38 Onslow Square – next door to Thackeray's old home, and presently conjoined with it – is a GLC plaque to the hydrographer and meteorologist **Admiral Robert FitzRoy** (1805–1865) ⑩ . A grandson of the 3rd Earl of Grafton, FitzRoy entered the Navy in 1819 and commanded HMS *Beagle* for the expedition of 1831–36 on which Charles Darwin formulated his theory of evolution – an association that gave the devoutly creationist FitzRoy 'the acutest pain'.[11] He was the second Governor of New Zealand (1843–45), and briefly superintended the Woolwich naval dockyard before being appointed Meteorological Statist (statistician) at the newly established government Meteorological Department in 1854. As set out in his *Weather Book* (1863), FitzRoy advocated the use of the barometer to predict storms, and the rapid dissemination of this information by semaphore. He was careful to warn that such 'forecasts' – the notion of which, when first mentioned in the House of Commons, raised a hearty laugh – were not 'prophecies or predictions', a view that his successors at the Met Office would surely endorse.[12] Always prone to depression, FitzRoy died in Upper Norwood by his own hand, the stigma of which may have led to his relatively low historical profile until recently. His plaque went up in 1981 at 38 Onslow Square, his London residence from 1854 – the year of his second marriage – until shortly before his death. Another, bluer (and deeper) memorial followed in 2002, when the shipping forecast sea area formerly known as Finisterre was renamed FitzRoy.

At 27 Sumner Place (formerly 8 Sumner Terrace), SW7, lived **Joseph Aloysius Hansom** (1803–1882) ⑪ , the architect and founder-editor of *The Builder*, whose name is more readily associated with the Hansom cab (see fig. 246). Born in York, where he trained as an architect, Hansom was declared bankrupt following the building of Birmingham Town Hall (1832–34), which he designed with Edward Welch; when he registered a patent for a 'safety cab', in December 1834, it was with the aim of recovering solvency. Unwisely, he sold the rights to the invention – though what became known to posterity as the Hansom cab, with large wheels and driver's seat at the back, bore scant resemblance to his original design. Nor did Hansom benefit much financially as founder and editor of *The Builder* (1842–43); it was George Godwin who set the magazine on a secure footing. Hansom did, however, enjoy success as an architect of churches, working in partnership with various members of his family and, for a time, Edward Welby Pugin. One notable later commission was St Philip Neri (1870–73), now the Catholic cathedral, at Arundel, West Sussex. This building, in the French Gothic style, was completed during Hansom's time at the house in Sumner Place, where he was living with his wife Hannah (1809–1880) by 1873, if not the previous year, and remained until 1877. The plaque was unveiled in 1981 by the 17th Duke of Norfolk, then Britain's leading Catholic layman, who travelled to number 27 by Hansom cab.

Onslow Gardens, SW7, was built by SIR CHARLES FREAKE – on an imposing scale – in 1865. That same year the historian and man of letters **James Anthony Froude** (1818–1894) 12 took up residence at number 5. Froude made his reputation with a monumental twelve-volume history of Tudor England, published between 1856 and 1870, and cemented it in the 1880s with volumes dedicated to the life and works of his friend THOMAS CARLYLE, which set a new standard for candour in biography. Here, with his second wife Henrietta, née Warre (d. 1874), he held dinner parties 'famous for their brilliance and charm'.[13] Froude left the house in 1892, when he was appointed Regius Professor of Modern History at Oxford; as a young scholar, he had been effectively hounded out of the ancient university for his opposition to compulsory ordination, as expressed in his work of thinly disguised autobiographical fiction, *The Nemesis of Faith* (1849). He was not a man to hide his partialities: *The English in Ireland in the Eighteenth Century* (1872–74) was stridently unionist, and an 1879 article in favour of a federal South Africa was said by one contemporary critic to be marred by mistakes 'which would be scarcely pardoned in a "special" war correspondent hurriedly writing against time'.[14] In 1933 the Clerk of the LCC wrote in a similar vein that 'Froude's reputation cannot be said to be based on his historical accuracy', but upheld the literary merit of his work.[15] The council set up a plaque in the following year, at which time number 5 was owned by Froude's son, Ashley (1863–1949).

One of the most trenchant critics of FROUDE's views on Ireland was a near neighbour, the historian and essayist **W. E. H. Lecky** (1838–1903) 13 , who is commemorated at 38 Onslow Gardens. Lecky's review of *The English in Ireland* is a classic among historical controversies: 'With a recklessness of consequence that cannot be too deeply deplored . . . he has thrown a new brand of discord into the smouldering embers of Irish discontent', he thundered.[16] William Edward Hartpole Lecky, whose paternal family was Irish, moved to number 38 on his marriage to Elisabeth Boldewina van Dedem (d. 1912), just after correcting the draft of the second edition of his *The Leaders of Public Opinion in Ireland* (1871). Much of his time here was spent toiling on the eight-volume *History of England in the Eighteenth Century* (1878–90), which was, its title notwithstanding, most notable for its material on Ireland. In spite of their professional and political hostilities, Lecky and Froude appear to have maintained a degree of cordiality, and they attended the funeral of THOMAS CARLYLE together in 1881. Lecky later turned down the chair at Oxford that Froude accepted, and was elected to Parliament for Dublin University, his Alma Mater, in 1895. His later works included *Democracy and Liberty* (1896), a discursive perspective on the issues of the day. Lecky died in his study at Onslow Gardens; the plaque was erected by the LCC in 1955.

At 24 Onslow Gardens is an LCC plaque of 1958 to the Prime Minister **Andrew Bonar Law** (1858–1923) 14 . As a leading Conservative politician, Bonar Law was a harbinger of change merely by dint of having social origins far removed from the landed upper classes: born and raised in New Brunswick, he never completely lost his Canadian accent, and came from a background in business, having made his fortune as an iron merchant in Glasgow. Bonar Law entered Parliament in 1900, and in 1911 was elevated to the leadership of the Conservative – or, as it was then usually known, Unionist – Party. His move to Onslow Gardens in September 1921 was supposed to signal his retirement; he had just returned from a trip to convalesce in France after relinquishing the leadership of his party and resigning from the coalition Cabinet of LLOYD GEORGE, in which the highest office he held was Chancellor of the Exchequer. However, the political machinations of the following year saw Bonar Law make a comeback as Conservative leader, and return to Downing Street as Prime Minister in October 1922. Ill-health drove him to relinquish the premiership in May 1923 after just 209 days in office, and he returned to Onslow Gardens, where he died that October. A teetotaller who disliked music and dancing, Bonar Law made for a great contrast with his predecessor Lloyd George, though the brevity of his tenure at 10 Downing

SOUTH KENSINGTON

take up a fellowship at King's College London, and moved into Flat 22 at Donovan Court, a 1930s apartment block. Franklin isolated two forms of the DNA molecule before transferring to Birkbeck College in 1953, where her supervisor was J. D. BERNAL. She remained at Donovan Court until her death at the Royal Marsden Hospital in Chelsea, her life having been cut tragically short by cancer. Rosalind Franklin's work was crucial to the discovery of the structure of DNA by Francis Crick and James Watson, for which they – and Maurice Wilkins, her superior at King's – won the Nobel Prize in 1962. The extent to which Franklin was effectively written out of the story has been a matter of controversy since. The award of a blue plaque thirty years later, at the suggestion of members of Franklin's family, is evidence of a widening recognition of her part in a major scientific breakthrough.

At 1 Drayton Gardens, SW10, is an English Heritage plaque to **Mervyn Peake** (1911–1968) **16** , the author and artist. Peake was born in China, the son of a Con-

229 A photograph by Henry Grant showing Rosalind Franklin at work in a London laboratory in 1954. [© Museum of London]

Street gave him little time to make much impact. HERBERT ASQUITH is supposed to have quipped at his funeral in Westminster Abbey, 'It is fitting that we should have buried the Unknown Prime Minister by the side of the Unknown Soldier'.[17]

The story of a short life profitably lived lies behind the plaque at Donovan Court, Drayton Gardens, SW10. It records the residence of **Rosalind Franklin** (1920–1958) **15** , a pioneer of the study of molecular structures, including DNA (deoxyribonucleic acid), the material that carries genetic information (figs 229 and 230). Born in Notting Hill into a wealthy Anglo-Jewish family, Rosalind Franklin was educated at St Paul's Girls' School in Hammersmith, read natural sciences at Newnham College, Cambridge, and went on to carry out groundbreaking work in the emerging fields of molecular chemistry and biology. Having worked for a time in Paris, she returned to England in 1951 to

230 The English Heritage plaque to Rosalind Franklin at Donovan Court, Drayton Gardens, her home in 1951–58. [© English Heritage. Photograph by Derek Kendall]

gregationalist missionary doctor. His artistic gifts became apparent during his schooling in Kent, and he went on to paint and draw professionally, as well as to write poetry, plays and – most famously – novels and children's books, which he illustrated in his own appealingly grotesque style. Peake is best known for the Gormenghast 'trilogy', a gothic fantasy that has been filmed and adapted for television. The final part, *Titus Alone* (1959), was finished when he moved with his artist wife Maeve, née Gilmore (1917–1983) and their family to Drayton Gardens in May 1960. The house had 'enough large rooms for the paintings', and was deemed to be 'near enough to the Fulham Road and other centres of creative activity to be alluring'.[18] Sadly, Peake was already exhibiting signs of the debilitating illness – eventually diagnosed as Parkinson's disease – which brought a premature end to his professional career, though while living at the address he did manage to illustrate his earlier poem *The Rhyme of the Flying Bomb* (1962) and completed a commission from the Folio Society. After 1965, Peake was cared for in nursing homes, though his family preserved his ground-floor study at Drayton Gardens as he had left it. The plaque was proposed by Peake's son Sebastian, and was unveiled by him in 1996.

The sculptor **Frank Dobson** (1886–1963) **17** has a plaque at 14 Harley Gardens, SW10, a four-storey end-of-terrace house dating from the early 1860s. Born in London, Dobson started out as a painter, and spent much of his early career in Cornwall. He was linked with the younger members of the Bloomsbury Group; among his better-known works is a brass head of Sir Osbert Sitwell (1922), and he also designed the curtain for *Façade*, the performance collaboration between Osbert's sister EDITH SITWELL and the composer William Walton which was first staged in 1922. Dobson moved to Harley Gardens from his wartime bolt-hole in Hampshire in the winter of 1945, upon his appointment as Professor of Sculpture at the Royal College of Art, to which he commuted on an ancient bicycle. He remained at the house – which was attached to a spacious studio – until the lease ran out in January 1961; latterly, it was a playground for his young grandchildren, who stayed over in the small downstairs studio that Dobson otherwise used in the evenings for modelling small terracottas. By this time, Dobson was generally recognised as one of the most significant British

sculptors of his generation. Works completed at number 14 included the curvilinear statue *London Pride*, executed for the Festival of Britain in 1951; it was recast in bronze and set up outside the National Theatre in 1987. The unveiling of the plaque in 1993 was attended by three generations of Dobson's descendants.

At 9 (formerly 1) Gilston Road, SW10, is an English Heritage plaque to the plant collector **Robert Fortune** (1812–1880) **18** . Born in Berwickshire, Scotland, Fortune worked his way up from garden boy to become Superintendent of the Horticultural Society's hothouse in Chiswick from 1842. He made his first trip to China the following year, and – thanks to the Wardian case, an innovative portable greenhouse (fig. 231) – brought many now-familiar plants to Britain for the first time, including the kumquat, the Japanese anemone and several species of azalea, rhododendron and chrysanthemum. After a spell as Curator of the Chelsea Physic Garden (1846–48), Fortune set out for China once again, this time charged by the East India Company with bringing back samples of the tea plant. In 1851 these were successfully transplanted to north-western India – a botanical triumph that had far-reaching economic consequences, and effectively ended China's monopoly of tea. The element of espionage in Fortune's work – and the sentiments of the Chinese about this – were made plain in the title of the 2002 film *Robert Fortune: The Tea Thief*. From 1857 Fortune lived in Gilston Road, along with his wife Jane and their two children; the house, built by GEORGE GODWIN, was almost new when he moved in. While here, Fortune published several travelogues, including *A Residence among the Chinese* (1857) and *Yedo and Peking* (1863); his later years were blighted by illness

231   A drawing of a Wardian case – a portable greenhouse – in c.1870. It was thanks to cases such as this that Robert Fortune introduced to Britain such plants as the kumquat and the Japanese anemone. [© Mary Evans Picture Library]

SOUTH KENSINGTON

associated with the privations endured on his travels. Fortune died at this address, and is buried in nearby Brompton Cemetery.

Redcliffe Gardens, SW10, is a boulevard that runs between the Old Brompton and Fulham roads. At number 57, a large yellow-brick house of about 1870, is a plaque to **Sydney Monckton Copeman** (1862–1947) ⑲, the immunologist and developer of the smallpox vaccine. Born in Norwich, where his father was a clergyman, Copeman trained at St Thomas' Hospital in London and spent his career in public health, working first for the Local Government Board and later for the Ministry of Health. Once a mass killer, smallpox was eradicated worldwide in 1977, an achievement for which Copeman is entitled to much credit, even though he built on the work of others, most notably Edward Jenner. Copeman's chief innovation, which he first publicly advocated in 1893, was the use of glycerine to keep the calf-lymph vaccine sterile: hitherto, vaccination had carried a risk of bacterial infection. Sir Joseph Lister took an avuncular interest, and financed Copeman's early research. Redcliffe Gardens was his home – where he lived with his wife Ethel, née Boord (1869–1944) and their young family – from about 1903 to 1909, during which time, thanks to Copeman's breakthrough, the government's vaccination programme was gearing up. The plaque was proposed by his grandson and fellow medical man, Dr Peter Copeman; it was unveiled in 1996 on the 200th anniversary of Jenner's discovery of vaccination against smallpox.

At 10 Redcliffe Street, SW10, on the corner with Westgate Terrace, is a plaque to the poet and essayist **Austin Dobson** (1840–1921) ⑳ . Dobson was born in Plymouth, and had a day job as a clerk at the Board of Trade for forty-five years; appropriately, his first prose work was entitled *The Civil Service Handbook of English Literature* (1874). He had moved to Redcliffe Street the year before, when the house was barely three years old; it was also in 1873 that he published his first verse collection, *Vignettes in Rhyme*, which was followed in 1877 by *Proverbs in Porcelain*. Dobson later wrote a well-regarded series of biographies of eighteenth-century figures, beginning with William Hogarth in 1879. In 1880 he moved to Ealing, where he remained until his death, spending most of the intervening period at 75

Eaton Rise (demolished). 'Ealing possessed no citizen more regular in his habits or more blameless in his conduct', remarked his friend and one-time colleague at the Board of Trade, Sir Edmund Gosse.[19] Dobson was a retiring and modest man: 'Fame is a food that dead men eat / I have no stomach for such meat', he wrote in 1906.[20] When his name was first proposed, the LCC committee dismissed him as being of insufficient stature. However, representations from the proposer – Mr C. A. S. Dobson, Austin's grandson – brought about a change of heart. The Redcliffe Street address was selected – Ealing being outside the county of London – and the plaque was erected in 1959, at which point number 10 was being used by the LCC as a maternity and child welfare clinic; it is now a doctors' surgery.

Another plaque to have gone up after initial rejection was that for the painter **Sir William Orpen** (1878–1931) ㉑ at 8 (formerly 5) South Bolton Gardens, SW5, which was installed at his centenary in 1978 (figs 232 and 233). Orpen was primarily a painter of portraits – among his best-known works are the self-portrait *Orpsie Boy* (1924) and his 1927 study of Lloyd George. He is also renowned for his work as an official war artist, notably the contentious *To the Unknown British Soldier in France* (1922–27). Orpen was born in County Dublin, but trained at the Slade and spent much of his career in London, about which he had mixed feelings: 'Every decent man in London has to be drunk by seven o' clock', he once declared, a conviction that probably foreshortened his life.[21] He was himself recalled as 'an extremely entertaining companion, high spirited, droll, and brimful of songs and stories'.[22] In 1906

232   A photograph of 1930 showing the façade of 8 South Bolton Gardens, dominated by the windows of the studio. A privately erected plaque to Sir Hugh Lane, seen just above the balcony, was joined by one to Sir William Orpen in 1978, the painter's centenary year. [© Country Life]

233 *Summer Afternoon* (*Artist in his Studio with a Model*), a painting of c.1913 by Sir William Orpen. The studio windows of 8 South Bolton Gardens form an impressive backdrop. [Photograph © 2008 Museum of Fine Arts, Boston]

234 The LCC plaque to the singer Jenny Lind (Madame Goldschmidt), positioned in the pediment above the entranceway of 189 Old Brompton Road. [© English Heritage. Photograph by Derek Kendall]

tranged him further from his wife Grace and their children, 8 South Bolton Gardens became his principal residence as well as his workplace.

In a pediment above the entranceway to 189 Old Brompton Road (formerly 1 Moreton Gardens), SW7 – on the elevation facing Boltons Place – is a wreathed LCC plaque to the singer **Jenny Lind** (**Madame Goldschmidt**) (1820–1887) **22** (fig. 234). Lind was born in Sweden, where she made her first stage appearance at the age of ten. She came to prominence as a singer on the Continent before making her London debut in 1847. At the height of her fame, her popularity was analogous to that of a modern pop star, with sell-out concert series and an extensive range of what would now be termed tour merchandise. In 1858, having retired from the stage, Lind settled in England with her husband Otto Goldschmidt (1829–1907), a former pupil of Jenny's friend Felix Mendelssohn. They lived first in the Wimbledon Common area before relocating in 1874 to what was then 1 Moreton Gardens, a substantial, newly built house. This move coincided with Otto's appointment as Vice-Principal of the Royal Academy of Music under their friend, the composer Sir William Sterndale Bennett. In 1883 Jenny became the first Professor of Singing at the Royal College of Music, and took classes at her home, which had good-sized ground-floor rooms well suited to the purpose. In the drawing room were held early soprano rehearsals of the Bach Choir, of which Otto was the first musical director and which continues to flourish. The house – which became 189 Old Brompton Road in 1937 – remained the couple's home until their respective deaths. The LCC considered the possibility of including Lind's popular nickname 'the Swedish Nightingale' on the plaque, but instead opted to add

Orpen took a studio at the recently built 8 South Bolton Gardens, a house in a quiet cul-de-sac which until that year had been numbered 5. From 1907 to 1909 he sub-let space to his fellow Irishman Sir Hugh Lane (1875–1915), later the Director of the National Gallery of Ireland, who has a private plaque on the building. Their next-door neighbours at number 9 were the artists Charles Ricketts and Charles Shannon. Orpen later bought this adjacent property, and remodelled the houses as a single unit in 1929; the striking white stucco frontage and large first-floor windows, which helped to make the vast, airy studio 'as light as an operating theatre', date from this time.[23] Orpen's success as a society painter enabled him to maintain family homes elsewhere in Chelsea and Kensington – at addresses including 13 Royal Hospital Road – but latterly, as his dependence on drink es-

SOUTH KENSINGTON

235 An item of publicity material for the Theatre Royal, Haymarket, which was managed and owned by Sir Herbert Beerbohm Tree for about ten years from 1887. [© Getty Images]

her married name. Lind's son Walter and daughter Jenny were present at its installation in 1909; the former relayed to the LCC their 'appreciation of the tablet and the great care and trouble with which it was placed in position'.[24]

The author **George Borrow** (1803–1881) 23 is commemorated at 22 Hereford Square, SW7. Originally from Norfolk, Borrow travelled widely in Europe and mastered many languages, which gave him a useful sideline as a translator. His particular affinity with Romany peoples was reflected in the subject matter of two of his best-known books, *Lavengro* (1851) and its sequel, *The Romany Rye* (1857). Borrow's earthy tales were written in conscious contrast to 'genteel' novels; by the time he moved to Hereford Square in 1860, it was not a voguish style. Hence the travelogue *Wild Wales* (1862) was little noticed by contemporaries, though it came to be seen by some as a classic. A genuine eccentric, Borrow found plenty to inspire him in London, 'where odd characters were far more numerous than in East Anglia, or Wales, or Cornwall', and he enjoyed frequent trips to the 'countryside' of Wimbledon Common and Richmond Park.[25] He felt keenly the loss of his wife Mary, née Clarke (d. 1869), and left number 22 for an earlier home – Oulton, Suffolk – in 1872. The wreathed blue plaque was erected by the LCC in 1911, a year later than planned as the first tablet cracked in the kiln. The house – which is part of a stuccoed terrace dating from about 1850 – suffered bomb damage in the Second World War, and was reconstructed behind the façade in 1949.

The unusual rectangular plaque that adorns 31 Rosary Gardens, SW7, was put up in 1950 to mark the residence of **Sir Herbert Beerbohm Tree** (1853–1917) 24 , the actor-manager (figs 235 and 236). Tree's real name was Herbert Draper Beerbohm; his younger half-brother was SIR MAX BEERBOHM. He lived in London for most of his life, though most of his residences – including 77 Sloane Street, Chelsea, his longest-term address – have since been rebuilt. Tree was at 31 Rosary Gardens between spring 1886 and 1888, when the four-storey brick terrace of which it is part was only a few years old. This was a brief yet significant period in his life, as it saw not only a revival in his acting career – begun in the late 1870s – but his first foray into theatre management: Tree took over the Comedy Theatre in

236 The rectangular LCC plaque to Sir Herbert Beerbohm Tree at 31 Rosary Gardens, his home between 1886 and 1888. [© English Heritage. Photograph by Derek Kendall]

Panton Street, near Leicester Square, in April 1887. That autumn he moved on to the Haymarket Theatre (the Theatre Royal), where he stayed for ten years and enjoyed great success. The profits he made helped to finance the building of Her Majesty's Theatre, also in Haymarket, which opened in 1897; Tree managed the theatre from that year until his death, during which time it enjoyed an international reputation. Tree was noted especially for his championship of Shakespeare; the theatre's productions were famous for their spectacular scenery and effects, and brought the plays before a wider audience. Offstage, he produced some memorable bons mots, including the observation that 'what a man would shrink from doing as an individual he wouldn't hesitate to do as a member of a committee'.[26] Tree – who founded the Royal Academy of Dramatic Art in 1904 – was supported in his many endeavours by his actress wife Maud, née Holt (1863–1937), whom he had married in 1882; he did, however, father six illegitimate children, including the film director Carol Reed. In 1897, by which time the couple were living in Sloane Street, Maud recalled Rosary Gardens as 'rather a mansion of a house in South Kensington'. It had, she continued, 'a pretty drawing-room, which I made from tulip-yellow walls and light green curtains, but on the whole the house was too Lincrustan and anaglyptic for us. We never could enter into the spirit of its staircase. So we fled from its splendours'.[27]

Field Marshal Edmund Henry Hynman, Viscount Allenby (1861–1936) 25 is commemorated with a

237 One of the most striking buildings to have been commemorated in London is 39 Harrington Gardens, built for Sir W. S. Gilbert in the early 1880s. It is shown here in a positioning photograph of 1929. [© City of London, LMA]

important capture of Jerusalem in December 1917 and the victory of the Battle of Megiddo in autumn 1918. He was made a field marshal and viscount in 1919; the worsening of his volcanic temper as he ascended the ranks led to his being nicknamed 'the Bull', though as High Commissioner for Egypt from 1919 to 1925 he displayed a sensible pragmatism. In retirement, Allenby and his wife Mabel, née Chapman (1869/70–1942) lived first in grace-and-favour accommodation at Deal Castle in Kent, but, finding it 'too cold', moved in 1928 to the 'conveniently sized and comfortable house' in Wetherby Gardens; it dates from the 1880s, and is notable for its elaborately decorated porch.[28] The couple travelled widely, mostly within the Empire, and Allenby served as President of the British National Cadet Force; he also enjoyed fishing and bird watching, sharing the latter interest with his wife. His death occurred at number 24 just after he had returned here with supplies for the aviary that he had constructed in the back garden. The plaque, which went up in 1960, was suggested by the Kensington Society.

One of the most striking London houses to bear a plaque is 39 (formerly 19) Harrington Gardens, SW7, where the dramatist **Sir W. S. Gilbert** (1836–1911) ㉖ (see also pp. 548–9) is commemorated (figs 237 and 238). William Schwenck Gilbert wrote many conventional plays, but is generally remembered as the librettist for the Savoy Operas, written with Arthur Sullivan and promoted by RICHARD D'OYLY CARTE. Tradition has it that he used the proceeds from one of their collaborations, *Patience* (1881), to finance the construction of this magnificent dwelling, which is built in the Flemish style with an enormous stepped gable. Its flamboyance was, in the words of one architectural historian, 'perfectly suited to its owner'.[29] Gilbert commissioned the house from Ernest George and Harold Peto, who designed the row of six to which it belongs, and informed the contractors, Stephens and Bastow, that he would take up residence in October 1883 regardless of progress. Accordingly, curious neighbours who took a peek inside the shell were met by Gilbert himself, who watched the finishing touches being applied around him; he had electric lighting installed from the outset by the company founded by COLONEL CROMPTON. It was in the Harrington Gardens house, numbered 19 until 1887, that he completed the libretto for *The Mikado* (1885) – perhaps the most enduring of

plaque at 24 Wetherby Gardens, SW5. Allenby saw active service in the Boer War, and commanded the Third Army in the First World War on the Western Front, in which theatre of conflict he lost his only son, Michael. It is for his dynamic leadership of the Egyptian Expeditionary Force that Allenby is chiefly celebrated; this was instrumental in the symbolically

238 The 'smoky grey' coloured plaque to Sir W. S. Gilbert at 39 Harrington Gardens; it was installed by the LCC in 1929 [© English Heritage. Photograph by Derek Kendall]

the Savoy Operas – and wrote those for *The Yeoman of the Guard* (1888) and *The Gondoliers* (1889). Gilbert planned his scripts using model figures, in his study on the first floor, from preference between the hours of 11pm and 3am, when 'no one can interrupt you, unless it be a burglar'.[30] The sailing ship on top of the gable was intended to allude to his claimed descent from the seafarer Sir Humphrey Gilbert – who went down with his ship, the *Squirrel*, in 1583 – rather than to *HMS Pinafore* (1878): 'Sir, I do not put my trademark on my house', Gilbert barked at one unfortunate visitor who assumed the latter.[31] He and his wife Lucy (1847–1936) left number 39 in 1890 for Grim's Dyke in Harrow. The wreathed plaque in Harrington Gardens went up in 1929, an instance of the twenty-year rule being waived; its 'smoky grey' colour was chosen in deference to the leaseholder's particular wish.

North of the Cromwell Road at 6 Grenville Place, SW7, is commemorated **Charles Booth** (1840–1916) ㉗, the pioneer in social research. Born into a Liverpool mercantile family, Booth went into partnership with his brother Alfred in 1860, founding the Booth Steamship Company; Charles remained active in the firm for over forty years. His real interests, however, lay elsewhere. In 1871 Booth married Mary (1847–1939), the niece of the historian THOMAS BABINGTON MACAULAY and granddaughter of ZACHARY MACAULAY; later, she became an important social reformer in her own right. After a spell in Switzerland for the benefit of Charles's health, the couple took a fifteen-year lease on 6 Grenville Place in 1875. The four-storey terraced house was a speculative new build, and suffered from both smoking chimneys and faulty drains. Booth's niece BEATRICE WEBB recalled it as 'dark and airless', and her

256

uncle as 'tall, abnormally thin, garments hanging as of on pegs' with 'the complexion of a consumptive girl'.[32] A more recent writer has contrasted the 'solid and settled' appearance lent to Booth's former home by the LCC plaque – erected in 1951 – with his personal circumstances when he took up residence here: his health remained precarious and his plan to open a London office of the Booth shipping line was opposed by his family.[33] Time vindicated Charles, and his increasing wealth financed his trailblazing social studies, famous for their colour-coded maps showing the relative prosperity of districts (fig. 239). Booth also coined the term 'poverty line'. While carrying out fieldwork in the winter of 1887–88, he took temporary additional lodgings in, among other places, Chester Street in Bethnal Green and Eldon Street, Finsbury; overall, he found the experience surprisingly congenial. The first of the seventeen volumes of Booth's *Life and Labour of the People in London* (completed 1902) appeared in April 1889, just as the family were moving from Grenville Place to 24 Great Cumberland Place, Marylebone, a house destroyed in the Second World War.

The 'man of letters' **Andrew Lang** (1844–1912) (28) lived for over thirty-five years at 1 Marloes Road, W8, as is commemorated by an LCC plaque of 1959, placed here at the prompting of the Kensington Society. Behind its quaint description of Lang's occupation lies the story of an extraordinarily prolific and versatile

239 Charles Booth's poverty map for the South Kensington area, from a series first produced in 1889 and revised in 1898–99. The coloured shading identifies this as a wealthy area: yellow represents the middle classes and red the upper-middle and upper classes. [Courtesy of RBKC Libraries]

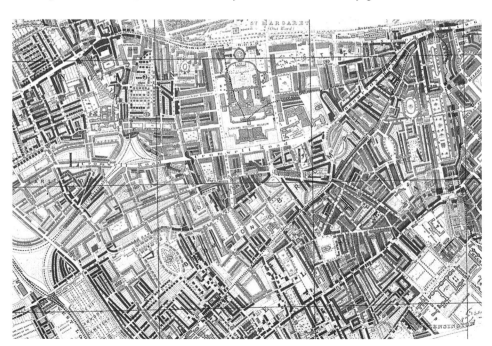

writer. Scottish by birth, and a one-time Fellow of Merton College, Oxford, he wrote poetry, fiction, history, biography, newspaper leader columns and literary criticism – 'a la-dy, da-dy, Oxford kind of Scot', in the words of his friend Robert Louis Stevenson.[34] The LCC report written in the 1950s on Lang's reputation highlighted his translation of Homer's *Odyssey* (1879). Since then, however, he has gained wider repute as a pioneering anthropologist: the two-volume *Myth, Ritual and Religion* (1887) drew links between folk customs and beliefs in disparate parts of the globe, and he was a founder member of the Folk-Lore Society in 1878. Lang lived at Marloes Road with his wife Leonora, née Alleyne, also a writer and translator, from 1876 until his death. He often walked home from his journalistic assignments in the City, which took him an hour and a half. 'Walk up the Cromwell Road until you drop – and then turn right', he would instruct potential callers.[35] The house is at the end of a terrace built by Samuel Juler Wyand, one of the most prolific builders in the area, and was new when the Langs moved in.

The actor David Suchet unveiled a plaque in 2005 to the playwright **Sir Terence Rattigan** (1911–1977) (29) (fig. 240), who was born at 100 Cornwall Gardens (formerly 3 Cornwall Mansions), SW7; the house was named Lanarkslea by his grandfather, Sir William Rattigan (1842–1904), after the Lanarkshire constituency that he represented in Parliament. At the time of Rattigan's birth here in June 1911, the opulent house – built in 1877–79 – belonged to Lady Evelyn Rattigan, his formidable widowed grandmother. It was at 3 Cornwall Mansions – as the house was then known – that Terence and his elder brother Brian were brought up, in 'an isolated world of starched aprons and prim mouths, of strict teatimes and prayers before bed'; their parents, Frank and Vera Rattigan, were abroad on diplomatic postings.[36] The young Rattigan's passion for the stage was first awakened in November 1918 by the pantomime *Cinderella*; he is said to have announced his wish to be a playwright shortly afterwards. In 1920 he left Cornwall Gardens to attend a prep school at Cobham in Surrey; after Oxford, he had his first West End hit with *French without Tears* (1936). Twenty years of stage success followed, including hits such as *The Winslow Boy* (1946), *The Deep Blue Sea* (1952) and *Separate Tables* (1954). Rattigan also wrote and co-wrote

SOUTH KENSINGTON

240 The actor David Suchet and Loyd Grossman, Chairman of the Blue Plaques Panel, at the unveiling of the English Heritage plaque to Sir Terence Rattigan. The plaque marks 100 Cornwall Gardens, Rattigan's birthplace. [© PA Photos]

1929; the novelist **Dame Ivy Compton-Burnett** (1884–1969) moved into Flat 5 here in 1934 with her companion Margaret Jourdain (1876–1951), a furniture expert (fig. 241). The following year saw the publication of Compton-Burnett's sixth novel, *A House and its Head*, one of her typical tales of domestic power struggles reflecting her own turbulent upbringing: her mother was an overbearing social climber, one brother died of pneumonia, another was killed in the First World War, and her two youngest sisters later perished in a suicide pact. Compton-Burnett preferred to write in one of the armchairs that sat on either side of the Adam fireplace that she and Jourdain had imported from their previous home in Linden Gardens, Bayswater. This feature apart, their first-floor flat was spartan in its furnishings, and grew still less homely after Margaret's death: one visitor of 1967 – the year that Ivy Compton-Burnett was made a dame – described it as 'bare, shabby and dark'.[37] By contrast, the window boxes on the balcony were always colourfully planted out; Compton-Burnett liked to grow from seed, and favoured 'little twopenny petunias from Woolworths'.[38] She died at the flat after living here for thirty-five years, despite having a rapacious landlord, whom she once described as 'frightfully friendly...I believe it's because of the enormous rent I pay him'.[39] The plaque, installed in 1994, is on the western elevation of the mansion block, which Margaret Jourdain compared to Balmoral.

The artist **Samuel Palmer** (1805–1881) is commemorated with a GLC plaque of 1972 at 6 Douro Place, W8. Palmer was one of The Ancients, a group of artists associated with WILLIAM BLAKE and in particular with the village of Shoreham in Kent. There Samuel lived between 1826 and 1832, producing the distinctive pastoral scenes with which his name is most readily associated. Palmer moved to Douro Place with his wife Hannah (1818–1893), the daughter of the artist JOHN LINNELL, in 1851; his son Alfred later recalled the house, which was built in 1846, as being 'about the most complete antithesis to his ideal of a residence that could have been devised. It was a hideous little semi-detached house, with a prim little garden at the back and front, and an ample opportunity of profiting by the next door neighbours' musical proclivities'.[40] The house was in fact of a respectable size, although city life clearly did not suit the asth-

screenplays, including those for the films *Brighton Rock* (1947), *Breaking the Sound Barrier* (1952) and *The Prince and the Showgirl* (1957). In the mid-1950s, Rattigan's reputation went into eclipse with the rise of the Angry Young Men – his plays were perceived as too 'comfortable' – but later recovered, and he was knighted in 1971.

The north-western part of Cornwall Mansions, Cornwall Gardens, had been renamed Braemar Mansions by

241 A portrait by Cecil Beaton of Ivy Compton-Burnett in 1949. It was probably taken in her flat at 5 Braemar Mansions, Cornwall Gardens. [Courtesy of the Cecil Beaton Studio Archive at Sotheby's]

SOUTH KENSINGTON

matic Palmer, who complained that he had to lean out of an attic window in order to get a breath of fresh air. As there was no studio, Palmer worked in the south-facing drawing room, though – never one to be bound by artistic convention – this was an arrangement he preferred. Of his later output, his water-colours and etchings have remained the most popular; they did not pay the bills, however, and Palmer continued to be financially reliant on his overbearing father-in-law. The Palmers left Douro Place in 1861 for the sake of the health of their eldest son, Thomas; the

boy sadly died not long after the family's arrival at Leith Hill in Surrey.

An English Heritage plaque records the residence of the poet **T. S. Eliot** (1888–1965) 32 at 3 Kensington Court Gardens, Kensington Court Place, W8, a ground-floor flat in an unremarkable apartment block built in 1887–89. Born in St Louis, Missouri, USA, Thomas Stearns Eliot married his first wife, Vivien Haigh-Wood, and settled in London in 1915, becoming a naturalised Briton – and an enthusiastic Anglican convert – in 1927. His

242 A view of the spectacular staircase at 17 Kensington Square, built in the late seventeenth century and marked with a plaque to Hubert Parry. [© City of London, LMA]

reputation was established by the epic poem *The Waste Land* (1922), and reinforced by the drama *Murder in the Cathedral* (1935) and the poetry collection *Four Quartets* (1943). Eliot lived at a number of addresses in West London and Regent's Park before moving to Kensington Court Gardens in April 1957, shortly after he had wed his erstwhile secretary Valerie Fletcher (b. 1926). The marriage came as a bolt from the blue to Eliot's circle, but it was a happy one, and when he died at number 3 a little short of nine years later, it was with Valerie's name on his lips. In his later years Eliot wrote almost no poetry, but did complete the play *The Elder Statesman* (1958) while living here, and continued to work for three afternoons a week as an editor at Faber & Faber in Russell Square. In this capacity Eliot introduced the work of many up-and-coming poets to the public, among them Ted Hughes, later Poet Laureate, who unveiled the plaque in 1986. Less to be expected was his association with Groucho Marx, the comic. Marx had dinner with the Eliots at Kensington Court Gardens in June 1964. Seeking to impress 'my celebrated pen pal' with his literary erudition, Groucho had read and re-read a couple of Eliot classics; he found, however, that the poet – 'tall, lean and rather stooped over' – was far more interested in discussing Marx Brothers films, of which he was a devotee.[41] At a popular level, Eliot is remembered especially for the nonsense verses in *Old Possum's Book of Practical Cats* (1939), adapted for Andrew Lloyd Webber's hit musical *Cats* in 1981.

Kensington Square, W8, is an island of antiquity in a sea of nineteenth-century development, being a speculation of the late 1680s by a joiner named Thomas Young. Young leased out many of the plots in King's Square, as it was first called, but was himself responsible for the building of number 17, the largest of the original houses, which was under construction in 1686. Exactly two centuries later, it was bought by the composer and musician **Hubert Parry** (1848–1918) **33**, who maintained the house as his London establishment until his death (fig. 242 and see fig. 40). He christened his new drawing room 'with a Brahms song', and number 17 proved to be conducive to composition, if not to domestic bliss; according to his son-in-law, Parry's wife Maude, née Herbert (1851–1933) was unsupportive and 'never cared for his music'.[42] Although Parry wrote symphonies, chamber music and oratorios – *Prometheus Unbound* (1880) is his best-

known early work – he is largely remembered for *Jerusalem* (1916), his setting of the poem by WILLIAM BLAKE. This was composed to be sung at a rally of Fight for Right – a pro-war movement – but the campaign for female suffrage and the Women's Institute took it up, and it has since become the unofficial English anthem, sung at the last night of the Proms. Parry, who was Director of the Royal College of Music from 1895, was knighted in 1898 and made a baronet in 1902. The honour, along with his unused first name of Charles, were omitted from the plaque's inscription at the particular request of his daughter, Lady Dorothea Ponsonby (b. 1876), who was living at the house when it was put up in 1949. The rectangular design was chosen as the most suitable for the available space; Lady Ponsonby would have preferred it to be round, 'which is so much more artistic, but I accept the fact that it could not be done satisfactorily'.[43]

Next door, at 18 Kensington Square, is a wreathed LCC plaque of 1907 – unusual, in that it is green in colour – commemorating the philosopher **John Stuart Mill** (1806–1873) **34** (fig. 243). Mill moved to Kensington

LCC

JOHN STUART
MILL
1806–1873
Philosopher
Lived Here

SOUTH KENSINGTON

243 The green LCC plaque to John Stuart Mill at 18 Kensington Square. [© English Heritage. Photograph by Derek Kendall]

Square with his mother Harriet (1782–1854) and eight younger brothers and sisters in 1837, following the death of his father, the philosopher James Mill. Here, John Stuart Mill continued to tutor his siblings according to the demanding curriculum prescribed by his father, and it was at Kensington Square that he wrote two of his most important works, *A System of Logic* (1843) and *Principles of Political Economy* (1848), the overarching themes of which were social progress and the relation of the individual to society. One visitor to the house, the diarist Caroline Fox, recalled Mill's 'charming library and . . . immense herbarium; the mother so anxious to show everything, and her son so terribly afraid of boring us'.[44] The close-knit family was blown apart in 1851 when Mill became engaged to the recently widowed Harriet Taylor, with whom he had been in love for more than twenty years. Mill and

Harriet moved to 113 Blackheath Park, SE3, and he took umbrage at – as he perceived it – the reluctance of his family to acknowledge his new wife; the drawing room at number 18 was the scene of a painful attempt at reconciliation. The house dates from 1686–87, and was built by Stephen Emmett, a bricklayer of the parish of St Margaret's, Westminster. It was associated with the Mill family until about 1857.

There are plaques on adjacent houses on the north side of Kensington Square. At number 40 – another house dating from the 1680s – resided the pioneer of public health **Sir John Simon** (1816–1904) ③⑤ , who moved to the square partly to please his wife Jane, née O'Meara (1816–1901), an inveterate social animal who was not enjoying life in far-flung Blackheath. Simon was the inaugural appointment as Medical Officer of

244 *The Lament* (1865–66) by Sir Edward Burne-Jones, one of the works executed during the artist's time at 41 Kensington Square. [William Morris Gallery, Walthamstow, UK / The Bridgeman Art Gallery]

Health to the City of London in 1848; he had made his name three years earlier with a paper on the thymus gland. In 1855, following the retirement of EDWIN CHADWICK, Simon was appointed Chief Medical Officer to the Board of Health; he then relinquished private medical practice, but held concomitant lecturing and surgical posts at St Thomas' Hospital until his retirement in 1876. The plaque to Simon was proposed in 1956 by Dr J. A. Scott, then the LCC's Chief Medical Officer, who asserted that Simon had 'perhaps more than any other one individual . . . moulded the form which the public health service of the country has taken'.[45] The resident of number 40 at the time, another doctor, was equally enthusiastic, and the plaque duly went up three years later. In Simon's time the house's interior decor was a product of the advanced artistic social circles in which he moved, with WILLIAM MORRIS wallpaper and paintings by the likes of TURNER and RUSKIN. The atmosphere was said to be 'overwhelmingly cerebral', and Simon's young nieces and nephews were 'cowed by Aunt Jane's formidable appearance and ferocious intelligence, and

amazed by Uncle John who quoted poetry at such length'.[46] It was at the house that Simon died.

At 41 Kensington Square is an English Heritage plaque put up in 1998 to honour the artist **Sir Edward Burne-Jones** (1833–1898) **36** (see also p. 60) (figs 244 and 245). In 1860 – the year after Burne-Jones left the Red Lion Square address where he is commemorated alongside WILLIAM MORRIS and D. G. ROSSETTI – he married Georgiana Macdonald (1840–1920), and during the period that followed established himself as a painter and designer of stained glass. It was in January 1865 that 'Ned' and 'Georgie' moved to number 41 with their young son Philip (1861–1926). Burne-Jones reported, 'We are settling fast, even looking a bit comfortable – Topsy [William Morris] has given us a Persian prayer carpet which amply furnishes one room. I have a little crib which I call a library because there I keep my tobacco and borrowed books'.[47] The garden – today much reduced – was then 'just large enough for a game of bowls'; a drawback was that the rooms with a north aspect were small.[48] The house

who was introduced to him by RUSKIN. By the time the Simons moved next door, however, the Burne-Joneses were gone, having been obliged to move out of number 41 in June 1867 after the house was sold from under them. They decamped to The Grange, North End Road, Fulham; the house, where Burne-Jones died in 1898, was marked with an LCC plaque in 1928 but demolished thirty years later.

The novelist **William Makepeace Thackeray** (1811–1863) 37 (see also pp. 218–19 and p. 248) has a plaque at 16 Young Street, W8 (fig. 246). It was at this address – then numbered 13 – that the author resumed family life after his wife Isabella became mentally ill; she was confined in a private asylum from 1842 and died in 1893. His two surviving daughters, Anne (1837–1914) and Minny (1840–1875), who had lived for a while with their grandmother in Paris, were brought by Thackeray in autumn 1846 to live with him in Young Street, his home since the previous August; three servants and a small black cat completed the household. Thackeray credited the happy reunion with inspiring him to complete the novel that made (and perpetuated) his name: *Vanity Fair*, published serially between January 1847 and July 1848, which had – remarkably – been turned down by five publishers. Thackeray also wrote *The History of Pendennis* (1848–50) and *The History of Henry Esmond* (1852) at Young Street – the latter he dictated in the first-floor bedroom 'while whiffing his cigar'.[49] The house, a yellow-brick detached building, cost Thackeray £65 a year in rent; a survivor of semi-rural Kensington, it dates from about 1815. The projecting segmental bays reminded Thackeray of a feudal castle: 'I'll have a flagstaff put over the coping of the wall, and I'll hoist a standard up when I'm at home!',

245 Number 41 Kensington Square and its English Heritage plaque to Sir Edward Burne-Jones. [© English Heritage. Photograph by Derek Kendall]

Right 246 A nineteenth-century drawing of William Makepeace Thackeray's former home at 16 Young Street, marked with a plaque by the LCC in 1905. [© Mary Evans Picture Library]

dates from 1804–5, and required extensive restoration after bomb damage in the Second World War. During his time here Burne-Jones worked hard on his technique, the fruits of which can be seen in such paintings as *The Lament* (1865–66) and *Cupid Delivering Psyche* (1867) – the latter being one of several works originally conceived for an abortive illustrated edition of *The Earthly Paradise* by Morris. Burne-Jones's social circle also included the poet ALGERNON SWINBURNE, the painter FORD MADOX BROWN and SIR JOHN SIMON,

SOUTH KENSINGTON

247   Colonel R. E. B. Crompton in
c.1902, seated in his White's
steam car outside Thriplands, 48
Kensington Court, his home from
1891 until 1939. [Courtesy of the
Institution of Mechanical
Engineers]

he quipped.[50] He left the address for Onslow Square in 1854. Apparently there was a private plaque to Thackeray at Young Street even before the LCC put up its wreathed, chocolate-coloured plaque in 1905.

On the side elevation of 48 Kensington Court, W8, is an English Heritage plaque of 2000 to the pioneering electrical engineer **Colonel R. E. B. Crompton** (1845–1940) 38 (fig. 247). Rookes Evelyn Bell Crompton, whose interest in engineering innovations pre-dated a spell with the Indian Army, formed a company in 1886 to supply electricity to the new housing development of Kensington Court. The firm, later the Kensington and Knightsbridge Electric Supply Company, laid cables in subterranean conduits that led from a purpose-built electricity generating station – now 46 Kensington Court – and carried direct current (DC), a system that eventually lost out to the rival alternating current (AC) system promoted by Sebastian Ziani de Ferranti. The architect of the power station was John Slater, who also built (in 1888–89) the house in front – number 48 – for Crompton, who moved here in 1891 with his wife Elizabeth (d. 1939). He named it Thriplands after a beautiful spot on his family's Yorkshire estate. The five-storey red-brick house, which has been described as 'unexceptional Tudor' in style, was, Crompton declared, 'one of the earliest to be built in England on the modern principle of framed steel girders on which the inner and outer brickwork is supported'.[51] The upper two floors of the house served as his laboratory; 'the scene of a great variety of experimental works', they were visited by Lord Kelvin.[52]

Crompton – who was an enthusiastic early motorist, and advised the War Office on the development of mechanical transport – remained at the house until 1939; he then returned to his native Yorkshire, where he died the following year.

NOTES

1   Ruth Richardson, 'George Godwin of *The Builder*', *Visual Resources*, vol. VI (1989), p. 123

2   John Physick, *The Victoria and Albert Museum: The History of its Building* (Oxford, 1982), p. 161

3   Constance Babington Smith, *Champion of Homoeopathy* (London, 1986), p. 99

4   *Homoeopathy*, vol. XLIX, no. 1 (1999), p. 15

5   Ibid, p. 12

6   Henriette de Witt, *Monsieur Guizot in Private Life* (London, 1884), pp. 253–54

7   *DNB, 1931–1940* (Oxford, 1949), pp. 701–2

8   Giles Playfair, *My Father's Son* (London, 1937), p. 17

9   Report of 12 August 1960 on blue plaque file.

10 *William Makepeace Thackeray: Memoirs of a Victorian Gentleman*, ed. Margaret Forster (London, 1980), p. 272

11 John and Mary Gribbin, *FitzRoy: The Remarkable Story of Darwin's Captain and the Invention of the Weather Forecast* (London, 2003), p. 266

12 Robert Fitzroy, *The Weather Book* (London, 1963), p. 171

13 Herbert Woodfield Paul, *The Life of Froude* (London, 1905), p. 434

14 James Martineau, *Life and Correspondence of Sir Bartle Frere* (London, 1895), vol. II, p. 367

15 Report of 31 January 1933 on blue plaque file.

16 Waldo Hilary Dunn, *James Anthony Froude* (Oxford, 1963), p. 364

17 Robert Blake, *The Unknown Prime Minister* (London, 1955), p. 531

18 John Watney, *Mervyn Peake* (London, 1976), p. 208

19 *West London Press*, 28 August 1959, p. 2

20 *The Oxford Dictionary of Quotations*, ed. Angela Partington (Oxford, 1992), p. 249

21 Bruce Arnold, *Orpen: Mirror to an Age* (London, 1981), p. 260

22 *DNB, 1931–1940, Supplement* (Oxford, 1949), p. 662

23 *Country Life*, vol. LXVIII, 20 September 1930, p. 344

24 Letter of 12 July 1909 on blue plaque file.

25 R. A. J. Walling, *George Borrow: The Man and his Work* (London, 1908), p. 233

26 Hesketh Pearson, *Beerbohm Tree* (London, 1936), p. 216

27 *Strand Magazine*, vol. XIII (1897), p. 257

28 Archibald Percival Wavell, *Allenby in Egypt* (London, 1940), p. 132

29 *Survey of London*, vol. XLII: *Southern Kensington*, ed. Hermione Hobhouse (London, 1986), p. 189

30 W. Archer, *Real Conversations* (London, 1904), p. 131

31 Lesley Baily, *The Gilbert and Sullivan Book* (London, 1952), p. 29

32 Beatrice Webb, *My Apprenticeship* (London, 1926), p. 221 and p. 219

33 Belinda Norman-Booth, *Victorian Aspirations: The Life and Labour of Charles and Mary Booth* (London, 1972), p. 47

34 Roger Lancelyn Green, *Andrew Lang: A Critical Biography* (Leicester, 1946), pp. 177–78

35 Ibid, p. 56

36 Geoffrey Wansell, *Terence Rattigan* (London, 1995), p. 17

37 Hilary Spurling, *Secrets of a Woman's Heart: The Later Life of Ivy Compton-Burnett, 1920–1969* (London, 1984), p. 283

38 Kay Dick, *Ivy and Stevie* (London, 1971), p. 16

39 Ibid, p. 19

40 Raymond Lister, *The Life and Letters of Samuel Palmer* (London, 1972), pp. 100–1

41 Lyndall Gordon, *Eliot's New Life* (Oxford 1988), p. 257

42 Jeremy Dibble, *C. Hubert H. Parry: His Life and Music* (Oxford, 1992), p. 247 and p. 497

43 Letter of 31 May 1949 on blue plaque file.

44 Michael Packe, *The Life of John Stuart Mill* (London, 1954), p. 265

45 Letter of 24 December 1956 on blue plaque file.

46 Royston Lambert, *Sir John Simon and English Social Administration* (London, 1962), p. 487

47 Georgiana Burne-Jones, *Memorials of Edward Burne-Jones*, vol. I (London, 1904), p. 287

48 Ibid, p. 289

49 Eyre Crowe, *Thackeray's Haunts and Homes* (London, 1897), p. 50

50 Ibid, p. 49

51 *Survey of London*, vol. XLII: *Southern Kensington*, p. 75; R. E. B. Crompton, *Reminiscences* (London, 1928), p. 139

52 Crompton, *Reminiscences*, p. 139

248 Number 7 Addison Bridge Place and its plaque to Samuel Taylor Coleridge, who stayed here intermittently between 1810 and 1811. [© English Heritage. Photograph by Derek Kendall]

WEST KENSINGTON AND EARLS COURT

West Kensington describes that part of Kensington to the west of Earls Court Road, and the term is also applied to the adjacent area further to the west, which lies in the borough of Hammersmith and Fulham. The earliest residential developments, such as Edwardes Square and Addison Bridge Place, were undertaken in the early 1800s, close to the arterial Kensington High Street and Hammersmith Road. Development to the south towards Earls Court, much of which belonged to the Edwardes estate of the earls of Kensington, proceeded apace as the nineteenth century wore on. Earls Court itself, a hamlet in 1820 and mostly given over to market gardening, was entirely built over by the 1880s. The District and Metropolitan railways had by this time arrived, as had the exhibition centre. The entire area's status was one of an *arriviste* addendum to Kensington proper; of the figures commemorated here, it is notable that some of the most prominent – EDWARD ELGAR, RIDER HAGGARD and WILLIAM ROTHENSTEIN – lived in the district at the outset of their careers. In Earls Court, in particular, many houses have now been subdivided into flats or converted into hotels, and the district has become renowned as a refuge for antipodean émigrés.

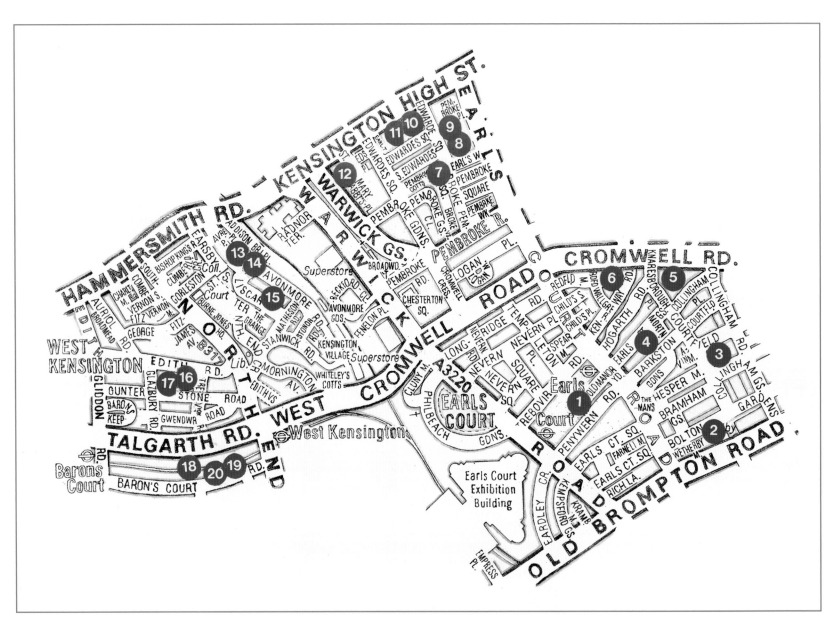

At 16 Penywern Road, SW5, is commemorated **Sir Norman Lockyer** (1836–1920) ❶ , the astronomer, physicist and founder of the journal *Nature* (fig. 249 and see fig. 47). It was Lockyer who, in 1868, identified and named helium using spectroscopic observation of the sun, nearly thirty years before it was isolated in a laboratory. Although he made this discovery as an amateur and while working as a civil servant at the War Office, Lockyer was already known for his pioneering studies of the sun's composition. A further scientific neologism for which he was responsible was chromosphere, the name he gave to a gaseous layer of the sun's atmosphere. Scientific education was another of Lockyer's interests: in 1869 he became the founding editor of *Nature*, which still flourishes as a leading scientific journal. In 1875 Lockyer was given a government secondment to the South Kensington-based Department of Science and Art; seven years later, he landed a lectureship at the associated Normal School of Science. When this became the Royal College of Science in 1890, Lockyer was made Director of its Solar Physics Observatory. His work there, which included ground-breaking research on the correlation of sunspot activity with the weather, continued until its move to Cambridge in 1911. He moved into the newly built 16 Penywern Road, which is on the Edwardes estate, in 1876, paying the

249 Number 16 Penywern Road in a photograph of April 1904, taken during the residence of Sir Norman Lockyer. Today, the house forms part of a hotel. [© RBKC Libraries]

then astronomical price of £2,700. The house, which is now part of a hotel, was kept on by Lockyer until his death; this occurred at Salcombe Regis, Devon, where he had set up an observatory. His plaque was unveiled in 2003 by the science minister, Lord Sainsbury.

The poet and journalist **Sir Edwin Arnold** (1832–1904) ❷ has a plaque at 31 Bolton Gardens, SW5. Arnold is chiefly known for *The Light of Asia* (1879), an account rendered in luxuriant verse of the life and teachings of the Buddha, Siddhartha Gautama. This went through scores of editions and was a crucial element in the growth of interest in Buddhism in the West. Arnold drew on his experience of India from 1857 to 1861, during which time he was principal of a college in Poona. On returning to England he worked at the *Daily Telegraph*, of which he was a chief editor from 1873 to 1889. His triumphs there included the part-financing of the expedition of HENRY MORTON STANLEY to find David Livingstone. As a poet Arnold was prolific, but he was disappointed in his reported expectation of being made Poet Laureate on the death of TENNYSON. From the mid-1870s he lived at several addresses in Earls Court and Kensington, including three in Cromwell Road. Arnold moved to 31 Bolton Gardens in 1898; the following year was published *The Queen's Justice*, a story set in the Indian subcontinent and dedicated to his Japanese third wife, Tama Kurokawa, who was forty years his junior. Arnold died at the house in 1904; it was recorded that 'he maintained his cheerfulness and his interest in life and literature to the last'.[1] His commemoration was suggested by his son and namesake; the wreathed LCC blue plaque of 1931 shows up particularly well against the dark red brick of the house, which is part of a development dating from 1894–96.

At 19 Collingham Gardens, SW5, a street developed by Ernest George and Harold Peto in the 1880s, is an English Heritage plaque honouring the Egyptologist and discoverer of the tomb of Tutankhamun, **Howard Carter** (1874–1939) ❸ (fig. 250). Carter, the son of an artist, was trained as a draughtsman, in which capacity he went to Egypt in 1891. Between 1893 and 1899 he was employed in recording the painted reliefs of a temple in Thebes; the results were published in the six-volume *The Temple of Deir el Bahari* (1894–1908). Having been inspired to take up archaeological exca-

250 Howard Carter and one of his workmen examine the mummy and solid gold funeral mask of Tutankhamun in the antechamber of the tomb in the Valley of the Kings, October 1925. [© Griffith Institute, University of Oxford]

vation while working under SIR FLINDERS PETRIE, Carter was appointed as the first Inspector in Chief of the monuments of Upper Egypt and Nubia at the age of just twenty-six. It was after leaving this post – and through the private patronage of his friend the 5th Earl of Carnarvon – that Carter made the discovery that in 1922 brought him to international attention: the treasure-filled 'lost' tomb of the boy-pharaoh Tutankhamun in the Valley of the Kings. A ten-year programme of its clearance and conservation then began. Number 19 Collingham Gardens, which belonged to Carter's brother Samuel (b. 1860/1), was Howard's London base for much of the 1920s, and for some time he had a self-contained flat here, numbered 19B. Fra-

ternal relations did not always run smooth, and a breach occurred in August 1930 after the bibulous Samuel broke into Howard's drinks cabinet, lamely insisting that he needed brandy for his sick wife. Soon afterwards, Howard moved to a flat at 49 Albert Court, Kensington Gore, SW7, where he lived until his death; but for the objections of the residents, it is this longer-term residence that would have been commemorated. The plaque was proposed by T. G. H. James, Carter's biographer, who was present at its unveiling in 1999 by John Carter, his subject's great-nephew. It was placed on the side elevation of the building, facing Laverton Place, owing to the lack of sufficient space on the main frontage.

251 The actress Ellen Terry in a portrait by George Frederic Watts, her first husband, painted in c.1864. [© National Portrait Gallery, London]

252 'The Alcove' of Ellen Terry's house at 22 Barkston Gardens, from a *Strand Magazine* article of 1892. The room was described as 'one of the prettiest corners in the whole house'.

The actress **Dame Ellen Terry** (1847–1928) ④ has a plaque at 22 Barkston Gardens, SW5 (figs 251 and 252). Born in Coventry, Terry was the daughter of actors and was herself a seasoned theatrical performer by the age of twelve. It was while at the height of her stage career, between 1889 and 1902, that she lived in Barkston Gardens; during this period she played numerous leading roles with distinction, including most of the Shakespearean canon. Much of Terry's work was performed at the Lyceum under HENRY IRVING; by 1881 she had two failed marriages behind her – Terry wed her first husband, the artist G. F. Watts, at the age of sixteen – and she and Irving were widely assumed to be lovers. It was also while living in Barkston Gardens that she conducted her famous correspondence with GEORGE BERNARD SHAW. Terry shared the terraced house, which dates from 1886, with a lady companion, Mrs Rumball – affectionately known as 'Boo' – and Prince, a singing bullfinch. During her residence the exterior was notable for lavish floral displays on the balcony and window sills. Very much the grande dame, Ellen Terry was afforded lavish and deferential treatment in the monthlies. 'My little home!', she simpered to one interviewer, 'only full of twopenny-halfpenny things; but I love them all for dear associations' sake'.[2] Her collection of gewgaws included Sarah Bernhardt's lace handkerchief, and eyeglasses that had belonged to Sir Arthur Sullivan, Irving and WHISTLER. Terry lived afterwards in King's Road, Chelsea. Her plaque at number 22, which is located below a first-floor window, was erected in 1951; then, as now, the house formed part of a hotel.

The plaque to the film director **Sir Alfred Hitchcock** (1899–1980) ⑤ at 153 Cromwell Road, SW5, was unveiled in 1999 by his daughter, Patricia Hitchcock O'Connell (fig. 253). Born in Leytonstone, Essex, Hitchcock made his debut as a director of feature films with *The Pleasure Garden* (1925); four years later he directed *Blackmail*, the first British full-length 'talkie', in which he made one of his trademark cameo appearances. Over the following years, Hitchcock cemented his reputation for cinematic innovation and suspense-filled plotlines with film successes such as *The Thirty-Nine Steps* (1935) and *The Lady Vanishes* (1938). Hitchcock's first home after his marriage in December 1926 to the film editor Alma Reville (1900–1982) was a modest two-bedroom flat on the top floor of 153 Cromwell Road, part of a mid-Victorian terrace; their wedding reception took place in the newly leased apartment. Hitchcock designed the furniture and fittings for the flat, which he retained as his London base despite his rising fortune and fame; 'I never felt any desire to move out of my own class', he once remarked.[3] 'Hitch' liked to hone his scripts at home, and callers often found him hard at work still wearing his favourite silk pyjamas and dressing gown. In March 1939, disillusioned with the lowly artistic standing of the cinema in Britain, Hitchcock and his wife left the Cromwell Road for Hollywood. As war then appeared inevitable, this move prompted much criticism – notably from MICHAEL BALCON – and the propagandist content of Hitchcock's subsequent film, *Foreign Correspondent* (1940), has been viewed as a gesture of atonement. He took American citizenship in 1955 – by which time he had made films such as *Rebecca* (1940), *Spellbound* (1945), *Notorious* (1946) and *Strangers on a Train* (1951) – but the rules then in force regarding dual nationality meant that he was fully entitled to bear the knighthood conferred on him very shortly before he died. The unveiling of the plaque took

WEST KENSINGTON AND EARLS COURT

253   The plaque to Sir Alfred Hitchcock, installed during his centenary year at 153 Cromwell Road. [© English Heritage. Photograph by Derek Kendall]

(1936), the verse written by W. H. Auden. In November 1935 Britten and Beth moved to a flat in West Hampstead: 'Anything to get away from boarding houses', he told a friend.[5] Although he is most readily associated with Suffolk – especially Aldeburgh, where he and his partner, the tenor Peter Pears, started the famous music festival – Britten kept a London base for much of the rest of his life. His English Heritage plaque was unveiled in 2001 by the concert pianist Marion Stein.

place on the exact centenary of Hitchcock's birth; by an appositely ominous quirk of the calendar, this fell on Friday the thirteenth.

The composer **Benjamin Britten, OM** (1913–1976) **6** has a plaque at 173 Cromwell Road. Britten, who is probably best known for the opera *Peter Grimes* (1945) and the *War Requiem* (1962), lived here while he was studying composition under JOHN IRELAND at the Royal College of Music. Built in 1873, number 173 was then a boarding-house, and Britten moved here in September 1931 along with his sister Beth (1909–1989), who was training to be a dressmaker. They had adjacent rooms on the top floor; Paul Wright, a fellow singer in the New Madrigal Choir, recalled listening to Britten's ingenious musical improvisations while seated in one of the 'uncomfortable, rickety armchairs' in his eyrie, and summed up his youthful host's persona as 'formidable'.[4] When not playing tennis – an abiding passion – Britten spent many hours at his digs practising and composing at the piano, on occasion to the irritation of fellow lodgers. His first professional performance was in 1933, when the BBC broadcast of *Phantasy* (1932) featured LÉON GOOSSENS as oboe soloist. Britten returned to his Suffolk home in Lowestoft that autumn, but was back in his Cromwell Road lodgings a year later on landing a job with the GPO FILM UNIT, in which capacity he provided the soundtrack for *Night Mail*

Just behind the south-eastern corner of Edwardes Square lie Pembroke Cottages, W8, an attractive semi-detached pair of villas dating from about 1840. At number 1 is the English Heritage plaque erected in 2000 to record the residence of the painter and writer **Sir William Rothenstein** (1872–1945) **7** . Born in Bradford of German parents, Rothenstein studied art at the Slade and in Paris, and made his name as a portraitist with the illustrations he produced for the book *Oxford Characters* (1896). He followed this up with *English Portraits* (1898), and became a leading member of the New English Art Club, with a wide circle of acquaintances in literary and artistic London. In 1899 Rothenstein married Alice Mary Knewstub (1869–1955), who had acted under the name Alice Kingsley, and the couple took 1 Pembroke Cottages as their first London home. That year he began perhaps his best-known painting, *The Doll's House*, for which the models were his wife and their friend AUGUSTUS JOHN. Rothenstein once lent the house for a spell to Augustus and his sister Gwen John; being forgetful of such worldly encumbrances as house keys, John fell into the habit of entering through a window. In the face of the imminent birth of a second child, the Rothensteins moved in November 1902 from the 'delectable cottage', as William described it, to a larger house – 26 Church Row, Hampstead, NW3.[6] From 1912 they lived principally in Gloucestershire, where Rothenstein suffered much prejudiced abuse during the First World War for his slight German accent and for his name, which he chose not to anglicise – unlike his brothers Charles and Albert, who took the English name of Rutherston. For similar reasons, he was once mistakenly arrested as a spy while working as an official war artist. Rothenstein was Principal of the Royal College of Art from 1920 to 1935, and his books *Men and Memories* (1931–32) and *Since Fifty* (1939) are invaluable as sources of information about the art and artists of his generation.

An earlier victim of national chauvinism was Louis Léon Changeur, the French developer of Edwardes Square, W8 (fig. 254). It was falsely claimed that Changeur planned the development in 1811 for the quartering of French officers following a successful Napoleonic invasion – an invasion that, by that date, was no longer a realistic threat. The venture bankrupted the Frenchman, who returned home leaving many houses unfinished, including number 19, which lies on the eastern side of the square. An early resident of the house was **Ugo Foscolo** (1778–1827) ⑧, the Italian poet and patriot. Foscolo's dreams of Italian nationhood had led him to support Napoleon against Austria, and he was a soldier in the army assembled by the Emperor to invade Great Britain. However, following Napoleon's defeat, it was as an exile – not a conqueror – that Foscolo came to London in 1816, following a spell in Switzerland. Lionised by leading Whig politicians, including Lord Holland of nearby Holland House, Foscolo lived extravagantly, and moved frequently to avoid his creditors; his stay at 19 Edwardes Square from September 1817 to April 1818 was, by his standards, a settled spell of residence. During this time

he produced the first of an important pair of essays on Dante for the *Edinburgh Review*, and collaborated uneasily with the Whig politician and writer John Cam Hobhouse on an essay on the state of Italian literature. The latter stirred up some controversy, and Hobhouse, who had taken pity on Foscolo on finding him sick and in dire financial straits, felt his embarrassment turn to outrage when his half-sister became the object of a marriage proposal from the libidinous Italian. The fusion of poetry, polemic and romantic patriotism in the work of Foscolo – who is best known for his poems *I Sepolcri* (1807) and the unfinished *Le Grazie* (1822) – has led to comparisons with Byron; another point in common was their success with titled ladies, and this despite Foscolo being, in the words of Sir Walter Scott, as 'ugly as a baboon'.[7] Foscolo died in poverty at Turnham Green; his plaque was erected in 1998.

A few doors down, at 11 Edwardes Square – one of the houses that Changeur did manage to complete – lived the author and humanist **G. Lowes Dickinson** (1862–1932) ⑨ (fig. 255 and see fig. 254). An active commentator on history and politics from the 1890s, Goldsworthy Lowes Dickinson opposed the First World War as a needless bloodbath, a view he expounded in such works as *War: Its Nature, Cause and Cure* (1923) and *The International Anarchy, 1904–14* (1926). He had held a fellowship of King's College, Cambridge, since 1887, and also taught at the London School of Economics from 1896; he used the Edwardes Square address as a London pied-à-terre from 1912 until he retired from lecturing in 1920. Only weeks after the outbreak of the war, Dickinson called for the establishment of a 'league of nations'. He may have been the first to use this term, and travelled abroad to promote the scheme; in the 1920s he advised the Labour Party on international affairs. A prolific writer on topics ranging over many epochs and continents, 'Goldie' Lowes Dickinson was a great influence on the writers and thinkers of Bloomsbury. E. M. FORSTER wrote a biography of him in 1934, the coyness of which was shown up only by the belated publication of Dickinson's disarmingly frank autobiography in 1973. If the revelation that he was homosexual caused no great surprise, the free admission of his masochistic boot fetish certainly did. Dickinson's plaque – a blue ceramic roundel – is unusual in that it was erected by private subscription in 1956 and immediately incorpo-

254   The east side of Edwardes Square in a photograph of February 1941. The buildings shown include number 19, the former home of Ugo Foscolo, and number 11, the former home of G. Lowes Dickinson. [Reproduced by permission of English Heritage. NMR]

273

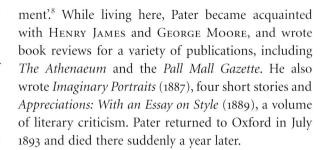

255 The plaque to G. Lowes Dickinson was erected by private subscription in 1956 and immediately incorporated by the LCC into the official scheme. Hence, it bears the name of no administrative body. [© English Heritage. Photograph by Derek Kendall]

256 A view of the Chalees Satoon in the Fort of Allahabad on River Jumna, India, from Thomas Daniell's *Oriental Scenery: Twenty-Four Views in Hindoostan, taken in the years 1789 and 1790* (1795). [© 2008 The British Library]

rated by the LCC into the official scheme; hence, it bears the name of no administrative body.

Earls Terrace, W8, which is situated to the north of Edwardes Square and occupies a prominent position on the south side of Kensington High Street, was built in the first decade of the nineteenth century as another part of Louis Léon Changeur's development. Two of its houses bear English Heritage plaques: the first, erected at number 12 in 2004, commemorates the aesthete and writer **Walter Pater** (1839–1894) **10** . Born in Stepney, Pater was elected in 1864 to a fellowship in classics at Brasenose College, Oxford, where his writings stirred controversy on account of their sceptical angle on religion and their implicit apologia for homosexuality. He became a leading aesthete: his credo, 'art for art's sake', had a considerable influence on Oscar Wilde and the younger Decadents. Pater – who lived with his sisters Hester ('Totty'; 1837–1922) and Clara (*c.* 1841–1910), the latter a tutor of modern languages and the classics – moved to number 12 in August 1885, a few months after the appearance of his novel *Marius the Epicurean*; he hoped to find fresh stimulus in London literary circles, though he remained in Oxford during term-time. For this reason, perhaps, visitors to Earls Terrace were struck by 'the extreme barrenness of the house, for there was in it neither ornament nor attempt at orna-

ment'.[8] While living here, Pater became acquainted with Henry James and George Moore, and wrote book reviews for a variety of publications, including *The Athenaeum* and the *Pall Mall Gazette*. He also wrote *Imaginary Portraits* (1887), four short stories and *Appreciations: With an Essay on Style* (1889), a volume of literary criticism. Pater returned to Oxford in July 1893 and died there suddenly a year later.

Two doors along, at 14 Earls Terrace, a plaque honours the topographical artist **Thomas Daniell** (1749–1840) **11** . Daniell was born in Kingston-upon-Thames and was apprenticed to a coach-builder before finding work with Charles Catton, coach-painter to King George III and a founder member of the Royal Academy. It was at the academy – no doubt assisted by this connection – that Daniell first exhibited in 1772. He is best known for the serially published *Oriental Scenery* (1795–1808), which features aquatints derived from the drawings made with his nephew William Daniell during his lengthy travels in India (1785–94) (fig. 256); apparently, he never lost his suntan. In later life, Thomas worked up these drawings into full-scale oil paintings for sale. This is the work that would have engaged him during his time in Earls Terrace, to which he moved in 1819, having lived previously at several addresses in Fitzrovia. Daniell carried out little work after exhibiting at the RA in 1828, and died at Earls Terrace twelve years later. As the first European landscape artist to work in India, Daniell was a pioneer; a contemporary critic commended his works for their 'truth and beauty'.[9] There is evidence to suggest that his employment of Indian assistants in printmaking may have impacted on the indigenous artistic tradition, and many of his oils still hang in Calcutta. In England, Daniell's experiences abroad fed into projects such as the Indian-inspired design of the house and gardens of Sezincote, Gloucestershire (begun *c.* 1805). The plaque was first proposed by the Kensington Society in 1978, and the suggestion was renewed nearly twenty years later by Dr Maurice Shellin, compiler of a catalogue of Daniell's works. It was installed in 1999.

The poet, novelist and critic **Gilbert Keith Chesterton** (1874–1936) **12** spent his formative years at 11 Warwick Gardens, W14, where a plaque on the side of the house – a stuccoed semi-detached villa with Italianate features, dating from the early 1850s – is easily visible thanks to the curve of the road. As Chesterton's sister-in-law Ada recalled, the house 'stood out from its neighbours. As you turned the corner of the street you had a glimpse of the flowers in dark green window boxes and the sheen of paint the colour of West Country bricks, that seemed to hold the sunshine'. On the inside, books lined the walls from floor to ceiling 'in a phalanx of leather'.[10] From the age of three or four, 'G. K.' – the son of Edward Chesterton (d. 1922), an estate agent, and his wife Marie Louise, née Grosjean (d. 1933) – spent a happy childhood here immersed in literature, political argument, writing and drawing; the five-year-old Chesterton reportedly greeted the advent of his brother Cecil (1879–1918), later a notable journalist, with the words 'Now I shall always have an audience'.[11] Ada Chesterton speculated that Gilbert's preference for writing in enclosed spaces could be traced to the scene of his childhood play in tiny upstairs 'cubbyholes' at the house. While still living here, in 1900, Chesterton published two collections of poems; one of these early verses, 'The Donkey', became a favourite anthology piece. It was also in that year that he met his literary ally HILAIRE BELLOC; they were collectively dubbed 'Chesterbelloc' by GEORGE BERNARD SHAW. Following his marriage in June 1901, Chesterton and his wife Frances moved a short distance away to 1 Edwardes Square, before moving on to Battersea and, in 1909, to Beaconsfield in Buckinghamshire; by this time 'G. K. C.' had become an established writer, with novels such as *The Man Who Was Thursday* (1908). Chesterton's plaque was put up in 1952; he had been dead for only sixteen years, but the LCC judged that his reputation was already 'sufficiently assured'.[12] Since then his star has waned, partly because of the anti-Semitic language that disfigures some of his work, though his Father Brown detective stories (1911–35) – inspired by a Roman Catholic priest who had been instrumental in Chesterton's own conversion – remain highly popular examples of their genre.

Addison Bridge Place, W14, runs southwards from near the point at which Kensington High Street becomes Hammersmith Road; it lies, like the remaining entries in this chapter, in the borough of Hammersmith and Fulham. The District Line runs on the eastern side of this cul-de-sac; the western side has a terrace of brown-brick, three-storey houses dating from the early nineteenth century. Two are adorned with plaques:

number 5 was the home of **Harold Laski** (1893–1950) ⬤13 , the teacher and political philosopher, from autumn 1926 until his death at St Mary's Hospital, Paddington. He shared the house with his wife Frida, née Kerry (1884–1977), with whom he had eloped at the age of eighteen, much to the chagrin – at least initially – of his Jewish family, for she was nine years his senior and a gentile. Laski, who was born in Manchester, was an intellectual prodigy. Following a spell as an editor at Harvard, he taught politics and government at the London School of Economics from 1920, becoming Professor of Political Science in his early thirties; he remained at the LSE until his death. It was partly Frida's influence that led Laski into politics, first as a supporter of women's suffrage; he went on to become a leading member of the FABIAN SOCIETY and theoretician for the Labour Party, of which he was Chairman in 1945–46. Along with John Strachey and Victor Gollancz, he started the Left Book Club in 1936, which published, among many other works, *The Road to Wigan Pier* (1937) by GEORGE ORWELL. His own publications included *A Grammar of Politics* (1925), *Liberty in the Modern State* (1930) and *Democracy in Crisis* (1933). Over time, Laski's political thought tacked between liberal socialism and Marxism. His interest in the latter creed brought him into conflict with more cautious Labour figures such as the party leader CLEMENT ATTLEE, and made him a particular target for Conservative attacks. Following the publication of *The American Democracy* (1948), Laski became a victim of the 'red scare' in the United States; the book charted what he saw as the corruption of democratic ideals by the overweening influence of big business. The plaque was erected by the GLC in 1974.

Frida Laski was a keen supporter of the plan – executed by the LCC in 1950 – to put up a plaque two doors down at 7 Addison Bridge Place (formerly 7 Portland Place) to **Samuel Taylor Coleridge** (1772–1834) ⬤14 (see also p. 512–13), the poet and philosopher (fig. 248). This had first been mooted in 1904, when the house's then owner declined a plaque on the grounds that Coleridge's residence here was 'an open question'.[13] There is no room for doubt, however, that Coleridge stayed at the address intermittently as a guest of John Morgan (1775?–1820), a lawyer friend from Bristol, between late 1810 and autumn 1811. Coleridge continued to live mostly with the Morgan

257 A detail from Sir Edward Elgar's manuscript for the overture *Froissart* (dated 25 May 1890), one of the works he composed during his time at 51 Avonmore Road. [Courtesy of the Elgar Birthplace Museum & Elgar Will Trust]

family after they moved from this address – then known as 7 Portland Place – to Berners Street, off Oxford Street. At that time Coleridge was at a creative and personal nadir: ravaged by opium addiction – according to Robert Southey, he was consuming a pint of laudanum a day – he was deeply wounded by the discovery that his friend William Wordsworth had privately expressed no hope for him. When Coleridge put pen to paper, it was only to denounce Wordsworth and to justify his own Christian faith, though he did manage to lecture at the London Philosophical Society. During 1811 Coleridge also worked for the *The Courier* newspaper; it was his stated intention to save money on carriage fares by walking from Hammersmith to the paper's office in the Strand, though it is not known that he actually did so. A reconciliation with Wordsworth took place in 1812, and soon after Coleridge entered the most creative phase of his life, publishing works including 'Kubla Khan' (1816), which he had written twenty years earlier.

At 51 Avonmore Road, W14, is the plaque to the composer **Sir Edward Elgar** (1857–1934) **15** . Born in Worcester, Elgar is so closely associated with nearby Malvern that some eyebrows were raised when a London plaque was put up in 1962. It is true that he lived at number 51 for little more than a year – from March 1890 to June 1891 – and that residence in London did not bring the instant recognition that had been hoped for by his wife Alice, née Roberts (1848– 1920); her belief in her husband's talent was crucial to his eventual success. The Elgars came to the house after brief sojourns in Marloes Road, Kensington, and at Upper Norwood; Alice Elgar sold her pearls in order to secure the tenancy. While here, Elgar had violin and organ pieces accepted for publication, and – significantly – composed the overture *Froissart* (fig. 257), which received its first performance at the Worcester Festival in September 1890, conducted by Elgar himself. This piece marked a step-change in his development as a composer, and for this reason the LCC's decision to grant him a plaque in the capital seems a sound one. Although important in his career, it was not a happy time or place for Elgar: he described the winter of 1890 as 'truly awful: the fogs here are terrifying and they make me very ill'.[14] Wider recognition came later – with the *Enigma Variations* (1899), and the first two *Pomp and Circumstance* marches (1901),

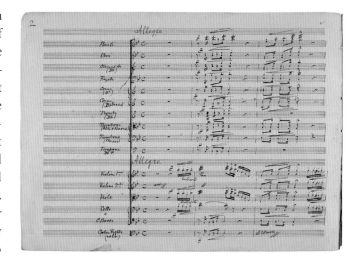

featuring 'Land of Hope and Glory' – though despite his success and identification with the quintessence of Englishness, Elgar never entirely lost his sense of 'outsider' status, partly owing to his being a Roman Catholic. From Avonmore Road – where their daughter Carice (1890–1970) was born – the Elgars moved to Malvern, and thence to Hereford, before returning to London for another spell from 1912 to 1920. This was spent in a house in Netherhall Gardens, Hampstead, designed by RICHARD NORMAN SHAW and now demolished.

One of the young composers who benefited from ELGAR's encouragement and advice was Sir Eugène Goossens (1893–1962); now better remembered as a conductor, he was a member of the **Goossens family** of musicians **16** commemorated at 70 Edith Road, W14, part of a terrace dating from the 1870s (fig. 258). Elgar also wrote specifically for Eugène's brother, the oboist Léon Goossens (1897–1988), an internationally known musician who was noted for his courageous – and successful – efforts to re-learn his instrument after his face muscles were damaged in a car accident in 1962. Léon survived the First World War thanks to a fortuitously placed silver cigarette case that deflected a bullet; his brother Adolphe (1896–1916), a promising horn player, was not so lucky, and perished at the Somme. The family was of Belgian origin, and came to England in the late nineteenth century. Eugène Goossens senior (1867–1958) – a violinist and conductor who was known especially for his work with opera companies – moved with his wife Annie Cook (1860– 1946), an opera singer, and their family to Edith Road

258   Members of the Goossens family in the garden of 70 Edith Road, their home from 1912 to 1927. From the left are Eugène junior, Eugène senior, Annie, Marie and Sidonie. [Courtesy of Jennie Goossens]

from Liverpool in 1912; they stayed until 1927. The couple's daughters, Marie (1894–1991) and Sidonie (1899–2005), were both harpists; all the Goossens siblings attended the Royal College of Music, where Léon and Sidonie later held professorships. Eugène junior conducted the first London performance of Stravinsky's *Rite of Spring* in 1921, and in the same year Sidonie made her professional debut at a Prom concert; exactly seventy years later she became the oldest person to perform at the Last Night. When the idea of a plaque to her siblings was first mooted in 1987, Sidonie was delighted: 'Eugène [junior] spent a very important part of his life in that house – rehearsing string quartets and other musical activities – I am sure the atmosphere in that house must still be saturated with our music', she wrote.[15] The plaque was unveiled in 1999 by Eugène's daughter Anne Obermer, in the presence of other family members; sadly, Sidonie was not well enough to attend the event.

Number 69 Gunterstone Road, W14, is a three-storey terraced house of the 1880s in a Gothic-influenced style. Outwardly, it seems an unlikely setting for the gestation of some of the best-known African adventure stories, a fact indicated by the plaque of 1977 to the novelist **Sir Henry Rider Haggard** (1856–1925) **17**. Haggard enjoyed an exciting early life in South

Africa, first in the colonial service and later, following a romantic disappointment, as an ostrich farmer. Having married Louisa ('Louie') Margitson (1859/60–1943), who, like him, came from Norfolk gentry stock, he returned to London and qualified as a barrister in 1885. Haggard found the work stultifying, however, and took to writing to alleviate the boredom. Challenged by his brother to write a boys' adventure tale as good as Robert Louis Stevenson's *Treasure Island* (1881–82), Haggard wrote *King Solomon's Mines* (1885) in just six weeks at the Gunterstone Road house, to which he had moved his young family that year. Two more novels were complete by the end of 1885: *Allan Quatermain* (largely written in Norfolk) and *Jess*. Both were published in 1887, along with *She*, which Haggard committed to paper during February and March 1886 'almost without rest . . . it came faster than my poor aching hand could set it down'.[16] Not being short of self-esteem, he took the manuscript to his agent and announced it as his gift to posterity. Having made the fortunate decision to take royalties rather than a publisher's advance, he was able to abandon the legal profession in 1887 and move his family to more salubrious accommodation at Redcliffe Square, West Brompton, in May 1888. Later, following the death of his only son in 1891, he retired to Ditchingham, Norfolk, where he established himself as an authority on agriculture and rural life. For a time he kept a pied-à-terre at 26 Ashley Gardens, Westminster, SW1, and it was in a London nursing home that he died.

Talgarth Road, W14, is part of the busy A4 trunk route out of London. Drivers caught in traffic jams should turn their heads to look at number 53, part of a terrace dating from the 1860s or 1870s, which bears a plaque marking the final residence of **Marcus Garvey** (1887–1940) **18**, the Pan-Africanist leader. Marcus Mosiah Garvey was born in Jamaica, where he founded the Universal Negro Improvement Association in 1914, soon after making his first visit to London. He moved to New York in 1916, where he founded the Black Star Line steamship corporation, a pioneering black business enterprise, and started a militant weekly, *Negro World*. Garvey was later found guilty of fraud arising from the promotion of Black Star, and served time in a US prison. He was deported to Jamaica in 1927 and, after making another short visit to London in 1928, moved to the capital permanently in 1935, though he

259   A photograph of 1903 showing Mahatma Gandhi as a practising attorney in South Africa, seated in front of a window bearing his name. It was while studying law in the 1880s that Gandhi lived at 20 Baron's Court Road. [© Getty Images]

was unimpressed with the opportunities on offer to black people at that time, and found that the damp climate worsened his bronchitis and asthma. A regular at Speakers' Corner in Hyde Park, he had offices at 2 Beaumont Crescent, Hammersmith, and lived in nearby Talgarth Road from around 1937, initially with his wife Amy Jacques (1896–1973) and their children and later with his secretary and nurse, Daisy Whyte; it was here that he died on 10 June 1940. Garvey was, and remains, a controversial figure. Behind his promotion of the 'Back to Africa' movement were separatist assumptions that do not chime with the societal ideals generally held today. However, his encouragement of black pride and self-confidence was an inspiration to many, and in Jamaica he is regarded as a national hero. Garvey's connection with London remains a lesser-known aspect of his life, though the English Heritage plaque – erected in 2005 at first-floor level, where he had his bedroom and library – has done something to rectify this.

At 20 Baron's Court Road, W14, is a house in which **Mahatma Gandhi** (1869–1948) 19 (see also pp. 327–8) lived as a law student in the late 1880s. Gandhi was first commemorated within six years of his death at an address in Tower Hamlets where he had stayed in 1931. In 1983 it was decided that a second plaque was justified, given the distance – in both the temporal and geographical senses – between Gandhi's first and last London sojourns. Number 20 Baron's Court Road was apparently the address in the capital where he stayed the longest; nineteen-year-old Mohandras Karmchand Gandhi – the designation 'Mahatma', meaning 'great soul', came much later – was here by 6 November 1888, the date of his formal admission to the Inner Temple. Some five weeks earlier he had landed at Tilbury, and spent most of the intervening period in Richmond. Board and lodging in Baron's Court Road cost Gandhi thirty shillings a week; the widowed landlady, Elizabeth Fanny Turner, had herself lived in India, but struggled to cater for his meatless diet; the dinners provided were, he recalled, 'third rate', and he was often left hungry.[17] Mrs Turner did tell him, however, of vegetarian restaurants in London, where he discovered one of his life's great causes: the promotion of a meatless diet. The lessons he took in dancing, elocution and French proved less enduring, though Gandhi continued to affect the smart dress of an aspiring lawyer –

including a top hat – for some time after leaving Baron's Court Road (fig. 259). This move took place after about eight or nine months, for reasons of economy and his dietary preference. Gandhi's subsequent addresses included 15 St Charles Square, northern Kensington, W10, and 52 St Stephen's Gardens (formerly St Stephen's Square), Bayswater, W2. Gandhi returned to India in June 1891, but came back to England on four occasions, and declared in 1909 that 'next to India, I would rather live in London than any other place in the world'.[18] The plaque of 1986 was one of the last to be put up by the GLC; like Gandhi's plaque in Bow, it bears no descriptor, it having been agreed that 'any attempt to describe his achievements in the usual short phrase would be superfluous'.[19]

Number 32 Baron's Court Road, a tall terraced house dating from the mid-Victorian period, bears an English Heritage plaque erected in 2001 to the aircraft designer **Sir Geoffrey de Havilland** (1882–1965) 20 (fig. 260). De Havilland lived here in Flat B from March 1909 – the year of his marriage to Louise Thomas (1881–1949) – until January 1911, rather than 1910 as is stated on the plaque. The house was conveniently close to the work-

260 Geoffrey de Havilland in his office in December 1942, surrounded by models and drawings of aeroplanes. [© Popperfoto / Getty Images]

fabric and make tea, but I think she had doubts about the outcome of our work and would have preferred something more down-to-earth'.[20] From an early age, de Havilland had displayed an obsession with mechanical engineering; he taught himself to fly in 1910, and went on to become chief designer of the Aircraft Manufacturing Company (Airco), which provided almost a third of British and American aircraft during the First World War. In 1920 he founded the De Havilland Aircraft Company, which – at its factory at Stag Lane Aerodrome, Hendon – produced the Moth series of planes, including the Tiger Moth, the favoured training plane of the RAF, and the Comet Racer, a monoplane that won the 1934 England to Australia race. The Mosquito was the firm's most important Second World War design, and was followed by a series of jet fighters. One of the great names of British aviation, Sir Geoffrey remained actively involved in the De Havilland Aircraft Company until 1955. Although Longcote, Tanglewood Close, Stanmore, was de Havilland's home for the last nineteen years of his life, its secluded position ruled it out for a blue plaque; his other London addresses, in Stanmore and Edgware, were found to have been demolished.

shop in Bothwell Street, off Fulham Palace Road, where he – together with Frank Hearle, an engineer and his future brother-in-law – constructed his first aeroplane in 1908–9. De Havilland later recalled how his wife Louise used to come to the workshop 'to sew the wing

NOTES

1 *The Times*, 25 March 1904, p. 8
2 *Strand Magazine*, vol. IV (July–December 1892), pp. 489–90
3 John Russell Taylor, '*Hitch*' (London, 1978), p. 81
4 Humphrey Carpenter, *Benjamin Britten: A Biography* (London, 1992), p. 45
5 *Letters from a Life: The Selected Letters and Diaries of Benjamin Britten, 1913–1976*, ed. Donald Mitchell, vol. I (London, 1991), p. 379 (23/24 October 1935)
6 Sir William Rothenstein, *Men and Memories*, vol. II (London, 1832), p. 28
7 *Journal of Sir Walter Scott*, eds J. G. Tait and W. M. Parker (Edinburgh and London, 1950), p. 12
8 Thomas Wright, *The Life of Walter Pater*, vol. II (London, 1907), p. 91

9 *ODNB*, vol. V, p. 484
10 Ada Chesterton, *The Chestertons* (London, 1941), p. 19
11 Michael Coren, *Gilbert: The Man who was G. K. Chesterton* (London, 1989), p. 13
12 Report of 3 July 1951 on blue plaque file.
13 Letter of 11 July 1904 on blue plaque file.
14 Michael Kennedy, *Life of Elgar* (Cambridge, 2004), p. 38
15 Letter of 6 April 1987 on blue plaque file.
16 Henry Rider Haggard, *The Days of My Life*, vol. I (London, 1926), pp. 245–46
17 James D. Hunt, *Gandhi in London* (New Delhi, 1978), p. 24
18 Ibid, p. 143
19 Report of 9 July 1984 on blue plaque file.
20 Geoffrey de Havilland, *Sky Fever: The Autobiography of Sir Geoffrey de Havilland* (London, 1961), p. 53

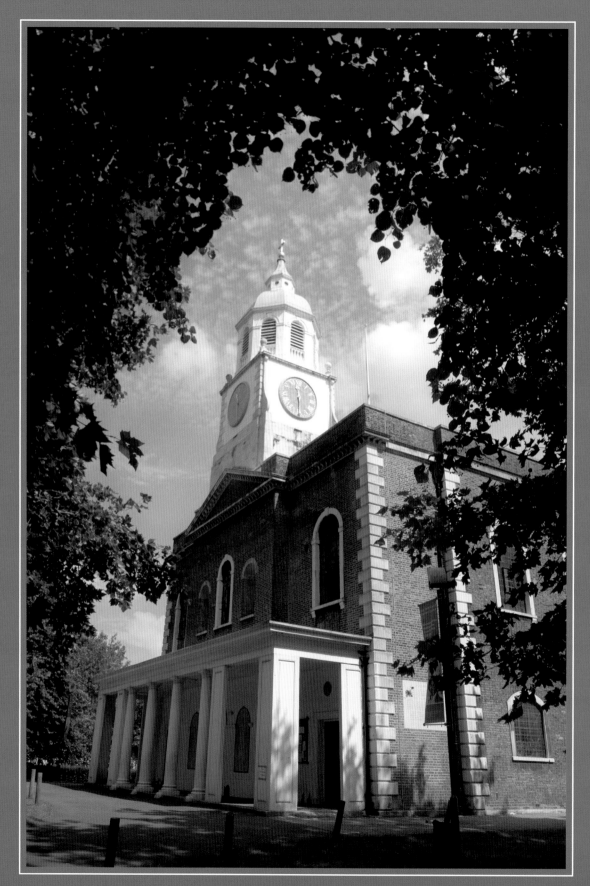

261 Holy Trinity Church on Clapham Common North Side was built in 1774–76. In the decades around 1800 it became the centre of the Clapham Sect, a fact commemorated by a blue plaque erected in 1984. [© English Heritage. Photograph by Derek Kendall]

LAMBETH

Lambeth is today one of the most densely populated parts of Britain, yet as recently as the mid-eighteenth century the area covered by the borough was largely uninhabited. The opening of new bridges across the Thames at Westminster (1750) and Blackfriars (1769) made the south side of the river more accessible. Ribbon development followed the main roads to Kennington, Wandsworth, Clapham and Brixton, while those keen to benefit from peace and fresh air built villas on the higher ground of Herne Hill, Streatham and Norwood. The Victorian period wrought radical changes to the area. North Lambeth descended to the state of a slum, overshadowed by industry, and the new railways brought outlying villages within the embrace of London; two of these – Clapham and Streatham, long since built up – were added to the borough in 1965. The twentieth century has been notable for vast amounts of new public housing, especially after the Second World War, so that by the early 1980s nearly half Lambeth's housing stock was council owned. This process of regeneration was epitomised by the Festival of Britain in 1951, which swept away the industrial buildings on the south bank of the Thames and began the transformation of the site into a centre for the arts.

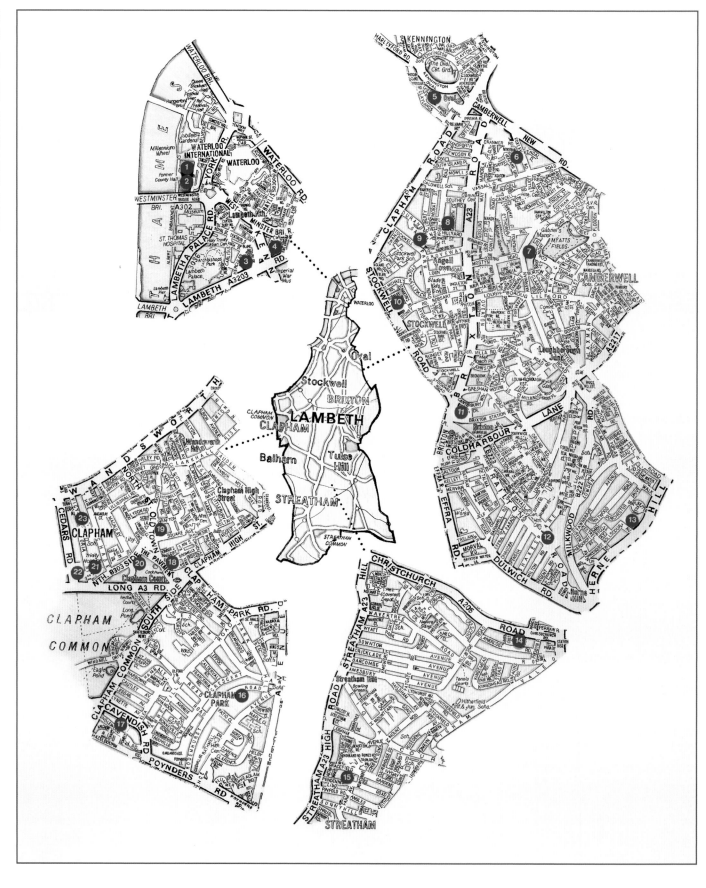

LAMBETH

NORTH LAMBETH

At the extreme north of the borough, the riverside is lined with a series of monumental buildings associated with business and local government as well as leisure and entertainment. The southernmost of these is **County Hall** ❶ (fig. 262), a vast edifice fronting onto the Embankment, with Westminster Bridge Road, SE1, to the south; it covers roughly five acres (2 ha) with a river frontage of just over 700 ft (213 m), and contains over five miles (8 km) of corridors. It now houses hotels, galleries, restaurants and the London aquarium, but two wreathed blue plaques flanking the east entrance in Belvedere Road reveal the past life of this building. The inscription on the first of these plaques commemorates County Hall as 'the Home of London Government from 1922 to 1986' and gives the life-dates of the capital's two ruling bodies – the London County Council (1889–1965) and the Greater London Council (1965–86). Designed by Ralph Knott, County Hall was begun as a purpose-built headquarters for the LCC in 1909, and was opened thirteen years later by King George V, although the original building was only completed in 1933; it was later expanded in phases until the 1970s. Among County Hall's many occupants were the staff responsible for running the blue plaques scheme, who largely formed part of the Clerk's Department. The immensity of the building meant that separate departments often worked in isolation; one member of staff found its size 'oddly liberating by reason of the anonymity it bestowed'.[1] Meanwhile, council members and the public frequently became hopelessly lost. The tradition of London-wide local government was ended – at least temporarily – by the abolition of the GLC in 1986, and the dispersal of its responsibilities among the London boroughs and among other bodies, including English Heritage. Faced with the GLC's imminent dissolution, a number of council members and officials decided that a blue plaque on County Hall would be an appropriate memorial to what was being lost. Angry at the manner of the authority's abolition, their principal aim was 'to leave some *permanent* record which it will be virtually impossible for the successor authority to obliterate'.[2] To make the plaque distinctive, a decorative border of laurel leaves was added to the standard design, and the arms of the GLC and LCC were placed at top and bottom (see fig. 45).

Once preparations were underway for the plaque honouring the LCC and the GLC, the **Inner London Edu-**

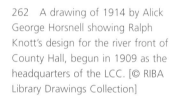

262   A drawing of 1914 by Alick George Horsnell showing Ralph Knott's design for the river front of County Hall, begun in 1909 as the headquarters of the LCC. [© RIBA Library Drawings Collection]

LAMBETH

cation Authority ❷ , also housed in County Hall (see fig. 262), decided that it would like to follow suit. ILEA came into being in 1965 as a special committee of the GLC to oversee schooling in the twelve inner London boroughs; the authority inherited the educational responsibilities of the LCC, which had themselves been taken over in 1904 from the London School Board. ILEA – the most notable leader of which, in 1970–81, was Ashley Bramall – was abolished in 1990, when its duties passed to the relevant London boroughs. The design of the plaque to ILEA was conceived alongside that commemorating the LCC and the GLC; both were unveiled on 27 March 1986, the last working day of the GLC, by the council's leader, Ken Livingstone.

The old village of Lambeth was clustered around Lambeth Palace – the London seat of the archbishops of Canterbury since the twelfth century – and the Church of St Mary, now the Museum of Garden History. In Lambeth Road, SE1, there are still a handful of the late Georgian terraces that signified the village's evolution into a London suburb. Number 160, a tall brick house of *c.* 1800 set back from the road, bears a plaque to the doyen of early twentieth-century theatre, the actor-manager **Sir Philip Ben Greet** (1857–1936) ❸ . It was unveiled in 1960 by the actress DAME SYBIL THORNDIKE, who had made her debut under his management in 1904 (fig. 263). The son of a naval captain, Philip Barling Ben Greet was born on board his father's ship *Crocodile* while it was moored on the Thames, and was educated at the Royal Naval School in New Cross, Lewisham. After a brief spell as a schoolteacher, he became an actor and then, in 1886, entered theatre management. Greet made his name staging open-air performances of Shakespeare in Oxford and Cambridge colleges. In 1914 he went into partnership with LILIAN BAYLIS, the manager of the Old Vic Theatre in Waterloo, where he introduced thousands of London schoolchildren to Shakespeare through his innovation of matinée performances. 'B. G.' – as he was generally known – began staying with his friend John William Keys and his family at 160 Lambeth Road during the early years of the First World War, when air raids prevented him from travelling home to 123 Charlton Church Lane, SE7, where he lived with his parents. As the plaque states, he lived permanently at number 160 from 1920 – together with the Keys family – until his death sixteen years later, which took place at a nearby nursing home.

Facing the grounds of the Imperial War Museum (built in 1811–14 as Bethlehem Hospital) is another Georgian terrace, originally known as Durham Place, which was built in c. 1794. The first resident of 3 Durham Place – now 100 Lambeth Road – was **William Bligh** (1754– 1817) **4** , Commander of the *Bounty*, who was commemorated with an LCC plaque in 1952. The address, shared with his wife Elizabeth, née Bentham (1754?– 1812), remained his London home until c. 1813. Bligh was born in Plymouth and, as a young seaman, took part in the second voyage around the world (1776–80) of Captain Cook. In 1787 – while living at 14 Moore Place, Kennington (demolished) – Bligh was appointed to the command of the *Bounty* for another expedition to the South Seas to export breadfruit – intended as high-energy food for slaves – from Tahiti to the British West Indies. It was during this voyage that the famous mutiny led by Fletcher Christian occurred in 1789, apparently incited by Bligh's violent temper and authoritarian leadership, but also exacerbated by his crew's incompetence and restiveness. The incident was famously portrayed in the film *Mutiny on the Bounty* (1935), starring Charles Laughton. Set adrift in an open boat, together with the eighteen men who had remained loyal, Bligh succeeded in navigating 3,600 miles (5,800 km) across the Pacific to Timor, while the mutineers either settled on Pitcairn Island or were arrested. In 1806 Bligh took up the post of Governor of New South Wales; he did not return to England until 1810, in the meantime having been embroiled in another mutiny which led to his imprisonment on board a ship moored at Hobart, Tasmania. In about 1813, after the death of his wife, Bligh left Lambeth for Farningham, Kent; he died, however, at a house in Bond Street and was buried at St Mary's, Lambeth.

KENNINGTON AND STOCKWELL

Kennington is best known today for the Oval cricket ground, established in 1845 as the home of Surrey County Cricket Club. Facing the south side of the cricket ground at 52–54 Kennington Oval, SE11, and screened by trees, is a substantial mid-nineteenth-century villa – with a distinctive neo-Tudor porch – that was originally the vicarage of St Mark's Church. It is now an arts centre known as Oval House and bears an English Heritage plaque commemorating the birth here of the Second World War hero **Field Marshal Viscount Montgomery of Alamein** (1887–1976) **5** . Bernard Law Montgomery was the fourth child of Henry Hutchinson Montgomery (1847–1932), vicar of St Mark's from 1879 to 1889, and Maud, née Farrar (1865–1949). When in 1889 his father was appointed Bishop of Tasmania, the family left Kennington for Hobart. Montgomery, who returned with his family to England in 1901, entered the Army in 1908 and proved an outstanding, though idiosyncratic, leader of men during the First World War. However, it is for his achievements during the Second World War that 'Monty' is largely remembered. As Commander of the British Eighth Army in North Africa, he was responsible for the Allied victory at the Battle of El Alamein (1942), a vital turning point, and went on to mastermind and command the D-Day landings at Normandy in 1944. Montgomery served as Chief of the Imperial General Staff from 1946 – the year he was raised to the peerage as viscount – until 1948; on retiring ten years later he moved to Alton, Hampshire, where he died. The suggestion to commemorate Oval House – the only surviving building in London associated with Montgomery – was first made by his younger brother Brian, who duly unveiled the plaque in 1987, the centenary of Monty's birth.

In the 1880s, when Montgomery's father was vicar of this parish, it was an inner-city area. Just sixty years earlier, when the artist **David Cox** (1783–1859) **6** came to live at 34 (formerly 9) Foxley Road, SW9, Kennington was on the fringes of London and largely undeveloped. Cox was born in Deritend, on the outskirts of Birmingham, and led a peripatetic life, obliged for most of his career to seek employment as a drawing master in order to supplement his earnings as a painter. He first came to London in 1804, finding work as a scene painter for Astley's Theatre in Lambeth and taking lodgings near what is now Elephant and Castle. He exhibited for the first time at the Royal Academy in 1805 and – immediately after his marriage in 1808 to

LAMBETH

264   *The Sea Front at Blackpool*, a painting of 1840 by David Cox. The artist lived at 34 Foxley Road between 1827 and 1841. [Private Collection / © Agnew's, London, UK / The Bridgeman Art Library]

his landlady's daughter, Mary Agg (1770/1–1845) – moved to Dulwich Common. From 1814 Cox worked as a drawing master in Hereford, but returned to London in spring 1827, when he and his family took up residence at what was then numbered 9 Foxley Road. The fine row of linked houses, in which Cox and his family resided until summer 1841, was built in 1824. Although Cox complained in later life of being unjustly neglected by the art world of the day, his reputation was assured by the late 1830s and he is now recognised as one of the great artists of the golden age of English watercolour (fig. 264). An LCC plaque was placed on number 34 in 1951, and has survived in spite of the dereliction that afflicted this and many other houses in the area during the 1970s.

At 56 Akerman Road, SW9, there is a plaque to a figure who, by contrast, enjoyed great fame and public esteem for almost all of his short life: the music-hall comedian **Dan Leno** (1860–1904) **7** , who lived here from 1898 to 1901 (fig. 265). This was one of half a dozen houses in South London in which Leno resided during the last decade of his life, by which time he had become the biggest star in the world of popular theatre. Born George Wild Galvin into a family of entertainers, Leno took to the stage at the age of four as a tumbler and contortionist, and in his teens became an expert clog-dancer, winning the world championship in 1880 and 1883. After his triumphant London debut as a solo artist in 1885 at the Foresters' Music

265   The music-hall comedian Dan Leno in a photograph of c.1900, probably taken in the conservatory of 56 Akerman Road, his home between 1898 and 1901. [© Getty Images]

Hall, Mile End, he specialised in the role of pantomime dame; Christmas 1899, for instance, saw him playing Dame Trot in *Jack and the Beanstalk* at Drury Lane. While living at Akerman Road, he also started to make films with his comedy partner Herbert Campbell. At

266 A photograph of 1972 showing the dilapidated exterior of 56 Akerman Road, which was then threatened with demolition. In 1974 the plaque to Dan Leno was removed for safekeeping, but – after the house was reprieved – it was replaced five years later. [© City of London, LMA]

267 A drawing of 87 Hackford Road, where Vincent van Gogh lodged in 1873–74. It is said to have been executed by van Gogh and made as a present for Eugenie Loyer, the daughter of his landlady. Number 87 is the second house from the left. It now forms the end of the terrace, the three houses to its right having been demolished. [© Amsterdam, Van Gogh Museum (Vincent van Gogh Foundation)]

Sandringham in 1901, Leno performed at the request of King Edward VII, yet within three years he was dead; the cause – syphilis – was not made public at the time. Leno was lauded by the thousands who attended his funeral, and his work went on to influence, among

others, Charlie Chaplin. In 1968, six years after the plaque had been erected, 56 Akerman Road was threatened with demolition as part of a massive redevelopment programme. As a result, it stood empty for a long time (fig. 266), and in 1974 the plaque had to be removed for safekeeping. Happily, the house was reprieved, and the plaque was re-erected in 1979.

In August 1873 – two months after having been sent to work at the London branch of his employers, the Dutch art dealer Goupil & Co. – a young Dutchman called **Vincent van Gogh** (1853–1890) ❽ came to Stockwell in search of cheap lodgings. He found them at 87 Hackford Road, SW9, a three-storey terraced house dating from *c.* 1840 that was the home of Mrs Sarah Loyer and her daughter Eugenie (fig. 267 and see figs 14 and 28). Van Gogh enjoyed the family atmosphere at his lodgings, writing to his brother, 'I now have a room such as I always longed for without a slanting ceiling and without blue paper with a green border. I live with a very amusing family now'.[3] His happiness was, however, marred by his unrequited love for Eugenie Loyer; he eventually left number 87 in summer 1874 after declaring his feelings and discovering that she was already engaged. Van Gogh moved to new lodgings at Ivy Cottage, 395 Kensington New Road, where he remained until he was recalled to the Paris branch of Goupil & Co. the following May. In April 1876 van Gogh returned to England, teaching at a school in Ramsgate and moving with it to Isleworth; he left England for the last time at Christmas 1876. Only twenty when he first arrived in London, van Gogh had not yet found his vocation as a painter; the works for which he became famous date largely from the last five years of his life, and include *Sunflowers* (1888) and *Starry Night* (1889). He is, however, known to have been influenced by the works published in the *Illustrated London News* and other such journals, and carried a sketchbook on his walks around South London. A drawing of 87 Hackford Road, which – it is said – he made as a present for Eugenie, shows that it has changed very little, although the terrace visible to the right of the house no longer exists.

Number 27 Stockwell Park Road, SW9, a double-fronted house of *c.* 1850, was the home of **Lilian Baylis** (1874–1937) ❾, the manager of the Old Vic and Sadler's Wells theatres. Born in Marylebone, Baylis was

LAMBETH

287

one of the outstanding personalities in the chequered history of the Old Vic Theatre, Waterloo. Her aunt, EMMA CONS, had saved the theatre from ruin by turning it into a temperance music hall, but Baylis – who became acting manager in 1898 and took full responsibility following Cons's death in 1912 – was able to establish its reputation for high-quality theatrical performance. Together with BEN GREET, Baylis is credited with putting Shakespeare back at the heart of the English repertoire. Performances continued throughout the First World War, despite the threat posed by Zeppelin attacks, which she dismissed with characteristic bravado, declaring, 'What's an air raid when my curtain's up!'.[4] Such stars as DAME SYBIL THORNDIKE, Sir John Gielgud and DAME EDITH EVANS established their reputations at the Old Vic during her time. In the 1920s Baylis realised the need for a second venue, and by 1931 had successfully raised funds to turn Sadler's Wells Theatre into a home for her ballet and opera companies. The proposal to commemorate Baylis was made following the demolition in 1971 of Surrey Lodge, 6 Morton Place, Lambeth, where an LCC plaque of 1952 had marked the residence of both Baylis and Emma Cons. Number 27 Stockwell Park Road was Baylis's home from 1914 until her death, and was shared with her aunt, Ellen Cons (1840–1920), a governor of the Old Vic. The GLC plaque at the address was unveiled by Dame Flora Robson in 1974, as part of the celebrations to mark the centenary of Baylis's birth.

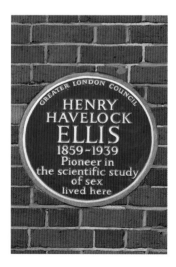

268 The GLC plaque to Henry Havelock Ellis at Dover Mansions, Canterbury Crescent. [© English Heritage. Photograph by Derek Kendall]

At 18 Burnley Road, SW9, a plaque commemorates the residence of the secret agent **Violette Szabo**, **GC** (1921–1945) **10** , the first British woman to be awarded the George Cross; as the plaque records, she gave her life for the French Resistance. Born in Paris to an English father, Charles George Bushell, and a French mother, Reine Leroy, Violette moved to 18 Burnley Road with her family in 1935 and attended the LCC school in Stockwell Road. The Bushells' home consisted of the basement, ground floor and a room on the first floor of the house. When the war came, Violette was still living at number 18 and was working in the perfume department of the Bon Marché store in Brixton, but her ordinary life was soon transformed. In 1940 she met and married a French officer of Hungarian parentage – Étienne Szabo – who almost immediately joined the Free French Forces in North Africa. Violette continued living with her parents until early 1942, when

she moved to a flat at 36 Pembridge Villas, Notting Hill, W11, which was to be her last home; her daughter Tania was born in June 1942. Following her husband's death in action in October of that year, Szabo – described by her father as 'always the tomboy ready for excitement and adventure' – was recruited into the French section of the Special Operations Executive (SOE).[5] Known as a crack shot, and for her striking good looks, she was sent into occupied France on two occasions: first in April 1944, and for the second and final time two months later, when, shortly after her arrival, Szabo was captured by the Germans; after months of captivity – and refusing to speak under interrogation – she was executed along with two SOE colleagues at Ravensbrück concentration camp. Szabo was awarded the GC posthumously; the award was presented to her infant daughter in 1946. Her story reached a wider audience with the 1958 film *Carve Her Name with Pride*, which featured several scenes filmed in Burnley Road (fig. 269). The plaque was unveiled in 1981 at a ceremony attended by Tania Szabo, who wrote to the GLC that 'the blue plaque remains as a silent, beautiful and significant acclaim to the courage of Violette Szabo and the many who worked with her. I shall remember that day and everything that took place forever'.[6]

BRIXTON, HERNE HILL, TULSE HILL AND STREATHAM

In Canterbury Crescent, SW9, in the heart of Brixton, is Dover Mansions, a red-brick, five-storey block of flats with a distinctive corner turret. At the east end of the block, on the first floor, is a GLC plaque of 1981 commemorating the residence of **Henry Havelock Ellis** (1859–1939) **11** , pioneer in the scientific study of sex (fig. 268). Born in Croydon, Ellis spent his teenage years in Australia before returning to London to train as a doctor at St Thomas' Hospital. He lived according to his creed – that sexual freedom brought happiness – and in 1884 formed an intense liaison with OLIVE SCHREINER, which lasted until she returned to South Africa in 1889. Ellis kept Flat 14 at Dover Mansions from autumn 1909 to 1928, sharing it with his bisexual wife – the lecturer and writer Edith Oldham Lees (1861–1916) – until her death, though much of their time was spent at their Cornish home, Carbis Bay. During this period, Ellis carried out some of his most influential work, which was published as the ground-

269   The film *Carve Her Name with Pride* (1958) – in which Virginia McKenna (shown here) plays Violette Szabo – featured several scenes shot in Burnley Road. Number 18 was the home of Szabo from 1935 to 1942. [© ITV plc / Granada International. Source: BFI]

breaking, seven-volume series *Studies in the Psychology of Sex* (1897–1928). Controversial at the time, Ellis's work as a sexologist brought him international fame. He focused particularly on the biological origins of human behaviour, asserting that nothing based in nature could be considered inherently wrong (homosexuality, for instance). Ellis lent his support to campaigns for sex reform, and gave advice to the many people who wrote to him about sexual matters. In 1928

he moved to 24 Holmdene Avenue, Herne Hill, SE24, with Françoise Lafitte-Cyon, known as Delisle – his partner since 1918 – and her two sons, but by the time of his death he was living in Suffolk.

Beyond Brixton are the 'railway suburbs', built over the Surrey hills in the late nineteenth and early twentieth centuries. Railton Road, SE24, once infamous as the 'front line' of the Brixton riots of 1981, is a long street

LAMBETH

270   C. L. R. James in his second-floor flat at 165 Railton Road, 1981. [© Val Wilmer]

271   The plaque to C. L. R. James being unveiled at 165 Railton Road as part of Black History Month, 2004. The cord was pulled by the journalist and political activist Darcus Howe, James's nephew. [© PA Photocall]

of modest Victorian brick terraces and modern housing developments, connecting Brixton with Herne Hill. In October 2004, during Black History Month, a blue plaque was placed on number 165 – on the corner of Railton Road and Shakespeare Road – to mark the former residence of **C. L. R. James** (1901–1989) 12 , the Trinidadian writer and political activist (figs 270 and 271). Cyril Lionel Robert James lived here from 1981 until his death eight years later. He first came to England in 1932 at the invitation of his fellow Trinidadian, the cricketer Learie Constantine, and made his name reporting on cricket matches for the *Manchester Guardian*. While living in London, James carried out much of the work that resulted in his most famous publication, *The Black Jacobins* (1938), a history of Haitian independence. In 1938 he moved to the United States, where he became deeply involved in Trotskyist politics, but as the years went by his thinking roamed more widely across history, literature and philosophy. London became James's home again in 1953, and he spent five years living in Hampstead and Willesden before returning to Trinidad, where he became involved in the island's independence movement and edited the political newspaper *The Nation*. By the 1980s, James enjoyed iconic status among the West Indian community in Britain and was internationally renowned. As he became increasingly housebound, his cramped second-floor flat in Brixton –

located above the offices of the journal *Race Today* – became a place of pilgrimage for students, journalists and politicians. The plaque was placed on the Shakespeare Road elevation of the building, close to James's front door and the staircase that ascended to his flat.

Between Herne Hill and Denmark Hill is an area deeply associated with the influential critic, artist and man of letters, **John Ruskin** (1819–1900) 13 . He lived here for nearly fifty years in three different houses, and retained a lifelong connection with the place. In the front garden of 26 Herne Hill, SE24, to the left of the drive, is a post with a rectangular bronze plate mounted upon it, indicating the site of Ruskin's family home from 1823 to 1842. This plaque dates from 1925, and was put up the following year; it replaces one erected in 1909 and lost without trace when his home, 28 Herne Hill, was demolished and replaced by two new houses, numbers 26 and 28. In order to be visible to passers-by, the 1920s plaque was placed in the front garden rather than on one of the new dwellings. An only child, Ruskin was born at 54 Hunter Street, Bloomsbury; from 1900 the house bore a Society of Arts plaque, but was demolished in 1969. When he was four years old, his father – John James Ruskin (1785–1864), a prosperous sherry merchant – decided to move with his wife Margaret (1781–1871) to somewhere more salubrious, outside the city. The house he found was a substantial semi-detached property dating from the late eighteenth century, with large front and back gardens (figs 272 and 273); it was set in a tranquil spot looking south to the hills of Norwood and north to the valley of the Thames, 'with Windsor

telescopically clear in the distance, and Harrow, conspicuous always in fine weather to open vision against the summer sunset'.[7] In his autobiographical study *Praeterita* (1885–89), Ruskin recalls the property as a sort of paradise, in which he passed a happy but very sheltered childhood. After taking his degree at Oxford in 1842, he returned to Herne Hill to embark on his earliest major work, the first volume of *Modern Painters* (1843), a passionate defence of J. M. W. Turner. In autumn 1842 his family moved to a larger house – 163 Denmark Hill (demolished) – where Ruskin was based until 1872; he lamented that 'we never were so happy again'.[8] This period was productive, seeing the publication of works including *The Seven Lamps of Architecture* (1849) and *The Stones of Venice* (1850–53). Ruskin also lived for a time at 30 Herne Hill (demolished), and retained the lease on number 28, using it partly as a store for his collection of mineral specimens, 'out of the way of the tidiness of his mother's household'.[9] The lease of the house was made over to his cousin Joan Agnew and her husband Arthur Severn as a wedding gift in 1871, and Ruskin was an occasional visitor, staying – and writing – in the room that had been his nursery. His last stay took place in December 1888, by which time his main home was Brantwood, Cumbria.

272   A drawing by John Ruskin of 28 Herne Hill, his family home from 1823 to 1842. [© Ruskin Foundation (Ruskin Library, Lancaster University)]

Far right 273   John Ruskin's house at 28 Herne Hill in a photograph of 1900. The building was marked with an LCC blue plaque in 1909, but was demolished in the early 1920s. Its site was commemorated in 1926. [© City of London, LMA]

At 27 Lanercost Road, SW2, in the suburb of Tulse Hill, a blue plaque of 1991 marks the home of the journalist, author and topographer **Arthur Mee** (1875–1943) **14** . Born in Nottinghamshire to Baptist parents, he served his apprenticeship on the *Nottingham Daily Express*, quickly rising to become editor of the paper's *Evening News* at the age of twenty. In the same year he starting writing for George Newnes's national weekly, *Tit-Bits*, and – after taking a permanent job editing Newnes's new weekly, *Home Magazine* – moved to London in late 1896. Mee first lived in lodgings, but by 1899 he and his wife Amy (b. 1877) had become the first occupants of 27 Lanercost Road, a semi-detached villa that was originally called Redcot. Professional success and a permanent position with the *Daily Mail* enabled him to move in 1902 to a larger house in West Norwood – 18 Elmcourt Road (formerly Court Road), SE27 – before he left London for good in 1905. Mee later earned fame as the writer of numerous educational works for children, most notably the *Children's Encyclopedia* (1908–10) and the *Children's Newspaper* – begun in 1919 and edited by Mee until his death – and as the editor of the series of guidebooks *The King's England*, published from 1936. Dubbed by LORD NORTHCLIFFE the 'little champion of the Nonconformist Conscience', Mee was a temperance campaigner as well as an ardent patriot and imperialist.[10]

The development of Streatham followed the pattern for Lambeth as a whole: a settlement aggrandised by villa development, followed by more and more intensive infilling in the later nineteenth century. Off Streatham High Road is Pendennis Road (formerly Angles Road), SW16, a typical street of the 1870s. At number 13 an English Heritage plaque commemorates one of the street's early residents, **Sir Arnold Bax** (1883–1953) **15** , the composer and poet. His parents – Alfred Ridley Bax (1844–1918) and Charlotte Ellen Lea (1860–1940) – had married in 1882 and this was their first home; Arnold, their eldest child, was born here on 8 November 1883. The family left number 13, or Heath Villa as it was then known, in 1884 but only went as far as the next-door house, 15 Pendennis Road. They lived at two further addresses in South London before settling in 1896 at Ivy Bank, Haverstock Hill, Hampstead (demolished). Encouraged by his mother, Bax discovered an early talent for music, and studied at the Hampstead Conservatoire and the Royal Academy of Music, where he

was taught the piano by TOBIAS MATTHAY. Although best known for his orchestral tone poems, most notably *Tintagel* (1917–19), Bax wrote seven symphonies and a wide variety of chamber music and piano pieces. His music was strongly imbued with the history and language of Ireland, and he published fiction and verse under the pseudonym Dermot O'Byrne. Knighted in 1937, Bax was appointed Master of the King's Musick in 1942 and, in his later years, composed music for films including David Lean's *Oliver Twist* (1948).

CLAPHAM

The area known as Clapham Park is a grand development begun in 1825 by THOMAS CUBITT, the developer of Belgravia. By the early twentieth century, most of the original houses had gone – including Cubitt's own home – and streets such as Rodenhurst Road, SW4, had been raised in their place. Towards the north end of this thoroughfare, at number 13, is the house in which the statesman **Arthur Henderson** (1863–1935) **16** lived from 1909 to 1921. The house dates from *c.* 1901, and bears an enamelled steel blue plaque of 1980 – unusually, but attractively, placed in the pediment over its front door. Born in Glasgow, Henderson became involved in the trade union movement while working in the iron-founding industry in Newcastle. In 1903 he was elected MP for Barnard Castle and, together with Keir Hardie and RAMSAY MACDONALD, was instrumental in leading the newly created Labour Party. He was Secretary of the party from 1912 to 1934, a period during which Labour became established as a political force and formed its first two governments, and served as Home Secretary (1924) and Foreign Secretary (1929–31). 'Uncle Arthur', as he was known, first moved to Clapham in 1906 and, while living at 13 Rodenhurst Road, served in the wartime Cabinets of both ASQUITH and LLOYD GEORGE; he also led the Labour Party for the second of three terms, between 1914 and 1917. When the party split over MacDonald's decision to join the National Government in 1931, Henderson took over as leader once again, resigning in October 1932. His last years were devoted to the cause of international disarmament, for which he was awarded the Nobel Peace Prize in 1934.

At the southern corner of Clapham Common is Englewood Road, SW12, where a plaque at number 17 – one

274 A signed photograph of Jack Hobbs and Andrew Sandham. The pair stand in front of the scoreboard recording the Surrey record opening stand in the match against Oxford University at The Oval in 1926. Hobbs's contribution to the record 428-1 was a mammoth 232, while Sandham made 183. [© Popperfoto / Getty Images]

of the last erected by the GLC – honours the cricketer **Sir Jack Hobbs** (1882–1963) ⑰ (fig. 274), generally recognised as the pre-eminent batsman of his day and the greatest since W. G. GRACE. John Berry Hobbs was born in Cambridge and started playing for his home county in 1904. He subsequently played for Surrey (1905–34) and for England (1908–30), his accomplished and seemingly effortless batting earning him the sobriquet 'The Master'. Hobbs, his wife Ada (d. 1963) and their children lived in Englewood Road between 1912 and 1927, the years of Hobbs's greatest achievement and fame. From here, it was a short journey up Clapham Road to Surrey's home ground at the Oval. It was while living at number 17 that Hobbs established his sporting goods business, Jack Hobbs Ltd, using the proceeds of his benefit season of 1919. In fact, his small shop in Fleet Street provided a much better income than his famous exploits on the cricket pitch, and enabled him to move in 1927 to Woodthorpe, Atkins Road, Clapham Park (demolished) and then to 23 Dunstall Road, Wimbledon, SW20. By the time of his retirement in 1934, Hobbs had scored more first-class runs (61,237) and

more first-class centuries (197) than any other cricketer, and in 1953 became the first British cricketer to be knighted. He spent his final years in Hove, where he died at the age of eighty-one.

Number 5 The Pavement, SW4, opposite Clapham Common Underground Station, was the home from c. 1804 to 1818 of **Zachary Macaulay** (1768–1838), the philanthropist, and his son **Thomas Babington Macaulay** (1800–1859) ⑱, afterwards Lord Macaulay, the historian and man of letters (fig. 275). Scottish by birth, Macaulay senior first moved to Clapham in 1800 with his wife Selina, née Mills (d. 1831). His political and moral opinions had been strongly influenced by his experiences as overseer of a plantation in Jamaica (1784–89) and then as Governor of Sierra Leone (1794–99). By the turn of the century, Zachary was committed to the campaign for the abolition of slavery, and between 1802 and 1816 edited the *Christian Observer*, the journal of the CLAPHAM SECT. It was his success as a businessman – Macaulay traded with Africa and the East Indies – that led the family to leave The Pavement for a smarter address near Sloane Square in 1818. Ten years later, however, Macaulay senior was facing bankruptcy; at his death, he was living in humble lodgings in Clarges Street, Mayfair. Thomas Babington Macaulay – the eldest of nine children – was a precocious boy who took an interest in all kinds of literature and in nature, observed on long walks around the then wild common. He attended Mr Greaves's Academy at 14 Clapham Common North Side from 1807 to 1812, before continuing his education at a private school in Cambridgeshire and then at Trinity College, Cambridge. Macaulay served for over twenty years as an MP, speaking in favour of the Reform Bill in 1832 and the abolition of slavery in 1833, but it was his *History of England* (1848–61) that has earned him lasting fame. First proposed in 1903, this LCC plaque was not erected until 1930 because of concerns about visibility, a large projecting shopfront having been added to number 5, a late eighteenth-century property. Lord Macaulay's nephew, Sir George Trevelyan, described the house as 'a roomy comfortable dwelling, with a small garden behind, and in front a very small one indeed, which has entirely disappeared beneath a large shop thrown out towards the roadway'.[11] To aid legibility, a large rectangular stone plaque was used instead of the standard blue roundel. This is now the only official tablet to

275   A photograph of 5 The Pavement in 1929 showing the proposed position – at second-floor level – of the rectangular stone plaque to Zachary Macaulay and his son Thomas Babington Macaulay. The tablet was installed the following year. [© City of London, LMA]

commemorate Thomas Babington Macaulay, an earlier LCC plaque of 1903 having been removed from the site of Holly Lodge, Campden Hill, Kensington – his last home – in 2003.

Around the corner is a handsome set of town houses of *c.* 1706. The first of these, 43 Old Town, SW4, has since 1950 carried a blue plaque to the architect **John Francis Bentley** (1839–1902) 19 . He and his wife Margaret, née Fleuss (1857–1939) moved here in 1876, after the house had been thoroughly renovated and furnished with a mixture of antique pieces and an oak dining suite designed by Bentley himself. When he moved away in August 1894, it was only as far as 3 The Sweep (demolished), another house in the Old Town, the site of which is now occupied by Trinity Close; it was there that he died. Born in Doncaster, Bentley set

up in practice as an architect in 1860, and two years later converted to Roman Catholicism. His work was mostly confined to churches, principally of his own denomination; it culminated in his *magnum opus*, Westminster Cathedral (1895–1903). Described by RICHARD NORMAN SHAW as 'beyond all doubt the finest church that has been built for centuries', Bentley's cathedral was designed in the Byzantine style and was greatly inspired by a visit to St Mark's, Venice.[12] Other works executed by Bentley – who also designed internal decoration, stained glass and furnishings such as organ cases and altars – include the seminary of St Thomas, Hammersmith (1876–88) and additions to his parish church, Our Lady of Victories in Clapham Park Road (completed 1895). The erection of the plaque at number 43 was delayed because of the need, in 1949, to repair war damage to the building.

Holy Trinity Church on Clapham Common North Side, SW4 (fig. 261), was built in 1774–76 by Kenton Couse to serve the area's growing population. Between 1792 and 1814 – when John Venn (1759–1833) was rector – the church became the centre of the **Clapham Sect** **20**, a group of evangelical Anglicans led by **William Wilberforce** (1759–1833) (see also pp. 177–8 and pp. 337–8). A blue plaque commemorates the successful campaigning by Wilberforce and the Clapham Sect that eventually resulted in the abolition of slavery in the British Dominions in 1834, the year after the Act of Parliament received royal assent; the apprenticeship system, which bound slaves to their ex-owners, was finally abolished in 1838. The 'Saints' – as they were known in their day – were also concerned to improve moral standards in Britain and to spread the Christian message abroad. The group – composed largely of figures who lived in Clapham, including Charles Grant (1746–1823), Director of the East India Company, and ZACHARY MACAULAY – was involved in the founding of the Church Missionary Society (1799) and the Bible Society (1804), and set up its own evangelical journal, the *Christian Observer*, in 1802. From 1792 until 1797 Wilberforce himself lived nearby at Battersea Rise – the home of fellow Saint, the banker Henry Thornton (1760–1815), and the principal base for the Sect – before moving to Broomfield, on the west side of Clapham Common. The plaque was placed on Holy Trinity in 1984, under the portico on the west front which had been added in 1812. Although it is very unusual for a church to be marked in such a way, in this case it allowed a number of significant individuals to be commemorated together in a place that was important for them all.

The architect **Sir Charles Barry** (1795–1860) **21** is commemorated by a plaque at 29 Clapham Common North Side. Barry's home – then known as The Elms, but now Trinity Hospice – is a much grander affair than that of his fellow architect, JOHN FRANCIS BENTLEY. The large three-storey house, built in 1754 but with many later additions – including some by Barry himself – stands back from the road behind railings and looks out across Clapham Common. Barry was born at 2 Bridge Street, Westminster (demolished), the son of a bookbinder, and served his apprenticeship with a firm of surveyors in Paradise Row, Lambeth. In 1818–20 he was greatly impressed by a tour he made of

Italy, Greece, Egypt and Syria, and – returning to England – he set up his architectural practice and home in Holborn. Barry's work as an architect was wide-ranging in type and style but typically reflected the wealth and power of England in the mid-nineteenth century. It included the Travellers Club (1829–32) and the Reform Club (1838–41) in Pall Mall, but is exemplified above all by the Houses of Parliament, the building of which dominated the last twenty years of his life. The foundation stone was laid in 1840 by Barry's wife Sarah, née Rowsell (1798–1882); the following year, he moved his home to Great George Street, Westminster, so that he could supervise his greatest project at close hand. In 1852 the Houses of Parliament were opened by Queen Victoria, though the clock tower (Big Ben) and Victoria Tower were only completed in 1858 and 1860 respectively. In 1853 Barry took up residence at The Elms, Clapham Common, where he devoted his last years to devising an ambitious scheme of 'Metropolitan Improvements' (1857) that would have transformed Westminster into the 'palatial quarter' of the capital.[13] As his son later wrote, Barry 'never cared to leave London', for 'all his interests were in town; he rejoiced in its bustle and society; and nothing would have compensated him for a banishment from it'.[14] He died at The Elms after a sudden seizure following a day out at the Crystal Palace.

The Norwegian composer **Edvard Grieg** (1843–1907) **22** is commemorated by an English Heritage plaque at 47 Clapham Common North Side (formerly 5 The Cedars), part of two matching blocks of enormous houses in the French Renaissance style that flank the entrance to Cedars Road; they were built in 1860 to designs by James Thomas Knowles junior. Born in Bergen, Grieg established his reputation as the leading Norwegian composer of his day with works such as his Piano Concerto in A Minor (1868) and the incidental music for Henrik Ibsen's *Peer Gynt* (1874–75); his work has a pronounced nationalism, and was often based on the melodies and rhythms of Norwegian folk songs. Number 47 – the entrance of which faces onto Cedars Road – was the home of Grieg's publisher George Augener (1830–1915), who played host to the composer and his wife, the singer Nina Hagerup (1845–1935), on their visits to England in the 1880s and 1890s (fig. 276); the Norwegian flag is said to have been flown outside when the composer was in residence. In

LAMBETH

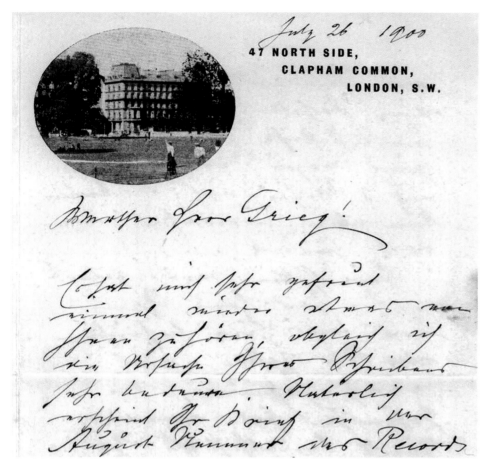

July 26 1900
47 NORTH SIDE,
CLAPHAM COMMON,
LONDON, S.W.

276   A detail of a letter written to Edvard Grieg by his publisher, George Augener, on 26 July 1900. During Grieg's visits to England in the 1880s and 1890s, he regularly stayed with Augener at 47 Clapham Common North Side, shown here in a vignette.
[© Bergen Public Library, The Grieg Archive]

those years Grieg was in great demand among English audiences as both conductor and performer, making his first public appearance in London at the Philharmonic Society Concert at St James's Hall in May 1888. At his Clapham 'home from home' he could rehearse for his many concerts and recitals, relax between engagements and entertain visitors such as Sir George Grove, compiler of the famous dictionary of music. Grieg also loved travelling by tram from Clapham into the West End and the City. In all, his stays at North Side totalled just under five months; his final visit lasted from 10 October to 23 December 1897. Grieg's last performance in London was given nine years later at Buckingham Palace.

The Chase, SW4, is a long street running north from Clapham Common, lined on both sides with large, mainly late nineteenth-century houses. At one such house – 81 The Chase, which dates from *c.* 1884 – there is an English Heritage plaque to one of Japan's greatest writers, the novelist **Natsume Soseki** (1867–1916) 23 , who lodged here between 20 July 1901 and 5 December 1902. Born in what is now Tokyo, he had been sent to London in 1900 by the Japanese Ministry of Education to study English literature, at a time when Japan, once a closed society, was opening up to the cultural and commercial influence of the West. Although he suffered from homesickness and neurosis for much of his stay, it was in London that Soseki first conceived the idea of writing fiction himself, and the knowledge he gained of Shakespeare would be a key influence on his work. It has been said that 'without his restricted but intense experience of London, Soseki would not have become so great a writer. Without it, Japanese literature would have been poorer'.[15] Number 81 The Chase was Soseki's fifth and last address in just over two years in the city, and was where he spent the longest time; he lived in a room at the rear of the second floor, the paying guest of the sisters Priscilla and Eliza Leale. In March 1902 he wrote, '[I] made up my mind to write a book, and to this end reading, taking notes, and jotting down my own thoughts are my daily chores'.[16] Soseki's stay in the capital inspired a number of short stories, including *Rondon To* (The Tower of London; 1905), and on returning home he wrote the first of a string of popular novels, *Wagahai wa Neko de aru* (I am a Cat; 1905). The writer's years in London are celebrated in the Soseki Museum, based at 80B The Chase, opposite his former lodgings. The plaque was unveiled in 2002 by the Japanese Ambassador, Masaki Orita, in the presence of Soseki's granddaughter, Professor Yoko Matsuoka-McClain.

NOTES

1 *Survey of London*, Monograph 17: *County Hall*, ed. Hermione Hobhouse (London, 1991), p. 118

2 Letter of 14 August 1985 on blue plaque file.

3 *The Complete Letters of Vincent van Gogh*, vol. I (London, 1958), p. 13 (13 September 1873)

4 Sybil and Russell Thorndike, *Lilian Baylis* (London, 1938), p. 59

5 Marcus Binney, *The Women Who Lived for Danger* (London, 2002), p. 219

6 Letter of 13 July 1981 on blue plaque file.

7 LCC, *Indication of Houses of Historical Interest in London*, vol. III (London, 1912), pp. 22–23

8 John Ruskin, *Praeterita. Outlines of Scenes and Thoughts perhaps worthy of Memory in my Past Life*, ed. Kenneth Clark (London, 1949), p. 287

9 W. G. Collingwood, 'John Ruskin', in H. B. Baildon *et al.*, *Homes and Haunts of Famous Authors* (London, 1906), p. 92

10 John Hammerton, *Child of Wonder: An Intimate Biography of Arthur Mee* (London, 1946), p. 140

11 LCC, *Indication of Houses of Historical Interest in London*, vol. VI (London, 1938), pp. 44–45

12 Winefride de L'Hôpital, *Westminster Cathedral and its Architect*, vol. II (London, 1919), p. 308

13 A. Barry, *Life and Works of Sir Charles Barry RA, FRS* (London, 1867), p. 299

14 Ibid, p. 324

15 Kii Nakano, 'Soseki's Stay in London', in Natsume Soseki, *The Tower of London* (Brighton, 1992), p. 20

16 Beongcheon Yu, *Natsume Soseki* (New York, 1969), p. 27

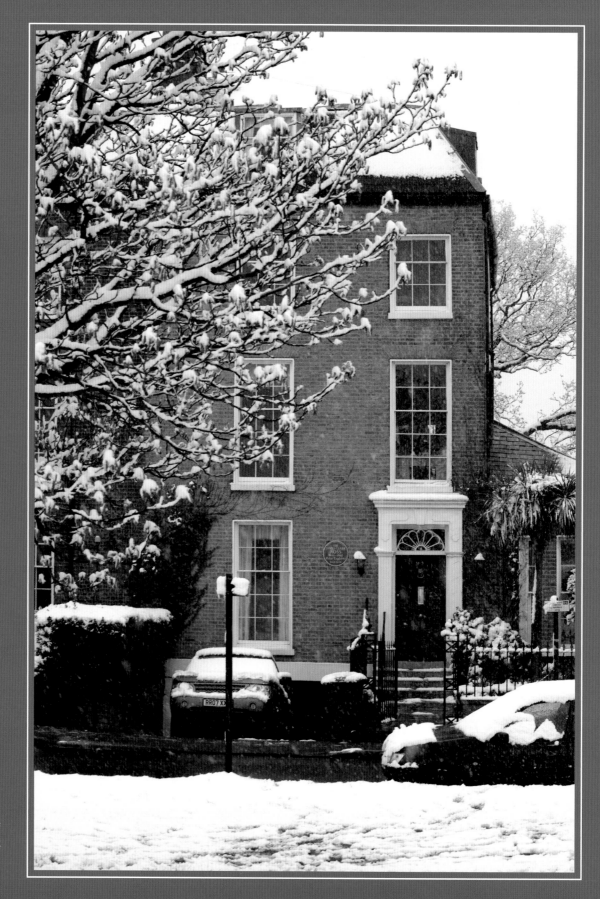

277 View of a snow-covered 2 Eliot Place, the former home of the polar explorer Sir James Clark Ross. [© English Heritage. Photograph by Derek Kendall]

LEWISHAM

Modern Lewisham forms a rough triangle from Thames-side Deptford to Sydenham in the south-west and Grove Park in the south-east. The area, once part of Kent, was more recently divided into the metropolitan boroughs of Lewisham and Deptford. The home of King Henry VIII's royal dockyard, Deptford was also the first coaching stop on the road to Dover; by the beginning of the nineteenth century, it had long been a thriving town. In the countryside to the south, Lee and Lewisham were merely the most significant of several villages. The latter, a straggling settlement along the road to Bromley, was unkindly dubbed 'long, lazy, lousy Lewisham', though it was home to numerous opulent London merchants and traders.[1] From the wharves of Deptford Creek to the silk and corn mills upstream, the River Ravensbourne was the area's most important commercial artery until the arrival of the railway; five lines bisect the borough, with Deptford being the first London suburb to have a station, in 1836. As elsewhere, this gave a huge impetus to suburban development, though the biggest expansion in population came in the last two decades of the 1800s. Most of the area's new inhabitants belonged to the burgeoning middle classes, with Blackheath and Sydenham being the most 'aspirational' of the new suburbs.

LEWISHAM

New Cross Road, SE14, is part of the ancient London to Dover road. At number 233, one of a mid-nineteenth-century semi-detached pair, is a GLC plaque to **John Tallis** (1817–1876) **1** , the publisher of *London Street Views* (fig. 278). The son of a Birmingham bookseller – also named John Tallis – the younger Tallis moved the family business in the direction of publishing, and between 1838 and 1840 released his famous *London Street Views*.[2] These were produced for seventy-four of the principal streets of the West End and the City, and consisted of illustrations of the elevations of each building in the street along with a map of the immediate area, historical notes, a street directory and advertisements. In the days before the *A–Z* and similar directories, these promised 'to assist strangers visiting the Metropolis, through all its mazes without a guide'.[3] It was asserted in *The Times* that 'Among the list of Cheap Periodicals none equal "Tallis's London Street Views" for price, – and for the great novelty of the plan it stands unrivalled; – the older it gets the more it will be esteemed'.[4] Encouraged by such plaudits, Tallis went on to produce a number of maps, atlases and street views of other towns and cities, which were noted for their accuracy and attractiveness. However, having greatly expanded his father's business, he decided to sell up, and went bankrupt in 1861 after an unsuccessful venture into newspaper publishing. It was in 1870 – following the death of his young son – that Tallis moved from Greenwich to New Cross, which was not then a fashionable area. He stayed here for the remaining six years of his life, during which time he was occasionally obliged to take

278 A page from John Tallis's *London Street Views* (1838–40), showing Newgate Street. It was near here that Tallis spent much of his working life. [© City of London]

in lodgers to pay his rates, and when he died number 233 was sequestrated to pay his debts.

The suburb of Brockley is characterised by large semi-detached houses in tree-lined streets that run in parallel south from Lewisham Way. At 6 Tressillian Crescent, SE4, a plaque of 1960 marks the residence of the writer **Edgar Wallace** (1875–1932) **2** . Born and bred in south-east London, Wallace tried his hand at soldiering and then journalism before he turned to writing fiction. He liked to live in style but, when he moved to Tressillian Crescent with his wife Ivy (1880?–1926) and their two children early in 1908, Wallace was heavily in debt, and the move was largely driven by economy. The back door of the house was often left open, so that Wallace could stealthily evade any calling creditors. An upturn in his fortunes came with *Sanders of the River* (1911), a collection of imperial adventure stories that were immediately popular, and he developed a sideline as a racing correspondent and tipster; this was ironic, given that his money problems were partly traceable to poor investments in the turf. The room at the back of the first floor of the house was Wallace's study, where he dictated his stories while chain-smoking cigarettes. In the early years of the First World War, the family moved to a flat near Regent's Park, lent to Wallace by a friend, and his long connection with this part of London came to an end. After the war, Wallace's books, such as *The Crimson Circle* (1922) and *The Gaunt Stranger* (1925), became phenomenally successful, and he was dubbed by his publishers the 'King of Thrillers'. In 1931 Wallace moved to

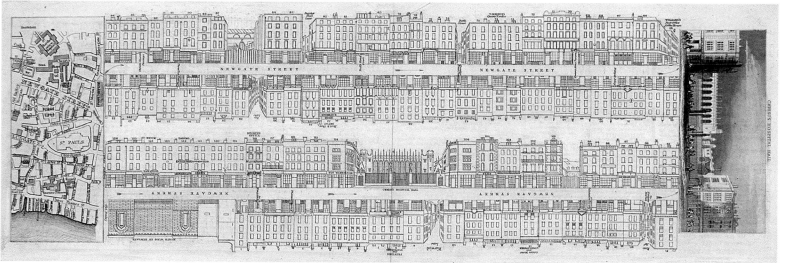

LEWISHAM

279 The carte-de-visite of James Glaisher and his fellow aeronaut Henry Tracey Coxwell, 1862. [© National Portrait Gallery, London]

280 The plaque to James Glaisher at 20 Dartmouth Hill, his home from c.1862 until 1893. [© English Heritage. Photograph by Derek Kendall]

America to work in the film industry; at the time of his death the following year, he was working on the story and screenplay of *King Kong* (1933), though the end-product owed more to his co-writers.

On the west side of Blackheath, at 20 Dartmouth Hill (formerly 1 Dartmouth Place), SE10, is a GLC plaque of 1974 to **James Glaisher** (1809–1903) ③ , the astronomer, meteorologist and pioneer of weather forecasting (figs 279 and 280). Born in Rotherhithe and brought up in Greenwich, Glaisher became interested in meteorology while working for the Ordnance Survey in Ireland in 1829–30. In 1833 he became assistant to Professor George Airy at the Cambridge University observatory and followed him to Greenwich on Airy's appointment as Astronomer Royal two years later. As head of the Magnetical and Meteorological Department at the Royal Observatory from 1838, Glaisher organised a nationwide network of volunteers to make observations, which he compiled as authoritative quarterly reports on the British weather. In the 1860s Glaisher made several balloon ascents for the purpose of making meteorological observations at high altitudes. A near-fatal accident during one ascent in 1862 was widely reported – and satirised – and made Glaisher a well-known public figure. At about this time he moved with his wife Cecilia, née Belville (1828–1892), a noted artist and photographer, to what was then 1 Dartmouth Place; it remained his home until 1893. The three-storey house dates from the late eighteenth century, and forms a pair with number 22 next door. Glaisher retired from the Royal Observatory in 1874 but continued to make his quarterly weather reports almost until his death, which occurred at his later residence in Heathfield Road, Croydon.

From 1859 until late 1863 **Samuel Smiles** (1812–1904) ④ , the author of *Self Help*, lived in Granville Park, Blackheath, SE13. In 1959 a plaque was erected by the LCC on number 11. However, subsequent research has shown that it marks entirely the wrong building. The cause of the confusion stemmed from the renumbering of the street in 1870–72: Smiles's home – originally 6 Granville Park Terrace – survives across the road as 12 Granville Park; the house that currently bears the plaque was formerly 6 Granville Park. Born in Scotland, Smiles qualified as a doctor at Edinburgh University, but was drawn to writing and lecturing on

general topics and was appointed editor of the radical *Leeds Times* in 1838. Seven years later he moved into railway work, and relocated to London in 1854 on his appointment as Secretary to the South Eastern Railway; from Granville Park, he commuted to an office at London Bridge. Meanwhile, Smiles continued to lecture and write, and actively championed the education of ordinary people. Following the publication in 1859 of *Self Help, with Illustrations of Character and Conduct*, he became a reluctant celebrity. This book, which grew out of a lecture Smiles had given in 1845, preached the virtues of hard work and thrift, and warned against the dangers of excessive government intervention. It caught the mood of the times, selling thousands of copies around the world and prompting Smiles to produce a series of similar works, but later came to be seen as an expression of the worst kind of Victorian materialism and individualism; Smiles's biographies – notably of the engineer George Stephenson (1857) – have better weathered the passage of time. The success of *Self Help* provided Smiles with the money to build a new family home, West Bank, Dartmouth Row (demolished), on the west side of Blackheath; a house-warming party was held at the house in January 1864.

Number 2 Eliot Place, SE3, is an early nineteenth-century house overlooking Blackheath that bears an LCC plaque to the polar explorer **Sir James Clark Ross** (1800–1862) ⑤ (fig. 277). Ross joined the Navy in 1812 and served under his uncle, John Ross, accompanying him on his first Arctic voyage in 1818. James Clark Ross returned to that polar region in four expeditions led by William Edward Parry, and was present on the voyage – led by his uncle – that located the position of the North Pole in 1831. Having conducted a systematic magnetic survey of Britain, Ross set out in 1839 for the Antarctic, where he made a number of important observations and located, but did not quite reach, the South Pole. There, he discovered Victoria Land and what became known as the Ross ice shelf; also named after him are the Ross Sea in the Antarctic and Ross's gull, a native of the Arctic region. His achievements were rewarded with a knighthood in 1844. Ross rented the house in Eliot Place after his marriage in 1843 to Ann Coulman (d. 1857), to whom Ross reputedly gave a promise to forsake polar exploration. It was in Blackheath that he started to set down his experiences,

281 The young James Elroy Flecker with his parents, the Rev. William Herman Flecker and and Sarah Flecker, née Ducat. [Courtesy of Dean Close School, Cheltenham]

which were published as *A Voyage of Discovery and Research in the Southern and Antarctic Regions* (1847). In 1845 Ross left the capital to live at Aston Abbotts, near Aylesbury, Buckinghamshire, where he died just short of his sixty-second birthday.

At the suggestion of Lewisham Local History Society, the GLC put up a plaque in 1986 to the poet and dramatist **James Elroy Flecker** (1884–1915) ❻ at 9 Gilmore Road, SE13, near Lewisham High Road (fig. 281). It was on a foggy 5 November that Flecker was born at the house, a detached villa then not long built. His parents had been resident here since August of that year, his father – the Rev. William Herman Flecker (1859–1941) – having been appointed Headmaster of the City of London College School, as well as curate of Holy Trinity Church in Lee. The infant Flecker was baptised Herman Elroy – the second name being a product of his Jewish heritage – and only adopted the name James while at Oxford University. His mother, Sarah, née Ducat, later recalled that as a baby, 'his masses of long black hair, gave him an elf-like look'.[5] The family left Gilmore Road in 1886, when the Rev. Flecker was made Headmaster of the newly opened Dean Close School, Cheltenham. After Oxford, James joined the consular service and was posted to Constantinople and later Beirut. Meanwhile, he produced several volumes of lyrical Romantic verse, starting with *The Bridge of Fire* (1907), and some of his poems were included in the anthologies *Georgian Poetry*. Flecker's most enduring work is *The Golden Journey to Samarkand* (1913), on which the time he had spent in the Near East was a palpable influence. By the time of its publication he was living in Switzerland, where he had gone to seek a fresh air cure for the tuberculosis that eventually cut short his life.

The publisher **Sir Stanley Unwin** (1884–1968) ❼ was born at 13 Handen Road, Lee, SE12; this late Victorian semi-detached house remained Unwin's home until 1890. Stanley was the youngest of the nine children of the printer Edward Unwin (1840–1933) and his wife, Elizabeth, née Spicer (1840–1921), whose family owned a paper firm; another relative, T. Fisher Unwin, was a successful publisher. Stanley Unwin started publishing on his own account when he formed George Allen & Unwin Ltd just as war broke out in 1914. He was soon producing books for a serious audience – including

many titles that reflected his own pacifist views – by authors such as George Lansbury, BERTRAND RUSSELL, LEONARD WOOLF and his early neighbour JAMES ELROY FLECKER. Unwin's reinvigoration of the insolvent publishing house of Allen was achieved by rigorous economies on overheads and by what his nephew recalled as his 'compelling, almost mesmeric force in argument'.[6] He became a figure of enormous importance within his industry, serving as President of both the Publishers Association of Great Britain and the International Publishers Association, and expanded his interests by taking a stake in the publishing house of Bodley Head Ltd. Although fiction did not form a large part of the output that Unwin superintended, he did enjoy great success with J. R. R. Tolkien's *The Hobbit* (1937) and *The Lord of the Rings* (1954–55). Unwin spent most of his adult life in Hampstead, but his longest-standing address there, in Oak Hill Park, is no longer extant, while the home of his early manhood – The Mount, 42 May's Hill Road, Bromley, BR2 – lies in a quiet and secluded location. Hence the choice of 13 Handen Road to bear the plaque, which went up on the exact centenary of Unwin's birth.

LEWISHAM

The high ground of Sydenham and Forest Hill was valued in the nineteenth century for its fresh air and fine views, and many large mansions were built here. At 100 London Road, Forest Hill, SE23, where the **Horniman Museum and Gardens** now stand ⑧, lived the tea merchant and founder of the museum, FREDERICK JOHN HORNIMAN (1835–1906) (see also pp. 575–6). Horniman was born in Somerset and in 1868 became Chairman of his father's business, Horniman & Co., which he ran with his brother William; by 1891 it was said to be the largest tea firm in the world. In 1868 Horniman moved to Surrey House, 100 London Road (fig. 282), which he filled with the collection of natural history and anthropological specimens he had gathered on his travels abroad. In December 1890 the house was opened for three days a week to the public – without charge – as the Surrey House Museum, Horniman and his first wife Rebekah (1825–1895) having decamped – supposedly at her insistence – to a nearby house, Surrey Mount, in order to escape their overstuffed abode. Such was the museum's success, and the expansion of its collections, that in 1897 Horniman decided to demolish his former residence and commissioned a purpose-built structure from the architect Charles Harrison Townsend, who had lately designed Whitechapel Art Gallery. Completed in 1901, the Horniman Museum incorporates elements of both the Arts and Crafts and the Art Nouveau styles, and has been described as 'one of the boldest public buildings of its date in Britain' (fig. 283).[7] As is recorded on the GLC plaque placed at the base of Townsend's clock tower in 1985, the building and its collections were given by Horniman to 'the people of London' in 1901, and placed in the care of the LCC. Since then the museum has been extended repeatedly, and now contains almost 350,000 artefacts, many of which have been acquired since Horniman's death. Additionally, the house and 9.5-acre (3.8 ha) estate of Surrey Mount were given over as the Horniman Gardens, which were almost doubled in size thanks to the acquisition of further land between 1901 and 1935. Surrey Mount itself was in use as a refreshment room by about 1905, and survived until 1960, when it was demolished following war damage.

Number 12 Westwood Hill (formerly West Hill), Sydenham, SE26, a detached house which stands next to St Bartholomew's Church, was the boyhood home of **Sir Ernest Shackleton** (1874–1922) ⑨, the Antarctic explorer. Shackleton was born in County Kildare and it was in 1885 that his father – Henry Shackleton (1847–1921), a general practitioner – brought his family to number 12, then known as Aberdeen House, in this prosperous suburb. Ernest, the second of ten children, was sent first to a nearby preparatory school and then to Dulwich College as a day-boy in 1887. At home, the young Shackleton's chief recreation was carpentry, 'his most ambitious effort being the erection of a wooden hut in the garden . . . big enough for grown-up people to enter'.[8] The house too provided opportunities for adventure: 'The top of the steeply-sloping roof of Aberdeen House is flat. To this lofty and unrailed deck Ernest and the other children were not long in finding a way; and in their surreptitious antics there they earned many a thrill of real danger, escaped by luck rather than circumspection'.[9] On leaving school in 1890, Shackleton was apprenticed to the White Star Line, and spent the next decade working on a number of ships in the Merchant Navy. Returning home to number 12 from a voyage in 1895, he brought with him a nest of young alligators, which he kept as household pets until – under threat of a revolt from the domestic staff – they were donated to a zoo. Two years later, on another home visit, he met his future wife Emily Dorman, a neighbour and a friend of one of his sisters. Shackleton's ascent to the pantheon of *Boy's Own* heroes started with the National Antarctic Expedition of 1901–4, on which he accompanied CAPTAIN SCOTT to within 500 miles (805 km) of the South Pole. Having returned to England, Shackleton married in April 1904 and set up his first home away from Sydenham. Later triumphs of exploration – the British Antarctic Expedition of 1907–9 and the Imperial Trans-Antarctic Expedition of 1914–17 – cemented his fame, and earned him a knighthood. It is a measure of Shackleton's status that he was commemorated with a wreathed LCC blue plaque just six years after his death (see fig. 46).

NOTES

1 John Coulter, *Lewisham* (Stroud, 1994), p. 36

2 It is now accepted that Tallis was born in 1817, rather than in 1816, as is stated on the plaque.

3 From Tallis's original prospectus, reproduced in John Tallis's *London Street Views, 1838–1840*, introduced by Peter Jackson (London, 1969), opposite p. 10

4 Ibid, frontispiece

5 Charles Williams, *Flecker of Dean Close* (London, 1946), p. 36

6 Philip Unwin, *The Publishing Unwins* (London, 1972), p. 91

7 Bridget Cherry and Nikolaus Pevsner, *The Buildings of England, London 2: South* (New Haven and London, 1994), p. 418

8 Hugh Robert Mill, *The Life of Sir Ernest Shackleton* (London, 1923), p. 22

9 LCC, *Indication of Houses of Historical Interest in London*, vol. VI (London, 1938), pp. 4–5

LEWISHAM

284 The plaque to George Myers at 131 St George's Road. The Roman Catholic St George's Cathedral – built by Myers in 1841–48 to designs by A. W. N. Pugin – is reflected in the window. [© English Heritage. Photograph by Derek Kendall]

SOUTHWARK

The modern borough of Southwark stretches along the south bank of the River Thames from the Oxo Tower to Rotherhithe and inshore to Peckham and Dulwich. It was created in 1965 by the amalgamation of the three metropolitan boroughs of Southwark, Bermondsey and Camberwell. The building of London Bridge, the first – and, until the mid-eighteenth century, only – bridge across the Thames, generated a busy medieval settlement at the southern approach to the capital that became one of England's larger towns on its own account. Southwark became known for its inns, prisons, breweries and theatres, which included the Rose, the Swan and the Globe. Later, the growth of the port brought development of the docks to the east, and was accompanied by a population explosion that spawned some of London's most notorious slums. These were gradually replaced, with some of the most intense and prolific council housing development in post-war London taking place in Bermondsey, Camberwell and Peckham. The southerly reaches of the borough retained a rural character for the longest, and – though they have long been infilled and suburbanised – reminders of the area's past can be found in the refined rusticity of Camberwell Grove and Dulwich Village.

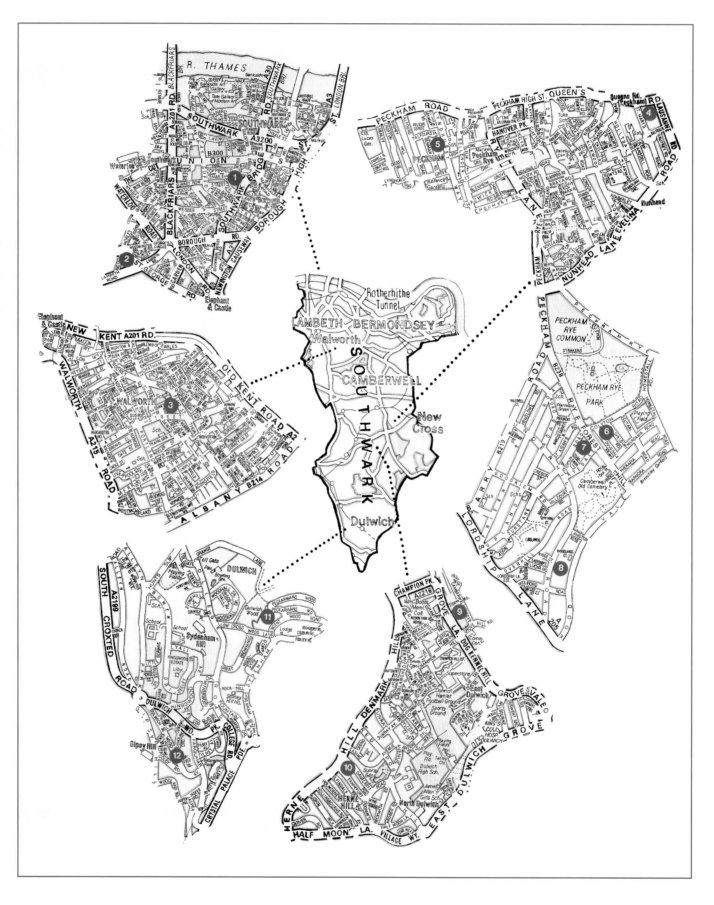

SOUTHWARK

lowing year he was appointed Superintendent of the London Fire Engine Establishment, which became the Metropolitan Fire Brigade in 1866. Shaw transformed London's fire service: under his supervision, the number of fire stations more than quadrupled, and its firemen gained an international reputation for their discipline, organisation and thoroughness. Number 94 Southwark Bridge Road was chosen as the brigade's headquarters after the service had outgrown its former premises in the City. The pre-existing block of Winchester House was extended in several directions, including the building in 1883 of an imposing Gothic range – fronting onto Southwark Bridge Road – which was demolished around the 1950s; the new premises included a training school (with practice tower), a fire station and officer accommodation. Shaw lived at Winchester House in some style, entertaining – among others – the Prince of Wales and his family. Some of his more down-at-heel neighbours were less hospitable, and the wall to the rear of the site had to be raised to prevent brickbats being thrown into the yard. Being something of an autocrat, Shaw found it difficult to get along with the LCC – formed in 1889 and responsible for the Metropolitan Fire Brigade – and carried through a threat to retire in 1891, by which time he had overseen attendance at some 55,000 fires and suffered serious personal injury at two major incidents; he was knighted on his last day in service. It was in 1886, while living here, that Shaw was cited as a co-respondent in the much publicised divorce case of Lady Colin Campbell, though no impropriety was ever proved, and the episode did no obvious damage to his reputation. Winchester House and its neighbouring buildings remained the fire brigade headquarters until 1937, and now house the Southwark Fire Training Centre and the London Fire Brigade Museum. Shaw's English Heritage plaque went up in 2000.

285   The funeral of Sir Eyre Massey Shaw, first Chief Officer of the Metropolitan Fire Brigade, in 1908. The imposing range of buildings on the right of the picture previously divided Winchester House from Southwark Bridge Road, but was demolished around the 1950s. [© London Fire Brigade]

Set back from the street, at 94 Southwark Bridge Road, SE1, is Winchester House, built as St Saviour's Workhouse in 1777, probably to designs by George Gwilt senior. It was later used as a hat factory, before becoming in 1878 part of the headquarters of the Metropolitan Fire Brigade and home to its first Chief Officer, **Sir Eyre Massey Shaw** (1828–1908) **1** (fig. 285).[1] Born in Ireland, Shaw pursued a military career before being appointed Superintendent of police and fire services at Belfast in 1860. Such was his success that in the fol-

A terrace of elegant mid-nineteenth-century houses faces the Roman Catholic St George's Cathedral in St George's Road, Southwark, SE1. A plaque at number 131 (formerly 9 Laurie Terrace) commemorates the home from 1842 to 1852 of the cathedral's builder, **George Myers** (1803–1875) **2** (fig. 284). Known as 'Pugin's builder', Myers first met the architect A. W. N. Pugin at Beverley Minster in 1827; their prolific partnership began with the construction of the Roman Catholic St Mary's Church in Derby ten years later. Myers executed

SOUTHWARK

almost all of Pugin's subsequent commissions, including the Roman Catholic cathedrals in Birmingham (1839–41), Nottingham (1841–44), Newcastle (1841–44) and Southwark (1841–48). The last commission brought Myers to London, where he and his wife Judith (d. 1891) stayed briefly in Chelsea before moving in 1842 to number 131, a newly built house then known as 9 Laurie Terrace. A few years later, he established a national contracting business and workshops at Ordnance Wharf, near Westminster Bridge, Lambeth, which assumed a leading role in the building boom of the 1850s and 1860s. Between 1837 and his retirement in 1873, it is estimated that Myers built an average of three churches a year; he worked for many denominations though, like Pugin, he died a Roman Catholic. His other projects ranged from Mentmore, Buckinghamshire (1852–54), the country house built for Baron Mayer de Rothschild, to Broadmoor Hospital, Berkshire (1858–63). Myers has been described as 'the rock on which Pugin built the Gothic revival'; their last collaboration was over the medieval court at the Great Exhibition (1851), and it was Myers who carved the effigy on the architect's tomb in Ramsgate (c. 1853).[2] Myers's English Heritage plaque was erected in 1999, following a suggestion made by his biographer, Patricia Spencer-Silver.

On the Dawes Street elevation of 153A East Street, Walworth, SE17, a nineteenth-century terraced house, a plaque of 1988 commemorates **Dr Charles Vickery Drysdale** (1874–1961) **3** , a founder of the Family Planning Association. Both Drysdale's parents – Charles Robert Drysdale and Alice, née Vickery – were ardent campaigners for birth control, women's suffrage and against the institution of marriage, while his uncle, George Drysdale, was another early promoter of contraception. Drysdale junior followed his father, both in pursuing a career in engineering – in which subject he gained his doctorate – and in becoming a founder member of the Men's League for Women's Suffrage in 1907. Like his parents and his uncle, however, Charles Vickery Drysdale is best remembered as a vociferous advocate of family planning, and effectively inherited from them the leadership of the Malthusian League. This organisation – of which he was President from 1921 to 1952 – was the first to promulgate birth control as a remedy for overpopulation and poverty, against a background – as Drysdale put it – of 'smug conven-

tionality and silence on the part of the comfortable classes'.[3] Spurred on by the success of Marie Stopes, Drysdale opened his first clinic at number 153A in November 1921; at the time, he was Superintendent of the Admiralty Research Laboratory in Teddington, a post he held until becoming the Admiralty's Director of Scientific Research in 1929. Drysdale's clinic was successively known as the East Street Welfare Centre and the Walworth Women's Welfare Centre, and provided maternity and child welfare services as well as contraceptive advice. It is now a Brook Advisory Centre, while the committee originally appointed to oversee it – known as the Society for the Provision of Birth Control Clinics from 1924 – had, by 1939, transmuted by amalgamation into the Family Planning Association. At his death, Drysdale was described by a correspondent to *The Times* as one who had 'fought hard for many years for ideas whose truth is now accepted by most of the civilised world'.[4]

Number 164 Queen's Road, Peckham, SE15, one of a pair of early nineteenth-century villas, served as the home and medical practice of the campaigner for racial equality **Dr Harold Moody** (1882–1947) **4** (see fig. 17). Moody came from Jamaica in 1904 to study medicine at King's College London. Having been denied a hospital appointment out of racial prejudice, he set up on his own as a GP, establishing a practice in King's Road (now King's Grove), Peckham, in 1913 – shortly after his marriage to Olive Mabel Tranter (1889–1965), 'a warm, affectionate English nurse'.[5] In 1922 he moved to nearby 164 Queen's Road, where he lived, worked and died. The Moodys' house was 'open to all the travelling black people who couldn't find a room or a meal elsewhere'; lodgers included the Jamaican writer and feminist Una Marson (1905–1965), whose bedroom 'looked out on to a grass tennis court and the colourful, rose-filled back garden'. She remembered number 164 as 'a comfortable, four-storey property with a middle-floor entrance leading to a small, often cluttered hall, and beyond that, large dining and drawing rooms'.[6] From it, Moody ran the League of Coloured Peoples – founded in 1931 – under which banner he published a newsletter, *The Keys*, and lobbied trade unions, the Civil Service and Parliament for the improvement of race relations. He fought for causes including employment rights for black merchant seamen, fair pay for the Trinidadian oil workers

286 A demonstration of air-to-air refuelling, as Sir Alan Cobham and Squadron Leader W. Helmore make a test over the south coast in anticipation of their non-stop flight to India, September 1934. [© Topfoto]

and the lifting of the implicit colour bar in the British Armed Forces that had prevented the appointment of black officers. Moody's influence reached its zenith in 1943, when he was appointed to a government advisory committee on the welfare of non-Europeans; a devout Congregationalist Christian, he also took the chair of the London Missionary Society that year. The League of Coloured Peoples did not long survive the death of the charismatic Moody, who was honoured with a plaque by English Heritage in 1995.

Also in Peckham, at 78 Denman Road (formerly 4 Hetley Terrace), SE15, is an English Heritage plaque of 2003 commemorating **Sir Alan Cobham** (1894–1973) ❺, the aviator and pioneer of in-flight refuelling (fig. 286). It was in this Victorian house, known as 4 Hetley Terrace until 1901, that Cobham was born and lived until he was twelve years old, when the family – his father, Frederick Cobham, was a tailor – moved to Streatham. While living here he attended a local council school, where he conceived an early passion for geography. 'It was one way of coming to know the nature and story of England, and to me it was not so much work as high romance', he recalled.[7] Soon, Cobham was seeing the world laid out like a map: he served with the Royal Flying Corps in the First World

War, and was commissioned in the newly formed Royal Air Force as a flying instructor in 1918. After the war, Cobham became a committed promoter of flight as a safe and practical mode of transport – he gave thousands their first taste of the air through a series of aviation displays – and, while employed by De Havilland's during the 1920s, completed a series of dramatic long-distance flights; a journey to and from Australia in 1926 – which ended in the landing of his seaplane on the Thames outside the Houses of Parliament – earned him a knighthood. In 1927 – by which time he was living in Frognal Lane, Hampstead – he established Alan Cobham Aviation Ltd, and in the 1930s began to develop practical ways of carrying out air-to-air refuelling; in 1934 he founded Flight Refuelling Ltd, which was based first in Sussex and later in Dorset. By the 1950s, the company – of which Cobham served as Managing Director until 1964 – was the European leader in air-to-air refuelling technology, while it also designed and manufactured fuel-system equipment and undertook large-scale aircraft repair programmes. Cobham died in the British Virgin Islands, where he lived from 1968.

Number 5 Colyton Road, Peckham Rye, SE22, is an attractive late Victorian semi-detached house which was the home and workplace of **Percy Lane Oliver** (1878–1944) ❻, the founder of the first voluntary blood donor service. A local government officer with Camberwell Borough Council, Oliver – together with his wife Ethel, née Grace (1879–1973) – was a dedicated Red Cross volunteer, and provided food, clothing and shelter to Belgian refugees during the First World War; this contribution earned each of the Olivers an OBE. In 1921, in his capacity as Honorary Secretary of the Camberwell Red Cross Division, Percy Oliver was asked by King's College Hospital if the division could provide a blood donor to save a stricken patient. At that time, giving blood was a novelty, but the mission was accomplished, and Oliver – with the assistance of his wife – was thus inspired to establish a panel of London-wide donors that became the world's first voluntary blood donation service. Such was the scheme's success that, in May 1928, he moved his family from 210 Peckham Rye to a roomier house in nearby Colyton Road. From here, Oliver ran the Greater London Red Cross Blood Transfusion Service – as it became known – until his death, having taken early

287 Boris Karloff in the title role of *The Mask of Fu Manchu* (1932), written by Sax Rohmer. [© MGM / The Kobal Collection]

At 36 Forest Hill Road, Peckham Rye, SE22, an unpretentious terraced house of the 1880s, an English Heritage plaque commemorates the actor **William Henry Pratt** (1887–1969) **7** , better known by his alias **Boris Karloff** (fig. 287). Here Pratt was born – he was the youngest of the nine children of Edward John Pratt and Eliza, née Millard – and spent the early years of his life, before moving with his family to Enfield in 1894. Initially, William intended to enter the consular service, but the smell of greasepaint proved more alluring, and he emigrated to Canada in 1909 to pursue his acting ambitions. Adopting the name of Boris Karloff, he spent much of his early acting career in repertory theatre and, after moving to Hollywood in 1917, took minor film roles as a generic 'baddie', to which his sinister appearance was amply suited. His big break came in the form of Frankenstein's monster, a part he played in the eponymous film of 1931, directed by James Whale. Karloff reprised the role in *The Bride of Frankenstein* (1935) and *Son of Frankenstein* (1939), having cemented his place in horror movie legend by his performances in *The Mummy* (1932) and *The Ghoul* (1933). Karloff's villainous potential was exploited in *The Mask of Fu Manchu* (1932), and he also enjoyed stage and television successes such as *Arsenic and Old Lace* (1941) and the 1950s series *Colonel March of Scotland Yard*. In later years he lived in Sussex and Hampshire, where he indulged his passion for cricket. Karloff's plaque was unveiled on the house – which, perhaps appropriately, is just in front of Camberwell Old Cemetery – on what would have been his 111th birthday, in the presence of his daughter Sara-Jane and the actor Christopher Lee. The ground floor of number 36 now functions as a restaurant.

retirement from the council in 1933 in order to devote himself full-time to promoting and extending the scheme. While here, he also supported the formation in 1932 of the Voluntary Blood Donors Association. The National Blood Transfusion Service was set up in 1946, two years after Oliver's death, while the Oliver Memorial Fund also continued his work by making awards to doctors, scientists and laypersons for outstanding merit in the advancement and promotion of blood transfusion. Oliver's plaque was erected by the GLC in 1979, at which time number 5 was tenanted by his daughter, Mrs Marjorie Hardy.

The novelist **C. S. Forester** (1899–1966) **8** is honoured with a plaque at 58 Underhill Road, East Dulwich, SE22, a semi-detached house of the late nineteenth century. Born Cecil Lewis Troughton Smith in Cairo – the son of a schoolmaster, George Foster Smith (1863–1947), and his wife Sarah, née Troughton (d. 1949) – he returned with his family to England in 1903 and moved from 37 Shenley Road, Camberwell, SE5, to Underhill Road in 1915. Following a spell at Dulwich College, Cecil began medical training at Guy's Hospital, but soon left to try his luck as a writer; by this time, he had already formed the habit of reading at least one book a day. Members of the family recall

long after his marriage in 1926 to Kathleen Belcher (1903–1987), moving in 1932 to Sydenham. Forester's first notable success was *Payment Deferred* (1926), which was partly set in Dulwich. It was adapted for the stage, while *The African Queen* (1935) made a famously successful transfer to the screen in a 1951 production starring Humphrey Bogart and Katharine Hepburn. While at number 58, Forester completed a biography of ADMIRAL NELSON (1929); later, between 1937 and 1962, he wrote the popular series of twelve novels featuring a fictitious naval hero, Captain Horatio Hornblower. During the Second World War, Forester served as a propagandist for both Britain and the United States, where he had settled by 1945 and died in 1966. Forester's English Heritage plaque was unveiled in 1990 by Margaret Stephens, his literary agent, in the presence of several family members.

The birthplace of the statesman **Joseph Chamberlain** (1836–1914) ❾ (see also pp. 170–1) at 188 Camberwell Grove (formerly 3 Grove Hill Terrace), Denmark Hill, SE5, is marked by a rectangular tablet of Hopton Wood stone, painted white and with lead inlaid lettering, a choice of materials that was intended to enhance its visibility (fig. 288). Such was Chamberlain's stock at the time that the LCC agreed to its installation less than a year after his death, and the plaque was put up in 1920. For the first nine years of his life he lived with his parents – Joseph Chamberlain (1796–1874) and Caroline, née Harben (1808–1875) – in this tall yellow-brick house of the late Georgian era, then numbered 3 Grove Hill Terrace; one biographer has described it as 'elegant but unpretentious'.[9] The locality was then a leafy suburb; it is said that it was possible to see the Palace of Westminster from the upper windows of the house on a clear day. The young Joseph was educated at the school of Miss Charlotte Pace, which was just a few doors away from number 188; Miss Pace commented that her pupil 'didn't like being behind anybody, and when he did fight he was in earnest about it'.[10] In 1845 the family moved to Highbury in North London, and in 1854 'Joe' Chamberlain was sent to Birmingham to represent his father's business interests in screw manufacturing. His involvement in politics began with his stint as Mayor of Birmingham between 1873 and 1876, when he was elected to Parliament. A leading Liberal, Chamberlain's aversion to the concept of Home Rule for Ireland led him to take the

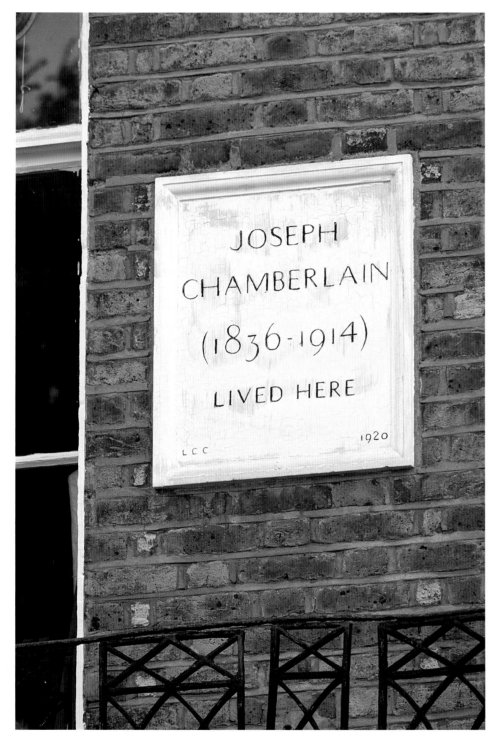

288   The stone LCC plaque erected in 1920 at the birthplace of Joseph Chamberlain, 188 Camberwell Grove. It was hoped that the inlaid lead lettering would enhance the plaque's visibility. [© English Heritage. Photograph by Derek Kendall]

Cecil's father giving him use of the attic at number 58 – then a claustrophobic and gloomy room with narrow windows, reached by a steep staircase – and one year to prove his mettle as an author. The reaction to his son's choice of pseudonym, which he adopted in 1923, was reportedly, 'Forester? Forester? What sort of a name is that?'.[8] He remained at the family home

breakaway Liberal Unionists into alliance with the Conservatives in 1886. However, after almost twenty years he split the Unionist coalition by his advocacy of protectionist tariffs, and it was partly owing to the divisions thus engendered that the Liberals won a landslide victory in the election of 1906.

At 51 Herne Hill (formerly 6 Danecroft Gardens), SE24, an Edwardian end-of-terrace house on the corner of Danecroft Road, a GLC plaque marks the home of **Arthur Henry Ward** (1883–1959) ❿ , best known as **Sax Rohmer**, the creator of Dr Fu Manchu (see fig. 287). Born in Birmingham to Irish parents, Ward started out as a newspaper reporter, and also worked as a ghost-writer for the music-hall comedians George Robey and 'Little Tich' (HARRY RELPH). His interest in Egyptology and the occult inspired him to produce one of his first short stories, *The Mysterious Mummy* (1903), written under the name Arthur Sarsfield Ward. It was following the Chinese revolution of 1911 that Ward – writing under the pseudonym Sax Rohmer – created his most famous fictional character, who first appeared in print in *The Mystery of Dr Fu Manchu* (1913). An inscrutable criminal genius, Fu Manchu seems uncomfortably like a racial stereotype today, but the books were immediately popular with contemporaries. Rohmer authored another fourteen

stories featuring the character – who is always outwitted by his nemesis Nayland Smith – and Fu Manchu also appeared in radio programmes, television shows and films, some starring BORIS KARLOFF. Many of the Fu Manchu stories – including *The Devil Doctor* (1916) and *The Si-Fan Mysteries* (1917) – were written at 51 Herne Hill, to which Rohmer moved in 1910, following his marriage to Rose Elizabeth Knox (1886–1979), a variety-act juggler and the sister of a member of the Crazy Gang. They were the first occupants of the house, known as 6 Danecroft Gardens until 1913, which they shared with Sax's father, Bill (d. 1932). However, as the couple were childless, they found the place 'a trifle larger than they really needed', and in 1919 left for Bruton Street, Mayfair.[11]

A GLC plaque commemorates the television pioneer **John Logie Baird** (1888–1946) ⓫ (see also p. 505) at 3 Crescent Wood Road, Upper Sydenham, SE26 (fig. 289). Both house and area were intimately connected with Baird and his pioneering development of television. He moved here in summer 1933, at the same time as his company's studios, workshops and offices moved to the Crystal Palace (which was destroyed by fire three years later); atop the 284-foot (87 m) high South Tower, the company built aerials to transmit high-resolution pictures. Baird's wife Margaret, née Albu (1907–1996), a concert pianist, described their detached mid-nineteenth-century home as 'vast, with acres of bare floors and windows high out of reach'.[12] With an eighty-foot (24 m) frontage and nearly three acres (1.2 ha) of land, it was a far cry from the top-floor front room Baird had occupied in Ealing on first arriving in London from Scotland in the mid-1920s. To Baird, the most attractive feature of number 3 – aside from its proximity to the Crystal Palace – was its capacity to accommodate a private laboratory. This, centred on the former stables, coach house and kitchen, was the scene of numerous experiments and discoveries, while the house was used for meetings, demonstrations and press conferences. Having been declared unfit for military service, Baird continued to live and work here during the Second World War, though he regularly joined his family in Cornwall, and – with the increasing dilapidation of the Sydenham property – began to stay in hotels nearby. In late 1945 he joined his family at a rented house in Bexhill, Sussex, though the house in Sydenham was kept up until his death.

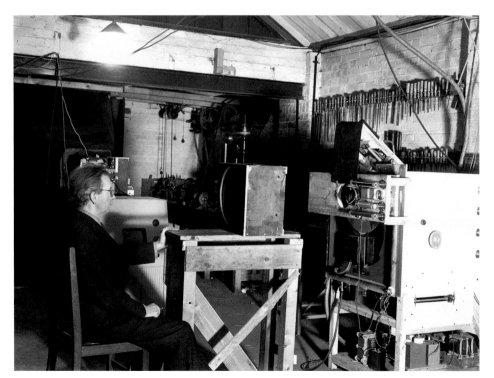

289 John Logie Baird demonstrating stereoscopic television in his laboratory at 3 Crescent Wood Road in December 1941. The room, centred on the former stables, coach house and kitchen, was the scene of numerous experiments and discoveries. [© Getty Images]

it, was 'hypocrisy or expulsion. I chose the latter'.[13] Annie Besant came to the small house then numbered 26 Colby Road early in 1874, along with her daughter Mabel (1870–1952), her ailing mother Emily – who died very shortly afterwards – and their maid. Nearby lived Thomas Scott, a friend and fellow freethinker, who introduced Besant to Charles Bradlaugh, sometime President of the National Secular Society. Soon she was contributing to the society's paper, the *National Reformer*, and in August 1874 she gave her first public lecture; its subject was the political status of women. Besant left the house in October of that year, initially to take up a domestic post in Folkestone; her later, longer-term London addresses in Paddington, Hampstead and St John's Wood have been demolished. In July 1888 Besant organised the strike by the female matchmakers – 'matchgirls' – employed by Bryant and May. She was also a member of the London School Board that introduced free secular education and free school meals, and secured its adoption of a policy only to purchase goods made under trade union-approved conditions. In the late 1880s Besant became a convert to theosophy, and – in tune with the movement's emphasis on the study of Eastern religions – lived mostly in India from 1893. There she founded the Central Hindu College in Benares and briefly suffered internment as a result of her strong advocacy of Indian self-determination. Annie Besant died at Adyar in 1933; her plaque was erected by the LCC thirty years later.

The Victorian semi-detached house at 39 (formerly 26) Colby Road, Gipsy Hill, SE19, was home to the social reformer **Annie Besant** (1847–1933) ⑫ , the sister-in-law of SIR WALTER BESANT (fig. 290). Annie Wood was born in the City into a wealthy family, and married Frank Besant, a clergyman, in 1867. However, her loss of religious faith led to a separation from her husband in 1873; her choice, as she later summarised

NOTES

1 It is now accepted that Shaw was born in 1828, rather than in 1830, as is stated on the plaque.
2 *ODNB*, vol. IL, p. 62
3 *The Malthusian*, 15 May 1921, p. 34
4 *The Times*, 11 February 1961, p. 8
5 Delia Jarrett Macauley, *The Life of Una Marson, 1905–1965* (Manchester, 1998), p. 46
6 Ibid
7 Alan J. Cobham, *A Time to Fly* (London, 1978), p. 7

8 Letter of 20 April 1989 on blue plaque file.
9 Denis Judd, *Radical Joe: A Life of Joseph Chamberlain* (London, 1977), p. 1
10 LCC, *Indication of Houses of Historical Interest in London*, vol. V (London, 1930), p. 32
11 Cay Van Ash and Elizabeth Sax Rohmer, *Master of Villainy: A Biography of Sax Rohmer* (London, 1977), p. 67
12 Antony Kamm and Malcolm Baird, *John Logie Baird: A Life* (Edinburgh, 2002), p. 252
13 Annie Besant, *An Autobiography* (London, 1893), p. 99

SOUTHWARK

291 Unique among London's plaques is that erected by the LCC in Shadwell's King Edward VII Memorial Park in 1922. It commemorates a group of explorers and navigators who 'set sail from this reach of the River Thames near Ratcliff Cross to explore the northern seas'. [© English Heritage. Photograph by Derek Kendall]

TOWER HAMLETS

The borough of Tower Hamlets is situated immediately east of the City, the 'hamlets' being those that lay beyond the Tower of London in the large parish of Stepney. This was largely rural until London's seventeenth-century growth established the area as the working end of what was already becoming Europe's greatest commercial city. Much early industry was of a maritime nature, shipbuilding along the Thames continuing until the 1860s. Inland, silk weaving was the principal activity, encouraged by the skills of Huguenot refugees. In the nineteenth century the wholly urban area, where there was poverty, disease and overcrowding, became the 'East End', the 'other' or dark mirror to the prosperous West End. Late nineteenth-century Jewish immigration transformed the inner districts, while the twentieth century saw population decline, wartime bombing, the closure of docks and new, predominantly Bengali, immigration. Despite its long-standing importance in the history of London, Tower Hamlets has relatively few blue plaques, largely because so many of the area's older buildings have been demolished. The LCC and GLC made conscious efforts to redress this imbalance, dealing flexibly with the selection criteria and installing a number of plaques on workplaces and sites.

TOWER HAMLETS

North of Tower Hill is Trinity Square, EC3. At number 43 (formerly 42) – a large late eighteenth-century house which functions as the vicarage and parish house of All Hallows by the Tower – an English Heritage plaque commemorates the **Reverend P. T. B. 'Tubby' Clayton** (1885–1972) ❶ , the founder of Toc H. Born in Australia, Philip Thomas Byard Clayton grew up in the City of London; he was nicknamed 'Tubby' during his university years, despite being no such thing. As an army chaplain during the First World War, he established Talbot House, a rest house at Poperinghe, Belgium, to give soldiers respite from the horrors of the Front. Abbreviated to TH, which became Toc H in Morse signallers' slang, Clayton's wartime brotherhood transferred to peacetime London, where his magnetic personality helped make it a hugely successful movement: formally founded in 1920, Toc H grew to have a thousand British branches, and many more overseas. Clayton described the principle of the movement as binding 'in a single tether those who would else be poor for their ignorance of one another'.[1] In 1922 the Archbishop of Canterbury offered Clayton the living of All Hallows by the Tower, then in a state of 'unrelieved decay'.[2] The church quickly became the spiritual focus for Toc H, while Tubby lived on 'The Hill' from 1923. Six years later, Charlotte Tetley presented All Hallows with what was then 42 Trinity Square; renamed Talbot House, this became the headquarters of Toc H's overseas commissioners as well as Clayton's home. The building housed a canteen, club room, skittle alley and other social amenities, which attracted tens of thousands of people a year. In 1938 it was joined via a passageway to 6 The Crescent, which contained rooms for staff and visitors. In 1940 All Hallows was seriously damaged by bombs. Clayton was despondent: 'That was the missus and the kids to me', he said.[3] He moved next door to a flat on the top floor of number 41 in 1948/9, and devoted himself to seeing the church rebuilt, work which was completed in 1957.

On the former Whitechapel Public Library, 77 Whitechapel High Street, E1, a PASSMORE EDWARDS benefaction of 1891–92 that stands immediately above one of the entrances to Aldgate East station, there is a plaque of 1987 to **Isaac Rosenberg** (1890–1918) ❷ , the poet and painter (fig. 292); it records that he 'lived in the East End and studied here', and was unveiled by the writer Emanuel Litvinoff. The son of poor Russian

Jewish immigrants, Rosenberg moved in 1897 from Bristol to London, where he studied at the Slade. He lived at a number of addresses in and around Stepney (including 58 Jubilee Street and 87 Dempsey Street) but, by 1983 – when the poet Geoffrey Hill suggested Rosenberg for a plaque – all the buildings had been demolished. It was thought vital that commemoration should be in the East End, to celebrate the local Anglo-Jewish culture from which Rosenberg had sprung. The only option was to commemorate Rosenberg at the library, which – after leaving school at fourteen and being apprenticed to a firm of engravers – he used regularly as a place to read and write poetry, there being nowhere to work at home. Rosenberg – whose interests and abilities were encouraged by the librarian, Morley Dainow – told a friend that his greatest joy 'was to run off to the library whenever he could, to read . . . anything he could find about poets and poetry'.[4] The library also became the meeting place for his circle of friends, known as the Whitechapel Group, which included the artists DAVID BOMBERG and MARK

292 The exterior of Whitechapel Public Library in 1929. A Passmore Edwards benefaction of 1891–92, the building was marked in 1987 with a plaque to Isaac Rosenberg, who studied here. [Tower Hamlets Local History Library and Archives]

TOWER HAMLETS

1932

293   Dr Jimmy Mallon – seated second from the right in the bottom row – amongst a group outside Toynbee Hall, 1932. [Reproduced by permission of the Barnett Research Centre, Toynbee Hall]

294   A detail of a robe made from brocaded satin designed by Anna Maria Garthwaite in c.1740, during her time at 2 Princelet Street. [© V&A Images / Victoria and Albert Museum, London]

GERTLER. Next door to the library was the Whitechapel Gallery, where Rosenberg exhibited. Despite a pacifist upbringing, he enlisted in 1915, not through patriotism but rather poverty: 'I thought if I joined there would be the separation allowance for my mother', he stated.[5] While serving in the trenches, Rosenberg wrote his finest poetry, most notably 'Daughters of War' and 'Dead Man's Dump'; he was killed on a night patrol of no-man's-land at the age of only twenty-seven.

On Toynbee Hall, 28 Commercial Street, Whitechapel, E1, is a plaque to **Dr Jimmy Mallon**, **CH** (1874–1961) ③ , who was Warden of Toynbee Hall and a champion of social reform (fig. 293). Like 'TUBBY' CLAYTON, he was an exponent of fellowship, but his was rooted in the Labour movement rather than the Church. Born in Manchester of Irish parents, Mallon moved to Toynbee Hall in 1906, when he was appointed Secretary of the National League to Establish a Minimum Wage. In October 1919 he became Warden of Toynbee Hall, the pioneering universities' settlement and base for experiments in social policy which had been founded in 1884 by CANON SAMUEL BARNETT and DAME HENRIETTA BARNETT in memory of ARNOLD TOYNBEE. Mallon strengthened the institution's community and educational roles, helping to

establish it as 'the poor man's university'. Jimmy (never James) had an effervescent character and was remembered as 'the most popular man east of Aldgate Pump'.[6] He served as resident Warden for thirty-five years, retiring in 1954. The plaque was unveiled by Len Murray of the TUC in 1984 – the centenary of Toynbee Hall – and was placed on the main building, designed by Elijah Hoole and built in 1884–85. Originally, Toynbee Hall was screened from the road by a range of tall warehouses and was entered through a gatehouse; these were destroyed during the Second World War, and the building is now set back behind what has become Mallon Gardens. Sadly, the plaque can no longer be easily seen from Commercial Street owing to the construction of a boundary wall.

In 1975 the historian Natalie Rothstein proposed a plaque to commemorate **Anna Maria Garthwaite** (1688–1763) ④ , the designer of Spitalfields silks, at 2 Princelet (formerly Princes) Street, E1, a substantial corner property of c. 1722 that had become one of the area's 'distressed houses' (figs 294 and 295).[7] For a long time the owners could not be traced, and when the plaque was eventually erected in 1998 Spitalfields had been thoroughly gentrified. Brought up a rector's

295   A view from 2 Princelet Street – the home of Anna Maria Garthwaite – towards the upper storeys of houses in neighbouring Wilkes Street, with the spire of Christ Church, Spitalfields, in the background. [© English Heritage. Photograph by Derek Kendall]

daughter in Lincolnshire, Garthwaite came to London in her early forties, settling in this house with her sister, the widowed Mary Dannye (d. 1763), and their niece Mary Bacon (d. 1765); it remained Anna's residence and workplace until her death. Here, Garthwaite established herself as a celebrated designer of fashionable fabrics, with a particular flair for botanical forms. At her peak, in the 1730s and 1740s, she was producing eighty designs for brocaded silks a year, and helped to introduce the 'principles of painting' into the loom. Garthwaite kept meticulous records of her designs and her customers, the greater part of which have survived and are now among the collections of the Victoria and Albert Museum.

Above a café at 12 Hanbury Street, Spitalfields, E1, there is a plaque to **Bud Flanagan** (1896–1968) ⑤, the comedian and leader of the 'Crazy Gang', who was born and brought up here as Reuben Weintrop, the youngest of the ten children of the Polish Jewish immigrants Woolf and Yetta ('Kittie') Weintrop. Flanagan later described the street of his birth as 'a patchwork of small shops, pubs, church halls, Salvation Army hostels, doss houses, cap factories and sweat shops', and noted that

it 'was typical of the Jewish quarter in the '90s'.[8] At number 12, a re-fronted house of *c.* 1712–13, his family ran a fried fish shop until the mid-1920s. As a boy, he anglicised his name to Bud Robert Winthrop and, age ten, found work as a callboy at the Cambridge Music Hall in nearby Commercial Street. In 1910 Bud walked to Southampton and worked his passage to New York, where he became involved with vaudeville, before returning in 1915 to join the Royal Field Artillery. At the rest house founded by 'Tubby' Clayton in Belgium, Bud met Chesney Allen, with whom in 1926 he formed a lasting comedy double act, taking the name Flanagan as revenge on a sergeant major of that name who had persecuted him for being Jewish. In 1932 the duo joined with others at the London Palladium to form the Crazy Gang, with Flanagan as the lynchpin of what was then innovatively anarchic and vulgar comedy. With his recordings of 'Underneath the Arches' (1937), 'We're Going to Hang out the Washing on the Siegfried Line' (1939) and 'Run, Rabbit, Run' (1939), Flanagan became a household name. Although Allen retired in 1945, the Crazy Gang kept going until 1962. One of Flanagan's last contributions to comedy was a recording of his 'Who Do You Think You Are Kidding, Mr Hitler?' for

TOWER HAMLETS

the title sequence of the television series *Dad's Army*. The plaque was unveiled in 1996, the centenary of Flanagan's birth, by the President of the British Music Hall Society, Roy Hudd, who wore Bud's battered old straw hat.

On a house of 1725 at 32 Elder Street, Spitalfields, E1, there is a plaque to the painter **Mark Gertler** (1891–1939) **6** ; it was unveiled in 1975 by the artist's son, Luke Gertler. Born in Spitalfields, the son of poor East European Jewish immigrants, Gertler was inspired by pavement art and by the autobiography of W. P. Frith to find his way to the Slade, where – between 1908 and 1912 – his talent shone among a cohort that included Stanley Spencer, Paul Nash and Isaac Rosenberg. In 1912 he boasted, 'I am a very promising artist – one who is likely to make a lot of money'.[9] In April of that year he moved with his brother and sister-in-law, Harry and Ann, to what was then a dilapidated house in Elder Street; here he remained – 'continually struggling against being overcome by the sordidness of my surroundings and family and by poverty' – until his move to Hampstead in January 1915.[10] Based in two rooms on the top floor, Gertler was increasingly lonely: 'By my ambitions I am cut off from my own family and class . . . They do not understand me nor I them'.[11] However, while at number 32 he produced much of his most original and powerful work, concentrating on Jewish subjects, including *Rabbi and Rabbitzin* (1914). His output was inspired first by the artist (Dora) Carrington, with whom he was in love, and later by the war; angered by the suffering, he aimed 'to paint a picture in which I hope to express all the sorrow of life'.[12] Through the patronage of Lady Ottoline Morrell, Gertler came into contact with the Bloomsbury Group, but from 1920 he struggled with tuberculosis, and his later career was a disappointment; depressed and isolated, he gassed himself at the age of forty-seven. A coal-hole cover on the pavement below the plaque bears a representation of Gertler's best-known painting, *The Merry-Go-Round* (1916).

Mary Hughes (1860–1941) **7** , described on the plaque as a 'friend of all in need', is commemorated at 71 Vallance Road, Bethnal Green, E1, a late nineteenth-century corner building that was formerly the Earl Grey public house, a notoriously bad haunt (fig. 296). Hughes took over the then vacant building in 1926 and converted it as the teetotal 'Dewdrop Inn: For Education and Joy', which she lived in and ran as 'a centre of helpfulness', a refuge for any in need of a roof over their heads. Known to those among whom she lived simply as 'Comrade', Mary was the daughter of Thomas Hughes, the author of *Tom Brown's Schooldays* (1857) and a founding Christian Socialist. Although born into comfortable circumstances in Mayfair, Mary was brought up to believe that service to the poor was a primary obligation: 'She didn't want to *visit* the poor. She wanted to be *with* the poor and to be poor herself'.[13] In 1896 she went to work as a voluntary social worker in Whitechapel, and from 1915 chose to live in solidarity with the outcast. She professed that 'indignation keeps me warm!', and was unhappy when brought a bath, preferring to use the public facilities with other locals.[14] In 1938 number 71 was altered for Mary by the architect Grylls Wilson, who described it as 'a four-storied building with scarcely a right-angle anywhere', its glass windows 'pasted up with every sort of political and religious propaganda'.[15] The basement became a recreation room, the former bar a canteen and meeting room, and a ground-floor scullery near the main door was converted into a tiny unheated room for Mary's own use. Number 71's upper rooms were originally intended to teach students of social conditions how the poor lived – Mary considered that nearby Toynbee Hall (see Jimmy Mallon) was 'far too luxurious'.[16] Hughes remained at the address until moving further along the street to St Peter's Hospital a few weeks before her death. Thereafter, the Dewdrop was renamed Mary Hughes House, in memory of one of the East End's 'most lovable and unforgettable characters'.[17] The plaque was unveiled by the philanthropist Sir Basil Henriques in 1961, at the earliest opportunity allowed by the twenty-year rule.

In Whitechapel Road, E1, is the Royal London Hospital, founded in 1740 and granted royal patronage in 1990; the front block was designed by Boulton Mainwaring and dates from the 1750s. On it a plaque to **Edith Cavell** (1865–1915) ⑧, pioneer of modern nursing in Belgium and heroine of the Great War, records that she trained and worked here from 1896 to 1901. The plaque was moved to this position in 2006 following the demolition of a late Victorian nurses' home to the rear of the hospital. Cavell came to nursing late, at the age of thirty, having been brought up comfortably as the daughter of a Norfolk clergyman. She entered 'the London' on 3 September 1896, and spent the next four and a half years hard at work: nurses were on duty around twelve hours a day, had few holidays and 'little or no social life'.[18] Initially, Cavell was a probationer on the wards, attending lectures by FREDERICK TREVES, among others. By the end of her two years' training, she was not spoken of especially highly by the matron, Miss Eva Lückes, who recommended she join the private nursing staff. Her third year was thus spent outside 'the London', though she returned in autumn 1899 as a junior staff nurse before leaving for a post at the St Pancras Infirmary in January 1901. Cavell entered the most vital period of her career in 1907, when she went to Brussels to help introduce modern nursing practice. In 1914 she took sole charge of the St Gilles Hospital, which became a centre of resistance to Belgium's German occupiers. Arrested and court-martialled, she was executed by the Germans on 12 October 1915, causing international outrage. Cavell became a heroine, a martyr and an instrument of propaganda for military recruitment.

Behind the Royal London Hospital, and converted as its medical school library, is the Church of St Philip, established as Stepney Chapel in 1818–23 and rebuilt in 1888–92. At 38 Newark Street, E1, is the church's Gothic vicarage of 1864, by A. W. Blomfield, which bears a plaque to the historian **John Richard Green** (1837–1883) ⑨ (see also pp. 404–5), who was vicar here in 1866–69 (fig. 297). Green was commemorated in 1909–10 by two LCC plaques, the first in Marylebone, the second here, the duplication an acknowledged excep-

tion even at that date. The wreathed chocolate-coloured plaque in Newark Street describes him as a 'historian of the English people', deriving from Green's own epitaph for himself: 'The historian of the English people. He died learning'. It also reflects Green's high reputation in the early twentieth century as a founder of social and cultural approaches to history; he was among the first to consider the role of the masses in great historical changes. Despite consumptive frailty, Green insisted on spending the 1860s in the East End as a minister among the poor, learning at first hand through a 'gruelling regimen of social work' what life was like for ordinary people.[19] 'One never realises what the monotony and narrowness of the life and thoughts of the ordinary shopkeeper is, till one spends a whole day in the midst of them'.[20] At Easter 1869, worn out and disillusioned with the Church, Green resigned his benefice – '*Won't it be jolly to have no sermons to preach on Sundays!*', he wrote – and took up the librarianship of Lambeth Palace, moving on to writing, to Marylebone and to growing radicalism.[21] His *Short History of the English People* (1874) sold half a million copies.

On the Clergy House in Wapping Lane, E1, there is a plaque to **Lincoln Stanhope Wainwright** (1847–1929) ⑩, the vicar of St Peter's, London Docks, who lived here from 1884 until his death. The church was begun in 1865–66 by Father Charles Lowder, a seminal figure in the rise of Anglo-Catholicism, whose success in Wapping helped to ensure the acceptance of High-Church ritual within the Church of England. St Peter's is screened from the street by the Sisters' House and the Clergy House, added in 1881 in Lowder's memory to designs by Bowes A. Paice. Wainwright, who was ordained a priest in 1872, arrived in Wapping the following year to become assistant curate under Lowder; he succeeded him as vicar in 1884, never leaving the parish for a single night thereafter. Like many others commemorated in Tower Hamlets, Wainwright – who founded the Church of England Working Men's Society – chose to give his life to the relief of East London's poverty at a time when the state did not provide social services. His funeral procession is said to have been followed and watched by hundreds of working men and women, sailors, dockers and shopkeepers. He was so well remembered that in 1961 the LCC took the unusual step of commemorating a vicar who was never more than a local hero.

297 The wreathed LCC plaque to John Richard Green, installed in 1910 at 38 Newark Street, the vicarage of the Church of St Philip. [© English Heritage. Photograph by Derek Kendall]

TOWER HAMLETS

In front of the round ventilator shaft of the Rotherhithe Tunnel in Shadwell's King Edward VII Memorial Park, E1, there is a Portland stone tablet with inset painted tiles depicting three galleons (fig. 291). Designed by the LCC architect G. Topham-Forrest, it commemorates the explorers **Sir Hugh Willoughby** (d. 1554), **Stephen Borough** (1525–1584), **William Borough** (1536–1598), **Sir Martin Frobisher** (1535?–94) and other navigators who 'set sail from this reach of the River Thames near Ratcliff Cross to explore the northern seas' **11** . Ratcliff's connection with English maritime history was established early – there were shipbuilding yards here by at least the time of King Edward III – but the area's importance became established during the later sixteenth century. It was from here, for instance, that Willoughby's three ships – the *Bona Esperanza*, the *Bona Confidentia* and the *Edward Bonaventure*, the crew of the last including the Borough brothers – sailed in 1553 to find a northern passage to China. Willoughby died near Murmansk the following year; the Boroughs sailed on to 'discover' Russia. In 1576 Frobisher set off from Ratcliff on the first of three north-westerly voyages that took him to Baffin Island via Greenland. The tablet originated in Stepney Borough Council's wish of 1913 to commemorate the site of Ratcliff Cross, a historic place then being destroyed by the building of the tunnel. The focus of discussion shifted to the mariners and, following a suggestion made by the politician Sir John Benn, the tablet was instead installed here, as part of the formation in 1922 of the first park in Stepney; this occupies the riverside site of a fish market cleared for the tunnel works.

Number 2 Butcher Row, Limehouse, E14 – a large brick sugar-merchant's house of 1795–96, later used as a vicarage – bears an English Heritage plaque to the priest and social reformer, the **Reverend St John Groser** (1890–1966) **12** . The building is the home of the Royal Foundation of St Katharine, which was founded in 1147 and – as a Royal Peculiar – survived the Reformation. Its buildings were located by the Tower of London until 1825, when they made way for St Katharine Docks and moved to Regent's Park. After the Second World War, the foundation's move to Butcher Row – site of the bombed St James's Ratcliff – was masterminded by Father Groser. Born in Australia, Groser had moved in 1922 to the East End, where he served at St Michael and All Angels, Bromley-by-Bow,

and Christ Church, Watney Street, Stepney. He was committed to helping the poor and homeless; known as 'the apostle of the unemployed', he was a Christian Socialist and a friend of MARY HUGHES.[22] Groser took up the position of Warden on the reopening of St Katharine's in summer 1948, by which time the welfare state was supplanting his vocation. In 1956 Groser became Master of the foundation, remaining here until 1962 and making it 'a kind of early "think-tank" and centre of commitment to the health and welfare of the East End'.[23] He oversaw the building of a radically furnished chapel in 1950–54, incorporating some magnificent medieval and later fittings from the foundation's earlier buildings.

Number 58 Solent House, Ben Jonson Road, Stepney, E1 – built as part of the Ocean Estate, begun in 1948 – carries a plaque of 1953 commemorating a figure intimately associated with the East End: **Doctor Barnardo** (1845–1905) **13** . As the plaque records, it was on this site, in what was then Hope Place, that Barnardo began his work for children in 1866 (fig. 298). Born and brought up in Dublin, Thomas John Barnardo discovered his Christian mission as a teenager. He came to the East End in 1866, intending to travel to China as a missionary. While waiting, he visited and prayed with those struck down by an outbreak of cholera, enrolled as a student at the London Hospital, taught at the Ernest Street ragged school and preached in the streets. Barnardo started his own teaching of poor children in an 'old, disused, and transmogrified donkey-shed' on the west side of Hope Place; there, he had his 'first indication of and inspiration towards what proved to be my life's work'.[24] By March 1868 he had raised enough funds to buy two cottages across the road; these he made the East End Juvenile Mission – 'seed-bed of the Barnardo Homes' – running classes and services for boys, girls and their parents.[25] By the following year he had acquired two further cottages on either side of his mission centre, which attracted hundreds of children each day. In 1870 Barnardo decided that preaching and teaching were not enough: he wanted to give the children more permanent care, and later that year opened the first of his homes for boys at nearby 18 and 20 Stepney Causeway (closed 1922). By night, he would search the streets with his lantern looking for destitute children. Barnardo, known as the 'child's champion', had rescued 60,000 boys and girls by the end of his life,

298 The former donkey shed in Hope Place in which Dr Barnardo began his teaching of poor children. By 1869, he had acquired several buildings in the street and here founded the East End Juvenile Mission, 'seed-bed of the Barnardo Homes'. [© Barnardo's]

TOWER HAMLETS

though he never did complete the studies that would have made him the doctor that he adopted as a title.

At 88 Mile End Road, E1, there is a large slate tablet commemorating the site of the residence of **Captain James Cook** (1728–1779) 14 , the circumnavigator and explorer. Cook was a labourer's son whose life at sea began in the North Sea coal trade. He enlisted in the Navy in 1755, and spent most of the Seven Years War in

the waters of North America, where his surveys of the St Lawrence River in 1758–59 established his reputation as a navigator. He moved to London in 1762, married Elizabeth Batts (1741–1835), the daughter of a Wapping publican, and found a home in the humble mariners' suburb of Shadwell. Two years later he acquired a newly built house in the more genteel district of Mile End Old Town, long a place of retreat for marine commanders and merchants. The property, then known as

Captain Cook
88 Mile End Road

Cook at 88 Mile End Road, but the house fell into decay and was demolished in 1959. The plaque was shipped to Australia as a gift to the Trustees of Captain Cook's Landing Place. A decade later, the Australian High Commission asked the GLC to put up a new plaque on the site to commemorate the bicentenary of Cook's landing at Botany Bay, New South Wales, in 1770. Objections of principle from officers were overruled for the sake of good Antipodean relations, but a non-standard slate tablet was chosen as a means of signifying its exceptional nature; it was unveiled in 1970 by Sir Alexander Downer, the High Commissioner for Australia.

At 288 Old Ford Road, E3, part of a terrace of *c.* 1870 near Victoria Park, there is a plaque to the writer and philanthropist **Israel Zangwill** (1864–1926) **15** , who lived here from 1884 to 1887. Born in Aldgate, Zangwill was the son of a Russian Jewish immigrant, and lived at number 288 while a pupil teacher at the Jews' Free School, Bell Lane, Spitalfields. During his final year at number 288, Zangwill collaborated with a fellow teacher, Louis Cowen, in writing *The Premier and the Painter* (1888), published under the pseudonym J. Freeman Bell. After an early career as a journalist, Zangwill came to notice with *The Children of the Ghetto* in 1892, a compelling account of East End Jewish life, which was followed by other works including *Ghetto Tragedies* (1893). When Dr Theodor Herzl came to London in 1896 to plead the Zionist cause, he won immediate and active support from Zangwill, much of whose later life was devoted to Zionism. In 1963 the Zangwill Centenary Committee asked the LCC to commemorate him, but it proved difficult to find a surviving address. Several of Zangwill's childhood homes in East London had been demolished and, in a situation that provoked intense feeling, it was felt inappropriate to select one of Zangwill's later addresses outside the East End. Finally, research carried out by the LCC historian Ida Darlington brought to light Zangwill's connection with Old Ford Road. In 1965 a plaque was unveiled – from behind the Union Jack and the Israeli flag – by Professor Oliver Zangwill, Israel's son, on what would have been his father's 101st birthday.

7 Assembly Row, was at the end of an irregular terrace, next to a baker's shop and a cartway leading to wine-vaults (fig. 299). As an ambitious seaman, Cook – most famous for charting the coasts of New Zealand, the east coast of Australia and the Pacific coast of North America – was seldom at home, though he is said to have doted on his family when he was; there were six children in thirteen years. After Cook's death in Hawaii, the widowed Elizabeth stayed on at Assembly Row until moving in 1788 to Clapham. In 1907 the LCC installed a terracotta-coloured wreathed plaque to

In Grove Road, Mile End, E3, there is a plaque on the north face of the west pier of a railway bridge. It commemorates the first **Flying Bomb** on London **16** ,

300 Photograph showing the damage caused by the flying bomb which fell on Grove Road on 13 June 1944, a week after D-Day. Six people were killed and forty-two injured. [Tower Hamlets Local History Library and Archives]

which fell here on 13 June 1944, a week after D-Day, seriously damaging houses in Antill Road, Burnside Street and Bellraven Street, and destroying the train line from Liverpool Street to Stratford (fig. 300); six people were killed and forty-two injured. A local recalled, 'After it went off we were all sworn to secrecy but the news got out soon enough'.[26] Remarkably, railway traffic was restored within forty hours on a temporary bridge that served until 1948. The arrival here of the V1, doodlebug or buzz bomb, a new departure in the use of jet propulsion, marked a significant and sinister new phase of the war for Londoners, who quickly learned to run for cover at the moment when the motor cut out. Allied troops overran the main launching sites in France before the end of summer 1944, but over two thousand V1s – launched from the ground or from piloted aircraft – had reached London. The area most affected was Croydon, where more than a thousand houses were destroyed. An enamelled steel plaque was put up in Grove Road by the GLC in 1985 following a proposal from Joseph V. Waters, a lifelong East Ender, one of whose brothers had been injured by the bomb; it was unveiled on 13 June, forty-one years after the bomb fell. Stolen in 1987, it was replaced with a standard English Heritage ceramic plaque the following year.

At Kingsley Hall, Powis Road, Bow, E3, a plaque commemorates **Mahatma Gandhi** (1869–1948) ⓱ (see also

301 Mahatma Gandhi during his visit to Bow in 1931, surrounded by local people. [© Popperfoto / Getty Images]

p. 278) (fig. 301). This, the first plaque to honour an Indian figure, was put up in 1954 by the LCC, which waived the twenty-year rule in recognition of 'one of the greatest men of his time'.[27] It is one of the few plaques not to mention the individual's achievements; it was felt that Gandhi's 'fame was such that it was unnecessary to describe him and that in fact it would do him most honour to let his name stand alone'.[28] Kingsley Hall was built in 1926–28 to the designs of Charles Cowles-Voysey. Originally established in 1915 in Eagling Road, Bow, by Muriel Lester (1883–1968) and her sister Doris, it commemorated the things their brother Kingsley had 'cared for and had worked for in his brief life', and developed into a Christian Socialist community centre for the East End poor.[29] It later transferred to Powis Road, where Muriel Lester – who met Gandhi in India in 1926 – worked as Warden. In 1931 Gandhi came to England to attend the Round Table Conference at St James's Palace that aimed – but failed – to establish a new constitution for India. During his stay, which lasted from 12 September to 5 December, he and his party were the guests of Lester at

TOWER HAMLETS

302 A photograph of November 1857 showing the *Great Eastern* nearing completion on the foreshore of the Thames. Its designer, Isambard Kingdom Brunel, can be seen in the foreground, wearing a top hat. [Reproduced by permission of English Heritage. NMR]

Kingsley Hall. Gandhi, with his spinning wheel, occupied one of the four 'cell-bedrooms' – that nearest the stone staircase – on the building's flat roof; his son Devadas (1900–1957) stayed in another.[30] Gandhi, who 'enjoyed living among his own kind, the poor people', explored the surrounding area on foot in the mornings.[31] His visitors included MARY HUGHES; Muriel Lester later recalled that the pair were 'about the same in spirit, and almost the same in stature and fragility (only an apparent fragility)'.[32] It has been said of his stay

in England – which included trips to Lancashire and Cambridge – that 'By his mere presence Gandhi had changed the attitude of the English people to India.'[33]

Adjoining 262 Westferry Road, Millwall, E14, there is a works office building of the early 1850s that bears the legend 'J. Scott Russell & Co'. On an adjacent archway leading into the Thames-side yard known as Burrell's Wharf is a plaque commemorating the **Great Eastern** (launched 1858) 18 (fig. 302), the largest steamship of the nineteenth century, conceived and designed by ISAMBARD KINGDOM BRUNEL and built by John Scott Russell (1808–1882), whose works stood on this site. The *Great Eastern*, designed in 1852–53, has been described as 'an engineering dream, a triumph of design over function, of ambition over common sense even'; it was Brunel's 'ultimate triumph, and his greatest folly', and has been said to have hastened his death.[34] At a time when the average length for a ship was about 300 ft (91 m), the *Great Eastern* – known as *Leviathan* while it was being built – was 692 ft (211 m) long, with room for 4,000 passengers and 3,000 tons of cargo; it was nearly fifty years before another ship, the *Lusitania*, outstripped her in size. In 1854 Scott Russell leased the Napier Yard next door to his own premises so as to have as much room as possible for the ship's construction. The hull of the 'monster steamer' was built on a huge gridiron of massive beams set on piles driven into the foreshore, and was complete by November 1857.[35] Its sideways launch into the Thames was an epic struggle, but the ship was finally afloat by 31 January 1858; remains of the gridiron can still be seen immediately adjacent to Burrell's Wharf. The *Great Eastern* never operated on the Far East routes for which she was designed: days after she left Millwall, she was seriously damaged by an explosion. In 1885 the ship suffered the ignominious fate of being moored in the Mersey and converted for entertainment use. In 1888 she was sold to ship breakers; it took two hundred men two years to take the hull apart. The plaque honouring this extraordinary ship was put up by the LCC in 1954 close to the boundary between the two yards in which it was constructed, but was removed prior to demolition of the sheds to the north in 1974; it was reset in its present location in 1992, following the conversion of some of the Burrell's Wharf buildings into housing.

NOTES

1 Tresham Lever, *Clayton of Toc H* (London, 1971), p. 104

2 Ibid, p. 116

3 Ibid, p. 228 (8 February 1941)

4 Jean Moorcroft Wilson, *Isaac Rosenberg: Poet & Painter* (London, 1975), p. 37

5 Quoted by Bernard Kops, *Guardian*, 20 November 1990, p. 37

6 *The Times*, 13 April 1961, p. 18

7 It is now accepted that Garthwaite was born in 1688, rather than in 1690, as is stated on the plaque.

8 Bud Flanagan, *My Crazy Life* (London, 1961), p. 10

9 *Mark Gertler: Selected Letters*, ed. Noel Carrington (London, 1965), p. 36 (19 June 1912)

10 Ibid, p. 78 (January 1915)

11 Ibid, p. 49 (December? 1912)

12 *The Grove Dictionary of Art*, ed. Jane Turner (London and New York, 1996), vol. XII, p. 493

13 Rosa Hobhouse, *Mary Hughes: Her Life for the Dispossessed* (London, 1949), p. vi

14 Ibid, p. 57

15 Ibid, p. 99 and p. 108

16 Ibid, p. 89

17 Ibid, p. 123

18 Rowland Ryder, *Edith Cavell* (London, 1975), p. 41

19 *ODNB*, vol. XXIII, p. 514

20 *The Letters of John Richard Green*, ed. L. Stephen (London, 1901), p. 196 (6 August 1868)

21 Ibid, p. 228 (February 1869)

22 Hobhouse, *Mary Hughes*, p. 87

23 *ODNB*, vol. XXIV, p. 75

24 Norman Wymer, *Father of Nobody's Children: A Portrait of Dr Barnardo* (London, 1954), pp. 51–52

25 Ibid, p. 67

26 *The Times*, 14 June 1985, p. 30

27 Letter of 15 November 1951 (from Mr H. S. L. Polak) on blue plaque file.

28 Letter of 27 June 1953 (from the Clerk of the LCC) on blue plaque file.

29 Hobhouse, *Mary Hughes*, p. 56

30 Ibid, p. 112

31 Louis Fischer, *The Life of Mahatma Gandhi* (London, 1951), p. 306

32 Letter of 4 March 1960 on blue plaque file to Mary Hughes.

33 Robert Payne, *The Life and Death of Mahatma Gandhi* (London, Sydney, Toronto, 1969), p. 416

34 Steven Brindle, *Brunel: The Man who Built the World* (London, 2005), p. 215

35 *David Napier, Engineer, 1790–1869: An Autobiographical Sketch*, ed. D. Bell (Glasgow, 1912), p. 22

TOWER HAMLETS

303 The GLC plaque to John
Walter at 113 Clapham Common
North Side. The plaque – which
features a typeface used by *The
Times* in the late eighteenth
century – is flanked on the right by
a recessed roundel containing a
bust of Shakespeare. [© English
Heritage. Photograph by Derek
Kendall]

WANDSWORTH

This large London borough extends from the River Thames south to Tooting and – to the west – as far as Wimbledon Common and Richmond Park. These expanses of open land, together with Battersea Park and Clapham and Wandsworth commons, have long given the borough a rural character and popular appeal. The nineteenth century saw the area's transformation from a largely agricultural settlement, with industrial activities centred on the Thames and the River Wandle, to built-up London suburbs. The pace of development quickened with the building of Chelsea (1858) and Albert (1873) bridges, and the opening in 1863 of Clapham Junction Station – the name of which belies its situation in mid-Battersea. The borough's character is varied: Battersea, in the north, was long associated with the skilled working classes, while areas such as Roehampton and Clapham – much of the latter falling within the borough of Lambeth – were noted for their large mansions and villas, and formed retreats for prosperous gentlemen and businessmen.

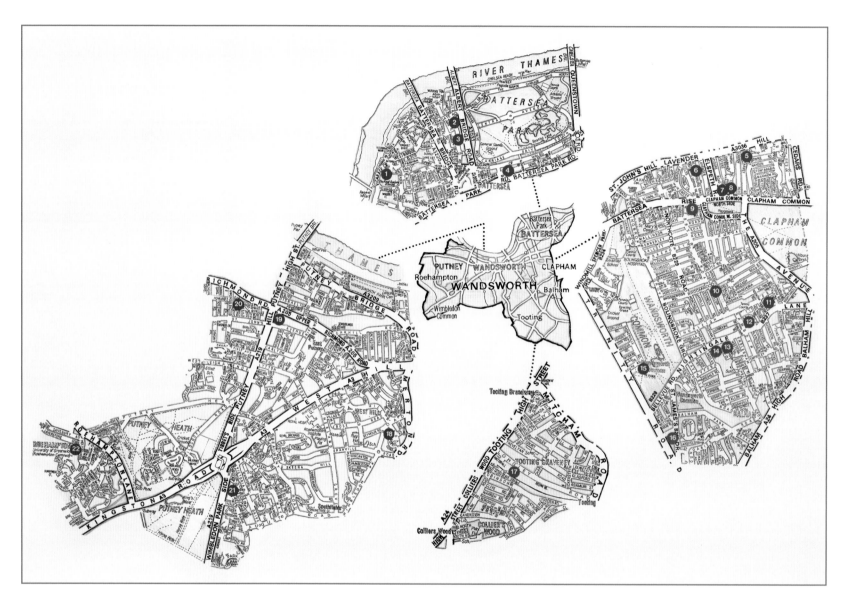

WANDSWORTH

BATTERSEA

St Mary's Vicarage, 42 Vicarage Crescent, SW11, is a handsome building of the mid-eighteenth century, extensively altered *c.* 1808. Formerly known as Caius House, it bears a wreathed LCC blue plaque of 1935 commemorating **Edward Adrian Wilson** (1872–1912) **1** , the Antarctic explorer and naturalist (fig. 304). Born in Cheltenham, Wilson read natural sciences at Cambridge before embarking on medical training in London in 1895. In November the following year, Wilson's journal records that he 'packed everything into a four-wheeler and came down to live with the Leighton-Hopkins' at Caius House, Battersea Square. This change will open my eyes to another phase of life which I think will have a good deal of interest . . . Living here in Battersea is really a good healthy change for me, as I hate Society, and here I shall have to learn to put up with a certain amount every day'.[1] Number 42 was then in use as a mission house, run jointly by Gonville and Caius College, Cambridge – which

Wilson had attended – and St Mary's Church, Battersea; its Warden was the Rev. W. L. B. Hopkins. Wilson at once became involved in the mission's work, spending his evenings 'talking, praying and singing in a positive reek of Battersea children'.[2] It was here, in the drawing room, that he met his future wife, Oriana Souper, the daughter of a rector. However, Wilson's health soon gave out under the stress of his lifestyle; in March 1898 he discovered that he was suffering from tuberculosis, and his connection with Caius House came to an abrupt end. Once recovered, Wilson joined the National Antarctic Expedition (1901–4) under CAPTAIN SCOTT as junior surgeon, zoologist and artist, and accompanied Scott and SHACKLETON to the 'Farthest South'. In 1910 he was invited by Scott to join his new Antarctic expedition as chief of the scientific staff; Wilson was one of the party of five to reach the South Pole on 18 January 1912, only to find that the Norwegian explorer Roald Amundsen had been there a month before. Weakened by the disappointment and the harsh conditions, Wilson and his colleagues were dead by March of that year.

Albany Mansions, Albert Bridge Road, SW11, is an imposing block built in about 1910. Flat 63 – on the first floor – was the home from 1913 to 1917 of the writer **Norman Douglas** (1868–1952) **2** . Born in Austria, Douglas worked for the Foreign Office in the 1890s before taking up writing professionally in 1907. The period 1910–17 – spent mainly in London – saw the publication of three works on southern Italy and Tunisia: *Siren Land* (1911), *Fountains in the Sand* (1912) and *Old Calabria* (1915). Douglas's most famous work, *South Wind*, was completed in Capri in 1917. Much of the author's life was spent abroad, where his notorious pederasty was less subject to censure. His almost four-year residence at Flat 63 was therefore, for him, a record in one house in London. Douglas chose the flat largely on account of its situation, facing the greenery of Battersea Park. The façade of the block created a problem for the plaque's design; it was finally decided to use a non-standard rectangular steel plaque, which was installed in an inset area beneath a first-floor window in 1980.

Further south along Albert Bridge Road – at number 67, a stuccoed semi-detached house of the mid-1800s – a plaque was unveiled in 2000 to the Yorkshire-born

WANDSWORTH

305 Charles Sargeant Jagger's masterpiece: the Royal Artillery Memorial, Hyde Park Corner, executed in 1921–25. Behind rises the façade of St George's Hospital, begun in 1827 and converted in c.1990 as the Lanesborough Hotel. [© Crown copyright. NMR. Photograph by Derek Kendall]

sculptor **Charles Sargeant Jagger** (1885–1934) ③. Unlike many war memorial artists, Jagger experienced life on the Western Front at first hand: he joined the Artists' Rifles at the outbreak of the First World War, abandoning an already promising career as a sculptor, and went on to win the Military Cross. It was while convalescing in England that he heard that the British War Memorials Committee was employing sculptors; Jagger's first commission was for a relief, the *First Battle of Ypres* (1918–19), for a proposed hall of remembrance. Other commissions followed, including *No Man's Land* (1919–20), the Great Western Railway

Memorial (1922) at Paddington Station and, Jagger's masterpiece, the Royal Artillery Memorial at Hyde Park Corner (1921–25) (fig. 305). By autumn 1923 Jagger was living at Anhalt Studio, Anhalt Road, to the rear of 117 Albert Bridge Road, a building that continued to be his home following his marriage in 1925 to Evelyn Isabel Wade. In 1930 the couple moved to the nearby 67 Albert Bridge Road, and it was here that Jagger died four years later. He was productive until the end, producing works for a wide circle of private patrons that included Edward, Prince of Wales; his last uncompleted project, a statue of King George V for the city of New Delhi, India, was part of a public works collaboration with the architect SIR EDWIN LUTYENS.

Between 1898 and 1902 some 950 mansion flats were built in Battersea, many around Battersea Park, which had been laid out in 1854. One of these imposing blocks, Overstrand Mansions, Prince of Wales Drive, SW11, bears a plaque to the playwright **Sean O'Casey** (1880–1964) ❹ , who lived at Flat 49 (fig. 306). O'Casey was born in Dublin into a Protestant family, and worked mainly as a casual labourer before writing his first plays in his thirties. He is best known for his three earliest works, *The Shadow of a Gunman* (1923), *Juno and the Paycock* (1924) and *The Plough and the Stars* (1926), all staged at Dublin's Abbey Theatre. In 1927 O'Casey moved to England, following the controversial production of *The Plough and the Stars*, set at the time of the 1916 Easter Rising; his rift with his native land was confirmed after the publication of his experimental anti-war play *The Silver Tassie* (1928), which was rejected by the Abbey Theatre. Flat 49 – a five-room apartment at third-floor level – was O'Casey's home from late 1934 until September 1938, when he moved to Devon. O'Casey's wife, Eileen, née Reynolds (1900–1995) – who sang and acted under the name Eileen Carey – described 'Sean's big room, overlooking

Battersea Park' as 'a near-copy of his other rooms, the desk so placed that he could pull round his chair to the fire'.[3] Here, O'Casey – who 'had the trick of singing a good deal' when considering an idea for a new play – completed *The Flying Wasp* (1937) and worked on the first volume of his autobiography, *I Knock at the Door* (1939), and his play *The Star Turns Red* (first performed 1940).[4] The plaque was unveiled in 1993 by his widow Eileen and their daughter, Siobhan.

CLAPHAM, BALHAM AND TOOTING

Just north of Clapham Common, stretching towards Lavender Hill, is Sugden Road, SW11. Here, at number 24, lived **Fred Knee** (1868–1914) ❺ , the London Labour Party pioneer and housing reformer. Knee spent a life dedicated to the working class from which he had sprung. Born and raised in Somerset, he moved to London in 1890, and soon joined both the FABIAN SOCIETY and the Social Democratic Foundation. When he entered local government in 1900 as Alderman for Battersea Council – a position he held until 1906 – Knee was already a prominent figure, having founded the Workmen's National Housing Council in 1898. Through his vigorous campaigning, the public provision of housing was extended, especially by the building of cottage estates. His greatest achievement was the central role he played in the founding of the London Labour Party in 1914; on 28 November of that year, just ten days before his death, Knee was confirmed as Secretary of the provisional committee of the party, and it is generally accepted that – had he lived – he would have become a major figure in national politics. Knee moved in 1898 to 24 Sugden Road – then newly built – with his wife Annie and their young family in order to be close to his friend and colleague Robert Phillimore; he remained here until moving to Hertfordshire in late 1901. The plaque, one of the last installed by the GLC, was unveiled in 1986 by Alf Dubs, then Battersea's Labour MP.

Of a similar date to 24 Sugden Road, though much larger in scale, is 33 Lavender Gardens, SW11. Here lived the author **G. A. Henty** (1832–1902) ❻ from 1894 until the year of his death. Born near Cambridge, where he later studied classics, George Alfred Henty was commissioned into the Army on the outbreak of the Crimean War, and from 1865 found work as a war cor-

306 The crowd gathers for a photograph following the unveiling of the English Heritage plaque to Sean O'Casey at Overstrand Mansions, Prince of Wales Drive, in 1993. The plaque was unveiled by O'Casey's widow Eileen (centre, foreground) and their daughter, Siobhan. [© John Neligan]

respondent. His accounts of such happenings as the Franco-Prussian War and the Spanish Civil War were published in the *Illustrated London News* and other journals, and brought him to widespread public attention. These experiences abroad also fed into the works for which Henty is best remembered, his historical adventure stories for boys; these books, which appeared at the rate of three or four a year and were notable for their historical accuracy, included *Out on the Pampas* (1868), *In Times of Peril* (1881) and *With Moore at Corunna* (1898). During his time at number 24, where he lived with his second wife Elizabeth, née Keylock (1854–1926), Henty wrote three of his best-selling novels: *With Buller in Natal* (1901), *With Roberts in Pretoria* (1902) and *With Kitchener in the Soudan* (1903). By the time of his death, which took place on board his yacht in Weymouth harbour, Henty had become an institution, encouraging an interest in history among countless schoolboys. Of the installation of the plaque by the LCC in 1953, *The Times* mused, '"G. A. who?" may ask some youthful and ignorant creature . . . Elder persons, however, may shed a tear for that friend of their boyhood and deem the memorial well deserved'.[5]

Clapham Common North Side, SW4, was much developed in the eighteenth century, when the area became a desirable suburban retreat. Number 113 dates largely from *c.* 1763, and is known as Gilmore House after the sister of WILLIAM MORRIS, Deaconess Isabella Gilmore (1842–1923), who lived here from 1891. It was originally one of an identical pair known as the 'Sister Houses', separated by a tree-lined avenue; the right-hand 'Sister' was demolished in 1895 and on its site was built what is now number 110. The surviving, left-hand 'Sister' – 113 Clapham Common North Side – bears a plaque commemorating **John Walter** (1739–1812) **7**, the founder of *The Times* (fig. 303). Walter was born in the City of London, where he carried on his father's business as a coal merchant before venturing into insurance in 1781. Heavy losses forced him into bankruptcy, and in about 1783 he was obliged to give up his town house in Queen Square, Bloomsbury, and 113 North Side, where he had lived with his wife Frances, née Landen (d. 1798) since 1773 and had 'expended a considerable sum of money, the fruits of many years industry'.[6] By the time Walter left, however, he had become interested in typography, and in 1782 bought

the patent to the logographic system, which was said to speed up the printing process; two years later, he founded the Logographic Press in Blackfriars. By this time, Walter had also conceived the notion of a newssheet, the *Daily Universal Register*. The first issue appeared on 1 January 1785, the name being changed to *The Times* three years later. The newspaper really came into its own under the ownership and editorship of Walter's son John (1776–1847), born at number 113; he assumed sole control of the paper in 1803, and by the time of his death had established *The Times* as one of the world's most influential broadsheets. For the design of the plaque, the GLC decided to use an 'appropriate' typeface for the words *The Times*, based on that used by the newspaper in the late eighteenth century. It was unveiled in 1977 by Sir Denis Hamilton, Chairman and Editor-in-Chief of Times Newspapers Ltd.

Number 110 Clapham Common North Side, a substantial gabled house of 1895, was the last home of the politician and statesman **John Burns** (1858–1943) **8** (fig. 307). Born in Lambeth, Burns was the sixteenth child of a Scottish engineer, and endured a childhood of relative poverty. It was around 1881 that

THE COLOSSUS OF BATTERSEA.

THE RIGHT HON. JOHN BURNS (*to his native borough*). "SHIFT ME, AND YOU BECOME A 'BLASTED HEATH'!"

["If he were defeated the borough would never recover from the indelible stigma of rejecting him."—*Report, in "The Times," of Mr. John Burns' speech at the Battersea Town Hall.*]

308 A photograph showing the proposed position of the plaque to Edward Thomas at 61 Shelgate Road. It was installed by the LCC in 1949. [© City of London, LMA]

he converted to socialism, reputedly after reading *Principles of Political Economy* by John Stuart Mill. Burns's apprenticeship in public speaking was served on Clapham Common, where he was arrested for the first of a number of times in 1878, and by the mid-1880s he was known as a powerful and persuasive orator. Burns came to widespread notice as one of the organisers of the great London Dock Strike of 1889. The same year, he was elected to represent Battersea on the newly created LCC – the only councillor with truly working-class origins. Three years later he became MP for Battersea and in 1905, at the invitation of Campbell-Bannerman, joined the Cabinet as President of the Local Government Board. In 1914, in protest at the war with Germany, Burns passed out of public life and moved with his wife Martha (d. 1936) to Alverstoke, 110 North Side, having previously lived at nearby 108 Lavender Hill and 37 Lavender Gardens. His remaining years were spent at number 110, where he collected books on Shakespeare, Sir Thomas More and London, a modest end to a pioneering career. A rectangular blue plaque was erected to Burns in 1950, the twenty-year rule having been waived due to his close connection with London and the LCC.

At 61 Shelgate Road, SW11, a plaque of 1949 commemorates the essayist and poet **Edward Thomas** (1878–1917) **9** (fig. 308). The suggestion for a plaque, made four years earlier, had the support of Walter de la Mare, who described Thomas as an 'ardent lover of England and Englishness'.[7] Although much of his work was inspired by the countryside, Thomas spent the greater part of his life in the boroughs' of Lambeth and Wandsworth. Born in Stockwell – the son of Philip Henry Thomas (1854–1920), a clerk at the Board of Trade, and his wife Mary (b. 1855) – he lived in Battersea from the age of two. Number 61 Shelgate Road was Thomas's family home from 1889 until November 1900, when, having recently graduated from Oxford, he moved with his wife Helen, née Noble (1877–1967) and their young son to Earlsfield; in 1901 he left London altogether, moving to Kent and later to Hampshire. Greatly inspired by the work of Richard Jefferies, Thomas penned his first book, *The Woodland Life* (1896), during his time at number 61. In the first decade of the twentieth century he wrote reviews and critical and biographical studies, but was known especially for his country books, which included *The Heart of England*

(1906) and *The South Country* (1909). From 1914 Thomas's literary talents were dedicated to poetry; he began writing in this form even before enlisting in the Artists' Rifles in summer 1915, and by the time of his sudden death – Thomas was killed during the first hour of the Battle of Arras – he had composed nearly 150 poems, many in a similar style to that of Wilfred Owen.

In 1904 the attentions of the LCC were turned towards Broomwood House (formerly Broomfield), then in the course of demolition, and its association with the opponent of slavery **William Wilberforce** (1759–1833) **10** (see also pp. 177–8 and p. 295) (fig. 309). Plans were immediately put in place for the erection of a plaque; this, a decorative rectangular tablet made up of a series of chocolate-coloured tiles, was affixed in 1906 to the side of the recently completed 111 Broomwood Road, SW11, which occupies the site of Wilberforce's former home (fig. 310). Wilberforce entered Parliament as Member for Hull, the town of his birth, in 1780. Seven years later he took up the question of the abolition of slavery, a matter with which he remained inti-

WANDSWORTH

309 Broomwood House (formerly Broomfield) shortly before its demolition in 1904. William Wilberforce spent a great deal of time here between 1797 and 1808. [© City of London, LMA]

Wilberforce's life: he dedicated himself to the promotion of the bill for the abolition of the slave trade, and – after a series of setbacks – saw it passed by Parliament in 1807. He also became the leading light of the CLAPHAM SECT, a group that included Henry Thornton, Granville Sharp and ZACHARY MACAULAY.

Gus Elen (1862–1940) **11** , the music-hall comedian, is commemorated at Edith Villa, 3 Thurleigh Avenue (formerly Thurleigh Road), SW12, a semi-detached house of the late nineteenth century; the plaque was unveiled in 1979 by Don Ross, widower of the popular entertainer Gertie Gitana. Ernest Augustus Elen was born in Pimlico and, according to his own account, 'grew up singing'.[10] He began his career performing at 'sing songs' in public houses such as the Magpie and Stump in Battersea, and by 1884 was appearing as a black-face singer. Elen made his name for his perfection of the coster character, adopting a persona that was closer to the real-life costermonger (fruit and vegetable seller) than the self-consciously idealised coster routine of his contemporary and rival, ALBERT CHEVALIER. Elen became a huge music-hall star during the 1890s and early 1900s, and remained popular until his retirement during the First World War. He made a brief comeback in the 1930s, appearing at the Royal Variety Performance of 1935 and recording some of his songs; the most famous of these included 'It's a Great Big Shame', 'If it Wasn't for the 'ouses in Between' and ''Arf a Pint of Ale'. From 1898 Elen lived largely in Balham, where he 'bred poultry and took up photography'.[11] By 1900 he was residing at Edith Villa, and it was here that he died forty years later.

mately concerned for the rest of his life. Wilberforce had a long and close association with Clapham. He lived for a time at his friend Henry Thornton's residence, Battersea Rise House; in 1797, the year of his marriage to Barbara Spooner (1777–1847), he began to use Broomfield – newly built by Thornton in the grounds of Battersea Rise House – as an 'occasional retreat'.[8] Over the next eleven years, until his removal in 1808 to Gore House, Kensington – Wilberforce's home until 1821, it was demolished in 1857 – he spent a great deal of time at Broomfield, which was within easy reach of London and was endeared to him 'by much happiness enjoyed in it, as well as by its own beauty'.[9] These years were the most active and important of

At 40 Nightingale Lane, SW12, a brick house of the 1880s, an English Heritage plaque of 1997 commemorates the cartoonist **H. M. Bateman** (1887–1970) **12** . Born in Australia, Henry Mayo Bateman came to England as a child, in 1888. Declared unfit for service in the First World War, he was able to devote his time to art and to the fulfilment of his earliest and most enduring ambition, 'to draw and make people laugh'.[12] Bateman's sharply humorous drawings began to be published in *The Sketch*, *Punch* and elsewhere, and were to become some of the most famous and popular cartoons of the twentieth century. Using his powers of observation, Bateman – himself a shy man – made a speciality of seizing on social absurdities and basic

310 The brown LCC plaque – made up of a series of Minton tiles – on the side elevation of 111 Broomwood Road. It marks the site of Broomwood House, the former home of William Wilberforce. [© English Heritage. Photograph by Derek Kendall]

On the site behind this house stood until 1904 Broomwood House (formerly Broomfield) where WILLIAM WILBERFORCE resided during the CAMPAIGN against SLAVERY which he successfully conducted in Parliament

311 'The Guardsman who Dropped It' by H. M. Bateman, first published in *The Tatler* in 1922. [© H. M. Bateman Designs Limited / ILN / Mary Evans Picture Library]

human failings. He produced thousands of humorous drawings – perfecting the comic strip without words – but is perhaps best known for 'The Man Who . . .' series, which illustrated agonising social gaffes wit-

nessed by goggling onlookers; these were published as double-page cartoons in *The Tatler* from 1922, beginning with 'The Guardsman who Dropped It' (fig. 311) and culminating in 'The Guest who Called "Pâté de Foie Gras" Potted Meat'. Bateman lived at 2 Bonneville Road, Clapham, SW4, until 1910, when he moved to Parkstone, 40 Nightingale Lane, his home for about four years; the rest of his life was spent largely outside of London. While at number 40, Bateman had his first one-man show, at the Brook Street Gallery (1911); his experiences of the Clapham area fed into later work including the collection *Suburbia* (1922).

At Queen Elizabeth House, 99 (formerly 59) Nightingale Lane, is a bronze LCC plaque to the preacher **Charles Haddon Spurgeon** (1834–1892) ⑬. Born in Essex, Spurgeon taught in schools before becoming pastor in 1852 of a congregation at Waterbeach, Cambridgeshire. Two years later he was appointed to the New Park Street congregation in Southwark, where great crowds were soon drawn to his ministry. The chapel became so popular that larger premises were needed, and the Metropolitan Tabernacle at Newington Butts (Elephant and Castle) was duly opened in

WANDSWORTH

312   The boxer Ted 'Kid' Lewis
during training in about 1920. The
last four years of his life were
spent at Nightingale House, 105
Nightingale Lane. [© Getty Images]

1861. Spurgeon ministered at the tabernacle until his death; only illness late in life curbed the vigour of his preaching. The bronze plaque now at number 99 has had a chequered history. It was first erected in 1914 at 75 Great Dover Street, Southwark, Spurgeon's home in 1854–56. Following the demolition of the house in 1953, it was moved to 217 New Kent Road (formerly 3 Bengal Place), the preacher's home in 1856–57, and – again after demolition – was finally transferred in 1971 to Helensburgh House, 99 Nightingale Lane. The seclusion of Helensburgh House was 'a great attraction' to Spurgeon, who 'felt the need of absolute quiet and rest after the labours and toils of the day'.[13] He moved here in 1857 with his wife Susannah, née Thompson (1832–1903) and their twin sons. Soon, however, the Spurgeons found the house 'altogether too small and inconvenient for a man whose work needed a very large library', and in 1869 it was completely rebuilt; the work was undertaken – largely at the expense of devoted admirers of the preacher – by William Higgs, the builder of the Metropolitan Tabernacle, to plans by his eldest son, also William.[14] Spurgeon – who declared that the new Helensburgh House was 'founded in love, walled with sincerity, roofed in with generosity' – remained here until summer 1880, a period Susannah later referred to as 'the least shadowed by care and sorrow of all the years of our married life'.[15] The family then relocated to Westwood, 49 Beulah Hill, Upper Norwood, a house in substantial grounds which was Spurgeon's home until his death.

At neighbouring Nightingale House, 105 Nightingale Lane, a building of 1871, a plaque commemorates the world champion boxer **Ted 'Kid' Lewis** (1893–1970) ⑭ (fig. 312). Lewis was born Gershon Mendaloff to a Jewish cabinetmaker's family in the East End. At the suggestion of a police officer – who had witnessed his performance in a street brawl – he entered the boxing ring in 1909, making his debut as 'Kid' Lewis at the Judaean Club, Whitechapel. In 1913, at the age of nineteen, he became the youngest ever British featherweight champion, and between 1914 and 1922 won numerous further titles, including European featherweight, British, Empire (now Commonwealth), European and world welterweight, and British, Empire and European middleweight. The fights between Lewis and the Irish-American Jack Britton for the world title were particularly notable; their relationship has been de-

scribed as one of the greatest rivalries in boxing history, and it was said that 'they winced and ducked every time they heard the other man's name'.[16] In 1929 – a worldwide celebrity – Lewis fought the last of nearly three hundred bouts, winning by a knockout; over the course of his career, he lost only thirty times. A nomad for much of his life, the widowed Lewis resided from 1966 at Nightingale House, the Home for Aged Jews, and died here at the age of seventy-seven. These were among the happiest years of his life, according to his son Morton, who unveiled the plaque in 2003.

At 3 Routh Road, SW18 – a large late Victorian house on the west side of Wandsworth Common – a plaque marks the home of the Prime Minister **David Lloyd George, Earl Lloyd-George of Dwyfor** (1863–1945) ⑮ , one of the outstanding political figures of the twentieth century. Born in Manchester, Lloyd George was brought up in Wales, where he took an early interest in politics. In 1890 he successfully stood for Parliament as a Liberal; he was to represent his constituency, Caernarfon Boroughs, for the next fifty-five years. Lloyd George was appointed to his first political office, President of the Board of Trade, in 1905. Three years later he became Chancellor of the Exchequer, a post in which his passion for social welfare came to the fore; Lloyd George's achievements included the 'People's Budget' of 1909 and the National Insurance Act of 1911. In 1916, on the resignation of ASQUITH, Lloyd George was appointed Prime Minister and formed a new coalition government. He guided the war effort for the remaining two years, and retained the premiership until 1922; although he continued to sit in the House of Commons for over twenty years, Lloyd George never again held political office. He was closely associated with the Wandsworth area: 179 Trinity Road (demolished) was Lloyd George's home from late 1899 until about 1903, when he and his wife Margaret, née Owen (1866–1941) moved to 3 Routh Road. It was while here that he was appointed President of the Board of Trade; in December 1905 he commented that his office was 'large enough to contain the whole of Number 3 Routh Road'.[17] It was here also that, in November 1907, Lloyd George's seventeen-year-old daughter Mair died. His grief was such that he left the house shortly afterwards, and in January 1908 moved with his family to Chelsea. The plaque, as erected in 1967, mistakenly gave Lloyd George's year of birth as 1865; a new, correct, plaque was installed by English Heritage in 1992.

313   A photograph of members of the Lauder family, taken in Tooting in c.1906. On the left, beside Harry Lauder, is his mother, Isobella. On the right are Lauder's wife Nance (Annie) and the couple's son, John, with his bulldog.

The poet and novelist **Thomas Hardy** (1840–1928) 16 (see also p. 376) lived at 172 Trinity Road (formerly 1 Arundel Terrace), SW17. Articled at the age of sixteen to an architect in Dorchester, Hardy left Dorset in 1862 to seek his fortune in London, where he entered the offices of the architect Arthur William Blomfield. In his spare time he indulged his passion for literature and in 1867 wrote his first novel, *The Poor Man and the Lady*. In 1873 Hardy turned to writing full-time; his most celebrated works of the following years included the novels *Far From the Madding Crowd* (1874), *The Mayor of Casterbridge* (1886), *Tess of the d'Urbervilles* (1891) and *Jude the Obscure* (1895). He also produced verse collections such as *Wessex Poems* (1898). Hardy moved on 22 March 1878 to The Larches, 1 Arundel Terrace, a house at the corner 'where Brodrick Road crosses Trinity Road towards Wandsworth Common Station, the side door being in Brodrick Road'.[18] Here, Hardy and his wife Emma, née Gifford (1840–1912) settled down to a London literary life; his residence saw the publication of *The Return of the Native* (1878), *The Trumpet-Major* (1880) and *A Laodicean* (1881). However, the writer never felt completely comfortable in the capital – complaining of a strange feeling of proximity to 'a monster whose body had four million heads and eight million eyes' – and, after a period of serious illness, left Tooting for Dorset in late May 1881.[19] The original plaque – brown in colour and of the experimental new design – was put up in March 1940, just before wartime economies prompted the LCC's seven-year closure of the scheme; it soon became badly worn, however, and was replaced with a blue roundel in 1962.

At 46 (formerly 24) Longley Road, SW17, backing onto the River Graveney and the railway, a plaque of 1969 honours the music-hall artiste **Sir Harry Lauder** (1870–1950) 17 (fig. 313). Born near Edinburgh, Lauder early showed a talent for singing and comedy, and decided to take up a stage career. After appearing in Scottish music halls, he came at the age of thirty to London, where he made his debut at Gatti's and rapidly became a favourite with audiences. In 1908 Lauder gave a command performance before King Edward VII, and during the First World War took part in many troop concerts, often on the Western Front. It was for these services that he was knighted in 1919. Lauder's act consisted of songs – almost all of which

WANDSWORTH

314 Holly Lodge, 31 Wimbledon Park Road, in a photograph of 1904. George Eliot lived here between 1859 and 1860, a period which saw the completion of *The Mill on the Floss*. [© City of London, LMA]

he wrote himself – with a heavily Scottish flavour, interspersed with comic patter; they included 'Keep right on to the End of the Road', 'Roamin' in the Gloamin'', 'Donald, where's your trousers?' and 'I Love a Lassie'. Lauder and his wife Annie (1873/4–1927) went to live at what was then known as Athole House, 24 Longley Road, in 1903, and stayed here until 1911; a double-fronted, detached house of *c.* 1890, it was his only permanent London home. In 1907 Lauder wrote, 'A Scotsman's house, they say, is his castle. My castle is a very modest villa out Tooting way. I'm never so truly happy as when at home in the bosom of my wife and "me family". On these occasions one or the other of us is seldom far away from the piano – and I often think it's a good job that we live in a self-contained house'.[20]

WANDSWORTH, PUTNEY AND ROEHAMPTON

The first blue plaque erected in South London can be found at Holly Lodge, 31 Wimbledon Park Road, SW18; its inscription records that the novelist **George Eliot** (1819–1880) **18** (see also pp. 191–2) lived here (fig. 314).

Born Mary Anne Evans in Warwickshire, she published her first full-length novel – *Adam Bede* – in 1859, and by the 1860s she enjoyed a flourishing literary career, accepted as one of the greatest writers of her time. Holly Lodge, a semi-detached brick house of the mid-nineteenth century, was Eliot's home between February 1859 and September 1860, and it was here that she wrote one of her most celebrated novels, *The Mill on the Floss* (1860). She moved to the house with the critic George Henry Lewes (1817–1878), who – despite being already married – lived openly with Eliot. She expected Holly Lodge to be their home 'for years to come', describing the house to her friend Sara Hennell as being 'very comfortable, with far more of vulgar indulgences in it than I ever expected to have again; but you must not imagine it a snug place, just peeping above the holly bushes. Imagine it rather as a tall cake, with a low garnish of holly and laurel'.[21] The couple enjoyed the suburban lifestyle, and entertained friends such as CHARLES DICKENS, WILKIE COLLINS and Edward Bulwer Lytton. However, Eliot soon became discontented; desperate to maintain her anonymity in the face of new-found success, she felt Holly Lodge to be overlooked by 'houses full of eyes', and found its situation 'inconvenient'.[22] By late September 1860, she was living in Marylebone. A blue plaque, of the LCC's standard wreathed design, was erected at Holly Lodge in 1905.

At 11 (formerly 2) Putney Hill, SW15, a blue plaque commemorates the poet **Algernon Charles Swinburne** (1837–1909) (see also p. 191) and his friend **Theodore Watts-Dunton** (1832–1914), the poet, novelist and critic 19 (fig. 315 and see fig. 182). It was put up at the suggestion of Clara Watts-Dunton, Theodore's widow, who was still living in the house when the plaque was erected in 1926; it remained her home until her death in 1938, at which point the property was sold and its contents – including various 'Pre-Raphaelite Relics' – were dispersed.[23] Swinburne developed his literary tastes at Eton and Oxford, and in London mixed in a circle that included D. G. Rossetti and Edward Burne-Jones. He suffered much from

315 The front of The Pines, 11 Putney Hill, in an undated photograph. Algernon Charles Swinburne looks out of the upper window, and Theodore Watts-Dunton appears below. [© Mary Evans Picture Library]

ill-health and alcoholism, and in 1879 was taken in by his friend Theodore Watts-Dunton, who encouraged discipline, and abstention, in the poet's life. The pair lived at The Pines, Putney Hill, a 'large double block of a building' of c. 1870, from September 1879 until their respective deaths; even Theodore's marriage in 1905 'did not change the quiet, ordered life at The Pines'.[24] Swinburne, whose health showed instant signs of improvement under his friend's rigorous care, occupied 'one room on the first floor, looking out upon the beautiful back garden . . . and a bedroom on the floor above, with a "commanding view" of Putney Hill from the top window in front of the house'.[25] Clara Watts-Dunton commented that it 'would be difficult to imagine a greater contrast between the idiosyncrasies of two men living under the same roof than that presented by the difference between Swinburne's tidy retreat upstairs and Walter's untidy workroom downstairs'.[26] While at The Pines, Swinburne enjoyed a regular routine, of which his walk across Wandsworth Common was 'the great event of the day'; 'Here I am,' he wrote, 'like Mr Tennyson at Faringford [sic], "Close to the edge of a noble down," . . . and yet within an easy hour's reach of Hyde Park Corner'.[27] Creatively, this was a productive period for him: it saw the publication of works including the verse collections *Songs of the Springtides* (1880) and *Astrophel* (1894), and a novel, written by 1862, *Love's Cross-Currents* (1904). Meanwhile, Watts-Dunton produced writings such as *The Coming of Love, and Other Poems* (1897) and the novel *Aylwin* (1898).

The President of Czechoslovakia **Dr Edvard Beneš** (1884–1948) 20 lived at 26 Gwendolen Avenue, SW15, a detached house of c. 1900. Born in what was then Bohemia, Beneš became, during the First World War, a diplomat and patriot in the cause of Czech nationalism. From 1918 to 1935 he was Foreign Minister of the new Czechoslovak State and served as its premier between 1921 and 1922, before holding the office of President in 1935. In autumn 1938, after the Munich Agreement ceded the Sudetenland to Germany, Beneš went into exile in London, where he led the movement for Czech freedom and, in 1940, became President of Czechoslovakia-in-exile. He was confirmed in office on his return to the liberated republic in 1945, and continued as President until the year of his death. Number 26 Gwendolen Avenue was Beneš's London home from

October 1938 until November 1940, when the Blitz forced the President and his Cabinet to leave the capital for Aston Abbotts, Buckinghamshire; apparently, a bomb fell on the garden of the house only days after Beneš's departure. A plaque was installed on 28 October 1978, the 60th anniversary of the founding of the state of Czechoslovakia.

A gatepier of Fairlawn, 89 Wimbledon Park Side, SW19 – a substantial detached house of 1853, built to the designs of Rawlinson Parkinson (fig. 316) – bears an English Heritage plaque of 1997 commemorating **Sir Edwin Saunders** (1814–1901) **21**, dentist to Queen Victoria. Saunders, who was born in London, was articled to a local dentist at a time when the profession had not yet developed as a medical discipline. He first came to notice in 1837, when he published *The Teeth, a Test of Age*, in which he demonstrated that the age of children could be accurately determined by observation of their teeth. From 1839 to 1854 he worked as a dental surgeon and lecturer on dental surgery at St Thomas' Hospital, and in 1840 co-founded an institution for the treatment of the teeth of the poor. Six years later Saunders took over the well-established practice of Alexander Nasmyth, as well as his premises at 13A George Street (now St George Street), Hanover Square. It was in so doing that he acquired the position of dentist to Queen Victoria – and other members of the royal

family – which he held for almost forty years. Saunders played an important part in the development of dentistry from the 1850s to the 1870s; the Odontological Society was formed at his Mayfair home in 1856 – he initially served as the society's Treasurer and later as President – and he was a trustee of the Dental Hospital of London, opened at 32 Soho Square in 1858. Saunders also played a leading part in the founding of the British Dental Association in 1880 and, three years later, became the first dentist to be knighted. Fairlawn, built for Saunders in 1853, became his permanent home from about 1894, following his retirement; it was here that he died at the age of eighty-seven.

Manresa House (formerly Parksted), overlooking Richmond Park, was built for the 2nd Earl of Bessborough in the 1760s to designs by Sir William Chambers, and was altered in the nineteenth and twentieth centuries. For about a hundred years from 1861, the building housed the country's leading Jesuit training college; one of its resident students was the poet **Gerard Manley Hopkins**, SJ (1844–1889) **22**, whose plaque can be seen on a modern gatepost at Holybourne Avenue, SW15. Hopkins was born into a High Anglican family of comfortable means. At Oxford, he came under the influence of J. H. Newman and converted to Roman Catholicism. In 1868 he entered the Jesuit order as a novitiate, resolving 'to write no more, as not belonging to my profession'.[28] However, barely ten years later, Hopkins produced his most famous work, the ode 'The Wreck of the *Deutschland*' (1875), commemorating a shipwreck in which five nuns lost their lives. Having broken his literary silence, Hopkins continued to write, though his work remained virtually unpublished before a full collected volume was brought out in 1918 by his friend Robert Bridges. Hopkins lived at Manresa House during three separate periods: as a novitiate (1868–70), as a teacher (1873–74) and to serve his tertianship, the third and last year of his noviceship (1881–82). Manresa House, the only building associated with Hopkins to survive in London, was owned by the GLC at the time when the plaque was erected in 1979. Its name, bestowed by the Jesuits, derives from the 'place where St Ignatius lived for a year doing penance in a cave'.[29] The plaque was re-erected on a new gatepost in 2004.

1   George Seaver, *Edward Wilson of the Antarctic: Naturalist and Friend* (London, 1963 edn), p. 21
2   Ibid, p. 32
3   Eileen O'Casey, *Sean* (London, 1990 edn), p. 145
4   Ibid, p. 147
5   *The Times*, 2 April 1953, p. 9
6   Ibid, 25 November 1977, p. 3
7   Letter of 24 November 1945 on blue plaque file.
8   Robert Isaac Wilberforce and Samuel Wilberforce, *The Life of William Wilberforce*, vol. II (London, 1838), p. 221
9   Ibid, vol. V (London, 1838), p. 387
10 Tony Barker, 'Gus Elen', *Music Hall Records*, no. 5, p. 85
11 *ODNB*, vol. XVIII, pp. 29–30
12 *The Times*, 13 February 1970, p. 12
13 C. H. Spurgeon, *The Early Years: 1834–1859* (London, 1962), p. 498
14 Charles Ray, *Mrs C. H. Spurgeon* (London, 1903), p. 56
15 *C. H. Spurgeon's Autobiography, Compiled from his Diary, Letters, and Records, by his Wife and his Private Secretary*, vol. III (London, 1899), p. 182; ibid, vol. II (London, 1898), p. 291
16 *The Times*, 21 October 1970, p. 19
17 Bentley Brinkerhoff Gilbert, *David Lloyd George: A Political Life*, vol. I: *The Architect of Change: 1863–1912* (London, 1987), p. 283 (12 December 1905)
18 Martin Seymour-Smith, *Hardy* (London, 1994), p. 242
19 Ibid, p. 261
20 Sir Harry Lauder, *Harry Lauder at Home and on Tour* (London, 1907), p. 123
21 *George Eliot's Life as Related in her Letters and Journals*, ed. J. W. Cross, vol. II (Edinburgh and London, 1885), p. 81 (6 February 1859); ibid, p. 83 (19 February 1859)
22 Ibid, p. 120 (23 July 1859); ibid, p. 266 (14 July 1860)
23 *The Times*, 7 March 1939, p. 27
24 *The Swinburne Letters*, vol. IV: *1877–1882*, ed. Cecil Y. Lang (New Haven and London, 1960), p. 95 (27 September 1879); LCC, *Indication of Houses of Historical Interest in London*, vol. V (London, 1930), p. 101
25 Thomas Hake and Arthur Compton-Rickett, *The Life and Letters of Theodore Watts-Dunton*, vol. II (London and New York, 1916), pp. 103–4
26 Clara Watts-Dunton, *The Home Life of Swinburne* (London, 1922), p. 49
27 *The Swinburne Letters*, vol. IV, pp. 111–12 (21 November 1879)
28 *ODNB*, vol. XXVIII, p. 56
29 Robert Bernard Martin, *Gerard Manley Hopkins: A Very Private Life* (London, 1991), p. 184

LCC
SIR
JULIUS
BENEDICT
(1804-1885)
MUSICAL
COMPOSER
Lived and
died here

WESTMINSTER

The City of Westminster is the administrative hub of the United Kingdom: within its boundaries lie the seat of Parliament, the chief London residence of the reigning monarch and the Royal Courts of Justice. Its importance dates back to before the Norman Conquest, when Edward the Confessor chose the riverside village as the site of a royal palace. The modern city – its charter was granted as recently as 1900 – also includes most of the West End, London's theatreland and leisure playground, with major retail thoroughfares such as Oxford Street and Regent Street. Within Westminster are some of the capital's earliest surviving residential developments outside the City of London – such as St James's and Soho – and, in the case of Belgravia and Mayfair, some of the smartest. Since 1965 Westminster has also encompassed the former metropolitan boroughs of Paddington and Marylebone, taking the boundary as far north as St John's Wood and including more socially mixed districts such as Westbourne Park and Kensal Rise. The oldest surviving blue plaque – to the French Emperor Napoleon III – lies in St James's, and overall Westminster contains far and away the largest number of blue plaques of any London borough.

Manchester Square, Marylebone, and the LCC plaques to Sir Julius Benedict (at number 2) and John Hughlings Jackson (at number 3) (see pp. 408–9). [© English Heritage. Photograph by Derek Kendall]

317 The expanse of Eaton Place, laid out by Thomas Cubitt between c.1826 and 1850. The thoroughfare boasts three blue plaques; that on the left of the picture, at number 29, commemorates Sir John Lubbock, Baron Avebury. [© English Heritage. Photograph by Derek Kendall]

BELGRAVIA

Socially and architecturally, Belgravia has always been one of London's grandest districts, and thanks to the stewardship of the Grosvenor Estate it remains one of the most complete examples of late Georgian and early Victorian town planning in the capital. The Grosvenor family owned the land from 1677, but development remained piecemeal until the 1820s, when Robert Grosvenor, 1st Marquess of Westminster – whose statue gazes across Belgrave Square – commissioned the master builder THOMAS CUBITT to provide an ambitious plan based upon a grid enlivened by magnificent squares and terraces. The area's streets take their names from the Grosvenor estates in Cheshire, and are characterised by handsome, stucco-fronted houses. Proximity to Buckingham Palace, the Royal Parks and the Palace of Westminster has ensured that Belgravia attracted a mix of fashionable, aristocratic and, more recently, plutocratic residents; it has, in particular, long been popular with leading politicians.

BELGRAVIA

Wilton Place, SW1, was constructed from 1824 to provide a link between Belgravia and Knightsbridge. Number 25 was the home of **George Bentham** (1800–1884) ①, one of the greatest systematic botanists England has produced. The nephew of the philosopher and jurist Jeremy Bentham, to whom he acted as secretary for a time, George spent many years in France – where he first became interested in botany – before settling back in England in 1826. Following his marriage to Sarah Brydges (d. 1881) in 1833, Bentham dedicated himself full-time to botany; under his auspices the Horticultural Society at Kew flourished, both scientifically and financially, and he was also active in the LINNEAN SOCIETY, serving as President in 1862–74. Having previously resided nearby at 91 Victoria Street, Bentham took a lease on 25 Wilton Place late in 1861 – three years earlier than the plaque's inscription suggests – and died here twenty-three years later. During this time, his daily routine was well established: he caught the train to the Royal Botanic Gardens at Kew, where he worked in the herbarium from ten until four in the afternoon; returning home he would write up his notes and dine quietly, seeing only intimate friends. The fruits of Bentham's labours during the years he lived here included the *Genera Plantarum* (1862–83), compiled with Sir Joseph Hooker, which gives a revised definition of every genus of flowering plant. It marked a new epoch in botanical studies, was a model of scientific accuracy and remains the standard classifica-

tion used by the world's botanists. Bentham's plaque – suggested by a serving botanical officer at Kew Gardens – went up in 1978.

In the year 2000 HRH The Prince of Wales unveiled a plaque at 2 Wilton Crescent, SW1, the residence from 1950 until their deaths of his great-uncle and great-aunt, the **Earl** (1900–1979) and **Countess Mountbatten of Burma** (1901–1960) ②, the last Viceroy and Vicereine of India (fig. 318). Born Prince Louis of Battenberg, Mountbatten abandoned his German title during the First World War and the family name was anglicised; to relations, he was known as 'Dickie'. Mountbatten followed his father into the Navy and took a leading part in the Second World War, serving from 1942 as Chief of Combined Operations. The apogee, but by no means the end, of his public service came in 1946, when he was appointed Viceroy of India to oversee the country's independence and, as it turned out, partition. The 1950s and 1960s saw Mountbatten become Admiral of the Fleet and Chief of Defence Staff, and he was still playing a role in public life when he was killed by an IRA bomb. Edwina Ashley, whom he married in 1922, was known for her wartime emergency relief and charitable work. Their marriage was a tempestuous one, but Mountbatten was devastated by her early death, which took place in Borneo while on an inspections tour for the St John Ambulance Brigade. The couple acquired 2 Wilton Crescent after their return from India in 1948, and made it their London home from 1950. Here, following his appointment as First Sea Lord in 1955, the Earl held working breakfasts with the Board of Admiralty, amid the many treasures that Lady Mountbatten had inherited from the Park Lane mansion of her grandfather, Sir Ernest Cassel. In the mid-1960s, Mountbatten moved into the mews property at the rear of Wilton Crescent – 2 Kinnerton Street – which remained his London address until his death. The plaque on 2 Wilton Crescent, which became part of the Singapore High Commission in 1969, was unveiled the day after the centenary of Mountbatten's birth.

The flamboyant French Renaissance style and monumental scale of Grosvenor Place, SW1, forms a dramatic contrast with the classical sobriety of the rest of Belgravia. Number 6, which lies on the corner with Halkin Street, was from 1878 to 1904 the residence of

318 HRH The Prince of Wales unveils a plaque at 2 Wilton Crescent in 2000. It was the residence from 1950 until their deaths of his great-uncle and great-aunt, the Earl and Countess Mountbatten of Burma. [Reproduced by permission of English Heritage]

B E L G R A V I A

319 The unveiling in 2005 of the plaque to Field Marshal Viscount Gort at 34 Belgrave Square. The ceremony was performed by Baron Hermann von Richthofen, a former German Ambassador in London, seen here (on the left) with Gort's grandson, Viscount De L'Isle. In the foreground are members of the Grenadier Guards, Gort's regiment. [© English Heritage. Photograph by Derek Kendall]

the Prime Minister **Sir Henry Campbell-Bannerman** (1836–1908) ❸ , for whom Ernest George and Harold Peto decorated the interior when he and his wife Charlotte (d. 1906) took up residence. Born in Glasgow, Campbell-Bannerman represented Stirling Burghs in Parliament from 1868 until his death, first achieving Cabinet rank under GLADSTONE as Secretary of State for War. He spent parliamentary sessions at number 6, but during the summer would sometimes decamp to the Lord Warden Hotel in Dover. Campbell-Bannerman's career blossomed while he lived in Grosvenor Place: he was elected Liberal leader in the Commons in 1899 and – after leaving Grosvenor Place and spending a brief period in Belgrave Square – moved to 10 Downing Street as Prime Minister in December 1905, at the age of sixty-nine. He was the first Prime Minister to officially bear that name, the formal title of the office having hitherto been First Lord of the Treasury. In early 1906 the Liberals were confirmed in office by a landslide election victory, though heart problems prompted 'C-B' to give up the premiership in April 1908, and he died less than three weeks later, while still in residence at 10 Downing Street. His period in office saw the foundations laid for House of Lords reform and the introduction of old-age pensions; a recent profile has denominated him 'Britain's first and only radical prime minister'.[1] Campbell-Bannerman's plaque was erected in 1959, having been proposed by the occupiers of an adjacent property, the Ladies' Carlton Club – a noble gesture given the club's strong links to the Conservative Party.

Belgrave Square, SW1, 'the great showpiece of Belgravia', was developed from 1826 to designs by GEORGE BASEVI, and is dominated by large stuccoed houses, many of which are now embassies, institutions or offices.[2] Despite its long connection with figures of note, the square boasts only one blue plaque: that at number 34 – part of the south-western terrace – to **Field Marshal Viscount Gort VC** (1886–1946) ❹ , the Commander-in-Chief at Dunkirk. Born John Standish Surtees Prendergast Vereker, Viscount Gort enjoyed an outstanding military career spanning both world wars. During the First World War, he was awarded the Victoria Cross for his remarkable bravery at the Canal du Nord in September 1918. In 1937 Gort was made Chief of the Imperial General Staff, and two years later was given command of the British Expeditionary Force in

France. His greatest achievement came in 1940, when – in defiance of his orders – he conducted the withdrawal of the BEF to Dunkirk. This paved the way for the legendary evacuation of nearly 340,000 British and French troops. Gort also masterminded the heroic defence of Malta in 1942 during the Second Siege, and proved an able diplomat in Gibraltar and Palestine. Number 34 Belgrave Square was Gort's London base from 1920 until 1926. He lived here with his wife – and second cousin – Corinna, née Vereker (1891–1940), known as 'Kotchy', and three children; their departure was prompted by the couple's divorce in 1925, following his wife's affair with an official from the nearby Spanish Embassy. Ironically, number 34 is now part of the German Embassy; the English Heritage plaque was unveiled in 2005 by Baron Hermann von Richthofen, a former German Ambassador in London and a friend of Gort's grandson, Viscount De L'Isle (fig. 319).

The first occupant of 37 Chesham Place, SW1, from 1841 to 1870, was **Lord John Russell**, **1st Earl Russell**

320 The plaque to Thomas Cubitt at 3 Lyall Street being unveiled by Lord Ashcombe, Cubitt's great-grandson, in 1959. [© Getty Images]

(1792–1878) **5** , twice Prime Minister, who came to prominence as the architect of the 1832 Reform Act. He moved to this newly built four-storey town house, which lies at the corner with Lowndes Place, in the year that he married his second wife, Lady Fanny Elliot (1815–1898), and was returned as one of the MPs for the City of London. The newly-weds were joined here by Russell's two daughters and four stepdaughters from his previous marriage to Adelaide, Lady Ribblesdale; John Russell (1842–1876), later Viscount Amberley, the eldest of his four children with Fanny, was born at the house. While at number 37, Russell occupied two of the highest offices in the land: Foreign Secretary (1852–53 and 1859–65) and Prime Minister (1846–52 and 1865–66). Among the liberal measures he promulgated as premier were the extension of poor relief provision in famine-hit Ireland and the imposition of a legal limit on the hours to be worked in factories. For his own part, as Lady Russell noted approvingly, her husband 'never but once worked after dinner . . . he always came up to the drawing room with us, was able to cast off public cares, and chat and laugh'.[3] In 1847 Russell accepted Queen Victoria's offer of the use of Pembroke Lodge in Richmond Park; this became his main residence, and it was there that he died. Lady Russell noted that the move 'obliged us to give up most dinner engagements in London and we regretted the . . . loss of society'.[4] Shortage of money caused Russell to let number 37 in 1857, and it was let again from 1870. He was created an earl in 1861; his grandson and eventual successor to the title was the philosopher BERTRAND RUSSELL. The blue plaque, bearing the LCC's wreathed border, was installed in 1911.

Lyall Street, SW1, was laid out in 1838 by the master builder **Thomas Cubitt** (1788–1855) **6** , who had his last London house and office at number 3 from 1847 to 1855. Born near Norwich, the son of a carpenter, Cubitt followed his father's trade before going into business as a building contractor in London with his brother, William. In 1824 he received an important commission for development of part of the Bedford estate in Bloomsbury, and went on to create Belgravia and Pimlico, the latter being known to contemporaries as 'Mr Cubitt's District'. While working from Lyall Street, he built two separate additions to Buckingham Palace (1846–50 and 1852–56); he had earlier worked on the remodelling (1845–48) of Osborne House on the Isle of

Wight, and Queen Victoria and Prince Albert commonly referred to him as 'our Cubitt'. Cubitt is known for his transformation of the building trade from the haphazard employment of a mass of individual craftsmen to the system of centralised contracting known today. In his working life, Cubitt was peripatetic: he would use a house in a developing street as his office, and moved premises about a dozen times in Belgravia alone. At 3 Lyall Street, his office was a large one, divided into Law Business, General Office and Confidential; the house then incorporated the adjacent property, now number 4, and the stables and workshops in the mews behind. Cubitt continued to work here until two months before his death, which took place at his Surrey home. The plaque was unveiled in 1959 by Lord Ashcombe, Cubitt's great-grandson and the President of the Cubitt Group of companies (fig. 320).

Eaton Place, SW1 – which takes its name from Eaton Hall, Cheshire, the ancestral home of the Grosvenor family – was laid out by THOMAS CUBITT (see above) between *c.* 1826 and 1850 and comprises a series of terraces, all in the classical tradition but with slight differences in style and material (see fig. 317). At 15 Eaton Place, an English Heritage plaque of 1996 commemo-

B E L G R A V I A

rates the London home from 1899 to 1907 of **Lord Kelvin** (1824 –1907) **7** , the physicist and inventor (fig. 321). Born William Thomson in Belfast, he was for over fifty years Professor of Natural Philosophy at the University of Glasgow; from his laboratory came a stream of epoch-making papers on heat, the movements of fluids and thermometric scales – he gave his name to that which measures absolute temperature. Kelvin's acquisition of number 15 as a London base was linked to his elevation in 1892 to the House of Lords. He attended debates quite regularly, speaking mostly on maritime matters, and served on an Admiralty committee on the design of battleships in 1904–5; he had once been a keen yachtsman, and a marine sounding device and a compass featured in his long list of patents. Kelvin was appointed to the Order of Merit and sworn of the Privy Council in 1902. Having relinquished his professorship at Glasgow in 1899, he was elected its Chancellor in 1904, and continued to publish papers at a prolific rate until his death at Netherhall, his Scottish country seat. Kelvin was buried in Westminster Abbey, alongside Isaac Newton.

The reformer **William Ewart** (1798–1869) **8** (see also pp. 585–6) was the first occupant of 16 Eaton Place, to which he moved early in 1830 after his marriage, and left eight years later for Rose Hill, Hampton, where he is also commemorated. This removal was prompted by the death of his wife, and first cousin, Mary, née Lee (1805–1837), who had given birth to five children in the preceding six years. On the death in September 1830 of his friend William Huskisson, Ewart was elected MP for Liverpool – his birthplace – and, bar a short spell out of the House in 1837–39, was an active parliamentarian until the year before his death. His career was distinguished by his progressive views: while resident in Eaton Place, Ewart succeeded in carrying a bill that abolished the penalty of hanging in chains, and another that did away with capital punishment for cattle stealing and sacrilege. He also began, in 1836, to become involved in the promotion of education and public libraries, which became a major part of his work thereafter. The plaque was originally erected in 1952 at 6 Cambridge Square, Paddington, Ewart's residence from 1843 until his death. When that building was demolished, the plaque was re-erected in its present location in August 1963 (see fig. 19), almost exactly a hundred years after Ewart had risen in the Commons to propose the founding of what became the blue plaques scheme (see p. 4 and pp. 9–10).

Number 29 Eaton Place was the birthplace of **Sir John Lubbock**, **Baron Avebury** (1834–1913) **9** (fig. 317), whose parents – Sir John William Lubbock (1803–1865), 3rd baronet, and Lady Harriet, née Hotham (d. 1873) – were among the earliest residents of Belgravia. Lubbock's long and distinguished career embraced the worlds of banking, politics, science and archaeology. He spent much of his early boyhood at Eaton Place prior to his father's inheritance of High Elms, Bromley, in 1840; a reported infant query, posed by the fireside – 'Where do burnt things go to?' – hinted at the line of critical inquiry that Lubbock carried into adult life.[5] He was the engine for important reforms of the banking system, and wrote numerous popular books on science. As a Liberal MP, he drafted the bill of 1871 that brought about the first secular bank holiday, then the first Monday in August and popularly called St Lubbock's Day. He was also President of the London Chamber of Commerce (1888–93), chaired the LCC (1890–92) and founded the organisation that

lowing year. Such was the range of his achievement that the council recommended that they should 'let the name speak for itself': hence the plaque features no descriptor.[6]

At 9 Upper Belgrave Street, SW1, an English Heritage plaque commemorates the residence of **Alfred, Lord Tennyson** (1809–1892) 🔟 , who was Poet Laureate from 1850 until his death (fig. 322). Tennyson's works, such as *In Memoriam* (1850) – written on the death of his close friend Arthur, son of HENRY HALLAM – *Maud, and Other Poems* (1855) and *Idylls of the King* (1859–85), drew deep at the well of High Victorian emotions. He is perhaps most readily associated with Farringford on the Isle of Wight, but he was no stranger to London; a private plaque records his residence at 15 Montpelier Row, Twickenham, TW1, while another of his homes in the capital – 225 Hampstead Road, near Euston – was marked by an LCC plaque from 1914 until its destruction during the Second World War. Number 9 Upper Belgrave Street was rented in 1880 and 1881; here, Tennyson lived with his wife Emily, née Sellwood (1813–1896), their son Hallam (1852–1928) – his father's secretary, and later Governor-General of Australia – and ten servants. It was while here that Tennyson was painted by JOHN MILLAIS, who reportedly regarded the portrait as among his finest; Tennyson, however, disliked it, while THOMAS HARDY, a visitor to Upper Belgrave Street, commented that the poet had 'a genial human face, which all his portraits belied'.[7] Tennyson told Hardy that he and his family spent a month or two every year in London – though he essentially disliked the capital – because they all 'got so rusty' on the Isle of Wight.[8] Despite the relative brevity of his connection with Upper Belgrave Street, it was felt that Tennyson's eminence was sufficient to justify commemoration of the house, and a plaque was erected in 1994.

322 Alfred, Lord Tennyson in an undated photograph by Barraud. On his lap is a copy of the *Odyssey of Homer*. [© The Rob Dickins Collection, Watts Gallery, Compton]

became the Electoral Reform Society. Lubbock was a conservationist too: when raised to the peerage in 1900 as Baron Avebury, he took his title from the Wiltshire prehistoric site that had featured in his campaign to preserve ancient monuments. His second wife was Alice Fox Pitt, daughter of his fellow archaeologist AUGUSTUS PITT-RIVERS. Proposed for commemoration in 1934, the centenary of his birth, Lubbock was honoured with a blue wreathed LCC plaque the fol-

Number 12 Upper Belgrave Street, one of a pair of stuccoed houses of *c.* 1830, was the residence from 1861 to 1870 of **Walter Bagehot** (1826–1877) 1️⃣1️⃣ , the writer, banker and economist. Today Bagehot is best remembered for *The English Constitution* (1867), which still influences interpretations of the role of the monarchy; originally published as nine essays in the *Fortnightly Review* in 1865–67, it was written while Bagehot was living at number 12. Bagehot – pronounced 'Baj-et', as if to trap the unwary – became editor in 1861 of *The Economist*, founded in 1843 by his father-in-law, James Wilson, and continued in the post until his death. This appointment – along with Bagehot's work for the London office of Stuckey's Bank, owned by his family – prompted his move from Cleveden, near Bristol, to Belgravia, where he lived with the family of his wife Eliza, née Wilson (d. 1921). His sister-in-law, Emilie Wilson (1841–1933), later Emilie Barrington, remembered how in Bagehot's company 'Ordinary conversation became extraordinarily stimulating', and that he was 'especially talkative at breakfast. It was flattering to hear him say that he found it more amusing to breakfast with his sisters-in-law than to join breakfast parties to which he was asked, given by Gladstone and other notable people'.[9] Bagehot himself entertained extensively in Upper Belgrave Street; during his time here he counted not only GLADSTONE, but also THACKERAY and MATTHEW ARNOLD among his friends, and stood unsuccessfully for Parliament three times. His GLC plaque – which is on the Wilton Street elevation – was proposed by Norman St John Stevas MP, who was then editing Bagehot's *Collected Works*. It was unveiled in 1967 by the then Prime Minister, Harold Wilson.

Henry Gray (1827–1861) **12** , the anatomist, lived and died at 8 Wilton Street, SW1, part of one of the earliest brick and stucco terraces in Belgravia, work on which started in *c*. 1813 (see fig. 41). Gray's early life is obscure: some authorities date his birth to 1825, while his place of birth – once thought to have been Wilton Street – is now more generally reckoned to have been Windsor. It has been established, however, that his father William Gray (1787–1834) was a messenger in the king's service, and that Gray lived in Wilton Street, at first with his parents, from about 1830 until his untimely death here thirty-one years later. While still a medical student, in 1848, he won a prize from the Royal College of Surgeons for a pioneering study of the eye. Gray was admitted a Fellow of the Royal Society at the age of just twenty-five, and held various surgical posts – including lecturer in anatomy – at St George's Hospital, London (see fig. 305). Gray's *Anatomy, Descriptive and Surgical*, notable for its fine illustrations and painstaking detail, was published in 1858 (fig. 323); perhaps no medical text has ever been so extensively used by medical students and surgeons. Gray was working on

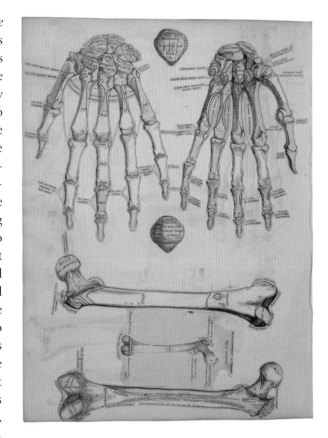

a second edition in 1861 when he became fatally ill with smallpox, contracted while attending the sickbed of his nephew. The plaque was first proposed in 1937, but the Second World War intervened and it was not erected until ten years later; it is one of only four surviving examples of the LCC's experimental brown series of plaques.

Eaton Square, SW1, was laid out from 1825, initially by THOMAS CUBITT, in the picturesque tradition established by John Nash in Regent's Park. An elongated oblong in shape, it is one of the most elegant 'squares' in London and has six official plaques. The Prime Minister **Stanley Baldwin**, **Earl Baldwin of Bewdley** (1867–1947) **13** has a GLC plaque at number 93, the centrepiece of a terrace of twenty by Cubitt, and the London house in which he lived the longest. On the face of it, Belgravia was an unlikely address for Baldwin, a Worcestershire man who successfully cultivated the image of a pipe-smoking, tweed-wearing countryman. His spell here began in 1912; the house was purchased to satisfy the aspiring Conservative politician's need for more reception rooms. During the years that followed, Baldwin's fortunes were in the ascendant; he became a junior minister at the Treasury in 1917, and it was at Eaton Square that the Prime Minister, ANDREW BONAR LAW, informed him of his appointment as Chancellor of the Exchequer in 1922. It was also while he was living here, in May 1923, that Baldwin first became Prime Minister, having assumed the leadership of the Conservative Party ahead of the more experienced Foreign Secretary, LORD CURZON, who famously derided his rival as 'a man of the utmost insignificance'.[10] Baldwin resigned as premier following the Conservatives' poor election showing that December – and briefly returned to live at number 93 – but went on to hold the highest office twice more, in 1924–29 and 1935–37. The property was sold not long after his second spell at 10 Downing Street began in November 1924. Latterly, Baldwin spent much time at his country home, Astley Hall, Worcestershire, though after his retirement in 1937 – in which year he was created Earl Baldwin of Bewdley – he took another house in Eaton Square: number 69.

A near contemporary and sometime political colleague of STANLEY BALDWIN was the statesman, Viceroy of India and Foreign Secretary **Edward Wood, 1st Earl of Halifax** (1881–1959) **14**, who inherited 88 Eaton Square in 1905; the house has since been incorporated into number 86. It remained the London residence of Halifax and his wife Dorothy (1885–1976) – daughter of the 4th Earl of Onslow – until the outbreak of the

Second World War; his family seat was at Hickleton, near Doncaster, Yorkshire. Halifax's public life began in 1910 with his election to Parliament, and culminated during England's darkest hour in 1940, when he became British Ambassador in Washington, a crucial posting at that critical juncture of the war; he saw the USA join the Allies in late 1941, and held the post until 1946. Halifax's efforts to cement Anglo-American relations won him admirers, as had his conduct as Viceroy of India (1926–31), in which capacity he presided over a turbulent period of resistance to British rule from the Indian National Congress. He had been raised to the peerage as Baron Irwin in 1925, inherited his father's viscountcy in 1934 and was created an earl in 1944. Halifax's plaque was suggested by his biographer, Andrew Roberts, and was unveiled in 1994 by Douglas Hurd, then Foreign Secretary, a position Halifax had held in 1938–40. In this capacity Halifax is inevitably associated with the ill-omened strategy of appeasing Hitler, as promoted by NEVILLE CHAMBERLAIN; recent historians have judged that he realised the folly of this policy sooner than many, and he has been credited with inspiring the firmer line taken by the government from early 1939.

George Peabody (1795–1869) **15**, the philanthropist, died at 80 Eaton Square on 4 November 1869, en route to the south of France for an intended recuperative holiday; his last words were, 'It is a great mystery, but I shall know all soon'.[11] Born in South Danvers (renamed Peabody in 1868), Massachusetts, George Peabody made his fortune trading in dry goods and settled in London in 1837. By the mid-1840s he was a successful merchant banker, specialising in American securities, and in 1854 took a new business partner, JUNIUS S. MORGAN, to whom Peabody handed over the company ten years later. By this time, the philanthropic work with which his name is still synonymous was well under way on both sides of the Atlantic. It was Lord Shaftesbury who persuaded him to direct his bounty towards the provision of better housing for the working classes and, by means of the Peabody Donation Fund – established in 1862 and today administered by the Peabody Trust – he applied much of his fortune to the construction of the estates that still bear his name (fig. 324); the first block of such housing was opened in Commercial Street, Spitalfields, in 1864. Peabody, a lifelong bachelor, occupied several houses

324 Peabody Square, Westminster, in a view of 1869. It was one of the many housing blocks built thanks to the philanthropy of George Peabody, who died at 80 Eaton Square. [© Illustrated London News Ltd / Mary Evans Picture Library]

BELGRAVIA

ENGLISH HERITAGE
VIVIEN
LEIGH
1913~1967
Actress
lived here

325   The English Heritage plaque to Vivien Leigh before its installation at 54 Eaton Square in 1996. [© English Heritage]

in the capital; that which bears the plaque was the home of his friend Sir Curtis Miranda Lampson (1806–1885), another American-born businessman. Peabody stayed here during the autumn of 1867 – when he sat in the back drawing room for the preliminary sketches for the statue of him that stands in Threadneedle Street, City of London – and during the spring of 1868. His final visit in the autumn of 1869 lasted four weeks. Number 80, part of a terrace built by CUBITT in 1841–55, is the only London address associated with Peabody that is known to survive; the plaque was erected in 1976 at the suggestion of a US cultural attaché.

At 54 Eaton Square, an English Heritage plaque commemorates the actress **Vivien Leigh** (1913–1967) **16**, who kept Flat D as her London base from 1958 until her death (fig. 325). Born Vivian [*sic*] Hartley in India, Leigh began acting professionally in her twenties, making her screen debut in *Things Are Looking Up* (1934) and signing a contract with the film director ALEXANDER KORDA in the following year. While

making *Fire Over England* (1937), she formed an intense relationship with her co-star, Sir Laurence Olivier, and the pair were married three years later. Leigh came to international attention for her Oscar-winning portrayal of Scarlett O'Hara in the film *Gone with the Wind* (1939) (fig. 326), a role that has somewhat overshadowed her reputation as an outstanding classical actress. At the time she moved to Eaton Square – alone, though she furnished a study for Olivier – she was still one of the most famous actresses in the world, but her private life was darkening. She was suffering from manic depression and her marriage was almost over; she and Olivier were divorced in 1960. Nonetheless, the last decade of Vivien's life continued to bring her acclaim as a star of stage and screen, particularly as the heroine of *The Roman Spring of Mrs Stone* (1961) and the rejected fading beauty in *Ship of Fools* (1965). By May 1967, the state of Leigh's health was such that she was rehearsing the Edward Albee play *A Delicate Balance* from her bed, where NoëL COWARD found her 'pale but lovely, and smoking, which she shouldn't have

326   An iconic film still from *Gone With the Wind* (1939), in which Vivien Leigh played Scarlett O'Hara. [© John Springer Collection / CORBIS]

been doing'.[12] She died of tuberculosis here a month later, with her beloved pet cat, Poo Jones, by her side, and a portrait of Olivier on her bedside table. Vivien Leigh was the first actress of her generation to be honoured under the blue plaques scheme. The home she shared with Olivier, Durham Cottage, 4 Christchurch Street, Chelsea, SW3, might have been preferred for commemoration had it not been screened from the roadway. So it was that a plaque at Eaton Square came to be unveiled by her close friend Sir John Mills in 1996, with Dame Diana Rigg and Vanessa Redgrave among those in attendance.

Number 44 Eaton Square – part of a block built in *c.* 1831–46 to the designs of Seth Smith – bears a GLC plaque commemorating the five-month stay of **Prince Metternich** (1773–1859) ⑰ , the Austrian statesman. Born in Koblenz, the son of a diplomat, Klemens Wenzel von Metternich rose quickly to public prominence, holding a series of senior diplomatic and political posts which culminated in his appointment as Chancellor in 1821. Made a Prince of the Austrian Empire in 1813, Metternich attended the Congress of Vienna – held in 1814–15, following the defeat of Napoleon – where he oversaw the formation of a European order that endured for many years. The Metternich system was, however, an oppressive and illiberal one, and in 1848 it collapsed in Europe-wide revolutionary movements. Its architect was forced to flee Vienna, and arrived in London in April. Metternich moved to Eaton Square on 6 May 1848, taking a four-month lease on number 44 from the Earl of Denbigh; it was, wrote Metternich's third wife Melanie (1805–1854), 'très-jolie, mais horriblement chère'.[13] Metternich liked England, which he thought 'the freest country in the world because it is the most orderly', and was astounded at the growth of London, which he had last visited almost half a century before.[14] At Eaton Square, his visitors included the Duke of Wellington, Lord Aberdeen and the rising political star Benjamin Disraeli, a particular admirer. Queen Victoria and Prince Albert, who apparently blamed Metternich's predicament on his own intransigence, steered clear, much to his chagrin: to his fellow exile François Guizot, whom he encountered on the steps of the British Museum, he declared – apropos their shared predicament – 'Error has not come into my mind'.[15] Metternich left Eaton Square in September 1848, and lived successively in Brighton and Richmond before returning to the Continent in October of the following year.

At 37 Eaton Square, a plaque commemorates the residence from 1923 to 1935 of the Prime Minister **Neville Chamberlain** (1869–1940) ⑱ (see fig. 1); apart from Downing Street, this was his only permanent London residence. Born in Birmingham, the son of Joseph Chamberlain, he enjoyed a long career in business, and became active in local government soon after his marriage in 1911 to Anne Vere Cole (1883–1967). Chosen as Lord Mayor of Birmingham in 1915, he was elected to Parliament in 1918, at the age of forty-nine. Chamberlain's rise thereafter was rapid, though his prevarication over buying a London home was due partly to a certain diffidence about national politics. He served in the Conservative ministries of Stanley Baldwin as Minister of Health in 1923 and again in 1924–29; having briefly been made Chancellor of the Exchequer in August 1923 – just as he was moving into number 37 – he held the office again from 1931 to 1937. Both posts allowed him to give practical expression to his concern with social reform, but the achievements of these years have been overshadowed by his reputation as the Prime Minister who appeased Hitler. His elevation to the highest office took place in 1937, two years after he moved from Eaton Square, and he resigned three years later – following the unsuccessful Norway campaign – to be succeeded by Winston Churchill. When, in 1962, Chamberlain, Ramsay MacDonald and Rufus Isaacs were proposed for commemoration, an LCC historian ventured that this would be premature, given that 'the merits of their various policies are still very much a matter of controversy'.[16] These concerns were evidently set aside, as all three were approved for commemoration; a blue plaque to Chamberlain was erected later that year. Owing to restoration works, the plaque only became visible in 1963, when – on the ninety-fourth anniversary of Chamberlain's birth – it was unveiled.

Number 16 South Eaton Place, SW1, forms part of a row of stucco houses dating from the 1830s, although its added attic storey marks it out from its neighbours. The house bears two blue plaques to complementary and associated figures (fig. 327), the earliest commemorating **Viscount Cecil of Chelwood** (1864–1958) ⑲ ,

BELGRAVIA

327 Number 16 South Eaton Place and its plaques to Viscount Cecil of Chelwood and Philip Noel-Baker, installed by the GLC and English Heritage respectively. [© English Heritage. Photograph by Derek Kendall]

better known as Lord Robert Cecil, who was instrumental in creating the League of Nations. Edgar Algernon Robert Cecil – to give him his full name – lived here from 1922 until the time of his death in Kent; it was the last and most fashionable London house occupied by the Viscount and his wife, Lady Eleanor, née Lambton (1868–1959). The son of the 3rd MARQUESS OF SALISBURY, the Conservative Prime Minister, Robert Cecil served as his father's private secretary and, perhaps inevitably, entered Parliament in 1906. Early in the First World War, his service with the Red Cross in France persuaded him that the prevention of armed conflict was 'the only political object worth while'.[17] As a junior foreign minister in the wartime coalition government from 1915 – with a Cabinet seat as Minister of Blockade in 1916–18 – Cecil was one of the first leading politicians to support the premise of a 'league of nations' to promote peace and international understanding. After the First World War he helped to bring the idea into being, serving as adviser to Britain's delegation at the Paris peace conference; there, he played a vital part in establishing the League of Nations, which was constituted by the first part of

the Treaty of Versailles, signed in June 1919. Cecil – who was awarded a viscountcy in 1923, and later won the Nobel Peace Prize (1937) – also took an active and prominent role in a supporter organisation, the League of Nations Union; by 1931 this had more than 400,000 members. For all that it promised, the league could not prevent the outbreak of the Second World War, and at its final session in 1946 Cecil declaimed, 'The League is dead; long live the United Nations'.[18] The plaque was proposed by PHILIP NOEL-BAKER, and was unveiled by him in 1976 on what was then his own house.

The second plaque at 16 South Eaton Place (see fig. 327) commemorates **Philip Noel-Baker** (1889–1982) [20], the Olympic sportsman and campaigner for peace and disarmament, who took over the lease following the death of VISCOUNT CECIL. Noel-Baker lived at nearby 43 South Eaton Place from the 1920s, and had resided at number 16 with his friend Cecil – to whom he acted as private secretary for a time – since the time of the Second World War. Among Cecil's bequests to Noel-Baker were his favourite chair; he had judged that the younger man possessed 'almost every intellectual gift

international relations. During the 1920s Noel-Baker – who adopted the additional surname following his 1915 marriage to Irene Noel – held a chair in international relations at the University of London and was involved in the work of the League of Nations. Having been elected to Parliament in 1929, he went on to hold several ministerial portfolios in the post-war Labour government, including Secretary of State for Commonwealth Relations (1947–50). In 1959, a year after the publication of his most famous book, *The Arms Race: A Programme for World Disarmament*, Noel-Baker was awarded the Nobel Peace Prize. Ennobled in 1977, he died at number 16 five years later. Noel-Baker is given his more familiar designation as a commoner on the plaque, which was erected in 1992 below that which honours Cecil.

Chester Square, SW1, a dignified series of stucco terraces, was built between *c.* 1832 and the late 1840s as an afterthought to the 'grand design' of Belgravia. At number 2, a house reflecting the relatively modest means of its occupant, lived **Matthew Arnold** (1822–1888) **21** , the poet and critic (fig. 328). Arnold had no fixed abode in the capital until he moved here in late 1858 with his wife Frances Lucy (1825–1901), known as 'Flu', and their family; he wrote that the house was 'a very small one, but it will be something to unpack one's portmanteau for the first time since I was married, now nearly seven years ago'.[20] The place was, he told his sister, 'delightful inside, and very pleasant to return to, though at present I cannot quite forgive it for not being twenty miles out of London'.[21] By the time he moved here, Arnold was already a noted poet: his first verse collection, '*The Strayed Reveller', and Other Poems*, had been published in 1849, and was followed by successes such as 'Dover Beach'. His long poem 'Empedocles on Etna', withdrawn from print in 1852, was finally published fifteen years later. Arnold – who subsidised his literary efforts with work as an Inspector of Schools between 1851 and 1886 – ventured into the field of literary criticism with *On Translating Homer* (1861), a tilt at the pedantry and antiquarianism he regarded as rife in academia. While living in Eaton Square, he had great success with the collection *Essays in Criticism* (1865), a landmark of its genre, and was also a noted social and religious critic, producing his best-known work, *Culture and Anarchy*, in 1869. Arnold left 'the dear little house' in Chester Square in

328 The LCC plaque to Matthew Arnold at 2 Chester Square, a house which he considered to be 'very small'. [© English Heritage. Photograph by Derek Kendall]

that a politician can desire coupled with unsparing devotion to the cause of peace'.[19] Born Philip John Baker in Brondesbury Park, West London, he was a finalist in the 1912 Olympics and, in 1920, was Captain of the British Olympic team and a silver medallist in the 1,500-metre race; he retained a profound belief in the positive role that sport could play in fostering good

March 1868 for Harrow, in pursuit of better schooling for his sons.[22] Commemoration of number 2 was proposed by the LCC in 1908 but, as the then owner of the building disliked plaques, Arnold was honoured only in 1954.

The author of *Frankenstein*, **Mary Shelley** (1797–1851) ㉒ , lived at 24 Chester Square – a location far removed from her radical roots – from 1846 until her death, the most prosperous if not the most productive years of her life. The daughter of two writers – the champion of women's rights Mary Wollstonecraft and the political philosopher William Godwin – Mary was accounted by her father 'singularly bold, somewhat imperious, and active of mind'.[23] In 1814 she met and fell in love with the poet PERCY BYSSHE SHELLEY, who left his wife for Mary; the couple were married in London two years later. Much of their life together was spent in Italy and Switzerland; it was in Geneva, at the age of just nineteen, that she wrote her masterpiece, *Frankenstein* (published 1818), one of the classics of English literature and the subject of numerous screen adaptations. After Shelley's death in a sailing accident in 1822, Mary returned to England, where she published other, less successful novels, and edited and helped to popularise her late husband's works. In 1845 she purchased number 24, and early the following year became the house's first resident; it was acquired in order to introduce her son Percy (1819–1889) – the heir to the Shelley baronetcy and estates – into society, though Mary spent much time at the family's country estate, Field Place, Sussex. They moved here from Putney, where Mary had been 'seized with a nervous rheumatism of a distressing kind'.[24] Chester Square provided little in the way of respite; in August 1846 she wrote from a German spa town, 'The very thought of that place makes me ill . . . if Chester Sq – were burned down I believe I should get well but it lies like a Million lb. weight round my neck'.[25] Mary Shelley recovered her health and spirits sufficiently to restart work on a biography of her husband, but further bouts of ill-health put paid to its completion, and she died here of a brain tumour. A plaque was first suggested in 1975, but the house was then being used as a vicarage, and concerns were raised at the prospect of having the word Frankenstein 'emblazoned' on it, the preferred wording being 'Author and Wife of the Poet, Percy Bysshe Shelley'.[26] The GLC refused to give way, and so

a private plaque was erected instead. In 2003 this was replaced with an English Heritage blue plaque, unveiled by Mary's biographer, Miranda Seymour.

Grosvenor Gardens, SW1, in the French Renaissance style, was laid out in the 1860s on ground to the northwest of the Grosvenor Hotel, adjacent to Victoria Station. From 1886 until 1895, number 4 was the home of the anthropologist and archaeologist **Lieutenant General Augustus Henry Lane Fox Pitt-Rivers** (1827–1900) ㉓ . Born Augustus Henry Lane Fox, Pitt-Rivers owed his fortune – and the name by which he is usually known – to an enormous inheritance from his cousin Horace Pitt, 6th Baron Rivers, who died in 1880. This enabled him to exchange a house in Earls Court for a mansion in Belgravia – which he did with alacrity – and provided the resources for the excavations he carried out over the succeeding twenty years. Pitt-Rivers's interest in archaeology had begun in the 1860s while he was in the Army. During the 1870s he and his son-in-law – SIR JOHN LUBBOCK, later Lord Avebury – introduced legislation that resulted in the Ancient Monuments Protection Act of 1882; Pitt-Rivers was the first holder of the office of Inspector of Ancient Monuments, and transacted much of his official business at Grosvenor Gardens. His extensive collection of ethnographic material formed the core of the Pitt Rivers Museum in Oxford, which opened in 1884, and his archaeological fieldwork set the pattern for modern excavation methods and techniques. Less enduring have been his attempts to apply the evolutionary theories of CHARLES DARWIN to the development of culture and society. In the 1890s Pitt-Rivers spent more time at his Wiltshire seat of Rushmore, and let 4 Grosvenor Gardens; one tenant was VISCOUNT WOLSELEY, who gave up the lease early following Pitt-Rivers's objections to his proposal to sub-let the house. The plaque was unveiled in 1983 by a descendant, Michael Pitt-Rivers.

Distinguished by its tall dome and mansard roof, 32 Grosvenor Gardens was the appropriately exuberant London residence of the lawyer and statesman **F. E. Smith**, **1st Earl of Birkenhead** (1872–1930) ㉔ . He lived here – with the exception of a spell during the First World War, when he lent the property to the American Red Cross – from 1913 until his death seventeen years later, together with his wife, Margaret, née

329 Ian Fleming in a portrait by Cecil Beaton, October 1962. It was earlier in his life – before the Second World War – that he lived at 22B Ebury Street. [Courtesy of the Cecil Beaton Studio Archive at Sotheby's]

Gardens', before leaving abruptly to catch a train.[28] At the unveiling of the plaque, his son – Frederick, 2nd Earl of Birkenhead (1907–1975) – recalled that number 32 'was a most impracticable house . . . my father took it because there was a huge room on the first floor large enough to take his books'. Apparently, the authorities 'made a big fuss' when 'F. E.' installed a bath in the corner of his bedroom, behind a screen.[29] The plaque was erected by the LCC in February 1959, within days of that to CAMPBELL-BANNERMAN.

Ebury Street, SW1, was built up mainly in the early nineteenth century on the site of Ebury Farm and is architecturally one of the less distinguished streets in Belgravia. It does, however, contain one of the area's most idiosyncratic buildings, the Greek Revival number 22, built in 1830 as Pimlico Grammar School, to designs by J. P. Gandy Deering, and later used as a literary institute. Following its conversion into flats, the apartment denominated 22B Ebury Street became the residence of **Ian Fleming** (1908–1964) **25** , the creator of James Bond (figs 329 and 331). Fleming took over the lease in late 1936, while he was working as a stockbroker in the City. His overbearing mother considered his choice of residence 'stupid', but Fleming set about transforming the apartment into a suitably louche setting in which to entertain his gang of Old Etonian men about town, known as 'Le Cercle Gastronomique et des Jeux de Hasard', and his numerous girlfriends.[30] The living room, converted from the top half of the chapel-like interior, was painted grey; concealed lighting was installed, a lavatory was fitted into an alcove, and the gallery above was converted into the bedroom; perhaps fortunately, his plans to feature an autobiographical diorama never came to fruition. Fleming, who served with the Naval Intelligence Division during the Second World War, was obliged to move out of Ebury Street during the Blitz as the roof skylight – despite his having had it glazed dark blue – did not conform to blackout restrictions; he stayed at clubs and hotels until settling in late 1941 in a flat at Athenaeum Court (now the Athenaeum Hotel), 116 Piccadilly, W1. 'So the orchid has left the orchid house', remarked the writer Peter Quennell.[31] The plaque was unveiled in 1996 by Desmond Llewellyn, Q in so many Bond films, having first been suggested by Fleming's brother Peter, also a writer, and revived by his nephew Nicholas. Consent had been withheld by the owners of

Furneaux (1878–1968) and their children. Frederick Edwin Smith – often known simply as 'F. E.' – was one of the most successful barristers of his time, known particularly for his successful defence of Ethel le Neve, mistress of the murderer Dr Crippen, and renowned for his maverick approach to public life. As Attorney-General from 1915 to 1919, he was responsible for the prosecution for treason of Sir Roger Casement and, as Lord Chancellor from 1919 to 1922, he made a name for himself as a legal reformer. 'F. E.' took the title of Baron Birkenhead from his birthplace, and was elevated to an earldom in 1922. STANLEY BALDWIN made him Secretary of State for India two years later, but he left politics in 1928, being unable to support his lavish lifestyle on a minister's salary: according to WINSTON CHURCHILL, 'He burned all his candles at both ends'.[27] Smith was noted for his wit: after a long and boring introduction at one public meeting, concluded with the words 'Mr Smith will now give his address', he is supposed to have stood up and announced '32, Grosvenor

B E L G R A V I A

the first address chosen for commemoration – 16 Victoria Square, SW1 – which was Fleming's London home from 1952, the year of his marriage to Ann Rothermere, until his death. It was during this later period that the series of fourteen Bond books – beginning with *Casino Royale* (1953) and ending with *Octopussy and The Living Daylights* (1966) – were written.

Number 109 Ebury Street was the childhood home of **Dame Edith Evans** (1888–1976) 26 , the actress. She was born at the now-vanished 12 Ebury Square and moved in 1890 to 109 Ebury Street with her parents – Edward and Caroline Evans – living here until around 1912; in that year, she made her professional stage debut for the producer William Poel in a production of the sixth-century Hindu classic, *Sakuntala*. Prior to this, Edith had attended the nearby St Michael's Church of England School, Chester Square, and had been apprenticed to a milliner, Mr Blackaller, in Buckingham Palace Road. She made her amateur debut – playing Viola in *Twelfth Night* – in October 1910. The daughter of a minor public servant, Edith was brought up in a household unmarked by either privilege or privation: she recalled that, 'I always had a bedroom to myself'.[32] Next door, at number 111, lived the young NOËL COWARD, whose mother ran a boarding-house; Edith's mother decided to follow suit, prompting the actress's recollection that 'the lodgers seemed happy enough but it was a hell of a hard job'.[33] Evans, who was appointed DBE in 1946, enjoyed an exceptionally long and successful career, appearing on stage and screen until the mid-1970s. She is perhaps most widely remembered for her incredulous enunciation of two words – 'a Handbag!' – as Lady Bracknell in the stage (1939) and film (1952) productions of WILDE's *The Importance of Being Earnest*, an association that she came to abhor. Dame Edith was honoured with a plaque unveiled in 1997 by Sir John Gielgud, in the presence of a phalanx of stage and screen luminaries.

One who early spotted the talent of EDITH EVANS – and, being somewhat smitten, secured her an engagement at the Royalty Theatre in Dean Street, Soho – was her neighbour **George Moore** (1852–1933) 27 , the author. He moved by April 1911 to the early nineteenth-century terraced house at 121 Ebury Street (fig. 330); a 'little hole in which to carry on my authorship', as he called it.[34] Geographically it placed him close to his

artistic friends in Chelsea, such as PHILIP WILSON STEER and Henry Tonks, for whom he sat for a portrait in Ebury Street. It was also handy for visits to his lover Maud Cunard, the society hostess, who lived in Grosvenor Square. Born in County Mayo, Moore studied art before turning to writing, a move prompted partly by a meeting in Paris with EMILE ZOLA. His attempts to introduce naturalism into English literature bore fruit in works such as *A Mummer's Wife* (1885). Moore spent the first decade of the century living in Dublin but, disappointed in his hopes of leading the Irish literary revival, he returned to live permanently in London and died at his house in Ebury Street. A prolific man of letters, he completed some dozen works while living here, including the

364

331   The English Heritage plaque to Ian Fleming at 22 Ebury Street, built in 1830 as Pimlico Grammar School and subsequently converted into flats. [© English Heritage. Photograph by Derek Kendall]

three volumes of his autobiography, *Hail and Farewell* (1911–14), the novel *The Brook Kerith* (1916) and a volume of literary criticism with the appropriate title of *Conversations in Ebury Street* (1924). Moore was accustomed to write in the dining room on the ground floor; he had the front bay window put in for better light, though its external appearance did not accord with his intentions. Next to it, his plaque was erected by the LCC in 1937, replacing one the council had put up the previous year that erroneously gave his birth year as 1851 and that described him, incompletely, as a novelist.

One of the earliest houses in Belgravia, 180 Ebury Street dates from around the 1720s; under the more bucolic street name of Five Fields Row, it was the residence for several weeks in 1764 of **Wolfgang Amadeus Mozart** (1756–1791) 28 . As the plaque records, the eight-year-old musical prodigy composed his first symphony here. Mozart, his father Leopold (1719–1787) and his elder sister Maria Anna (1751–1829), known as 'Nannerl', were in London on a European grand tour. This then semi-rural lodging, owned by a Dr Randal, was chosen as a suitable place for Leopold Mozart's convalescence after a minor illness had been exacerbated by medical intervention, and he moved his family here on 6 August. To expedite his recovery, no instrument could be played in the house: so it was that, in the words of his sister, 'in order to occupy himself, Mozart composed his first symphony for all the instruments of the orchestra, especially for trumpets and kettledrums'.[35] It seems that the work she referred to is lost, but the symphony now known as Mozart's first (K.16 in E flat major) was also written at this time, being one of the precocious works aired at the Haymarket Little Theatre in February 1765. Not long after this, Queen Charlotte gave the boy composer – who had made himself quite a favourite at court – a much-needed present of fifty guineas, having been presented with an engraved edition of six sonatas. Following Leopold Mozart's recovery, the family moved back to central London in September 1764, when they took lodgings at 20 Frith Street, Soho. There they remained until leaving England in July 1765; Leopold Mozart, a musician and teacher, regarded the country as a godless, expensive, culinary wasteland, and particu-

larly deplored the English habit of 'guzzling solidified fat', by which he presumably meant dripping.[36] After 20 Frith Street was dismissed as unsuitable for commemoration due to substantial rebuilding, a sepia brown tablet with cream lettering – the first of a new series with a simplified design (see pp. 27–8) – was installed by the LCC in Ebury Street in 1939. The plaque was re-erected in 1951, following war damage.

In 1914, 180 and 182 Ebury Street were combined into one house by the architect EDWIN LUTYENS and occupied by **Harold Nicolson** (1886–1968) and **Vita Sackville-West** (1892–1962) 29 , the writers and gardeners; the house belonged to Vita's mother, Victoria, Lady Sackville (1862–1936). It was here – and at their country retreat, Long Barn, Kent – that both husband and wife laid the foundations of their literary careers, Harold with *Paul Verlaine* (1921) – the first of his six literary biographies – and Vita with her first novel, *Heritage* (1919), and the poem *The Land* (1926). 'I became quite sociable', Vita later recalled, and reckoned this time 'the only period in my life when I achieved anything like popularity'.[37] Following the First World War, their marriage nearly foundered on the rock of Vita's infatuation for fellow writer Violet Trefusis, and in 1922 VIRGINIA WOOLF first dined at Ebury Street, beginning her long intimacy with Vita. Harold likewise strayed into homosexual affairs, but by the time the couple ceased their intermittent residence at Ebury Street in 1927 their relationship had turned to one of affectionate companionship, the fruits of which would be the creation of one of the most influential gardens of the twentieth century at Sissinghurst Castle, Kent, their home from 1930. Harold, who had a later career in politics, described Ebury Street as being 'rather stern and prim and quiet', though his wife thought it was haunted, having once felt 'a warm feminine hand close gently over her own as it rested on the banister rail'.[38] Lutyens's garden dining room and other additions were destroyed by bombing in 1941, and the two houses are now once more separated. The couple's son, the writer Nigel Nicolson (1917–2004), who was born here, unveiled the English Heritage plaque in 1993; it was specially coloured brown to match the one to MOZART next door (see fig. 42).

NOTES

1   *ODNB*, vol. III, p. 718

2   Simon Bradley and Nikolaus Pevsner, *The Buildings of England, London 6: Westminster* (New Haven and London, 2003), p. 739

3   Sir Spencer Walpole, *Life of Lord John Russell*, vol. I (London, 1889), p. 434

4   Ibid, p. 449

5   Horace G. Hutchinson, *Life of Sir John Lubbock* (London, 1914), p. 6

6   Report of 1 May 1934 on blue plaque file.

7   F. E. Hardy, *The Early Life of Thomas Hardy* (London, 1928), p. 178

8   Charles Tennyson, *Alfred Tennyson* (London, 1950), p. 449

9   Emilie Isabel Barrington, *Life of Walter Bagehot* (London, 1914), p. 354 and p. 357

10   *DNB*, 1941–50 (Oxford, 1959), p. 44

11   Franklin Parker, *George Peabody* (Nashville, 1971), p. 181

12   *The Noël Coward Diaries*, eds Graham Payn and Sheridan Morley (London, 1982), p. 651 (2 July 1967)

13   *Mémoires, documents et écrits divers laissés par le prince de Metternich*, eds A. Klinkowstroem, C. L. W. Metternich-Winneburg and R. C. J. L. H. Metternich-Winneburg, vol. VIII (Paris, 1884), p. 19

14   Arthur Herman, *Metternich* (London, 1932), p. 380

15   Alan Palmer, *Metternich* (London, 1972), p. 317

16   Report of 3 July 1962 on blue plaque file.

17   Viscount Cecil, *A Great Experiment* (London, 1941), p. 189

18   Viscount Cecil, *All the Way* (London, 1949), p. 240

19   Cecil, *A Great Experiment*, p. 105

20   George Saintsbury, *Matthew Arnold* (Edinburgh, 1899), p. 71

21   *Letters of Matthew Arnold*, ed. George W. E. Russell, vol. I (London, 1895), p. 76 (4 November 1858)

22   Ibid, p. 239

23   *ODNB*, vol. L, p. 194

24   *Letters of Mary Wollstonecraft Shelley*, ed. Betty T. Bennett, vol. III (London and Baltimore, 1988), pp. 285–86 (May/June 1846)

25   Ibid, pp. 292–93 (25 August 1846)

26   Letter of 17 October 1975 on blue plaque file.

27   W. S. Churchill, *Great Contemporaries* (London, 1937), p. 183

28   John Campbell, *F. E. Smith, First Earl of Birkenhead* (London, 1981), p. 260

29   *Evening Standard*, 18 February 1959

30   John Pearson, *The Life of Ian Fleming* (London, 1966), p. 75

31   Andrew Lycett, *Ian Fleming* (London, 1995), p. 123

32   Bryan Forbes, *Ned's Girl* (London, 1977), p. 7

33   Charles Castle, *Noël* (London, 1972), pp. 35–36

34   Joseph Hone, *The Life of George Moore* (London, 1936), p. 364

35   H. C. Robbins Landon, *The Mozart Essays* (London, 1995), p. 82

36   Ruth Halliwell, *The Mozart Family* (Oxford, 1990), p. 91

37   Victoria Glendinning, *Vita: The Life of Vita Sackville-West* (London, 1983), p. 74

38   *Vita and Harold: The Letters of Vita Sackville-West and Harold Nicolson*, ed. Nigel Nicolson (London, 1992), p. 57 (22 May 1916); Nigel Nicolson, 'The Ghosts of Ebury Street', *The Spectator*, 29 May 1993

332 A view south along Craven Street, showing the bronze LCC plaques to Benjamin Franklin (at number 36) and Heinrich Heine (at number 32). [© English Heritage. Photograph by Derek Kendall]

COVENT GARDEN, THE STRAND AND THE ADELPHI

The Strand – on the north bank of the River Thames – has long formed a significant part of the route between the cities of London and Westminster, and from the thirteenth to the seventeenth centuries was a prestigious place of residence for churchmen, aristocrats and courtiers. Of the many great houses that formerly graced the thoroughfare, the last survivor was Northumberland House (see fig. 9), controversially demolished in 1874. The area to the north of the Strand – land that once belonged to the abbey (or convent) of St Peter at Westminster – was developed as Covent Garden in 1629–37, to designs by Inigo Jones. Based around an Italianate piazza, with a church on its west side, Covent Garden was – and still is – one of London's liveliest districts. Noted for its coffee-houses, taverns, lodging-houses and theatres, the area was especially popular with artists, writers and dramatists, a fact reflected by its plaques, an unusually high number of which commemorate groups rather than individuals. Above all, Covent Garden is associated with its market. Once the largest fruit and vegetable market in England, it had overwhelmed the residential character of the area by the early nineteenth century; the market house, constructed in 1828–30, served its original function until the market moved to Nine Elms, Battersea, in 1974. Its rescue and subsequent conversion to commercial units has been acknowledged as a triumph of conservation.

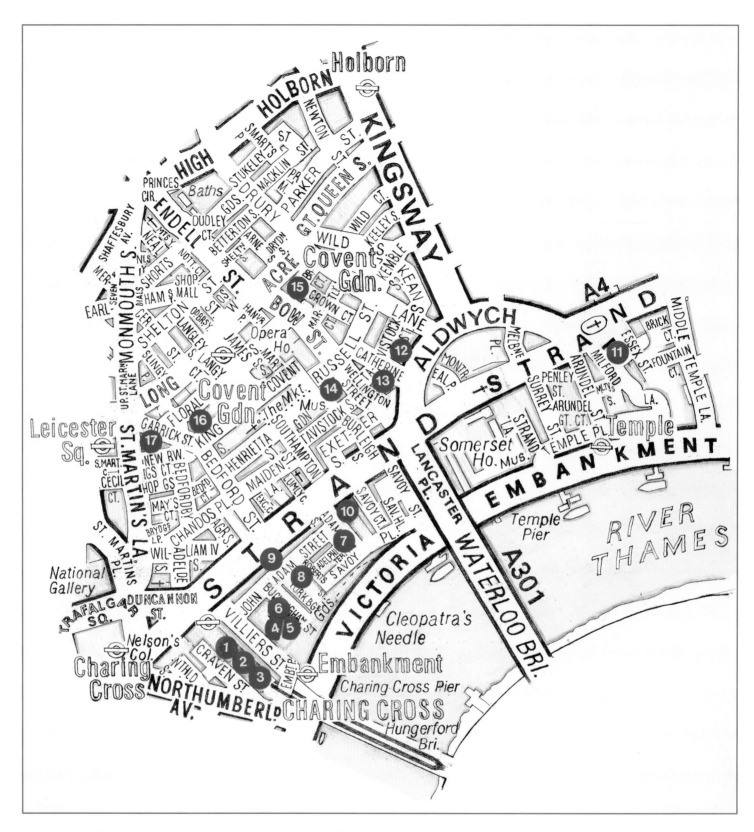

COVENT GARDEN, THE STRAND
AND THE ADELPHI

THE STRAND AND THE ADELPHI

Craven Street, WC2, was created by the Hon. William Craven from 1730, and today stands in the shadow of Charing Cross Station, built in 1863–65. By the time of the station's construction, the street had become noted in particular for its lodging-houses. Perhaps its most famous overseas resident was **Benjamin Franklin** (1706–1790) ➊, the American statesman, writer and scientist, who lodged at 36 (formerly 7 and later 27) Craven Street, a house of 1732–33 (fig. 332). Born in Boston, Massachussetts, Franklin trained as a printer and by the 1730s had become a highly successful writer and newspaperman. Meanwhile, he developed his scientific interests, which led him to retire from printing in 1748; Franklin's work on electricity and his many inventions – including bifocal glasses and the lightning rod – earned him international acclaim. He was also active in the political arena, chiefly in Pennsylvania, where he lived from the 1720s. It was diplomatic work that took Franklin to London for two vital periods: 1757–62 and 1764–75. During these years, as agent of the Pennsylvania Assembly, Franklin encouraged pro-American sympathies, continued his scientific experiments, mixed in circles that included JAMES BOSWELL and JOSEPH PRIESTLEY, and was active as a writer. Following his return to Philadelphia, he assisted in the preparation of the Declaration of Independence of 1776 and later became President of Pennsylvania (1885–88). Franklin's years in London were spent at two addresses in Craven Street; the most significant of these, then numbered 7, was a lodging-house run by Margaret Stevenson. Here, in 1757–62 and 1764–72, Franklin occupied four comfortable rooms shared with his son and assistant, William ('Billy') (1730/1–1813) – later Governor of New Jersey – and their two slaves, Peter and King. Franklin was amazed by the 'dearness of living' in the capital and in 1758 wrote to his wife, 'The whole Town is one great smoky House, and every Street a Chimney, the Air full of floating Sea Coal Soot'.[1] In October 1772 he – and Mrs Stevenson – moved to 1 Craven Street (demolished), which was his home until his return to America three years later. Franklin was first commemorated in 1869, when the Society of Arts installed a plaque at 7 Craven Street. However, research carried out by SIR LAURENCE GOMME showed that this identification was incorrect: the number 7 in which Franklin had resided had later become number 36. The LCC marked the latter (correct) house with a bronze plaque in 1914; for a short time, until the demolition of number 7, the two plaques to Franklin rather embarrassingly stood on opposite sides of the street. Number 36 has since been restored and was opened to the public as the Benjamin Franklin House on 17 January 2006, the 300th anniversary of his birth.

A few doors away, at 32 Craven Street, a similar bronze LCC plaque records the stay of **Heinrich Heine** (1799–1856) ➋, the German poet and essayist (see figs 37 and 332). Heine was born in Düsseldorf into a Jewish family, and studied law before turning to a career in literature. His first collection of poems appeared in 1821, and he had particular success with *Buch der Lieder* (Book of Songs; 1827), published two years after his conversion to Protestantism. Heine's poetry inspired composers such as Schumann, Mendelssohn and Wagner, though his works – like others of the Young Germany movement – were banned in his homeland in the mid-1830s. The writer had long wished to see London, but his sole visit to the capital – from April to early August 1827 – was not a success, due largely to Heine's weakened state of mind and body. In a letter of 23 April, written from his rooms at number 32, Heine complained of the dearness of living and of there being 'nothing but fog, coal-smoke, poets and Canning'.[2] 'It is so fearfully damp and uncomfortable here', he wrote, 'and no one understands me, and no one understands German'.[3] Recalling his experiences in 'English Fragments', part of the fourth volume of *Reisebilder* (Travel Pictures; 1831), Heine stated, 'Send a philosopher to London: but, on pain of your life, not a poet! . . . The mere seriousness of everything, the colossal uniformity, the machine-like movement, the shrillness even of joy – this over-driven London oppresses fancy and rends the heart'.[4] Thinking perhaps of Craven Street, he continued, 'I expected great palaces and saw nothing but little houses. But the very monotony of them, and the infinite number of them, make a powerful impression'.[5] In 1831 Heine settled in Paris, where he became a major literary figure, renowned for such works as *Französische Zustände* (Conditions in France; 1833) and *Atta Troll* (1847); he died there at the age of fifty-eight. His plaque was erected in 1912, a subscription to cover its cost having been raised by interested locals.

COVENT GARDEN, STRAND, ADELPHI

At 25 Craven Street, an end-of-terrace house of 1791–92, a plaque records the stay of another overseas visitor, **Herman Melville** (1819–1891) ❸ , the author of *Moby Dick*. Born in New York, Melville spent much of his early life at sea; it was his experiences in the Pacific, where he sailed on board the whaler *Acushnet* in 1841, that formed the basis of many of his works, including *Typee* (1846) and *Omoo* (1847). Melville came to London in autumn 1849 to secure a publishing deal for his new novel *White-Jacket, or, the World in a Man-of-War* (1850), and to gather material for an account of the American revolutionary Israel Potter (published 1855). Living in cheap lodgings in Craven Street on 6–27 November and 13–25 December 1849 – stays separated by a brief visit to the Continent – Melville was an indefatigable partygoer and sightseer; in his diary, he recorded visiting the Lord Mayor's Show, a public hanging, the British Museum, the National Gallery and London Zoo. On returning home to Massachusetts, Melville wrote his best-known work, *Moby Dick, or, The Whale* (1851), dedicated to his friend Nathaniel Hawthorne; it subsequently became one of the first American novels to attain classic status, though it flopped completely on first publication. The failure of this work – and of its satirical successor, *Pierre* (1852) – brought about a mental breakdown from which Melville never entirely recovered. Largely forgotten by literary society, he became a New York customs inspector, and abandoned fiction for poetry, save for a last – unfinished – novel, *Billy Budd* (published 1924).

Villiers Street, WC2, was built mainly in 1674–75 on the site of York House, formerly the residence of George Villiers, 1st Duke of Buckingham; like Craven Street, it is now dominated by Charing Cross Station. At Embankment Chambers, 43 (formerly 19) Villiers Street, a plaque honours the poet and story writer **Rudyard Kipling** (1865–1936) ❹ (figs 333 and 334). Kipling was born in Bombay and, having settled in England in 1871, displayed precocious literary ability; his earliest collection of verse, *Schoolboy Lyrics*, was published in 1881. The following year, Kipling returned to India, where he became a highly successful journalist and writer, publishing such works as *Plain Tales from the Hills* (1888). He lived at Embankment Chambers – in three second-floor rooms above an establishment of Harris the Sausage King – between 1889,

when he was newly arrived from Calcutta, and 1891, the year before his marriage to Caroline Balestier. In *Something of Myself* (1937), Kipling recalled, 'My rooms were small, not over-clean or well-kept, but from my desk I could look out of my window through the fanlight of Gatti's Music-Hall entrance, across the street, almost to its stage. The Charing Cross trains rumbled through my dreams on one side, the boom of the Strand on the other, while, before my windows, Father Thames under the Shot Tower walked up and down with his traffic'.[6] While living here, Kipling wrote *The Light that Failed* (1890), a novel with passages recording his early impressions of London. It was in America, then home to his wife's family, that Kipling wrote the works for which he is most widely remembered: *The Jungle Book* (1894) and *The Second Jungle Book* (1895). In 1897 he settled in Sussex, where he enjoyed huge literary renown and produced *Stalky & Co.* (1899), *Kim* (1901) and the *Just So Stories* (1902). Kipling was first commemorated in 1940, only four years after his death, with one of the LCC's experimental, brown-coloured series of plaques; it had become so badly weathered by 1957 that it was replaced using the standard blue design.

335 An oil painting showing Buckingham Street in 1854, with the York Water Gate, the Thames and the Hungerford Suspension Bridge in the distance. Samuel Pepys lived at two addresses on the west (right) side of the street. [© Museum of London]

Buckingham Street, WC2, begun shortly before 1680, was originally known as York Buildings, like all the premises raised on the site of York House, the former residence of the Dukes of Buckingham (fig. 335). Until the creation of the Victoria Embankment by BAZALGETTE in 1864–70, it ran down to the river's edge, the position of which is marked by the York Water Gate of 1626–27. Number 14, at the south-west corner of Buckingham Street, bears a brown-coloured rectangular LCC plaque of 1908 (see fig. 23). It states that 'in a house formerly standing on this site' lived the diarist **Samuel Pepys** (1633–1703) and the statesman **Robert Harley, Earl of Oxford** (1661–1724), and that 'in this house' lived the painters **William Etty** (1787–1849) and **Clarkson Stanfield** (1793–1867) ⑤ . As the wording of the plaque suggests, the original late seventeenth-century building was so radically altered in the 1790s as to be unrecognisable today. Here Pepys lived from around March 1688, the year before his resignation as Secretary to the Admiralty, until August 1701, when he

336 The interior of Pepys's library at 14 Buckingham Street in a drawing of 1693 by Sutton Nicholls. [© The Pepys Library, Magdalene College, Cambridge]

337 The plaque to Samuel Pepys at 12 Buckingham Street. One of the brown experimental series of plaques manufactured before the Second World War, it was erected by the LCC in 1947. [© English Heritage. Photograph by Derek Kendall]

paintings for exhibition at the Society of Arts, just around the corner in John Adam Street. Meanwhile, Stanfield had taken up lodgings in the first-floor rooms vacated by Etty in 1826; he and his family remained here until 1832, when they moved to Mornington Crescent, Camden Town. During this time, Stanfield was best known for his work as scene painter at the Theatre Royal, Drury Lane, and for his easel paintings, which included *The Opening of New London Bridge* (1832), a work commissioned by King William IV.

The fact that **Samuel Pepys** (1633–1703) (see above) ⑥ had lived at number 12 as well as 14 Buckingham Street was unearthed by Ida Darlington, a historian with the Survey of London, as part of the compilation of its Strand volume of 1937. Two years later, one of the LCC's experimental brown tablets was manufactured. It was installed at number 12 – a house completed in 1677 and immediately taken by Will Hewer (1642–1715), a friend and former employee of Pepys – in 1947, after the plaques scheme was resumed following the Second World War (fig. 337). Born near Fleet Street, Pepys worked at the Exchequer and the Navy Board before being promoted, in 1673, Secretary to the Admiralty. In 1679, however, he resigned amidst accusations of 'Piracy, Popery and Treachery', and in May was imprisoned in the Tower of London. It was on his release, in July of that year, that the widowed Pepys found refuge with Hewer, receiving from him 'all the Care, kindness and faithfulness of a Son'.[9] While living at number 12 – adjacent to number 11, then used as the King's Wardrobe – Pepys was in his heyday: here, he continued to amass his library – which contained his famous diary, covering the period 1660–69 – and in 1684 began his second stint as Secretary to the Admiralty. It seems

moved to the Clapham home of his friend Will Hewer. Visitors to number 14 – which housed his extensive library (later acquired by Magdalene College, Cambridge) (fig. 336) – included John Evelyn. Pepys was immediately succeeded at number 14 by Robert Harley, who was at that time Speaker of the House of Commons, a position he retained until 1705. Later, in 1710, he became Chancellor of the Exchequer and in 1711, the year which saw him raised to the peerage as 1st Earl of Oxford and Mortimer, he was appointed Lord Treasurer. Harley remained in Buckingham Street until 1714, and while here built up the nucleus of his famous collection of manuscripts, now part of the collections of the British Library. Etty and Stanfield both lived at 14 Buckingham Street after it had been rebuilt as residential chambers in the late eighteenth century. Etty, wanting to be close to the river, moved to rooms on the first floor of the house in mid-1824, but 'the top-floor was the watch-tower for which our Artist sighed'.[7] When it fell vacant in 1826, he moved upstairs and stayed there for twenty-two years, until he left London for his native York in 1848. In his rooms, 'of which I love in my heart every stick, hole, and corner', he received artists such as FUSELI, Flaxman, CONSTABLE and TURNER and painted works including *The Combat* (1825) and *The Sirens and Ulysses* (1837).[8] In 1849 the dismantled lodgings were used as his headquarters while he gathered together a large collection of his

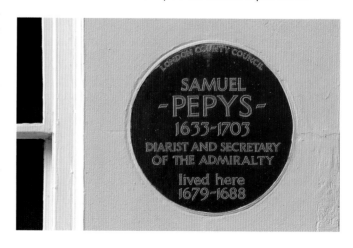

338 A photograph of July 1913 showing Adelphi Terrace, built by the Adam brothers in 1768–74. Just visible is the plaque to David Garrick, erected at number 5 by the Society of Arts in 1876. In 1914, this was joined by an LCC plaque to Robert and James Adam at number 4. Both were lost during the demolition of the terrace in 1936. [© City of London, LMA]

COVENT GARDEN, STRAND, ADELPHI

that number 12 was used as an office in connection with this post, and in 1688 – possibly due to the consequent reduction in living space – Pepys transferred to 14 Buckingham Street, a larger house with a fine prospect of the river. As the latter has since been rebuilt, number 12 – which features an original seventeenth-century oak staircase – is the only one of Pepys's London residences to survive.

On a pier on the river side of Adelphi Terrace, WC2, an inscription of 1951–52 commemorates **the Adelphi** and some of its former inhabitants 7 (fig. 338 and see fig. 12). A speculative development of prestigious housing built in 1768–74 between the Strand and the Thames, the Adelphi was one of the most notable works of the **Adam Brothers**: Robert (1728–1792) (see also p. 376) and James (1732–1794). With its fine river frontage and neoclassical

375

339 Mr W. H. Sharpington colouring the inscribed plaque commemorating the Adelphi and some of its former inhabitants, November 1951. The wording was subsequently altered to take in the full title of the London School of Economics and Political Science. [© Getty Images]

death here in 1901; during this time, he was famously in partnership with GILBERT and Sullivan, producing such works as *The Yeomen of the Guard* (1888) and *The Gondoliers* (1889). These productions were most closely associated with the Savoy Theatre on the Strand, opened in 1881 by D'Oyly Carte, who also built the Savoy Hotel, completed eight years later. Hardy, meanwhile, worked as a draughtsman in the office of the architect Arthur William Blomfield, based on the first floor of number 8 in 1864–68, and Shaw lived at number 10 from 1898 until 1927 with his wife Charlotte, née Payne-Townshend (1857–1943). Charlotte had leased the two upper floors of the property in summer 1896 from the **London School of Economics and Political Science**, co-founded the previous year by a group including Bernard Shaw. The LSE was based at number 10 until 1900, when it joined the University of London; two years later, the school moved to its present site north of Aldwych. The final name on the plaque is that of the **Savage Club**, a gentlemen's club founded in 1857; it had its premises at 6 and 7 Adelphi Terrace from 1890 to 1936, during which time members included SIR CHARLES WYNDHAM and SIR HENRY WOOD.

detailing, the Adelphi – despite being something of a financial failure – transformed what had been a derelict site into an address popular with the wealthy and distinguished. Largely demolished in 1936, it is one of London's greatest architectural losses. In the years after the Second World War, the LCC decided to commemorate the area and some of its residents, three of whom – DAVID GARRICK and the two Adam brothers – had been named on earlier plaques, installed by the Society of Arts and the LCC respectively. As a standard tablet was too small to contain the long inscription, the words were cut directly into the stonework of a 1930s pier on the site of Adelphi (originally Royal) Terrace, the pinnacle of the Adam development. As is stated in the inscription – which was carved and coloured by Mr W. H. Sharpington (fig. 339) – former residents of the terrace included the book collector **Topham Beauclerk** (1739–1780), his wife, the artist **Lady Diana Beauclerk** (1734–1808), the actor **David Garrick** (1717–1779) (see also p. 585), the theatrical impresario **Richard D'Oyly Carte** (1844–1901), and the writers **Thomas Hardy** (1840–1928) (see also p. 341) and **George Bernard Shaw** (1856–1950) (see also p. 80). The Beauclerks lived at 3 Adelphi Terrace in 1772–76 and Garrick at number 5 from 1772 until his death here; his wife, Eva Maria, née Veigel, continued to reside at the house until her death in 1822. D'Oyly Carte lived at number 4 from the time of his marriage in 1888 to the businesswoman Helen Lenoir (1852–1913) until his

At 1 Robert Street, WC2, a rectangular blue plaque of 1950 commemorates the eminent residents of this building and the adjacent numbers 2 and 3, all of which formed part of the Adelphi development and survived the demolition of the 1930s. Since the early twentieth century the three buildings have been conjoined, and were known as Adelphi Terrace House. Those inhabitants named on the plaque are the architect **Robert Adam** (1728–1792) (see above), the poet **Thomas Hood** (1799–1845) (see also pp. 493–4), the novelist and playwright **John Galsworthy** (1867–1933) (see also pp. 106–7) and the novelist and dramatist **Sir James Barrie** (1860–1937) (see also pp. 459–60) **8**. Adam moved to 3 Robert Street in 1778, having lived previously at 4 Adelphi Terrace with his brother James. He remained until his move to Albemarle Street, Mayfair, in 1785, during which time he was involved in works that included the rebuilding of Portland Place, Marylebone (1776–90). The adjacent number 2 is, along with number 1, an early example of purpose-built, high-status flats. Here lived Thomas Hood between 1828 and 1830, when he and his wife Jane (1791–1846) moved to Winchmore Hill, Enfield. By the time Galsworthy took up residence, the buildings had become known as Adelphi Terrace

340 J. M. Barrie in 1930, standing before the windows of his flat at 3 Adelphi Terrace House, which overlooked the Thames. [Courtesy of Great Ormond Street Hospital for Children, London]

341 Thomas Rowlandson's 'Dr Syntax and the Bees' from *The Second Tour of Dr Syntax*, published by Rudolph Ackermann in 1820. The engraving displays Rowlandson's flair for both comedy and architectural perspective. [© Mary Evans Picture Library]

House. He lived here in 1917–18, publishing in the latter year a successful collection of short stories, *Five Tales*, though he was known – at that time – chiefly as a playwright. His friend and fellow dramatist J. M. Barrie lived at 3 Adelphi Terrace House – just across from BERNARD SHAW – from November 1909 until his death, initially in a third-floor flat and, from 1917, in a more spacious fourth- (top) floor flat, altered for him by LUTYENS (fig. 340). This period saw the publication of *Peter and Wendy* (1911) and the creation of plays including *The Adored One* (1913), *Dear Brutus* (1917) and *Mary Rose* (1920).

At 16 John Adam Street (formerly John Street), WC2, just to the west of the headquarters of the Royal Society of Arts, a plaque marks the site of the house once occupied by the London-born artist and caricaturist **Thomas Rowlandson** (1757–1827) ⑨ . For the last twenty-seven years of his life, Rowlandson lived in attic rooms at 1 James Street (now Durham House Street), an eighteenth-century corner house demolished in 1904; its site is now occupied by 16 John Adam Street, which was built in 1908. During his time at the address, where he kept a printing press, Rowlandson worked chiefly as an illustrator of books, most notably those produced by Rudolph Ackermann's firm, the Repository of Arts. Based nearby, at 101 Strand, the firm published works including *The Microcosm of London* (1808–10), an illustrative collaboration between Rowlandson and the artist A. C. Pugin. Rowlandson's range was remarkable – he was adept at portraiture, and architectural and topographical drawing – but he is best remembered for his distinctive, humorous work based on scenes from everyday life. In his day, he was renowned in particular for his animated and satirical drawings in *The Three Tours of Doctor Syntax*, published in three volumes in 1812, 1820 and 1821, with verses by William Combe (fig. 341). Rowlandson was first proposed for commemoration in 1914, but the LCC decided not to further the suggestion on the grounds that the original James Street house had been demolished. Thirty-five years later, the council came to a different decision, and a plaque was erected in 1950.

Number 8 Adam Street, WC2 (fig. 342), was the London home from 1788 to 1792 of the industrialist and inventor **Sir Richard Arkwright** (1732–1792) ⑩ ,

342 The GLC plaque to Sir Richard Arkwright at 8 Adam Street, part of a terrace built in 1768–74 to designs by Robert Adam. [© English Heritage. Photograph by Derek Kendall]

a figure most strongly associated with Lancashire, Derbyshire and Nottinghamshire, where the textile industry was based. Born in Preston, the son of a tailor, Arkwright began his career as a barber and wigmaker, settling in Bolton in 1750. The catalyst for his future achievements and wealth was his co-invention in 1767 of a roller-spinning machine that revolutionised the manufacture of cotton. Putting his pioneering device into operation, he set up mills in Nottingham and Cromford, Derbyshire, and was soon known as the 'father of the factory system'. From about 1780, Arkwright became involved in a series of trials regarding his various patents, which he tried to enforce rigorously. It was this that drew him to London, where he spent much of the last five years of his life. Arkwright found that 8 Adam Street was ideally situated, close as it was to the lawyers in the Inns of Court and the law courts at Westminster Hall. Within view of the house was the Society of Arts, the Secretary of which – Samuel More – was among those who spoke on Arkwright's behalf at his lawsuits. Number 8 signified Sir Richard's wealth and position, and was furnished accordingly: its contents included a portrait of Arkwright painted by the American artist Mather Brown in 1790. Arkwright died at his home in Cromford, where he had established a mill in 1771; the buildings have since been restored by the Arkwright Society. His London residence was sold by his son, another Richard Arkwright, in 1794. The proposal for a plaque was

made by Derbyshire County Council – coincidentally, the authority then owned 8 Adam Street – as part of the celebrations surrounding the 250th anniversary of Arkwright's birth. A temporary plaque of enamelled steel was put up at number 8 for a ceremony held in March 1983; it was replaced with a permanent ceramic plaque the following year.

Towards the eastern end of the Strand, beyond Somerset House – the masterpiece of Sir William Chambers – is a plaque commemorating the historical associations of a whole street: **Essex Street**, WC2 ⑪ (fig. 343). The thoroughfare, which runs south from St Clement Danes towards the river, was laid out by **Nicholas Barbon** (*c.* 1637–*c.* 1698) in 1675 on the grounds of Essex House, formerly the home of two favourites of Queen Elizabeth – Robert Dudley, Earl of Leicester, and Robert Devereux, 2nd Earl of Essex. The rectangular LCC plaque, of inscribed Portland stone, is embedded in the façade of Essex Hall, 1–6 Essex Street, a mid-twentieth-century building; originally erected at 7 Essex Street in 1962, it was moved to this location two years later following number 7's demolition. Essex Street was a popular place of residence for lawyers and other professional men. Those named on the plaque are the Lord Keeper **Sir Orlando Bridgeman** (1609–1674), the novelist **Henry Fielding** (1707–1754) (see also p. 381 and pp. 591–2), the Lord Mayor of London **Brass Crosby** (1725–1793) and the architect **James Savage** (1779–1852).[10] Also named are the Young Pretender **Prince Charles Edward Stuart** (1720–1788), who stayed at a house in the street in 1750, the Unitarian minister the **Rev. Theophilus Lindsey** (1723–1808), who founded the Essex Street Chapel here in 1774, and the writer **Dr Samuel Johnson** (1709–1784) (see also p. 62 and p. 381), who established an evening club at the Essex Head in December 1783. Of those named, Bridgeman was the earliest resident; he lived in the part of Essex House that survived Barbon's development – its site is now represented by Essex Hall – from 1651 until his death. Fielding lived at 24 Essex Street for a brief period from 1739 to 1740, when he was called to the Bar. Bonnie Prince Charlie was an even more short-lived resident: during a six-day visit to London in September 1750, he stayed with Lady Anne Primrose (d. 1775) in a house in Essex Street. Brass Crosby moved to 17 Essex Street in about 1773, three years after he was elected Lord Mayor; he remained until about

343 A view of Essex Street from the north, painted by Thomas Colman Dibdin in 1851. The myriad associations of the street as a whole were commemorated by a rectangular LCC plaque originally installed in 1962. [© City of London]

COVENT GARDEN, STRAND, ADELPHI

1780, though latterly his house was probably used for business purposes only. Meanwhile, Theophilus Lindsey had founded a meeting house in the surviving portion of Essex House, which was altered for use as a chapel; the first service was held in April 1774, when over two hundred people were present, including JOSEPH PRIESTLEY and BENJAMIN FRANKLIN. Lindsey resigned his ministry in 1793, five years after the rebuilding of the Essex Street Chapel, but remained in an adjacent house until his death. The chapel itself was remodelled in 1886 as Essex Hall, a venue used by groups including the FABIAN SOCIETY; it was completely rebuilt after being destroyed by a flying bomb in 1944. On the opposite side of the road, at what was – by the late nineteenth century – 40–41 Essex Street, Dr Johnson established a club; 'The terms', he wrote in a letter to REYNOLDS, 'are lax, and the expences [sic] light . . . We meet thrice a week, and he who misses forfeits two-pence'.[11] The sole resident of the nineteenth century to be named on the plaque is James Savage; known for buildings such as St Luke's, Chelsea (1820–24) and St James's, Bermondsey (1827–29), he

lived at 31 Essex Street from c. 1827 until c. 1852. Today, only six buildings in Essex Street – none of them mentioned above – pre-date the mid-eighteenth century.

A lifetime spent professionally and physically in the theatre is uniquely represented by the plaque to **Ivor Novello** (1893–1951) 12 , the composer and actor-manager, who lived for thirty-eight years at 11 Aldwych, WC2, in a flat on the fourth (top) floor of the building, above the Strand Theatre (fig. 344). Born in Cardiff as David Ivor Davies, he imbibed a strong interest in music and the world of theatre from his mother, Clara Novello Davies (1861–1943), who taught singing. In 1927 David changed his name to Ivor Novello by deed poll, having already begun to make his mark with works such as the 1914 song 'Keep the Home Fires Burning (Till the Boys Come Home)'. He made his debut as an actor in the silent film *The Call of the Blood* (1920), and enjoyed subsequent success on stage and screen, works including *The Rat* – a play of 1924 which he co-wrote, and which was made into a film the following year – and HITCHCOCK's *The Lodger*

344 The interior of Ivor Novello's flat above the Strand Theatre (now the Novello Theatre) at 11 Aldwych, in a photograph taken during his residence. This corner area, with its raised dais and piano, was a focus at many riotous parties.

guest books include Douglas Fairbanks Junior, PAUL ROBESON and VIVIEN LEIGH. The plaque at number 11, now aptly known as the Novello Theatre, was unveiled in 1973 by Olive Gilbert, who lived in the flat beneath Ivor's and had appeared in many of his productions.

At 36 Tavistock Street (formerly 4 York Street), WC2, a house of 1733, a plaque honours **Thomas De Quincey** (1785–1859) 13 .[14] It was here – as the inscription records – that he wrote *Confessions of an English Opium Eater* (1821), an account of his addiction to opium, a drug then exciting much interest in society. De Quincey was born in Manchester, and first visited London in his teens; according to his *Confessions*, it was in the capital, in 1804, that he had his first taste of opium, then readily and legally available. In 1807 De Quincey met COLERIDGE, Wordsworth and Robert Southey, and thenceforth dedicated himself to literature. He spent an important and prolific – if miserable – part of his career in London, where he arrived in mid-1821, leaving his wife Margaret and their family at home in the Lake District. Shortly afterwards, he moved into lodgings at what was then 4 York Street, a thoroughfare rather less salubrious than it appears today. Here – reputedly in a small room at the rear of the property – he completed his *Confessions*, published in the *London Magazine* in September and October 1821. The work, which appeared in book form the following year, made De Quincey's reputation. It is unclear how long he remained at number 36, which was occupied in 1831–67 by the bookseller and publisher H. G. Bohn (1796–1884). De Quincey was beset by debt, and frequently went into hiding from his creditors; he also returned for periods to his home in Grasmere. However, it would seem that number 36 remained his base for much of the period 1821–25. From that time on, De Quincey resided largely in Edinburgh, where he contributed essays to such journals as *Blackwood's Magazine*. He was first honoured with a blue plaque in London in 1909, when the LCC commemorated 61 (formerly 58) Greek Street, Soho, consent having been refused for a plaque in Tavistock Street; number 61, which was De Quincey's home in 1803, was demolished in about 1937. The GLC plaque at number 36 was unveiled by the actor Donald Sinden in 1981, shortly after the renovation and re-opening of nearby Covent Garden market.

(1926). Novello was best known for his succession of brilliant musical shows, the bulk of which were composed with Christopher Hassall as lyricist and starred Novello himself; almost all staged at the Theatre Royal, Drury Lane, they included *Glamorous Night* (1935), *Careless Rapture* (1936), *The Dancing Years* (1939) and *King's Rhapsody* (1949). Novello and his mother ('Mam') settled in 1913 at 11 Aldwych, part of a block built in 1905 to the designs of W. G. R. Sprague and situated adjacent to the Waldorf Hotel, on the corner of Catherine Street. The flat – which was also sometime home to Novello's father, David Davies (1852?–1931) – remained Ivor's London residence until his death here, in the presence of his lifelong companion, the actor Bobbie Andrews. Novello was noted for his hospitality; he entertained regularly both in London and at his country home, Redroofs, near Maidenhead, Berkshire. 'The Flat', as it was known to theatrical London, was the setting for a number of sparkling parties, which were 'a signal for general rejoicing'.[12] In his memoirs, NOËL COWARD described how it was accessed either by an ancient and unreliable lift or by seven long flights of stairs. 'The big room of the flat had a raised dais running across one end. Upon this, there were sometimes two, at other times no grand pianos . . . The high spots of the parties were reached in this room. Charades were performed, people did stunts . . . Visiting musicians were subtly lured to the piano. Native musicians rushed to it'.[13] Names written in Novello's

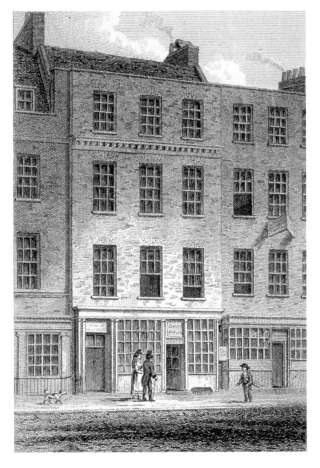

345 Number 8 Russell Street in an engraving of *c*.1810. It was here, in a bookshop owned by Thomas Davies, that Dr Samuel Johnson first met James Boswell, in May 1763. [© City of London]

On the other side of Bow Street, at 8 Russell Street, WC2 (fig. 345) – built in 1759–60 – a GLC plaque commemorates the first meeting of the author **Dr Samuel Johnson** (1709–1784) (see also p. 62 and pp. 378–9) and his biographer, **James Boswell** (1740–1795) (see also pp. 516–17) **14** . The encounter took place in 1763 in the back parlour of what was then a bookshop owned by a former actor, **Thomas Davies** (*c.* 1712–85), who lived at number 8 until his death. On the evening of Monday 16 May, after Boswell had finished drinking tea with Mr and Mrs Davies, Johnson unexpectedly came into the shop. Boswell recalled that Mr Davies, 'having perceived him through the glass-door in the room in which we were sitting, advancing towards us', announced 'somewhat in the manner of an actor in the part of Horatio, when he addresses Hamlet on the appearance of his father's ghost, "Look, my Lord, it comes"'.[15] Despite an initial snub from Johnson, who was known for his prejudice against Scots, Boswell – then just twenty-two – made an immediate impression; the pair talked for three hours, and Davies noted, when seeing Boswell out, 'I can see he likes you very

well'.[16] Shortly afterwards, Boswell called on Johnson at his lodgings at 1 Inner Temple Lane (demolished), on the south of Fleet Street, beginning the friendship that would last until Johnson's death. In his *Life of Johnson* (1791) – one of the most famous of all biographies – Boswell noted that he had never since passed by 8 Russell Street 'without feeling reverence and regret'.[17] A plaque was erected in 1984 as part of the Johnson bicentenary celebrations.

At 19–20 Bow Street, WC2 – on the façade facing onto Broad Court – is a white rectangular tablet of 1929 commemorating the historic importance of **Bow Street** as a whole **15** (fig. 347). Built from 1637, Bow Street was – like Essex Street – home to a number of illustrious individuals, especially in the seventeenth and eighteenth centuries; it is now dominated by the Royal Opera House (built 1857–58), the site of which was occupied by the Covent Garden Theatre from 1732. The LCC chose to mention on the plaque only those seven former inhabitants who then appeared in the *Dictionary of National Biography*: the novelist **Henry Fielding** (1707–1754) (see also p. 378 and pp. 591–2), the magistrate **Sir John Fielding** (1721–1780), the woodcarver **Grinling Gibbons** (1648–1721), the actor **Charles Macklin** (1699?–1797), the physician **John Radcliffe** (1650–1714), the poet **Charles Sackville**, **Earl of Dorset** (1643–1706) and the dramatist **William Wycherley** (1641–1716). The link between Bow Street and the Fieldings is of particular note. Henry Fielding moved to a house on the street's west side in December 1748 – just as his literary masterpiece, *Tom Jones*, was being printed. The following year he became magistrate for Middlesex at the Bow Street office, based at number 4 until it was replaced in 1880 by a purpose-built police station and courthouse on the street's east side. Shortly after taking up this position, he established the Bow Street Runners, an important shift towards modern policing. In 1751 Fielding's blind half-brother, John, became a magistrate for Westminster, and succeeded him as court justice on his retirement in 1754; in that year, John took over Henry's house, living at the address until his death. Together, the Fieldings did much to improve conditions at a time when lawlessness and crime were rife in London. Grinling Gibbons was an earlier resident, living at a house on the east side of Bow Street from about 1678; following its collapse in 1702, the house was rebuilt, and remained Gibbons's home

such successful comedies as *The Country Wife* (1675) and *The Plain Dealer* (1676) – who lived in Bow Street from *c.* 1678 until his death. Macklin, a regular performer at the Drury Lane theatre, lived on the west side of the street in about 1743–48, at the property adjacent to that subsequently occupied by the Fieldings. All of these buildings have been demolished.

Number 31 King Street, WC2, on the west side of Covent Garden piazza, was the home of **Thomas Arne** (1710–1778) **16** , the composer (fig. 346). The son of an upholsterer, Thomas Arne (d. 1736), and his second wife Anne, née Wheeler (d. 1757), the younger Thomas was born at number 31. In 1712 the house – newly built – was destroyed by fire, and the present building was put up on its site the following year; it remained the Arne family home until 1733. Thomas loved music from his early years but, as his father disapproved of such studies, he is said to have practised secretly at home, muffling the strings of his spinet with cloths. It was only when his abilities had reached an advanced stage that his father discovered Thomas's subterfuge and sanctioned his chosen career. Arne went on to enjoy great fame: he composed music for some ninety theatrical works, many for the Drury Lane and Covent Garden theatres, including a setting of Milton's *Comus* (1738) and the opera *Artaxerxes* (1762). Arne worked frequently with his sister Susannah (1714–1766) – a singer and actress who married the successful playwright Theophilus Cibber in 1734 – and his brother Richard (b. *c.* 1719), also a singer and actor; another actress, Cecilia Young, became Arne's wife in 1737. He is best known for 'Rule, Britannia', written by the poet JAMES THOMSON and set to music by Arne for his opera *Alfred* (1740). Arne lived in Covent Garden for most of his life, but 31 King Street is the only one of his houses to survive; given a stucco front in 1860, it bears an English Heritage plaque of 1988, the shape of which was specially adapted to fit a narrow space on the building's façade.

346 Number 31 King Street and its English Heritage plaque to Thomas Arne. Erected in 1988, its shape was specially adapted to fit a narrow space on the building's façade. [© English Heritage. Photograph by Nigel Corrie]

until his death, a period which saw the execution of his greatest work, including that at St Paul's Cathedral. Among Gibbons's neighbours was Charles Sackville, who lived in Bow Street in 1684–85, and John Radcliffe, who lived here from 1684 until 1702, during which time he prospered as a physician to members of the royal family. Another resident was Wycherley – author of

St Martin's Lane, WC2, the western boundary of Covent Garden, was once a centre of the furniture-making industry, a fact reflected by a bronze LCC plaque at number 61 marking the site of the workshop of the cabinetmakers **Thomas Chippendale** (1718–1779) and his son, another **Thomas Chippendale** (1749–1822/23) **17** . The elder Thomas Chippendale

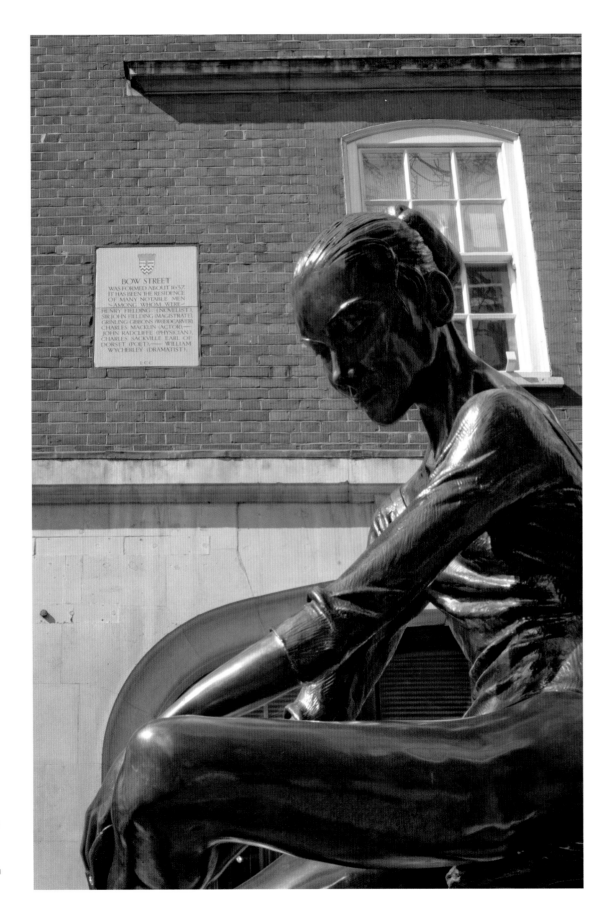

347 The white rectangular plaque commemorating the historical associations of Bow Street, erected by the LCC in 1929. It is seen here behind the statue of a ballerina, *Young Dancer*, by Enzo Plazzotta. [© English Heritage. Photograph by Derek Kendall]

348   A plan of the Chippendale premises in St Martin's Lane as they were in 1803, redrawn for the Survey of London from a fire insurance plan. A plaque commemorating the associations of this site was installed by the LCC in 1952. [Reproduced by permission of English Heritage]

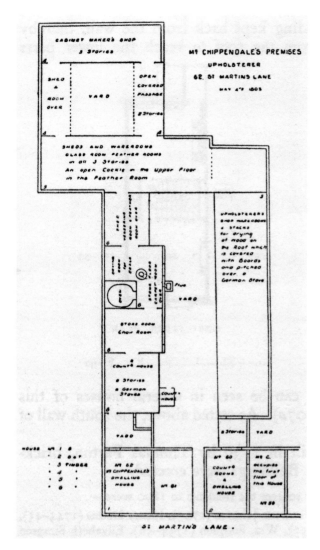

partner, James Rannie (d. 1766). That year also saw the publication of his furniture pattern book *The Gentleman and Cabinet-Maker's Director*, which established Chippendale's reputation and proved enormously influential. Copies were for sale at his house, 60 St Martin's Lane, which stood to the right of a covered way, leading to a rear yard enclosed by workshops and warehouses; these accommodated a team of craftsmen, including cabinetmakers, upholsterers, gilders and polishers. On the left-hand side of the cartway was 61 St Martin's Lane, the ground floor of which housed the firm's shop. The adjacent number 62 was earlier thought to have been the home of James Rannie, but this is now known not to have been the case; it was occupied by various tenants and, between 1793 and 1813, was the residence of the younger Thomas Chippendale, who also made use of the first floor of number 59. The Chippendale firm worked for a broad range of patrons from the aristocracy and gentry, carrying out lavish furnishing programmes at such houses as Nostell Priory, Newby Hall and Harewood House, all in Yorkshire. Some of these projects were continued by Thomas junior, who was active in the family firm by the time of his father's retirement in 1776 and took over its management three years later, working in partnership with the bookkeeper Thomas Haig (d. 1803) until the mid-1790s. A distinguished designer in his own right, the younger Thomas Chippendale remained at St Martin's Lane until 1813, when he and his business moved to Haymarket, on the other side of Leicester Square. Of the original eighteenth-century buildings, only 62 St Martin's Lane now survives. Numbers 60 and 61 date from the late nineteenth century, and were marked with a plaque in 1952, the LCC having finally given in to a proposal first made in 1929.

was born in Yorkshire, the son of a joiner, and moved to London in the late 1740s. It was in late 1753 that he sub-let the substantial premises in St Martin's Lane that his firm would occupy for sixty years (fig. 348). A formal lease was signed in 1754, when Chippendale moved into the buildings with his new business

NOTES

1 *Survey of London*, vol. XVIII: *The Strand (The Parish of St Martin-in-the-Fields, Part II)*, eds Sir George Gater and Walter H. Godfrey (London, 1937), p. 38; S. Morgan, *Benjamin Franklin* (New Haven and London, 2002), p. 106 (19 February 1758)

2 *Heinrich Heine's Memoirs, from his Works, Letters, and Conversations*, ed. Gustav Karpeles, trans. Gilbert Cannan, vol. I (London, 1910), p. 194

3 Ibid

4 Ibid, pp. 192–93

5 Ibid, p. 193

6 Rudyard Kipling, *Something of Myself* (London, 1951), pp. 79–80

7 Alexander Gilchrist, *Life of William Etty, RA* (London, 1855), vol. I, p. 221

8 Ibid, vol. II, p. 248

9 *The Letters of Samuel Pepys and his Family Circle*, ed. Helen Truesdell Heath (Oxford, 1955), p. 74 (14 July 1679)

10 It is now accepted that Bridgeman was born in 1609, rather than in 1606, as is stated on the plaque.

11 *Boswell's Life of Johnson*, ed. George Birkbeck Hill, rev. L. F. Powell, vol. IV (Oxford, 1934), p. 254 (4 December 1783)

12 Noël Coward, *Present Indicative* (London, Toronto, 1937), p. 141

13 Ibid, pp. 141–42

14 The plaque spells his name 'De Quincy', in error.

15 *Boswell's Life of Johnson*, vol. I (Oxford, 1934), p. 392

16 Ibid, p. 395

17 Ibid, p. 390 note 2

349 Number 3 Spanish Place, dating from the 1780s, and its two LCC plaques, the first (uppermost) commemorating Captain Frederick Marryat and the second commemorating George Grossmith. [© English Heritage. Photograph by Derek Kendall]

MARYLEBONE

Marylebone takes its name from the medieval parish church of St Mary-le-Bourne, which was built in the heart of Tyburn village in about 1400. Bounded by Portland Place to the east and Edgware Road to the west, Marylebone lies to the north of Oxford Street, which was developed from the late 1600s. The whole area was open countryside – and a notorious haunt of highwaymen – when, in 1708, John Holles, Duke of Newcastle, bought part of the manor; within ten years his son-in-law, Edward Harley, 2nd Earl of Oxford and Mortimer, began developing a new residential quarter that fanned out from Cavendish Square. This estate was subsequently conveyed by marriage into the hands of the dukes of Portland, and passed in 1879 to Lord Howard de Walden. Building in the west of Maryle-bone began when the Portman family laid out Portman Square in 1764, and continued with the creation in the early nineteenth century of Bryanston, Montagu and Dorset Squares. Having shaken off its early disreputability, this largely Georgian townscape attracted many pioneering and reforming figures in the fields of politics, literature, architecture and medicine, as well as a host of cultural institutions. Since 1867, when Marylebone received the capital's first blue plaque – that to Lord Byron (lost through demolition in *c.* 1889) – over sixty plaques have been erected, thanks in part to the vigorous efforts of the St Marylebone Society, formed in 1948. This total gives the area the highest tally of plaques in London.

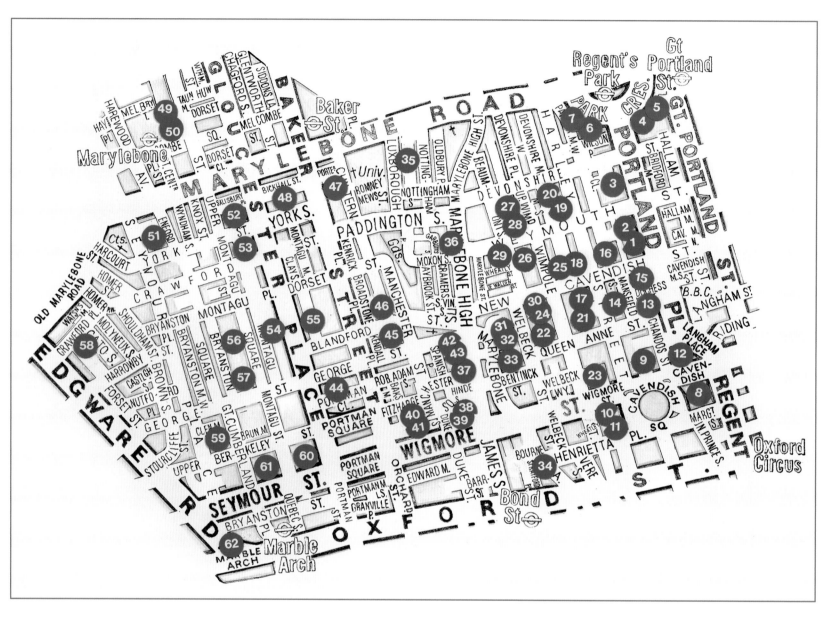

MARYLEBONE

350 The stone LCC plaque to Earl Roberts, erected at 47 Portland Place in 1922. Its unusual design seems to have been considered most appropriate for the rusticated façade of the building. [© English Heritage. Photograph by Derek Kendall]

FROM PORTLAND PLACE TO MARYLEBONE HIGH STREET

Portland Place, W1, was laid out for the 3rd Duke of Portland by the ADAM BROTHERS from the mid-1770s, and was later incorporated by John Nash into his grand scheme linking Carlton House to the newly laid out Regent's Park. The English Heritage plaque at 41 (formerly 22, later 29 and 54) Portland Place commemorates **Thomas Gage** (1719/20–1787) ❶, the Commander of British forces in North America.[1] Gage was the first resident of this large terraced house, which was designed and built in about 1776. The son of the 1st Viscount Gage, Thomas entered the Army in his early twenties, purchasing a lieutenancy in 1741. He served from 1754 and throughout the Seven Years War (1756–63) in North America, where, despite a series of defeats, he won the respect of his fellow officers, including GENERAL JAMES WOLFE. In 1763, at the outbreak of the Pontiac War, Gage was appointed Commander-in-Chief of British forces in North America, with headquarters in New York; he spent the next ten years trying – and failing – to contain the growing discontent of the American colonies. Gage was on leave in London when the Boston Tea Party of December 1773 escalated the crisis, and he floundered when full-scale rebellion was sparked off by the skirmish at Lexington in April 1775. In October of that year, Gage was discharged from his duties and returned to England with his American wife, Margaret, née Kemble (c. 1734–1824) and their children. In 1779 he moved to what was then 22 Portland Place, which remained his home until his death here eight years later; this period saw him briefly command the defences of Kent against French invasion (1781) and his promotion to full general (1782). Gage's widow lived at the house until 1791.

At 47 Portland Place, on the corner of Weymouth Street, a discreet rectangular plaque commemorates the Field Marshal **Earl Roberts** (1832–1914) ❷, hero of the Second Anglo-Afghan War and the South African War (fig. 350). Born in Cawnpore, India, Frederick Sleigh Roberts followed his father into the service of the East India Company, and was commissioned into the Bengal Artillery in 1851. He enjoyed a highly distinguished career in India, rising to become Commander-in-Chief first of Madras (1881–85) and then of all India (1885–93), and was honoured for his service

during the Second Afghan War. Having returned to England from India in 1893, Roberts was promoted field marshal in 1895 and, four years later, was sent to South Africa with LORD KITCHENER to rescue the British Army, which had suffered a series of devastating defeats by the Boers. Roberts fought a blistering campaign and within ten months had gained possession of the Orange Free State and the Transvaal. He returned to England to serve as Commander-in-Chief of the British Army (1900–4) – succeeding his arch rival, VISCOUNT WOLSELEY – and from 1902 to 1906 lived with his wife Nora Henrietta, née Bews (1838–1920) at 47 Portland Place, the only house in London he ever owned. Despite introducing the Enfield rifle – along with khaki uniform – into the Army, Roberts believed that Britain was hopelessly unprepared for the war with Germany and supported the National Service League's campaign to introduce conscription. The proposal to commemorate Roberts, who had been created an earl in 1901, was made the year after his death and was strongly backed by figures such as WINSTON CHURCHILL and HERBERT ASQUITH. In 1922 the LCC erected a Hopton Wood stone tablet with lettering picked out in lead that oddly omitted the council's initials; this unusual design was presumably considered most appropriate for the boldly rusticated façade of number 47.

At 63 Portland Place is a GLC plaque to the writer **Frances Hodgson Burnett** (1849–1924) ❸. Born in Manchester, the daughter of Edwin and Eliza Hodgson, Frances spent her early adulthood in the United States, where her first novel, *That Lass o' Lowrie's*, was published in 1877; her reputation as a children's author was established a decade later with *Little Lord Fauntleroy* (1886). Following her marriage

MARYLEBONE

in 1873 to Swan Moses Burnett, an American ophthalmologist, Frances divided her time between Washington and London, and was often separated from her family; her marriage finally ended in divorce in 1898. In autumn 1893 Burnett rented 63 Portland Place, which was at times also home to her son Vivian (1876–1937) and her sister Edith Fahnestock (1852–1931); this large 1770s house, with its long chilly passages and cavernous cellars, provided the inspiration for her historical novel *A Lady of Quality* (1896). Somewhat in awe of the house's grandeur, she described how she wanted 'to use these big drawing rooms until they are so filled up with the atmosphere of being lived and talked and thought in that they will no longer wear stately airs and graces and suggest that they are great and lofty and that they were built a century ago'.[2] However, Burnett – who enjoyed an opulent lifestyle – struggled to pay the bills and manage her servants, as she documented in her short story *The Captain's Youngest* (1894). It was with some relief that she moved in spring 1898 to the country, renting Maytham Hall in Rolvenden, Kent; the rose garden of this house inspired her best-known literary work, *The Secret Garden* (1911). By the time of the novel's publication, Burnett had taken American citizenship, and she died in Long Island, New York, thirteen years later. Proposed for commemoration by her biographer, Ann Thwaite, Burnett was awarded a plaque in 1979, but its erection on the wrong house – number 65 rather than number 63 – caused consternation and panic among the GLC's historians. The plaque was hastily removed the following day, before the mortar had set, and was placed in its correct position next door.

At the top of Portland Place, almost hidden behind the ground-floor colonnade of number 98 (formerly 5 Upper Portland Place), is a GLC plaque marking the location of the **United States Embassy** from 1863 to 1866 and the residence of the US historian **Henry Brooks Adams** (1838–1918) ❹ . Number 98 is the end house of the terrace which forms the eastern half of the quadrant known as Park Crescent. The early nineteenth-century building was restored after severe bomb damage in the Second World War, and the present façade is a facsimile of the original. Adams was born in Boston into a political family; his great-grandfather was John Adams and his grandfather was John Quincy Adams, respectively the second and sixth Pres-

idents of the USA. Henry Brooks Adams arrived in London in 1861 as private secretary to his father, Charles Francis Adams (1807–1886), who was Ambassador to the United Kingdom from 1861 to 1868; both father and son lived at this address – then the US Embassy, and known as 5 Upper Portland Place – between 1863 and 1866. In all, the younger Adams spent seven years in England, during which time he formed a crucial friendship with fellow Marylebone resident CHARLES LYELL, who fired his enthusiasm for history and instilled in him an appreciation of the evolutionary theory regarding human history. He was also active as a journalist, writing as the anonymous London correspondent to the *New York Times*. Following his return to the USA in 1868, Adams became a distinguished professor at Harvard University and gained fame for his nine-volume history of his nation, published in 1889–91. Proposed by the American Embassy, the plaque was erected in 1978.

Park Crescent, W1, built in 1812–22 as the first part of John Nash's Regent's Park development, comprises two sweeping terraces of stuccoed houses, with single-storey colonnades (fig. 351). At number 12, in the east quadrant, a bronze LCC plaque commemorates the surgeon **Joseph**, **Lord Lister** (1827–1912) ❺ (fig. 352). Lister was educated at University College London, but it was in Glasgow and Edinburgh that he pioneered the use of antiseptics in surgical operations, thereby dramatically increasing patient survival rates. He moved from Scotland after being appointed to the chair of clinical surgery at King's College Hospital in 1877, settling at Park Crescent. This was not a favoured address for professionals, partly because of a prohibition on the brass door nameplates then considered de rigueur. Lister, who probably felt no need to advertise, chose it for its proximity to green spaces; he kept a laboratory at the house, where he devoted the early mornings to experiments, assisted by his wife Agnes, née Syme (1834–1893). The medical establishment in London was initially unconvinced of Lister's methods, which involved the use of carbolic acid: at his first operation, one distinguished surgeon remarked that 'when this poor fellow dies, someone ought to proceed against that man for malpraxis'.[3] Lister was vindicated and, as one of the most celebrated medics of the age, was raised to the peerage in 1897. He remained at Park Crescent until 1909, when he retired

351 A view of Park Crescent in 1822, the year of its completion. The sweeping terraces were built as the first part of John Nash's Regent's Park development. [© Museum of London]

352 The plaque to Lord Lister as unveiled at 12 Park Crescent in a ceremony of 1966. It had originally been erected at the address in 1915, but was removed due to war damage and was reinstalled following the completion of rebuilding works. [© Getty Images]

to Walmer, Kent. The plaque was erected in 1915, just three years after Lister's death, but Park Crescent was seriously damaged during the Second World War. In the early 1960s the crescent was rebuilt, with a façade that stayed faithful to the original design. The Lister plaque had been sold illicitly for scrap, but was located thanks to an article in *The Lancet* and was re-erected in 1966.

At 19 Park Crescent, part of the street's western quadrant, the scientist and inventor **Sir Charles Wheatstone** (1802–1875) ⑥ has a plaque. Wheatstone took over his uncle's musical instrument making business in

1823, moving it in 1829 to 20 Conduit Street, Mayfair, where it remained for over eighty years. His early inventions were musical, and included the exotically named flute harmonique and the acouryptophone ('enchanted lyre'); the concertina, which he patented in 1844, has proved to be longer lived. The physics of sound was a parallel interest for Wheatstone, and he is credited with demonstrating the viability of mass communication by telegraph. It was in the vaults beneath King's College on the Strand – where Wheatstone held a professorship in experimental philosophy from 1834 – that he made this breakthrough, using about four miles (6.4 km) of suspended copper wire. He was also responsible for numerous other inventions and discoveries, and his name is perpetuated in 'Wheatstone's bridge', an electric circuit that measures resistance. Ironically for a man who helped to take the world into the era of mass communication, Wheatstone was such a reluctant public speaker that MICHAEL FARADAY was conscripted to deliver his Royal Institution lectures. His commemoration was first suggested in 1906, but the LCC felt that a plaque to Wheatstone was not a priority; after the proposal was revived by a member of the International Concertina Association, the plaque was erected in 1981 at Park Crescent, where Wheatstone lived from 1866 until his death.

At 24 Park Crescent is a plaque of 1972 marking the residence of the actress **Dame Marie Tempest** (1864–1942) ⑦ (fig. 353). Born Mary Susan Etherington in the Marylebone Road, Marie Tempest took her stage name from a member of the aristocratic Vane-Tempest family whom she described as her godmother. Her early roles were in musical comedy, and she moved to Park Crescent in 1899 following her advantageous marriage to Cosmo Charles Gordon-Lennox (1869–1921), a member of the Duke of Richmond's family. Within number 24, Tempest kept a 'pretty chintz-covered boudoir where a little green parrot calls her "Marie".'[4] The couple lived here for three years, during which time Gordon-Lennox had a hand in *Becky Sharp* (1901), a stage adaptation of THACKERAY's *Vanity Fair*; Tempest took the title role, which brought her to prominence as a serious actress. Her stage career lasted fifty-five years: significant later roles included Judith Bliss in *Hay Fever* (1925) by NÖEL COWARD, which allowed her to send up her drawing-room comedy persona of yore. In her early career Tempest had some-

353 'The charming Miss Marie Tempest at home, with her husband, Mr Cosmo Stuart', in a photograph published in *The Sketch* on 25 October 1899. The couple lived at 24 Park Crescent between 1899 and 1902. [© Illustrated London News Ltd / Mary Evans Picture Library]

veiled in 1965 by his grandson and namesake, who became Baron Hailsham of St Marylebone in 1970. Having made a fortune as a sugar merchant and businessman, the London-born Hogg devoted his life to educational philanthropy, starting a ragged school in Charing Cross (1864–65) and a Youths' Christian Institute in Covent Garden (1878). He is best known for transforming the Royal Polytechnic Institution, which was founded in 1838 under the chairmanship of SIR GEORGE CAYLEY. Having leased the institution's site at 309 Regent Street for £15,000 in 1881, Hogg opened the building to two thousand students in September of the following year, offering instruction and recreation to men and women of working and trade backgrounds. The Polytechnic – intended to educate mind, body and spirit – flourished under his direction, becoming London's largest adult education provider, but Hogg's personal finances suffered from his philanthropic impulses; to celebrate his silver wedding in 1896, his friends rallied round and raised nearly £15,000 to relieve this pressure. Hogg moved into 5 Cavendish Square – which backs onto the Polytechnic – in autumn 1885, with his wife Alice (d. 1918) and their five children, and built a bedroom and bathroom in the passage connecting the two buildings. He and his family moved out of number 5 in 1898, selling it four years later, but Hogg retained use of the modest rooms to the rear, which were linked to the Polytechnic; it was here that he died in January 1903, accidentally asphyxiated by fumes from the gas heater in his bathroom. Since the death of its founder, the Polytechnic – which was completely rebuilt in 1911 – has continued to grow, becoming part of the Polytechnic of Central London in 1970 and the University of Westminster in 1992.

Number 15, on the northern side of Cavendish Square, was home for nearly forty years to the surgeon, scientist and teacher **Sir Jonathan Hutchinson** (1828– 1913) **9** . After training at the York School of Medicine and St Bartholomew's Hospital, London, Hutchinson settled in Finsbury Circus, Islington; in 1861 he and his wife Jane, née Pynsent West (1835–1887) took a larger house in the circus – number 4 – where his lodger for three years was his great friend and fellow doctor JOHN HUGHLINGS JACKSON. In 1874 Hutchinson moved to 15 Cavendish Square, a house of the early 1800s placed between two eighteenth-century buildings, one of which (number 16) was occupied by

thing of a reputation for petulance, and later admitted to having been 'a self-important little baggage, with a hot temper'.[5] A leading force in the foundation of Equity, the actors' union, she was made a dame in 1937.

Cavendish Square, W1, was the first square to be laid out north of Tyburn Road (now Oxford Street) in 1717, but it was only completed around fifty years later. The LCC plaque at number 5, a house of the 1740s, commemorates **Quintin Hogg** (1845–1903) **8** , the founder of the Polytechnic, Regent Street; it was un-

his illustrious medical colleague, Sir Andrew Clark. He acquired the freehold three years later – thereby severely testing the family finances – and stayed here until 1907, when he moved permanently to his country home in Haslemere, Surrey. Hutchinson came to attention as a surgeon and professor of surgery at the London Hospital in Whitechapel, where he worked from 1859 to 1883 and specialised in ophthalmology, dermatology, neurology and venereology. He was also on the staff of institutions including the Royal London Ophthalmic Hospital and the Royal Lock Hospital, and was Hunterian Professor of the Royal College of Surgeons in 1879–83. The first postgraduate medical college in London had its origins in Hutchinson's 'polyclinic' at 22 Chenies Street, Bloomsbury, where he stored his medical collections and gave public lectures and demonstrations. Hutchinson's research into syphilis proved to be of particular importance, unlike his theory that leprosy was chiefly caused by eating rotten fish, which has not stood the test of time. Hutchinson held strongly to the view that women should not be doctors, and dismissed as 'too absurd' the notion of ELIZABETH GARRETT ANDERSON practising medicine.[6] The GLC plaque was unveiled in 1981 by the President of the Royal College of Surgeons, Sir Alan Parks.

Number 18 Cavendish Square – which dates from 1756 – was the home of another medical figure, the Nobel Laureate and discoverer of the mosquito transmission of malaria, **Sir Ronald Ross** (1857–1932) **10** . Born in

India to a Scottish family, Ross trained as a doctor in London and pursued a conventional career in the Indian Medical Service in the 1880s, which allowed him time to investigate the causes of malaria. In 1894, while on leave in London with his wife Rosa (d. 1931), he met the great expert on tropical medicine, PATRICK MANSON, who inspired him to research the possible link between mosquitoes and malaria. On his return to India, Ross discovered that the malarial parasite was transmitted to human beings by the blood-sucking *Anopheles* mosquito. In 1902, in recognition of this vital breakthrough, Ross – by then lecturer at the Liverpool School of Tropical Medicine – became the first Briton to receive the Nobel Prize, an honour that soured his friendship with Manson. Ross left Liverpool in 1912, and worked as a consultant at King's College Hospital and for the War Office while living at 18 Cavendish Square, his home between 1913 and 1916. In 1926 he founded the Ross Institute and Hospital for Tropical Diseases in Putney, where he died; the institute was subsequently incorporated into the London School of Hygiene and Tropical Medicine. The plaque to Ross was installed in February 1985, four days after that to Manson.

Also on the western side of Cavendish Square is number 20, the home of the Yorkshire-born statesman **Herbert Henry Asquith, 1st Earl of Oxford and Asquith** (1852–1928) **11** (fig. 354). An MP from 1886, he moved here in 1895, following his marriage the previous year to his second wife, Margot Tennant (1864–1945). Their life at number 20 – with their two surviving children, Elizabeth (1897–1945) and Anthony (1902–1968) – proved happy. These years saw Asquith rise to the top of the Liberal Party: he was appointed Chancellor of the Exchequer when the Liberals were returned to power in 1905, and then succeeded CAMPBELL-BANNERMAN as Prime Minister in April 1908, when he left Marylebone for Downing Street. His lasting achievement was the Parliament Act of 1911, which ended the House of Lords veto on financial legislation, and the subsequent introduction of National Insurance. Asquith proved a less able leader in war than in peace, and resigned in favour of LLOYD GEORGE in December 1916. He then returned to 20 Cavendish Square, which remained his home until 1920, when a shortage of funds forced a move to a cheaper house in Bedford Square, Bloomsbury. Asquith died at The

354   Herbert Henry Asquith in his study at 20 Cavendish Square in c.1906. It was the exterior of this room that was marked with a blue plaque in 1951.

MARYLEBONE

355 The exuberant Gothic Revival interior of St James-the-Less, Pimlico, built to designs by G. E. Street in 1859–61. [© English Heritage. Photograph by Derek Kendall]

Wharf, Sutton Courtenay, Oxfordshire, his country home since 1912. Although number 20 dates from 1729, it was re-fronted to designs by Sir Edwin Cooper after being bought in 1922 by the Cowdray Club. The LCC plaque to Asquith, erected in 1951, marks the ground-floor room that served as his study.

The architect **George Edmund Street** (1824–1881) ⑫ lived at 14 Cavendish Place, W1, on the corner of Chandos Street, from February 1870 until his death. One of the great champions of High Victorian Gothic, Street learned his craft in the office of GEORGE GILBERT SCOTT in the 1840s; fellow pupils were G. F. BODLEY and William White. Street, who set up in practice in 1849 and settled permanently in London in 1856, excelled in building subtly monumental churches; these included St Philip and St James, Oxford (1858–65) and St James-the-Less, Pimlico (1859–61) (fig. 355), both of which were influenced by the eclectic range of styles Street witnessed during his travels on the Continent. He moved to this mid-eighteenth-century house while engaged on his grandest and most important project, the Royal Courts of Justice, built in 1871–82. During the decade he lived here, Street suffered the death of his first wife, Mariquita (d. 1874), and his second, Jessie (d. 1876), and reluctantly considered moving to a smaller and more manageable house. When the deal fell through, Street wrote to his only son, 'I felt as if I had been reprieved after a sentence of death. All my happiest associations are with these rooms, and I begin to think I should be less happy anywhere else'.[7] President of the Royal Institute of British Architects at the time of his death, Street was proposed for commemoration in 1913 by the RIBA, but it was not until 1980 that he was honoured with a GLC plaque.

Number 2 Mansfield Street, W1, is a large mansion block of 1923 that bears an English Heritage plaque to **Sir Robert Mayer** (1879–1985) 🔟3️⃣ , the philanthropist and patron of music, who lived in Flat 31 from 1953 until his death. Born and educated in Mannheim, Germany, Mayer settled in Britain in 1896 and forged a career in the metal industry; as a naturalised British citizen, he served in the British Army during the First World War. A talented musician, Mayer was encouraged by his wife Dorothy Moulton (d. 1974), a soprano singer, to use his private wealth to institute a concert series for children. The first season, conducted by ADRIAN BOULT, opened in 1923, and the concerts – mostly under the baton of SIR MALCOLM SARGENT – became an annual fixture not only in London but also in provincial cities; Mayer remained in control until the BBC took over in 1973. He and SIR THOMAS

BEECHAM founded the London Philharmonic Orchestra in 1932, and five years later Mayer was knighted for services to music. Tireless in his promotion of classical music to wider audiences, Mayer documented his philanthropic activities in an autobiography, *My First Hundred Years* (1979). Following his death at the age of 105, Mayer was proposed for a blue plaque by his second wife, Jacqueline, who was present when the plaque was unveiled in 1997 by Sir Claus Moser, then Chairman of the Royal Opera House, Covent Garden.

Number 13 Mansfield Street was home to two distinguished architects, **John Loughborough Pearson** (1817–1897) and **Sir Edwin Landseer Lutyens** (1869–1944) 1️⃣4️⃣ ; the pair are commemorated on a joint plaque erected by the LCC in 1962 (fig. 356). Part of an Adam speculation, the house dates from about 1773. Pearson, who moved here in May 1881, designed intricately crafted pieces of furniture to suit the Adam interiors rather than to reflect his own Gothic aesthetic. He was then at the height of his powers, having established himself as one of the foremost proponents of Gothic architecture with a large number of church commissions, including Holy Trinity, Bessborough Gardens, Pimlico (1849–52; demolished), and St Augustine's, Kilburn (1870); these and other works brought him the prestigious commission to design Truro Cathedral in 1878. Pearson died at number 13 at the age of eighty. A later resident of the house was Sir Edwin Lutyens (fig. 357), who moved here in 1919 from 31 Bedford Square, Bloomsbury, WC1. Lutyens had made his name designing country houses that blended vernacular styles with classicism, and famously collaborated with the garden designer Gertude Jekyll; his many works include Castle Drogo, Devon (1912–30). When Lutyens and his wife, Lady Emily, née Bulwer-Lytton (1874–1964), took up residence in Mansfield Street, he was working on his most ambitious commission, the creation of a new Indian capital city, New Delhi (1913–31). Together with Herbert Baker, he planned and designed this scheme of government and residential buildings, which were placed within a setting of parks and wide, tree-lined streets, with the magnificent Viceroy's House as a focal point. In July 1919 Lutyens accepted LLOYD GEORGE's commission to design a 'catafalque' to commemorate the British war dead. The resulting stone Cenotaph in Whitehall, which was unveiled on Armistice Day 1920, is still the

356   A view from Mansfield Street, showing number 13 and its LCC plaque jointly commemorating John Loughborough Pearson and Sir Edwin Lutyens. In the distance is the plaque to Alfred Waterhouse at 61 New Cavendish Street. [© English Heritage. Photograph by Derek Kendall]

MARYLEBONE

Number 20 Mansfield Street was the home of the reformer and inventor **Charles Stanhope**, **3rd Earl Stanhope** (1753–1816) ⑮ , who lived here from 1787 to 1795. Stanhope married Hester, the sister of WILLIAM PITT THE YOUNGER, in 1774, and was elected an MP six years later. Having become Lord Mahon at the age of ten, he inherited the earldom on his father's death in 1786. Stanhope used his seat in the House of Lords to campaign for parliamentary reform, the abolition of the slave trade and religious liberty, notably for Roman Catholics. He was dubbed 'Citizen Stanhope' for sympathising with the revolutionaries in France, even after Britain declared war on that country, and having been viewed as an eccentric, became known as a political fanatic. On the night of 11 June 1794, his home in Mansfield Street – which he shared with his second wife, Louisa, née Grenville (1758–1829), a cousin of Hester and William Pitt – was set on fire by the mob, but without causing lasting damage. Stanhope – who escaped unscathed – became disillusioned with politics and seceded from the House of Lords for five years from 1795, the same year that he left this house to live principally at his country estate, Chevening, Kent. He

focus of the annual service held on Remembrance Sunday. Despite running an internationally renowned architectural practice – based from 1910 at 17 Queen Anne's Gate, Westminster, and from 1931 at 5 Eaton Gate, Belgravia – Lutyens and his wife struggled to maintain this large London town house, with its complement of ten servants. In the early 1930s the architect created a more convenient layout by moving the kitchen and dining room to the first floor, which enabled the couple to manage with fewer staff and thereby live more economically, and transferred his studio to a building at the rear of the property. At the same time, the basement was converted into a flat for their daughter, the composer Elisabeth Lutyens (1906–1983). From his studio in the house, Lutyens masterminded the construction of Queen Mary's Dolls' House, which involved the work of sixty artists and over 250 craftsmen (fig. 358); it was unveiled to the press in 1924 in the drawing room, and is now on display at Windsor Castle. Lutyens died at number 13 on New Year's Day, 1944, surrounded by his (unexecuted) designs for the Roman Catholic cathedral at Liverpool.

359 The plaque to Charles, 3rd Earl Stanhope, at 20 Mansfield Street. It was unveiled in 1951 by a descendant, James, 7th Earl Stanhope (shown here). [© Getty Images]

the Victoria University of Manchester). In 1865 he moved to London, and established both his home and his architectural practice at this house, then numbered 8 New Cavendish Street. It was from here that he designed his two most famous buildings – Manchester Town Hall (1867–77) and the Natural History Museum at South Kensington (1872–81) (fig. 360) – confirming his place as one of the most successful and popular architects of the day. His lavish rebuilding of Eaton Hall, Cheshire, for the 1st Duke of Westminster in the 1870s attracted a number of other country-house clients, but Waterhouse is especially known for his institutional commissions, a late addition to which was University College Hospital, London (1896–1906), and for his commercial work, most notably the twenty-seven buildings he designed for the Prudential Assurance Company, including its headquarters in Holborn (1876–1901). His outstanding commissions were completed by his son Paul (1861–1924), who lived at the New Cavendish Street house with Waterhouse and his wife Elizabeth, née Hodgkin (1834–1918) and who inherited his father's architectural practice on his

was equally well known for his scientific experiments; as early as 1777 – four years after his election to the Royal Society – Stanhope advocated the use of stucco in architecture, pointing to its value in rendering buildings fireproof, and demonstrated the value of lightning conductors. He also built several model steam-powered ships, but his most successful invention – of 1805 – was a stereotype process of printing, which was taken up by Oxford University Press and *The Times*. The LCC plaque was unveiled in 1951 by his descendant, James, 7th Earl Stanhope (fig. 359).

Number 61 (formerly 8, then 20) New Cavendish Street, W1 (see fig. 356) – one of a pair of houses built by John Johnson in 1776–77 – was the London base of the architect **Alfred Waterhouse** (1830–1905) **16** from 1865 until 1901. After buying the house in 1864, he remodelled the upper floors, adding iron verandas and balconies, to create a family home, and converted the ground floor into his office. Liverpool-born, Waterhouse began his career in Manchester, where he designed a succession of public buildings including the Assize Courts (1859–64; demolished), Strangeways Prison (1866–68) and Owens College (1870–1902; later

360 Alfred Waterhouse's design for the entrance to the Natural History Museum, South Kensington, c.1872. The building was completed in 1881. [© RIBA Library Drawings Collection]

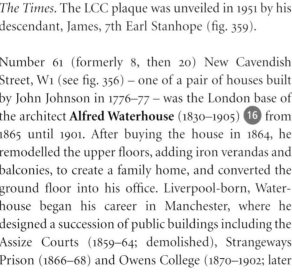

MARYLEBONE

retirement in 1901. Alfred Waterhouse spent the last part of his life at his country house – Yattendon Court, Berkshire, built to his own designs in 1878–81 and since demolished – and died there at the age of seventy-five.

To the west lies perhaps the best known of all Marylebone thoroughfares, Harley Street, W1, a name now synonymous with the world of private medicine. Planned in the 1720s, the street was built from 1752 onwards. An English Heritage plaque at 63 Harley Street commemorates the Scottish ophthalmologist **Sir Stewart Duke-Elder** (1898–1978) **17** , who was based here for over forty years (fig. 361). This was the third address in Harley Street occupied by Duke-Elder, who had lived at numbers 37 and 59 in the late 1920s and early 1930s. When he moved in 1934 to number 63, he demolished the existing house and rebuilt it to accommodate his home and flourishing practice, allowing room for two medical student lodgers and his secretary. While living at number 63 – an address he shared with his wife and fellow ophthalmologist, Phyllis, née Edgar – Duke-Elder wrote in flowing longhand the bulk of his seven-volume *Text-book of Ophthalmology* (1932–54), known to students as 'the Ophthalmologists' Bible'. Knighted in 1933, he served as first President of the Faculty of Ophthalmology at the Royal College of Surgeons (1945–49) and played a lead role in the founding in 1947 of the Institute of Ophthalmology, London; students were fondly nicknamed 'Duke-Elderberries'. In 1963 Duke-Elder took a house at 28 Elm Tree Road, St John's Wood (demolished), but he continued to use number 63 until his retirement in 1976. Duke-Elder was commemorated with a plaque in 2002.

At 73 (formerly 53) Harley Street, a blue wreathed LCC plaque of 1908 commemorates two great Victorians: the geologist **Sir Charles Lyell** (1797–1875) and the statesman **W. E. Gladstone** (1809–1898) (see also pp. 468–9 and pp. 471–2) **18** , who lived in a house on this site. The original number 73 was built in the 1770s and demolished in 1905; the present house was designed by W. H. White. Lyell – who was born in Scotland, the son of a botanist – moved to what was then number 53 in autumn 1854, having lived previously at 24 (formerly 11) Harley Street (demolished). While living here, he wrote *The Antiquity of Man* (1863) and prepared new editions of his most influential

works, *Principles of Geology* (1830–33) and *Elements of Geology* (1838); he was created a baronet in 1864. Despite his growing physical frailty, Lyell – a mentor and close friend of Charles Darwin – continued to make geological tours both at home and abroad, and, after the death in 1873 of his wife Mary, née Horner, he dedicated himself wholly to his studies. He wrote, 'I endeavour by daily work at my favourite science to forget as far as possible the dreadful change which this has made in my existence'.[8] Two years later, he died in his bedroom at Harley Street. Lyell was succeeded at the house – renumbered 73 in 1866 – by William Ewart Gladstone who, having resigned as leader of the Liberal Party in 1874, moved here in May 1876. During his four years at this address, Gladstone at first distanced himself from politics, taking refuge in literary pursuits in his sparsely furnished study, with its fireplace tiled with Homeric subjects. However, the issue of the 'Bulgarian atrocities' – a series of outrages committed by the Turks against Christians in their Balkan territories – saw him renew his attacks on Disraeli. This culminated in the famous Midlothian campaign (1879–80), which won Gladstone a seat in the Commons and swept him back into 10 Downing Street for his second term as Prime Minister (1880–85). Contrary to the inscription on the plaque, which states that he lived here until 1882, Gladstone moved his home to Downing Street in May 1880, but retained the lease on number 73 until two years later.

In 2003 an English Heritage plaque was erected at 109 Harley Street (formerly 49 Upper Harley Street) to the architect **George Frederick Bodley** (1827–1907) **19** . A superb proponent of late Victorian Gothic, Bodley was Britain's leading ecclesiastical architect in the late nineteenth century and was responsible for churches around the country. The son of a Hull doctor who ended up practising in Harley Street, Bodley spent much of his life in Marylebone. Soon after the completion of his five-year apprenticeship (1845–50) in the office of George Gilbert Scott – where he worked with G. E. Street – Bodley moved to Wimpole Street. He lived with his mother Mary (1790/1–1883) at what was then 49 Upper Harley Street from 1862 until his marriage to Minna Reavely in September 1872, whereupon the newlyweds moved to 24 Church Row, Hampstead, NW3; the plaque erroneously states that the architect lived here until 1873. During his years at

361 Number 63 Harley Street, rebuilt in 1934 to accommodate the home and flourishing practice of the ophthalmologist Sir Stewart Duke-Elder. It was marked with an English Heritage plaque in 2002. [© English Heritage. Photograph by Derek Kendall]

362 Sir Arthur Pinero's former home at 115A Harley Street, which fronts onto Devonshire Street and was built in 1898. The playwright lived here between 1909 and 1934. [© English Heritage. Photograph by Derek Kendall]

writer, he made his debut with *£200 a Year* (1877) and, his first full-length play, *La Comète* (1878). Pinero, who in 1883 married the actress Myra Holme (1851/2–1919), forged his reputation with a series of comedies – the so-called 'Court' farces – which included *The Magistrate* (1885) and *Dandy Dick* (1887). He had further success with *The Second Mrs Tanqueray* (1893), a bold denunciation of contemporary sexual double standards, while his time at number 115A saw the production of plays including *The Big Drum* (1915) and *The Enchanted Cottage* (1922). However, Pinero's work was generally out of fashion after the First World War and, when proposed for a plaque in 1965, doubts were expressed about his lasting stature. Nevertheless, a GLC plaque was erected in 1970 on number 115A, the house in which he had lived the longest.

Number 28 Queen Anne Street, W1, dating from *c.* 1770, served as the home and workplace from December 1912 to 1941 of the paediatrician **Sir George Frederic Still** (1868–1941) **21**, the first professor of paediatric medicine in England. Through his work as a private practitioner, and as physician for diseases of children (1899–1906) at King's College Hospital and then professor (1906–33) at King's College London, he established child health as a distinct branch of medicine. A somewhat reserved bachelor, Frederic Still enjoyed a special rapport with children: he delighted in his ward rounds and filled the waiting room at number 28, where his private practice was based, with toys to entertain his young patients. His pioneering research into childhood arthritis – Still's disease is named in his honour – was followed by seminal texts on other childhood conditions and a *History of Paediatrics* (1931). Still led a successful campaign to found the British Paediatric Association, now the Royal College of Paediatrics and Child Health, and presided over the association's first meeting, held at his house in 1928. He retired from active practice four years later – when he was presented with a portrait of himself painted by fellow Marylebone resident, Sir Gerald Kelly – but served from 1937 as Physician-Extraordinary to King George VI. The English Heritage plaque was unveiled by the President of the British Paediatric Association, Sir David Hull, in 1993.

number 109, which served as both home and office, Bodley worked on some of his most important early commissions, including St Salvador's, Dundee (1865–74) and St John the Baptist, Tuebrook, Liverpool (1867–70). Following a serious illness in 1868–69, Bodley went into partnership with Thomas Garner, a collaboration that lasted until 1897 and which produced works including St Augustine's, Pendlebury, near Manchester (1870–74), and Holy Angels, Hoar Cross, Staffordshire (1872–76). Bodley continued to practise until his death, which occurred at his country home in Oxfordshire.

Number 115A Harley Street, fronting onto Devonshire Street, is a delightful Queen Anne villa dating from 1898 (fig. 362). It was the home of the playwright **Sir Arthur Pinero** (1855–1934) **20** from 1909 – the year he was knighted – until the time of his death. Born near Sadler's Wells Theatre, Arthur Wing Pinero took up acting while in his teens, and performed in provincial repertory before being engaged in 1876 at London's Lyceum, where he supported Henry Irving. As a

A GLC plaque at 58 (formerly 27) Queen Anne Street commemorates the visit of the celebrated French com-

364 A Bedford Lemere photograph of the drawing room at 6 Wimpole Street, taken in 1892, during the residence of Sir Frederick Treves. [Reproduced by permission of English Heritage. NMR]

poser **Hector Berlioz** (1803–1869) 22 to London for the Great Exhibition in the summer of 1851 (fig. 363). Born near Lyon, Berlioz devoted himself to composition from the 1820s; it was during the following decade that he produced his most popular works, including *Symphonie Fantastique* (1830), *Harold en Italie* (1834) and *Roméo et Juliette* (1839), while he also made his name as a conductor, and in 1843 published the important *Grand Traité d'Instrumentation et d'Orchestration Modernes*. In 1851 Berlioz made the second of five trips to London, lodging in an apartment above the New Beethoven Rooms at 58 Queen Anne Street, an eigh-

teenth-century house altered in about 1840–50, where the Beethoven Quartet Society held its meetings from 1845. Rather than conducting his own works, Berlioz was entrusted with 'the stupid job of examining the musical instruments sent to the [Great] Exhibition'.[9] Early each morning he walked across Hyde Park to the Crystal Palace at South Kensington, and on some evenings he listened to the concerts held in the drawing room below his room at number 58. He described one such occasion in a letter home: 'I could easily hear the whole performance by simply opening my door. One evening I heard Beethoven's trio in C minor being played. I opened my door wide, Come in, Come in, welcome proud melody! How fine and beautiful it is'.[10] Berlioz returned to London in 1852, 1853 and, for the final time, in 1855, conducting a series of performances of his works.

Wimpole Street, W1, was developed by the Portland Estate in the second half of the eighteenth century. At number 6, an English Heritage plaque commemorates the surgeon **Sir Frederick Treves** (1853–1923) 23 , who lived and worked here from 1886 to 1907 (fig. 364). A brilliant student at the London Hospital – the staff of which then included JOHN HUGHLINGS JACKSON and JONATHAN HUTCHINSON – Treves initially practised in Derbyshire before qualifying as a surgeon and returning to work at the hospital where he had trained. He remained there until 1898, enjoying great celebrity as the foremost practitioner of anatomy and abdominal surgery in the country. Treves once boasted that his operating coat 'was so stiff with congealed blood after many years of use that it would stand upright when placed on the floor'.[11] By the time of his death, he could count three monarchs among his patients, and his consulting rooms at number 6 – a house he shared with his wife Anne, née Mason (1854–1944) and their two daughters – were among the most famous in England; he was created a baronet in 1902. Treves is primarily remembered today for his involvement with Joseph Merrick, whom he rescued from being exhibited as 'the Elephant Man' in freak shows and found, in 1886, a permanent residence at the London Hospital. When Merrick asked to see inside a family home, Treves brought him to 6 Wimpole Street, which Merrick examined in the minutest of detail and 'with untiring curiosity'.[12] From 1908 onwards Treves lived at Thatched House Lodge in Richmond Park, a grace-

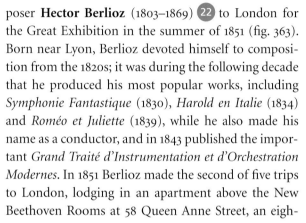

MARYLEBONE

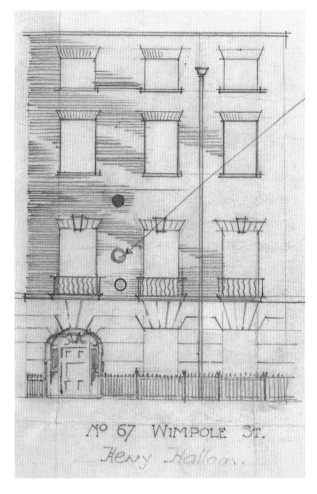

365   A drawing showing alternative positions for the plaque to Henry Hallam at 67 Wimpole Street. The occupant of the building thought that the lower position (marked in red) would not be visible, and was in favour of the position marked with an arrow. The LCC concurred, and installed the plaque in 1904. [© City of London, LMA]

N⁰ 67 WIMPOLE ST.

Henry Hallam.

This was written in memory of his close friend Arthur Henry Hallam (1811–1833), Henry's eldest son, who died suddenly while the family were in Vienna. Hallam's time at number 67 was also marked by the deaths of his daughter Eleanor (d. 1837) and his wife Julia, née Elton (1783–1840), after which he moved to 24 Wilton Crescent, Belgravia, SW1.

An English Heritage plaque at 36 Wimpole Street honours the colonial administrator **Evelyn Baring, 1st Earl of Cromer** (1841–1917) **25** . Born into a family of bankers at Cromer Hall in Norfolk – the name of which he adopted as his title when he was created an earl in 1901 – Baring spent much of his long career in Egypt. He first went to the country to advise on the financial crisis of 1876, returned as one of two Controller-Generals in 1879, and was appointed Consul-General in 1883, with orders to reform the civil administration. An advocate of British withdrawal from Egypt, Baring only reluctantly supported General Gordon's mission to Khartoum, and devised the eventual peace settlement between France and Britain (1904). Most of his energies were concentrated on transforming the railway network and the irrigation, education and justice systems, all towards the goal of modernising Egypt. Baring's stay in London was restricted to the years following his retirement in May 1907, during which he was extremely industrious: while living at number 36 – from 1908 until his death – he wrote several books, including a defence of his policies, *Modern Egypt* (1908), and a comparison of ancient and modern empires, *Ancient and Modern Imperialism* (1910). Invited in summer 1916 to preside over the Dardanelles Commission, he collapsed and died at number 36 the following January.

and-favour house granted to him by King Edward VII, though after the First World War he lived mainly abroad, and died at Lausanne.

Number 67 Wimpole Street was the home of the historian **Henry Hallam** (1777–1859) **24** , who was commemorated in 1904 by a wreathed blue plaque, the fifth erected by the LCC (fig. 365). Born in Windsor into a clerical family, Hallam abandoned a legal career in order to concentrate on historical scholarship. Politically a Whig, he enjoyed a high reputation throughout the nineteenth century for his *Constitutional History of England from the Accession of Henry VII to the Death of George II* (1827), which was written while he was living at number 67. Hallam's final work, also written at this address, was *Introduction to the Literature of Europe in the Fifteenth, Sixteenth, and Seventeenth Centuries* (1837–39). Number 67 Wimpole Street, Hallam's home from 1819 to 1840, was immortalised by TENNYSON as 'Dark house, by which once more I stand / Here in the long unlovely street' in his poem *In Memoriam* (1833).

High up on the rebuilt façade of 50 Wimpole Street is a chocolate-brown Society of Arts plaque to the poetess **Elizabeth Barrett Barrett** (1806–1861) **26** (see also pp. 415–16), who, as the inscription records, was afterwards the wife of Robert Browning (figs 366 and 367). The plaque was first erected in 1899 to commemorate her residence from May 1838 to September 1846 in the house of her widowed father, the plantation owner Edward Barrett Moulton Barrett (1785–1857). After the eighteenth-century house was demolished in 1936, both the RSA and the LCC declined the offer of the plaque, which was therefore re-erected on the new

comment that its shadowy walls looked 'so much like Newgate's turned inside out'.[13] She was confined by chronic illness to her room on the third floor at the back of the house, which was gloomily decorated with dark green wallpaper and heavy curtains, while a large ivy blocked out the light from the window. It was in this room that 'EBB' completed her highly successful two-volume collection of *Poems* (1844), which included the verses 'A Drama of Exile' and 'Lady Geraldine's Courtship'. It was also here, on 20 May 1845, that she first met the poet Robert Browning; the pair had corresponded about poetry – Browning was a devoted admirer of Elizabeth's work – and were soon to embark on a passionate love affair. Mr Barrett's resolute refusal to sanction the couple's engagement compelled the lovers to elope; they were married in old St Marylebone Church on 12 September 1846. Elizabeth was never reconciled with her father, who returned all her letters unopened, and spent the rest of her life largely in Italy, where she died in 1861.

The nursing reformer **Ethel Gordon Fenwick** (1857–1947) 27 is commemorated with an English Heritage plaque at 20 Upper Wimpole Street, W1 (fig. 368). After training in Nottingham and Manchester, Ethel Gordon Manson worked as a sister at the London Hospital, and at the young age of twenty-four was appointed Matron and Superintendent of Nursing at St Bartholomew's Hospital. She resigned her post on marrying Dr Bedford Fenwick (1855–1939) in July 1887, and the couple set up house at number 20. Mrs Bedford Fenwick, as she became known, thereafter devoted her energies to improving the status of British nurses. At a meeting of matrons and doctors held in the drawing room of her house in November 1887, it was agreed to establish the British Nurses' Association, which in 1891 became the first women's professional body to receive a royal charter. Fenwick's most important achievement was the state registration of nurses, enacted in 1919 after twenty-five years of determined campaigning. Fittingly, hers was the first name listed in the Register of Nurses in England and Wales, and she was appointed to the new statutory body, the General Nursing Council. Fenwick's remaining years were coloured by a long-running feud with the College of Nursing (established 1916), and its campaign to legitimise assistant nurses by enrolling them. In 1926 she set up a rival institution, the British College of Nurses.

frontage. To prevent any misunderstanding that the house was her original home, an additional inscription – describing her by her married name, Elizabeth Barrett Browning – was carved into the stonework at ground-floor level, making it clear that she lived in a house on this site. Grief-stricken at the death of two of her brothers in 1840, Elizabeth – who usually signed her name 'EBB' and was familiarly known as 'Ba' – was initially unhappy in Wimpole Street. Her first impression of the thoroughfare had provoked her to

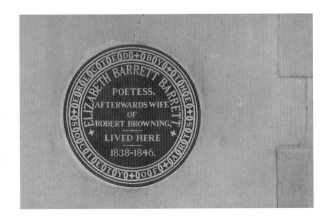

MARYLEBONE

368 Number 20 Upper Wimpole Street and its English Heritage plaque installed in 1999 in honour of Ethel Gordon Fenwick. The (Royal) British Nurses' Association was founded at a meeting held here in 1887. [© English Heritage. Photograph by Derek Kendall]

Fenwick moved away from number 20 in late 1924 or early 1925 to 12 Barton Street, Westminster, SW1, where she continued living until 1940, even after separating from her husband.

The historian **John Richard Green** (1837–1883) **28** (see also p. 323) was first honoured with an LCC plaque at 4 Beaumont Street, W1, in 1909; the plaque was re-erected after the late eighteenth-century house was demolished in 1924, but was damaged in the process and so was replaced in 1964 by another LCC plaque. Since then the house has twice been rebuilt, and the plaque is now on a building of 1988. Formerly a vicar in Stepney, Green moved to number 4 in spring 1869, having taken up the less onerous position of Honorary Librarian at Lambeth Library; he wrote

happily to a friend, 'I enjoy even the cleaner streets, and above all my morning's trot through the Parks. It is such a change too to get a chat when one likes, to be able to get a peep at good pictures, and to have one's mind free for the things one cares about . . . I am getting on with work as well . . . in fact, I am getting into the literary rut pretty well'.[14] It was while living at number 4 that Green wrote *A Short History of the English People* (1874), which outsold all similar works except the *History of England* by THOMAS BABINGTON MACAULAY and helped shape a generation's understanding of the country's history. Buoyed by this success, Green planned to write a series of historical biographies, which, he argued, 'would do a great deal for the historic education of English people who – poor souls – cry aloud for decent histories, and can't

404

get 'em'.[15] Green moved out of 4 Beaumont Street in 1876, the year before his marriage to Alice Stopford, also a historian, and spent his last years writing *The Making of England* (1882).

An LCC plaque at 1 Wheatley Street (formerly 1 Chesterfield Street, later Great Chesterfield Street), W1, marks the site of the family home of the divine and hymn writer **Charles Wesley** (1707–1788) and his two sons, the musicians **Charles Wesley** (1757–1834) and **Samuel Wesley** (1766–1837) **29** ; the building, on the corner of Wesley Street (formerly Little Weymouth Street), is adjacent to a public house. Like his elder brother John Wesley, Charles Wesley senior spent much of his life as a peripatetic preacher spreading the Methodist message across the country, and was also an active poet and writer; it is said that, in old age, he could compose hymns on horseback in shorthand. In 1771 Wesley and his wife Sarah, née Gwynne (1726–1822), an accomplished amateur musician, left Bristol for London, taking a lease on 1 Chesterfield Street. Here they lived with their two sons and a daughter, Sarah (1759–1828). Both boys exhibited musical abilities from an early age: Charles was a fine harpsichordist and organist, and Samuel became one of the most important English composers of the period, producing works such as the *Ode to St Cecilia* (1794; first performed 1799). The brothers gave subscription concerts at number 1, attracting fashionable audiences, and continued living here with their mother after their father's death; Sarah Wesley finally left the house in 1806. The Wesleys' home was demolished around forty years later and rebuilt in the 1860s, a fact which led the proposal for a plaque to be shelved initially on the grounds that the 'historical surroundings and atmosphere [were] quite lost'.[16] Submissions from the International Methodist Historical Society and the Methodist Church persuaded the LCC to change its view in 1951, and a plaque was erected two years later.

At Welbeck Mansions, 35A Welbeck Street, W1 – a late Victorian block of flats on the corner of New Cavendish Street – there is an English Heritage plaque to the cartoonist **Victor Weisz** (1913–1966) **30** , better known by his pen name of '**Vicky**'. Born in Berlin, of Hungarian-Jewish descent, Weisz escaped from Nazi Germany and arrived in London in 1935. He quickly found a niche working as an artist for broadsheets including the *News Chronicle*, where his personal experience of Nazi brutality gave his cartoons a darkness and urgency that was lacking in the work of most of his English contemporaries. After the Second World War, Vicky also worked for the *Daily Mirror* and the *New Statesman*, and in 1958 moved to the *Evening Standard*, where he succeeded his fellow cartoonist and rival David Low. Vicky produced some of his best work while living in Marylebone in the post-war period. This included his most famous caricature: the portrayal of the Prime Minister Harold Macmillan as 'Supermac', an enduring image that summed up the political optimism of the 1950s and early 1960s, which Weisz – a committed socialist – felt compelled to satirise. Vicky – who was apparently 'exactly like the miniature of himself which frequently figured in his cartoons as the puzzled little man bewildered by events' – shared his flat with, in turn, the second (Lucielle) and third (Zlata) of his four wives.[17] By 1954 Weisz had moved to a flat at nearby 22 Upper Wimpole Street, where – suffering from depression – he committed suicide twelve years later, taking an overdose of the sleeping tablets upon which he had relied for so long. The plaque was unveiled in 1996 by his sister Elizabeth Weisz and the Labour politician Michael Foot. Subsequent research, however, has revealed that Vicky lived in a maisonette flat on the upper floors of the neighbouring property – 35 Welbeck Street – rather than at Welbeck Mansions. This was his home between 1949 and 1953, but has since been rebuilt as 33 Welbeck Street.

At 48 Welbeck Street, a house of *c.* 1780, an LCC plaque of 1951 commemorates the man of science **Thomas Young** (1773–1829) **31** ; it replaced an earlier light-green wreathed council plaque of 1905, which had deteriorated. An extraordinarily precocious child, Young matured into an impressive polymath and developed a lifelong fascination with languages: he was one of the first to attempt to understand Egyptian hieroglyphics, and successfully deciphered some two hundred characters of the ancient Egyptian Rosetta Stone, discovered by the French in 1799. After completing his medical training at Cambridge – where he earned the sobriquet 'Phenomeon Young' – he set up in practice in early 1800 as a physician at 48 Welbeck Street, where he remained until 1825, sharing the house with his wife Eliza, née Maxwell (1785–1859). During these years, he was as active in science as he was in medicine, and was briefly Professor of Natural Philosophy (1801–3) at the newly founded Royal Institution. Today, Young is regarded as the founder of physiological optics, owing to his research into the mechanics of the eye, which also led him to pioneering attempts at formulating a wave theory of light and sound. Sir Humphry Davy wrote of him, 'had he limited himself to any one department of knowledge, he must have been the first in that department. But as a mathematician, a scholar, a hieroglyphist, he was eminent, and he knew so much that it was difficult to say what he did not know'.[18]

Two doors away, at 50 Welbeck Street, a GLC plaque honours **Sir Patrick Manson** (1844–1922) ❸❷ as the 'Father of Modern Tropical Medicine'. Manson's discovery of the intermediary role played by bloodsucking insects in transmitting disease paved the way for the breakthrough made by Ronald Ross in deducing that the malarial parasite developed in the mosquito. A Scot, Manson spent most of his life working as a doctor in China and Hong Kong, but he returned to Britain in 1889 and resumed private practice in London for financial reasons. For the next twenty years he lived and worked at 21 Queen Anne Street, Marylebone (demolished) and, from there, successfully lobbied government to improve its colonial medical service. In 1899 Manson founded the London School of Tropical Medicine, where he worked as administrator, lecturer and physician. His *Tropical Diseases: a Manual of the Diseases of Warm Climates* (1898) remained the principal authority on the subject for many years. Knighted in 1903, Manson lived at 50 Welbeck Street from 1910 until his retirement in 1912, and died in London ten years later. His plaque was installed in 1985, at the same time as that to Ross; a reception was held by the Royal Society of Tropical Medicine and Hygiene, which Manson had co-founded in 1907.

In 1964 the LCC erected a plaque at 7 Bentinck Street, W1, the site of the former home of the London-born historian **Edward Gibbon** (1737–1792) ❸❸ (fig. 369). Gibbon lived at this address, in some opulence, from early 1773 until his move to Switzerland in 1783, years during which he published to great acclaim the first

three volumes of his masterpiece, *The History of the Decline and Fall of the Roman Empire* (6 vols; 1776–88). Before moving in, Gibbon had the house redecorated, paying particular attention to his library: 'the paper of the Room will be a fine shag flock paper, light blue with a gold border, the Book cases painted white, ornamented with a light frize [*sic*]: neither Doric nor Dentulated . . . but Academic'.[19] He was delighted with the results, proudly declaring that 'my little Palace . . . is absolutely the best house in London'.[20] The Society of Arts erected a plaque on the original house in 1896, but this was taken down when the building was demolished in 1908–9. A proposal to 'medallionize' the rebuilt address came to nothing in 1925, but in 1949 the question arose again and – as it concerned a site rather than a surviving residence – provoked considerable debate. It was ultimately agreed that since number 7 was the only house in London connected with Gibbon, an exception to the usual rules could be made. However, the building's owner, Mrs Lizzie Elaine Winter, refused to give consent for the plaque, expostulating that she 'was astounded to think the LCC wanted to waste more public money now when the County is on the verge of bankruptcy'.[21] Despite the best efforts of the LCC, the owner stood her ground, and the plaque had to wait until 1964 – following a change of ownership – to be installed.

Just north of Oxford Street is Stratford Place, W1, part of a grand cul-de-sac built around 1771–80 by Richard Edwin for the Hon. Edward Stratford on the site of the Lord Mayor's banqueting house. At number 7, a GLC

370 'Spring' – representing a passage from William Morris's *The Earthly Paradise* – in a piece of painted glass by Charles Eamer Kempe, installed at Wightwick Manor, Wolverhampton, in 1887. [© NTPL / Derrick E. Witty]

was President of the United States from 1837 to 1841, but his hard-headed attitude to the deep economic depression of 1837 put paid to his chances of re-election. He spent the rest of his life largely in retirement at his home in Kinderhook, New York.

MARYLEBONE HIGH STREET TO EDGWARE ROAD

The regimented layout of Marylebone is pleasingly interrupted by the bustling Marylebone High Street, which runs north from Oxford Street, past the site of old St Mary's, to Marylebone Road, where the new St Mary's was built in 1813–17 to the designs of Thomas Hardwick. To the west, high up on 37 (formerly 28) Nottingham Place, W1 – now a hotel – an English Heritage plaque marks the building in which the stained-glass artist **Charles Eamer Kempe** (1837–1907) ③⑤ lived and worked. Initially a student of the architect G. F. BODLEY, the ardently Anglo-Catholic Kempe turned to stained glass in 1864, working as an apprentice to the renowned firm of Clayton & Bell; two years later he founded his own business – the Kempe Studio for Stained Glass and Church Furniture – at his lodgings at 47 Beaumont Street, Marylebone, and made his name in 1869 with his decoration of Bodley's St John the Baptist, Tuebrook, Liverpool. Inspired by Flemish and German masters of the sixteenth century, Kempe developed a style of glass that was characterised by rich colours and soft, clear light (fig. 370). He moved his flourishing studio to Nottingham Place in 1886 and remodelled the building to create a small flat in the rooms above, where he lived when in London. The exterior of this late eighteenth-century house – together with the rest of the terrace – was embellished with bay windows, red-brick trimmings and a gable in 1891–92 by E. Keynes Purchase. In the first-floor studio, Kempe worked with his assistants – who included ARTHUR HUGHES – to produce the large-scale cartoons for the glass made at the factory he had established in 1874 at 2 Millbrook Place, Camden Town (demolished). It was at Nottingham Place that Kempe died in 1907, though since 1875 he had owned an Elizabethan manor house in Lindfield, Sussex, where he entertained friends and colleagues. His firm was based at number 37 for a further twenty-seven years – until its closure in 1934. The plaque – of a smaller size than usual so as to fit onto the building's façade – was

plaque honours the eighth US President, **Martin van Buren** (1782–1862) ③④ . He lived here as American minister to Great Britain from September 1831 until April 1832, when he returned to the United States to accept the vice-presidential nomination under Andrew Jackson. Van Buren's stay in this elegant pilastered terrace was a happy and formative period in his career, and van Buren, known for his charm, gained the close friendship of his Legation Secretary, WASHINGTON IRVING. A lawyer of Dutch descent, van Buren – nicknamed 'Old Kinderhook' after the town of his birth –

MARYLEBONE

371 An undated portrait of Octavia Hill, the housing reformer and co-founder of The National Trust. She is commemorated with a plaque at 2 Garbutt Place, where her reforming work began. [© NTPL]

unveiled in 1994 by Margaret Stavridi, the daughter of Kempe's chief designer, John Lisle.

The housing reformer and co-founder of The National Trust, **Octavia Hill** (1838–1912) 36 (fig. 371), also lived in Nottingham Place – at number 42 (formerly 14; demolished) – from 1860 to 1890, but she has been commemorated further south, at 2 Garbutt Place (formerly Paradise Place), W1. Octavia Hill was born in Wisbech, Cambridgeshire, and from an early age was moved with the spirit of reform. Following her family's move to central London in 1852, she came into contact with a circle that included F. D. Maurice and John Ruskin. It was a loan from Ruskin that enabled Hill to acquire, in spring 1865, this small terrace of early nineteenth-century cottages, then known as Paradise Place. Here, as the plaque's inscription records, she began her reforming work. Hill transformed these cramped slum dwellings into neat, well-maintained lodgings for seasonal and casual workers, and created a playground for their children in the surrounding space. She both managed the buildings and acted as a social worker and counsellor to her tenants, helping them find work and arranging classes; in this, she was assisted by others including Emma Cons. Hill went on to rescue other properties in nearby Freshwater Place and St Christopher's Place and also in areas such as Walworth and Southwark, and campaigned to preserve precious open space in London, crucially saving Parliament Hill Fields from developers. She pioneered the idea of a 'green belt' around London in her article 'More Air for London' (1888), and together with Canon Hardwicke Rawnsley and Sir Robert Hunter founded The National Trust; this was first conceived in 1893 and was incorporated in January 1895. Hill died at her home, 190 Marylebone Road, but since neither this nor any of her residences in London are still standing, English Heritage decided to celebrate this remarkable woman by erecting a plaque in Garbutt Place in 1991.

High up on the stuccoed façade of Hinde House, 11–14 Hinde Street, W1, an English Heritage plaque marks the second-floor flat once occupied by the writer **Rose Macaulay** (1881–1958) 37 . Born in Rugby, Emilie Rose Macaulay – a descendant of the historian Thomas Babington Macaulay – was educated at Oxford and published her first novel, *Abbots Verney*, in 1906. She first moved to Marylebone in 1913 after winning a lit-

erary competition with her novel *The Lee Shore* (1912), and was introduced into London's literary circles by her childhood friend, Rupert Brooke. A string of successes, such as *Potterism* (1920), *Crew Train* (1926) and *Keeping Up Appearances* (1928), established Macaulay as one of the most popular women novelists of her day. After being bombed out of her flat in Luxborough Street during the Blitz in March 1941, Macaulay moved nearby to Flat 20, Hinde House. Here she wrote the last – and best known – of her twenty-three novels, *The Towers of Trebizond* (1956). Awarded a DBE in 1958, Macaulay died in her flat in October that year, leaving fragments of her last novel, *Venice Besieged*, which was published together with her *Letters to a Sister* in 1964. The writer and critic A. N. Wilson – long a member of English Heritage's Blue Plaques Panel – paid tribute to Macaulay's 'delicate, book-filled, witty mind' when he unveiled the plaque in 1996.[22]

Hinde Street leads into one of the loveliest of London's squares, Manchester Square (built 1776–88), W1, the home of the Wallace Collection at Hertford House. In 1934 the LCC erected a wreathed blue plaque at 2 Manchester Square to commemorate the musical composer **Sir Julius Benedict** (1804–1885) 38 , who moved here in 1845 and died here forty years later (fig. 372). The son of a wealthy German banker, Benedict studied music with Jan Hummel in Stuttgart and with Carl Maria von Weber in Dresden, through whom he met Beethoven and Mendelssohn. He came to London in 1835, and became conductor first of the Italian Opera at the Lyceum and then at Drury Lane, where he premiered his own compositions; these included *The Gipsy's Warning* (1838), *The Bride of Venice* (1843) and *The Crusaders* (1846). Although his oratorios and his later opera, *The Lily of Killarney* (1862), met with some success, Benedict was renowned more for his performances of works by his contemporaries, especially those by Balfe and Mendelssohn, and was known as an accomplished pianist. He was particularly active at provincial festivals, conducting at the one in Norwich every year between 1845 and 1878. Benedict became a naturalised British citizen before receiving a knighthood in 1871, awarded in recognition of his role in popularising classical music.

At 3 Manchester Square, a similar wreathed LCC blue plaque honours Benedict's neighbour, the physician

372　The wreathed LCC plaques to Sir Julius Benedict and his neighbour John Hughlings Jackson at 2 and 3 Manchester Square. [© English Heritage. Photograph by Derek Kendall]

John Hughlings Jackson (1835–1911) **39** (see fig. 372). Jackson moved to this address in 1871 with his wife (and cousin) Elizabeth, née Jackson (1836/7–1876), and died here in October 1911. After training in York and at St Bartholomew's Hospital, Jackson was helped by Jonathan Hutchinson to obtain a position at the Metropolitan Free Hospital in 1859. Within a few years he was working as a physician at the London Hospital in Whitechapel and the National Hospital for the Paralysed and Epileptic in Queen Square, Bloomsbury; he remained on the staff of these hospitals until 1894 and 1906 respectively. In his clinical practice, Jackson investigated diseases of the nervous system that caused fits and paralysis, most notably epilepsy, and transformed contemporary understanding of how the brain controlled voluntary movements of the body. For this pioneering work, Jackson has been hailed as the 'father of modern neurology'. He was proposed for commemoration in 1930 by the Royal College of Physicians, who argued that 'his name was second to none in the list of physicians of the Victorian period'.[23] The LCC delayed erecting the plaque until 1932, so as to allow twenty years to pass from the time of his death.

Number 14 Manchester Square was the London home of the German-born statesman **Alfred**, **Lord Milner** (1854–1925) **40** during the last four years of his life. Milner was a controversial figure whose reputation today is overshadowed by his imperialist and racist views. After coming under the influence of Arnold Toynbee, and helping to set up Toynbee Hall (see Jimmy Mallon) in the East End, he entered politics in 1884 as secretary to the Liberal Unionist politician G. J. Goschen. An able administrator, Milner served in the

Ministry of Finance in Egypt (1889–92) and as High Commissioner in South Africa (1897–1905), where he took a hard-line stance against the Boers. In the ensuing war of 1899–1902, Milner worked with Lord Roberts to achieve his long-term political goal of bringing the Orange Free State and the Transvaal under British rule. He gathered around him a group of young civil servants – known as 'Milner's kindergarten' – to implement his imperialist vision in the post-war reconstruction of the colony, of which he served as Governor (1901–5). Milner was created a baron in 1901, and raised to the viscountcy the following year; he was later a chief author of the Balfour Declaration (1917), and was Secretary of State for War (1918–19) and for the Colonies (1919–21). He moved to 14 Manchester Square in 1921, shortly after marrying the widowed Violet, Lady Edward Cecil (1872–1958), and divided his retirement between this house and his country seat, Sturry Court, Kent, where he died in 1925; his widow remained at number 14 until 1939. A self-proclaimed 'British Race Patriot', Milner was nonetheless approved for commemoration by the GLC after being proposed by the tenants of number 14, and the plaque was erected in 1967.[24]

Number 4 (formerly 27) Duke Street, W1 – to the south of Manchester Square – bears a plaque commemorating **Simón Bolívar** (1783–1830) 41 as 'the liberator of Latin America'. The plaque was unveiled in 2002 by the Venezuelan Ambassador, Alfredo Toro-Hardy. Bolívar enjoyed a privileged upbringing on his family's plantation in Caracas, and in his early adulthood travelled extensively in Europe, where he imbibed the post-revolutionary principles of national self-determination. In June 1810 he landed in England, one of a deputation from Caracas seeking British support in the fight for Latin American independence – Andres Bello was another of the party. Both Bolívar and Bello lodged at Morin's Hotel at what was then 27 Duke Street from July to mid-September, during which time they met Francisco de Miranda, who was also active in the independence movement. Returning home in late 1810, Bolívar went on to liberate Caracas from the Spanish in 1813, upon which he was named 'El Libertador'. Over the next twelve years he won independence for Colombia, Venezuela, Ecuador, Peru and Upper Peru, which changed its name to Bolivia in his honour. Declared President of the federation known as Greater (Gran)

Colombia in 1821, Bolívar proved to be a dictator in peacetime, fuelling conflict with neighbouring states and alienating his erstwhile supporters at home. He survived an assassination attempt in 1828 and died two years later, soon after resigning his presidency. The English Heritage plaque at number 4 supplements a rectangular marble tablet, erected in 1971 by the Anglo-Colombian Society, which more fully describes Bolívar's achievements.

Number 3 Spanish Place, W1, a house dating from the 1780s, is adorned with two plaques at ground-floor level (fig. 349). Unveiled in 1953, the upper plaque commemorates the novelist **Captain Frederick Marryat** (1792–1848) 42 , who lived here from 1841 to 1843. A tearaway in his youth, Marryat joined the Navy at the age of fourteen, and over the next twenty-four years served in the Mediterranean, the West Indies, the North Atlantic and the Far East. He proved an able and courageous officer, who saved over a dozen lives at sea; he also designed a new lifeboat, for which he was awarded a gold medal by the Royal Humane Society in 1821. Marryat exploited his naval experiences to good effect in his subsequent literary career, and wrote a stream of best-selling adventure stories, such as *The Naval Officer* (1829), *The King's Own* (1830), *Newton Forster* (1832) and *Mr Midshipman Easy* (1836). While living at 3 Spanish Place, he published works including *Percival Keene* (1842) and ventured into writing for children; his first book in this genre was *Masterman Ready, or, The Wreck of the Pacific* (1841). However, the best known of his novels is not a naval yarn but a tale of Roundheads and Cavaliers, *The Children of the New Forest* (1847). Number 3 was Marryat's last home in London, for in 1843 his marriage to Catherine Shairp ended and he moved to Langham, Norfolk, where he died five years later. His daughter and biographer, Florence (1837–1899), recalled how 'it was here [at number 3] that, in the tiniest of houses, furnished according to his own taste, a very gem in point of its adornment – rich in pictures and *objets d'art*, clothed in velvet and decorated with hot-house flowers – he received visitors who made the little room brilliant with their conversation and their wit'.[25]

Florence Marryat was a family friend of the second notable inhabitant of 3 Spanish Place, the actor-manager **George Grossmith** (1874–1935) 43 (see fig.

349). His plaque was unveiled in 1963 on the same day as a plaque was unveiled to his father, another GEORGE GROSSMITH, elsewhere in Marylebone. Born in London, the younger Grossmith devoted his life to the theatre, first appearing on stage at the age of eighteen in his father's operetta *Haste to the Wedding* (1892). However, it was his creation of the 'dude-y' role of Bertie Boyd in the comedy *The Shop Girl* (1894) that established him on the London stage, and he went on to star in numerous light comedies at the Gaiety Theatre in Aldwych. Grossmith also turned his hand to writing and producing shows, including some of the first revues to be performed in Britain, *Rogues and Vagabonds* (1905), *Hullo . . . London!* (1910) and *The Bing Boys Are Here* (1916). In 1919 he and Edward Laurillard opened a new theatre, the Winter Garden in Drury Lane, which scored a number of musical hits, such as *Kissing Time* (1919), and pioneered cabaret in London in the 1920s. Grossmith continued to act, both on stage and in the movies, and enjoyed great success as Billy Early in the musical *No, No, Nanette* (1925). He lived at 3 Spanish Place from 1909 until 1935 – sharing the house with his wife Elizabeth, née Rudge (1873–1951), known during her acting career as Adelaide Astor – and died at a nursing home in nearby Beaumont Street.

The LCC plaque to the Irish poet **Tom Moore** (1779–1852) **44** at 85 (formerly 44) George Street, W1, was unveiled in 1963 by the Irish Ambassador, C. C. Cremin. The plaque had originally (in 1953) been affixed to 28 Bury Street, St James's, but was removed when the building was demolished in 1962 and was re-fixed at number 85. Born in Dublin, Moore first arrived in London in spring 1799 to study law at the Middle Temple, and took lodgings at 85 George Street. In a letter to MARY SHELLEY, he described it as 'the first house I ever inhabited in London – where I began with a single room on the second floor at 7s. 6d. a week, but was, in process of time, promoted downstairs, and where some adventures befell me that would not tell badly in a confessional'.[26] It is likely that number 85 remained Moore's London home until 1801, during which time he began publishing poems and songs, such as *Poetical Works of the Late Thomas Little* (1801). Although his poetry proved extremely popular – in particular, his exotic romance *Lalla Rookh* (1817) and his verse satire *The Fudge Family in Paris* (1818) –

Moore often courted controversy. His *Epistles, Odes, and other Poems* (1806) provoked one reviewer to denounce the writer as 'the most licentious of modern versifiers', and his *Memoirs of Captain Rock* (1824) contained a scathing attack on the misgovernment of Ireland.[27] Moore also wrote biographies of two of his heroes, RICHARD BRINSLEY SHERIDAN (1825) and Lord Byron (1830), and a pioneering *History of Ireland* (1835–46). In 1812 Moore and his wife Bessy left London for good, setting up house five years later at Sloperton Cottage, Bromham, Wiltshire, where he died.

Sir Francis Beaufort (1774–1857) **45** , the admiral and hydrographer, is commemorated at 51 Manchester Street, W1, where he lived from 1822 to 1832. Born in County Meath, Beaufort joined the Navy at the age of fifteen and immediately sailed to Indonesia on East India Company business. It was on this voyage that he started to write a daily weather diary, which he kept up until six days before his death. Beaufort served throughout the wars with France, rising to the rank of commander in 1800, and found time to chart the Rio de la Plata in South America (1807) and the Turkish coast (1810–12). In May 1829, aged fifty-five, he was appointed Hydrographer to the Navy, with a salary of £500 plus continuance of his half-pay, and in 1833 was given a seven-room official residence at 7 Somerset Place (now Somerset House) in the Strand. He wrote of his delight: 'I think I can be of use in my generation, and that is a charming feeling. 2ndly It is a proud situation for an insulated unconnected individual like me to find myself absolutely at the *head* of a department, and that in a country which . . . places her hydrographical department at the head of all others'.[28] In 1831 Beaufort commissioned the *Beagle*, under the command of ROBERT FITZROY, to survey the western shores of Patagonia, and arranged for a naturalist – the young CHARLES DARWIN – to keep him company. During this expedition, Beaufort's scale for measuring the strength of wind, which he had devised in 1805, was used for the first time; the Beaufort scale remains the internationally accepted measurement of wind force. Beaufort moved out of 51 Manchester Square after his beloved wife Alicia (1782–1834) developed cancer in summer 1832. After his second marriage in 1838, he took up residence nearby at 48 (formerly 11) Gloucester Place, his home for the next seventeen years. Appointed rear admiral in 1846 and knighted in 1848,

MARYLEBONE

373 The Society of Arts plaque – set in a mount – commemorating Michael Faraday's time at 48 Blandford Street. The tablet was set up in 1876, and is the oldest to survive in Marylebone. [© English Heritage. Photograph by Derek Kendall]

Above right 374 An advertisement for George Riebau's bookbinding business at 2 (now 48) Blandford Street. Michael Faraday lived and worked here as an apprentice between 1805 and 1812. [© City of Westminster Archives Centre]

375 The design for the first LCC plaque to William Pitt (Pitt the Younger). Erected at 120 Baker Street in 1904, the final plaque was actually pale green – rather than blue – in colour. It was lost when the building was remodelled in 1925 and in 1949 was replaced with a blue plaque of the standard design. [Reproduced by permission of English Heritage]

he retired in 1855 and moved to Hove, where he died two years later. The LCC chose to commemorate Beaufort at 51 Manchester Street rather than 48 Gloucester Place because the latter address already bore a plaque to JOHN ROBERT GODLEY, and there was no space for a second. The plaque was unveiled in 1959 on Beaufort's birthday, 27 May, by the Admiralty Hydrographer, Rear Admiral Kenneth St Barbe Collins.

The oldest plaque in Marylebone is that commemorating **Michael Faraday** (1791–1867) 46 , 'Man of Science', at 48 (formerly 2) Blandford Street, W1, a building of *c.* 1790–1800 (figs 373 and 374; see fig. 21). This chocolate-brown plaque, placed in a white plaster mount, was erected by the Society of Arts in 1876 on the house where Faraday worked and lodged as an apprentice to the bookbinder George Riebau from October 1805 to October 1812. Here he first came into contact with books on science, in particular Jane Marcet's *Conversations on Chemistry* (1805). Riebau was keen to encourage his young apprentice, and provided space at the back of his shop for Faraday to make scientific instruments. In spring 1812 Faraday introduced himself to the chemist Humphry Davy, who arranged for him to be appointed laboratory assistant at the Royal Institution on 1 March 1813. Faraday went on to discover electromagnetic rotation (1821) and electromagnetic induction (1831), which laid the foundation of all present-day applications of electricity. He was an extremely popular lecturer, and in 1826 founded Friday Evening Discourses and the Christmas Lectures for children, which are still the mainstay of the Royal Institution's education programme. Described by his biographer as 'one of those rare figures whose distinction was always recognized by contemporaries and by posterity', Faraday has given his name to both the unit for measuring electrical charge (faraday) and that for measuring capacitance (farad).[29] In 1858 he left his rooms at the Royal Institution – his home and place of work for forty-five years – for a grace-and-favour house, now known as Faraday House, Hampton Court Road, KT8; it was there that he died nine years later.

Number 120 Baker Street (formerly 14 York Place), W1, was the home of the Prime Minister **William Pitt the Younger** (1759–1806) 47 from April 1802 to May 1804 – rather than from 1803 to 1804, as is stated on the

plaque. A pale-green LCC plaque was put up at this address in 1904, but it disappeared when the house was remodelled in 1925 (fig. 375). There were plans to replace it with a brown plaque of the LCC's experimental series (see fig. 39), but in the end – war having intervened – a blue roundel of the standard design was installed in 1949. Born at Hayes Place in Bromley, William Pitt followed in the political footsteps of his father, WILLIAM PITT, EARL OF CHATHAM, and in 1783 – at the age of twenty-four – became Britain's youngest Prime Minister. During his seventeen years in office he took the country to war against revolutionary France, and made a lasting impact on domestic politics with his introduction of income tax in 1799 and the union with Ireland of 1800. It was his failure to persuade King George III to agree to Catholic emancipation that forced his resignation on 3 February 1801.

Pitt moved from 10 Downing Street to 12 Park Place, St James's, SW1, and then in April 1802 to what is now 120 Baker Street, a house of 1789. Here he was preoccupied with the parlous state of his own finances, which were alleviated by the generosity of his friends and by the sale of his country seat, Holwood House, Kent. Pitt returned to office as Prime Minister in May 1804, but chronic ill-health and the strain of waging war against Napoleon brought about his death in January 1806, at the age of forty-six.

The LCC plaque at 20 (formerly 10) York Street, W1, marks the home of the painter **George Richmond** (1809–1896) **48** . The son of a miniature painter, Richmond trained from 1824 at the Royal Academy Schools, where he was taught by HENRY FUSELI; in about 1825 he joined the circle of young artists centred around WILLIAM BLAKE and SAMUEL PALMER, known as 'The Ancients'. Richmond initially painted landscapes in Palmer's visionary style but, in need of a steady income to support his wife Julia (1811–1881) – the daughter of the architect Charles Heathcote Tatham – and their growing family, he turned to portraiture. His first major commission was a portrait of WILLIAM WILBER-FORCE (1833), which launched his career as one of the most popular portrait painters of his day. Richmond moved to what was then 10 York Street in February 1843, and during his first few months in the house he painted Elizabeth Fry, JOHN RUSKIN and W. E. GLAD-STONE and his wife Catherine. His son John later wrote that, 'Few houses in London can have been visited by a greater variety of interesting people, ranging from F. D. Maurice, the Duke of Wellington to Mrs Manning, the murderess, who came as lady's maid to the Duchess of Sutherland!'.[30] Another son, William Blake Richmond (1842–1921), became a successful painter, and was knighted in 1897. George Richmond has been criticised for flattering his subjects, for he adhered to the ideal of portraiture as 'the truth lovingly told', and deliberately engaged his sitters in conversation so that their expressions would be animated rather than stiff and unnatural.[31] He worked at a phenomenal rate: in 1847 alone he produced nearly a hundred portraits, yet was rarely satisfied with the results and longed to concentrate on his real passion, which was landscape painting. Richmond died at number 20 aged eighty-six. Although first proposed for commemoration in 1910 by his son John, his case was not then eligible and

was only formally considered in 1959; the plaque was erected in 1961.

At 24 Dorset Square, NW1, a plaque honours **Sir Laurence Gomme** (1853–1916) **49** , a renowned folklorist and historian who served as Clerk to the London County Council from 1900 until 1914 (see fig. 22). In this role, he oversaw the transfer of the blue plaques scheme from the Society of Arts to the LCC in 1901 and played a major part in establishing procedures and standards (see pp. 12–13); the scheme's continued success is due in no small part to Gomme. Associated with London for all of his life, George Laurence Gomme entered, at the age of twenty, the service of the Metropolitan Board of Works, absorbed into the newly created LCC in 1889. He served as Statistical Officer before being promoted to Clerk, a senior administrative post that he held until his retirement. Gomme's achievements during his forty-one years of government service were prodigious: he oversaw huge transfers of authority, and aimed to make London's administration the most perfect in Britain. In his own right, Gomme was important as an historian of London, antiquarian and writer; it has been said that his enthusiasm for the capital led to a new reverence for things of the past, especially historic buildings. In 1878 Gomme co-founded the Folklore Society; he was also closely involved in the early history of the Survey of London – the first volume of which was published in 1900 – and played a part in founding the Victoria County History (1899). Gomme lived at 24 Dorset Square with his wife Alice, née Merck (1853–1938), also a notable folklorist, from 1895 until March 1909. This early nineteenth-century house has since been thrown together with the neighbouring number 25. The plaque was unveiled in 2006 by the architectural historian Professor Andor Gomme, a grandson of Sir Laurence.

A few doors away, at 28 Dorset Square, an LCC plaque of 1963 commemorates the actor and author **George Grossmith** (1847–1912) **50** , who lived here from 1885 to 1902. At this house, which dates from 1815–20, he wrote with his brother Weedon Grossmith *The Diary of a Nobody*, which was serialised in *Punch* in 1888–89 and was first published as a book in 1892 (fig. 376). This great comic novel chronicled the life – in all its mundane triviality – of Charles Pooter of The Laurels, Brickfield Terrace, Holloway, and poked fun at Pooter's

Mr. and Mrs. Charles Pooter and their son Lupin.

376 One of the drawings from *The Diary of a Nobody*, written by the brothers George and Weedon Grossmith and first published as a book in 1892. It shows Mr and Mrs Charles Pooter and their son Lupin, who has just announced his engagement. [© Mary Evans Picture Library]

377 Number 136 Seymour Place and its GLC plaque to Emma Cons. The building – formerly the Walmer Castle public house – was acquired by Cons in 1879 and converted into a coffee tavern. [© English Heritage. Photograph by Derek Kendall]

rather endearing snobbery and social aspirations, which were continually thwarted by his rather tiresome neighbours, Cumming and Gowing, and the antics of his incorrigible son Lupin. The novel's continuing success has almost eclipsed Grossmith's fame as an actor, for he was one of the most popular entertainers of his day. After making his name with solo shows, he was engaged in 1877 by RICHARD D'OYLY CARTE, and created many of the leading comic roles in the Savoy operas by GILBERT and Sullivan; these included John Wellington Wells in *The Sorcerer* (1877), the Lord Chancellor in *Iolanthe* (1882), Ko-Ko in *The Mikado* (1885) and Jack Point in *The Yeoman of the Guard* (1888). Despite having only a passable singing voice, Grossmith excelled in performing Gilbert and Sullivan's famous 'patter songs'. He returned to one-man entertaining in the 1890s, and toured Britain and America with his highly successful 'humorous and musical recitals'.[32] Grossmith lived at 28 Dorset Square with his wife Emmeline Rosa, née Noyce (d. 1905) and their children, one of whom was GEORGE GROSSMITH junior. Said to be 'a house that bubbled with life and laughter', it remained the family's home until 1902; seven years later, Grossmith retired to Folkestone, Kent, where he died.[33]

Just south of Marylebone Road lies Seymour Place, W1, where a plaque at number 136 marks the building

in which **Emma Cons** (1837–1912) 51 , the philanthropist and founder of the Old Vic, lived and worked (fig. 377). Although trained as an artist, Cons became a volunteer at a young age in the housing projects of OCTAVIA HILL, and helped to manage Hill's properties in Paradise Place, Freshwater Place and Drury Lane. In 1879 Cons founded the South London Dwellings Company, which in 1884 built a quadrangle of model dwellings in Morton Place, Lambeth, known as Surrey Lodge; this was her home and office from 1889 until her death. A lifelong temperance campaigner, Cons founded in 1879 the Coffee Music Hall Company, with the aim of developing the coffee tavern as an attractive non-alcoholic alternative to pubs and gin-palaces. Her first venture was the Old Vic in Waterloo Road, which opened as the Royal Victoria Coffee Music Hall in 1880, and nine years later also became the venue for Morley College's evening classes for working-class men and women. Cons passed the management of the Old Vic to her niece, LILIAN BAYLIS, in 1899; ten years earlier, she had become one of only three female members of

378 Sir Gerald Kelly in his studio at 117 Gloucester Place, his home for over fifty years. The photograph was taken in early 1950, shortly after Kelly's appointment as President of the Royal Academy. [© Popperfoto / Getty Images]

Festus Kelly – the founder of Kelly's Post Office Directories – and the son of a curate, Gerald Kelly was born in Paddington and grew up in Camberwell. After being given an ultimatum by his father to 'be a painter or nothing', Kelly went to study art in Paris, where he came under the influence of Monet, Degas, Sargent and SICKERT.[34] A year in Burma (1908–9) inspired him to paint his first series of oriental dancers, which were reproduced as highly popular prints. In 1916 Kelly moved to 117 Gloucester Place, which he had leased the previous year as a home for his retired father, Frederic. Here he exploited his flair for painting likenesses – which is apparent in his early portrayal of his great friend SOMERSET MAUGHAM as *The Jester* (1911) – and turned his house into 'a portrait factory'; among his sitters were M. R. James (1937), SIR MALCOLM SARGENT (1948) and RALPH VAUGHAN WILLIAMS (1953).[35] In 1945, the year he was knighted, the artist completed portraits of King George VI and Queen Elizabeth II. Kelly worked in the large studio he had built in the garden, and while he painted he entertained his sitters with a wide repertoire of songs. Elected RA in 1930, Kelly proved to be an enterprising President of the Royal Academy (1949–54). He and his wife Jane, née Ryan – a favourite model of the artist – were greatly attached to their home, and when the lease was due to expire in 1955 Kelly sold manuscripts, proofs and first editions given to him by Somerset Maugham in order to buy the freehold; thereafter he lived on the top floor and rented out the rest of the property. Sir Gerald died at number 117 in January 1972, at the age of ninety-two.

the newly formed London County Council. An LCC plaque to both Cons and Baylis was erected at Surrey Lodge in 1952, but after the building was demolished in 1971 the only surviving address associated with Cons was 136 Seymour Place, where the GLC erected a plaque in 1978. This former public house – the Walmer Castle, dated 1873 – was acquired by Cons in 1879 and converted into a coffee tavern; she occupied rooms above the establishment until 1889 – when she moved to Surrey Lodge – and managed a block of cheap accommodation at the rear of the building.

In 1993 English Heritage erected a plaque in honour of the portrait painter **Sir Gerald Kelly** (1879–1972) 52 at 117 (formerly 65) Gloucester Place, W1, where he lived for fifty-six years (fig. 378). The grandson of Frederic

At 99 (formerly 74) Gloucester Place is a discreet bronze plaque to the poet **Elizabeth Barrett Browning** (1806–1861) 53 (see also pp. 402–3), who lived here with her family from December 1835 to May 1838. This unusual plaque was erected by the LCC in 1924, after the freeholder, the Portman Estate, requested 'some smaller tablet or bronze plate' rather than the standard blue ceramic roundel.[36] It places ready public understanding before historical accuracy: during her time here, Elizabeth was known by her maiden name, Barrett Barrett, or – as she signed herself – 'EBB'. The family – headed by Edward Barrett Moulton Barrett (1785–1857), a plantation owner, who had been widowed in 1828 – moved here from Sidmouth, Devon. At first Elizabeth desperately missed the countryside, and described how she had grown 'a double rind thicker and thicker on my spirit'.[37] However, in May 1836 she met Wordsworth and struck up a close friendship with a fellow author, Mary Russell Mitford, who introduced her to the writings of Robert Browning; the couple were to wed in 1846, and spent the rest of their married life on the Continent. While living at what was then 74 Gloucester Place, 'EBB' worked on a collection of ballads and verses that was published in June 1838 as *The Seraphim, and other Poems*, the first work to bear her name on the title-page. By the time of its appearance, Elizabeth had moved with her family to 50 Wimpole Street (see fig. 366), which became their permanent London residence.

The home of the novelist **William Wilkie Collins** (1824–1889) 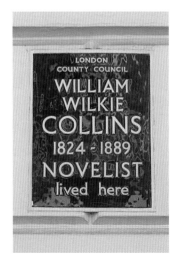 at 65 (formerly 90) Gloucester Place is marked with a blue rectangular LCC plaque (fig. 379). Collins lived here from 1867 to 1888, and in his first year of residence wrote *The Moonstone* (1868), now hailed as one of the first detective novels in the English language. Named after his godfather, the painter Sir David Wilkie, Collins was born at 11 New Cavendish Street, and lived in or near Marylebone for most of his life. The success of his first novel, *Antonina* (1850) – together with the encouragement of his close friend and mentor, CHARLES DICKENS, whom he met in 1851 – convinced him to write for a living. Collins moved to what was then 90 Gloucester Place while at the height of his powers, having made his reputation with a string of 'sensation novels', the best known of which are *The Woman in White* (1860), *No Name* (1862) and *Armadale* (1866). This, however, proved a turbulent period in his private life, for his mistress, Caroline Graves (1829–1895), left him to marry Joseph Clow in 1868 on discovering his affair with another woman, Martha Rudd. Although Collins had three children with Martha, Caroline returned to live with him at Gloucester Place in 1870, and her daughter Harriet Graves continued to supervise the running of his household; he maintained his relationships with both women until his death. During his twenty-one years in this house, Collins wrote ten novels – including *The Law and the Lady* (1875) and *The Fallen Leaves* (1879) – together with numerous short stories, plays and stage adaptations. In April 1888 he moved to nearby 82 Wimpole Street, where he died the following year. His reputation declined sharply thereafter and, when considering his case for commemoration in 1910, the Clerk of the LCC advised that Collins's writings 'were not of a high order'.[38] The proposal was not resurrected until 1949, and the plaque was put up two years later.

John Robert Godley (1814–1861) **55**, founder of Canterbury, New Zealand, moved in 1858 to 48 (formerly 11) Gloucester Place – having lived previously at number 109 (then 69) in the same street – and died here on 17 November 1861. His widow, Charlotte, née Wynne (1821–1907), continued to live in the house until her death. Born in Ireland and educated at Oxford, Godley became deeply interested in the issue of colonisation, and in 1847 joined forces with Edward Gibbon Wakefield – the co-founder of Wellington – to plan a new settlement on the South Island of New Zealand. Intended as an Anglican colony, the settlement was named Canterbury in honour of one of its principal backers, the Archbishop of Canterbury, while its capital city, Christchurch, took its name from Godley's Oxford college. As chief agent of the Canterbury Association, Godley travelled in 1849 to New Zealand, where he oversaw land sales to settlers and presided as magistrate, but progress was slow and financial problems beset the project. His resignation in 1851 paved the way for the fledgling colony to become a self-governing province the following year. On his return to London in 1853, Godley worked for the Inland Revenue and at the War Office, and championed the cause of colonial self-sufficiency and nationalism. As part of Canterbury's centenary celebrations in 1951, the LCC plaque to Godley was unveiled by F. W. Doidge, the High Commissioner for New Zealand.

GODLEY's statue in Christchurch was admired by a fellow Marylebone resident, the novelist **Anthony Trollope** (1815–1882) **56**, while on a visit to New Zealand in 1873. On returning to London later that year, Trollope – with his wife Rose, née Heseltine (1820–1917) – settled at 39 Montagu Square, W1, which remained their home until 1880. An employee of the Post Office from the age of nineteen, Trollope made his most significant contribution to the organisation in 1852, when he pioneered the use of roadside pillar boxes, which were soon set up throughout the United Kingdom. He began writing his first novel, *The Macdermots of Ballycloran* (1847), while stationed in Ireland on Post Office duties, and followed it with the six-part

379 The rectangular plaque to William Wilkie Collins at 65 Gloucester Place, installed by the LCC in 1951. [© English Heritage. Photograph by Derek Kendall]

380 The GLC plaque to Mustapha Reschid Pasha at 1 Bryanston Square. It was unveiled in 1972 by the Turkish Ambassador, Zeki Kuneralp. [© English Heritage. Photograph by Derek Kendall]

Barchester Chronicles (1855–67), which included *The Warden* (1855), *Barchester Towers* (1857) and *The Last Chronicle of Barset* (1867). Trollope's satirical portrayal of the Church of England clergy in the fictional county of Barsetshire proved to be phenomenally popular, and his most brilliant characters, such as Mrs Proudie and Mr Slope, became household names. Able to command fees of up to £3,000 for his novels, Trollope resigned from the Post Office in 1867 to concentrate on his writing. He had already started a second series – the Palliser novels – that were more political in tone than the Barchester Chronicles. While living at 39 Montagu Square, a house of *c.* 1810–11, he completed the last three novels in the Palliser series – *Phineas Redux* (1874), *The Prime Minister* (1876) and *The Duke's Children* (1880) – and wrote the longest and most serious of his novels, *The Way We Live Now* (1875), which is partly set in nearby Welbeck Street. In 1880 Trollope moved to Sussex, but later returned to Marylebone, where he died in a nursing home. When his name was proposed in 1913, the owner of 39 Montagu Square, a Miss Joseph, initially refused to give her consent for the plaque as she was of the opinion that Trollope was not one of those 'very great or famous persons'.[39] She finally relented, but insisted on a small plaque that was in keeping with the building. A bronze tablet was agreed upon and duly erected at first-floor level in 1914; it was later moved to a more prominent position beneath the ground-floor bay window.

Number 1 Bryanston Square, W1, was home to the Turkish statesman and reformer **Mustapha Reschid Pasha** (1800–1858) **57**, Turkish Ambassador to London in 1836–37 and 1838–39 (fig. 380). The plaque was unveiled in 1972 by the Turkish Ambassador, Zeki Kuneralp, who had originally proposed Reschid for commemoration. Reschid, who was born in Constantinople, entered public service at an early age, and served as Ambassador in Paris – a post he later held twice more – before travelling to England in 1836. His stay in London was mostly spent at 1 Sussex Place, Regent's Park, NW1, but by April 1839 he and the Turkish Embassy had moved to 1 Bryanston Square, a magnificent five-storey stuccoed house built in 1811 to designs by Joseph Parkinson; he stayed here for the next four and a half months, and it continued as the embassy until the late nineteenth century. Reschid's diplomatic work was directed towards improving rela-

tions between Britain and Turkey. However, he failed to secure the aim of his second mission, which was to form an alliance between the two countries, and he helped to embroil Britain in the Crimean War. After returning to his homeland in August 1839, Reschid held the office of Grand Vizier six times between 1845 and 1857, and is regarded as one of his country's most outstanding statesmen. His most notable reform was the wholesale remodelling of Turkish administration and legislature, the Tanzimat, which brought about an end to slavery and enshrined the principle of equality in the constitution.

The discovery in 1820 of the **Cato Street Conspiracy** **58** is commemorated at 1A (formerly 6) Cato Street, W1 (fig. 381 and see fig. 13). This GLC plaque, erected in 1977, marks a former stable building in a mews, which is entered via an archway from Crawford Place. The Cato Street Conspiracy was a plot to assassinate the British Cabinet, which was believed to be dining at the Earl of Harrowby's home, 44 Grosvenor Square, Mayfair, on the night of 23 February 1820. It was con-

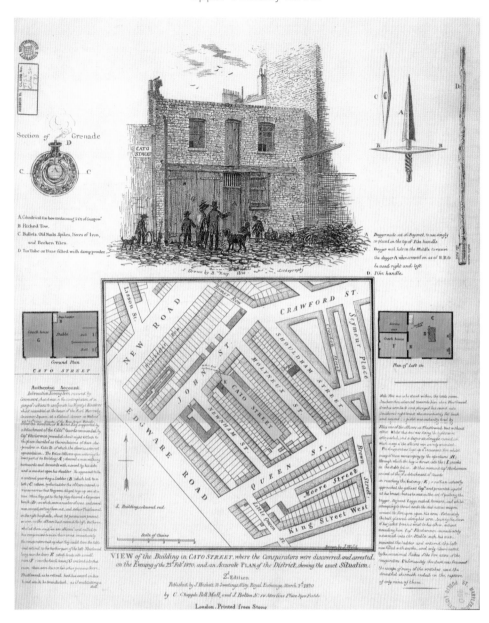

and beheaded at Newgate on 1 May 1820, and the five other conspirators were transported. By using an agent provocateur to set up the conspiracy, Lord Liverpool's government successfully discredited the radical movement and bolstered public support for the repressive legislation passed in the wake of the Peterloo Massacre of 1819. Crowds of people flocked to Cato Street to view the dilapidated premises where the conspirators had met; the thoroughfare's notoriety was such that shortly after 1820 the residents changed its name to Horace Street, and it remained known as such until 1937.

The first woman to qualify as a doctor in Britain, **Elizabeth Garrett Anderson** (1836–1917) 59 , lived at 20 Upper Berkeley Street, W1, from 1865 to 1874. The elder sister of MILLICENT GARRETT FAWCETT, Elizabeth Garrett joined the Langham Place Group in the mid-1850s and campaigned for extending women's employment. After meeting Elizabeth Blackwell, an Englishwoman who had gained an MD in the United States, she became determined to train as a doctor. She sidestepped the ban on female medical students at universities and hospitals by studying privately, and exploited a loophole that allowed her to qualify as a Licentiate of the Society of Apothecaries in 1865; her name was duly entered on the medical register. Later that year, Elizabeth Garrett moved to 20 Upper Berkeley Street, where she set up in practice and gave lectures on physiology to a female audience. In June 1866 she moved her practice around the corner to 69 Seymour Place, which opened as the St Mary's Dispensary for Women and Children. This 'nucleus of a hospital' received its first in-patients in 1871, and as the New Hospital for Women moved to a larger building in Marylebone Road in 1874, and then to purpose-built premises in Euston Road in 1890.[40] It was the first hospital in Britain to be staffed entirely by women, and appropriately was renamed after its founder in 1918. Elizabeth Garrett married the shipowner J. G. S. Anderson (1838/9–1907) in 1871, and three years later – the year of the founding of the London School of Medicine for Women, of which she served as Dean (1883–1902) – moved further down the street to 4 Upper Berkeley Street. This was the Andersons' London home until 1902, when they retired to Aldeburgh, Suffolk. In 1908 Elizabeth Garrett Anderson was elected Mayor of Aldeburgh – an office previously held by her husband – thereby becoming Britain's first

381 A print produced in 1820, shortly after the discovery of the Cato Street Conspiracy. It includes details such as a plan and elevation of 1A (formerly 6) Cato Street, where the conspirators were discovered and arrested. [© City of Westminster Archives Centre]

ceived by a government spy, George Edwards (c. 1787–1843), who had infiltrated a group of insurrectionist London radicals, nearly all of whom had been involved in the Spencean Philanthropists, organisers of the Spa Fields meetings of 1816. The conspiracy was foiled when, on the evening of 23 February, the police raided the loft above the stables at 1A Cato Street, where the plotters met. In the ensuing fray, the conspirators' leader, Arthur Thistlewood (1774–1820), killed one of the Bow Street constables, Richard Smithers. Ten conspirators were subsequently arrested and put on trial for high treason; Thistlewood, John Thomas Brunt (b. 1782), James Ings (bap. 1794), Richard Tidd (bap. 1773) and William Davidson (b. 1786) were publicly hanged

female mayor. The plaque was unveiled by her grandson, Sir Colin Anderson, in 1962.

The musical composer **Michael William Balfe** (1808–1870) 60 lived at 12 (formerly 7) Seymour Street, W1, from 1861 to 1864, by which time he was regarded as one of Britain's foremost composers and opera conductors. Dublin-born, Balfe first came to London in 1823 to study music under Charles Edward Horn, and travelled in the mid-1820s to Italy and France, where his career as an opera singer took off under the patronage of Cherubini and Rossini. While in Italy, Balfe staged three of his own operas, and after returning to England in 1834 achieved notable success with *The Siege of Rochelle* (1835), *The Maid of Artois* (1836) and *Falstaff* (1838). His most popular opera, *The Bohemian Girl* (1843) – with its well-known ballad, 'I dreamt that I dwelt in marble halls' – remained a hit for over a century. At this address – which he shared with his wife, the Hungarian singer Lina Roser (d. 1888) – Balfe completed some of his last operas, *The Puritan's Daughter* (1861), *The Armourer of Nantes* (1863) and *Blanche de Nevers* (1864), and wrote the cantata *Mazeppa* (1862). In 1864 he and Lina Roser moved from Seymour Street to a country estate, Rowney Abbey, Hertfordshire, where Balfe died six years later. When the composer was put forward for commemoration in 1910, the owner of 12 Seymour Street, A. Forbes Siveking, objected to the style and size of the proposed stone plaque, commenting that 'Balfe's merits as a composer . . . however undeniably popular his melodies may be, would be more satisfactorily represented by a less architecturally important Tablet'.[41] A more discreet lead tablet – bearing the date 1911 – was installed by the LCC in January 1912.

Number 30 Seymour Street (formerly 16 Upper Seymour Street) was briefly home to the peripatetic artist and writer **Edward Lear** (1812–1888) 61 (fig. 382). The LCC plaque at this address was installed in 1960, at a time when Lear was recognised as an outstanding watercolourist, as well as the 'laureate of nonsense'. Born in Holloway, Lear started working as an ornithological illustrator in the 1820s, drawing the parrots in London Zoo for his first publication, *Illustrations of the Family of Psittacidae, or Parrots* (1830–32). Invited by Lord Stanley, later 13th Earl of Derby, to draw his menagerie at Knowsley Hall, Cheshire, he

came across a book of limericks that inspired him to write more of the nonsense poems – or 'old persons' as he termed them – that he had been writing since childhood. These were published, together with charming pen-and-ink drawings, as *A Book of Nonsense* (1846), which has since become a much-loved collection of limericks. Lear's most famous poem, 'The Owl and the Pussy-cat', was published in *Nonsense Songs, Stories, Botany and Alphabets* (1871). He never settled for long at any of his many London addresses, for chronic ill-health compelled him to abandon 'Foggopolis' virtually every winter for the Mediterranean and he spent much of the 1840s in Italy. While abroad, he painted landscape views, published in a series of illustrated travel journals, the first of which was *Views in Rome and its Environs* (1841). In 1848 Lear left Italy and travelled east to Corfu, Greece, Turkey, Albania and Egypt, where he continued to produce an astonishing number of landscape watercolours, including *The Monastery of St Paul* (1856). He was in London once again in May 1857, 'having taken a redboom at Hamsens 16 Upper Seymour Street, Squortman Pare',

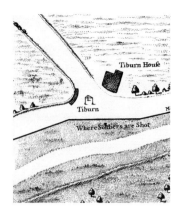

383 The gallows at Tyburn, in a detail of John Rocque's map of London, 1746. The triangular structure was capable of hanging up to twenty-four prisoners at once.

but by mid-November of that year he had left for Corfu.[42] Lear travelled further afield to Lebanon and Palestine before finally settling in 1869 at San Remo, Italy, where he lived until his death.

In 1964 the LCC placed a plaque in the ground of the traffic island at the junction of Edgware Road and Bayswater Road, W2, to mark the exact **Site of Tyburn Tree** 62 (figs 383 and 384). This circular Portland stone plaque, which has inscribed bronze lettering around a central cross, replaced an earlier triangular plaque in the road put there by the LCC in 1909 – together with an explanatory bronze tablet at Marble Arch – that had been displaced by road improvements.

Thousands of public executions took place at these notorious gallows, which stood next to the Tyburn brook, at the junction of four manors: Paddington and Lillestone in the north, Hide and Eyebury in the south. The earliest recorded execution was that of William FitzOsbert ('Longbeard') in 1196; later victims included Perkin Warbeck (1499), Elizabeth Barton, 'the Holy Maid of Kent' (1534), Claude Duval (1670), Jack Sheppard (1724) and Laurence Shirley, 4th Earl Ferrers (1760). The dead bodies of Oliver Cromwell, Henry Ireton and other regicides were dug up and hung here in 1661. The last hanging – of the highwayman John Austin – took place on 3 November 1783. The lower branches of one of the celebrated elms of Tyburn

384 A photograph taken in 1964, soon after the installation of the LCC plaque commemorating Tyburn Tree. Placed in the ground of the traffic island at the junction of Edgware Road and Bayswater Road, it replaced an earlier triangular plaque of 1909.
[© Getty Images]

formed the first gibbet, but in 1571 huge triangular gallows were built, capable of hanging up to twenty-four prisoners at once. Replaced by moveable gallows in 1759, the former Tyburn Tree was converted into stands for beer butts in the cellars of a nearby public house. On hanging days, the condemned travelled in open carts from Newgate Prison along Oxford Street to Tyburn, where immense crowds gathered to watch them die on the gallows. The usually raucous and carnivalesque mood occasionally gave way to silent sympathy if the crowd believed the criminal to be innocent, as happened in 1777 at the execution of Dr

William Dodd, who had been convicted of forgery. One spectator recorded that 'every visage expressed sadness; it appeared indeed, a day of universal calamity . . . Thousands sobbed aloud, and many women swooned at the sight . . . Tens of thousands of hats, which formed a black mass, as the coach advanced, were taken off simultaneously'.[43] Fear of public disorder and rioting persuaded the government to move executions to Newgate Prison in 1783, but Tyburn remains 'probably the most blood-saturated spot in London'.[44]

NOTES

1   It is now accepted that Gage was born in 1719/20, rather than in 1721, as is stated on the plaque.
2   Gretchen Gerzina, *Frances Hodgson Burnett* (London, 2004), p. 176
3   G. T. Wrench, *Lord Lister* (London, 1913), pp. 278–79
4   Hector Bolitho, *Marie Tempest* (London, 1936), p. 96
5   Ibid, p. 89
6   Herbert Hutchinson, *Jonathan Hutchinson: Life and Letters* (London, 1946), p. 114
7   Arthur Edmund Street, *Memoir of George Edmund Street, RA 1824–1881* (London, 1888), p. 232
8   *Life, Letters and Journals of Sir Charles Lyell*, ed. Mrs Katharine Murray Lyell, vol. II (London, 1881), p. 451 (7 July 1873)
9   A. W. Ganz, *Berlioz in London* (London, 1950), p. 93
10 Ibid, pp. 93–94
11 Stephen Trombley, *Sir Frederick Treves: The Extra-Ordinary Edwardian* (London, 1989), p. 29
12 Frederick Treves, *The Elephant Man, and other Reminiscences* (London, 1923), p. 30
13 *The Brownings' Correspondence*, eds Philip Kelley and Ronald Hudson, vol. III (Winfield, Kansas, 1985), p. 203 (7 December 1836)
14 *Letters of John Richard Green*, ed. Leslie Stephen (London, 1901), pp. 232–33 (24 April 1869)
15 Ibid, p. 249 (April 1870?)
16 Letter of 27 February 1950 on blue plaque file.
17 *ODNB*, vol. LXII, p. 959
18 'Characters, by Sir Humphry Davy', *Gentleman's Magazine*, vol. CXXXVII (1837), p. 367
19 *The Letters of Edward Gibbon*, ed. J. E. Norton, vol. I (London, 1956), p. 353 (15 December 1772)
20 Ibid, p. 364 (5 May 1773)
21 Letter of 31 October 1949 on blue plaque file.
22 Letter of 25 November 1992 on blue plaque file.
23 LCC Local Government Committee minutes of 27 March 1931, on blue plaque file.
24 Alfred Milner, '"Credo." Lord Milner's Faith', *The Times*, 27 July 1925, p. 13
25 Florence Marryat, *Life and Letters of Captain Marryat*, vol. II (London, 1872), p. 115
26 *The Letters of Tom Moore*, ed. W. S. Dowden, vol. II (Oxford, 1964), p. 586 (26 November 1827)
27 Francis Jeffrey, 'Review of *Epistles, Odes, and Other Poems*', *Edinburgh Review*, vol. VIII (1806), p. 456
28 Alfred Friendly, *Beaufort of the Admiralty: The Life of Sir Francis Beaufort, 1774–1857* (London, 1977), p. 244
29 *ODNB*, vol. XIX, p. 36
30 Letter of 20 July 1910 on blue plaque file.
31 *The Works of John Ruskin*, eds E. T. Cook and A. Wedderburn, vol. XXXVI (London, 1909), p. xxvii
32 *ODNB*, vol. XXIV, p. 88
33 Ibid, p. 87
34 *The Times*, 6 January 1972, p. 12
35 Derek Hudson, *For Love of Painting: The Life of Sir Gerald Kelly, KCVO, PRA* (London, 1975), p. 37
36 Letter of 23 January 1924 on blue plaque file.
37 Margaret Forster, *Elizabeth Barrett Browning* (London, 1988), p. 79
38 File note of 20 September 1910 on blue plaque file.
39 Letter of 13 November 1913 on blue plaque file.
40 Elizabeth Crawford, *Enterprising Women: The Garretts and their Circle* (London, 2002), p. 50
41 Letter of 9 March 1911 on blue plaque file.
42 Vivien Noakes, *Edward Lear: The Life of a Wanderer* (London, 1968), p. 150 (1 May 1857)
43 Henry Angelo, *Reminiscences of Henry Angelo* (London, 1828), vol. I, p. 460 and p. 475
44 LCC press release, 'In memory of Tyburn Tree' (25 September 1964), on blue plaque file.

MARYLEBONE

385 The plaque commemorating Nancy Mitford at her workplace, Heywood Hill's bookshop, 10 Curzon Street. [© English Heritage. Photograph by Derek Kendall]

MAYFAIR

Bounded by Oxford Street, Regent Street, Piccadilly and Park Lane, Mayfair takes its name from the annual fair held until the mid-1700s in what were then open fields. The largest and most important high-class London development of its time, Mayfair was built up from the early to the mid-eighteenth century on six principal estates: Burlington, Millfield, Conduit Mead, Berkeley, Curzon and – the largest of all and the only one to survive – Grosvenor. Its grand, luxurious houses represented the height of fashion, and their designers included renowned architects such as Roger Morris, Sir Robert Taylor and COLEN CAMPBELL. As completed, the area boasted three large squares, a church and streets interspersed with mansions; it remained largely residential until the twentieth century, when the balance shifted markedly towards office use. From the outset, Mayfair attracted professional men and the aristocracy; SYDNEY SMITH said that the area enclosed 'more intelligence and human ability, to say nothing of wealth and beauty, than the world has ever collected in such a space before'.[1] Mayfair's long association with figures of means and significance is reflected in one of the capital's highest concentrations of plaques. However, as – in the early twentieth century – the Duke of Westminster preferred his own plaques to those of the LCC, coverage on the Grosvenor estate is somewhat sporadic.

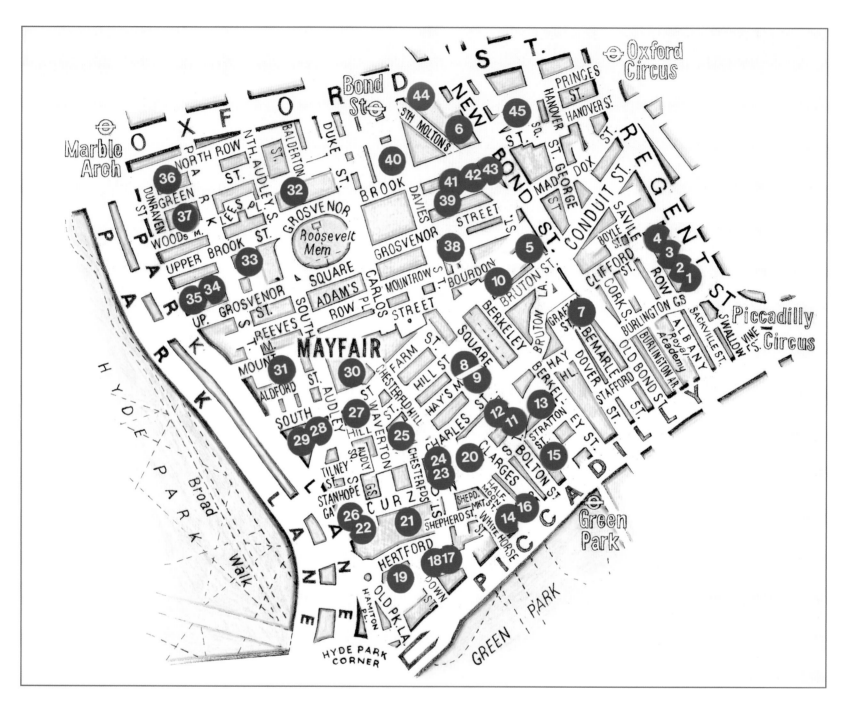

MAYFAIR

Savile Row, W1, takes its name from Lady Dorothy Savile, wife of the 3rd Earl of Burlington. Built in the 1730s, the houses originally occupied only the east side of the street, and faced gardens on the west. The most famous inhabitants of Savile Row – the tailors – are relatively recent arrivals, having become established from the mid-nineteenth century onwards. The southernmost of Savile Row's plaques, at number 11, is also the latest in date; erected by the GLC in 1979, it commemorates the residence of the Bristol-born physician **Richard Bright** (1789–1858) **①** . Bright decided that the street suited him perfectly – 'it does not remove me too far from my old residence [14 Bloomsbury Square]', he wrote, 'and yet puts me decidedly in the west'.[2] It was, in addition, an extremely popular location with other men of his profession: a writer of 1870 stated that Savile Row was 'now almost entirely inhabited by eminent physicians and surgeons'.[3] A physician at Guy's Hospital from 1820 until 1844, Bright came to the house in September 1831 – on the publication of the second volume of his internationally acclaimed *Reports of Medical Cases* (1827–31) – and stayed until his death. While living at number 11 – with his second wife Eliza, the sister of the lawyer Sir William Webb Follett, and their children – he carried out some of his

most important work; in 1837 he was appointed Physician-Extraordinary to Queen Victoria, and the following year was honoured for his identification of what became known as Bright's disease, an ailment of the kidneys. After retiring from Guy's, he concentrated on his considerable private practice; among Bright's patients were Lord TENNYSON and ISAMBARD KINGDOM BRUNEL. After Bright's death, his house was acquired by his most noted pupil, Sir George Johnson (1818–1896), who lived here from 1859 until he died. Number 11 Savile Row, like the houses it adjoins, was built in 1732–35; the fourth storey was added in 1836, during Bright's occupancy.

The historian **George Grote** (1794–1871) **②** , a contemporary and neighbour of BRIGHT, is commemorated with a brown, wreathed LCC plaque at 12 Savile Row (fig. 386). A friend of the philosophers Jeremy Bentham, James Mill and JOHN STUART MILL, Grote came to prominence as a politician; in the 1830s he was a leading spokesman for the philosophic radicals, authoring the *Essentials of Parliamentary Reform* (1831), and between 1832 and 1841 was MP for the City of London. He was also – according to a friend, the psychologist Alexander Bain – 'a Greece-intoxicated man'.[4] The first four of the twelve volumes of Grote's *magnum opus*, *A History of Greece* (1846–56), were written during his time at 4 Belgrave Place (formerly 4 Upper Eccleston Street), Belgravia, SW1, his home from 1834 until May 1848. The work was completed at 12 Savile Row, Grote's home of twenty-three years and the place of his death. While here, he also wrote *Plato, and the other Companions of Sokrates* (1865) and the posthumously published *Aristotle* (1872). In 1848 Grote's wife Harriet, née Lewin (1792–1878) described number 12 as 'a convenient, roomy house, in a quiet situation, especially adapted to Mr Grote's purposes and pursuits'.[5] Harriet Grote herself was a noted hostess and woman of letters, and was especially celebrated for her musical receptions; visitors to the house included FREDERIC CHOPIN and JENNY LIND. Erected in 1905, the plaque was raised to first-floor level and set in a mount late the following year upon the conversion of the ground floor to commercial premises.

One of the most moving episodes in Savile Row's history centres on number 14 and its occupant of 1813–16, the dramatist **Richard Brinsley Sheridan** (1751–

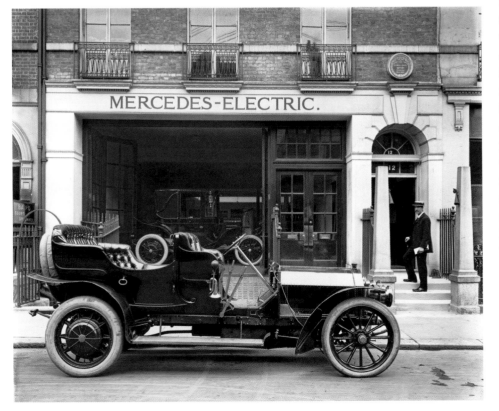

386 A Bedford Lemere photograph of 1907 showing the LCC plaque to George Grote at 12 Savile Row, with Mercedes showrooms at ground-floor level. [Reproduced by permission of English Heritage. NMR]

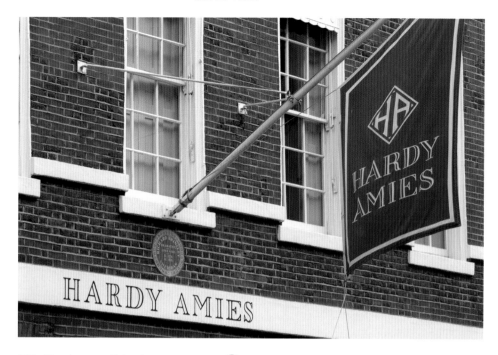

388 Number 17 Savile Row and its LCC plaque to the architect George Basevi. [© English Heritage. Photograph by Derek Kendall]

1816) ③ (see also p. 434) (fig. 387). Sheridan, born in Dublin, penned a number of brilliant comedies, including *The Rivals* (1775) and *The School for Scandal* (1777), and was a leading figure in the Whig party, with a seat in Parliament almost continuously between 1780 and 1812. From 1776 he managed the Theatre Royal, Drury Lane, but its rebuilding in 1791–94 – followed by its destruction by fire in 1809 – effectively bankrupted him, and he was excluded from involvement in the new theatre that opened in 1812. By the time of Sheridan's residence at number 14, Mayfair had long been his London home but, following the decline in his fortunes, he was forced out of his own property and fell back on houses provided by friends; 17 Savile Row was lent to him by Lord Wellesley for a time. At number 14, despondent and in failing health, Sheridan's condition reached rock bottom; a visitor found 'all the reception rooms bare, and the whole house in a state of filth and stench that was quite intolerable'.[6] In his final days, he narrowly avoided arrest and being carried off to a sponging house (a debtors' prison); in desperation he wrote, 'They are going to put the carpets out of the window, and break into Mrs S's room and *take me*'.[7] The bailiff's officers were deterred only by the physician's insistence that any move would kill Sheridan. The politician and dramatist died here on 7 July 1816, in the presence of his second wife, Hecca (*c.* 1775–1817), who was herself seriously ill; against his name in the rate book is written, 'Goods distrained by Sheriff, Dis-

traint resisted. Dead and Insolvent'.[8] Sheridan's plaque, chocolate-brown in colour and placed in a plaster mount, dates from 1881, and is one of the earliest to survive. Since 1946, number 14 has been the base of the fashion house of Hardy Amies.

The architect **George Basevi** (1794–1845) ④ is commemorated with a plaque set up at 17 Savile Row by the LCC in 1949 (fig. 388). Born in London into a Jewish family, Basevi became a pupil of John Soane in 1810, and completed his training six years later. His family connections – Benjamin Disraeli was a cousin – brought him a steady stream of commissions, including work at Gatcombe Park, Gloucestershire (*c.* 1820), the country home of David Ricardo. In 1825 his relatives William and George Haldimand took over the development of Belgrave Square from Thomas Cubitt and appointed Basevi as surveyor. Between that year and 1840, the square's terraced houses were

built to his design; success there led to similar work in South Kensington, including Pelham Crescent (1833) (see fig. 227) and Thurloe Square (1840–45). The work for which Basevi is best remembered is the Fitzwilliam Museum in Cambridge, begun in 1837; it was completed after the architect's death by C. R. COCKERELL, though work continued into the 1870s. Basevi lived in Savile Row from 1829 until the time of his grisly end: while supervising repair work in Ely Cathedral's bell tower, the architect slipped through a hole in the scaffolding and fell to his death.

Bond Street, W1, has always been predominantly commercial. In the eighteenth and nineteenth centuries, as now, it was a luxury shopping street and a fashionable promenade for the beau monde. Old Bond Street, running from Piccadilly to Burlington Gardens, was built from 1684; New Bond Street followed to the north after 1700. The thoroughfare is associated with a figure of immense fame: **Horatio**, **Lord Nelson** (1758–1805) **5** **6** , the naval commander and hero of the Battle of Trafalgar. Nelson has not one but two plaques in New Bond Street. The first was erected in 1876 by the Society of Arts at number 147 (formerly 141); the plaque, which states that Nelson 'fell at Trafalgar', has since been set into the building's stonework, hiding its distinctive decorative border. The second plaque, at number 103 (formerly 96), was installed by the LCC in 1958. Norfolk-born, Nelson entered the Navy in 1771, and came to prominence as a commander in the 1780s; encounters of the following decade included that at Santa Cruz, Tenerife, when Nelson was wounded in his right arm. It was in order to convalesce following its amputation that he returned to London, in low spirits, and in mid-September 1797 moved to number 147, then a lodging-house run by a Mr Jones. Happily, by 11 December he could describe himself as being 'perfectly recovered'.[9] After spending a month or so in Bath, Nelson and his wife Fanny (1761–1831) returned to Bond Street in early February 1798, taking up residence at number 103. This building is notable in being the only one of Nelson's London residences to remain intact, number 147 having been rebuilt in the nineteenth century. On 16 March 1798, two days after taking his leave of King George III, Nelson received orders to proceed to Portsmouth and left Bond Street, sailing to rejoin the British fleet near Cadiz. On 1 August of that year he was responsible for a crushing naval victory against the French at the Battle of the Nile; triumph at the Battle of Trafalgar, during which Nelson lost his life, followed in October 1805. During his time in Bond Street, Nelson had not yet scandalised society by involving himself in a *ménage à trois* with Sir William and Lady Hamilton. Their relationship was to develop from late 1798 onwards, when Nelson was regularly at the Hamiltons' home, 23 (later 103) Piccadilly (demolished). Interestingly, the 1958 plaque to Nelson was conceived alongside one for Emma, Lady Hamilton; 11 Clarges Street, Mayfair, her residence in 1803–6, was commemorated by the LCC the same year, but the building was demolished some five years later.

At 15A Grafton Street, W1 – on the corner of New Bond Street and Grafton Street, above the shop premises occupied by Asprey's since 1848 – is the flat in which **Sir Henry Irving** (1838–1905) **7** , the actor, lived from December 1872 to June 1899 (fig. 389). Born John Henry Brodribb in Somerset, he used the name Henry Irving from the time of his first professional appearance in 1856 and found fame after joining the company at London's Lyceum Theatre in 1871. Having triumphed in roles such as Hamlet and Shylock in *The Merchant of Venice*, Irving took over management of the Lyceum in 1878. Thus began a period that saw the theatre become famous worldwide. Irving's productions were noted in particular for their high-quality design, and he established such practices as the darkening of an auditorium so as to focus attention on the stage. In 1895 Irving became the first actor to be knighted, the triumph of his long crusade to see the theatre recognised as an art form. He remained associated with the Lyceum, where his acting partner was ELLEN TERRY and his colleagues included BRAM STOKER, until its closure in 1902. Irving moved to Grafton Street a year after separating from his wife, Florence – who had scorned his profession – and lived a bachelor existence in rooms on the first and second floors, somewhat sombre in character due to the presence of stained glass windows. A contemporary commented that, 'Nowhere could be found a more perfect example of the confusion and neglect of order in which the artistic mind delights'.[10] Irving's dining room, which overlooked Bond Street, featured busts of John Philip Kemble and Dante; other chambers included a cigar room, a drawing room and a study, where the actor planned his performances. In 1899

MAYFAIR

lands to the north of Piccadilly soon after the Restoration. The square was originally laid out in the 1730s, but was built up gradually due to differences over leases and building contracts, and was only completed in the years just before the Second World War. Although a favourite haunt of criminals, Berkeley Square was immediately fashionable: number 44 was built in 1742–45 by William Kent for Lady Isabella Finch, while HORACE WALPOLE lived from 1789 at number 11 (formerly 40; demolished). Number 45 Berkeley Square – on the square's west side – was the last home of **Lord Clive of India** (1725–1774) ⑧ , the soldier and administrator; the house was built – along with number 46 – in *c.* 1744–45, to the designs of Henry Flitcroft. The son of a Shropshire squire, Robert Clive is best remembered as the victor of the Battle of Plassey (23 June 1757), in which the French were driven out of Bengal. This victory paved the way for British rule in India, and catapulted Clive to wealth and success. Returning to Britain in summer 1760, he was created Baron Clive of Plassey, and in early 1761 he moved with his wife Margaret, née Maskelyne (1735–1817) into this grand house in Berkeley Square, which in 1763–67 was redecorated in the height of fashion by William Chambers. The only London building associated with Clive, number 45 was not continuously his residence: he was away in 1764–67, serving once again as Governor of Bengal and Commander-in-Chief of the Army, though his wife continued to live in Berkeley Square; in 1765 she held a musical reception at which the young MOZART made an appearance. Clive's fame and wealth were to earn him powerful enemies: on his return from India in 1767, he was accused of bribery and corruption. Although he was acquitted in 1773, Clive was left broken in heart and health, and the following year he died at number 45, having taken a large dose of opium. The case for commemorating Clive was first made in 1908, but the then owner of number 45 – George Herbert, 4th Earl of Powis, a descendant of Lord Clive – did not see the need for a plaque. Permission was finally granted in 1951, when the owners suggested that a rectangular tablet would be more appropriate for the stonework of the building than the usual roundel. The plaque, manufactured by Doulton, was put up two years later.

Irving was advised by his doctors to move to sunnier quarters, and he took up residence in a flat at nearby 17 Stratton Street, which remained his home until his death. The plaque was originally manufactured in 1939, but a mistake in the residency dates – corrected by Irving's grandson – meant that a new roundel had to be made; this was installed in 1950, after the resumption of the scheme following the Second World War.

Berkeley Square, W1, is generally regarded as the most picturesque of Mayfair's open spaces. It takes its name from the 1st Lord Berkeley of Stratton, who acquired

At 50 (formerly 3) Berkeley Square there is a GLC plaque to the statesman **George Canning** (1770–1827)

390 A view from the hallway of 50 Berkeley Square towards the open space beyond. The former home of George Canning, the address is now the base of the antiquarian booksellers Maggs Bros Ltd. [© City of London, LMA]

391 Norman Hartnell in the mirrored salon at 26 Bruton Street in 1955. The three models look radiant in their Hartnell dresses. [© Getty Images]

moved house frequently. Over the last twenty-seven years of his life, he had fifteen different addresses in the capital, only two of which survive: 50 Berkeley Square (fig. 390) and 24 Bruton Street, Mayfair. Although Bruton Street was Canning's London home for about a year (1808–9), number 50 was chosen for commemoration as it preserved its domestic appearance and had been relatively unaltered. Canning kept this town house for several months in 1806, not long before his appointment as Foreign Secretary in March 1807; his two years in office were marked by his determined handling of foreign policy relating to the Napoleonic Wars, and he became the effective leader of the House of Commons. In 1822, on the death of VISCOUNT CASTLEREAGH – whom he had famously fought in a duel in 1809 – Canning was appointed Foreign Secretary for a second time; he held the post for five years, before briefly taking the highest office, heading a coalition of Tories and Whigs. Number 50 Berkeley Square, completed in about 1744, was to become notorious during the Victorian period as the most haunted house in London; stories of ghostly sightings began in about 1840, and intensified in the later decades of the century, when the house was occupied by an eccentric recluse. It was said in 1879 in the society magazine *Mayfair* that, 'The very party walls of the house, when touched, are found saturated with electric horror'.[11] Today, any stories of hauntings have generally been forgotten, number 50 becoming better known as the home of the antiquarian booksellers Maggs Bros Ltd, proposers of the plaque in 1977.

, who served as Prime Minister for only 119 days before dying of pneumonia at Chiswick House. Born in London to Irish parents, Canning – who was seldom out of public office between 1796 and 1827 –

Mayfair has long been associated with the fashion industry, a fact reflected by the English Heritage plaque at 26 Bruton Street, W1 – immediately to the east of Berkeley Square – to the court dressmaker **Sir Norman Hartnell** (1901–1979) 10 (fig. 391). Born in a public house in Streatham Hill, Hartnell rose to become one of the most famous of British couturiers. His fabulous dresses, renowned for their glamour and ability to reflect the personality of the wearer, clothed women of fame and high society for five decades; clients included Greer Garson and VIVIEN LEIGH. From the late 1930s, Hartnell worked increasingly for the royal family; the highlights of his career included commissions to design Princess Elizabeth's wedding dress (1947) and the dress for her coronation (1953). He was also active at the other end of the spectrum, designing a series of

MAYFAIR

392 The principal façade of Lansdowne House in c.1914, prior to its remodelling as the Lansdowne Club, which opened in 1935. The building then faced onto a large garden, occupying the south side of Berkeley Square, but now fronts directly onto Fitzmaurice Place. [© Country Life]

utility dresses for the mass market during the Second World War and later designing uniforms, such as that for female officers of the Metropolitan Police. Hartnell's long association with Bruton Street began in 1923, when he opened a couture establishment at number 10 (demolished). In 1935 his business moved to 26 Bruton Street, where it was to remain for the rest of his life. From at least the mid-1950s, the property also served as Hartnell's residence, the couturier having given up The Tower House, 12 Park Village West, Regent's Park, NW1, his home for around twenty years; between 1934 and the mid-1960s, his country residence was Lovel Dene, Windsor. Number 26, which dates from the mid-eighteenth century, was altered for Hartnell in 1934 by the architect and designer Gerald Lacoste. It was one of the most celebrated salons of its day, with elaborate glass and mirror panelling; the showrooms were on the ground floor, the main salon was at first-floor level and the large, airy workshops were to the rear, entered via Bruton Place.

Immediately to the south of Berkeley Square, in what is now Fitzmaurice Place, W1, stands one of the most important houses to survive in Mayfair; Edward Hamilton, a visitor of the 1880s, described it as 'one of the most charming houses – if not *the* most charming house, in London'.[12] Lansdowne (formerly Shelburne)

House (fig. 392) was begun in 1762 for the 3rd Earl of Bute, to designs by ROBERT ADAM. Three years later it was sold, incomplete, to **William Petty, 2nd Marquess Shelburne and 1st Marquess of Lansdowne** (1737–1805) ⑪, the Dublin-born Prime Minister and supporter of American independence; he is commemorated by the first of the two English Heritage plaques which flank the entrance. Shelburne, who lived here from 1768 until his death, oversaw the completion of the house, employing architects and craftsmen such as GEORGE DANCE THE YOUNGER. Despite being widely disliked by his contemporaries – who found him arrogant and deceitful, and knew him as the 'Jesuit of Berkeley Square' – Shelburne was a figure of importance, especially for his consistent and outspoken opposition to the war with America. During his time as Prime Minister (1782–83), Shelburne oversaw the signing of a provisional peace treaty between Britain and America – the so-called Treaty of Paris – which he and BENJAMIN FRANKLIN drafted at Lansdowne House in November 1782. However, Shelburne's fall from power was rapid; resigning as premier on the establishment of the coalition headed by CHARLES JAMES Fox and Lord North, he never returned to political favour. In his later years, having been created Marquess of Lansdowne in 1784, he became an important patron of literature and the fine arts; his collection of manuscripts was acquired by the British Museum after his death. Visitors to Lansdowne House included DAVID GARRICK, SAMUEL JOHNSON and Jeremy Bentham, while JOSEPH PRIESTLEY was employed as librarian and philosopher both here and at Shelburne's country home, Bowood in Wiltshire.

Given SHELBURNE's associations with America, it is rather appropriate that the last tenant of Lansdowne House (see fig. 392) was the department store magnate and entrepreneur par excellence, **Harry Gordon Selfridge** (1858–1947) ⑫, commemorated with a plaque in 2003. Born in rural Wisconsin, USA, Selfridge joined the Chicago department store of Field, Leiter & Co. at the age of twenty-one; in 1890 he was made a junior partner of the firm, which had become Marshall Field & Co. in 1881. Determined to go it alone, he moved in 1906 to London, where – three years later – he opened his pioneering Oxford Street department store; featuring 130 departments, a library, roof garden, restaurants and a 'bargain basement', it quickly set the standard for retailing practice. During his period of residence at Lansdowne House – which he leased from early 1921 until 1929 at a cost of £5,000 a year – Selfridge was at the height of his fame and fortune. The profits from his department store reached a peak in 1925, enabling him to live extravagantly; Selfridge bought racehorses, Rolls Royces and Highcliffe Castle, Hampshire, and lavished money on entertaining London's elite at his Mayfair home. He was famed for his parties led by the Dolly Sisters, the Hungarian-American cabaret artistes who gave demonstrations of dances such as the Black Bottom and the Charleston. Selfridge's life never reached the same heights again: increasingly beset by debt, he lost control of his business in 1939, retired as President in 1941 and spent his last years in poverty, dying at a small flat in Putney, 2 Ross Court, West Hill, SW15. The fortunes of Lansdowne House itself were also to change: in 1929 the building was sold and was subsequently extensively altered to form the Lansdowne Club, which opened in 1935. In order to allow the creation of Fitzmaurice Place, the whole façade was demolished and moved forty feet (12 m) further back, requiring the dismantling of the front tier of rooms; two of these were shipped intact to America, where they survive in museums.

High up on the May Fair Hotel, Stratton Street, W1, on the corner of Berkeley Street, a plaque honours the popular dance band leader **Bert Ambrose** (*c.* 1896–1971) ⑬ (fig. 393), who lived and played here

between 1927 and 1940. Little is known about the early life of London-born Benjamin Baruch Ambrose, though music was clearly an abiding passion. Originally a violin player, he came to prominence as a musical director in New York in 1917–20, and then made his mark in London with his Embassy Club orchestra. In March 1927, on the opening of the May Fair Hotel – a building begun in 1924, to designs by W. H. White – Ambrose took the job of musical director, which allowed him to broadcast on the radio on Saturday nights and to make some eighty records a year. The deal also included a flat at the hotel, which Ambrose retained even when he returned to the Embassy Club in Old Bond Street in 1933–36. Ambrose – whose signature tune was 'When Day is Done' – soon came back to the May Fair. He and his band appeared here for the last time between September 1939 and August 1940, by which time his band was nationally famous and had featured vocalists such as Sam Browne and Vera Lynn; Ambrose's arrangers and band members included Lew Stone, Sid Phillips, Billy Amstell and Ted Heath. Exasperated with the air raids, he subsequently retired to Hertfordshire and, with the decline of big bands, spent much of the rest of his career managing other performers, notably the singer Kathy Kirby. Ambrose's plaque was unveiled in 2005 at a ceremony attended by a huge crowd of fans.

The north side of Piccadilly and the streets running north into Mayfair have long been popular, positioned

393   Bert Ambrose with his orchestra in a photograph of the 1940s. He lived and played at the May Fair Hotel in Stratton Street between 1927 and 1940.
[© Popperfoto / Getty Images]

MAYFAIR

as they are close to the seat of government and areas of open parkland. Only a few of the great houses that once faced onto Piccadilly now remain, the most notable being Burlington House (which houses the Royal Academy of Arts), originally built in *c.* 1664–68. Another survivor is Cambridge (or Egremont) House at 94 Piccadilly, W1, occupied from 1866 to 1999 by the Naval and Military Club and familiarly known as the 'In and Out' from the lettering on the gateposts. Built in 1756–58 by Matthew Brettingham for the 2nd Earl of Egremont, Cambridge House takes its name from Prince Adolphus, Duke of Cambridge (1774–1850), who acquired the property in 1829 and died here twenty-one years later. The building was the home of the Prime Minister and Foreign Secretary Henry John Temple, **Lord Palmerston** (1784–1865) **14** (see also pp. 472–3 and pp. 528–9), from 1855 until the time of his death. This fact, and number 94's royal association, is recorded on an LCC plaque erected on the boundary wall in 1960, shortly after the completion of rebuilding works necessitated by severe bomb damage. During his residence at Cambridge House, Palmerston – who, like other early premiers, never lived at 10 Downing Street – served as leader of the House of Commons and Prime Minister, a position he held for all but one year of the period 1855–65; his spells as Foreign Secretary had come earlier, in 1830–34, 1835–41 and 1846–51. A Liberal, Palmerston was notable for his tough approach to foreign policy, and was committed to the suppression of the international slave trade. While at Cambridge House, Emily, Lady Palmerston (1787–1869) continued to hold the celebrated social 'assemblies' that had become such a famous feature of their home in Carlton Gardens. The two gateways of number 94 served to direct the flow of guests, who included politicians, ambassadors and society beauties.

At 11 Bolton Street, W1, there is a chocolate-brown plaque to the authoress **Madame D'Arblay (Fanny Burney)** (1752–1840) **15** (fig. 394). This is notable for its early date – it was installed by the Society of Arts in 1885 – and its status as the second plaque to commemorate a woman; the first, to the actress Mrs Sarah Siddons, was put up in 1876 at 27 Upper Baker Street, Marylebone (demolished in 1905). Born in King's Lynn, the daughter of the musician and writer Dr Charles Burney, Fanny moved with her family to London in 1760, and was propelled into the limelight

by the publication of her novel *Evelina* (1778). Fêted by Samuel Johnson and David Garrick, she consolidated her literary reputation with *Cecilia* (1782) and, after five eventful years (1786–91) as Second Keeper of the Robes to Queen Charlotte, wrote the most profitable of her works, *Camilla* (1796). Burney's writings are said to have inspired Jane Austen, and led to her being described by Virginia Woolf as the mother of English fiction. Fanny moved to number 11 on 8 October 1818, following the death of her husband, the French émigré Alexandre D'Arblay. She intended the house to provide a London home for their son, Alexander (1794–1837), and described it in her journal as 'my new and probably last dwelling'.[13] Burney was, in fact, to move a further three times, always within Mayfair: on 1 November 1828 she left Bolton Street for 1 Half Moon Street; in 1837 she transferred to 112 Mount Street; and in 1839 she moved to her final address, 29 Lower Grosvenor Street. The greater part of her time at Bolton Street was dedicated to assembling the three-volume *Memoirs of Doctor Burney* (1832).

Number 46 (formerly 44) Clarges Street, W1, a terraced house of *c.* 1730, bears a wreathed plaque to the statesman **Charles James Fox** (1749–1806) **16** (fig. 395); erected here in 1950, it has a complicated history. In 1904 the LCC looked into Fox's various London addresses – most in Mayfair and St James's – and decided to commemorate him at 9 Arlington Street, just south of Piccadilly, his London home from 1804 until 1806. However, the occupier strongly objected to the letters 'LCC' being placed on the plaque, which had, alas, already been made. Anxious to please, the council went to the lengths of covering its initials with blue glass, rendering them completely invisible; the now happy lessee gave his consent, and the plaque went up in 1912. In the 1940s the house was pulled down, and the LCC was forced once again to consider possible locations for the plaque. It was found that only two of Fox's London addresses were known to survive: Holland House, Kensington, his family home, and 46 Clarges Street, his residence for a short period in 1803. The latter was eventually chosen, and the old plaque was re-erected, the glass triumphantly removed. Fox was born in Mayfair, the son of Henry Fox, later 1st Baron Holland, and became an MP at the age of nineteen. A powerful orator, he grew to be

395 The wreathed plaque to Charles James Fox at 46 Clarges Street. Originally installed in 1912 at 9 Arlington Street, St James's – with the initials 'LCC' covered over at the owner's request – the restored plaque was re-erected in Clarges Street in 1950. [© English Heritage. Photograph by Derek Kendall]

radical in outlook, supporting the French Revolution and the cause of American independence. Antipathy between Fox and King George III put paid to his chances of high office; his most senior office was Foreign Secretary, a post he first held in 1782. In the following year, the King conspired to undermine the coalition Fox had formed with Lord North, thereby paving the way for their rival, WILLIAM PITT THE YOUNGER, to begin his long stint as premier. By 1803, Fox – doyen of the Whigs – was living largely in retirement at St Anne's Hill, Surrey, and was only prompted to make his brief return to London by talks surrounding the resumption of the war between Britain and France. In 1806 he came to office – for the second time – as Foreign Secretary, but died shortly afterwards.

Hertford Street, W1 – one of the narrow streets in the area to the east of Park Lane – became one of the most fashionable thoroughfares in London in the early 1830s. It has three plaques, two of them on the same house: 10 Hertford Street, built in *c.* 1768–69 by the elder Henry Holland and his son. The two plaques were proposed by the building's then owner, an advertising firm, and were installed in 1954–55 (fig. 396). The first commemorates **General John Burgoyne** (1723–1792) **17**, nicknamed 'Gentleman Johnny', who enjoyed a threefold career as soldier, politician and dramatist.[14] He first came to attention during the Seven Years War and in 1762 – a year after his election to Parliament – saw action in Portugal, for which he was promoted colonel. In 1775 he was appointed to join GENERAL GAGE in North America, and was later given the command of the Canadian Army. Burgoyne is best known as the general who surrendered to the Americans at Saratoga, New York, on 17 October 1777, one of the major turning points of the War of Independence. Returning – with George Washington's permission – to Britain the following year, he re-entered Parliament and, with CHARLES JAMES FOX and EDMUND BURKE, became a fierce spokesman against the war. Burgoyne's military career continued despite his failure in America – he served as Commander-in-Chief of Ireland in 1782–84 – but his later years were dedicated chiefly to literary work; his first play, *The Maid of the Oaks*, produced by GARRICK in 1775, was followed by *The Heiress*, staged at the Drury Lane theatre in 1786 and described by HORACE WALPOLE as 'the best

MAYFAIR

illustrious former occupant, GENERAL BURGOYNE, and remained here until 1802 (see fig. 396). Irish-born, Sheridan moved with his family to London and, in 1770, to Bath, where he met the famous singer Elizabeth Linley; they were married in 1773, but had all but separated by the time of her death in 1792. It was on his second marriage, to Esther ('Hecca') Ogle (*c*. 1775–1817), that Sheridan took up residence in Hertford Street; their son Charles (1796–1843) was born the following year. By this time, Sheridan was well established as a politician; first elected to the House of Commons in 1780, and famed for his parliamentary oratory, he was a leading Whig and a friend of CHARLES JAMES FOX. He was also known as a highly successful dramatist and theatre manager. While here, Sheridan wrote his last work, the tragedy *Pizarro* (presented in 1799), and continued to manage the Theatre Royal, Drury Lane, the company of which included John Philip Kemble, Mrs Siddons and MRS JORDAN. However, Sheridan invested greatly in the theatre's rebuilding in 1791–94, and his financial position – always precarious – reached a crisis point in 1802, prompting the bailiffs to seize his Hertford Street home.

Number 20 Hertford Street was the home of **Sir George Cayley** (1773–1857) **19**, the scientist and pioneer of aviation, and the first man to lay down the principles of heavier-than-air flight; he is now widely regarded as the father of aeronautics (fig. 397). Cayley, the 6th baronet, was born at Scarborough and succeeded to the family estates in 1792, thereafter living mainly at Brompton Hall, Yorkshire, where his scientific researches were carried out. By 1799 he had already sketched a machine that established the basic configuration of the modern aeroplane. His studies, published in *Nicholson's Journal* in 1809–10, form the basis of modern aerodynamics. In

396   A contractor installs the plaque to Richard Brinsley Sheridan at 10 Hertford Street in 1955. Above is the plaque to General John Burgoyne, erected the previous year. [© Getty Images]

Right 397   An early design for a helicopter by Sir George Cayley. It dates from 1843, during Cayley's time at 20 Hertford Street. [© Getty Images]

modern comedy'.[15] Burgoyne acquired number 10 in 1769, and commissioned ROBERT ADAM to carry out alterations. He and his wife Lady Charlotte (d. 1776) – daughter of Edward Stanley, 11th Earl of Derby – moved in two years later, and it remained Burgoyne's residence until his death here in 1792, the most important years of his career.

The dramatist and statesman **Richard Brinsley Sheridan** (1751–1816) **18** (see also pp. 425–6) moved to 10 Hertford Street in 1795, three years after the death of its

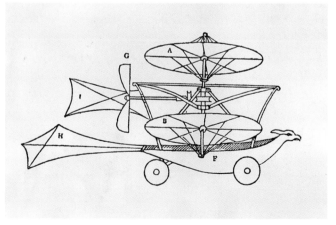

1853, about fifty years before the 'flying machine' was officially patented by the American brothers Orville and Wilbur Wright, Cayley saw the successful flight of the first man-carrying glider in history, which he had built close to his Yorkshire home; it was supposedly piloted by his coachman. Cayley's pioneering work did not end there: he also invented the caterpillar tractor, the hot-air engine and the tension wheel (later to become the modern bicycle wheel), and carried out original work on land reclamation, railway engineering, acoustics, optics and electricity. He was also important as an educator, serving as first Chairman of the Polytechnic Institution (see QUINTIN HOGG) from 1838 until his death. Number 20 Hertford Street was Cayley's town house from 1840 until c. 1850. Dating from the eighteenth century, the building was heavily re-faced in about 1890. However, as the major surviving building in London associated with the scientist, the LCC decided to erect a plaque here, and it duly went up in 1962.

One of the most important thoroughfares in south Mayfair is Curzon Street, W1, developed from the 1720s onwards around the gardens of Crewe House and Chesterfield House. It was just south of here, at what is now Shepherd Market, that the original May fair [sic] took place. At 10 Curzon Sreet, an English Heritage plaque marks Heywood Hill's bookshop, the workplace of the writer **Nancy Mitford** (1904–1973) **20** from March 1942 until late summer 1945 (fig. 385). The eldest of the six Mitford girls, the well-known daughters of Lord and Lady Redesdale, Nancy is best remembered for her novels *The Pursuit of Love* (1945) and *Love in a Cold Climate* (1949), the latter written in France, where she settled in 1946. During the Second World War, she worked at the fashionable Curzon Street bookshop run by Heywood Hill (1906–1986) and his wife Anne (b. 1912). After Hill was called up in December 1942 and Anne left to have her first baby, Mitford took over the running of the shop, in which she was ably assisted by Mrs Mollie Friese-Green [sic], daughter-in-law of the pioneering cinematographer. The bookshop soon became a meeting place and refuge for the literati, and was a favourite haunt of writers of Mitford's generation, including EVELYN WAUGH, Anthony Powell and Osbert Sitwell. Such associations led the Mitford family to suggest that Curzon Street was a far more appropriate place to commemorate Nancy than her home at 12 Blomfield

Road, Maida Vale, W9, where she lived for most of the period 1936–46 but which was rebuilt after the war. Number 10 Curzon Street, which has mid-eighteenth-century origins, remains largely as it was in 1945, with a fine bowed shop front of the first half of the 1800s. The plaque was unveiled in 1999 by Nancy's sister, Deborah, Duchess of Devonshire.

On the south side of Curzon Street, at number 32, there is a GLC plaque to **Rufus Isaacs**, **1st Marquess of Reading** (1860–1935) **21** , the lawyer and statesman. Isaacs was born in the City of London, the son of a Jewish fruit merchant, and rose to become a leading advocate and a close friend of LLOYD GEORGE. Having enjoyed a highly successful career as a barrister, he served as Solicitor-General and Attorney-General in quick succession before becoming Lord Chief Justice in 1913. This post, which Isaacs held until 1921, was interrupted by his time as Ambassador to the United States (1918–19), where – with characteristic tact and diplomacy – he persuaded America to become more closely involved in the war. Isaacs was Viceroy of India between 1921 and 1926, when he was created Marquess of Reading, the seat he had represented in Parliament for nearly ten years (1904–13). His final political appointment came in 1931, when RAMSAY MACDONALD made him Foreign Secretary. Isaacs moved from Park Lane to 32 Curzon Street in mid-1910 and lived here until his death twenty-five years later, with the exception of the years he spent in America and India. He loved the house, which dates from the late eighteenth century, sharing it with his wife Alice, née Cohen, who died here in 1930, and their son Gerald (1889–1960). After 1931 it became home to Isaac's second wife, Stella, née Charnaud (1894–1971), who in 1938 founded the Women's (Royal) Voluntary Service. At first the LCC encountered difficulties with the plaque: in 1962 the owner of the building – the politician Francis Curzon, 5th Earl Howe – refused consent for its installation. After his death, his son proved more amenable, and the plaque was put up in 1971.

Number 19 Curzon Street, part of a terrace of c. 1763–65, was the last home of **Benjamin Disraeli, Earl of Beaconsfield** (1804–1881) **22** (see also pp. 58–9), the Victorian statesman and Conservative Prime Minister (fig. 398). The chocolate-brown wreathed

398 Number 19 Curzon Street as it appeared in 1881. Benjamin Disraeli died at the address in April of that year. [© Illustrated London News Ltd / Mary Evans Picture Library]

Far right 399 The 'leader of fashion' Beau Brummell in a portrait by Robert Dighton. It dates from 1805, around the time that Brummell left 4 Chesterfield Street. [Private Collection / The Bridgeman Art Library]

plaque, erected by the LCC in 1908, was the second to commemorate Disraeli, and marks the house where he lived for four months and died on 19 April 1881. The writer Francis Espinasse, who visited Disraeli shortly before his death, described the reception rooms as having 'a look of spick and span newness'.[16] At the time the LCC was considering Disraeli's case, there was another contender for commemoration – 93 Park Lane (formerly 1 Grosvenor Gate, and then 29 Park Lane), where he lived for twenty-nine years (1839–72). However, the Duke of Westminster's then monopoly on commemorative tablets on the Grosvenor estate led to its being ruled out by the council. Disraeli acquired 19 Curzon Street in November 1880 – using part of the proceeds of his recently published novel, *Endymion* – and moved in on 15 January 1881. By this time, Disraeli had retired from politics – he resigned as Prime Minister in April 1880 following the electoral triumph of his Liberal rival, GLADSTONE – and hoped to spend his time writing novels; a work now known as *Falconet*, a sequel to *Lothair* (1870), was left unfinished at his death. However, Disraeli's ambitions were halted due to a sharp downturn in his health. During his final illness, he famously declined the offer of a visit by

Queen Victoria, stating, 'No it is better not. She would only ask me to take a message to Albert'.[17] On 31 March – three weeks before his death – he corrected his last speech for *Hansard*, asserting that he would 'not go down to posterity talking bad grammar'.[18]

Chesterfield Street, W1, which extends north from Curzon Street, dates from the mid-eighteenth century, and is one of the least altered streets in Mayfair. At number 4, a GLC plaque of 1984 celebrates the dandy and leader of fashion **Beau Brummell** (1778–1840) 23 (fig. 399). The son of a private secretary to the Prime Minister Lord North, George Bryan ('Beau') Brummell moved to Chesterfield Street in 1799, having inherited money on coming of age and having recently left the Army. By then he was already close to George, Prince of Wales – whom he had first met at the age of sixteen – and had begun to impose on society his strong views on fashion. Always smart and self-assured, Brummell set a new standard for his friends and contemporaries by scorning the typically ostentatious dress of the eighteenth century. His style – which became known as dandyism – relied on fine-quality cloth, precise cutting and understated elegance, and was epitomised, above all, by the starched cravat. Brummell's house in Chesterfield Street thronged with members of the aristocracy and the so-called 'Dandiacal Body', who anxiously hoped to gain access to the inner sanctum, Beau's front dressing room. The Prince is said to have called nearly every morning to discuss matters of dress. However, the pair's friendship was soon under strain and ended with a famous exchange in 1813: while walking with Lord Moira in St James's, and having been snubbed by the Prince, Brummell – known for his cutting wit – asked his colleague, 'Pray, who is your fat friend?'. By this time, Brummell had left Chesterfield Street – his home until around 1804 – and occupied at least three other Mayfair addresses, all since demolished: 18 Bruton Street (c. 1804–8), 22 South Street (1810) and 13 Chapel (now Aldford) Street (1812–16). In 1816 mounting gambling debts forced him to flee to France. Brummell died there in a paupers' lunatic asylum in 1840, at the age of sixty-two.

Two doors away, at 6 Chesterfield Street, a plaque of 1975 commemorates a very different figure: the novelist and playwright **William Somerset Maugham** (1874–1965) **24** . Born in Paris, Maugham qualified as a doctor in London in 1897 but – having written his

first novel while still a student – chose to make literature his career, and went on to become well known as a satirist of British society. Maugham moved house regularly and enjoyed long spells abroad between 1895 and 1927, the year he left London for France. While in Chesterfield Street, his home from 1 April 1911 until 31 March 1919, Maugham enjoyed great success, writing his most famous novel, *Of Human Bondage* (1915), and holding supper parties for the casts of such of his plays as *Caroline* (1916). This period of his life, though productive, was partly shrouded in mystery: Maugham's experiences as a British espionage agent during the First World War were later recounted in *Ashenden* (1928), while his regular trips to the Pacific Islands and the Far East resulted in works including *The Moon and Sixpence* (1919). While at Chesterfield Street, Maugham began his long relationship with Gerald Haxton, an Anglo-American with whom he served in the First World War. From here, in 1917, he also embarked on his ill-fated marriage to the interior designer Syrie Wellcome, née Barnardo (1879–1955). The couple later lived in Marylebone – at 2 Wyndham Place and 43 Bryanston Square, W1 – and then at 213 King's Road, Chelsea, SW3. They were divorced in 1929, by which time Maugham was living in France with Haxton. The Second World War left numbers 5 and 7 Chesterfield Street gutted; the two houses were subsequently incorporated with number 6, which had survived intact.

At 20 Charles Street, W1, an LCC plaque marks the birthplace of Archibald Philip Primrose, **5th Earl of Rosebery** (1847–1929) **25** , the Prime Minister and first Chairman of the London County Council (fig. 400). The eldest son of Lord Dalmeny (1809–1851) and his wife Lady Wilhelmina, née Stanhope (1819–1901), and the grandson of the 4th Earl of Rosebery, Archibald Primrose succeeded to the earldom in 1868 and made his maiden speech in the House of Lords three years later. A Liberal, Rosebery was appointed Lord Privy Seal in 1885; he then served as Foreign Secretary in 1886 and 1892–94, before becoming Prime Minister on the resignation of GLADSTONE in 1894. Despite being one of the most celebrated and wealthy figures in England, Rosebery was a disappointment as premier and felt himself unsuited to the role, resigning in 1895. More successful had been his brief term as first Chairman of the LCC (1889–90); Rosebery Avenue, Islington, the first of the council's street

400   The dining room of 20 Charles Street, in a photograph of 1897 by Bedford Lemere. Archibald Philip Primrose, later 5th Earl of Rosebery, was born at the house in 1847. [Reproduced by permission of English Heritage. NMR]

MAYFAIR

improvements, was named in his honour and was opened by him in 1890; he later (in 1903) unveiled the first of the council's blue plaques, erected in honour of LORD MACAULAY. Rosebery was long and closely associated with the area of his birth: he lived at 20 Charles Street for the first year of his life, at 2 Berkeley Square in 1869–78, then at Lansdowne House before settling in 1888 at 38 Berkeley Square, his London home until his death. As all but the first of these properties had been rebuilt, it was felt that 20 Charles Street – which dates from the mid-eighteenth century and was re-fronted in c. 1840 – was the most appropriate for commemoration. The plaque was unveiled in 1962 by his son, Harry Primrose, 6th Earl of Rosebery.

One of Mayfair's most celebrated thoroughfares, South Audley Street – together with the neighbouring streets – was home to a remarkable collection of famous figures, especially during the nineteenth century. The southern part of the street was long dominated by Chesterfield House, the mansion built in 1747–50 by Philip Stanhope, 4th Earl of Chesterfield, and demolished in the 1930s. In its shadow, at 5 Stanhope Gate (formerly Great Stanhope Street), W1, lived **Lord Fitzroy Somerset, 1st Baron Raglan** (1788–1855) **26** , Commander during the Crimean War. Number 5 was his home from 1834 to 1854; he had previously lived, between 1821 and 1828, at 85 Pall Mall (demolished). Raglan was one of several eminent military men put

forward in 1908 for commemoration by the LCC; others were LORD CLIVE, Sir James Outram, the Duke of Wellington and GENERAL WOLFE. Three years later, Raglan's blue wreathed plaque was erected here, his final address in England. The house dates from c. 1760, but was re-faced in stone and heightened around the first decade of the twentieth century. Lord Fitzroy Somerset – as he was known before being raised to the peerage in 1852 – spent most of his long military service as the right-hand man of Arthur Wellesley, Duke of Wellington, whose niece – Emily Wellesley-Pole (1792–1881) – he married in 1814. Somerset served with him almost continuously from 1807 until the Duke's death in 1852, and was with him at Waterloo, where he was wounded and then lost his right arm. After a period as Master-General of the Ordnance, Raglan was appointed British Commander in the Crimea, and in April 1854 – a month after the outbreak of war – left Mayfair for Turkey. Although he saw victory at the battles of Alma and Inkerman, Raglan came under increasing censure, especially for his part in the disastrous Charge of the Light Brigade of October 1854. The following year, shortly after the failure of an assault made as part of the Siege of Sevastopol, Raglan died at camp, worn out by anxiety and disappointment.

The intersection of Hill Street and South Audley Street, W1, marks the southern boundary of the Grosvenor estate. Just beyond this point, at 14 South Audley Street – a house built in c. 1736 by a carpenter, Roger Blagrave – is an LCC plaque of 1955 commemorating the sculptor **Sir Richard Westmacott** (1775–1856) **27** (fig. 401). Having studied sculpture with his father – of the same name – and later in Italy, Westmacott first exhibited at the Royal Academy in 1797, and thereafter became a regular contributor. By the time of his death, Westmacott had produced nearly three hundred works and was known as Britain's foremost official sculptor. He produced a large body of portrait and funerary sculpture and monumental classical works; these include the bronze statue of Francis Russell, 5th Duke of Bedford in Russell Square (1809), the monument to CHARLES JAMES FOX in Westminster Abbey (1810–23), *Achilles* in Hyde Park (1814–22) and, his last known commission, the group in the pediment of the British Museum (1851). Westmacott was associated with Mayfair throughout his life: he spent his youth at 25

401 A view by George Johann Scharf showing Sir Richard Westmacott lecturing on sculpture at the Royal Academy, Somerset House, in 1830. [© Royal Academy of Arts, London]

402   Number 10 South Street as it appeared in 1929, shortly before its demolition. Florence Nightingale lived in the house for forty-five years and died here in 1910. [© Grosvenor Collection, City of Westminster Archives Centre]

Mount Street, and lived next door at 24 Mount Street from 1796 to 1818. In the latter year, requiring larger premises, Westmacott moved to 14 South Audley Street, which was altered for him and served as his residence, studio and gallery; the sculptor remained here until his death thirty-eight years later. While at number 14, Westmacott completed some of his greatest works, and, in 1827, succeeded John Flaxman as Professor of Sculpture at the Royal Academy, a position he held until his death. He lived with his wife, Dorothy, née Wilkinson (d. 1834), and their large family; his eldest son – also Richard Westmacott (1799–1872) and another successful sculptor – lived here until 1830.

Almost opposite, at 72 South Audley Street, there is an English Heritage plaque to **Charles X** (1757–1836) **28**, the last Bourbon King of France. Charles-Philippe – known from his birth as the Comte d'Artois, and later simply as 'Monsieur' – was the younger brother of Louis XVI and Louis XVIII and the grandson of Louis XV. A devout Roman Catholic, the Comte was also a notorious womaniser, known for his wit, charm and good looks, and came to be a close friend of his sister-in-law, Marie Antoinette. Following the storming of the Bastille in 1789, Louis XVI ordered the Comte to leave France, and he went into exile, first in Germany, then in Italy and finally in Britain. After three years (1796–99) at Holyrood House, Edinburgh – lent to him by King George III – he settled in London, where he was to remain until the fall of Napoleon in 1814; his brother, later Louis XVIII, was also in exile in Britain, but was not permitted to reside in London. Charles lived at two addresses in the capital: 46 (later 85) Baker Street, Marylebone (demolished), from late 1799 to 1805, and 72 South Audley Street, from 1805 to 1814. During this period – saddened by the death in 1804 of his beloved mistress, Louise de Polastron – he generally lived a quiet and retired life. Following his return to France on the restoration of the monarchy, and the death of Louis XVIII, Charles acceded to the throne in 1824. A reactionary figure, largely unpopular in his own country, he ruled until 1830, when revolution forced his abdication and drove him once again into exile; the Crown subsequently passed to a cousin, Louis-Philippe, Duc d'Orléans. Number 72, a house of the 1730s much altered in the nineteenth century, was marked with a plaque in 2000.

403   Florence Nightingale in a photograph of 1910. It was probably taken in her bedroom at the back of the second floor of 10 South Street. [© Illustrated London News Ltd / Mary Evans Picture Library]

In South Street, W1, is a plaque that may be considered one of London's least successful, given its modern context. Installed by the LCC in 1955, and re-erected in 1978, it straddles the party wall of numbers 10 and 14 (see fig. 26); the former is part of a block of flats built in c. 1935–38 that stands on the site of the home of **Florence Nightingale** (1820–1910) **29**, the nurse and heroine of the Crimean War (figs 402 and 403). Named after the Italian city in which she was born, Nightingale came to prominence when, in 1854, she took a party of nurses to a hospital in Scutari, Turkey; there she was based until 1856 and her return – a heroine – to England. Nightingale played a major part in reducing deaths in the Army, in the improvement of health care and in the establishment of nursing as a profession; she designed hospitals, and in 1860 founded the Nightingale School of Nursing at St Thomas' in London. Number 10 (formerly 35) South Street was acquired for Florence by her father William in 1865, and she died here forty-five years later. Cecil Woodham-Smith wrote that, 'To enter her house was to receive an instant impression of whiteness, order and light'.[19] Nightingale, who was unmarried, spent almost all her time in her bedroom, at the back of the second floor; she never saw visitors except by appointment. During these years, she was 'treated with an

MAYFAIR

almost religious deference – ministers, kings, princesses, statesmen waited at her door, and her utterances were paid the respect due to an oracle'.[20] Among Nightingale's neighbours were her sister and brother-in-law, Sir Harry and Lady Parthenope Verney, who lived at 4 (formerly 32) South Street from 1859 until 1890. Number 10 was marked with a plaque by the Duke of Westminster in 1912, but was demolished in 1929–30. In 1954 the LCC decided to commemorate its site, Nightingale's fame being seen as sufficient justification for this departure from the rules; the plaque was unveiled the following year by Mary, The Princess Royal, Patroness of the Florence Nightingale Hospital in Lisson Grove.

Number 43 South Street – part of an imposing terrace designed by J. J. Stevenson and built in 1896–98 – was the home from 1918 to 1940 of **Albert Henry Stanley**, **Lord Ashfield** (1874–1948) **30** , the first Chairman of London Transport. Born in Derbyshire, Albert Henry Knattriess – the name Stanley was adopted in the mid-1890s – moved with his family to America in 1880. There he enjoyed a successful career in transport before returning to England in 1907 to take up the post of General Manager of the Underground Electric Railways Company of London (UERL). Three years later, he became Managing Director, and oversaw an important series of mergers from 1912. After a period as President of the Board of Trade (1916–19) – which earned him a peerage – Ashfield returned to become Chairman as well as Managing Director of UERL; the subsequent growth of the group is reflected in its large and imposing headquarters building at 55 Broadway, Westminster, built in 1927–29 to the designs of Charles Holden. Together with Herbert Morrison and Frank Pick, Ashfield masterminded the inauguration in 1933 of a unified transport system for the capital, the London Passenger Transport Board (later simplified to London Transport). As Chairman from 1933 to 1947, he oversaw the development of services and provisions at a time of major expansion for London's suburbs. The plaque, conceived in conjunction with that to Pick, was unveiled in 1984; the sans serif designed by Edward Johnston was used as the typeface, as it had been on the plaques to Pick and Johnston himself, thus completing what the GLC described as 'a coherent group of plaques in commemoration of the early days of London Transport'.[21]

A contemporary of Lord Ashfield, **John Gilbert Winant** (1889–1947) **31** , the United States Ambassador in 1941–46, was commemorated by the GLC in 1982. The plaque is at 7 Aldford Street, W1, on the corner of Rex Place, originally a stable building serving 14 and 16 Park Street (fig. 404); the whole block was built in 1896–97 to designs by Eustace Balfour and H. Thackeray Turner. Born in New York, Winant served in the 1920s and 1930s as Governor of New Hampshire and first Chairman of the new Social Security Board before being appointed Ambassador to Britain by President Franklin D. Roosevelt. During his years in London, Winant made a great impact on the British public and press. People from all walks of life were affected by his energy and his promotion of justice, freedom and truth; during air raids on London, he walked the streets at night offering support and encouragement, and took a close interest in British trade unions. During the war years, Winant lived in a

404   The plaque to John Gilbert Winant at 7 Aldford Street, built in 1896–97 on the corner of Rex Place. [© English Heritage. Photograph by Derek Kendall]

flat above the American Embassy, then at 1 Grosvenor Square (now the Canadian High Commission), which he described in his volume of memoirs, *A Letter from Grosvenor Square* (1947). In June 1945, soon after the end of the war, Winant moved to a 'small house down the street' at 7 Aldford Street, also taking a lease on the neighbouring property, 9 Rex Place.[22] By this time, he was a broken man; the death of his friend and benefactor President Roosevelt in April 1945 had come as a blow, and in March the following year he resigned as Ambassador, left Mayfair, and in May returned to the US. Increasingly despondent, and weighed down with financial worries, Winant was driven to suicide, a sad end to a varied and distinguished career.

Grosvenor Square, W1, laid out in *c.* 1725–31, was long one of the grandest addresses in Mayfair, if not in the capital as a whole, and in size is exceeded among London's squares only by Lincoln's Inn Fields. In 1790 it was home to six earls, including Earl Grosvenor. However, the twentieth century wrought radical changes: with only three of its pre-1900 houses remaining, the square is now dominated by flats and hotels built between the 1920s and 1960s and, on the west side, by the United States Embassy (1957–60). Given this wholesale rebuilding, it is perhaps unsurprising to find that the square has only one blue plaque, that to the aircraft designer and manufacturer **Sir Frederick Handley Page** (1885–1962) **32** . Handley Page kept Flat 3 at 18 Grosvenor Square – part of a block built in 1933–35 on the north side of the square – from 1952 until his death. This was considered the only address suitable for commemoration, given the secluded position of Limes House, Warren Lane, Stanmore, his home for about forty years, from the early 1920s until 1962. Born in Cheltenham, Handley Page was notable as an engineer and a businessman and, later, as an educator. His company, Handley Page Ltd, the first in Britain to be registered specifically to manufacture aeroplanes, was founded in 1909, and became known for its bombers produced during the First World War, including the O/400 of 1918. Its most successful aeroplane of the Second World War was the Halifax bomber, the first of which flew in September 1939. Alongside this, a smaller company, Handley Page Transport Ltd, was set up in 1919; five years later it became part of Imperial Airways, Britain's first national airline service. From 1911, Handley Page lectured in aeronautics at the North-

ampton Polytechnic Institute (later the Northampton Engineering College), and in 1946 helped to found the College of Aeronautics at Cranfield, Bedfordshire. At the time of Handley Page's death – which took place at his flat in Grosvenor Square – his original company was still independent; it was finally wound up eight years later, in 1970.

A plaque at 51 Upper Brook Street, W1, is testament to Mayfair's international character: it commemorates the Greek Ambassador, poet and Nobel Laureate **George Seferis** (1900–1971) **33** (fig. 405). Born Yeorgios Seferiadis in Smyrna (now Izmir, Turkey) and educated in Athens and Paris, Seferis enjoyed successful careers in both the literary and political arenas. He was active as a writer from his twenties; his first poetry collection, *Strophe* (Turning Point), appeared in 1931, and he came to prominence in 1935 with the publication of *Mythistorema* (Novel), a fusion of ancient Greek epic and modernism. The works that followed, including the poems *Kichli* (The Thrush; 1947) and *The King of Asine* (1948), led to his gaining wide regard as the T. S. ELIOT of Greece; Seferis was awarded the Nobel Prize for Literature in 1963. He was also promi-

405 George Seferis in Piccadilly Circus in 1932, the year after the publication of his first poetry collection, *Strophe* (Turning Point). Between 1931 and 1934 Seferis served as Vice-Consul and then Consul in the London Embassy. [Courtesy of the George Seferis Photographic Archive of the Cultural Foundation of the National Bank of Greece]

MAYFAIR

nent as a diplomat, having joined the Royal Greek Ministry of Foreign Affairs in 1926. Seferis, a great Anglophile, served as Vice-Consul and then Consul in the London Embassy in 1931–34, as Counsellor of the Embassy in 1951–52 and, from 1957 to 1962, as Ambassador to the Court of St James's. During this latter period, Seferis's longest stay in England, he and his wife Maro (d. 2000) lived at 51 Upper Brook Street – a stone-fronted building of 1905–6 designed by R. G. Hammond – which has been the official residence of the Greek Ambassador since 1921. Here, Seferis received literary friends such as T. S. Eliot, Lawrence Durrell and Sir Steven Runciman, and worked at consolidating Anglo-Greek relations. The plaque was unveiled in 2000 by the Greek Ambassador, Alexandros Sandis, as part of the celebrations surrounding the centenary of Seferis's birth.

Number 16 Upper Grosvenor Street, W1, is significant in having been the town house of the Peel family for over two decades. The building, completed in *c.* 1730 and stuccoed in 1881, was leased from 1800 to 1822 by the first **Sir Robert Peel** (1750–1830) **34** , the manufacturer and reformer, who was – as the owner of a flourishing calico-printing business – one of the pioneers of the Industrial Revolution. It was here that his famous son – **Sir Robert Peel** (1788–1850), the Prime Minister and founder of the Metropolitan Police – spent the formative years of his youth and early adulthood. Number 16 is now the only surviving London home of the younger Sir Robert, his other addresses having been demolished: the principal of these was 4 Whitehall Gardens, Westminster, Peel's residence from 1824 until his death, commemorated by the LCC in 1904 and redeveloped in 1938. Born near Manchester and brought up for a career in politics by his father – who he is said to have resembled in many ways – the younger Peel spent intermittent but important periods of his life at number 16; it was during his time here, in 1805 – between Harrow and Oxford – that he first began to frequent the House of Commons. In 1809, at the age of twenty-one, Peel entered politics; his long and successful career was crowned by two periods as Prime Minister (1834–35 and 1841–46). It was in 1829, during his second posting as Home Secretary, that Peel established the Metropolitan Police Force, based at Scotland Yard. He is also remembered for repealing the Corn Laws (1846), which split the Tory party that he had led

for so long, and for continuing the efforts made by his father to reform working conditions in factories. The plaque, erected by English Heritage in 1988 – the bicentenary of the younger Peel's birth – was proposed and unveiled by the Home Secretary, Douglas Hurd.

Park Lane, W1, overlooking Hyde Park, reached its peak as one of London's most fashionable streets from *c.* 1820 to 1830. Sadly, many of its original houses have been lost through redevelopment. It is thus all the more fitting that one of those that survive – number 99, part of a block of bow-windowed houses – is marked with a blue plaque. Built in 1823–25 to the designs of John Goldicutt, 99 Park Lane (formerly 7 Grosvenor Gate and 35 Park Lane), on the corner of Culross Street, was the home for sixty years of the philanthropist and Jewish leader **Sir Moses Montefiore** (1784–1885) **35** . Montefiore was the house's first occupant – he was granted a lease in 1824 and moved in two years later – and kept the house until the time of his death. It is interesting to note that among Montefiore's neighbours was Benjamin Disraeli, who lived at 93 Park Lane in 1839–72. With the Rothschilds, Moses Haim Montefiore was pre-eminent among England's nineteenth-century Jewish leaders, whose abilities and work brought the Jewish community into the mainstream of public life. His marriage in 1812 to Judith Cohen (1784–1862) led to his becoming the stockbroker of her brother-in-law, Nathan Mayer Rothschild; by the time of Rothschild's death in 1836, Montefiore had become exceedingly wealthy, and was knighted during his term as Sheriff of London (1837–38). In a position to retire from active business at the age of forty, he devoted his energies to philanthropic work on behalf of oppressed Jews, both at home and abroad. His many missions – Montefiore visited Palestine seven times, as well as countries including Russia and Morocco – brought him international respect and fame. A year after Montefiore's hundredth birthday – a cause of widespread celebration – he died at East Cliff Lodge, Ramsgate (demolished), his country estate from the 1830s. The plaque was unveiled by the President of Israel, Chaim Herzog, in 1984, the bicentenary of Montefiore's birth.

At 17 Dunraven (formerly Norfolk) Street, W1, is an English Heritage plaque to the writer **P. G. Wodehouse** (1881–1975) **36** (fig. 406). Interestingly, the suggestion

406   P. G. Wodehouse in his study at 17 Dunraven Street, from a *Strand Magazine* article of 1929. The writer lived at the house between 1927 and 1934.

Wooster and his factotum Jeeves as much-loved fictional characters, Wodehouse became Britain's best-selling author, with an unrivalled reputation as a humorist; the Jeeves and Wooster series finally came to an end with *Aunts Aren't Gentlemen* in 1974. Wodehouse and his wife Ethel, née Newton (1885–1984) lived in what was then Norfolk Street – in a Neo-Georgian house built in 1897–98 to the designs of Sidney R. J. Smith – for rather sporadic phases between early 1927 and summer 1934, the period of his greatest success. Of his typical daily routine, his stepdaughter Leonora wrote, 'He writes in the afternoon, when he must on no account be disturbed. It is understood that he is thinking deep thoughts and planning great novels, but when all the smoke has cleared away it really means that he is either asleep or eating an apple and reading Edgar Wallace'.[24] During his time at number 17, Wodehouse wrote ten books, usually in his bedroom, which he found 'really jolly'; these included *Summer Lightning* (1929), *Very Good, Jeeves* (1930) and *Right Ho, Jeeves* (1934).[25] The house, looked after by a retinue of servants, was described by Wodehouse's nephew Patrick as 'homely and warm, with a dotty Edwardian flavour just like the books Uncle Plum spent all his time writing'.[26] After 1940 Wodehouse's life and standing were to change. While living in France, he was captured by the Germans, and in Berlin naively made a series of broadcasts to an American audience. These led to Wodehouse being denounced as a traitor and Nazi propagandist – accusations now known to have been completely without basis – and he was permanently exiled from Britain. Wodehouse spent the rest of his life in America. A knighthood in 1975 was the first major symbol of forgiveness. The unveiling of Wodehouse's plaque in 1988 by Queen Elizabeth, The Queen Mother, could perhaps be seen as another.

for a plaque had been given Wodehouse's blessing the year before his death: he told the proposer that he liked 'the idea very much'.[23] Born in Guildford, Pelham Grenville ('Plum') Wodehouse initially embarked on a career in banking, before turning to writing full-time at the age of twenty. His early successes included *Mike* (1909) – featuring Psmith (the 'P' being silent) – and *Something Fresh* (1915), the first of the Blandings Castle series. In the 1920s, with the establishment of Bertie

Number 46 Green Street, W1 – another substantial Neo-Georgian property, built in 1913–15 to designs by Wimperis, Simpson and Guthrie – bears a plaque unveiled in 1998 to the aviator and aircraft manufacturer **Sir Thomas Sopwith** (1888–1989) **37** . Born at 92 Cromwell Road, Kensington, SW7, Sopwith was interested in flying and mechanics from an early age, and went on to stand at the forefront of military aircraft development for over fifty years. His name has been immortalised by the aircraft produced by the firm he headed after 1912: the Sopwith Aviation Company Ltd.

During the First World War, over 18,000 Sopwith aircraft entered service with the Allied air forces; these included the Tabloid, the Triplane, the Pup and – most famous of all – the Camel. Following the firm's closure in 1920, Sopwith founded the H. G. Hawker Engineering Company Ltd (later known as Hawker Aircraft Ltd); in 1934 this became part of the Hawker Siddeley Group Ltd, which – by the time of Sopwith's retirement as Chairman in 1963 – also included firms such as A. V. Roe & Co. and the De Havilland Aircraft Company. During this period, Sopwith's flair for producing high-performance machines for the RAF continued unabated. Under the design team headed by Sydney Camm, the Hawker company produced aircraft such as the Hart, the Hurricane – famously used in the Battle of Britain (1940) – the Typhoon, the Tempest and the revolutionary Harrier, capable of vertical take-off and landing. It was during the key period of his career – from 1934 to 1940 – that Sopwith lived in Green Street with his second wife, Phyllis, née Gordon (d. 1978); he had previously lived (in *c.* 1929–31) across the road at 32 Green Street. Sopwith, who was knighted in 1953, died at the age of 101 at his Hampshire home, Compton Manor, King's Somborne, acquired in 1945.

Grosvenor Street, W1, was one of the earliest streets laid out on the Grosvenor estate; in 1734 it was described as 'a spacious well built Street, inhabited chiefly by People of Distinction'.[27] It remained fashionable until the First World War, when commerce began to take over. Today, only about a quarter of the original houses survive. Number 60 (originally 59) Grosvenor Street was the home from 1725 until her death five years later of the actress **Ann Oldfield** (1683–1730) **38** . One of the leading figures on the London stage in the early eighteenth century, Oldfield was – as the plaque records – the first occupant of this house, which was built in 1723 and damaged by fire in 1897; a shop front was inserted at ground-floor level in the twentieth century. Oldfield's time in Mayfair marked the culmination of her career, and reflected her status as the respectable mistress of General Charles Churchill (*c.* 1678–1745), nephew of the 1st Duke of Marlborough; Churchill is thought to have stayed here with Oldfield much of the time, though he maintained a separate residence. Having first joined the Drury Lane company on the recommendation of John Vanbrugh in 1699, when she

was barely sixteen, Oldfield went on to appear in over a hundred roles, embracing both tragedy and comedy; these included Lady Betty Modish in *The Careless Husband* (1704), a part written for her by Colley Cibber. A legendary beauty, she made her last stage appearance on 28 April 1730 in Vanbrugh's *The Provok'd Wife* and died at number 60 six months later; Oldfield was buried in Westminster Abbey, the only actress to receive such an honour. The house was left to her second son, Charles Churchill, who died here in 1812. The plaque was erected on the façade – all that survives of the original house – in 1992.

Almost directly opposite, at 21/22 Grosvenor Street – originally built in 1898–99 to the designs of Balfour and Turner – is an English Heritage plaque marking the workplace of another figure associated with the performing arts: the film producer **Sir Alexanda Korda** (1893–1956) **39** . Born Sándor Lázló Kellner in Hungary, of a Jewish family, Korda directed his first film in 1914, and went on to become a major figure in the Hungarian film industry before leaving the country for Vienna in 1919. Having made a series of films in Germany and Hollywood, Korda moved in November 1931 to London, where in February the following year he founded London Film Productions. The company's activities were centred on Denham Studios, Buckinghamshire, built by Korda in 1935–36 and then the most advanced film studios in Europe. Korda had his first major hit with *The Private Life of Henry VIII* (1933), starring CHARLES LAUGHTON and Merle Oberon, whom he was to marry in 1939. This was followed by the films which brought him, and the British film industry, worldwide fame: *The Scarlet Pimpernel* (1934), *The Four Feathers* (1939) – directed by his brother, Zoltán Korda – *The Thief of Baghdad* (1940) and *The Third Man* (1949), directed by Carol Reed. It was both for his contribution to the film industry and for his wartime undercover work for British Intelligence that Korda was knighted in 1942. Initially, it was hoped that a plaque to Korda could be placed on his home of 1954–56, 20B Kensington Palace Gardens, W8. When consent was refused by the building's owners, Korda's Grosvenor Street workplace – the headquarters of London Films from February 1932 until autumn 1936 – was selected instead. Korda's home of 1932–40, 81 Avenue Road, St John's Wood, was demolished in the 1950s.

private and public buildings together with his own designs, and set out the architectural principles that were to be taken up by Lord Burlington and his circle. Sir John Summerson commented that, during this time, Campbell 'set up the models upon which the whole of Palladianism in England was to depend'.[28] From about 1719, the year he was appointed architect to the Prince of Wales, Campbell found favour with a number of aristocratic and wealthy patrons, including SIR ROBERT WALPOLE, for whom he designed Houghton Hall, Norfolk (1722–35). Other country-house commissions included Stourhead, Wiltshire (*c.* 1720–24) and Mereworth Castle, Kent (*c.* 1720–25). Campbell was also active in town, remodelling Burlington House, Piccadilly, in 1717–20 and designing a number of houses in Mayfair, including 76 Brook Street. On its completion in 1726, the architect became the property's first occupant, and died here three years later.

A little further along the street, on the corner of Avery Row, is 39 (formerly 49 and then 50) Brook Street, the home of the architect **Sir Jeffry Wyatville** (1766–1840) ④ (fig. 407). Born in Staffordshire, Jeffry Wyatt changed his surname in 1824 in order to distinguish himself from his illustrious relatives, the Wyatt family of architects and artists. He enjoyed the greatest years of his career during his residence in this house, from 1799 to 1840. During this time, Wyatville's work included alterations of 1820–41 at Chatsworth, Derbyshire, for the 6th Duke of Devonshire, and a spectacular reconstruction of Windsor Castle for King George IV from 1824; the work at Windsor continued until about 1840, and earned him a knighthood. Wyatville is said to have designed or restored at least a hundred other buildings; these were mostly country houses, though he was also active in his local area, altering buildings such as 5 Grosvenor Square (1810; demolished) and Chesterfield House, South Audley Street (1811–13; demolished). The house in Brook Street, the core of which dates from 1720–23, served as Wyatville's home and London office, and remained the residence of his daughter Emma Knapp (1801–1883) until 1876. After the Tyburn brook, which runs beneath Avery Row, caused damage to the property, it was remodelled by Wyatville in 1821–23; work included the creation of the distinctive curved corner and the construction of a new wing to the rear, containing the

407 The plaque to Sir Jeffry Wyatville at 39 Brook Street, in a photograph of 1984. The property, dating from the early eighteenth century, was remodelled by Wyatville in 1821–23; additions included the distinctive curved corner. [© City of London, LMA]

Running parallel to Grosvenor Street is Brook Street, W1, named after the Tyburn brook, which forms the eastern boundary of the Grosvenor estate. At number 76 is a GLC plaque to a figure closely associated with the development of Mayfair, the architect and author of *Vitruvius Britannicus* **Colen Campbell** (1676–1729) ④ . Scottish by birth, Campbell had abandoned a legal career to become an architect by 1712, when he received his first – and perhaps most important – commission, that for Wanstead House, Essex (*c.* 1714–20; demolished 1824). He found fame as the author of *Vitruvius Britannicus* – published in three volumes between 1717 and 1725 – which included engravings of

The House in Lower Brook Street (at present, 1839, numbered 57), in which Handel lived and died;– as it appeared before the front of the Attic Story was raised.

408   Handel's house at 25 Brook Street in a watercolour of 1839 by John Buckler. The ground floor of the building is now a shop, and the attic storey has been raised. [© The Handel House Collections Trust]

own occupation which still survives relatively unaltered'.[29] The case for commemorating Wyatville was first considered in 1972, but was rejected by the GLC's Historic Buildings Board; this decision seems to have been due largely to the views of one of the committee's members – the architectural historian Sir John Summerson – who felt that Wyatville was 'a second-rank architect'.[30] However, the GLC came to a different decision in 1981, and a plaque was duly unveiled three years later by the politician Sir Woodrow Wyatt, a descendant of Sir Jeffry; the reception was hosted by the interior decorating firm Colefax and Fowler, which has been based at number 39 since 1945.

Number 25 (formerly 57) Brook Street – an early eighteenth-century terraced house with a late nineteenth-century attic floor and a shop front added in 1905 – bears a plaque to the composer **George Frideric Handel** (1685–1759) 42 (fig. 408). Born in Halle in what is now Germany, Handel was a talented musician by the age of seven and saw the staging of his earliest opera, *Almira*, at the age of twenty. Five years later he paid his first visit to London, and settled in the capital permanently in 1712, becoming a naturalised British citizen in 1727. Handel moved to 25 Brook Street in July 1723, when the property was newly built, and remained here until his death thirty-six years later. This was the period of Handel's greatest eminence; here, he wrote masterpieces including *Israel in Egypt* (1739), 'Zadok the Priest' (composed for the coronation of King George II, 1727), *Messiah* and *Samson* (both 1741) and 'Music for the Royal Fireworks' (1749). Number 25 was conveniently placed: from here, Handel could walk to the King's Theatre, Haymarket, where many of his operas were performed, and to St James's Palace, where he served as Composer of Music for the Chapel Royal. Unmarried, and a lover of good food and wine, he held frequent dinner parties, but suffered increasingly from poor health in his later years, and died at the age of seventy-four. Number 25 was first commemorated, by the Society of Arts, in 1870. However, by the middle of the twentieth century the plaque – chocolate-brown in colour – had become illegible and so was replaced by the LCC in 1952. In 2001 English Heritage replaced the plaque again, taking the opportunity to correct the anglicisation of Handel's middle name – given as 'Frederick' – and to move the plaque lower down on

architect's drawing office at ground-floor level and a gallery above for the reception of clients. The exterior of the house survives much as Wyatville designed it, with the exception of shop fronts added in 1926–27; a GLC historian wrote that the house 'is one of very few in London designed by a pre-Victorian architect for his

409   Jimi Hendrix and his girlfriend Kathy Etchingham in an undated photograph, taken at their flat at 23 Brook Street. Hendrix lived at the address in 1968–9. [© Eric Harlow / Mirrorpix]

the façade. Later the same year, the Handel House Museum opened in numbers 25 and 23, with rooms restored to their early Georgian appearance.

In 1997 HANDEL's plaque was joined by that to the guitarist and songwriter **Jimi Hendrix** (1942–1970) ④ at 23 Brook Street, creating one of the most famous pairings of blue plaques in London. Born in Seattle, Washington, USA, James Marshall Hendrix spent the most successful years of his working life in London. He first arrived in the capital in September 1966, three months after having been 'discovered' by the British musician Chas Chandler, who had been impressed by Hendrix's innovative guitar style and dynamic stage presence. By October, the Jimi Hendrix Experience had been created – with Noel Redding on bass and Mitch Mitchell on drums; the band's first single, 'Hey Joe', was met with acclaim, while the second, 'Purple Haze', became Jimi's signature tune. In

1968, after an extended tour and the release of the album *Are You Experienced?*, Hendrix joined his girl-friend Kathy Etchingham (b. 1946) at the flat she had taken in June on the top two floors of number 23 (fig. 409). Jimi lived in the flat for some months – assisting in its refitting and redecoration – before leaving to tour the USA in March 1969. The flat now forms part of the Handel House Museum and its 1960s appearance has been partially recreated. Several journalists interviewed Hendrix in Brook Street, and many commented upon the neighbouring plaque to Handel: to one Jimi con-fessed, 'I didn't even know this was Handel's pad. And, to tell you the God's honest truth, I haven't heard much of the fella's stuff'.[31] Hendrix was to return to London for only brief spells in 1970, spending his last night at the Samarkand Hotel, 22 Lansdowne Crescent, Notting Hill, W11, where he died of a drug overdose at the age of just twenty-seven. The unveiling of Hendrix's plaque was one of the most impressive events of its kind: the traffic was stopped while the curtain's cord was pulled by Noel Redding together with Pete Townshend of The Who, in the presence of a huge crowd that included Jimi's father, James Al Hendrix, and the musicians Jimmy Page and Ray Davies.

Running north-west from Brook Street is South Molton Street, W1, now predominantly commercial. At Stratford Mansions, 34 South Molton Street, at the junction with Oxford Street, is an English Heritage plaque to **Ernest Bevin** (1881–1951) ④ , the trade union leader and statesman. Born on the edge of Exmoor, the illegitimate child of a village midwife, Bevin rose to become one of the most powerful trade union leaders of the twentieth century. Originally associated with the Dockers' Union – he was known as the 'Dockers' KC' for the part he played in advocating dockers' rights in a dispute of 1920 – Bevin was General Secretary of the Transport and General Workers' Union in 1922–45. In 1940 he entered national politics, first as wartime Minister of Labour and National Service (1940–45) under WINSTON CHURCH-ILL, and later as Foreign Secretary (1945–51) under CLEMENT ATTLEE. Bevin is of particular note for the part he played in containing Soviet expansion in post-war Europe; the creation of the North Atlantic Treaty Organisation (NATO) in 1950 was partly a result of his efforts. Initially, it was hoped that Bevin's plaque could be erected at Phillimore Court, Kensington High

MAYFAIR

Street, W8, where he lived in 1946. Consent was, however, refused due to a disagreement about the proposed inscription – the flats' management company felt Bevin should be described simply as 'statesman' – and the final choice rested on Stratford Mansions; Bevin lived here in Flat 8 from 1931 to 1939. The plaque was unveiled on Bevin's birthday, 9 March 2001, by the Foreign Secretary, Robin Cook.

On the east side of Bond Street is the earliest of Mayfair's three great piazzas, Hanover Square, W1, laid out from 1713 for the 1st Earl of Scarborough. Like Berkeley Square and Grosvenor Square, it was home to 'Noblemen, and Gentlemen of the first Quality', though only a few of the original houses survive today.[32] Number 21 Hanover Square, formerly known as Downshire House, was the residence of **Prince Talleyrand** (1754–1838) 45 , the French statesman and diplomatist, from 28 October 1830 until 19 August 1834, when he returned to Paris. Charles Maurice de Talleyrand-Périgord was born in Paris and was ordained a priest in 1779; despite his aristocratic heritage, he supported the revolutionary cause, and was instrumental in organising the *coup d'état* by which Napoleon came to power. Talleyrand is perhaps best remembered as Napoleon's Minister for Foreign Affairs (1799–1807), but he later recommended the restoration of the Bourbons, and became a trusted servant of Louis XVIII and Louis-Philippe. He was the chief French representative at the Congress of Vienna (1814–15) and served as his country's Prime Minister in 1815. Talleyrand spent two periods in London: the first was in 1792–94, when he attempted to dissuade the British government from entering war with France, and the other was in 1830–34, when he served as French Ambassador under Louis-Philippe. Talleyrand shared his Hanover Square mansion with his niece, Dorothée, Duchesse de Dino (1793–1862), whose charm and intelligence assisted him 'in conciliating that very exclusive English society'; she was described as Talleyrand's 'confidant, counsellor, and private secretary'.[33] The pair were famed for their sparkling hospitality, and held many sumptuous receptions at 21 Hanover Square, where visitors included the Duke of Wellington; Dorothée told a friend that her dinners 'were making gastronomic history in London'.[34] Number 21, built in *c.*1718, was converted into a bank in 1856–57; its ground floor was re-faced in stone in the late nineteenth century. The plaque, which marks the building's Brook Street elevation, was put up by the GLC in 1978.

NOTES

1 Ian Kelly, *Beau Brummell: The Ultimate Dandy* (London, 2005), p. 158

2 Pamela Bright, *Dr Richard Bright (1789–1858)* (London, Sydney, Toronto, 1983), p. 168

3 Reginald Colby, *Mayfair: A Town within London* (London, 1966), p. 35 (quoting H. B. Wheatley)

4 Alexander Bain, *John Stuart Mill: A Criticism: with Personal Recollections* (London, 1882), p. 94

5 Mrs [Harriet] Grote, *The Personal Life of George Grote* (London, 1873), p. 185

6 Madeleine Bingham, *Sheridan: The Track of a Comet* (London, 1972), p. 365

7 *The Letters of Richard Brinsley Sheridan*, ed. Cecil Price, vol. III (Oxford, 1966), p. 246 (15 May 1816)

8 *Survey of London*, vol. XXXII: *The Parish of St James Westminster: Part Two*, ed. F. H. W. Sheppard (London, 1963), p. 525

9 *The Dispatches and Letters of Vice Admiral Lord Viscount Nelson*, ed. Nicholas Harris Nicolas, vol. II (London, 1845), p. 458 (11 December 1797)

10 Austin Brereton, *The Life of Henry Irving*, vol. I (London, New York, Bombay, Calcutta, 1908), p. 218

11 Elliott O'Donnell, *Ghosts of London* (London, 1932), p. 27 (quoting article in *Mayfair*, 10 May 1879)

12 Robert Rhodes James, *Rosebery: A Biography of Archibald Philip, Fifth Earl of Rosebery* (London, 1963), p. 123

13 *Diary and Letters of Madame D'Arblay (1778–1840)*, ed. Charlotte Barrett, vol. VI (London, 1905), p. 377

14 It is now accepted that Burgoyne was born in 1723, rather than in 1722, as is stated on the plaque.

15 W. Fraser Rae, *Sheridan: A Biography*, vol. II (London, 1896), p. 23

16 LCC, *Indication of Houses of Historical Interest in London*, vol. II (London, 1909), p. 64

17 Robert Blake, *Disraeli* (London, 1966), p. 746

18 Ibid

19 Cecil Woodham-Smith, *Florence Nightingale 1820–1910* (London, 1950), p. 575

20 Ibid

21 Report of 19 January 1983 on blue plaque file.

22 John G. Winant, *A Letter from Grosvenor Square: An Account of a Stewardship* (London, 1947), p. 2

23 Letter of 3 September 1974 on blue plaque file.

24 Leonora Wodehouse, 'P. G. Wodehouse At Home', *Strand Magazine*, vol. LXXVII (January 1929), p. 20

25 *The Letters of P. G. Wodehouse*, ed. Frances Donaldson (London, Sydney, Auckland, Johannesburg, 1990), p. 114 (17 May 1927)

26 *Daily Mail*, 4 June 1988

27 Robert Seymour, *A Survey of the Cities of London and Westminster*, vol. II (London, 1734), p. 667

28 John Summerson, *Architecture in Britain: 1530 to 1830* (Harmondsworth, 1983 edn, 1986 repr.), p. 333

29 Report of 10 September 1981 on blue plaque file.

30 Note of 18 April 1972 on blue plaque file.

31 *Evening Standard*, 13 March 1995

32 Seymour, *A Survey of the Cities of London and Westminster*, vol. II, p. 666

33 *Memoirs of the Prince de Talleyrand*, ed. Duc de Broglie, vol. III (London and Sydney, 1891), p. 233; J. F. Bernard, *Talleyrand: A Biography* (London, 1973), p. 536

34 Jean Orieux, *Talleyrand: The Art of Survival* (London, 1974), p. 587

410 Chester House, Clarendon Place, designed for his own use by Sir Giles Gilbert Scott and completed in 1926. The architect lived here for the rest of his life. [© English Heritage. Photograph by Derek Kendall]

PADDINGTON AND BAYSWATER

As recently as 1800, the Paddington and Bayswater districts contained few houses outside the three ancient villages of Paddington Green, Westbourne Green and Bayswatering, the last situated where the Westbourne stream crosses the Bayswater Road. Seven years later, development started close to what is now Marble Arch, the former public execution site of Tyburn, next to the Tyburn brook. It was dubbed Tyburnia as a result, but is now usually referred to more demurely as the Hyde Park estate. Originally laid out by Samuel Pepys Cockerell, the father of the architect C. R. Cockerell, the area developed most rapidly in the twenty years from 1835, with the opening of the Great Western terminus

at Paddington in 1854 acting as a spur. Further west, the building of houses in Bayswater followed on apace, as it did in the slightly less salubrious Westbournia, to the north. The area south of the railway was entirely urbanised by 1870 and was popular, even if Tyburnia never quite matched Belgravia as a fashionable address. The contemporary journalist George Augustus Sala characterised the inhabitants as 'mushroom aristocrats, millionaires . . . people of that sort', an observation that resonates with some – but not all – of the figures commemorated in Paddington and Bayswater as a whole.[1]

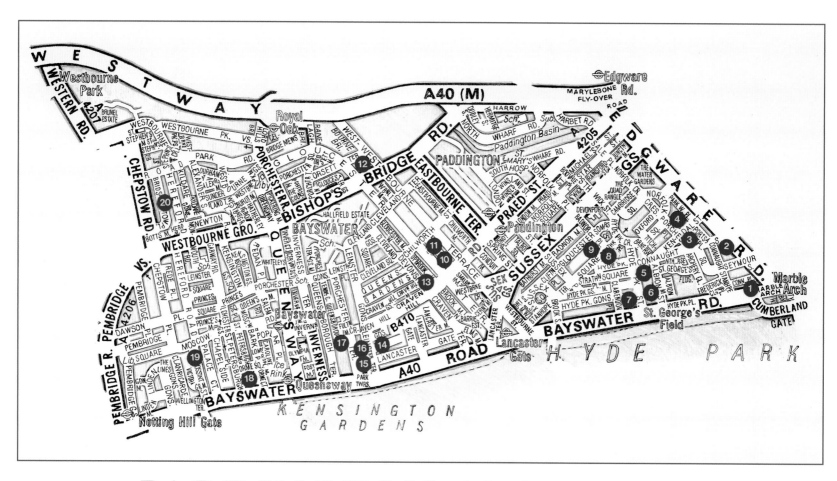

PADDINGTON AND BAYSWATER

411 The plaque to Lord
Randolph Churchill being unveiled
by his grandson and namesake at
2 Connaught Place in 1962. It was
re-sited by the GLC in 1985 after
the building had been altered.
[© PA Photos]

Far right 412 Marie Taglioni in *La
Sylphide*, the ballet for which she
was best known. [© ArenaPAL /
Topfoto]

PADDINGTON AND BAYSWATER

Described as a statesman on his plaque at 2 Connaught Place, W2, **Lord Randolph Churchill** (1849–1895) ❶ was one of the most flamboyant public figures of his era – and not an invariably statesmanlike one. The father of Britain's Second World War Prime Minister Winston Churchill – who lived at number 2 when he was young – Randolph Churchill entered the House of Commons in 1874. He took much credit for reviving the moribund Conservatives with his oratory, and was made Secretary of State for India after the party came to power in 1885. In this capacity Churchill was largely responsible for the annexation of Upper Burma – the final addition to British India. A strong supporter of the union between Great Britain and Ireland, it was Churchill who coined the phrase, apropos the unionists in the north of Ireland, 'Ulster will fight, Ulster will be right'. However, he lasted only months as Chancellor of the Exchequer in 1886 before resigning over defence expenditure. Churchill moved to Connaught Place, which is part of the early nineteenth-century Tyburnia development, early in 1883. His American wife Jennie, née Jerome (1854–1921), who keenly set about a refurbishment, asserted that it was 'the first private house in London to have electric lights'; power was generated by a dynamo in the cellar, the noise of which 'greatly excited all the horses as they approached our door'.[2] The proximity to the gallows at Tyburn led her to wonder 'if the house would be full of wailing ghosts; but frankly I never saw or heard one'.[3] By early 1893 the Churchills had moved to Grosvenor Square, Mayfair, where Randolph died (probably of syphilis) two years later. The plaque was unveiled in 1962 by his grandson and namesake (fig. 411), by which time number 2 had been conjoined with number 1. The plaque was re-sited by the GLC in 1985 after the building was altered. Misleadingly, the position chosen is part of the former number 1; the house where Randolph Churchill lived comprises the two westernmost bays of the present building and the entrance porch, on which the plaque was originally sited.

The ballet dancer **Marie Taglioni** (1804–1884) ❷ (fig. 412) is commemorated at 14 Connaught Square, W2, a house built in 1821–30.[4] Born in Stockholm into a family of choreographers and dancers, Marie made her debut in 1822 in *La Réception d'une jeune nymphe à la* *cour de Terpsichore*, a ballet choreographed by Taglioni's Italian father to music by Rossini. A pioneer of dancing *sur les pointes*, she was widely admired for the grace and lightness of her technique; among those who lionised her were Victor Hugo and WILLIAM MAKEPEACE THACKERAY. Taglioni was widely renowned by the time of her first performance in London in 1829; three years later, she appeared at Covent Garden in the ballet for which she became best known, *La Sylphide*. She retired in 1847, and spent time in Italy before returning to London, where she worked as a teacher of deportment, her fortune having been dissipated through bad investment and the economic impact of the Franco-Prussian War. Taglioni lived at two addresses on the eastern side of Connaught Square – at number 14 from about 1875 to 1876, and at number 6 from about 1877 to 1880. On account of the reluctance of the owner of number 6 to allow the installation of a plaque, the final choice rested on number 14, commemorated by the LCC in 1960.

The author **Olive Schreiner** (1855–1920) ❸ is commemorated at 16 Portsea Place, W2. Born in South Africa, Schreiner was the daughter of a German-born missionary and his English wife, and endured a tough upbringing. She drew on this for her most famous work, *The Story of an African Farm* (1883), a novel originally published under the pseudonym of Ralph Iron. Among Schreiner's works of non-fiction were a collection of feminist and socialist allegories entitled *Dreams* (1890) and the treatise *Woman and Labour* (1911). Her freethinking and anti-imperialist beliefs led to a breach with most of her family and friends in South Africa and she spent two long spells in England, in 1881–89 and 1913–20, staying at numerous London lodgings. The selection of an address at which to commemorate Schreiner was fraught: the first chosen – 9 Porchester Place, Edgware Road, W2, her home between 1918 and 1920 – was then earmarked for demolition, and owner consent was not forthcoming for the second – 19 Russell Road, Kensington, W14 – where she lived for a time in 1897. So it was that in 1959 the plaque was put up at 16 Portsea Place, where Schreiner lodged from August 1885 to January 1886. Shortly after moving in, she told her friend and lover HAVELOCK ELLIS that she was going through 'a very dark and bitter moment of my life', and was thinking fondly of her South African home.[5] Schreiner returned there in 1889, and became increasingly involved in pol-

itics despite her failing health. Works of this period included *Closer Union* (1909), the articles published as *Thoughts on South Africa* (1923) and her last, uncompleted, novel, *From Man to Man* (published in 1926).

On the Kendal Street elevation of Park West, Edgware Road, W2 – a vast complex of flats dating from 1936 – is a plaque to the lyric tenor **Richard Tauber** (1891–1948) ❹ , who lived at Flat 297. Born in Austria, the son of an actor of Jewish ancestry, Tauber made his debut in *The Magic Flute* in 1913, and became famed for his performances in the operettas of Franz Lehár; one such featured Tauber's best-known song, 'You are my Heart's Delight'. From 1922 he worked for the Vienna and Berlin state operas; the rise of the Nazis saw him flee Germany abruptly for his native Austria in 1933. Tauber, a contemporary of JOHN MCCORMACK, first lived in London after his marriage to the English actress Diana Napier in 1936. He raised spirits during the Second World War with radio broadcasts of such tunes as 'We'll Gather Lilacs' by IVOR NOVELLO, and also composed several works, including the operetta *Old Chelsea* (1943). Tauber became a naturalised British citizen in 1940, and moved in the summer of 1947 to 297 Park West – on the ninth floor – telling his partly estranged wife Diana that, 'My new flat is very sweet and cosy, very quiet and away from the noise'.[6] Conveniently, it was also directly above the abode of his mistress, Esther Moncrieff. As well as having a complicated personal life, Tauber was beset by financial and health worries. His performance in *Don Giovanni* at Covent Garden in September 1947 turned out to be his last, as he died at a Marylebone clinic the following January. The proposal to commemorate Tauber came from the Richard Tauber Opera Society, and the English Heritage plaque was erected in 1998.

An imperial phenomenon, the last Rajah of Sarawak **Sir Charles Vyner Brooke** (1874–1963) ❺ is commemorated with a GLC plaque at 13 Albion Street, W2. The Brooke dynasty of white rajahs was founded by James Brooke, who was granted the title in 1841 by Rajah Muda Hassim, uncle of the Sultan of Brunei, in acknowledgement of his assistance in quelling a rebellion in Sarawak, on the island of Borneo. Charles Vyner Brooke, his great-nephew, succeeded as the third Rajah on the death of his father in 1917, though his appetite for the business of government was slender. He shared

413 The W. H. Smith bookstall at King's Cross Station in 1910. [Courtesy of the W. H. Smith Archive]

highly profitable station bookstalls – initially to be found on the route of the London and North-Western Railway – were his idea (fig. 413); from his refusal to sell books he regarded as unsuitable, Smith – a devout Christian who had considered entering the Church – became known as the 'North-Western Missionary'. He used his position as a highly successful and much admired businessman to make the transition into politics. Smith was elected Conservative MP for Westminster in 1868, and went on to hold several offices in the Cabinets of DISRAELI and SALISBURY. It was his appointment as First Lord of the Admiralty in 1877 that provoked W. S. GILBERT to write the song 'When I was a lad' in *HMS Pinafore* (1878), with its mocking chorus about the landlubber who becomes 'ruler of the Queen's Navee'. A notable philanthropist, Smith rendered a lasting service to Londoners by securing Victoria Embankment Gardens as a public open space in 1875. His plaque was originally erected in 1961 at 3 Grosvenor Place, Westminster, where he lived for the last nine years of his life, during which time he served as First Lord of the Treasury and leader of the House of Commons (1887–91). In 1964, just three years later, the building was redeveloped, and the tablet was re-erected in 1966 at 12 Hyde Park Street, which is the sole survivor of a terrace built in about 1840. Smith lived here for twenty years following his marriage to the widowed Emily Leach (1828–1913) in 1858.

power with his brother Bertram and later with his nephew Anthony, and devolved many functions to his adviser, Gerard MacBryan, and a committee of administration. Brooke's major achievement was the establishment of Sarawak's first constitutional government in September 1941, the centenary of his family's rule. This was ended by the Japanese invasion three months later, upon which Brooke took refuge in Australia before coming to London in 1943. Apart from a brief trip back to Sarawak in 1946, he remained in the capital for the rest of his life. After the war, Brooke controversially ceded power to the British Crown, and lived after 1949 in the modest brown-brick terraced house in Albion Street, which dates from the 1830s. Stories of a handsome pay-off from the British government were apparently untrue, and he survived on his Sarawak pension. Brooke died in Albion Street just a few months before Sarawak became part of the Federation of Malaysia.

The London-born bookseller and statesman **W. H. Smith** (1825–1891) ❻ , whose most conspicuous memorial is a nationwide chain of stores, has a plaque at 12 (formerly 1) Hyde Park Street, W2. The 'Son' of W. H. Smith & Son, William Henry Smith became a partner in his father's business in 1846. The firm's

The architect **Sir Giles Gilbert Scott** (1880–1960) ❼ has an English Heritage plaque at Chester House, on the east side of Clarendon Place, W2, a 'restrained villa' designed by Scott himself in 1925–26 (fig. 410).[7] It was here that he lived – along with his wife Louise, née Hughes (1888–1949) and their two sons – for the rest of his life, remaining active as an architect until the end. Born in Hampstead into a family of architects – his grandfather was SIR GEORGE GILBERT SCOTT – Giles won the competition to design a new Anglican cathedral in Liverpool, despite being aged just twenty-two – and a Roman Catholic. Consecrated in 1924, it was finally completed eighteen years after his death, the refinement of the design having been a constant in Scott's career. Knighted in 1924, he was also responsible for designing numerous churches, including the Roman Catholic church at Sheringham, Norfolk (1909–14) and St Andrew's, Luton, Bedfordshire (1931–32). From his offices in Gray's Inn, Scott acted as con-

PADDINGTON AND BAYSWATER

sultant architect for the university libraries at Cambridge (1930–34) and Oxford (1935–46), and for the power stations at Battersea (1930–33) and Bankside (1947–63); the latter, having closed in 1982, opened as Tate Modern in 2000. He took charge of the rebuilding of the House of Commons after it was damaged in the Second World War, and was also responsible for the two most famous models of the red British telephone box – the dome-topped Kiosk 2 design of 1926 and the squarer Kiosk 6 or Jubilee design of 1935. Scott, who served as President of the Royal Institute of British Architects from 1933, steered a middle course between modernism and traditionalism, and his approach both to design and the use of materials was pragmatic. Of his brick-built Neo-Georgian home, Chester House, one critic commented that its restrained design recalled Scott's exhortation 'to do all things in measure, even if in these commonplace times there is more money in being surprising'.[8]

At 43 (formerly 40) Gloucester Square, W2, a house on the corner with Hyde Park Square, there is a plaque to **Lady Violet Bonham Carter**, **Baroness Asquith of Yarnbury** (1887–1969) **8** , the politician and writer. The daughter of one Liberal leader, HERBERT HENRY ASQUITH, she was the mother-in-law of another, Jo Grimond, and was herself the first female President of the Liberals (1945–47); she had earlier served as President of the Women's Liberal Federation (1923–25 and 1939–45). Violet's talent as a public speaker brought her to prominence in her father's bid to revive his political career in the early 1920s, and she became a notable voice against the appeasement of Hitler in the following decade. CHURCHILL, a friend, made her a governor of the BBC, and she later wrote a biography of him, *Winston Churchill as I Knew Him* (1965). Given a life peerage in 1964, Lady Bonham Carter campaigned for, among other causes, family allowances and an end to arms sales to Nigeria in the wake of the Biafran crisis. Tony Benn wrote approvingly in his diary that she belonged 'to the "couldn't care more" brigade'.[9] She was twice defeated in pursuit of a Commons seat, but – in an early harbinger of a Liberal revival – saw her son Mark (1922–1994) elected at a by-election in 1958; it was he who later proposed her for a plaque. Violet's husband was Sir Maurice Bonham Carter (1880–1960), known as 'Bongie', who was principal private secretary to her father. Together with

their children, they occupied the entirety of this substantial house – then numbered 40 Gloucester Square – from 1935 until 1952; the building dates from 1844, and is externally little altered. From January 1953, after it was converted into apartments, the Bonham Carters lived on the first floor. 'The flat is spacious & will be delightful when we get it straight. But oh for Cupboards!', sighed Violet.[10] She remained at the flat – which was informally known as 21 Hyde Park Square – for the rest of her life, and it was here that she died. The blue plaque was unveiled by the Liberal Democrat peer Baroness Seear of Paddington in 1994, in the presence of members of the Bonham Carter family – including Helena, the actress, who is Violet Bonham Carter's granddaughter.

At what is now 35 Gloucester Square, a brown wreathed plaque records that the engineer **Robert Stephenson** (1803–1859) **9** 'died here'. The building that it presently adorns actually dates from the interwar years; a supplementary plaque records that the tablet was re-fixed in 1937, Stephenson's house – which was numbered 34 – having been demolished. The son of the railway pioneer George Stephenson, Robert was only nineteen when he set up in business with his father and others. The firm, Robert Stephenson & Co., had its works in Newcastle – the first locomotive works in the world – and became known for its exceptionally high-quality engines, including *Locomotion* (1825), *Rocket* (1829) and *Planet* (1830) (fig. 414). In 1833 Stephenson was appointed Chief Engineer of the London to Birmingham Railway (opened 1838), and moved to London. He was especially celebrated for his railway bridges, notably the high-level crossing of the Tyne at Newcastle (completed 1849), the Britannia Bridge over the Menai Strait (1850) and, further afield, the Victoria Bridge over the St Lawrence River in Montreal, Canada (1859). Stephenson moved to Gloucester Square in 1847, the year of his election to Parliament for Whitby, in his native north-east. Surprisingly for a man so identified with the Industrial Revolution, Stephenson was a protectionist Tory. His drawing room conformed more to type, with shelves 'so liberally stocked with works of curious contrivance, and philosophical toys, that they had almost the appearance of a museum. Singularly constructed clocks, electric instruments, and improved microscopes . . . were arranged on all sides'.[11] The

414 A nineteenth-century trade card for Robert Stephenson & Co., which was based in Newcastle. Stephenson himself lived at 34 Gloucester Square for the last two years of his life. [© National Railway Museum / Science & Society Picture Library]

widowed Stephenson was a convivial host of Sunday lunches 'at which many chiefs of literature and science were in the habit of meeting', but he became prone to depression after the death of his brother-in-law and close friend John Sanderson in 1853.[12] He died in Gloucester Square at the age of fifty-five, a month after the death of his friend and fellow engineer, ISAMBARD KINGDOM BRUNEL. The plaque originated with a suggestion passed on by the Society of Arts to the LCC, and was first erected in 1905.

At 44 Westbourne Terrace, W2, a plaque of 1987 marks the family home of **Susan Lawrence** (1871–1947) ⑩ , the social reformer, who was born at the house and lived here until 1917, when – following the death of her mother – she moved to the East End. The property forms part of an impressive terrace of stuccoed houses dating from the 1840s, and reflects Susan Lawrence's comfortable background: her father, Nathaniel Tertius Lawrence (1823/4–1898), was a successful solicitor, while her mother Laura, née Bacon (1833/4–1917) was the daughter of a judge. Having studied mathematics at University College London and at Cambridge, Susan Lawrence was elected to the LCC in 1910. Two years later she abandoned her Conservative allegiance for Labour, and returned to the council under her new colours for Poplar. In 1921 Lawrence was one of the Poplar councillors imprisoned for their refusal to pay what they regarded as unfairly weighted dues to the

LCC. Her main grouse about incarceration in Holloway Prison was that she was forbidden to smoke. Lawrence, a member of the executive of the FABIAN SOCIETY between 1913 and 1945, became one of the first three women Labour MPs when she was elected for East Ham North in 1923. She held junior office in the first two Labour governments, and was the first woman to chair the party conference in 1930. With her upper-class accent, monocle and legendary indifference to matters sartorial, 'our Susan', as she was known, cut an unmistakable figure: Beatrice Webb, a critical admirer of Lawrence, wrote that she belonged 'to the old order of irreproachable female celibates'.[13] Latterly, frustrated in attempts to return to Parliament after her defeat in 1931, she became a champion of the early kibbutzniks in Palestine. For many years, Lawrence lived in a flat at 41 Grosvenor Road, Pimlico (demolished), the former home of SIDNEY and BEATRICE WEBB. Bombed out during the Blitz, she moved to Berkshire, before returning to London after the war; her final address was 28 Bramham Gardens, South Kensington, SW5.

Number 60 Westbourne Terrace, part of the same 1840s block as number 44, was the home of the civil engineer **Charles Manby** (1804–1884) ⑪ . Manby's father Aaron owned the Horseley ironworks in Staffordshire, and the young Charles assisted his father in building what is said to have been the world's first iron steamboat, the modestly christened *Aaron Manby*. This vessel sailed for France in 1822, with Charles Manby on board as chief engineer. The following year, Manby was given charge of the gas supply company established in Paris by his father, and he went on to manage an ironworks in South Wales before establishing himself in London in 1835 as a specialist in heating and ventilation systems. As the first permanent Secretary of the Institute of Civil Engineers from 1839 to 1856, Manby was given much credit for raising the status of his profession. In 1856 he became the London representative for Robert Stephenson & Co., and was a member of the international commission on the feasibility of constructing the Suez Canal. Manby lived in Westbourne Terrace from about 1870 to 1876 with his second wife Harriet, née Willard (b. 1817/8) and his stepson, Arthur Robert Hood (b. 1851). The address was chosen for commemoration as it had been so little altered, and the plaque was installed in 1961. The costs

415   The GLC plaque to Alexander Herzen at 1 Orsett Terrace, an Italianate villa built in 1843–48. [© English Heritage. Photograph by Derek Kendall]

1843–48. A comparatively low, two-storey profile was adopted for the building so that it did not dwarf Holy Trinity Church, which formerly lay behind, on Bishop's Bridge Road. As a plaque placed in a blind window records, the house was the residence of the Russian political thinker **Alexander Herzen** (1812–1870) **12** (fig. 415). Known as the 'father of Russian socialism', Herzen was first exiled to London in 1852, in the wake of the revolutions of 1848. He originally intended to stay no more than a month, and told a friend in 1855 that life in the capital was 'about as boring as that of worms in a cheese'.[14] The indefatigability of Polish exiles shook Herzen out of his torpor, however, and – using the Russian Free Press that he had set up in 1853 – he produced underground publications for circulation in his homeland, the most influential of which was the journal *Kolokol* (The Bell), published between 1857 and 1867. This attacked the autocratic tsarist regime, and advocated the abolition of serfdom and censorship. As the son of a nobleman, Herzen was wealthier than most refugees, and he extended traditional Russian hospitality to visitors, many of whom were fellow exiles. He lived at Orsett Terrace from November 1860 until June 1863, making it the longest standing of his many addresses in the London area. It was here that Herzen played host to the writers Tolstoy, Dostoevsky and Turgenev, as well as the anarchist Michael Bakunin. Fellow revolutionary émigrés KOSSUTH and MAZZINI were among his other associates in England. Herzen left the country in 1865 for Switzerland, and died five years later in Paris. The plaque went up in 1970, having been suggested in a leading article in *The Times* eight years earlier.

The radio comedian **Tommy Handley** (1892–1949) **13** has a GLC plaque of 1980 at Amersham House, 34 Craven Road, W2, where he lived in Flat 1 with his wife Rosalind (d. 1958), a singer. Liverpool-born, Thomas Reginald Handley was in the Royal Naval Air Service in the First World War, and joined a concert party while on active duty. Soon he was a regular performer in variety programmes, both on stage and on the fledgling BBC radio, and enjoyed particular success with his sketch *The Disorderly Room*. Handley is widely remembered as the star of *ITMA*, an acronym for 'It's That Man Again' – the 'man' being a veiled reference to Adolf Hitler. The show, scripted by Ted Kavanagh, ran for 310 episodes over the ten years from 1939; much

of its manufacture and fixing were met mostly by the Newcomen Society, dedicated to furthering the study of the history of technology and engineering.

Number 1 Orsett Terrace, W2 – formerly known as Orsett House – is a detached stuccoed Italianate villa, built to the designs of George Ledwell-Taylor in

of its comedy centred on bureaucratic obstructiveness and incompetence, and relied heavily on memorable catchphrases, including Handley's own 'TTFN' ('Ta ta for now'). A large part of the show was in the tradition of innuendo-laden British humour, as in the phrase 'Can I do you now, sir?', uttered by the charlady character of Mrs Mopp. The fun was cut short by Handley's untimely death, which was the occasion for much public grief: thousands turned out to pay their respects. Handley was living at 34 Craven Road by autumn 1936 and remained here throughout the war years, displaying, in the words of his biographer, 'the typical tenacity of the north countryman in hanging on to his home'.[15] A bomb blast of 1941 threw him out of bed, after which he is said to have dusted himself down and given an impromptu performance for a resting fire crew. On the whole, however, Handley was a private man; the poet P. J. Kavanagh, son of Tommy's scriptwriter, recalled that 'He was either on-stage in the public eye or invisible, gone'.[16] Handley was still living in Craven Street at the time of his death, which occurred in a private nursing home nearby.

The end house of a grand terrace dating from 1865, 74 Lancaster Gate, W2, was the home of the American writer **Francis Bret Harte** (1836–1902) **14**. The plaque, which is on the Leinster Terrace elevation of the building, was suggested by the United States Embassy, and was put up by the GLC in 1977. Harte was born in Albany, New York State, and moved in 1854 to California, where he turned to writing and journalism. He produced parodies of famous contemporaries such as DICKENS and DISRAELI but is better remembered for his stories of frontier life in the American West, such as 'The Luck of Roaring Camp' (1868) and the ballad 'The Heathen Chinee' (1870) – an anti-racist morality tale – both first published in *Overland Monthly*, of which he was editor. When his home audience tired of the formula, Harte found a new readership in Europe, where he obtained consular appointments in Germany and, from 1880, in Glasgow. Frequent absenteeism in London led to the loss of the latter post, and he settled permanently in the capital in 1885. Harte lodged with a Belgian diplomat, Arthur Van de Velde (d. 1892), and his wife Marguerite (d. 1913), first at 152 Hamilton Terrace (formerly 15 Upper Hamilton Terrace), St John's Wood, NW8, and, from 1893, at 109 Lancaster Gate. Marguerite assisted Harte, both in translating his

works into French and in adapting several for the stage. Late in 1895 he moved alone to 74 Lancaster Gate, where he continued to write plays and articles for the London monthlies. Bret Harte remained here for the rest of his life, though he died not here, as stated on the plaque, but at Marguerite Van de Velde's country home, the Red House, near Camberley, Surrey. He was then impoverished, but *Salomy Jane* (1898), based on one of his earlier stories, was a posthumous West End hit in 1907, and the plotlines and characterisations of his Wild West stories inspired many cowboy films of the silent era.

At 100 Bayswater Road, W2, is the plaque to the novelist and dramatist **Sir James Barrie** (1860–1937) **15** (see also pp. 376–7) (fig. 416). Better known as J. M. Barrie, he worked as a journalist in Nottingham before settling in 1885 in London, where he first made his name with his sketches of life in his native Scot-

416 A photograph by William Nicholson showing J. M. Barrie in the garden of his house at 100 Bayswater Road in October 1904. Barrie's dog Luath was the prototype for Nana in *Peter Pan*. [Courtesy of Great Ormond Street Hospital for Children, London]

land, *Auld Licht Idylls* (1888). In June 1902 he moved with his wife, the actress Mary Ansell (b. 1862), to Leinster Corner, as number 100 was then known – being at the south-west corner of Leinster Terrace. Barrie's play *Quality Street*, the name of which is perpetuated in a chocolate-box selection, was produced at the Vaudeville Theatre that September, and *The Admirable Crichton* premiered in November. It was at number 100, in a study fitted out above a stable-cum-garage building at the bottom of the back garden (now demolished), that Barrie wrote *Peter Pan* (1904) and *Peter Pan in Kensington Gardens* (1906). The gardens, which lie opposite, were a place of inspiration and refuge for him, as was his occasional country retreat, Black Lake Cottage, near Tilford, Surrey. The models for the Darling family were the children of Arthur and Sylvia Llewellyn Davies, for whom Barrie later acted as guardian; with Sylvia – the sister of GERALD DU MAURIER – Barrie became infatuated. This, and his wife's affair with a young actor, led to the final breakdown of their unsuccessful marriage; sensationally, for the time, they were divorced in October 1909, and Barrie left Bayswater Road for a flat at 3 Adelphi Terrace House, south of the Strand. Created a baronet in 1913 and appointed to the Order of Merit in 1922, Barrie died at Adelphi Terrace House at the age of seventy-seven. Number 100 Bayswater Road is one of a pair of villas dating from 1824; a GLC architect noted in 1970 that the houses were 'virtually the last pre-Metropolitan survival of the former Uxbridge Road'.[17]

They have been threatened with demolition several times; the plaque to Barrie, installed in 1961, was cited in the most recent campaign for their preservation.

Another exceptional building marked with an LCC plaque is 3 Porchester Terrace, W2, the home of the landscape gardeners **John Loudon** (1783–1843) and **Jane Loudon** (1807–1858) **16** (fig. 417). As the plaque – which features a special foliate motif – attests, 'Their horticultural work gave new beauty to London squares'. An advocate of open spaces in the expanding city, John Claudius Loudon was instrumental in having the wall around nearby Hyde Park replaced by a fence, to promote its enjoyment by the public. His 'Hints Respecting the Manner of Laying out the Grounds of the Public Squares in London', published soon after his arrival in the capital in 1803, led to the introduction of the plane, sycamore and almond trees to the city. Numbers 3 and 5 Porchester Terrace were built in 1823–25 to John Loudon's own design at a cost of over £5,000 and feature a prominent conservatory topped with a wrought-iron dome, a form which he recommended. He later described the 'double detached Suburban Villa' design in *The Suburban Gardener and Villa Companion* (1838) as two houses 'which should appear as one, and have some pretensions to architectural design'.[18] At the rear of the house was the office of Loudon's *Gardener's Magazine*, started in 1826; beyond, in a hothouse, pineapples, melons and guavas were cultivated. The garden, 'thickly coated over with the best London stable dung', was planted out with 2,000 different species of plants.[19] Loudon – who was active as a landscape gardener mainly in London and his native Scotland – lived at number 3 (the conjoined number 5 being let) initially with his mother, Agnes (d. 1831), and after 1830 with his young wife Jane, née Webb. She was the author of the early science fiction work *The Mummy! A Tale of the Twenty-Second Century* (1827), a publication which made John Loudon anxious to meet her. Jane went on to act as his amanuensis, and herself wrote popular horticultural books including *Instructions in Gardening for Ladies* (1840). She did so partly from necessity, as the production of her husband's monumental *Arboretum et Fruticetum Britannicum* (1838) – in which he was assisted by JOHN LINDLEY – had saddled them with vast debts. The indefatigable John Loudon, who had conquered laudanum addiction – developed after the

417   John Loudon's perspective view of 3–5 Porchester Terrace and their gardens, as published in *The Suburban Gardener and Villa Companion* (1838). The pair were built in 1823–25; number 3 was marked with a plaque in 1953. [© Royal Horticultural Society, Lindley Library]

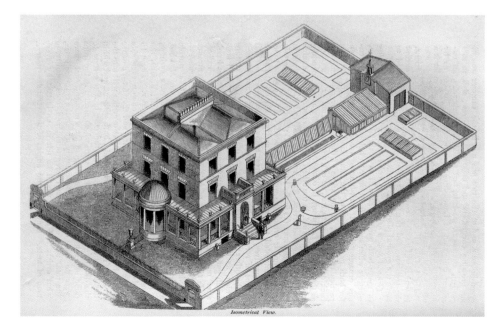

Isometrical View.

amputation of an arm in 1825 – died at Porchester Terrace: he collapsed into his wife's arms shortly after he had finished dictating *Self-Instruction for Young Gardeners* (1845). Jane was granted a civil-list pension, and died here fifteen years later.

Sir William Sterndale Bennett (1816–1875) **17** , one of the most important composers of the nineteenth century, is commemorated at 38 Queensborough Terrace, W2. Bennett's father was the organist of Sheffield parish church, and he himself was a musical prodigy who was early championed by Mendelssohn, whom he visited in Germany. Bennett was settled in London from 1837, initially in Fitzrovia; among his early successes was *The Naiades* (1836), a popular orchestral work, and *Suite de Pièces* (1841), for piano. He was an excellent pianist too, and many of his best compositions were written for the instrument. Teaching took up much of Bennett's time after his marriage in 1844 to Mary Anne Wood: in 1856 he was elected Professor of Music at Cambridge and from 1866 he was Principal of the Royal Academy of Music, where his pupils included Arthur Sullivan. It was in autumn 1865 that the widowed Bennett moved to 38 Queensborough Terrace, a mid-Victorian house. He lived here

until 1870, when he let the property for two years and moved to 18 Porchester Terrace, immediately to the rear, which he had acquired in 1866. Knighted in 1871, Bennett returned briefly to number 38 in 1872 before moving to St John's Wood in September 1873. During his time in Queensborough Terrace, Bennett enjoyed a creative renaissance, with such well-received works as the sacred cantata *The Woman of Samaria* (1867) and the piano sonata *The Maid of Orleans* (1873). The plaque went up at the house, which is now part of a hotel, in 1996, having been proposed by one of his descendants. It is sited somewhat misleadingly, the original façade of Bennett's house being represented by the two bays immediately to the right of the plaque.

The chocolate-brown wreathed LCC plaque at 1 Orme Square, W2, marks the former home of the postal reformer **Sir Rowland Hill** (1795–1879) **18** (see also p. 97) (fig. 418); the plaque was erected in 1907 at the suggestion of his daughter – and biographer – Eleanor Smyth. Born in Worcestershire, Hill was in his forties when he became interested in postal reform; at that time, England's postal system was cumbersome and expensive, with postage costs being charged to the recipient. He wrote his influential work *Post Office Reform: Its Importance and Practicability* in 1837, while living at 2 Burton Crescent (now Cartwright Gardens), Bloomsbury; the owner of this property refused a plaque and the building was later demolished, its site now being occupied by the University of London's Commonwealth Hall. Hill was living at Orme Square when the Penny Postage Act passed into law, having moved here with his wife Caroline, née Pearson (d. 1881) in the summer of 1839; one of a pair of stucco-fronted houses, it had been built not long before. In 1840, as a result of Hill's work, the world's first official postage stamps were issued: the penny black and the twopenny blue. When the in-coming government of Sir Robert Peel dispensed with his services in 1842, Hill countered the loss in income by 'vigorous retrenchment', recording that with the 'zealous and most efficient co-operation of my dear wife, our expenditure was soon brought within very narrow limits'; this was achieved without 'any change of house or diminution in number of servants'.[20] Hill did eventually relocate – to Brighton – after being taken on by the London and Brighton Railway in 1843. Three years later he was able to resume his great cause of Post

418 Number 1 Orme Square, the former home of Sir Rowland Hill, in a photograph of c. 1906. The building was commemorated with an LCC plaque in 1907. [© City of London, LMA]

Office reform, after another change of government saw him appointed Secretary to the Postmaster-General. Between 1854 and his retirement ten years later, Hill served as Secretary to the Post Office, and in 1860 was knighted for his contribution to postal reform.

The poet and essayist **Alice Meynell** (1847–1922) ⑲ is commemorated at 47 Palace Court, W2. Alice Thompson, as she was before her marriage in 1877, spent much of her early life in Italy. She was a Catholic convert, and religious themes imbue her poetry, the first volume of which – *Preludes* – was published in 1875, with illustrations by her sister Elizabeth, soon to become Lady Butler. Among the admirers of her verse were COVENTRY PATMORE and GEORGE MEREDITH but, although there was even a suggestion that she might succeed TENNYSON as Poet Laureate, Alice herself believed that her best work was in prose. She wrote for numerous periodicals, including a regular column for the *Pall Mall Gazette* from 1893, and – together with her husband, the journalist Wilfrid Meynell (1852–1948) – edited the *Weekly Register* and a monthly, *Merry England*. Seven of their children survived infancy; one, the typographer Sir Francis Meynell (1891–1975), was helpful in providing information relating to the LCC plaque. The five-storey house in Palace Court dates from 1890, and was designed for the Meynells by Leonard Stokes, who is better known for his churches.

Their daughter Viola (1885–1956), a successful writer, recalled that 'Its red brick, its tall gable, its small paned windows made a surprising contrast with the prevalent greyness and squareness'; most of the Meynells' work was carried out at their dining-room table.[21] The couple's Sunday 'at homes' attracted figures such as OSCAR WILDE, AUBREY BEARDSLEY and W. B. YEATS; a regular visitor, the writer Charles Lewis Hind, recalled 'arriving at about half-past three, staying till midnight, and meeting in the course of the year most of the literary folk worth knowing'.[22] Alice lived here from 1890 until 1905, when the house was let; Wilfrid later returned, and was still living here in 1947, when the LCC granted permission for a temporary plaque to be unveiled on the centenary of Alice's birth. A permanent tablet went up the following year.

At 71 Hereford Road, W2, an LCC plaque honours **Guglielmo Marconi** (1874–1937) ⑳ , the pioneer of wireless communication (fig. 419). Marconi was born in Bologna to an Italian father and an Irish mother, and it was in his home country that he carried out his first experiments in wireless transmission. He came to London in February 1896, at the age of twenty-one, and lived at the commemorated address for some eighteen months in 1896–97; it was from here that, on 2 June 1896, he filed his famous patent for 'Improvements in Transmitting Electrical Impulses and Signals and in Apparatus therefor', which was accepted in July of the following year. Part of a terrace dating from the 1850s, number 71 was then a guest-house run by a Mrs Sophia Gerstner; another occupant recalled being shown Marconi's 'large room at the top of the house facing the road', which apparently had 'wires all round it'.[23] This suggests that Marconi conducted experiments here; he certainly brought from Italy his apparatus, which was damaged by the rough hands of HM Customs, and during his stay in England made a series of demonstrations, including the transmission of signals across the Bristol Channel. In July 1897, while still in London, he founded the firm that became Marconi's Wireless Telegraph Company (now Marconi). Four years later he made the first transatlantic wireless transmission, confounding those experts who insisted that electromagnetic waves travelled only in straight lines. Marconi, co-recipient of the Nobel Prize for Physics in 1909, settled permanently in Italy in 1914, following the outbreak of the First World War. One blot on his career

419 Guglielmo Marconi with his radio transmitter in a portrait of c.1896, taken around the time of his residence at 71 Hereford Road. [© Getty Images]

was his subsequent support for Mussolini and defence of the Italian invasion of Abyssinia; a 1935 visit to London saw Marconi denied airtime to propound the latter case by Sir John Reith (later LORD REITH). However, when he died in Rome in July 1937 all radio transmitters in the world were silent for two minutes as a mark of respect. The blue plaque was set up in 1952 on Marconi's birthday – 25 April – but turned out to be defective, and was replaced two years later.

NOTES

1. Edward Walford, *Old and New London*, vol. V (London, 1892), p. 202
2. Mrs G. Cornwallis-West (Jenny Churchill), *The Reminiscences of Lady Randolph Churchill* (London, 1908), p. 102
3. Ibid, p. 101
4. It is now accepted that Taglioni was born in 1804, rather than in 1809, as is stated on the plaque.
5. *Olive Schreiner Letters*, volume I: *1871–1899*, ed. Richard Rive (Oxford, 1988), p. 66
6. Charles Castle, *This was Richard Tauber* (London, 1971), p. 188
7. Bridget Cherry and Nikolaus Pevsner, *The Buildings of England, London 3: North West* (London, 1991), p. 688
8. Raymond McGrath, *Twentieth Century Houses* (London, 1934), p. 84
9. Tony Benn, *Years of Hope: Diaries, Letters and Papers, 1940–62* (London, 1994), p. 256
10. Violet Bonham Carter, *Daring to Hope: The Diaries and Letters of Violet Bonham Carter, 1946–1969*, ed. Mark Pottle (London, 2000), p. 399 (12 January 1953)
11. J. C. Jeaffreson, *The Life of Robert Stephenson* (London, 1864), p. 160
12. Ibid, p. 159
13. *Beatrice Webb's Diaries*, ed. M. I. Cole (London, 1952), p. 150
14. E. H. Carr, *The Romantic Exiles: A Nineteenth-Century Portrait Gallery* (London, 1933), p. 134
15. Ted Kavanagh, *Tommy Handley* (London, 1949), p. 242
16. P. J. Kavanagh, *People and Places: A Selection, 1975–1987* (Manchester, 1988), p. 105
17. Report of 24 November 1970 on blue plaque file.
18. J. C. Loudon, *The Suburban Gardener and Villa Companion* (London, 1838), p. 325
19. Ibid, p. 327
20. G. B. Hill, *Life of Sir Rowland Hill* (London, 1980), vol. I, p. 480
21. Viola Meynell, *Alice Meynell* (London, 1929), p. 72
22. Philip Waller, *Writers, Readers, and Reputations: Literary Life in Britain 1870–1918* (Oxford, 2006), p. 556
23. Letter of 17 April 1952 (from Leonora M. S. Churchill) on blue plaque file.

PADDINGTON AND BAYSWATER

420   The wreathed blue plaque to Sir Isaac Newton, marking the site of his former home at 87 Jermyn Street. As is recorded by a supplementary tablet, the plaque was re-erected here in 1915, following demolition of the original building. [© English Heritage. Photograph by Derek Kendall]

ST JAMES'S

It was in the 1660s that Henry Jermyn, 1st Earl of St Albans, created a high-class residential area adjacent to St James's Palace, built by King Henry VIII in about 1531–40. A grand, French-style piazza – St James's Square – was developed for 'Noble men and other Persons of quality'; dominated to the north by SIR CHRISTOPHER WREN's Church of St James Piccadilly (1676–84), the square remains the centrepiece of one of the most fashionable parts of Westminster.[1] St James's has one of the highest concentrations of listed buildings in England, ranging from the grandeur of Carlton House Terrace and the private mansions bordering Green Park to the more modest buildings to the west of Haymarket. Throughout the eighteenth and nineteenth centuries, its proximity to Court and government ensured that St James's was home to many public figures, a fact reflected in the remarkably high number of plaques to politicians. St James's has traditionally been the centre of gentlemen's clubs, from the gambling clubs of the 1700s to dignified institutions such as the Travellers Club and Reform Club in Pall Mall, both outstanding examples of nineteenth-century architecture. In the early 1900s the area's character began to change rapidly, with the advent of offices and residential chambers. It is now perhaps best known as a centre of fine-art galleries and gentlemen's outfitters.

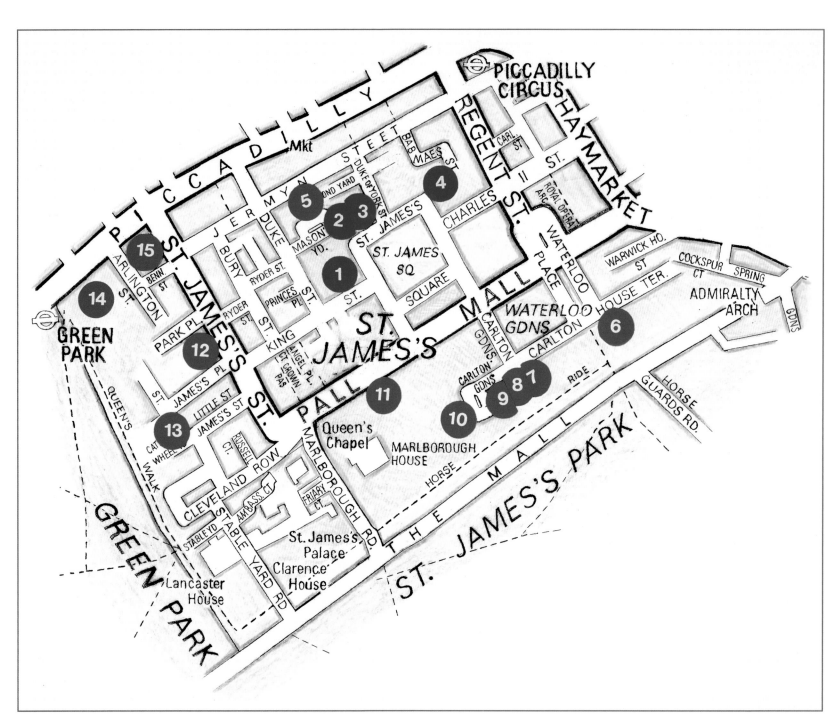

ST JAMES'S

and, like other members of his family, was exiled from France after the Battle of Waterloo (1815); he spent the years that followed in Switzerland, Germany, Italy, America and London, where he resided briefly at 1 Carlton Gardens, SW1. On his return to France in 1840, Louis Napoleon was imprisoned for life, but six years later he managed to escape and fled to England. In February 1847 he took a lease on a newly built house in King Street and transformed its interior into a shrine to the Bonapartes, installing a portrait of Napoleon I by Delaroche, uniforms worn by his uncle and other relics that survived the fall of the dynasty. The Prince became a leading figure in London society: he was given honorary membership of some of the most celebrated clubs in St James's, and enrolled as a special constable during the Chartist riots of 1848. Greater disturbances across the Channel in this year of revolutions led to the overthrow of the French monarchy, and in September 1848 he departed for France. Louis Napoleon seems to have left King Street in some haste: his landlord found 'the Prince's bed unmade and his marble bath still full of water'.[2] Back in Paris, he was elected first President of the Second Republic in December 1848; the Prince remained President until 1852 when, on the restoration of the French Empire, he took his place as Emperor. As Napoleon III, he was noted for his industrial modernisation of France and his rebuilding of Paris – inspired in part by his observations of London – though his foreign policy was less successful: in 1870 he embarked on the Franco-Prussian War, and the following year was captured by the enemy at the Battle of Sedan. Exiled once again to England, Napoleon moved with his wife and son to Camden Place, Chislehurst, Kent, where he died two years later.

421 Number 1C King Street in a photograph of the 1920s. Its blue plaque, commemorating the stay of Napoleon III, was installed in 1867 and is the earliest to survive in London. [© City of London, LMA]

Number 1C (formerly 3A) King Street, SW1, is of interest not only because it was the residence of **Napoleon III** (1808–1873) ❶ , the last Emperor of the French, but also because it bears London's earliest surviving blue plaque (fig. 421 and see fig. 20). Manufactured by Minton Hollins & Co. and put up by the Society of Arts in 1867, it is the only plaque to have been installed during a candidate's lifetime, and is notable in bearing the imperial eagle, used as a symbol of empire by both Napoleon I and his nephew and heir, Napoleon III. Prince Louis Napoleon Bonaparte was born in Paris

Nothing remains of the twenty-two uniform red-brick houses which, when built in the 1660s, made up the first St James's Square, SW1. Nonetheless, a large enough number of the town houses of the nobility survive to preserve the square's domestic scale, and the impact of over-sized development is softened by the garden, enlarged by John Nash in 1817–18 and laid out again in 2000. Number 12 (formerly 10) St James's Square bears an English Heritage plaque to the pioneer of computing, **Ada**, **Countess of Lovelace** (1815–1852) ❷ , who lived here from 1837 until winter 1846. The house, built in 1836 for Ada's husband – William,

mathematics and science. In 1833, probably through the scientific writer Mary Somerville, Ada met Charles Babbage, the inventor of the first general computer, a calculating machine or 'analytical engine'. At once, she began to collaborate with him and mixed in his circle of friends and acquaintances, who included Sir Charles Wheatstone. In 1843, while she was living at number 12, the Countess of Lovelace translated a paper by an Italian, L. F. Menabrea, on Babbage's analytical engine, and added her own extensive notes; 'I do *not* believe', she wrote to Babbage, 'that my father was (or ever could have been) such a *Poet* as I *shall* be an *Analyst*; (& Metaphysician)'.[3] This work, published in September of that year, has led to her being described as one of the world's first computer programmers. Her contribution remains widely acknowledged: in 1979 the United States Department of Defense chose to name its new software Ada in her honour, and a blue plaque was erected in 1992.

Number 10 (formerly 8) St James's Square – known as Chatham House, a name adopted by its occupant, the Royal Institute of International Affairs – is singular in having been the London residence of three Prime Ministers: **William Pitt**, **Earl of Chatham** (1708–1778), **Edward Geoffrey Stanley**, **Earl of Derby** (1799–1869) and **William Ewart Gladstone** (1809–1898) (see also p. 398 and pp. 471–2) ❸ , all of whom are commemorated by an LCC blue plaque, unique in design, which was erected in 1910 (fig. 422). Numbers 9, 10 and 11 St James's Square were built in 1735–36 to the designs of the architect Henry Flitcroft. Originally, the three houses presented a uniform stock-brick façade towards the square. Number 10, owned by the Heathcote family from 1736 until 1890, survives as a good example of a Palladian town house; the principal feature of its interior, and one which would still be recognised by the three Prime Ministers, is the fine full-height staircase. Pitt the Elder – created an earl in 1766 – occupied the house from 1759 until late 1761, when at the apogee of his power and glory, nominally as Secretary of State for the Southern Department but in effect Prime Minister. During this time, Pitt – powerful, highly celebrated and immensely popular – presided over a series of military victories that effectively marked the creation of the British Empire and ensured Britain's success in the Seven Years War (1756–63). He left St James's Square at about the time of his

422   The LCC plaque to three Prime Ministers – Pitt the Elder, the Earl of Derby and W. E. Gladstone – at Chatham House, 10 St James's Square. The plaque, erected in 1910, is of a unique design, its wreathed border being made up of a series of individual Minton tiles. [© English Heritage. Photograph by Derek Kendall]

Baron King (1805–1893), created Earl of Lovelace in 1838 – is an early example of the Italianate style of Thomas Cubitt. Built of brick with stucco decorations, it forms a marked contrast to its more sober neighbours. Born in Piccadilly, Augusta Ada was the only (legitimate) child of the poet, Lord Byron. She was brought up by her mother Annabella, née Milbanke, who supervised her education and encouraged her interest – one rare in a woman of the time – in

423 The upper part of the main staircase at 4 St James's Square, built in 1726–28. It was the London home of the Astors between 1912 and 1946. [© City of London, LMA]

resignation as Secretary of State in October 1761, and went on to serve as premier between 1766 and 1768. Lord Derby, three times Prime Minister (1852, 1858–59 and 1866–68), was in opposition when he took up residence here in late 1837. He began his second stint as Colonial Secretary in 1841, in the administration of Sir Robert Peel, and in 1852 – the year after he succeeded to his father's earldom – he formed, but was unable to maintain, a ministry. Derby left the address in about 1854, moving to 23 (now 33) St James's Square, which was his town house until the time of his death. Gladstone occupied number 10 during the parliamentary session of 1890, towards the end of his political career. During this time, he was leader of the opposition, and was particularly active in promoting the cause of Irish Home Rule; he went on to serve his fourth, and last, term as Prime Minister in 1892–94. In 1909 the LCC proposed erecting a plaque to Pitt and Derby, but at the suggestion of number 10's occupant, Arthur, Lord Kinnaird (1847–1923) – a notable figure in the development of association football – decided also to commemorate Gladstone. Due to the long

inscription, and the difficulty of manufacturing large roundels, the LCC's traditional wreathed border was placed on a series of individual surrounding tiles. After the plaque had been erected, Alma, Lady Kinnaird (d. 1923) remarked upon its 'very ugly bright blue colour, shewing so badly on this old house'.[4] She was assured by the council that it would soon tone down in the atmospheric conditions of London, as indeed it has.

The oldest building to survive in St James's Square is number 4, which bears an English Heritage plaque to **Nancy Astor** (1879–1964) ❹ , the first woman to sit in Parliament (figs 423 and 424; see fig. 3). Built in 1726–28 for the 1st Duke of Kent, and now the Naval and Military Club, this terraced mansion has a Palladian façade of stock brick. Nancy Witcher Langhorne, born in Virginia, USA, came to England in 1904 and two years later married fellow American Waldorf Astor (1879–1952), the wealthy politician and newspaper proprietor. In 1912 the couple acquired this house in St James's Square, the London addition to a portfolio of

4, having been damaged by bombs and requisitioned during the Second World War, was finally sold in 1946, a moment which heralded both the end of Nancy's political career and the tradition of a great London house as a centre of political influence. The plaque was unveiled in 1987 by the then Prime Minister, Margaret Thatcher, who praised Astor's courage – from which she herself had taken heart – for going into 'that totally male-dominated place'.[6]

Sir Isaac Newton (1642–1727) **5** , one of England's greatest natural philosophers, is honoured with a plaque on the site of his former home at 87 Jermyn Street, SW1, a thoroughfare completed in the 1680s and now known for its gentlemen's shops (fig. 425 and see figs 25 and 420). Newton was born in Lincolnshire and studied at Cambridge, where he made his first scientific discoveries. He came to international attention on the publication of his *Philosophiae Naturalis Principia Mathematica* (1687), a work which introduced the three laws of motion and the law of universal gravitation; it has been said that the *Principia* 'may have done more to shape the modern world than any other [work] ever published'.[7] Newton moved to London –

properties that included their most famous home, Cliveden, Buckinghamshire. Number 4's magnificent reception rooms provided a glittering setting for entertainment: at a time when such splendour was becoming rare, Lady Astor gave dinner parties for fifty, two or three balls a season for up to six hundred guests – the house's first floor is dominated by a huge ballroom – and receptions for as many as a thousand people. Nancy apparently 'liked to pose at the top of the staircase, sparkling with jewels, to welcome her guests'.[5] Her campaigning spirit and enthusiasm for politics were formidable: she sat in the House of Commons as Conservative member for Plymouth for over twenty-five years (1919–45). The champion of many causes on behalf of underprivileged women and children, Astor was – for example – a keen supporter and benefactor of the nursery schools of Margaret McMillan. Number

426 Workmen repaint the Mall frontage of Carlton House Terrace, in a Bedford Lemere photograph of 1898. The terrace was designed by John Nash and built in 1827–33; notable former residents include W. E. Gladstone and Lord Curzon. [Reproduced by permission of English Heritage. NMR]

1908, was thus the second to honour Newton, the LCC having deemed it a worthy case despite the fact that demolition of the late seventeenth-century house was imminent. In 1915 the plaque was re-erected on the new building occupying the site, a fact recorded by a supplementary tablet.

Carlton House Terrace, SW1, was built in a monumental Graeco-Roman style by John Nash in 1827–33 – on the site of the royal palace of Carlton House – and forms an impressive backdrop to the Mall and St James's Park (fig. 426). Number 11, completed in the 1860s – and joined, in part, to number 10 since 1924 – bears a fine, highly coloured plaque in honour of the statesman **William Ewart Gladstone** (1809–1898) ⑥ (see also p. 398 and pp. 468–9) (fig. 427). Liverpool-born, Gladstone moved to London in 1833, on taking his seat in the Commons, and was closely associated with the area of St James's: he lived with his wife Catherine, née Glynne (1812–1900) at 13 Carlton House Terrace (1840–48), 6 Carlton Gardens (1848–53) and 4 Carlton House Terrace (1855–56) before moving in April 1856 to 11 Carlton House Terrace, his London home until April 1875. These years saw him attain the high offices he was to hold for much of his life: he began his second stint as Chancellor of the Exchequer in 1859, was leader of the House in 1865–66 and became Prime Minister in 1868. Gladstone's government was defeated over proposals for Irish Home Rule in 1874, and he resigned as Liberal Party leader the following year. With retirement and economy in mind, he retreated to his country home, Hawarden Castle, Wales, though he was later to return three times to the office of Prime Minister (1880–85, 1886 and 1892–94). Gladstone preferred Carlton House Terrace to any of his official residences. He occasionally used the property for Cabinet business and entertained here extensively: his breakfast parties were celebrated, and in 1865 he gave a ball for the Prince of Wales. Gladstone installed what he referred to as a 'modest' picture gallery, and displayed here his considerable collection of Wedgwood and other china. In 1875, having (reluctantly) left the address, he wrote that he 'had grown to the house, having lived more time in it than in any other since I was born, and mainly by reason of all that was done in it'.[8] A plaque was first proposed in 1907, but the building's lessee, the politician Arthur Edward Guinness, Lord Ardilaun (1840–1915), refused consent

and to Jermyn Street – in 1696, on his appointment as Master of the Mint, a position he held until his death. He lived at number 88 until 1700, when he moved next door to the larger number 87, where he remained until autumn 1709. This period saw Newton hold a series of important appointments: he was Lucasian Professor at Cambridge until 1702 and President of the Royal Society in 1703–27; Newton was knighted by Queen Anne in 1705. In 1704 he published *Opticks*, a work which drew upon research he had carried out largely in the 1660s and 1670s, and in 1713 completed the second edition of his *Principia*. After a brief period in Chelsea, Newton settled at 35 St Martin's Street, Leicester Square, his home from 1710 to 1725 (see fig. 10). The house, which had a rooftop observatory built by the scientist, was commemorated with a Society of Arts plaque in 1881, but was demolished in about 1913. The wreathed blue plaque at 87 Jermyn Street, erected in

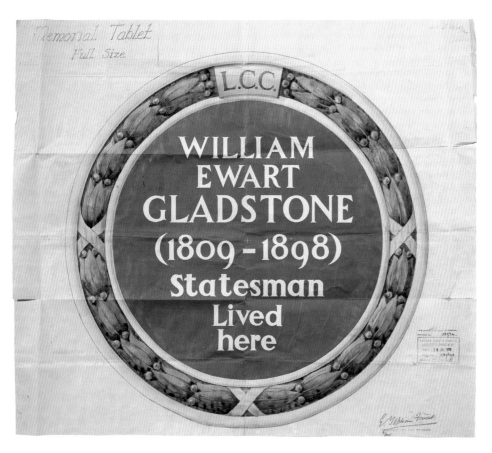

427   The spectacular design for the plaque to William Ewart Gladstone, installed in 1925 at 11 Carlton House Terrace. The statesman lived at this address from 1856 to 1875. [Reproduced by permission of English Heritage]

for its installation. In 1924 the LCC made a second attempt; the building's new occupant, the Union Club, was more amenable, and a plaque was erected the following year.

Number 1 Carlton House Terrace (see fig. 426) bears a GLC plaque erected in 1976 in honour of **George Nathaniel Curzon**, **Marquess Curzon of Kedleston** (1859–1925) **7** , the statesman and Viceroy of India. An MP from the age of twenty-seven, Curzon was noted for his interest in and knowledge of Asia, and in 1891 was appointed Under-Secretary for India. In 1898, shortly before he left England to take up the post of Viceroy of India, Curzon acquired number 1; it was intended as a London base for himself and his much-loved wife, Mary, née Leiter (1870–1906), during their period abroad. In March 1906, soon after his resignation as Viceroy and return to England, Curzon settled permanently at the house. His first months in Carlton House Terrace were dedicated to the care of his ailing wife, who died here in July 1906. Later, out of office until 1915, he devoted himself to his interest in the arts and conservation: he restored Bodiam Castle, Kent, and

Tattershall Castle, Lincolnshire, both of which he bequeathed to the nation, and drafted reports that shaped the future of the National Gallery and the Tate Gallery. In May 1914 the coming-out ball of Irene (1896–1966), one of Curzon's three daughters, was held in the house. It was one of the last great pre-war events of its kind; a supper room seventy feet (21 m) long was erected in the garden, and the ROBERT ADAM silver was brought from Kedleston, Derbyshire, Curzon's ancestral home. Curzon returned to office in 1915 in the coalition Cabinet, and four years later became Foreign Secretary under LLOYD GEORGE. His greatest achievement was the Treaty of Lausanne (1923), which effectively established the modern state of Turkey. In that year Curzon was passed over for the Conservative leadership – and the premiership – in favour of STANLEY BALDWIN. He remained at the Foreign Office until 1924, and died at Carlton House Terrace the following year.

Carlton Gardens, SW1, is a secluded terrace laid out by John Nash in the 1820s as part of the southern termination of his classical *via triumphalis*. Number 4, a stone-built office block of 1933–34 by Sir Reginald Blomfield & Son, bears two plaques. The first is a brown wreathed LCC plaque commemorating the statesman **Lord Palmerston** (1784–1865) **8** (see also p. 432 and pp. 528–9), who lived at a house on this site from late 1846 until January 1855. Henry John Temple, 3rd Viscount Palmerston, was one of the most colourful and commanding of Victorian politicians. An MP from 1807, he sat in sixteen Parliaments – at first as a Tory, later as a Liberal – and, tireless in his defence of British interests, is best remembered for his use of 'gunboat diplomacy'. Palmerston became Foreign Secretary – for the third time – in the year he moved from 5 Carlton House Terrace to 4 Carlton Gardens. His maverick approach to the niceties of diplomacy frequently brought him into conflict with Queen Victoria and Prince Albert, and the Court seized the pretext of his unofficial recognition of NAPOLEON III to secure his dismissal from office in 1851, though he was subsequently appointed Home Secretary (1852–55). Palmerston's wife – Emily, née Lamb (1787–1869), sister to the former Prime Minister Lord Melbourne – lent powerful support to her husband's career by holding a sophisticated and cosmopolitan salon at Carlton Gardens; it has been said that she 'surrounded his political existence with a social charm which gave to his hospitality an attraction that at once enthralled his friends and softened his opponents'.[9] In 1855 Palmerston began the first of two spells as Prime Minister, and left Carlton Gardens for 94 Piccadilly. When the plaque was erected at number 4 in 1907, it was the residence of Arthur Balfour (1848–1930) – Prime Minister in 1902–5 – who had acquired the property in 1870. The house was demolished in 1933; three years later, the plaque – together with a supplementary tablet recording its history – were installed on the imposing new structure built on its site.

The second plaque at 4 Carlton Gardens was put up by the GLC to commemorate **General Charles de Gaulle** (1890–1970) 9 (fig. 428), President of the French National Committee – the temporary government-in-exile – who set up the headquarters of the Free French Forces here in late July 1940; the forces were associated with this building until mid-1944, though their headquarters was moved to Algiers in 1943. The plaque commemorates the associations of the site as much as the person; under the selection criteria, de Gaulle was not yet eligible when the proposal was made in 1983. Born in Lille, de Gaulle pursued a military career, and was promoted brigadier-general not long after the outbreak of the Second World War. He served briefly as Under-Secretary of State for War, but rebelled against

the government led by Marshal Pétain – which sought a truce with Nazi Germany – and fled to London. On 18 June 1940, the day after his arrival, de Gaulle used the BBC radio service – with the support of WINSTON CHURCHILL – to deliver his famous address, encouraging his countrymen to continue to fight occupation; the broadcast was concluded with the words, 'Whatever happens the flame of French resistance must not and shall not be extinguished'.[10] Sentenced to death *in absentia*, de Gaulle set about organising the so-called Free French Forces, which – by the end of 1944 – numbered one million individuals. Following liberation, he became head of the French Provisional Government, and in 1958 founded the Fifth Republic, becoming first President, a post he held until 1969. Initially, it was intended that the plaque be placed on 3 Carlton Gardens, a building of *c.* 1828 that housed, at first-floor level, de Gaulle's private office, where he slept on occasion. However, at the suggestion of the Foreign and Commonwealth Office, it was placed on the neighbouring number 4, alongside the rectangular tablet of black marble set up by the Free French of London to record de Gaulle's rallying call of 18 June 1940. The blue plaque was unveiled by Queen Elizabeth, The Queen Mother, in the presence of the French Ambassador and veterans of the Free French Forces; the event took place on 5 June 1984, just hours before the fortieth anniversary of the D-Day Landings.

Number 2 Carlton Gardens bears a wreathed LCC plaque to **Field Marshal Earl Kitchener of Khartoum, KG** (1850–1916) 10 , perhaps best known from the First World War recruiting posters that bear his image. Kitchener was born in Ireland to English parents, and entered the Army in 1871. He spent his entire military career abroad, coming to public attention as Commander-in-Chief (Sirdar) of the Egyptian Army (1892–99); in this capacity, he saw victory at the Battle of Omdurman (1898), avenging the death of General Gordon at Khartoum and earning himself a baronetcy – an earldom followed in 1914. Kitchener later held posts including Governor-General of Sudan (1899), Chief of Staff under LORD ROBERTS and then Commander during the Second Boer War (1899–1900), Commander-in-Chief in India (1902–9) and British Consul-General in Egypt (1911–14). Number 2 Carlton Gardens, a splendid semi-detached house with views over the Mall and St James's Park, was lent to him –

428 General Charles de Gaulle in his office at Carlton Gardens in 1943. The Free French Forces were associated with number 4 between 1940 and 1944. [© Popperfoto / Getty Images]

429 An undated watercolour of Schomberg House, 80–82 Pall Mall. Dating largely from 1698, the building was divided into three properties in 1769. Thomas Gainsborough occupied number 80 – on the right of the illustration – from 1774 until his death in 1788. [© City of Westminster Archives Centre]

with domestic staff – by his friend Harriet, Lady Wantage (1837–1920). He lived at this house, with his personal secretaries Captain Oswald Fitzgerald (d. 1916) and (Sir) George Arthur (1860–1946), towards the end of his long and distinguished career, from August 1914 until February 1915, when he moved to York House, St James's Palace. On the outbreak of war in 1914, Kitchener was appointed Secretary of State for War, and while living in Carlton Gardens advised the Cabinet on military strategy and prepared plans for the expansion of the British Army. This laid the foundations for the victory he did not live to see: Kitchener drowned when the ship carrying him on a special mission to Russia struck a German mine in June 1916. News of the death of this popular hero was greeted with universal mourning and in 1924, only eight years later, the LCC honoured his residence at Carlton Gardens with one of the earliest of Doulton's new high-glaze blue plaques.

Number 80–82 Pall Mall, SW1, a handsome brick building known as Schomberg House (fig. 429), bears a plaque to the artist **Thomas Gainsborough** (1727–1788) , who lived here from midsummer 1774 and died here fourteen years later. Rebuilt for the 3rd Duke of Schomberg in 1698, the building was subdivided into three properties in 1769; Gainsborough occupied the western house (the present number 80). Born in Suffolk, Gainsborough set up as an artist in the mid-1740s; he exhibited at the newly founded Royal Academy from 1769, by which time he was living in Bath. Returning to London in 1774, Gainsborough received the patronage of King George III and immediately became the most fashionable portrait painter of the age. At his home in Pall Mall, he built a large painting room over the garden, above which was a salon used as another studio and also for the display of paintings; here, the artist produced works such as the portraits of the Duke and Duchess of Cumberland (1777) and Mrs R. B. Sheridan (1785), and his series of 'fancy pictures'. On a visit to Gainsborough, the painter William Beechey saw his then unappreciated landscapes ranged in long lines from his hall to his painting room; he commented that 'they who came to sit for their portraits rarely deigned to honour them with a look'.[11] After Gainsborough's disagreement and then break, in 1783, with the Royal Academy – headed by his great rival, SIR JOSHUA REYNOLDS – the display of pictures at Schomberg House assumed greater importance, and patrons and critics were regularly admitted to his galleries. The artist held his first private exhibition here in 1784; the last took place in 1792, shortly before the tenancy of Gainsborough's widow, Margaret, née Burr (c. 1728–98), came to an end. She left number 80 for good in 1793, as did Gainsborough Dupont (c. 1754–97), the artist's nephew and studio assistant. Gainsborough's house, then located a few doors away from Christie's salerooms, has subsequently been rebuilt behind a reconstructed façade. A tablet erected by the Society of Arts in 1881 had become illegible by the mid-twentieth century; in 1951 it was replaced with an LCC plaque unveiled by the painter Sir Alfred Munnings.

St James's Place, SW1, is an unusual L-shaped road that owes its configuration to the fact that it was laid out at two distinct periods over ground belonging to different owners. Number 4 dates from the development of 1685–86; originally part of a brown-brick terrace, it was stuccoed in the early nineteenth century and re-faced in the 1970s. The building bears a GLC plaque of 1981 recording that from this house, in 1848, **Frederic Chopin** (1810–1849) (12) went to the Guildhall to give his last public performance. Born near Warsaw to a French father and a Polish mother, Chopin was an accomplished musician by the age of seven and made his debut in Vienna in 1829. Two years later, he settled in Paris, where he made his name as a great Romantic pianist-composer, working particularly in the genres of nocturne, étude, waltz and mazurka. A fervent Polish nationalist, Chopin embarked on an affair with the novelist George Sand (Madame Dudevant) in 1838; the couple's relationship broke down nine years later, accelerating a decline in Chopin's health. In 1848, in flight from revolutionary Paris, he travelled to England with his Scottish pupil Jane Stirling, taking lodgings from April to August at 48 Dover Street, Mayfair (demolished). On 31 October of that year, following a trip to Scotland, he settled at 4 St James's Place, his home until 23 November. Chopin's residence here, marred by illness, came at a particularly poignant moment towards the end of his life and career. On 19 November 1848 he wrote, 'Since Nov. 1st I have been in my room, in my dressing-gown, and have been out only on the 16th, to play for my compatriots'.[12] It was on this occasion that he braved the London fogs to drive to the Guildhall to give his very last public performance at a gala benefit for the Friends of Poland. Chopin left London for Paris a few days later, suffering from the final stages of the consumption that would kill him the following year.

Further along, in the shadow of Spencer House (built 1756–58), stands 28 St James's Place, a late seventeenth-century stock-brick house rebuilt by Henry Holland in 1794. It bears an LCC plaque of 1962 to the statesman **William Huskisson** (1770–1830) (13). He moved here from Mayfair in 1804, the year he became MP for Liskeard and was appointed joint Secretary to the Treasury, and left the property in 1806, the year that saw his temporary retirement into opposition. Huskisson, an ally of GEORGE CANNING and a fellow liberal Tory, subsequently enjoyed a distinguished and varied political career. Admired particularly as an administrator and man of business, he served as President of the Board of Trade and Treasurer of the Navy from 1823 until 1827. In 1823 he succeeded Canning as MP for Liverpool, and went on to become Colonial Secretary (1827–28) and leader of the House of Commons (1827–

28); it was thought that he might go on to become Prime Minister. Sadly, Huskisson's political successes as a promoter of free trade tend to be overshadowed by the circumstances of his death. Always accident prone, he was Britain's first railway casualty, killed by a train at the ceremonial opening of the Liverpool and Manchester Railway on 15 September 1830.

Number 22 Arlington Street, SW1 – known as Wimborne House from its owners of 1871–1947, the lords Wimborne – was the residence of **Henry Pelham** (1694–1754) (14) during his time as Prime Minister.[13] The house, of considerable significance as a survival of William Kent's work in London, was begun in 1740, but was only finished shortly before Pelham's death here in March 1754; its interiors are among the most magnificent in St James's, and were used as a setting for Pelham's many levées. The first part of the house was sufficiently complete for Pelham and his wife, Lady Katherine, née Manners (1700/1–1780), to take up residence in May 1743; shortly afterwards, Pelham's near neighbour, HORACE WALPOLE, commented that Arlington Street had become 'absolutely the ministerial street'.[14] Soon after moving in, Pelham – politically a Whig, and a protégé of SIR ROBERT WALPOLE – became First Lord of the Treasury, Chancellor of the Exchequer and leader of the House of Commons; he died in office, and was succeeded as Prime Minister by his elder brother, Thomas, Duke of Newcastle. His premiership is best remembered for his efforts to bring about the Treaty of Aix-la-Chapelle (1748), ending Britain's involvement in the War of the Austrian Succession. Number 22, a testament to Pelham's passion for architecture, was considerably altered in the twentieth century. In the late 1970s, Eagle Star Insurance – based here since 1947 – demolished and redeveloped the range facing Arlington Street, and restored the building facing Green Park to its eighteenth-century form. Partly because of this, and partly because of visibility, English Heritage chose to place the plaque – erected in 1995 – on the secondary, Green Park elevation, facing onto Queen's Walk.

Number 5 Arlington Street was first commemorated in 1881, when the Society of Arts installed a plaque to **Sir Robert Walpole**, **Earl of Orford** (1676–1745) (15). Sir Robert, regarded as the first British statesman to hold the office with which the title of Prime Minister is now associated, lived in Arlington Street from his fall from power in 1742 until his death, having moved here from 10 Downing Street, granted to him by King George II. During his long term of office – Walpole was First Lord of the Treasury and Chancellor of the Exchequer in 1715–17 and again in 1721–42 – he dominated the Commons and became famous as a master in the art of parliamentary management. Earlier in his career, between 1715 and 1732, Sir Robert had lived at a different house on the western side of Arlington Street, number 17 (demolished in the 1930s to make way for Arlington House); it was there that his son Horace was born, the youngest of Walpole's children with Catherine, née Shorter. By 1976 the Victorian plaque at number 5 had become badly weathered and the GLC took the opportunity to replace it, adding the name of Sir Robert's famous son, the connoisseur and man of letters **Horace Walpole** (1717–1797). Renowned as an author, aesthete and wit, Horace is remembered especially for the creation of the 'little Gothic castle' of Strawberry Hill, Twickenham (1749–66), a striking contrast to the magnificence of Houghton Hall, Norfolk, built by his father in 1721–35.[15] Horace filled his house at Arlington Street with part of his collection. Paintings and antiquities jostled for space with his 'curious cabinets of limnings, enamels, and his col-

lection of English heads &c.', together with 'a number of antique coins, medals, medallions, etc.', which a contemporary newspaper valued at 'near £3000'.[16] Such wonders made the house a meeting place for London's dilettanti, but also attracted unwelcome visitors: in 1771 the property was rifled by burglars. While living in Arlington Street, Walpole published his Gothic romance *The Castle of Otranto* (1764), and between 1762 and 1780 produced his *Anecdotes of Painting in England*; his famous correspondence was published after his death. Research carried out by English Heritage since the replacement of the plaque at number 5 has shown the Walpoles' connection with Arlington Street to be more complicated than was first thought. Number 5 was, in fact, the residence of Horace alone – it was acquired for him by Sir Robert in 1742 – though while he was living here the property was intimately joined to his father's larger house at number 4. After Sir Robert's death in 1745, Horace moved to the more spacious of the two houses, and number 5 was re-divided and let in the 1750s. Horace, a lifelong bachelor, lived at number 4 until 1779, when he moved to 11 Berkeley Square, Mayfair (demolished). Number 4 Arlington Street is probably a late seventeenth-century building, partly re-fronted in 1786–87, while the house bearing the plaque actually dates from 1795–97.

NOTES

1. Simon Bradley and Nikolaus Pevsner, *The Buildings of England, London 6: Westminster* (New Haven and London, 2003), p. 582
2. Ivor Guest, *Napoleon III in England* (London, 1952), p. 96
3. *Ada, The Enchantress of Numbers: A Selection from the Letters of Lord Byron's Daughter and her Description of the First Computer*, ed. Betty Alexandra Toole (Mill Valley, California, 1992), p. 215 (30 July 1843)
4. Letter of 30 November 1910 on blue plaque file.
5. *ODNB*, vol. II, p. 799
6. *The Independent*, 24 November 1987, p. 6
7. *ODNB*, vol. XL, p. 723
8. John, Viscount Morley, *The Life of William Ewart Gladstone*, vol. II (London, 1903), p. 522
9. Evelyn Ashley, *The Life and Correspondence of Henry John Temple, Viscount Palmerston*, vol. I (London, 1879), p. 401
10. *The Times*, 19 June 1940, p. 6
11. *Gainsborough*, eds Michael Rosenthal and Martin Myrone (London, 2002), p. 37
12. *Chopin's Letters*, ed. E. L. Voynich (London, 1932), p. 398
13. It is now accepted that Pelham was born in 1694, rather than in *c*. 1695, as is stated on the plaque.
14. David Watkin *et al.*, *A House in Town: 22 Arlington Street, its Owners and Builders* (London, 1984), p. 108
15. *The Yale Edition of Horace Walpole's Correspondence*, ed. W. S. Lewis, vol. XX (London and New Haven, 1960), p. 111 (10 January 1750)
16. Morris R. Brownell, *The Prime Minister of Taste: A Portrait of Horace Walpole* (New Haven and London, 2001), p. 77; *Horace Walpole's Correspondence*, ed. Lewis, vol. XXIII (London and New Haven, 1967), p. 285 note (*St James's Chronicle*, 21–23 March 1771)

430   The English Heritage plaque
to Alan Turing at his birthplace,
Warrington Lodge, 2 Warrington
Crescent, now the Colonnade
Hotel. [© English Heritage.
Photograph by Derek Kendall]

ST JOHN'S WOOD, MAIDA VALE AND LISSON GROVE

The first houses were constructed on the lands now comprising St John's Wood, Maida Vale and Lisson Grove in the early 1800s. By the middle of the century, St John's Wood in particular had become an immensely popular residential area, noted for its clean air and for its detached and semi-detached villas set in substantial grounds; these, the first of a kind, represented a revolutionary change from the terraces and squares of the 1700s. The relative remoteness of St John's Wood was an attraction for many – the area was known as a haven for mistresses, courtesans and exiled activists – and, combined with its uninterrupted north light, provided a perfect setting for those connected with the arts, a fact reflected by the area's blue plaques. One of the earliest residents of 'the Wood' was the artist Sir Edwin Landseer, who lived at 1 (later 18) St John's Wood Road (demolished) for nearly fifty years (1825–73) and spearheaded an influx of others of his profession. Despite the destruction caused by the building of the Great Central Railway in the 1890s, St John's Wood could still be described in 1913 as 'the district *par excellence* for interesting people'.[1]

ST JOHN'S WOOD, MAIDA VALE
AND LISSON GROVE

On the Rossmore Road elevation of 116 Lisson Grove (formerly 1 St John's Place, then 58 Lisson Grove), NW1, a plaque jointly commemorates the painter **Benjamin Haydon** (1786–1846) and the sculptor **Charles Rossi** (1762–1839) ① (fig. 431). The precise connection between the pair and number 116 was the subject of considerable research. The LCC eventually proved that the house had been built soon after 1808 by John Charles Felix Rossi, who lived here – and probably also in the adjoining houses, numbers 112 and 114 – and owned the property until his death; this period saw the completion of such of his works as the monument to Admiral Lord Rodney in St Paul's Cathedral (1810–15) and the caryatids of St Pancras New Church (1819–22). In 1817–23 B. R. Haydon leased and occupied the Rossmore Road side of number 116 – then known as 1 St John's Place – and used as his studio a building on the site of the existing Evangelical church at 1 Rossmore Road (originally 22 Lisson Grove North); Rossi carried out alterations in order to suit the buildings to Haydon's needs. The Plymouth-born painter – a former student of HENRY FUSELI – recalled that 'the quiet and peace of having a painting-room and a parlour to live in with my books around me was heavenly'.[2] During his time in Lisson Grove, Haydon produced some of his most famous work, including the immense paintings *Christ's Entry into*

Jerusalem (1814–20) and *The Raising of Lazarus* (1820–23). It was also here – 'with Jerusalem towering up behind us as a background' – that, on 28 December 1817, he held a celebrated dinner party for LAMB, KEATS and Wordsworth.[3] Rossi – who was sculptor from 1797 to the Prince of Wales, later King George IV, and then to his brother King William IV – was something of a strict landlord; Haydon wrote of his 'appetite for bricks and mortar', and described how he had 'sunk the whole of his money on this place'.[4] The increasingly penurious Haydon was threatened with expulsion in 1822, a year after taking a wife, the widow Mary Cawse Hyman. Having been imprisoned for debt in 1823 – 'A year of more misery than any I have endured since my birth' – he left by January 1824 for Connaught Terrace, near Edgware Road.[5] The joint plaque at number 116 – a house which has been much rebuilt since the early nineteenth century – was unveiled in 1959 by Sir James Mann, Director of the Wallace Collection.

At 17 Cunningham Place, NW8, part of an early to mid-nineteenth-century terrace, a plaque commemorates the residence of **Emily Davies** (1830–1921) ②, the founder of Girton College, which has formed part of the University of Cambridge since 1948. Born in Southampton and raised in Gateshead, Davies came with her mother Mary, née Hopkinson (d. 1886) to London in January 1862, following the death of her father. The pair – with a cook and a housemaid – moved immediately into 17 Cunningham Place, a house found for them by Emily's brother Llewelyn. It was apparently 'small but cheerful', with 'a minute garden in which Mrs [Mary] Davies could potter about to her heart's content', and its position was described by Emily as 'ideal'.[6] It continued to be her home until shortly after her mother's death in 1886. While here, Davies became actively involved in furthering the rights of women. Working with her friends Barbara Leigh Bodichon, ELIZABETH GARRETT ANDERSON, FRANCES MARY BUSS and others, she pressed for the opening of university courses and professional careers to women, and was also active in the campaign for women's suffrage. In 1866 she published her successful book *The Higher Education of Women*, and later the same year the London Schoolmistresses' Association was founded at number 17, with Emily as Secretary. Most notably, Davies's work of this period included the founding in 1869 – with Bodichon – of Girton College,

431   A positioning photograph of 1958 for the joint plaque to Benjamin Haydon and Charles Rossi at 116 Lisson Grove, on the corner of Rossmore Road. The site of Haydon's studio is now occupied by an Evangelical church, shown on the far left of the picture. [© City of London, LMA]

ST JOHN'S WOOD, MAIDA VA., LISSON GRO.

based initially at Hitchin, Hertfordshire, and from 1873 on the edge of Cambridge. Girton, a residential college where women took the same courses and exams as men, remained a major part of Davies's life until 1904, and survives as her greatest memorial. The plaque was erected in 1978, International Women's Year.

At 10 Howley Place, W2, a semi-detached house of the 1840s, a plaque commemorates the nine-month stay of **Lokamanya Tilak** (1856–1920) ❸ , the Indian patriot and philosopher (fig. 432). Bal Gangadhar Tilak, known as Lokamanya – meaning 'beloved of the people' – is a figure of major significance in Indian history: he was named 'the Father of the Indian Revolution' by Nehru and 'the Maker of Modern India' by Gandhi. Born in the Ratnagiri district, Tilak was an ardent opponent of British rule and a central figure in the extremist party. In 1918–19 – towards the end of his life – he stayed in London, where he gave evidence to a parliamentary committee on behalf of the All India Home Rule League, and mixed with such figures as Ramsay MacDonald, Arthur Henderson and George Bernard Shaw. His first plaque, unveiled in

432 Lokamanya Tilak in a portrait taken during his residence at 10 Howley Place in 1918–19.

1961 by Kwame Nkrumah at 60 Talbot Road, Bayswater (see fig. 34), provoked a stream of protests from those who felt Tilak to be a 'seditionist'. The scene was somewhat calmer when, in 1988 – following the demolition of 60 Talbot Road – an English Heritage plaque was unveiled at 10 Howley Place by J. S. Tilak, Lokamanya's grandson. Tilak moved to number 10 – a house found for him by his colleague and countryman, Joseph Baptista – on 29 October 1918, following his arrival in London. He and four colleagues had six rooms at their disposal, two on each floor, and were well looked after by a Mr and Mrs McNalty; such was the couple's mastery of curry preparation that they later opened an Indian restaurant. Tilak remained at this house – known at the time as 'No. 10 Indian Downing Street' – until early August 1919, when he moved to Talbot Road, his home for about two months.[7] At the time of writing, Tilak's plaque at Howley Place – positioned on the wall to the right of the entrance bay – is joined by one commemorating the artist Canaletto, placed on the front of the house; although this bears the name of the LCC, it was not authorised by that council, and there is no connection between the artist and the building, which post-dates Canaletto's life.

Number 30 Maida Avenue (formerly Maida Hill West), W2, a semi-detached house of c. 1830 that overlooks the Regent's Canal, was the London home from 1907 to 1912 of **John Masefield**, OM (1878–1967) ❹ , the Poet Laureate. During his time at number 30 – a house he shared with his Irish wife Constance, née Crommelin (1866/7–1960) – Masefield completed some of his finest work, including his first novel, *Captain Margaret* (1908), the play *The Tragedy of Nan* (1909), the collection *Ballads and Poems* (1910) and his narrative poems *The Everlasting Mercy* (1911) and *The Widow in the Bye Street* (1912). The location of the house – then known as 30 Maida Hill West – is an indication of Masefield's love of water: his teenage years were spent at sea, and it was his *Salt-Water Ballads* (1902) – which includes the popular 'Sea-Fever', set to music by John Ireland – that first brought him to literary attention. After 1909, when Masefield acquired Rectory Farm, Great Hampden, Buckinghamshire, his time was divided between London and the country. Although he and his family left number 30 in 1912 for 13 Well Walk, Hampstead, NW3 (see H. M. Hyndman), Masefield

433ˊ Sir Ambrose Fleming's original thermionic valve of 1889, crafted around the time he moved to 9 Clifton Gardens. He later developed valves such as this for use in detecting radio signals. [© Science Museum / Science & Society Picture Library]

and successful career, Fleming was closely involved with the development of important applications of electrical science, including the telephone, electric lighting and wireless telegraphy. The work which brought him worldwide fame was his development in 1904 of the thermionic valve, which was used to detect the strength of radio signals (fig. 433); this valve was quickly taken on and adapted by MARCONI – to whom Fleming served as scientific adviser – and was to become one of the essentials of electronics during the first half of the twentieth century. It was originally hoped that a plaque could be erected at the house where Fleming was living at the time of the valve's invention, 212 Finchley Road (formerly 2 Langland Place), West Hampstead, his home in 1896–1910. However, as that property had been demolished, and as The Pryors – the block of flats in East Heath Road, Hampstead, where Fleming had lived from 1911 until his retirement to Devon in 1926 – proved unsuitable for a plaque, the GLC settled on 9 Clifton Gardens. This mid-nineteenth-century terraced house was the home of Fleming and his wife Clara, née Pratt (1856/7–1917) from 1889 until 1896, a period that saw the publication of works including *The Alternate Current Transformer* (1889–92) and *Electric Lamps and Electric Lighting* (1894). At the time the plaque was put up in 1971, number 9 formed part of the Worsley Hotel; it is now part of a residential conversion, Connaught House.

Alan Turing (1912–1954) **6** , the code-breaker and pioneer of computer science, is one of those rare people who can justifiably be said to have fundamentally changed the way in which we live. An English Heritage plaque commemorates his birth in a nursing home at Warrington Lodge, 2 Warrington Crescent, W9, a mid-nineteenth-century stuccoed building which occupies part of an island site closed on the north by Formosa Street (fig. 430). The son of the civil servant Julius Mathison Turing and his wife Ethel, née Stoney, Alan was interested in science from his youth and entered Cambridge in 1931. By the age of twenty-four, he had published his vital paper 'On Computable Numbers' (1936) and developed the concept of the 'universal Turing machine', now seen as embodying the principle of the modern computer. During the Second World War, he worked as a cryptanalyst at Bletchley Park, Bedfordshire, where he made his vital – and, at the time, top-secret – contribution to the deciphering

spent much of the rest of his life outside London, and moved permanently to Oxfordshire in 1917. There, he reached his zenith of creativity with the much-loved poem *Reynard the Fox* (1919), which drew on his childhood in Herefordshire. Eleven years later, Masefield was appointed Poet Laureate; he held the position for thirty-seven years, longer than any of his predecessors except TENNYSON. Number 30 was marked with a plaque in 2002, at a ceremony organised by the John Masefield Society.

The pioneering scientist and electrical engineer **Sir Ambrose Fleming** (1849–1945) **5** has a plaque at 9 Clifton Gardens, W9, erected at the suggestion of two successive provosts of University College London. Born in Lancaster, Fleming worked as a science teacher before studying under JAMES CLERK MAXWELL at Cambridge. In 1885 – after a period with the Edison & Swan United Electric Light Company – he was appointed Professor of Electrical Technology at UCL, where he remained until his retirement in 1926. During his long

of the German Enigma code. In 1945 – the year he received an OBE – Turing joined the National Physical Laboratory at Teddington, where he designed and was instrumental in the development of the Automatic Computing Engine (ACE), regarded as the world's first universal computing machine. In 1948 he was invited to join the Manchester Computer Laboratory – working under the mathematician Max Newman, whom he had known from Bletchley Park days – and two years later he settled in nearby Wilmslow. However, his final years were marked by tragedy: in 1952 Turing was prosecuted for his relationship with another man and, despite having always been open about his sexuality, came to be regarded by his employers as a security risk. The ensuing phase of depression ended with his suicide by cyanide poisoning at the age of forty-one; the half-eaten apple found next to Turing's bed is said to have inspired the name and logo of Apple Computers. A plaque was unveiled at 2 Warrington Crescent by Turing's biographer, Andrew Hodges, on 23 June 1998, the eighty-sixth anniversary of Turing's birth. The sole survivor of the two London addresses associated with Turing, the building is now the Colonnade Hotel.

At 75 Warrington Crescent, a plaque commemorates the residence from 1920 to 1921 of **David Ben-Gurion** (1886–1973) **7** , the first Prime Minister of Israel. Ben-Gurion was born in what was then Russian Poland, where anti-Semitism was endemic. He dedicated his life to the Zionist cause, believing passionately that the establishment of a Jewish homeland was necessary if his people were to be freed from victimisation. Galvanised by the pogroms, Ben-Gurion moved to Palestine in 1906, and later transferred to Turkey; expelled from the country at the outbreak of the First World War, he sailed for New York and subsequently fought in the Jewish Legion of the British Army. In summer 1920 – the year which saw him play a key part in the formation of Histadrut, the General Federation of Jewish Workers – Ben-Gurion came to England with his wife Paula, née Munweis (1892–1968), in order to promote good relations and attract more settlers to Palestine. The couple rented a modest flat at number 75, located in an area in which there was a high proportion of Jewish immigrants. From here, Ben-Gurion travelled by Underground to the offices of Poale Zion, the organisation of Labour Zionists for

which he worked, at 27 Sandys Row, Spitalfields. In August 1920, while they were living in Warrington Crescent, the Ben-Gurions' son Amos was born in Stockwell. The family subsequently lived at addresses including 24 Westbourne Square, Paddington (demolished), before returning in 1921 to Palestine. There, Ben-Gurion's remaining years were spent, though he returned to London in 1940, living for several months at a house in Church Row, Hampstead. The culmination of Ben-Gurion's efforts came on 14 May 1948, when he proclaimed the independent state of Israel in Tel Aviv. He was made Prime Minister, a position he held – except for the period 1953–55 – until 1963, and also served as Minister of Defence. Ben-Gurion, long the 'prophet and statesman, the leader and father of his people', finally retired from politics in 1969, when he settled on his kibbutz and dedicated himself to writing.[8] The plaque was proposed by Reg Freeson MP on behalf of Poale Zion, and was unveiled during Ben-Gurion's centenary year, 1986; it bears the name of the GLC but was installed after the scheme had transferred to English Heritage.

The Greek poet and patriot **Andreas Kalvos** (1792–1869) **8** , one of the foremost champions of Hellenic culture in the West, is commemorated with an English Heritage plaque at 182 Sutherland Avenue (formerly 7 Sutherland Gardens), W9. Born on the island of Zakynthos and brought up in Tuscany, Kalvos spent most of his life in Italy and England. He wrote his first works soon after becoming secretary to the writer Ugo Foscolo in 1812, and is best known for his twenty patriotic odes published in two parts, *The Lyre* (1824) and *New Odes* (1826). Works such as these raised popular awareness across Europe of the cause of Greek nationalism, and excited an upsurge of philhellenism that played an important role in the creation of the modern Greek state. Kalvos first came to England with Foscolo in 1816, and married Theresa Thomas in London two years later. After her early death in 1820, he spent time in Florence, Geneva and Paris before settling in 1826 in Corfu, then a British territory. There, Kalvos worked intermittently for the Ionian Academy, and also supported himself by running a school. After he moved permanently to England in 1852 and married an Englishwoman, Charlotte Wadans, Kalvos returned to this occupation; in partnership with his wife and Miss Georgina Keating, he set up and ran a school for

434 Sir Joseph Bazalgette – standing top-right – in a photograph of 1862, showing the building of the Northern Outfall Sewer below Abbey Mills pumping station in East London. [© Getty Images]

ST JOHN'S WOOD, MAIDA VA., LISSON GRO.

young ladies at 7 Sutherland Gardens, then newly built, where he based himself from 1857 to 1865. In the latter year, Kalvos and his wife left for Louth, Lincolnshire, where they founded another school; it was there that he died, at the age of seventy-seven. The plaque at number 182 was unveiled in 1998 by the Greek Ambassador, Vassilis S. Zafiropoulos, who had proposed Kalvos for commemoration.

Number 17 (formerly 48, then 83) Hamilton Terrace, NW8, a brick villa off St John's Wood Road, was the boyhood home of **Sir Joseph William Bazalgette** (1819–1891) **9**, the civil engineer (fig. 434). It has been said that Bazalgette 'created more of London, above and below ground, than anyone else'.[9] Born in Enfield, he was apprenticed as an engineer in Ireland, and entered the service of the Metropolitan Commission of Sewers in London in 1849. As Chief Engineer to the Metropolitan Board of Works from 1856 until his retirement in 1889, Bazalgette was responsible for the design and construction of some of the most important components of London's infrastructure. In the 1850s, London's sewage drained directly into the Thames, causing foul odours and frequent outbreaks of disease. In 1858 a hot summer led to a crisis known as 'The Great Stink', which forced action; in a remarkably short space of time – from 1858 to 1875 – Bazalgette developed and built a comprehensive and extensive new sewage system. His treatment works, pumping stations and more than eighty miles (129 km) of intercepting sewers remain in full use today. His many other works included the construction of the Albert (1868), Victoria (1870) and Chelsea (1874) embankments, the design of river crossings such as Hammersmith Bridge (1887) and the building of new thoroughfares, among them Shaftesbury Avenue (1886) and Charing Cross Road (1887). Number 17 Hamilton Terrace is the only one of Bazalgette's London residences to survive. It was his family home – his father, Captain Joseph Bazalgette (1783–1849), was a naval officer – from c. 1831, when the house was newly built, until c. 1844. The plaque was unveiled in 1974.

On the other side of the road, at 20 (formerly 7) Hamilton Terrace, an LCC plaque commemorates the painter and etcher **William Strang** (1859–1921) **10**, who lived here from 1900 until the time of his sudden death at a hotel in Bournemouth. Strang was a Scot who came to London in 1875, and studied art at the Slade. He took to printmaking under the influence of his professor, Alphonse Legros, and made his name with illustrative etchings such as those for *The Pilgrim's Progress* (1885), *The Ancient Mariner* (1896) and *Don Quixote* (1902). For most of Strang's years in Hamilton Terrace, however, he was active primarily as a painter, producing works including *Bank Holiday* (1912) and *Lady in a Red Hat* (1918), a depiction of VITA SACKVILLE-WEST. He was especially renowned for his portrait drawings, his sitters including ALMA-TADEMA (1908), LORD KITCHENER (1910) and JOHN MASEFIELD (1912). When the plaque was installed in 1962, number 20 was still the home of his son, the artist David Strang (b. 1887). The house, which dates from *c.* 1830, also bears a plaque erected by the Society of Musicians in 1895 to the composer Sir George Macfarren (1813–1887), who lived and died here.

An English Heritage plaque at 10 Hall Road, NW8, an early nineteenth-century semi-detached house, honours the painter **John William Waterhouse** (1849–1917) ⑪ . Like STRANG, Waterhouse moved to St John's Wood in 1900, when he was at the height of his fame, and remained at number 10 until his death; he lived here with his wife, Esther Kenworthy Waterhouse (1857–1944), who was also an artist. Waterhouse was born in Rome, and settled in South Kensington with his family in 1854; both his parents were artists, and he followed their profession by entering the schools of the Royal Academy in 1870. He became known in particular for his paintings of classical scenes, including *The Favourites of the Emperor Honorius* (1883), and for his skilful depiction of women, as in *Marianne* (1887). From Primrose Hill Studios, which he leased from 1878, Waterhouse produced a stream of successful works in the romantic vein popular at the time; these include *The Lady of Shalott* (1888), *Ophelia* (1889), *Ulysses and the Sirens* (1891), *St Cecilia* (1895) and *Hylas and the Nymphs* (1896). In his studio at number 10 – which occupied the lower-ground floor of the house, expanded by its previous occupant, the sculptor Harry Bates (1850–1899) – Waterhouse turned increasingly to non-narrative subjects, producing works such as *Song of Springtime* (1913). *The Enchanted Garden*, which stood on his easel at the time of his death, is believed to have been inspired by the garden at Hall Road. The plaque was unveiled in 2002 by John Physick, Waterhouse's great-nephew.

435   The unveiling in 2001 of the English Heritage plaque to Madame Marie Tussaud at 24 Wellington Road. The cord was pulled by Anthony Tussaud, Marie's great-great-great grandson, in the presence of Tussaud's wax-work self-portrait. [© English Heritage. Photograph by Derek Kendall]

Among the few early nineteenth-century villas to survive in Wellington Road, NW8, number 24 (formerly number 12) – set back behind a boundary wall – was the home in 1838–39 of **Madame Marie Tussaud** (1761–1850) ⑫ , the artist in wax (fig. 435 and see fig. 2). Born in Strasbourg, France, Marie Grosholtz learned her trade in Paris at the waxworks museum established by her mentor and guardian, Dr Philippe Curtius. Having lived for nine years at the Palace of Versailles, where she modelled Louis XVI and Marie Antoinette, Marie survived the revolution by manufacturing death masks of victims of the guillotine. By the time of her marriage in 1795 to François Tussaud, a civil engineer, she had inherited Curtius's museum, with which she left France for England in 1802, spending the next thirty years touring Britain with her ever-expanding collection. In 1835 Madame Tussaud's museum settled at the Bazaar, Baker Street, where it soon grew into one of London's most popular attractions; it remained in this location until 1884, when it moved to Marylebone Road. Tussaud herself led an itinerant life. Her case for a blue plaque was first raised in 1902, but nothing was done due to the demolition of what was then her only known London residence – 58 (later 59) Baker Street, where Tussaud lived from *c*. 1840 until her death. By 1966, evidence of her occupation of what was then 12 Wellington Road had come to light, but the GLC was not convinced that her brief residence justified a plaque. English Heritage came to a different conclusion, commemorating Tussaud at number 24 in 2001; since then the house has been greatly rebuilt.

On a gatepier at 31 Grove End Road, NW8, a plaque commemorates the conductor and impresario **Sir Thomas Beecham, CH** (1879–1961) **13** (fig. 436). Born in St Helen's, Lancashire – where his grandfather, also Thomas Beecham, set up his pill manufactory in the 1860s – Beecham made his debut as a conductor at the age of twenty. During his long and successful career,

Greater London Council

MEMORANDUM

To 31 Grove End Road NW 8 room

from room

tel. date

436 A sketch of 1983 showing the position initially proposed for the plaque to Sir Thomas Beecham at 31 Grove End Road. In the end, the plaque was installed on a gatepier, a position favoured by the building's owners. [Reproduced by permission of English Heritage]

he trained and conducted three new orchestras, the Beecham Symphony Orchestra (founded 1909) and the London Philharmonic (1932) and Royal Philharmonic (1946) orchestras. Knighted in 1916, he produced some 120 operas, sixty of them new to the country, and was England's leading champion of the works of Richard Strauss and FREDERICK DELIUS. Beecham led something of a nomadic life, residing in at least five London properties, most in the Regent's Park and St John's Wood areas. The original choice for commemoration was 39 Circus Road, NW8, his home in 1946–48, but consent for a plaque was refused by the building's owners. Shirley, Lady Beecham – Sir Thomas's widow – suggested as an alternative 31 Grove End Road, his home from 1950 to 1954. The house, a handsome villa of about the 1820s, had six rooms, plus servants' quarters, and was filled with the Beechams' fine furnishings; Sir Thomas lived here with his second wife, the pianist Betty Humby (1908–1958), who 'did what she could to cram a quart into a pint pot'.[10] During his time at number 31, Beecham made a number of gramophone records at the nearby Abbey Road Studios; it was these studios which served as the venue in 1985 for the unveiling celebrations, hosted by Lady Beecham.

Almost opposite, a GLC plaque on the boundary wall of 44 (formerly 17) Grove End Road commemorates **Sir Lawrence Alma-Tadema, OM** (1836–1912) **14** , one of the most famous painters of his time (figs 437 and 438). Dutch by birth, Alma-Tadema trained as an artist in Antwerp and established his reputation on the Continent. His fascination with Roman history was fostered by his first trip to Italy in 1863; thenceforth, he made his name as a painter of scenes from classical antiquity. Alma-Tadema moved to London in 1870, and soon afterwards established his home at Townshend House in Regent's Park with his wife and former pupil, Laura, née Epps (1852–1909). In November 1886 the couple took up residence at what was then 17 Grove End Road, purchased from the French painter Jean-Jacques Tissot (1836–1902). Rebuilt 'practically . . . from its foundations' to Alma-Tadema's own designs, the house – entered by a covered entrance (now number 44A) – was transformed into a sumptuous temple of the arts and a home to the painter's collection of antique and exotic furnishings.[11] It was, for a time, the most talked-about house in London, and was described in 1899 as

437 The extraordinary interior of Sir Lawrence Alma-Tadema's studio at 44 Grove End Road. This photograph, with others, appeared in the Christmas supplement of the *Art Journal* in 1910.

438 Alma-Tadema's *The Roses of Heliogabalus* (1888), one of the many paintings he completed during his time at 44 Grove End Road. [© Christie's Images / CORBIS]

of Wales and Tchaikovsky. Alma-Tadema strove to make his residence 'so picturesque and decorated in such diverse styles and feeling that, even if at any time I should not be inclined to work, my eyes must of necessity, in passing from one room to another, fall upon some object exciting enough, in colour or form, as to make me wish to paint'.[13] A visitor commented, 'His house is a glimpse of his work; it is his soul seen from the interior. Whoever understands his house learns to cherish his art'.[14] Number 44, his home until his death at a German spa, incorporated studios both for Alma-Tadema and for Laura, a painter in her own right. That used by Sir Lawrence was an enormous galleried room featuring a semi-dome lined with aluminium, providing the effect of silvery light so central to his oeuvre. Here, Alma-Tadema completed a prodigious number of paintings, among them *The Roses of Heliogabalus* (1888), *Spring* (1894), *Coign of Vantage* (1895) and *The Baths of Caracalla* (1899).

'a home which more than any other in London illustrates the artistic beauty of domiciles such as Horace and Cicero knew'.[12] The 'at homes' held on Monday afternoons, and the Tuesday dinners and concerts, were crowded with persons of distinction, such as the Prince

Number 16 (formerly 9) Langford Place, NW8, a substantial house of *c.* 1890, is notable for its association with the painters **Dame Laura Knight** (1877–1970) and **Harold Knight** (1874–1961) (fig. 439). Both Laura, née Johnson, and Harold hailed from Nottinghamshire; they met at Nottingham School of Art in 1890, though it was only in 1903 that they were married. After a period at Newlyn in Cornwall, the Knights moved to London and in 1922 took a long lease of what was then 9 Langford Place, where each had a studio. Sixteen years later, Harold purchased the freehold of number 16 (which had been renumbered in 1930), together with the adjoining numbers 12 and 14, all of which had previously been associated with the sculptor John Adams-Adam (1830–1910). By this time, both were highly successful artists: Harold was known for his portraits, while Laura – appointed DBE in 1929 – made her name with her paintings of ballet and circus life, such as *Charivari* or *The Grand Parade* (1928). In 1936 she became the first woman to be elected a full Royal Academician – the honour was extended to Harold a year later – and in 1946 was commissioned to produce a pictorial record of the war criminals' trials at Nuremberg. Following Harold's death in Colwall, Herefordshire – used as a country retreat by the Knights since before the Second World War – Laura continued to live in Langford Place; she died here in 1970 at the age of ninety-two. When the plaque was

439 Laura Knight's *Spring in St John's Wood* (1933), depicting the view from a front window of 16 Langford Place. [© Reproduced with permission of the Estate of Dame Laura Knight DBE RA 2009. All Rights Reserved. Courtesy of The Bridgeman Art Library]

erected by the GLC in 1983, number 16 was the home of the clarinettist Gervase de Peyer (b. 1926).

The biologist **Thomas Henry Huxley** (1825–1895) 16 has a wreathed blue plaque of 1910 at 38 (formerly 4) Marlborough Place, NW8 (fig. 440). Although Huxley was not then strictly eligible for consideration,

the LCC felt that his fame was 'likely to be enduring'.[15] The council even felt that a second plaque was justified: 88 (formerly 58) Paradise Street, Rotherhithe, where Huxley worked for a brief period as a medical assistant in 1841, was commemorated in 1912, but was demolished in 1931. An immensely influential figure, Huxley was the first great populariser of science. He

championed the importance of scientific education among a wide variety of the public and did much to promote CHARLES DARWIN's theory of evolution, becoming known as 'Darwin's bulldog'. An early resident of St John's Wood, he lived in the area from the time of his marriage to Henrietta ('Nettie') Heathorn (1825–1914) in 1855. In December 1872 he moved with his wife and children to what was then 4 Marlborough Place, a house altered for the Huxleys by the architect James Knowles. The family remained for the next eighteen years in this early nineteenth-century villa, which was the focus of an active social life; visitors included MATTHEW ARNOLD, HENRY JAMES and Darwin, a great friend of Huxley. According to his son LEONARD HUXLEY, the house 'was built for comfort, not beauty; designed, within stringent limits as to cost, to give each member of the family room to get away by himself or herself if so disposed'.[16] During his time here, Huxley was occupied mainly with official duties – he was, for example, President of the Royal Society in 1883–85 – though he continued to write and lecture until his retirement. He was connected in particular with the Science Schools at South Kensington – now part of Imperial College – where he and his laboratory were based from the early 1870s. In 1890, having suffered for some time from failing health, Huxley moved to Eastbourne; it was there that he died five years later.

At 13 Blenheim Road, NW8, a wreathed blue plaque of 1935 marks the house in which the singer **Sir Charles Santley** (1834–1922) **17** lived and died (fig. 441). Santley was described by GEORGE BERNARD SHAW as 'the best baritone singer with whom the London public is familiar', and was hailed in *The Times* as one of the 'brightest ornaments' of England's musical world.[17] Born in Liverpool and trained in Italy, he

made his debut in Pavia in 1857 and first appeared in an opera in London two years later; he found particular success as Valentine in CHARLES GOUNOD's *Faust* (1863). Santley remained active as an operatic performer until 1876, when he transferred his success to the concert stage, only retiring in 1911. In 1907, when Santley was celebrating his jubilee as a singer, he became the first of his profession to be knighted. At the time of the proposal for his commemoration in 1934, the customary twenty years from death had not yet elapsed, but the LCC felt sure that Santley's reputation was unlikely to 'diminish in the next eight years'; since then it must be admitted that his name has lost some lustre.[18] Santley lived at five houses in St John's Wood; his longest residence was at 5 Upper Hamilton Terrace, his home in 1872–92, but the LCC chose to commemorate 13 Blenheim Road, to which Santley moved from 62 Carlton Hill in about 1911 and where he died eleven years later. Since the installation of the plaque, number 13 has been substantially altered.

Number 6 Carlton Hill, NW8, was the home from 1895 to 1899 of the architect and designer **C. F. A. Voysey** (1857–1941) **18**, who was commemorated with an English Heritage plaque in 1995. Charles

442   C. F. A. Voysey's design of 1898 for Broadleys, Windermere, Cumbria, commissioned by Arthur Currer Briggs. It was one of a number of works executed during the architect's time at 6 Carlton Hill. [© RIBA Library Drawings Collection]

Francis Annesley Voysey was born near Hull and became a pupil of the architect J. P. Seddon in 1874, later joining the office of George Devey. He set up his own practice in 1881, but was initially better known for his distinctive wallpaper and textile designs; these – inspired by the work of figures such as A. H. Mackmurdo – were part of a larger oeuvre which included the design of furniture, carpets, ceramics and metalwork. Voysey received his first architectural commission in 1888, for The Cottage, Bishop's Itchington, Warwickshire. Between 1890 and 1914 he enjoyed a flourishing career as an architect in the Arts and Crafts style, principally designing country and suburban houses. Voysey's characteristic and highly influential buildings, with their steeply pitched roofs, domestic massing and emphasis on horizontal lines, include New Place, Haslemere, Surrey (1897), and Broadleys (1898–1900) (fig. 442) and Moorcrag (1899–1900), Windermere, Cumbria. These houses and their fittings were all designed in his studio at 6 Carlton Hill, to which Voysey had moved from nearby 11 Melina Place, a house ruled out for commemoration on account of its modern alterations. In 1899 he and his wife Mary Maria, née Evans (b. 1864) left St John's Wood for a house of his own design, The Orchard, Chorleywood, Hertfordshire, where they remained until 1906. For the last twenty-four years of his life, Voysey lived in a block of chambers at 73 St James's Street, off Piccadilly, SW1.

Clifton Hill, NW8, has a well-preserved sequence of villas and terraced houses, three of them bearing blue plaques. Number 42, the former home of the psycho-analyst and pioneer of child analysis **Melanie Klein** (1882–1960) ⑲ , was commemorated by the GLC. Born to Jewish parents in Vienna, Melanie – whose surname was Reizes before she married Arthur Klein at the age of twenty-one – became interested in psychology on reading Sigmund Freud's *On Dreams* in about 1914. By 1919, she had begun the work for which she would become best known – analysis of children; the first psychoanalyst to work in this area, she published her first paper – 'The Development of a Child' – in 1921. In that year, Klein moved to Berlin and, in summer 1925, came to London to give a series of papers on her work. Invited back by Ernest Jones, she settled permanently in the capital in 1926, and became a British citizen in 1934. Klein quickly established herself as a leading light of the British Psycho-Analytical Society, and her theories and approach, especially her play technique, attracted widespread attention; her most important publication, *The Psychoanalysis of Children*, appeared in 1932. Three years later, Klein moved to 42 Clifton Hill, a semi-detached house of *c.* 1840. Interestingly, the address was not far from Maresfield Gardens, West Hampstead, the home from 1938 of Anna Freud, Klein's professional rival; so strong was the split between the two women and their respective camps that it had a permanent impact on British psychoanalysis. Klein turned to another Freud, Sigmund's son Ernst, to rework number 42's interior; the result of this, his first commission in England, was 'rather Bauhaus, very attractive in its way, but some people felt it unsuitable for a Regency house'.[19] At the unveiling of the plaque in 1985, the house was described by Dr Hanna Segal, Chairman of the Melanie Klein Trust, as 'a cradle of new generations of analysts and new ideas'; it was apparently 'the home she was most attached to'.[20] Klein's visitors here included Virginia Woolf, who described her host as a 'bluff grey haired lady, with large bright imaginative eyes', though she noted an underlying 'subtlety' in her character.[21] Number 42 remained Klein's residence until 1953, when – aged seventy-one – she moved to her last home, a first-floor flat at 20 Bracknell Gardens, Hampstead, NW3.

On the left gatepost of the entrance to Clifton Hill Studios, 95A Clifton Hill – a building of 1881, set back from the road – an English Heritage plaque of 2001 commemorates the sculptor **Sir William Reid Dick** (1878–1961) ⑳ (fig. 443). He worked here from about

ST JOHN'S WOOD, MAIDA VA., LISSON GRO.

ENGLISH HERITAGE
SIR
WILLIAM
REID DICK
1878-1961
Sculptor
worked here in
Studio 3
1910-1914

1908 until shortly before his marriage to Catherine Treadwell in 1914, initially in Studio 6 and, after 1910, in Studio 3. Born in Glasgow – where he learned his trade as apprentice to a firm of stonemasons – Reid Dick moved to London in 1907 and exhibited at the Royal Academy from the following year. He made his reputation as an exponent of the twentieth-century classical school of sculpture with a number of memorials, including those to Field Marshal LORD KITCHENER (1922–25) in St Paul's Cathedral and President Roosevelt (1948) in Grosvenor Square; he was also noted for his architectural sculpture, including that for Unilever House, Blackfriars (1932), and for his portraits. Reid Dick served as President of the Royal Society of British Sculptors between 1933 and 1938; in the latter year, King George VI appointed him Sculptor-in-Ordinary for Scotland, a position he held until his death. The case for a plaque to Reid Dick was strengthened by a connection of almost sixty years with the St John's Wood area. His most notable residence was 16 Maida Vale, the former home of the sculptor Sir Alfred Gilbert, where Reid Dick lived from 1937 until his death. As this building had been demol-

ished in 1966, the favourite for commemoration was 31 Grove End Road, Reid Dick's home in 1921–37. However, the owners of the property wished to limit themselves to the one plaque that had already been erected to SIR THOMAS BEECHAM. Attention consequently turned towards Clifton Hill Studios, in which the sculptor worked at the beginning of his career. His period here saw the completion of works including a portrait of the music-hall artiste HARRY LAUDER (1911) and a group piece, *Femina Victrix* (1913). Reid Dick's enthusiasm for the commemoration of greatness later surfaced in an interest in blue plaques, and he was invited to write the introduction to a guide to the scheme published in 1953 (see p. 1).

Number 114 Clifton Hill was the home of the painter **W. P. Frith** (1819–1909) **21** . Born in Yorkshire, William Powell Frith entered the Royal Academy Schools in 1837 and quickly established himself as an artist of the historical and literary genre; in 1842 he was commissioned by DICKENS – a lifelong friend – to paint characters from his novels. He is best known, however, for his panoramas of scenes from modern life. The first painting of this type, *Life at the Seaside* or *Ramsgate Sands* (1854), was purchased by Queen Victoria; it was followed by *Derby Day* (1856–58) – of which it has been said that 'Few paintings have ever earned such universal acclaim' – and *The Railway Station* (1860–62).[22] These, and Frith's other most notable works, were painted at 7 (formerly 10) Pembridge Villas, Bayswater, where Frith lived for over thirty years (1854–88) but which had been demolished by 1968, when the GLC first considered his case for commemoration. Frith's second-longest residence was at 114 Clifton Hill; he moved into this mid-nineteenth-century property in 1896, following the death of his second wife, and died here at the age of ninety. The plaque was erected in 1973.

An English Heritage plaque of 2004 at 31 Marlborough Hill, NW8, put up at the suggestion of a London cab driver, commemorates the residence of the forensic pathologist **Sir Bernard Spilsbury** (1877–1947) **22** . Born in Warwickshire, Spilsbury studied medicine at St Mary's Hospital, Paddington, and subsequently worked there under the pathologist A. J. Pepper. He first came to widespread notice for his clear, confident and persuasive evidence at the murder trial of Dr

444 A selection of Sir Bernard Spilsbury's case cards. Many of these were written up in the ground-floor study of his home at 31 Marlborough Hill. [© Topfoto]

Crippen in 1910, testimony which found favour with Sir Edward Henry, Commissioner of the Metropolitan Police. Appointed Honorary Pathologist to the Home Office soon afterwards, Spilsbury had a hand in the conviction of nearly all of the early twentieth century's most notorious murderers – figures including the poisoner Frederick Henry Seddon and the 'Brides in the Bath' murderer, G. J. Smith. During his long career, Spilsbury gave evidence at countless trials – the public flocked to see him in action – and carried out more than 25,000 post-mortems; it was perhaps fortunate that he lost his sense of smell after the 1920s. By the 1930s Sir Bernard had reached the peak of his career, established as the founding father of forensic pathology and – for many – the epitome of the 'scientist-detective'. He moved to Marlborough Hill with his wife Edith, née Horton (b. 1878/9) and their growing family in 1912; they remained here until 1940, when the bombing of London forced their departure. A back room on the top floor was equipped as Sir Bernard's laboratory, while on the ground floor was his study, where he wrote up what eventually resulted in a total of six thousand case cards (fig. 444). The last years of Spilsbury's life were beset by tragedy and sadness: while living at the Langdorf Hotel, 20 Frognal, West Hampstead, NW3 – his home from c. 1940 – he suffered the death of both of his sons and, depressed and unwell, took his own life in his laboratory at University College London.

At 3–21 Finchley Road, NW8 – built from 1827 as a major access route onto the Great North Road – a block of flats, Eyre Court, bears a plaque of 1986, the first erected by English Heritage. Placed on the section of the block which projects at the north, close to the junction with Finchley Place, it commemorates the painter **Oskar Kokoschka** (1886–1980) 23 , who lived here in Flat 120. Born in Austria to a Czech father, Kokoschka studied art in Vienna and soon established himself as a painter of portraits. During the second decade of the twentieth century, he became a leader of the Expressionist movement in Germany and in 1919–23 served as Professor of Painting at the Kunstakademie, Dresden. The 1920s were dedicated largely to travel, during which Kokoschka produced landscapes and townscapes including *Large Thames View I* (1926). In 1934 he left Vienna for Prague, and four years later came to London to escape the Nazi invasion of Czechoslovakia; he became a British citizen in 1947. Despite his early success on the Continent, Kokoschka achieved prominence in Britain mainly in the post-war period, with works such as the two triptychs *The Prometheus Saga* (1950) and *Thermopylae* (1954). The artist is especially renowned for the series of London panoramas that ended with the completion in 1970 of *London View with St Paul's Cathedral*. Kokoschka moved to 120 Eyre Court – part of a block built in 1930 to designs by T. P. Bennett & Son – with his wife Olda, née Palkovská (b. 1915) in the winter of 1946/7. The flat had recently been vacated by Olda's parents, who had lived in London since 1940; Kokoschka had spent four months here in 1940–41. It remained Oskar and Olda's home until 1953, when the couple moved to a house of their own design overlooking Lake Geneva, Switzerland; number 120 was retained as their London base until at least 1980.

A little further north along Finchley Road (formerly Finchley New Road), at number 28, there are not one but two plaques to the London-born poet **Thomas Hood** (1799–1845) 24 (see also pp. 376–7), an early resident of the area. Hood's career in journalism began in 1821, when he was appointed sub-editor of the *London Magazine*. A friend of Hazlitt, Dickens and Lamb, he quickly became known for his serious and,

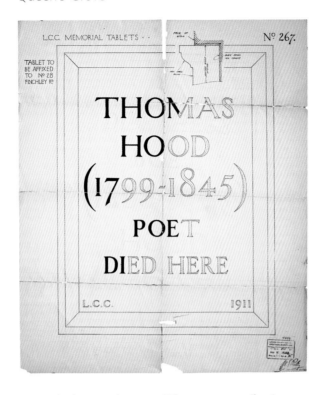

445 The design for the LCC plaque to Thomas Hood, made of Hopton Wood stone and erected at 28 Finchley Road in 1912. The plaque, at first-floor level, had become illegible by 1960 and in 2001 was supplemented with an English Heritage blue roundel, placed on the storey below. [Reproduced by permission of English Heritage]

in particular, comic verse. His many contributions to journals such as *Punch* were brought together in collections including *Whimsicalities* (1844). Hood was often in debt, and – in order to economise – spent five years on the Continent. In winter 1841, soon after his return, he moved to 17 Elm Tree Road, close to Lord's cricket ground, calling himself 'Hood of the Wood'; there, he wrote the popular poem 'The Song of the Shirt' (1843), highlighting the plight of underpaid seamstresses. A plaque was erected at number 17 by the LCC in 1908, but the house was demolished in 1936. In January 1844, in increasing financial straits and declining health, Hood moved with his wife Jane (1791–1846) – sister of the writer John Hamilton Reynolds – and their two children to the recently built 28 Finchley New Road, which he named Devonshire Lodge, 'in remembrance of the exceeding generosity and kindness, which . . . he received from the late Duke of Devonshire'.[23] In a letter to Dickens, Hood described the house as being located 'just two or three doors short of the turnpike beyond the Eyre Arms'.[24] While here, he launched *Hood's Magazine*, but publication ceased

abruptly on his death at Devonshire Lodge in May 1845. It was in 1912 that a plaque was first erected at number 28, which was occupied between 1900 and 1961 by the St John's Wood Arts Club. The club expressed a preference for a 'circular blue medallion' – opining that 'a little colour would look better and also be seen better' – but the LCC opted instead for one of its rectangular tablets of Hopton Wood stone (fig. 445).[25] This had become eroded and illegible by 1960. In 2001 English Heritage decided to affix a standard blue plaque to the ground floor of the building, leaving the LCC's stone tablet *in situ* between the windows of the storey above.

Queen's Grove, NW8, features a number of handsome detached villas of *c.* 1830–40. One of these, number 32, bears a plaque to the sculptor **George Frampton** (1860–1928) **25** . The son of a stonemason, Frampton studied in London and Paris, and enjoyed early success with works such as *An Act of Mercy* (1887) and *Mysteriarch* (1892). He is known above all for his statue *Peter Pan* (1912) in Kensington Gardens, but produced a large body of public sculpture and also carried out architectural decoration at buildings including the Victoria and Albert Museum (1909); he was knighted in 1908. Frampton was proposed for commemoration by the sculptor Arthur Fleischmann, who lived in the original studio of 90 (now 92–96) Carlton Hill, NW8, Frampton's home from 1909 until his death. The GLC was eager to commemorate this house, which was rebuilt for Frampton and included the studio in which he completed *Peter Pan*. However, the building was found to be set back from the road and obscured by trees. A suitable alternative was 32 Queen's Grove, where Frampton lived and worked from 1894 to 1908. Here, in a studio and workshop built to the rear of the property, he executed some of his most important work, including the statues of the philanthropists Dame Alice Owen (1897) and QUINTIN HOGG (1906). Frampton lived at number 32 with his wife, the painter Christabel Cockerell (1863–1951), and their son Meredith (1894–1984), who also became an artist.

NOTES

1. Richard Tames, *St John's Wood and Maida Vale Past* (London, 1998), p. 5 (quoting Alan Montgomery Eyre)
2. *The Autobiography and Journals of Benjamin Robert Haydon*, ed. Malcolm Elwin (London, 1950), p. 308
3. Ibid, pp. 316–17
4. Ibid, p. 308
5. Ibid, p. 383
6. Daphne Bennett, *Emily Davies and the Liberation of Women 1830–1921* (London, 1990), p. 30
7. D. V. Tahmankar, *Lokamanya Tilak: Father of Indian Unrest and Maker of Modern India* (London, 1956), p. 287
8. *The Times*, 3 December 1973, p. 17
9. Stephen Halliday, 'The Great Stink of London – Sir Joseph Bazalgette and the Cleansing of the Victorian Metropolis', *Journal of The London Society*, Spring 2002, p. 13
10. Charles Reid, *Thomas Beecham: An Independent Biography* (London, 1961), p. 227
11. *Strand Magazine*, vol. XVIII (December 1899), p. 612
12. Ibid, p. 604
13. Luigi Arditi, *My Reminiscences*, ed. Baroness von Zedlitz (London, 1896), p. 498
14. Vern G. Swanson, *Sir Lawrence Alma-Tadema: The Painter of the Victorian Vision of the Ancient World* (London, 1977), p. 27
15. Report of 10 November 1909 on blue plaque file.
16. Leonard Huxley, *Life and Letters of Thomas Henry Huxley*, vol. I (London, 1900), p. 383
17. *ODNB*, vol. XLVIII, p. 955; *The Times*, 23 September 1922, p. 10
18. Report of October 1934 on blue plaque file.
19. Phyllis Gross-Kurth, *Melanie Klein: Her World and her Work* (London, Sydney, Auckland, Toronto, 1986), p. 200
20. Transcription of the speech made by Dr Segal, on blue plaque file.
21. Gross-Kurth, *Melanie Klein*, p. 237
22. *ODNB*, vol. XXI, p. 46
23. F. F. Broderip, *Memorials of Thomas Hood. Collected, Arranged, and Edited by his Daughter*, vol. II (London, 1860), p. 194 note
24. *The Letters of Thomas Hood*, ed. Peter F. Morgan (Edinburgh, 1973), p. 586 (January 1844)
25. Undated latter (of *c.* December 1911) on blue plaque file.

446 A detail of the imposing façade of 41–43 Wardour Street, built for the theatrical wigmaker Willy Clarkson in 1904–5. [© English Heritage. Photograph by Derek Kendall]

SOHO AND LEICESTER SQUARE

This area – at the heart of the West End – has, perhaps more than any other in London, experienced a radical transition in character from residential to commercial. Developed in the late seventeenth and early eighteenth centuries, Soho and Leicester Square were desirable places to live for the titled and successful; residents, beyond those set out in this chapter, included Sir Isaac Newton and William Hogarth, both of whose houses – formerly marked with Society of Arts plaques – have since been demolished. However, by the mid-1700s residents had begun to move to grander houses elsewhere – in recently developed Mayfair, for instance, just to the west of Regent Street. In Soho, a new wave of residents arrived – artists, craftsmen, tradesmen and immigrants from the Continent, especially French Huguenots, who started settling here from as early as the 1680s. By the middle of the nineteenth century, the area was notorious as one of the most overcrowded and densely populated in the capital, with its once neat terraces turned into slum tenements. The nineteenth and twentieth centuries brought further change. Leicester Square – invaded by theatres, shops, restaurants, cinemas and hotels – gained its reputation as London's centre of entertainment. Soho – which is here taken to extend into the part of the City of Westminster that falls north of Oxford Street – saw programmes of mass demolition, and the development of the commercial premises that dominate the streetscape today.

PALL MALL TO
SHAFTESBURY AVENUE

447 *The Fairy Feller's Master-Stroke* (1855–64), one of the paintings for which Richard Dadd is best known. [© Tate, London 2008]

The terrace comprising 12–17 Suffolk Street, SW1, was designed by Lewis Wyatt in about 1823, and forms part of John Nash's Regent Street development. At number 15 – part of the block closing the north end of the street – a plaque commemorates the painter **Richard Dadd** (1817–1886) ❶ , who lived here with his family from 1833 until about 1839. The house was used as a base for the gilding and ormolu manufacturing business run by his father, Robert (1788/9–1843). Dadd entered the Royal Academy Schools in 1837, and was soon exhibiting paintings a few doors down from his home, at 6¹/₂ Suffolk Street, the galleries of the Society of British Artists. He established his reputation as a fairy painter with two scenes from *A Midsummer Night's Dream*: *Titania Sleeping* and *Puck* (both 1841). Soon after, however, Dadd began to suffer from mental delusions, and in 1843 achieved notoriety by murdering his father in Cobham, Kent. Dadd escaped to France, but was arrested and returned to England, where he was certified insane. He was confined, firstly in Bethlem Hospital, Southwark, and later in Broadmoor, Berkshire, though his artistic output remained undiminished; during this period of over forty years, Dadd produced works including *Contradiction: Oberon and Titania* (1854–58) and *The Fairy Feller's Master-Stroke* (1855–64) (fig. 447), both notable for their rich and painstaking level of detail. Dadd's work was largely unknown until an exhibition was held at the Tate Gallery in 1974, the year in which he was proposed for commemoration. Three years later, a GLC plaque was erected at 16 Suffolk Street; this was subsequently found to be the wrong house – the wholesale mid-twentieth-century rebuilding of 15–17 Suffolk Street, in a neo-Regency style, had caused confusion – and the plaque was moved to neighbouring number 15 in 1980.

The statesman **Richard Cobden** (1804–1865) ❷ spent the last weeks of his life at 23 Suffolk Street, a house on the street's west side (fig. 448). Cobden was born in Sussex, and began his career as a man of business. While living in Manchester, he published his first work, *England, Ireland and America* (1835), and became involved in the campaign to repeal the Corn Laws; from 1841, with his friend John Bright, Cobden led the Anti-Corn Law League, founded in Manchester two years earlier. In the same year, he entered Parliament as a Liberal MP; he played a major part in the repeal of the Corn Laws in 1846, and campaigned tirelessly for retrenchment, non-intervention, and educational and colonial reform. Among his achievements was the Cobden-Chevalier trade treaty of 1860 between England and France. In November 1864, after addressing a Rochdale constituency meeting, Cobden's health

SOHO AND LEICESTER SQUARE

cared for by his wife Kate, née Williams (1815–1877) at his lodgings; however, his condition soon worsened and he died here on 2 April. The following year, the Cobden Club was founded in his honour, its motto being 'Peace, free trade and goodwill among nations', and in 1905 the LCC commemorated him with one of its wreathed blue plaques, set high up on the façade of number 23.

Number 27 Whitcomb Street, WC2, just beside the National Gallery's Sainsbury Wing, was the last home of the Glasgow-born archaeologist **Sir Mortimer Wheeler** (1890–1976) ❸ . Wheeler was instrumental in establishing archaeology as a popular subject, and in the 1950s became well known as a television and radio personality. He first took up archaeology in 1913 and, seven years later, became Keeper of Archaeology at the National Museum of Wales; he was promoted to Director in 1924. Along with his wife Tessa, née Verney, who died in 1936, Wheeler excavated sites including Caerleon, Gwent (1926), Verulamium, St Alban's, Hertfordshire (1930–34), and Maiden Castle, Dorset (1934–37); inspired by the work of PITT-RIVERS, he set new standards for excavation and recording. Returning to the capital as Keeper of the London Museum from 1926, Wheeler established, with Tessa, the Institute of Archaeology, which opened in 1937. Subsequently, he became Director-General of the Archaeological Survey of India (1944–48) and Secretary of the British Academy (1949–68). Number 27 Whitcomb Street was chosen for Wheeler in 1958 by his devoted secretary, Molly Myers – it was said to have been a brothel previously. Myers organised the move while Wheeler was excavating in Charsada, Pakistan. He lived here for nearly twenty years – from 1958 until shortly before his death – during which time he wrote his memoirs, *Alms for Oblivion* (1966), and *My Archaeological Mission to India and Pakistan* (1976). Wheeler's flat – on the upper floors – was furnished with his oriental rugs and Persian plates, and yellow curtains from Liberty's. He became 'a familiar figure in and about Piccadilly as he walked between his little house, the Academy, or Antiquaries and the Athenaeum'.[1] In his final years, Wheeler was looked after by Myers, and died at her house in Leatherhead, Surrey. The plaque was unveiled in 1993 by Barry Cunliffe, then President of the Society of Antiquaries, an office Wheeler held in 1954–59.

448   The wreathed LCC blue plaque to Richard Cobden, high up on the façade of 23 Suffolk Street. The house forms the return to the north side of Suffolk Place and was built in 1822–23 as part of John Nash's development. [© English Heritage. Photograph by Derek Kendall]

deteriorated, and he was confined to his home in Dunford, Sussex, to which he had moved permanently in 1853. The following spring, on 21 March 1865, he travelled to London to attend the House of Commons and, rather than staying with friends, he took lodgings at number 23, which was conveniently situated near to Parliament and his club, the Athenaeum. On arriving in London, Cobden had an asthmatic attack and was

CRIBB'S PARLOUR. *Tom introducing Jerry and Logic to the Champion of England*

Pub.d by Sherwood Neely & Jones, Jan, 1 1821.

449   The interior of the Union Arms public house (now the Tom Cribb), Panton Street. Known as 'Cribb's Parlour', it is shown here in a view by George Cruikshank from Pierce Egan's *Life in London: The Adventures of Tom and Jerry* (1821). Tom of the book's title introduces 'Jerry' and 'Logic' to the boxing champion of England. [© Mary Evans Picture Library]

450   A postcard showing Sir Joshua Reynolds's former home and studio at 47 Leicester Square. It was first marked with a plaque by the Society of Arts in 1869, but this was removed when the house was demolished in 1937. Its site was commemorated by the LCC in 1947. [Reproduced by permission of English Heritage. NMR]

At 36 (formerly 26) Panton Street, SW1, on the corner of Oxendon Street, is a public house formerly known as the Union Arms and now named after **Tom Cribb** (1781–1848) **4** , the bare-knuckle boxing champion. Cribb, who entered his first public fight in Wood Green in 1805, was champion from 1809 until 1822, and is remembered particularly as the master of 'milling on the retreat', the technique of attacking and then stepping away. Under the rigorous training of Captain Robert Barclay, his skill was quickly honed, and he won a dramatic fight against the Bristol-born boxer Jem Belcher in 1809. Cribb's most famous fight was with the black American champion Tom Molineaux in 1811 at Thistleton Gap, Leicestershire; it was watched by around 20,000 people, and the victorious Cribb was received back in London as a public hero. Soon afterwards, Cribb underwent the then typical metamorphosis from pugilist to publican: having run public houses in Southwark and St James's, he managed the Union Arms in Panton Street – which became known as 'Cribb's Parlour' – from about 1819 to 1839 (fig. 449). Referred to in works such as *Vanity Fair* (1847–48) by THACKERAY and *Rodney Stone* (1896) by CONAN DOYLE, it was a popular meeting place for both the aristocracy and for prizefighters, reflecting the importance of the Leicester Square area to the boxing profession in the early nineteenth century. It was while he was here that Cribb retired from boxing in 1821 and

received the champion's belt, which he was allowed to keep for the rest of his life. His last years were marred by financial and domestic problems, and gambling debts forced him to give up the pub to his creditors. In 1846 he moved to the house of his son at 111 Woolwich High Street, SE18, where he died two years later. Cribb's plaque was erected in Panton Street in 2005.

Leicester Square, WC2, was laid out – under the name of Leicester Fields – in 1670 by Robert Sidney, 2nd Earl of Leicester (fig. 451); it was placed to the south of the Earl's residence, Leicester House, built in 1631–35 and demolished in about 1791. The square was lined with spacious houses, number 47 being the home for thirty-two years of the portrait painter **Sir Joshua Reynolds** (1723–1792) **5** (fig. 450). Its site is now occupied by 43–50 Leicester Square, an office block of the 1930s. Born in Devon, Reynolds made his first recorded portrait at the age of twelve, and had an established business by 1744, four years after his move to London. He had settled in the area of Leicester Square by 1747, and

Here (47, Leicester Sq., London) lived Sir Joshua Reynolds, Painter, from 1761 to 1792.

451   Leicester Square from the south, in a hand-coloured engraving of 1753. The home of Sir Joshua Reynolds was at number 47, on the square's west (left) side. [© Museum of London]

in summer 1760 moved to number 47, a late seventeenth-century house on the square's west side. He immediately set about modernising it, building an extension to accommodate a series of studios and a picture gallery; his painting room was octagonal in shape and lit by a single window, positioned high up in the wall. It was during his time here that Reynolds enjoyed his greatest success, and established himself as the leading portrait painter of the day. His celebrated sitters included his friends EDMUND BURKE, Oliver Goldsmith and DAVID GARRICK. Appointed first President of the Royal Academy in 1768 – a position he held until his death – Reynolds was knighted in 1769 and in 1784 became Principal Painter in Ordinary to King George III. Number 47 was the centre of Reynolds's active social life: regular visitors included DR JOHNSON, with whom he founded the Literary Club here in February 1764; the club continued to meet, mostly at the nearby Turk's Head in Gerrard

Street, until 1784. Reynolds employed a series of pupils and was looked after by a housekeeper, a role fulfilled first by his sister Fanny (1729–1807) and, from the late 1770s, by his niece, Mary Palmer, both of whom were talented artists. A descendant recalled that, 'Everybody in the house painted . . . the coachman and the man servant Ralph and his daughter, all painted, copied and talked about pictures'.[2] In 1789, when his eyesight began to fail, Reynolds retired from painting, and he died at number 47 three years later. The first plaque to Reynolds was one of the earliest erected by the Society of Arts; it was set up at 47 Leicester Square in 1869, but was removed when the artist's house was demolished in 1937 to make way for Fanum House, designed by Andrew Mather as the headquarters of the Automobile Association. In 1947 one of the LCC's new experimental brown plaques was put up, but this was taken down ten years later when the building was extended. It was re-erected at first-floor level by the LCC in 1960; a

452 Number 41–43 Wardour Street during the time of Willy Clarkson, who lived and worked here from 1905 until his death nearly thirty years later. [Reproduced by permission of English Heritage. NMR]

453 The Society of Arts plaque to Edmund Burke, installed in 1876 at 37 Gerrard Street, seen here in the modern context of Chinatown. [© English Heritage. Photograph by Derek Kendall]

duplicate, metal plaque was placed in a more visible location at street level by the AA in 1965.

The magnificent building at 41–43 Wardour Street, W1 – to the south of the intersection with Shaftesbury Avenue – was where the theatrical wigmaker **Willy Clarkson** (1861–1934) ❻ lived and worked from 1905 until his death (fig. 452 and see fig. 446). The premises were designed for Clarkson's expanding business by H. M. Wakley; bronze plaques were erected on either side of the entrance to record the laying of the foundation stone by Sarah Bernhardt in 1904 and the coping stone by Sir Henry Irving in 1905. Clarkson's origins are obscure, but he seems to have been born in London, the son of a perruquier – possibly of Jewish ancestry – and inherited his father's business at the age of twelve. Clarkson recalled that he 'never 'ad any toys like an ordinary kid. Father used to give me a wig to play with'.[3] For over fifty years, the announcement 'Wigs by Clarkson' appeared on theatre programmes everywhere; at the height of his success, Willy was hiring out 10,000 wigs each Christmas. He also made his name as a theatrical costumier, a development which came after he was granted a royal appointment by Queen Victoria in 1888. It was to Clarkson's premises that the most famous actors of the day came for their costumes, while others hired clothes for the military tournaments and fancy-dress balls popular at the time. One of Clarkson's specialities was the provision of disguises: it was said that 'he may have – he was almost certain he had – disguised Jack the Ripper himself, besides the detectives and medical students who went to search for him'; another client was Dr Crippen.[4] Clarkson was one of the most colourful characters of his time. A small, thickset man, with curly hair and a beard, he spoke in an accent which 'was at once Cockney, Jewish and guttural French'; it has been said that he 'was hardly real, in the sense of ordinary, everyday humanity, but was something essentially of the theatre'.[5] His living quarters in Wardour Street were, by the time of his death, 'crammed with the junk of a make believe life time'.[6] The LCC plaque – set up high, at the centre of the façade – was erected in 1966, under the aegis of the GLC, at the suggestion of Clarkson's god-daughter, Mrs Diana Evans. The proposal was supported by many thespians who had known Clarkson, among them Sir Laurence Olivier and Dame Sybil Thorndike.

Gerrard Street, W1, laid out from 1677 and now in the heart of Chinatown, features two plaques put up by the Society of Arts in the scheme's earliest years. At that time, research facilities and procedures were not well established, and the identification of both buildings with the plaques' recipients has since been questioned. At number 37, a plaque commemorates the author and statesman **Edmund Burke** (1729–1797) ❼ , who lived here – or near here – between 1787 and 1790 (fig. 453). Dublin-born, Burke entered Parliament as a Whig MP in 1766, ten years after the publication of his first book, *A Vindication of Natural Society*. An outstanding orator, he is said to have been 'gentle, mild and amenable to argument in private society', but 'was often intemperate and even violent in Parliament'.[7] Burke was a part of the intellectual and gifted group of friends centered on The Club, formed by Dr Johnson and Joshua Reynolds, which from 1764 to 1783 met across the road at the Turk's Head, 9 Gerrard Street, a building of the 1750s that still stands. It was while living in Gerrard Street, with his wife Jane, née Nugent (1734–1812), that Burke's career reached a crisis point: his long friendship with fellow Whig Charles James Fox was increasingly under strain, and ended altogether in 1791, when Burke transferred his alle-

giance to the Tory PITT THE YOUNGER. In *Reflections on the Revolution in France* (1790), Burke condemned the French Revolution – which had been supported by Fox – and set out his belief in the values and virtues of the British constitution. The book provoked enormous controversy, and there were a number of responses, including Tom Paine's *Rights of Man* (1791). Burke died a few years later at his country estate of Gregories, Beaconsfield, Buckinghamshire, acquired in 1768. Number 37 forms part of a terrace built in 1737. By 1974 the house was in such poor condition that all but the ground floor was demolished. The chocolate-brown plaque, set in a white plaster mount, was erected in 1876, but was removed and re-erected when a new building – designed in a Georgian style – was constructed in 2002.

In 1870 a plaque was placed on 43 Gerrard Street to mark the home of the poet **John Dryden** (1631–1700) **8** ; it is unique among surviving Society of Arts plaques in its colour – white, with blue lettering – and, like the plaque to BURKE, is set in a plaster mount. Subsequent research found that Dryden actually lived – from about 1687 until his death – in a house on the site of neighbouring number 44, which he shared with his wife Elizabeth (*c.* 1638–1714), the sister of the politician Sir Robert Howard. Dryden was born in Northamptonshire, and settled in London in about 1660. Three years later, his first play, *The Wild Gallant*, was staged at the Theatre Royal, Drury Lane. For much of his career Dryden was best known for his dramatic works – these included satires such as *Marriage à-la-mode* (first performed 1671) and the tragedy *All for Love* (1678) – but he is now best remembered for his poetry and translations. Dryden's years in Gerrard Street were difficult: his conversion to Catholicism in *c.* 1685 meant that he was unable to take the oath of allegiance after the Glorious Revolution of 1688 and lost his position as Poet Laureate, one he had held for twenty years. He found himself in financial difficulties, but remained highly active in London's literary world. Dryden usually worked in the front ground-floor room of the house, and it was here that he completed his last play, *Love Triumphant* (1694), the poem *Alexander's Feast, or, The Power of Musique* (1697) and translations such as *The Works of Virgil* (1697); in its preface, Dryden likened himself to Virgil in his 'Declining Years, struggling with Wants, oppress'd with Sickness'.[8] Number 44

was built in about 1681 and re-fronted in 1793, before being redeveloped in about 1901. At the same time, number 43 was demolished, a deed described in the press as 'a hideous and wanton act of vandalism'.[9] The plaque, though damaged, was immediately re-erected on the new structure.

SOHO

The rear façade of the Lyric Theatre in Great Windmill Street, W1, is all that remains of the home and museum of the Scottish anatomist **Dr William Hunter** (1718–1783) **9** (fig. 454). William and his younger brother JOHN HUNTER were two of the greatest physicians and anatomical collectors of their time. Moving in 1740 to London, where he was assisted for some years by John, William quickly became known as a teacher of anatomy, with a popular school in Covent Garden and, later, in Jermyn Street; he was also an accomplished man-midwife, and in 1762 was appointed Physician-Extraordinary to Queen Charlotte, becoming Professor of Anatomy at the Royal Academy six years later. In 1767 he built a house at 16 Great Windmill Street; it was designed by the Scottish architect Robert Mylne, who was related to Hunter by marriage. The building incorporated a lecture theatre, dissecting room and library, and a museum containing a varied collection of anatomical specimens, coins, minerals, shells, corals, insects and paintings. The museum, at the rear of the

454   An undated watercolour showing the principal façade of Dr William Hunter's house in Great Windmill Street, built in 1767. It was greatly altered in 1888 as part of its incorporation into the Lyric Theatre, Shaftesbury Avenue. [© The Royal College of Surgeons of England]

property, was described in 1812 as 'a room admired for its proportions, of great size, with a handsome gallery running round'.[10] The first anatomical lecture was held in the house in October 1767, and Hunter took up residence the following year. His museum was open to the public, and following his death here in 1783 its contents were bequeathed to Glasgow University, later becoming the Hunterian Museum. Hunter's house passed to his nephew and pupil, Matthew Baillie (1761–1823), who lived here with his sister Joanna Baillie until 1791 and owned the building until 1808. It continued in use as a school of anatomy until 1831. In 1888 the property was greatly altered as part of its incorporation into the Lyric Theatre, Shaftesbury Avenue, newly built to designs by C. J. Phipps. C. Robert Rudolf, Curator of the Hunterian Society, noted that 'The stage door is the door through which the bodies were taken and they were dissected on what corresponds to the stage of the theatre today'.[11] The plaque was unveiled by Hunter's great-great-great niece, Dorothea Oliver, in 1952.

455   A crowd and a rather precariously balanced cameraman gather to watch the unveiling of the plaque at 22 Frith Street in 1951. It was here, in 1926, that John Logie Baird first demonstrated television.
[© City of London, LMA]

Two attic rooms at 22 Frith Street, W1, were rented by the engineer **John Logie Baird** (1888–1946) ⑩ (see also p. 314) as his laboratory between November 1924 and February 1926; a plaque erected by the LCC in 1951 records that it was here, in 1926, that he first demonstrated television. Born in Scotland, Baird studied electrical engineering in Glasgow, and in 1922 began to

formulate ideas about how to transmit and receive pictures. With only limited resources, he set about investigating his theories, and by 1925 had made excellent progress; in March of that year, he began a three-week series of demonstrations of moving silhouette images at Selfridge's in Oxford Street. On 2 October, working from his Frith Street laboratory, he managed to transmit the first television picture with tone gradation, first using the head of a ventriloquist's dummy and then moving on to a human face. Baird's subject was William Edward Taynton, a twenty-year-old office boy, who later recalled that 'Mr Baird rushed downstairs in baggy flannels, a pair of carpet slippers, and no socks. He almost dragged me into his workroom and sat me in front of his machine, a mass of wires and enormous electric light bulbs'.[12] The occasion that the plaque commemorates took place on 26 January 1926, when Baird – repeating his experiment of October 1925 – made a formal demonstration of his 'televisor' in front of forty members of the Royal Institution. A *Times* journalist reported that the image as transmitted was 'faint and often blurred, but substantiated a claim that through the "Televisor" . . . it is possible to transmit and reproduce instantly the details of movement, and such things as the play of expression on the face'.[13] Further demonstrations followed – in 1928, for example, Baird sent a television picture across the Atlantic and demonstrated colour television for the first time – and in early 1927 the world's first television sets were offered for sale in Selfridge's. From 1929 Baird's system was trialled by the BBC, which inaugurated the country's first thirty-line television service in August 1932, but it was the rival Marconi-EMI system that was eventually adopted, in 1937. Baird's plaque at 22 Frith Street was unveiled on the twenty-fifth anniversary of the demonstration by Sir Robert Renwick, President of the Television Society; those present included William Taynton, the first person ever to have been televised. Naturally, the plaque's unveiling was captured on film (fig. 455).

At 6 Frith Street, a house built in 1718, the essayist **William Hazlitt** (1778–1830) ⑪ took lodgings in early 1830 (fig. 456). Hazlitt was born in Kent into an Irish dissenting family; moving to London in his teens, he decided to become a painter – like his elder brother John – and mixed in the circle that included Wordsworth, Coleridge, and Charles and Mary

456 The light-green wreathed LCC plaque to William Hazlitt at 6 Frith Street, now in use as a hotel. [© English Heritage. Photograph by Derek Kendall]

LAMB. However, in 1812 he turned to lecturing and journalism, writing for newspapers and periodicals such as the *Morning Chronicle* and *The Examiner*, founded by LEIGH HUNT. His first collection of essays, *The Round Table*, was published in 1817, and was followed four years later by *Table-Talk*. Hazlitt had his greatest success with *The Spirit of the Age, or, Contemporary Portraits* (1824), a collection of biographical studies of such figures as Lord Byron and Jeremy Bentham. By the time of his move to Frith Street, however, Hazlitt was living in considerable poverty, and had been briefly placed under arrest for debt. The appearance of the third and fourth volumes of his *magnum opus*, a biography of his hero Napoleon, had been delayed owing to the publisher's bankruptcy – they appeared shortly after his death – and his health was also a concern; it formed the subject of his brief essay 'The Sick Chamber', published in the periodical *The Atlas* in August 1830. The following month Hazlitt was confined, dangerously ill, to his bed – in a small room at the back of number 6. There he died, with his son William and Charles Lamb at his bedside. A light-green wreathed LCC plaque was put up in 1905, but by 1909 the front wall of number 6 had been rebuilt – as an inexact copy of the original – and the plaque re-erected. Number 6 now forms part of the popular hotel, Hazlitt's.

Soho Square (formerly King Square), W1, was laid out in 1677 and was largely complete by 1691. It was greatly altered in subsequent centuries, and both of the plaques in the square commemorate houses now demolished. That at number 20, a bronze tablet erected by the LCC, marks the site of the London home of **Arthur Onslow** (1691–1768) ⑫ , Speaker of the House of Commons from 1728 to 1761 – a record thirty-three years (fig. 457). Onslow lived at this address in moderate splendour from about 1753 until 1761, when he retired from Parliament due to ill-health and moved to Great Russell Street, Bloomsbury. Born in Kensington, Onslow initially trained for a legal career, but in 1720 became a Whig MP. Eight years later he was elected

457 The original 20 Soho Square, in a photograph of c.1908. The late seventeenth-century building was marked in 1912 with a plaque to Arthur Onslow, but was demolished twelve years later. A plaque marking its site was erected by the LCC in 1927. [© City of London, LMA]

nearby Argyll Street, the son of a Lincolnshire land-owner, Banks returned to the capital after leaving Oxford, and soon became a Fellow of both the Royal Society and the Society of Antiquaries. In 1766 he set sail as naturalist on an expedition to Labrador and Newfoundland and, from 1768 to 1771, accompanied CAPTAIN JAMES COOK to the Pacific, a voyage that brought both men international acclaim. Banks acquired what was then 30 Soho Square in 1777, and it was his London home for the rest of his life; 'a virtual research institute', it housed both his library and his extensive botanical collections.[15] While he was living in Soho Square – with his wife Dorothea, née Hugessen (1758–1828) and his sister Sarah (1744–1818), also a collector – Banks established himself as the leader of the British scientific community. He welcomed visitors, and his frequent soirées and gatherings were attended by men of letters and men of science from all over Europe. A wreathed blue plaque was erected by the LCC in 1911, but it was removed when the house was demolished in 1937. When a stone tablet was affixed to the new building in 1938, it was decided to add the names of two prominent Scottish botanists, both protégés of Banks: **Robert Brown** (1773–1858) and **David Don** (1799–1841).[16] With Banks, these men were closely associated with 32 Soho Square, a building described by the LCC as being 'for a period of eighty years . . . a mecca for students of Natural History'.[17] Robert Brown, who first met Banks in about 1798, came to attention as naturalist on the Australian expedition led by MATTHEW FLINDERS in 1801–5. On his return, Brown was appointed librarian of the Linnean Society, and from 1810 was Banks's personal librarian at Soho Square. When Sir Joseph died, he bequeathed Brown a life interest in his collections, which subsequently passed to the British Museum. Brown lived at 17 Dean Street – the building to the rear of number 32, which housed Banks's library and collections – until his death, by which time he had amassed one of the world's greatest herbariums. David Don, born into a family of botanists and gardeners, succeeded Brown as librarian of the Linnean Society in 1822. He was later Professor of Botany at King's College London (1836–41), and died at number 32. The plaque's inscription refers also to the **Linnean Society**, founded in 1788 by James Edward Smith (1759–1828) – a friend of Banks – for the study of natural history, and named after the eighteenth-century Swedish naturalist Carl Linnaeus,

Speaker, becoming the third member of his family to hold the position. A close friend of SIR ROBERT WALPOLE, Onslow has been described as 'a man of rare integrity in an age of corruption'; by the time of his retirement, impartiality and authority had become established elements of the Speaker's role.[14] The original house at number 20 was built in the 1680s for Earl Fauconberg and was – at the time Onslow lived here, with his wife Anne, née Bridges (1703–1763) – one of the finest in the square. Onslow held parliamentary levées at the house, and entertained contemporaries such as the printer and novelist Samuel Richardson. A stone tablet was erected at number 20 in 1912, but was removed when the building was demolished twelve years later. As the old plaque was considered unsuitable for re-fixing, a newly made bronze tablet was placed on the new structure – built as the offices of Crosse & Blackwell – in 1927.

An inscribed stone tablet at 31–32 Soho Square – built at the square's south-west corner in 1937–38 as offices for Twentieth Century Fox – marks the site of number 32 (formerly 30), the London home of the botanist **Sir Joseph Banks** (1743–1820) **13** , President of the Royal Society from 1778 until his death (fig. 458). Born in

507

458 Sir Joseph Banks's house at 32 Soho Square, which was marked with a plaque by the LCC in 1911. This photograph dates from January 1937, shortly before the building's demolition. [© City of London, LMA]

Born in Prussia into a Jewish family, Marx made his first visit to England in 1845, arriving with his friend and collaborator, FRIEDRICH ENGELS. He came again two years later – shortly before the publication of his *Communist Manifesto* (1848) – and, having been expelled from his homeland, settled permanently in London in 1849 with his wife Jenny, née von West-phalen (1814–1881) and their family. Although Marx earned a small income from 1851 as London corre-spondent for the *New York Daily Tribune*, he lived at number 28 in considerable poverty. Two of his young children died during their time here, though the period also saw the birth of a daughter, Eleanor (1855–1898), later to become an important socialist cam-paigner. Marx initially had only two rooms on the second floor of the house; at the back was a bedroom, used by the whole family, while the front room served as a kitchen and living room. Marx later rented a third room for use as a study. The whole ensemble was described by Jenny Marx as 'the evil frightful rooms which encompassed all our joy and all our pain'.[18] Despite the cramped conditions, Marx was politically active: friends and fellow radicals and refugees who visited number 28 included Wilhelm Wolff and Ernst Dronke. He was also busy writing the first volume of his most famous work, *Das Kapital* (1867), regularly carrying out research at the library of the British Museum. In September 1856, with the help of Engels and an inheritance received by Jenny, Marx finally left Dean Street and moved to Kentish Town, where he remained until his death. It was at his last address – 41 Maitland Park Road, his home from 1875 – that the first plaque to Marx was erected, in 1935. However, the LCC plaque and its replacement were both vandalised soon after installation, and the owner of the house declined a third. The house was later demolished, and attention turned to 28 Dean Street, where a GLC plaque was unveiled in 1967 by Andrew Rothstein, then Chairman of the Marx Memorial Library. The plaque omits any descriptor, reflecting both its elevated position on the building and the immense fame of Karl Marx, whose ideas and writings exerted such a powerful influence in the years after his death.

MARX's neighbours in Dean Street included the health care reformer **Dr Joseph Rogers** (1820–1889) 15 , who lived and worked at number 33 – a house of *c.* 1734 on the corner of Bateman Street – between 1851 and 1885.[19]

whose collection Smith had acquired in 1784. Brown leased the front part of number 32 to the society – of which he served as President in 1849–53 – from summer 1822, although the group had met at the house since May of the previous year. It remained the society's headquarters until 1857, when it moved to larger premises at Burlington House, Piccadilly.

High up on the façade of 28 Dean Street, W1, a plaque marks the lodgings in which **Karl Marx** (1818–1883) 14 lived from 1851 until 1856 (see fig. 129). Marx moved here from 64 Dean Street (demolished), where he lodged for a few months in the winter of 1850–51.

459 Thomas Sheraton's trade card, dating from between 1793 and 1795, the years he was based at 163 (formerly 106) Wardour Street. [© The Trustees of the British Museum]

After qualifying as a doctor at the Middlesex Hospital Medical School, Rogers joined his brother's practice in Soho in 1844. Seven years later, he set up his own surgery at number 33, but his growing practice was destroyed in 1854–55 by the effects of a cholera epidemic. In 1855 Rogers was appointed medical officer to the Strand Union Workhouse in Cleveland Street, Fitzrovia, where he was appalled by the disgraceful state of medical provision for the poor. For the rest of his life, he led a determined campaign for improvements in conditions for the sick and for medical officers. His successes, achieved with the backing of medical journals such as *The Lancet*, included the founding of the Association for the Improvement of London Workhouse Infirmaries, which was launched at a dinner held at number 33 in 1866. With the support of CHARLES DICKENS and FLORENCE NIGHTINGALE, the association's lobbying led in 1867 to the Metropolitan Poor Bill, under the terms of which twenty hospitals were provided for workhouse inmates. These were in effect the first public social hospitals built in London, and were absorbed into the National Health Service when it was set up in 1948. In 1868 Rogers helped to found the Poor Law Medical Officers' Association, of which he served as first Chairman, and in 1872 he was appointed to the Westminster Infirmary in nearby Poland Street, a post he held until his retirement in 1886. His plaque was erected in 1996 at the suggestion of the Soho Society.

The furniture designer **Thomas Sheraton** (1751–1806) ⑯ lodged at 163 (formerly 106) Wardour Street, W1, from 1793 to 1795 (figs 459 and 460). A cabinetmaker from County Durham, Sheraton moved to London in about 1790; the following year, he began to publish his first important work, *The Cabinet Maker and Upholsterer's Drawing-Book*, in weekly parts. Intended as an aid to craftsmen, the book explained proportion, perspective and geometry, and also included a number of Sheraton's own designs. Typically less English in inspiration than those of THOMAS CHIPPENDALE, these designs were to become widely influential, both in Europe and America, though Sheraton did not enjoy the rewards during his lifetime: he struggled to make a living as a draughtsman, author, publisher and teacher of drawing – work which he carried out alongside his career as a Baptist minister – and died in poverty. While lodging at what was then 106 Wardour

Street, Sheraton published the second edition of his *Drawing-Book* (1794), and also produced *Scriptural Subjection to Civil Government in an Exhortation to Real Christians* (1794). From about 1798 to 1800, he and his wife Margaret, née Mitchinson lived at another address in Wardour Street, number 98 (now part of 147), and – after a spell in County Durham – settled in about 1802 at 8 Broad Street (later 32 Broadwick Street; demolished); it was there that Sheraton died, three years after publishing a second book, *The Cabinet Dictionary*, and in the process of completing a third. The plaque – proposed by a descendant, Richard Sheraton – was erected by the LCC in 1954.

460 A photograph of 1982, redolent of Soho, showing 163 Wardour Street and its plaque to Thomas Sheraton. [Reproduced by permission of English Heritage. NMR]

SOHO AND LEICESTER SQUARE

In 1811 the poet **Percy Bysshe Shelley** (1792–1822) **17** and his friend Thomas Jefferson Hogg (1792–1862) took rooms at 15 Poland Street, W1. The two of them had been expelled from Oxford on 25 March of that year for writing the pamphlet *The Necessity of Atheism* (1811). Hogg – who later wrote a biography of Shelley – relates that they left for London where, soon after, they went in search of accommodation: 'we came to Poland Street; [which] reminded [Shelley] of Thaddeus of Warsaw and of freedom. We must lodge there, should we sleep even on the step of a door'.[20] A notice declared that there were lodgings to let at number 15. At first-floor level there was a sitting room, 'somewhat dark, but quiet', and, opening off it, a bedroom which Shelley took as his own; Hogg's bedroom was on the floor above.[21] The pair were particularly impressed with the 'delightful' wallpaper, which bore a pattern based on grape vines and trellises. Touching it, Shelley declared, 'We must stay here; stay for ever!'.[22] However, in early May 1811 – after just over a month – he returned to his family's home in Sussex. It was in London that the poet met the sixteen-year-old Harriet Westbrook, with whom he eloped later that year. It was also in London – three years later – that Shelley fell in love with Mary Wollstonecraft Godwin (see MARY SHELLEY), who became his second wife in 1816. In 1818 the couple left England for Italy, where Shelley wrote some of his best work, including *Prometheus Unbound* (1820) and *Adonais* (1821), an elegy on the death of KEATS. Shelley was never to return to his homeland: in 1822 he was tragically drowned in a sailing accident at the age of twenty-nine. The poet was first considered for commemoration in 1905 but, as his various London residences were so brief – he occupied as many as nineteen different lodgings – it was decided that none qualified. In 1931 evidence came to light of a three-month stay (1814–15) at 26 Nelson Square, Southwark, and an LCC plaque was duly erected there the following year; the building was demolished in 1950. In 1979 an enamelled steel plaque was put up by the GLC at 15 Poland Street – a late eighteenth-century house much altered inside. This was replaced in 2000 with an English Heritage plaque, likewise made of enamelled steel and surface-mounted on account of the poor condition of the façade's brickwork, which had been damaged by an IRA bomb in 1976.

In 1984 a GLC plaque was unveiled by the Lord Mayor of Westminster at 54 Broadwick Street (formerly 19 Broad Street), W1, the home of the landscape gardener **Charles Bridgeman** (d. 1738) **18** from 1723 until his death. HORACE WALPOLE was probably correct in seeing Bridgeman as the first English gardener to move away from the rigid 'square precision of the foregoing age' to the more natural landscape gardening of the Georgian period.[23] This transition was exemplified above all by his work for the 1st Viscount Cobham at Stowe, Buckinghamshire, where between *c.* 1713 and *c.* 1725 Bridgeman created one of the most important landscape gardens of the age, collaborating with architects such as John Vanbrugh and William Kent. Five years after moving with his wife Sarah (d. 1743/4) to what was then 19 Broad Street – a terraced house built by Bridgeman's brother-in-law, John Mist, in 1722–23 – he was appointed Royal Gardener; responsible for a portfolio of properties including Hampton Court, St James's Palace and Windsor Castle, he worked for Queen Caroline at Kensington Gardens, designing the Round Pond (1728) and the Serpentine (1731). Other commissions included the gardens at Claremont, Surrey, and Amesbury, Wiltshire. It seems likely that he produced designs for such works from his home at number 54: the inventory made of the property's contents at the time of his death – which occurred at his official residence in Kensington – records two drawing boards, a theodolite and 'a wooden Case for taking Prospects'.[24] Number 54 was rebuilt following wartime bomb damage, and was restored in 1983–84 by the architect Quinlan Terry.

The Venetian painter **Antonio Canal** (1697–1768) **19** , known as **Canaletto**, lodged in about 1746–55 at 41 Beak Street (formerly 16 Silver Street), W1, a house then owned by a cabinetmaker, Richard Wiggins (fig. 461). Born in Venice, the son of a painter, Canaletto made his name with the views he painted of his native city from about 1725; many of these were commissioned by English aristocrats making the Grand Tour, while Joseph Smith – British Consul in Venice – was his principal patron and agent. Canaletto reached his artistic peak in the 1730s, but the outbreak of the War of the Austrian Succession (1740–48) – which restricted travel to Venice – created a temporary hiatus in his career. As his English patrons could not come to him, Canaletto decided to go to them, arriving in London in May 1746; the artist stayed in the capital for around

461 The Doulton plaque installed in 1925 at 41 Beak Street. The Venetian painter Canaletto lived at the address in about 1746–55, when it was known as 16 Silver Street. [© English Heritage. Photograph by Derek Kendall]

462 One of the paintings exhibited by Canaletto at his Beak Street lodgings was a view of St James's Park, possibly this – *The Old Horse Guards, London* (c. 1749). [© The Andrew Lloyd Webber Art Foundation]

nine years, returning briefly to Italy in 1750–51. During his time in England, Canaletto painted about fifty views, initially of London and the Thames and later of country houses such as Syon House, Middlesex, and Alnwick Castle, Northumberland. In order to increase his sales, he used his London address – then known as 16 Silver Street – for exhibiting his work; the show held here in summer 1749 included his *View of St James's Park* (fig. 462), and a second exhibition was staged at the property in summer 1751. Number 41 is typical of the houses built in Soho in the 1680s, though it has been altered in succeeding centuries. The high-glaze plaque, with its distinctive coloured wreath, is one of the series made by Doulton, and dates from 1925.

Golden Square, W1, begun in 1675, was one of London's fashionable new squares for the gentry, but by 1740 the original residents had been superseded by foreign artists and legations such as those of Bavaria, Brunswick, Genoa and Russia. These, in their turn, gave way to boarding-houses and hotels in the nineteenth century, and by 1900 to manufacturers and merchants. Today, the character of the square is predominantly commercial; only two of the original seventeenth-century houses remain, both much altered – numbers 21 and 23. The latter building, together with number 24, was in use as the **Portuguese Embassy** in 1724–47 **20** . From 1739 to 1744 the two houses also served as the residence of the Portuguese Ambassador and statesman Sebastião José de Carvalho e Mello, the **Marquess of Pombal** (1699–1782), who, after returning to his homeland, became one of Portugal's most famous politicians. He was chief minister under King Joseph I, and ruled as effective dictator from the time of the disastrous Lisbon earthquake of 1755 until the King's death in 1777. Created Count of Oeiras in 1759 and Marquess of Pombal eleven years later, the minister supervised the reconstruction of Lisbon – featuring some of the world's first earthquake-proof buildings – and enacted reforms that were aimed at establishing an English type of commercial system, the success of which he had witnessed during his stay in London. Number 24, dating originally from *c.* 1675, was one of the earliest houses to be built in Golden Square; it was re-fronted in about 1730 and rebuilt behind its façade in 1959. The adjacent number 23 was built in about 1684 and, though it retains its original staircase, has been much altered internally since the 1700s. The two buildings backed onto a Catholic chapel, specifically established for the use of the Portuguese Embassy; it continued to be used by the Bavarian Legation – which occupied numbers 23 and 24 in 1747–88 – before being demolished and replaced with the late eighteenth-century chapel of Our Lady of the Assumption and St Gregory, Warwick Street. A GLC plaque was erected between numbers 23 and 24 in 1980 at the suggestion of the Portuguese Ambassador, Armando Martins.

In lodgings at 31 (formerly 30) Golden Square lived the Scottish surgeon **John Hunter** (1728–1793) **21** from 1765 to 1768. He moved in 1748 to London, where he studied surgery and anatomy while assisting his elder brother Dr William Hunter, before serving as a

surgeon in the Seven Years War (1756–63). It was while living at number 31 that Hunter began the anatomical research and lecturing that earned him election as a Fellow of the Royal Society in 1767. The following year, he became a member of the Company of Surgeons and joined the surgical staff of St George's Hospital, Hyde Park Corner (see fig. 305). It was also at about this time that Hunter began to collect anatomical specimens; the rapid expansion of this collection, and the success of his private practice, led him to move to a house in Jermyn Street, St James's, that had previously been occupied by his brother William. In 1783 Hunter moved again – with his wife, the poet Anne, née Home – to his last London address, 28 Leicester Square (demolished). Following Hunter's death, his natural history collection was purchased by the government, and was presented to what was soon to become the Royal College of Surgeons. In 1813 a purpose-built Hunterian Museum was opened at the college's headquarters in Lincoln's Inn Fields, where it can still be found today. A chocolate-brown wreathed LCC plaque was erected in 1907 at 31 Golden Square, a house built in the 1680s. When the building was redeveloped in 1931, the plaque was re-erected, a fact recorded by a supplementary tablet. This building was itself demolished in 1998, and both plaques were positioned on the new structure in about 2000.

Just south of Oxford Street lies Argyll Street, W1, where a plaque was put up on number 8 in 1983 at the suggestion of Wayne Wilcox, Cultural Attaché at the US Embassy. It commemorates one of his predecessors, the American writer **Washington Irving** (1783–1859) 22 . Irving lived in this house, which dates from the 1730s, from about 1830 until his return to America in 1832. Born in New York, Irving travelled in 1829 to London, where he served as Secretary to the American Legation at 9 Chandos Place, just off Oxford Street. By this time, he was already a published author: Irving had his first major success with *The Sketch Book of Geoffrey Crayon* (1819), a collection which includes the popular stories 'Rip van Winkle' and 'The Legend of Sleepy Hollow'. At number 8, he put the finishing touches to *The Alhambra* (1832) – published in London under the pseudonym of Geoffrey Crayon – a product of his trip to Spain in 1826–29. One of his last journeys in England was to visit the Nottinghamshire home of his hero, Lord Byron, which he described in *Abbotsford and Newstead Abbey* (1835). On his return to America,

Irving was greeted as a celebrated man of letters and went on to become one of the country's major literary figures, renowned for such works as *The Adventures of Captain Bonneville* (1837).

A GLC plaque at 10 (formerly 12) Argyll Street marks the building in which the founder of the Ordnance Survey, **Major-General William Roy** (1726–1790) 23 , lived from 1779 until his death. Roy, born in Lanarkshire, started working for the Military Survey of Scotland in 1747, by which time he was an accomplished surveyor and map-maker. Moving south in 1755, he joined the Army and carried out a reconnaissance survey of southern England. In 1765, after service in the Seven Years War, Roy was put in charge of military surveys in Britain; he was promoted major-general in 1781. The beginnings of the Ordnance Survey came about in 1783 – during Roy's time in Argyll Street – when it was proposed that the trigonomic connection between the observatories of Paris and Greenwich be accurately established to determine the difference in longitude. The President of the Royal Society, Sir Joseph Banks, commissioned Roy to take charge of the English survey. The starting point for this was a line, stretching for five miles (8 km) eastwards from King's Arbour on Hounslow Heath, and known as the 'Hounslow Heath base'. By 1789 Roy had completed all the triangulation work between the base and the Kentish coast, making use of a theodolite specially crafted by the instrument maker Jesse Ramsden. He died at Argyll Street, having all but finished the last of three papers for *Philosophical Transactions* which described his surveying work . However, Roy's achievements did not end there. As early as 1763, he had suggested that a survey of Britain be undertaken at public cost. His fieldwork in southern England was to provide the foundations for just such a survey, set up in 1791 – the year after Roy's death – by the Board of Ordnance. Originally termed the Trigonometrical Survey, it produced its first map – of Kent – in 1801 and, as the Ordnance Survey, continues to flourish to this day.

NORTH OF OXFORD STREET

High up on the Berners Street façade of the Plaza Centre, W1 – formerly the Bourne & Hollingsworth department store – is a plaque to the Devon-born poet and philosopher **Samuel Taylor Coleridge** (1772–1834)

463 Number 71 Berners Street, the former home of Samuel Taylor Coleridge, in a photograph of December 1904. It was commemorated the following year with an LCC plaque, but was demolished in 1908 to make way for an extension of the Bourne & Hollingsworth store. [© City of London, LMA]

24 (see also pp. 275–6). Coleridge lived in a house on this site – 71 Berners Street (fig. 463) – for about eighteen months in 1812–13, sharing it with his Bristol friend John Morgan (?1775–1820) and Morgan's family. Coleridge had, by this time, established himself as a writer; perhaps his most famous poem, 'The Rime of the Ancient Mariner', had appeared in 1798 in *Lyrical Ballads*, a collection co-written with his friend William Wordsworth. However, his fortunes had taken a turn for the worse: Coleridge – who separated from his wife Sara in 1808 – was suffering increasingly from poor health and an addiction to opium, was in financial straits, and had quarrelled with Wordsworth. In Berners Street, he made an attempt to recover himself; a reconciliation with the Lake District poet was enacted in May 1812 and, while here, Coleridge also began to give a series of literary lectures and had some success with his play *Remorse*, staged at the Drury Lane theatre in January 1813. By autumn of that year, the bankruptcy of Morgan forced Coleridge to leave Berners Street, and he began a peripatetic existence until settling at the Highgate home of his doctor, James Gillman, in 1816. This was a momentous year, during which Byron read what is perhaps Coleridge's most famous poem – 'Kubla Khan' – and induced John Murray to publish it with another piece, 'Christabel'. Coleridge, who died in Highgate at the age of sixty-one, was first considered for commemoration in 1904; the LCC decided that the most suitable location for a plaque was 3 The Grove, Highgate, N6 (see J. B. PRIESTLEY), the poet's home from 1823, but the prospect that the building might be demolished meant that nothing was done. As it happened, number 3 was reprieved, but by that time the council had chosen another location for its chocolate-brown wreathed plaque – 71 Berners Street, which was commemorated in 1905. Three years later, following the demolition of the house to make way for an extension of the Bourne & Hollingsworth store, the plaque was re-erected with a rectangular supplementary tablet recording its history; both were replaced on a new façade in 1928 after a larger store was built to designs by Slater & Moberly. The moves took their toll on the condition of the tablet, and in 1966 it was replaced – under the aegis of the GLC – with a standard LCC blue plaque.

At 28 Newman Street, W1, lived the painter and illustrator **Thomas Stothard** (1755–1834) **25**, from 1793 until his death. Newman Street was then a popular place of residence for artists: Stothard's neighbours included Thomas Banks, John Bacon and Benjamin West, President of the Royal Academy. Stothard was born in Covent Garden, the son of a publican, and trained initially as a silk weaver. In 1777 he entered the Royal Academy Schools, where he became a friend of John Flaxman and WILLIAM BLAKE. Stothard found success primarily as a book illustrator, contributing to such works as John Bunyan's *Pilgrim's Progress* (1788–89), ALEXANDER POPE's *The Rape of the Lock* (1798) and Samuel Rogers's *Italy* (1830). However, it was the

464 Joseph Nollekens with his bust of Charles James Fox, in a portrait of c.1797 by Lemuel Francis Abbott. The painting once hung in the sculptor's corner studio in Mortimer Street. [© National Portrait Gallery, London]

money he inherited on the death of his father in 1770 – rather than this lucrative source of income – that enabled him to purchase 28 Newman Street in 1793. In his painting room at the house, which he shared with his wife Rebecca, née Watkins (1760/1–1824) and their six children, Stothard produced a large and varied body of work, including *The Pilgrimage to Canterbury* (1806); engraved in 1817, it became one of the best-known prints of the nineteenth century. In 1814, as part of the celebrations surrounding the peace with France, Stothard designed the silver shield presented to the Duke of Wellington by the merchants and bankers of the City of London. The Duke took a keen interest in the designs, visiting Stothard at his home to inspect the drawings. A handsome rectangular lead tablet was erected at number 28 by the LCC in 1911; it was re-erected when a new façade was given to the building in 1924.

At 44 Mortimer Street, W1, built as a hostel in 1903 to designs by Beresford Pite, an LCC plaque marks the site of the home of **Joseph Nollekens** (1737–1823) **26** ; one of the most successful sculptors of his time, he lived here from 1770 until his death over fifty years later. The son of a painter, Nollekens was born at 28 Dean Street (see Karl Marx), and at the age of thirteen was placed in the studio of the sculptor Peter Scheemakers. In 1762 he left London for Rome, where he made copies of antique sculpture and began to produce the portrait busts for which he became renowned; the first, depicting David Garrick, was completed in 1764. On his return to England in 1770, Nollekens settled at what was then 9 Mortimer Street, a substantial house on the corner of Great Titchfield Street that had previously been occupied by the portrait painter Francis Newton (1720–1794). His modelling room was visited by some of the greatest and most fashionable figures of the time, drawn by the lure of his portrait busts; Nollekens produced more than 170 such works in all, including those of Dr Johnson (1777), Charles James Fox (1791 and 1802) and Pitt the Younger (1806) (fig. 464). He also created mythological, or 'poetical', works such as the *Judgment of Paris* (1773–76) and *Venus Chiding Cupid* (1778). Nollekens was described in an LCC report as being 'small in stature, of grotesque appearance and eccentric in his behaviour'.[25] Despite his wealth – Nollekens left a fortune of around £200,000 – he and his wife Mary (1742/3–1817) were notoriously parsimo-

nious, and some of their habits approached squalor: old shaving lather was, for instance, retained for use at home. The sculptor's studio was a corner room, which featured – above the chimney piece – the portrait of Nollekens painted by Lemuel Francis Abbott in *c.* 1797 (see fig. 464). The sculptor died in the first-floor drawing room in 1823. His house, renumbered 44 in 1879, was demolished about twenty years later, and a plaque was placed on the new building in 1954. Among those present at the unveiling was the sculptor Sir William Reid Dick.

The short-story writer **Hector Hugh Munro** (1870–1916) **27** , alias '**Saki**', rented rooms on the third floor of 97 Mortimer Street from *c.* 1908 until he enlisted at the outbreak of the First World War. Born in Burma, Munro published his first book (and only serious historical work), *The Rise of the Russian Empire*, in 1900, and soon began to contribute characteristically satirical and witty stories to leading periodicals under the pen name 'Saki'. Between 1902 and 1908, as special correspondent for the *Morning Post*, he travelled to the Balkans, Warsaw, St Petersburg and Paris. On his return to London, when he moved to number 97,

465 Henry Fuseli's *Titania and Bottom* (1790), one of the works completed during the artist's time at 37 Foley Street. It was painted for John Boydell's popular Shakespeare Gallery in Pall Mall. [© Tate, London 2008]

Munro entered the most creative phase of his career. The short stories he produced for periodicals including the *Westminster Gazette* and the *Morning Post* were later collected and published as *The Chronicles of Clovis* (1911), *Beasts and Super-Beasts* (1914), *The Toys of Peace* (1919) and *The Square Egg* (1924). While living here, Munro also wrote two novels: *The Unbearable Bassington* (1912) and *When William Came* (1913). Saki, a name thought to derive from a character in *The Rubáiyát of Omar Khayyám*, was smart, handsome and urbane. His pied-à-terre at number 97, a building of the late nineteenth century, was convenient for his favourite haunts – the British Museum, the shops in Regent Street, the Cocoa Tree Club in St James's Street and the Turkish baths in Jermyn Street. Munro left Mortimer Street in 1914 never to return: two years later, at the age of forty-five, he was killed by a sniper's bullet during the final assault at the Battle of the Ancre on the Western Front. His English Heritage plaque was unveiled in 2003 by the writer Will Self.

At 37 Foley Street, W1 – formerly known successively as 72, 75 and 37 Queen Anne Street East – an LCC plaque marks the home from 1788 to 1803 of the artist **Henry Fuseli** (1741–1825) **28** . Born Johann Heinrich

Füssli in Zurich, Switzerland, he inherited a love of art from his father, though initially trained as a minister. In 1768, on his second trip to London, he met REYNOLDS, who encouraged him to become a painter and to study in Italy. Fuseli duly did so, and in 1779 returned to England, where he began to establish himself as an artist. Works of this period included *The Death of Dido* (1781), *The Nightmare* (1782) and *The Three Witches* (1783); reflecting his interest in mythology and the supernatural, they proved influential on younger artists such as WILLIAM BLAKE. In 1788 Fuseli married the young society beauty Sophia Rawlins (1762/3–1832) and moved to what was then 72 Queen Anne Street East. During his time at the house, the artist enjoyed a period of success. It was here that he completed a series of paintings for John Boydell's popular Shakespeare Gallery in Pall Mall, which opened in 1789; these included *Titania and Bottom* (1790) (fig. 465). In 1799 Fuseli – newly created Professor of Painting at the Royal Academy – attempted to emulate Boydell's success with his own Milton Gallery; he exhibited nearly fifty paintings inspired by Milton's life and work at the gallery's premises in Pall Mall. However, it was a financial failure; many paintings went unsold and remained in his studio until his death. In 1803 Fuseli moved to nearby 13 Berners Street (demolished), which had been designed and occupied by Sir William Chambers, and the following year – on his appointment as Keeper of the Royal Academy – moved to Somerset House, his home until his death.

The plaque to the Shakespearean scholar **Edmond Malone** (1741–1812) **29** was unveiled on the 150th anniversary of his death by Professor F. P. Wilson, President of the Malone Society. Malone lived at 40 Langham Street, W1 – formerly known successively as 55 Queen Anne Street East, 58 Queen Anne Street and 23 Foley Place – from 1779 until his death thirty-three years later. Born in Ireland, he became a lawyer, writer and editor, and in 1777 – on the publication of his new edition of the works of Oliver Goldsmith – settled permanently in London. Shortly afterwards, he became involved in the edition of the *Johnson-Steevens Shakespeare* (1778), writing supplements in 1780 and 1783. Malone was among the first scholars to base his research on Shakespeare on original documents, and drew widely on his celebrated library of Elizabethan literature; the greater part of his books

SOHO AND LEICESTER SQUARE

and manuscripts were presented to the Bodleian Library, Oxford, after his death. While living at number 40, Malone – a lifelong bachelor – researched his monumental ten-volume edition of the works of Shakespeare, published in 1790 to great acclaim. He also provided invaluable assistance to Boswell with his *Tour to the Hebrides with Samuel Johnson* (1785) and *Life of Johnson* (1791). Malone held frequent dinner parties for his friends, among whom were Edmund Burke, Joseph Banks, Edward Gibbon, Charles James Fox and Joshua Reynolds, whose collected works he edited in 1797–98. Inhibited in his later years by fading eyesight, he left unfinished a new

octavo edition of Shakespeare, which was published in 1821. The interiors of Malone's late eighteenth-century house remain largely unaltered, although the façade was rebuilt and additional floors were added in about 1900, possibly after the death of a later resident – David Edward Hughes.

At 94 Great Portland Street, W1 – on the corner of Langham Street – an English Heritage plaque commemorates **David Edward Hughes** (1831–1900) (30), the scientist and inventor of the microphone (see fig. 32). Born in London, Hughes moved with his family to America in about 1838. His early talent for music – which he taught from 1850 – soon gave way to experimental science; in 1856 he patented his printing telegraph, which was adopted throughout Europe over the course of the next ten years. Having lived for a time in France, Hughes settled in about 1878 at 94 Great Portland Street, where he devoted himself to electrical experiments. It was in that year that he made his most important invention, the microphone; demonstrations of the device were given at number 94 before an audience of distinguished scientists. While at the house, Hughes also invented the induction balance – later used in metal detectors – and worked at developing a form of 'wireless' communication; walking up and down Great Portland Street, holding a microphone in one hand and a telephone to his ear in the other, he was able to hear at some distance the sounds made by a transmitter left at home. In February 1880 – shortly before Hughes was appointed a Fellow of the Royal Society – he invited the society's President and secretaries to witness his experiments, but they 'pooh-poohed all the results' and, disheartened, he abandoned his researches.[26] Thus, though Hughes was the first person to achieve radio communication, its development was left to Heinrich Hertz, Guglielmo Marconi and others. By 1881, Hughes had moved the very short distance to 108 Great Portland Street, and he later lived – and died – just around the corner, at 40 Langham Street, the former home of Edmond Malone.

At 122 (formerly 47) Great Portland Street, a wreathed blue plaque marks the site of the last home of the biographer **James Boswell** (1740–1795) (31) (see also p. 381) (fig. 466). Born in Edinburgh – the son of Lord Auchinleck, a successful judge – Boswell followed his

466 The wreathed LCC plaque to James Boswell at 122 Great Portland Street in a photograph of 1937, taken the year after its installation. [© City of London, LMA]

father's wishes by pursuing a legal career, though he indulged his passion for literature whenever possible. He first visited London in 1760, when he met David Garrick and Laurence Sterne, and returned two years later; in May 1763 he was unexpectedly – but fatefully – introduced to Dr Johnson, and shortly afterwards conceived the idea of the biography that would become his greatest work. Boswell moved permanently to the capital on being called to the English Bar in 1786 and, having been widowed in 1789, took up residence in January 1791 at what was then 47 Great Portland Street, close to his friend and associate Edmond Malone. His time at the address – where he died four years later – witnessed his greatest triumph: the publication on 16 May 1791 of the *Life of Johnson*. 'I really think it will be the most entertaining collection that has appeared in this age', wrote Boswell in April of that year.[27] But the period was also marked by a deterioration of mind and body. A contemporary described how 'Convivial society became continuously more necessary to him, while his power of enchantment over it continued to decline'.[28] By the time of his death, Boswell's notorious 'wine bibbing' and whoring had become the talk of the town. He was first considered for commemoration in 1903. Two years later, the LCC erected a plaque at 56 Great Queen Street, Covent Garden, the last of Boswell's London homes to survive unaltered; he had lived there from 1786 to 1789, during which time he wrote part of the Johnson biography. Following the demolition in 1915 of number 56 – a fine house of 1637 – attentions turned on 122 Great Portland Street, originally excluded from consideration as it had been so completely rebuilt; a plaque was erected here in 1936.

The American painter, and inventor of the Morse Code, **Samuel Morse** (1791–1872) ㉜ , lived at 141 Cleveland Street (formerly 8 Buckingham Place), W1, from 1812 to 1815. Born in Massachusetts, the son of a Calvinist minister, Samuel Finley Breese Morse became a pupil of the painter Washington Allston in 1811, and accompanied him to England later the same year. In London, Morse studied under Benjamin West, the American-born President of the Royal Academy, and by August 1812 had settled with his fellow pupil Charles Robert Leslie (1794–1859) at what was then 8 Buckingham Place, 'in the very centre of all the artists in London'.[29] Leslie told a friend, 'Morse and I find our-

selves very comfortable in our new lodgings', which became the setting for evening parties attended by other pupils of West.[30] During his time at the house, Morse studied at the schools of the Royal Academy, where he exhibited works such as *Dying Hercules* (1812–13), and became friends with figures including Wordsworth, Turner and Coleridge. Returning to America in 1815, he made his name as one of the most important of the early United States artists; a successful portraitist, Morse also continued to produce history paintings such as the *House of Representatives* (1822–23), and in 1825 co-founded the National Academy of Design in New York. However, it was his subsequent work as a scientist that brought him international renown. In 1832 Morse conceived the idea of a recording telegraph, which transmitted a series of electromagnetic impulses. These were of short and long duration – 'dots' and 'dashes' – and were combined by Morse into arrangements representing the letters of the alphabet. Although Morse was not the first to develop the electric telegraph – a patent was taken out for similar technology in 1837 by Charles Wheatstone and William Fothergill Cooke – it was his system that was universally adopted after 1851. Honoured as a hero during his lifetime, Morse was commemorated with an LCC plaque in 1962.

Another American, the broadcaster **Edward R. Murrow** (1908–1965) ㉝ (fig. 467), lived from 1938 to 1946 in Flat 5, Weymouth House, 84–94 Hallam Street, W1, on the second floor of this block built in about 1927. During his career, which spanned a quarter of a century, Ed Murrow made more than 5,000 broadcasts, and did much to shape the format of modern television news. Born in North Carolina, he joined Columbia Broadcasting System (CBS) in 1935 as Director of Talks and Education. Two years later, he left America as European Director of CBS and quickly assumed a front-line reporting role, making his first broadcast in Vienna during the *Anschluss*. He soon settled in London, where he worked with a team of reporters – who came to be known as the 'Murrow Boys' – and was encouraged and supported by the BBC. Throughout the Second World War, Murrow's news broadcasts – which famously began 'This is London' – conveyed the true horror of the Blitz, and helped to rally American public opinion to Britain's side. Murrow displayed courage in the pursuit of the best angle on a story:

SOHO AND LEICESTER SQUARE

517

467 Edward R. Murrow in a characteristic pose, with CBS microphone, cigarette and memo pad. The photograph was taken in January 1939, during Murrow's time in London. [© Getty Images]

during raids, he regularly gave broadcasts from rooftops – including that of Broadcasting House – and also flew on a number of bombing missions. At the height of the Blitz, he was one of only three occupants who remained in Weymouth House, where he lived with his wife and fellow broadcaster Janet, née Huntington Brewster (1910–1998). Murrow was frequently obliged to walk the short distance to the BBC and CBS offices in Portland Place in the blackout, sometimes while a raid was in progress; he would arrive 'often out of breath, occasionally dusty, very occasionally on all fours'.[31] After returning to the United States in spring 1946, Murrow was appointed to CBS's Board of Directors, and in 1948 launched the radio series *Hear it Now*; this was transferred to the screen as *See it Now* (1951–58). The series – which essentially created the prototype TV documentary – tackled a host of controversial subjects, and was the vehicle for Murrow's celebrated attack on the virulent anti-Communist Senator Joseph McCarthy, broadcast in 1954. Their clash formed the focus of George Clooney's film *Good Night, and Good Luck*, released in the UK in 2006, shortly after the blue plaque was unveiled by Richard C. Hottelet, last of the Murrow Boys.

A wreathed LCC blue plaque commemorating the birthplace of the poet and painter **Dante Gabriel Rossetti** (1828–1882) 34 (see also p. 60 and p. 191) was erected in 1906 at 110 Hallam Street (formerly 38 Charlotte Street), W1. In 1928, following the demolition of the eighteenth-century building and its replacement with a large block of flats, the plaque was re-erected, together with a supplementary tablet recording its history. Rossetti was born at 38 Charlotte Street – then 'dingy' and 'mostly unrespectable' – the son of Gabriele Rossetti (1783–1854), a writer and teacher of Italian, and his wife Frances, née Polidori (1800–1886).[32] Rossetti's siblings – Maria (1827–1876), William Michael (1829–1919) and CHRISTINA (1830–1894), all of whom became writers – were also born at the house, which was described by William as 'a fairly neat but decidedly small one: it is smaller inside than it looks viewed from outside'.[33] Despite its size, it welcomed frequent visitors – William wrote that it 'seems hardly an exaggeration to say that every Italian staying in or passing through London, of a Liberal mode of political opinion, sought out my father'.[34] While here, Rossetti – baptised Gabriel Charles Dante, a name he changed after the death of his godfather, CHARLES LYELL – displayed an early interest in literature and art. He wrote his first poem 'towards the age of five', and at the age of about four 'he stationed himself in the passage leading to the street-door, and with a pencil of our father's began drawing his rocking-horse'; a passing milkman commented that he had seen 'a baby making a picture'.[35] The house remained the Rossetti residence until 1836, when the family moved to a larger property on the opposite (west) side of the road, 50 Charlotte Street (demolished). While there, Dante embarked on his artistic training at the Royal Academy. He finally left the family home in 1848, the year which saw the creation of the PRE-RAPHAELITE BROTHERHOOD, which he co-founded with others including his brother William, MILLAIS and HOLMAN HUNT.

NOTES

1 J. Hawkes, *Mortimer Wheeler: Adventurer in Archaeology* (London, 1982), p. 370
2 *ODNB*, vol. ILVI, p. 558
3 *The Times*, 24 December 1976, p. 7
4 Ibid, 7 January 1936, p. 17
5 Ibid, 24 December 1976, p. 7; A. J. Nathan, *Costumes by Nathan* (London, 1960), p. 139
6 *The Times*, 24 December 1976, p. 7
7 N. W. Wraxall, *Historical Memoirs of My Own Time* (London, 1904), p. 358
8 J. Dryden, *The Works of Virgil* (London, 1697), p. 621
9 Algernon Ashton, *Truth, Wit and Wisdom: A Mine of Information: 525 Letters to the Press 1887–1903, from the Pen of Algernon Ashton* (London, 1905), p. 295
10 *Survey of London*, vol. XXXI: *The Parish of St James, Westminster: Part II: North of Piccadilly*, ed. F. H. W. Sheppard (London, 1963), p. 50
11 Letter of 4 December 1950 on blue plaque file.
12 *News Chronicle*, 23 October 1951
13 *The Times*, 28 January 1926, p. 9
14 *ODNB*, vol. ILI, p. 874
15 Ibid, vol. III, p. 693
16 It is now accepted that Don was born in 1799, rather than in 1800, as is stated on the plaque.
17 Undated report (of 1937) on blue plaque file.
18 David McLellan, *Karl Marx: His Life and Thought* (London and Basingstoke, 1973), p. 265
19 It is now accepted that Rogers was born in 1820, rather than in 1821, as is stated on the plaque.
20 Thomas Jefferson Hogg, *The Life of Percy Bysshe Shelley* (London, 1906), p. 177
21 Ibid
22 Ibid, p. 178
23 Horace Walpole, *The History of the Modern Taste in Gardening* (New York, 1995), p. 42
24 Peter Willis, *Charles Bridgeman and the English Landscape Garden* (London, 1977), p. 161
25 Press release of 7 July 1954 on blue plaque file.
26 G. Burniston Brown, 'David Edward Hughes, FRS, 1831–1900', *Notes & Records of the Royal Society of London*, vol. XXXIV, no. 2 (March 1980), p. 234
27 *Letters of James Boswell*, ed. Chauncey Brewster Tinker, vol. II (Oxford, 1924), p. 435 (19 April 1791)
28 LCC, *Indication of Houses of Historical Interest in London*, vol. VI (London, 1938), p. 108
29 Charles Robert Leslie, *Autobiographical Recollections*, ed. Tom Taylor (Boston, 1867), p. 185
30 Ibid, p. 179 (6 August 1812)
31 Ann M. Sperber, *Murrow: His Life and Times* (New York, 1987), p. 170
32 William Michael Rossetti, *Some Reminiscences* (London, 1906), p. 3
33 LCC, *Indication of Houses of Historical Interest in London*, vol. I (2nd edn, London, 1915), p. 105
34 Ibid, p. 106
35 Ibid, p. 107

468　A view along Queen Anne's Gate, which boasts a total of six plaques. Those shown here commemorate Lord Palmerston (at number 20), William Smith and Lord Fisher (both at number 16) and Charles Townley (at number 14). [© English Heritage. Photograph by Derek Kendall]

WESTMINSTER AND PIMLICO

Westminster has been at the heart of national government since the eleventh century. It is here, in the Houses of Parliament and in the imposing office buildings lining the broad sweep of Whitehall, that the business of state is carried out. Many of the offices date from the nineteenth century, and reflect the growth of government and London's status as a world city. Whitehall itself has traditionally been ruled out for blue plaques; this is largely due to its association with so many important figures, as well as its status as an area of work rather than domesticity. There are, however, notable clusters of plaques around the nearby eighteenth-century terraces of Smith Square and Queen Anne's Gate. From the mid-1800s, a new commercial centre grew up between Parliament Square and Victoria Station. This bustling quarter is characterised by tall blocks of mansion flats, department stores and offices, and by the Byzantine magnificence of the Roman Catholic Westminster Cathedral. Built to designs by J. F. BENTLEY in 1895–1903, it makes for a contrast with the Gothic grandeur of medieval Westminster Abbey at the other end of Victoria Street. Pimlico, to the west, was built up in the mid-Victorian era as a genteel suburb for professional men; it aspired to – but never quite matched – the social standing of neighbouring Belgravia. The area's stuccoed Italianate terraces and squares are now intermingled with post-war local authority housing and subsequent developments.

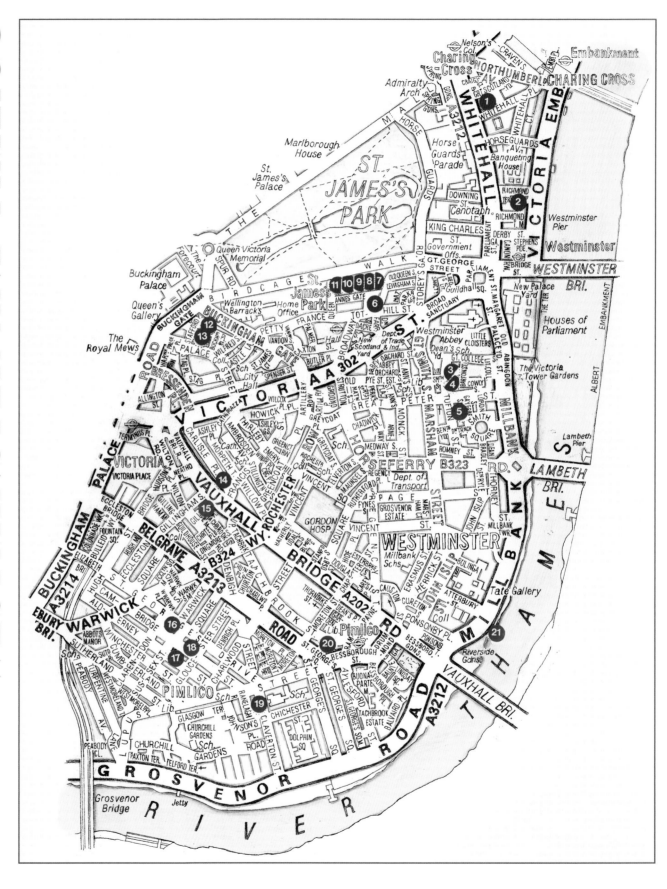

469 Scotland Yard, Whitehall –
the headquarters of the
Metropolitan Police from 1829 to
1890 – in a view of c.1850.
[© City of Westminster Archives
Centre]

One of the two blue plaques in the Whitehall area commemorates the site of **Scotland Yard** ❶, the headquarters of the Metropolitan Police from its creation in 1829 until 1890 (fig. 469 and see fig. 30). Unveiled in 1979 – the 150th anniversary of the founding of the Police Force – the plaque marks the former Board of Agriculture Building, now part of the Department of the Environment, Food and Rural Affairs (DEFRA), at 3–8 Whitehall Place, SW1. This occupies the site of the former 4 Whitehall Place, one of a row of small houses built in about 1820 and taken over in September 1829 by the Home Secretary SIR ROBERT PEEL for use as the headquarters of his newly founded police force. The Metropolitan Police's early nicknames – the 'blue army' and the 'raw lobster gang' – were soon superseded by 'Peelers' and 'bobbies', both of which derived from the force's founder; Peel himself lived from 1825 until his death at nearby 4 Whitehall Gardens, a fact recorded by an LCC plaque until the house was demolished in 1938. At the rear of 4 Whitehall Place, which backed onto Great Scotland Yard, an extension served as a section house – a police barracks. It was the entrance to this, rather than to that of the main build-

ing, which was used by the public and the press, leading to the whole building becoming popularly known as Scotland Yard from the early 1840s onwards. By 1888, the police headquarters had overflowed into several adjacent buildings, including numbers 3, 5, 21 and 22 Whitehall Place, 8–9 Great Scotland Yard and 1–3 Palace Place, all of which have been demolished. It was clear that a new headquarters was needed, and in November 1890 the police moved to the purpose-built New Scotland Yard on Victoria Embankment, now known as the Norman Shaw Building after its eminent architect (see NORMAN SHAW). The Met moved again in 1967 into a twenty-storey tower at 10 Broadway, off Victoria Street, designed by Max Taylor of Chapman Taylor Partners; once again, the headquarters retained the original name.

Number 6 (formerly 2) Richmond Terrace, SW1, was the London home of the explorer and writer **Sir Henry Morton Stanley** (1841–1904) ❷ from 1890 to 1904. At present, its plaque may only be seen distantly through the security barriers from Whitehall. The house forms part of a terrace built in 1822–25 to designs by Henry

WESTMINSTER AND PIMLICO

523

Harrison, which was demolished and reconstructed behind a retained façade in 1984–86 for the Department of Health. Stanley was born John Rowlands in Denbigh, North Wales; he was illegitimate, and such education as he received was in the workhouse at St Asaph. After emigrating to the United States in 1859, he was adopted by a cotton trader named Henry Hope Stanley, and eventually found work as a journalist. Stanley was famously sent by the *New York Herald* to Africa in search of the explorer David Livingstone; in 1871 his search was successful, though Livingstone politely refused to accompany him back to Britain. Stanley returned to face a disbelieving public – his accounts of hardship and adventure were widely ridiculed – but his book *How I found Livingstone* (1872) proved enormously successful. Between 1874 and 1877 Stanley was once again in Africa, an expedition described in his best-selling book *Through the Dark Continent* (1878). In 1879–84 he played a major part in opening up the Congo, using forced labour to do so; later, under the Belgian King Leopold, the country was the subject of some of the worst excesses of colonial exploitation, in which Stanley's complicity has been much debated. In 1887 he embarked on an expedition to relieve Emin Pasha, the beleaguered Governor of the Egyptian province of Equatoria. On his return in 1890, Stanley settled in England, married the painter Dorothy ('Dolly') Tennant (1855–1926) and was re-naturalised as a British subject. At the insistence of Dorothy's formidable mother Gertrude (1820–1918), the couple went to live with her at what was then 2 Richmond Terrace. This was convenient for Parliament when, in 1895, Stanley was elected Liberal Unionist MP for North Lambeth. However, he made little mark as a politician: 'I am too old to change my open-air habits for the asphyxiating atmosphere of the House of Commons', he reflected.[1] Stanley continued to travel and lecture widely, and wrote another travelogue, *Through South Africa* (1898). In 1899 he was knighted and bought a country estate, Furze Hill, Pirbright, Surrey; Stanley and his wife continued to stay in Richmond Terrace on visits to London. It was here – with a reflection on the nature of time occasioned by hearing the chimes of Big Ben – that he died.

Barton Street, SW1, just to the south of Westminster Abbey and the Houses of Parliament, is a rare early Georgian survival of an almost complete run of

brown-brick terraced houses; it was developed by the actor Barton Booth in 1722. A plaque records the stay at number 14 of **T. E. Lawrence** (1888–1935) ③ , 'Lawrence of Arabia' (fig. 470); it was here, between March and August 1922 – while serving as a political advisor at the Colonial Office – that Lawrence worked on the final draft of the *Seven Pillars of Wisdom* (1926). This colourful – some have since said fanciful – tale of his adventures as a solider and diplomat during the Arab revolt against Turkish rule (1916–18) forms the basis of Lawrence's reputation as a patriotic paragon. Number 14 served as the office of the successful architect Sir Herbert Baker (1862–1946), whose works include the rebuilding of the Bank of England (1921–42) and Church House, Dean's Yard, Westminster Abbey (1936–40). Baker, an associate from Oxford, offered Lawrence the use of the simply furnished attic as a refuge from the celebrity that resulted from his wartime exploits. Lawrence found it 'the best-and-freest place I ever lived in', and was delighted that 'nobody has found me . . . despite efforts by callers and telephones'; he stayed here again for short spells

470   A pencil sketch of T. E. Lawrence (Lawrence of Arabia) by Augustus John. Intended for the subscriber's edition of the *Seven Pillars of Wisdom*, the portrait dates from *c*.1926. [Private Collection / © Philip Mould Ltd, London / The Bridgeman Art Library]

in 1923, 1926 and 1929, while serving in the RAF. Baker, who left number 14 in 1934, recalled that Lawrence was largely nocturnal, and 'refused all service and comfort, food, fire or hot water'; he 'ate and bathed when he happened to go out', and otherwise subsisted on chocolate – 'it required no cleaning up, he said'. Baker added, 'We who worked in the rooms below never heard a sound; I would look up from my drawing-board in the evening sometimes to see him watching, gnomelike, with a smile; his smile that hid a tragedy'.[2] From 1924, Lawrence spent much time at his country retreat, Clouds Hill, near Wareham, Dorset, close to which – at the age of forty-six – he died in a motorcycle accident. The plaque was erected by the GLC in 1966, four years after the release of David Lean's epic film *Lawrence of Arabia*.

Number 6 Barton Street was the home of **Lord Reith** (1889–1971) **4** , the first Director-General of the BBC. Born in Scotland, a son of the manse, John Charles Walsham Reith became General Manager of the fledgling British Broadcasting Company in 1922, and the first Director-General when it became a public corporation in 1926, an appointment that brought him a knighthood. Barton Street – to which Reith moved in June 1924 with his wife Muriel, née Odhams (d. 1977) – was within walking distance of the BBC offices, based from 1923 in Savoy Hill, just off the Strand; a purpose-built headquarters, Broadcasting House, Portland Place, was opened in 1932. It was from his study at number 6 that Reith himself announced the beginning of the General Strike in 1926 – a 'very impressive performance', he noted, with a characteristic horror of false modesty.[3] The Reiths left Barton Street, the birthplace of their son Christopher (b. 1928), for Buckinghamshire in March 1930; they had tired of the 'dirt and confinement' of London, but would later return to a flat in Lollards Tower, Lambeth Palace.[4] Reith left the BBC in 1938, just as the television age was dawning, in order to become Chairman of Imperial Airways. Raised to the peerage in 1940, he held a series of appointments in CHURCHILL's War Cabinet; afterwards he chaired the Colonial Development Corporation (1950–58) and held numerous directorships. The plaque which was unveiled in 1994 by Marmaduke Hussey, Chairman of the BBC, is not that which adorns number 6 today. Reith's second forename had been omitted from the original inscrip-

tion, and as he was, in the words of his son, 'such a stickler for absolute correctness in every detail', it was decided to have a new plaque made with a simplified wording; this was erected in 1995.[5] Owing to a concern about the thinness of the main brick façade of the house, the plaque is situated on the building's Cowley Street elevation.

Just off Marsham Street, at 5 Tufton Court in Tufton Street, SW1, lived from 1940 to 1945 the pioneer of family allowances, **Eleanor Rathbone** (1872–1946) **5** . Born into a wealthy Nonconformist shipping family, the daughter of the philanthropist and politician William Rathbone, Eleanor first came to prominence as a dedicated feminist and reformer in her native Liverpool. She was Secretary of the Liverpool Women's Suffrage Society from 1897, strove to improve working conditions in the city's docks, and in 1909 became the first woman elected to Liverpool City Council. In 1919 she succeeded MILLICENT FAWCETT to the presidency of the National Union of Societies for Equal Citizenship and moved to London, where she lived at 50 Romney Street – around the corner from Tufton Street – with her lifelong friend and companion Elizabeth Macadam (1871–1948), a fellow social reformer. Ten years later, Rathbone was elected to Parliament for the Combined English Universities as an Independent, and held the seat until her death; hers was among the voices raised early against the threat posed by Nazi Germany. The Romney Street house, later demolished, was severely bomb damaged in 1940, forcing Eleanor and Elizabeth to move to 5 Tufton Court – a flat on the ground floor of a new purpose-built seven-storey block. In the same year, Rathbone published *The Case for Family Allowances* (1940); she had long advocated state support for mothers and children, and the passage of the Family Allowances Act five years later has been described as a 'notable personal triumph in legislation'.[6] In April 1945 Eleanor and Elizabeth moved to 26 Hampstead Lane, Highgate, N6, where Rathbone died suddenly in January of the following year. The plaque was erected by the GLC in 1986, having originally been suggested by Rathbone's biographer, Mary Stocks.

In Queen Anne's Gate, SW1, there are a total of six plaques – one of the largest concentrations in London – most of them commemorating political figures (fig.

WESTMINSTER AND PIMLICO

468). Until 1873 it was two separate streets: Queen Square was to the west and Park Street to the east; the former intersection is now marked by a statue of Queen Anne. Number 3 Queen Anne's Gate – built in 1776 as part of Park Street and variously numbered 8, 12 and 13 – was the London home of **Sir Edward Grey, Viscount Grey of Fallodon** (1862–1933) ⑥ , Foreign Secretary from 1905 to 1916 in the Liberal governments of CAMPBELL-BANNERMAN and ASQUITH. Grey, who belonged to the same political dynasty as the Prime Minster Earl Grey, began his political career in 1884 as Private Secretary to SIR EVELYN BARING. The following year, he entered Parliament as Liberal MP for the Berwick division of his native Northumberland, a seat he retained until 1916. As Foreign Secretary, Grey was largely responsible for negotiating the pre-First World War agreements between Britain, France and Russia for mutual defence in case of attack by Germany. In February 1906, facing a crisis over Morocco that threatened to erupt into a European conflict, he suffered the tragic death of his wife Dorothy in a coaching accident. She had just secured the lease on 3 Queen Anne's Gate, where Grey was installed by early spring. 'I am left alone and have no wish to live', he told a friend; when time permitted, he found solace in the country pursuits – such as birdwatching – that he and Dorothy had once enjoyed together.[7] The last person to use number 3 as a private residence – now used as offices, it is conjoined with number 1 – Grey moved in 1913 to 33 Eccleston Square, Pimlico, SW1, the former home of WINSTON CHURCHILL. He returned to Queen Anne's Gate to lodge with his friend VISCOUNT HALDANE during the dramatic days leading up to the outbreak of war: 'The lamps are going out all over Europe; we shall not see them lit again in our life-time', he famously commented, after the final ultimatum to Germany was drafted.[8] Haldane wrote of Grey 'sparing no effort to avoid the catastrophe', though his failure to do so inevitably drew criticism: according to RAMSAY MACDONALD, he 'combined a most admirable intention with a tragic incapacity to drive his way to his own goal'.[9] He was ennobled as Viscount Grey of Fallodon in 1916, and the plaque was put up by the GLC in 1981 (fig. 472).[10]

Number 14 Queen Anne's Gate (originally 7 Park Street) once housed one of the largest and most famous collections of classical antiquities in the coun-

try. It was amassed by the antiquary and collector **Charles Townley** (1737–1805) ⑦ – born into a Catholic family in Lancashire – during and after his three visits to Italy between 1767 and 1777 (fig. 471). Townley had the house built by Michael Barratt from 1775 to the designs of Samuel Wyatt, for the express purpose of displaying his collection of mostly Roman statuary; he acquired the lease of the house in 1777, and moved in early the following year. His treasures, which also included terracottas, bronzes, coins, gems and drawings, were put on permanent display here, with servants under instruction to admit 'all individuals of respectability who desired to see them'; some of the six to seven hundred annual visitors were given guided tours by Townley himself.[11] Townley, who was unmarried, entertained regularly at number 14 – he was famed for his Sunday dinners, and welcomed friends such as JOSEPH NOLLEKENS, SIR JOSHUA REYNOLDS and JOHANN ZOFFANY – and continued to amass antiquities right up until his death, which occurred here in 1805. The house remained in the possession of his heirs; his cousin Edward Towneley [sic] was still here in 1843. Meanwhile, most of Townley's antiquities were acquired by the British Museum, and were

471 A painting by Johann Zoffany of Charles Townley and friends in the gallery at 14 Queen Anne's Gate (originally 7 Park Street), 1781–83. [© Towneley [sic] Hall Art Gallery and Museum, Burnley, Lancashire / The Bridgeman Art Library]

472   The GLC plaque to Sir Edward Grey, Viscount Grey of Fallodon, who lived at 3 Queen Anne's Gate from 1906 to 1913. The handsome doorcase, in an early Georgian style, post-dates his residence, having been added by Holland & Hannen & Cubitts in the mid-twentieth century. [© English Heritage. Photograph by Derek Kendall]

installed in a specially built gallery in 1808; this was lost in later rebuilding, though in 1984 the Townley marbles were once again afforded their own dedicated gallery space. The LCC turned Townley down for commemoration – opining that he was 'not of sufficient merit to warrant the erection of a tablet in his memory' – but the GLC decided differently, and installed a plaque in 1985 (see fig. 468).[12]

Next door, at 16 Queen Anne's Gate (formerly 6 Park Street) – another house of the 1770s – are two plaques, placed either side of the central first-floor window; both were erected by the GLC in 1975 (see figs 7 and 468). One commemorates **William Smith MP** (1756–1835) **8** , and designates him a 'pioneer of religious liberty' – perhaps 'promoter' might have been a more felicitous term. A Unitarian, and a Whig MP from 1784, Smith was a leading light in securing the abolition of laws that deprived dissenters of their full civil rights, culminating in 1828 with the repeal of the Test and Corporation Acts, which had largely barred Nonconformists from holding office under the Crown. Between 1805 and 1832, he held the important post of Chairman of the Dissenting Deputies, and worked to secure the passing of the Unitarian Toleration Act of 1813. More widely, Smith played an important part in the struggle for social and parliamentary reform, and his support for the French Revolution drew him into controversy. He was particularly active in the anti-slavery movement led by his friends William Wilberforce and Thomas Clarkson, which in 1807 brought about the end of the slave trade in British territories; in 1823 Smith helped to found the London Society for the Abolition of Slavery in Our Colonies. Having lived for many years in Clapham, Smith moved in 1794 to what was then 6 Park Street with his wife Frances, née Coape (1758–1840) and their large family; Smith's grandchildren included Florence Nightingale, the campaigner for women's rights Barbara Leigh Bodichon and the Arctic explorer Benjamin Leigh Smith. A patron of the artists John Sell Cotman and John Opie, Smith owned a collection of paintings including Reynolds's *Mrs Siddons* and Rembrandt's *The Mill*, and he had a fine library too. His books and art were largely sold off in 1819, along with the house, after he suffered a series of business reverses, including a fire at the Millbank distillery of which he was a partner. The plaque was erected at the suggestion of Smith's biographer, R. W. Davis, who first identified 16 Queen Anne's Gate as Smith's residence.

The second plaque at 16 Queen Anne's Gate commemorates the Admiral of the Fleet **Lord Fisher**, **OM** (1841–1920) **9** (see figs 7 and 468), who had his official residence here during his stint as First Sea Lord between October 1904 and January 1910; he briefly returned to this post, though not to this address, between October 1914 and May 1915. The son of an army captain, John Arbuthnot Fisher entered the Navy at the age of thirteen, and rose through the ranks to take the helm of the senior service, in which capacity he pursued a vigorous policy of modernisation. As First Sea Lord, he initiated a construction programme of fast, heavily armed battleships; the first and most famous of these, HMS *Dreadnought*, was launched in 1906, while the world's first battlecruiser, HMS *Invincible*, entered service the following year. Appropriately, Fisher – awarded the Order of Merit in 1905 – chose the motto 'Fear God and Dread Nought' on his elevation to the peerage in 1909. A forceful, confident personality, he advocated pre-emptive strikes against the navies of Germany and Japan; this caused consternation, not least to Edward VII, who had concerns about Fisher's over-dedication, commanding him 'to do *no* work on *Sundays*, nor go near the Admiralty'.[13] The injunction had little effect. 'Jacky' Fisher's daily routine was to walk to the Admiralty in Whitehall via Westminster Abbey, where he said his morning prayers. It was there that he was given a public funeral in 1920.

At 20 Queen Anne's Gate (formerly 4 Park Street), a blue wreathed plaque commemorates the birthplace of the Prime Minister **Lord Palmerston** (1784–1865) **10** (see also p. 432 and pp. 472–3) (fig. 473 and see fig. 468). It was once thought that Henry John Temple, later to become 3rd Viscount Palmerston, was born at his family's estate at Broadlands, Hampshire; the plaque, the second to commemorate him, was put up in 1927 after the LCC investigated – and proved – the claim that he had been born in London. The crucial evidence was afforded by an entry in his father's diary, which describes a journey to London before noting, 'Lady P. indifferent', 'Lady P. ill' and finally, on 20 October 1784, 'Lady P. brought to bed of a son at seven in the evening'.[14] Henry Temple (1739–1802), the 2nd Viscount, and his second wife Mary, née Mee (1754–1805) were in

473 The wreathed LCC plaque to Lord Palmerston, erected in 1927 at 20 Queen Anne's Gate, his birthplace. [© English Heritage. Photograph by Derek Kendall]

474 Visitors to 28 Queen Anne's Gate included Albert Einstein, seen here being photographed in the garden in 1921. His host, Lord Haldane, is second from the left. [© Ullstein / Topfoto]

colour'.[15] Number 20 forms part of a terrace built between 1775 and 1778, and was the London home of the 2nd Viscount Palmerston from 1778 until 1791.

The earliest terraced houses in Queen Anne's Gate, built in about 1704–5, originally formed part of Queen Square and are among the most important early eighteenth-century domestic buildings to survive in London. Number 28 (formerly 10 Queen Square) was from 1907 until his death the London home of the statesman, lawyer and philosopher **Lord Haldane** (1856–1928) **11** . Richard Burdon Haldane, born and educated in Edinburgh, lived here during the most significant period of his life; he served as Secretary of State for War from 1905 until 1912, then – after being created Viscount Haldane of Cloan – as Lord Chancellor until 1915. Briefly, he held the same office again in 1924, having switched allegiance from the ailing Liberals to ascendant Labour. At the War Office, Haldane instituted a number of important reforms: he introduced the concept of an expeditionary force in 1906 – the British Expeditionary Force was finally established in 1914 – and founded the Imperial General Staff and the Territorial Army in 1907. In another guise, he had helped to establish the London School of Economics in 1895, and was an accomplished philosopher, translating works by SCHOPENHAUER and writing a number of his own, including *The Reign of Relativity* (1921). A man with a wide range of intellectual interests, Haldane commissioned EDWIN LUTYENS – whose office was then on the opposite side of the road at number 17 – to improve his house by the addition of a library. His guests included LORD KITCHENER, LORD CURZON, Albert Einstein (fig. 474), EDMUND GOSSE and Kaiser Wilhelm II, who had lunch with Haldane here in May 1911 and, as his host later recalled, chaffed 'about the small size of 28 Queen Anne's Gate, which he called my Dolls' House'.[16] Haldane was unfairly criticised for being pro-German; for a time, a story – now known to be unfounded – circulated that he had one of number 28's keystone masks carved with a likeness of the Kaiser. While the Foreign Secretary SIR EDWARD GREY was his guest in the turbulent days of July 1914, Haldane acted as a gatekeeper for despatches delivered at night, in order that Grey could get some rest and respite. After Haldane – a lifelong bachelor – died at Cloan at the age of seventy-two, the house was altered by the architect Aston Webb, whose office was at 19

London so that the elder Palmerston – an MP for forty years from 1762 – could sit for a portrait by SIR JOSHUA REYNOLDS; it was, however, never completed. The younger Palmerston, who went on to be Foreign Secretary three times (in 1830–34, 1835–41 and 1846–51) and Prime Minister twice (1855–58 and 1859–65), was baptised at St Margaret Westminster on 23 November 1784. A magnificent ball was thrown at Winchester to celebrate the birth, and the heir to the peerage was described four years later as 'quite stout, with a fine high

475 A photograph of c.1940 showing Lord Hore-Belisha crossing Whitehall in safety, thanks to one of the beacons named in his honour. [© Hulton-Deutsch Collection / CORBIS]

Anne King (1837–1917) – the daughter of ADA, COUNTESS OF LOVELACE – and was driven by similar passions for verse, exotic travel, radical politics and women. He embarked on a diplomatic career at the age of eighteen, but retired after the death of his brother in 1872. Blunt thereupon inherited Crabbet Park, the family estate in West Sussex, where – six years later – he and Anne founded a famous stud breeding Arab stallions. There, it was said, weekend guests played tennis in the nude. He and his wife spent much time travelling in Spain, Turkey, North Africa and the Middle East, and in 1882, during their time at number 15, bought a small estate near Cairo in Egypt. An anti-imperialist, Blunt campaigned for causes such as Egyptian and Irish self-determination; his efforts to promote the latter landed him in gaol for a spell during 1888. He was also active as a writer, publishing works including *Sonnets and Songs by Proteus* (1875) and *Satan Absolved* (1899). A notorious womaniser – Blunt's mistresses included Catherine Walters ('Skittles') and Lady Gregory – he kept a private diary throughout his adult life. An entry for 1880 records the renting of a flat opposite Victoria Station as a love nest; his wife eventually lost patience, and left him in 1906. Blunt's dark good looks and occasional bids for political martyrdom led one contemporary to observe, 'The fellow knows he has a handsome head and he wants it to be seen on Temple Bar'.[17] His plaque was put up by the GLC in 1979.

Close to Buckingham Palace is 16 Stafford Place, SW1, where a plaque was installed in 1980 by the GLC to the statesman **Lord Hore-Belisha** (1893–1957) 13 (fig. 475), who bought the house in the summer of 1936 and lived here until his death. Born in London, the son of a Jewish businessman, Hore-Belisha began his parliamentary career in 1923 as MP for Plymouth Devonport, a seat he held until 1945. He is largely remembered for the Belisha beacon, a road safety innovation introduced in 1934 while he was Minister of Transport; despite an initial surge of vandalism, the beacons – characterised by a flashing orange globe, then made of glass – soon became widespread, and had a significant impact on road safety. In 1937 NEVILLE CHAMBERLAIN appointed Hore-Belisha Secretary of State for War; he piloted important army reforms, but his relations with the top brass – notably VISCOUNT GORT – were problematic, and he resigned in 1940 rather than take a different ministerial post. A

Queen Anne's Gate; Webb removed Lutyens's library and reinstated an early eighteenth-century-style doorcase. The LCC plaque was put up in 1954 in a recessed brick panel on the far right of the building's façade.

Opposite Wellington Barracks is 15 Buckingham Gate (formerly 10 James Street), SW1. This mid-eighteenth-century terraced house was the London home from about 1878 until 1887 of the diplomat, poet and traveller **Wilfrid Scawen Blunt** (1840–1922) 12 , who – as the plaque records – founded the Crabbet Park Arabian Stud. Blunt married Lord Byron's grandchild

476 The imposing Italianate façade of 22 Carlisle Place as it appeared in 1913, the year before the installation of the plaque to Cardinal Manning. It was built in c.1867 as the Guardsmen's Institute, and was later known as Archbishop House. [© City of London, LMA]

wife Cynthia, née Elliot (1916–1991) after their marriage in 1944. Chips Channon, who had visited in May 1938, described the interior decor as 'a horror... though arranged with care, it shows an astonishing lack of taste or humour. Wedgwood plaques cover the walls... old ones, small ones, good ones, bad ones. And his bedroom he [Hore-Belisha] has turned into a sort of "Chapelle ardente" to his mother's memory'.[19]

The Francis Street elevation of 22 Carlisle Place, SW1, bears an unusual LCC lead plaque, inscribed with the date of its erection – 1914. It honours **Cardinal Manning** (1808–1892) 14, the second Roman Catholic Archbishop of Westminster, who lived in the building – now known as Manning House – from 1873 until his death (fig. 476). Henry Edward Manning was ordained an Anglican deacon in 1832, having studied at Oxford, and in 1840 – three years after the death of his young wife, Caroline, née Sargent – was appointed Archdeacon of Chichester. However, in 1851 he followed John Henry Newman in converting to Roman Catholicism, and fourteen years later succeeded Cardinal Wiseman as Archbishop of Westminster. In a city where anti-Catholic sentiment had been widespread a generation earlier, Manning won regard for his social concerns, becoming known as the 'Cardinal of the Poor'. The doors of Archbishop House, as it was known during his residence, were open to all. The building, a vast brick Italianate palazzo designed by H. A. Darbishire in about 1867, was described by Lytton Strachey as 'more like a barracks than an Episcopal palace'.[20] It was actually built as the Guardsmen's Institute, and came into Manning's hands in 1872 as part of the proposed development of Westminster Cathedral (built 1895–1903); the Archbishop apparently favoured 'the austerity of its bareness and openness'.[21] During his residence, Manning added a bedroom on the upper storey and used one of the large rooms on the first floor as a living room, where he worked surrounded by his books and papers on the floor and tables; writings of this period include *The Eternal Priesthood* (1883). From a bedroom window, Manning – once an aspirant politician – could at that time see the Houses of Parliament: 'If I had been able to have my own way and to go there, what a rascal I should have been by this time!', he wrote in old age.[22] In the days immediately after his death here in January 1892, Manning's body lay in state at Archbishop House. It was reported

factor in his departure was his conviction that the German Army would circumvent French frontier defences, in which he was shortly vindicated. Hore-Belisha, a Liberal who eventually joined the Conservatives, never achieved high office again, and was awarded a peerage in 1954. 'What a bore the old boy has become... the tragedy of a good mind unharnessed', the politician and diarist Sir Henry 'Chips' Channon had lamented the previous year.[18] Number 16 is part of a brick-built terrace of the early nineteenth century; according to his biographer, Hore-Belisha was only its third occupant, as its first owner – Lady Catherine Coke, a lady-in-waiting to Queen Victoria – was exceptionally long-lived. Edwin Lutyens remodelled the entrance hall and added panelling in the dining room for Hore-Belisha, who lived here with his

that the crowds who queued to see him brought traffic to a halt in Victoria Street. The building remained the residence of the archbishops of Westminster until 1901.

In Gillingham Street, SW1, between Wilton Road and Vauxhall Bridge Road, there is a modest row of terraced houses built in 1827. At number 17, a blue plaque was unveiled in 1984 to the novelist **Joseph Conrad** (1857–1924) 15 by his grandson, Philip Conrad. Joseph had rooms here from early 1891 until his marriage in March 1896 to Jessie Emmeline George; thereafter he lived mostly outside London. Born Józef Teodor Konrad Korzeniowski in the Ukraine, he suffered exile in a remote Russian province for his family's Polish nationalist beliefs and came to Britain in 1878 to join the British mercantile marine; in 1886 Conrad gained both his master mariner's certificate and British nationality. By the early 1890s, with steam superseding sail, he was finding it difficult to get work and embarked on a literary career with the help of a bequest from an uncle. Conrad's first novel, *Almayer's Folly* – begun at his previous lodgings not far away at 6 Bessborough Gardens (demolished) – was completed in his 'snug bachelor quarters' in Gillingham Street in 1894 and was published the following year.[23] It was followed by numerous other influential and widely read works, including *Heart of Darkness* (1902), *Nostromo* (1904), *The Secret Agent* (1907) and *Under Western Eyes* (1911). *Heart of Darkness* was based on Conrad's own nightmarish experiences of a trip up the Congo river in 1890, which left him with a life-threatening malarial fever, for which he was treated at the German Hospital in Dalston just prior to his arrival at Gillingham Street. Conrad encouraged a prospective visitor to the house with the observation that, 'The country is quiet just now hereabouts and the inhabitants have given up the practice of cannibalism, I believe, some time ago'.[24]

Number 95 Cambridge Street, SW1, bears an English Heritage plaque to **Jomo Kenyatta** (*c.* 1894–1978) 16 , first President of the Republic of Kenya, who stayed here for a short spell in 1930 and made the house his settled residence between 1933 and 1937 (fig. 477). Born Kamau wa Ngengi in east Africa, the son of a Kikuyu farmer, he took the name Kenyatta – after the Kikuyu word for a type of beaded belt he wore – during his twenties; his adopted first name, Johnstone, was exchanged for Jomo in the late 1930s. Kenyatta embarked on his political career in 1928 as General Secretary of the Kikuyu Central Association (KCA), a body that sought to represent the community's grievances, and travelled widely during the following years. His first visit to Britain was in 1929; he returned the following year, finding lodgings at number 95, and in 1931 arrived once again in England, where he spent the next fifteen years, before settling permanently in Kenya after the war. In 1933 Kenyatta returned to his lodgings in Cambridge Street; while here, he represented the KCA, became associated with Pan-Africanists such as C. L. R. JAMES, wrote works such as the seminal *Facing Mount Kenya* (1938) and studied at institutions including the London School of Economics. Money was very short; he often owed rent to his landlady at number 95, Mrs Hocken, and sold the stamps from mail he received from Kenya in order to buy penny buns. In the autumn of 1934 Kenyatta supplemented his income by working as an extra in the film *Sanders of the River*, which starred PAUL ROBESON. Having spent the war years in Sussex, Kenyatta returned to Africa in 1946, where he became an outspoken nationalist. In 1953 he was unjustly convicted for involvement in the Mau Mau rebellion and was imprisoned for almost nine years. However, when Kenya won self-government from Britain in 1963 Kenyatta was named as Prime Minister, and he became President of the new Kenyan republic a year later. Having worked to unify the nation, he died in office in 1978.

477   The plaque to Jomo Kenyatta following its unveiling at 95 Cambridge Street in 2005. Shown from the right are Mr Najib Balala, Kenya's Minister of State for National Heritage, Mr Uhuru Kenyatta, leader of the official opposition and the grandson of Jomo Kenyatta, and Mr Joseph Muchemi, High Commissioner of Kenya. [© English Heritage. Photograph by Nigel Corrie]

478 Aubrey Beardsley's 'The Climax of Salome' (1893) – an illustration for Oscar Wilde's *Salome* – was one of the works that the artist produced during his two years at 114 Cambridge Street. [© V&A Images / Victoria and Albert Museum, London]

WESTMINSTER AND PIMLICO

Number 114 Cambridge Street, opposite St Gabriel's Church, was the home of the artist **Aubrey Beardsley** (1872–1898) **17** . He lived here with his sister Mabel (1871–1916) and their mother, Ellen, née Pitt (1846–1932), between June 1893 and June 1895. Its lease was partly bought with the proceeds of Beardsley's precocious successes; hitherto, the family had been mired in genteel poverty, and lived in short-term lodgings. His commissions from this time included the now-famous illustrations for Thomas Malory's *Morte d'Arthur* (1893–94) and OSCAR WILDE's *Salome* (1894) (fig. 478). The two connecting rooms on the first floor in Cambridge Street were used by Beardsley as a drawing room-cum-studio; in his memoirs, the artist WILLIAM ROTHENSTEIN recalled that 'the walls . . . were distempered a violent orange, the doors and skirtings were painted black; a strange taste I thought; but his taste was all for the bizarre and exotic'.[25] Another of Beardsley's affectations was an insistence on working by candlelight, behind heavy curtains. This was all of a part with the artist's intense, disturbing work – 'I see everything in a grotesque way', he once admitted.[26] Visitors to 114 Cambridge Street included his friends MAX BEERBOHM, WALTER SICKERT and Oscar Wilde. In 1894 Beardsley was employed by John Lane as art editor of *The Yellow Book*, but he was sacked the following year in the aftermath of the downfall of Oscar Wilde – a victim of guilt by association. With his main source of income gone, Beardsley put the Cambridge Street house up for sale in May 1895, and with his sister Mabel – later the inspiration for 'Upon a Dying Lady' (1919) by W. B. YEATS – moved to 57 Chester Terrace (now Chester Row), Belgravia, SW1. By the close of 1896, Beardsley was recuperating on the south coast from consumptive attacks; as his health further declined he moved to France, where he died at the age of just twenty-five. The plaque was unveiled on the fiftieth anniversary of Beardsley's death by John, the son of William Rothenstein and Director of the nearby Tate Gallery. It was the first blue plaque of the LCC's new 'modern' design to be erected (see pp. 27–8).

The English Heritage plaque erected in 2004 at 63 St George's Drive (formerly St George's Road), SW1, commemorates **Swami Vivekananda** (1863–1902) **18** , the Hindu philosopher, who stayed in this house from early May until mid-July 1896. Born in Calcutta as Narendranath Datta, the monk (or swami) Vivekananda became a leading spokesman for modern Hinduism and an early proponent and apologist for the faith in the West. He embarked upon his first Western Mission in 1893 and later, on his lecture tour of 1895–96, stayed at several London addresses including 63 St George's Drive, part of a stucco terrace built in about 1870. The house was let to him furnished by Mortimer Reginald Margesson (1861–1947) and his wife Lady Isabel (d. 1946), who was interested in the Swami's teachings. Vivekananda held regular classes in the first-floor double drawing room, which was said to have seated about a hundred people. The hub of his everyday life was the ground-floor parlour, fronting onto the street, while he slept in a windowless room immediately to the rear; other parts of the house were given over to his entourage, which included his stenographer Josiah

Goodwin (d. 1898), the theosophist Henrietta Müller (1845/6–1906) and Swami Saradananda (1865–1927), who was – like Vivekananda – a disciple of the leading proponent of the Hindu revival, Sri Ramakrishna. Although the Swami's stay at this address was relatively brief, it was clearly significant in the westward spread of his – and Ramakrishna's – teachings, and blazed a trail that many proponents of Eastern religions have followed since. On 24 June 1896 Vivekananda wrote, 'What will be the good of my going home? This London is the hub of the world. The heart of India is here'.[27] He did, nevertheless, return to India in December 1896, after a ten-week stay at Flat 14, Greycoat Gardens, Greycoat Street, Westminster, SW1 – where consent for a plaque to Vivekenanda was refused. Back in his homeland, Vivekananda established the Ramakrishna Mission; still based in Calcutta, it seeks to propagate Ramakrishna's principles and translate them into practical social action.

At 15 Ranelagh Road, SW1, a mid-nineteenth-century stuccoed terraced house built by THOMAS CUBITT, lived **Douglas Macmillan** (1884–1969) **19** , the founder of Macmillan Cancer Relief. Macmillan moved from Somerset to London at the turn of the twentieth century, and enjoyed a long career as a civil servant. A Strict Baptist convert, he started a monthly periodical, *The Better Quest*. In the August 1911 issue, Macmillan wrote about the death of his father from cancer, an event that prompted him the following year to found the Society for the Prevention and Relief of Cancer. An early priority – which continues to this day – was the training of specialist cancer nurses. The society was based at the Ranelagh Road house Macmillan shared with his wife Margaret, née Miller (1868–1957); she had initially been his landlady at the address, where he was apparently living as a lodger by about 1902. They were married in 1907 and lived here, running the society virtually unassisted, until they moved to 11 Knoll Road, Sidcup, in 1924. The offices of the charity – which changed its name to the National Society for Cancer Relief that year – remained in Ranelagh Road until 1936, when it moved to 47 Victoria Street. The widowed Macmillan relocated from Sidcup to his native Somerset in 1966, on discovering that he was suffering from cancer of the stomach. A total of three blue plaques were manufactured: the first contained a spelling error, and the second was made redundant when the fund changed its name from Cancer Relief Macmillan Fund to Macmillan Cancer Relief. Since the third and final plaque to Macmillan was put up in 1997, the charity he started has continued to grow in size and scope and has changed its name once more, to Macmillan Cancer Support.

On a corner of St George's Square, SW1, is number 33, part of a stuccoed terrace built in about 1850 as part of the development by CUBITT. It was the London home of **Major Walter Clopton Wingfield** (1833–1912) 20 , the father of lawn tennis, for the last ten years of his life; it was here, too, that he died. Born in Wales, Wingfield served in the 1st Dragoon Guards, and gained the rank of major in the Montgomeryshire Yeomanry

THE GAME OF

SPHAIRISTIKÈ,

DEDICATED TO THE

Party assembled at Nantclwyd

IN DECEMBER, 1873.

BY

Walter Wingfield

HARRISON AND SONS, 59, PALL MALL.

[ENTERED AT STATIONERS' HALL.]

479   The title page of Major Walter Clopton Wingfield's book *The Game of Sphairistike* (1874), which introduced the rules of lawn tennis. [© Topfoto]

Cavalry. Of greater significance to posterity was his career as an amateur inventor. Wingfield is best known for patenting the game of lawn tennis in 1874 (fig. 479). Its basic principles were not new, but it was he who had the idea of formalising rules and standardising a tennis set that included racquets, balls, posts and a net. Wingfield called the sets 'Sphairistike', derived from the Greek for ball-game, a name ripe for lampoon and which never caught on; the sets were sold at five guineas a throw by Messrs French & Co. at nearby 46 Churton Street, off Belgrave Street. Lawn tennis – to use the supplementary name given to it by Wingfield as an afterthought – quickly became a very popular and sociable open-air pursuit for the middle classes. By 1877 the All England Croquet Club at Wimbledon had added lawn tennis to its title, and many croquet lawns were turned into tennis courts. However, the game developed rapidly from Major Wingfield's original rules, which envisaged an hour-glass shaped court and a higher net than modern players would recognise. Later in life, Wingfield tried (and failed) to repeat his success by developing group bicycle riding in time to martial music, as described in his book *Bicycle Gymkhana and Musical Rides* (1897). The plaque was suggested by a member of the Major Wingfield Club, a US-based association of tennis aficionados. Erected in 1987, it was one of five plaques manufactured by the GLC and put up by its successor body, English Heritage.

On the Thames Embankment side of Millbank, SW1, nearly opposite the entrance to Tate Britain, is a large cylindrical granite block with a bronze plaque commemorating **Millbank Prison** 21 (fig. 480). One of the last LCC plaques, it was fixed under the aegis of the GLC in May 1965. It is unique among London's official plaques in marking a fragment of a structure: the stone, which was moved from its original position, was formerly a bollard at the head of the river steps to Millbank Prison or Penitentiary. From here, between 1843 and 1867, prisoners sentenced to transportation to penal colonies in Australia and elsewhere embarked on their journeys. Millbank was the first national prison, and when built was the largest of its type in Europe. It was begun by the architect Thomas Hardwick, to designs by William Williams, but the foundations failed on the marshy ground. In 1816 ROBERT SMIRKE took over the project, constructing an innovative concrete base and completing the building in 1821. The

WESTMINSTER AND PIMLICO

480   A colour aquatint of c.1823 showing Millbank Prison on the north bank of the Thames. The prison – built on a radial plan – was completed in 1821, and was then the largest of its type in Europe. [© City of Westminster Archives Centre]

prison – which included 1,100 cells for offenders of 'secondary turpitude' – was founded on the humane and rational principles of classification, employment and reason, and its radial plan was in part influenced by ideas expounded by Jeremy Bentham in his *Panopticon, or, the Inspection-House* (1791); its design also drew on the work of the prison reformer JOHN HOWARD. As a penitentiary it was essentially a failure, however, and – apart from being a holding house for transportation – Millbank was variously used after 1843 as a military gaol and a general purpose prison, in which both male and female convicts were confined. It closed in November 1890, and most of the buildings had been demolished by 1893. Over the course of the following two decades, the vast site was developed as the Tate Gallery, the Royal Army Medical College (now Chelsea College of Art and Design), the Queen Alexandra Military Hospital (now used as offices by the Tate) and, on the north, the LCC's Millbank estate.

NOTES

1 Richard Hall, *Stanley: An Adventurer Explored* (London, 1974), p. 348

2 John E. Mack, *A Prince of Our Disorder: The Life of T. E. Lawrence* (London, 1976), pp. 283–84

3 Ian McIntyre, *The Expense of Glory: A Life of John Reith* (London, 1994), p. 141

4 Ibid, p. 183

5 Letter of 15 October 1994 on blue plaque file.

6 Hilary Land, 'Eleanor Rathbone and the Economy of the Family', in *British Feminism in the Twentieth Century*, ed. H. Smith (Aldershot, 1990), p. 104

7 G. M. Trevelyan, *Grey of Fallodon* (London, 1937), p. 371

8 Viscount Grey of Fallodon, *Twenty-Five Years: 1892–1916*, vol. II (London, 1925), p. 20

9 Richard Burdon Haldane, *An Autobiography* (London, 1929), p. 273; Keith Robbins, *Sir Edward Grey: A Biography* (London, 1971), p. 370

10 The title, which derives from Grey's Northumberland estate, is unfortunately misspelled 'Falloden' on the plaque.

11 *Gentleman's Magazine*, vol. LXXI, part 1 (1805), p. 184

12 Report by the Clerk of the Council, 6 April 1950, on blue plaque file.

13 *Fear God and Dread Nought: The Correspondence of the Admiral of the Fleet Lord Fisher of Kilverstone*, ed. Arthur J. Marder (London, 1952), p. 17 (8 January 1905)

14 Unpublished diary cited in LCC report of 4 November 1926 on blue plaque file.

15 Philip Guedella, *Palmerston* (London, 1926), p. 16

16 Haldane, *An Autobiography*, p. 224

17 Wilfrid Scawen Blunt, *My Diaries* (London, 1932), p. xii

18 *Chips, The Diaries of Sir Henry Channon*, ed. R. R. James (London, 1975), p. 471

19 Ibid, p. 155

20 Lytton Strachey, *Eminent Victorians* (London, 1918), p. 109

21 LCC, *Indication of Houses of Historical Interest in London*, vol. IV (London, 1923), p. 36

22 Shane Leslie, *Henry Edward Manning: His Life and Labours* (London, 1921), p. 472

23 *Letters from Joseph Conrad*, ed. E. Garnett (Indianapolis, 1928), p. 5

24 Ibid, p. 31 (4 January 1895)

25 W. Rothenstein, *Men and Memories* (London, 1931), pp. 134–35

26 Matthew Sturgis, *Aubrey Beardsley* (London, 1998), p. 220

27 Marie Louise Burke, *Swami Vivekananda in the West: New Discoveries, The World Teacher: Part Two* (Calcutta, 1986), p. 237

481 The plaque to David Garrick on the boundary wall of Garrick's Villa, a building greatly altered in *c.* 1775 by Robert Adam. The villa's prospect of the Thames is now somewhat interrupted by Hampton Court Road, which was built across what were formerly its riverside gardens. [© English Heritage. Photograph by Derek Kendall]

OUTER LONDON

Before 1965 – when the administrative area of Greater London was created – the outlying portions of the capital were part of the counties of Middlesex, Surrey, Kent, Hertfordshire and Essex. As such, they were beyond the geographical remit of the LCC and the blue plaques scheme. This position changed with the transfer of the scheme to the newly created GLC; the council first entered previously uncharted territory in 1967, when a plaque was erected in the borough of Redbridge in honour of ALBERT MANSBRIDGE. From this time onwards, there was a concerted effort to broaden the scheme's geographical range – with plaques being erected in areas as diverse as Wimbledon and Edmon-

ton – though coverage remains patchy; there is, for instance, only one official plaque in Sutton, and there are none at all in Hillingdon. As a group, the plaques of outer London reflect two key aspects of the capital's history: the status of areas such as Chiswick and Richmond as retreats from the strains of metropolitan life, and the development of the capital's outer suburbs from the 1870s onwards. With the coming of the railways – and, later, the extension of the Underground network – outer London became increasingly accessible, and attractive, to those who worked in the centre of the city.

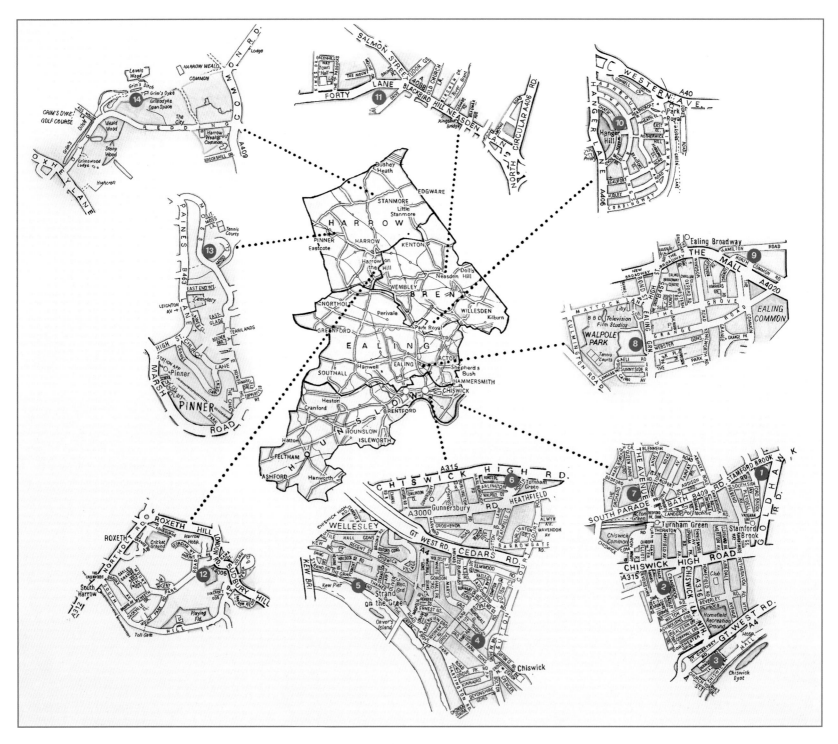

HOUNSLOW, EALING, BRENT
AND HARROW

THE BOROUGH OF HOUNSLOW

In 1976 a plaque to the painter, printer and wood engraver **Lucien Pissarro** (1863–1944) ❶ was erected by the GLC at The Brook, 27 Stamford Brook Road, Ravenscourt Park, W6. Lucien was born in Paris, the eldest son of the Impressionist painter Camille Pissarro. During the Franco-Prussian War, the family fled to England and lived at Upper Norwood, returning to France in 1871. The links with England were, however, retained, and Lucien divided his time between the two countries, settling in England in 1890, marrying Esther Bensusan (1870–1951) in 1892 and moving to The Brook in 1902. Here, in the words of their daughter Orovida (1893–1968), 'having been attracted by a derelict 18th-century farmhouse behind a little green overshadowed by some ugly tall flats . . . they turned the stable into a printing room, [and] the "brewhouse" into a studio'.[1] The house was the headquarters of the Eragny Press, founded in 1894 at the Pissarros' cottage in Epping and named after the Normandy home of Lucien's family; the press published thirty-one books, many illustrated by Lucien, and featured a specially designed typeface, named 'The Brook' after the couple's Chiswick home. After the closure of the press in 1914, Pissarro concentrated increasingly on his paintings (fig. 482); predominantly landscapes, they included views of local scenes such as *Well Farm Bridge, Acton* (1907). He moved in artistic circles, and was a founder member of both the Camden Town Group (1911) and the London Group (1913); in 1919 he co-founded the Monarro Group to represent artists inspired by the work of the French Impressionists Monet and Camille Pissarro. A naturalised British citizen from 1916, Lucien died in 1944 at Hewood, Dorset, whither he and his wife had retreated during the Second World War; afterwards, Esther Pissarro returned to The Brook, which remained her home until her death.

On 25 January 2004, the 125th anniversary of the Battle of Rorke's Drift, a plaque was unveiled at 62 Cranbrook Road, Chiswick, W4, the former home of one of the heroes of the battle, **Private Frederick Hitch**, **VC** (1856–1913) ❷ . Hitch's outstanding bravery achieved popular recognition through the 1964 film *Zulu*, starring Michael Caine. A builder's labourer, Hitch enlisted at the age of twenty and – as a private in the 24th Regiment of Foot – was sent to South Africa. There, in January 1879, he saved the life of his commanding officer, helped to keep the enemy at bay while the field hospital was evacuated and, despite having a shoulder shattered by a Zulu bullet, continued to pass ammunition to his comrades. Hitch received one of the eleven Victoria Crosses presented for the defence of Rorke's Drift, the largest number ever awarded for a single action. Following demobilisation, left disabled by his wound, Hitch returned to civilian life. He worked variously as a labourer, a publican and a cab driver, and lived at numerous London addresses, including the vanished Little Durweston Street, Marylebone, where he ran a pub, and Epirius Mews, Fulham. After the death of his wife Emily in 1909, he

482 *My Studio Garden*, painted by Lucien Pissarro in June 1938, shows the view from his studio at The Brook, 27 Stamford Brook Road, Ravenscourt Park.
[© Ashmolean Museum, University of Oxford]

HOUNSLOW TO HARROW

483 The English Heritage plaque to Alexander Pope at the Mawson Arms public house, 110 Chiswick Lane South. The poet lived in this early eighteenth-century terrace between 1716 and 1719. [© English Heritage. Photograph by Derek Kendall]

A plaque to the poet **Alexander Pope** (1688–1744) ③ was erected by English Heritage in 1996 at the Mawson Arms public house, 110 Chiswick Lane South, Chiswick, W4 (fig. 483). Pope may hold the record for the longest wait to be commemorated by an official plaque. In 1902 *The Estates Gazette* included a drawing of a Society of Arts plaque suggested for erection at 9 Berkeley Street, Piccadilly, to record Pope's supposed residence there. In 1908 the LCC dismissed the claims made for Berkeley Street and concentrated instead on Bolingbroke House, Battersea, which was then reputed to be the place where Pope wrote his *Essay on Man* (1733–34). However, the building proved to be hidden from public view, and was subsequently demolished in 1922. Pope's famous riverside villa at Twickenham having been pulled down in 1808 (leaving only the vandalised grotto), the only option was Mawson's Buildings, a terrace of five houses built in *c.* 1715, where Pope lived from 1716 to 1719 'under the wing of my Lord Burlington' of nearby Chiswick House.[2] Also resident here were his mother, Edith, née Turner (1643–1733), his old nurse Mary Beach and – briefly – his father, also named Alexander Pope (1646–1717). The house in which the Popes lived is thought to have been the end building, converted in 1897 to a public house. Born in the City of London to Roman Catholic parents, Pope was active as a poet from his youth, and by the time of his move to Chiswick had published two highly acclaimed works, the *Pastorals* (1709) and *The Rape of the Lock* (1712). His time in Mawson's Buildings saw the publication of his *Works* (1717), including two new compositions, 'Elegy to the Memory of an Unfortunate Lady' and 'Eloisa to Abelard'. Meanwhile, Pope was hard at work on his translation of Homer's *Iliad*, which appeared between 1715 and 1720. The substantial profits he received enabled him to acquire, in 1719, land at Twickenham on which to build his villa; it was there that Pope died, unmarried, at the age of fifty-six.

The Olympic rowing champion **Jack Beresford** (1899–1977) ④ (fig. 484) is honoured with a plaque at 19 Grove Park Gardens, Chiswick, W4. Jack Beresford Wiszniewski, as he was originally known, was born a short distance away at 36 St Mary's Grove; his father Julius (1868–1959) – a Polish émigré furniture manufacturer – was himself a keen oarsman, and was to win a silver medal at the 1912 Olympics. The family moved in 1903 to Belfairs, 19 Grove Park Gardens, a large

lodged with friends at 62 Cranbrook Road, a modest two-storey terraced house of the 1880s; it was here that he died of pneumonia at the age of fifty-six. Hitch's funeral was a noteworthy affair: a cavalcade of over 1,500 cab drivers, together with the local fire brigade, district councillors and Boy Scout troop, accompanied the hearse to the nearby churchyard of St Nicholas.

484 Jack Beresford (shown on the left) with Dick Southwood, winning the double sculls event at the infamous Berlin Olympics of 1936. [© AFP / Getty Images]

detached property built a few years earlier. Beresford remained here until his marriage in 1940, and his lengthy spell at the address encompassed all his sporting triumphs. His first taste of Olympic success was a silver medal at Antwerp in 1920, when he missed winning gold by a second in a legendary race against the Irish American, Jack Kelly. In all, Beresford competed at five consecutive Olympic Games, winning medals at all of them, a record surpassed only in 2000 by the rower Steve Redgrave. The last of Jack's medals – and the third of his golds – was won in the double sculls at the infamous Berlin Olympics of 1936. In front of Adolf Hitler, Beresford and his colleague Dick Southwood beat the highly fancied German team, who nicknamed their ageing English rival 'The Old Fox'. For Beresford's part, he proclaimed it 'the sweetest race I ever rowed in'.[3] Beresford also won the Wingfield Sculls, the amateur sculling championship of Great Britain, every year from 1920 to 1926, and was a frequent victor at Henley. In later years, he lived in Oxfordshire, and worked as a coach and sports administrator. The unveiling ceremony for the plaque in 2005 was hosted by Thames Rowing Club, based on the Putney Embankment; during the 1970s Beresford had

served as President of the club, to which his father had also belonged.

On a picturesque bank of the River Thames, at 65 Strand-on-the-Green, Chiswick, W4, is a GLC plaque to the painter **Johann Zoffany** (1733–1810) **5** (fig. 485). Born near Frankfurt as Johannes Josephus Zauffaly, he first came to England in the late 1760s. In the beginning, he struggled, but soon won the patronage of the actor DAVID GARRICK, producing such works as *The Farmer's Return* (1762), and became renowned as a master of the 'conversation piece', the genre of group portrait in which figures are depicted in lively interaction. Commissions from the royal family followed; the favour he enjoyed from Queen Charlotte – by whose command he painted the *Tribuna of the Uffizi* (1771–78) – may have owed much to their shared first language of German. Zoffany occupied three houses in Strand-on-the-Green: from 1764 he lived at the now-demolished London Style House, and from 1779 at number 69, in some splendour – waited on by servants liveried in scarlet, gold and blue. He had passed much of the 1770s in Italy, and it was after a six-year sojourn in India that he and his wife Mary, née Thomas (*c.*

485 Number 65 Strand-on-the-Green and its plaque to Johann Zoffany, as seen from the river. The painter lived in this early eighteenth-century house for the last twenty years of his life. [© English Heritage. Photograph by Derek Kendall]

The novelist **E. M. Forster** (1879–1970) **6** has a plaque at Arlington Park Mansions, Sutton Lane North, Turnham Green, W4, his only surviving London residence. Born in Marylebone, Edward Morgan Forster kept a London flat from 1925, though he spent much of his life with his widowed mother Lily in Surrey; it was at Harnham (now Revard), Monument Green, Weybridge, their home in 1904–25, that all of his six novels were completed. Forster moved from Bloomsbury to Arlington Park Mansions in October 1939, partly to escape central London following the outbreak of war, and partly to be closer to his friend Bob Buckingham in Shepherd's Bush. The block was built in 1905, and Forster occupied a top-floor flat – number 9 – 'with a lovely view over Turnham Green'.[5] He had written most of his novels – including *A Room with a View* (1908) and *Howards End* (1910) – during an early burst of creativity; *A Passage to India*, his last, was published in 1924. After this Forster continued to write reviews and articles, was a regular broadcaster and dedicated himself to causes such as the National Council for Civil Liberties. Perhaps his most significant later work was the libretto for the BENJAMIN BRITTEN opera *Billy Budd* (1951), which he co-wrote with Eric Crozier. In 1945 Forster was elected a Fellow of King's College, Cambridge, but continued to spend one or two days a week in London, invariably travelling with his small Gladstone bag by bus and train, since he regarded taxis as 'a vulgar extravagance'.[6] He retained the flat at Arlington Park Mansions as a pied-à-terre until his death. The plaque, which was erected in 1983, is only twelve inches (30.5 cm) in diameter; made of enamelled steel, it was specially commissioned in order to fit into the narrow space to the right of the ornamental porch.

THE BOROUGH OF EALING

There is a plaque to **John Lindley** (1799–1865) **7** , the botanist and pioneer orchidologist, on the rear façade of Bedford House, The Avenue, Acton Green, W4, just inside the borough of Ealing (fig. 486). The house, which has been much altered since Lindley's day, was built in about 1793 to designs by John Bedford; it was he who gave his name to Bedford Park, the garden suburb that was built around it some eighty years later. Lindley lived in the house from 1836 until his death, and had lived in the area since 1822, when he became

1755–1832) settled in 1790 at the commemorated address, which dates from the early eighteenth century and is usually considered 'the finest in the row'.[4] Known since as Zoffany House, it was here that the artist died twenty years later. Among the works he executed while living at number 65 was *The Plundering of the King's Cellar at Paris* (1794), an expression of his horror at the violence of the French Revolution.

486 Bedford House, The Avenue, Acton Green, in a drawing of 1845 by Sarah Lindley, daughter of the botanist John Lindley. The building has subsequently been much altered. [Image PDP09787 courtesy of the Royal British Columbia Museum, British Columbia Archives]

Assistant Secretary of the Horticultural Society's garden at Chiswick. Born in Norfolk, the son of a nurseryman, he gained a propitious introduction to Sir Joseph Banks, then the country's leading botanist, who in 1819 made Lindley his assistant librarian at his residence in Soho Square. Lindley went on to become the first Professor of Botany at the University of London in 1829 – a post he held for over thirty years – and was the author of numerous books on botany and horticulture, including *Elements of Botany* (1841) and *The Vegetable Kingdom* (1846). With works such as *The Genera and Species of Orchidaceous Plants* (1830–40) and *Orchidacae Lindenianae* (1846), he laid the foundations of modern orchidology, and was responsible for naming many species. All this was accomplished in

487 Sir Michael Balcon on the set of *A Run for Your Money* (1949), directed by Charles Frend and filmed at Ealing Studios. Balcon was co-producer with Leslie Norman. [© Getty Images]

spite of his having lost the sight in one eye; a recent biographer has commented that he 'saw more detail in plants with one eye than most people ever do with two'.[7] During his time at Bedford House, where he lived with his wife Sarah, née Freestone (1791–1869) and their family, Lindley lectured at the Chelsea Physic Garden and was closely involved in the Horticultural Society; after his death, his collection of books passed to the society as the Lindley Library. The plaque, which went up in 2005, was proposed by the Keeper of the Herbarium, Royal Botanic Gardens, Kew. It was Lindley's report of 1838 on the then decaying gardens that led to their development as a national and international centre for the study of botany.

In the minds of many people, the name of Ealing is most readily associated with the eponymous film studios on Ealing Green, W5. Film-making took place at this site from the first years of the twentieth century, though the present buildings – in outward appearance, at least – date from the early 1930s. For the next quarter of a century, the studios were a powerhouse in film-making. The man behind much of this success was the film producer **Sir Michael Balcon** (1896–1977) **8** (fig. 487), who is commemorated with an English Heritage plaque on the White House building, a nineteenth-century house remodelled in 1931. Born into a Jewish family in Birmingham, Balcon migrated in the early 1920s to London, where he co-founded Gainsborough Pictures and gave Alfred Hitchcock his first break as a director. Following stints with Gaumont-British and MGM, he became Head of Production at Ealing Studios in 1938 – with an office in the rear part of the White House – and oversaw the studio's wartime productions, which included *The Next of Kin* (1942), a dark warning about the danger of fifth columnists that Winston Churchill tried to ban as a threat to public morale. After the war – having secured a distribution deal with the Rank Organisation – Balcon explicitly set out to make films 'reflecting Britain and the British character'.[8] The results included such classic comedies as *Passport to Pimlico* (1949), *Kind Hearts and Coronets* (1949), *The Lavender Hill Mob* (1951) and *The Ladykillers* (1955), as well as the occasional epic such as *Scott of the Antarctic* (1948) and dramas including *The Blue Lamp* (1950). Following tensions in the relationship with Rank, the studios were sold in 1956 to the BBC, which retained ownership of the buildings for about forty years. Balcon, who had been knighted in 1948, left Ealing and led his team into exile to the Borehamwood studios of MGM; the last Ealing film appeared in 1959. Having served latterly as Chairman of the British Film Institute's Production Board, he died at Upper Parrock, East Sussex, his country home since the time of the Second World War.

The first female sporting personality to be commemorated under the scheme was the lawn-tennis champion **Dorothea Lambert Chambers** (1878–1960) ⑨ (fig. 488), whose English Heritage plaque is at 7 North Common Road, Ealing, W5. It was unveiled in 2005 at a ceremony organised by the Ealing Lawn Tennis Club, to which Dorothea Douglass, as she was born, had belonged. She made her Wimbledon debut in 1900 and won the singles title seven times between 1903 and 1914. This remains the record for a Briton and, on the international scoreboard, puts her behind only Helen Wills Moody and Martina Navratilova. Between 1903 and 1910, Dorothea also won the Wimbledon ladies' doubles twice and the mixed doubles on three occasions; she was awarded an Olympic gold medal for the

488 Dorothea Lambert Chambers during the 1903 Wimbledon final, at the age of twenty-four. She defeated Ethel Thomson to clinch her first championship win. [Courtesy of Wimbledon Lawn Tennis Museum / AELTC]

ladies' singles in 1908, was a badminton champion and played hockey for Middlesex. In 1919, at the age of forty, Mrs Lambert Chambers – as she was known after her marriage of 1907 – narrowly lost a legendary final to Suzanne Lenglen, a Frenchwoman half her age, who had the temerity to play in an outfit that revealed not only her forearms but her ankles as well. Lambert Chambers went on to captain the British Wightman Cup team and to work as a coach. The commemorated address was – and remains – the vicarage of St Matthew's Church next door. Dorothea's clergyman father, the Rev. Henry Charles Douglass (d. 1916), moved his family in 1887 to the newly built house, the walls of which are said to have been used by the young Dorothea (familiarly known as 'Dolly') for hitting practice. She moved out twenty years later on her marriage to Robert Lambert Chambers, a merchant, the ceremony having been conducted by her father at St Matthew's. The couple spent about ten years at Bryn-y-Mor, 12 Queen's Road, Ealing, W5, and later lived in central London.

The electronics engineer and inventor **Alan Dower Blumlein** (1903–1942) ⑩ has a plaque at 37 The Ridings, Ealing, W5, a detached property dating from the 1930s. Blumlein has been described as 'possibly the greatest British electronics engineer of the twentieth century'.[9] Born in Hampstead to a German father and a Scottish mother, he undertook pioneering work on the development of television, and in sound recording and reproduction; the significance of his work on stereophonic sound was only apparent many years later. From 1939, Blumlein was co-opted to work on radar – in particular on-board technology for aircraft, which enabled pinpoint raids to be made on key German industrial targets. He was killed on a test flight in June 1942, aged thirty-eight, but so effective was his prototype that the technology was put into service within months. Blumlein had settled in Ealing on his marriage to Doreen Lane (1908–1989) in 1933, and this was his home at the time of his vital war work and untimely death. The plaque was erected by the GLC in 1977 – the first to go up in the borough. Present at the unveiling was the nuclear physicist Sir Samuel Curran, a former colleague of Blumlein, who revealed, for the first time, that had it not been for a late change of plan, he – not Blumlein – would have been on the fateful flight.

THE BOROUGH OF BRENT

At 11 Forty Lane, Wembley, HA9, is a plaque of 1978 to **Arthur Lucan** (**Arthur Towle**) (1885–1954) **11** , the entertainer and creator of the character 'Old Mother Riley'.[10] Born in Boston, Lincolnshire, Towle was active in the theatre from an early age. However, the disapproval of his family forced him to run away, and he soon travelled to Ireland, where he was adopted by the comedians Danny and Vera Clifton. In 1910 Towle cast the thirteen-year-old singer and actress Kitty McShane (1897–1964) in the title role of *Little Red Riding Hood*, in which he was playing Granny. Three years later – after Arthur had taken his stage name from the village of Lucan, near Dublin – the couple were married. 'Lucan and McShane', as they were billed, performed together for the next forty years as 'Old Mother Riley and her daughter Kitty'. The knockabout routine of an elderly washerwoman and her sophisticated daughter was popular with stage and radio audiences alike, and the pair also appeared in fifteen films between 1936 and 1951, including *Old Mother Riley's New Venture* (1949). Offstage, their relationship was notoriously volatile, and Lucan was touring alone when he died in the wings of Hull's Tivoli Theatre just before curtain up. The couple were living at the house in Forty Lane – a substantial detached property dating from the early 1920s – by 1946, though it appears that Lucan himself may have moved out a couple of years before his death. The decision to give Lucan a plaque was a controversial one, and passed by the GLC's Historic Buildings Board on the Chairman's casting vote. It was condemned by one councillor as 'a misguided effort to curry popular favour'; while it may be true that Lucan's own fame has proved somewhat transitory, the name of his character has certainly remained part of the lexicon.[11]

THE BOROUGH OF HARROW

Three plaques were erected by the GLC in Harrow as a result of suggestions from the local borough council. That honouring **R. M. Ballantyne** (1825–1894) **12** , the author of books for boys, is at Duneaves, Mount Park Road, Harrow on the Hill, HA1, and was put up in 1979. Born in Edinburgh into a family of prominent printers and publishers, Robert Michael Ballantyne spent five years working for the Hudson's Bay Company in Canada. His experiences in the frozen north inspired the autobiographical *Hudson's Bay, or, Every-day Life in the Wilds of North America* (1848) and a number of subsequent adventure stories, such as *The Young Fur Traders* (1856). Ballantyne preferred to base his boys' adventure stories on personal experience; for example, he lived off the coast of Scotland with the lighthouse keepers on Bell Rock as research for *The Lighthouse* (1865). *The Coral Island* (1858), perhaps his best-known book, was an exception to the rule, and Ballantyne was mortified to discover that he had committed an egregious error concerning the appearance of unharvested coconuts. For the sake of the health of his family, he left Edinburgh for Europe in 1873; he settled in Harrow six years later, when his two sons were allocated day places at the public school. With the aid of a bank loan, Ballantyne bought land in what is now Mount Park Road, and had Duneaves – a large detached house, now divided into flats – built on the gently sloping site. With his tall, dark features, neat beard and silk top hat, Ballantyne became a well-known local figure, and lived at the house until shortly before his death.

The illustrator and comic artist **W. Heath Robinson** (1872–1944) **13** lived at Moy Lodge, 75 Moss Lane, Pinner, HA5, where a plaque commemorating him was put up in 1976. William Heath Robinson, who belonged to an artistic family, attended the Royal Academy Schools in the 1890s. Having failed to realise his ambition to be a landscape painter, he found a niche as an illustrator of children's books, including two of his own composition: *The Adventures of Uncle Lubin* (1902) and *Bill the Minder* (1912). It was, however, for his humorous drawings for weekly magazines, featuring complicated and improbable 'contraptions' with whimsical applications – such as for peeling potatoes or testing artificial teeth – that Heath Robinson became well known (fig. 489); their appeal has proved enduring, and his name is still used as an adjective to describe an unlikely mechanical arrangement. The first of these contraptions appeared in 1906; two years later, Heath Robinson and his wife Josephine, née Latey (1878–1974) moved from Holloway to Hatch End, Pinner. His brother Tom – also an artist – was already living in the area, having conceived the idea of 'taking possession and founding a colony on the banks of the River Pin'.[12] Heath Robinson lived and worked at Moy Lodge – a detached house dating

HOUNSLOW TO HARROW

489   A cartoon of 1940 by W. Heath Robinson: 'Sixth Column Strategy: Stout patriots dislodge an enemy machine-gun post from the dome of St Paul's'. [© The Estate of Mrs J. C. Robinson c/o Pollinger Limited and ILN / Mary Evans Picture Library]

SIXTH COLUMN STRATEGY: STOUT PATRIOTS DISLODGE AN ENEMY MACHINE-GUN POST FROM THE DOME OF ST. PAUL'S.

Stout patriots in every sense of the word may come in useful against Fifth Column devilment! At least, that's W. Heath Robinson's opinion, for he here forecasts a very weighty effort by means of which an enemy machine-gun post might be dislodged from such a point of vantage as the dome of St. Paul's Cathedral.

DRAWN BY W. HEATH ROBINSON.

from the turn of the twentieth century – from 1913 to 1918. Much of his output during these years related to the First World War, and relied on the kind of deadpan absurdist humour indicated by the title of the collection *The Saintly Hun: A Book of German Virtues* (1917).

490   Richard Norman Shaw's design for Grim's Dyke, Old Redding, 1872. [© Royal Academy of Arts, London]

'I really have a secret satisfaction in being considered rather mad,' he admitted at about this time.[13] Other works completed here were illustrations for *The Water Babies* (1915) by CHARLES KINGSLEY and *Peacock Pie* (1916) by WALTER DE LA MARE. In 1918, desiring greater peace and quiet, Heath Robinson moved to Surrey, though he later returned to London, where he produced such works as *How to Live in a Flat* (1936), the first of the popular 'How to . . .' series.

At Grim's Dyke, Old Redding, Harrow Weald, HA3, a GLC plaque commemorates three luminaries: the building's architect, **R. Norman Shaw** (1831–1912) (see also p. 113), and two of its residents, the painter **Frederick Goodall** (1822–1904) and the playwright and librettist **W. S. Gilbert** (1836–1911) (see also pp. 255–6) 14 . Richard Norman Shaw is renowned for his houses in the 'Old English' style, of which this, with its half-timbered gables and tall, irregularly placed chimneystacks, is a fine example (fig. 490). Shaw, who spent all his life in London, was commissioned to build Grim's Dyke by the painter Frederick Goodall, known especially for his Egyptian landscapes, such as *Early Morning in the Wilderness of Shur* (1860). Hailed as 'an artistic house by an artist for an artist', it took its name from a nearby prehistoric earthwork, but was first known by the daintier variant Graeme's Dyke.[14] Goodall moved here on its completion in 1872, shortly after his marriage to his second wife Alice, née Tarry (1849/50–1913), a fellow artist who was twenty-seven years his junior. She, along with their daughter Rica (b. 1876), were the models for *Palm Sunday* (1876), which was posed in one of the house's oriel windows. A keen horticulturist, Goodall laid out thirty acres (12 ha) of landscape garden; however, feeling isolated from the art world, he sold the house in 1883 and moved to Avenue Road, Swiss Cottage. William Schwenck Gilbert, a more prominent figure, bought Grim's Dyke – as he re-designated it – in 1890, and commissioned George and Peto to carry out alterations (fig. 491). The most fruitful years of Gilbert's collaboration with Arthur Sullivan had by then passed, though his time here saw two final joint works, *Utopia (Limited)* (1893) and *The Grand Duke* (1896). A JP for Middlesex from 1891, Gilbert died at Grim's Dyke, having suffered a heart attack after nobly diving into the artificial lake to save a girl who he believed to be drowning. Gilbert's wife, Lucy, née Blois Turner (1847–

491 An undated photograph of the interior of the studio at Grim's Dyke. The fireplace is by George and Peto, who were commissioned to carry out alterations by W. S. Gilbert soon after he acquired the house in 1890. [Reproduced by permission of English Heritage. NMR]

1936), remained here until her death, looked after by their adopted daughter, the American singer Nancy McIntosh (1874–1954). The grand house, situated up a winding driveway, has been a hotel since 1970, and the plaque is visible only from the hotel car park. It was set into the wall in 1976, but – because the building was undergoing a refurbishment – was not unveiled until nearly two years later.

HOUNSLOW TO HARROW

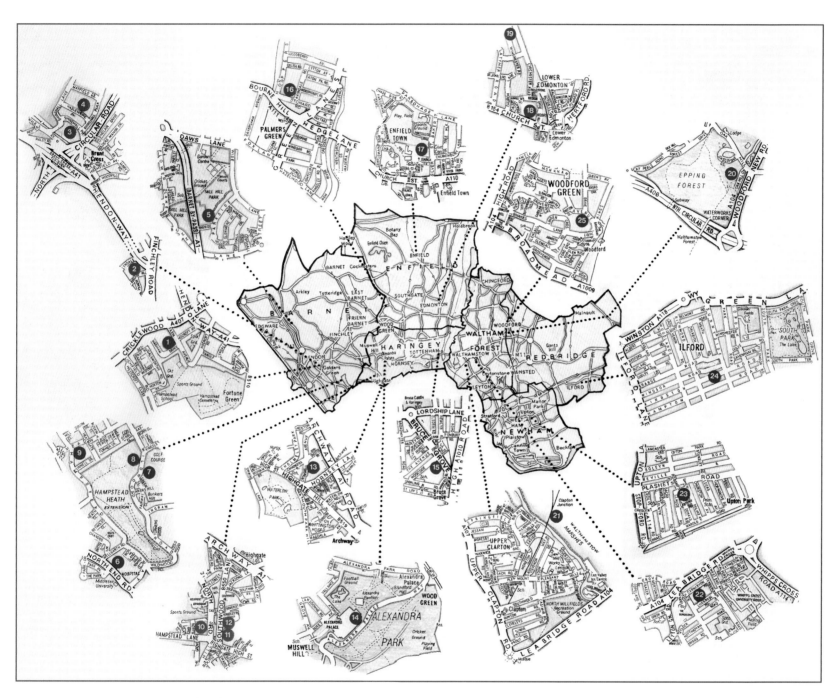

BARNET, HARINGEY, ENFIELD, WALTHAM FOREST, NEWHAM AND REDBRIDGE

492   The pioneering aviator Amy
Johnson in a portrait of
c.1933–35. [© Popperfoto / Getty
Images]

THE BOROUGH OF BARNET

An English Heritage plaque at 38 Harman Drive, Cricklewood, NW2 – a little-altered semi-detached house in a quiet cul-de-sac – commemorates **Henry Hall** (1898–1989) ❶ , the dance band leader and broadcaster. Hall was the first occupant of the house, which was originally known as Rutland; he took up residence here in 1932 and stayed until 1959, when he moved to Maida Vale. Born in Peckham, Hall had his first break in 1922, when he found work as a relief pianist at the Midland Hotel in Manchester. Within a year, he was musical director of the hotel band, and by 1931 was in charge of all the bands in the thirty-two hotels owned by the London Midland and Scottish Railway group. In 1932 the BBC invited Hall to become resident dance band leader and form a new orchestra. In their enormously popular daily broadcasts, the orchestra played Hall's best-known hits, which included 'Here's to the Next Time', 'The Sun Has Got His Hat On' and 'The Teddy Bears' Picnic'. In 1934 Hall founded *Henry Hall's Guest Night*; the 'first chat show on British radio', it ran for over twenty-three years and featured celebrities such as NOËL COWARD and Gracie Fields.[15] A star by the mid-1930s, Hall left the BBC in 1937 to concentrate on touring with his band, and he later moved successfully into the new medium of television, hosting the show *Face the Music*. Hall's greatest years were spent at number 38, which he shared with his wife Margery, née Harker (1894–1976) and their two children; while here, he wrote his autobiography, *Here's to the Next Time* (1955). It was Hall's son, Michael, who unveiled the plaque in 2003.

The pioneering aviator **Amy Johnson** (1903–1941) ❷ (fig. 492) is commemorated at Vernon Court, Hendon Way, Cricklewood, NW2, a sprawling half-timbered block of the inter-war period that stands close to the junction with Finchley Road. Johnson was born in Hull, and moved in 1927 to London, where she worked as an assistant in a legal firm. It was in her spare time that she developed her passion for flying; in 1927 Johnson was a founder of the Women's Engineering Society and joined the London Aeroplane Club at Stag Lane, Edgware, and by the end of 1929 she had become the first woman in Britain to qualify as a ground engineer. She soon turned her sights on record-breaking. On 5 May 1930, when Johnson set off

from Croydon in a second-hand De Havilland Gipsy Moth, *Jason*, she was virtually unknown. Nineteen days later, on arriving at Port Darwin, she became the first woman to fly solo from England to Australia, and was hailed as an international celebrity and a model of courage and determination. In November 1930, at the height of her fame, Johnson – dubbed 'Queen of the Air' – moved to Flat 15 in the newly built Vernon Court, located within easy reach of Stag Lane Aerodrome. It was her pied-à-terre until about June 1932, the month before her marriage to fellow aviator and record-breaker, Jim Mollison. Throughout the 1930s, Johnson continued to make pioneering flights, some with her husband; in 1931, for instance, she flew from Britain to Japan in record time. Soon after the outbreak of the Second World War, she became a pilot with the Air Transport Auxiliary. It was on a routine flight in January 1941 that she encountered difficulties in poor weather conditions, and bailed out over the

BARNET TO REDBRIDGE

Thames estuary; her body was never recovered. Johnson's plaque – the fifth installed by English Heritage – was unveiled in 1987 by Michael Spicer, Minister for Aviation.

Beyond the North Circular Road, at 93 Shirehall Park, Hendon, NW4, a GLC plaque marks the house in which the music-hall comedian **Harry Relph** (1867–1928) ③ , better known as 'Little Tich', lived and died (fig. 493). As a child, Relph – who never grew taller than four feet six inches (137 cm) – was nicknamed 'Young Tichborne', after his supposed resemblance to the claimant in the celebrated Tichborne inheritance case of 1871–72. Soon after making his London debut in 1884, he adapted an abbreviated version as his stage name; it was later said that 'so famous was the name that innumerable under-sized boys and men throughout the country have been nick-named Tich by their mates'.[16] Harry Relph – 'Tich he was in public and Relph in private' – enjoyed a long and highly successful career in music hall and comic theatre.[17] His influ-

ential, and acrobatic, act consisted largely of impersonations of various characters – from sailors to Spanish dancers – and invariably ended with his famous 'Big Boot Dance'; the boots, around twenty-eight inches (71 cm) in length, seemed almost as long as he was tall. Little Tich was known internationally, and has been described by Jacques Tati as 'the father of all film comedy'.[18] Number 93 Shirehall Park was newly built when Relph and his second wife, Winifred Emma Ivey (1892–1973) – who acted under the name of Ivey Latimer – took up residence in October 1925. At the time the plaque was unveiled – in 1969 – number 93 was still the home of his widow and daughter Mary (b. 1918), and was run as the Shirehall Park Hotel; it was sold by the Relphs in 1971.

Harry Relph's near neighbour, the football manager **Herbert Chapman** (1878–1934) ④ , is honoured with an English Heritage plaque at 6 Haslemere Avenue, Hendon, NW4 (fig. 494). He moved into this newly built house in 1926 with his wife Annie, née Poxon (b. 1880/1), and died here eight years later. Chapman was born in a mining town near Sheffield. He became a professional footballer in 1901 and, after a rather unremarkable career as a player with clubs such as Sheffield United and Tottenham Hotspur, moved into football management. During his five years (1907–12) as Manager of Northampton Town, Chapman made a strong impression, leading the club to the top of the Southern League. This success continued at Huddersfield Town, which he managed between 1921 and 1925, a period that saw an FA Cup and two League Championship victories. His years in Haslemere Avenue were the greatest of his career: appointed Manager of Arsenal in mid-1925, Chapman did everything he could to put football – and especially his club – in the public eye, and encouraged a new brand of professionalism in the sport. Among his many innovations were the introduction of rubber studs on boots, numbers on players' shirts and floodlit matches; he also improved the club's Highbury ground, and in 1932 arranged for the name of the closest Underground station to be changed from Gillespie Road to Arsenal, in order to attract crowds. The results were immediate – Arsenal won the FA Cup in 1929–30 and the League Championship in 1930–31 and 1932–33. After Chapman's untimely death – probably hastened by overwork – the team he built went on to win two further

493   A characteristic portrait of Little Tich, wearing his famous 'big boots'. Born Harry Relph, he lived at 93 Shirehall Park, Hendon, from 1925 until his death three years later. [© Topfoto]

494 English Heritage contractor Ernie Butler and his grandson George install the plaque to Herbert Chapman at 6 Haslemere Avenue, Hendon, in 2005. [© English Heritage. Photograph by Nigel Corrie]

495   The blue plaque to Graham Hill – the first to commemorate a racing driver – was installed in 2003 at 32 Parkside, Mill Hill. [© English Heritage]

496   Graham Hill and the young Damon Hill in a photograph taken by Lewis Morley at 32 Parkside during the 1960s. The address was the family home between 1960 and 1972. [© Lewis Morley Archive / National Portrait Gallery, London]

League titles in succession. The club has remained famous worldwide, and it was its Chairman – Peter Hill-Wood – who unveiled the plaque in 2005.

Another famous sporting personality, the world champion racing driver **Graham Hill** (1929–1975) ⑤ , is commemorated at 32 Parkside, Mill Hill, NW7, a detached house of the inter-war period (figs 495 and 496). Hill – who grew up at 20 Vaughan Avenue, Hendon, NW4 – fell by chance into the career in which he would find fame. In 1953 he took up a magazine offer to drive laps in a racing car at Brands Hatch and met Colin Chapman, who offered him full-time work as a mechanic at his Lotus car works in Hornsey. In 1958, at Monaco, Hill drove his first Formula One race for Team Lotus. Two years later he transferred to British Racing Motors (BRM), and in 1962 won his first Grand Prix; later that year, after a tense battle with the Lotus driver Jim Clark, Hill emerged as world champion, the first British driver to achieve this success in an all-British car. Having finished as runner-up in the ensuing three seasons, he returned to Lotus in 1967 as joint lead driver with Clark. Hill's second world championship followed in 1968 – an achievement partly overshadowed by the sudden death of his teammate

that April – and he went on to win his fourteenth, and last, Grand Prix the following year. By the time of his retirement as a driver in 1975, Hill had competed in a record-breaking 176 races, and had also achieved the 'triple crown' of victory at Formula One (1962, 1968), Indianapolis (1966) and Le Mans (1972); he remains the only driver to have done so. Many of Hill's triumphs date from his time at 23 Parkside; he moved here from Belsize Park in November 1960 with his wife Bette and their children. Bette wrote of the house, 'when I walked in I knew it was the one I wanted. It was pretty and had a pleasant atmosphere, five bedrooms plus a study for Graham, and a large garden which backed onto the park'.[19] It remained the family's home until their move to Hertfordshire in 1972, three years before Hill's untimely death in a flying accident with members of his Embassy Hill team. Number 23 was the childhood home of Graham's son Damon Hill (b. 1960), another world champion racing driver, who unveiled the English Heritage plaque in 2003.

Number 145 North End Road, Golders Green, NW11 – on the edge of Hampstead Heath – was the family home of the writer **Evelyn Waugh** (1903–1966) ⑥ . Described by him as a 'typical unpretentious house of its period', number 145 – originally named Underhill – was built in 1907 by the writer's father, the publisher and editor Arthur Waugh (1866–1943).[20] It was the family residence from September 1907 until 1931, when the Waughs moved to 14A Hampstead Lane, Highgate, N6. Although Evelyn came to dislike the house, he spent much time here, even after his marriage to Evelyn Gardner in 1928. The family's years of residence saw the emergence of Waugh's literary interests, and the publication of his biography of D. G. ROSSETTI (1928), his first novel, *Decline and Fall* (1928), and his first major success, *Vile Bodies* (1930), which satirised the 'bright young things' of the day. The house was also home to Waugh's elder brother, Alec (1898–1981), another popular novelist and one of the stars of Evelyn's film *The Scarlet Woman* (1925), shot in number 145's garden. In 1937, following his divorce from his first wife, Waugh married Laura Herbert and settled at Piers Court, Gloucestershire. It was while he was in the Army during the Second World War that he wrote his best-known work, *Brideshead Revisited* (1945). This was followed by novels such as *The Loved One* (1947), the *Sword of Honour* trilogy (1952–61) and

497 The writer Auberon Waugh unveiling a plaque to his father Evelyn at 145 North End Road, Golders Green, in 1993. [© English Heritage]

498 A photograph of 1940 showing Myra Hess at the piano at 48 Wildwood Road, Hampstead Garden Suburb, her home from 1936 to 1953. The windows of the room were criss-crossed with sticky tape as a wartime precaution against flying glass. [© Getty Images]

in his twenties, 'chiefly in the desire to get away from it into the elegant salons of Brideshead'. Auberon hoped that the plaque would 'act as a beacon of hope to the people of Golders Green, assuring them that with honest effort and application they too can end their days in a West Country manor house'.[21]

Hampstead Garden Suburb was founded in 1907 by DAME HENRIETTA BARNETT and laid out by Sir Raymond Unwin and Barry Parker. Its houses, most of an 'informal, picturesque vernacular idiom', were home to a number of notable figures, three of whom are honoured with blue plaques.[22] The pianist **Dame Myra Hess** (1890–1965) **7** was commemorated by English Heritage at 48 Wildwood Road, NW11 (fig. 498). Hess was born in West Hampstead into a prosperous Jewish family. She studied first at the Guildhall School of Music and later at the Royal Academy of Music, where she was taught by TOBIAS MATTHAY, an important influence and a lifelong friend. Myra made her official London debut in a 1907 concert conducted by THOMAS BEECHAM, but only established her reputation at about the time of the First World War. During her long and successful career – which lasted until 1961 – Hess built up a large and wide-ranging repertoire, but specialised in performing works by MOZART, Beethoven and Schumann. She is perhaps best remembered for her role as the organiser of the daily chamber music concerts held at the National Gallery, the only regular performances of music in London during the Second World War. These ran for six and a half years and made a vital contribution to public morale, earning Hess a DBE in 1941. Unmarried, she worked from number 48, a Neo-Georgian house of *c.* 1912 which was her home from 1936 until 1953, when she moved to St John's Wood.

On the other side of the street, at 15 (formerly 8) Wildwood Road, a GLC plaque commemorates **Frank Pick** (1878–1941) **8** as the 'Pioneer of Good Design for London Transport'. Born in Lincolnshire, Pick joined the North Eastern Railway Company in 1902 and, four years later, moved on to the Underground Electric Railways Company of London. There, he became associated with A. H. Stanley, later LORD ASHFIELD, and enjoyed thirty-four years of increasing influence over the capital's public transport: Pick served as Commercial Manager of the Underground from 1912, Joint Manag-

the semi-autobiographical *Ordeal of Gilbert Pinfold* (1957), all of which were written at Piers Court and Combe Florey House, Somerset, Waugh's home from 1956. The plaque was unveiled in 1993 by Waugh's son Auberon (fig. 497), also a writer, who explained the 'profound effect' number 145 had exerted on his father

BARNET TO REDBRIDGE

499 A photograph showing the proposed position of the plaque to Robert Donat, installed in 1994 at 8 Meadway, Hampstead Garden Suburb. Dominating the centre of the picture is the garage, almost certainly that designed for the Donats by C. F. A. Voysey; this allowed Robert to reach his car without being mobbed by fans. [© English Heritage]

ing Director from 1928 and then as Vice-Chairman and Chief Executive of the newly created London Passenger Transport Board from 1933 until his retirement in 1940. In collaboration with Lord Ashfield, he changed the face of the capital's transport system, merging the Underground, the London General Omnibus Company and more than 150 independent transport undertakings into the largest and – at the time – most efficient urban transport system in the world. Pick had a passion for good design: he set new standards for poster art, and in 1916 commissioned EDWARD JOHNSTON to design a new typeface for use on the Underground. He is associated, in particular, with the architect Charles Holden, whose designs for stations on the extensions of the Piccadilly and Northern lines remain models of their kind. Between 1932 and 1934, Pick served as President of the Design and Industries Association, and in 1934 was the first Chairman of the Council for Art and Industry. He lived at 15 Wildwood Road, a detached red-brick house, from about 1914 and died here twenty-seven years later. The plaque was installed in 1981; notably, the sans serif typeface Pick commissioned from Johnston was used for its lettering.

At 8 Meadway, Hampstead Garden Suburb, NW11 – one of a group of four houses built in 1908 to designs by M. H. Baillie Scott – a plaque marks the home of the actor **Robert Donat** (1905–1958) 9 (fig. 499). The son of a civil engineer of Polish descent, Donat studied drama in his native Manchester before embarking on a career as an actor in 1924. He had his first theatrical triumph playing Gideon Sarn in a 1931 adaptation of Mary Webb's *Precious Bane*, and went on to enjoy a number of other stage successes. After appearing as Thomas Culpepper in KORDA's *The Private Life of Henry VIII* (1933), Donat played the lead role in *The Count of Monte Cristo* (1934), which established him as a major film star. Soon after being offered the part, Donat moved to 8 Meadway, where he lived with his first wife Ella, née Voysey (b. 1902), the niece of the architect C. F. A. VOYSEY. Donat's time here, from 1934 to 1937, saw the burgeoning of his career: in 1935 he starred in HITCHCOCK's *The Thirty-Nine Steps* and Korda's *The Ghost Goes West*. Such was his popularity that 'Uncle Charles' Voysey was commissioned to build a garage in front of the house, allowing Donat to reach his car without running the gauntlet of the fans who gathered outside. Soon after moving out, Donat scored

his greatest screen hit – and his first Oscar – with the title role in *Goodbye, Mr Chips* (1939), from the novel by JAMES HILTON. His home at number 8 was not forgotten: in 1939 Donat set up the Meadway Company, named after the address, to 'loan' his services to film companies and theatres. The plaque – proposed by number 8's then owner, the writer Bernard Lott – was unveiled in 1994 by Donat's son John in the presence of other family members.

THE BOROUGH OF HARINGEY

Byron Cottage, 17 North Road, Highgate, N6 – a fine early eighteenth-century terraced house named after a governor of Highgate School, situated opposite – bears a GLC plaque to the poet and scholar **A. E. Housman** (1859–1936) 10 (fig. 500). As the inscription records, it was here that Housman wrote his most famous collection of poems, *A Shropshire Lad*. Born and raised in Worcestershire, Alfred Edward Housman studied at Oxford, and moved to London in 1882 to take up a clerkship at the Patent Office. Alongside this work, he published a large number of papers and returned to academia in 1892, when he took up the chair of latin at University College London, a position he held for nearly nineteen years. Later, from 1911 until the time of his death, he held a professorship at Cambridge. Although Housman anticipated that his greatest memorial would be his work as a classical scholar – he produced editions of Ovid (1894), Manilius (1903–30), Juvenal (1905) and others – it is as a poet that he is best remembered. His time at Byron Cottage

500 Byron Cottage, 17 North Road, Highgate, and its GLC plaque to A. E. Housman, author of *A Shropshire Lad*. [© English Heritage. Photograph by Derek Kendall]

moved with her, remaining there until he transferred to Cambridge in 1911.

There are two blue plaques in Southwood Lane, N6, which links Highgate High Street and Archway Road. At number 22, set back behind railings, a plaque of 1975 commemorates the traveller and ethnologist **Mary Kingsley** (1862–1900) 11 , who lived here as a child from about 1864 until 1879. Mary was born in Islington, the daughter of the physician and traveller Dr George Kingsley (1826–1892) and the niece of the writer CHARLES KINGSLEY. As her father was often away, she grew up largely in the company of her mother – Mary, née Bailey (d. 1892) – and her brother Charles (b. 1866) in this detached villa of *c*. 1830, which stood adjacent to the Highgate Tabernacle, from which hymns issued at regular intervals, 'much to George's agnostic annoyance'.[23] At number 22, Kingsley educated herself – taking a particular interest in her father's anthropological studies – and caused minor domestic disasters by experimenting with gunpowder and the household plumbing. She later recalled that, 'The whole of my childhood and youth was spent at home, in the house and garden. The living outside world I saw little of, and cared less for'.[24] This sense of seclusion was intensified by the house's aspect: all but one of its front windows were blind, as they remain today. Following the death of her parents in 1892, Kingsley was able to indulge her desire to travel, and between 1893 and 1895 made two pioneering voyages to West Africa, where she gathered natural specimens and information about indigenous religious beliefs and practices. Hailed as an intrepid adventurer on her return to England in 1895, Kingsley used her celebrity status to educate her countrymen about West African culture and politics: she lectured and published two books, *Travels in West Africa* (1897) and *West African Studies* (1899). In March 1900 Mary went to Cape Town as a volunteer nurse in the South African War; she contracted typhoid and died three months later. Soon after, the (Royal) African Society – envisaged by Kingsley in 1897 – was founded to continue the work that she had begun.

– he lived here from 1886 until 1905 – saw a burst of creative energy that produced *A Shropshire Lad* (1896), *Poems by Terence Hearsay* (1896) and the majority of the works published in *Last Poems* (1922). Here, he lived a bachelor life, and was served devotedly by his landlady, Mrs Trim; when in November 1905 Mrs Trim moved to 1 Yarborough Villas, Pinner, Housman

At 50 Southwood Lane is an English Heritage plaque to the poet, translator and orientalist **Arthur Waley** (1889–1966) 12 . Arthur was born in Kent, the son of the economist David Frederick Schloss and his wife

BARNET TO REDBRIDGE

Rachel Sophia, née Waley, whose maiden name was adopted by the family in 1914 as a response to anti-German sentiment. In 1913, after studying at Cambridge, he became an assistant in the new Sub-Department of Oriental Prints and Drawings at the British Museum, under Laurence Binyon. Waley quickly taught himself Chinese and Japanese, initially in order to catalogue the paintings in the museum's collection. In 1916 he published his first translations of Chinese verse, some of which were included in his highly successful collection *A Hundred and Seventy Chinese Poems* (1918). Further publications – including *The Nō Plays of Japan* (1921) and a translation of the tenth-century *Tale of Genji* (1925–33) – ensured Waley's reputation as one of Europe's most distinguished oriental scholars. Having lived for a long period in Clive Bell's house at 50 Gordon Square, Bloomsbury, WC1, Waley acquired the Southwood Lane residence in 1960. Alison Grant Robinson (1901–2001), to whom he had been romantically attached for many years, moved in immediately. In 1962, after the death of his long-term partner Beryl de Zoete, Waley joined Alison at number 50. The couple were finally married in 1966, a month before Waley's death here at the age of seventy-six. As the Gordon Square house already bore a plaque – erected by Camden Borough Council in honour of Clive Bell – English Heritage chose to commemorate Waley's Highgate residence; the plaque was unveiled in 1995 by Alison Waley, who was still living at the house.

Just north of Waterlow Park is 65 Cromwell Avenue, Highgate, N6, a substantial detached house on the corner of Cromwell Place. Built in the 1880s and inaugurated as India House on 1 July 1905 – with a speech by H. M. Hyndman – it was intended as a hostel for Indian students in London, and between June 1906 and July 1909 was the home of the Indian patriot and philosopher **Vinayak Damodar Savarkar** (1883–1966) **13** . He had been born near Nasik in the province of Bombay, and at the age of twelve vowed to carry on the struggle for Indian independence. In 1906 Savarkar came to England on a scholarship arranged by his fellow nationalist Shyamaji Krishnavarma and supported by Lokamanya Tilak. He entered Gray's Inn, and was called to the Bar in 1910. Savarkar's four years in London were critical to his development as a Hindu nationalist and revolutionary leader. While living at

India House, set up by Krishnavarma, he mixed with other fighters for Indian independence, among them Gandhi, who spent the night here on 20 October 1906. Meanwhile, Savarkar developed his literary interests: in 1907 he translated into Marathi the autobiography of Mazzini, his European hero, and carried out research for *The Indian War of Independence of 1857* (1909), a publication banned in India until 1946. In 1910 Savarkar was implicated in the murder of a British official in Nasik, which he allegedly helped to organise. Following a dramatic chase by police, he was arrested and extradited to India, where he was convicted. During his years in prison, 'Veer' (heroic) Savarkar became a committed Hindu nationalist, writing the influential pamphlet *Hindutva: Who is a Hindu?* (1923). On his release in 1937, he entered politics, encouraging the militarisation of Hindus and campaigning against untouchability. The controversy that dogged him throughout his life reached a peak after the assassination of Gandhi in 1948, a crime which he is said to have co-organised, though he was acquitted by the courts. The GLC plaque, put up at the suggestion of the Savarkar Centenary Celebration Committee, was unveiled in 1985 by the former MP Lord Fenner Brockway.

At the base of the south-east tower of Alexandra Palace, Wood Green, N22 – one of North London's most prominent landmarks – a GLC plaque commemorates the BBC's inauguration on 2 November 1936 of **the world's first regular high definition television service** **14** (fig. 501). The wording of the inscription was chosen with care as a number of experimental and sporadic television transmissions had already been made, some of them by the British Broadcasting Corporation itself. It was in 1935 that the BBC began to search for a suitable site from which to pilot its first television transmissions. In order to have the greatest range, the site had to occupy high ground not far from central London. In summer of that year, the BBC chose Alexandra Palace, built in 1873–75 to the designs of Alfred Meeson and John Johnson; known originally as the 'People's Palace', it was intended to rival the Crystal Palace as a public recreation and entertainment centre. At the south-east corner of the building, the BBC constructed offices and two studios, and a transmission mast – 220 feet (67 m) tall – was raised above the existing corner tower. In 1936 Major

501 Alexandra Palace in August 1936, with – in the foreground – a Marconi-EMI instantaneous television camera transmitting the view over London. The mast and transmitting aerials mark the position of the BBC offices and studios at the south-east corner of the building. [© Getty Images]

502 An early nineteenth-century cloud study by Luke Howard showing an aggregate cumulus in different stages. Howard, the 'namer of clouds', was commemorated with a plaque at 7 Bruce Grove, Tottenham, in 2002. [© Royal Meteorological Society / Science & Society Picture Library]

George Tryon, the Postmaster-General, performed the opening ceremony, and the world's first television programme was broadcast; initially, the Baird and the Marconi-EMI systems were used alternately, with the latter ultimately selected. The range of broadcast was estimated to be some twenty-five miles (40 km); all of London was covered, though only a tiny fraction of the population had purchased television sets to view the two separate hours of broadcasting on offer each day. It was only after the Second World War – during which transmissions were suspended – that televisual broadcasting got into its stride; the screening of Queen Elizabeth's coronation in 1953 is generally taken to mark the start of the television age. At the time of the plaque's unveiling in 1977 by Ian Trethowan – then Director-General designate of the BBC – Alexandra Palace was owned by the GLC. In 1980 it passed to Haringey Council, and later the same year was damaged by fire; following a remodelling, the building was reopened in 1988. Alexandra Palace was the main transmitting centre for the BBC until 1956, after which time it was used exclusively for news broadcasts. The building ceased to be used by the corporation in 1981, though its mast continues to transmit local broadcasts.

Tottenham's only blue plaque – at 7 Bruce Grove, N17 – marks the home of **Luke Howard** (1772–1864) ⑮ , poetically described as the 'namer of clouds' (fig. 502). Born in Clerkenwell, the son of a Quaker tinsmith, Howard enjoyed a successful career as a manufacturing chemist. In his spare time, he cultivated other scientific interests, and was one of the founders of the London-based philosophical group the Askesian Society in 1796. A regular contributor of scientific papers, Howard presented his now-famous 'On the Modification of Clouds' in 1803. This indicated the nature and height of clouds, and set out a system of classification and nomenclature – cirrus, stratus, cumulus and nimbus – which remains in international use today. His work was much admired: the German poet and scientist Goethe was so impressed that he wrote a poem, *Howard's Ehrengedächtnis* (1817), in his honour. In 1818–20 Howard published further meteorological findings in *The Climate of London*, which influenced figures including JOHN CONSTABLE, and later wrote *Seven Lectures on Meteorology* (1837). There was a veritable Howard (and Quaker) community in Bruce Grove, then one of Tottenham's 'prettiest . . .

spots'.[25] Luke Howard lived from 1837 at number 4 – now fronted by a shop – next door to his sister Elizabeth, at number 6. In 1852, on the death of his wife Mariabella, Howard went to live over the road with his eldest son Robert (1801–1871) at 7 Bruce Grove. This house of the 1790s had been in Luke Howard's ownership since at least the mid-1820s, and had been Robert's home from soon after that time. Luke also owned 14 Bruce Grove, where his daughter and son-in-law lived. It was at number 7 that Luke Howard died; members of his family remained at the house until 1892. The plaque was unveiled in 2002 by the TV weatherman Michael Fish on the part of the building that dates from the mid-nineteenth century.

THE BOROUGH OF ENFIELD

The poet **Stevie Smith** (1902–1971) **16** is commemorated with a plaque at 1 Avondale Road, Palmers Green, N13, an end-of-terrace house built in about 1904 (fig. 503). Florence Margaret Smith – known as 'Stevie' from the 1920s – was born in Hull. In 1906,

503   Number 1 Avondale Road, Palmers Green, the home for a remarkable sixty-five years (1906–71) of the poet Stevie Smith. [© English Heritage. Photograph by Derek Kendall]

after her father joined the Merchant Navy, she moved with her family to Palmers Green, then a rural village near London. She lived at number 1 from that year until the time of her death – a remarkable residence of sixty-five years. This 'house of female habitation' – described in Smith's poem 'A House of Mercy' (published 1966) – was shared with her elder sister Molly (1901–1975), her mother Ethel, née Spear (1876–1919) and, most enduringly, her aunt, Margaret Spear (d. 1968).[26] 'The Aunt' cared for Stevie for much of her life, and appeared in her writings as the 'Lion of Hull'. Stevie Smith's first work of fiction, the autobiographical *Novel on Yellow Paper* (1936), was written on the copying paper of the firm where she worked as a personal secretary, and from which she retired only in 1953. An immediate success, it was followed by two similar works, *Over the Frontier* (1938) and *The Holiday* (1949). However, it was as a poet that Smith excelled. Her verse – witty, bizarre, sad, sometimes caustic – reached a wide audience and brought her immense success; it appeared, most famously, in the volume *Not Waving but Drowning* (1957), illustrated – like her other poetry collections – with her own line drawings. Smith was awarded the Queen's Gold Medal for Poetry in 1969, and died during a trip to Devon two years later. The English Heritage plaque – unveiled in 2005 by the Poet Laureate, Andrew Motion – replaced a surface-mounted plaque installed by Enfield Council some years previously.

White Lodge, 68 Silver Street, Enfield, EN1 – a handsome weatherboarded building dating from the eighteenth, and possibly even the seventeenth, century – faces the modern Civic Centre, and bears a plaque to **Joseph Whitaker** (1820–1895) **17** , the London-born publisher and founder of *Whitaker's Almanack*. Whitaker's entrepreneurial flair came to the fore in 1849, when he founded the *Penny Post*, a monthly church magazine. By 1855, he was well established as a religious and theological publisher, and between 1856 and 1859 edited the *Gentleman's Magazine*. In 1858 Whitaker founded *The Bookseller*, a monthly journal for the publishing and bookselling business that continues to operate today. Ten years later, he first published the work that made his name familiar throughout the English-speaking world – *Whitaker's Almanack*, the comprehensive reference book that has been published annually since 1868. Whitaker took a

504 A detail of an engraving of 1883, showing Lamb's Cottage, Church Street, Edmonton. Charles Lamb lived here for just over a year (1833–34), while his sister Mary stayed on at the house until 1841. [© Illustrated London News Ltd / Mary Evans Picture Library]

505 Number 133 Chichester Road, Edmonton, the home of Charles Coward between 1945 and 1976. [© English Heritage. Photograph by Derek Kendall]

lease on White Lodge in June 1862, acquiring the property in 1875 and living here until his death, when the editorship of the *Almanack* passed to his twelfth child, Cuthbert (1873–1950). Since 1901, the house has been used as a doctors' surgery; it was marked with an English Heritage plaque – made of enamelled steel due to the building's timber-facing – in 1998.

A plaque at Lamb's Cottage (formerly Bay Cottage), Church Street, Edmonton, N9 – opposite the Charity School founded in 1778 – commemorates the writers **Charles Lamb** (1775–1834) (see also pp. 167–8) and **Mary Lamb** (1764–1847) **18** (fig. 504). Charles and his sister Mary were born in London and, after their respective educations, supported their ageing mother and increasingly senile father, Mary by needlework and Charles with a clerkship in the East India Company. The siblings were thrown firmly together in 1796, when Mary – in one of her fits of insanity – killed their mother with a table knife. She was put on trial and, being found insane, entrusted to the care of her brother. This involved great self-sacrifice on Charles's part, though the pair shared literary interests: their collaborations included the books *Tales from Shakespear* [*sic*] (1807) and *Poetry for Children, Entirely Original* (1809). In 1825 Charles dedicated himself full-time to

writing, and decided to move with his sister to Enfield. However, the quiet provincial life did not – as he had hoped – prevent Mary's bouts of mental illness. In May 1833 – the year that saw the publication of one of Charles's greatest works, *The Last Essays of Elia* – he moved with Mary to what was then Bay Cottage, a house kept as a discreet private asylum by Mr and Mrs Walden, who – Charles wrote – 'arranged to lodge and board us only'.[27] Here, Charles lived 'in a half-way purgatory', witnessing the rapid deterioration of his sister.[28] Soon after moving in, he wrote of Mary to William Wordsworth, 'I see little of her; alas! I too often hear her'.[29] Three days before Christmas 1834, Charles had a fall in nearby Fore Street, and died shortly afterwards. Mary lived on at Bay Cottage until 1841, and on her death was buried alongside her brother in the churchyard of All Saints', on the opposite side of Church Street. The modest early eighteenth-century house in which they lived – set back behind high railings and a narrow garden – was marked with a blue plaque in 1999.

At 133 Chichester Road, Edmonton, N9 – a wonderfully ordinary inter-war end-of-terrace house – a plaque commemorates the remarkable **Charles Coward** (1905–1976) **19** as the 'rescuer of prisoners from Auschwitz' (figs 505 and 506). Coward's wartime experiences – partially brought to the screen in *The Password is Courage* (1962), starring Dirk Bogarde – earned him widespread recognition, especially in Israel, where he has a tree at Yad Vashem, the Holocaust memorial in Jerusalem. Having entered the Army in 1937, Coward was captured at the fall of Calais three years later, and became notorious for his repeated attempts to escape captivity. He vowed to make himself a nuisance to the Nazis, and to help his fellow prisoners. Posted to the Auschwitz complex of labour and death camps in Upper Silesia, Sergeant Major Coward witnessed at first-hand the atrocities committed by the Nazis. There – based at the labour camp E715, next to the I. G. Farben plant – he was appointed Red Cross Trustee responsible for British prisoners of war, and was able to operate without the usual restrictions. Coward repeatedly risked his own life in order to smuggle prisoners out of Auschwitz, by swapping the identities of inmates for those who had died in the camp; he also brought in arms and explosives and sent regular coded letters, providing information to the

THE BOROUGH OF WALTHAM FOREST

At 42 Oak Hill Gardens, Woodford Green, IG8 – an early twentieth-century end-of-terrace house on the edge of Epping Forest – a plaque commemorates **James Hilton** (1900–1954) **20** , the novelist and scriptwriter. Born in Leigh, Lancashire, Hilton moved in 1902 with his family to London, where his father John (1872–1955) – one of the models for Mr Chips – was employed as a master by the Walthamstow School Board. Having attended boarding school in Cambridge, Hilton entered the university in 1918; it was as an undergraduate that he published his first novel, *Catherine Herself* (1920). On leaving Cambridge in 1922, he moved to his parents' new home at 42 Oak Hill Gardens – which they had named Leigh – and dedicated himself to writing. While here, he penned novels including *Terry* (1927) and *And Now Goodbye* (1931), but did not find fame until 1933, about a year after leaving number 42, when he published *Lost Horizon*. Soon after came another triumph, *Goodbye, Mr Chips*, written in just four days and published in book form in 1934. On the strength of these two works, Hilton was invited to Hollywood, where he worked on the film versions of his stories and on other screenplays, such as that for *Mrs Miniver* (1942). He lived for the rest of his life in California, though he often returned to London to visit his ageing and widowed father, who lived at number 42 until the 1950s. By 1997, when the plaque was put up, the house had been named Shangri-la, the fictional utopia Hilton had created in *Lost Horizon*.

506   Charles Coward giving evidence at the I. G. Farben trials at Nuremberg in 1947, with a plan of Auschwitz displayed behind him. During his internment at the camp, he helped to rescue hundreds of prisoners. [© Paul M. Hebert Collection, Paul M. Hebert Law Center Library, Louisiana State University]

British government. On one occasion, he exchanged places with an inmate of the nearby concentration camp, and had a night-long experience of the horrific conditions. The number of Jews rescued by Coward is said to have numbered in the hundreds. Liberated in 1945, he moved to 133 Chichester Road; shared with his wife Florence and their five children, it was his home until the year of his death. It was from here that Coward set out to give crucial – and, at the time, sensational – testimony at the I. G. Farben trials at Nuremberg in 1947. He also gave evidence at a trial in Germany in 1953, enabling thousands of survivors from Auschwitz to file lawsuits for compensation against their former oppressors.

On the east side of the railway arches that carry the Chingford line over the River Lea – the Walthamstow Marsh Railway Viaduct, E17 – a surface-mounted plaque commemorates the site where the pioneering aircraft designer and manufacturer **Alliott Verdon Roe** (1877–1958) assembled his Avro No. 1 triplane **21** , now on display at London's Science Museum (fig. 507). Born in Manchester, Roe began to study the problems of flight in the early twentieth century, and in 1907 won a prize for a model aeroplane. A full-scale version tested at Brooklands the following year, but it was only in 1909 that Roe managed a substantial flight. Beneath two arches on Walthamstow Marshes, he built his triplane; this succeeded in flying a hundred feet (30 m)

COPYRIGHT:
HALFTONES L:-

507 A. V. Roe's No. 1 triplane, assembled in arches beneath the railway line at Walthamstow Marshes in summer 1909. It made the first all-British powered flight – travelling a distance of 100 feet (30 m) – on 13 July of that year. [© Science Museum / Science & Society Picture Library]

on 13 July 1909 – the first all-British powered flight – and over 900 feet (274 m) ten days later. The arches were, Roe recalled, damp, muddy and poorly lit; he wrote that, 'We had boarded up the ends of two of them, but it was hardly an ideal workshop, for there were no windows and it was necessary to take down the shutters if we wanted light . . . The machine would be wheeled out and pushed to a suitable corner of the ground, amid occasionally excited expressions, sometimes jeers and sometimes rude remarks of lookers-on'. After the engine had been started and warmed, 'I would give the signal: "Let go", and the machine then tore over the ground followed by my helpers carrying tools, pieces of timber, and other necessary appliances

to cope with the repairs necessary after the almost inevitable "crash"'.[30] This was just the beginning of Roe's successful career: in 1910 he set up A. V. Roe & Co. with his brother, H. V. Roe, in Manchester. The firm's first great triumph was the Avro 504, the leading military plane of the First World War. Roe was knighted in 1929, the year after he sold his share in his company to Armstrong Siddeley; his later years were dedicated to flying boats, such as the Saunders-Roe Princess (launched 1952). The plaque was originally proposed by the pupils of Mandeville Primary School, Clapton, who were carrying out a project on flight; it was unveiled in 1983 by Sir Alliott's son, Geoffrey Verdon Roe.

The black South African writer and campaigner for African rights **Solomon T. Plaatje** (1876–1932) 22 has a GLC plaque at 25 Carnarvon Road, Leyton, E10, a late nineteenth-century terraced house. Plaatje was born into the Setswana-speaking BaRolong people in the Orange Free State, South Africa, and in 1894 entered the Cape Civil Service. In 1902 he left to become a newspaper editor, and in 1911 began to write articles for English-language papers. The following year, iPlaatje was one of the founders of the South African Native National Congress, later the African National Congress, and was appointed General-Secretary. It was as a member of a congress deputation sent to protest against the Natives' Land Act of 1913 – which deprived Africans of the right to acquire non-African land – that he made his first trip to London, between May 1914 and January 1917. Shortly after his arrival, Plaatje found lodgings with a Mrs Timberlake at 25 Carnavon Road, and this remained his home until mid- to late 1915, when he moved to 33 Alfred Road, Acton, W3. While at number 25, Plaatje wrote most of *Native Life in South Africa* (1916). His second major work, the historical novel *Mhudi*, was largely completed in London in 1920 – during Plaatje's second of three visits to the capital – though it was only published ten years later; this was the first novel in English known to have been written by a black African. By the time of his death, Plaatje was regarded as a major spokesman for his people, and had played a pioneering role in the emergence of African literature.

THE BOROUGH OF NEWHAM

The borough of Newham's sole official plaque commemorates a figure intimately associated with the area: **Will Thorne** (1857–1946) 23 , the trade union leader and Labour MP, who lived at 1 Lawrence Road, West Ham, E13, a Victorian end-of-terrace house that has its entrance front in Claude Road. Born in Birmingham, Thorne worked as a labourer from the age of six and became involved in his first labour protest at Saltley Gasworks. In the early 1880s, a few years after his marriage to Harriet Hallam, the daughter of a fellow gasworker, he took up work at Beckton Gasworks in London, and joined the Social Democratic Federation – coming into contact with figures such as H. M. HYNDMAN. Helped by Ben Tillett, he established in 1889 the National Union of Gasworkers and General

Labourers; this soon chalked up its first success by persuading gas companies to introduce the eight-hour day, an achievement that preceded the famous London Dock Strike of August 1889. Thorne was Secretary of the organisation until 1934, by which time it had become known as the National Union of General and Municipal Workers. Through it, he became involved in the TUC. Aside from trade unions, Thorne's other great loyalty was to West Ham; he was a member of the Town Council from 1891 until his death, and was MP for the area from 1906 to 1945. A GLC plaque – erected under the aegis of English Heritage – was unveiled in 1987 in the heart of Thorne's constituency at 1 Lawrence Road, his home from 1907 until his death. In a tribute to Thorne, HAROLD LASKI wrote, 'The mean streets of West Ham are less mean because he lived there'.[31]

THE BOROUGH OF REDBRIDGE

At 198 Windsor Road, Ilford, IG1, a plaque honours **Albert Mansbridge** (1876–1952) 24 , the founder of the Workers' Educational Association (WEA). His case for commemoration was treated somewhat exceptionally, a fact that doubtless reflects the influence of its proposer, the Chairman of the GLC Sir Harold Shearman. In order for a plaque to be awarded, the standard twenty years from death – required under the selection criteria – was specially reduced to ten years (see p. 18). The case subsequently progressed from suggestion to plaque in what was, for the scheme, remarkable speed – a little under two years. Mansbridge moved from Gloucester to London with his family in 1880, and grew up in Battersea. In his twenties, he became closely involved in the co-operative movement, and was active as a writer and orator. The work for which he is chiefly remembered – the founding, with his wife Frances, née Pringle, of the WEA – took place in 1903, the year prior to the couple's move from Clapham to 198 Windsor Road. This ordinary end-of-terrace house of the late nineteenth century served as the association's central office until late 1906, and remained the Mansbridges' home until about 1909. The WEA – originally the Association to Promote the Higher Education of Working Men – brought Mansbridge, its General Secretary, to the forefront of his field, and had widespread significance. By the outbreak of the First World War, there were nearly 180 WEA branches, with over 2,500 affiliated societies, all of them committed to organis-

508 Neil Kinnock, then leader of the Labour Party, unveils the plaque to Clement Richard Attlee at 17 Monkhams Avenue, Woodford Green, in 1984. On his left is Mrs Olive Fisher, the occupant of the house. [© City of London, LMA]

ing lectures, courses and tutorials in order to raise standards of education. After his retirement as Secretary in 1915, Mansbridge remained committed to his cause, and was a founder of the Church Tutorials Classes Association (1917), the World Association for Adult Education (1919) and, with LORD HALDANE, the British Institute of Adult Education (1921). The font of the plaque was specially adapted to enable the full title of the WEA to appear on one line rather than two; it was installed by the GLC in 1967.

The Prime Minister **Clement Richard Attlee** (1883–1967) 25 is commemorated at 17 Monkhams Avenue, Woodford Green, IG8, a substantial Edwardian semi-detached house. Attlee, the son of a solicitor, was born

and brought up in Putney. After a conventional middle-class education at public school and Oxford, he read for the Bar but – after witnessing deprivation in the East End – joined the Stepney branch of the Independent Labour Party in 1908, and decided to devote himself to socialism and politics. He worked as Secretary of Toynbee Hall (see JIMMY MALLON) and as a lecturer on social work before enlisting in the Army at the outbreak of the First World War. In 1922 Attlee was elected MP for Limehouse – a seat he held until 1950 – and in 1931 was chosen as deputy leader of the Labour Party under George Lansbury. At about this time, he developed the political ideas embodied in his book *The Will and the Way to Socialism* (1935), published in the year that he became party leader. In 1940 Attlee agreed to serve with WINSTON CHURCHILL in the War Cabinet and two years later became Deputy Prime Minister, playing a major part in the wartime government. The surprise Labour victory of 1945 brought Attlee to power as premier, and he began to implement a massive programme of national re-organisation, based on taking many utilities and industries into public ownership; abroad, his most notable achievement was the granting of full independence to India in 1947. Attlee remained Prime Minister until 1951, and leader of the party until 1955, when he retired and was elevated to the peerage. He moved from Limehouse to 17 Monkhams Avenue shortly after his marriage to Violet Millar (1896–1964) in January 1922, and lived here until October 1931, when, largely in order to meet the needs of a growing family, he moved to Stanmore. Number 17 is one of the only London addresses associated with Attlee to survive; in 1984 it was marked with a GLC plaque, unveiled by the then leader of the Labour Party, Neil Kinnock (fig. 508).

BARNET TO REDBRIDGE

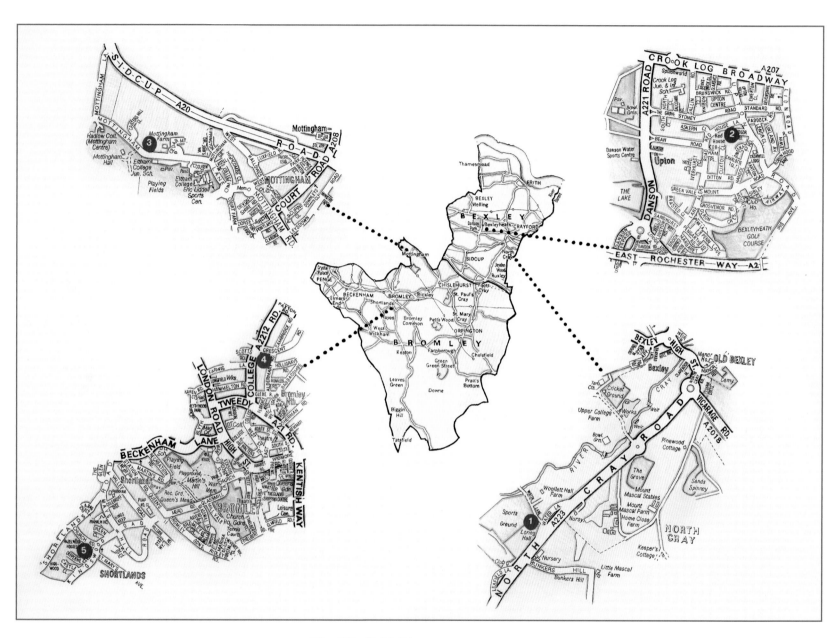

BEXLEY AND BROMLEY

THE BOROUGH OF BEXLEY

Loring Hall, 8 Water Lane, North Cray, Sidcup, DA14, is a modest mid-eighteenth-century farmhouse on the edge of London where the statesman Robert Stewart, **Viscount Castlereagh** (1769–1822) ❶ , lived and died. Castlereagh took a lifelong lease on the house – then known as North Cray Farm or Cottage – in the summer of 1810. He had the place enlarged, and bred Merino sheep on its forty acres (16 ha) of grazing land, while his wife Amelia, née Hobart (1772–1829), daughter of the 2nd Earl of Buckinghamshire, kept a small zoo. Castlereagh loved the country and pursuits such as fishing, which provided relief from the strains of high political office. Born in Dublin, he began his career as Chief Secretary for Ireland (1798–1801), and played a key role in the passage of the Act of Union between Britain and Ireland (1801). In 1812, in the midst of the Napoleonic Wars, he became Foreign Secretary and was responsible for negotiating the vital peace treaties of 1814 and 1815. He remained in office as Foreign Secretary and leader of the House of Commons until 1822, the year after he became 2nd

Marquess of Londonderry on the death of his father. Posterity knows him as Castlereagh, and for contemporary opponents of the government it was a name synonymous with unpopular policies such as detention without trial. The strain of a difficult parliamentary session in 1822 made Castlereagh ill, and in the summer recess – feverish and delusional – he retreated to North Cray. His pistols and razors were taken away lest he harm himself, but on the morning of 12 August 1822, briefly left alone, he went into his dressing room and committed suicide by cutting his throat with a penknife; it has been suggested, though never proved, that he was a victim of blackmail. It is a measure of Castlereagh's unpopularity that his funeral cortège was actually jeered en route to Westminster Abbey, but posterity has been rather kinder, especially about his talent in the diplomatic arena. His English Heritage plaque, set into a boundary wall by the entrance, was erected in 1989.

'More a poem than a house . . . but an admirable place to live in', said D. G. Rossetti of **Red House**, Red House Lane, Bexleyheath, DA6 ❷ (fig. 509).[32] This

509 The east front of Red House, Bexleyheath, designed by the architect Philip Webb for his friend William Morris and completed in 1860. [© NTPL / Andrew Butler]

BEXLEY AND BROMLEY

architectural gem, now surrounded by inter-war suburbia, was, as the plaque records, designed by the architect **Philip Webb** (1831–1915) for his friend **William Morris** (1834–1896) (see also p. 60), the poet and artist. The house was conceived by Morris in summer 1858, the year before his marriage to Jane Burden (1839–1914), as a retreat for himself, his family and their friends, away from the smoke and dirt of London. For its site Morris chose an orchard of cherry and apple trees in the remote hamlet of Upton. The building, with its red-tiled roof and orange-red brick walls, was revolutionary in design and plan, and was essentially the prototype of all domestic architecture in the Arts and Crafts style; it has been contended, nonetheless, that it displays the influence of G. E. STREET and WILLIAM BUTTERFIELD. It was ready for occupation by June 1860, and the Morrises, with help from friends such as EDWARD BURNE-JONES and his wife Georgiana, set about decorating it. This challenge prompted Morris to co-found in April 1861 the decorative furnishing firm of Morris, Marshall, Faulkner & Co., the partners of which included Webb, Rossetti and Burne-Jones. The early days at Red House fitted Morris's ideal of life: friends living, working and playing together in an idyllic rural setting, into which two daughters, Jenny and May, were born in 1861 and 1862. Soon, however, the work of Morris's London-based firm was taking up most of his time, and in 1865 he and his family left Red House for 26 Queen Square, Bloomsbury (demolished). Much of his notoriously monumental furniture had to be left behind, being too heavy to shift; Morris himself could never bring himself to revisit Red House, which was sold. The plaque – set into one of the brick gatepiers – was erected by the GLC in 1969, at which time Red House was the residence of Ted Hollamby (1921–1999), a civic architect who worked for the LCC and for Lambeth Council. The property, which survives virtually unaltered, was taken into the ownership of The National Trust in 2003.

THE BOROUGH OF BROMLEY

In 1966 the GLC erected a plaque to the cricketer **W. G. Grace** (1848–1915) ❸ at his last residence, a detached late Victorian villa called Fairmount in Mottingham Lane, Mottingham, SE9, now a retirement home. William Gilbert Grace (fig. 510) was born near

Bristol and imbibed a love of cricket from his family; two of his brothers, E. M. Grace and G. F. Grace, went on to play first-class cricket, but it was Gilbert who became one of the game's iconic figures, and was recognised internationally as a sporting genius. In a first-class career that lasted over forty years, he turned batting from an accomplishment into a science and helped to elevate cricket from a mere pastime to a national institution. Grace was nominally an amateur, being a doctor by training and profession, and it was this work that prompted his move to London in 1898. The following year, he played his last test match for England and transferred from Gloucestershire CC to the new London County Club, based at Crystal Palace, of which he also became Manager. In 1909, the year after he retired from first-class cricket – with a career total of nearly 55,000 runs – 'W. G.' moved with his wife Agnes, née Day (1853–1930) to Fairmount. While here, Grace – affectionately known as 'The Old Man' – remained a keen sportsman, playing golf, bowls and curling as well as cricket; however, at the outbreak of the First World War he wrote to *The Sportsman* urging players to abandon the county season and to enlist. In October 1915 Grace suffered a stroke while working in Fairmount's garden – in which he grew the choicest asparagus – and died at home a few days later. It was said that distress caused by Zeppelin raids contributed to his demise; Grace complained that, unlike the deliveries from fast bowlers, it was a threat that he could not see coming. The plaque to Grace had originally been erected by the LCC in 1963 at 7 Lawrie Park Road, Sydenham – his home in 1898–1909 – but the following year that building was demolished. The plaque was salvaged and re-erected by the GLC at Fairmount, making it a curiosity – an LCC plaque placed beyond that authority's geographical boundaries.

Number 6 Crescent Road, Sundridge Park, BR1, is an ordinary semi-detached house near the centre of Bromley that was once the home of the theorist of anarchism **Prince Peter Kropotkin** (1842–1921) 4 , a fact commemorated by an English Heritage plaque of 1989. Scion of an old aristocratic Russian family, Kropotkin was born in Moscow and became a committed anarchist after a visit to western Europe in 1872. Fourteen years later he took refuge in England, having been imprisoned for his political activities in both Russia and France. He worked as a scientific journalist while living a life of blameless respectability on the fringes of London. In the summer of 1894 Kropotkin moved from Acton to Crescent Road in Bromley, and while here wrote a number of influential books, including *Fields, Factories and Workshops* (1899), his autobiography, *Memoirs of a Revolutionist* (1899), and *Mutual Aid: A Factor of Evolution* (1902), which expounded a peaceful, gradualist theory of anarchism. Although they had little money, Kropotkin and his wife Sofiya, née Ananyeva-Rabinovich (1856–1938) were generous hosts and entertained a wide circle of friends and acquaintances every Sunday afternoon at the house. This was then called Viola, and was unkindly described by FORD MADOX FORD as 'troglodytic'.[33] Its walls were

covered in vines; among his Bromley neighbours, Kropotkin was chiefly reputed as a keen and able gardener. In the front room, the chief adornments of which were natural science specimens, Kropotkin would entertain his guests at the piano with renditions of revolutionary songs; another political theorist, G. D. H. Cole, recalled that his playing was 'atrocious'.[34] The Kropotkins left Bromley in the autumn of 1907 for Muswell Hill Road, Highgate, and afterwards lived in Brighton; latterly, Kropotkin's delicate health prompted him to winter in Switzerland. He returned to Russia in the wake of the February Revolution of 1917.

At 20 Church Road, Shortlands, BR2, on the corner of Kingwood Road, is a GLC plaque to **Alexander Muirhead** (1848–1920) 5 , a Scottish electrical engineer whose specialism was telegraphy. Despite a childhood accident that left him deaf in one ear – and therefore prone, at that time, to being unfairly regarded as having a learning disability – Muirhead enjoyed an outstanding academic career at University College London, where he studied chemistry. At St Bartholomew's Hospital he undertook pioneering work on the electrocardiogram, before being appointed scientific adviser to his father's firm of telegraph engineers; an early achievement for Muirhead in this field was a patent for duplexing wireless signals in submarine cables – that is, rendering them capable of receiving and transmitting simultaneously. Later he set up his own business manufacturing electrical equipment, Muirhead & Co., which moved to Elmers End near Bromley in 1896. Three years earlier, Muirhead had married Mary Elizabeth Blomfield (1858–1930) and settled at number 20, known as The Lodge, an appropriately grand home for an important local employer. In 1894 he began to take an interest in wireless, and this led to the formation in 1901 of the Lodge-Muirhead Wireless Syndicate, a business co-founded with the physicist Oliver Lodge that was bought by MARCONI in 1911. Muirhead died at home in Church Road in December 1920. The plaque was unveiled by his niece, Norah Twinberrow, in 1981.

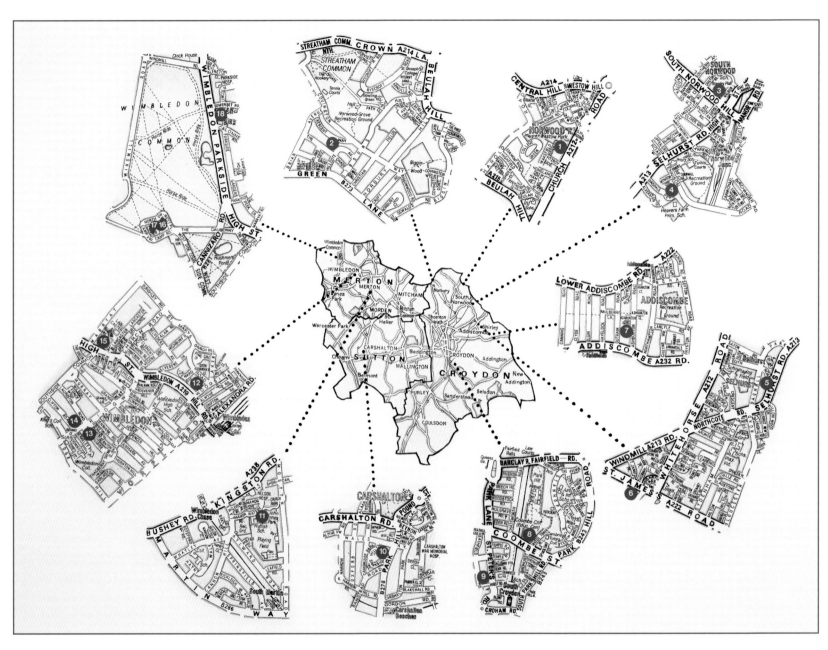

CROYDON, SUTTON AND MERTON

THE BOROUGH OF CROYDON

At 122 Church Road, Upper Norwood, SE19, close to the northern edge of Crystal Palace Park, stands the ornate Italianate Queen's Hotel of 1853–54, designed by F. Pouget; here, a plaque records the residence of the French novelist **Emile Zola** (1840–1902) ❶ in 1898–99. Zola is regarded as the founder of the literary naturalist movement that sought to de-romanticise the portrayal of human life. He is best known for his series of twenty novels chronicling the life of a family during the French Second Empire, *Les Rougon-Macquart* (1871–93); these, like other of his works, were based on first-hand observation of all levels of society. In 1897 Zola's literary career was interrupted by the Dreyfus Affair: Captain Alfred Dreyfus, a French-Jewish army officer, was tried for treason, and Zola was among those who protested his innocence, publishing a fierce denunciation of the French general staff, 'J'Accuse' (1898), as an open letter in the newspaper *L'Aurore*. Zola was subsequently found guilty of libel. While awaiting retrial on appeal, he fled to England in July 1898 and briefly stayed at the Grosvenor Hotel, Victoria, before he was advised by his friend and publisher, Ernest Alfred Vizetelly, to move to a more secluded location. During his stay at Oatlands Park Hotel in Walton, he was spotted by a *Daily Mail* reporter, and so moved again. By October 1898, Zola – who adopted the persona of M. Jean Richard – had settled at the Queen's Hotel, living first in rooms overlooking the garden and then in a suite on the raised ground floor at the front. Here, he wrote *Fécondité* (1899), one of the series of novels known as *Les Quatres Evangiles*. Zola was visited in turn by his wife, Gabrielle Meley (1839–1925), and by his mistress, Jeanne Rozerot (1867–1914), the latter accompanied by their two young children. In his leisure, Zola cycled around Upper Norwood and took photographs of the locality, especially of Crystal Palace. When he heard that Dreyfus was to be retried, Zola returned to his homeland in June 1899 and received a pardon from the government in 1900. He died from carbon monoxide poisoning, caused by a blocked chimney, two years later. The plaque was unveiled in 1990 by Lord Montagu, then Chairman of English Heritage, in the presence of several of Zola's descendants.

Number 45 The Chase, Norbury, SW16, one of a cluster of inter-war detached houses, was the home from 1927 to 1934 of **Will Hay** (1888–1949) ❷, the comic actor and astronomer. Born in County Durham, William Thomson Hay had a peripatetic childhood, but returned to the north of England in his twenties, living mostly in the Manchester area. Following his marriage in 1907 to Gladys Perkins (b. 1889), he embarked on a music-hall career, taking inspiration from his sister's teaching anecdotes to develop his schoolmaster comedy persona. His routine – above all, his sketch 'The Fourth Form at St Michael's' – soon became widely loved, and his role as a shambolic blustering boss also saw him lampooning the police and the prison service. Hay acted in nineteen films in the 1930s and 1940s, a few of which he also directed; these are epitomised by *Oh, Mr Porter!* (1937), set at the fictitious Buggleskelly railway station in rural Ireland, and also included *My Learned Friend* (1944). Hay had long been interested in astronomy and in 1932 brought this hobby into a more public domain, joining the British Astronomical Association and becoming a Fellow of the Royal Astronomical Society. It was while living at 45 The Chase, using his home-made observatory in the back garden, that Hay discovered a white spot on Saturn in 1933. He left number 45 after his marriage broke down in 1934 and subsequently lived at the White House, 6 Great North Way, Mill Hill, NW4, where he rebuilt his observatory. Hay's final years were spent with his partner, Randi Kopstadt, in a flat on the Chelsea Embankment. The English Heritage plaque was unveiled in 2000 by the comedian Roy Hudd, then King Rat of The Grand Order of Water Rats.

At 12 South Norwood Hill, South Norwood, SE25, lie Stanley Halls and Technical Trade School. These handsome brick buildings – a main hall and gallery, a smaller hall and a trade school – were all founded and designed by the inventor, manufacturer and philanthropist **W. F. R. Stanley** (1829–1909) ❸, and were built between 1901 and 1909 (fig. 512). They were marked with an English Heritage plaque in 1993. Born in Islington, the son of a mechanic, William Ford Robinson Stanley grew up in Hertfordshire, and his natural aptitude for mathematics and science soon led to a career designing scientific instruments. In 1854 he set up a small shop in Holborn, where he sold drawing instruments and, later, tools for surveying, such as a simplified theodolite. In 1865 Stanley moved to South Norwood and two years later established his own

511   A photograph of 12 Tennison Road, South Norwood, taken during the residence of Arthur Conan Doyle, between 1891 and 1894. In his study – to the left of the front door – he wrote eighteen Sherlock Holmes stories. [Reproduced with the kind permission of the Royal College of Surgeons of Edinburgh]

factory in Belgrave Road, where it remained until a business merger in 1926 brought about a move to Eltham. Also in 1867, he and his wife Elizabeth Ann, née Savory took up residence at Stanleybury, 74 Albert Road (demolished), one of a group of three semi-detached houses that were built according to his specifications. In 1878 Stanley moved to a much larger detached house, Cumberlow Lodge, Chalfont Road, South Norwood, which he also designed. As Cumberlow Lodge – his home until his death – could not be seen from the road, the plaque was placed on nearby Stanley Halls. A visionary thinker, a polymath and an inveterate student, Stanley produced a blueprint for an ideal community – Stanleyton – in *The Case of the Fox: A Political Utopia* (1903), which was set in 1950. In keeping with his principles, he invested hugely in Stanley Halls, which he intended should serve as a secular meeting place and a technical education centre. Described by Bridget Cherry and Nikolaus Pevsner as 'the most memorable buildings in South Norwood', Stanley Halls and Technical Trade School remain in use by the local community, though Cumberlow Lodge was demolished by a property developer in 2006.[35]

At 12 Tennison Road, South Norwood, SE5, a GLC plaque of 1973 commemorates **Sir Arthur Conan Doyle** (1859–1930) **4**, the creator of that most famous of British detectives, Sherlock Holmes (fig. 511). Born in Edinburgh, Conan Doyle studied medicine at the city's university, where he was greatly influenced by his professor, Joseph Bell, a master of deduction. After graduating, he established a medical practice in Southsea, Hampshire, but in spring 1891 moved to London with his wife Louise, née Hawkins (1856/7–1906) and their daughter Mary (b. 1889); the family took lodgings at 23 Montague Place, Marylebone (demolished), while Conan Doyle set up in practice nearby at 2 Upper Wimpole Street, hoping to establish himself as an eye specialist. However, his time was increasingly devoted to writing, which had long been his passion. Conan Doyle first came to attention with *A Study in Scarlet* (1887) and its sequel *The Sign of the Four* (1890), which introduced the characters of Sherlock Holmes and Dr Watson. By the end of summer 1891, Conan Doyle had moved his family to 12 Tennison Road – 'a prettily-built and modest-looking red-brick residence' dating from *c.* 1887 – and turned his attentions to writing full-time.[36] His Holmes stories, meanwhile, were trans-

ferred to the newly established *Strand Magazine*, through which they found immense popularity. In his study, to the left of the front door, Conan Doyle wrote eighteen such stories, including 'The Boscombe Valley Mystery' (1891), 'The Speckled Band' (1892) and 'The Musgrave Ritual' (1893), while the area inspired later works such as 'The Norwood Builder' (1903). In this 'quiet corner', decorated with paintings by his father, he worked 'between the hours of breakfast and lunch, and again in the evening from five to eight, writing some three thousand words a day'.[37] However, as the fame of his literary creation grew, Conan Doyle became uneasy; when demands for outrageous writing fees failed to avert requests for further Holmes tales, he decided to put an end to the stories, with the apparent death of the detective in 'The Final Problem' (December 1893). Conan Doyle left Tennison Road the following year, although the house was not sold until spring 1895. He and his family settled at Undershaw in Hindhead, Surrey, which was specifically designed to benefit Louise Doyle's health. There, under further pressure from his publisher, Conan Doyle wrote *The Hound of the Baskervilles* (1902) and reprised his creation for another series of *Strand* stories, collected as *The Return of Sherlock Holmes* in 1905. The last Holmes collection, *The Case-Book of Sherlock Holmes*, appeared in 1927, by which time Conan Doyle had authored such works as *The Lost World* (1912) and had turned his energies to spiritualism.

Number 30 Dagnall Park, South Norwood, SE25, a small brick semi with a neat hedge and garden, was once the home of **Samuel Coleridge-Taylor** (1875–1912) **5**, composer of the *Song of Hiawatha*. He was

512 Stanley Halls, 12 South Norwood Hill, and the English Heritage plaque commemorating their founder, W. F. R. Stanley. [© English Heritage. Photograph by Derek Kendall]

the first black recipient of a blue plaque, which was erected in 1975. Born at 15 Theobald's Road, Holborn (demolished), the son of a Sierra Leonean father, and brought up in Croydon by his English mother, Coleridge-Taylor displayed musical talent at an early age and by 1891 he was studying the violin at the Royal College of Music. In 1893 he won a scholarship that enabled him to continue his education for a further four years, during which time his abilities as a composer became apparent. In 1898 the college hosted the first performance of Coleridge-Taylor's most famous work, *Hiawatha's Wedding Feast*, which was an immediate success and was first performed at the Albert Hall in 1900; it inspired further pieces including *The Death of Minnehaha* (1899) and *Hiawatha's Departure* (1900), which completed his three-part cantata *Scenes from 'The Song of Hiawatha'*. Early in 1900, after marrying Jessie Fleetwood Walmisley (1869–1962) – who had also studied at the Royal College of Music – Samuel moved to 30 Dagnall Park; the couple and their son Hiawatha (1900–1980), later a musician, remained here until 1901. Coleridge-Taylor's career flourished, and his compositions were much performed, both in Britain and America. He spent several years teaching at Trinity College of Music (1903–10) and the Guildhall School of Music (1910–13), and was active as a conductor in London and New York. Coleridge-Taylor became increasingly interested in African folk music and composed several works on this theme, including *African Romances* (1897) and *24 Negro Melodies* (1905). His popularity was partly responsible for his demise: overwork brought on pneumonia, leading to his untimely death at the age of thirty-seven at Aldwick, 6 St Leonard's Road, Duppas Hill, SW14, where he had lived since 1909. As Aldwick had been greatly altered in appearance, the GLC decided to commemorate 30 Dagnall Park instead.

In 2005 English Heritage installed a plaque at 144 St James's Road (formerly 5 Edinburgh Villas), Croydon, CR9, the birthplace of the all-round sportsman **C. B. Fry** (1872–1956) **6** . The son of Lewis John Fry, a civil servant, and his wife Constance, née White, Charles Burgess Fry became interested in cricket at the age of seven and was also a gifted athlete who, by 1889, had taught himself to jump a distance of twenty feet (6 m). He later became a top-class sprinter and hurdler, was a fine swimmer, golfer and horseman, ventured into

rugby, played football for England in 1901 and was an FA Cup finalist for Southampton the following year. However, it was as a cricketer that Fry rose to international prominence. He was a member of the Sussex County Cricket team between 1894 and 1908, a member of the Hampshire team in 1909–21 and took part in twenty-six test matches for England, often partnered with K. S. Ranjitsinhji. Over the course of his career in first-class cricket – which came to a close in 1922 – Fry, noted especially for his batting abilities, reached an aggregate of 30,886 runs and made ninety-four centuries. A prolific writer, he turned increasingly to sports journalism, and from 1904 to 1911 edited and directed *Fry's Magazine of Sports and Outdoor Life* from offices in Southampton Street, Covent Garden. Much of Fry's life was spent outside London, notably in Sussex, Kent and Hampshire; he spent over forty years in the last-mentioned county, as Director of the training ship *Mercury*, which he ran with his wife Beatrice. The only suitable address for commemoration in the capital was 144 St James's Road – originally 5 Edinburgh Villas, St James's West – a mid-nineteenth-century detached house modernised in the later 1900s. It was the Fry family home only briefly, though his birth and residence here qualified 'C. B.' to join the Surrey County Cricket team in 1891. The plaque was unveiled by Fry's grandsons, Jonathan and Charles, on the anniversary of his birth.

At 20 Outram Road, Addiscombe, CR0, a GLC plaque marks the home of the electrical engineer **Frederick George Creed** (1871–1957) **7** , inventor of the teleprinter (fig. 513). Born in Nova Scotia, Canada, the son of a Scotsman, Creed worked as a Morse telegraph operator in the Americas, but became frustrated by the laborious process of manipulating the three-key perforator that punched in the code, which eventually caused permanent damage to his right hand. He came to Britain in 1897 and settled in Glasgow with his wife Jeannie, née Russell (1868/9–1945); it was while working for the *Glasgow Herald* that he developed a tape perforating machine that he adapted from a typewriter keyboard. He then developed equipment to record and print incoming signals, which consisted of a reperforator and a printer to translate the tape into letters. The first transmission, in 1898, reached a speed of sixty words per minute; by 1912 Creed's 'high speed automatic printing telegraphic system' was in use

513 A photograph of October 1924, showing workers at the GPO's Central Telegraph Office waiting to receive election results by teleprinter. The machine's inventor, Frederick George Creed, lived at 20 Outram Road, Addiscombe, from 1939 until his death. [© Getty Images]

across the globe and could transmit up to two hundred words per minute. His invention – which was adopted by the *Daily Mail* in 1912 and the Press Association in 1920 – revolutionised the diffusion of news. Creed's long association with Croydon began in 1909, when he and his business partner, Harald Bille, moved to the area in order to be nearer to the Post Office – an important client – and set up a workshop at Creed's home, which was then in Selsdon Road. In 1915 he moved the business to larger premises in east Croydon, which he named Telegraph House. It was there that he refined his system and in 1923 produced the first teleprinter, which recorded and printed incoming signals directly as letters, rather than as a series of dots and dashes, thereby eliminating the need for a reperforator. A strict Evangelical, Creed insisted that his staff abstain from alcohol, and in 1931 he resigned from the board of Creed & Co. – which had been acquired three years earlier by the International Telephone and Telegraph Corporation – because of a dispute over the use of company sports fields on Sundays. He devoted

much of his retirement to designing a twin-hulled ship, and in 1939 moved to 20 Outram Road – a detached villa built in 1863 – which remained his home until his death here at the age of eighty-six. Creed's second wife, Valerie (1906–1994), who proposed him for commemoration, was still living at number 20 in 1973, when the plaque was installed, alongside a stone emblem taken from Creed's factory.

At Coombe Cliff, Coombe Road, Fairfield, CR0 – an imposing Italianate villa on the corner of Water Tower Hill – an English Heritage plaque of 1988 commemorates **John Horniman** (1803–1893) and his son **Frederick John Horniman** (1835–1906) ⑧ (see also p. 304), the tea merchants, collectors and public benefactors. The suggestion to commemorate the pair at this address was initially rejected in favour of the HORNIMAN MUSEUM in Forest Hill, marked with a plaque in 1985. However, Coombe Cliff's significance as the only surviving home of the Horniman family finally won through and, exceptionally, a second plaque was erected. Born in Berkshire, John Horniman set up in business as a grocer and is generally credited with selling the first sealed packets of tea in 1826, although it was not until the 1840s that he started trading as a tea merchant on the Isle of Wight. In 1852 he settled in Croydon with his wife Ann, née Smith (1800–1900) and their family; Horniman had acquired land in Coombe Road in 1850 and three years later commissioned the building here of a rural residence. This house, designed by E. C. Robins and named Coombe Cliff, was John Horniman's home from at least 1860 until his death thirty-three years later. Frederick, meanwhile, had entered his father's firm at the age of fourteen; on John Horniman's retirement in 1868, the business passed to Frederick and his elder brother, William. Shortly after his marriage to Rebekah Emslie, Frederick moved to Forest Hill, where his extensive collections became the core of a museum, first opened in 1890. Three years later, on the death of his father, Frederick inherited Coombe Cliff, although he also kept a flat in town, firstly 2 Whitehall Court, Westminster, SW1, and then from 1898 at Falmouth House, 20 Hyde Park Gate, SW7. His collections spilled over into Coombe Cliff, which he owned until 1902 and which featured a large conservatory, built in 1894 to house his assortment of rare and exotic plants; this was derelict by the 1980s, when it was dismantled and re-erected adjacent to the Horniman Museum. In keeping with the Hornimans' philanthropic and educational interests, Coombe Cliff is now an adult education centre and, though hidden from the road by trees, can be viewed from the drive. Its extensive gardens were merged into the neighbouring Park Hill in the 1960s, and are open to the public.

Number 44 St Peter's Road, South Croydon, CR0 – formerly known as Pen-y-Bryn – was the home from 1880 to 1881 of the naturalist **Alfred Russel Wallace** (1823–1913) **9** . Born near Usk, Monmouthshire, Wallace first worked as a land surveyor and then as a schoolmaster in Leicester, where he met H. W. Bates. Their shared interest in natural history – manifested in bug hunts in the locality and a common knowledge of the writings of CHARLES DARWIN – prompted an expedition to the Amazon basin to describe the wildlife and to collect specimens. They set out in 1848 but parted company two years later; Wallace returned to Britain in 1852 and published his account of the voyage the following year. Between 1854 and 1862 he carried out

research in the Malay Archipelago, where he identified the delineation between oriental and Australian fauna, known subsequently as the Wallace Line. From amassing and studying thousands of specimens, he formulated an evolutionary theory on 'the survival of the fittest' that was comparable with Darwin's theory of natural selection. Wallace and Darwin corresponded about their similar ideas, and their papers on the subject were jointly presented to the LINNEAN SOCIETY in 1858. Darwin's *On the Origin of Species* was published the following year, while Wallace is known principally for his 1876 work *The Geographical Distribution of Animals*. Wallace – who settled in England in 1862, four years before his marriage to Annie (1845/6–1914), the daughter of the botanist William Mitten – lived at a number of different addresses. Having moved to Croydon in 1878, he and Annie took up residence at the newly built Pen-y-Bryn in 1880 – the year that saw the publication of his work *Island Life* – and left the area for good a year later. A committed spiritualist since 1866, Wallace wrote widely on the subject and also became increasingly absorbed in socio-political causes such as land nationalisation and the anti-vaccination movement. A campaign by the Croydon Natural History and Scientific Society led to Wallace's commemoration at 44 St Peter's Road in 1979; at the request of the house-owner, a surface-mounted plaque of enamelled steel was chosen, rather than a standard ceramic model, and the plaque was installed by the owner himself.

THE BOROUGH OF SUTTON

Number 19 Park Hill, Carshalton, SM5, was commemorated by the GLC in 1979 as the house built and lived in by the novelist **William Hale White** (1831–1913) **10** , best remembered by his pen name 'Mark Rutherford'; the plaque was unveiled by his grandson, Mark White. From a Nonconformist family, White was born and educated in Bedford and began training for the ministry at New College, St John's Wood. His literary career began after he was expelled in 1852 for expressing unorthodox views about the Bible, and ran in parallel with his work as a civil servant at Somerset House. After living in a succession of unsatisfactory rented houses with his wife Harriet, née Arthur (d. 1890), White was able to commission the construction of this house in the 1860s. Built to the design of Charles Vinall, a pupil of Philip Webb, number 19 – then known as Wensum Lodge – was White's home from 1868 until 1889, when he moved to Ashstead, Surrey. The street was also home to his father, who lived at number 5, and his brother-in-law, John Arthur, whose house at number 11 may have been designed by either Vinall or Webb. While living in Park Hill, White wrote his best-known works – *The Autobiography of Mark Rutherford: Dissenting Minister* (1881), *Mark Rutherford's Deliverance* (1885) and *The Revolution in Tanner's Lane* (1887). These semi-autobiographical novels, 'edited by his friend Reuben Shapcott', traced the agonies of a man losing his faith, just as White had during his time at New College, and drew on his experience of Nonconformity. His honest and candid self-analysis, and the quality of his writing – exhibited in these and later works, such as *Catharine Furze* (1893) and *Clara Hopgood* (1896) – ensured that his reputation continued beyond his lifetime. White's admirers included the writers D. H. LAWRENCE and ARNOLD BENNETT, while frequent visitors to the house were Philip Webb, WILLIAM MORRIS (working nearby at Merton Abbey) and ARTHUR HUGHES, to whom he was related by marriage.

THE BOROUGH OF MERTON

In Watery Lane, SW20, is Rutlish School, which forms part of a small suburb – the Merton Park estate – built by **John Innes** (1829–1904) ⑪ , the founder of the John Innes Horticultural Institution. A GLC plaque

was erected in 1978 on the Manor House, which was originally a farmhouse bought by Innes in 1867; between *c.* 1870 and 1900 it was completely rebuilt by the architect H. G. Quartermain, according to Innes's eclectic tastes, to form a rambling country home. The son of a West Indies merchant who became an abolitionist, John Innes formed the City of London Real Property Company with his elder brother James in 1864. The company amassed a considerable portfolio of properties, including land in Merton and Morden. With Quartermain, Innes undertook the development of the Merton Park estate as an early garden suburb, with generous plots, a variety of building types and a profusion of trees and holly hedges. The settlement, built between the 1870s and 1904, reflected Innes's political and social outlook in boasting a temperance house (rather than a pub), a masonic hall and a boys' club. On his death here in 1904, Innes – Lord of the Manor since *c.* 1872 – bequeathed his home and estate to charitable purposes, in particular horticultural research and technical instruction. Six years later, in 1910, the John Innes Horticultural Institution was founded in a separate building on the site, under the directorship of William Bateson, a pioneer in plant breeding and genetics. In the 1930s the institution developed the now-famous Innes compost to provide its scientists with a precise and well-balanced growing medium for research. Between 1946 and 1953 the institution moved to Bayfordbury, Hertfordshire, leaving the Manor House and other buildings to Rutlish School, which Innes had helped to found. In 1967, renamed the John Innes Institute, the organisation transferred to Colney, Norfolk, where it remains today. A hero to the amateur gardener everywhere, Innes would surely be pleased that his enthusiasm and generosity have benefited suburbs well beyond South London.

Number 3 St Mary's Road, Wimbledon, SW19 – a large yet unassuming detached house dating from *c.* 1905 – bears an English Heritage plaque erected in 2000 to commemorate **Air Chief Marshal Lord Dowding** (1882–1970) ⑫ , Commander-in-Chief of Fighter Command (fig. 514). Born Hugh Caswall Tremenheere Dowding in Moffat, Dumfriesshire, he first served in the artillery, spending six years (1904–10) in India which he regarded as the happiest of his career. Dowding learnt to fly in 1913 and joined the

514 The English Heritage plaque to Air Chief Marshal Lord Dowding, erected in 2000 at 3 St Mary's Road, Wimbledon. [© English Heritage. Photograph by Derek Kendall]

Royal Flying Corps on the outbreak of the First World War, but was mostly given ground duties; by 1922 he had reached the rank of brigadier general. As Director of Training in the Air Ministry from 1926, he worked with Hugh Trenchard, Chief of the Air Staff, and in 1930 joined the Air Council. In 1936 – a year before his promotion to Air Chief Marshal – Dowding became leader of the newly created Fighter Command, based at Bentley Priory, Stanmore; when first appointed, Dowding lived at home in Wimbledon Hill and travelled to and from Stanmore daily, but an official residence was soon purchased, namely Montrose House, Gordon Avenue, Stanmore (demolished). In the years that followed, Dowding oversaw the transformation of the RAF into a modern fighting force employing monoplanes – the Hurricane and the Spitfire – and establishing radar stations along the English coast. His resistance to sending squadrons to France as part of the ill-fated expeditionary force was vindicated when his fighters repelled the Luftwaffe's onslaught during the Battle of Britain (1940), effectively thwarting Nazi invasion plans. Dowding resigned from Fighter Command later that year and retired from the Armed Forces in 1942; he was raised to the peerage as Baron Dowding of Bentley Priory the following year. He spent the ten years between 1941 and 1951 at 3 St Mary's Road, exploring his interest in spiritualism and publishing several books on the subject, including *Many Mansions* (1943) and *Lychgate* (1945). After marrying his second wife, Muriel Whiting, in September 1951, Dowding moved to her home in Tunbridge Wells, which is where he died; 3 St Mary's Road was his sister Hilda Dowding's home until her death in 1960.

Number 4 Berkeley Place, Wimbledon, SW19, just off the Ridgway, was the home of the actress **Dame Margaret Rutherford** (1892–1972) 13 from 1895 to 1920. Born at 15 Dornton Road, Balham, SW12, Rutherford moved in about 1895 with her parents to India, where her mother committed suicide the same year. Her father, William Rutherford (formerly Benn) – who had suffered from acute mental illness for some time, had murdered his own father and would spend the rest of his life in asylums – was unable to look after her. So it was that on returning from India later in 1895 the young Margaret was sent to live with her maternal aunt, Bessie Nicholson (d. 1925), at 4 Berkeley Place.

This late nineteenth-century brick house remained her home until 1920, when she and her aunt moved to nearby 2 St John's Road. Rutherford's teenage hopes of an acting career were fostered by her aunt, who paid for private drama lessons, but were not fully pursued until Bessie died in 1925, leaving Margaret a small income. That year she gave up her career as a music teacher to join the Old Vic Company as a trainee actress, and in 1927 she was recruited by Nigel Playfair for the Lyric, Hammersmith. Numerous roles followed, and in 1933, aged forty-one, Rutherford made her West End debut. Her big break followed six years later when she played Miss Prism in Oscar Wilde's *The Importance of Being Earnest* opposite Edith Evans and John Gielgud. Another successful role, later to be reprised on screen (1945), was the spiritualist Madame Arcati in *Blithe Spirit* by Noël Coward. Rutherford's enduring popularity resulted above all from her appearances in films such as *Passport to Pimlico* (1949), *The Happiest Days of Your Life* (1950) and *The VIPs* (1963), for which she won an Oscar; she was also renowned for her portrayal of Miss Marple, the amateur detective created by Agatha Christie. One of the finest comedy actresses of her generation, Rutherford was appointed a DBE in 1967. In later life she and fellow actor Stringer Davis – whom she had married in 1945 – lived in Buckinghamshire, first in Gerrards Cross and then in Chalfont St Giles. Rutherford's plaque was erected by English Heritage in 2002; it is of a smaller size than usual, so as to fit onto the building's façade.

At 1 Lauriston Road, Wimbledon, SW19 – a substantial brick building, on the corner of the Ridgway, that was formerly known as Red Branch House – an English Heritage plaque records the birth of the writer **Robert Graves** (1895–1985) 14 . Unveiled by his daughter Lucia, in the centenary year of his birth, the plaque marks the house which was built in 1893–94 and designed by T. G. Jackson to the specifications of Graves's German mother, Amy, née Ranke (1857–1951). The son of an Anglo-Irish poet and educationist, Graves was brought up in a literary environment; of his siblings, Clarissa (b. 1892) and Charles (1899–1971) were also to become writers. Robert's first poems were published while he was at Charterhouse, but he deferred his academic career to join the Royal Welch Fusiliers upon the outbreak of the First World War; in

France, he formed a friendship with SIEGFRIED SASSOON and penned the works that were collected as *Over the Brazier* (1916). Twice mentioned in dispatches and wounded several times, he managed to return home safely, disproving the announcement of his death given in *The Times* in 1916. He did, however, suffer from shell shock, which weakened his health for the rest of his life. In 1918 Graves married Nancy Nicholson, sister of the artist BEN NICHOLSON, and moved to Oxfordshire, but much of his life was to be spent overseas. In 1929, after the publication of his autobiography, *Goodbye to All That* – written while he was living at 35 St Peter's Square, Hammersmith, SW8 – Graves moved with the American poet Laura Riding to Majorca. It was there that he wrote his acclaimed historical novels *I, Claudius* (1934) and *Claudius the God* (1935). The years of the Second World War were spent in Devon, but in 1946 Graves returned to Majorca, where he died at the age of ninety. During this later part of his career he produced works including *The White Goddess* (1948) and *Homer's Daughter* (1955), but poetry was always his passion. He once said that 'Prose books are the show dogs I breed and sell to support my cat'.[38] Graves lived with his family in Lauriston Road from the time of his birth until 1909, when he was sent to boarding school. He held the area in little affection, describing it in his autobiography as 'a wrong place . . . neither town nor country . . . I didn't like thinking of Wimbledon'.[39]

Eagle House, a fine gabled building of 1613 set back from Wimbledon High Street, SW19, served as Wimbledon School from 1789 to 1805 and continued in educational use until 1887, when it was bought and restored by the architect T. G. Jackson. One of the school's most famous pupils, the German philosopher **Arthur Schopenhauer** (1788–1860) **15**, was commemorated with a plaque in 2005. Born in Danzig (now Gdánsk), Schopenhauer accompanied his parents, Heinrich Floris and Johanna, on an extensive European journey in 1803, arriving at Dover in May of that year. His six-month stay in England was to prove one of the most important formative experiences of his life, especially the three months spent at Wimbledon School, then run by the Rev. Thomas Lancaster. Schopenhauer studied here from 30 June until 20 September, while his parents were touring Britain; though he found the regime miserable and the curriculum

tedious, it has been said that 'perhaps no other writer has been so profoundly influenced by the experiences of a single term or been so much the product of such rapidly acquired youthful likes and dislikes'.[40] Back in Germany, Schopenhauer was much influenced by his mother – widowed in 1805, she was a notable writer and a friend of Goethe – and in 1809 entered the University of Göttingen, where he studied metaphysics and psychology. He soon made a name for himself as an outstanding philosopher. Schopenhauer's principal work, *Die Welt als Wille und Vorstellung* (The World as Will and Idea), was published in 1819. Further writings, produced in Frankfurt, where Schopenhauer settled in 1833, included *Über den Willen in der Natur* (On the Will in Nature; 1836) and *Über die Grundlage der Moral* (On the Basis of Morality; 1840). By the time of his death, Schopenhauer – known as the 'philosopher of pessimism' – had attracted worldwide recognition. His thought has affected the ideas and methodologies of vitalism, life philosophy, parapsychology and anthropology, and influenced figures such as SIGMUND FREUD.

At the south-west corner of Wimbledon Common, enjoying an uninterrupted vista of woodland, is the aptly named North View, SW19. On adjacent houses are two English Heritage blue plaques. The first, erected in 2003 at number 9, commemorates the biochemist and developer of penicillin **Sir Ernst Chain** (1906–1979) **16**, who lived here from 1973 until his death. Born in Berlin to Jewish parents, Chain came to Britain in 1933 to work in the Department of Biochemistry at Cambridge University, but two years later joined Oxford's antibacterial research team, headed by the Australian scientist Howard (later Lord) Florey. Around 1938 he and Florey began the work that brought them to prominence: the isolation and concentration of pure penicillin. Famously discovered by ALEXANDER FLEMING in 1928, penicillin had up to that time been of little practical value. It was Chain's work, in collaboration with that of the team headed by Florey, which bridged the gap between its laboratory use and its clinical use, and demonstrated that penicillin was of enormous medical benefit, as proved the case during the Second World War. In 1945 Fleming, Florey and Chain were jointly awarded the Nobel Prize in recognition of their work, and Chain was knighted in 1969. In 1948 Chain left Oxford for Rome, where he

CROYDON TO MERTON

worked with his wife, Anne Beloff-Chain (1921–1991), on the mode of action of insulin and oversaw research into antibiotics. In 1961 he became Professor of Biochemistry at London's Imperial College, a position he held until 1973. Upon retirement Chain moved to 9 North View, a large mid-twentieth-century detached house, but he spent 'whatever time he could spare from London' at the home he built in Mulranny, County Mayo, which is where he died.[41]

Number 8 North View, a tall end-of-terrace house dating from the late 1880s, was marked in 2001 with a plaque to **Josephine Butler** (1828–1906) **17** , the champion of women's rights (fig. 515). Born in Northumberland into a family of wealthy political reformers

515 A watercolour by Malcolm Fowler of 8 North View, Wimbledon, and its English Heritage plaque commemorating Josephine Butler. [© Malcolm Fowler]

– the Whig Prime Minister Earl Grey was a cousin of her father – Josephine Grey was mostly educated at home, where she was encouraged in liberal thinking. In 1852 she married the academic and Anglican clergyman Dr George Butler, who shared her hatred of social injustice. George's career took them first to Oxford, then to Cheltenham and, in 1864, to Liverpool, where Josephine became increasingly involved in women's rights. In 1867 she became President of the North of England Council for Promoting the Higher Education of Women, and was a supporter of the Married Women's Property Act (passed 1882). In 1869 – a year after the publication of her first pamphlet, *The Education and Employment of Women* – Mrs Butler was appointed Secretary to the Ladies' National Association for the Repeal of the Contagious Diseases Acts. Introduced in the 1860s to reduce venereal disease and regulate prostitution, these laws – especially the provision for compulsory medical examinations – were seen as humiliating to women by many, including Mrs Butler; after a long and ardent campaign, the acts were finally repealed in Britain in 1886. In subsequent years, Josephine continued to lobby for causes including Irish Home Rule, women's suffrage and the problem of underage prostitution; she also led a campaign to end regulation of prostitution in India. Dealt a blow by her husband's death early in 1890, Josephine moved from Winchester to look for a house in London with her son George Grey Butler (1852–1935). They were settled at 8 North View by August 1890. Josephine relished her new home's situation near Wimbledon Common, writing that 'There is perfect freedom to walk out at all times, without "dressing up", and in a few minutes one can find oneself in a retreat surrounded by purple heather and bracken . . . where the solitude and silence towards evening makes it difficult to realise that one is so near London'.[42] After her son's marriage in 1893, she moved to 29 (now 93) Tooting Bec Road, Wandsworth, SW17, then travelled abroad and spent three years living in Cheltenham before settling in 1903 at her final home in Northumberland.

Beech Holme, 49 Wimbledon Parkside, SW19 – a large stuccoed Italianate villa which now forms part of Parkside Hospital – is marked with an English Heritage plaque honouring the aural surgeon **Joseph Toynbee** (1815–1866) and his son **Arnold Toynbee** (1852–1883), the social philosopher **18** . Following a grammar-school education, the Lincolnshire-born Joseph Toynbee was apprenticed to a London surgeon, and expanded his medical expertise at St George's and University College hospitals. In 1843 he was appointed surgeon to St George's and St James's Dispensary, Mayfair, and seven years later he moved his highly regarded practice – which specialised in ear conditions – to 18 Savile Row (demolished). In 1851 Joseph was appointed aural surgeon and lecturer on ear diseases at St Mary's Hospital, Paddington. He distilled his experience in the highly regarded textbook *Diseases of the Ear: Their Nature, Diagnosis and Treatment* (1860). So great was Toynbee's success that a grand house such as the newly built Beech Holme was well within his means. He and his wife Harriet, née Holmes moved here in 1854, and stayed until the time of his death in 1866, when the property was sold. The Toynbees' time here saw the birth of a number of children, including their third son, Paget (1855–1932), later an expert on Dante, and a daughter, Grace (1858–1946), later a bac-

teriologist. Arnold, the second of Toynbee's four sons, had been born in Savile Row and, after growing up at Beech Holme, enjoyed a successful academic life at Oxford, which he entered in 1873. He went on to teach at Balliol College; his active interest in philanthropy prompted him to give extramural lectures, specialising in industrial history, and to undertake educational work among East London's poor. Following his early death at the Wimbledon home of his mother-in-law, Arnold's friends Canon Samuel Barnett and Henrietta Barnett founded the first university settlement, which they named Toynbee Hall in his honour (see Jimmy Mallon). Toynbee's reputation as a historian was established posthumously by the publication of his *Lectures on the Industrial Revolution in England* (1884); edited by his widow, Charlotte, née Atwood, this was the first serious study of the social and economic changes brought about by technological advances in the eighteenth and nineteenth centuries.

CROYDON TO MERTON

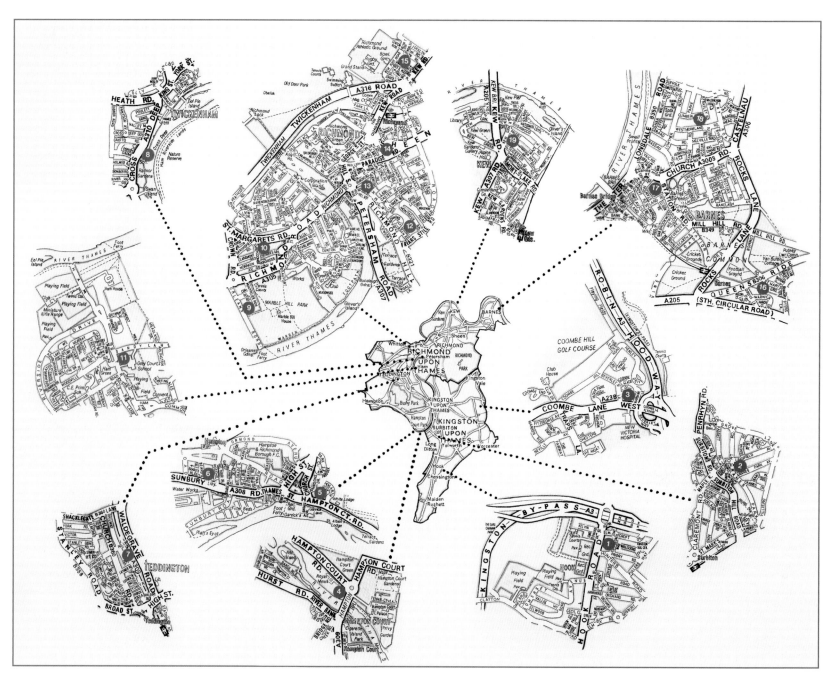

KINGSTON AND RICHMOND

THE ROYAL BOROUGH OF KINGSTON UPON THAMES

Number 207 Hook Road, Chessington, KT9 – a late Victorian detached house formerly known as Southernhay – was, for four years, the home and workplace of the children's writer **Enid Blyton** (1897–1968) ❶ (fig. 516). Born in East Dulwich, Blyton turned to writing in her teens, but decided in 1915 to train as a teacher. In January 1920 she was engaged as a governess by Horace and Gertrude Thompson – relatives of Enid's friend Mabel Attenborough – who had lived at Southernhay since their marriage. The Thompsons' four sons – David, Brian, Peter and John – were Blyton's charges until she left Southernhay in April 1924, shortly before her marriage to Major Hugh Pollock, an editor in a publishing firm. It was while at Southernhay – where she was given her own small room at the back of the house – that Blyton first blossomed as a storyteller. She later wrote to Brian of being 'so happy' at the house, and described her time here as 'the foundation of all my success'.[43] Blyton's charges were quickly joined by other local children, forming a small 'school', and it was on this group that she 'practised', writing and reciting plays, poems and songs for their education and enjoyment; the group, in turn, provided her with further inspiration.[44] Locking her door when the day's duties were done, she produced

works including her first success, the poetry collection *Child Whispers* (1922). A full-time writer from 1924, Blyton was extraordinarily prolific, her many bestsellers including the Secret Seven, the Famous Five, the Faraway Tree and the Malory Towers series. The majority of these books were written at Green Hedges, Beaconsfield, Buckinghamshire (demolished), her home from 1938. The plaque was unveiled by Blyton's eldest daughter, Gillian Baverstock, on the centenary of Enid's birth.

An English Heritage plaque marks 58 Cranes Park, Surbiton, KT5, the home for thirty years of **Alfred Bestall** (1892–1986) ❷ , the illustrator of Rupert Bear. Born in Burma, Alfred Edmeades Bestall came to England at the age of five. He studied art in Birmingham and London before serving on the Western Front, and took up work as a full-time illustrator from 1919. Having worked for *Punch* and contributed to children's books including *The Play's the Thing* (1927) by ENID BLYTON (see above), Bestall had his big break in 1935, when he succeeded Mary Tourtel as writer and artist of the Rupert Bear strip published in the *Daily Express*. Tourtel had created her 'Little Bear Lost' – with his distinctive checked trousers and scarf – in 1920, and Bestall sustained this persona, developing Rupert's adventures in Nutwood. The thirty years (1935–65) during which Bestall produced the strip saw Rupert rise to international stardom; Bestall continued to illustrate the Rupert Annuals until 1973. Based in Surbiton from 1920, he moved to Stavordale, 58 Cranes Park – a detached house of the 1920s – on his father's death in December 1936, living here with his mother Rebecca (d. 1964) and sister Maisie (b. 1895). Bestall described the house as 'nothing very interesting . . . just an old-fashioned suburban place with a garden', but it was highly significant for his life and career: while here, working regularly in an attic room at the front of the house, the illustrator produced many of the cartoons for which is he best known.[45] In 1966, following the death of his mother, Bestall sold number 58, though he remained in Surbiton – a much-loved member of the local community – until 1980, when he moved permanently to North Wales.

Coombe, on the southern edge of Richmond Park, was once a favoured place of residence for the wealthy due to its combination of clean country air and easy access

516 Enid Blyton at Southernhay, 207 Hook Road, Chessington, where she was employed as a governess between 1920 and 1924. She is surrounded by her pupils – the four Thompson boys – together with Terry and Mollie Sayer. [Courtesy of Barbara Stoney]

517   The Old Court House, Hampton Court Road, and its blue plaque to Sir Christopher Wren, installed in 1996. [© English Heritage. Photograph by Derek Kendall]

to London. Its early twentieth-century residents included Lord and Lady de Grey (later Marquis and Marchioness of Ripon), who were prominent in society and held many famous entertainments at their home, Coombe Court. Lady de Grey was a friend and sponsor of the Australian operatic soprano **Dame Nellie Melba** (1861–1931) ③, who is commemorated with an English Heritage plaque at Coombe House (formerly Coombe Cottage), 187 Coombe Lane West, KT2. This house was built for the banker E. C. Baring in about 1863, to designs by George Devey, and was altered in 1870–74. Born Helen Mitchell, and known as 'Nellie' from childhood, Melba is said to have coined her stage name in honour of Melbourne, her native city. Having trained under the celebrated teacher Mathilde Marchesi, she made her operatic debut in Brussels aged twenty-six and first appeared in London in 1888. For the next twenty years, she reigned supreme as the prima donna of Covent Garden, and also enjoyed a brilliant career in Europe and America. Her immense success led, famously, to the creation by the chef Auguste Escoffier of the dessert Peach Melba, first served in London in 1892. Melba's position allowed her to move in exalted social circles, and she gained a rep-

utation as a snob and shameless name-dropper. In 1906 she rented Coombe Cottage from her friend Admiral Lord Charles Beresford; her country retreat, it provided the name and inspiration for the house she built in Coldstream, Australia, which became her principal base after 1909. Melba's most significant London home – 30 Great Cumberland Place, Marylebone, where she lived in about 1901–8 – has been demolished.

THE BOROUGH OF RICHMOND UPON THAMES

Overlooking Hampton Court Green – and backing onto the Thames – is the Old Court House, Hampton Court Road, East Molesey, KT8, the boundary wall of which bears an English Heritage plaque to **Sir Christopher Wren** (1632–1723) ④, arguably Britain's greatest architect (fig. 517). Born in Wiltshire, Wren entered Oxford in 1650, where he excelled as a scientist, mathematician and astronomer. However, it is for his numerous and highly influential architectural works that he is best remembered. On the completion of his first major work, the Sheldonian Theatre, Oxford (1664–69), Wren was appointed Surveyor-General of the King's Works, a position he held until 1718. He took charge of rebuilding the City of London after the Great Fire, designing numerous churches – such as St Stephen Walbrook (1672–80) – and oversaw the building of St Paul's Cathedral, his crowning achievement, between 1675 and 1711. Wren's secular works included the library of Trinity College, Cambridge (1676–84), the Royal Hospital, Chelsea (1682–92) and the Royal Naval Hospital, Greenwich (begun 1696), while he also supervised rebuilding work at royal palaces, such as that carried out at Hampton Court from 1689. During this time, his official residence was the Old Court House, owned by the Crown. In 1706 Wren requested a lease on the then decayed building, and this was duly granted two years later by Queen Anne; Wren carried out major alterations here from 1710 onwards. The house was by turns the home of Wren, his son Christopher (1675–1747) and his grandson Stephen (b. 1722); it has undergone many changes since, but some of Wren's work survives, and it remained a grace-and-favour house associated with the palace until 1958. When he retired from the Office of Works in 1718, Wren left his home in Scotland Yard, Whitehall (demolished), and came to live here more permanently; he spent his remaining years in Hampton Court, 'free from worldly affairs', passing his time 'in contemplation and studies', before dying at his son Christopher's house in St James's Street, off Piccadilly, at the age of ninety.[46] The plaque – proposed by the owner of the Old Court House, Toby Jessel MP – was unveiled in 1996 by Virginia Bottomley, Minister for National Heritage.

The social status of Hampton in the eighteenth century was boosted by the arrival of the actor **David Garrick** (1717–1779) **5** (see also p. 376), one of the celebrities of the age, who is commemorated on the boundary wall of Garrick's Villa, Hampton Court Road, TW12 (fig. 481); the building's mathematical tiling (tile-facing on timber) ruled out a plaque on its façade. From the time of his debut in 1741, Garrick made a sensational impact on the London stage with his dynamic and expressive acting and was also a successful manager, running the Drury Lane theatre from 1747 until his retirement in 1776. DR JOHNSON, an old friend, said that his 'profession made him rich and he made his profession respectable'.[47] Garrick and his Austrian wife Eva Maria, née Veigel (1724–1822) rented what was then named Fuller House in Hampton in January 1754, purchasing the property eight months later and remaining until their respective deaths. ROBERT ADAM was employed to make alterations to the house, including the building of the façade with its central portico facing the river. The gardens, which sloped down to the Thames, featured 'a grateful temple to Shakespeare', whose reputation Garrick did much to foster (fig. 518).[48] The house was the Garricks' summer retreat, their main residences being 27 Southampton Street (from 1749) and 5 Adelphi Terrace (from 1772), off the Strand, both since demolished. In Hampton, the couple entertained lavishly – their 'night fêtes' were famous – and on one day each year they opened the grounds to local people. Such was the sweetness of life at Hampton that Johnson was moved to say, 'Ah, David, it is the leaving of such a place that makes a death-bed terrible'.[49] The house was sold at auction after Eva Garrick's death; the plaque was installed by the GLC in 1970, shortly after the building had been converted into flats.

At Rose Hill, situated between Rosehill and Upper Sunbury Road, Hampton, TW12, an English Heritage plaque jointly commemorates the singer **John Beard** (c. 1717–91) and the promoter of public libraries

518   David Garrick and his wife Eva Maria, shown standing by their Thames-side temple to Shakespeare in a painting of c.1762 by Johann Zoffany. The temple, which survives, was a notable feature of the gardens of Garrick's Villa. [Yale Center for British Art, Paul Mellon Collection, USA / The Bridgeman Art Library]

KINGSTON AND RICHMOND

519 The south (garden) front of Rose Hill. The house is said to have been built for John Beard in the second half of the eighteenth century, and was the home of William Ewart between 1838 and 1842. Today it functions as a library. [© English Heritage. Photograph by Derek Kendall]

William Ewart (1798–1869) (see also p. 354) ⑥ (fig. 519). The house is said to have been built for Beard soon after the middle of the eighteenth century and became known as Rose Hill in the 1820s; it has since been altered and, rather appropriately given its connection with Ewart, has since 1902 functioned as a public library. Beard made his name in HANDEL's opera company at Covent Garden – he sang more parts under the composer than any other singer. A successful actor, he appeared regularly at Drury Lane and Covent Garden, and was perhaps best known for playing Macheath in John Gay's *The Beggar's Opera*, revived in 1737. As a singer, Beard was equally at home with operas, oratorios and traditional English songs such as 'The Early Horn', a popular favourite. In 1761 he took over the patent for the Covent Garden Theatre from his late father-in-law, John Rich. He sold it six years later for £60,000 and retired to Hampton, living close to his friend DAVID GARRICK. Beard acquired what is now Rose Hill in April 1774 and died here seventeen years later; his widow, Charlotte (1726–1818), remained at the house until her death. From 1838 to 1842, Rose Hill was the home of William Ewart MP, then recently widowed; an important figure among Liberal reformers, he was involved in a number of causes, including the establishment of public museums and art galleries, and was also an important force behind the founding of the plaques scheme in the 1860s (see p. 4 and pp. 9–10). Particularly notable is the part Ewart played in securing the Libraries Act of 1850; this established what ultimately became a national system of free libraries. Ewart's years at Rose Hill saw him elected Member for Dumfries Burghs, a seat he held until his retirement in 1868.

A far cry from the houses of the great and the good along the river is 131 (formerly 5) Waldegrave Road, Teddington, TW11, a late Victorian semi-detached house that bears a plaque commemorating the birthplace of the actor, playwright and songwriter **Sir Noël Coward** (1899–1973) ⑦ . The house, then known as Helmsdale, had been the home of his parents – Arthur (1856–1937) and Violet, née Veitch (1863–1954) – since their marriage in 1890. His mother and father were both musical and had met in the choir at nearby St Alban's Church; it was there that Coward was christened in February 1900. Eighteen months after his birth, the family left Helmsdale – 'An unpretentious abode / Which, I believe, / Economy forced us to leave / In rather a hurry', wrote Coward many years later – and moved to another house close by.[50] They left Teddington altogether in 1904, a year that marked the start of a series of short sojourns in various South London suburbs. Coward's mother was a devotee of the theatre and was keen to encourage her son to be a performer. A child prodigy, he went on to establish himself as an internationally renowned playwright and composer with works such as *The Vortex* (1924), *Hay Fever* (1925) and *Private Lives* (1930), and during the Second World War he wrote and co-produced the classic films *In Which We Serve* (1942), *Brief Encounter* (1945) and *Blithe Spirit* (1945), which was based on his play of 1941. In later years, he remained the epitome of pre-war style and glamour while reinventing himself as a cabaret singer, introducing his own songs – among them 'Mad Dogs and Englishmen' – to a new audience, and making guest appearances in such films as *The Italian Job* (1968). Coward's plaque was erected in 1995 at the suggestion of the Twickenham Society and local residents. His principal base during his greatest years (1930–56) – 17A Gerald Road, Belgravia, SW1 – had been privately commemorated in 1979, and Coward spent the last twenty-five years of his life largely in Jamaica. The plaque was unveiled by Sir Noël's biographer, Philip Hoare, after a speech by the actor Donald Sinden, who stepped in after Coward's long-term partner, Graham Payn, was sadly unable to attend.

On the banks of the Thames is Pope's Villa, 19 Cross Deep, Twickenham, TW1. Now St James's Independent School for Boys, this sprawling mansion was built in 1842–43 to designs by H. E. Kendall junior near the site of the famous residence of ALEXANDER POPE, demolished in 1808. The house was much rebuilt for the radical MP and journalist **Henry Labouchere** (1831–1912) ⑧ , who lived here with his wife, the actress Henrietta Hodson (1841–1910), from 1881 until they moved to Florence in 1903. The Laboucheres used Pope's Villa mainly in summer, hosting gatherings of figures influential in politics, finance and the arts; their central London residence for much of this period was 24 Grosvenor Gardens, Belgravia, SW1. Taking advantage of the associations of Pope's Villa, Labouchere's staff showed 'the bedroom to sightseers as the identical room in which the poet died', reaping 'a considerable benefit from the lie'.[51] Born in London to a Huguenot family, Henry Du Pré Labouchere rose to become a highly successful journalist; he wrote for papers such as the *Daily News* and in 1876 founded the journal *Truth,* which specialised in exposing corruption and hypocrisy in the establishment. From 1880, Labouchere became famous as one of the most outspoken and colourful politicians of the late nineteenth century, and was famed for his cynical wit. Never afraid of controversy, 'Labby' spoke out against the monarchy, the constitution and imperialism. He was also responsible for a clause in the Criminal Law Amendment Act of 1885, known as 'Labouchere's

Amendment', which made sexual activity between men explicitly illegal. This remained in force until 1967, and – even allowing for the moral climate in which Labouchere lived – is generally regarded today as a black mark on his reputation.

On the garden wall of South End House, Montpelier Row, Twickenham, TW1 – a fine building of *c.* 1720 at the far end of a cul-de-sac, overlooking Marble Hill Park – is a plaque of 1995 to the poet **Walter de la Mare** (1873–1956) ⑨ . The two upper floors of the house were his home from 1940 until his death. Born in Charlton, South London, de la Mare came to public attention with the poetry collection *The Listeners* (1912), and achieved immense success with his collection of children's verse, *Peacock Pie* (1913). By the time he moved from Buckinghamshire to South End House, de la Mare was an established literary figure with a high reputation as a poet, anthologist and short-story writer. While living here, he produced works such as the anthology *Love* (1943) and the long poems *The Traveller* (1946) and *Winged Chariot* (1953). He was deeply attached to South End House and its garden, continuing to live here through the war and after the death of his wife Elfrida, née Ingpen (1862–1943). According to Theresa Whistler, de la Mare's biographer, South End House was his 'longest and best-loved home, saw the years of his greatest fame, the visits of a multitude of friends, and had a character and beauty more expressive of his imagination and personality than any other he lived in'.[52] By the time of his death in Montpelier Row – where he received visitors including T. S. ELIOT, JOYCE GRENFELL and AUGUSTUS JOHN – de la Mare was a Companion of Honour and a recipient of the Order of Merit.

An oddity among Twickenham's ranks of suburban houses is 40 Sandycoombe Road, TW1, originally designed for himself as a country villa by the painter **J. M. W. Turner**, **RA** (1775–1851) ⑩ (figs 520 and 521). Born in Covent Garden, Joseph Mallord William Turner entered the Royal Academy Schools at the age of fourteen, and was soon recognised as an artist of genius. In 1807, by which time he had produced acclaimed works such as *The Shipwreck* (1805), Turner bought for £400 a plot of land in Twickenham and worked on the design of the house over the next five years. Construction began in 1812, under Turner's own

520 Some of the many designs for Sandycombe Lodge, Twickenham, which appear in J. M. W. Turner's Sandycombe and Yorkshire sketchbook. The drawings date from c.1810–11; work on the house began in 1812. [© Tate, London 2008]

KINGSTON AND RICHMOND

521   A view of Sandycombe Lodge by William Havell (engraved by W. B. Cooke). It was published in 1829, three years after the house was sold by J. M. W. Turner. [© Mary Evans Picture Library]

supervision, and was completed early the following year. The finished house, which featured a large sitting room-cum-studio overlooking the garden, was initially named Solus Lodge but soon became Sandycombe [*sic*] Lodge. Turner's main base was in Marylebone – at 47 (later 23) Queen Anne Street (demolished), his home from 1810 until his death – but, as a successful painter with a professorship at the Royal Academy, he was able to afford a retreat away from the city. Here he entertained friends from the art world, while his father William (1745–1829) – with whom he shared the house – enjoyed working in the garden. Turner painted many local scenes, most notably in the large canvas *England: Richmond Hill on the Prince Regent's Birthday* (1819). Yet long tours in England and on the Continent took Turner away from Twickenham a great deal; as early as 1815, he wrote, 'Sandycombe sounds just now in my ears as an act of folly, when I reflect how little I have been able to be there this year'.[53] This and other reasons compelled Turner to sell the house in 1826. Commemorated with a plaque in 1977, Sandycombe Lodge is Turner's only significant residence to survive unaltered.

In 1981 the GLC erected a plaque on the ground floor of Grey Court, a large late eighteenth-century house in Ham Street, Ham, TW10, which is now part of Grey Court School. It commemorates **John Henry Newman** (1801–1890) ⑪ , later **Cardinal Newman**, recording that it was here that he 'spent some of his early years'. Grey Court was the country home of Newman's parents – the banker John Newman (d. 1824) and his

wife Jemima, née Fourdrinier (d. 1836) – from before his birth until September 1807. Between 1803 and 1822, the family's principal home was at 17 Southampton Street (now Southampton Place), Bloomsbury, WC1, where a bronze plaque was erected by the Duke of Bedford in 1908. Ordained in 1824, Newman came to prominence in the 1830s as a leading figure in the Oxford Movement, a group of High Church Anglicans, several of whom later converted to Catholicism. Having produced such works as *Parochial Sermons* (1834–42), Newman himself joined the Roman Catholic Church in 1845, established the Birmingham Oratory in 1848 and that in London in 1849, and was made a Cardinal in 1879. Newman's writings, which proved widely influential, included his first novel, *Loss and Gain: The Story of a Convert* (1848), and *Apologia Pro Vita Sua* (1864), a religious autobiography which set out the motivation behind his conversion. Although the Cardinal's association with Ham was brief, the area was etched strongly on his memory. He recalled that, 'When, at school, I dreamed of heaven, the scene was Ham', and noted in 1861 that he knew more about Grey Court 'than any house I have been in since, and could pass an examination on it. It has ever been in my dreams'.[54] He remembered in particular his family's celebration of the victory of Trafalgar (1805), when candles were placed in the house's windows, and apparently watched wayfarers with lanterns on their nightly journeys to and from Teddington Lock; it has been suggested that these memories inspired 'Lead, Kindly Light', which was written by Newman in 1833 and later became a popular hymn.

At 5 Montague Road (formerly Montague Villas), Richmond, TW10, is a plaque erected in 1992 in honour of the public-health reformer **Sir Edwin Chadwick** (1800–1890) ⑫ .[55] Chadwick had first been considered for a plaque by the LCC in 1910, but – largely on account of the demolition of 9 Stanhope Terrace (formerly 4 Stanhope Street), Bayswater, his home in 1839–54 – nothing was done until the late 1980s, when attention turned towards Richmond. Born near Manchester, Chadwick moved with his family to London in 1810. He was active as a reformer from 1832, when – as assistant to the political economist Nassau Senior – he became involved with the Royal Commission on Poor Laws. Appointed a Commissioner the following year, Chadwick played a key part in the passing of the Poor Law Amendment Bill in 1834, and was also instrumental in seeing the Factory Act become law in 1833. From 1838 his energies were directed towards sanitary reform. His most significant accomplishment was to bring to public attention the conditions in which a large part of the urban population of Britain lived, and to instigate vital improvements; it has been said that Chadwick's 'achievements live on in every home and under every street in Britain'.[56] Key to this reform was Chadwick's *Report on the Sanitary Condition of the Labouring Population of Great Britain* (1842), which created a sensation and led to the first Public Health Act of 1848. In that year, the government created the General Board of Health, and Chadwick was made a Commissioner. However, known for his combative and authoritarian nature, he did not last long: having lost his political backing, Chadwick was forced out of his post in 1854 as part of a general reorganisation. The following year he settled, with a pension of £1,000 per annum, at 5 Montague Villas, a semi-detached Italianate house of *c.* 1840. Chadwick's long retirement was spent advocating various initiatives for the public good, such as state ownership of railways, and making unsuccessful attempts to win a seat in Parliament. In 1869 he left Richmond for his last home, Park Cottage,

East Sheen (demolished); there he died, a year after having been knighted.

One of Richmond's more unexpected residents, commemorated with an English Heritage plaque in 1994, is **Bernardo O'Higgins** (1778–1842) 13 , a man of Irish and South American parentage who rose to become a general, statesman and the liberator of Chile. The plaque was installed on the boundary wall of Clarence House, 2 The Vineyard, TW10, a building of 1696 set back from the roadway, which is – at the time of writing – undergoing considerable renovation. In the 1790s the building was in use as a Roman Catholic school, under the headmastership of Timothy Eeles. O'Higgins was a boarder here from 1795 to 1798, having been sent to England by his father, Ambrosio O'Higgins – then Governor of Chile – to learn English and to finish his education. In addition to his formal schooling, Bernardo gained an introduction to the revolutionary politics of his native continent when he met Francisco de Miranda and José de San Martín in London. After leaving England in 1799, and returning to Chile in 1802, O'Higgins joined the fight for independence from Spanish rule. With the aid of San Martín, he and his revolutionary army were victorious at the Battle of Chacabuco on 12 February 1817; four days later O'Higgins was declared Supreme Director, the first to head independent Chile. He led his country for six years, before being deposed in a coup in January 1823 and exiled to Peru, where he died. Today, O'Higgins is revered as one of the great nineteenth-century liberators of South America, and the unveiling of his plaque, organised by the Embassy of Chile, was attended by many diplomatic representatives from the continent (fig. 522); the cord was pulled by the Chilean Ambassador, Hernán Errázuriz.

In early 1915 the author and political activist **Leonard Woolf** (1880–1969) and his wife, the writer **Virginia Woolf** (1882–1941) (see also pp. 80–1) 14 , moved from 17 The Green, Richmond, to nearby Hogarth House, 34 Paradise Road, TW9. They had seen and fallen 'in love with' the house at the end of 1914, and were to remain here for almost exactly nine years; it was, wrote Virginia, 'far the nicest house in England'.[57] At that time the building, which dates back to *c.* 1748, was divided in two: the Woolfs initially occupied the eastern half, Hogarth House, though in December 1919

522 The unveiling of the plaque to Bernardo O'Higgins at 2 The Vineyard, Richmond, in 1994. The ceremony was organised by the Embassy of Chile, and was attended by many diplomatic representatives from that continent. [© John Neligan]

KINGSTON AND RICHMOND

they also acquired the western half, Suffield House. The early months of the Woolfs' residence here were dominated by Virginia's mental breakdown, but her health gradually improved, and their years in 'the tranquil atmosphere' of Hogarth House became a time of great activity for both of them.[58] Virginia wrote her second novel, *Night and Day* (1919), its successor *Jacob's Room* (1922) and much of *Mrs Dalloway* (1925), while Leonard was busy with his work on international relations for the FABIAN SOCIETY and later the Labour Party. In 1917, as the plaque records, the couple decided to set up a printing press in the house, partly as a hobby but also as a way of publishing their own writing. It became a serious concern: between 1917 and 1923 the Hogarth Press published thirty-two books, seventeen of which – including *The Waste Land* (1923) by T. S. ELIOT – were printed and bound here by the Woolfs. Looking back, Virginia wrote, 'nowhere else could we have started the Hogarth Press . . . Here that strange offspring grew & throve; it ousted us from the dining room . . . & crept all over the house'.[59] On 13 March 1924 the Woolfs returned to Bloomsbury – Virginia had begun to feel 'tied, imprisoned, inhibited' in Richmond – and the press, relocated to the basement of their house in Tavistock Square, continued to flourish; it was finally acquired by Chatto & Windus in 1946.[60] From 1919 the couple spent much time at Monk's House, Rodmell, Sussex; it was near there that Virginia committed suicide, and there that Leonard died. The plaque at Hogarth House was unveiled by PHILIP NOEL-BAKER – a close associate of Leonard Woolf – in 1976, shortly after a separate plaque was installed at Virginia's early home in Fitzroy Square.

At the Royal Hospital, Kew Foot Road (formerly Lane), Richmond, TW9, an English Heritage plaque commemorates **James Thomson** (1700–1748) **15** , the poet and author of 'Rule, Britannia'. Born in Scotland, Thomson came in 1725 to London, where his first play, *Sophonisba*, was staged in 1730. That year also saw the publication of his first, and most successful, poetical work: *The Seasons*, a collection of verses begun in 1726 that led Thomson to become one of Britain's most widely admired poets in the century after his death, praised by figures including COLERIDGE and HAZLITT. Thomson was living in Kew Foot Lane by spring 1736, and in 1739 the profits from his play *Edward and Eleonora* enabled him to move to a more substantial

house in the same road (fig. 523). This house, situated next to Richmond Gardens, was enlarged by Thomson, and formed the perfect rural retreat for his writing; works composed here included the ode 'Rule, Britannia' – first performed in Thomson's *Alfred: A Masque* in 1740, with music by THOMAS ARNE – and a revised and enlarged edition of *The Seasons* (1744). A frequent visitor was ALEXANDER POPE, who lived nearby in Twickenham. After Thomson's death here, the house was sold to his friend George Ross (1708/9–1786), who enlarged the property and named it Rossdale Cottage. As Rosedale, it became the home from 1787 of Frances Boscawen (1719–1805), widow of the well-known admiral; a celebrated literary hostess, she created a shrine to Thomson, one of her favourite poets. For much of the nineteenth century, it was known as Shaftesbury House after its resident, the 6th Earl of Shaftesbury (1768–1851). In 1867 – two years after the death of his widow – the house began to be used as a hospital, and as such was extensively altered. The plaque marks the eighteenth-century building, five bays wide, which survives at the core of the Royal Hospital. The room at the front on the left is said to be that 'in which Thomson breathed his last, being his bedchamber', while that on the right was 'his sitting room, where he passed his time'.[61]

Number 3 St Mary's Grove, Barnes, SW13, a late nineteenth-century detached house set back from a quiet road near Richmond Park, bears an English Heritage plaque to the railway and tunnelling engineer **James Henry Greathead** (1844–1896) **16** , who helped create today's London Underground. Born in South Africa, Greathead came to England at the age of fifteen, and in

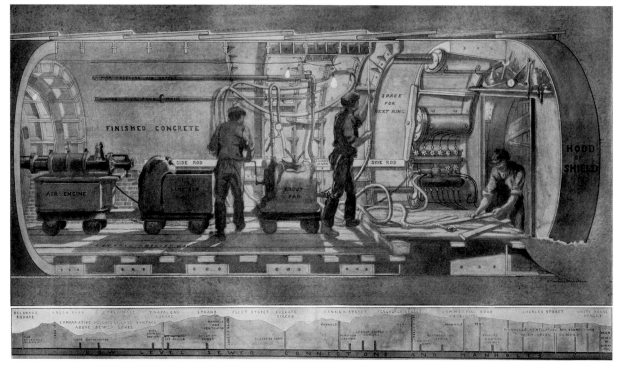

524 The 'Greathead Shield', seen on the right of the illustration, being used in the construction of a sewer from Belgrave Square to Barking in 1910. [© Illustrated London News Ltd / Mary Evans Picture Library]

1864 began an apprenticeship with the civil engineer Peter W. Barlow, the brother of W. H. BARLOW. In 1869, aged only twenty-four, Greathead was entrusted with the construction of the Tower Subway, a pedestrian tunnel under the Thames; completed in 1870, it was constructed using a cylindrical boring device designed by Greathead that enabled tunnels to be driven through soft, waterlogged ground. He continued to develop this machine, which came to be known as the 'Greathead Shield' (fig. 524) and was used again from 1886 when work started on the City and Southwark Subway. This grew into the City and South London Railway, the world's first underground electric railway, which eventually opened in 1890 and is now part of the Northern Line. Greathead was resident engineer on the Hammersmith and Richmond extension of the Metropolitan District Railway, and was also involved in the construction of the Blackwall Tunnel (opened 1897) and the Waterloo and City Line (opened 1898). In 1884 Greathead married Blanche Emily Caldecott Coryndon (1862–1912) and the following year came to live at Birchwood, 3 St Mary's Grove, remaining in the house until the family moved to Streatham in 1889. The plaque was unveiled in 2000 by Greathead's grandson, Jim.

On the west side of Barnes Green – overlooking the village pond – is Milbourne House, 18 Station Road, SW13, on the corner of Essex Court. This fine building, re-fronted in the eighteenth century, bears a GLC plaque to the novelist **Henry Fielding** (1707–1754) ⑰ (see also p. 378 and p. 381). Born in Somerset, Fielding earned his living as a dramatist before turning to a legal career in 1737. He continued to write, however, producing a series of works which culminated in his masterpiece, *Tom Jones* (1749). By this time, Fielding had been appointed magistrate for Middlesex; based in Bow Street for over five years, until his retirement in 1754, he watched 'the long parade of wretchedness and villainy' pass before him, and did much to reduce crime in the metropolis.[62] While this work demanded Fielding's presence in town, his fragile health – he suffered from gout, asthma and dropsy – led him to seek the fresh air and tranquillity of the countryside. After living in what is now Holly Road (formerly Back Lane), Twickenham, he took Milbourne House as a country retreat in *c.* 1750–52, dividing his time between Bow Street and Barnes; the latter was conveniently situated near to his sisters, who lived in Turnham Green, and his friend George Bubb Doddington, who lived in Hammersmith. It is thought that, while here, Fielding devoted much of his time to writing his last and best-selling novel, *Amelia* (1752), which draws on his experiences to depict a lawless London with corrupt courts and squalid prisons. By February 1753 Fielding and his second wife,

525 *Relief in Relief* (c.1942–45), one of the works executed by Kurt Schwitters during his time at 39 Westmoreland Road. It incorporates driftwood salvaged from the River Thames. [© DACS 2008 / Tate, London 2008]

Mary, née Daniel (d. 1802), had moved to Fordhook, Ealing (demolished), a 'little house . . . in the country'; a year later he left England for Portugal, where he died.[63]

In 1984 the GLC erected a plaque at 39 Westmoreland Road, Barnes, SW13, a semi-detached house of the inter-war period which was the home of the artist **Kurt Schwitters** (1887–1948) **18** . Born in Hanover, Germany, Schwitters came under the influence of Cubism during the First World War. In 1919 he formulated his own interpretation of Dada – Merz – which involved the assembly of pieces of discarded ephemera into collages, applied to canvas and to buildings. Labelled 'degenerate' by the Nazi regime, Schwitters left Germany for Oslo in 1937 and, three years later, fled Norway in advance of the Nazi invasion. Seeking refuge in Britain, he was initially interned in a camp on the Isle of Man and came to London on his release. From August 1942 until June 1945, Schwitters rented 39 Westmoreland Road, sharing the house with his son Ernst (1918–1996) and an émigré friend, Gert Strindberg, a great-nephew of the celebrated Swedish writer and artist August Strindberg. Here, the 'walls were soon covered with paintings, the loft was filled with collages and constructions, and the garden shed became his studio'; material for the artist's collages was collected on London's streets or picked out of the Thames (fig. 525).[64] In 1944 Schwitters suffered a stroke, and an English friend, Edith Thomas (1915–1991) – known as 'Wantee' – moved into number 39 to look after him. Together they moved to Ambleside in the Lake District in 1945. It was while creating his last work, now known as the Elterwater Merzbarn, that Schwitters died in 1948. He was then largely unappreciated – 'English people', mused Schwitters, 'don't understand art at all' – but is now recognised as one of the most influential figures in twentieth-century art.[65]

At Eastside House, 22 Kew Green, Kew, TW9, there is an English Heritage plaque to the London-born Pre-Raphaelite painter **Arthur Hughes** (1832–1915) **19** . In the early 1850s, while a student at the Royal Academy Schools, Hughes was inspired by the work of a group of older artists, the PRE-RAPHAELITE BROTHERHOOD,

and he soon became part of their social and artistic circle; in 1852 Hughes's *Ophelia* was hung at the Royal Academy with a painting of the same subject by MILLAIS. In the following years Hughes produced his best-known works, *The Long Engagement* (1853–59) and *April Love* (1856), the latter acquired by WILLIAM MORRIS. From the 1860s he established himself as a leading illustrator, providing designs for – most notably – the works of GEORGE MACDONALD, as well as TENNYSON's *Enoch Arden* (1865) and Thomas Hughes's *Tom Brown's School Days* (1869). Hughes, his wife Tryphena, née Foord (c. 1828–1921) and their children moved house frequently before settling in the 1870s at Wandle Bank (now 284 London Road), Wallington, Surrey. Their last move brought them in 1891 to Eastside House, an early nineteenth-century property on Kew Green. By this time, Hughes's popularity and reputation as a painter had been in decline for many years, though he continued to exhibit, producing such works as *The Door of Mercy* (1893) and *The Rescue* (1908). Having outlived all the major figures of the Pre-Raphaelite movement, Hughes died at Eastside House at the age of eighty-three.

1   Letter of 29 July 1957 on blue plaque file.

2   *The Correspondence of Alexander Pope*, ed. G. Sherburn, vol. I (Oxford, 1956), p. 339 (20 April 1716)

3   *ODNB*, vol. V, p. 327

4   *Victoria County History, A History of the County of Middlesex*, vol. VII, ed. T. F. T. Baker (London, 1982), p. 63

5   Nicola Beauman, *Morgan: A Biography of E. M. Forster* (London, 1993), p. 361

6   P. N. Furbank, *E. M. Forster: A Life*, vol. II (London, 1978), p. 279

7   William T. Stearn, *John Lindley, 1799–1865: Gardener, Botanist and Pioneer Orchidologist* (Woodbridge, 1998), p. 18

8   *ODNB*, vol. III, p. 435

9   Ibid, vol. VI, p. 331

10   It is now accepted that Towle was born in 1885, rather than in 1887, as is stated on the plaque.

11   *Evening News*, 9 June 1975

12   Langston Day, *Life and Art of William Heath Robinson* (London, 1947), p. 120

13   Percy V. Bradshaw, *The Art of the Illustrator* (London, 1918), p. 15

14   *Building News*, 6 September 1872, p. 182

15   *ODNB*, vol. XXIV, p. 616

16   *Observer*, 12 February 1928

17   Ibid

18   *Sunday Times*, 24 March 1968

19   Bette Hill, with Neil Ewart, *The Other Side of the Hill* (London, 1978), p. 36

20   Evelyn Waugh, *A Little Learning* (London, 1964), p. 42

21   *Daily Telegraph*, 16 October 1993

22   Bridget Cherry and Nikolaus Pevsner, *The Buildings of England, London 4: North* (London, 1998), p. 144

23   Katherine Frank, *A Voyager Out: The Life of Mary Kingsley* (London, 1987), p. 21

24   Ibid, p. 23

25   Frederic Fisk, *The History of Tottenham* (London, 1913), p. 175

26   *The Collected Poems of Stevie Smith*, ed. James MacGibbon (London, 1985), p. 410

27   *An Edmonton Heritage: Being an Anthology of Verse and Prose Relating to Edmonton*, comp. G. W. Sturges (London, 1947), p. 101 (late May 1833)

28   Ibid, p. 103 (31 May 1833)

29   Ibid, p. 101 (late May 1833)

30   Alliott Verdon-Roe, *The World of Wings and Things* (London, 1939 edn, repr. 1980), pp. 55–56

31   Giles and Lisanne Radice, *Will Thorne: Constructive Militant* (London, 1974), p. 54

32   Bridget Cherry and Nikolaus Pevsner, *The Buildings of England, London 2: South* (New Haven and London, 1994), p. 138

33   George Woodcock and Ivan Avakumović, *The Anarchist Prince: A Biographical Study of Peter Kropotkin* (London, 1950), p. 249

34   Ibid, p. 251

35   Cherry and Pevsner, *London 2: South*, p. 230

36   'A Day with Dr. Conan Doyle', *Strand Magazine*, vol. IV (July–December 1892), p. 183

37   Ibid

38   *The Guardian*, 24 June 1995, weekend supplement, p. 14

39   Robert Graves, *Goodbye to All That* (London, 1929, repr. 1966), p. 33

40   Patrick Bridgwater, *Arthur Schopenhauer's English Schooling* (London, 1988), preface

41   Ronald W. Clark, *The Life of Ernst Chain: Penicillin and Beyond* (New York, 1985), p. 198

42   Jane Jordan, *Josephine Butler* (London, 2001), p. 258

43   Barbara Stoney, *Enid Blyton: The Biography* (London, Auckland, Sydney, 1992 edn), p. 61

44   Ibid

45   Caroline G. Bott, *The Life and Works of Alfred Bestall, Illustrator of Rupert Bear* (London, 2003), p. 91

46   Christopher Wren, *Parentalia; or, Memoirs of the Family of the Wrens* (London, 1750), p. 344

47   *Boswell's Life of Johnson*, ed. George Birkbeck Hill, vol. III (Oxford, 1934), p. 371 note

48   Ian McIntyre, *Garrick* (London, 1999), p. 233

49   Ibid, p. 216

50   Noël Coward, *Collected Verse*, eds Graham Payn and Martin Tickner (London, 1984), p. 40 ('Personal Reminiscence')

51   Hesketh Pearson, *Labby: The Life and Character of Henry Labouchere* (London, 1936), p. 235

52   Letter of 5 February 1993 on blue plaque file.

53   A. J. Finberg, *The Life of J. M. W. Turner, RA* (2nd edn, Oxford, 1916), p. 227 (1 August 1815)

54   *The Letters and Diaries of John Henry Newman*, vol. XV, eds Charles Stephen Dessain and Vincent Ferrer Blehl (London, 1964), p. 397; vol. XX, ed. Charles Stephen Dessain (London, 1970), p. 23 (5 August 1861)

55   It is now accepted that Chadwick was born in 1800, rather than in 1801, as is stated on the plaque.

56   *ODNB*, vol. X, p. 839

57   Leonard Woolf, *Beginning Again: An Autobiography of the Years 1911–1918* (London, 1964), p. 171; *The Question of Things Happening: The Letters of Virginia Woolf*, vol. II: *1912–1922*, ed. Nigel Nicolson (London, 1976), p. 60 (22 February 1915)

58   Leonard Woolf, *Downhill all the Way: An Autobiography of the Years 1919–1939* (London, 1975), p. 16

59   *The Diary of Virginia Woolf*, vol. II: *1920–1924*, ed. Anne Olivier Bell (London, 1981), p. 283

60   Woolf, *Downhill all the Way*, p. 117

61   E. B. Chancellor, *The History and Antiquities of Richmond, Kew, Petersham, Ham, &c.* (Richmond, 1894), p. 246

62   Martin C. Battestin with Ruthe R. Battestin, *Henry Fielding: A Life* (London and New York, 1989), p. 446

63   Ibid, p. 584

64   Gwendolen Webster, *Kurt Merz Schwitters: A Biographical Study* (Cardiff, 1997), p. 333

65   *The Guardian*, 7 October 1981

LIST OF THE DATES OF THE PLAQUES INCLUDED IN THIS BOOK AND THE ORGANISATIONS RESPONSIBLE FOR THEIR INSTALLATION

This list sets out the dates when the plaques were first installed.
For details of any subsequent re-erections of plaques,
see the information provided in the main body of the text.

CAMDEN

Bloomsbury and Holborn

Augustus Siebe	EH	2000
George du Maurier	LCC	1960
Randolph Caldecott	GLC	1977
T. H. Wyatt	GLC	1980
Bertrand Russell	EH	2002
Dr Robert Willan	LCC	1949
Sir Hans Sloane	LCC	1965
Lord Eldon	LCC	1954
Ram Mohun Roy	GLC	1985
William Butterfield	GLC	1978
Sir Anthony Hope Hawkins	GLC	1976
Thomas Wakley	LCC	1962
Thomas Hodgkin	GLC	1985
Sir Harry Ricardo	EH	2005
Henry Cavendish	adopted by GLC (1983)	1903 (Bedford Estate)
Pre-Raphaelite Brotherhood	EH	1998
Millicent Garrett Fawcett	LCC	1954

Lady Ottoline Morrell	GLC	1986
James Robinson	EH	1991
George Dance the Younger	GLC	1970
Charles Darwin	LCC	1961 (replacing LCC plaque of 1906)
Giuseppe Mazzini	LCC	1950
Hugh Price Hughes	EH	1989
John Maynard Keynes	GLC	1975
Lytton Strachey	GLC	1971
Robert Travers Herford	EH	1990
Christina Rossetti	adopted by GLC (1974)	c. 1913 (Bedford Estate)
Samuel Romilly	adopted by GLC (1983)	1919 (Bedford Estate)
Paul Nash	EH	1991
Thomas Carlyle	LCC	1907
R. H. Tawney	GLC	1980
Sir Syed Ahmed Khan	EH	1997
W. R. Lethaby	GLC	1979
V. Brittain and W. Holtby	EH	1995
Charles Dickens	LCC	1903
Sydney Smith	LCC	1906 (replacing LCC plaque of 1905)
John Howard	LCC	1908
Dorothy L. Sayers	EH	2000
Benjamin Disraeli	LCC	1948 (replica of LCC plaque of 1904)
Sir Hiram Maxim	GLC	1966
W. R. Lethaby	LCC	1957
D. G. Rossetti, W. Morris and E. Burne-Jones	LCC	1911
John Harrison	LCC	1954
Thomas Earnshaw	LCC	1948
Spencer Perceval	LCC	1914
William Marsden	GLC	1986
Dr Samuel Johnson	SoA	1876

Camden Town and Kentish Town

Sir Nigel Gresley	EH	1997
George Cruikshank	SoA	1885
Walter Sickert	GLC	1977
George MacDonald	EH	2005
John Desmond Bernal	EH	2001
Dylan Thomas	GLC	1984
Tom Sayers	EH	2002
Ruth First and Joe Slovo	EH	2003
William Daniell	EH	2000
Theodor Fontane	EH	2005
Frances Mary Buss	EH	2000
George Orwell	GLC	1980
'Father' Henry Willis	GLC	1986
Ford Madox Brown	GLC	1976
Kwame Nkrumah	EH	2005

Charles Laughton	EH	1992
Coventry Patmore	LCC	1960
Sir Robert Smirke	GLC	1979
George Bernard Shaw	adopted by GLC (1975)	1951 (St Pancras Borough Council)
Virginia Stephen (Woolf)	GLC	1975
R. G. Cecil (Marquess of Salisbury)	LCC	1965
Sir Charles Eastlake	GLC	1985
A. W. Hofmann	EH	1995
Captain Matthew Flinders	LCC	1961 (later re-erected)
Francisco de Miranda	EH	1996
Andres Bello	EH	1996
Fabian Society	GLC	1985
Henry Mayhew	LCC	1953
Constant Lambert	EH	1997
W. W. Jacobs	EH	1998
Sir Henry Wellcome	EH	1989
Sir John Maitland Salmond	EH	2002
C. R. Cockerell	EH	1989
Frederick Denison Maurice	GLC	1977
Sir Charles Wyndham	LCC	1962 (later re-erected)
Dr Ernest Jones	GLC	1985
Francis Turner Palgrave	GLC	1976
José de San Martín	LCC	1953
E. H. Shepard	EH	1993
Ralph Vaughan Williams	GLC	1972
Anthony Salvin	EH	1990
H. G. Wells	GLC	1966
Earl Dundonald and Earl Beatty	GLC	1974

Hampstead

Sir Rowland Hill	SoA	1893 (later re-erected)
John Heartfield	EH	2004
Lee Miller and Sir Roland Penrose	EH	2003
John Keats	SoA	1896
Ben Nicholson	EH	2002
Sir Harry Vane	SoA	1898
Dame Edith Sitwell	EH	1998
Sir Arthur Bliss	EH	1993
K. Mansfield and J. M. Murry	GLC	1969
John Constable	LCC	1923
H. M. Hyndman	GLC	1972
Karl Pearson	GLC	1983
Sir Gerald du Maurier	GLC	1967
Sir Flinders Petrie	LCC	1954
Baron Friedrich von Hügel	GLC	1968

Rabindranath Tagore	LCC	1961
D. H. Lawrence	GLC	1969
J. L. and Barbara Hammond	GLC	1972
Paul Robeson	EH	2002
John Galsworthy	LCC	1950
Sir George Gilbert Scott	LCC	1910
George du Maurier	adopted by LCC (1959)	1900 (private)
Joanna Baillie	SoA	1900
George Romney	LCC	1908
Sir Henry Dale	GLC	1981
Sir Walter Besant	LCC	1925
Hugh Gaitskell	GLC	1986
Tamara Karsavina	EH	1987
Kathleen Ferrier	GLC	1979
Sir Harold Gillies	EH	1997
Kate Greenaway	LCC	1949
Dennis Brain	EH	1995
Tobias Matthay	GLC	1979
Richard Norman Shaw	EH	2006
John Passmore Edwards	EH	1988
Sidney and Beatrice Webb	GLC	1981
Sigmund Freud	EH	2002 (replacing LCC plaque of 1956)
Anna Freud	EH	2002
Cecil Sharp	GLC	1985
Martina Bergman Österberg	EH	1999
David Bomberg	EH	1996
Alfred Harmsworth (Viscount Northcliffe)	GLC	1979
Sir Adrian Boult	EH	1998
Leonard, Julian and Aldous Huxley	EH	1995
John McCormack	EH	2005
Sir Ronald Aylmer Fisher	EH	2002
W. H. Lever (Viscount Leverhulme)	EH	2002
Michael Ventris	EH	1990
John Linnell and William Blake	GLC	1975
Henrietta and Samuel Barnett	GLC	1982
J. B. Priestley	EH	1994

Primrose Hill and Belsize Park

Humphrey Jennings	EH	2006
William Roberts	EH	2003
Roger Fenton	EH	1991
Friedrich Engels	GLC	1972
Dr Jose Rizal	GLC	1983
Sylvia Plath	EH	2000
W. B. Yeats	LCC	1957
Alfred Stevens	LCC	1924
Arthur Rackham	GLC	1981

Sir Henry Wood	GLC	1969
Dame Clara Butt	GLC	1969
Robert Polhill Bevan	EH	1999
Henry Noel Brailsford	GLC	1983
Frederick Delius	EH	1999
Ramsay MacDonald	LCC	1963
David Devant	EH	2003
Henry Moore	EH	2004
Piet Mondrian	GLC	1975

GREENWICH

C. Day-Lewis	EH	1998
Benjamin Waugh	GLC	1984
General James Wolfe	LCC	1909
Earl of Chesterfield	LCC	1937
Viscount Wolseley	LCC	1937
Sir Frank Dyson	EH	1990
W. H. Barlow	EH	1991
Ettore Schmitz (Italo Svevo)	EH	1999
Herbert, Lord Morrison	GLC	1977
Richard Jefferies	GLC	1986
Sir Arthur Eddington	GLC	1974
Donald McGill	GLC	1977
GPO Film Unit	EH	2000
Nathaniel Hawthorne	LCC	1953
Charles Gounod	LCC	1961

HACKNEY

Priory of St John and The Theatre	LCC	1920
P. H. and Sir Edmund Gosse	GLC	1983
Marie Lloyd	GLC	1977
Joseph Priestley	GLC	1985
Daniel Defoe	LCC	1932
Ebenezer Howard	EH	1991

HAMMERSMITH AND FULHAM

Sir Frank Brangwyn	EH	1989
George Devine	EH	1992
T. J. Cobden-Sanderson	GLC	1974
Eric Ravilious	EH	1991
Edward Johnston	GLC	1977
Sir Emery Walker	LCC	1959
Sir Alan Herbert (A. P. H.)	EH	1990
'Ouida' (Marie Louise de la Ramée)	LCC	1952
C. Whitworth Whall	GLC	1983

The Silver Studio	GLC	1981
Sir Frank Short	LCC	1951
Gustav Holst	EH	2004

ISLINGTON

William Caslon	LCC	1958 (later re-erected)
John Wesley	LCC	1926
John Groom	EH	1997
Joseph Grimaldi	EH	1989
Edward Irving	GLC	1982
T. H. Shepherd	GLC	1976
Charles Lamb	LCC	1907
Caroline Chisholm	GLC	1983
Collins Music Hall	GLC	1968
George Leybourne	GLC	1970
Louis MacNeice	EH	1996
Samuel Phelps	LCC	1911
Joseph Chamberlain	LCC	1915

KENSINGTON AND CHELSEA

Chelsea

Sir Charles Wentworth Dilke	LCC	1959
William Wilberforce	LCC	1961
Dorothy Bland (Mrs Jordan)	GLC	1975
Lillie Langtry	GLC	1980
Sir George Alexander	LCC	1951
Count Edward Raczyński	EH	2004
Arnold Bennett	LCC	1958
Sir Archibald McIndoe	EH	2000
Earl Jellicoe	GLC	1975
Percy Grainger	GLC (erected by EH)	1988
Princess Seraphine Astafieva	GLC	1968
Dame Sybil Thorndike	EH	1998
Charles Kingsley	GLC	1979
William and Evelyn De Morgan	LCC	1937
John F. Sartorius	LCC	1963
Sir Stafford Cripps	EH	1989
Joyce Grenfell	EH	2003
Augustus John	GLC	1981
A. A. Milne	GLC	1979
George Meredith	GLC	1976
John Ireland	EH	1996
Sylvia Pankhurst	GLC	1985
Philip Wilson Steer	GLC	1967
John Tweed	GLC	1985

Walter Greaves	GLC	1973
Hilaire Belloc	GLC	1973
Sir Marc I. Brunel and I. K. Brunel	LCC	1954
James Abbott McNeill Whistler	LCC	1925
Mrs Gaskell	LCC	1913
D. G. Rossetti and A. C. Swinburne	LCC	1949
George Eliot	LCC	1949
Sir Alexander Fleming	GLC	1981
Chelsea China and Tobias Smollett	LCC	1950
Leigh Hunt	LCC	1905
Jane, Lady Wilde	EH	2000
Robert Falcon Scott	LCC	1935
George Gissing	GLC	1975
G. F. S. Robinson (Lord Ripon)	LCC	1959
Oscar Wilde	LCC	1954
P. A. Heseltine (Peter Warlock)	GLC	1984
Samuel L. Clemens (Mark Twain)	LCC	1960
Bram Stoker	GLC	1977
Jerome K. Jerome	EH	1989

Holland Park and Campden Hill

Mohammed Ali Jinnah	LCC	1955
Chaim Weizmann	GLC	1980
Sir Hamo Thornycroft	LCC	1957
Marcus Stone	EH	1994
Sir Luke Fildes	LCC	1959
William Holman Hunt	LCC	1923
Lord Leighton	LCC	1958
Phil May	GLC	1982
Sir David Low	EH	1991
Kenneth Grahame	LCC	1959
Sir Henry Newbolt	EH	1994
Ford Madox Ford	GLC	1973
Ezra Pound	EH	2004
Walter Crane	LCC	1952
Radclyffe Hall	EH	1992
Sir Charles Stanford	LCC	1961
James Joyce	EH	1994
Jean Sibelius	EH	1995
Dame Agatha Christie	EH	2001
Prebendary Wilson Carlile	GLC	1972
Sir Edward Henry	EH	2001
Frank Bridge	EH	1989
Muzio Clementi	LCC	1963
Dame Marie Rambert	EH	1997
John McDouall Stuart	LCC	1962
Charles Morgan	EH	1992

Siegfried Sassoon	EH	1996
Evelyn Underhill	EH	1990 (replacing GLC plaque of 1975)
Aubrey House	LCC	1960
Maharajah Duleep Singh	EH	2005
Percy Wyndham Lewis	GLC	1983
Sir Max Beerbohm	GLC	1969
James Clerk Maxwell	LCC	1923
King Haakon VII	EH	2005
W. M. Thackeray	SoA	1887

Knightsbridge and Hyde Park Gate

Stéphane Mallarmé	LCC	1959
Francis Place	LCC	1961
E. F. Benson	EH	1994
Sir B. Thompson (Count Rumford)	EH	1999
Bruce Bairnsfather	GLC	1981
Sir Francis Galton	adopted by LCC (1959)	c. 1931 (private)
Lord Lugard	GLC	1972
Junius S. and John Pierpont Morgan	EH	2004
Sir Malcolm Sargent	EH	1992
Robert Baden-Powell	GLC	1972
Sir Leslie Stephen	LCC	1960
Sir Winston Churchill	GLC	1985
Enid Bagnold	EH	1997
Sir John Everett Millais	LCC	1926
Henry James	LCC	1949

Notting Hill and Ladbroke Grove

Hablot Knight Browne (Phiz)	EH	2001
W. H. Hudson	adopted by LCC (1938)	1938 (Hudson's Friends Society of Quilmes)
S. V. J. Patel	EH	1991 (replica of GLC plaque of 1986)
Jawaharlal Nehru	EH	1989
Howard Staunton	EH	1999
C. Ricketts, C. Shannon, G. Philpot, *et al.*	GLC	1979
Louis Kossuth	LCC	1959
Sir William Crookes	GLC	1967
Emmeline and Dame Christabel Pankhurst	EH	2006
Lao She	EH	2003
Albert Chevalier	LCC	1965

South Kensington

George Godwin	GLC	1969
Sir Henry Cole	EH	1991
Dr Margery Blackie	EH	2004

Sir John Lavery	GLC	1966
Sir Charles James Freake	GLC	1981
François Guizot	EH	2001
Sir Nigel Playfair	LCC	1965
Béla Bartók	EH	1997
W. M. Thackeray	LCC	1912
Admiral Robert FitzRoy	GLC	1981
Joseph Aloysius Hansom	GLC	1981
James Anthony Froude	LCC	1934
W. E. H. Lecky	LCC	1955
Andrew Bonar Law	LCC	1958
Rosalind Franklin	EH	1992
Mervyn Peake	EH	1996
Frank Dobson	EH	1993
Robert Fortune	EH	1998
Sydney Monckton Copeman	EH	1996
Austin Dobson	LCC	1959
Sir William Orpen	GLC	1978
Jenny Lind (Mme Goldschmidt)	LCC	1909
George Borrow	LCC	1911
Sir Herbert Beerbohm Tree	LCC	1950
E. H. Hymnman (Viscount Allenby)	LCC	1960
Sir W. S. Gilbert	LCC	1929
Charles Booth	LCC	1951
Andrew Lang	LCC	1959
Sir Terence Rattigan	EH	2005
Dame Ivy Compton-Burnett	EH	1994
Samuel Palmer	GLC	1972
T. S. Eliot	EH	1986
Hubert Parry	LCC	1949
John Stuart Mill	LCC	1907
Sir John Simon	LCC	1959
Sir Edward Burne-Jones	EH	1998
W. M. Thackeray	LCC	1905
Col. R. E. B. Crompton	EH	2000

West Kensington and Earls Court

Sir Norman Lockyer	EH	2003
Sir Edwin Arnold	LCC	1931
Howard Carter	EH	1999
Dame Ellen Terry	LCC	1951
Sir Alfred Hitchcock	EH	1999
Benjamin Britten	EH	2001
Sir William Rothenstein	EH	2000
Ugo Foscolo	EH	1998
G. Lowes Dickinson	adopted by LCC (1956)	1956 (private)
Walter Pater	EH	2004

Thomas Daniell	EH	1999
G. K. Chesterton	LCC	1952
Harold Laski	GLC	1974
Samuel Taylor Coleridge	LCC	1950
Sir Edward Elgar	LCC	1962
Goossens family	EH	1999
Sir Henry Rider Haggard	GLC	1977
Marcus Garvey	EH	2005
Mahatma Gandhi	GLC	1986
Sir Geoffrey de Havilland	EH	2001

LAMBETH

County Hall	GLC	1986
ILEA	GLC	1986
Sir Philip Ben Greet	LCC	1960
William Bligh	LCC	1952
Montgomery of Alamein	EH	1987
David Cox	LCC	1951
Dan Leno	LCC	1962 (later re-erected)
Vincent van Gogh	GLC	1973
Lilian Baylis	GLC	1974
Violette Szabo	GLC	1981
Henry Havelock Ellis	GLC	1981
C. L. R. James	EH	2004
John Ruskin	LCC	1926 (replacing LCC plaque of 1909)
Arthur Mee	EH	1991
Sir Arnold Bax	EH	1993
Arthur Henderson	GLC	1980
Sir Jack Hobbs	GLC	1986
Zachary and Thomas Babington Macaulay	LCC	1930
John Francis Bentley	LCC	1950
Clapham Sect and William Wilberforce	GLC	1984
Sir Charles Barry	LCC	1950
Edvard Grieg	EH	2004
Natsume Soseki	EH	2002

LEWISHAM

John Tallis	GLC	1978
Edgar Wallace	LCC	1960
James Glaisher	GLC	1974
Samuel Smiles	LCC	1959
Sir James Clark Ross	LCC	1960
James Elroy Flecker	GLC	1986
Sir Stanley Unwin	GLC	1984
Horniman Museum and Gardens	GLC	1985
Sir Ernest Shackleton	LCC	1928

SOUTHWARK

Sir Eyre Massey Shaw	EH	2000
George Myers	EH	1999
Dr Charles Vickery Drysdale	EH	1988
Dr Harold Moody	EH	1995
Sir Alan Cobham	EH	2003
Percy Lane Oliver	GLC	1979
W. H. Pratt (Boris Karloff)	EH	1998
C. S. Forester	EH	1990
Joseph Chamberlain	LCC	1920
A. H. Ward (Sax Rohmer)	GLC	1985
John Logie Baird	GLC	1977
Annie Besant	LCC	1963

TOWER HAMLETS

Rev. 'Tubby' Clayton	EH	1995
Isaac Rosenberg	EH	1987
Dr Jimmy Mallon	GLC	1984
Anna Maria Garthwaite	EH	1998
Bud Flanagan	EH	1996
Mark Gertler	GLC	1975
Mary Hughes	LCC	1961
Edith Cavell	EH	1988 (later re-erected)
John Richard Green	LCC	1910
Lincoln Stanhope Wainwright	LCC	1961
H. Willoughby, S. Borough, *et al.*	LCC	1922
Rev. St John Groser	EH	1990
Dr Barnardo	LCC	1953
Capt. James Cook	GLC	1970 (replacing LCC plaque of 1907)
Israel Zangwill	LCC	1965
Flying Bomb	EH	1988 (replacing GLC plaque of 1985)
Mahatma Gandhi	LCC	1954
Great Eastern	LCC	1954 (later re-erected)

WANDSWORTH

Edward Adrian Wilson	LCC	1935
Norman Douglas	GLC	1980
Charles Sargeant Jagger	EH	2000
Sean O'Casey	EH	1993
Fred Knee	GLC	1986
G. A. Henty	LCC	1953
John Walter	GLC	1977
John Burns	LCC	1950
Edward Thomas	LCC	1949

William Wilberforce	LCC	1906
Gus Elen	GLC	1979
H. M. Bateman	EH	1997
Charles Haddon Spurgeon	LCC	1914 (later re-erected)
Ted 'Kid' Lewis	EH	2003
David Lloyd George	EH	1992 (replacing GLC plaque of 1967)
Thomas Hardy	LCC	1962 (replacing LCC plaque of 1940)
Sir Harry Lauder	GLC	1969
George Eliot	LCC	1905
A. C. Swinburne and T. Watts-Dunton	LCC	1926
Dr Edvard Beneš	GLC	1978
Sir Edwin Saunders	EH	1997
Gerard Manley Hopkins	GLC	1979 (later re-erected)

WESTMINSTER

Belgravia

George Bentham	GLC	1978
Earl and Countess Mountbatten	EH	2000
Sir Henry Campbell-Bannerman	LCC	1959
Viscount Gort	EH	2005
Lord John Russell	LCC	1911
Thomas Cubitt	LCC	1959
Lord Kelvin	EH	1996
William Ewart	LCC	1952 (later re-erected)
Sir John Lubbock (Baron Avebury)	LCC	1935
Alfred, Lord Tennyson	EH	1994
Walter Bagehot	GLC	1967
Henry Gray	LCC	1947
Stanley Baldwin	GLC	1969
Edward Wood (Earl of Halifax)	EH	1994
George Peabody	GLC	1976
Vivien Leigh	EH	1996
Prince Metternich	GLC	1970
Neville Chamberlain	LCC	1962
Viscount Cecil	GLC	1976
Philip Noel-Baker	EH	1992
Matthew Arnold	LCC	1954
Mary Shelley	EH	2003
Augustus Pitt-Rivers	GLC	1983
F. E. Smith (Earl of Birkenhead)	LCC	1959
Ian Fleming	EH	1996
Dame Edith Evans	EH	1997
George Moore	LCC	1937 (replacing LCC plaque of 1936)
Wolfgang Amadeus Mozart	LCC	1939 (later re-erected)
Harold Nicolson and Vita Sackville-West	EH	1993

Covent Garden, the Strand and the Adelphi

Benjamin Franklin	LCC	1914
Heinrich Heine	LCC	1912
Herman Melville	EH	2005
Rudyard Kipling	LCC	1957 (replacing LCC plaque of 1940)
Samuel Pepys, Robert Harley, *et al.*	LCC	1908
Samuel Pepys	LCC	1947
The Adelphi	LCC	1952
Robert Adam, Thomas Hood, *et al.*	LCC	1950
Thomas Rowlandson	LCC	1950
Sir Richard Arkwright	GLC	1984
Essex Street	LCC	1962 (later re-erected)
Ivor Novello	GLC	1973
Thomas De Quincey	GLC	1981
Dr Johnson and James Boswell	GLC	1984
Bow Street	LCC	1929
Thomas Arne	EH	1988
Thomas Chippendale, sen. and jun.	LCC	1952

Marylebone

Thomas Gage	EH	1996
Earl Roberts	LCC	1922
Frances Hodgson Burnett	GLC	1979
US Embassy and Henry Brooks Adams	GLC	1978
Joseph, Lord Lister	LCC	1915 (later re-erected)
Sir Charles Wheatstone	GLC	1981
Dame Marie Tempest	GLC	1972
Quintin Hogg	LCC	1965
Sir Jonathan Hutchinson	GLC	1981
Sir Ronald Ross	GLC	1985
Herbert Henry Asquith	LCC	1951
G. E. Street	GLC	1980
Sir Robert Mayer	EH	1997
J. L. Pearson and Sir Edwin Lutyens	LCC	1962
Charles Stanhope	LCC	1951
Alfred Waterhouse	EH	1988
Sir Stewart Duke-Elder	EH	2002
Sir Charles Lyell and W. E. Gladstone	LCC	1908
G. F. Bodley	EH	2003
Sir Arthur Pinero	GLC	1970
Sir George Frederic Still	EH	1993
Hector Berlioz	GLC	1969
Sir Frederick Treves	EH	2000
Henry Hallam	LCC	1904
Evelyn Baring (Lord Cromer)	EH	1998

Elizabeth Barrett Barrett	SoA	1899 (later re-erected; supplementary inscription added by LCC in 1937)
Ethel Gordon Fenwick	EH	1999
John Richard Green	LCC	1964 (later re-erected; it replaced an LCC plaque of 1909)
The Wesleys	LCC	1953
Victor Weisz	EH	1996
Thomas Young	LCC	1951 (replacing LCC plaque of 1905)
Sir Patrick Manson	GLC	1985
Edward Gibbon	LCC	1964 (replacing SoA plaque of 1896)
Martin van Buren	GLC	1977
Charles Eamer Kempe	EH	1994
Octavia Hill	EH	1991
Rose Macaulay	EH	1996
Sir Julius Benedict	LCC	1934
John Hughlings Jackson	LCC	1932
Alfred, Lord Milner	GLC	1967
Simón Bolívar	EH	2002
Captain Frederick Marryat	LCC	1953
George Grossmith (jun.)	LCC	1963
Tom Moore	LCC	1953 (later re-erected)
Sir Francis Beaufort	LCC	1959
Michael Faraday	SoA	1876
William Pitt the Younger	LCC	1949 (replacing LCC plaque of 1904)
George Richmond	LCC	1961
Sir Laurence Gomme	EH	2006
George Grossmith (sen.)	LCC	1963
Emma Cons	GLC	1978
Sir Gerald Kelly	EH	1993
Elizabeth Barrett Browning	LCC	1924
William Wilkie Collins	LCC	1951
J. R. Godley	LCC	1951
Anthony Trollope	LCC	1914 (later re-erected)
Mustapha Reschid Pasha	GLC	1972
Cato Street Conspiracy	GLC	1977
Elizabeth Garrett Anderson	LCC	1962
Michael William Balfe	LCC	1912
Edward Lear	LCC	1960
Site of Tyburn Tree	LCC	1964 (later re-erected; it replaced an LCC plaque of 1909)

Mayfair

Richard Bright	GLC	1979
George Grote	LCC	1905
Richard Brinsley Sheridan	SoA	1881
George Basevi	LCC	1949

Horatio, Lord Nelson (1)	SoA	1876
Horatio, Lord Nelson (2)	LCC	1958
Sir Henry Irving	LCC	1950
Lord Clive of India	LCC	1953
George Canning	GLC	1979
Sir Norman Hartnell	EH	2005
William Petty (Lord Shelburne / Lansdowne)	EH	2003
Harry Gordon Selfridge	EH	2003
Bert Ambrose	EH	2005
Lord Palmerston	LCC	1960
Madame D'Arblay (Fanny Burney)	SoA	1885
Charles James Fox	LCC	1912 (later re-erected)
General John Burgoyne	LCC	1954
Richard Brinsley Sheridan	LCC	1955
Sir George Cayley	LCC	1962
Nancy Mitford	EH	1999
Rufus Isaacs	GLC	1971
Benjamin Disraeli	LCC	1908
Beau Brummell	GLC	1984
William Somerset Maugham	GLC	1975
5th Earl of Rosebery	LCC	1962
Lord Fitzroy Somerset (Baron Raglan)	LCC	1911
Sir Richard Westmacott	LCC	1955
Charles X	EH	2000
Florence Nightingale	LCC	1955 (later re-erected)
A. H. Stanley (Lord Ashfield)	GLC	1984
John Gilbert Winant	GLC	1982
Sir Frederick Handley Page	EH	1999
George Seferis	EH	2000
Sir Robert Peel (sen.) and Sir Robert Peel (jun.)	EH	1988
Sir Moses Montefiore	GLC	1984
P. G. Wodehouse	EH	1988
Sir Thomas Sopwith	EH	1998
Ann Oldfield	EH	1992
Sir Alexander Korda	EH	2002
Colen Campbell	GLC	1977
Sir Jeffry Wyatville	GLC	1984
George Frideric Handel	EH	2001 (replacing LCC plaque of 1952, which replaced SoA plaque of 1870)
Jimi Hendrix	EH	1997
Ernest Bevin	EH	2001
Prince Talleyrand	GLC	1978

Paddington and Bayswater

Lord Randolph Churchill	LCC	1962 (later re-erected)
Marie Taglioni	LCC	1960
Olive Schreiner	LCC	1959

Richard Tauber	EH	1998
Sir Charles Vyner Brooke	GLC	1983
W. H. Smith	LCC	1961 (later re-erected)
Sir Giles Gilbert Scott	EH	1990
Lady Violet Bonham Carter	EH	1994
Robert Stephenson	LCC	1905 (later re-erected)
Susan Lawrence	EH	1987
Charles Manby	LCC	1961
Alexander Herzen	GLC	1970
Tommy Handley	GLC	1980
Francis Bret Harte	GLC	1977
Sir James Barrie	LCC	1961
John and Jane Loudon	LCC	1953
Sir William Sterndale Bennett	EH	1996
Sir Rowland Hill	LCC	1907
Alice Meynell	LCC	1948
Guglielmo Marconi	LCC	1954 (replacing LCC plaque of 1952)

St James's

Napoleon III	SoA	1867
Ada, Countess of Lovelace	EH	1992
W. Pitt, E. Stanley and W. E. Gladstone	LCC	1910
Nancy Astor	EH	1987
Sir Isaac Newton	LCC	1908 (later re-erected, with supplementary tablet of 1915)
W. E. Gladstone	LCC	1925
George Nathaniel Curzon	GLC	1976
Lord Palmerston	LCC	1907 (later re-erected, with supplementary tablet of 1936)
General Charles de Gaulle	GLC	1984
Earl Kitchener	LCC	1924
Thomas Gainsborough	LCC	1951 (replacing SoA plaque of 1881)
Frederic Chopin	GLC	1981
William Huskisson	LCC	1962
Henry Pelham	EH	1995
Sir Robert and Horace Walpole	GLC	1976 (replacing SoA plaque of 1881)

St John's Wood, Maida Vale and Lisson Grove

Benjamin Haydon and Charles Rossi	LCC	1959
Emily Davies	GLC	1978
Lokamanya Tilak	EH	1988
John Masefield	EH	2002
Sir Ambrose Fleming	GLC	1971
Alan Turing	EH	1998
David Ben-Gurion	GLC (erected by EH)	1986
Andreas Kalvos	EH	1998

Sir Joseph William Bazalgette	GLC	1974
William Strang	LCC	1962
John William Waterhouse	EH	2002
Madame Marie Tussaud	EH	2001
Sir Thomas Beecham	GLC	1985
Sir Lawrence Alma-Tadema	GLC	1975
Dame Laura and Harold Knight	GLC	1983
T. H. Huxley	LCC	1910
Sir Charles Santley	LCC	1935
C. F. A. Voysey	EH	1995
Melanie Klein	GLC	1985
Sir William Reid Dick	EH	2001
W. P. Frith	GLC	1973
Sir Bernard Spilsbury	EH	2004
Oskar Kokoschka	EH	1986
Thomas Hood	EH	2001 (supplementing LCC plaque of 1912)
George Frampton	GLC	1977

Soho and Leicester Square

Richard Dadd	GLC	1977 (later re-erected)
Richard Cobden	LCC	1905
Sir Mortimer Wheeler	EH	1993
Tom Cribb	EH	2005
Sir Joshua Reynolds	LCC	1947 (later re-erected; it replaced a SoA plaque of 1869)
Willy Clarkson	LCC (erected by GLC)	1966
Edmund Burke	SoA	1876 (later re-erected)
John Dryden	SoA	1870 (later re-erected)
Dr William Hunter	LCC	1952
John Logie Baird	LCC	1951
William Hazlitt	LCC	1905 (later re-erected)
Arthur Onslow	LCC	1927 (replacing LCC plaque of 1912)
J. Banks, R. Brown, D. Don and the Linnean Society	LCC	1938 (replacing LCC plaque of 1911)
Karl Marx	GLC	1967
Dr Joseph Rogers	EH	1996
Thomas Sheraton	LCC	1954
Percy Bysshe Shelley	EH	2000 (replacing GLC plaque of 1979)
Charles Bridgeman	GLC	1984
Antonio Canal (Canaletto)	LCC	1925
Portuguese Embassy and Marquess of Pombal	GLC	1980
John Hunter	LCC	1907 (later re-erected, with supplementary tablet of 1931)
Washington Irving	GLC	1983
Major-General William Roy	GLC	1979
Samuel Taylor Coleridge	LCC (erected by GLC)	1966 (replacing LCC plaque of 1905)
Thomas Stothard	LCC	1911 (later re-erected)

Joseph Nollekens	LCC	1954
Hector Hugh Munro (Saki)	EH	2003
Henry Fuseli	LCC	1961
Edmond Malone	LCC	1962
David Edward Hughes	EH	1991
James Boswell	LCC	1936
Samuel Morse	LCC	1962
Edward R. Murrow	EH	2006
D. G. Rossetti	LCC	1906 (later re-erected, with supplementary tablet of 1928)

Westminster and Pimlico

Scotland Yard	GLC	1979
Sir Henry Morton Stanley	GLC (erected by EH)	1987
T. E. Lawrence	GLC	1966
Lord Reith	EH	1995 (replacing plaque of 1994)
Eleanor Rathbone	GLC	1986
Sir Edward Grey	GLC	1981
Charles Townley	GLC	1985
William Smith	GLC	1975
Lord Fisher	GLC	1975
Lord Palmerston	LCC	1927
Lord Haldane	LCC	1954
Wilfrid Scawen Blunt	GLC	1979
Lord Hore-Belisha	GLC	1980
Cardinal Manning	LCC	1914
Joseph Conrad	GLC	1984
Jomo Kenyatta	EH	2005
Aubrey Beardsley	LCC	1948
Swami Vivekananda	EH	2004
Douglas Macmillan	EH	1997
Major Walter Clopton Wingfield	GLC (erected by EH)	1987
Millbank Prison	LCC (erected by GLC)	1965

OUTER LONDON

Lucien Pissarro	GLC	1976
Private Frederick Hitch	EH	2004
Alexander Pope	EH	1996
Jack Beresford	EH	2005
Johann Zoffany	GLC	1973
E. M. Forster	GLC	1983
John Lindley	EH	2005
Sir Michael Balcon	EH	2005
Dorothea Lambert Chambers	EH	2005
Alan Dower Blumlein	GLC	1977
Arthur Lucan (Arthur Towle)	GLC	1978

R. M. Ballantyne	GLC	1979
W. Heath Robinson	GLC	1976
R. Norman Shaw, F. Goodall and W. S. Gilbert	GLC	1976
Henry Hall	EH	2003
Amy Johnson	EH	1987
Harry Relph	GLC	1969
Herbert Chapman	EH	2005
Graham Hill	EH	2003
Evelyn Waugh	EH	1993
Dame Myra Hess	EH	1987
Frank Pick	GLC	1981
Robert Donat	EH	1994
A. E. Housman	GLC	1969
Mary Kingsley	GLC	1975
Arthur Waley	EH	1995
Vinayak Damodar Savarkar	GLC	1985
Television (Alexandra Palace)	GLC	1977
Luke Howard	EH	2002
Stevie Smith	EH	2005
Joseph Whitaker	EH	1998
Charles and Mary Lamb	EH	1999
Charles Coward	EH	2003
James Hilton	EH	1997
A. V. Roe and Avro No. 1 triplane	GLC	1983
Solomon T. Plaatje	GLC	1986
Will Thorne	GLC (erected by EH)	1987
Albert Mansbridge	GLC	1967
Clement Richard Attlee	GLC	1984
Viscount Castlereagh	EH	1989
Red House, P. Webb and W. Morris	GLC	1969
W. G. Grace	LCC	1963 (later re-erected)
Prince Peter Kropotkin	EH	1989
Alexander Muirhead	GLC	1981
Emile Zola	EH	1990
Will Hay	EH	2000
W. F. R. Stanley	EH	1993
Sir Arthur Conan Doyle	GLC	1973
Samuel Coleridge-Taylor	GLC	1975
C. B. Fry	EH	2005
Frederick George Creed	GLC	1973
John and Frederick John Horniman	EH	1988
Alfred Russel Wallace	GLC	1979
William Hale White	GLC	1979
John Innes	GLC	1978
Air Chief Marshal Lord Dowding	EH	2000
Dame Margaret Rutherford	EH	2002
Robert Graves	EH	1995
Arthur Schopenhauer	EH	2005

Sir Ernst Chain	EH	2003
Josephine Butler	EH	2001
Joseph and Arnold Toynbee	EH	2004
Enid Blyton	EH	1997
Alfred Bestall	EH	2006
Dame Nellie Melba	EH	2000
Sir Christopher Wren	EH	1996
David Garrick	GLC	1970
John Beard and William Ewart	EH	1992
Sir Noël Coward	EH	1995
Henry Labouchere	EH	2000
Walter de la Mare	EH	1995
J. M. W. Turner	GLC	1977
John Henry Newman	GLC	1981
Sir Edwin Chadwick	EH	1992
Bernardo O'Higgins	EH	1994
Leonard and Virginia Woolf	GLC	1976
James Thomson	EH	2005
James Henry Greathead	EH	2000
Henry Fielding	GLC	1978
Kurt Schwitters	GLC	1984
Arthur Hughes	EH	1993

LIST OF BLUE PLAQUES PUT UP BY ENGLISH HERITAGE SINCE JUNE 2006 AND NOT INCLUDED IN THIS BOOK

1 June 2006	DENNIS GABOR 1900–1979 Physicist and Inventor of Holography lived here	79 Queen's Gate, South Kensington, SW7 (Royal Borough of Kensington and Chelsea)
6 June 2006	Dame NINETTE DE VALOIS O.M. 1898–2001 Founder of the Royal Ballet lived here 1962–1982	14 The Terrace, Barnes, SW13 (Borough of Richmond upon Thames)
26 June 2006	GUY GIBSON V.C. 1918–1944 Pilot Leader of the Dambusters Raid lived here	32 Aberdeen Place, St John's Wood, NW8 (City of Westminster)

29 June 2006	JOSEPH MICHAEL GANDY 1771–1843 Architectural Visionary lived here 1833–1838	58 Grove Park Terrace, Chiswick, W4 (Borough of Hounslow)
15 September 2006	Sir JOHN BETJEMAN 1906–1984 Poet lived here 1908–1917	31 Highgate West Hill, Highgate, N6 (Borough of Camden)
21 September 2006	THOMAS SMITH TAIT 1882–1954 Architect lived here	Gates House, Wyldes Close, Hampstead, NW11 (Borough of Barnet)
23 October 2006	KATHLEEN ('KITTY') GODFREE née McKANE 1896–1992 Lawn Tennis Champion lived here 1936–1992	55 York Avenue, East Sheen, SW14 (Borough of Richmond upon Thames)
25 October 2006	CETSHWAYO *c.*1832–1884 King of the Zulus stayed here in 1882	18 Melbury Road, Holland Park, W14 (Royal Borough of Kensington and Chelsea)
19 April 2007	SIR MICHAEL COSTA 1808–1883 Conductor and Orchestra Reformer lived here 1857–1883	59 Eccleston Square Belgravia, SW1 (City of Westminster)
3 May 2007	EDWARD ARDIZZONE 1900–1979 Artist and Illustrator lived here 1920–1972	130 Elgin Avenue, Maida Vale, W9 (City of Westminster)

10 May 2007	HERTHA ARYTON 1854–1923 Physicist lived here 1903–1923	41 Norfolk Square, Paddington, W2 (City of Westminster)
17 May 2007	HAROLD ABRAHAMS 1899–1978 Olympic Athlete lived here	Hodford Lodge, 2 Hodford Road, Golders Green, NW11 (Borough of Barnet)
26 September 2007	SIR THOMAS FOWELL BUXTON 1786–1845 Anti-Slavery Campaigner lived and worked here	The Directors' House, Old Truman Brewery, 91 Brick Lane, Spitalfields, E1 (Borough of Tower Hamlets)
24 October 2007	IRA ALDRIDGE 1807–1867 Shakespearian Actor 'The African Roscius' lived here	5 Hamlet Road, Crystal Palace, SE19 (Borough of Bromley)
5 November 2007	SIR NIKOLAUS PEVSNER 1902–1983 Architectural Historian lived here from 1936 until his death	2 Wildwood Terrace, Hampstead, NW3 (Borough of Camden)
22 November 2007	FRANK MATCHAM 1854–1920 Theatre Architect lived here 1895–1904	10 Haslemere Road, Crouch End, N8 (Borough of Haringey)
29 November 2007	MARY SEACOLE 1805–1881 Jamaican Nurse Heroine of the Crimean War lived here	14 Soho Square, W1 (City of Westminster) [NB re-erection by EH of a GLC plaque, originally installed in 1985 at 157 George Street, Paddington (demolished)]

10 December 2007	GILBERT BAYES 1872–1953 Sculptor lived here 1931–1953	4 Greville Place, St John's Wood, NW6 (City of Westminster)
12 December 2007	SRI AUROBINDO 1872–1950 Indian Spiritual Leader lived here 1884–1887	49 St Stephen's Avenue, Shepherd's Bush, W12 (Borough of Hammersmith and Fulham)
15 December 2007	SIR FRANCIS PETTIT SMITH 1808–1874 Pioneer of the Screw-Propeller lived here 1864–1870	Fountain House, 17 Sydenham Hill, Sydenham, SE26 (Borough of Southwark)
9 February 2008	DAME LUCIE RIE 1902–1995 Potter lived and worked here from 1939 until her death	18 Albion Mews, Bayswater, W2 (City of Westminster)
28 February 2008	SIR KARL POPPER 1902–1994 Philosopher lived here 1946–1950	16 Burlington Rise, East Barnet, EN4 (Borough of Barnet)
23 July 2008	ALASTAIR SIM 1900–1976 Actor lived here 1953–1975	8 Frognal Gardens, Hampstead, NW3 (Borough of Camden)
9 September 2008	ELEANOR MARX 1855–1898 Socialist Campaigner lived and died here	7 Jews Walk, Sydenham, SE26 (Borough of Lewisham)
25 September 2008	JAMES SMITHSON 1764–1829 Scientist Founder of the Smithsonian Institution lived here	9 Bentinck Street, Marylebone, W1 (City of Westminster)

18 December 2008   DAME CELIA JOHNSON   46 Richmond Hill,
                              1908–1982   Richmond,
                               Actress   TW10
                            was born here   (Borough of
                                                       Richmond upon Thames)